1001 FOODS
YOU MUST TRY BEFORE YOU DIE

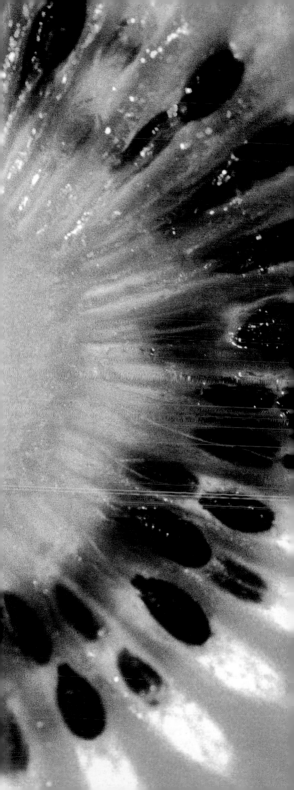

Elderflower

Found all over Europe, Asia, and North America, the elder—*Sambucus nigra* in Europe, *Sambucus canadensis* in northern North America—is a neglected plant. Yet provided they are cooked, both flowers and berries are a boon.

The flowers in their characteristic wide flat clusters have a distinctive fragrance, which may be added to sorbets and desserts or used to flavour gooseberry jelly. The Austrian preference for making fritters from the sprays and serving them with icing sugar is said to have caught on after World War II, when starving families gleaned what food they could from the fields and hedgerows, although elderflower fritters have a heritage that stretches back to medieval times.

The berries make a fine jam popular in Hungary and other parts of central Europe; they are also used as an ingredient in an Austrian compote called *hollerröster*, and in Scandinavian mixed fruit soups. In England, elderflowers are often used to make cordial or a mildly vinous champagne; elsewhere they are infused in boiling water as a cold remedy. **GM**

Taste: Elderflowers have a sickly, gooseberry-like scent and flavour. Elderberries taste somewhere between a blackberry and a ripe plum, but with a strong bitterness.

Rose Petal

In Iran, the scent of rose petals provides a mysterious background to dishes both sweet and savoury. According to Margaret Shaida's *The Legendary Cuisine of Persia* (2002): "Just as the rose is as much a part of Persian literature as the nightingale, so its delectable fragrance is as much a part of Persian cuisine as the lemon and saffron."

The Mohammadi roses grown around the city of Kashan south of Tehran are prized because the hot desert air enhances their scent. Dried or powdered petals may be mixed with *polows* (Persian cooked rice dishes), included in the spice blends known as *advieh*, added to sweet preserves, or made into jams. It takes 90 pounds (40 kg) of their pink or red petals—a day's work for professional pickers—to extract 0.3 fluid ounces (10 ml) of essential oils.

Rose water spread with the influence of Persian cuisine west to Turkey and east to India. It brings exoticism to Turkish Delight (*lokum*), and is sometimes used in ice creams, rice puddings, sherbets, cakes, and sweets throughout South Asia and the Middle East. **MR**

Taste: Rose petals have little taste, but their perfume infuses a dish so fast that they call for subtle dosing. Used in rose water, they add a note of the exotic to many dishes.

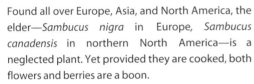

Roses are traditionally picked at dawn to preserve the freshness of their petals. »

Blackcurrant

It is odd that a flavour which is now summoned to describe the taste of the finest Bordeaux *crus* could have spent so much of its existence as a poor relation of redcurrants and white currants. But *Ribes nigrum* suffered this until the last century and remains, despite a vitamin C content far higher than lemons, relatively rare except in liqueurs such as the Burgundian *crème de cassis*, and Ribena, the branded fruit syrup which guzzles almost three-quarters of the United Kingdom's commercial crop.

Yet gardeners know that the small berries have more to offer than juice. While some varieties are plumper and sweeter, others are sharper and more intensely flavoured, all come into their own as a culinary fruit. Harvested in early summer, they are bottled, jammed, or mixed with other fruits in a compote, where they deliver a distinctive aroma. In professional cuisine, the currants are often used to add punch to sauces, for example those served with roasted duck fillets. Blackcurrants are suited to mixing with blander ingredients: in ice cream, in sorbets, or as a topping for cheesecakes. **MR**

Taste: *The aroma of fresh blackcurrant is powerful and fragrant. The berries contain a sharp juice and seeds that benefit from poaching in syrup to unwrap their berry tang.*

Mountain Huckleberry

Like a super-charged blueberry, rich in aroma, flavour, sugar, and antioxidants, yet with a deep purple colour that continues even under its skin, the mountain huckleberry is the most frequently harvested and highly coveted of the dozens of varieties of wild huckleberries that grow in North America. A member of the same genus as the blueberry and cranberry, *Vaccinium membranaceum* is typically found in the northwest United States, where it goes by a whole range of names. The huckleberry remains culturally important to Native Americans who have relied on it as a food source.

Low elevation picking begins in early July and can continue into late September. Pickers regard huckleberry patches a closely-guarded secret, and will move to elevations as high as 10,000 feet (3,048 m) to continue harvesting as the season progresses. It is believed that millions of pounds of huckleberries are harvested each season. Because of concerns that demand is outstripping supply, there are current attempts to domesticate the plant, which has proven difficult to grow in cultivation. **CLH**

Taste: *The taste is similar to blueberries but juicier with both sweet and tart notes. Huckleberries are used in desserts, preserves, and sweets, and as a sauce for meats.*

Berry-picking is one of the pleasures of a northwestern American childhood. »

Cranberry

An essential part of American Thanksgiving turkey dinners, these sour little scarlet berries are native to both the Old World and the New World, and local varieties are prized every bit as much in Scandinavia as they are in the United States.

Yet it is the North American cranberry, *Vaccinium macrocarpon*, that has made its mark on the world. High in bezoic acid, a natural preservative that enables the berries to be stored for months without deteriorating, the berries were a staple in the diets of Native Americans, who used them fresh and dried, or pounded with meat into the trail mix known as pemmican. They became, in turn, a valued food of the early settlers and of colonial sailors, who carried them on voyages stored in barrels of water. When, in 1677, the colonists sent a gift of their choicest products to placate Charles II, King of England, cranberries went along with the cod and corn; by 1689 they were being eaten at Thanksgiving.

Gathering in the commercial cranberry crop takes the form either of dry harvesting, when the berries are combed off the vines with rakes, or, more spectacularly, wet harvesting. In the latter case, the cranberry fields are flooded and special machinery is employed to beat the berries off the vines. The floating red berries are then gathered together and collected for worldwide distribution.

Old World cranberries are mostly used in sauces, jams, preserves, and liqueurs. The sauces also pair well with game. In North America berries are used for sauces, famously cranberry sauce, the traditional accompaniment to the Thanksgiving turkey, and also in pies, salads, and cakes. Cranberries are high in vitamin C and their juice is also popular. **SH**

Cloudberry

Found in the far northern regions of Europe and North America, cloudberries are circumpolar in distribution. For centuries, these bright berries, which resemble yellow raspberries, have played a major role in the diet of Scandinavians, the northern Sami tribes of Lapland, and the Inuits of Alaska and Canada, where the berry is known as the baked-apple berry or bakeberry.

The natural habitat of the cloudberry, *Rubus chamaemorus,* is peaty bogs and marshes. The low, creeping plant sprouts small white flowers, then forms red berries that turn a deep yellow colour as they ripen in late summer. Cloudberries are as yet largely uncultivated, and so must be laboriously harvested from the wild, which makes them both exclusive and expensive. Once gathered, however, they can be frozen and stored for long periods.

Cloudberries are highly valued in Scandinavia, where a rich heritage of gathering and using wild berries still thrives today. The Swedish botanist Carl Linnaeus praised the berry in his masterpiece *Flora Lapponica* (1737) and reported how copious amounts of preserved cloudberries were transported every year to the tables of the Swedish capital. The Finns, who call them *lakka*, use them to make a liqueur and eat them with a Lappish farm cheese. In Sweden, cloudberries are often made into a jam and eaten with pancakes or ice cream. The Inuits traditionally mixed them with fat and snow to make *akutaq*, known as Eskimo ice cream. Aside from their delicious taste, cloudberries are appreciated for health reasons. High in vitamins, including vitamin C, they were historically eaten by Nordic seafarers to prevent scurvy. **CC**

Taste: *Very firm with crunchy flesh, cranberries have a pungent, tart, acidic taste which requires sweetening. Some varieties have a distinctive taste of pine.*

To wet-harvest cranberries in the autumn,
⊗ *farmers flood the bogs in which they grow.*

Taste: *Cloudberries have an intense freshness, unique tangy flavour, and juicy texture that is best enjoyed freshly picked and carefully warmed up, with a pinch of sugar.*

Wild Raspberry

Stretching across Europe and Asia, and into North America, the raspberry (*Rubus idaeus*) thrives in thickets, open woods, and hedgerows and has been harvested wild for thousands of years. The ancient Greeks were most likely the first to cultivate the fruit, and according to Pliny named it after Mount Ida because the plants grew so thickly on its slopes.

Wild raspberries may be red, yellow, white, or shades in between: like their cultivated relatives, they are slightly hairy and are plucked easily from the thorny bush. Like blackberries, they are not botanically berries, but clusters of tiny individual stone fruit, or drupelets, set around a central core. This "receptacle" stays on the branch when the raspberry is picked, leaving a small, cup-like fruit.

Raspberry's fruit, leaves, and bark have long been used to treat ailments or minor wounds: the leaves, in particular, have a long history of usage during pregnancy and childbirth. Once harvested, the berries can deteriorate quickly, making them difficult to transport: those that do not survive the journey may be used in jams, pastries, pies, or teas. **CLH**

Black Mulberry

Myth attaches itself to this most luscious but fragile of fruits, the best tasting of the many varieties of mulberry. "And the gods touched their parents. Ever after / Mulberries, as they ripen, darken purple." This, according to Ovid, explains how the bloody suicide of the star-crossed lovers Pyramus and Thisbe, next to a mulberry bush, led to the white mulberry becoming the black mulberry (*Morus nigra*).

The mulberry is native to southwest Asia but has been grown in Europe since classical times, and was probably introduced into Britain, France, and Spain by the Romans. It has also been successfully introduced into the Americas and Australia. It is not a true berry, but a cluster of berries, and harvest is challenging. The fruit tend to collapse when picked, and can stain a virulent purple: some prefer to wait until the fruit ripen sufficiently to fall from the tree.

Mulberries rot very quickly and should only be washed immediately before eating, but any surplus can be made into a delicious jelly. In Afghanistan, they are dried, powdered, and mixed with flour to make bread. **AMS**

Taste: *Wild raspberries are sweet, tart, and highly aromatic. The berry is fragile and juicy, and the flavour of some varieties found in the wild can be spectacular.*

Taste: *The black mulberry is very sweet but has sufficient acidity to give a burst of flavour that is comparable to a blackberry, but less "pippy" in both taste and texture.*

Black mulberries are white when young, but turn black; the white mulberry is a separate species. »

Boysenberry

Marionberry

Softer and larger than blackberries, with a sweeter flavour, smaller seeds, and a colour closer to maroon or indigo than black, boysenberries have a rather complicated heritage. They are named after Rudolph Boysen, a California farmer who developed the fruit in 1923 but failed to sustain a crop, and are a cross between blackberries, raspberries, and loganberries—which are in turn believed to be a hybrid of a blackberry and a raspberry.

Similar to the blackberries found growing wild around the globe, although some varieties have no thorns, boysenberries are grown commercially in Chile, New Zealand, Australia, and parts of the United States, where they are a popular ice cream flavour. Good raw, when they can top breakfast cereals and adorn green salads, their flavour is enhanced by being lightly cooked. Chefs use them to create sauces and purées to accompany meats and poultry, sometimes paired with ingredients such as ceps. Boysenberries also do well in jams, jellies, pies, tarts, and cobblers, or simply served fresh with cream, and perhaps a hint of sugar. **SH**

While in Britain and northern Europe blackberries are still often left to be picked wild from the hedgerows, in North America their cultivation is a serious business. Marionberries are a succulent type, a cross between two modern breeds of blackberries with some raspberry heritage: shiny black in colour, they are moderately firm and relatively large in size, with a very fruity fragrance. Marionberries were developed and grown in Oregon during the 1950s, as part of a selective breeding programme, and take their name from Marion County in that state.

Marionberries are available fresh for only about a month, typically between 10 July and 10 August, although they are sold frozen at other times. They make delicious jellies, jams, ice creams, and sorbets, and work well as an addition to pancakes and waffles. The purée makes a flavourful marinade and appears in sweet-and-sour sauces. American chefs offer dishes such as an oat and nut granola over honey yoghurt with Marionberry purée. Innovative cooks have even made a glaze from the berries for rattlesnake, a most unlikely pairing. **SH**

Taste: *Boysenberries have a rich, sweet flavour with tart undertones. They have hints of blackberry, strawberry, and raspberry in their flavour.*

Taste: *Marionberries have an intense blackberry flavour that is sweet and a little musky. At their best they strike a perfect balance between sweet and tart.*

Fresh boysenberries should be eaten within three days of picking because they deteriorate quickly.

Alpine Strawberry

The French name *fraises des bois*, like the Italian *fragole di bosco*, suggests that these tiny, delectable strawberries are a wild fruit. But while they are indeed found wild, they are more often cultivated by gardeners, as they have been since the fourteenth century. The French king Charles V had his gardener plant 12,000 sets as early as 1386.

Unlike their larger cousins, alpine strawberry plants (*Fragaria vesca*) fruit right through the summer. In size they may be smaller than a currant or the size of a manicured little fingernail. Some may be drier or juicier or sweeter than others, but they are always strongly fragrant and distinctive.

Alpines are highly perishable so rarely make a commercial crop. Sensitive fingers are required when picking, for they bruise easily and discolour. During the seventeenth century, plants were dug up in the wild for replanting in gardens; during the British Regency, fruiting plants were placed on tables for diners to eat at will. Although alpines shine in a *tarte aux fraises des bois* and make a luxurious sorbet, the taste of the fresh fruit cannot be bettered. **MR**

Taste: *Alpines are best enjoyed as a handful of perfectly ripe fruit. Individual fruit may be a little sour, but a mouthful gives a complete, intense berry flavour.*

Alpine strawberries are at their best picked fully ripe from the garden or the wild.

Mara des Bois Strawberry

For many millennia, tiny, alpine strawberries were beloved in Europe. They were picked 8,000 years ago and the Romans valued them highly. Yet the discovery of America revealed sturdier, larger species that were introduced to Europe and hybridized with existing fruit. Faced with this competition, the soft, low-yielding alpines began to fall from favour.

In 1991 a French laboratory created the Mara des Bois strawberry, a hybrid of four different strains of berry, with the aim of capturing the fragrance and flavour of an alpine strawberry and packaging it in a berry with the firm texture of contemporary varieties. Available on the market for an extended growing season, from springtime until the first frosts, this fantastically fragrant fruit fetches a premium price and accounts for about a tenth of France's strawberry harvest. The colour ranges from brick red to pinkish purple, while the berries may be as small as a pea or as large as a plum. Cultivation is expanding from its heartland in southwest France to California, the United Kingdom, and beyond. **HF-L**

Taste: *Combining the musky fragrance of wild strawberries with the firm-fleshed attributes of its genitors, a balance of sweetness and acidity marks this melt-in-the-mouth berry.*

Casseille

Hybridizing fruit is hardly a new science. Pears can be crossed with apples. Tangelos are part mandarin orange, part grapefruit. Known botanically as *Ribes x culverwellii*, the casseille or jostaberry is a relatively recent example: a happy marriage between a blackcurrant and a gooseberry, usually credited to Dr. Rudolph Bauer in Germany in the early 1970s.

The berries look like outsize blackcurrants, but the pulp has the texture of gooseberries. They are easy to pick from bushes, with none of the awkward hanging bunches associated with currants or the spikes common to gooseberries. Their size, similar to small Muscat grapes, is ideal for the kitchen.

In Britain, where the gooseberry is relatively widely grown, the fruit has not yet made an impact, however, the French have been quick to seize the opportunities presented by a fruit that is much more than a novelty. Although it can be eaten raw, the main attraction is as a very versatile ingredient that lends itself well to jams, preserves, compotes, bavarois, sorbets, and ice creams, as well as the branded liqueur known as crème de casseille. **MR**

Taste: A casseille conserve has a less assertive taste than blackcurrant, but similar. It is fresher, lighter on the palate, and less cloying than blackcurrant's syrupy intensity.

Gooseberry

What is sauce for the goose is sauce for the mackerel. The English name "gooseberry" and the French name—literally "mackerel currant"—both point to the early use of the European gooseberry as a base for sauces where its tartness offset the oiliness of meat or fish. However, the berries are not necessarily sour. Picked mature they are sweet and juicy. They come in four colours: yellow, green, red, and "white." Some are furry, others prickly, others smooth; some are as pale as pearls, others almost black.

Ribes grossularia has attracted little interest on mainland Europe, but in northern England and especially in the county of Cheshire it has been highly prized. Annual competitions to judge the largest gooseberry of the year date back to 1786, and by the mid-nineteenth century there were 250 amateur gooseberry societies in Britain: the record-holding fruit weighs more than 2 ounces (60 g).

In Britain, home-made gooseberry pies and jams are popular. In the most typical of British dishes, gooseberry fool, gooseberry is mixed with whipped cream, sometimes flavoured with elderflowers. **MR**

Taste: Under-ripe gooseberries picked for cooking are hard and sharp. In ripe fruit, the plentiful seeds are coated in a slippery pulp with a taste that is sweet and refreshing.

Hairy gooseberry fruit with their many seeds have a unique texture when baked whole in desserts. ◗

Miracle Berry

Native to West Africa, where it grows on small, azalea-like shrubs, the intensely sweet miracle berry gets its name from the miraculin it contains, although any weight-watcher with a sweet tooth will assert that it is a genuine miracle worker, too. Used for hundreds of years in its homeland, the fruit was brought to the attention of the West by U.S. explorer David Fairchild in the 1930s.

Miraculin is a type of protein that persuades the taste buds that sour foods are actually sweet. This attribute was exploited to the full in 1995 by a Tokyo café that claimed the unique selling point of having no dish on the menu containing more than 100 calories. The Japanese dieters who packed the tables happily tucked into cakes and desserts made from mouth-puckering quantities of lemons and limes after having eaten just one berry beforehand. Miraculin works by binding its active glycoprotein molecule with some trailing carbohydrate chains to receptors of the taste buds; the molecule changes their function for a short time. The fruit does not make sweet food taste sweeter, because it is not a sweetener in itself; its effects depend on what is eaten afterwards, and it has been used to make bitter medicines more palatable.

The scarlet berries, also known as miracle fruits and serendipity berries, are grape-sized and develop from small, white flowers. Although they have been used by West Africans as a sweetener for centuries, they long remained unknown elsewhere because the bushes do not flourish in cooler climes and the berries were impossible to export since they rotted quickly. Freeze-drying has changed all that, and the berries can now be enjoyed around the world. **WS**

Taste: *Discard the pip and chew the vaguely sweet but bland flesh of a miracle berry and everything you eat, however sour, will taste sweet for the next couple of hours.*

Sea Buckthorn

This spiky plant (*Hippophae rhamnoides*), with its bright orange berries, is native to northern Asia and Europe and was one of the first to establish itself in Scandinavia after the Ice Age. Hardy and vigorous, it is a pioneer species, tolerant of exposure, that grows in sandy mountains and coastal areas. The fruit of this plant has long been praised for its health-giving properties, mentioned in ancient Tibetan medical texts and also in Chinese traditional herbal medicine and in Indian Ayurvedic medicine. Today the fruit of sea buckthorn, phenomenally rich in vitamins C and E, is being newly marketed as a "super berry," with research being carried out into it as a source of cholesterol-lowering compounds.

The hardy bush is covered by long thorns, a fact reflected in its common names of sea buckthorn, Alpine sandthorn, and Siberian pineapple. This natural defence makes the berry difficult to pick and harvest, although thornless varieties are cultivated in Russia. In Scandinavia, a special tool is used to press the juice out of the berry while it is still on the spiky bush; in other places, the bushes are shaken— mechanically or by hand—to loosen the berries.

In Scandinavia, the sour-sweet berries are a particularly special delicacy. They have appeared at the prestigious Nobel Prize dinner, as a main ingredient in the traditional ice cream. The juice is used as an ingredient in desserts, jams, sauces, and alcoholic drinks, such as schnapps. Health-food shops sell dried sea buckthorn berries in powdered form, to add to smoothies or sprinkle over yoghurt and porridge, and it is also available as a juice, often mixed with other fruit juices. The plant is also used in herbal medicine and skin-care products. **CC**

Taste: *Sea buckthorn has a unique, citric taste and a fresh aroma that has been likened to passion fruit. Many prefer it as a juice blended with sugar rather than a raw fruit.*

The fruit-covered branches of sea buckthorn fan out to form a pleasing ornamental plant. ❯❯

Açaí

Riberry

Known as the "purple pearl of the Amazon," the açaí is deep violet, almost black in colour, with firm flesh surrounding a sturdy stone. Yet its culinary potential would have gone unnoticed if indigenous tribes had not realized centuries ago that the pulp required processing. The resulting thick purée forms a wonderful base for juices, mousses, and ice creams, and lasts far longer than the fresh fruit.

Açaí grows in bunches from a tall, leafy palm, *Euterpe oleracea*, which can reach a height of 65 feet (20 m) or more, deep in the rainforest around the Amazon River and its tributaries. Locals pick the fruit daily and send it down-river for sale at markets such as Ver-o-Peso (See-the-Price), the colonial covered market in the regional capital of Belém.

Açaí makes a great, energy-charging breakfast; however, sophisticated chefs in Rio and São Paulo, who are keen to encapsulate different facets of their country in their cuisine, use it as a base for sauces to accompany roast meats and desserts such as crème caramels and ice creams. Outside Brazil, it is gaining increasing renown as a super-food. **AL**

Botanically related to the common spice clove, the riberry (*Syzygium leumannii*) is a small rainforest tree originally found in northern New South Wales where it was a forage food of the Bundjalung people and other local clans. It is now commonly used as a decorative urban planting all along the east coast. Ten-year-old plants and even potted specimens can bear impressive bunches of rose to scarlet heart-shaped fruits in the few months around Christmas. The fruits are hand-picked, stemmed, then washed and cleaned. They are then either stored frozen or made into preserves such as spreads and vinegars.

Delicious in desserts, particularly in combination with chocolate—commercial riberry confit pairs wonderfully with a rich chocolate mousse—they are equally at home in a riberry vodkatini or tossed through stir-fries. A classic Australian combination is kangaroo cooked medium rare with a port wine *jus* and riberry confit. The sweetness of the sugar-cured fruits can be offset with red wine vinegar; drained of their syrup, preserved riberries are ideal with cheese. **VC**

Taste: *The acidity of açaí fruit and the discreetly bitter notes, which some compare to chocolate, come into their own when balanced with sugar or honey.*

Taste: *The seedless fruits have a refreshing watermelon texture and aromatics of cinnamon and clove; clove is more dominant in seeded varieties.*

Extravagant claims are made for the health benefits of this rainforest fruit, used by indigenous tribes.

Marula

Traditional wisdom has it that elephants become intoxicated from eating the slightly fermented fallen fruits of the marula tree: certainly elephants are partial to the fruit and in South Africa the marula is known as the "elephant tree." Be that as it may, marula (*Scelerocarya birrea*) has fed a diversity of creatures in southern Africa, possibly from as early as 10,000 BCE. Thriving in dry, sandy soils and drought-resistant, the tree is a familiar sight in the savannah and the veldt today.

The marula is considered a sacred tree in many parts of Africa and is attributed with many powers, including those of fertility and virility. Among the Venda people, the bark was used to select the sex of an unborn child: an infusion of bark from a male tree was believed to produce a son, while an infusion from a female tree would summon a daughter. Given the tree's sacred status, the harvesting of marula fruits from the wild is the cause for celebration and harvest festivals.

The marula is a prolific tree, bearing many fruit, historically a valued food source in many parts of Africa. The fruits are about the size of a golf ball, ripening from green to pale yellow, and contain several times as much vitamin C as an orange. The smooth, shiny, yellowish skin surrounds white flesh. When completely ripe, marula fruit are used in various jams and jellies. The fruit is also used to make wine, beer, the South African moonshine brandy known as *mampoer,* and as an ingredient in the cream liqueur, Amarula. The hard, brown nut inside the fruit contains edible kernels also prized as a foodstuff, used in porridge or as a flavouring. Oil extracted from the kernels is used in cosmetics. **HFi**

Mazhanje

Highly valued in Africa as a cash crop, mazhanje is the tropical fruit of *Uapaca kirkiana,* an indigenous tree that grows at medium altitudes in areas that receive good rainfall and are free of frost. Antelopes and elephants are also partial to fruit that has fallen to the ground and is fermenting. Popular in Zimbabwe, the fruit owes its name to the Shona language; it is known as wild loquat in English and by a host of different names across Africa.

The fruit tree grows in the Miombo ecological zone of woodland in southern Africa that takes in countries such as Zimbabwe, Angola, Namibia, Botswana, South Africa, Zambia, Tanzania, and Mozambique. The berry-like fruit can be up to 1.5 inches (4 cm) across and has a bitter, reddish-brown skin and a yellow-brown pulp embedded with several hard, white seeds. The flesh can be eaten raw, but the tough skin, which contains bitter tasting tannins and seeds, is discarded. A ripe fruit can weigh up to 1.75 ounces (50 g). Mazhanje is low in fat and high in potassium, and is highly regarded as an important famine food.

The fruit is usually collected from the wild by women and children, either from low-lying branches or from the ground, and is then sold at roadsides. The ripe fruit pulp is used to sweeten maize-meal porridge and is also made into a variety of local beers, cakes, and a jam that is eaten with bread. It is common for the jam to be sold a spoonful at a time. The tropical fruit also may be broken up, placed in water, and left to ferment to make a sweet, heady wine. In Malawi the fruit is used to produce an opaque beer called "napolo ukana" and a gin called "kachasu." **CK**

Taste: *Marula has an earthy, fruity scent. Remove the skin, then pop the central stone and the pulp around it into your mouth. The flesh has a refreshing, sweet-and-sour taste.*

Taste: *The ripe flesh of the mazhanje fruit has a honey sweet flavour that tastes like a cross between an orange and a pear; it has a fleshy, squash-like texture.*

Fermenting marula berries are known to intoxicate wild animals, and are also used to make beer.

Barhi Date

Mamoncillo

The fruit of a palm tree, *Phoenix dactylifera*, which grows in clusters in hot climates from North Africa to California, the date has been cultivated since prehistoric times. By the beginnings of the ancient civilizations in Egypt and Mesopotamia it was already a staple, and in the Middle East and North Africa it is still a vital fruit.

The maturation cycle is known around the world by its Arabic names. Khalal denotes a date that has reached full size but is still hard and pale; bisr is when the fruit begins to colour; during rutab the date begins to soften at the tip; at tamr the dates are ready to be packed. Barhi dates are one of few cultivars that are enjoyable to eat at the khalal stage.

Barhis, which probably originated in Basra, Iraq, are popular across the Arab world, and have been grown in California since the early twentieth century. Firm, round, pale yellow, and as crunchy as an apple at the khalal stage, they are naturally high in sugar. During the rutab stage they become known as "honey balls" for the sweet liquid that pools inside their fragile surface. **FC**

Mamoncillo fruit begs to be plucked and eaten on the spot from the roadsides of Central and South America and all across the Caribbean. Clusters of these emerald green, round fruits ripen during the tropical summers on the native trees, which also conveniently offer a shady place to snack. On scorching hot afternoons the juice and flesh of the fruit can be slurped out of hand. The fruit also finds its way into the desserts, salsas, and cocktails that are served on the sun-drenched beaches.

Known by many other names including genip, honeyberry, and "Spanish lime," *Melicoccus bijugatus* belongs to the same family as rambutan and longan. Physically similar to these relatives, its orange-pink opaque flesh surrounds a large oval seed. Wrapped in an inedible leathery shell that almost cracks when bitten or pierced, the inner fruit is slippery and releases easily with a gentle squeeze.

Mamoncillo is available preserved in syrup, but the fresh fruit offers the best flavour. Enterprising chefs toast the inner seeds and use them in much the same way as nuts or pumpkin seeds. **TH**

Taste: *Barhi dates are crisp, firm, and slightly fibrous, with a mild astringency until the flavours open up. Expect notes of sugarcane, cinnamon, cooked fruit, and candied nuts.*

Taste: *Mamoncillo is slightly tarter than either lychee or longan, but maintains a fruity sweetness that is an unusual yet refreshing cross betwen mango and grape.*

In many regions, dates are still hand harvested
⊗ *by pickers who hazardously shin up the palms.*

Rainier Cherry

Griotte

All cherries that are grown today descend from two wild species: *Prunus avium*, the ancestor of all "sweet" cherries, and *Prunus cerasus*, the ancestor of the "sour" type. Harold Fogle, a scientist at Washington State University, developed the intensely sweet Rainier variety in 1952 by crossing two cherry strains: the Bing and the Van. The result? A delicate cherry with yellow flesh, yellow skin, and a bright red blush, pretty enough for little girls to wear as earrings. He named it after Mount Rainier in the state's Cascade Mountains.

Rainier cherry skin bruises easily, making the plants extremely sensitive to weather, especially wind and rain: they also react badly to heat. Their delicacy makes them hard to pick and challenging to transport, so that the crop is never as large as that of other cherries, making the fruit expensive—doubly so when they have to be imported. Rainier cherries can be used in dishes calling for any kind of cherry, but they are at their best eaten fresh out of hand. Commercially they are dried and coated with dark chocolate to make a delectable sweet. **SH**

The wild sour cherry is supposedly named after the Turkish town of Cerasus, although it has since spread further north. When raw, sour cherries are sharp, so rather than eaten fresh, they find themselves destined for cooking where the requisite sweetening can lift their flavour. They star not only in the jams, compotes, and liqueurs of central and northern Europe but in *meggyleves*, the Hungarian sour cherry soup, and *Schwarzwälder kirschtorte* (Black Forest gateau). They may be preserved whole in a kirsch-based liquid, and sold as *griottines*, or coated in icing and dipped in couverture chocolate for a Christmas treat. In Belgium, they are made into a kind of wine, and also a fruit beer. Served fresh from the tree and made into a clafoutis, they are to die for.

Any confusion should not distract from the fact that griottes are fruit, rarely sold over the counter raw because of their sourness, but common in both orchards and gardens. Their juiciness lends them to cooking and they are better suited to the classic roast duck with cherries than the sweeter, paler cherries recommended in some cookery books. **MR**

Taste: *Sweetest of the sweet cherries, Rainier cherries have firm, juicy yellow flesh and a rich fruity taste. Drying concentrates the flavour even further.*

Taste: *Packed with juice, griottes vary in size, shape, and colour. All varieties are pleasantly tart, with an entrancing fruitiness, delivering notes from coffee to sweet, red fruits.*

Acerola

The world's richest natural source of vitamin C, a ripe acerola contains, weight for weight, around twenty to thirty times as much ascorbic acid as an orange. When you consider that the tree can bear three crops of fruit a year with ease, small wonder it has a reputation as a miracle fruit.

With its vivid, orangey scarlet hue, acerola looks rather like a brightly coloured cherry, and is reputed to come from the Caribbean island of Barbados—hence its alternative names of "Barbados cherry" and "West Indies cherry." In fact, it is originally from Central America, yet reached Brazil from its adoptive Bajian homeland. In the 1950s, it was established in the United States due to interest in its vitamin C content, but has since failed to take off.

Malpighia emarginata, a remarkable tree, stands up to 10 feet (3 m) tall and—in the tropics—can flower for most of the year. In the hands of skilled confectioners, its fruit becomes a magical ingredient for cakes, compotes, jams, and ice creams. Acerola's physical beauty has also led canny chefs to use it for decorating salads and main dishes. **AL**

Taste: *Acerola is highly aromatic. It has a pleasantly sour cherry taste with a hint of lime. Wonderful au naturel, it is fantastically refreshing served as a juice or as a drink.*

Pitanga

Small, aromatic, and extremely sweet, with seven or eight distinctive "ribs," this elegant fruit grows wild across a swathe of Latin America, but was named by the Tupi peoples of Brazil's Atlantic coast. Most commonly blazing scarlet, it can also take on other hues, darkening to a purple or near-black.

The pitanga's skin is remarkably delicate considering the fleshy, fragile pulp it has to protect, which makes it a fruit for gardens and domestic orchards only: its fragility means that it is rarely found in markets. All the same, as its other names, which include "Surinam cherry," "Brazilian cherry," "Cayenne cherry," and "Florida cherry," indicate, it has spread widely across the world, from the United States to Sri Lanka and even China.

However, the pitanga is larger than a cherry, with a taste that is stronger and tarter than its namesake. It is great in juices, ice creams, jams, and chutneys. In northeastern Brazil, housewives patiently await the pitanga season from October to January to make a liqueur that is reputed to have aphrodisiac properties. **AL**

Taste: *The pulp of the pitanga is soft and more intensely sweet, yet also sharper than a cherry. The sweetness is rounded off with a refreshing hint of bitterness.*

Davidson's Plum

Jamun

Native to the rainforests of southeast Queensland, the fruit known by Aborigines as "ooray" hangs in clusters amid the dark green, leathery leaves of *Davidsonia pruriens*. It starts off green, deepens to a dark purple or brilliant burgundy upon ripening, and varies when mature from 1 to 2 ½ inches (2.5–6 cm) in diameter. Like the European plum, to which it is not related, the Davidson's plum is soft and juicy, although its firm skin—but for the few sparse hairs that scatter it—is more similar to that of a date. The twin seeds, which together form a teardrop-shaped whole, are densely coated with short fibres.

The rich colour and brilliant pink juices make Davidson's plum a desirable ingredient in otherwise less colourful preparations, while its tang provides balance to chutneys, jams, and sauces. It is one of Australia's most versatile native foods with a pleasantly acid character that, like lemon, works equally well in sweet and savoury dishes. Limited wild harvest supplies are being replaced by cultivated sources from the coasts of Queensland and northern New South Wales. **SC-S**

As much a part of an Indian summer as strawberries are of Western summers, the scorching afternoon siestas of a blazing June are often punctuated by itinerant fruitsellers singing out, "Jamun kah-ley, kah-ley!" (black, black jamuns). Hordes of children come scampering out to buy handfuls of the deep purple berries and wolf them down with a sprinkling of rock salt.

Jamuns are about the size and shape of large black olives and grow on tall, shady trees, which are a popular summer refuge from the heat and sun. Ripe jamuns hang down in bunches and annual contracts are given out to harvest them from trees in public areas, as from June the ripe fruit fall with every gust of wind to be crushed underfoot, staining the streets a livid purple.

Also known as jambul, jambolan, and java plum, *Syzygium cumini* grows over much of the Indian subcontinent and into South East Asia, and is found as far afield as Hawaii and Zanzibar. Besides being a summer snack, the dried and powdered fruit may be used as a digestive or to flavour gravies. **RD**

Taste: *Davidson's plums are sour on their own. Simply stew them in their own weight of sugar to tame the acidity and soften the grass, resin, and green pepper notes.*

Taste: *Varying from sweet to tart, jamuns are mouth-puckeringly astringent when even slightly unripe. Either way, they stain the mouth a deep shade of violet.*

An Indian labourer with his harvest of jamuns. The berries turn from green to nearly black as they ripen. ❯

Illawarra Plum

The Illawarra plum, or brown pine (*Podocarpus elatus*), belongs to an ancient species. A southern hemisphere conifer, it stands tall and proud in dense subtropical riverine, and seashore rainforests along Australia's east coast. Its family name, *Podocarpus*, comes from the Greek for "foot" and "fruit," a reference to the fleshy dark edibles that are botanically the stem of the fruit, yet in culinary terms the fruit itself.

Aborigines and the early settlers of southern New South Wales valued Illawarra plums highly but in Queensland, where there was a greater variety of bush fruit, they were usually left to the possums. The tree produces its plums prolifically: they are a grape-like swelling of juicy flesh that may be up to 1 ¼ inches (3 cm) long, with a hard, inedible, smaller seed attached to their outside edge.

Most supplies of this classic wilderness food come from wild harvest. The plums are used in both sweet and savoury foods but are most often enjoyed in preserves, fruit compotes, baking, and sauces. Chilli and sugar make happy accompaniments. **SC-S**

Taste: The fleshy part of the fruit is subtly sweet with a mild, pleasantly resinous quality. The core is resinous and the flesh closest to it tastes so piny it should be avoided.

Cashew Apple

The cashew apple (or cashew fruit) is one of Brazil's most enticing fruits. With the cashew nut sprouting from one end of its fleshy, almost pear-shaped growth, this pseudo-fruit conceals a lot of juice below its fibrous peel. The intense aroma spreads easily and can perfume a kitchen within seconds.

Widely cultivated along the coast of Brazil's stunning northeast region, to which it is probably native, the cashew apple has long been a favourite of the indigenous population. Ancient tribes used it to make a thick, creamy wine called *mocororó*, which was served at festivals; today the cashew apple makes one of Brazil's most popular fruit juices, found fresh in snack bars and processed in supermarkets.

Anacardium occidentale is also the base ingredient in an unusual juice drink called *cajuína*, made by filtering the juice and cooking it in a bain-marie. It is enjoyed in ice creams, mousses, trifles, jams, and chutneys; reduced on a low heat for many hours it produces the dark, very sweet syrup known as cashew honey. In Goa, the cashew apple is used to produce a liqueur called Fenny. **AL**

Taste: Cashew apples range in colour from pale yellow to vermilion, and have a tangy, sour, astringent bite. If under-ripe, the tannins will cause an unpleasant after-taste.

The cashew nut is removed from the cashew apple and processed as soon as the fruit is harvested. »

Lucuma

This fruit (pronounced loo-ku-mah) is known as the "gold of the Incas"; its Latin name is *Pouteria lucuma*. Although mainly found in Peru, lucuma is also grown in Chile, Brazil, and Ecuador, and it is next to impossible to find it fresh away from these countries. Lucuma is referred to as one of the "lost crops of the Incas"; these are indigenous foods that are now being introduced to the West for the first time.

Similar to a small mango in appearance, lucuma is green-skinned when young, ripening to a warm red. Round or oval in shape, the fruit has golden flesh and a distinct, fragrant flavour, said to be similar to that of maple syrup. The unripe fruit contains a bitter white latex. In South America, lucuma is revered as an ancient and well-loved food, commonly included in celebratory feasts and banquets. One tree can produce as many as 500 fruits in the course of a year, helping to sustain people when field crops are out of season or damaged by drought. At such times the species literally becomes the tree of life.

The fruit can be eaten fresh when ripe and is also consumed in the form of a refreshing drink. Most lucuma is dried and powdered and used in ice creams and other sweets. In Peru, lucuma is one of the most popular flavourings for ice cream. Lucuma pulp is also frozen for export.

Like most golden fruits, lucuma is an excellent source of beta-carotene, as well as being rich in iron and niacin. Powdered lucuma has been gaining popularity among health-conscious Westerners as a low-glycaemic, delicious sweetener for cakes and biscuits. Its syrupy, shortbread flavour makes it an ideal substitute for wheat when making gluten-free versions of traditional treats. **KMW**

Taste: *Usually eaten fresh, out of hand, the highly juicy flesh is slightly fibrous, with an exquisite aroma and a delicate, caramel-like flavour.*

Red Mombin

In conditions as varied as the torrential downpours of the Amazon forest and the dry heat of the savannah, the red mombin flourishes across Latin America under a bewildering range of names—most notably jocote in parts of Mexico (from the Aztec *xocotl*), ciruela, and Spanish plum. Many varieties grow throughout the region—more than twenty in Mexico's Yucatan region alone. The Spanish introduced the fruit to the Philippines also, where it grows well and is known as siniguelas. In the Philippines the fruit is eaten raw or features as an ingredient in the traditional sour stew, sinigang.

With its delicate, thin skin, the red mombin has a simplicity typical of wild fruits: a pleasant, sweet flavour, with contrasting sour nuances, balanced by a citric fragrance. The fruit is small, only 1 to 2 inches (2.5–5 cm) in length, and ranges in shape from rounded to oval, like an olive. It grows on the tree singly or in clusters of two or three and comes in many varying colours, from yellow and orange to deep red or violet. Red mombin fruit is generally harvested from the wild, but research is being undertaken into its potential for cultivation because the tree is easy to propagate and fast-growing.

Naturally juicy and refreshing, *Spondias purpurea* yields a juice perfect for energizing the body on hot days. In Brazil, the juice forms a base for ice creams; in Costa Rica, it is the star of a preserve called "jocote honey." In Nicaragua, where the Pacific Coast was famous for its red mombins back in colonial times, the fruits are also enjoyed "green," before they ripen. To make the most of their intense acidity, they are seasoned with salt and sold by the bagful on the streets of cities such as the capital, Managua. **AL**

Taste: *With the concentrated sweetness of yellow plums and a light acidity reminiscent of a sour orange, the red mombin is fantastic raw, in ice cream, and in cocktails.*

Latin America is seeing greater consumption of red mombin, mainly supplied by local markets. »

Ambarella

Originally native to the Society Islands of the South Pacific, the ambarella fruit (*Spondias dulcis*) is now widely grown in tropical and subtropical areas including South-East Asia, India, Sri Lanka, Australia, Jamaica, Trinidad, and Venezuela. It is consequently known by a bewildering host of names, including golden apple, pomme cythere, Otaheite apple (which derives from Otaheite, the old name for Tahiti), Tahitian quince, hog plum, Brazil plum, Polynesian plum, and Jew plum.

The oval, egg-sized ambarella fruit grows on a handsome, tall, glossy-leafed tree, borne in hanging clusters of between two to ten fruits. The fruit, which is sometimes likened to an inferior mango, has a thin but tough skin with a rough, knobbly surface that ripens from green to a yellowy orange, and contains a few small pale seeds embedded in the centre.

In many countries the fruit is often eaten when unripe, enjoyed for its tangy sourness and crisp texture. Its juice is extracted for cold drinks (often mixed with the juice of other tropical fruits). The flesh can be stewed, sweetened, and then sieved to make a sauce to accompany meat. The ripe flesh is also used to make a cinnamon-flavoured preserve similar to apple butter. The unripe fruit is made into pickles, chutneys, and relishes, used to flavour stews and soups, and added to curries in Sri Lanka. High in pectin, it is often used in jams. In Indonesia, where it is called *kedongdong*, the crisp, sour flesh of the green, unripe fruit is used in *rujak*, a traditional salad dish of raw vegetables tossed with a salty-sweet dressing; the young leaves are steamed and served with salted fish and rice. Sliced and dipped in salt and chilli powder, it is a popular street snack. **CK**

Wampee

A distant relative of the orange, wampee (*Clausena lansium*) looks like a large grape and grows in bunches of up to eighty fruit, each fruit having five segments of soft, highly aromatic flesh. The dense wampee trees with their dark green leaves are native to southern China but provide much-needed shade throughout South East Asia. The tree also grows well in greenhouses in England.

The fruit has many local names, including *wang-pei* in Malaysia, *galumpi* in The Philippines, *hong bi* in Vietnam, and *som-ma-fai* in Thailand, where the wampee has been recognized as the country's finest fruit. In Vietnam and China the halved, sun-dried, immature fruit is used as a remedy for coughs and bronchitis. Dried wampee fruit is very popular in Thailand where it is eaten as a sweet preserve.

Wampee fruits turn yellow when ripe. Although the skin is thin, papery, and easily peeled, it is also minutely hairy, resinous, and quite tough, and therefore should be peeled away before eating. Each fruit contains one or more large seeds, but a seedless variety has been developed in recent years.

In China, wampee is served to accompany meat dishes, and the fruits are also made into pies, jams, and drinks, including a champagne-like aperitif made by fermenting the fruit with sugar and then straining off the juice. A fully ripe, peeled wampee can be eaten fresh, after discarding the large seed or seeds. Jelly can be made only from the acidic under-ripe fruit. The fruit is reputed to have a cooling effect, and the Chinese also prize the fruit as a digestive aid—contending that "When too many lychees have been eaten, wampee will counteract any adverse effects." **WS**

Taste: *Crisp and firm in texture, ambarella fruit has a pleasant, juicy, slightly sour taste. Its flavour and musky aroma are similar to an under-ripe pineapple.*

Taste: *The jelly-like flesh varies from sweet and tangy to sharp and almost sour. Freshly picked, wampees are thirst quenching, refreshing, and a delightful palate cleanser.*

Islands in the South Pacific offer fruit and vegetable species yet to make an impact in the wider world.

Mirabelle

These golden, honey-sweet, walnut-sized plums were first recognized as a separate variety in a seventeenth-century French tract, Lectier's *Catalogue of Cultivated Garden Trees*. Although the fruit is widely grown, Mirabelles have been most closely identified with Lorraine in France, where there are two specific varieties. Both the smaller Mirabelle de Nancy and its sister the Mirabelle de Metz fall under an E.U. Protected Geographical Indication (PGI) that guarantees their provenance. They are grown in orchards and ripen in midsummer. Their smooth skins are often speckled with reddish dots.

When baked, Mirabelles have a sticky, lip-smacking taste that is at its best in *tarte aux mirabelles*. The halved plums are packed on top of a pastry prepared with a yeast dough, then baked in a hot oven until the fruit is lightly caramelized, when it is sprinkled with a little sugar and cinnamon and given a final glaze. Mirabelle sits alongside kirsch and Poire William as one of the eaux-de-vie for which Alsace and Lorraine are most celebrated: the fruit is also popular in jams, jellies, and preserves. **MR**

Taste: *At the peak of maturity, Mirabelles have a syrupy, almost cloying sweetness that is unlike any other plum. Their flavour in an open tart is incomparable.*

Greengage

The story goes that the carrier who was delivering the first greengage trees from France to England thought that the label Gage on his consignment of green plums was the name of the fruit. So while many Europeans know the fruit by some variation on Reine Claude, the wife of Francis I of France (1494–1547), Anglo-Saxons memorialize William Gage, who imported them to Suffolk in 1724.

Not botanically distinct from other plums, most greengages have green skins with especially sweet green or yellow flesh. Round rather than oval, they tend to be smaller than other European plums. (Some, such as the Oullins gage, can be red or green, and larger than the average plum.) They were developed in France and Italy from the domestic plum, possibly crossed with a wild green plum from Asia Minor; France still grows more greengages than anywhere else in the world. Fruit produced in volume for transport can be tasteless compared to those found in a home garden or picked fresh from the orchard. The season in western Europe extends from early July until late September. **AMS**

Taste: *Greengages are best eaten raw and very fresh. Their rich and honeyed sweetness comes as a surprise, in contrast to the acidity their skin colour suggests.*

Blenheim Apricot

Nectarine

Cultivated in China for more than four millennia, over the centuries the apricot has traversed the globe. By the first century CE, cuttings had reached Europe by way of the Middle East. Later, Spanish colonists brought the fruit to Mexico and from there to California. By the turn of the twentieth century, a burgeoning apricot industry was in place in the state, and groves of California's trademark variety, the Blenheim, flourished all around San Jose. But acreage was lost to development, as communities grew, and the farmers moved out to poorer land. Although prized for its flavour and scent, the Blenheim is particularly delicate, and does not hold up well to transport or storage, so during the second half of the century it gave way to sturdier varieties.

By the close of the twentieth century, the Blenheim was in danger of extinction, but the current interest in heirloom fruit varieties is helping rescue it from the brink. Small, often organic, farms are creating a new generation of enthusiasts to support this delicate fruit, seeking it out at farmers' markets or orchard stands in early summer. **CN**

This succulent fruit, produced in orchards around the world, has suffered from its popularity. Few varieties are grown commercially and those are too often picked and marketed under-ripe. But rare varieties such as the yellow-fleshed Vaga Loggia duracina, which grew in Thomas Jefferson's garden, enjoy a special reputation for their flavour.

Peaches were probably first domesticated in China 3,000 years ago. Nectarines evolved from them as a kind of sport or genetic anomaly. With their smooth skins, they look a little like large plums but are not at all related: their English (and French) name, probably comes from German or Dutch and points to the nectar-like sweetness and juiciness of their flesh. Their popularity grew, in Europe, during the seventeenth century. Louis XIV was especially partial to those growing in his *potager* at Versailles.

As with peaches, there are cultivars with white fruits and yellow, with freestones and clingstones. They are best eaten as a table fruit, though many recipes exist, notably the luxurious nectarines macerated in champagne. **MR**

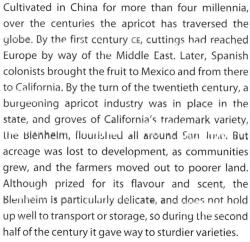

Taste: *Not as juicy-sweet as a peach, apricots tend to have a lovely flavour between sweet and tart. The Blenheim has a rich, full flavour that is remarkably potent for an apricot.*

Taste: *Ripe nectarines have a smooth skin and buttery-textured pulp that is juicy but denser than most peaches. The flavour is perfumed and sweet, with a hint of acidity.*

Pêche de Vigne

Pêche de vigne appears for a fleeting few weeks during late summer, most often in the orchards around the Rhone valley. Its greyish, fuzzy exterior conceals fragrant red or pink flesh that connoisseurs consider the very best peach on the planet.

The name means "peach of the grapevine" and some say it derives from French *vignerons*, who would plant young peach trees at the end of their rows so that they would contract diseases or pests before the grapevines did—rather like a canary in a coal mine. Others say it comes from the colour of the flesh, which can be as bright as red wine lees.

The peach originated in China over 3,000 years ago; there the peach tree symbolizes immortality and springtime. The fruit found its way to the West via the silk roads to Persia—hence its botanical name, *Prunus persica*—which is most likely where Greeks under the leadership of Alexander the Great discovered it and brought it to Europe.

Best simply peeled and eaten au naturel, pêches de vigne are also wonderful sliced and submerged in red dessert wine or a rich rosé. **LF**

Taste: *The sweet-smelling flesh of pêche de vigne combines the light but slightly musky flavour of a juicy white peach with the spirit of sun-kissed raspberries.*

Prunus persica *peach trees blossom in spring.* ❯❯

Green Mango

Alphonso Mango

Any mango (*Mangifera indica*) is called a green mango in its unripe state. The deliciously sour flavour makes this a popular fruit throughout South and South East Asia, where the mango has been cultivated for millennia, although it is now grown and enjoyed in tropical and subtropical climates around the world.

In India, where they are a symbol of imminent richness, green mangoes play an important role in harvest and New Year feasts across the nation, which coincide with the fruit's annual debut around March or April. The tangy, tender fruit are sliced or diced and added to lentils, vegetables, or fish dishes in summer; pickled in mustard oil and spices to last throughout the year; or sun-dried and powdered to become the sour spice amchur. In Thailand, they are used in salads and as a souring agent; in the Philippines, green mango juice is sought-after; in Central America, they are served with salt and spices.

Green mangoes are best plucked fresh from the tree, peeled, and eaten with a sprinkling of chilli powder or rock salt. The sour tang is addictive. **RD**

Mangoes have been a part of India's mystique for millennia, referenced in ancient Hindu scriptures, Chinese Buddhist chronicles, and by countless visiting Europeans down the centuries. This varietal of *Mangifera indica* is known as Haphoos locally, a corruption of its name Alphonso, supposedly after the Portuguese nobleman-adventurer Afonso de Albuquerque who arrived in Goa in 1504 CE.

The Alphonso is western India's pride and joy, dubbed "the king of mangoes" in a nation that grows nearly 70 per cent of the world's mangoes in more than 135 varieties. It appears in Indian fruit stores early on in the mango season, reaching its peak from mid-May to mid-June, and, because it travels well, is increasingly found elsewhere.

No Indian summer can start without biting into a luscious Alphonso then chasing the juice that runs down the forearm with your tongue. Simply cut off the two "cheeks" of the fruit by slicing vertically from stem to tip on either side of the seed, score the flesh in a grid pattern (without piercing the skin), push the skin up to turn out the flesh—and tuck in! **RD**

Taste: *Green skin encloses white or pale yellow flesh. The texture varies from hard to spongy, whereas the flavour can be mouth-puckeringly astringent or delightfully sour.*

Taste: *The Alphonso's deep orangey-saffron flesh covers the large flat seed. The vanilla aroma provides sweet citrus hints; the buttery-sweet flavour offers a dash of tartness.*

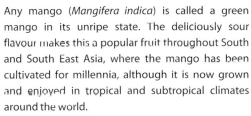

Firmer than their ripe siblings, green mangoes have a sour tang that is valued in many cultures.

Salak

Longan

Known as snakeskin fruit because of their leathery, scaly skin, salak or zalak are native to Indonesia, but also grow in Thailand and Malaysia. The fruit grows in bunches at the base of a short-stemmed palm and is similar in size and shape to a fig or small pear, with a plump, rounded base, and pointed tip. The easiest way to peel salak is to pinch the tip to loosen the thin, reddish-brown skin so it can be pulled away to reveal three segments of creamy, ivory flesh that closely resemble fat cloves of peeled garlic. Each segment contains a hard, inedible seed.

The texture of the different varieties of salak range from moist and juicy to very dry. General consensus holds that the best salak grow on the island of Bali, where they are refreshingly crunchy. Salak from the Yogyakarta region of Java, known as *pondoh,* is thought to have the sweetest flesh, but its pungent aroma is offputting to some. Sweet and acidic, salak are usually eaten fresh, but they are also pickled or tinned in syrup. Their texture makes them good in cooked desserts and they are often added to pies and puddings. **WS**

As the spring comes to a close in southern China, country farmers seem to defy gravity as they travel into the cities with overloaded baskets strapped to all sides of their bicycles. Branches bejewelled with the treat of fresh longan fruit are taken straight from the tree at higher altitudes to hungry city dwellers by makeshift couriers in what has become a seasonal culinary tradition.

Handfuls of the fruit (*Dimocarpus longan)* are the perfect snack and can be had for only a few yuan. The size of large grapes, longans have hard shells that must be pierced to allow the slippery flesh to escape. The art is part skill and part comedy but streets become littered with remnants of the game.

Sometimes called "dragon's eyes," longans are best fresh from the tree or the nearest farm vendor but can also be found dried, jellied, canned in syrup, and even distilled into a mildly alcoholic cordial. While exported to, and increasingly grown in, Western markets, the sweetness of the fruit diminishes in transport compared to China, where numerous cultivars are grown. **TH**

Taste: *Salak tastes like pineapple crossed with the sharp crunchiness of a Granny Smith apple. Its tangy character becomes more pronounced the dryer the flesh becomes.*

Taste: *The fruit is sweet and musky, sometimes, although not always, sharp, but reminiscent of lychees and kiwis. The soft, juicy flesh is completely sealed within the shell.*

The dense clusters of longan fruits are simply cut from the tree during harvesting. »

Lychee

The fruit of a tall evergreen, *Litchi chinensis*, and native to the subtropical parts of Asia, the lychee's mesmerizing qualities are clear from early Chinese lore. The tenth-century writer Ts'ai Hsiang devoted a treatise to the subject; the emperor Hsuan Tsung was reportedly brought down by his concubine's fondness for the fruit; from the first century ce, fast horses used to carry lychees to the imperial court.

Scarlet when ripe on the tree, and—more or less—heart-shaped, this aromatic little fruit has long been associated with romance and credited with aphrodisiac powers, too. The skin has a rough, leathery texture which is easily broken by slight pressure, revealing the translucent whitish flesh around the smooth brown seed at its core.

Like most fruits, lychees are best eaten fresh. However, unlike many fruits, they keep much of their natural flavour even when they are canned or made into juice. The refreshing quality of lychees is savoured in the humid conditions of their subtropical homeland, and has led to their being cultivated in similar climates around the world. **JN**

Taste: *Lychees are sweet and have delicate floral notes with hints of melon. The texture is similar to firm grapes that are plump with juice, although a little more glutinous.*

Rambutan

If the lychee is the blowsy diva of the tropical fruit world, the rambutan is the elegant, honey-voiced recitalist. That said, the appearance of *Nephelium lappaceum* is pure music hall, with a flashy scarlet or yellow coat covered in thin, green-tipped hairs. Native to Malaysia but now grown more widely across Asia, in Australia, and in parts of the Americas, rambutans are valued for their pearly, succulent flesh and their sheer sweetness, accented with a lightly citric tang in some varieties. Like peaches, they come in clingstone and freestone types.

They are best bought fresh and ripe and eaten out of hand the same day: cooking and canning both attenuate their flavour, and adding sugar overwhelms their natural taste. Despite their appearance, they are easy to peel, making them a perfect fruit for snacking. A close cousin of the rambutan called pulasan (*Nephelium mutabile*) has thicker, juicier flesh that when perfectly ripe may even better that of rambutans. Neither rambutans nor pulasans travel well, and are hard to find outside their growing regions. **CTa**

Taste: *A pure burst of sweetness distinguishes the first bite of a ripe rambutan; successive bites reveal a faint, almost lily-like perfume. Sweet-sour cultivars add a lemony note.*

Thailand's floating markets have become a big
⊗ *tourist attraction as well as an outlet for local produce.*

Passion Fruit

The passion fruit is the fruit of a tropical vine, *Passiflora edulis*, which is native to Brazil, although members of the same family are found in tropical regions around the globe. The name, which suits its extraordinary flavour, originates with Christian missionaries who named the flower the "passion flower" in the belief that the shapes of its various parts were symbolic of the crucifixion of Christ: its five stamens supposedly represent the five wounds of Christ, and its three styles the nails that pinned him to the cross.

On plantations, a single vine will easily produce around one hundred fruits each year. The darker, purple-brown passion fruits, which wrinkle when ripe, are better for eating than the prettier, smoother, yellow varieties. Cut open, the fruit reveals a golden-orange pulp, which clusters in teardrop-shaped arils around edible black seeds. The flavour and aroma carry well, making passion fruit a popular flavouring for desserts, drinks, and fragrances. It is probably best enjoyed, however, scooped raw from the half-shell with a spoon. **FC**

Pomegranate

The fruit whose seeds, in ancient Greek mythology, led to Persephone's captivity by Hades, the god of the underworld, has been cultivated in its Asian homeland for several millennia, and has acquired iconic and religious status in many cultures. It is cited in the Koran as an example of the good things God provides, and prescribed as adornment for priestly robes in the book of Exodus. It is a national symbol of Armenia, where folklore suggests that it contains 365 seeds, one for each day of the year.

The pomegranate is the fruit of a small tree, *Punica granatum*, and varies widely in shape and colour. Those that are best for eating have a hard rind coloured anywhere between a mild yellow and a bright crimson, while the interior is laced with clusters of glassy-looking, crystalline arils coloured on a spectrum between white and scarlet and separated by yellowish, pithy membranes. Used in cooking throughout the Caucasus and Middle East, the flavour is often harnessed as a juice or syrup: many commercial versions in the United States and Europe gain their taste from other red berries. **FC**

Taste: *The intensely sharp flavour has notes of mandarin, orange, and pineapple. Most enjoy the contrast of the succulent pulp and the crunch of the mild-flavoured seeds.*

Taste: *Pomegranate pulp is tart, reminiscent of a sweeter cranberry. The skin encasing each aril is firm, delivering a satisfying burst; the seeds have a distinct bitterness.*

All varieties of Passiflora produce spectacular flowers, but the fruits are not equally appealing.

Mangosteen

Known in parts of Asia as "The Queen of Fruits," with the durian as its king, the mangosteen is the fruit of *Garcinia mangostana*, a tall, ultra-tropical tree that can take fifteen years to reach maturity. Airfreighted fruit can be found in luxury food stores in many countries, although these are smaller and less flavoursome than those picked fresh from the tree.

The mangosteen inspires lyricism wherever it is encountered: Queen Victoria allegedly offered a knighthood to anyone who could bring her a mangosteen that had survived its long journey to England and was ready to eat. The hard, maroon rind, whose juice can easily stain, contains between four and eight elegant segments of soft, snow-white flesh; some contain a gelatinous, edible seed.

Mangosteens are best eaten raw, cut neatly in half so that the white fruit rests within the cup of the crimson half-shell and can be carefully extracted with the fingers. However, unripe mangosteens are preserved in Malaysia, and mangosteen juice has been used as a common folk remedy in parts of Asia and marketed with medicinal claims in the West. **FC**

Taste: The creamy flesh is light and sweet, with a delicate sharpness reminiscent of mandarin oranges, and light floral hints of lychee, peach, and strawberry.

In transit, the delicate flesh of the mangosteen is
⊗ *protected from bruising by its thick, fibrous shell.*

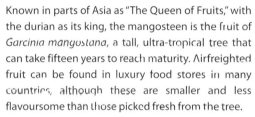

Pequi

There are perhaps few fruits with a scent or flavour as intense as that of the pequi (*Caryocar coriaceum*), which is native to the central savannah region of Brazil. The fruit, which ranges in colour from white to egg yolk yellow, is a highlight of Goiás state's most typical landscape—scrubland dominated by small and twisted trees—and of its home cooking. It stars in two signature dishes, pequi rice (a type of country risotto) and chicken pequi (a traditional chicken stew). Many chefs enjoy the challenge of creating new dishes that combine this aromatic fruit with other ingredients without letting it dominate.

When using the pequi whole in dishes, caution is required beyond the strictly culinary. The flesh must be carefully chewed, as it conceals a stone bristling with spikes which can damage the mouth and tongue. (Most chefs opt to use the flesh with the stone removed.) In addition to savoury dishes, pequi is also used to make an aromatic liqueur for rounding off meals: this can linger on the palate for many hours. Cultivated pequi fruit are preferable to the wild sort, which are under pressure. **AL**

Taste: Pequi's musky aroma is almost untamable and its balsamic oiliness unmistakable. Using it requires care to stop other ingredients next to it from becoming bit players.

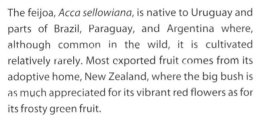

Feijoa

Golden Kiwi Fruit

The feijoa, *Acca sellowiana*, is native to Uruguay and parts of Brazil, Paraguay, and Argentina where, although common in the wild, it is cultivated relatively rarely. Most exported fruit comes from its adoptive home, New Zealand, where the big bush is as much appreciated for its vibrant red flowers as for its frosty green fruit.

Also known as the pineapple guava, each fruit is a smooth or knobbly barrel measuring 3 to 4 inches (7–10 cm), not dissimilar to a small avocado, but with a sensual, intensely perfumed aroma and flavour. The slippery, coated seeds in the translucent central core, the granular texture of the creamy white flesh, and the distinct aroma of guava demonstrate its relationship to the fruit whose name it bears. As with the quince, just a few can scent a room.

Traditionally the feijoa was made into a savoury jelly or bottled to eat during the winter. Today, its unique flavour is appreciated when cooked with apples under a crumble topping or in deep pies, although many prefer to halve the chilled fruit and simply scoop the flesh out raw. **GC**

The kiwi fruit is indigenous to the Yangtze River basin, China, where its local names include monkey peach, macaque peach, and sun peach. It reached its adoptive home, New Zealand, with missionaries at the turn of the last century. *Actinidia deliciosa* originally produced a small, cigar-shaped fruit that New Zealanders tended to cook, producing a gooseberry-like flavour—hence the name, Chinese gooseberry. The fruit's modern success began in the 1960s when the locally bred Hayward variety, with bigger fruit like a flattened barrel, was renamed the kiwi fruit. Today it is grown in many countries.

Golden kiwi fruit, a variety developed in New Zealand, has a yellow flesh speckled with tiny black seeds at the white core. It has a sweeter, more intense tropical flavour than those with the bright green flesh. The kiwi fruit is unique, although sliced or segmented it can become a garnishing cliché. Halved and spooned out, sliced on to cakes, pavlova, or fruit salad, it remains popular. Avoid misuse in ice creams and sorbets; if the seeds are broken by a liquidizer they become particularly bitter. **GC**

Taste: *The scented, full palate combines pineapple and guava, with an initial sweetness that mellows to leave a slightly citric herbal flavour.*

Taste: *The rich, full, honeyed flavour of ripe golden kiwi fruit is initially reminiscent of apples but develops unique sweet aromas and a deliciously long, acidic finish.*

The flowers make the feijoa a most attractive evergreen
❦ *shrub; its fruits should not be eaten if over-ripe.*

Strawberry Guava

With its intense aroma and surprising sharpness on the palate, this cousin of the guava is considered by many gastronomes the best and tastiest fruit in the guava family. Native to Brazil, where it grows wild in some states and is a great countryside delicacy, *Psidium cattleianum* is a spectacularly fertile plant. An evergreen tree, it bears two crops a year in some locations, and fruits virtually year-round in others: a habit that would make it a true plant of the future, but for its tendency to colonize new habitats, wiping out competing native vegetation, which means that many countries now class it as an invasive weed.

The round fruit looks like an egg with skin that can vary from green to red, although yellow types are the best, with juicy, "seedy," white pulp. Delicious eaten unaccompanied and particularly appetizing when fresh, it is also excellent used in jams and sweets: *araçazada* is a popular Brazilian sweet, prepared using purée and cut simply into tablets. The strawberry guava appears in ice creams, liqueurs, juices, jellies, jams, pastes, and sherbets, and also works well in cocktails such as punch. **AL**

Taste: *The juicy pulp has a sourness not usually found in this type of fruit, and the taste is sharp and refreshing, a little like melon mixed with touches of lime.*

Carambola

Pastry chefs adore *Averrhoa carambola* for the decorative five-pointed stars it can be sliced into. To South East Asian palates, carambola has the same ineffably cooling aura as watermelon or papaya. Sweltering tropical humidity or an overheated constitution are agreeably countered by a serving of star fruit juice or slices, carefully seasoned with a pinch of salt.

Carambola's juicy bite makes it a good appetite stimulant and palate cleanser: in countries including Singapore, Malaysia, and Taiwan, it is even considered a cure for sore throats. Today, the star fruit is extensively cultivated outside its homeland, from Australia to China via Latin America and Israel: in the United States, some wine-makers have produced crisp white wines from its juice.

Carambolas are often confused in literature with a close relative, *Averrhoa bilimbi*. Bilimbis taste very similar to carambolas, except more acidic and astringent; they are used to sour curries, pickles, and chutneys in India and South East Asia. Both fruits are also often candied in sugar syrup. **CTa**

Taste: *Barely ripe carambola has a verjuice-like sharpness. As it ripens, it acquires notes of pear, melon, and gooseberry, with a balance of flavours that is lightly sweet and sour.*

Averrhoa carambola *deserves its nickname of "star fruit" for more than its physical shape.* »

Date Plum

Reputed to be the fabled food eaten by the lotus-eaters in Homer's *Odyssey*, the date plum (*Diospyros lotus*) is sometimes confused with the American persimmon, which is a close cousin. The potential confusion is further increased by the fact that another persimmon variety, the kaki (*Diospyros kaki*), is also sometimes called a date plum.

The date plum's precise origins are not clear, but it grows today, both in the wild and in cultivation, in in southeastern Europe and as far east as Japan, China, and Korea. The size of a large cherry, the fruit varies in colour—from yellow to brown-blue-black—depending on ripeness—and has a flavour that is sweet and astringent at the same time. Most fruits contain flat, brown seeds.

Date plums can be eaten raw or cooked. Raw, they can be eaten out of hand, but, unless they are fully ripe, they will be overly harsh and astringent. The fruit can also be used to make jams, puddings, and other fruit desserts. In Asia, the date plum is often dried, when it assumes a more recognizable date-like flavour. **SH**

Taste: *Neither a plum nor a date, a ripe date plum has a very soft flesh and a rich, sweet, slightly spicy taste, similar to that of a persimmon, but less astringent.*

Loquat

Native to China, in the United States and Europe, the loquat is also known as a Japanese medlar—*nèfle du Japon* in France, *nespola giapponese* in Italy—or even, sometimes, just plain medlar. In China, *Eryobotrya japonica* is also known as the pipa, after the ancient Chinese four-string "lute."

Oval shaped, the loquat has a beautiful colour, similar to a ripe apricot or mango, depending on the variety. They have been cultivated in China for over 1,000 years and have been popular in Japan for centuries, but, although they are grown in other parts of the world—notably in Turkey, the Americas, and Australia—they are not an easy fruit to find. When ripe, the loquat bruises very easily and visibly, making it difficult to transport: the skin, which is peeled rather than eaten, is rather thin. The tree is sometimes grown as an ornamental plant.

Delicious raw, the loquat is also dried or cooked, as all the fruit on a tree ripens within a very short time. It can be made into preserves, jellies, syrups, and liqueurs, while in China both the leaves and the dried fruit are used in treatments for coughs. **KKC**

Taste: *The flesh of the loquat has a sweetness, texture, and fragrance that brings apricots to mind. However, the taste is different—both juicier and sharper.*

Loquat fruit trees thrive in the fertile valleys of southern Spain. »

Cape Gooseberry

Agbalumo

Jane Grigson memorably captured the beauty of "the orange-red berry glimmering through its dried out, gauzy calyx" and long before Europeans arrived Native Americans were extracting these pretty round fruit from their papery, parchment-like husks and eating them out of hand or drying them for the winter. It was Australian settlers in the early nineteenth century who christened the Cape gooseberry, however, after the Cape of Good Hope in South Africa, from where it had travelled to them.

Cape gooseberries belong—like other physalis fruits—to the Solanaceae (nightshades), and should not be confused with *Physalis ixocarpa*, the tomatillo. Today they are highly popular and widely cultivated in Hawaii, where they are known as poha berries and used for both sweet and savoury dishes: combined with couscous and coriander, they form an accompaniment to scallops. In Colombia and Andean countries, they feature in yoghurts, ice creams, and savoury sauces, whereas in Brazil and some parts of Europe, they are dipped in chocolate and served as petits fours. **SH**

One of the foods Nigerians are most likely to miss when they live far from home is agbalumo, a fruit that is highly prized for its sweet-sour qualities. The fruit of a tropical canopy tree, *Chrysophyllum albidum*, that is found in lowland mixed rainforest areas in such African countries as Sudan, Kenya, Ghana, Sierra Leone, Uganda, Cameroon, Cote d'Ivoire, and of course Nigeria where the tree is cultivated. The fruit is also known as the "white star apple," after its five-pointed-star-patterned flesh.

Round in shape with a slight point, the fruit measures about 1 inch (2.5 cm) in diameter. The green-grey fruit turns to orange-red, yellow-brown, or yellow, sometimes with speckles, when it is ripe. Agbalumo has a red fleshy interior and creamy white core. It is very popular with children, who as well as eating the flesh, play games with the flat, bean-like, inedible brown seeds. The fruit also takes on the texture of chewing gum when continually chewed. Agbalumo is eaten raw and the pulp is also used to make jams and jellies. Locals also ferment and distil the fruit to produce wine and spirits. **CK**

Taste: *Bittersweet, slightly tart, and quite juicy, Cape gooseberries have some of the acidity of a cherry tomato and notes of citrus fruits, pineapple, peaches, and cherries.*

Taste: *The soft luscious flesh of the ripe agbalumo fruit has a mouthwatering, creamy texture and a sweet-and-sour flavour that is distinctly more-ish.*

Each Cape gooseberry develops inside a
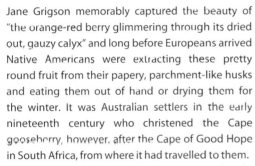 *calyx that is brightly coloured when young.*

Bael

When British botanists visited India in the early nineteenth century they encountered a bewildering array of unfamiliar exotic fruits and they renamed many of them, such as the pineapple and custard apple, as variations of the English apple. The bael, which is also known as bilva, Buddha fruit, holy fruit, and Bengal quince, was dubbed "wood apple."

The thorny bael tree is native to India but grows all over South East Asia. The tree is sacred in the Hindu religion; the god Shiva is said to live under a bael tree and its oval, pointed leaves are used in religious rituals. The tree is prized for its medicinal properties and is used to treat a range of maladies from dysentery to the common cold.

Related to the citrus family, the bael makes a popular breakfast in Indonesia where it is sweetened with palm sugar. In Bangkok, a family-run cottage industry turns dried bael into a tangy syrup with a subtly, smoky flavour. In India, the seeded fruit pulp is mixed with sugar and sometimes tamarind to make a refreshing drink. The fruit can also be made into fruit teas, jams, pickles, and even toffee. **WS**

Cherimoya

The lumpy exterior of this pear-shaped fruit belies the creamy, elegant interior that has led it to be called "the jewel of the Incas." Mark Twain described it as "the most delicious fruit known to men."

Native to Ecuador and Peru, the cherimoya (*Annona cherimola*) is now cultivated not only in Hawaii, where Twain encountered it, but in many subtropical areas around the world, as well as the California coast and New Zealand. Its name is from the language that the ancient Incas spoke—Quechua—and means "cold seeds." The cherimoya is one of several fruits that can also be called "custard apple," because of the custardy texture of its flesh.

When ripe, cherimoyas yield to slight pressure. They can then be halved or sliced, and the flesh scooped out with a spoon. (The seeds and skin are not edible.) Cherimoyas make a valuable addition to a fruit salad of apples, berries, and bananas, or give an interesting flavour contrast when served with red or white wine. Delicious served with ice cream or yoghurt, or mixed with cream into a fool, they also make a good ice cream or sorbet. **SH**

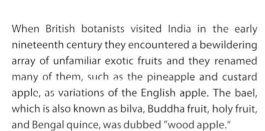

Taste: *The pale orange pulp smells sweet but has a citric, refreshing taste that has a cooling effect on the body. Wild fruits are quite tannic compared with cultivated varieties.*

Taste: *The cherimoya's delicious, creamy white flesh tastes like a gentle blend of banana, papaya, and pineapple with subtle hints of coconut, mango, and vanilla.*

Bael fruit is used in Ayurvedic medicine as an
ingredient of remedies for numerous ailments.

Cupuaçu

A first taste of the cupuaçu is an experience to challenge the senses. Initially, this Amazonian fruit is extremely sweet, but soon a subtle acidity creates a wonderfully refreshing feel, alongside a curious, yet not unpleasant, effect on the palate that could be compared to a mild dose of chloroform.

This relative of the cocoa bean looks as extraordinary as it tastes, with the unrefined look of a fruit normally found growing in dense, unexplored rainforest. The trees can exceed heights of 50 feet (15 m), although farmed varieties seem to shrink to around 10 feet (3 m). The Tupi people of the Amazon called the cupuaçu "big fruit" and *Theobroma grandiflorum* can reach a length of 10 inches (25 cm) and weigh as much as 9 pounds (4 kg).

On opening, the hard, brown shell unleashes an inebriating aroma and reveals a fleshy pulp that varies in colour from white to yellow and hides five rows of seeds. The pulp most often becomes a simple, delicious cream that is used as a base for drinks, liqueurs, ice creams, jams, and superb chocolate-covered sweets. **AL**

Duku

The nondescriptly beige skins of the duku fruit (*Lansium domesticum*) give no hint of the delicious treat they hide. Once peeled, the segments of jelly-like duku flesh burst when bitten into, flooding the mouth with sweet juice. Found across South East Asia under various names, the duku fruit is seasonal and highly perishable once ripe so it is typically enjoyed fresh when available, and is seldom (if ever) cooked.

Duku are round and the size of a golf ball, with thick skins covered in a peach-like fuzz; their white or pink flesh tastes predominantly sweet. A variety of duku, langsat (also classified as *Lansium domesticum*) is smaller, egg-shaped, and has a thinner skin that bleeds a sappy latex when broken open. Langsat taste more tart than duku, and often have bitter seeds. In Thailand, the fruit grows in tightly packed clusters and is known as *longkong*.

Langsat are called *lanzones* in the Philippines, where their flesh is sometimes preserved in syrup. Filipinos also dry the skins, which are then burnt to produce a smoke that repels mosquitoes. **CTa**

Taste: *The inebriating intensity of the cupuaçu becomes fuller on tasting the cream made from it. This mix of fresh cream, sugar, and fruit pulp should be served very chilled.*

Taste: *Good duku have a lavish sugariness. Some prefer the taste of langsat, the sweetness of which is balanced by a tartness reminiscent of grapefruit or carambola.*

Sapodilla

Native to Mexico and Central America, this exotic fruit's first claim to fame was the white, chewy, chicle sap extracted from the bark of its tree, and used to make chewing gum: today the fruit of the sapodilla is also prized. Next to the more glamorous pineapple, mango, or star fruit, *Manilkara zapota*—or sugardilly, tree potato, naseberry, chiku, sapota, nispero, or marmalade plum as it is known elsewhere—would struggle to win any votes in a beauty pageant. Egg-shaped, about the size of an apricot and with a scruffy brown skin when ripe, the kindest description of a sapodilla is that it resembles a raw, rather wrinkly, potato.

Looks can deceive, however, and beneath its unpromising exterior, the sapodilla is sweet and delicious. The flesh ranges from yellow to toffee brown, from smooth and creamy to granular like a ripe pear. The shiny, flat black seeds need to be picked out before eating as each has a small hook at the top that can scrape the back of the throat if swallowed. Eat with a splash of lime, rum, or coconut, or enjoy in ice cream, West Indian style. **WS**

Taste: *The exceptionally sweet flesh of a sapodilla tastes of honey and caramel: some have described it as a cross between brown sugar and root beer.*

Mamee

This unassuming brown fruit, a relative of the mangosteen, grows from the majestic heights of a tree that can reach up to 60–70 feet (18–21 m) high. It has many different names—notably mamey and mamee apple—and a lot of them, for example the English San Domingo apricot, the Brazilian Portuguese *Abricó do purá*, and the French *abricot d'Amerique*, refer to it as apricot. Yet despite the golden colour and peachy texture of the delicious flesh which nestles within leathery skin, the mamee is related to neither the apricot nor the peach.

A native of the West Indies, and probably also Central America, from where it is exported to a range of countries, *Mammea americana* flourishes in the humidity of the equatorial rainforest. The fruit yields large amounts of thick juice and is generally enjoyed au naturel, cut into thick slices, although the pulp finds its way into jams, compotes, ice creams, and preserves. The tree resembles a magnolia, and in the French West Indies mamee flowers add their scent to an aromatic liqueur; in the Dominican Republic, the pulp is used to make a sort of sorbet. **AL**

Taste: *The orange pulp, best eaten plain, is sweet, tangy, and aromatic, similar to a ripe mango, but with hints of vanilla and caramel. It is sometimes compared to apricot.*

Smyrna Fig

Medlar

Like the figs that were first cultivated more than four millennia ago, these sensuous fruit are the product of a peculiar synergy between a small wasp, a semi-wild fig tree known as a caprifig, and a cultivated tree. The wasp hatches in the caprifig, which is not edible, and fertilizes the Smyrna tree that is planted nearby.

Smyrna figs take their name from the Greek form of the Turkish port of Izmir, on the Aegean, and in the Mediterranean may produce two crops a year. The fruit from the second of these crops is generally smaller and sweeter, and best enjoyed straight from the tree. Figs bred for transport and distribution through the modern food chain are tougher and less succulent. The skin colour can vary from green to deep violet, but the pulp is always red and full of "seeds" (botanically, tiny individual fruit).

When the fruit is dried, the seeds add a nuttiness or crunchiness that is not found in other kinds of fig. The boxes in which they are packed sometimes contain a bay leaf to repel weevils, which might otherwise burrow into the dried fruit. **MR**

When ripe, the medlar or *Mespilus germanicus* is the wizened brown fruit of the eponymous tree. The seed boxes are exposed at the rear end, hence its historic English name of openarse. A similar insult is levelled at it in France, where it is called *cul de chien* (dog's bottom). Its official title, however, derives from the Greek *mespilon*, although the Greeks themselves acquired the fruit from the ancient Persians: it is still highly valued in Iran.

The medlar is famous for the fact that it must be eaten in late autumn when the fruit is in a state of putrescence. French writer Jean-Anthelme Brillat-Savarin recognized as much when he classified it among foods eaten in a state of decomposition in *The Physiology of Taste* (1825). Not to everyone's taste, D.H. Lawrence called medlars "wineskins of brown morbidity, autumnal excrementa." However, pigs are fond of medlars, and in the Edwardian writer Saki's story *The Boar-Pig* the malevolent animal is disarmed by a "handful of over-ripe medlars." The Victorians used them to make medlar cheese and jelly, but they are much less common today. **GM**

Taste: *Smyrna figs have a surface texture that is plump but slightly yielding. The pulp, which contains the small seeds, is juicy and melting, and the taste is honeyed.*

Taste: *Medlars come into their own when picked after the frosts. The flesh is opaque, gelatinous, and very sweet, reminiscent of very sugared reinette apples in a tart.*

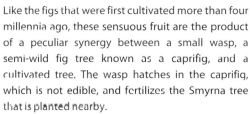

Figs were among the fruits that the ancient Egyptians offered to their gods.

Tamarillo

Naranjilla

Taste a tamarillo and you will remember it always. Smooth scarlet or golden eggs, the fruits hang by threads from a bush that emits the musky scent common to many other Solanaceae. *Cyphomandra betacea* was once called the tree-tomato, and is known as *tomate de arbol* in parts of South America: when cut, it looks very much like a tomato.

A native of the Peruvian Andes, the tamarillo was cultivated in the United States in 1913 and reached New Zealand shortly afterwards. As the intense acid-sweet flavour is too much for many to eat raw, the tamarillo is generally found cooked. It excels in both sweet and savoury guises and, if problems with its fragile skin were to be solved, many believe it could have greater international success than the kiwi fruit.

The golden flesh between the skin and seed-pulp belies what happens when the fruit is chopped, liquidized, or heated; it magically creates the most vibrant blood-red juice that survives cooking beautifully. The name has nothing to do with its origins but was invented as a marketing ploy. **GC**

Deliciously refreshing, with striking pale emerald pulp, the naranjilla (*Solanum quitoense*) thrives in the tropical heat of Peru, Colombia, and, in particular, Ecuador where it is the national fruit. In contrast to the leaves, which are large and covered with a velvety purple down, the fruit of the naranjilla (or lulo) measures only 2 ½ inches (6 cm) or so across and has a bright-orange skin and a hairy coating, which can easily be scuffed off.

Inside, a fleshy membrane divides the pulp into quarters, each studded with tiny seeds, and the flesh is so juicy that the easiest way to eat a freshly picked naranjilla is to remove its stalk and five-point calyx, rub off the fuzzy coat, cut the fruit in half, and squeeze the pulp straight into the mouth.

Rich in minerals and vitamins A and C, naranjilla can be made into ice cream or jam, added to pies, distilled as a wine, or mixed with banana, piled back in the shell, and baked, but it is most popular served as a drink. The pulp is liquidized and strained, then sweetened and poured into long glasses over plenty of ice for a foamy, pastel-green cooler. **WS**

Taste: *Tart, tangy, even sour, tamarillos are best enjoyed with sugar. Their sharpness makes them outstanding poached, in crumbles, sorbets, or savoury relishes.*

Taste: *Fully ripe naranjillas combine the sharp tang of lemon with the mellow sweetness of fresh pineapple. The flesh is soft, very juicy, and has a slightly acidic taste.*

The hairy coating protects the naranjilla until it is ripe, after which the fuzz can be rubbed off. ❯❯

Comice Pear

Nashi Pear

The mid-nineteenth century was a golden age for pomologists. In 1838 the Comice Horticole (Horticultural Association) was founded in Angers, central France, to develop new strains of fruit and flowers. In 1842 it organized the first exhibition of roses in the country. Seven years later it produced a pear variety that has outlasted the multifarious and many-flavoured pears other nurseries offered, and that has stood the test of time as one of Europe's best-loved fruit.

The Comice is a large, rounded pear with a distinct neck. The skin is thin and greenish yellow, sometimes with a rosy blush, and the white flesh is extraordinarily juicy. It forms a favourite partnership with cheese—aged Parmigiano Reggiano or ripe Gorgonzola especially—and retains its shape and taste well when cooked. Pastry chefs bake it on a bed of frangipane for their *tartes aux poires*, and it is also suitable for the popular dessert "pears in red wine." Like other pears, it must be consumed perfectly ripe. It is hard and uninteresting when under-ripe; when over-ripe it is mushy. **MR**

The nashi (or Asian) pear originated in China and has been known in Asia for millennia, in many different varieties and under many different names: nashi is its Japanese name. Unlike Western pears that have to be picked while under-ripe, Asian pears ripen on the tree and can remain there for several weeks, still firm, before being eaten straight after picking.

Nashi pears (*Pyrus pyrifolia*) come in a range of colours, shapes, and sizes. Great care is taken not to bruise or otherwise damage the fruit, which is often sold at extortionate prices for gift purchasers. Popular varieties include Kosui (water of happiness), a small, flat bronze russet; Hosui (water of abundance), which is bronze-skinned but larger, juicy, and sweet with low acidity; and Shinseiki, which is round, yellow, and medium to large in size.

The skin on nashi is always thick and a little rough, so the fruit is peeled. A popular dish in Korea is *yukheo*—shredded nashi pear mixed with raw meat and an egg. In China they are filled with honey and jujube, steamed, and served as dessert; the Japanese eat them chilled with a dusting of salt. **SB**

Taste: Strikingly sweet and juicy with an almost buttery texture; its characteristic flavour note is ratafia-almond. The fruit bruises easily but this does not mar the taste.

Taste: Combining the juiciness of pears and the crispness of apples, nashi pears are exceptionally sweet and crunchy, but dripping with juice.

Valuable as gifts in China, nashi pears are carefully wrapped before transportation. »

Cox's Orange Pippin

Reine des Reinettes

Cox's Orange Pippin is widely regarded as the finest English table apple. Although closely related to the Ribston Pippin, a variety introduced from France in the seventeenth century, the Cox takes its name from a retired brewer who is credited with raising it in about 1825. According to the fruit farmer, David Atkins, "It is like a fragile English girl who can only be pollinated with loving care, a warm bed, and gentle handling." Its survival is a testimony to the skill of British growers.

Medium-sized and 2 to 3 inches (5–8 cm) in diameter, the yellowish green skin is flecked with reddish brushmarks; the flesh is creamy, firm, and very juicy; and the aroma is often described as "spicy." Some connoisseurs believe that the apples should not be harvested in the autumn but left on the trees until winter to allow the complex flavours a chance to develop. However, fruit held in storage for sale throughout the year loses the edge that makes it so special. Cox's apples make a delicious monovarietal apple juice but the fruit is not ideally suited to cooking. **MR**

Despite its status as the most admired table apple in France, it is likely that the Reine des Reinettes in fact originated either in Holland or the German state of Hanover. According to André Leroy's *Dictionary of Pomology* (1873), its original name derives from the daughter of a Hanoverian duke—Louise von Mecklenburg-Strelitz—who became queen of Prussia in 1793. It is probably, he suggests, the same apple as an earlier Dutch variety: the Kroon Renet.

A very pretty round apple, its smooth skin flecked with red and orange, the Reine des Reinettes is harvested late, from October to the end of November, but can be stored naturally until Christmas and beyond. Although eaten raw, it is ideally suited to cooking: slices that are quartered or cut for a *tarte aux pommes* keep their shape well.

The term "reinette" is often used indiscriminately, but there are dozens of different related reinettes, notably the Reinette du Mans, Reinette d'Orléans, and Reinette du Canada. Many of these are delicious but difficult to find outside of private gardens or scattered localities where they survive. **MR**

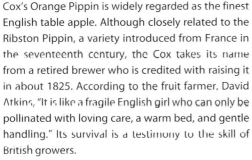

Taste: *"Mango," "melon," and "freshly squeezed Florida orange"—none of these tasting experts' terms adequately describes a fruit so juicy, sweet, crisp, and distinctive.*

Taste: *A crisp, sweet apple with white, juicy flesh. It does not have a marked fragrance, but when cooked it gives off a seductive, honeyed aroma, almost like that of quince.*

In season and freshly picked, the Cox's
❸ ***Orange Pippin has unbeatable flavour.***

Quince

Babaco

Lumpen and yellow, ripe quinces have one of the most delightful fragrances of any fruit: historically, they were sometimes used to scent rooms. The fruit of a small, deciduous tree, *Cydonia oblonga*, it is closely related to the apple and the pear, but was popularized internationally long before the apple: its botanical name derives from Cydonia, now Chania in Crete, where the Greeks developed a superior strain.

The quince has been cultivated for at least 3,000 years and, like other ancient fruits, has acquired layers of cultural symbolism along the way. It was most likely the "golden apple" that Paris awarded to Aphrodite, the Greek goddess of love, sparking the Trojan war; It figures in the Song of Solomon; and it was probably the fruit with which the serpent tempted Eve in the Garden of Eden.

Despite the promise of its honeyed, musky, and floral perfume, most varieties of quince are too sour and astringent to be eaten raw. Quince preserves are popular throughout much of Europe, and the fruit is cooked as an accompaniment to meat in many Middle Eastern cuisines. **FC**

Unknown in the wild, this unusual tropical fruit probably originated as a naturally occurring hybrid of two different types of papaya. Indigenous to Ecuador, babaco (*Carica pentagona*) is now grown commercially elsewhere, but, despite its striking, pentagonal profile and unique flavour, it is farmed only In small quantities, and is considered a rare fruit.

Probably size is part of the issue. Around 8 to 12 inches (20–30 cm) long and 4 inches (10 cm) in diameter, it is a substantial fruit that generally weighs around 2 pounds (1 kg): a size and price that discourages impulse buying and makes it hard to find except in speciality markets.

The babaco turns from green to yellow, and becomes very fragrant when fully ripe. Both the skin and the seedless flesh are edible. Because its flesh has an effervescent quality, babaco is sometimes referred to as "champagne fruit." It is best eaten raw, cut into thick, crosswise slices and sprinkled with lemon juice and sugar. Babaco juice has long been a refreshing breakfast drink in Ecuador. Mixed with ice cream or yoghurt, it makes delicious milkshakes. **SH**

Taste: Cooked with sweeteners, the flavours develop into a supercharged blend akin to an abstract essence of apples and pears, while the colour becomes rich sunset.

Taste: The riper and softer the fruit, the better the flavour. Slightly acidic and not too sweet, babaco's unique taste blends notes of papaya, strawberry, and pineapple.

Quince is delicious made into a paste, dusted
◉ *with sugar, and served in cubes as a sweetmeat.*

Crabapple

Cicely Mary Barker's Crabapple Fairy hymned her trademark flower thus: "Crab-apples, Crab-apples, out in the wood, / Little and bitter, yet little and good!" And these tiny sour apples, when cooked, far out-perform their distinctive sourness when raw.

Species of crabapples, wild or cultivated, are found in North America, Europe, and Asia, although it is Anglo-Saxons who seem to like them best. In Britain they can be found growing wild in woods (mostly oak woods) and hedgerows. In Northumbria they are known as "scroggs." They can vary in size from that of a plump cherry to that of a golf ball, and tend to have long stalks, which makes them look rather like cherries. Their colour can vary from deep pink to yellow-green, depending on the variety. Because the Latin word for apple tree is *malus* and the Latin word for evil is also *malus*, the apple has long been associated with Adam and Eve and their exit from paradise. Yet alongside these sinful associations, the apple has also been considered the fruit of health: in England, an apple a day is still said to keep the doctor away.

Crabapples are extremely tart, but have a high content of pectin (a natural setting agent). Combining them with low-pectin fruits is a way of ensuring jam has a good set. In medieval England, crabapples were cooked with honey and spices for use as a pie filling. They make a delightful jelly that is delicious spread on scones or toast, and which also pairs beautifully with savoury foods such as roast game and meats. They can be added to pies and chutneys, or made into a potent crabapple wine. In the United States they are spiced and preserved whole to serve alongside pork and poultry. **LF**

Ber

Also known as Indian jujube or Chinese date, ber is one of the subcontinent's most ancient and highly prized fruits. Ber trees can grow to a height of 40 feet (12 m), and the fruits vary in colour from green to reddish purple to dark brown. The fruits' size and shape vary, too: wild fruits tend to be small, around 1 inch (2.5 cm) in length, whereas cultivated fruit grow to 2 inches (5 cm) long, and they can be round, oval, or oblong. The fruits ripen at different times, even those growing on a single tree.

Believed to be native to tropical India, ber has migrated to other parts of the world, being cultivated in Australasia and Africa, where it is an important crop. In China, it has been cultivated for more than 4,000 years. American explorer David Fairchild encountered the fruit for the first time in 1938 on a boat leaving Shanghai, observing that "Ripe jujubes when eaten raw are amusing rather than delicious and have a crisp, sprightly flavour different from other fruits."

Most Indians believe that ripe ber fruit is best eaten fresh, but it can also be boiled with rice or millet and stewed or baked. Ber is also used in sweet dishes, drinks, butters, and spreads, or candied as sweetmeats. Sour, unripe fruit is not allowed to go to waste, although it has to be pickled to make it palatable. The fruit is easily digestible, but it can act as a mild laxative. The leaves from the ber tree can be eaten as a vegetable with couscous.

Ripe ber has a high sugar content, is rich in carotene, vitamin A, phosphorus, and calcium, and has one of the highest levels of vitamin C of all fruits. Ber fruits have a short storage life and should be kept in a cool, dry place. **WS**

Taste: *Raw crabapples are an acquired taste: pleasantly crunchy but distinctly acerbic. Crabapple jelly is wobbly, lustrous, sharp, and fantastic with roast pork.*

Taste: *A ripe ber fruit is rich, juicy, and deliciously sweet with a hint of mild acidity. Some varieties of ber have soft pulp, whereas others have crisp, firm flesh.*

Often considered purely ornamental,
◖ *crabapples make a delicious jelly.*

Jabuticaba

Some see the jabuticaba as an extravagance of nature, a fruit bequeathed from father to son. It takes over a decade for the tree, a native of the Brazilian Atlantic rainforest, to reach sufficient maturity for the delicately flavoured, small fruit to sprout from its trunk and branches, coloured from violet to black and little larger than a grape. And, in the manner of the ancient grapevines from which the Brazilian grape tree takes its name, the older the tree, the better the fruit.

After picking, the jabuticaba has a life of no longer than thirty hours before it spoils, becoming sour and inedible. Housewives from the state of Minas Gerais use it to make jams, compotes, a liqueur, and a spirit that is not distilled industrially, but created and recreated using household recipes passed on from mother to daughter. The jabuticaba also has its place in haute cuisine. French chefs living in Brazil, such as Claude Troisgros, son of the legendary Pierre Troisgros, have used it to create sauces to accompany *magret de canard* and game. This is a perfect combination. **AL**

Kyoho Grape

In Japan, Kyoho grapes are considered the essence of grapes. The short season, exceptional flavour, and regal appearance of these large, dark purple fruits mean they come with a hefty price tag. This makes them more desirable to the Japanese, who prize exclusivity and cost in their gifts. The grapes are given as gifts during the traditional August season.

A cross between the varieties Campbell and Centennial, Kyoho originate from Kyushu, Japan's southern island. The name means "great mountain" and the best still grow in the region of Tanushimaru on the fertile Chikugo Plain at the base of the Mino Mountains. The best Japanese Kyoho grapes are the size of small plums with a thick velvety skin, spectacularly sweet flesh, and large seeds that are bitter and inedible. Served cold, peeled, and unadorned, they make a luxurious dessert. They are also at the heart of the exclusive Kyoho wine.

Kyoho grapes are now cultivated outside Japan, notably in Korea, Taiwan, California, and Chile, which means they are available outside Japan, for a longer season, and at less phenomenal prices. **SB**

Taste: *The white pulp around the large stone is fabulously sweet, and the skin deliciously tannic. The aroma and flavour of the whole is reminiscent of red grapes.*

Taste: *The flesh is very sweet with a strong "grapeyness." The high sugar content means the texture is soft and slightly sticky; the scent is like super-charged Muscat.*

Muscat Grape

Muscadine

These honeyed fruit may be the world's oldest cultivated grape variety. They probably originated in Greece, but passed via the Roman Empire to what is now France. During the reign of the Emperor Charlemagne, Muscat grapes were being exported from the Frankish port of Frontignan. The name could be linked to the Islamic port of Muscat, once a part of Arabia, now part of Oman, or simply be a reference to their distinctive musky aroma

There are more than 200 cultivars of Muscat—and counting. Different types are grown around the world both for eating and for wine-making: fruits can be coloured "white," black, green, red, and amber, can have thinner or thicker skins, come with seeds, and without. Some, notably the famous Belgian Muscats that are delivered to Buckingham Palace, are grown under glass, others are ripened by the sun. Although the vast majority of table grapes are grown for convenience rather than flavour, Muscat varieties are always recognizable as such, regardless of the strain or the provenance, so long as they are harvested ripe and eaten at once. **MR**

When European navigators explored the coasts of North Carolina, they remarked on the many grapes that grew there. In 1584, Walter Raleigh's juniors remarked that "In all the world, the like abundance is not to be found." The native muscadine, however, is a very different species from the European grape. *Vitis rotundifolia* is larger and sturdier, with a thicker skin: it loves heat and humidity, and dislikes cold weather. Once part of the diet of Native Americans, who some say knocked grapes from the vines with a stick rather than harvest them, the grapes have a musky, intense flavour, which lends them to eating out of hand. Also known as scuppernong, they were used for wine as early as the sixteenth century, although vintages tend to the bland and sweet.

Home cooks usually turn the purple, bronze, or pale gold fruit into sauces, jellies, and preserves, but chefs use them in soups or relishes, or as garnishes for meats, poultry, and fish. Varieties of muscadine are known as "southern fox," and commercial products often return home as souvenirs with visitors to the South. **SH**

Taste: *Muscat grapes are always honeyed, sweet, and floral, yet with a distinctly musky air. They often have nuances of attar of roses or orange-flower water.*

Taste: *Muscadine pulp tastes more like wine than other grapes. It is juicy, sweet, and intense. The thick skin is tart: when eaten out of hand, the pulp is squeezed from the skin.*

Honey Jack

Durian

Although multifarious varieties of jackfruit can be found growing throughout South East Asia and in other tropical areas of the world, it is the honey jack or *peniwaraka*, as it is also known, that is the most highly prized for its sweet flavour.

The largest of all tree fruits, jackfruit can grow to a staggering 3 feet (90 cm) long and sometimes weigh up to 90 pounds (41 kg). They are thought to have originated in the rainforests of the Western Ghats, a mountain range running down the southwest coast of India. In South India, jackfruit are an important part of the local diet, being eaten both unripe as a vegetable and ripe as a fruit.

The ripe fruit has a noxious scent of rotting onions and is best prepared outdoors. When the fruit is cut open, copious amounts of sticky gum flow out and will coat the knife and the hands of the person preparing the fruit unless both are rubbed with vegetable oil first. Because of this jackfruit is often sold ready to eat, canned or in shrink-wrapped plastic trays. Inside the honey jack small, yellow-gold bulbs enclose a seed that is edible when boiled. **WS**

Known by many as the "king of fruits," the durian is the fruit of a tall tree, *Durio zibethinus*, which is native to Malaysia and cultivated in other South East Asian countries. The name derives from the Malay word for spike, *duri*, and this exotic-looking creature is coated in them. The large, thorny shell that encases the creamy fruit looks for all the world like a spiky football. It is never picked, but is allowed to ripen fully then collected once it has fallen from its branches into the canopy nets below.

The durian is known primarily for its offensive and confronting odour, which is often compared with the stench of spoiled meat and has resulted in its prohibition from hotels and public transport systems in its home territories. Yet this remains a fruit that inspires devotion, and its flesh is highly valued for its unique flavour. It is used in both sweet and savoury dishes across South East Asia.

Some Western countries import snap-frozen durians for immediate consumption, although nothing compares with cracking open a fresh durian at a roadside stall in the blazing tropical heat. **JN**

Taste: *Ripe jackfruit are soft and sweet with the honey jack being the sweetest and most aromatic of all—a luscious cross between a pineapple and a banana.*

Taste: *The flesh is eaten off the seed like ice cream from a cone. The texture is creamy and reminiscent of custard, with a subtle sweetness that offers hints of rum and raisin.*

Most hotels in South East Asia ban durian because of its pungent odour. »

Charentais Melon

Shizuoka Melon

What is in a name? In France, the terms "Charentais" and "Cavaillon" are almost interchangeable as a signifier of quality. They refer respectively to melons grown in the Charentes, a *département* in the west of the country, and those from northern Provence. Both are direct descendants of the Cantaloupe melons that monks introduced from Italy during the sixteenth century, though the word Cantaloupe was not used until the fruit had developed from a rare epicurean treat into a more widespread delicacy some 200 years later. By the early nineteenth century Charentes was recognized as an area that produced some of the best crops.

Round, and 6 to 10 inches (15–25 cm) in diameter, the Charentais was once recognizable by a coarse irregular network of lines on its surface. Modern hybrids have a smoother skin with stripes running down the sides. The flesh varies from orange to pink, but is always soft and very juicy. Choosing a ripe melon requires a good sense of smell, and those in the know press around the peduncle (stalk) in search of the subtle give that indicates ripeness. **MR**

Renowned for its precious muskmelons grown under glass, Shizuoka is a Japanese prefecture west of Tokyo. Only the costly price tag is likely to deter people from sampling the delectable Shizuoka melon (*Cucumis melo*). In Japan fruits such as melons, grapes, cherries, peaches, and pears are specially grown and given as luxury gifts. The practice is most popular at the two peak gift-giving seasons, at the end of the year or mid-summer, to friends, family, and business clients.

Shizuoka melons are meticulously cultivated in high-tech, air-conditioned greenhouses to ensure their perfectly formed appearance. The melon vines are planted in soil bedding that is separated from the ground so as to regulate moisture levels, and temperatures are carefully and continually monitored to optimum levels. The vines are trimmed so that only three melons grow on each plant; when the baby melons reach the size of a human fist, two are removed to allow the most promising melon to take all the nourishment from the vine and mature into the juicy delicacy that is a Shizuoka melon. **CK**

Taste: *More than other kinds of melon, a Charentais at its peak has an exotic, sweet, almost musky perfume. The flesh stays tender right down to the rind.*

Taste: *A Shizuoka melon has a sweet taste that is finely balanced with a slight hint of sourness. The melon has an appealing musky aroma and a perfectly round shape.*

The Japanese offer Shizuoka melons in elegant wooden boxes as presents. »

YOKOHAMA MIZUNOBU **Fruit gift**

静岡県産

温室マスクメロン

2個

税込 **¥20000**

Cassabanana

Watermelon

Few plant species have a fragrance as distinct as cassabanana. Its deep, involving aroma emanates not just from the fruit but from the flowers of this perennial creeper. Of Brazilian origin, *Sicana odorifera* is now found in almost all of tropical America. Long, cylindrical, and reminiscent of a giant cucumber—hence its alternate name "musk cucumber"—it comes in festive colours of orange, red, purple, or indigo, and assails the nose with an aroma like super-charged fresh melon.

The fruit shares a number of characteristics with its pumpkin relatives: it is protected by a hard skin and has orange, fleshy pulp with strips of flat seeds. Due to its refreshing taste, the cassabanana should be enjoyed pure, either in its natural state or chilled; cut into small pieces with the seeds removed, it tastes good in a fruit salad. Brazilians prefer to add sugar, even at the fully ripe stage. A versatile ingredient, cassabanana can be found in jams, chutneys, and other compotes, as well as a variety of sweets. While under-ripe it works well as a vegetable, simply sliced and added to soups and stews. **AL**

Mark Twain called watermelon "chief of this world's luxuries . . . When one has tasted it, he knows what Angels eat." Native to central Africa, *Citrullus lanatus* was cultivated and eaten in Egypt long before 2,000 BCE. It probably came to Europe when the Moors invaded Spain; it reached the New World on slave ships. Although in most of the Western world watermelon is considered a dessert, in arid countries it has long been used as a source of water as well as a vessel for carrying water.

In general, the watermelon is a large fruit: most varieties come to market weighing 10 to 25 pounds (5–11 kg), although some, such as Sugar Baby and Bambino, are considerably smaller. The flesh may be red, pink, or yellow. The rind, which may be striped or plain, is completely edible and often pickled; the seeds, which may be brown or black, can be toasted and eaten out of hand.

In 1981 a farmer from Zentsuji, Japan, developed a square watermelon for easy storage where space was at a premium. These curios are now beginning to be available elsewhere. **SH**

Taste: *Nothing beats eating the cassabanana fresh and ripe. The potent fragrance leads to a clean taste with melon to the fore and banana nestled discreetly behind it.*

Taste: *Sweet but somewhat bland, with a grainy texture that collapses refreshingly in the mouth. When chilled, it seems as much a beverage as a fruit.*

Watermelons can grow in arid terrain such as deserts, providing a welcome source of refreshment. ⊗

Lacatan Banana

When the first bananas reached Europe, in the sixteenth and seventeenth centuries, they acquired names such as Adam's fig or *figue du Paradis* (Paradise fig), raising the intriguing possibility that the banana was the fruit of the Tree of Knowledge, and that Adam's modesty was preserved with a comfortably-large banana leaf rather than the more delicate fig. But, despite its apparent resemblance to a small palm, the banana plant is not a tree but a herb that dies back at the end of the growing season and must produce a new trunk each year.

Today numerous varieties of banana plant grow in the tropics, but many consider the Lacatan from the Philippines one of the best in the world. On the small side, or at least to European and North American eyes, the Lacatan is a delicate, yet disease-resistant hybrid that is now also grown in Jamaica, other Caribbean islands, and parts of Latin America. Like other bananas destined for export, Lacatans are picked when two-thirds ripe: while bananas ripen well off the stem, the flavours of those picked fresh from the "tree" are the best. **WS**

Taste: *Highly fragrant, the Lacatan banana has sweet firm flesh that is equally delicious eaten raw or baked. The flesh turns a golden orangey yellow when ripe.*

Red Banana

In 1889 an advertisement for bananas informed the U.S. public that "there are two kinds, the yellow and the red. The latter is considered the best." Despite their price being twice that of ordinary bananas—a fact that caused detractors to mutter darkly about "customers paying for their colour"—red bananas soon became popular. By the early twentieth century *The Boston Cooking School Cookbook* recommended them for a dessert entitled "Tropical Snow."

Red bananas continue to be prized above yellow-skinned varieties, and are still found in the United States, although most are so frail and short-lived they stay in the Caribbean and Asian regions where they grow. They can replace yellow bananas in any cooked dish but their superior flavour means most people prefer to eat them raw. Red bananas range in colour from orange or reddish brown to maroon or purple—some are variegated, with green stripes. As they ripen, like other bananas, they give off ethylene (a gas that helps some fruit develop colour and ripeness) in such large quantities that they can help a hard avocado ripen overnight. **WS**

Taste: *When fully ripe, the luscious flesh of red bananas is a creamy pink and very sweet. The rich flavour combines classic banana notes with strawberry.*

Banana plantations have spread over vast areas of tropical lowlands. ⟫

Abacaxi Pineapple

Azores Pineapple

Long, long before Columbus arrived on the continent, the indigenous people of the Brazilian lowlands were already enjoying the delights of a tough-looking fruit with a seductive, citric aroma: the pineapple. It was soon domesticated, and spread from Brazil to the hotter parts of South and Central America, getting as far as Mexico, where its allure was immediately noticed by European colonizers.

The Abacaxi is a particularly succulent, fragrant type of pineapple, with white or pale yellow flesh and only a tiny core. A tall and beautiful fruit, from the same family as many of the world's most beautiful flowers, it grows as a cluster of individual fruitlets amid a crown of sharp, pointed leaves.

There is no substitute for an Abacaxi served fresh and perfectly ripe. It makes fine desserts, from tarts and cakes to bon bons. Its well-balanced acidity makes it an ideal garnish for roasted meats, either pure or in a sweet sauce. Although dismissed by many, the skin is used to make an excellent drink in Brazilian homes, simply boiled in water, strained, sweetened, and served chilled. **AL**

A taste of the past, the Azores pineapple (DOP) is grown with great care under glass, like the fruit so lovingly tended in the hothouses of grand homes during the eighteenth century. The Azores, a cluster of nine volcanic islands stranded in the mid-Atlantic, belong to Portugal and have been inhabited since the fifteenth century. Until 250 years ago, the principal export crop was oranges. When these were ravaged by disease, the islanders switched to growing pineapples, especially for the luxury English market where they were the most fashionable fruit. This unique, year-round harvest is still valued today.

São Miguel is the main producer of a type of Smooth Cayenne pineapple called St. Michael. The Gulf Stream flows past the islands, so the climate is temperate all year round, but there are differences in sweetness between winter pineapples and those that ripen in summer. The latter are eaten as a dessert whereas those harvested in January or February are served mostly as a vegetable to accompany grilled beef or the lightly smoked black pudding that is served in the *tascas*, or bars. **MR**

Taste: *The Abacaxi has an intense citric perfume and a sweet flavour. Best enjoyed au naturel, it is also excellent grilled and sprinkled with a touch of sugar and cinnamon.*

Taste: *Large, juicy, and tender, Azores pineapples are sweet-and-sour in winter and sugary in summer. Both kinds have a potent scent and are never sold under-ripe.*

The English named the pineapple after the pine cone, a reference to its bumpy skin.

Kumquat

In China, just before the start of the Lunar New Year, small kumquat trees are positioned at the doors of homes and businesses to bring good luck and prosperity. For the Chinese, it is impossible to think of New Year without kumquats: the little, glossy orange citrus is as essential to the festival as lion dancers, peach blossoms, and children waving their scarlet packets of "lucky money."

The small fruit rarely reach more than 1 ¼ inches (3 cm) in diameter, and have a bittersweet flavour that is the reverse of most citrus fruits: rather than the pulp being sweet and the rind bitter, it is the kumquat's skin that is sweet, and the flesh that is sour. Round varieties tend to be sweeter than the oval ones.

Fresh kumquats are usually eaten whole so the sweet and sour flavours balance one another. They are delicious candied or preserved in syrup, and make vibrantly coloured marmalades. They can also be used in relishes or pickles. In China, a powder of salt-cured kumquat is dissolved in hot water and sipped to soothe sore throats; some bartenders infuse the fruit in vodka to use in cocktails. **KKC**

Yuzu

The most cold-resistant of all the citrus fruits, yuzu is about the size of a mandarin, and some believe it originated as a hybrid of one. It grows wild in Korea and Tibet, but is most associated with Japan, where it was introduced over 1,000 years ago.

Yuzu is mainly used in Japan for its uniquely fragrant peel, which is added at the last minute to soups, salads, and simmered dishes. Sweet white miso flavoured with yuzu is a popular dressing for *aemono*; while the well-known dipping sauce ponzu is made with the juice of either yuzu, or the sour green fruits sudachi (*Citrus sudachi*) and kabosu (*Citrus sphaerocarpa*). Koreans make a sweet yuzu marmalade which is diluted with hot water to create an aromatic and vitamin C-laden tea. Western chefs have also discovered the joys of yuzu, and both the juice and the zest are used to flavour ice creams, brûlées, biscuits, and all manner of dishes, both Japanese and fusion.

It is traditional in Japan to put a whole yuzu or two, or its skin, in the bath on the day of the Winter Solstice to protect against winter colds and flu. **SB**

Taste: *Popped into the mouth fresh, the bittersweet aroma of the thin, honeyed skin gives way to a satisfying and extremely sour citrus burst of pulp and pips.*

Taste: *Although lime and lemon are often prescribed as substitutes for this sharp, acidic fruit, yuzu has a distinctive highly fragrant aroma. This is released on gentle heating.*

The kumquat tree's size made it a table-top dessert ❸ for the Victorians, and a staple of Chinese New Year.

Clementine

Sorrento Lemon

It is unclear precisely how this delicious little citrus fruit originated: some believe a priest named Père Clément cross-bred it from a mandarin orange and a sour orange in Algeria some time around 1900. Others think it is just a type of tangerine.

Unlike other citrus fruits such as oranges, limes, and lemons, clementines have a fleeting season: they are usually only available for a few months in the winter. They are small, generally a little larger than a golf ball, with a bright orange hue and very thin skin, which, as with tangerines, satsumas, and mandarin oranges, is loose and easy to peel.

The clementine is rather expensive to use as a common source for juice, and has a low yield compared to oranges. Cooking with the juice destroys its elusive flavour, while the thin skin is unsuitable for marmalade. The clementine is, however, delicious when the peeled fruit, broken apart into segments, is frozen for about thirty minutes—just long enough for the membrane to freeze so it turns shatteringly crisp and delicate, creating a fine contrast to the juicy flesh within. **KKC**

Sunshine yellow, egg-shaped, and distinctively knobbly, Sorrento lemons (PGI) have been appreciated for their exceptional flavour and aroma for centuries. Known to the locals as *sfusato amalfitano*, wall paintings and mosaics uncovered at Pompeii and Herculaneum suggest that these most prized lemons were being cultivated as long ago as the first century. Like other lemons, the parent stock most likely originated in northern India, and arrived by way of the Middle East.

The fruits' pronounced lemony flavour, highly scented skin, and juicy, sparsely seeded flesh ooze vitamin C, and this exceptional combination has earned them a shining reputation worldwide. Traditionally, they were grown along steep terraces, and matured under straw mats known as *pagliarelle*. Today it is nets, not mats, that ensure the fruit are protected from the elements. Their PGI status means that Sorrento lemons must be grown within a designated geographical area, and only fruits weighing 3 ounces (80 g) or more may be sold under the name. **LF**

Taste: *The sweet, juicy, refreshing flesh has a delicate membrane and is usually seedless. Both the skin and the flesh are wonderfully fragrant. Pure pleasure to eat.*

Taste: *Fragrant, thin-skinned, sweet, and tangy, with concentrated citrus oils very much in evidence, the raw fruit is often eaten dusted with icing sugar, skin and all.*

A Sorrento lemon grove in Campania, southern Italy, shares its territory with brilliant red poppies. »

Key Lime

Finger Lime

Widely grown in tropical regions around the world, the Key lime (*Citrus aurantifolia*) is the lime that started it all. But despite its association with the Florida Keys and the Caribbean, it originated in Malaysia. It was most likely the Arabs who carried the fruit into Europe: it was known and cultivated not only in Spain but in Italy and possibly France by the middle of the thirteenth century. European colonists brought it to south Florida and other parts of the New World three centuries later, although the Miami hurricane of 1926 wiped out commercial Key lime production in Florida, and today Mexico and Malaysia are two of the bigger producers.

About the size of a golf ball, these neat little fruits are more yellow than green when ripe. They are most prized for their juice, which can be used as a marinade, in cooking, or as a beverage: whether paired with salt, as in the classic margarita formulations, or sugar, in limeade or cordials. Key lime pie is the most famous dish made from the juice: a creamy pie topped with a dollop of whipped cream and garnished with a lime slice. **SH**

Named because of their resemblance to chubby digits, these Australian native citrus fruits are gaining popularity among chefs as much for their flavour as their appearance, which ranges in colour from purple or black to green, yellow, and bright pink. Yet the fruit have not always been so highly regarded. Although we can assume Aborigines ate the species known as *Citrus australasica*, and the early settlers to Australia used them for marmalade, farmers in the fertile Northern Rivers region of New South Wales and southeast Queensland worked hard to rid their lands of the spiny, sprawling tree that interfered with their cattle grazing.

Dubbed "caviar lime," the fruits have jewel-like, colourful vesicles that burst from the skin upon cutting like tiny citrus bath balls. These are housed in about six equal-sized loculi, and make an attractive addition to dressings and drinks, and a flavoursome contribution to curd, sauces, jams, or chutneys. The aromatic skin has a glossy appearance and a slightly greasy texture due to surface oil cells; it can be dried and used like any other citrus peel in cooking. **SC-S**

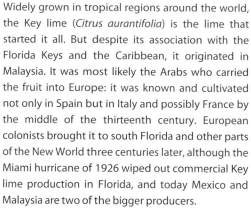

Taste: *Extremely fragrant and pale in colour, Key limes have a delicate citrusy lime flavour that is slightly acidic. They are tart, but with an underlying hint of sweetness.*

Taste: *The vesicles have a citrus tang with a subtle hint of turpentine. The slightest pressure from the teeth pops the casing and delivers a refreshing burst of juice.*

Calamansi

Citron

Most likely descended from a mandarin-kumquat cross of old and obscure origins, the calamansi barely reaches 1 inch (2.5 cm) in width, but its small form hides a citrus flavour that combines the sourness of lime with the sunny notes of tangerine.

A popular, easily grown tree across South East Asia, x *Citrofortunella microcarpa* are enjoyed for their fragrant flowers and glossy foliage as well as their fruit. In Indonesia, Malaysia, Singapore, and the Philippines, calamansi is treated as a type of lime. It harmonizes well with other key Asian ingredients, such as coconut milk, fish sauce, soy sauce, shrimp paste, and chilli. Grilled or barbecued seafoods, especially if doused in spicy sambals, are often served with calamansi on the side, and it works wonderfully in the Filipino marinated fish salad kinilaw. Calamansis are juiced to make drinks, squeezed over cut fruit, and are often a default garnish for street food, such as fried noodles, whose rich ingredients require a sour foil. Modern pastry chefs are harnessing calamansi's palate-cleansing power in sorbets and a variety of desserts. **CTa**

Unusually for a fruit, the citron is valued not for its flesh, which is quite dry and hard to separate from its outer skin, but for its peel. It looks like a large, very knobbly lemon, but was popular long before its rival, finding its way from the perfumeries of ancient India to the household altars of China and Japan. The earliest written reference to citron is in the Indian *Vajasaneyi Samhita*, from before 800 BCE: Kubera, the Hindu god of wealth, often carries the fruit in his hand.

Most citrons are roughly egg-shaped—some can reach as much as 1 foot (30 cm) long—but one variety has a particularly spectacular appearance. Grown mainly in Japan and China, the Buddha's Hand Citron sprouts from its stem many separate, or nearly separated, lobes. Although highly fragrant, it contains little pulp.

While the juice and flesh found uses in older times, today it is the peel that finds most use. Candied, it is used in confectionery and baking: it may be an ingredient in fruit cake, plum pudding, and similar products, and makes a delicious addition to panforte. **SH**

Taste: *Calamansi juice rounds out the tart zip of lime with fruity notes of tangerine and musk. Its aromatic zest has a similarly wonderful fragrance, but with bitter notes.*

Taste: *The peel of the citron is thick, and aromatic, almost resinous, with bittersweet, citrusy, and lemon zest flavours that respond well to candying. The flesh is unremarkable.*

Jaffa Orange

Blood Orange

Some say this is the only orange in the world worth eating. Called Shamouti or Khalili in the Near East and Jaffa in the Western world, this extremely fragrant fruit appeared near Jaffa in the mid-nineteenth century—some say in 1844—when the area, part of the Ottoman Empire, was known as Palestine. Although cultivated elsewhere in the eastern Mediterranean, today it is most closely linked with its original home in what is now Israel.

A medium to large orange, the Jaffa is believed to have first appeared as a "limb sport"—a mutation whereby one branch of a tree bears different fruit from the rest—on a type of local orange. It was exported to England early on, during British rule in Palestine, and became very popular. In the 1930s, it gave its name to the sponge, dark chocolate, and tangy orange creations sold as Jaffa cakes.

Nearly seedless with a thick, easy-to-peel skin, the Jaffa is a good orange for eating out of hand. In Israel the peel is candied, dipped in chocolate, and served as a sweet snack. The intense orange flavour makes it work well in desserts such as cheesecakes. **SH**

Citrus fruit aficionados consider the blood orange to be one of the world's most superb dessert oranges. Generally smaller than its other cousins, it derives its red-coloured flesh and faintly blushed peel from anthocyanin, a pigment commonly found in many flowers and red fruits, but not typically in citrus fruits. The first mutations were probably discovered in Sicily in the seventeenth century and most still grow in the Mediterranean area today.

Each of the three main varieties, Tarocco, Sanguinello, and Moro, has its own unique qualities. Seedless Tarocco is the sweetest, and its lightly flushed pulp contains more vitamin C than any orange in the world, largely due to the fertile soils around Mount Etna on which it grows. The sparsely seeded Sanguinello is the oldest, whereas the Moro has the most pronounced hue: its pulp can vary from scarlet through to burgundy, or even almost black.

Blood oranges can be used in most recipes that would contain ordinary orange juice, such as cakes, ice creams, and sorbets, but are particularly special simply squeezed and served as a drink. **LF**

Taste: *The Jaffa orange has light, firm flesh which is juicy and sweet. The flavour is authentically and intensely "orangey" and comes across beautifully in juice.*

Taste: *The tender flesh yields a glorious juice with a well-balanced flavour, oozing the sweet mouth-watering spirit of the orange but hinting at sun-ripened raspberries.*

The Jaffa orange is the crowning glory of centuries
⊙ *of citrus cultivation in the eastern Mediterranean.*

Pink Grapefruit

Pomelo

More attractive to some because of its colour, pink grapefruit is quite similar to white or golden varieties in both quality and taste, yet richer in nutrients. All colours of grapefruit (*Citrus paradisi*) derive from the pomelo, but precisely how is not known.

The grapefruit arrived in the United States via Florida in 1823. In 1907, a pink bud shoot (a branch or flower distinctly different from the rest of the plant) was discovered and subsequently propagated. All of today's pink grapefruit varieties are descended from a single sport that appeared in 1913.

So named, some say, because the fruits grow in clusters like grapes, most grapefruits are eaten in their raw state. For breakfast, grapefruit halves are sprinkled with sugar and eaten with a special serrated spoon that easily removes the segments. Pink grapefruit, in particular, is an attractive addition to salads, either combined with other fruits or on top of greens with seafood. Grapefruit are rarely used in cooking because their flavour can easily come to dominate, but they are delicious topped with sugar, cinnamon, and butter, then grilled. **SH**

The pomelo is often called a Chinese grapefruit and the two fruits are related, but it is widely accepted that the pomelo came first. As its botanical name, *Citrus grandis*, would suggest, it is the largest fruit in the citrus family: some grow to over 8 inches (20 cm) in diameter.

Like the grapefruit, the flesh of the pomelo can range from pale yellow to light ruby, with a flavour that can vary from mouth-puckeringly tart to sweet with hints of strawberry. The spongy skin is much thicker than a grapefruit's, and it is best peeled by scoring almost to the flesh: the segments inside are divided by a tough, inedible membrane that also needs to be removed. The segments are composed of myriad juicy "beads," which are beginning to find favour as a garnish with Western chefs.

As with many other citrus fruits, the skin of the pomelo is edible, although it takes time and effort to make it delicious. In Cantonese cuisine, it is often steamed or braised in superior stock with Chinese ham or dried shrimp roe. It can also be candied in the same way as orange and lemon peel. **KKC**

Taste: *A tangy, tart-sweet flavour a little reminiscent of orange, with a distinctive bitterness that is increased by the bitter pith and membrane that encases the segments.*

Taste: *There are many pomelo cultivars, but all share aromatic skin. The taste is similar to grapefruit, but the beads separate easily and burst satisfyingly in the mouth.*

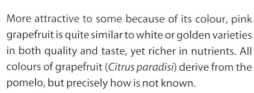

Pomelos often arrive at market in the nets that help support their weight as they grow. »

Champagne Rhubarb

Although grown in Europe, the United States, and parts of Asia, rhubarb is perhaps quintessentially English. As a fruit, this vegetable reaches its apex in the form of "forced" rhubarb, rebranded by modern marketers as "champagne" rhubarb.

The stem of a leafy plant, whose leaves are mildly toxic, rhubarb was introduced to the British Isles as a medicinal plant during Tudor times. Champagne rhubarb is grown indoors, out of the light and away from the cold, so that it matures in winter. Its stems turn a bright lipstick pink rather than a fibrous green.

Victorian gardeners used straw and upturned buckets or cloches to blanch conventional rhubarb as it emerged from the ground. While home gardeners use this method today, commercial crops are grown in Yorkshire in heated barns. Forced rhubarb needs sweetening and has special affinities with orange zest, strawberries, and star anise. In England, it is used in pies, crumbles, and fools, while Anglo-Saxon chefs are also reinventing vegetable treatments popular further east. **MR**

Sugar Cane

Humans' natural love of sweetness carried sugar cane around the world many thousands of years ago, but the wild ancestor of *Saccharum officinarum* probably originated in New Guinea. Cultivation began in parts of Asia and spread throughout the ancient world and on, in time, to the New World. Today it is grown in temperate regions around the globe and, despite the ascent of the sugar beet, remains the world's largest source of sugar.

A gigantic fibrous grass, sugar cane looks a bit like bamboo. Its centre, though, is not hollow but filled with a sweet sap or juice that can be pressed or sucked out. In South Asia, it was originally grown for chewing. It is still enjoyed that way in parts of Asia, the Caribbean, and Hawaii, optimally picked fresh from the field and eaten out of hand.

Fresh sugar cane juice, sometimes mixed with fresh ginger, lemon, or lime juice, is considered a delicacy and often used in cocktails in Latin America. The stalks can also be peeled and used as skewers for cooking, as in Thailand, where they impart a subtle sweetness to meat and dumplings. **SH**

Taste: *The stems are slender, tender, and nicely sour when cooked. The aroma, like the taste, is green but lightly perfumed. After poaching, the stems should remain intact.*

Taste: *The best part of sugar cane is the juice or nectar. Not excessively sweet, it has a refreshing, grassy flavour. The fibrous stalk is usually chewed rather than swallowed.*

A worker harvests sugar cane by hand in Brazil, one of the world's biggest producers. »

Moscatel Raisin

Prune d'Agen

While humans have almost certainly eaten grapes that have withered on the vine for hundreds of thousands of years, these crumpled gems, the flavourful dried fruit of Moscatel (Muscat) grapes, are without a doubt the royalty of the raisin world.

Large in size and a plummy brown in colour, they come complete with seeds: the best are Malaga raisins, grown in an area of Andalusia that runs from southwest Axarquia through to the foothills of the Montes de Malaga. The countryside around this 39-mile (62 km) stretch of land—known as "The Route of the Raisin"—is speckled with traditional drying beds for the fruit that has changed little since nineteenth-century travellers praised it.

Malaga raisins follow a traditional drying process and are trimmed by hand; the finest, known as Malaga clusters, are dried on their stalks. These are served as a dessert rather than used as a cooking ingredient, and have a great affinity with cheese. Soaked in sweet Malaga wine, ideally one made using Moscatel grapes, lesser grades of Moscatel raisin also make the most divine ice cream. **LF**

Dark bluish violet plum trees were introduced to France by Crusaders returning from the Holy Land. They became known as the *pruniers d'Ente* (grafted trees), and the name has endured for centuries. Agen, a medium-sized town east of Bordeaux, was never an important growing area, but its port on the River Garonne made it a major distribution centre.

Originally the prunes—dried plums—were sun-dried. Now they are dehydrated at a low temperature for twenty-four hours. It takes 4 pounds (2 kg) of fruit to make 1 pound (450 g) of the large, black, wrinkled Pruneaux d'Agen. "Giants"—the largest of the three official sizes—weigh just under ½ ounce (15 g).

Anglo-Saxons often treat the fruit as little more than a laxative; the French regard them as a jewel in their gastronomic crown. Steeped in Armagnac, stuffed with almond paste, flavouring the batter puddings called *fars,* and as the base of a world-beating ice cream, they figure in many classic desserts. They also figure in savoury recipes like *lapin sauté au pruneaux,* a rabbit stew thickened with gingerbread and a hint of bitter chocolate. **MR**

Taste: *Aromatic, lightly chewy, and sweet with a delicate crunch of seeds, Malaga raisins are deliciously rich with flavours of dark toffee, chestnut honey, and figs.*

Taste: *Larger and more succulent than most prunes, Pruneaux d'Agen share the dark, glutinous sweetness of others of their species.*

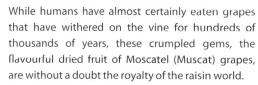

***Spread out on slanted beds called* paseros,**
Ⓚ *Moscatel grapes are dried in the sun.*

Hachiya Persimmon

One of the most spectacular sights of a Japanese winter is the leafless persimmon tree, its laden branches bending under the weight of shiny orange fruit, bright against the snow. Persimmons or kaki (*Diospyros kaki*)—both *shibugaki*, the astringent type that are inedible when merely ripe, and the sweet type known as *amagaki*—have been cultivated for many centuries.

The Hachiya persimmon is a kind of astringent persimmon characterized by its oval, acorn-like shape and a mouth-puckering quality so intense that, as the haiku poet Issa remarked a couple of centuries ago, only a mother's love can bear it. Yet once "bletted"—or rotted in a controlled fashion—the tannins in Hachiya persimmons give way to a rich, honeyed sweetness. In Japan, it is most often eaten dried and strings of persimmons, covered in their white, powdery sugar coating—drying in the winter sun—used to be a common sight in rural areas. Another rather pleasing way of removing the astringency of *shibugaki* is to soak them in the alcoholic drink known as *shochu*. **SB**

Taste: *Fresh but bletted, the Hachiya persimmon is sticky, sweet, and so soft that it needs to be eaten with a spoon. The flavour is like apricot with echoes of pumpkin.*

Pala Manis

Native to Indonesia, nutmeg was so prized by both the Dutch and Portuguese, who colonized the islands in the early seventeenth century, that their rivalry led to bloodshed. The British, who later occupied the Moluccas, took the nutmeg tree to the West Indies, where it is now cultivated, particularly on the island of Grenada.

The fruit of the nutmeg tree, pala manis, looks like a large apricot. When split open, it reveals a shiny, chestnut-brown oval kernel encircled with lacy, red arils. Both are dried to produce spices; the tendril-like arils become mace and the hard inner kernel, nutmeg. In Indonesia, the fruit's outer flesh is crystallized to make a popular sweet called *manisan pala*. In Sri Lanka, a jam is made from the fruit.

Serious cooks like to grate their own nutmeg kernel, which has a superior flavour to the pre-packed, ground version. Only a little nutmeg is needed in sweet or savoury dishes—using too much will overwhelm other flavours. Also, as the English herbalist Nicholas Culpeper (1616–54) warned, it can induce delirium in those who over-indulge. **WS**

Taste: *Dried pala manis is a little like crystallized ginger in appearance and taste. Freshly grated nutmeg is warm, nutty, and sweet, and adds an exotic lift to milky puddings.*

A pala manis splits open on the branch, revealing the red arils that are dried as mace. ❯❯

Hunza Apricot

Quandong

High up in the Karakoram Mountains, in northern Pakistan, lies a land of lofty peaks and terraced valleys, of isolated villages and snowy winters: Hunza. The Hunzakuts who live here are renowned for their good health and longevity, which some attribute to the magnificent Hunza apricot. In fact, so revered is the apricot that a family's economic standing can be measured in apricot trees.

The Karakorams are at the western end of the Himalayan massif, and on the Silk Road that distributed Chinese silk across the continents: it may have been silk traders who brought the apricot from its Chinese homeland, too. The Hunzakuts enjoy their apricots fresh in season, but also dry vast quantities of them. Dried, they may be eaten as they are, cooked into savoury or sweet dishes, or puréed and mixed with snow to make a sort of ice cream.

Fresh apricots are highly difficult to transport, so in the West the dried Hunza is the one to look out for. Vastly different from the squishy neon-orange types that are typically treated with sulphur as a preservative, the Hunza apricot is dark brown. **LF**

The scorched, parched wilderness of central Australia seems an inhospitable place for food to grow, but the desert yields delicacies that have been harvested by indigenous Australians for centuries. The quandong—also known as the "wild" or "desert" peach—is so high in vitamin C that many early Australian explorers would have died of scurvy had they not stumbled upon this rich native food. Its English common name derives from *guwandhang*, the word used by the Wiradjuri people of the Lachlan River in New South Wales.

As traditional "bush tucker" becomes a popular sustainable food source, the farming of quandong is growing. The fresh fruit is about the size of a small apricot, coloured brilliant red, with white or pale yellow flesh. Indigenous people dry it in the sun to preserve it for later use: frozen or dried it can last up to eight years without loss of flavour. The kernel is rich in oil and can be baked to give an almond-like nut, but some are bitter and unpalatable. The wood of the quandong tree releases a pleasant sandalwood scent when burnt. **RH**

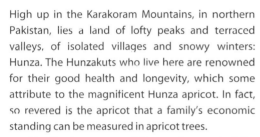

Taste: The dried Hunza apricot is pleasantly chewy with a deep, slightly bosky, honeyed fruit aroma and a flavour that hints at dark toffee on the finish.

Taste: Acidic when fresh, quandong has a slight peach and apricot flavour, with rhubarb notes. Preparing it as a confit or preserving in brandy and sugar offsets the tartness.

Hunza apricots flourish in the awe-inspiring surroundings of the Himalayan massif.

Guarana

Tamarind

Of all the fruits of the Amazon, the guarana berry is probably the best known, thanks to the fizzy pops and "energy drinks" which are made from its fruit. The pretty fruit, which resembles an open eye coloured in red, white, and black, is a legacy from indigenous people, whose origins are lost in time. Portuguese colonizers learned of it from the Sateré-Maués tribe as early as the seventeenth century.

From then until this day, the drink has been produced in the same way. Harvested from *Paullinia cupana*, a creeping shrub, the fruit is dried, toasted, and crushed to form a smooth paste. This is moulded into rods which can then be grated to a powder and diluted with water, creating a liquid with a high caffeine content.

Guarana began to appear on the shelves of health food shops and pharmacies some years ago. It has been marketed in various forms—from syrups, concentrated extracts, and capsules, to traditional rods for grating. Its followers see it as an ideal remedy for everyday stress; other enthusiasts even claim aphrodisiac effects. **AL**

A world without tamarind would be bereft of Worcestershire sauce, HP sauce , countless chutneys, and innumerable curries from almost every tropical region, which is ample reason for venerating this tall, shady tree. Originating from Africa, *Tamarindus indica* has grown in India since prehistoric times and, thankfully, is now widely cultivated in many other tropical parts of the world.

Filipino cooks simmer the unripe green pods in soups and stews, while Indian cooks turn them into pickles and preserves. The brown pulp of mature pods is blended with water and strained of its seeds and fibres to make a paste or "juice" that bring tamarind's delicious souring qualities to South Indian and South East Asian kitchens. As it is one of those rare ingredients at home in both savoury and sweet dishes, tamarind appears in drinks and sorbets as well as relishes, braised meats, and soups. In Vietnam and Thailand a sweet-sour cultivar is eaten straight from the pod as a snack, or cooked with sugar and chilli into spicy sweetmeats: this is sold in some Western markets as "sweet tamarind." **CTa**

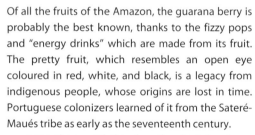

Taste: *Guarana is best tried as a drink, hand-prepared with the concentrated extract. It has hints of vanilla and orange flavour, wrapped up in a fabulous sweetness.*

Taste: *Ripe tamarind has a fruity sourness with notes of apple, plum, quince, and carob: in sweet cultivars, the flavour is also tangy and sherbety. Young pods taste sharp.*

As the tamarind ripens, the fruit dries naturally within its brown husk. »

Honeyed Jujube

Khalasah Date

Dubbed "food of harmony" because they are reputed to strengthen the body and cleanse the blood, jujubes have been cultivated in China for over 4,000 years. Also known as honey dates or red dates, they are not in fact true dates. Their size varies from small and round to long and thin; they can be cherry-sized or larger, more like plums.

Jujubes have creamy, white flesh, a hard, single stone, and thin skins that turn from green to red as they ripen. Eaten fresh, the fruits are considered to be at their best before they become fully ripe, when they start to dry out and lose their succulence.

As well as eating jujubes fresh, the Chinese also dry, pickle, and smoke them. However, it is as a candied bonbon that they become an irresistible treat capable of satisfying the sweetest tooth. The fruit is first boiled in syrup and then dried for up to two days. This boiling and drying process is repeated twice more, the skins being slit for the final boiling which is done in a more concentrated syrup often flavoured with honey. The candied fruits are then dried until they are no longer sticky. **WS**

"Khalasah" is the Arabic word for quintessence, and date connoisseurs the world over consider this famous beauty exactly that. The epitome of date perfection, its gorgeous glossy skin shrouds sticky, irresistible, bright amber flesh. This cultivar of the date palm is grown in the Al-Ahsa province of Saudi Arabia, near one of the largest oases in the world.

The date palm (*Phoenix dactylifera*) is thought to have originated in the Persian Gulf, and has been cultivated since at least 5,000 BCE, even before the Sumerians and Babylonians made the date palm their sacred tree. The ancient Romans loved dates but imported them from North Africa; it was the Moors who brought the fruit to Spain, and Spaniards who then took them to Mexico and California. Today, a huge number of different varieties of date are grown around the world, but the Khalasah is routinely pronounced top of the crops.

Dates are best eaten like good chocolate, that is, left on the tongue so that the outer skin simply slips off and the soft flesh slowly melts, releasing a glorious complexity of flavours. **LF**

Taste: *Fresh jujubes have crisp, sweet flesh with a flavour and texture similar to a dessert apple. Candied they are soft and mellow, with a luxurious honeyed sweetness.*

Taste: *Dissolving slowly on the tongue, the Khalasah surrenders a complex swirl of honey and caramel, with notes of fresh sugar cane and hints of honeycomb toffee.*

Khalasah dates mature on the palm for many weeks before being carefully harvested. »

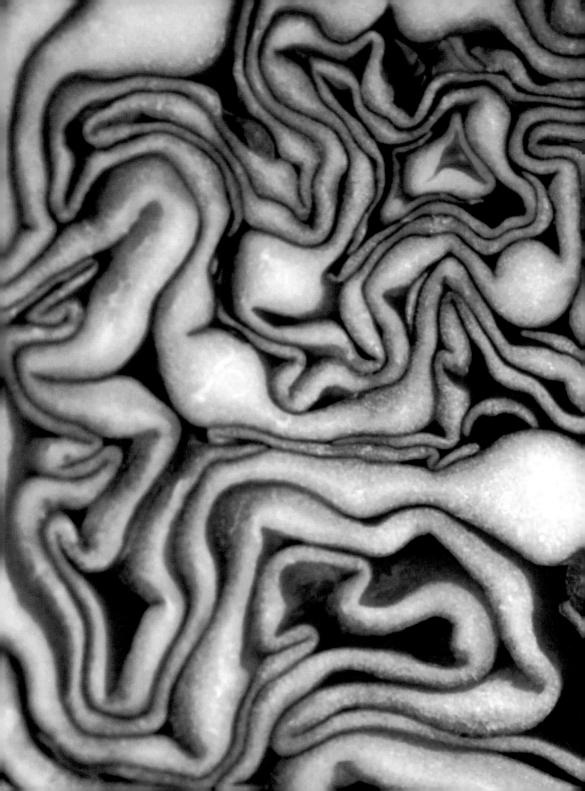

Nasturtium

Nasturtium or *Tropaeolum majus* is a completely edible plant prized both in the garden and in the kitchen for its brilliant red, orange, and yellow flowers. It is native to the jungles of Mexico and Peru, where the Incas grew it as an ornamental and cultivated a relative for its roots, hence its alternate name of Indian cress. Spanish conquistadores brought the plant home in the sixteenth century. It was widely grown in colonial America.

Among the most common of edible flowers, nasturtium blooms are used both fresh and dried as garnishes, in salads, and on open-faced sandwiches. A delicious salad combines dried flowers with fresh radicchio, chives, and spinach under a dressing of champagne vinegar, Dijon mustard, salt, pepper, and olive oil. Fresh, the blossoms make a striking and flavoursome casing for everything from cheese spreads to Mediterranean vegetable blends. The flower buds, when pickled, are an inexpensive substitute for capers, while the spicy leaves are good used sparingly in salad, and even the stems may be served boiled in soups. **SH**

Taste: *Mildly pungent and peppery, nasturtium blossoms have a sweet-spicy flavour similar to watercress. Those grown in full sun and picked later taste more intense.*

Courgette Blossom

The courgette blossom is the pretty yellow flower of the courgette, also known as the zucchini, a young summer marrow (*Cucurbita pepo*), from the same family as cucumber and melon. Stuffed and fried or simply sizzled in a crisp golden tempura-style batter, the blossoms were once a speciality of Italian and French restaurants, but are now seen as a delicacy all over the world. The blossoms are quite fragile and must be used within a day or two of being picked.

Interestingly, courgettes may be male or female, and both duly flower. The female blossom opens first, but once fertilized crinkles and collapses as the fruit grows; by the time the courgette is ready to be picked, the flower has wasted away. However, the male blooms vigorously from a single thin stem but never develops into a courgette.

Typically, male flowers are larger and stay open longer than their female counterparts. Once the bees have done the job of collecting the pollen and transferring it to the female flower, nature has no further use for the male blossom, and so it is the preferred flower for stuffing. **LF**

Taste: *Courgette blossoms are mild and sweet in flavour and can be stuffed or eaten raw in salads. The smaller female flowers are favoured for deep-frying in batter.*

A male courgette flower awaits a bee to carry its pollen to the female flower nearby.

Palm Heart

These prized ingredients are the tender, creamy cores of a number of different types of palm: the very top and centre of the green shoots of a brand new tree. With many varieties of palm, this excision kills the parent plant, making the heart a true luxury—hence its role in dishes with titles such as "millionaire's salad," a speciality of Mauritius.

The hearts of the cabbage palm, *Sabal palmetto*, which grows around the Caribbean and Central America, are known as "swamp cabbage" in the state of Florida. There they are traditionally sliced thin, simmered in water with salt pork or bacon, and served with pepper vinegar. Because harvesting kills this palm, it is now a protected species in Florida.

Instead, palm hearts are harvested from *Bactris gasipaes*, the peach palm or *pejibaye*, which is native to the Amazon. In the wild it was a staple in the lives of Indians in the region; today it is cultivated for its hearts, which, as it produces multiple shoots, can be harvested without killing the parent trees. In Brazil, the Assai palm is cultivated for its hearts, which are often are used as a filling for empanadas. **SH**

Taste: *Soft, yet with a many layered texture, palm hearts have a sweet, nutty flavour, often described as a blend of artichokes, asparagus, and mushrooms.*

The cabbage palm is the state tree of Florida,
⊗ where harvesting of its heart is prohibited.

Cardoon

Like its close relative, the globe artichoke, the cardoon (*Cynara cardunculus*) belongs to the thistle family and originated in the Mediterranean, where it has been eaten for millennia. Unlike the artichoke, however, the cardoon is generally appreciated for its edible stalk, which Roman aristocracy stewed in fish sauce, and peasants apparently ate raw.

Today cardoons are grown in a similar way to most celery plants, with banks of earth raised around the growing stems to lighten their look and flavour. Unlike celery, however, these stalks remain too bitter to be enjoyed raw, although once cooked they become tender and take on an exquisite delicate flavour. Today they are popular in Spain, southern France, and Italy; although they arrived in England to a mixed reception, they were popular with the New England colonists across the Atlantic. In Provence, cardoons are a favourite dish at Christmas. In the north of Italy, they are served with the hot dip of olive oil, anchovies, and butter known as *bagna cauda*. They are roasted, used to make soup, or fried in a crisp, light, tempura-style batter. **LF**

Taste: *Eaten raw, cardoons have spicy, celery-like aspects that hint of fennel. Cooked until tender, the bitterness subsides to reveal a fine artichoke flavour.*

Pacaya

The edible flower bud of a tropical palm tree (*Chamaedorea tepejilote*), pacaya grows in Central America. The fleshy yellow flowers of the male plants resemble long thin ears of corn and are harvested while young and tender, and still enclosed in the spathes. Grown in Guatemala for the last two centuries, pacaya is harvested in the wild and from cultivated plants, often for export to North America. The tricky process of flower collection provides vital income to people living in poor, rural communities.

Also known as vegetable squid because of the snaking tendrils coiled in its large petals, pacaya can be eaten raw in salads. It is also often boiled and eaten as a vegetable; fried in an egg batter and served with tomato sauce, black beans, rice, and tortillas; or added to scrambled eggs and stir-fries. Pacaya is one of the fifty-odd ingredients found in *fiambre*, a salad served in Guatemala at the beginning of November for *El Día de los Muertos* (the Day of the Dead), when people honour their ancestors at cemeteries. In El Salvador, it is eaten stuffed with cheese as *pacaya rellena de queso*. **CK**

Flor de Izote

With an impressive flower spike reaching up to 3 feet (0.9 m) high and, in summer, covered in a stunning mass of fragrant, white flowers, flor de izote is a yucca plant belonging to the agave family. The edible, bell-shaped flowers of this plant are considered a delicacy in Mexico, Costa Rica, Guatemala, and especially El Salvador, where it is the national flower. When the plant is semi-mature, bell-shaped flowers appear that can be harvested for eating, either as they open or just before they open. The ancient Maya boiled the flowers to make an energy-boosting herbal tea.

Rich in calcium, the flowers need soaking for twenty minutes or washing and blanching before cooking, to remove some of their bitterness. Locals use the flowers in *huevos revueltos* (scrambled eggs), tamales, and in dishes containing tomatoes, onions, or garlic, and even in barbecue sauce. They can also be a welcome ingredient in a salad, casserole, soup, or just fried in butter with a little salt and pepper. In El Salvador, the flowers are used to stuff *pupusas*, which are similar to a corn tortilla or pitta bread. **CK**

Taste: *The tender petals of pacaya enclose chewy inner tendrils. The buds have a hearty, slightly bitter flavour a little like asparagus.*

Taste: *After careful soaking and blanching flor de izote has a pleasantly bitter flavour. Even when cooked the flowers should still be slightly crunchy in texture.*

A single yucca flower spike bears a substantial crop of edible blooms. ⊗

Banana Flower

Roman Artichoke

Bullet-shaped, heavy, and sheathed in ridged outer leaves of crimson purple, the banana flower or banana bud looks rather formidable. Yet its tough exterior hides an ingredient of surprising delicacy, often compared to artichoke. The thick outer leaves unfold to reveal tightly packed softer leaf bracts, pale pink or burgundy in hue, interspersed with small finger-like blossoms that are immature bananas. Both taste faintly earthy and astringent, and the blossoms bear a hint of bitterness.

Banana flowers are a common sight at markets in Vietnam, Thailand, the Philippines, and Cambodia, where they are eaten raw or lightly blanched in salads dressed with vinegar or citrus, cooked until tender in soups or coconut milk sauces, or shredded as a garnish for noodle dishes and the fondue-style sharing dishes known as "steamboats."

Small, rounded flowers are said to taste better than larger, more pointed specimens. They can discolour to a muddy brown extremely rapidly when sliced, and thus are usually soaked in acidulated water immediately after being cut. **CTa**

The *carciofo romanesco del Lazio* (IGP), or Roman artichoke, is an exquisite type of globe artichoke with a large, spherical, tightly packed head and green leaves tinged a rosy violet colour. A native of the Mediterranean, the exact history of *Cynara scolymus* is a little hazy: some think it was developed in ancient Sicily, others that the plant the ancient Greeks and Romans knew was a type of cardoon. It then disappeared only to reappear in Italy during the Renaissance; many varieties grow there today.

For the most part, the Roman artichoke is cultivated along the Lazio coast around Rome and on towards Civitavecchia. Artichokes thrive in salty climes and the coastal soil offers ideal growing conditions. The season is from late winter to early spring, and, as with so many things edible and Italian, its arrival is a signal to party. Every April, the coastal town of Ladispoli holds a festival that sees the town's restaurants vying to produce the best Roman artichoke dish; at the Velletri festival, the artichokes are cooked over a fire fuelled by their own dried shoots. **LF**

Taste: Banana flowers have the crisp texture of a palm heart, fortified by more fibre; their lightly nutty flavour is reminiscent of raw artichoke, mushroom, and courgette.

Taste: Prized for being more tender than its cousins, the Roman artichoke has a smooth, creamy flavour followed by a slightly metallic aftertaste with patches of sweetness.

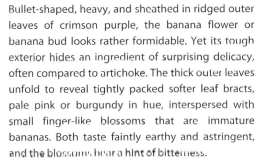

The heavy flower weighs down the shoot,
✪ *and the young bananas sprout upwards.*

Lumignano Pea

Mange-tout

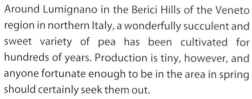

Around Lumignano in the Berici Hills of the Veneto region in northern Italy, a wonderfully succulent and sweet variety of pea has been cultivated for hundreds of years. Production is tiny, however, and anyone fortunate enough to be in the area in spring should certainly seek them out.

It was apparently Benedictine monks who brought the peas to the hills, about 1,000 years ago. By accident or design, they selected an ideal microclimate: the sheer rock faces held the warmth from the sun as if in a storage heater, reflecting it back on the plants, while the sun shone down from above, meaning the peas ripened sweet and early. Over the centuries, farmers carried on what the monks had started, adapting growing methods, and building steep terraces to access the best positions: everything, from the stones to the harvest, were hauled up and down the slopes on the farmers' backs.

Today the peas are harvested from April to May, and a festival—the Sagra dei Bisi—is held each May to celebrate. The peas perform wonderfully in the famous Venetian soup *risi e bisi* (rice and peas). **LF**

One of the pod peas, so named because both the pod and the immature peas are edible, mange-tout or "snow peas," one expression of *Pisum sativum*, are picked in early spring, when many regions still have snow on the ground. They are even younger than the sugar-snap varieties designed to be eaten pod and all: mange-tout are eaten so flat and so young that the seeds have barely had time to develop.

Legumes, including peas of many varieties, were harvested in the wild many, many millennia ago. Peas probably originated in western Asia, not far from where the ancient Greeks were cultivating them around 400 to 500 BCE, and *Pisum sativum* was well-established in China by the seventh century CE. (More than 1,000 years later, mange-tout were one of the thirty-odd varieties of pea that Thomas Jefferson cultivated at Monticello in Virginia.)

Mange-tout can be eaten raw or lightly cooked. In addition to their role as an ingredient in stir-fried dishes throughout Asia, they add colour and texture to salads, soups, rice, and pasta dishes, or make an accompaniment to meat or fish. **SH**

Taste: *Crisp but tender, the fresh-flavoured pods reveal juicy, small, vivid green peas which surrender a delightfully clean sweetness on the tongue.*

Taste: *Mange-tout taste similar to garden peas, but are less starchy and have a sweeter flavour. Raw or quickly cooked, they have a clean, sweet, slightly grassy taste.*

French Bean

Green Flageolet

Despite their English name—in French they are *haricots verts*—these beans are native to Central America, where they have been domesticated for more than 5,000 years. (The name haricot is a corruption of the Aztec word *ayecotl*.)

The parent plant, *Phaseolus vulgaris*, grows in a frankly bewildering range of varieties that make it the most cultivated type of bean in Europe and the United States today. It was originally grown for its seeds alone, and many varieties—such as those which produce flageolets or dried haricots—still are. The bean reached Europe during the sixteenth century, but it was probably Italians who were the first to eat the whole pods, a century or two later. Today these slender beans have been carefully cultivated to produce tender pods with tiny seeds.

Fresh from the garden, French beans are crisp eaten raw. Steamed or boiled until crisp and tender, they have a starring role in *salad niçoise*, and make a lovely accompaniment to simple meat or fish dishes. More elaborate French recipes pair them with bacon, tomato sauce, or a rich cream sauce. **SH**

Sometimes referred to as the "Rolls-Royce" of beans for their smooth texture and subtle flavour, green flageolets—*flageolets verts* in French—are small beans with a low starch content, grown for their light green seeds. In nineteenth-century France, bean seeds were coloured red, white, yellow, or even black. It was not until the 1870s, however, that Gabriel Chevrier of Arpajon, a little town just south of Paris, developed a variety whose seeds stayed green long enough to be sold and dried while green. The "new" beans were very popular, and even today are sometimes known as *chevriers* in their creator's honour. Chevrier's original variety is now a heirloom breed and hard to find, but both it and its descendants remain a great delicacy in the kitchen.

Fresh green flageolets, when available, should be cooked in very little water over low heat for only a short time. The dried ones may be cooked like any dried bean. They pair especially well with braised or roasted lamb, which is the traditional way to serve them in France; slow-cooked lamb shanks and flageolets is a popular dish in England. **SH**

Taste: *French beans are at their best fresh, young, and straight from the garden—or at least a local supplier. Then they are sweet and crisp with a clean, "green" taste.*

Taste: *The beans have a very mild, very creamy flavour somewhat similar to but more delicate than edamame or small lima beans, with gentle chlorophyll notes.*

Edamame

The vegetarian influence of Buddhism means that the soya bean has long been an important food source in China, Japan, and South East Asia. It is known as "the meat of the fields" for its high protein content, but because it is tough and indigestible when dried, it is usually processed into products such as tofu and soy sauce. Immature beans, however, are a different matter. In Japan, where they are known as edamame, large bunches of the fuzzy green pods appear in shops from May to September. Boiled in the pod they make a lovely accompaniment to drinks, particularly sake, and a basketful of salted edamame, warm from the pot and tossed in salt, is one of the joys of a visit to any izakaya (drinking establishment) in Japan.

Edamame have become fashionable in parts of the West, where they are increasingly available both fresh and frozen. Chefs use the bright green beans as an ingredient in many dishes, while edamame mash is a popular Pacific Rim side dish. In Japan, the Tamba region of Hyogo is known for its kuromame—a larger, darker variety that is particularly delicious. **SB**

Broad Bean

For centuries these flat, green, greyish, or pink seeds were a major source of protein both in Europe and in parts of Asia and Africa. Also called fava beans—their botanical name is *Vicia faba*—broad beans have been cultivated for so long and so widely that any wild predecessors have been lost in antiquity.

Not everyone ate them, however. In ancient Egypt the upper classes considered the beans unworthy, although today a local variety is dried and used in the popular dish *ful medames*. The sixth-century BCE philosopher Pythagoras called them the "beans of the dead," conceivably because for a very small percentage of the population broad beans can be toxic. The Romans held them in higher regard, which may explain their use fresh and dried in Italian stews and casseroles. In the spring, tender broad beans are eaten raw with fresh pecorino cheese.

In China and Thailand, the beans, called "open mouth nut," are fried and served salted as a snack. Elsewhere, they are used in everything from frittatas and risottos to soups and salads, and as an accompaniment to meats, such as cooked ham. **SH**

Taste: *Sucking the salt off an edamame pod while squeezing the beans into your mouth is a real pleasure. The beans are tender, juicy, and subtly sweet, with a firm texture.*

Taste: *Broad beans have a robust, meaty, earthy taste somewhere between a lima bean and an edamame. In young beans this taste is muted by a delicate sweetness.*

A staple for millennia, broad beans still bless European gardens today. »

Petai Bean

Horseradish Pod

The beautiful spiralling pods—twist bean is a colloquial name—of petai (*Parkia speciosa*) look like something straight out of Tolkien. If their appearance is elven, however, their flavour is surely dwarven, with something of the sulphur mines about it: their other common name of stink bean is deserved because of the way their scent lingers about one's person after consumption, rather like garlic or asparagus.

The beans crunch softly between one's teeth and have nutlike nuances to their taste, and indeed they resemble jade-green marcona almonds, gently curved and ridged. In southern Thailand, where petai are called *sataw* or *sator*, two different varieties are eaten: *sataw kow*, which has twisted pods and sweeter beans, and *sataw darn*, which has straight pods and larger, stronger-smelling beans that are often pickled. Both there and across the border in Malaysia, petai are popularly stir-fried with prawns and a spicy chilli paste. Malaysians also enjoy petai as part of a typical meal centred on an assortment of herbs and vegetables eaten with sambals. **CTa**

Sometimes known as "drumsticks," the long, narrow pods of the horseradish tree contain seeds with a delicate, slightly hot flavour. The horseradish tree (*Moringa oleifera*) is no relation to the horseradish of the mustard family. Rather, the tree received its name because its pungent root is used as a substitute for horseradish. The tree is grown in semi-arid tropical and subtropical areas, and is native to the southern foothills of the Himalayas, Africa, and the Middle East, although it is also cultivated in Latin America, Sri Lanka, Malaysia, and the Philippines.

The outer part of the pod is inedible but the young, triangular seeds inside can be cooked as a vegetable similar to a green bean, and have a delicate flavour. They can be prepared in a variety of ways: fried; boiled; steamed; or made into a pickle. They are frequently made into soup and added to curries, dals, and stews. The mature pods can be stewed and eaten like an artichoke, by scraping away the inner pulp and discarding the remainder. When the mature pods are cooked, the flavour is similar to okra. **CK**

Taste: *Petai have an appealingly nutty, subtly sweet earthiness that brings to mind broad beans, but with an aura a little reminiscent of garlic.*

Taste: *Young horseradish pods are tender when cooked, and have a delicate flavour that has been compared to a combination of horseradish, asparagus, and peanut.*

The exotic appearance of twist beans is
❸ *matched by their remarkable pungency.*

Silver Queen Sweetcorn

For more than a half century, Silver Queen set the United States standard for corn that was eaten from the cob. But, although prized by chefs such as Thomas Keller, this corn with its delicate white kernels is becoming harder to find each day as growers turn to newer hybrids that hold their sweetness longer after picking.

Developed in 1955, Silver Queen can most likely trace its ancestry back more than 7,000 years to *teosinte*, a plant that grew wild in Mexico. Cultivation spread southwards to Peru and northwards into what would become the United States. Columbus found it in the New World and brought it back to Spain, although it was grown in Europe as a grain. Americans began cultivating sweetcorn—varieties of maize to be eaten when immature and still sweet—around 1800. Silver Queen remains a prime choice. Like all sweetcorn, it is best eaten within a day or so of being picked, before its sugar turns to starch. It is delicious boiled and slathered with butter, salt, and pepper or grilled and seasoned with herbs or spices like cumin. **SH**

Ackee

Ackee, also spelled akee, takes its Latin name *Blighia sapida* from the infamous Captain Bligh. The red, pear-shaped fruit, which grows in clusters on an evergreen tree, is indigenous to the forests of the Ivory Coast and Gold Coast of West Africa, and Bligh is said to have brought it on slave ships to Jamaica around 1793. Today it is Jamaica's national fruit and figures alongside salt cod in the country's national dish, ackee and saltfish.

Ackee must only be picked when it has turned completely red and has split fully open in the distinctive "yawn" or "smile" that reveals its black seeds and the creamy yellow, pulpy aril around them. Only the pulp is eaten. The rest of the ripened ackee and all unripened ackee are toxic and can be fatal. (Tinned ackee is readily available in many parts of the world and is completely safe to eat.)

Ackee looks, tastes, and feels very similar to creamy scrambled eggs. Some say it also looks like brains, hence its alternate name, vegetable brains. It is sometimes curried and used as a filling for patties, and can form part of a soup or a vegetarian stew. **SH**

Taste: *Silver Queen is the standard by which corn on the cob is measured. It has a well-balanced sweetness that remains "corny," not sugary, and a creamy, milky flavour.*

Taste: *Ackee has a mild flavour that picks up the taste of other ingredients in the dish. Its texture is smoother and more melting than that of scrambled eggs.*

Ackee display their "yawn" or "smile" when they are ripe for harvest. »

Tomatillo

Green Tomato

Tomatillos are a fruit related to the ground cherry and Cape gooseberry, although like their close relative the tomato, they are used as a vegetable. Smaller than a regular tomato, tomatillos are encased in a papery calyx or husk that is often removed before cooking. Usually green and mild flavoured, they can be eaten raw, but their flavour grows with cooking.

Tomatillos (classified as *Physalis ixocarpa* and *P. philadelphica*) are also known as husk tomatoes and, although they are sometimes called green tomatoes too, they should not be confused with green, unripe tomatoes. They originated in Mesoamerica and are still found in the wild and cultivated from the cool highlands of Guatemala to southern Texas. Tomatillos also grow in Australia, India, and East Africa. There are many different types of tomatillo prized throughout Latin America and distinguished by their colour and size.

A common ingredient in Latin American cuisines, they are cooked or puréed into sauces, especially the *salsa verdes* that go with grilled or roasted meats. They are also sometimes added to guacamole. **SH**

Green tomatoes may be unripe but they are not inedible. In fact, the immature state of this fruit, generally served as a vegetable, has a culinary culture all of its own. Green tomatoes take centre stage in the United States when summer gives way to autumn, and unripened tomatoes must be picked from the garden. Widely known and appreciated throughout the American South, the fruit achieved worldwide notice in the film based on Fannie Flagg's novel, *Fried Green Tomatoes at the Whistle Stop Cafe*.

Fried green tomatoes are a delicacy. Thick slices of green tomato are dipped in egg, coated with flour and breadcrumbs, and then fried in oil, to produce an appetizer or side dish. Green tomatoes are also used in soups, jams, relishes, salsas, and pickles.

Although most closely associated with the American South, green tomatoes also feature in Indian cooking. Prepared with mustard seeds, cumin, and other spices, they can be served over rice as a vegetarian main course or used as a side dish. They are also used to make chutney. Green tomato tarte tatin is a U.S. take on the French classic. **SH**

Taste: *Similar in texture to tomatoes, tomatillos have a refreshing acidic flavour with hints of apples and lemon that blends well with the heat of chillies.*

Taste: *Green tomatoes are best when they are truly green. Although the flavour is reminiscent of ripe tomatoes, they are much tarter. In their prime, they are firm and tangy.*

Cherry Tomato

San Marzano Tomato

As cherry tomatoes only became fashionable in the late twentieth century, it is easy to mistake them for a development of modern plant breeders. *Lycopersicon esculentum cerasiforme* was, in reality, cultivated by the Aztec civilization in Central America before the Spanish conquistadors brought it back to Europe. Like other tomatoes, it probably evolved from wild Peruvian ancestors.

Even though tomatoes were not generally eaten by Old World gourmets (who remained suspicious of the fruit's deadly nightshade lineage) until the end of the nineteenth century, many kinds of cherry tomato were being grown. The cultivars developed today have usually been conceived with the needs of multiple retailers in mind (thicker skins, long shelf-life). However, bright red "Gardener's Delight" is a delicious English variety and the golden Japanese "Sungold" is exceptionally mellow and sweet.

Cherry tomatoes are usually eaten raw, although they are increasingly being cooked. Lightly pan-fried and mixed with fresh herbs they make an instant summery pasta sauce. **MR**

When it comes to plum tomatoes, the San Marzano tomato has long carried the vote. Tomatoes have been cultivated in the southern Italian provinces of Naples, Salerno, and Avellino since the sixteenth century. When the San Marzano tomato arrived a couple of hundred years later, the volcanic ash from nearby Mount Vesuvius and the rich earth of the pre-Apennine hills combined with the sea air and created growing traditions to create a prized fruit.

Lauded for its intense flavour and vibrant colour, the San Marzano's skin is easy to peel, its pulp is firm, and it has few seeds, making it perfect for tomato sauces. Since 1996, the Pomodoro di San Marzano has carried DOP certification, which distinguishes it from San Marzano tomatoes grown to less strict standards in other parts of the world. Pomodoro di San Marzano tomatoes grow on specially trained vines and are hand-picked over multiple harvests. They are washed, peeled, and canned without any additives or preservatives. The unmechanized process makes them expensive in comparison to other varieties, but they are definitely worth it. **LF**

Taste: *The sweetness and acidity of a cherry tomato should be in balance. Juicy, with mellow acidity, and full of sweet flavour, it should have a subtle savoury scent.*

Taste: *San Marzano have a robust flavour that combines a complex sweetness with slightly acerbic notes. Canned, they exhibit a juicy excellence that is deliciously intense.*

Water Chestnut

After tasting fresh water chestnuts, the canned version will never seem the same again. Fresh water chestnuts have a lively, crisp, juicy texture and a subtly sweet taste; after canning, the experience is just a pale ghost of itself. The crunch remains but the flavour vanishes into thin air.

Fresh water chestnuts (*Eleocharis dulcis*) have an unassuming appearance. Being the tubers of an aquatic plant, they are usually covered in mud. Rinsing reveals a shiny, dark brown, hard shell, not dissimilar to its namesake chestnut, which is peeled to reveal the white flesh inside. When buying, look for unwrinkled specimens that are completely firm; the ones with soft spots will be mouldy inside. Unpeeled water chestnuts can be stored for several weeks in a plastic bag in the fridge; after peeling they can be frozen with no loss of texture or flavour.

Water chestnuts are ground into a lumpy flour that makes a beautiful, crisp, delicate crust when fried. This, combined with fresh water chestnuts, makes a chewy steamed pudding that is traditionally eaten at Chinese New Year. **KKC**

Taste: *Water chestnuts can be eaten raw or cooked. They are often used in dishes where their crisp texture contrasts with softer ingredients such as steamed minced pork.*

Water chestnuts feature in some Chinese stir-fries. »

Asian Aubergine

Mediterranean Aubergine

Browse the stalls selling aubergines in an Asian market and none of the varieties on offer are likely to resemble the shiny, deep purple beauties so ubiquitous in the West. Despite its starring role in Mediterranean cuisine, the aubergine is native to tropical Asia, where many varieties come in a host of different shapes, sizes, and colours.

The tiny, bitter variety popular in Thailand and known as *makhua puang*, grows in clusters and is the size, shape, and colour of a large pea. Other aubergines in South East Asia are small, round, and range in colour from white to pale green, and yellow to purple. In Japan and China, aubergines are long and slender with pale purple skins, sometimes streaked with white. These are good for stir-fries.

Asian cooking rarely calls for aubergines to be salted to rid them of bitter juices. Small, round aubergines are added whole or halved to Thai curries to contrast with rich coconut sauces, whereas pea aubergines add astringency. Japanese aubergines (*nasu*) make fine tempura. In India, aubergine is used in the hot pickle *brinjal*. **WS**

A member of the diverse family that encompasses potatoes, tomatoes, and deadly nightshade, aubergine (*Solanum melongena*) is eaten as a vegetable, but is botanically a berry. Although some Asian, African, and Spanish varieties have a colour and shape that explains the otherwise mystifying alternative name of eggplant, the Mediterranean varieties have shiny, smooth, dark purple skin and light flesh with pale brown seeds.

Probably originating in India, the aubergine travelled with the Arabs to Europe during the thirteenth century. Now a mainstay throughout the Mediterranean, aubergine makes its most celebrated appearance in the Turkish dish *imam bayildi*, stuffed with onions and cooked in copious quantities of olive oil. It is a key ingredient in Provençal ratatouille and in Greek moussaka, where it is layered with minced meat and white sauce. Roasted, it becomes the basis for numerous Greek and Middle Eastern dips, among them *baba ghanoush*. It may be served battered and fried, stuffed, pickled, in stews, as a relish, or in a myriad other ways. **SH**

Taste: *Tart pea aubergines are used to balance sweeter ingredients in Thai dishes. Long, thin Asian aubergines have fewer seeds and therefore the most mellow flavour.*

Taste: *When cooked, aubergine has a subtle, creamy taste, often with a smooth bitterness from the skin that adds an indefinable extra to the other ingredients.*

This vegetable display includes just a few of the
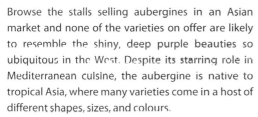 *aubergine varieties grown in South East Asia.*

Hass Avocado

Plantain

The fruit of a subtropical tree, the avocado (*Persea americana*) has been cultivated in Central and South America since about 7000 BCE. The Hass variety is smaller than many others, higher in oil, easier to peel, and richer in flavour: it is a hybrid of species originally from Mexico and Guatemala.

Developed by Rudolph Hass of California during the 1920s and patented by him in 1935, the Hass has pebbly skin that darkens as it ripens from green through to indigo or almost black. It is the most widely cultivated avocado in the United States and is also grown extensively in Mexico. (All Hass avocado trees trace their lineage back to a single mother tree, which died in 2002 aged seventy-five.)

Although no longer used as a butter substitute, as it was by seventeenth-century sailors—hence its names of midshipman's butter and butter pear—the avocado is still most often used raw. Guacamole, the simple mash that dates back to Aztec times, is by far the best known dish. But the avocado also has a starring role in Cobb salad, a blend created at Los Angeles' Brown Derby restaurant. **SH**

A staple in East and Central Africa and parts of Asia, plantains are, essentially, kinds of banana that can only be used for cooking: they are generally larger than dessert bananas, with a tougher skin, and a starch level that renders them unappealing until heat converts it into sugars. Edible plantains start green, turn yellow, get black spots, and when fully ripe are all black. They were probably known in South East Asia as early as the sixth century BCE.

When green and unripe, plantains have a starchy, potato-like flavour: they may be sliced and fried into chips or crisps. Once the interior is sweet and ripe, they lend themselves to mashing, sautéing, baking, boiling, sun-drying, and dishes from curries to the gloopy West African *fufu*. However, it is frying that suits plantains' glutinous sweetness best, and *platanos maduras fritos*—fried slabs of juicy, golden plantain—is a traditional Latin American and Caribbean side dish, served with rice and beans, meat, fish, or even breakfast. *Pazham pori*—plantain fritters—are popular in India, while crunchy plantain crisps are in vogue on several continents. **SH**

Taste: *Avocados have a sweet and nutty flavour. The Hass variety is especially rich. It has the subtle taste of room-temperature butter with a creamy aftertaste.*

Taste: *When green, plantains have a bland, starchy taste. Ripe plantains are sweet and have a distinctive flavour, with banana notes overlaying an almost carrot-like base.*

Women take unripe plantains to the open-air market in Mwika, Tanzania. »

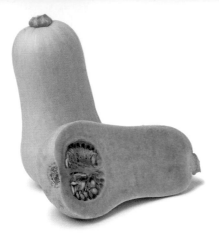

Butternut Squash

Spaghetti Squash

With its tan skin, long neck, and bulbous base, butternut squash looks like nothing so much as a very large pear. One of the most popular of the myriad varieties of squash that are grown around the world, it is a winter squash—the fruit is left to ripen on the vine until it develops a hard, thick rind.

Squash have long been eaten in their New World home: archaeological evidence shows that varieties were consumed at least 12,000 years ago and cultivated more than 9,000 years ago. Butternut belongs to the *Cucurbita moschata* family of squashes: remains of cultivated relatives dating back to 5,000 BCE have been found in Mexico. Colonists and Europeans adopted members of the family as early as the seventeenth century; today it is grown anywhere with a long, warm growing season.

Butternut squash is an extremely versatile vegetable that pairs particularly well with allspice, cinnamon, cloves, ginger, and other warming winter seasonings. It makes creamy soups and mashes, is baked and served with brown sugar, and can even be turned into puddings and pies. **SH**

Weight Watchers International put spaghetti squash, known as vegetable spaghetti in England, and also called noodle squash, on the culinary map when it introduced this low-calorie alternative to pasta to its members. A member of the extensive gourd family (*Cucurbita pepo*), spaghetti squash is loosely cylindrical, like a jumbo marrow. When ripe it has bright yellow skin and yellowish-white flesh.

The spaghetti squash is generally believed to have been developed around 1930 in North America but its history is uncertain, especially since it is known and grown in Japan. It takes its name from the ease with which the cooked flesh can be pulled away with a fork into strands resembling spaghetti. An orange-fleshed variety, called Orangetti, was developed in the later twentieth century.

Spaghetti squash can be boiled or baked. As its name implies, the tendrils are often treated like spaghetti and dressed with sauces, or butter, fresh herbs, garlic, and Parmesan cheese. When treated like a squash, the vegetable is often served stuffed. It can also be used in soups. **SH**

Taste: *Slightly sweet with nutty notes, yet with a dilute, gentle flavour, butternut squash tastes a little like a pumpkin and a bit like sweet potato or yam.*

Taste: *The fun of this rather bland vegetable is in its tendril-like texture. The taste is slightly sweet and nutty with a hint of lemon; the orange variety is slightly sweeter.*

Spaghetti squash becomes a fibrous mass when cooked.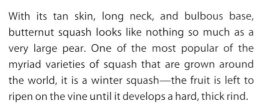

Pumpkin

Winter Melon

At the stroke of midnight, Cinderella's carriage most likely turned into a *Rouge Vif D'Estampes*, a large, French pumpkin, or *potiron*, coloured an orange so bright it is almost scarlet. But this stunningly flexible vegetable—which is technically a fruit—had its origins in Central America thousands of years ago.

When the first English explorers arrived in North America, they found Native Americans turning pumpkins into soup, stews, and other dishes. Centuries later, chefs have made pumpkin soup into a gastronomic classic, while pumpkin stews are popular from Africa to the Caribbean. The pumpkin's blandness means it can be treated both as savoury and sweet: in the U.S. Thanksgiving classic, pumpkin pie, it is blended with molasses, sugar, and spices.

In England and the United States, freakishly large pumpkins are grown for festivals and contests: some have reached over 220 pounds (100 kg) in weight. Neither these nor the types that are sold for carving into lanterns at Halloween make good eating: the fibrous texture makes them easy for children to cut but militates against flavour. **SH**

The large, waxy-skinned gourd known as winter melon is actually a misnomer, being neither sweet nor a winter fruit. It is, in fact, a squash that is harvested during the winter. It is also sometimes called wax gourd and ash gourd.

The winter melon (*Benincasa hispida*) is thought to have originated in Japan or Indonesia and is now popular all over South East Asia. Its white, waxy coating means that it can be stored for many months as long as it remains uncut. It can weigh up to 100 pounds (45 kg). The smallest melons are sold whole, whereas larger ones are cut and sold in slices. The winter melon looks a bit like an oblong watermelon and its colour varies from pale to dark green, although the flesh inside is white.

Winter melon is used in soups, curries, stir-fries, pickles, and preserves. At banquets, winter melon soup is served in a hollowed-out, whole small winter melon. Although often eaten as a vegetable in South East Asia, the flesh is also candied and is used to make a paste, along with almonds and sesame seeds, inside the popular pastries "wife's cakes." **KKC**

Taste: *Pumpkins taste earthy and sweet, a cross between butternut squash and sweet potato. The flavour intensifies with cooking, but also forms a good base for other flavours.*

Taste: *Winter melon has a mild, delicate taste, a little like courgette. Crisp and tender when cooked briefly, its texture becomes almost melting when cooked for longer.*

Pumpkins are grown on an agribusiness
❮ *scale across North America.*

Amaranth

Microleaf

Known to some as pigweed, to others as love-lies-bleeding, or Joseph's coat, amaranth in its various forms is a weed, a dye, an ornamental plant, a cereal, and a vegetable—not to mention an ingredient in Aztec blood rituals in Mexico. With more than fifty varieties, some of which can grow taller than a man, *Amaranthus* has been endlessly adapted as a food. In India, the spinach-like leaves, *chawli*, are mixed with dhal, in a bhaji (a kind of fritter), or into dry curries. The Chinese stir-fry the leaves or add them to soups. In Africa, under the name *morogo*—a generic word for vegetables—freshly picked leaves go straight into the pot. It is also one of the greens of the Caribbean soup or side dish, *callaloo*.

The shot-sized seeds are rich in protein and have been used as a cereal since Mayan times. In Mexico they are popped like popcorn and mixed with honey or sugar syrup to make a chewy confection called *alegria* (meaning happiness in Spanish). In the Himalayas, crushed grain is compacted with raw sugar to make the snack, *chikki*. Amaranth flour contains no gluten but is made into flatbreads. **MR**

The most delicate leaves of lettuces, herbs, and other greens, microleaves—or micro greens as they are called in North America—do not come in one variety but many, ranging from rocket and mustard to celery and radish. Other popular varieties include spinach, ruby chard, beet, and coriander.

Microleaves were "discovered" by enterprising chefs who, after sampling the intense flavours of tiny plant leaves, incorporated them into salads and used them as seasonings and garnishes. Many vegetables and herbs are grown specifically as microleaves and valued not only for their flavour but also for their colour. They can be bought individually or in mixtures, and many cooks grow their own.

Because there are so many varieties, there is a microleaf to suit most dishes. Several varieties make a good salad when topped with a light vinaigrette and they can be used like lettuce in sandwiches or wraps. Very quickly sautéed, they make a delicious base for salmon and other fish. They add flavour to soups when dropped in at the very last minute of cooking, and make a flavoursome garnish. **SH**

Taste: *Amaranth leaves cook like a spinach, but are milder tasting and not generally astringent. The grain is bland tasting with a texture similar to quinoa.*

Taste: *Microleaf rocket is mildly spicy and nutty; beet is earthy; broccoli is mildly peppery; mustard is tangy with a bite reminiscent of horseradish.*

According to Greek mythology, the amaranth flower ❸ *never faded no matter how little light or water it had.*

Wild Rocket

Lamb's Lettuce

Rocket, *Eruca sativa*, is also known as rugola, rucola, Italian cress, and arugula, but takes its English name from the French *roquette*. The plant was valued by the ancient Romans not only for the small, serrated leaves but for its seeds, which they used to flavour oils. (These were used in aphrodisiac mixtures as far back as the first century CE, and the plant was subsequently barred from monastery gardens.)

Long popular in Mediterranean Europe, particularly Italy, and in Egypt, where the varieties favoured are bland and cooked as a vegetable, it was in the 1990s that nations including Italy, India, Egypt, Turkey, and Israel pooled their resources of native strains to develop varieties that include the plant now rather misleadingly sold as "wild rocket."

Aromatic and with an assertive flavour, wild rocket is often combined with milder greens: its superb pairing with shaved Parmesan cheese has become a culinary cliché. Prepared in the style of a pesto, it makes a good accompaniment to pasta or boiled potatoes. Either raw or lightly sautéed in olive oil, it complements roast beef or grilled steak. **SH**

Under its French name *mâche*, lamb's lettuce (*Valerianella locusta*) was a trendy ingredient in the warm mixed salads that were popular in the 1980s. Although cultivated commercially in France, the wild plant is treated as a weed by most other gardeners. It grows as a small, spreading, tufty sprig of elongated, dark green leaves, and will produce small clusters of flower heads if left unpicked.

The wild leaves make an autumn or winter salad when lettuces are unavailable, but for cooks, lamb's lettuce has one mild inconvenience. Traces of grit tend to lodge at the base of each plant, and can be tricky to remove, even with careful rinsing. Once washed, the sprigs need careful drying or trapped water can spoil the dressing.

Although lost to Anglo-Saxon kitchens until a generation ago, lamb's lettuce was a regular salad ingredient in seventeenth-century Britain. King Charles II's chef, Robert May, recommended it, as did John Evelyn in *Acetaria: a Discourse of Sallets* (1699). Nowadays, lamb's lettuce is often a constituent of supermarket vacuum-packed salad mixtures. **MR**

Taste: *This attention-getting leaf is spicy, peppery, and rather mustardy in flavour, with intense, lightly bitter, green back notes and a deliciously tangy flavour.*

Taste: *Lamb's lettuce is tender, mild without bitterness or astringency, and delivers an accessible, mildly sweet flavour alongside an almost velvety mouthfeel.*

Watercress

Pea Shoot

Watercress is one of nature's most lovely greens. Mostly eaten raw, the bunching small green leaves make a refreshing, colourful addition to everything from soups to salads. Originally native to Europe and Asia, it now also grows in the ponds and brooks of North America, and is widely cultivated elsewhere.

Watercress gets its name in part from the fact that it grows in cold running water and, in general, the fresher and purer the water, the better the wild leaves. Despite its botanical name, *Nasturtium officinale*, it is a member of the same family as mustard, an entirely different genus from the nasturtium flower. Historically, watercress has been valued for its medicinal properties: the Greek general Xenophon made his men eat it as a tonic.

The British used to include watercress and/or cucumber sandwiches as part of afternoon tea. Watercress also makes a tasty salad, either alone and seasoned with fennel and balsamic vinegar or in combination with other greens, such as rocket. In France, *potage cressonnière* is a watercress and potato soup garnished with blanched watercress leaves. **SH**

This delicate vegetable, with its complex, elegant pea flavour, is the tender top leaves, stems, and tendrils of the young pea plant, and such a delicacy that from Shanghai to southern England plants are cultivated solely for their shoots. They can be eaten at stages varying from a thread-like stem only 2 inches (5 cm) long with leaves the size of a little fingernail, to young plants 6 inches (15 cm) long with leaves 1 inch (2.5 cm) in diameter.

It was probably the Hmong people of southern China and South East Asia who introduced pea shoots to a wider world. In China, where they are known as *dou miao* (Mandarin) and *dow miu* (Cantonese), they are served stir-fried, in soups, in salads, or in dumplings. In Japan and much of South East Asia, they are used in many contexts where other young greens might be.

Pea shoots are making an increased appearance in the West, where chefs harness the baby shoots as a pretty, surprisingly flavoured garnish to fish and meats, transform them into a salad, dressed with lemon, or sauté older shoots with garlic. **SH**

Taste: *Raw watercress has a pungent, spicy taste reminiscent of peppery radishes. When cooked, it loses some of its bite, but releases a heady, flowery aroma.*

Taste: *Young pea shoots have a vegetal sweetness like fresh petits pois. Older shoots have a stronger flavour, with hints of baby spinach, watercress, and mange-tout.*

Purslane

Purslane (*Portulaca oleracea*), also known by its Spanish name, *verdolaga*, is a succulent, spreading herb with clusters of jade-like leaves that grows wild and is also cultivated. Found in parts of Europe, southern Africa, Asia, and the Americas, it has slipped in and out of favour as a culinary ingredient. It was once very popular throughout the Arab world and, more recently, was adopted by French chefs during the nouvelle cuisine fashion of the 1980s. Although more commonly eaten raw it can also be cooked, when it will give a mucilaginous texture, rather like okra, to a sauce or soup. In Mexico, it is often served with hard cheese.

Purslane is enjoying a revival among the health-food lobby because it contains significant amounts of both Omega-3 fatty acids and vitamin E. The plant is used in traditional Chinese medicine as a treatment for diarrhoea, a strange choice since, eaten in quantity, it is an effective laxative. In Malawi, purslane's name translates as "buttocks of the chief's wife," a reference, no doubt, to the firm but springy texture of its leaves. **MR**

Taste: *The flavour is quite bland but gains characteristics from the soil where the purslane is grown, which can make it taste either lemony or salty.*

Long considered a weed by gardeners,
◖ *purslane is gaining favour as a salad leaf.*

Sorrel

There are several kinds of sorrel that have been eaten as a vegetable since ancient times; however, they share one common feature: they are all sour. Round-leafed or French sorrel (*Rumex scutatus*) is now the most widely cultivated kind. It has long been used to offset rich food and was the key ingredient of one of the most famous nouvelle cuisine dishes, *escalope de saumon à l'oseille*, a fillet of salmon lightly cooked with a cream and sorrel sauce, that was created by the chefs, the Troisgros brothers.

Sorrel, often grown as a potherb, has a long growing season and is available from early spring until early winter. In old English cooking, a green sorrel sauce was served with roast goose. A handful of the leaves transforms a soup made with onion and potato. In French cuisine, sorrel purée traditionally accompanied a pot-roasted cushion of veal. Cultivated sorrel leaves dissolve with prolonged cooking. They should not be chopped with carbon steel knives or stewed in iron pots, which will turn them black and bitter. **MR**

Taste: *Wilted for a few moments sorrel will turn from green to khaki. The level of sourness depends on the variety and the soil, but is always pleasant and lemony.*

Cos Lettuce

The lettuce of choice for Caesar salads, Cos may owe its name to the island of Cos in the Aegean Sea, where some say it originated. Other food historians and etymologists believe the word derives from *xus*, the Arabic word for lettuce, and a similar lettuce is pictured in an ancient Egyptian carving. Today, this dark green variety of lettuce with long, crisp leaves is often also known as Romaine, from the French *laitue romaine* and the Italian *lattuga romana*.

Part of the *Lactuca sativa* family, Cos is related to common garden flowers such as marigolds, asters, and zinnias. It usually grows to a weight of about 11 ounces (300 g), although the Little Gem variety, popular in Britain, weighs as little as 3 ½ ounces (100 g).

Like Beatrix Potter, whose Flopsy Bunnies became drowsy after eating lettuce, the ancient Greeks and early Romans believed that the leaves had a sleep-inducing, calming effect. Torn into bite-sized pieces, Cos blends well with fruits and other vegetables in both hot and cold salads and is a good replacement for cabbage in stir-fries. **SH**

Frisée

Traditionally known as endive, and more contemporarily as frisée, from the French *chicorée frisée* (curly chicory), this frilly green is one of many varieties of *Cichorium endivia*. Native to the Mediterranean and cultivated throughout southern Europe, frisée has been around for more than 300 years, and its bite is widely appreciated in salads.

The narrow, curly, fringed leaves, looking quite literally "frizzy," form a compact pale green to lime green head whose central leaves vary between yellow and white. In the United States, as in the United Kingdom before the rise of rocket, they are used as a garnish for grilled vegetables and meats.

Frisée is a common component of *mesclun*, the salad of baby greens that originated in southern France. It is often, like dandelion greens, paired with bacon, croutons, and sometimes egg in a *salade lyonnaise*. Combined with spiced walnuts and poached pears, it makes a fresh-tasting, light dessert. In salads, it makes a good counterpoint to blood oranges, tangerines, and other citrus fruits, and works beautifully with watercress. **SH**

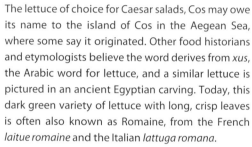

Taste: *The outer leaves of Cos have a slightly bitter taste. The centre leaves are sweeter and more delicate in flavour. When cooked, Cos tastes a little like asparagus.*

Taste: *Like most members of the chicory family, frisée has a slightly bitter taste with some nutty overtones. Its texture combines pleasant crispness with a frilly delicacy.*

Tudela Lettuce Heart

Chicory

Situated in northern Spain's fertile Ebro valley, the municipality of Tudela is famed for the quality of its fresh produce. For centuries, the glorious Navarra sunshine and the waters of the Ebro River have created an ideal microclimate in which to grow fruit and vegetables. Among them is the king of lettuces: Tudela lettuce hearts (or *cogollos* in Spanish).

Lettuce (*Lactuca sativa*), a member of the daisy family, began life as a humble weed over 4,000 years ago; Egyptian tomb paintings depict a plant that looks like lettuce and there are references to various types of lettuces in ancient Greece.

Tudela lettuce hearts have tightly packed leaves that are coloured light green to yellow. They carry a PDO certificate, which means that they must be grown within a specified zone and the seeds may not be sold outside that stipulated area.

Navarran cuisine often pairs *cogollos* in salads with anchovies, salmon, or prawns; they are also popular braised. The crisp leaves work equally well with punchy dressings made from oil, garlic, and anchovies, or simply a splash of good Spanish olive oil. **LF**

Although the bitter leaves of wild chicory were enjoyed in ancient Greece and Rome, it was not cultivated as a vegetable until the sixteenth century. Chicory (*Cichorium intybus*) is closely related to endive, (*C. endivia*), a member of the same family, and the two are often confused in French and English.

There are many varieties of chicory but the type often encountered today is known as *witloof* (white leaf). This cigar-shaped chicory is said to have originated in 1850 in Belgium, although it had a precedent in the *barbe de capucin* grown in the Low Countries since the sixteenth century. Belgian lore tells of a farmer who, returning to his fields after a prolonged absence, discovered that the roots of chicory plants he had covered with soil before leaving had developed heads of white, compact, pointed leaves. These *chicons* soon travelled to France under the name of endive, with a Belgian subtitle.

The crisp yet tender texture of chicory leaves makes them ideal in salads, but they can also be lightly braised or baked. When cooked, a pinch of sugar can offset any bitterness that remains. **MR**

Taste: *The compact hearts of Tudela lettuce yield delightfully crisp and fresh flavoured leaves that are both tender and sweet. They are good raw in salads or braised.*

Taste: *Raw, crunchy chicory has a delicate flavour with a hint of bitterness. Braised, it takes on the flavours of the ingredients with which it is cooked.*

Arrowhead Spinach

Swiss Chard

Spinach (*Spinacia oleracea*)—once called the "prince of vegetables" by the Arabs—has been cultivated since ancient times. Arrowhead or arrowleaf spinach is one of the prestige choices among gourmet chefs and is very popular in the United States, which is one of the world's biggest producers of spinach. In the 1920s, the vegetable was famously promoted there as the strength-building food of the cartoon character, Popeye the Sailor. (In fact, the absorption of spinach's high nutritional, particularly iron, content is inhibited by its oxalic acid levels.)

Often grown as a "baby" variety, hybrids of arrowhead spinach include Razzle Dazzle and Bordeaux. The latter has red stems that turn green with cooking. Some takes on the classic French *mesclun* or spring mix of green leaves include arrowhead spinach. It is also excellent on its own. New World chefs unite the leaves with any number of ingredients, including cherries, Mandarin oranges, cashews, and even wasabi dressing. Wilted arrowhead spinach is also a popular base for many other foods from venison to shellfish. **SH**

This tall leafy vegetable with thick, crunchy red, white, or yellow stalks and wide green fan-shaped leaves is grown widely throughout France's Rhône valley and used in many Mediterranean cuisines. However, this ancient plant has no known connection to Switzerland.

Swiss chard is a member of the beet family, as shown by its scientific name, *Beta vulgaris* var. *cicla,* and is probably the plant that Aristotle wrote about in the fourth century BCE under the name of beet. Other names include chard, leaf beet, seakale beet, white beet, and spinach beet.

The vegetable has a long history in Arab cuisines—it was quite possibly grown in the hanging gardens of ancient Babylon—and was an ingredient in many ancient Roman dishes. Today, it is widely used in Italy, sometimes as part of the filling in *tortelli di erbette*. The French use it to make *tourtes des blettes*, a sweet or savoury tart. Swiss chard, raw or quickly sautéed, goes well with beetroot and carrot in salads and can be used in most recipes calling for greens. **SH**

Taste: *Unlike older variants of spinach that have a stronger edge, arrowhead spinach has a delicately sweet flavour. The Razzle Dazzle hybrid is especially mild.*

Taste: *Spinach lovers adore Swiss chard. The leaves have a mild, sweet flavour that is reminiscent of spinach but slightly bitter. The stalks can be compared to asparagus.*

The stems of rainbow chard might even tempt vegetable-shy children to try them. »

Shungiku

The chrysanthemum is Japan's national flower. In autumn, chrysanthemum shows are held all over the country, while outsize dolls made entirely of the flowers used to be a common sight. Nevertheless, this does not deter the Japanese from eating a particular variety. Shungiku, the young leaves of the garland chrysanthemum (*Glebionis coronarium*) will add a taste of the East to any food. As with rocket, there are two types: a smaller, stronger, "wild" style with serrated leaves, and a milder type with broad leaves. Most varieties fall somewhere in between.

Young tender leaves can be eaten raw, or used in tempura, but mostly they are parboiled then refreshed in cold water. They are a key ingredient in *sukiyaki* and other stewed dishes, to which they are added at the last minute, as overcooking makes them bitter. Parboiled, they can be served *o-hitashi*-style with soy sauce, or with vinegar. In China, under their Cantonese name of *tong ho*, they are used in soups, stir-fries, and salads. The edible flowers—the best come from Aomori prefecture—are also dried and sold in thin flat sheets called *kikunori*. **SB**

Uzouza Leaf

Harvested from a wild evergreen climbing plant in the rainforest, the uzouza leaf is one of the most popular green leafy vegetables in Nigeria.

It is also eaten in other Central African countries where it is known by various names; in English it is sometimes called wild spinach. The leaf is collected in the wild by rural communities rather than cultivated, and then sold in markets across the region. The leaves are also exported to Europe and the United States for sale in African grocery stores.

Before being cooked, the leaves are cut into thin strips by rolling them and using a sharp knife to shave the ends into thin strips. The leaves are light green when fresh, and darken when dried or frozen. In Nigeria they are eaten raw in vegetable salads dressed with palm oil. The finely shredded leaves are also a common ingredient in hearty soups such as the spicy fish and meat soup *ofe-owerri*, the melon seed soup, *egusi*, and *ibaba*, a meat soup thickened with ground ibaba seeds. In Cameroon and the Central African Republic, the leaves feature in a stew made from beef and greens in a peanut sauce. **CK**

Taste: *The earthy, tangy taste has a slight bitterness like the scent of chrysanthemums. Both taste and texture are coarser than spinach, for which it may be substituted.*

Taste: *Aromatic and almost sweet smelling, pale green uzouza leaves have a mild, delicate taste reminiscent of spinach.*

Chrysanthemums flourish in the shade
◉ *of snow-capped Mount Fuji, Japan.*

Bok Choy

Celtuce

Bok choy belongs to the large brassica family of plants, which includes other vegetables popular in Asian cookery such as mustard greens and Chinese leaves, as well as broccoli, Brussels sprouts, and kale. It has as many different spellings—pak choi and bak choi are two of the most common—as it boasts different varieties. Trying to figure them all out can confuse even a botanist. Some have lighter green leaves and thicker stems, with others the leaves are heavily veined with white, and the sizes can range from just over 1 inch (2.5 cm) up to about 8 inches (20 cm). However, bok choy generally has a distinctive appearance: green, ruffled leaves contrast sharply with the smooth, juicy white stems that give the vegetable its name (bok is the Cantonese for "white").

The attractive white-green contrast means that the vegetable is often cooked whole, while slightly larger ones are halved or quartered lengthwise. The stems are juicy and crunchy whereas the thin leaves wilt quickly when cooked. Bok choy can be boiled, steamed, stir-fried, and used to fill dumplings. **KKC**

Also known as stem lettuce and asparagus lettuce, celtuce (*Lactuca sativa* var. *asparagina*) originated in China and is sometimes called Chinese lettuce. It is grown mainly for its thick, tender stem but its cos-like leaves can also be eaten. In spite of its name, it is not a cross between lettuce and celery. In China, it is known as *wosun* or *woju*.

When peeled to remove the bitter, milky sap in its outer edges, the stem can be sliced or diced and eaten raw in a salad or cut into pieces and served with a dip. In China, the stems are grilled or boiled, added to soups and used in stir-fries with meat, poultry, or fish. The Chinese also pickle celtuce. The stem can also be cooked and served like broccoli. Young, tender celtuce leaves can be added to salads or lightly sautéed. Once the plant has matured, the milky sap makes the leaves bitter and inedible.

Celtuce is grown as a commercial crop in China. It is believed to have been brought to the United States in the 1940s by a missionary. There and in the rest of the world, it is not widely known and is grown mostly in home gardens. **SH**

Taste: *The flavour of all bok choys are subtle compared to many other types of brassica—mildly sweet and sometimes with a faintly bitter undertone.*

Taste: *Cooked the stem tastes like a cross between squash and artichoke. Raw, it is crisp, moist, and mild flavoured. The young leaves have a chicory-like bitterness.*

Pristine, freshly harvested bok choy on
○ *offer to customers in Kowloon, Hong Kong.*

Melokhia

Turnip Top

Although the leaves of the melokhia plant are eaten as a vegetable in many parts of the world, including the Middle East and South America, it is in Egypt that melokhia has been an important staple of the national diet since the time of the Pharoahs.

Made into a wholesome soup called simply melokhia, the dish is still prepared in the same way as depicted in ancient tomb paintings. For centuries, generations of Egyptian women have balanced pots of the popular dish on their heads, carrying it out at lunchtime to their menfolk toiling in the fields.

Fresh, serrated-edged leaves can be bought in Egypt, but for any expatriate Egyptian longing for a taste of home, they are exported dried, canned, and frozen. Fresh leaves need to be washed, dried, and finely chopped before simmering in water for about ten minutes. The most basic soup is simply melokhia leaves cooked in a light vegetable stock, but in Syria and Egypt a thicker version is made using chicken stock. Bread is laid on plates and piled with rice and small pieces of boned chicken, before the thick melokhia broth is spooned over. **WS**

The turnip (*Brassica rapa*) is one of the earliest cultivated vegetables. Traditionally, turnip tops or turnip leaves were a seasonal vegetable, available only when the turnip crop was thinned out in spring. Plants are now cultivated exclusively for their leaves both in Europe and the United States.

Typically light green, thin, and hairy, turnip tops feature in many Mediterranean and other European recipes, particularly in the cooking of northern Portugal's Trás-os-Montes e Alto Douro region. The rustic cuisine of this mountainous area is characterized by strong flavours; here turnip tops are combined with *alheira*—a kind of sausage made from meat other than pork—and with cod. In neighbouring Galicia, in Spain, the leaves are served with pork, while further south in Portugal they appear in soup and rice dishes, and as a side dish for fried mackerel. In the Apulia region of Italy, turnip tops are used in pasta dishes. In the United States, turnip greens are a staple of Southern dishes, where they are cooked in a broth with a small portion of salt pork or ham hocks for seasoning. **DM**

Taste: *Melokhia leaves have a slightly bitter flavour similar to sorrel. Cooked they become glutinous, and have been described as a cross between okra and spinach.*

Taste: *Generally served boiled, the pungent leaves have a slightly bitter flavour, rather like mustard greens, which becomes milder with cooking.*

Turnip leaves flourish under protective netting on a farm in Suffolk, England. »

Rock Samphire

Marsh Samphire

Rock samphire (*Crithmum maritimum*) grows in nooks and crevices along the seashores of Europe. Edgar in Shakespeare's *King Lear* described harvesting it as a "dreadful trade," presumably because it involved dangerous clinging to cliff edges. In fact, it grows in more accessible areas too.

In the seventeenth century, rock samphire was hugely popular in England. During the eighteenth century, it was used mainly as a pickle: in *Food For Free* (1972) the author Richard Mabey described it being covered in spiced vinegar and left in a cooling baker's oven over the weekend. It was still popular in the nineteenth century, but fell out of fashion, despite a brief revival in the late twentieth century.

As with other wild plants, it is best gathered early in the season when the pointed leaves are still tender. Later the texture becomes coarse and the resinous odour overpowering. The leaves are mainly used today as a garnish, an accompaniment, a pickle, or an addition to a mixed seafood salad. The unusual flavour requires discreet handling to prevent it from dominating a dish. **MR**

Very different from its rocky namesake, this bright green vegetable, shaped like lots of miniature Arizona cacti, flourishes in the mud of salt marshes around the coastlines of England, France, and the Low Countries. Collecting and cleaning it is a messy and time-consuming business, but as soon as the first shoots emerge in June the foraging begins.

Marsh samphire (*Salicornia europaea*) probably takes its name from the old French term, *l'herbe de Saint Pierre*, but is also known as glasswort, and was once used in glassmaking. Today samphire and its relatives are seen as plants of the future because they will grow in salty conditions.

At the start of the season samphire may be eaten raw, but the saltiness is too much for many. It can be pickled, but this destroys the subtle green salinity. Blanched, it works well in light salads, and is the perfect seasonal partner to summer trout. In places where demand for samphire outstrips the local harvest, cultivated varieties are imported from Israel and the Gulf; *Salicornia virginica*, a related species, is harvested in the United States. **AMS**

Taste: *Lightly cooked, rock samphire is crunchy, but also, despite its saltiness, juicy. Its vaguely perfumed taste has been compared to carrots, but is individual and powerful.*

Taste: *Blanched without salt, dressed with butter, and eaten by pulling the succulent flesh off with the teeth, this briny delicacy lives up to its nickname "sea asparagus."*

Resilient to salt and drought, samphire is likely to have greater economic importance in the future. »

Dandelion

The French name for dandelion, *pissenlit*, echoes its seventeenth-century English name, "piss-a-bed." Its contemporary English name derives from the French *dent de lion* (lion's tooth), a reference to its serrated leaves. This edible weed (*Taraxacum officinale*), a relative of chicory, is, of course, popularly known as a diuretic, but it is also a salad green. The white dandelion was cultivated in Flanders, in the dark, in the same way as the poetically named endive *barbe de capucin* ("monk's beard"). It is a seasonal speciality at its best in March. Both the wild and cultivated kinds occur in salads, particularly *salade aux lardons*, where the leaves are mixed with bacon and a dressing of hot fat and vinaigrette.

The difference between wild and cultivated dandelion lies in the flavour. Except in the case of the youngest, most tender leaves, wild dandelion is bitter, to the point where it becomes unpleasant, whereas blanched leaves are much milder. Dandelion flowers, picked in spring, can be made into a golden, sweet preserve: *cramaillotte*, halfway between a honey and a jelly. **MR**

Taste: *Dandelion leaves have a bitterness that blends well with other, gentler salad leaves. The leaves can also be cooked in much the same way as spinach.*

Wild dandelions attract many insects due
❻ *to their high levels of pollen and nectar.*

Nettle

Widespread and abundant throughout Europe, the leaves of stinging nettles, with their serrated edges and hairy surfaces, are among the most common sight in the wild. The sting derives from formic acid, and it is this that makes nettles so difficult to treat as a vegetable: gloves are essential during harvesting and preparation, although any chance of being stung is destroyed by cooking.

Nettles flourish throughout the spring and summer, dying down in autumn, but are only edible in the spring when the leaves are tender. Then, they can be boiled or wilted or made into a soup—such as the soups enjoyed today in Ireland, Scandinavia, and Tibet. Later they will turn bitter. (When the English diarist Samuel Pepys wrote of eating "nettle porridge" in 1661, he was probably describing a thick soup rather than one made with oats.)

The use of nettles in ethnic cuisines is often disguised by the generic term "wild greens," for example in Greek cooking where the term *hortes* often includes nettle and dandelion leaves. In Italy, nettles are added to rustic risottos or frittatas. **MR**

Taste: *Although likened to spinach, nettles have a marked tang reminiscent of iodine. Freshly blanched they have a bright green colour unlike any other leaf vegetables.*

Wild Garlic Leaf

Fiddlehead

Wild garlic, also known as ramsons, appears in early spring over much of Europe, usually in damp woodland. Its Latin name, *Allium ursinum* (bear garlic), may reflect the fact that it appears around the time when bears emerge from hibernation.

Wild garlic bulbs are edible, but better left in the ground. Although the starry white flower spikes that appear once the leaves are past their best are flavoursome and beautiful, it is the young, slender leaves that appeal to cooks, including renowned chefs such as Marc Veyrat and Michel Bras. In Italian cuisine, wild garlic leaves flavour frittatas, are pounded to make a kind of pesto, and appear in stuffings and soups. Belgians chop them finely and mix them in with *fromage frais*. The tender leaves can also be added in small amounts to green salads.

What makes wild garlic leaves so attractive to cooks and chefs is their intense bright green colour after they have been blanched in boiling water. Some chefs also dry them, grind them to a powder with a little salt, and use the results as a versatile seasoning year-round. **MR**

Fiddleheads (*Matteuccia struthiopteris*) are a herald of the long-awaited New England spring. Tightly coiled, the bright green early shoots of the ostrich fern make their brief but dramatic appearance each spring in April and May.

Although increasingly available in grocery stores in the northern United States and Canada, fiddleheads remain a wild plant and are foraged rather than farmed. Harvesting must happen before the tightly coiled head unfurls, making the plant inedible, and the perishable young shoots are best eaten as soon after picking as possible.

Caution should be taken when foraging: some varieties of fern are dangerous and bracken shoots, although eaten as *warabi* in Japan, have been considered carcinogenic. Fiddleheads should not be eaten raw. They are traditionally boiled or steamed, then blanched, after which they are often sautéed in butter and served as an accompanying dish. The shoots are frequently added to salads or soups, and can even be served dipped in chocolate. In New Zealand, koru shoots are a similar delicacy. **CLH**

Taste: *Puréed wild garlic leaves taste less assertive than cultivated garlic bulbs, with a hint of chives. While garlicky, they do not have the strong odour of garlic.*

Taste: *Fiddleheads are best eaten on the day they are picked. They have a gentle taste with hints of asparagus and earthy artichoke, and are tender to the bite.*

Fiddleheads take their name from their close resemblance to the scrolled neck of a violin. ❯❯

Vaucluse Green Asparagus

Set in the heart of Provence, the Vaucluse enjoys a unique status for the quality of its fruit and vegetables, due partly to tourism but also to a climate that has adapted to growing outstanding raw materials. As a species, the green Vaucluse asparagus is no different from those grown elsewhere and its production is relatively recent. In his autobiography, written early in the twentieth century, the great chef Auguste Escoffier noted that in Provence all asparagus were white until he persuaded the farmers in Lauris to switch to green.

Green asparagus from the Luberon area of the Vaucluse is mainly grown in greenhouses or polytunnels in order to bring it to the market early in the year—the season can start in February. The spears (the French refer to the stems as *turions*) are left to grow out of the ground to a height of no more than one foot (30 cm) before they are cut off just below the surface of the soil. The secret of their taste lies in eating them (boiled in a steep-sided pan to let them stand vertically) within a day of picking, after which they start to lose their sweetness. **MR**

Bassano White Asparagus

In the spring, asparagus fever hits the pretty town of Bassano del Grappa in northern Italy. The wonderful white asparagus grown here has a unique flavour: so much so that it carries a DOC.

A member of the lily family, asparagus has been grown in Bassano for many years: it was valued as a delicacy even before Roman times. In the early sixteenth century, or so the story goes, a devastating hailstorm destroyed the town's asparagus crop. Faced with such destruction, the farmers had little choice but to harvest the part of the plant which had remained underground. The shoots were white because they lacked exposure to sunlight, but the asparagus was strikingly tender and flavoursome. The delighted farmers decided to cultivate the whole plant underground from that point on.

In late May every year, Bassano hosts a festival to celebrate its most prized crop. Farmers present their asparagus on the streets, while restaurants compete in A Tavola con l'Asparago DOC di Bassano to create the most spectacular succession of courses involving their beloved white asparagus. **LF**

Taste: *Green asparagus should be firm and veering towards al dente in texture. Its colour should be intense. Its characteristic taste is slightly sweet with a hint of sulphur.*

Taste: *The long, chubby spears have a notable succulence. The elegant, restrained sweetness is quite remarkable: it opens up over the entire tongue with each mouthful.*

These shoots of green asparagus illustrate
⊗ ***how the tips and scales can deepen to red.***

Marais Poitevin Angelica

Purple Sprouting Broccoli

Tall, waving fronds of musky scented angelica (*Angelica archangelica*) line the banks of the ancient waterways that criss-cross the swampy wilderness of Marais Poitevin, a marshy area close to Niort in France's Poitou-Charente region. This land provides the damp soil essential for the plant's growth. For centuries the people living there relied on the healing powers of angelica as an antidote to poisons.

A member of the parsley family, angelica is also grown in Italy, Scotland, Germany, Scandinavia, Russia, and parts of North America, although it is mainly cultivated in France. It is one of the few plants to withstand the harsh climates of Iceland, Greenland, and the Faroes, where it is still cooked and eaten as a vegetable. The fresh leaves can also be shredded in salads and used in omelettes and fish dishes, whereas the stems are often stewed with rhubarb or made into preserves and jams.

However, the most common use of angelica today is as a candied confection for use in cakes, sweet breads, cheesecakes, or, cut into diamond shapes, as a decoration for sweetmeats. **WS**

A sturdy and substantial brassica, broccoli is a traditional winter vegetable in many countries: yet it reaches its peak when young and newly budded in the spring. Like the cauliflower—to which it is botanically close—broccoli is a type of cabbage, topped with clusters of tiny buds that can range in colour from yellowish white to a very deep purple through various shades of green. The vegetable was almost certainly developed in Italy (the Italian name means "little shoots"). As its early French name of Italian asparagus shows, the stalks were enjoyed along with the flower heads.

Today, popular varieties are grown to produce the largest, most compact, and most consistently coloured flowering head, although the varieties that were historically popular are returning to favour. With their small, dark flower heads, crisp but tender stalks, and relatively delicate upper leaves, purple sprouting broccoli provides infinitely more flavour than blander mass market varieties, and is enjoyed whole, perhaps with butter or a dipping sauce such as the Italian *bagna cauda*. **FC**

Taste: *Fresh angelica leaves and stems taste of liquorice. The leaf stalks can be blanched and eaten like celery. After crystallization the stems turn a glorious acid green.*

Taste: *The blanched heads of purple sprouting broccoli have a meaty flavour, crisp texture, and slightly bitter, ferrous aftertaste. The tender stalks are slightly sweeter.*

Immature flowers form the heads of purple sprouting broccoli. »

Brussels Sprout

At their most flavourful and most widely available from September to March, Brussels sprouts (*Brassica oleracea*), are one of those foods you either love or hate. A member of the same family as cabbage, kale, broccoli, and other strong-flavoured vegetables with an equally assertive aroma, their tightly packed leaves make them look like tiny cabbages. Most are green, although a few varieties are purple.

Probably brought to Belgium by the Roman legions and most likely served at the medieval Burgundian court at Lille, Brussels sprouts have been grown near Brussels for more than four centuries. Today they are also cultivated in England, northern Europe, and the United States.

Brussels sprouts lend themselves to many cooking methods—steamed and dressed with balsamic vinegar and Parmesan cheese, or served with cream or cheese sauces. They are a traditional Christmas dinner dish in England, and are often paired with chestnuts along the lines of the French and Belgian *bruxelloise*, a garnish of stewed Brussels sprouts, braised chicory, and potatoes. **SH**

Taste: Brussels sprouts are best fresh and cooked until they are tender. Then, they have a sweet taste like young cabbage. Smaller is better as large ones can be bitter.

Kohlrabi

Although considered in many countries an Asian vegetable, kohlrabi originated in northern Europe, and the unusual name is German in origin. It means cabbage-turnip, and, like the common cabbage, broccoli, and Brussels sprouts, this curious vegetable is a subspecies of *Brassica oleracea (var. gongolydes)*. Kohlrabi is grown for its swelling, globe-shaped stem that resembles a turnip yet appears just above the ground: it may be greenish-white or purple. The few, cabbage-like leaves grow off long shoots above the globe. Those of young plants are edible, whereas mature leaves, like mature globes, are more traditionally used as animal fodder.

The globe can be diced and used in a stir-fry. It is often added to soups in China, and in Italy is sometimes made into a soup with rice. It is good mashed with potatoes, or puréed with butter. The youngest bulbs may be eaten raw, simply peeled and cut into matchsticks to add to a salad or a slaw. When very fresh and green, the leaves can be removed from their stalks, blanched, sautéed, and dressed with a little lemon juice or vinegar. **SH**

Taste: Kohlrabi globes that are no larger than a tennis ball are the mildest and sweetest, and taste like broccoli stems with a hint of radish. When raw, the taste is peppery.

Red Cabbage

It is hard to imagine the cooking of the Scandinavian countries, Germany, Hungary, Poland, and other Eastern European states without red cabbage. This heading cabbage, much like its green and white cousins except in colour, has been a long-standing staple in the cuisines of these countries, in part because it grows in cold weather. In the past, it was a survival food for many during the long and difficult winter months. Although perhaps peasant by reputation, with its shiny dark magenta leaves, red cabbage actually makes for an elegant presentation. Since the colour is only in the outer skin and stem, when cut it makes a pretty picture of red and white.

Red cabbage can be cooked just like green cabbage, but it has developed a group of recipes particular to itself. In the Ukraine, it is combined with apples, raisins, sugar, vinegar and other vegetables to make a sweet-and-sour soup. Throughout Eastern Europe, sweet-and-sour cabbage is a staple. *Rotkraut*, as it is called in Germany, is served with *sauerbraten*, a popular, savoury beef dish. A similar red cabbage preparation is served with ham in Sweden. **SH**

Taste: *There is little difference in flavour between red and green cabbage. Both are tender and juicy, although red cabbage is slightly more peppery.*

Braganza Cabbage

One of the more ancient vegetables that are still grown today, cabbages (*Brassica oleracea*) have most likely been cultivated since before recorded history. With its thick, chard-like stem and large, delicate, flaccid green leaves, Braganza cabbage is rather like the sea cabbages that grow wild along European coastlines. It has crinkly leaves that are loose, rather than forming a head, so belongs to the group of cabbages known as Savoy.

Braganza cabbage goes by several other names: sea kale cabbage, Portugal cabbage, or (in Portugal) *couve tronchuda*. Its flavour is sweet, and its leaves hold up well to cooking, retaining both colour and texture better than other varieties. Braganza cabbage is delicious steamed or braised, and it is the preferred choice of the Portuguese when they prepare their national dish *caldo verde*—a soup of vegetables, spicy linguica sausage, and shredded Braganza. Many people associate the soup with kale, but the flavour of Braganza is much more distinctive. The young leaves can be served raw in salads while the stems are often stir-fried. **LF**

Taste: *The fleshy leaves of Braganza cabbage have an exquisite, slightly sweet flavour, avoiding the sulphuric undercurrents often found in compact headed varieties.*

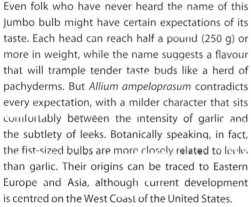

Elephant Garlic

Jersey Shallot

Even folk who have never heard the name of this jumbo bulb might have certain expectations of its taste. Each head can reach half a pound (250 g) or more in weight, while the name suggests a flavour that will trample tender taste buds like a herd of pachyderms. But *Allium ampeloprasum* contradicts every expectation, with a milder character that sits comfortably between the intensity of garlic and the subtlety of leeks. Botanically speaking, in fact, the fist-sized bulbs are more closely related to leeks than garlic. Their origins can be traced to Eastern Europe and Asia, although current development is centred on the West Coast of the United States.

Perhaps the best use of these garden giants reinforces their mild character: gentle slow roasting mellows and sweetens the taste yet further. Roasting also softens the flesh that can then be spread easily on toasts or used as a dip. Because of their size, the whole cloves can be sliced and sautéed in butter, allowing gentle caramelization of the natural sugars into faint memories of its overbearing common garlic cousins. **TH**

Like onions and garlic, shallots belong to the *Allium* family, but they are smaller and sweeter than an onion, much less pungent than garlic, and often the unsung heroes of the kitchen because of their ability to add a subtle but delicious flavour to all manner of savoury dishes.

The Jersey shallot is one of two main varieties of shallot; the other being the grey shallot. Whereas the grey shallot is also referred to as the "true shallot," the poor Jersey shallot has been saddled with the rather unflattering alternative name of "false shallot." Fortunately, this is less about flavour and more about the fact that the pinky coloured Jersey shallot has a more rounded bulb than its slightly milder cousin and was initially thought to be an onion simply impersonating a shallot.

Shallots are believed to have originated in central Asia more than 2,000 years ago. Crusaders returning from the Holy Land introduced them to Europe in the Middle Ages, where they became particularly prominent in French cuisine, flavouring such classic sauces as *beurre blanc* and *béarnaise*. **LF**

Taste: *Cooked, the mild garlic and onion character in both flavour and aroma is complemented by a marked sweetness. Raw, it is similar to common garlic.*

Taste: *Jersey shallots fuse the gentle flavours of sweet, red onion with suggestions of garlic. They are heavenly oven-roasted until caramelized and served as a vegetable.*

Elephant garlic grows near Gilroy in California,
◈ *home of the annual Gilroy Garlic Festival.*

Rosé de Roscoff Onion

Maui Onion

So special are the fragrant, rose-coloured Rosé de Roscoff onions (AOC) that they have not only a museum dedicated to them, but also their own two-day festival—the Fête de l'Oignon Rosé—to celebrate them, held every August in Roscoff, Britanny, when the pretty pink onions are harvested.

The onions first appeared on the shores of Brittany in the mid-seventeenth century, when monks brought seeds by boat from Portugal. The local microclimate—created by the combination of sandy soils, mineral rich seaweed, and warming Gulf air streams—meant that the onions flourished and before long a blossoming onion industry was born.

The good keeping qualities of these onions led agricultural labourers known as "Onion Johnnies" to travel to Britain to sell the unique pink onions door-to-door. Dressed in berets and striped shirts, and riding bicycles strung with the onions, they helped create the stereotypical image of the Frenchman.

Mild and fruity enough to be eaten raw, Rosé de Roscoff onions are also superb cooked in many dishes, including in soups, tarts, and breads. **LF**

Among the sweetest of onions, the Maui is white to golden yellow, juicy, and grown only in the rich, red earth of Haleakala, a dormant volcano on the island of Maui in Hawaii. It is one of the smallest of the sweet onion species and the earliest to mature, usually coming to market from April to June. It has a flattened sphere-like shape and a crisp texture.

First grown commercially by a cooperative of local farmers in 1943, these delicately flavoured onions are harvested by hand and then left to cure in the fields and dry in the mild trade winds. They were known only on the island until tourists began taking them back to the U.S. mainland. However, they are still not as widely available as other sweet onion varieties.

Maui onion ponzu dressing for salads and meats is produced commercially in Hawaii. Reflecting the strong Japanese influence on Hawaiian cuisine, it is citrus-based and made with Maui onions and soy sauce. The onions are a good addition to many Asian stir-fries and fish dishes. They are also excellent cut into rings, battered, and deep fried. **SH**

Taste: *Mild and sweet and delightfully crisp, Rosé de Roscoff are especially tasty when they are slow cooked or roasted, causing the natural sugars to caramelize.*

Taste: *All onions become sweeter when cooked. But Maui onions have a sweet, delicate flavour and none of the "hotness" of many other onions, even when raw.*

Uprooted Maui onions are allowed to dry on Maui's red volcanic soil. ❯❯

Spring Onion

Calçot

In the lily family, the genus *Allium* represents onions, as well as leeks and garlic. There are many types of onions, but spring onions as the English call them, are not one of them. What they are is the immature plant of many different kinds of globe or bulb onions. In the United States, they are most often called scallions or green onions.

Spring onions were probably first used in China as long ago as 100 BCE and they remain an important part of many Asian dishes. They are prized not only for their white roots, where the bulb is just beginning to form, but also for their long, straight green leaves. In Asian cooking, spring onions add a bite to stir fries and are mixed with finely chopped fresh ginger to make a condiment for seafood.

In the West, spring onions are generally eaten raw, either on their own or in salads. When sliced, the root of a spring onion separates into nearly transparent rings, and is often used as a garnish for salads and soups. Called *ciboules* in France, whole green onions often appear as crudités. They are also an integral ingredient of an antipasto tray. **SH**

The party animals of the *Allium* family, these delicious Catalan onions that look like giant spring onions or undersized leeks are traditionally grilled or roasted over vine cuttings and served with punchy garlic-laden sauces at fabulous local feasts known as *calçotadas*. The original festival, held in January in the town of Valls, southwest of Barcelona, plays host to around 30,000 revelling onion enthusiasts: a must-do for any visiting onionophile.

Calçot de Valls is a special variety of onion— Blanca Gran Tardía de Lleida to be precise. It was created in Valls in the late nineteenth century by an enterprising farmer who planted white onions and, as the young bulbs started to appear, dug them up, then repeatedly replanted them, each time keeping them covered with a protective layer of earth. This process, known in Spanish as *calzar* or "putting their boots on," blanches the onions and gives them their sweet flavour. Those first humble beginnings grew into an industry that now produces more than twenty million calçots every year, and has earned European Union recognition. **LF**

Taste: *Sweet to spicy and sometimes slightly hot, spring onions are less pungent than mature onions and have a savoury onion taste. The leaves are milder than the root.*

Taste: *Eating calçots is a delicious ritual. Pull away the charred outer leaves to expose the tender, sweet onion within, then dunk quickly into garlic-laced sauces.*

Spring onions, like most members of the Allium
❻ *family, produce highly ornamental flower heads.*

Ramp

Ramps, also known as wild leeks, wild onions, or wild garlic, are, like other onions, members of the lily family. They are highly prized for their combination of garlic and onion flavours.

Native to the mountains of eastern North America, ramps (*Allium tricoccum*) are among the first edible plants to appear in early spring before the forest canopy turns green. As one of the first signs of spring, they were fêted by the early settlers, who used them medicinally, and in the Appalachian region of the United States, festivals still celebrate their arrival. Highly aromatic, ramps can be foraged for only a brief seasonal window, and so are often frozen or pickled for later use.

Ramps can take up to seven years to mature, and are found in patches or colonies at heights over 3,000 feet (900 m). With their white roots they look a little like a spring onion, albeit one with a purplish stem and broader leaves: all parts of the plant are edible. The plant's growing popularity has caused over-harvesting in some areas, where ramps are now protected by legislation. **CLH**

Bleu de Solaise Leek

The Bleu de Solaise leek (*Allium porrum*) is a chunky, Goliath of a leek. It is highly prized for both its fabulous flavour and its resistance to frosts, the latter of which is a valuable characteristic given that it is a winter vegetable. Despite its quite hefty dimensions, it has attractive, bluey-grey, green sword-like leaves that turn violet in cold weather. A slow-growing heirloom variety, it originated around the French town of Solaise, near Lyon, on the eastern side of France in the nineteenth century.

Tomb drawings indicate that leeks were grown in ancient Egypt. Nero, the artistically bent but much troubled Roman emperor, was given the nickname *Porrophagus*, or leek eater, because he believed that eating leeks would improve his singing voice. The Romans introduced leeks to England and Wales, and though they are widely linked with those countries, France is one of the most important growers.

Leeks are not really suitable for eating when raw, but cooked they become tender and have a delicious flavour that is not as pronounced as the onion, although they belong to the same family. **LF**

Taste: *Sweet, but with pronounced flavours of both garlic and onion, ramps can be substituted for either in recipes. They are known for their strong and lasting aroma.*

Taste: *Bleu de Solaise leeks have a sweet yet mildly astringent flavour, similar to chives. A great base for soups, they are also exquisite coupled with cream and cheese.*

⊘ *Early ramps push through the previous season's leaf fall after the snow has melted.*

Celery Heart

Florence Fennel

These slender, almost white inner ribs of celery are valued for their crunchy stalks, their fragrant leaves, and, in some quarters, their low calorific content. *Apium graveolens* var. *dulce,* the cultivated version of a white-flowered plant that grows wild in Europe and Asia, is a dieter's delight. Consuming and digesting a single rib generally burns more calories than the food itself contains.

Cooks, though, have long valued celery for its aromatic properties and, until half a millennium ago, it was a bitter, potent plant used more as a herb than as a vegetable. The ancient Greeks used celery in garlands for their dead; the Romans wore garlands of it during drinking bouts for their strong fragrance, which masked less appealing aromas.

It was most likely the Italians who discovered celery's potential in the sixteenth century and began cultivating milder varieties. Today these are a staple in stockpots and roasting pans, and widely cultivated in temperate regions throughout the world. The hearts are prized for their fresh, clean taste, and are less stringy than outer ribs. **SH**

Florence fennel, one of the three key manifestations of *Foeniculum vulgare*, is sometimes called bulb fennel. But it is not a bulb and it probably originated far from Florence, in the Azores, volcanic islands stranded in the middle of the Atlantic.

The compact, layered, white or green fist that pokes out of the soil, with stalks protruding every which way, forms a versatile, liquorice-flavoured vegetable that developed from the wild herb. It is eaten both raw and cooked, in salads and braised, by itself and in composite dishes—it is often mixed with pasta. Perhaps on account of its sweetness, Florence fennel has an affinity with citrus flavours: many recipes call for a squeeze of lemon juice.

Although identified with Italy, fennel is grown and eaten throughout Europe and the Americas. The wispy leaves are used as a herb, while the stems may be thrown on the barbecue and charred when grilling oily fish like sardines or mackerel. In fashionable restaurants, slender, tender "micro" fennel is sometimes served, simply split, boiled, and brushed with oil or butter. **MR**

Taste: *When raw, celery has a slightly, but pleasantly, bitter taste, reminiscent of parsley and anise. When fried, sautéed, or steamed, their flavour becomes a little milder.*

Taste: *The texture of raw fennel is crunchy, but long stewing renders it soft like celery. Its aniseed taste is distinctive yet mild and refreshing when eaten as a crudité.*

Fennel roasted in olive oil and balsamic vinegar is served as a side dish or added to soup recipes. ❯❯

Beauty Heart Radish

Chioggia Beetroot

Although the swollen stems of *Raphanus sativus* have been eaten the world over since prehistory, the origins of radishes are obscure. Historians tend to place them in western Asia. After the fall of the Roman Empire, radishes disappeared from European literature, but they probably continued to grow.

Radishes come in many sizes, shapes, and colours. Among them the beauty heart radish—with its red flesh, white skin, and greenish shoulders—is one of the most distinctive. Known as *shinrimei* (meaning "beauty in the heart") in China, its other names include rose heart, Asian red meat, and red daikon. While related to the Japanese radish-like vegetable, the beauty heart is not a true daikon. It is also sometimes called watermelon radish, an apt name for when cut it looks like a slice of watermelon.

Because of their exceptional good looks, beauty heart radishes are valued sliced in salads and on sandwiches and as part of hors d'oeuvres platters. They can also be cooked like turnips and served with cream, braised, sliced, and added to stir-fries. In China, they are often pickled. **SH**

This heirloom variety of beetroot is strikingly pretty. Its magenta outer skin conceals an interior made up of concentric rings of alternating rose and white—hence its U.S. names of bulls-eye beet or candy stripe beet—rather than the block colour common to most beetroots. This arresting appearance is lost when cooked, so it is most often eaten raw.

Beetroot (*Beta vulgaris*) evolved from wild sea beet, which grew around coastlines from Europe to India. Although in classical times the plant was valued for its leaves more than for its roots, which were small, by the sixteenth century the spherical, bulbous root vegetable we know today had come into being, probably in Italy.

This beetroot takes its name from Chioggia, the coastal town on an island at the southern entrance to the Venetian lagoon, where it originated. Chioggia beetroot looks eye-catching when sliced crossways and served raw in salads. When boiled, the colours bleed; roasting is a better alternative, but again affects the colour. Cooking of any kind intensifies the sweetness, which is rather high. **LF**

Taste: *Unlike other radishes, beauty hearts get milder not hotter as they mature. Crisp, sweet, and mildly pungent, their outer edges are hotter than the colourful flesh inside.*

Taste: *Raw, young Chioggia has a sweet, but faintly earthy flavour with a crisp, juicy texture, and a subtle radish-like tang. Older roots have a more pronounced earthy flavour.*

Candy-striped and candy pink, Chioggia beetroot makes a striking addition to any salad. ⟫

Turnip

A European staple before potatoes had reached the Old World, turnips (*Brassica rapa*) were well established as a crop in early Greece and Rome. Later they were popular in Britain and northern Europe, whence they went to the United States in the early seventeenth century. They still account for considerable acreage in the United States, southern Europe, and Asia.

Small, young turnips have always been more favoured than their older, coarser siblings, and the current popularity of baby turnips is an extension of this trend. A member of the same family as cabbages and radishes, these crisp, white roots are very different from the matured root vegetable.

Throughout the world, turnips are a flavourful addition to soups and stews. It is mostly in French and Asian cuisines, however, that they escape the pot of boiling water in favour of braising, roasting, sautéing, and stuffing. Tetlow turnips, named after the town in Germany where they originated, are considered a delicacy. Kaku or Japanese turnips are hotter, like radishes. **SH**

Jicama

A member of the legume family and native to Mexico and Central America, jicama (also known as the Mexican potato, yam bean, and Mexican turnip) is a versatile vegetable that until recently had been limited in popularity to only the regions of its origin. Now it has also found favour with North American and Chinese cooks, who appreciate its neutral flavour profile. In China in particular, it is often an ingredient in stir-fries, although it can be used instead of water chestnuts in almost any Asian-style recipe.

In Mexico, its traditional home, the pleasingly crunchy jicama is often cut into matchstick-size pieces and used in salad. It is delicious eaten raw, with a squirt of lime juice, a sprinkling of salt, and dash of hot powdered chilli. It also goes well with fruit, and street vendors mix it with different melon chunks as a fruit salad.

Brown-skinned and shaped like a cross between a turnip and a beet, it can grow to up to 50 pounds (23 kg) in weight, although most that come to market weigh no more than about 5 (2.3 kg). **SH**

Taste: *Baby turnips have a sweeter, more delicate taste than mature ones, which are harvested in autumn and can be musty. Raw, the texture is crisp and refreshing.*

Taste: *Jicama's crunchy and juicy white flesh has a bland flavour with a light sweetness similar to an apple or a pear. Although it looks starchy, there is no strong starch flavour.*

The edible part of a turnip root protrudes above the ground; a long taproot supplies it with nutrients.

Celeriac

Arracacha

This winter vegetable, also called celery root or celery knob, is a type of celery (*Apium graveolens* var. *rapaceum*) that is grown solely for its tan to brown knobbly root. When peeled, it reveals an ivory white flesh with a firm but not necessarily hard texture. Believed to be derived from wild celery, celeriac was first cultivated in the Mediterranean area and gained popularity in the Middle Ages. Today, it is grown worldwide, although France, Germany, Belgium, and the Netherlands are the main producers.

Related to carrot, parsnip and fennel, celeriac should be peeled before using. Its leaves are usually discarded, but can be used as seasoning much like the leaves of its parent plant. Celeriac is popular in Europe, especially northern Europe, where it is cooked and combined with potatoes to serve as croquettes or a mash. The French julienne the vegetable and sweat it with a little butter and sugar, but much of the European crop is pickled.

Celeriac is generally under-used in the United States and Britain. When a part of the menu, it is most often shredded or grated raw into salads. **SH**

Native to the New World, especially the Andes Mountains region, arracacha (*Arracacia xanthorrhiza*) was once a food of the Incas. It belongs to the same family as carrot, parsnip, and celery, but has never been widely cultivated because of its susceptibility to disease and its short shelf life once harvested. Nevertheless, this tasty tuber is grown in Brazil and in other parts of South America and the Caribbean.

Sometimes called a Peruvian carrot, arracacha looks like a large, white carrot. Although the young, green stems can be boiled or eaten raw like celery, it is mainly used for its starchy root, which has a similar crisp texture to potato. The flesh ranges in colour from white to light yellow or purple and emits a fragrant aroma when being cooked.

Arracacha is almost always cooked before it is eaten. The yellow-fleshed variety turns orange when cooked, making it a colourful ingredient in dishes. The roots can be boiled, baked, fried, or added to soups and stews. It is a common component in the hearty Andean stews known as *sancochos*, which are very popular in Colombia and Venezuela. **SH**

Taste: *Celeriac tastes like a cross between strong celery and parsley. The roots can be as large as a cantaloupe. The smaller the root, the milder the flavour.*

Taste: *Arracacha has a pleasantly mild, slightly sweet flavour that is a combination of celery, carrot, and parsnip with hints of roasted chestnuts.*

Celeriac has great flavour and versatility, and ⊗ makes a useful non-starch substitute for potatoes.

Chantenay Carrot

Parsnip

An heirloom carrot widely grown up until the 1960s, Chantenay or Chantennay carrots later lost favour commercially in the United Kingdom to larger, mass-produced carrots. Fortunately, this squat, sweet-tasting variety has since made a strong comeback.

Wild carrots have grown throughout Asia and southern Europe for thousands of years. Early varieties were yellow, white, purple, or black, and the bright orange kind—a fine source of beta-carotene—was not developed until the seventeenth century by the Dutch. Chantenay carrots originated in France, probably in the late 1800s, when there are references to their medicinal use. Varieties include Royal Chantenay and Red Cored Chantenay, and both are good for home growing.

Chantenays are shorter but thicker in girth than other carrots, but are not a "baby" carrot. Some have purple-coloured "shoulders." Although they are not always uniform in size and are sometimes gnarled and knotty, they always taste good. As versatile as any root vegetable, they can be boiled, steamed, or roasted, as well as eaten raw or juiced. **SH**

An old root vegetable, the parsnip was the potato of Europe before the potato came along—and at times its sugar, too. A member of the same family as parsley, carrots, and celery, the sweet root of *Pastinaca sativa* was used in medieval Europe both as a vegetable and as a starchy base for puddings.

The wild plant was probably native to the eastern Mediterranean and areas northeast, including the Caucasus, and was cultivated by the ancient Greeks. Although the Romans generally preferred carrots, it was probably they who introduced the parsnip to Britain. From there it spread to Australasia and North America in turn. It is hardly grown at all in southern Europe.

Parsnips may be boiled, or added to soups and stews. (In Ireland, they were once used to make beer.) They make a nice alternative to mashed potatoes, when boiled and mashed with butter, or puréed with cream and spices such as cinnamon or nutmeg. Added to the pan when roasting meats or poultry, the sugars caramelize to distinctive effect. Unlike carrots, parsnips are not eaten raw. **SH**

Taste: *Arguably the best-tasting carrots grown, the Chantenay carrot is very sweet and is excellent for making carrot juice. The Red Cored variety is the most delicious.*

Taste: *Parsnips taste a little similar to carrots, although they are more sugary, with "rooty" undertones that are slightly reminiscent of turnips.*

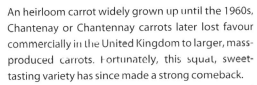

Sweet-tasting Chantenays need only to be scrubbed, not peeled, before eating.

Bellflower Root

Lotus Root

Korean people describe the taste of their food as "pleasingly sour, sweet, hot, burning hot, salty, bitter, and nutty." The agreeable bitterness of their cuisine comes from ginger, ginseng, herbs, seeds, and certain vegetables including a staple ingredient in Korean kitchens, the bellflower root. The root is also used in Japan and China, but mainly medicinally.

Called *toraji* in Korean, this long, milky white, earthy-looking root is in the same family as ginseng and looks similar. It has a crunchy, fibrous texture and is available both fresh and dried. The raw roots need parboiling and rinsing to expel any excessive bitterness. The dried form is easily reconstituted in water and works equally well in cooking.

Bellflower root is most often prepared as one of the cooked seasoned vegetables served at traditional family dinners. Bellflower root salad, a popular, spicy, cold dish, combines peeled strips of bellflower root along with salt, vinegar, red pepper, sesame oil, and other seasonings. The root is also pickled, used in stir-fries, added to rice and noodle dishes, and puréed as a tasty pancake topping. **WS**

The lotus is revered in many parts of Asia. Although it grows in muddy ponds and lakes, the plant produces graceful, delicate flowers that rise proudly above their humble, less than pristine home: this represents the enlightenment one can achieve through spirituality.

The beautiful flowers and large, flat leaves of *Nelumbo nucifera* conceal long, thick segments of root—actually a rhizome. This has air chambers running through its length, which form delicate patterns when thinly sliced. Combined with its white hue, this makes it an artistic ingredient for serving in salads or as a garnish; the holes can also be used to advantage during cooking, by chefs who stuff them with meat or glutinous rice.

Lotus root can be eaten raw and cooked, in sweet and savoury dishes; it can be dried, candied, ground into flour, or infused as a tea; it can be simmered for a long time without disintegrating and so is often added to soups and stews. In Japan, it is served in salads, stews, and as tempura; in Kashmir, under the name of *nedr*, it is often fried. **KKC**

Taste: *Korean cooks often flavour bellflower root with intense seasonings. On its own, it is mild, earthy, faintly sweet, and a little bitter.*

Taste: *When raw, lotus root has a subtly sweet, yet starchy taste similar to raw potato. The flavour becomes starchier when it is cooked, but candying intensifies the sweetness.*

Lotus petals fall away to reveal the large seedhead. The dried seeds are important in East Asian cuisine. »

Gobo

In Japanese vegetable markets, the long brown taproots of great burdock (*Arctium lappa*) are piled high, encrusted with soil, and it is chiefly in Japan that burdock is eaten as a vegetable. Burdock tolerates a range of temperatures, so is available all over Japan under the name of gobo: Oura gobo, from Oura near Tokyo, has shorter, thicker roots with a hollow centre, whereas Horikawa gobo, from the Kyoto region, has long thin roots.

Young, tender, tiny roots can be found in the pickle section of Japanese supermarkets. Although vacuum packed and coloured a somewhat artificial orange, they are crunchy and delicious. Mostly, though, gobo is cooked. Do not peel, but scrub or lightly scrape the skin, to retain maximum flavour and goodness, then place it in acidulated water to keep the flesh white and lessen any bitterness.

A common method of preparation is to shave pieces from the tip of the root as if you are sharpening a pencil. These can then be sautéed in sesame oil and flavoured with soy sauce and other aromatics to make the popular dish *kinpira*. **SB**

Taste: *Gobo tastes earthy like Jerusalem artichoke. It softens on cooking, yet keeps just enough bite. A salad of cooked gobo, mayonnaise, and sesame is a revelation.*

Sweet Potato

The root of a vine in the morning glory family, *Ipomoea batatas,* the sweet potato seems to have been eaten in Peru at least 10,000 years ago, and cultivated in its homeland of the tropical Americas since before the time of the Incas. Like other American tubers, it began its ascent to global popularity at the end of the fifteenth century.

Sweet potatoes come in a range of styles, with skin that varies from white to purple via orange, red, and brown, flesh along a continuum from white to red via orange, and texture that can be mealy, waxy, or simply mushy. Probably the most interesting kind are the sweet varieties with dark skin and bright orange flesh, such as Beauregard.

These nutrient-dense vegetables are always eaten cooked, and many like to accentuate their sweet nutty flavour with cinnamon or nutmeg. Sweet potatoes are a Thanksgiving tradition in the United States, where they are also served sweetened in desserts. Roasted whole in their skins, they are a popular street food in parts of China and Japan. They are good baked and served with a little butter. **SH**

Taste: *All sweet potatoes have a sweet, starchy taste, but Beauregards seem sweeter because of their softer, moister texture. Slightly nutty notes are evident.*

Hot weather lovers, sweet potatoes need to be harvested before or soon after the first signs of frost. ❯❯

Jerusalem Artichoke

Chinese Artichoke

Despite its name, the Jerusalem artichoke is not a member of the artichoke family and did not originate anywhere near Jerusalem. Native to the New World, *Helianthus tuberosus* is a tuber, and a member of the sunflower family, hence its alternative name, sunchoke. Some say its name originates from a mispronunciation of *girasole*, the Italian word for sunflower, coupled with the observation that its flavour resembles the globe or true artichoke. Its curious French title, *topinambour*, is a memento of a group of Brazilian Indians of the Topinambous tribe who were brought to France in 1613, creating a national sensation.

Packed with nutrients and relatively easy to grow, these awkward shaped tubers have creamy white flesh. Their skin colour varies, and most are knobbly, although varieties have been developed that are easy to peel. Jerusalem artichokes are good roasted, or in soups, or braised and served with butter and cream. The starch in Jerusalem artichokes is different to potato starch and not easily digestible by everyone. **SH**

About as long as a finger, these beady little tubers look rather like a caterpillar or a mismatched string of pearls, and are absolutely no relation of either globe artichokes or Jerusalem artichokes. They may also be known as knotroot, by their French name, *crosnes*, or by their Japanese name, *chorogi*.

The roots of *Stachys affinis*, a member of the mint family native to China and Japan, they found their way from Beijing to France during the 1880s, when a gentleman named Pailleux began growing them in his garden in the village of Crosnes. They retained some popularity until the 1920s, usually cooked in butter then dressed with *fines herbes* or cream, but are now something of a curio.

Chinese artichokes are still cultivated in China and Japan, where they are popular pickled. They had a renaissance in the United States at the beginning of the twenty-first century, where chefs serve them alongside everything from lobster to pork cheeks, and they are regaining some popularity in Europe. Their crunchy texture makes them a delightful snack when eaten raw and a good addition to salads. **SH**

Taste: *Raw they are crisp like radishes, with a sweet and nutty flavour. Cooked, their texture is between Irish potatoes and roasted onions, and their flavour intensifies.*

Taste: *Not really an artichoke at all, the Chinese artichoke has a sweet, nutty taste. Crisp, juicy, and a little peppery, the flavour offers hints of parsnip and apple.*

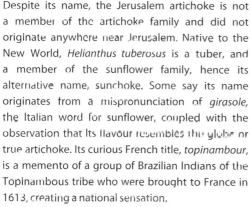

The Jerusalem artichoke's bright flower
◔ *accounts for its alternative name of sunchoke.*

Japanese Yam

Known in Japanese as *yamaimo* (mountain potato), and also as "mountain eel," the Japanese yam has been revered for its medicinal qualities in the Far East for thousands of years. In the past the Japanese have seen the long juicy root as an aphrodisiac, suitable only for men.

A member of the large and sprawling yam family, *yamaimo* is unusual for a yam in that it is most often eaten raw. Grated (when it is known as *tororo*), it is served on top of a bowl of noodles or with rice, and eaten on the third day of January after the excesses of the New Year, apparently to aid digestion.

In Japan, there are two main varieties: the long, thin *nagaimo* and the fist-shaped *ichoimo*. The latter is slightly denser and less watery than *nagaimo*. It grows wild both in Japan and in the United States, but Japanese varieties are now widely cultivated, and harvested in winter. They can be found in Japanese markets, sometimes packaged in straw or sand to protect the delicate flesh during transport. *Yamaimo* flour is sometimes used as a binder in other foods. **SB**

Taste: *Raw, grated yam is highly sticky—an acquired taste but one worth acquiring. Thinly sliced, with soy sauce and wasabi, it is crisp and juicy. Cooked, it is gluey and soft.*

Eddo

Also commonly called taro or taro root, this ancient tuber may have been cultivated in India or South East Asia as early as 5,000 BCE. It then spread to China, Japan, Egypt, and eventually Africa. Today, it is an important crop in all those places, as well as in Hawaii, the Caribbean, and other subtropical and tropical regions. Eddo has many varieties and numerous names, but generally can be recognized by its dark brown, hairy skin, which is similar to a coconut. Its flesh, coloured white to light grey and sometimes pink, is very filling and highly nutritious, and must be cooked before eating.

In Hawaii, the purple-fleshed variety is pounded into a thick paste to make *poi*, and used as a side dish or cooking ingredient. Vegetarians like to thinly slice eddo and fry it into chips. In the Caribbean, eddo is made into soups and stews, including cream of eddo soup. There, and in Africa, the leaves from the eddo plant are cooked and used like greens. Eddo can be boiled, steamed, baked, deep fried, or puréed and made into fritters. It must be eaten hot as it gets very sticky when it cools. **SH**

Taste: *Eddo has much more flavour than many other tubers. Its texture is similar to that of a white potato, but it has a nuttier and more earthy taste.*

A Hawaiian grinds eddo into thick paste, poi, for use during the Establishment Day festival. »

Jersey Royal Potato

By the middle of the nineteenth century, Jersey, the largest of the British Channel Islands, was exporting 20,000 tons of potatoes to England. These potatoes were not, however, the variety for which the island is famous today. Around 1880, a farmer, Hugh de la Haye, acquired two outsize potatoes of uncertain origin from a store; he divided them into sixteen pieces, planted each piece, and exhibited the results at a local show. The editor of a St. Helier newspaper dubbed them the "Royal Jersey Flukes," implying the role luck had played in their discovery. The name stuck and the variety has never changed.

Small, kidney-shaped, and waxy, with a skin that rubs off, the potato originally owed some of its quality to the rich Jersey soil, which was cultivated in the past with plentiful applications of seaweed, sometimes with additional guano. Today the pressure to produce two crops a year and the use of chemical fertilizers mean that not all Jersey Royal Potatoes (PDO) taste as good as they used to. They are best eaten immediately—freshly dug up and popped straight into the pot. **MR**

Taste: *Boiled then tossed in melted butter, Jersey Royals have a sweet taste and a distinctive firm texture. With their skin left on, there is a more earthy flavour.*

Ratte Potato

Rattes apparently earned their name from a shape that looks, arguably, like an earless rodent. However, when first introduced around 1872, these waxy potatoes had a more sympathetic name, Quenelles de Lyon. Like other French varieties, they have evolved, and the finest quality is now identified with the Normandy strain, Rattes du Touquet. Produced in sandy soil along the coast from Calais to Abbéville, these small, elongated, yellow-skinned potatoes with firm, creamy flesh are planted in spring and harvested in late August and September.

Rattes are often identified with the buttery *purée de pommes de terre* of the chef Joël Robuchon, but show to best advantage in two classic recipes: sliced potatoes sautéed from raw with onions (*pommes lyonnaise*) and *gratin dauphinois*, in which thin slices are baked in cream with a hint of garlic. In these dishes, their ability to keep their shape when cooked, allied to a depth of flavour, gives them an edge over other potato strains. Rattes, as a commercial variety, nearly became extinct a generation ago, but they are now grown in both Europe and North America. **MR**

Taste: *The texture is dense, firm, resistant to breaking down, and yet smooth. Not sweet like new potatoes, rattes have a nutty taste, often likened to chestnuts.*

Pink Fir Apple Potato

Elongated, often knobbly, with pink skins and yellow, waxy flesh, these salad potatoes were developed in England in Victorian times, and are closely related in size and appearance to American fingerlings. In the nineteenth century, English potato salads were quite sophisticated, mixed with red cabbage and beetroot, or cucumber, gherkins, and button onions, or chopped chives, capers, and hard-boiled eggs.

The pink fir apple's origin is uncertain; there are suggestions that it was already being imported into America in 1850 by British settlers, but it was only officially recognized as a variety there around 1870. During the twentieth century, it was not grown commercially, but survived precariously in private gardens, notably the country home of André Simon, president of the Wine and Food Society.

Best enjoyed with its skin on, this potato owes its revival to the charitable organization now known as the Henry Doubleday Research Association or Garden Organic. This charity works to restore heritage crops by collecting plant seeds and making them available to the public. **MR**

Peruvian Purple Potato

The versatile spud has a humble appearance, apart from when it is garbed in royal colours. Peruvian purple potatoes—purple both inside and out—are a food fit for royalty, and, indeed, legend has it that when harvested, they were kept for the Inca kings.

Some believe that Peruvian purples are the grandfathers of all potatoes. Potato cultivation in what is today southern Chile is thought to date back to 5000 BCE. Europeans did not encounter potatoes until the sixteenth century, when Spanish colonists in the New World described them as "truffles."

Peru has been dubbed the potato capital of the world, for its array of different sizes, shapes, and colours. Peruvian purples get their colour from the same antioxidant that makes blueberries blue. They are an heirloom member of the fingerling family of potatoes. Not to be confused with Okinawan or Hawaiian purple potatoes, which are actually sweet potatoes, Peruvian purples bring a touch of the exotic to the table. They can be cooked as other potatoes, but are impressive sliced into salads, made into French fries, or served as a colourful mash. **SH**

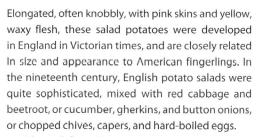

Taste: *Thickly sliced, pink fir apple potatoes are nutty, earthy, and full of flavour. They taste significantly better when eaten freshly dug from the ground.*

Taste: *Similar in taste to round red, round white, or other waxy potatoes, but with more complexity and depth of flavour. Peruvian purples have an earthy, creamy texture.*

Black Périgord Truffle

Although synonymous with them today, the Périgord region of southwest France was never the main source of the famed "black diamonds"—*Tuber melanosporum*. It was more of a processing hub for those found elsewhere, mainly in Provence around Carpentras. Like its sister fungus, the white Alba truffle, a symbiotic relationship with a host tree is essential to the truffle's slow ripening underground. The hunting season lasts from November to February.

Rossini called truffles the "Mozart of the kitchen" and they are a key flavouring and aromatic tool in haute cuisine. Gnarled and black on the outside, not unlike shagreen to the touch, grey and veined on the inside, they should not be confused with cheaper, less perfumed varieties such as *Tuber indicum*.

Freshly picked black truffles are infinitely better than processed ones and when cooking with them it is unwise to skimp. They may not be the aphrodisiac some have claimed, but truffles can create an intense emotional response—eating them can be a complex, mystic experience. They make powerfully aromatic sauces and the finest of omelettes. **MR**

White Alba Truffle

White Alba truffles, the *tartufi bianchi* of legend, sit near the top of the league of luxury, expensive foods. Smooth, yellowish, or ochre outside, greyish yellow on the inside, these wild fungi take their name from the Piedmontese town that has done so much to raise their profile. (Although strongly identified with this northern Italian province, *Tuber magnatum Pico* is also found in Croatia.)

Truffles have so far defied all efforts to grow them commercially and because of increasing scarcity truffle hunting is heavily regulated. During the season, which runs from October to December, trained dogs nose out the tubers that grow up to 1 foot (30 cm) underground.

Unlike black Périgord truffles, white truffles are never cooked. Instead, they are shaved over food using a kind of plane—an *affetta tartufi*. They have a special affinity with eggs and simple pasta dishes, such as the Piedmontese *agnolotti*. The intensity that distinguishes fresh truffles diminishes fast: oils, pastes, and cheeses sold under the name may contain chemicals rather than the real thing. **MR**

Taste: *Scientists have identified over one hundred aroma components in black truffles ranging from nutty and grassy to sulphurous with hints of vanilla, rose petal, and bergamot.*

Taste: *The aroma more than the taste, which could be likened to Parmesan cheese, is unique. The white Alba smells unforgettably intense and sulphurous.*

In most regions the truffle-hunting pig has been replaced by specially trained dogs. ❯❯

Huitlacoche

With a name that includes the Aztec word for dung, and a mode of life that involves growing on corn crops as a blight, huitlacoche (*Ustilago maydis*) is many, many times more delicious than a picture or description might lead one to believe. Also known as corn smut, and by more recent, market-friendly coinages such as "Aztec caviar," "Mexican truffle," and "corn mushroom," this naturally-occurring fungus disfigures growing maize. The neat white, yellow, or golden kernels swell and mutate into distorted silvery blue lumps with black interiors.

Mexican farmers have long embraced huitlacoche, but for years their U.S. counterparts—and some legislative bodies—regarded it as a pest to be eradicated. Increased demand has prompted farmers in Mexico, the United States, and Canada to find ways of cultivating it. Chefs prize it for its rich umami flavour and the way it adds an exotic black or grey colour to dishes. It can be difficult to source fresh huitlacoche outside Mexico, but speciality food stores in North America frequently stock flash-frozen or canned versions. **CLH**

Iwatake

The Japanese delicacy iwatake (*Gyrophora esculenta*) takes it name from *iwa* meaning "rock" and *take* meaning "mushroom." Yet this is misleading, in that iwatake is a lichen that grows on rocks high in the mountains of Japan, China, and Korea. It has been collected as a prized culinary delicacy for hundreds of years and is said to enhance longevity.

Iwatake is also a rarity because lichens are notoriously slow growing, and it may take up to 100 years for iwatake to grow to a size worth harvesting. The harvesting itself is a precarious process and not for the faint-hearted. Harvesters need considerable mountaineering skills to rappel down mountains to gather iwatake by prizing it from the cliff face with a sharp knife. The process is made even more dangerous because iwatake is best harvested in wet weather because moisture makes it less likely that the lichen will crumble when being removed.

In Japan, it is used as an ingredient in deep-fried tempura, soups, and salads. In Korea, rock mushroom is used in kimchi cabbage and radish soup, and is served with noodles or rice. **CK**

Taste: *Huitlacoche has a mushroom-like flavour with hints of corn and liquorice. It is usually sautéed with garlic and onion and used to flavour traditional Mexican dishes.*

Taste: *Raw iwatake has a slimy, slippery texture and virtually no flavour. It can be somewhat chewy and is at its best when made into a delicate tempura.*

North Americans have had some difficulty in accepting that huitlacoche is edible.

Enokitake

Although to many these delicate fungi are Japanese mushrooms and called by their Japanese name, they grow wild in both Europe and North America. Because they grow throughout the winter—or at least during its warmer spells—they are sometimes called winter mushrooms in English and *yukinoshita* (under the snow) in Japanese. In Japan, they are a common ingredient in *sukiyaki*, and other *nabemono* (one-pot dishes). Outside Japan, they are often eaten raw in salads, where their distinctive shape shows to advantage.

The wild and cultivated forms of *Flammulina velutipes* are noticeably different. The cultivated kind, grown on sawdust in cylinders and shielded from the light, are characterized by their thin and spindly white stems, up to 5 inches (12 cm) long, on top of which sits a sticky, cream-coloured cap about the size of a button—½ inch (1 cm) across. Wild specimens are thicker and bigger with darker coloured caps. In Japan, the wild variety are traditionally found on the wood of the Chinese hackberry tree, or enoki. **SB**

Taste: *Enokitake taste very mild and fresh, with a texture that is crisp for a mushroom, yet also chewy, and long stringy stems that can get caught between the teeth.*

Matsutake

In Japan, the matsutake is prized every bit as much as the truffles of Alba. It grows only in certain pine forests, and defies cultivation: those found in undisturbed mountain forests of Japanese red pine are deemed the best.

A potent symbol of autumn, *Tricholoma matsutake* has been depicted in haiku, painting, and other decorative arts since at least the Heian era (794–1185 CE); Matsuo Basho, the seventeenth-century haiku master, devoted a poem to it. Up until the 1940s, Japanese mushroom hunters were finding 12,000 tons a year, but by 2005 this had declined to under 40 tons, a fact reflected in the exorbitant price.

For a short period of two or three weeks in autumn, Japanese stores enter a kind of matsutake frenzy. Specimens are arranged on fronds of bracken; store assistants shout the virtues of matsutake rice or bento; sweet cakes are crafted into mushrooms. The best matsutake are eaten before the dark cap that tops the white stem is fully open. Served lightly grilled with a squeeze of the sudachi citrus, matsutake is one of the pinnacles of gastronomy. **SB**

Taste: *Pungent and fragrant with the scent of pine woods, the texture is meatily dense. The taste is earthy and nutty with an aftertaste that is almost spicy but never peppery.*

Presentation boxes of matsutake at a street market in Kyoto, Japan. »

Maitake

The Japanese name of this remarkable mushroom—maitake or "dancing mushroom"—apparently arose because when mushroom hunters come across a particularly good specimen they dance with joy. In feudal Japan, the maitake is said to have been worth its weight in silver, so with specimens known to grow to as much as 45 pounds (20 kg) in weight, dancing with joy would seem entirely appropriate.

Known in English as hen-of-the-woods (but not to be confused with the unrelated chicken-of-the-woods), the maitake forms a round mass of curly, overlapping, leaf-like fronds sprouting from a single thick white stem on hardwood, including oak. It has been used in oriental medicine for centuries and in recent years an extract has been marketed worldwide as a food supplement.

Fresh maitake makes superlative tempura because the batter clings nicely to the fronds. It is good in miso soup, with noodles or rice, in simmered dishes, and stir-fried; it can also be sautéed in butter or oil, Western style, or added to soups, omelettes, and risottos. **SB**

Taste: *Maitake has a mild mushroomy taste, a pleasant fragrance, and a robust but succulent texture with a little resistance to the bite, which is pleasing to most palates.*

Oyster Mushroom

More flavoursome than their cultivated relatives, the best oyster mushrooms (*Pleurotus ostreatus*) grow in clusters on tree stumps and decaying broadleaf wood. Unlike many other wild mushrooms, they have the advantage of being easily recognized and quite distinct from any of the toxic species.

Oyster mushrooms do not look or taste exactly like their namesake, but there is a similarity. Their flattened, lopsided caps in muted shades of grey and brown look a little like the oysters known as "natives" in England and *belons* in France, and may reach up to 5 inches (12.5 cm) across. When they are fried, their surface becomes slippery.

In England, at the turn of the twentieth century, these mushrooms were battered and fried, but the fashion has lapsed. Few cooks would look beyond cutting off the stubby, tough stalks and frying the sliced caps in butter or fat. In France or Italy, parsley, garlic, and lemon juice would be added, whereas an oyster mushroom goulash with paprika, onion, and tomato is a Hungarian speciality. Greek cooks grill them over charcoal and baste with olive oil. **MR**

Taste: *Some people can pick out a faint aniseed smell, but it is mixed up with a pleasant, musty woodland aroma. The texture delivers more bite than a field mushroom.*

Oyster mushrooms are often used in stir-fried Japanese and Chinese dishes. »

Oronge Mushroom

Saffron Milk Cap

This rare yet delicious mushroom is found in many parts of the world, but particularly France and Italy: it is especially prized in Italian cooking. The name comes from the Provençal dialect word *ouronjo*, which means orange and refers to the mushroom's distinctive colour. It is also known as Caesar's mushroom, or botanically *Amanita caesarea*.

The orange mushroom has a firm elliptical cap atop its yellow stem and gills and is found in oak and chestnut forests from June to October. Great care must be taken to distinguish it from its deadly relatives in the Amanitaceae family, such as the death cap mushroom. (Agrippina, wife of the Emperor Claudius, probably laced a plate of delicious orange mushrooms with poison extracted from the death cap in order to kill him.)

Lethality aside, oronge mushrooms have a firm texture and are superb eaten raw in salads. Pan-fried in a little oil or butter, they ooze delectable juices. Washing will leave the mushrooms waterlogged and compromise their flavour; with good quality specimens, a light brushing should suffice. **LF**

In Poland's national epic poem *Pan Tadeusz* (1834), the exiled romantic bard Adam Mickiewicz recalls a mushroom-picking outing back in the Napoleonic era: "But all hunt for milk caps which, though not very tall / And largely unsung, are the tastiest of all . . ." Even today, shawl-clad grannies hawking wicker baskets full of mushrooms are a common sight at rural roadsides in autumn.

Saffron milk caps are orange mushrooms (*Lactarius deliciosus*), which take their name from the milky reddish-orange liquid they exude. Young specimens have a slightly convex cap, which becomes concave as they mature: they can measure up to 5 inches (12.5 cm) across. They grow most abundantly in the clearings of pine forests, and are most highly valued in fungophile Eastern Europe, notably in Poland, Russia, Ukraine, and Slovakia.

Saffron milk caps may be pickled, used in soups, stewed in sour cream, or strung up to dry for future use. But connoisseurs—some of whom prefer them to ceps—insist pan-frying in butter is the only method that truly does them justice. **RS**

Taste: *Served raw, oronge mushrooms have a crisp, fresh earthiness and a deep, savoury-sweet flavour. They work particularly well in dishes with chestnuts or chestnut flour.*

Taste: *Fried in butter, saffron milk caps taste rich and mellow with faintly peppery undertones. They are delicious eaten straight off the pan with a rye bread to sop up the juices.*

*On this London stall, saffron milk caps are being sold under their French name of **lactaire**. »*

VARIETY: **Lactaire**

COUNTRY: **Spain**

PRICE: **20,- m por kg**

Chanterelle

Cep

One of the great culinary wild mushrooms, *Cantharellus cibarius* and its relatives—the family is found across Europe, North America, China, and in parts of Africa—are often sold in France under the name *girolles*. They emerge in small clusters, and the cream to apricot-coloured caps form ruffle-edged trumpets beneath which the gills stretch down to the stems. Although the gathering season is said to be autumn, they start appearing in Mediterranean markets as early as May. Freshly gathered, they should be crisp and dry, never viscous or blotchy.

Chanterelles figure on most gastronomic menus as a garnish and are at their best sautéed rapidly in hot butter. Care has to be taken that they do not stew in their own juices. Even more than with other mushrooms, it is important not to wash them; simply wipe or brush them, or pick off any detritus.

Chanterelles' close relation, the horn of plenty (*Craterellus cornucopioides*), looks similar, but for its black colour, and is as tasty. Budding mushroom hunters should always be wary of confusing true chanterelles with the toxic false chanterelle. **MR**

The gastronomic term cep (*porcino* in Italian) most often refers to a variety of mushroom, *Boletus edulis*, that is commonly called the "penny bun" in England and "king boletus" in North America. The name apparently derives from a Gascon word, appropriate since many of the best recipes, such as *cèpes à la Bordelaise*, fried with garlic, shallots, parsley, and breadcrumbs, come from southwest France.

Ceps grow in broadleaf woodland, often in small clusters, emerging from late summer until autumn. They have thick, stubby stems and tan to dark brown caps with pores—not gills—on the underside that are white and quite firm when young. They are at their best when smaller, firm, and rounded.

In northern Italy, dried *porcini* are used in many dishes, especially risotto and pasta, and there is a long tradition of preserving them in oil. Such store cupboard products have a place in the kitchen, but cannot match the fresh mushroom, so cep hunting expeditions are a popular hobby. Other varieties of boletus are equally good to eat, but need picking with care: the Satan Boletus is deadly poisonous. **MR**

Taste: *The intensity of the perfume, both sweet and musty, accords perfectly with the taste, and the texture has the right amount of bite.*

Taste: *Freshly foraged, ceps are strongly perfumed and meaty. The aroma differs from common mushrooms in its persistence: stews and sauces retain this distinctive note.*

The delicate flavour of chanterelles is best
❷ *preserved by quickly sautéeing them in butter.*

Shiitake

Morel

Easy to cultivate, and full of flavour, the shiitake has spread from Asia all around the world. Known botanically as *Lentinula edodes,* the shiitake grows in the wild around or on a type of chestnut oak called *shii* from which it takes its name. In both Japan and China, mushrooms harvested with the cap not quite open, during winter, are considered the best. When served fresh, a decorative cross is often cut into the cap, and the stem removed.

Unusually, the dried shiitake is more than just a preserved version of the fresh mushroom: it is a food in itself. The process of drying creates the amino acid sodium guanylate, which intensifies the aroma and taste of the flavoursome fresh mushroom, creating more of what the Japanese call "umami"—tastiness. The soaking liquid used to rehydrate the mushrooms has a sweet, earthy aroma, similar to dried porcini, that makes it an important element in *Shojin ryori,* the strict vegetarian cuisine developed in Japanese Buddhist temples. It adds flavour and goodness to the diet, and is used in a vegetarian version of dashi, the basic stock used in all Japanese cooking. **SB**

Prized in Asia, North America, and throughout Europe, the *Morchellus* tribe of fungi includes several edible varieties, some crinkly, others conical, some brown, and some black. All are spongy—the familiar Italian name is *spugnola*—with white funnel-like stems, and all grow in the spring.

Fresh morels are velvety to the touch, yet almost brittle as mushrooms go. Because of their commercial value, they are often exported dried from developing countries, the Indian subcontinent especially. Reconstituted morels lack the delicate scent of the fresh ones, and the caps may be leathery and uninteresting. Eaten raw, morels may cause stomach upsets because they contain traces of toxic helvellic acid: this is destroyed by cooking.

The honeycomb texture of the cap traps finely diced shallots, ham, and other ingredients beautifully during cooking. In the classic French *morilles à la crème,* the sauce clings to the mushroom enhancing the flavour. Chefs have stuffed morels with fine mousses or *paneer,* but this interferes with the texture and taste. **MR**

Taste: *The fresh mushroom is meaty with a mild, earthy taste. Dried and reconstituted shiitake is chewier, with a stronger mushroom taste, which is also sweet and aromatic.*

Taste: Morchella esculenta, *the best eating variety, has a fragrant mushroomy smell that grows in intensity when cooked with cream. The taste is delicate but persistent.*

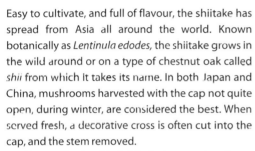

On this typical shiitake farm in Japan, logs inoculated with shiitake spores produce a wealth of mushrooms.

Kalamata Olive

This famous table olive, one of the oldest varieties in the world, comes from Greece, where olives have grown since very early times. In fact, Greek mythology tells of a contest between the goddess Athena and the god Poseidon: Zeus promised to give control of Attica to whoever provided the most useful gift. Athena produced an olive tree and won.

Kalamata olive trees grow throughout the Greek mainland, and around the town in the Peloponnese Peninsula after which they are named. They are graceful and willowy in shape, and the fruit is oval with a small pimple at the end. When fully ripe, Kalamata olives are as dark as an aubergine. Their high fat content, around 25 per cent, makes them particularly suited for table use. Very few are pressed for oil.

The ripe olives are harvested by hand, washed, and placed in barrels to be cured naturally in brine. They are ready to eat after seven to eight months. Some are stoned and stuffed, the best with fresh ingredients such as almonds, cloves of garlic, cubes of cheese, or cooked and chopped pimentos. **JR**

Taste: Kalamata olives are quite large and juicy and the flesh easily leaves the stone behind. The flavour is rich and strong but quite sweet in style without much bitterness.

Nyons Olive

The medieval fortress town of Nyons in Provence has been a centre of excellence for olives for many years, and gained its own *appellation d'origine contrôlée* in 1968. Olive trees, *Olea europea,* were first planted in this part of Provence by Roman settlers as Julius Caesar conquered Gaul during the 50s BCE. They have grown here ever since.

The local olive variety is La Tanche, a hardy tree that can withstand the winter frosts. Indeed, the cold extracts the moisture from the olive, wrinkling the skin and concentrating the flavour just before the harvest, which falls after the middle of November but before January. When they are fully ripe and black in colour, the olives are picked by hand.

The best olives are cured in a mixture of fresh brine and brine from the previous year. This method eschews the chemicals used to manufacture cheap "pizza" olives, and it takes six to eight months before the olives are fully cured. So seriously does the town take its olive trees that it is home to the Musée de l'Olivier (Olive Museum) and the Institut du Monde de l'Olivier (Global Olive Institute). **JR**

Taste: Nyons olives are quite large with lush, juicy flesh and slightly crunchy skin. They are not very salty but have an attractive bitterness underlying the full fruity flavour.

Bella di Cerignola Olive

Moroccan-style Olive

Sometimes known simply as "Cerignola," these olives are prized for their size: the largest are as big as the top joint of the human thumb. Oval in shape, and green or black in colour, they come from the Gargano Peninsula and other parts of Puglia in the "heel" of Italy, as specified in their *Denominazione di Origine Protetta* (DOP).

Green Bella di Cerignola are picked before the fruit has ripened and darkened on the tree; those that will become black olives mature further before harvest. Both types are hand-picked in small baskets carried at the waist and delivered to the processing plant as soon after harvesting as possible, which helps keep quality high.

Both the green and the black olives are cured in a saltwater solution that has had a small amount of vinegar added to it. They remain in this solution for six to seven months before they are ready to eat. Unlike Spanish Gordal olives, they are never cured in caustic soda or pasteurized before bottling. Both green and black olives are often served with local goat's or sheep's cheeses. **JR**

"A taste older than meat, older than wine" is how writer Lawrence Durrell described the olive, a tree fruit native to the eastern Mediterranean. Indeed, olives have been gathered from wild trees since prehistoric times. The olive tree began to be cultivated, in or near Syria, before 3000 BCE, and it probably reached North Africa via trade routes.

Olive trees still thrive on the arid North African plains and Morocco is a major olive producer. Masters in the use of spices, Moroccans preserve their olives in exquisitely aromatic marinades. As olives are harvested at each stage of ripeness, Moroccan markets feature huge bowls of gleaming green, pink, red, brown, and black fruit, all preserved in spicy blends including hot peppers, cumin, garlic, coriander, preserved lemons, and fennel.

Olives can be marinated either by first briefly heating the olive oil and spices until fragrant, and then adding the mix to the olives along with other ingredients such as garlic or preserved lemon, or by simply combining all the ingredients. The longer the olives are marinated, the better they will taste. **WS**

Taste: *Green Bella di Cerignola olives have a good crunchy but juicy texture, rather like fresh nuts. The black Cerignola are softer with a more meaty taste.*

Taste: *Moroccan olives are juicy, with a deliciously nutty flavour. Depending on the marinade ingredients, the taste ranges from savoury to sweet and pungent to aromatic.*

Frozen Pea

Freezing has been used to preserve food since time immemorial—since whenever the first human being dug a hole in the snow and left some meat to keep—but mechanical freezing of food did not come about until the 1840s. Even then, it took the best part of a century before the Brooklyn-born inventor, Clarence Birdseye, discovered the necessity of quick freezing, which meant that vegetables could be preserved without destroying their taste and structure.

Birdseye's frozen foods were first marketed as "frosted." Freezing has never had much cachet, yet garden peas benefit especially from the freezing process. Peas lose their quality soon after picking, as sugar turns to starch—and for industrially farmed "fresh" peas, which can travel thousands of miles before they reach the consumer, the consequences to both flavour and texture can be dismal. By contrast, peas that are blanched and then flash-frozen within hours of leaving the field keep their natural sweetness, resulting, probably uniquely among frozen vegetables, in a taste and texture that is fresh and lively. **SH**

Taste: *The best peas are grown in one's own garden or bought fresh from the vine. But good quality frozen peas offer a spring and summer flavour all year-round.*

Row upon row of pea plants bask in the California sun. »

Pickled Silverskin Onion

Lampascioni Onion

Also known as "cocktail" onions, these little things—often as small as ½ inch (1 cm) in diameter—are the delicacies one spears with a stick, transforming an everyday martini into the more exotic Gibson. They are small silverskin onions from varieties such as Pompeii and Paris, harvested young then pickled, traditionally in malt vinegar, sugar, salt, and spices.

The British are particularly fond of their pickled onions. Jars of onions as much as 1 ½ inches (3.5 cm) in diameter were once essential behind the bar of any self-respecting pub and de rigueur in every fish and chip shop. Their pungent flavour and sharp malt tang still pairs extremely well with full-flavoured cheese, freshly made bread, and a glass of ale, and they also figure alongside ice cream as a pregnancy craving. Today, however, smaller onions, lighter vinegars, and sweeter cures are becoming the norm.

Rakkyo onions, although a different species from Western onions, are similar. Pickled in vinegar, mirin, soy sauce, or some combination of the three, they are widely used in Japanese cuisine. Some are salt-cured before pickling. **SH**

Muscari comosum, a type of hyacinth, grows wild in the woods and meadows of Apulia, southern Italy, and blossoms each spring bearing beautiful purple-blue flowers. When grown to eat, however, the plant is harvested long before its blooms appear: the little russet bulbs known as lampascioni onions or *vampagioli* are the heart of the culinary experience. The ancient Greeks knew them as an aphrodisiac.

During the Middle Ages, lampascioni were considered a food for the poor and were consumed in large quantities by peasants and farmers. Now they are considered a delicacy and are prepared locally in a range of ways. Around the Murgia region of Puglia they are typically cooked under hot wood ashes before being dressed with olive oil and salt; they are also particularly delicious when stewed simply in extra virgin olive oil.

Outside Italy, lampascioni onions can be found preserved in oil and balsamic vinegar (pictured above); Sapori del Salento produce a delicious *Lampascioni alla brace*—grilled lampascioni preserved in extra virgin olive oil. **LF**

Taste: *Fresh silverskin onions have a mild onion flavour. Pickled, they are deliciously crunchy, with a sweet-and-sour tang. The precise taste is determined by the pickle.*

Taste: *The bitterness of raw lampascioni can be an acquired taste. Cooking brings out a mellow pairing of savoury and sweet, with a hint of almonds.*

The tassel grape hyacinth, whose bulbs are sold as "wild onions," a somewhat misleading term. »

Pantelleria Caper

Zesty and piquant, capers (*Capparis spinosa*) are the unopened buds of a flowering bush that has grown wild in the Mediterranean, and in particular Italy, since Roman times. Pantelleria in Sicily is considered to produce some of the very finest, thanks to the black, lavic soil that intensifies their distinctive aroma and flavour, and only capers from the region may be sold as Pantelleria capers.

The buds are harvested by hand between May and August. In their natural state they are hugely bitter so a process of salting and rinsing is used to remove the harsh flavour. The buds are dried in the sun and then packed in salt and left for eight days. After rinsing, the operation is repeated twice more.

As capers are sold preserved in salt or brine they need to be thoroughly washed before being eaten. They can be served alone with aperitifs but are also typically used in sauces, particularly in the tomato-based *puttanesca* sauce and the tuna and caper sauce that is a feature of the delicious Italian veal dish *vitello tonnato*. Capers also marry incredibly well with anchovies. **LF**

Caper Berry

Bud brothers of the better known caper, caper berries are the mature fruit of *Capparis spinosa*. While the lively little morsels known simply as "capers" are the unopened buds of the white flower the shrubs produce, caper berries are the actual fruit. Like most fruit, they are much larger than their flower buds, and look rather like a small green olive in size and colour, albeit with muted white lines along the surface. They have a lightly seeded interior and are usually sold with the stems intact.

Caper berries are particularly popular in Spain, but are nowhere near as high profile globally as their piquant younger siblings. Most often found in jars, pickled or preserved in brine, they have a milder flavour than capers, so do not usually make a good substitute in recipes. However, they are wonderful eaten in much the same way as olives, as part of a tapas plate or an antipasti course, or as a nibble with drinks: their stalks make the perfect tool for easy handling and elegant eating. Caper berries make an especially good accompaniment to cold cuts, particularly beef, lamb, game, rich pâtés and fish. **LF**

Taste: *Piquant and salty with a pungent, saliva-inducing, citrussy tang, capers are reminiscent of a tiny gherkin. They deliver a welcome punch to salads, sauces, and pizzas.*

Taste: *Spirited and tangy, yet slightly more restrained than its better-known sibling, the caper berry delivers pizzazz without pucker. Size matters, and small is best.*

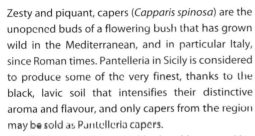
Caper plants grow well in arid areas. In Syria, nomads collect them by hand to supplement their income.

Pickled Gherkin

Cornichon

These small cucumbers from the Cucurbitaceae family—the same family as pumpkins, gourds, and watermelons—are possibly one of the oldest pickles on the planet. Eaten all around the world, they are very popular in the United States and are considered a delicacy in much of northern and Eastern Europe. They are also enjoyed, perhaps partly for their salt-replenishing qualities, in parts of the Middle East.

In the colder climes of northern Europe, the pickling liquid tends to be a flavour-packed concoction of vinegar laced with peppercorns, mustard seeds, dill, horseradish, salt, and spices such as chilli, cinnamon, cloves, and ginger. In Russia, salty, pungent slices often appear as part of the traditional appetizer selection known as *zakuski* that is served alongside shots of vodka. In warmer climates, such as Turkey and Lebanon, brine-cured variants are found with olives, pickled root vegetables, and pickled peppers as an appetizer. Across the Atlantic, the main flavouring is dill seed, the preference is for a sweeter, milder taste, and the results are more likely to be known as dill pickles. **LF**

Cornichons (French for gherkins) are often translated as gherkins, but these diminutive, pickled members of the cucumber family (*Cucumis sativus*) are somewhat different to the large, sweet-and-sour sausage-like gherkins popular in central Europe and the United States. The species of ridge cucumber is the same, but the fruit is picked before it is fully developed, normally when smaller than a little finger or less than 2 inches (5 cm).

In France, the two preferred varieties for pickling are the Vert Petit de Paris and the Cornichon Amelioré de Bourgogne. Good quality brands of cornichons are available, such as Maille, but some commercial brands can be overly tart. Home-made pickled cornichons can be made using a good white wine vinegar with shallots, onions, peppercorns, and possibly garlic and herbs. They will take around two months to reach their full potential.

Cornichons are a traditional partner to simple charcuterie such as pâté de campagne because they add contrast to the pork's fattiness. They also feature in the original recipe for tartare sauce. **MR**

Taste: *Crunchy on the outside, soft on the inside, a great gherkin will deliver a perky, tongue-tingling balance of sweet and sour. Flavours depend on precise recipes.*

Taste: *Cornichons give a neat and satisfying crunch in the mouth. Flavours vary according to the pickling ingredients, but should balance tart and sweet.*

Stallholders in Majorca display a tempting appetizer of crunchy and juicy pickled vegetables and olives. »

Sun-dried Tomato

Navarra Piquillo Pepper

For centuries, across the southern Mediterranean — in countries such as Italy, Spain, and Greece—plum tomatoes (*Lycopersicon esculentum*) have been sliced in half, sprinkled with salt, and dried in the sun for several days, before being packed into glass jars or clay crocks and covered with olive oil for use when fresh tomatoes are not in season.

Calabria is particularly associated with this intensely flavoured delicacy. There the rugged, mountainous terrain can make growing conditions difficult and the preservation of fruit and vegetables has long been traditional. Calabrians season their sun-dried tomatoes with garlic, basil, and oregano, for use in antipasti, risottos, and stews.

Although the age-old method is still used by home cooks and small producers, today most sun-dried tomatoes are preserved in dehydrators, a method which, although quicker, cannot match the flavour of those dried naturally in the sun. The technique was perfected in California in the mid-1980s. As a result, what was once seen as a gourmet item became highly popular across the globe. **MR**

Fire-roasted and hand-peeled piquillo peppers—*Pimientos del Piquillo*—are the speciality of an area of Navarra in the Basque region of Spain. These small, bright red peppers are named after their uniquely curved point, or *piquillo*. They grow in the fertile soils of the hills just north of the Ebro River, and are picked between September and November.

The best are immediately roasted over embers to loosen the outer skin, while retaining the firm flesh inside. Up to 60 per cent of the weight is lost at this stage, concentrating and intensifying the flavour. They are skinned, cored, and deseeded by hand, and then trimmed and packed in jars in only their own natural juices. The Lodosa *Denominación de Origen*, granted in 1987, guarantees not only the peppers' origin but this artisan mode of preparation.

Drizzled with a little olive oil, and maybe some garlic or parsley, these peppers do not need any further attention. Their ability to retain their shape even after cooking has led Basque chefs to stuff them with a variety of ingredients: crab, shrimp, salt cod, chorizo, and mushrooms among them. **JAB**

Taste: *Sun-dried tomatoes are chewy and sweet, with an intense tomato flavour. Those packed in olive oil should be tender, delicate, and deep red.*

Taste: *Sweet and only mildly spicy, these peppers have an initial sharpness followed by a sweet, rounded flavour from the natural oils and a smoky tang from fire-roasting.*

The superior quality of tomatoes dried naturally in the Calabrian sun justifies the heavy work involved.

Piquanté Pepper

What is small and red, and sweet and spicy at the same time? Answer: the sweet and spicy pickled peppers known as piquanté or sweet piquanté peppers, but also marketed worldwide as Peppadew™. These peppers—which look like a cross between a cocktail tomato and a small, plump bell pepper—were discovered growing wild in a holiday home garden in the Eastern Cape of South Africa, in the 1990s. Their discoverer, Johan Steenkamp, trademarked the name and came up with a secret preparation recipe which he patented.

The capsicum from which the peppers are prepared are thought to be native to Central America. Extensively farmed in the provinces of Limpopo and Mpumalanga, Peppadew™ come ready to use in jars, in either a hot or mild version. Their unique crisp texture is attributed to the brining process that uses no preservatives.

Fantastic in all types of cold salads, piquanté peppers add zing and brightness to numerous dishes, including pizzas and pasta sauces. They are also good stuffed with cheese as an appetizer. **HFi**

Chuño

For at least 1,000 years, people living in the Andes of South America have been preserving potatoes as chuño, both to protect against crop failures and to provide lasting sustenance that can be easily stored and transported. Possibly the world's first dehydrated food, chuño allowed the ancient Incas to fuel the workforce behind their sophisticated empire in Bolivia and Peru—and, subsequently, enabled the Spanish invaders to feed their troops and labourers.

Making chuño is a lengthy process that can take up to four weeks. Potatoes are exposed to frost overnight, which causes them to lose moisture. The frozen tubers are then trodden on to squeeze out the excess water before being dried in the sun. To make chuño *blanco*, the potatoes are peeled and soaked in running water. (Chuno *negro* is left in its dark brown skin.) The resulting chuño will keep for ten years or more without refrigeration. Chuño are re-hydrated in soups and stews, or prepared with cheese as a side dish. Chuño *blanco* are made into a dessert with molasses and fruit, *mazamorra*. **GR**

Taste: *Thin-fleshed but tantalizingly crisp, piquanté peppers taste peppery and pleasantly astringent with sweet, spicy undertones.*

Taste: *Like a fresh potato only lighter as it contains less water, chuño is bland and easily assumes other flavours. It can be bitter if it is not properly washed and peeled.*

The piquanté pepper, better known worldwide
⊘ *under its trademarked name of Peppadew™.*

Ja Choy

Mui Choy

In Chinese and South East Asian cuisine, the range of varieties of mustard greens cultivated—some for their leaves, others for their stems—is dazzling. Ja choy is one of the most addictive and mouth-watering versions, although, as a khaki-coloured lump of mustard stem covered in chilli paste, it is hardly the most attractive.

Ja choy (Sichuan pickled vegetable) is made by salting the fresh mustard stem to draw out excess moisture, covering it with chilli paste, and fermenting it in a sealed earthenware jar about 2 feet (60 cm) high. The jar is cast as a single piece, and to get at the vegetable, the top of the jar must be painstakingly broken off. In supermarkets ja choy is often sold sliced or julienned and wrapped in vacuum-sealed bags ready to eat; if buying from traditional Chinese grocers, tongs or long chopsticks are used to select the most tender pieces.

Ja choy may be eaten on its own or cooked with other ingredients: rinse off excess chilli paste (which stains), then pat dry before using. Take saltiness into account when seasoning. **KKC**

As with other preserved Chinese vegetables, mui choy tastes much better than it looks. The shrivelled, light brown stalks and floppy dark green leaves are salted, dried mustard greens—botanically *Brassica juncea*, and in Cantonese *gai choi* or *gai choy*.

There are two types: sweet and salty. Although the sweet type is also strongly salty, the other variety is so salty that it is heavily covered in salt flakes: in some dishes the two are used together so that their flavours balance each other out. Both types are available as whole pieces in plastic packs, or chopped in tins: they should always be soaked and rinsed in water to get rid of excess salt. Because of its chewiness, mui choy is usually finely chopped before being used in dishes: to soften and hydrate the vegetable, it can be steamed for about ten minutes before being soaked and rinsed. When cooking with mui choy, take its saltiness into consideration before seasoning the food.

Mui choy is frequently paired with braised pork belly or duck because the salty, sweet, and bitter flavours cut the fattiness of the meat. **KKC**

Taste: *The preserved vegetable is a good balance of salty, tangy, and spicy: the best is soft and tender. It stimulates the taste buds and helps increase the appetite.*

Taste: *Mui choy has an intense salty-sweet flavour— whether the salt or the sweet dominates depends on the type—and a slight bitterness like fresh mustard greens.*

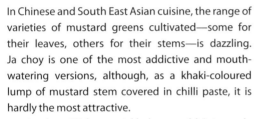

Mustard greens in California, where they are eaten raw or cooked more often than preserved. »

Wakame

Wakame (*Undaria pinnatifida*) is a saltwater-dwelling marine alga native to the waters around Japan and Korea, although a similar plant, alaria, occurs in Europe and North America in the Atlantic Ocean. The cultivation of wakame, where the spores grow on rope, was introduced relatively recently.

Wakame grows well in fast-moving waters, where it produces tender plants. It is usually harvested in March and the fresh leaves are blanched then chilled. This preserves the green colour and inhibits the growth of undesirable microorganisms, so it stays fresh for longer. In Japan, fresh wakame is on sale at harvest time, where it is piled high in salt-covered, stringy mounds in stores and markets. Dried wakame is widely available in Japan and overseas. A dull, grey-green colour when dry, it magically regains its vibrant green hue when soaked in cold water.

Used extensively in miso soup, wakame is frequently combined with seafood or cucumber in vinegared salads. Ita wakame is dried pieces of wakame pressed into a flat sheet rather like nori, and is used as a condiment with rice. **SB**

Taste: *With a mild flavour of the ocean, wakame is slightly slippery, but not off-puttingly so. It is a bit like lettuce, yet has a tender, melt-in-the-mouth texture.*

Wakame is an invasive seaweed as well as an important food. »

Hijiki

Nori

A user-friendly introduction to the world of sea vegetables, hijiki (*Hizikia fusiforme*) grows wild on the coasts of China, Korea, and Japan: the best is said to come from the Boshu Peninsula in eastern Japan. It appears just below the tide line in dense clumps of black, cylindrical strands. Young shoots picked early in the season—in February and soon after—are most tender and the highest grade: they grow to thicker strings, rather like bootlaces, as they mature.

The harvested hijiki is cooked, which turns it an attractive deep black, and dried, ready for sale. On reconstituting it expands to five times its dry volume. Hijiki's somewhat coarse texture lends itself well to sautéing in a little sesame oil together with root vegetables, while its colour is often used to create contrast, especially with carrots and lotus root. Cooked and flavoured with a little sugar and soy sauce, it keeps for several days, making it a perfect ingredient for a bento box. In 2004 there was concern over the levels of naturally occurring arsenic in some hijiki, although the Japanese and Koreans have been eating it for centuries with no obvious detriment. **SB**

The Japanese have been eating nori, the name for various seaweeds (and most famously, the wrapping used for sushi rolls) for at least 1,300 years, and farming it for four centuries or so. Yet its survival in cultivation is down to a Dr. Kathleen Drew, who brought her understanding of laver—the Welsh name for various members of the nori family—to Kyushu in the 1940s. She is commemorated by a bronze monument near the Bay of Shimbara, where nori is still seeded the way she suggested.

Nori is harvested in winter from inlets near the shore, where fresh water and seawater meet. To make sheet nori, it is washed and chopped to produce a thin sludge, which is pasted onto bamboo mats and dried. The different types of nori have various names depending on what species they come from and what they are used for: aonori, for example, is dried green laver sold in small flakes

In Wales, laver has been eaten for centuries, but prepared quite differently from the Japanese method: boiled to a sludge, combined with oatmeal, and made into little patties of "laverbread". **SB**

Taste: *Coarse and chewy with a texture more like land vegetables than slippery sea vegetables, hijiki is satisfyingly nutty and tastes strongly of the ocean.*

Taste: *Nori is mild, with only a faint taste of the sea, as it grows near estuaries. Crispy and savoury, it is a perfect accompaniment to soy sauce and, surprisingly, cheese.*

On the Japanese coast, clumps of hijiki
◎ are pegged out to dehydrate in the sea air.

Sauerkraut

Natto

It is difficult to find two words that are less likely to have anyone clambering to get to the dinner table than "fermented cabbage," but that is exactly what sauerkraut is. Love it or hate it, this traditional preserve has fans the world over, from China to Chile, and from the United States to Europe. Although frequently deemed a German invention, the fermentation of finely shredded cabbage actually goes back to ancient China.

Sauerkraut literally means "sour cabbage" and it is made by a very simple procedure involving wild fermentation, that is to say, it needs no live starter to begin the process. Salt is added to finely shredded cabbage and this draws out water from the vegetable. Naturally occurring bacteria present in the cabbage react with the resulting brine and this causes the cabbage to ferment and take on its sour flavour. Although it can be purchased in jars and cans, fresh sauerkraut has a superior flavour and texture.

Sauerkraut makes a refreshing side dish to salty meats such as sausages, ham, and bacon. It can also be eaten cold in salads and sandwiches. **LF**

The place of soya in Japanese culture is confirmed during the Setsubun festival that marks the start of spring, as soya beans rattle onto the streets, chasing away bad luck and evil spirits. High in protein, yet sometimes indigestible, soya beans have inspired almost as much culinary ingenuity as milk, and one of its many fermented products is natto.

Natto is one of those foods that divides people. Popular in Tokyo yet far too vulgar a taste for the refined folk of Kyoto, it is made of cooked soya beans. These are fermented, not with mould but with bacteria, into a pungent, sticky, and highly nutritious mass, where the beans retain their shape amid a viscous goo that forms fine threads like a sticky spider's web when stirred. Although claims made on Japanese television that natto is a weight loss panacea have proved unfounded, modern natto is not only high in protein but an important vegetarian source of vitamin B_{12} and B_2. In eastern Japan, it is a popular breakfast food, mixed with soy sauce, mustard, and sometimes a raw egg or chopped spring onion, and eaten with rice. **SB**

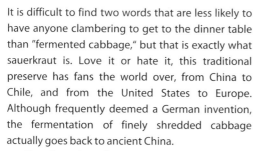

Taste: *Crunchy and pleasantly tart, sauerkraut has a clean but pleasantly sour flavour that is good at cutting through the fattiness of some meats.*

Taste: *The smell is highly pungent, like Gorgonzola with a whiff of ammonia; the texture is sticky and slightly slimy. Wrapped in a leaf and deep-fried, natto loses its stickiness.*

Silken Beancurd

Stinky Tofu

As its name suggests, silken beancurd is light, soft, and delicate. Unlike other types of fresh beancurd, which are pressed with weights to rid them of excess water, the coagulated soya bean liquid used for silken beancurd is poured into moulds and allowed to set, giving it a soft, moist, wobbly texture that is like the most fragile of custards. Because it is so delicate, silken beancurd is rarely cooked beyond being gently heated; stir-frying, even if done with great care, would break the beancurd into small, unattractive lumps. Even slicing it can be difficult.

Commercially made silken beancurd comes in small blocks, but if you find it freshly made in Chinese markets, the vendor will use the edge of a shallow metal or porcelain plate to both cut it and scoop it out of its container. In Japan, silken beancurd is usually eaten "as is" with a dash of soy sauce and chopped spring onions. It can also be made into desserts (usually served with sugar or ginger-flavoured syrup), steamed with a light sauce, or cut into small cubes and poached gently in a clear but flavourful broth. **KKC**

Never was there a food that better illustrated the saying that smell is nine-tenths of taste. Stinky tofu, known as *ch'ou doufu* in Mandarin, has a mild, faintly sour, beany flavour, but its aroma is monumental in stature, usually encountered before the *doufu* is within visual range.

To make it, assorted vegetables, herbs, shrimps, and sometimes other seafood items are fermented to produce a pungent brine, an initial step that takes days, if not weeks. Into this trenchant liquid, fresh beancurd cakes are added. After marinating for several hours, followed by a brief rest period out of the brine, they acquire a spongy texture. Regional variations abound in China, Taiwan, and Hong Kong, their colour and flavour varying with the make-up of both beancurd and brine.

Stinky tofu is often eaten as street food, perhaps for the sake of ventilation. Deep-fried until crusty on the outside, then dressed with spicy sauces, it is topped with chilli oil and garlic in Hunan, while Taiwanese vendors also add vinegar and pickles. It also appears in steamed and soup preparations. **CTa**

Taste: *Silken beancurd has a soft, smooth texture and a delicate flavour. As with other beancurd, it is a good source of protein and popular in vegetarian cuisine.*

Taste: *Stinky tofu seethes with hints of other microbe-enhanced foods, mainly tempeh and natto, with notes of Stilton and cider, plus a mushroomy dankness all its own.*

Goma Dofu

Yuba

Although goma dofu resembles tofu, it is actually made from sesame milk thickened with kuzu starch. Part of the Zen Buddhist vegetarian tradition known as *Shojin ryori*, it is often served at Japanese temples and monasteries at the start of a meal. Sesame seeds are high in calcium, and contain iron and vitamin B_1, making it is an important food for those on a dairy-free, no-meat diet, such as the Buddhist monks.

To make goma dofu, the sesame seeds are first dry roasted and then ground. The paste is then combined with water and thickened with kuzu. Another important ingredient, kuzu is also used as a thickener for sweets and jellies. Unlike other starches, it does not give off water when it sets, which makes it a superior, if expensive, thickener. Kuzu is added to the sesame milk, simmered for thirty minutes, and stirred vigorously until large elastic bubbles appear.

Goma dofu is usually served in a small square, anointed with a dab of wasabi and a drizzle of soy sauce. It is sometimes available ready-made in Japanese food stores. **SB**

It has been said that the fourteenth-century warlord Masahige Kusunoki used this high protein food to sustain his people during the long siege of Chihaya castle. Fresh yuba is a delicacy in Kyoto cuisine and plays an important role in *Shojin ryori*, the vegetarian cooking of Buddhist monks. The Buddhist monks of Rinnoji Temple in Nikko developed dried yuba as a portable, nutritious food to sustain them on retreats into the mountains. As tofu skin, yuba is still an everyday food in China, where it is known as *doufu*, and that is probably where it originated.

At Yuba Han, one of the few remaining original shops, they still prepare yuba daily, by heating large rectangular pans of soya milk. The delicate protein skin that forms is scooped off and hung up to air dry on long wooden rails. As it is so labour intensive and highly perishable, fresh yuba is now a gourmet food. In Kyoto, restaurants specializing in yuba cuisine use both dried and fresh yuba in a variety of ways—as a wrapper for vegetables, as a garnish for soups or sushi, or, best of all, freshly made yuba, just as it is, with a dab of wasabi and a little soy sauce. **SB**

Taste: *Goma dofu is nutty and creamy with a texture halfway between jelly and custard. It has a rich, satisfying flavour that is rather addictive.*

Taste: *Fresh yuba is slightly nutty with a faint taste of bean. It has a creamy, unctuous texture, with a little resistance to the bite. Dried yuba needs reconstituting.*

Iru

When fermented, this African locust bean makes a powerful condiment for flavouring dishes such as soups and stews. It is particularly popular with the Yoruba people of Nigeria, and in neighbouring countries whose cuisines are noted for their love of strong flavours. Similar to *ogiri* (fermented melon seeds), iru is an ingredient in two of Nigeria's most pungent national dishes: egusi soup, made from seafood, bush meat, and ground melon seeds, and the fiery ogbono soup, made from the kernels of the wild mango tree and hot chillies.

Iru is available both fresh and dried, the fresh usually being wrapped in moimoi leaves, large, shiny, oval leaves similar to banana leaves. When dried, iru is flattened into cakes. The drying process causes the fermented beans to lose some of their strong flavour, although when the dried iru is fried, much of this flavour is restored. High in protein, fat, and vitamins, iru is an important part of the diet of many West African people, particularly when meat is scarce. Fermenting the beans makes them easier to digest and increases their nutritional content. **WS**

Taste: *Iru is much more pungent than other fermented bean products and an acquired flavour. It is frequently compared to strong cheese, miso, and even stinky tofu.*

Tempeh Murni

This protein-rich soya bean cake comes originally from Indonesia but is now produced all over South East Asia. Tempeh is as versatile as meat and often replaces it in recipes as a cheaper alternative.

Tempeh can be cooked in all kinds of ways, being added to soups, stir-fries, braises, or salads and is even used in sandwich fillings. Like tofu, tempeh absorbs other flavours well so it is often marinated and grilled in the same way as a steak or hamburger. When sliced and deep-fried, its outer skin becomes golden and crisp, which makes a satisfying contrast to the creamy-white cake inside.

Many different types of tempeh exist: "murni" indicates that the soya beans have been fermented in a plastic bag. The whole beans are first soaked overnight and then skinned before being cooked. They are then packed into a plastic bag and left to ferment for two to three days in a hot, humid place. Tempeh is widely available in blocks, both fresh and frozen. Home cooks in Indonesia also prepare their own tempeh, the tropical climate being ideally suited to the fermentation process. **WS**

Taste: *Firmer than tofu with a denser, chunkier texture, tempeh has a slightly tart, nutty flavour, best described as a cross between red meat and a large field mushroom.*

Saikyo Miso

Miso, a paste made of fermented soya beans, often with other grains too, has existed in Japan since at least the eighth century CE, and comes in a wide range of colours, textures, and tastes. At the gentler end of the taste spectrum stands Saikyo miso, a sweet, smooth, white miso that lends itself almost as well to Western desserts as to classic Japanese dishes.

It is a speciality of Kyoto cuisine, or *Kyo ryori*, a style of cooking that developed under the twin influences of the Imperial Court and the vegetarian monks of the city's many Zen temples. In this refined and delicate cuisine, appearance is even more important than usual for Japan and lightness of colour is favoured: white miso, like light soy sauce, is favoured because it does not discolour the food.

Like almost all miso, Saikyo miso is made using soya beans mixed with either rice or barley, then fermented using *koji*—the mouldy starter used in making soy sauce and sake. However, the recipe contains more rice and less salt than is standard, meaning that Saikyo miso is high in natural sugars and so ferments in weeks rather than months. **SB**

Taste: *With a smooth and runny texture similar to lemon curd, and almost as sweet, Saikyo miso tastes delicate, fruity, and nutty with buttery caramel notes.*

Hatcho Miso

Probably the polar opposite of Saikyo miso—which has, in fact, been taken on all six Japanese expeditions to the South Pole—this rich, firm, savoury miso has an equally lofty pedigree, being a daily favourite of the late Emperor Hirohito.

Unlike other miso, it is made only from soya beans and salt. It also stands apart for being produced using a naturally-occurring mould, *Aspergillus hatcho*, which is unique to the Hatcho area of Okazaki. It is fermented for two to three cycles of the hot humid summers and mild winters of Aichi prefecture in central Japan.

Using organic soya beans, the Hatcho Miso Company in Okazaki has been making its miso for over 500 years. It is fermented under the weight of 3 tons of river stones in cedar vats that are 7 feet (2 m) high and can hold around 12,000 pounds (5,000 kg) of miso. The pressure from the stones effectively shuts out oxygen, creating the perfect growth environment for the microorganisms that make Hatcho miso a nutritional powerhouse. Perhaps it is one reason the Emperor lived so long. **SB**

Taste: *With a chunky texture so firm you can cut it with a knife, a rich brown colour and a deep savoury aroma, Hatcho miso gives a satisfying flavour to soups and stews.*

Huge vats turned on their sides wait to be filled once more at a Japanese miso factory. »

Cornish Clotted Cream

In traditional Cornish farmhouses, this ultra-rich cream was made in the kitchen, not the dairy, when the milk was at its richest and most abundant. The milk was heated without boiling to a gentle simmering temperature, then left to cool overnight. The next day, the cook would skim off the cream that had set on the surface like a blanket: a skilled maker would be able to roll it up like a Swiss roll.

Today the process is more mechanized. The cream is skimmed off the fresh milk and scalded in trays to achieve the desired consistency. With a minimum butterfat content of 55 per cent, or even more, clotted cream is very rich. At its best, the surface has a rough, partly crystalline, golden crust.

Also made in Devon, clotted cream is the cornerstone of the traditional English cream tea when it is served with warm scones and strawberry jam. *The Oxford Companion to Food* suggests that because of its similarity to the Near Eastern cream *kaymak*, it may have been introduced to Cornwall by Phoenician traders 2,000 years ago, but there is no evidence to support this attractive theory. **MR**

Taste: *The key to its taste is in the name—"clotted." The dense texture is unique, while the farmhouse product has a rich flavour that far exceeds that of commercial variants.*

The distinctive crust on clotted cream is produced by first ripening, then heating the cream.

Crème Fraîche d'Isigny

In 1932 forty-two dairy farmers around the town of Isigny-sur-Mer in Normandy formed a cooperative that has since expanded to represent farms in almost 200 communes along the English Channel. From their milk, it manufactures fresh and ripened cheeses including Camembert and Mimolette, and two AOC products under its brand name Isigny Sainte Mère: butter and crème fraîche.

The latter, as its title suggests, could once refer to any cream from freshly milked cows. Its richness varied with the time of year or the quality of animal husbandry. Its thickness, sweetness, or acidity depended on how it was handled. Nowadays, the term describes a specific kind of pasteurized cream, produced in a factory, that is thick, rich (Isigny contains 40 per cent butterfat) and lightly acidulated as a result of controlled ripening.

In France, crème fraîche is the workhorse of many classic cream sauces, particularly *sauce Normande*. Whipped and sweetened, it is the basis of Chantilly cream. To taste the difference from ordinary cream, however, it is best sampled fresh. **MR**

Taste: *Smooth textured, thick, and rich, crème fraîche d'Isigny is not cloying on the palate and the hint of acidity gives it a taste that is refreshing yet never sour.*

Smetana

This sour cream is an essential ingredient of cultured Russian cuisine. It is left on the table as part of the mixed hors d'oeuvres called *zakuski* that are eaten with shots of vodka. It accompanies blinis and caviar, enriches soups, dressings, and sauces, and figures in the many recipes for pashka. It spread, with Russian influence, across eastern and central Europe and through the former Soviet states, although it was not known in the West until the Crimean War (1853–56).

Just as cream in western Europe ranges from clotted cream to crème fraîche, so eastern European smetanas vary widely. Some are sweeter, whereas others are more sour; some have a butterfat content of around 20 per cent, others more than 40 per cent. A visit to the covered Besarabski market in Kiev gives a sense of this diversity as ladies ladle out portions of smetana from behind a long counter.

The best smetana is produced on an artisanal scale, and soured and thickened by natural bacterial action, as it was in the past. The industrial product is made with a stabilizer additive to give the cream body and, though thick and sour, is less rich. **MR**

Taste: *Artisan smetana looks smooth and velvety white. The sourness is always apparent and contrasts with the creaminess but not aggressively. It has a refreshing taste.*

Cottage Cheese

To most consumers cottage cheese is a generic term for industrially processed fresh curd made from skimmed milk or dried milk solids. Tasting mild with very low acidity, this lightly compacted mass of small, moist, rubbery gobbets is used for both salads and sandwiches.

Its origins, however, begin as a fresh, unpressed curd made either from naturally soured raw milk or with renneted fresh milk. Known in England as "green" cheese, because it was new (or "pot" cheese) it probably acquired the name "cottage" to point up the distinction between cheeses made from whole milk and those made from skimmed milks.

According to John Ayto's *The Diner's Dictionary* (1990), the usage first appeared in print in Bartlett's *Dictionary of Americanisms* in 1848. Artisan cheese-makers in the United States (among them Cabot Creamery, Vermont, and Sweet Home Farms, Alabama) still produce cottage cheese for sale in farmers' markets. Under craft conditions, the cottage cheese can be made "sweet" or "soured," in the latter case by the addition of buttermilk. **MR**

Taste: *The bland taste allied to its texture makes cottage cheese a good mixer rather than a cheese worth eating in its own right. It is partnered with foods such as pineapple.*

Russian dairy workers are celebrated by this ◀ *Soviet-era mosaic mural on Sakhalin Island.*

Labneh

Islamic cookery books from as early as the fourteenth century call for a "Persian milk" that may well be the forerunner of labneh. Also spelt "labne," "lebne," and "laban," this creamy, spreadable dairy product is closer to a yoghurt than a cheese, and still home-made throughout the Middle East, especially in Syria and neighbouring Lebanon.

Labneh can be made from cow's, goat's, or sheep's milk that is either whole or skimmed. Fresh yoghurt is strained through a cheese cloth for four or five hours until it reaches the desired texture, when it is generally salted. The results vary from a smooth dipping product to one that can, after extra straining, be shaped into small balls and preserved in olive oil. Spread on warm pitta bread and rolled up, labneh is called *arus* ("the bride"). As a meze, it is served with olive oil, lemon juice, and a sumac and thyme seasoning known as *zaatar*. For dessert, it is eaten with cinnamon and honey. In the Middle East, labneh is prepared from whole milk, but Western countries now produce low-fat versions. These lack the suave mouthfeel of the genuine item. **MR**

Taste: *The texture of labneh is always smooth with none of the furriness on the palate that is typical of manufactured dairy products. It should taste of clean, fresh milk.*

Sheep's Milk Yoghurt

Whether one terms it "Greek," as is popular in most Western supermarkets, or "Bulgarian," as a homage to the discovery of the *Lactobacillus bulgaricus* bacteria that ferment the milk, sheep's milk yoghurt is a delightfully creamy and rich dairy product.

Yoghurt is, in fact, a pan-Balkan speciality. In *The Melting Pot* (1999), Maria Kaneva-Johnson describes the sheep's yoghurt freshly made by Macedonian shepherds on Mount Bistra: "This mountain yoghurt was the finest that I have ever eaten—thick, rich, and delicately flavoured under its pale-golden crust of cream." There is special affection for yoghurt produced late in August when the sheep's milk is at its richest. In the Rhodope Mountains of Bulgaria, one yoghurt is famous under the name "gathered mad milk" because it ferments wildly and is made with milk from several milkings.

Export of commercial Greek yoghurt goes some way towards explaining its status today. More just renown is earned by the sublime coupling of the farmhouse yoghurt with Hymettus honey enjoyed by millions of visitors to Greece each year. **MR**

Taste: *The finest sheep's milk yoghurt is silky smooth and unctuous in texture. Faintly sweet, it should have no harshness or unpleasant acidity.*

Sheep grazing in Bulgaria's Rhodope Mountains produce milk for the local yoghurt kisselo mlyako. »

Skyr

This ancient dairy product was introduced to Iceland by the Vikings who settled the island more than a thousand years ago, and it remains a source of pride to Icelanders, who consider skyr a national speciality.

Although similar to yoghurt, and often marketed in a similar way—skyr is not, in fact, a yoghurt. Yoghurt is a form of soured milk containing bacteria that alter its texture while adding a measure of acidity. Skyr is a fresh, low fat cheese, made from milk that has been curdled using rennet and drained a little; it also has added bacteria similar to those found in yoghurt. Like yoghurt, it is digested far more quickly and more easily than milk: about 90 per cent of it is assimilated within an hour, as opposed to 30 per cent for milk. For this reason, and because of its low-fat content, it is considered to be a genuinely healthy food, and contains neither stabilizers nor the skimmed milk powder used in the manufacture of factory-produced, low-fat yoghurts. It is usually sweetened and softened with milk or cream to taste. Icelanders traditionally eat skyr at breakfast or with dessert. **MR**

Cuajada

Cuajada (meaning "curds") is a Spanish version of the old-fashioned nursery dessert junket, and is made by adding rennet to fresh milk. To make this wobbly wonder, the milk is heated gently, the rennet is added, and the mixture is poured into small earthenware or terracotta pots where it is left to set before being sweetened to taste.

Cuajada is popular in northern Spain, in the Basque Country and around the Navarre and Castilla y León regions, although it is possible to find it all over Spain these days. Traditionally, it was made with ewe's milk and set with a vegetable rennet, giving it a delightfully loose set and delicious mild flavour. The milk was heated using a red hot poker, which gave it a pleasant, vaguely burnt aftertaste. Now, it is more likely to be made from cow's milk and set with animal rennet, but artisan-made versions of the dessert are well worth seeking out.

Cuajada is typically served as a dessert and sweetened with honey or sugar, often accompanied by walnuts. It is also eaten for breakfast, again with honey and often alongside fresh fruit. **LF**

Taste: *Skyr is creamy but not smooth and quite dense. It has a clean taste of freshly soured milk. Softened with milk or cream, it resembles a slightly grainy fromage frais.*

Taste: *Light and silky with an engaging quiver, handmade cuajada has the lemony tang of ewe's milk. Distantly yoghurt-like, the consistency is somewhat more graceful.*

Most skyr is made in Iceland, where
flavoured versions are also available.

Beurre d'Échiré

Goat's Butter

Darling of Michelin-starred chefs, Beurre d'Échiré (AOC) comes from a creamery in Deux-Sèvres, a *département* of the Loire valley, that has run as a cooperative for over a century. The milk is supplied from sixty-six farms, all no more than 20 miles (32 km) away. Strict controls ensure that the traditional practices of butter-making continue. The fresh milk is kept between 46°F and 50°F (8–10°C), rather than at a chill temperature, to enhance the ripening of the cream, and is not pasteurized. The dairy has a special dispensation from the European Community to churn the butter in two giant teak butter-churns. The wood, chosen because it does not taint the cream with tannins, also contributes to the butter's texture. It is more fibrous than the smooth butters found on supermarket shelves, and is packaged in elegant boxes made from poplar wood.

Beurre d'Échiré finds its main use at the table but is the key ingredient of a good *beurre blanc*, the sauce made by reducing finely diced shallots and dry white wine to a glaze then whisking in small cubes of butter to form a warm emulsion. **MR**

The production of goat's milk in increasingly large herds on an agro-industrial scale is a recent phenomenon in both Europe and North America. Proponents claim that fewer people are allergic to goat's milk than to cow's milk. Although similar to cow's butter in its fat level and calorific content, goat's butter is indeed more digestible. The fat globules cluster differently from those in cow's milk, are more easily assimilated, and contain types of fatty acids that are more readily digested by intestinal enzymes.

The milk is marginally richer in fat than the average cow's milk, so lends itself to butter-making, particularly in those dairies where the cream is automatically separated and returned to the milk. Goat's butter leaves the churn white, yet producing farms often use annatto or carotene colourings to give it a pale yellow tint. Like other butters, it may be salted or unsalted, and is spreadable at room temperature and hard in the fridge. The level of "goaty" taste changes from producer to producer, but is significantly different from cow's butter. **MR**

Taste: *Beurre d'Échiré is distinctive in taste and texture. Spread on bread it seems more waxy than normal butter, while the taste of ripened cream lingers in the mouth.*

Taste: *The suggestion of goat's cheese in the taste is what makes goat's butter special. It spreads as easily and melts as fluently as more conventional butters.*

Aficionados of goat's milk products insist that the quality is superior from farms where goats roam free. »

Vologda Butter

Cadí Butter

Lying 250 miles (400 km) northeast of Moscow, the Russian town of Vologda is famous for three things: flax, lace, and butter. With a luxurious butterfat content of 82 ½ per cent, Vologda butter is truly a gourmet product. Only three dairies in the region have been making it since 1881.

With its roots in the mid-nineteenth century, Vologda butter owes its special qualities to Nikolai Vereshchagin, the founder of modern Russian dairy farming. Noticing the sour taste of some butter, he separated the sweet cream from the milk twice, instead of the usual once. This resulted in increased butterfat and a richer flavour. The butter was dubbed "Parisian butter" after it won a gold medal at the Paris Exhibition. Its name changed after the Russian Revolution and production declined under communism. But, since the 1990s, the world has rediscovered this fine butter, despite scurrilous attempts to pass off old government surplus butter under the Vologda name. An oval portrait of a milkmaid symbolizes the authenticity of the genuine butter, as does the name *Vologodskoye maslo*. **FP**

Cadí butter (DOP) or Mantega de l'Alt Urgell i Cerdanya is the sweet butter made by the Cadí cooperative in Catalonia in Spain. The breathtaking landscapes of the Pyrenees and the Cadí mountains protect vast expanses of leafy woodland and verdant meadows, thus providing a unique home for the cows whose milk produces this extraordinary butter. The cold, dry winters, spring rains, and hot arid summers react with the flora and fauna and create lush grazing that gives a distinctive flavour to the milk, and is captured perfectly in the butter.

The Cadí cooperative was set up in 1915 by a group of forward-thinking producers who wanted to farm in a way that was most compatible with the environment. Production began with just 420 pints (200 litres) of milk a day and, although the quantity has increased significantly over the years, output is limited to ensure that only the best milk is used. Cadí butter now carries a DOP certificate, which means that every stage of the production has to adhere to strict criteria, including the diet and geographical habitat of the cattle. **LF**

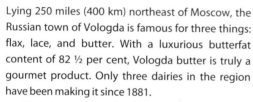

Taste: *Clean and fresh on the palate, Vologda butter has a creamy taste with a hint of walnut, and a melt-in-the-mouth texture. The best butter is sold in birch wood casks.*

Taste: *Cadí butter has a silky consistency, a creamy, sweet flavour, and a penetrating aroma of lush green pastures and mountain air. Particularly good with dark rye breads.*

The milk of cows that graze the Cadí mountains produces a unique butter. »

Mozzarella di Bufala Campana

Mozzarella di Bufala Campana (DOP) is easily recognizable by its green and red logo bearing the black face of a buffalo. The origins of this cheese can be traced back to the introduction of the buffalo to Italy, probably during early medieval times.

Fresh, soft textured, and porcelain white, Mozzarella di Bufala Campana is made from buffalo milk using age-old techniques and traditions in only seven provinces in the southwest of Italy. It has a barely noticeable rind and a delicate milky taste. When cut, it oozes a chalk-coloured, watery fluid with a gentle tang of milk enzymes.

Mozzarella belongs to the "stretched curd" family of cheeses and takes its name from the Italian word *mozzare*, which means "to cut off." Cheese-makers knead the curd by hand, in the same way that a baker kneads dough, until the stretched paste is smooth and shiny. A strand is then pulled out and "cut" using the finger and thumb to form a ball of cheese—a process known as *mozzatura*. The cheeses are put into brine baths and soaked until they take on a fibrous and elastic consistency. **LF**

Taste: *Mozzarella has a cool, sweet, milky flavour, melt-in-the-mouth texture, and fresh, delicately balanced, herbal qualities. It combines well with juicy fruits.*

Kneading mozzarella by hand gives the cheese its elasticity. »

Vacherin

There is nothing like food, and perhaps cheese in particular, to bring out a veritable rash of patriotism. Vacherin, a deliciously soft winter cheese from the mountains that form the border of France and Switzerland, is such an example. Once upon a time Vacherin (du) Mont d'Or could be either Swiss or French, thanks to a shared E.U. appellation: today Vacherin Mont d'Or can be made in Switzerland alone, and the French must sell their cheese as Mont d'Or or Vacherin du Haut-Doubs. Folk from either side of the border take great pride in their cheeses.

Both Vacherins are produced only during the cooler months of the year. The curd—which in France is made using the raw milk of specified cows—is poured into thin spruce hoops. These stay in place throughout the initial maturing process, during which the cheese may be washed in a light brine solution; it undergoes its final affinage in the pine box in which it will eventually be sold.

Ripened to perfection, Vacherin has a wavy, orange skin that contains a silky, almost runny inside, which is usually dished up with a spoon. **MR**

Langres

Steven Jenkins put it well in his *Cheese Primer* (1996): "Langres is excruciatingly delicious—it just shocks your tongue with its intense, spicy, creamy flavour."

A rich cheese that takes its flavour from the Marc de Champagne in which it is washed during the ripening process, Langres (AOC) has a unique appearance. Cylindrical in shape, the top forms a bowl into which, at one time, it was fashionable to pour *eau-de-vie*, an unnecessary practice that, like the one of pouring port into Stilton, has died out. The bowl originates with the earthenware moulds (*fromottes*) in which the curds were left to drain. These were shaped rather like the top half of a wine bottle; the whey would drip out through the "neck," leaving a hollow in the curd. But the critical part of the process takes place during the washing phase. Over several weeks the immature cheeses are washed in a cocktail of brine and alcohol.

Langres should be supple but soft and have a pungent aroma. Because it is unpasteurized and relatively young when eaten it cannot be exported to the United States. **MR**

Taste: *Maturing in spruce gives Vacherin a faintly resinous aroma. The cheese has a flavour that is deep rather than strong. The texture is soft enough to drop from a spoon.*

Taste: *Like many monastery cheeses, Langres has an in-your-face smell. Its aroma is matched by a texture that is denser than clotted cream, and a powerful flavour.*

Langres, like many French cheeses, has a texture that is as well-liked as its flavour. ❯❯

Limburger

Herve

This brick-shaped cheese with a powerful aroma emigrated from its lowland Belgian home to Germany and, once established there, crossed the Atlantic to create an outpost in Wisconsin.

It belongs, like Maroilles and Munster, to the family of Trappist cheeses that were first devised by monks. These are washed and wiped during their maturing to develop a tacky brownish or reddish coat. In Germany, where it is also known as *Backsteinkäse*, Limburger is made to both full fat and skimmed milk recipes. The potent aroma comes from bathing it up to eight times in a brine solution inoculated with Coryne bacteria. During this period the blocks are turned until they develop an even skin. This should be sticky but not slimy.

The version in the United States, made by the Chalet Cheese Cooperative in Monroe, Wisconsin, is indistinguishable from its European counterpart. It is served in a traditional deli sandwich on rye bread with raw onion. Although Limburger is often the butt of jokes about its pungent smell, it is not actually a strong-tasting cheese. **MR**

This small, bright orange, washed-rind cheese has a venerable history. Although there are references to cheese being produced in the Pays de Herve (a corner of Belgium that abuts the Dutch and German borders) before his time, Herve owes its existence to a law passed in the sixteenth century by Charles V, Holy Roman Emperor, forbidding the export of grain from the region. Peasant farmers converted their land from cereals to pasture and Herve was a by-product of the enforced switch.

To make Herve (AOC), the fresh curd is lightly pressed into bands between wooden boards. These are turned for four to five days before they are firm enough to be cut into blocks. The surface colour, known as *morge,* is obtained by washing the surface with a liquid containing the bacteria *Brevibacterium linens.* Thereafter, the texture and the taste depend on affinage. Cheesemongers may ripen Herve until sharp and spicy, keep it mild, or sell it at a degree of maturity between these two extremes. Locally, it is enjoyed with *sirop de Liège,* a sweet, sticky, black syrup made from boiled apples. **MR**

Taste: *The texture is quite springy, softer in the case of the full-fat cheese. The smell is reminiscent of dampness and decay, but the taste is round, sweetish, and mellow.*

Taste: *Like other washed rind cheeses such as Munster, which it closely resembles, Herve has a strong aroma of decay that belies a fruity flavour and a smooth texture.*

An ornately tiled panel from the renowned
Pfunds Molkeri cheese shop in Dresden, Germany.

Camembert Fermier

Camembert fermier is an increasingly rare product whose taste outshines all its imitators. Its creation is often credited to Marie Harel, a Normandy dairymaid, helped In some versions by a curate from Brie in 1791. However, there are references to Camembert cheese from at least a century before that, although no one is sure how it was made. Pierre Androuët observed in his magisterial *Guide du Fromage* (1971) that the crucial moment in Camembert's history occurred in 1891, when the wooden cylindrical box used to package it was invented. Until then it had been distributed in straw and was often spoiled.

Camembert fermier is an AOC, mould-ripened cheese from Normandy, made with unpasteurized milk on a farm. There is only one surviving farmer–producer, François Durand, still making the cheese in Camembert. The 9-ounce (250 g) disc is fatter than most factory cheeses. The white mould has hints of grey, brown, and orange. It has the usual aroma, but is more complex, mixed with the smells of fruit and chanterelles. It should not be runny when cut open but should have a smooth texture akin to Brie. **MR**

Taste: *The flavour of ripe farmhouse Camembert is milder than the factory-made products. One is conscious of the fresh milk from which it is made and the taste lasts longer.*

The flavours of Camembert fermier develop
◄ *during an ageing period of up to twenty-one days.*

Brie de Meaux

Brie de Meaux has a long pedigree and can claim with some justice to be the "king of cheese and the cheese of kings," since it traces endorsements back to the reign of Charlemagne in the eighth century.

This famous, mould-ripened cheese has various elements affecting its quality. The primary reference is its AOC status, which means it must originate from one of three *départements* near Paris: Seine-et-Marne, Meuse, and the Loiret. The second criterion is the use of unpasteurized milk: although some factories do use pasteurized, heat treatment alters the microbial flora in the milk. A third factor is the use of the *pelle à brie*—a hand tool—to ladle the curds into the hoops This gives a more delicate texture.

Affinage, the process of ripening the cheese, is as important as its making. Over a period of a month, mottled white-to-russet mould forms on the surface of the discs and the yellowish curd becomes more supple. Brie is ready to eat when there is no longer a chalky thread running through the middle, but aficionados prefer it not to be runny because it develops an ammonia smell when over-ripe. **MR**

Taste: *A perfectly ripe Brie bulges slightly but does not flow. It is almost fruity, but more tangy than the pasteurized factory-produced versions.*

Harzer

The beautiful mountain range of Harz lies deep in the German countryside, south of the town of Braunschweig in Lower Saxony. The area is well known for breeding canaries (a once-thriving industry), and for producing a strong smelling, sour milk cheese, known as Harzer.

Made from low-fat curd cheese, Harzer is a small, cylindrical cheese often delicately flavoured with caraway seeds. It is famed for its extremely strong smell that develops after maturing for only a few days. The distinctive aroma is considered pretty offputting by some, but belies its mildly piquant taste. The cheese can be kept in the fridge or at room temperature, and lasts for up to six weeks. The younger the cheese, the whiter it is at the core, and the more delicate it is in flavour. As the cheese ripens, the core turns a golden-yellow colour and the flavour strengthens.

Harzer is high in protein and contains only 1 per cent fat, and is therefore loved by those on a low-calorie diet. It is typically eaten with bread, pickled cucumbers, or mustard. **CK**

Taste: *Harzer cheese has a powerfully strong aroma and a slightly spicy flavour. It can be eaten young and firm, or ripe and soft according to preference.*

Crottin de Chavignol

Crottin de Chavignol has been made in the village of Chavignol since the sixteenth century and is probably the most famous cheese from the Loire valley. It is still produced on at least two dozen farms from raw goat's milk. The French word *crottin*, which means a small animal dropping, gives a clue as to its size: a small cylinder that fits snugly in the palm of the hand and weighs, according to its ripeness, somewhere around 2 ounces (60 g).

Chavignol's vigorous maturation is a key to why this cheese is such a gem. When still fresh, a week or so after draining and salting, it is pleasantly acid. As moulds start to develop on the surface, it grows drier and the flavours balance out. When the moulds turn blue and the crottins continue to dry out, the cheese becomes harder and more strongly flavoured. Finally, and these are not found outside the region, aged cheeses stored in earthenware jars develop a creamy texture allied to a powerful taste. In its early stages of maturity, Crottin de Chavignol is delicious thickly sliced, grilled, and served with a leafy salad dressed in old vinegar and hazelnut oil. **MR**

Taste: *Even when dry and strong, this wonderful cheese has a clean taste of goat milk that is never musty. Its natural accompaniment is a glass of Sancerre wine.*

The village of Chavignol makes Sancerre white wine as well as the eponymous cheese. »

CHAVIGNOL
VILLAGE
DE
RENOM

TRADITIONS-QUALITÉ

Rocamadour

Picodon

A place of pilgrimage to the Black Madonna, the village of Rocamadour clings to the tall cliffs that channel the Alzou River in southwestern France. It is a mysterious and romantic location, and the farmers and cheese-makers of the surrounding *départements* who produce the small, roughly 1 ounce (30 g) discs of goat's cheese trade on this reputation.

Its full title—Cabécou de Rocamadour—places it in a family of *fromages de chèvre* that take their name from a patois word for goat. Although it was once sometimes made with sheep's milk during the winter, its manufacture has been standardized by AOC regulation. Today it is a seasonal *chèvre* that must be made only from raw milk between April and November. Goats must get 80 per cent of their food from natural grazing and cannot be stocked at a greater density than ten animals per hectare.

Fresh cheeses appear for sale within a week of being made. They have a grid pattern on the surface from the racks on which they are stored. As they age, they develop a blotchy skin, while the creamy heart hardens and develops from soft to chewy. **MR**

In summer, the aroma of Picodon goat's cheese wafts through the village markets of the Drôme and the Ardèche, two French *départements* separated by the River Rhône. The small cylinders, weighing less than 3 ½ ounces (100 g), begin life fresh, white, and innocuous but will become hard, sharp, and pungent with full maturity.

In the local Langue d'Oc patois, Picodon bears the name Picaoudou, but the cheese was not considered a specific named variety until the mid-nineteenth century. Although it has benefited from an AOC since 2000, it remains very much a local cheese whose taste and quality depends on the husbandry and dairying skills of individual farmers.

There are two basic variations of the cheese. The Picodon de Dieulefit is washed during the ripening process and develops a blue-yellow mould on the rind whereas other Picodons are left to dry out. Both are seasonal, in their prime from April to August. Connoisseurs prefer them when the smooth texture is allied to a pleasant goatiness but has yet to develop the fiery quality appreciated by some habitués. **MR**

Taste: *Young Rocamadour has a soft texture and a clean, pleasant taste, reflecting the goat's diet of dry grass. As it ages, the cheese becomes more goaty, nutty, and sharper.*

Taste: *Fresh Picodon is similar to many other small goat's cheeses, but as it ripens it develops a marked earthy taste that should optimally include the scent of wild herbs.*

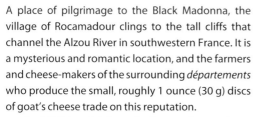

A Drôme dairyman adds another rack to his stock of freshly formed Picodon cheeses. »

Chabichou

Tiroler Graukäse

A goat's cheese from Poitou in central France, Chabichou du Poitou (AOC) has an etymology that links it to the Moors, who were driven out of France during the eighth century by Charles Martel. The "chabi" of its name derives from *chebli*, an Arabic word for goat.

    The farmhouse (*fermier*) version is prepared with raw milk, and is seasonal, made between the end of spring and the autumn. Currently, only six farms make the artisan cheese, although factory-produced Chabichou is available all year round. It is made with fresh curd from whole milk, and left for a minimum of ten days before salting: it matures for a further ten days before it is ready to eat as a young cheese.

    Chabichou's shape—small, cylindrical, and slightly truncated at the top—is referred to as a "bonde" in the local patois: each weighs 3 ½ ounces (100 g). The mould that covers the surface may be white, blue, grey, or all three, while the base of the cheese is embossed with the initials "CdP." During affinage, Chabichou continues to develop, becoming first supple then slightly crumbly. **MR**

Tiroler graukäse (PDO), or Tyrolean Grey Cheese, is a form of curd cheese made in the Zillertal valley in the Austrian Alps, northeast of Innsbruck. The cheese has been made from the milk of Tyrolean cows for centuries and was once an essential part of the peasant diet. Made from raw or pasteurized milk, the cheese is extremely low in fat at half a per cent. It takes between ten to fifteen days to mature, but the longer it matures the more spicy and acidic it tastes. Tiroler graukäse has a thin, blue-grey rind with slight cracks; inside the cheese is marbled with grey-green mould veins. The paste is dry with a gooey, white core that turns yellow as it matures. The cheese needs to be eaten within twenty-five days, because if it is left too long it can develop an unpleasantly sour after taste.

    Tiroler graukäse is often served in slices on rustic bread, or with vinegar, oil, and marinated onions. It is also used in salads and to make a sauce for dumplings. Locals add small cubes of it to a soup base of meat broth, flour, and whipped cream, which is then eaten with black bread. **CK**

Taste: *Chabichou fermier has a pronounced goaty smell. When young it is quite mild with an unctuous mouthfeel. It becomes sharper with prolonged affinage.*

Taste: *Dry at the edges, Tiroler graukäse has a fattier texture towards the centre. It has a strong aroma and a tart flavour that is slightly spicy and mildly acidic.*

A Tyrolean dairy cow greets visitors by means of its flowered headdress. »

Stinking Bishop

This modern British cheese was developed by the Gloucestershire cheese-maker Charles Martell in the 1990s. It takes its name from a Worcestershire pear that was in turn named after a cantankerous farmer called Bishop who once shot a kettle of hot water when it failed to boil. In appearance and style it is modelled on the French monastery cheeses such as Époisses and Pont l'Evêque.

Martell, a committed conservationist, is both a collector of pear trees and the main force behind saving the heritage breed of Gloucester cattle. Initially, he experimented with their milk to produce the unpasteurized flat discs of cheese that are washed in a brine and perry solution as part of the ripening process. The growing notoriety of the cheese (it featured in an Oscar-winning Wallace & Gromit film animation, *The Curse of the Were-Rabbit*) has meant that Martell now uses bought-in pasteurized milk. However, his own small herd of rare breed cattle continues to supply the raw material for traditional wheels of unpasteurized Single and Double Gloucester. **MR**

Taste: *Stinking Bishop lives up to its name. A significant part of this smooth cheese's attraction is the contrast between the subtle, creamy taste and the aggressive nose.*

Pears for the cheese's perry solution are sorted by hand. »

Torta del Casar

Serra da Estrela

Made from the milk of the Merino and Entrefina breeds of sheep that graze on the harsh, steppe-like plains of the province of Extremadura in central Spain, this organic, unpasteurized cheese is so soft when ripe that it is almost runny. Its size—from about 1 pound (500 g) up to more than 2 pounds (900 g)—makes it awkward to serve, so the top is normally sliced off and the contents dished out with a spoon or with a hunk of crusty white bread.

Once a seasonal cheese only produced at the end of winter and in early spring when the ewes were lambing, Torta del Casar (PDO) is now available throughout the year. The first half of its name refers to the shape—like a cake—the second to the town where it was originally produced, Casar de Caceres. Today it is made only by eight artisan dairies from whole milk curdled using the cuajo plant—a type of wild thistle known as *Cynara cardunculus*—as a flavoursome, vegetarian rennet. After ripening for at least sixty days, the paste becomes smooth and then unctuous. It is best left for some time at room temperature before being eaten. **MR**

The highest region of Portugal, Serra da Estrela, a mountainous spine running down the centre of the country, produces an eponymous DOP sheep's milk cheese. The predominantly black-coated, Bordeleira sheep is an autochthonous Iberian breed that would be in danger of extinction, but for its link to the "king of Portuguese cheeses."

Similar to the Torta del Casar, Serra da Estrela is a soft, runny cheese. Because there are no cattle in the region, the milk is curdled with rennet from the cardoon thistle, which is infused in the warm milk like a teabag then removed so that the curds can be stirred and broken by hand. These are then poured into cloth-lined hoops and the extra whey is squeezed out by hand. Formed into cylinders, the fresh cheeses are wrapped in muslin and left to mature for up to three weeks. Taken from the ripening room, they continue to mature until the paste inside turns to a fatty, tacky cream. When ready to eat, the rind on top of the cheese is sliced off and the contents are spooned onto a plate or the traditional cornmeal bread of the region, *broa*. **MR**

Taste: *The rich buttery paste of Torta del Casar has a dropping consistency. The sweetness of the sheep's milk is tempered by the herbal, vaguely bitter taste of the cuajo.*

Taste: *Mildly herbaceous, Serra da Estrela has a sweet taste with undertones of burnt toffee. Its aroma is intense and its soft, creamy texture is perfect for spreading.*

Portugal's black Bordeleira sheep is now rare, so milk from other species is increasingly used. »

Reblochon

Munster

This wonderful cheese from the Savoyard mountains in southeast France has an interesting name. It derives from a patois word, *re-blocher*, which means to squeeze the cow's teat a second time. This second milking would extract a richer liquid that could then be set aside, if in abundance, for cheese-making.

Coming from high alpine pastures, Reblochon (AOC) has a strong seasonal connotation, and is at its best in summer and autumn when the cattle graze extensively. Reblochon fruitier is produced in several hamlets using milk from cows that have not fed on silage, whereas the word "fermier" (farmer) on the label is a further sign of good provenance.

Reblochon is made as a 1 pound (500 g) disc and as a smaller "petit Reblochon" from whole and, at its best, untreated milk. During the ripening process it develops a rind about the colour of latte—possibly with hints of pink—which may in turn be covered with a light bloom. Ready at about two months old, the Reblochon cheese is smooth and velvety with a colour of aged ivory. It is resilient to the touch, almost elastic. **MR**

There are cheeses called Munster produced all over the world, but the Munster (AOP) made in and around Alsace stands out from the crowds. In this part of eastern France the food and the wines—like the names of towns and the language—are influenced by the proximity of the German border and by a history during periods of which the region was under German control.

"Munster kaes" is a monastery cheese (the word is itself a contraction of the Latin *monasterium*) whose pedigree goes back to the Middle Ages. It is sold as a small, flattish disc that must weigh at least 4.2 ounces (120 g), or in a larger version that weighs somewhere around 1 to 3 pounds (500–1500 g).

Munster—also known as Munster Géromé—is ripened in warm, very humid conditions, normally for only two or three weeks. During this time it is regularly wiped with a light brine. The surface develops an orange tinge, the inside of the cheese turns a buttery yellow, the texture changes to a soft consistency not unlike clotted cream, and the aroma builds to its characteristic intensity. **MR**

Taste: *The smell alone of Reblochon is enticing. Its taste is not aggressive but full, with a touch of grassiness. With 50 per cent butterfat, the finish is long and satisfying.*

Taste: *Ripe Munster has a decaying aroma, mixed with an appealing fruitiness. The taste is strong and tangy, but not in a harsh, acidic way—in fact, it is almost meaty.*

Azeitão

Postel

Nestled in the lush, herbaceous foothills of the Arrábida Mountains, the Portuguese village of Azeitão produces a lovely semi-soft cheese made from unpasteurized ewe's milk. Local legend places its origins in the nineteenth century, when a homesick farmer sent for a Serra cheese from his old flock of sheep and Azeitão adopted the cheese as its own. The cheese has PDO status and is artisan made in Setúbal, Sesimbra, and Palmela.

Rather than animal rennet, wild cardoon thistle flowers (*Cynara cardunculus*) are used to separate the curd from the whey. It is left by an open fire to curdle in huge clay pots lined with the thistle flowers, and then moulded into cloth-covered wheels. Azeitão varies in texture from soft and buttery to chewy and firm as it ages, with few or no holes. It has a strong, earthy aroma and the flavour intensifies as it matures. Azeitão is often eaten by cutting open the top, and scooping out the runny cheese with a small spoon. It is usually served with rustic, nutty bread, or with pine nuts and honey, and a glass of the local Moscatel. **CK**

Handmade by the Trappist monks at Postel Abbey in the Belgian municipality of Mol, Postel is a dense cow's milk cheese. To a certain extent the cheese has a French character, largely because the monks fled to Postel from France during Napoleon's anti-church campaign during the mid-nineteenth century. Today, the monks continue to make several cheeses at the abbey. Aged for a minimum of twelve months, Postel is a hard cheese that is suitable for grating. The paste is dark, slightly open, mustard yellow in colour, and tinged with brown towards the edges. It has a distinctive loaf shape that resembles a flattened barrel. It makes a delightful table cheese, but it is excellent for cooking, too.

Belgium now produces around 300 cheeses and, as with the country's beer, the monasteries have had a clear influence on the development of its cheeses. During the Middle Ages, there were fifty abbeys in Belgium making cheese to sell to the public, but now only the one at Postel continues to do so—other abbeys associated with cheeses do so simply by licensing their name. **LF**

Taste: *Azeitão has a tangy, slightly salty flavour with undertones of creamy sour milk and herbs. Ripe and at room temperature, it has a runny unctuous texture.*

Taste: *Postel cheese has a firm texture, an agreeable aroma, and an initial rich, nutty flavour that releases hints of warm spices such as cloves and nutmeg on the palate.*

Maroilles

One reason why Maroilles (AOC) produces such a buttery tasting cheese is that the milk is sourced from the Bretonne Pie Noire, a cow that has Jersey and Guernsey strains in its genetic inheritance. The cheese, however, comes not from Brittany, but from Pas-de-Calais, on the northern rim of France, next to the border with Belgium. This is a true monastery cheese, possibly first produced at an abbey (where St. Hubert is said to be buried) near the eponymous village. According to the French cheese bible, *Guide du Fromage* (1971), it was first known as Craquegnon. By the eighteenth century, it was a heavily salted cheese made on farms for sale in large towns such as Lille, where it was washed to desalt it.

In its classic incarnation today Maroilles is a washed rind cheese with an orange skin, shaped like a flattened brick roughly 5 inches (12.5 cm) square. However, there are a number of different sizes: the Monceau, the Mignon, and the Quart. Maroilles has a more elastic texture than some other "smellies," perhaps because it is washed only in a brine solution without any additional alcohol. **MR**

Taleggio

Although one of Italy's more venerable cheeses and today protected by a DOP, Taleggio did not officially exist by name until 1918. Until then it was one of several Lombardy cheeses known as *stracchino*, a dialect word that relates to milk from cattle tired after their seasonal droves from the alpine pastures into the valleys. It is still identified with the valleys of Taleggio and Valsassina, but is made across the north throughout the year.

A square, flat cheese, Taleggio weighs about 5 pounds (2.2 kg). Its reddish brown rind is stamped with four rings, three of which enclose a letter "T," the fourth a band. A full-fat cheese, it develops the powerful aroma, for which it is famous, during a ripening process that lasts over a month and sees the surface smeared with a brine solution inoculated with a mould and bacteria. When quite ripe the surface of the cheese should bulge like an over-filled corset. The off-white paste should be smooth like a springy butter. If it has a chalky core, it is under-ripe; if it is runny, it is over-ripe. The rind is edible, but is better scraped or sliced off the cheese. **MR**

Taste: *Although strong smelling, Maroilles has a clean aroma. The taste is strong, more of a cheese to eat with pain de campagne than at the end of a refined dinner.*

Taste: *Artisan Taleggios from Valtellina, Valsassina, and Valtaleggio have a distinctive taste that can be meaty, beefy, mushroomy, fruity, nutty, and salty, all at once.*

Maroilles cheeses acquire their distinctive criss-cross pattern as they are turned on the wire rack.

Tilsiter

Feta

Today Tilsiter (or Tilsit) is often thought of as a Swiss cheese but it is much travelled. In the nineteenth century it was made at Tilsit in eastern Prussia, by a Swiss, Otto Wartmann, who was possibly producing a cheese of Dutch origin. In 1893 he returned to his native Thurgau, set up the Holzhoff dairy in Bissegg, and returned to his profession as a cheese-maker, apparently after tinkering with the recipe he had borrowed. Made in 4 pound (2 kg) semi-hard wheels, Tilsiter is made in various versions, both raw and pasteurized, and may be aged for up to six months. The yellowish curd is pocked with pea-sized holes. German Tilsit is another kind of cheese: loaf shaped, with a washed rind, its semi-soft, springy paste is marked with small fissures. Although many are eaten sliced as a mild breakfast cheese, a strong farmhouse Tilsit can be similar to a Limburger.

The conflicting styles and confused history mean that there are effectively two quite different cheeses bearing the same name. Ironically, the town of Tilsit—renamed Sovetsk after the Russian Revolution—no longer exists. **MR**

Feta has been a staple part of the Mediterranean diet for centuries. In fact, some historians believe that Polyphemus, the one-eyed Cyclops encountered by Odysseus in Homer, was preparing an early precursor of this salty, white cheese.

Although Bulgaria and Turkey have a long heritage of producing feta and it has been made more recently in many other countries, in 2005, after fighting a long battle, Greece achieved PDO status for its emblematic cheese. As of October 2007, a feta cheese must be made in Greece from the milk of sheep, goats, or both. The pressed, sliced curd is salted and dried for twenty-four hours before maturing in a brine bath for about a month.

While much feta is mass-produced and has little but salt to define its taste, the best examples are still made in the country from the intensely flavoured, unpasteurized milk of animals that have grazed on the high, scrubby pastures of the mountains. Feta will keep almost indefinitely if submerged in brine but can dry out very quickly if exposed to air. Some soak it briefly in water to remove excess salt. **HF-L**

Taste: *Swiss Tilsiter is always made from excellent milk. It has an earthier flavour than, say, Gruyère. German Tilsit is a mild slicing cheese that can become more pungent.*

Taste: *Taken direct from its brine bath and consumed at room temperature, this tangy, pure white cheese is solid and crumbly, yet creamy, with a milky acidity.*

Ardrahan

Tomme de Savoie

Like Cashel Blue, Ardrahan belongs to the family of modern Irish cheeses that were pioneered during the 1980s. Eugene Burns began the business in his farmhouse in County Cork to the south of the island, making cheese with milk from the family's herd of pedigree Friesians.

Ardrahan is made as a pasteurized, semi-soft, washed rind cheese, using vegetarian rennet to coagulate the milk. The small—10 ounce (300 g)—and medium—2 pound (1 kg)—wheels owe their distinctive character to the bacteria inoculated into the brine with which they are wiped during early ripening, in this case *Brevibacterium aurantiacum*. Lightly pressed during making, the mild, springy cheese begins to bulge at the edges as it ages, at the same time developing both silkiness and potency.

Relatively low in both fat and cholesterol, it is a popular cooking cheese in its native Eire and has made waves internationally. Ardrahan's first outlet was a customer in Rungis, the celebrated Paris wholesale market, and it is regularly served at the White House on St. Patrick's Day. **MR**

With its light, sweet taste, Tomme de Savoie comes from the Savoy region of the French Alps. Originally a tomme was made from the skimmed milk remaining after the cream had been removed for butter-making, most often by farms working cooperatively. But until 1996, the name was borrowed by French manufacturers and used to market cheap factory cheese. An IGP label now guarantees its authenticity.

Today Tomme de Savoie can be produced using skimmed milk, full fat milk, or something in between: the fat content of the finished cheese varies between 20 per cent and 45 per cent. It is made in wheels that weigh 2 ½ to 4 pounds (1.2–2 kg), which are brushed regularly to prevent undesirable black mould forming and turned every other day during an affinage that lasts from one to three months. Invisible to the naked eye, hidden under the rind crust, tommes have a red label (indicating dairy manufacture) or a green label (for farmhouse manufacture). A good quality tomme will further specify *fabrication traditionelle au lait cru*. **MR**

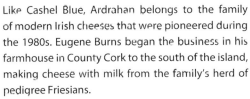

Taste: *When ripe, Ardrahan has a compact texture, more chalky in the centre than most other smeared cheeses. The earthy aroma is stronger than the silky smooth taste.*

Taste: *Tomme has an open texture, sometimes with small holes. The light flavour varies according to the fat content: cheese lovers will prefer the rougher, drier, higher fat kind.*

Olomoucké Tvarůžky

Olomoucké tvarůžky, or mature Olomouc (pronounced OH-la-mootz), is one of the Czech Republic's best-known traditional cheeses. It has been produced in the Haná region for hundreds of years, and is named after the town of Olomouc. It was first documented in the late fifteenth century, when it was reputed to be a favourite of Czech king Rudolf II, and the cheese was awarded a prize at the first Austrian Dairy Exhibition held in Vienna in 1872. It even has a museum dedicated to it in the town of Lotice. An application has been made for the cheese to be registered as an internationally Protected Designation of Origin product.

The cheese, which is very low fat at only 1 per cent, is made according to an ancient recipe from skimmed sour curd, which is crushed and mixed with ripening agents. Salt is the only added preservative. As it matures, Olomoucké tvarůžky develops a distinctive, powerful aroma, which some people dislike. Its surface is covered with a golden to orange smear, and the cheese is semi-soft in texture with a softer core. It is moist and slightly sticky, with a lustrous, translucent layer on the outside. The inside is firm and may be creamy white or pale beige. The cheese is usually moulded into short rolls, rings, wheels, or sticks weighing approximately ¾ to 1 ounce (20–30 g) each.

Intriguingly, the cheese was included in a Czech-Chinese banquet some years ago when Olomouc cheese dumplings in ginger sauce were served as a dessert. This flavoursome and nutritious table cheese is commonly eaten with bread, but it is also a staple ingredient of Czech cuisine. It is a popular Czech pub snack, and can be fried in batter. **CK**

Hoch Ybrig

The cheese Hoch Ybrig (pronounced hockh EE-brig) comes from the town of Kussnacht in the Swiss canton of Schwyz, high in the Swiss Alps. Created relatively recently, in the 1980s, the semi-hard cheese was modelled on Swiss Gruyère and shares its name with the picturesque alpine region.

The cheese is sold in wheels weighing around 15 pounds (6.8 kg); because of its limited availability it is expensive to buy. It is made in a single dairy during the summer months from unpasteurized milk from a number of herds of Simmenthal cows from small farms, where they graze on lush alpine pastures containing wildflowers and abundant herbs. The whey is removed from the cooked pressed curds, and the cheese is washed in a white wine brine once a week to help mould grow and to ripen the cheese, a process which gives the cheese its unique character and flavour. The wheels are brought to market aged eight months to one year. Young cheeses are slightly reddish, whereas more mature wheels have darker, harder rinds with a dusting of white mould and a strong earthy aroma. Year-old cheeses will have developed a deep golden interior and more powerful flavour, with pleasantly crunchy protein crystals, similar to those that develop in aged Parmigiano Reggiano.

Hoch Ybrig is best eaten after having been left at room temperature for about an hour, when the surface will glisten with drops of milk fat. It is delicious served with mostarda and a chunk of fresh baguette, and a glass of white wine or Amontillado sherry to enhance the nutty aroma of the cheese. It is also superb with crisp apple slices or grapes, and is an excellent cheese for fondue. **CK**

Taste: *Olomoucké tvarůžky has a yellowish colour and a savoury, piquant flavour. It is easily recognizable by its distinctive pungent odour.*

Taste: *Hoch Ybrig has a smooth, slightly granular texture similar to aged Parmigiano Reggiano, a musty aroma, and an exquisite sweet flavour tinged with a rich nuttiness.*

The milk of Swiss Simmenthal cows grazing in high alpen pastures is flavoured by the rich flora. »

Selles-sur-Cher

Fleur du Maquis

In the heart of Sologne, the region south of Orléans, the town of Selles-sur-Cher has lent its name to a goat's cheese of distinction that stands comparison with other classic *chèvres* of the Loire valley: Sainte Maure, Valançay, and Crottin de Chavignol.

Selles-sur-Cher was recognized as a specific style of cheese in the 1880s, when the *coquetiers* who travelled around farmhouses to buy for resale began distributing it. Made from whole, unpasteurized milk, it achieves its own personality through the care with which the milk is produced, the delicacy with which the curd is formed, and the attention paid to its affinage—a painstaking process for any cheese, but particularly for one as small as this.

Goats are mainly reared indoors on a diet of cereals and hay. Very little rennet is used to curdle the milk; the curd is ladled by hand into moulds. After it has settled, the flattish discs are coated by hand with a solution of salt and ash. Left for several weeks to harden and mature, the cheeses become drier, finer, smoother, and denser, achieving a beautiful balance. **MR**

The name alone of this Corsican cheese would make it attractive, redolent of the flowers and herbs that scent the island's rocky plains. Coated in rosemary and savory leaves, sometimes flecked with chilli pepper, it catches the eye on any counter or shelf.

Fleur du Maquis is a seasonal cheese, made between spring and late summer, most often using milk from the island's Lacaune ewes. It may be sold fresh or left for several months to ripen, by which time it will start to turn runny. Although it was probably conceived as a tourist cheese in the early 1950s, it has always been a craft product, made with raw milk, sometimes under its alternative names of Brindamour or Brin d'Amour.

When young the outside leaves retain their silver-green colour. As the cheese ages, they dry out and discolour, and mould forms under the surface. The best stage at which to sample Fleur du Maquis depends entirely on personal preference. Cheeses weigh from about 1 pound (450 g) and should be chosen with care. Check the label to see whether they have been made with sheep or goat's milk. **MR**

Taste: *On a ripe Selles-sur-Cher, the cheese under the ash coating is less than 1 inch (2.5 cm) thick. The flavour is distinctly but not aggressively goaty, with extreme length.*

Taste: *Scrape off the herbs on the surface before eating. Texture and taste ranges from sweet, pleasant, and herby in fresh cheese to strong, intense flavours in older cheese.*

Milk from Lacaune ewes is used in both Fleur du Maquis and Roquefort. »

Afuega'l Pitu

Afuega'l pitu is a historic, traditional cheese, made in the Asturias region of Spain, an area noted for its variety of cheeses, many of them artisanal. Afuega'l pitu is a cow's milk cheese, made from raw or pasteurized milk. The cheese's striking, colloquial name translates as "choke the cockerel," thought to be a reference to the cheese's distinctive texture or to its strong flavour. One of the area's oldest cheeses, it has the distinction of being legally protected; it has been given a Protected Denomination of Origin (PDO), a definition that recognizes the cheese's geographical origins and which restricts production to an area between the Nalan and Narcea rivers.

Afuega'l pitu has two authentic shapes, which may confuse some cheese aficionados. In the *atroncao* form it takes the shape of a cut-off cone, which is obtained by ladling the curds into moulds (*barreñas*). Alternatively, the curd may be hung up in small bags to drain, where it compresses and acquires a distinctive rounded form similar to a pomelo. Furthermore, the cheese is also available *blanco* (white) or *rojo* (red), the latter given colour and flavour through having either hot or sweet pimentón added to the curd.

The variety of forms afuega'l pitu can take also extends to its size and weight. The maturing time also varies, so the cheese ranges in texture and flavour from soft and mild when young to a stronger, more textured version when older. Some versions also feature moulds on the rind, adding to the depth of flavour. In Asturia, it is traditionally washed down with the dry cider for which the region is also known, and where local cheese-makers have a chance to show off their produce at an annual festival. **MR**

Casu Marzu

Squeamish readers may want to skip this entry. Casu marzu is a Sardinian cheese that, unless you hail from the island itself and consider it liquid gold as some older locals do, might politely be described as an acquired taste. (Indeed, it may rank as a food you would rather know of, than actually eat.) Casu marzu means "rotten cheese" and is literally riddled with live maggots. Banned even in its country of origin, it tends to be sold under the counter. In fact there is a large black market for the cheese and shepherds produce small quantities of it for niche markets, and also sell it to people who request it.

Casu marzu is an offshoot of Pecorino Sardo, a wonderful Sardinian cheese made from ewe's milk. In spring a few cuts are made into the rind, and the larvae of a cheese fly known as *Piophila casei* are introduced to the cheese. The grubs are allowed to grow inside the cheese paste to help encourage an advanced level of fermentation, one that most people would describe as decomposition. The developing grubs produce a spicy cream inside the cheese with a very soft melting texture, causing it to ooze beads of an aptly named liquid known as *lagrima*, which means "tears" in Sardinian.

The cheese is normally eaten with Sardinian bread (pane carasau) accompanied by Cannonau, a strong red wine. The translucent maggots (which should be alive when the cheese is eaten) are ⅓ inch (8 mm) long and can jump distances almost twice their length—diners might like to consider wearing eye protection. If the maggots are not wriggling, the cheese has become toxic. Some people prefer to remove the larvae before eating; others throw caution to the wind and devour the lot. **LF**

Taste: *Round Afuega'l pitu is open textured and granular, whereas the* atroncao, *rich at first, becomes firmer, almost brittle, when aged. The cheese is mildly acidic when young.*

Taste: *The maggots can be eliminated by sealing the cheese in a paper bag and waiting for them to die. What remains has a pungency that defies description.*

Before its exposure to maggots, casu marzu begins life as Pecorino Sardo cheese. »

Yarg

A Cornish cheese, created near the end of the twentieth century, Yarg is a kind of Caerphilly wrapped in stinging nettles. Allegedly it traces its pedigree back to an early seventeenth-century best-seller, *The English Housewife* by Gervase Markham, that describes how fresh cheeses were sometimes laid out on nettles while they aged.

Made only at Lynher Dairy, a boutique cheese-maker near Truro, using milk from its own farm, Yarg combines modern technology with handcrafting. After brining, each lightly pressed 6 pound (3 kg) cheese is coated by hand in a nettle layer before it goes to the maturing room to ripen. Generally the cheese is marketed young to multiple retailers and delicatessens where the spinach-coloured green leaves create an instant visual impact. For a handful of specialist cheesemongers, however, Lynher Dairy changes the recipe. It replaces vegetarian rennet with a traditional animal one. Extended ripening turns the leaves black. Moulds form on the surface. The cheese looks less appealing to an untutored eye, but the flavour becomes more distinctive. **MR**

Taste: *Young nettle Yarg has a pleasant, lightly acidic taste with a mushroom-like aroma. The nettle taste is only marginal. Aged nettle Yarg has more length and depth.*

Caerphilly

This crumbly, white cheese was once thought of as unique to Wales. It was considered a coal miners' cheese; they took chunks of it down the pits wrapped in cabbage leaves. The hot conditions may explain why Caerphilly was often more salty than other British cheeses. Yet Caerphilly was also made in Somerset, where dairy farmers found a ready use for excess milk. They exported it across the Bristol Channel because it never achieved much popularity in a county that had its own love affair with cheddar.

During World War II the Ministry of Food banned Caerphilly in the false belief that the cheese did not keep and when the war ended no Welsh cheese-makers were able to re-establish the craft commercially. An industrial version survived, but the handmade cheese almost died out. One Somerset dairy farmer, Chris Duckett, continues to make an authentic version. He, in turn, has trained Todd Trethowan, who has revived Caerphilly-making at Gorwydd in Wales. Duckett's Caerphilly is eaten at a few weeks old but Trethowan's is allowed to mature until it develops a rind. **MR**

Taste: *Duckett's Caerphilly is a milky curd cheese, open textured, lightly flavoured, and salty. The Gorwydd version is crumbly and lactic at the centre, but earthier under the rind.*

Cheeses made in the Caerphilly style are aged for two to eight weeks. »

Schabziger

Gjetost

If the moon were made of green cheese, as folklore once had it, it would have to be made of Schabziger. Hard, green, and shaped like a neat truncated cone weighing around 3 ½ ounces (100 g), this remarkable cheese comes from the eastern Swiss canton of Glarus. It may have been created by monks over a thousand years ago and the first recipe for it dates to 1463.

Schabziger has a stunningly low fat content for a cheese—around 3 per cent. It is made using skimmed cow's milk to produce a curd that is pressed, dried, ground into powder, then mixed with blue fenugreek (*Trigonella caerulea*), the herb that gives it its pale green colour and flavour. It is then pressed into small moulds and left to harden.

In Switzerland, Schabziger is traditionally grated and mixed with butter to make a kind of spread: pre-mixed Schabziger butters are now available. The cheese may also be used as a flavouring for noodles and *rösti*. However, its powerful and distinctive flavour means it is more commonly used as a seasoning, particularly in the United States where it is known (and sold) as Sapsago. **MR**

Gjetost is an unusual and distinctive cheese from Norway, with the texture of fudge and a flavour reminiscent of sweet—but still cheesy—caramel. It is made with cream and whey from the milk of both goats and cows, cooked under pressure until the lactose, or natural milk sugars, caramelize and the cheese develops its characteristic flavour and colour. It is then cooled in rectangular moulds.

Like many foods, Gjetost was the result of a happy accident. Over 130 years ago, Anne Hov, a farmer's wife from Norway's Gudbrandsdalen valley, had the bright idea of adding cream to the whey cheese she was preparing. The cheese commanded higher prices than her regular produce, and so Gjetost was born. The story goes that the resulting income saved the valley from imminent financial ruin.

Gjetost is best served in wafer-thin slices using a cheese plane. Typically, it is eaten with Norwegian flatbreads or grilled until melting and served with toast. It is delicious melted over a number of dishes and into sauces to accompany meats such as game. It also makes a tasty addition to a cheeseboard. **LF**

Taste: *Schabziger is so hard it has to be grated or ground before it can be eaten. Then its strong herby flavour with undertones of Cos lettuce or sage comes to the surface.*

Taste: *After the first bite, the caramel nature of Gjetost gives way to a fresh, slightly sour-sweet edge rather than the cloying qualities one might expect at first glance.*

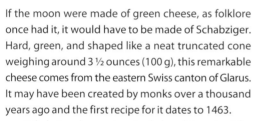

Everyday life in Gudbrandsdalen, Norway, around the time Gjetost was first created. »

Tête de Moine

Halloumi

Created by Swiss monks and originally known as Bellelay, this cheese may have an 800-year-old history, but today's producers recommend that it is best served directly from the fridge. This is because it is served in a unique way—pared very thinly, so that the air brings out maximum flavour from the cheese. This was once done with a knife held at right angles to the cheese, but is now achieved using a *girolle*, a device invented in 1982, which scrapes the surface in circles to create frilly curls. The colder it is, the thinner the cheese can be pared, but it must be eaten quickly or the air will decimate the flavour and texture of the fine curls.

Tête de Moine, or "monk's head," has an AOC status and is made by nine dairies, using raw unpasteurized milk, in the Jura region. Ripened for four to six months, the rind of the cheese is brine washed, creating a sticky red coating that gives the cheese its characteristic spicy, fruity aroma. Fine shavings of Tête de Moine are sometimes eaten with ground black pepper or cumin. It is also good with fruit and charcuterie, or shaved over salads. **GC**

A creamy white soft to semi-hard cheese with a fibrous, springy texture that is made from goat's and/or ewe's milk and a little mint. It was originally made by Bedouin in the Middle East, as its good keeping qualities made it ideal for their nomadic lifestyle. The popularity of the cheese led to its widespread production throughout Greece and Cyprus, where it remains a favourite cheese.

Halloumi is made in Cyprus using centuries old methods. It is such a key part of the culture that halloumi "police" visit stores and dairies to ensure that the time-honoured methods are being upheld. Halloumi can be eaten fresh or left to mature for one month. The finished cheese can be sliced but not crumbled, and it is at its best when cooked.

In Cyprus, thin slices of the cheese are cooked in a hot pan until the outside is crisp and golden and the inside is soft. Or it is grilled and drizzled with olive oil, and then served with salad and pitta bread. In Lebanon, where it is known as kebab cheese, it is cubed, threaded on skewers, and grilled over charcoal, then sold as a popular street snack. **CW**

Taste: *Tête de Moine has a spicy, mushroomy, nutty flavour with an elegant sweet finish on the palate. Its supple texture ranges from semi-hard to hard.*

Taste: *Salty, but mild, with a tangy flavour. Some halloumi is saltier than others and needs soaking in warm water or milk for a short time to remove excess salt.*

Wafer-thin layers of a Tête de Moine cheese
❮ *are sheared from its surface by a girolle.*

Mimolette Vieille

Aged Gouda

The name Mimolette hints that it was dreamt up by a marketing guru. "Mi" equals half; "molette" implies a measure of softness. However, it was not. The story goes that Jean Baptiste Colbert, one of Louis XIV's ministers, banned cheese imports from Holland during one of the recurring wars between France and its neighbour. In northern France, dairymaids then took to making their own version of a popular Dutch cheese. Shaped like a large cannonball—hence its alternative name "Boule de Lille"—this impressive *fromage* weighs in at 9 pounds (4 kg).

Mimolette is a pressed cheese that varies from semi-hard to hard. Its thick, crusty rind is attacked by mites. These tiny creatures serve to aerate the cheese, helping the bacteria and enzymes perform their flavour-giving miracle. Cheeses sold as Mimolette Vieille must be at least twelve months old, and Extra Vieille at least eighteen months old, although the cheese continues to develop taste beyond this. The principal manufacturer is Isigny-Sainte-Mère in Normandy. Its cheese benefits from the French quality mark Label Rouge. **MR**

This venerable cheese, like cheddar, has a worldwide reputation. It has been made in the Netherlands for at least eight centuries and much copied by the dairy industries of other countries over that time. In its young form, Gouda is a bland, mellow cheese made from whole milk by a technique known as "washed curd," where the solid curds are washed before pressing. It is springy, with quite a waxy texture, and the Dutch eat slices of it at breakfast.

Yet when it is aged. Ideally for as much as six years—this rather mundane raw material takes on entirely new identities. After one year, it can still be sliced with a sharp knife, but is starting to become brittle. At five or six years old, it can be as hard as a Parmigiano Reggiano, packed with a powerful, complex flavour and calcium lactate crystals that make it almost crunchy when chewed. When Gouda has reached this stage of maturity, the distinctive flavour and aroma is best savoured on its own or with a well-made bread and a glass of good Low Countries beer. It should not be treated as an alternative to Parmesan and used for cooking. **MR**

Taste: *Mimolette's scent is often likened to butterscotch. The taste of Vieille is nutty, with a lot more edge than the young cheese. The texture is hard, brittle, and quite waxy.*

Taste: *The aroma of aged Gouda can range from honey-like to butterscotch or dark caramel. Its taste, which should not be too salty, is sometimes likened to old whisky.*

Quite possibly related to the Edam family,
❰ mimolettes can undergo years of ageing.

Cheshire

Cheddar

In medieval England, Cheshire was the benchmark by which all other cheeses were measured. In the nineteenth and early twentieth centuries, it was the only British cheese, apart from Stilton, that the French knew by name. During the 1920s more than 1,200 farms were making Cheshire, and before World War II it accounted for 60 per cent of British cheese consumption.

Today this typical English hard cheese survives as a much-diluted factory product, and is made on a bare handful of farms. Only one of these, Appleby's of Hawkstone, still makes cloth-bound cylinders with unpasteurized milk from its own dairy herd. Cows graze on the Cheshire Plain, above mines that have produced rock salt for two millennia, which gives a saltiness to the cheese. It is usually eaten younger than cheddar, rarely at more than six months old. Some Cheshire cheeses have an orange tinge due to the addition of annatto. Appleby's makes versions with and without the use of this natural dye. Their method delivers a cheese that is less sour and more buttery than other Cheshires. **MR**

In the eighteenth century, when Daniel Defoe (creator of *Robinson Crusoe*) visited Cheddar, the village on the Somerset levels was already known for the large wheels of cheese produced there. The distinctive "cheddaring" process, however, where the fresh curd is cut into blocks and stacked then restacked so that it drains under its own weight, was not described until the mid-nineteenth century.

Today, cheddar is a generic term for a hard, pressed cheese that is made in English-speaking countries around the world. It covers everything from young, industrial cheeses to small-scale, artisan creations. The finest English cheddars still made in Somerset come from three farms: Montgomery's, Keen's, and Westcombe Dairy. These are the only ones to use unpasteurized milk from their own herds, animal rennet to separate the curds and whey, and a traditional starter to promote the acidity in the milk. The cheese wheels weigh more than 30 pounds (14 kg) each and are matured for between twelve and eighteen months. There is just one farmhouse producer based in Cheddar itself. **MR**

Taste: *Appleby's Cheshire cuts easily and is open-textured and flaky rather than crumbly. The taste is brightly sour, almost piquant, although never harsh or biting.*

Taste: *Mature cheddar has a typical nuttiness. Its compact texture is not too dense. It should never be harsh, hot, or acidic, but should cover the palate with its long flavour.*

At the start of the "cheddaring" process, fresh curd is placed on steel mesh to drain it of whey. »

Idiazabal

The fashion for Basque cuisine that began in the 1980s put the spotlight on a hard cheese produced with milk from the indigenous Latxa sheep, Idiazabal (DOP). In size and shape the cylinders resemble Manchego, but Idiazabal's character is all its own.

Traditionally, shepherds pastured their sheep in the Pyrenees in spring and summer, made their cheeses *in situ,* and brought them down with their flock at the outset of winter. They would, incidentally, store their cheeses in the open chimneys of their mountain huts. Today, outside the Basque country and Navarra where it is made, Idiazabal is thought of as smoked cheese, and is often gently smoked over beech, birch, or fruitwoods. This process gives the outer rind a patina of antique wood that transmits its flavour through the ripening curd.

Idiazabal is ready to eat at between two and four months old, but can be kept for much longer when it becomes hard enough to grate. Most Idiazabal is made in small factories from unpasteurized milk, but a handful of shepherds still make it in the time-honoured way. **MR**

Taste: *Unsmoked Idiazabal is sweet, buttery, and firm with a nutty flavour. The influence of the smoking is subtle rather than assertive, delivering an elegant complexity.*

Ossau-Iraty

More than a hundred shepherd-farmers, grazing flocks of between 200 and 400 ewes on the lower slopes of the French Pyrenees, still make this traditional French Basque sheep's milk cheese. Although protected by an AOC, Ossau-Iraty is less standardized in style than many other cheeses with a designated origin: in fact, its particular charm is that each cheese-maker will come up with a slightly different cheese from his or her neighbour.

It must be made using whole milk only from Basque sheep, during a season that generally runs from the New Year until the end of August. (It is illegal to make Ossau-Iraty in September or October.) The summer cheeses, produced when the sheep graze on high, wild pastures, are most desirable: during this time, farmers strain the milk over stinging nettles for extra herbaceous hints. The cylinders of cheese can weigh anything from 4 to 15 pounds (1.8–7 kg) and are matured—sometimes still in traditional cellars or caves—for over three months. All have a minimum butterfat level of 50 per cent, so are typically oily. **MR**

Taste: *Ossau-Iraty is firm but not hard, with a melting texture. The taste is fatty, sweet, and nutty: in its homeland it is paired with cherry jam, which enhances its flavours.*

Paški Sir

The Croatian sheep's milk cheese is a jewel of a hard cheese, bursting with both flavour and history. Pronounced pash-key seer, paški sir can be translated as "cheese (sir) of the island of Pag." Pag is one of Croatia's four Kvarner islands on the Adriatic Sea, and this quiet little island is becoming a popular tourist destination. Tourism apart, Pag is known for only four things: cheese, lamb, lace, and salt.

Paški sir is a delicacy that is seldom found outside Croatia. The cheese is made from the milk of seaside sheep whose origins date back to the eighteenth and nineteenth centuries, by the crossing of regional sheep varieties with imported merino sheep. These rugged sheep feast on salt-slaked grasses and sage brush that give their milk a distinctly herbaceous flavour. This is enhanced further through a curing process that involves brining the wheels in salt water, with some being rubbed with olive oil and ash. Young paški sir is aged for five months while old versions are aged for a year or longer. Only about eighty tons of this cheese is produced yearly, from the island's 40,000 sheep. **JH**

São Jorge

The Azores, which belong to Portugal, are a group of volcanic islands in the middle of the Atlantic. São Miguel, the largest, has a significant dairy industry, but it is São Jorge that has lent its name to a cheese that is exported across the Portuguese diaspora. It is a semi-hard cheese, generally eaten quite young and, when produced commercially, it is easy-going enough for Azorean hotels to serve it sliced for breakfast. In local *tascas*, a cross between tapas bars and bistros, small wedges are eaten as an aperitif.

São Jorge is a narrow rib of a pasture-matted isle. The Gulf Stream ensures a temperate climate that is ideal for dairying, and cattle graze all year round in small enclosures that shield them from Atlantic storms. Nowadays the cheese is made with milk from modern breeds of cattle, but the islands still have a few of the Ramón Grande breed that were brought here in the sixteenth century. Wheels of cheese weigh 12 to 22 pounds (5.4–10 kg) and have a yellowish rind. Aged São Jorge is still sold in the main market of São Miguel, but is generally exported at about four months old. **MR**

Taste: *A hard cheese that can melt at high temperatures, paški sir offers a Parmigiano Reggiano-like taste, only saltier and with a slightly more herbaceous flavour.*

Taste: *São Jorge has a lactic taste, crossed with a touch of sweetness. Connoisseurs claim to detect a hint of grassiness. Its texture is compact with a smooth finish.*

Boulette d'Avesnes

It seems unkind to describe a cheese as anti-social, but Boulette d'Avesnes does make its presence felt and should be treated with respect. Cone shaped and paprika coloured, it comes from the same corner of France as another "smelly," Maroilles, and is unusual in that it is both a washed rind cheese and a flavoured cheese. The first element of this pungent pairing derives from bathing in a beer brine during the early stages of ripening. The second is down to the pepper, tarragon, parsley, and, in some recipes, ground cloves that are stirred into the curd. Add a dusting of annatto and one has an item worthy of its nickname "the devil's suppository."

The first reference to Boulette d'Avesnes links it to the Abbaye de Maroilles in 1760. At that time farmers made it entirely with cooked whey. Today it is a full fat cheese that is made by artisans using the same basic process as for Maroilles, although it has to be hand-rolled to obtain its unique shape. A Boulette is 4 to 5 inches (10–12 cm) high and weighs about 7 ounces (200 g); it is matured for three months before it is sold over the counter. **MR**

Tartous Shanklish

This unusual looking cheese, which has been likened to a grubby tennis ball, is a speciality of the port of Tartous (or Tartus) which lies 137 miles (220 km) northwest of Damascus. Also known as *surke*, aromatic shanklish cheese is commonly, though not exclusively, made along the Syrian coast and into north Lebanon, either from cow's, goat's, or sheep's milk, but the Tartous version is the best known.

The cheese is traditionally made at home. Milk is fermented into yoghurt, then shaken in a ceramic container. Any fat is removed until a semi-skimmed yoghurt remains. This is heated until it separates and the white residue is hung in a cloth for twelve hours. What remains is known as *arish*, and this is salted and rolled into balls. The flavour can be enhanced with Aleppo pepper or *zaatar*, for example, (although aniseed or chilli can also add a kick). The balls are then left to ripen for anything from a week to a month.

Tartous shanklish is eaten as a meze dish or as a table cheese. Locals most often serve it in a salad of tomato with oil and finely chopped onion. **CK**

Taste: *On a cheeseboard this is the last one to sample as it is the most pungent. Apart from its assertive smell, the cheese will prickle the palate with added spice.*

Taste: *Tastes like an aged feta but with deep herby notes and a spicy kick. Flavour does depend on age: mature cheeses are darker, harder in texture, and more pungent.*

The Tartous area of Syria; its cheese can be made from the milk of cows, goats, or sheep. »

Churpi

Travellers to the Indian subcontinent—particularly Tibet, India, Nepal, and Bhutan, where nomadic herdsmen in hilly regions have depended on the shaggy-haired yak for thousands of years—are likely to encounter churpi.

Mainly made by yak farmers from sweet, rich yak's milk, although it can be made from buffalo or cow's milk, churpi is an unusual type of hard, dried cheese. While most hard cheese can be cut with a knife, churpi needs to be broken with a hammer. It must then be sucked or chewed over a long period of time—from ten minutes up to an hour or more—to get the distinctive flavour of the cheese. At first, churpi has no taste, but after an hour or more a milky taste coats the palate. The indigenous people carry it while they accompany their grazing herds of goats or sheep. It is portable, nutritious, and energy-giving.

Prior to the 1980s, Nepal was the world's leading yak cheese producer and churpi remains important to the rural economy there. Production methods have changed little over the years; the cheese is traditionally made using a special cylindrical churn made of wood and bamboo, before being moulded, pressed, and dried.

Churpi can be chewed as a snack, and is ideal for travellers. It is very popular in Nepal, where it is sucked and chewed rather like chewing gum. A Tibetan delicacy is made by lightly frying churpi with the young tendrils of a local fiddlehead fern called *ningro*. Yak cheese is beginning to be known across the world, thanks largely to China. There are varying styles of the cheese, and as the Chinese government puts its weight behind yak dairy initiatives in western China, more are likely to head west. **TB**

Taste: *Rock-hard churpi once patiently softened in the mouth has a creamy texture that coats the palate. It has a distinctive flavour that is slightly sweet and mildly salty.*

Yaks produce sweet, richly flavoured milk and cheese-making preserves it in a portable form.

Moose Cheese

The moose (the American name for the European elk) has an important place in Swedish culture and food. Although the animal is valued for its meat, there is, however, no tradition of eating moose cheese in Sweden. In 1996 Christer and Ulla Johansson decided to try something new to breathe life into the sleepy community of Bjurholm in northern Sweden and adopted a couple of abandoned moose. Their dairy farm is now home to more than a dozen moose and is the only moose dairy farm in Europe. The usually wild animals have been domesticated, making it possible to milk them.

People not only make the pilgrimage to the Johanssons' "Älgens hus" (Moose House) to stroke domesticated moose, they also visit to try the unique moose cheese that is made here. Moose only produce milk between May and September and the milking process can take up to two hours; each moose produces about a gallon (4–5 litres) of milk a day. The milk is kept refrigerated and curdling is done three times per year—yielding 660 pounds (300 kg) of cheese annually.

Moose milk is somewhat similar to cow's milk, but higher in protein and fat. It is very nutritious and reputed to have great health benefits. In Russia, moose milk is used to treat blood diseases and gastrointestinal ailments such as stomach ulcers. It is also becoming popular as a drink.

The extremely expensive price per pound means that moose cheese is for the lucky few. It is sold in upmarket restaurants and a few exclusive outlets in Sweden. The Johanssons make three different types of moose cheese, one of which is best described as a type of feta, and is stored in rapeseed oil. **CC**

Taste: *Moose cheese is less "crumbly" than feta and has a much smoother, broader, and deeper taste. The high price tag suggests it should be enjoyed on its own.*

Arzúa-Ulloa

Ubriaco

Traditionally known as "turnip-top cheese" and made in the provinces of La Coruña and Lugo in Galicia in northwest Spain, Arzúa-Ulloa is a delightful cow's milk cheese. Hugely popular in Spain, it is also known as *queixo do pais* or "cheese from the countryside." Young Arzúa-Ulloa has a soft paste and a mild flavour, whereas the cured version has a salty edge and a harder texture.

Artisan Arzúa-Ulloa carries a DOP certificate that lays down strict criteria governing the entire production of the cheese. It must be produced from the full-fat milk of specified breeds of cow, in particular Rubia Gallega (also known as Galician Blonde), Friesian, or Alpine Brown—all of which yield a deliciously sweet, dense milk that contributes towards making the special flavour of the cheese.

To make Arzúa-Ulloa, salt is added to the milk and the mixture is heated to 33°C (91°F), at which point the milk curdles and the curds are poured into moulds before being left to drain. Young cheeses are left to develop from six to fifteen days, but the cured variety matures for at least six months. **LF**

Ubriaco or "drunken" cheese comes from near the Piave River in the Veneto region of Italy. It is so called because the young cheese is literally soaked in wine and then covered with crushed grape skins before maturation. Ripening cheese in wine and grape must is a long tradition in Italy, thought to stem from times past when oil was scarce and expensive.

It is made between September and November by dunking pieces of Latteria, Asiago, Montasio, Marsure, or Fagagna—all cheeses made from full cream cow's milk and already seasoned for between six and twenty-four months, in the fresh marc of red wine, mainly Merlot, Cabernet, or Raboso. The cheese is immersed in the wine for between thirty-five and fifty hours, then dried and matured for between six and ten months. Consequently, the crust takes on a dark purple to light violet shade, depending on the wine used.

The taste of ubriaco cheese varies according to the cheese and wine used. A fine cheese eaten on its own, it is best accompanied by a young red wine of the same variety as the marc used in making it. **HFa**

Taste: *Young Arzúa-Ulloa has a clean, milky aroma and a mild, buttery taste. The mature cheese develops a harder texture with flavours hinting of vanilla and walnuts.*

Taste: *The best ubriaco has a firm, crumbly, open texture and is never rubbery. It has a nutty, slightly tangy taste with a characteristic hint of pineapple on the palate.*

Dry Jack

Provolone Valpadana

Sonoma County is home to the Vella Cheese Company and to its celebrated Dry Jack cheese. The name, or part of it, is borrowed from another Californian hard cheese, Monterey Jack. This was first produced in the nineteenth century by a Scot, David Jacks, who is said to have adapted a recipe that he obtained from a Franciscan monastery: the monks had most likely sought inspiration from Spain. The Vellas, who to complete this international tapestry originate in Sicily, have made cheese in Sonoma County since the 1930s and are considered pioneers of U.S. cheese-making.

Dry Jack is an unpasteurized, pressed cheese made with whole Guernsey milk. It becomes hard and flaky with ageing, rather like an Italian *grano*. Wheels of Bear Flag—the driest of their four "Jacks"—are aged for two years, weigh about 8 pounds (3.6 kg), and are coated in a mix of cocoa powder and oil to protect them from mites. Like Parmigiano Reggiano, the aged Jack can be eaten with fruit, but it is generally used in Italo-Californian cuisine, flaked on pasta or over salads. **MR**

Provolone Valpadana (DOP) belongs, like mozzarella, to the *pasta filata* family of cheeses, a name that refers to the practice of curd "spinning," which began in southern Italy during the Middle Ages. The high temperatures used for cheese-making would initially create an unstable curd that crumbled back into the whey. Yet it was noticed that if the curd was left to rest for some time, it tended to "spin"— develop a plastic texture, which could then, like wool, form threads if stretched. The end result was good and so the process was copied. The curds were left to rest on tables then stretched in hot water. The finished, aged cheese became known as provolone.

In time, the cheese-makers moved north to the lush and fertile plains of Lombardy and Provolone Valpadana was born. Today it is made according to strict DOP criteria, moulded into various traditional shapes, bound with strong twine, and hung in special caves to age for between two and four years. The result is a tangy cheese with a hard texture, which is especially good served in flakes in a similar way to Parmigiano Reggiano. **LF**

Taste: *Friable and dense, Dry Jack's texture is a little oilier than the Italian cheese with which it is often compared. The taste is rich and powerful with an acidic edge.*

Taste: *Full flavoured and firm, Provolone Valpadana has a tangy piquancy and a pleasing texture. Gutsy and with a clean edge, it makes an excellent table cheese.*

Karak Jameed

The time and care invested in making traditional cheeses is well known in Italy and France, but in the Middle East—specifically in the region surrounding the Jordanian city of Karak—cooks descended from Bedouin tribes practise the craft in their own unique fashion. Rather than the giant wheels seen in Europe, artisans there create small lumps of jameed, a pungent dairy product that straddles the line between cheese and yoghurt. It is said that Karak produces the country's very best jameed.

To make this unique dried yoghurt, goat's milk yoghurt, with added salt and sometimes herbs, is hung in cheesecloth. The cloth is repeatedly twisted to squeeze out any moisture so that it begins to form a ball shape. This flattens slightly as it dries until it is rock hard. If dried in the sun, the jameed acquires a yellowish hue; left in the shade it remains a milky colour. Nowadays, jameed is also produced in a state-of-the-art dairy in the town of Ader.

Jameed is famously used in the preparation of Jordan's revered rice and lamb dish, mansaf. This was originally a traditional Bedouin dish, made with the foodstuffs most plentiful to Bedouins: sheep or lamb meat and the yoghurt produced from sheep's milk. Mansaf is eaten on celebratory occasions and is served on a large platter; according to tradition it should be eaten standing up using one's hands, and no more than eight people should collect around the platter. The balls of jameed are reconstituted in water and crushed to yield a whey-like liquid that is used to make the accompanying sauce. From recent times, liquid jameed has been produced to speed up the sauce-making process. Jameed is also used to lend its distinctive tart tang to soups. **TH**

Taste: *Jameed is essentially the distilled essence of tangy goat's milk in a creamy soft base. It is like an extremely intense and salty feta with an almost feral smell.*

Xynotyro

In Greek, "xyno" refers to anything sharp tasting, such as lemons or yoghurt, that has an acidic flavour, while "tiri" means cheese. The name of this cheese therefore translates as "sour cheese," which does not accurately describe a flavour profile that includes both caramel and the sour taste of the whey. Like most Greek cheeses, it is made from ewe's or goat's milk, or a mixture of the two (but never from cow's milk as this would not produce the traditional flavour and colour), and is produced in the Cyclades islands of the Aegean Sea, especially Mykonos and Naxos. Greece has a long tradition of cheese-making, dating back thousands of years. In the *Odyssey*, Homer mentioned putting curdled goat's and ewe's milk into baskets to make cheese.

An unpasteurized, rindless, whey cheese with the low content of 20 per cent fat, xynotyro is traditionally drained and then left to mature for several days in reed baskets. This process accounts for the distinctive markings on the cheese's surface, caused when the surface of the cheese comes into contact with the basket. The need to stack xynotyro in baskets also accounts for the fact that the resulting cheeses are distributed in assorted shapes and sizes. Traditionally, after xynotyro has matured for three months the cheese is preserved in bags made of animal skin.

Xynotyro can be eaten when fresh and young or as a mature cheese after ripening. It may be eaten on its own, but it is more often served with a salad of cucumber, tomato, and black olives. As it shreds and melts easily, xynotyro also works well in baked dishes such as tarts and pies, including *tyropitakia* (filo pastry triangles filled with cheese). **CK**

Taste: *Xynotyro is a white cheese with a hard, flaky texture. It has a distinctive sweet-and-sour flavour with an undertone of burnt caramel.*

Xynotyro can be used in a number of Greek baked foods, such as cheese and spinach-filled **spanakopita.** ❯❯

Fiore Sardo

Parmigiano Reggiano

Sardinian pecorino, Fiore Sardo (DOP), has a number of unique selling points that make it different from other Italian ewe's milk cheeses. The race of sheep, *pecora sarda*, though widely distributed throughout Italy, is indigenous to the island. And the flocks graze on Mediterranean pastures that offer an unrivalled variety of wild grasses and herbs.

Fiore Sardo is the only Italian raw milk sheep's cheese that bears a European *Denominazione di Origine Protetta* certification. The main zone of production is Gavoi, although smaller amounts come from Ollolai, Ovodda, Lodine, Fonni, and Orgosolo. The raw milk is coagulated with a natural lamb's or goat's rennet, and the curds are broken by hand in open vats. Freshly formed cheeses are dry-salted then very lightly smoked using a combination of myrtle, wild oak, arbutus, and olive woods. They are left in maturing cellars for seven months, at which point they begin to approach their prime. By ten months, when they are usually marketed, they have turned into dry, hard cheeses with a butterfat content of around 75 per cent. **MR**

Undisputedly known as the king of Italian cheeses, Parmigiano Reggiano (DOP) has picked up an impressive array of fans. It was reputed to be Napoleon's favourite cheese, and the French playwright Molière was said to have a big soft spot for it—when stricken by the illness that eventually claimed his life, he apparently eschewed the more traditional broth in favour of Parmigiano.

Parmigiano belongs to the family of cheeses known as *grana* (grain) in its homeland, and is produced from raw milk in magnificent wheels, each of which weighs in at more than 66 pounds (30 kg). The name Parmigiano Reggiano is stencilled in small dots on the slightly oily, straw-coloured rind of each cheese, signifying it has been produced by artisans in specified zones of Emilia-Romagna in northern Italy.

Parmigiano Reggiano is fabulous shaved over salads and pizzas, stirred into risotto, pounded in pesto, or grated on to soups and pasta, but it is perhaps best of all simply served in bite-sized chunks before dinner. **LF**

Taste: *Sharp on the palate, Fiore Sardo has echoes of wild plants and a sweet taste reminiscent of dried fruit. A dense, hard cheese that can still be easily sliced.*

Taste: *Parmigiano Reggiano has a wonderful complexity of flavour. Initially salty and nutty, the taste opens up into an intense rich tang with surprisingly subtle fruity notes.*

The method of making Parmigiano today is based on techniques used during the Middle Ages. »

Manchego

Pecorino Romano

The flat, dry region of La Mancha in central Spain takes its name from the Moors, who called it Al Mansha (the waterless land). Burning hot in summer, icy in winter, it produces some of the world's finest saffron and a great cheese, Manchego (DOP).

Made with whole milk from Manchega ewes, this hard, pressed cheese is made in cylinders that weigh about 6 pounds (3 kg) each. The rinds are distinguished by zigzag, basket-weave indents that were originally a memento of the esparto grass moulds into which shepherds pressed their curd.

Manchego is produced both on an industrial and on a craft scale and so its quality ranges from outstanding to reliable. The colour varies from white to a pale lemon-yellow, depending on the season it was produced and the quality of the milk. When sold at about two months old (*fresco*), it is mild and sweet. By a year old (*curado*), it is drier and more complex. Aged for two years (*añejo* or *viejo*), a farmhouse Manchego develops into a powerful savoury cheese that marries perfectly with honey. Thin wedges are a basic part of Spanish tapas bar culture. **MR**

Probably one of the oldest cheeses in existence, Pecorino Romano (DOP) made its first literary appearance in the first century CE when the Roman agronomist Columella provided an account of how to make it, which still holds roughly true today. It is probably the most famous of the Italian Pecorino cheeses, all of which are made from sheep's milk, and take their names from the word *pecora* (sheep).

As the name would suggest, Pecorino Romano was created near Rome, but much production is now focused on Sardinia. It is matured for between eight and twelve months, and has an ivory-coloured paste that darkens and develops a saltier flavour as the cheese matures into a typical *grana* cheese, with a hard, granular texture and piquant taste.

Like its siblings, for example Pecorino delle Crete Senesi and the Sicilian Pecorino Canestrato, Pecorino Romano is ideal for grating and is typically used in pasta dishes and salads. The mature cheese is shaved thinly and served with cured meats, fruits, or breads. It also makes a superb dessert cheese, drizzled lightly with a little full-flavoured honey. **LF**

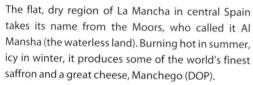

Taste: *The taste of Manchego is determined by its age and provenance. As it matures and hardens, a good farmhouse cheese develops fantastic intensity and length of flavour.*

Taste: *The fruity, zesty tang of the newly mature cheese develops into a well-defined piquancy. The potent flavour so typical of grana cheeses becomes more robust with age.*

Pecorino di Fossa

Italy offers literally hundreds of ewe's milk cheeses, but Pecorino di Fossa is absolutely unique. It is a *formaggio di fossa*, or buried cheese, which matures in a pothole covered with leaves or straw.

A speciality of Sogliano al Rubicone in southern Emilia-Romagna, the cheese was originally concealed to protect it during the internecine conflicts that were common before Italy became a single nation. Today it is entombed during August, wrapped in canvas, and sealed in a communal *fossa*, or "grave," until St. Catherine's Day in late November.

Pecorino cheeses are always hard and "sheepy." After three months in humid, airless environments, they emerge with a powerful pungency. But what comes out depends on what goes in. Cheeses that were part-ripened will be harder and drier than those that were still young, and there is no conformity in size, shape, or colour. The outsides may be russet, yellow, or dirty white; the paste can range from off-white to a pale straw hue. Although it is used as a cooking cheese, Pecorino di Fossa is best enjoyed by itself, accompanied by honey or fruit. **MR**

Taste: *In general, Pecorino di Fossa is sharp and tangy with a hint of bitterness that contrasts with the sweetness of ewe's milk, giving a complex taste experience.*

Leidsekaas

The arms of the southern Dutch town of Leiden, two crossed keys, figure on every authentic aged Leidsekaas. One of a family of large pressed cheeses, including Gouda and, from Friesland in the north of the Netherlands, Kanterkaas, it can be eaten young as part of a typical breakfast collation or aged for many years: it is sometimes coated in reddish wax.

What gives Leidsekaas its special character is flavouring with cumin, caraway, and occasionally cloves, too. The spices are only mixed with a part of the fresh curd and sandwiched between two other layers that contain cheese only. Leidsekaas is made both by creameries and in dairies on cheese-making farms: Boeren-leidsekaas (PDO), the farmhouse variety, is usually prepared from unpasteurized milk.

Ageing completely transforms these cheeses, making them even more interesting than their spice content might suggest. The wheels, which weigh about 17 pounds (8 kg), can easily be sliced at first, but a six-year-old cheese will be harder than an aged Parmigiano Reggiano. The taste and appearance will also reflect changes brought about by time. **MR**

Taste: *The young cheeses are springy, yellowish, and pleasantly flavoured by the raw spices. With age the colour darkens to burnt orange and the texture hardens.*

Roquefort

Bleu d'Auvergne

One of the world's "big three" blue cheeses, Roquefort (AOC) has acquired its fair share of legends. The most popular is that a young shepherd left his lunch of bread and ewe's milk cheese in a cave in southwest France while he visited his girlfriend. When it was later discovered, the bread had gone mouldy, as had the cheese, but the results were delicious. What does have a historical basis is that Charles VI gave a monopoly to the inhabitants of Roquefort-sur-Soulzon to make this cheese.

Between fact and fiction we have the main elements of what Roquefort is: ewe's milk cheese with a characteristic blue marbling, matured most often in caves. This marbling comes from an eponymous form of bacterium, *Penicillium roqueforti*, which has since been used as the base for diverse blue cheeses. Roquefort is a seasonal cheese, matured for at least three months, and available from the end of winter. It should have an ivory ground with even marbling; when cut it should not crumble. Seepage of serum from the cheese is not a bad sign. In fact, some experts prize it. **MR**

Often described as a cow's milk Roquefort because its veining was once achieved with the help of mouldy rye bread, Bleu d'Auvergne (AOC) is one of France's most widely eaten blue cheeses. It is also the first to have been manufactured industrially.

Auvergne was already known for its Cantal cheese in 1854, when a cheese-maker, Antoine Roussel, discovered he could induce blueing in his large Cantals by spiking them as they matured in his cellars. The taste of the marbled cheese was new and different, meaning he could sell it at a premium. (The link between *Penicillium roqueforti* bacteria and the blue veins was not understood scientifically until the early twentieth century.) As with other "blues," the milk is inoculated with bacteria and the fresh cheeses are pierced around their circumference to aerate them. During ripening, moulds form on the hand-salted rinds and an even network of marbling develops inside. A similar cheese, Bleu des Causses (AOC), is produced to the same recipe, always with unpasteurized milk, further south in the *départements* of Hérault and Gard. **MR**

Taste: *The smell of Roquefort is a pointer to the taste of this salty, powerfully flavoured cheese. The sharpness, paired with a subtle sweetness, is its main attraction.*

Taste: *Firm and fatty, Bleu d'Auvergne has a strong cheesy scent. The taste is potent and quite salty, with hints of sourness alongside subtle grassy, wildflower notes.*

*Natural draught passages—fleurines—ensure
that Roquefort maturing in caves is well ventilated.*

Stilton

Curiously, this celebrated English blue cheese may never have been made in the town from which it takes its name. The association derives from the landlord of the Bell Inn in Stilton, Cooper Thornhill, who agreed in 1730 with a dairy farmer from Wymondham in Leicestershire that he would market his blue cheese. As Stilton was on the main stagecoach route between London and the north of England, word of the inn and its cheese spread rapidly. Blue cheese had been popular in the Midlands for generations, however, and Stilton (PDO) may have developed from a family recipe produced on the Quenby Hall estate for Lady Beaumont.

Today Stilton is one of very few English cheeses to benefit from a Protected Designation of Origin. It is produced by six creameries in the counties of Leicestershire, Nottinghamshire, and Derbyshire, using whole pasteurized milk from local cows.

Stiltons are unctuous and richly flavoured. Today the blue veining that made its name is controlled by inoculation with *Penicillium roqueforti*, the mould with which Roquefort is made. **MR**

Smokey Blue

Marketed as Smokey Blue and created in 2005 by the Rogue Creamery in Central Point, Oregon, this award-winning cheese is believed to be the world's first, and only, smoked blue cheese. Established in the 1930s in Oregon's Rogue River valley, the creamery is dedicated to producing artisan cheeses and was the first to make blue cheese in caves west of the Missouri River.

The creamery specializes in blue cheeses and only uses milk from Brown Swiss and Holstein cows, which graze along the Rogue River on wild grasses, herbs, and flowers. The creamery took one of its own blue cheeses—Oregon Blue—and cold smoked it for sixteen hours over hazelnut shells. This bold move resulted in a nutty flavoured cheese that is less sharp and tangy than most traditional blue cheeses.

Made from full-cream milk, this unique cheese is best eaten at room temperature. It is good simply on a baguette with fresh tomato and basil, sliced or melted atop a grilled burger, or tossed with chives into a warm new potato salad. It is also a good conversation starter on a cheese plate. **SH**

Taste: *As it ripens, Stilton develops a buttery, nutty smoothness with a hint of sharpness from the marbling. The texture is creamy and the finish clean but lasting.*

Taste: *This semi-firm, buttery cheese has sweet caramel and hazelnut flavours, tempered with a sharp, saltiness and an understated smokiness.*

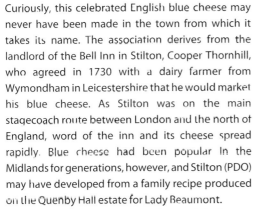

A "cheese iron" is used to extract a core from a Stilton in order to check its flavour and texture.

Cashel Blue

Gorgonzola

The Rock of Cashel stands high above Ireland's Tipperary plain, topped with the twelfth-century chapel of King Cormac. When Louis and Jane Grubb started making Cashel Blue on their family farm in the 1980s, they borrowed the iconic outcrop's name. Theirs was the first blue cheese to be made in Eire and its success helped inspire a string of new Irish cheeses—notably Milleens, Gubbeen, and Durrus.

The Grubbs intended Cashel to be a cheese for the local market, using milk from their Friesian herd to make something similar to Danish Blue. But it turned out closer to softer, creamier blue cheeses, and has grown into an internationally known brand that is exported to Europe and the United States. Today Cashel is made from pasteurized milk, in wheels weighing 3¼ pounds (1.5 kg), which are ripened for about four months. The best cheeses are made between April and early autumn when the cattle feed on the lush Irish pasture: these can be aged for longer. Another branch of the family produces a similar cheese, Crozier Blue, which is made from ewe's milk, like Roquefort. **MR**

Alongside Stilton and Roquefort, Gorgonzola (DOP) is one of the three greatest blue cheeses in the world today. Made from whole cow's milk, it belongs to the family of white, "uncooked" cheeses known as *stracchino*. Around the eleventh century, however, or so the story goes, a fortunate accident occurred when an innkeeper left a white cheese out in his kitchen and it became veined with mould. The results tasted so good that the idea stuck and Gorgonzola became a *stracchino verde*, with its characteristic marbling of green or blue mould. Today cheese-makers rely on *Penicillium* spores to create their mould, and use metal rods to create channels that ensure its even spread and growth.

Gorgonzola takes its name from a village near Milan, and the cheeses were originally thought to have been made there. Today it carries a DOP certification, which limits production to regions of Piedmont and Lombardy. Gorgonzola makes a wonderful table cheese, but also lends itself to cooking, having a particular affinity with walnuts, pasta, and peppery leaves like spinach and rocket. **LF**

Taste: *Milder, less salty, less sharp, and less blue than many blue cheeses, Cashel Blue stands out for its melt-in-the-mouth creaminess, to the point of being spreadable.*

Taste: *Semi-soft and creamy with a subtle salty edge, Gorgonzola develops a firmer texture and gathers a flavourful spiciness and peppery pizzazz as it ages.*

Making air holes in a cheese containing Penicillium spores promotes the characteristic "blue" veining. ❯❯

Cabrales

Given its name, and its reputation for pungency, the casual observer could be forgiven for thinking that Cabrales (DOP) was a goat's cheese. Although goat's milk is sometimes used in its recipe, mixed with cow's and even sheep's milk, it is its "blueness" that dominates Cabrales, not the creature that produced it. It is made in spring and summer in the Asturias region of northern Spain, and matured in limestone caves. The best is ripened for about four months. High, inaccessible pasturage gives the milk, which is generally unpasteurized, its special quality.

The cylinders of cheese, which weigh 5 to 9 pounds (2.3–4 kg), are not dissimilar to Roquefort, but Cabrales lacks the latter's sweaty texture and salty taste. The rind is crustier, the texture a little crumbly, and the veining a vivid blue, rather than the greenish persillage of the French cheese. Cheese deity Steven Jenkins waxes lyrical about the taste. "[The] flavour immediately electrifies the tongue with . . . blackberries and currants; bittersweet chocolate; grass and hay; leather and woodsmoke, walnuts and, yes, beef . . ." **MR**

Taste: *The white paste contrasting with clear blue veins points to the taste, which is intense and sharp-edged. The texture is open and crumbly, but smooth and rich.*

Cabrales matures in natural limestone caves. »

Fynsk Rygeost

Danes are very proud of this smoked cheese, which is arguably the only one of the cheeses invented in Denmark that did not take "inspiration" from somewhere else. Rygeost, both fresh and smoked, is believed to date back to a sour-milk cheese—one of the earliest sorts of cheese—that was first produced by the Vikings. Cattle have been raised in Denmark for centuries and butter, milk, and cheese have long been part of the Danish diet.

Rygeost traditionally comes from a small group of cheese-makers on the island of Fyn, Denmark's third largest island, which has a long tradition of producing foods. On the island, the cheese is only made at the Løgismose Dairy. As well as producing around 1,650 tons of commercial rygeost each year, islanders also like to make their own cheeses, smoke them in brick-built "ovens," and eat them as part of their picnics on lazy summer evenings. The cheese is made with whole cow's milk, buttermilk, and rennet, and is traditionally smoked quickly (in about thirty seconds) over nettles and oat straw, which gives it its characteristic smoky flavour. The straw is cut in a special way to prevent it from snapping, as this would spoil the smoking. The cheese rests on a grid during smoking, causing the large white discs rapidly to become crisscrossed with brown marks. Often, the cheeses are sprinkled with caraway.

Rygeost is usually eaten with radishes and chives on a piece of Danish rye bread, but it is also good on white bread with blackcurrant jam. It is often included in *sommersalat* (summer salad) with toasted rye bread, and is eaten around a bonfire on Midsummer's Night, which is always celebrated in Scandinavia, along with copious quantities of beer. **CTj**

Taste: *This creamy, crumbly cheese has a distinct and distinctive smokiness. The taste remains smooth and aromatic, combined with a slightly acidic finish.*

Leipäjuusto

The name of the Finnish cheese leipäjuusto, also known as juustoleipä, literally translates as "bread cheese," and derives from its manufacturing process, which can include baking to give it its characteristic golden-brown colour. Other dialects have various names, such as *narskujuusto*, that refer to the way in which the cheese "squeaks" while being eaten.

Leipäjuusto is a cheese steeped in centuries-old tradition and owes its high quality to the richness of Finnish cow's milk. Traditionally the cheese was made from cow's beestings, the rich yellow milk first taken from a cow that has recently calved. In the old days it was considered a festive food and was a common "repayment" to people who had helped with the harvest.

To extend its longevity, the cheese was left to dry and harden in rye bread. It could last for several years in this form, which most likely instigated the habit of dipping it in coffee to soften it. In Sweden, a few pieces are put into a cup and hot coffee poured over them to make *kaffeost*. The cheese can also be served with cloudberry jelly or fresh cloudberries. It is also sliced, with a little cream poured on top, followed by a sprinkling of sugar and cinnamon, and then grilled or baked for a few minutes and served with cloudberry jelly.

Today's leipäjuusto is typically soft and lasts for around a week in the fridge. It is round and flat with a slightly brown bread-like surface derived from the oven. Leipäjuusto has a "squeaky" consistency and is eaten cold or warm. Most connoisseurs prefer the homemade variety, although the ready-made product is more common today. Popular brands include Juustoportti, Valio, Ingman, and Arla. **CC**

Taste: *Somewhere in between unsalted halloumi and mozzarella but with a sweeter, more buttery flavour, leipäjuusto is popularly served with cloudberry jelly.*

Milk from Finnish cows has a richness that derives from their lush pastures. »

Oscypek

Parenica

This delightful smoked sheep's cheese comes from the Tatra Mountains, which form a natural border between Poland and Slovakia. It is traditionally made by Góral (highlander) shepherds from unpasteurized milk, using hand-carved moulds that create distinctive rustic, geometric patterns on the spindle-shaped cheeses. Afterwards, it is soaked in brine and smoked in tiny, rustic smokehouses.

In the days before refrigeration, the cheeses could then be indefinitely suspended from a cottage rafter, protected by their brownish crust. They were mentioned in an early fifteenth-century chronicle and the first recorded recipe appeared in 1748. Polish officials are currently campaigning to have oscypek recognized with a European Union PDO, a project challenged by the existence of a similarly named Slovak cheese called ostiepok.

Oscypek is a favourite breakfast and supper food for many Poles, served with rye or black bread and butter. Modern cooks might add it cubed to salads in place of feta or bread it, fry it, and serve it with cranberry jam. **RS**

Parenica (PDO)—which means "steamed cheese" in Slovakian—has been made by shepherds in a mountainous region of the Slovak republic, close to the borders of Poland, the Czech Republic, and the Ukraine since the early 1800s. It is a semi-firm cheese made from unpasteurized sheep's milk produced by the Wallachian, Cigaya, and East Friesian breeds, although this is sometimes mixed with cow's milk. The cheese is sometimes lightly smoked.

To make parenica cheese, the curdled cheese is moulded by hand into lumps, which are then left to ferment before being placed in wooden churns and steamed in hot water. Steaming darkens the colour of the outside of the cheese. The cheese is then pulled out of the water, stretched, and folded into strips. These are skilfully wound into two rolls that are connected in a distinctive S-shape and bound with cheese string. These distinctive spiral shapes were a popular decorative motif used by the ancient Slavs and parenica cheese always featured at the *jarmoks*, or annual fairs that traditionally took place in the Slovak Republic. **CK**

Taste: *Oscypek is a mild, slightly salty cheese with faintly smoky undertones. It is cream coloured and springy with a pleasantly squeaky texture on the teeth.*

Taste: *Parenica cheese has the odour of sheep's milk, a stringy, elastic texture, and a delicate, pleasantly salty flavour. The smoked version has a mildly smoky aroma.*

Oscypek is piled on a stall selling traditional
foods at a Christmas market in Krakow, Poland.

Burford Brown Egg

Pei Dan

Burford Brown eggs take their name from the pretty town of Burford in the Cotswolds. They acquired it early in the twentieth century, partly on account of their location and partly for their thick, rich brown shells. That said, both breed and shell have a rather minor influence on the quality of an egg: freshness, feed, and animal welfare are much more important.

There is no pedigree breed of hen called a "Burford," but the eggs are marketed by a specialist free-range egg supplier, Clarence Court, a brand created by farmer Philip Lee-Woolf in 1990. Although based in Cornwall, he has adopted the name and story, and uses hybrid hens that will lay eggs with the special character.

Compared to most other eggs that are sold through British multiple retailers, Burford Browns have the character that those familiar with eggs from traditionally reared barnyard fowl will recognize. In cooking, the advantages of the eggs compared to factory-farmed ones is marked: thicker custards, stiffer mayonnaise, better cakes, and lighter soufflés. **MR**

Pei dan—or good pei dan—looks as if it belongs in a museum rather than on a plate. The "white" ranges from golden amber to an unusual translucent black; the yolk contains merging rings of soft green, yellow, and grey; the centre is soft, dark, and oozing.

People unused to these wonderful preserved eggs tend to view them with horrified fascination, and, if they bother to taste them, are often repulsed. Perhaps it is names such as "thousand-year-old eggs" or "century eggs" that scare off the novices. In fact, most mass-produced eggs take less than a fortnight to "cure" while the better, more traditional eggs are cured under their coating of ash, tea, slaked lime, salt, and often earth for around three months.

Pei dan is usually eaten peeled but uncooked, often with pickled spring ginger. It may also be simmered with congee (rice pudding) and salted dried pork or steamed with spinach, garlic, and another type of Chinese preserved eggs (salted eggs). You can smell "bad" pei dan from across a room—the strong ammonia scent will make your eyes water. **KKC**

Taste: *Burford Brown eggs have a thicker yolk than standard free-range eggs, with a deep, orange-yellow colour and a much richer flavour.*

Taste: *A good pei dan tastes rich, complex, and pungent, like ripe blue cheese with a very faint hint of ammonia. The texture of the white is slightly rubbery while the yolk is soft.*

Salted duck eggs are sold in colourful nets at the annual Duanwu Festival in China. ❯❯

Unagi

The eel (unagi) has long been a valued food and a legendary source of "stamina" in Japan. The rich, fatty flesh of this fish is indeed high in proteins and vitamin A. In Japan, eel consumption traditionally rises during the period known as the "days of the bull," the two days after the rainy season in June, when the enervating humidity of summer creates a lethargy known as *natsubate*. This condition demands the consumption of energy-giving food, with a consequent rush on eel restaurants. Such is unagi's popularity in Japan that eels are farmed on a large scale. Historically, the farmed eels were housed in artificial ponds, but now they are raised in indoor tanks in temperature-controlled conditions. Natural eel populations are currently under threat and the food should be obtained from sustainable sources.

In Japan, the most popular way of eating eel is in the dish *kabayaki*, in which the eel is basted with sweetened soy sauce and then grilled over charcoal, resulting in deliciously contrasting crisp skin and succulent flesh. Japan has many restaurants offering only eel dishes, especially *kabayaki*. True unagi enthusiasts opt for *shirayaki*, eel grilled without sauce. *Unagi donburi*, a convenient, tasty, one-pot meal where the cooked eel is served on steamed rice, is said to have been invented to enable kabuki audiences to eat without interruption during the famously long performances.

In Japan's eastern Kanto area, the fins, tail, and head of the eel are removed before grilling; Kansai folk in the west prefer to leave them on. A common and delicious accompaniment everywhere is the tongue-numbing pepper and citrus *sansho*, which is commonly served with fatty foods. **SB**

Taste: *Cooked* kabayaki-*style, unagi is sweet and unctuous, with a pronounced fishy taste, and an underlying smokiness. It has a rich, creamy texture.

Unagi, cooked in the kabayaki-style as here, is costly
◉ *in Japan but highly valued for its nutritional content.*

Elver

Thinner than a pencil, as long as a finger, and almost transparent—hence their alternative name "glass eels"—elvers are fragile creatures. These immature eels cluster in shoals near the mouths of tidal rivers, visible mainly as a wriggling disturbance in the water. Mature eels spawn in the Sargasso Sea, in the middle of the North Atlantic, and it takes two or three years for the Gulf Stream to carry their leaf-like larvae (*Leptocephalus*) towards Europe. On arrival, the little creatures shift shape again and transform into what are recognizably miniature eels. Today, elvers are an expensive, highly prized delicacy.

In Britain, the tradition of eating both eels and elvers dates back to medieval times. The River Severn was long noted for its abundance of eels. Elvers there are trapped at night in fine-meshed nets placed across the river as they make their way upstream. Today, much of the elver catch is sold abroad to supply eel farms. English ways of eating elvers include elver pie (a type of pasty), frying them in bacon fat, and flouring and deep-frying them.

Elvers are also treasured in Spain, a country with a rich tradition of seafood dishes; the writer Ernest Hemingway wrote appreciatively of *angulas* "as tiny as beansprouts." A favourite Spanish way of preparing *angulas* is to fry them briefly in olive oil with garlic and a touch of chilli, and serve them sizzling hot to be eaten with a wooden fork. When the live elvers hit the hot pan, they lose their glassiness and turn an opaque cream hue; their eyes are seen as two black dots.

Sadly, with European eel populations at a historic low, consumption of this traditional delicacy cannot be justified at present. **MR**

Taste: *The delight of elvers is in their texture, which is rather like that of pasta, but creamier and with a little more bite. The taste is mild and delicate, not fishy.*

Tilapia

Mojarra

Tilapia has become one of the most farmed fish around the world, although it is not a new practice: records indicate that tilapia farming existed more than 2,000 years ago in ancient Egypt. Tilapia is the common name for around 100 different species worldwide, and it is becoming more and more popular as an eco-friendly fish. Both *Sarotherodon mossambicus*, also known as Mozambique tilapia, and the Nile tilapia (*S. niloticus*) are good for eating.

Tilapia have a hardy, adaptable constitution, thriving in fresh, brackish, and salt waters, as well as in crowded farming aquariums. Tilapia carefully farmed in controlled environments have more flavour than wild hybrid varieties. Tilapia is very popular in the United States where most of the supply is farmed in Central and South America.

A versatile fish, tilapia can be grilled, baked, fried, blackened, stir-fried, or added to a fish soup. Its mildness offers a blank canvas on which cooks can overlay a multitude of other flavours. It is particularly suited to Chinese cuisine, which allows seasonings such as garlic and ginger to really shine. **BF**

The mojarra is a tropical fish from the *Gerreidae* family, found in the Caribbean. It lives predominatly in shallow coastal areas to avoid larger predators, although it is also known to occasionally venture into rivers inland. There are many different species of mojarra and they can be difficult to identify unless very closely examined.

A silvery fish with a compressed body and a highly protruding mouth, it grows up to 13 ½ inches (35 cm) long. It is highly prized throughout Central America, and is popular in Colombia, Ecuador, Puerto Rico, Costa Rica, and Mexico where it is widely found in markets and restaurants.

Mojarra is served in numerous ways throughout Latin America. Fried as *mojarra frita* it has a tasty crusty skin and is accompanied with white rice and *tostones*, flattened fried plantain. It can be roasted whole including the head, tail, and bones, and served with white rice, avocado, lettuce, tomato, and lime juice. It is also enjoyed simply grilled over smoking coals, then eaten with hot chipotle pepper sauce and sautéed onions. **CK**

Taste: *Tilapia has lean, white flesh. Its mild, slightly sweet flavour makes it perfect for marinating and partnering with sauces and other ingredients.*

Taste: *The mojarra is a bony fish with flaky, meaty, white flesh. It has a mild, satisfying flavour that is a cross between tilapia and snapper.*

In a 1400–1390 BCE tomb painting, an official of Thutmose IV spears tilapia in marshland.

Spotted Sorubim

Few freshwater fish from south of the equator possess both the size and the supreme flavour of the spotted sorubim (or *pintado*), a native of the São Francisco, Prata, and Paraguay river basins in Brazil. The undisputed king of sorubims in South America, it has distinctive skin covered in black spots and can exceed 5 feet (1.5 m) in length and 176 pounds (80 kg) in weight. Despite feeding on crustaceans and small fish, which it ingests along with mud and thick sand, its white, fatty, bone-free flesh has a pleasant flavour, as well as a consistent texture. Either cut into thick slices or roasted whole, the spotted sorubim reigns in the *churrascarias* (barbecue grill restaurants) found all over Brazil; its qualities are enhanced by charcoal grilling.

With its flat head and round body covered in skin instead of scales, the spotted sorubim lends itself to many other culinary delights. It is often cooked in an oven with only a coarse salt seasoning to bring out the taste of the flesh, or in a clay pan, with the resulting juice used to make *pirão*, a salty paste thickened with fine cassava flour. **AL**

Taste: *As a fish rich in "good" fat, the spotted sorubim reveals its full glory when flame-grilled; its oil softens the flesh and the flames confer a delicious burnt aroma.*

Sterlet

Of the twenty-five species of sturgeon, sterlet is one of the smallest. It can reach about 20 inches (50 cm) in length and is about the size of a farmed salmon. The river-loving sterlet (*Acipenser ruthenus*) is found as far north as Siberia. It was once abundant in the estuaries that feed into the Black and Caspian Seas. But, sturgeon numbers have been decimated in the hunt for caviar and even the most ardent fish-eater should think twice before sampling a wild sterlet.

In times when it was plentiful, it was appreciated both for its taste and texture. Recipes for it appear in early Russian and Turkish cookery manuals. Although sturgeon farming has been developing in Europe and North America—mainly with a view to supplying caviar—the smaller sterlet has only recently been targeted by aquaculture industries.

The whole fish was served grilled to Presidents Putin and Bush when the U.S. leader stopped over in Moscow. Barbecued, baked, stewed, fried, in soups, and even raw, it often figures on the menus of Russia's new generation restaurants, but many of these have originated in fish farms. **MR**

Taste: *Praised as the "Queen of Sturgeons," wild sterlet is often compared to veal. Firm and meaty, it has a compact, flesh with a mild taste, reflecting its freshwater origin.*

This fish market stall in Astrahan, southern Russia, is entirely devoted to various forms of smoked sturgeon. »

Pike

Zander

Long, fast, and very savage, pike has been described as a freshwater barracuda. It can empty a lake or pond of other fish—even take aquatic birds. However, as a food, *Esox lucius* has had a reputation both as a delicacy and as inedible.

In the Middle Ages, it was much admired. A recipe by Taillevent from the fourteenth century *Le Viandier*, for pike dressed with ginger and saffron, begins with the advice to the cook to slap it on the grill. Today, Lyon has a particular liking for this fish, especially those that are caught in the historic fishponds of the neighbouring Dombes. Pounded and mixed with cream, they are the basis of the celebrated *quenelles de brochet*, which are served with the crayfish-based *sauce Nantua*.

Although specimens weighing up to 45 pounds (20 kg) have been caught, the preferred size for cooking is 2 to 4 pounds (900 g–1.8 kg). Pike has a thick layer of scales and sharp, pointed bones, so presents as much of a challenge to the cook as to the game fisherman. Opponents argue that it can taste very muddy if it has lived in stagnant water. **MR**

A much-prized fish gracing the tables of restaurants and riverside inns throughout Europe, zander (*Stizostedion lucioperca*) is a voracious predator known to grow to up to 3 feet 3 inches (1 m) long. It has exceedingly sharp teeth, and enjoys a diet of smaller fish, which gives it a full and meaty flavour.

Also known as pike-perch, zander is often incorrectly thought to be closely related to that other "wolf of the river," the mean and snappy pike. Zander also has a similar fin pattern to freshwater bream, but it is in fact not a hybrid of either of these fish. It is native to the fresh and brackish waters of Central and Eastern Europe and much of the fish landed there finds its way to the restaurants of the Netherlands, where it is considered to be a delicacy.

It was introduced into the United Kingdom, specifically East Anglia, primarily as a sport fish, but proved to be so damaging to other fish stocks that it was culled. It is still imported there in small quantities, but demand in Europe is so high that it is a rare find. In flavour, it is often compared with the North American walleye. **STS**

Taste: *Pike has white, firm, flaky flesh. Its taste lacks the sweet mineral aromas of some sea fish, but at its best has a flavour comparable to that of grey mullet or sea bass.*

Taste: *Zander flesh is quite firm and meaty with a full herbaceous flavour very similar to carp and almost indistinguishable from walleye.*

A plentiful catch of young pike—known as
◐ *kawakamasu in Japan—is dried in the sun near Chiba.*

Carp

Elephant Ear Fish

Widely esteemed in Asian, Eastern European, and Jewish cuisine—whether steamed, roasted, or poached in a seasoned stock—carp is served at family meals on high days and holidays. The fish is a particular delicacy in Poland, where it is roasted and served as a traditional festive dish on Christmas Eve. Carp is also beautiful cooked *au bleu*; that is, cooked immediately after being caught, usually by simmering in white wine with herbs, or in water containing salt and vinegar.

Muddy water leads to mud-flavoured fish, so if possible the best choice is fish that have been farmed on gravel. The common carp has a dark bronze back with gold sides and a yellow belly, and the body is fully covered with large scales. All members of the carp family have a thick natural slime that needs to be rinsed away prior to scaling; this is best done by a gentle soaking in acidulated water.

Species of carp are native to the Danube and Asia, but various types have been introduced to many countries worldwide. Carp is one of the most widely farmed freshwater fish in the world. **STS**

Given that Vietnamese cuisine is somewhat notorious among Westerners for delicacies such as dog or still-beating snake heart, the idea of elephant ear fish may not immediately be considered appetizing. In fact, elephant ear fish is a type of butterfly fish (*Chaetodon*) most noted for its flat shape, similar to bass.

The fish is popular throughout the Mekong River Delta. What is most notable about it, is how it is presented. Roughly the size of a large platter, the fish is gutted, fried, and then propped up between wooden chopsticks, sometimes dressed with fresh herbs and sculpted vegetables. Chopsticks are used to peel off the crispy, curling scales, and prize away the soft, white, flaky flesh. The flesh is then layered, along with local herbs such as mint, coriander, basil, and sometimes noodles and cucumber, in thin rice-paper pancakes. These are then rolled up, and dipped in *nuoc cham* fish sauce. The result is a wonderfully sweet and succulent dish, as the texture of the meaty, earthy, soft flesh is balanced by the light but chewy pancakes, and given a kick by the salty, hot chilli, garlic, and lime fish sauce. **CK**

Taste: *Carp are best known for their herbaceous, murky, almost woody flavour, but this will depend primarily upon the habitat in which they live.*

Taste: *The elephant ear fish is known for its wonderfully sweet and succulent taste; its notoriety comes from its appearance and name.*

Cooking simply with herbs and seasoning
⊗ *preserves and enhances the flavour of carp.*

Copper River King Salmon

Arctic Char

For a period that begins in mid-May and lasts a mere four weeks, hundreds of thousands of king salmon (*Oncorhynchus tshawytscha*) grapple their way upstream through 300 miles of Alaska's Copper River, from the Pacific to their spawning grounds. This huge effort translates into flesh that is firm yet packed with extra stores of flavour-bearing fat.

The first major wild Alaskan fish to come to market each spring, and the largest of the five Pacific salmon species, king salmon's fleeting availability and steep retail price catapult it into the realm of luxury, but salmon groupies swear the annual splurge is worth it. This was not always so.

While Copper River salmon had been fished for canning as early as 1889, the king salmon began its rise to prominence almost a century later. This was when former fisherman Jon Rowley convinced his peers that salmon could fetch a much higher price if they improved their onboard processing and brought the fish to market fresh. Today, king salmon are sustainably harvested using methods approved by the respected Seafood Watch Program. **CLH**

A close cousin of both salmon and trout, Arctic char (*Salvelinus alpinus*) is one of the most northerly freshwater fish. Slow to mature, it thrives in the icy polar regions of North America and Europe, including Canada, Iceland, and Russia: in the wild it rarely reaches more than 12 inches (30 cm) in length or 10 ounces (300 g) in weight.

Arctic char are unusual in that they can flourish both as resident populations or as anadromous, meaning some fish live permanently in land-locked lakes—notably in Scandinavia, the Alps, and the northern British Isles—whereas others reside in salt water, returning to freshwater rivers and streams to spawn and spend the winter.

The fish has a long history in Inuit culture, where it provided an integral food source for indigenous people. In England during the eighteenth and nineteenth centuries, Arctic char was highly prized and a status symbol of the wealthy. While abundant in the wild, its extreme habitat makes it difficult to economically bring to market, so much of what is found in restaurants and markets is farmed. **CLH**

Taste: *High in Omega-3 oils, Copper River king salmon is packed with flavour. Its large stores of fat deliver a velvety texture, without the mushiness of much farmed salmon.*

Taste: *Arctic char can range in colour from deep orange to pale pink. It has a delicate, mild flavour that resembles salmon or trout. It should be tender but not mushy.*

A woman with her catch of Arctic char in the North Slope of Alaska, where rivers flow over frozen tundra. »

Rainbow Trout

This sparkling, eye-catching fish is native to the rivers of the west coast of the Pacific, Alaska, Canada, northern United States, and Asia. Straight from the water, pan-fried or poached in a light *court bouillon* on the river bank, a wild rainbow trout is a gastronomic sensation.

Rainbow trout is a round fish with a deep body, a small head, and beady eyes. The skin colour is predominantly spotty, light green across the back shading down to a white belly and a striking pink stripe running parallel to the lateral line down the flank of the fish, giving the rainbow appearance. The colour of the flesh depends on the diet of the trout. A wild fish may feed on a freshwater shrimp diet, creating an orange-pink flesh. Farmed fish, on the other hand are fed a dye (from both natural and synthetic sources) that gives the flesh a deep orange colour.

The wild migratory rainbow species, caught in the Pacific, is the steelhead trout but, like salmon, spends only part of its life cycle at sea, returning to fresh water to spawn. **STS**

Taste: *The flavour of fresh trout depends on its habitat, but often has a slightly earthy note. The flakes of a wild fish have a delicate flavour reminiscent of herbs and fungi.*

Baking does not spoil the beautiful pink colouring on the skin of rainbow trout.

Ishkan Trout

One of the largest high-altitude lakes in the world, picturesque Lake Sevan in Armenia is home to a unique fish prized for its subtle flavour. Contrary to its name, ishkan trout (*Salmo ischchan*) is actually a member of the salmon family. In this land-locked country, ishkan trout is referred to as the "prince of fishes," reputedly because the spots on its head resemble a crown. Records show that the fish was served at a state banquet in 1919 surrounded with its own caviar and accompanied by a sauce made with the cream of water-buffalo milk, mixed with fresh peeled walnuts and a touch of horseradish. The fish is still served today with a walnut sauce.

Sadly, the Ishkan trout is endangered due to the introduction of competing fish such as common whitefish and Danube crayfish into Lake Sevan. However, it is now farmed locally, and it was also successfully introduced into Kyrgyz Republic's Issyk-Kul Lake in central Asia during the 1970s.

Ishkan trout is delicious grilled or poached. In Armenia, it is often stuffed with fruits such as prunes or apricots before being oven-baked. **CK**

Taste: *Ishkan trout has a mild, delicate flavour similar to trout. Its pink flesh is virtually boneless. The grilled fish is excellent served rolled up in the local lavash flatbread.*

Sardine

Sea Trout

All around the world silvery, soft-boned sardines have long provided fresh, barbecued suppers. Straight out of the water, still in rigor mortis, with bright convex eyes, and few loose scales, sardines are, at this stage, at their very best.

Although they have many fine bones, for which they are often criticized, sardines also offer lovely cream-coloured fillets when cooked. A quick scaling and gutting can easily be achieved with thumb and finger in place of a knife. They are best grilled, barbecued, or marinated and can also be eaten raw as an hors d'oeuvre. Traditional flavour partners include oregano, extra virgin olive oil, and lemon.

The term sardine varies depending on where you are in the world. In Europe, it is used to describe a young European pilchard, under about 4 inches (10 cm) in length. Any longer and it is just a pilchard. In the United States, it refers to any small, saltwater fish such as sprat, young pilchard, and herring.

Portugal, Spain, and France produce high-quality canned sardines, packed in extra virgin olive oil, which are a useful store cupboard staple. **STS**

Sea trout (*Salmo trutta trutta*), or salmon trout, are sleek, gleaming fish that are considered by many to outrank salmon both in looks and flavour. Like salmon, the flesh is soft-pink because of a diet of crustaceans, which contain the distinctive carotenoid pigment. The flavour too is similar, although sea trout is more creamy. The whole fish is often stuffed before cooking, but its taste is enhanced by simply poaching it in a lightly acidulated *court bouillon* and serving it with a hollandaise sauce.

The migratory form of the widely distributed brown trout, sea trout are found in the streams and rivers of northern Europe. They spend between one to five years in fresh water and their middle life at sea where they feed and grow, before returning to fresh water to spawn. Sea trout have been introduced to Chile, Argentina, New Zealand, Australia, and the eastern seaboard of North America.

Good brown and sea trout needs little flavouring and suits poaching, grilling, or frying. It is deliciously sweet and spicy grilled with honey, butter, salt, and plenty of freshly ground black pepper. **STS**

Taste: *Although sardines are high in Omega-3 oils, they are not overly "fishy" in taste. They are best eaten very fresh and are delicious grilled and simply lightly seasoned.*

Taste: *Sea trout is herbier than rainbow trout, but less earthy then the non-migratory brown trout. It is delicious fried, poached, or cooked en papillote.*

Freshly caught sardines, cooked over charcoal and
❰ *served with lemon, are popular beach fare in Spain.*

Shisamo

Whitebait

A small, saltwater fish, about 4 to 6 inches (10–15 cm) long, shisamo is common to the northern Pacific Ocean and the Atlantic Ocean, although it travels to fresh water to spawn. Indeed, it is traditionally caught in Japan at the Kushiro river mouth as it swims upstream in October and November. A rare and expensive delicacy, the roe carrying female fish are most prized, and those from Kushiro City and Mukawa particularly so. For a short period in the autumn, shisamo is served locally in Mukawa as sashimi and sushi.

Most usually, however, shisamo are salted, dried, and threaded, side-by-side with their mouths gaping open, along a bamboo skewer for grilling. This makes an impressive, if somewhat unnerving, sight in the street markets. The process not only preserves the fish, but salting followed by sun-drying breaks down protein, creating amino acids which deliver the delicious flavour known as *umami*. The aroma of charcoal-grilled shisamo wafting though Japanese streets, as late-night drinkers sip their sake, is a never-to-be-forgotten memory. **SB**

Small, silver-white, and translucent, whitebait are the young fry of various fish, caught during the first year of their life. In England, they are usually young herring or sprat; in New England, they are the fry of silverside or sand-eel; whereas in New Zealand, they are young freshwater fish such as inanga. In France, whitebait are known as *blanchailles* and in Italy as *bianchetti* or *gianchetti*, although the latter are usually the spawn of sardines and anchovies.

The culinary history of whitebait in England goes back to the early seventeenth century, when small fry swarmed the tidal waters of the Thames. These delicate little fish did not travel well, so diners had to go to them. Taverns along the river in Greenwich and Blackwall started to serve special whitebait dinners that proved hugely popular.

Then, as now, whitebait were fried whole. To prepare these delicious small fry, wash fresh whitebait in cold salt water, drain, toss in beaten egg, and lightly dust in well-seasoned flour before deep-frying in oil until golden. Simply serve with lemon wedges. **LW**

Taste: *Grilled shisamo are crispy, smoky, salty, and have a deeply savoury flavour, with a slightly bitter and burnt aftertaste. Their texture is chewy and meaty.*

Taste: *A mound of tiny silver fish, lightly battered, deep-fried to crispness, and doused with lemon juice delivers the intensified taste of a whole fish in one small mouthful.*

In Japan, reusable wooden crates are used to transport the catch to Tokyo's Tsukiji fish market.

Hong Kong Grouper

Hiramasa Kingfish

A delicacy in China and South East Asia, Hong Kong grouper (*Epinephelus akaara*) is found in shallow seas and around coral reefs throughout the Far East. This exotic fish is regarded as a gourmet food and since the region—and in particular Hong Kong—has become more prosperous, so has demand for the fish increased. This is threatening the survival of one of the oldest fish living on coral reefs.

Fishermen sometimes use cyanide to stun their catch of wild Hong Kong grouper. The fish are then packaged in bags of water before being delivered to seafood restaurants where they can be sold to eager locals at exorbitant prices. The endangered status of wild Hong Kong grouper has led to much effort being channelled into encouraging the local population to opt for farm-reared Hong Kong grouper instead.

In China and Hong Kong, grouper is believed to bring good luck and have medicinal value. The fish can be baked, fried, or grilled. In China, it is often served steamed and eaten whole. In South East Asia, it is also delicious wok-fried with lemongrass and stuffed with *belachan*, local shrimp paste. **CK**

Plucked from the waters encircling the South Pole, immediately killed by *iki jimi*—a Japanese method, where a spike through the brain minimizes pain and stress, and drains the blood resulting in whiter fillets—the most prized kingfish sashimi starts its journey north, cooled in a slurry of ice.

In Tokyo, *Seriola lalandi* (aka yellowtail kingfish, or gold-striped amberjack) is welcomed at the tables of the best restaurants and on the plates of the most discerning diners. Biodynamically farmed in a cool climate, off the south coast of Australia, it is firmer and tastier than that farmed in subtropical waters. Served as sashimi, hiramasa kingfish is firm, rich in oil, and sweet; its flesh is a pretty, pale pearl pink.

Hiramasa cooks to a moist opaque ivory, but the broad flakes can easily become dry and tough with overcooking. It stands up well in South East Asian curries and casseroles, where the flesh holds together firmly yet benefits from the moisture of a sauce. Although more delicate in flavour and texture, cooked hiramasa kingfish can be compared to a gentler tuna. **RH**

Taste: *The Hong Kong grouper is prized for its tasty, firm flesh. It has a magnificent fresh flavour when steamed. The farmed fish is an acceptable substitute for the wild.*

Taste: *Hiramasa is at its best raw. In sashimi, it is firm to the bite, with a fresh, marine aroma. Cooked, it has a meaty mouthfeel, with a taste that is mildly sweet and briny.*

Grouper sold in Hong Kong's busy night fish markets is now more likely to be farmed than wild-caught.

Coral Trout

In the aerated tanks of Cantonese restaurants, thick-lipped, fire engine-red fish sprinkled with iridescent blue spots swish slowly up to the glass through the bubbly water. Coral trout (*Plectropomus leopardus*), also known as leopard fish, flourish in subtropical waters around the reefs of Australia and throughout the Indo-Pacific. Their spectacular skin, which varies from red or bright orange to dark olive or brown, conceals a most succulent meat, with a mild sweet taste and gentle aroma.

While coral trout can grow to over 50 pounds (23 kg), it is small to medium fish, weighing upwards of 2 pounds (900 g), that make the best eating. The pale pink flesh cooks to a brilliant, almost ultraviolet white and forms large, mouth-watering flakes. Coral trout belong to the same family as sea bass and groupers, which gives an indication of the general taste and mouthfeel. While they suit many cooking styles—including steaming, sautéing, and deep frying—grilling the fillets simply with lemon and butter beautifully highlights both the taste and the texture of this sublime fish. **RH**

Silver Pomfret

Shaped like a plate with aerodynamic fins and a forked tail, silver pomfret (*Pampus argenteus*) swims off the Indian subcontinent, around the China seas, and as far as coastal Japan. Like many other fish prized for their taste, it risks extinction from over-exploitation, in part because its natural habitat is the muddy seabed of inshore waters. It belongs to a small genus of fish commonly known as "butterfish" (Stromateidae), a name that provides a clue as to its texture when cooked. Also known as white pomfret, it should not be confused with the black pomfret that belongs to a different species, and fetches less than a quarter of its price in Asian markets.

Chinese and South East Asian chefs generally cook it whole (the soft fins are eaten, too), but it fillets and skins easily, producing two lean, boneless strips of flesh. Down the west coast of India, from Mumbai to Goa, it is baked in a tandoor, while Thais prefer to fry it. Chinese and Malays like it best steamed with ginger and spring onions. Silver pomfret has not been farmed successfully, so it is an exclusive and increasingly rare luxury. **MR**

Taste: *The large, firm flakes are sweet in taste, velvety in texture, and devoid of a "fishy" taste or aroma. The skin can sometimes taint the flesh with a bitter flavour.*

Taste: *Silver pomfret has an ivory white flesh. Its texture when steamed is soft and melting. It is quite fatty too. Freshly caught, it is almost sweet, and not at all fishy.*

In South India, foods such as pomfret are served on banana leaf, which may also be used as a flavouring. »

Barramundi

Barracuda

Succulent, sweetly flavoured, healthy, inexpensive, easy to cook, available fresh locally all year round, and it leaves your environmental conscience clear. Impossible? No, barramundi.

Native to tropical northern Australian waters, the barramundi (*Lates calcarifer*) is one of the world's finest eating and sporting fish. To sample the mouth-watering delights of wild "barra"—the name is an Aboriginal word meaning large-scaled fish— aficionados travel down-under during the peak February to April season and battle these silver monsters, which can weigh between 65 and 130 pounds (30–59 kg).

Luckily modern aquaculture, and an eye to sustainability, provides an alternative for the rest of the planet. Fresh and saltwater farmed barramundi is available in the Asia-Pacific region, Europe, and United States. Packed with heart-healthy Omega-3 and Omega-6 fatty acids, barramundi is also light on bones and the fat content ensures it stands up to most forms of kitchen abuse, consistently producing a luscious, succulent result. **RH**

Positioned near the top of the seafood chain, the barracuda (*Sphyraena* species) is as good an eater as it is eaten. It is renowned as a voracious predator, and with its scary mouthful of fang-like teeth, it is easy to see why. It has a sleek aerodynamic body similar to the European freshwater pike and is extremely fast, possessing a characteristically forked tail to give it turn of speed. Barracuda swim in shoals and hunt in packs, and they corral their prey into a huge cylinder near the surface of the sea and then dart into the column to snap up their victims.

The barracuda has something of a reputation for attacking humans, although this probably has more to do with its aggressive appearance than actual fact. Of course, humans have the culinary advantage more frequently: pan-fried or barbecued, the excellent quality of the barracuda lends itself to rich and bold flavours.

In general, the barracuda's colour is dark bronze or steely grey above, chalky-white or silver along the belly, often with a row of darker cross-bars, chevrons, or black spots on each side. **STS**

Taste: *Wild barramundi has a sweet flavour, robust flakes, and an al dente mouthfeel, suggestive of an active life in open waters. Farmed barra is milder and finer textured.*

Taste: *Rich, meaty, and well-textured, the barracuda has a distinctive gamey flavour. It is excellent either filleted or cut into steaks.*

People associate the barracuda with Australia, but this is the Mediterranean species, Sphyraena sphyraena. ❯❯

Luvar

Dubbed the "Cadillac of fish" and the "best fish in the ocean," the only downside of the elusive luvar is its rarity. It is almost never seen in fish markets and seldom forms part of a fisherman's catch; when it does, it is most often instantly cooked and eaten as a treat by its lucky captor. Once or twice a year, fish suppliers on the west coast of the United States are able to offer luvar to their customers. The fish is also found in the Gulf of Mexico, where it is called the "emperador." Back in 1997 a particularly fine specimen went on sale in Sydney, Australia, and a few years ago one was caught in Newlyn in Cornwall, only to be stuffed for posterity.

The luvar, a large solitary fish, has been known to grow to almost 10 feet (3 m) long. It lives in the deep waters of the Atlantic and Pacific Oceans. While similar to members of the tuna family, the luvar is not directly related to any other species. It is the sole species in its family, Luvaridae.

Luvar is a beautiful, eye-catching fish, silver coloured with a brilliant pink lower body and a deep blue, dark-spotted upper body with scarlet fins and tail. The fish has a huge, bulging head similar to that of a Mediterranean dorade, with small, low-set eyes. Females produce huge numbers of eggs; one fish, 5 ½ feet (1.7 m) long, was estimated to contain 47.5 million eggs. The adult is entirely different from the young fish and goes through several characteristic stages of development. These changes have led to several of the stages being claimed at one time or another as distinct species of fish. For such a large fish, it has a tiny, toothless mouth that limits its diet largely to jellyfish and other gelatinous, planktonic animals. **WS**

Taste: *Similar in colour and texture to turbot and halibut, the flesh is white with big flakes that are firm, sweet, and succulent. A sublime fish by most fish lovers' standards.*

Flying Fish

Despite their striking name, flying fish, which belong to the family Exocoetidae, do not actually fly. Rather, they glide through the air, using their extremely large, wing-shaped pectoral fins and vibrating tail to help them. This striking action is achieved by the fish swimming very fast up to the surface of the sea and launching themselves upwards through the air, sometimes for 55 yards (50 m) at 30 miles (50 km) per hour. Found in warm tropical and semi-tropical seas, the fish rising out of the waves and soaring through the air make an arresting sight. Their distinctive gliding through the air is a strategy to evade underwater predators such as swordfish.

The flying fish is highly valued in the Caribbean, where it is associated particularly with the island of Barbados, nick-named "the land of the flying fish." Something of an island mascot, the fish features on Bajan stamps and coins. The flying fish industry has long been an important part of the island's economy and is a popular food. With its many tiny, fine bones, it is best eaten in fillet form. The national dish of Barbados is flying fish and *cou cou*—flying fish fillets, flavoured with lime juice, garlic, and pepper sauce, fried or steamed, served with cornmeal and okra. Most visitors to Barbados experience it fried in breadcrumbs with a squeeze of lime juice or as "fish and chips." Sadly, over-fishing has made the flying fish a rarity in Barbadian waters, leading to fishing disputes with nearby Tobago. There are now conservation initiatives to try and preserve flying fish stocks.

In Japan, the fine-grained, orange-red roe of the flying fish (*tobiko*) is used in sushi, often as garnish, valued for its crunchy texture. **MR**

Taste: *The texture is quite compact and dry for a small fish, not woolly as might be expected. Once the little bones have been negotiated, the taste is sweet and meaty.*

The long, wing-like pectoral fins of flying fish are seen in this catch, photographed off the coast of Barbados. »

Parrotfish

One of the most decorative and prettiest fish in the sea, parrotfish (so named because of its beak-like head and bright colouring) make a colourful splash. The fish requires scaling prior to gutting and cooking, and while the removal of the scales takes some of the gloss off the skin colour, it takes away nothing from the unique flavour. Parrotfish are often offered as a delicacy in the Caribbean, where they are pan-fried, grilled, or served with a rich, coconut curry sauce. The small blue parrotfish from Sri Lanka, meanwhile, has a very delicate white flesh and is generally considered to be the best flavoured.

Despite their appeal, parrotfish should perhaps be tried only once in a lifetime. They are known to graze on certain seaweeds that are threatening to destroy coral reefs; it is because of this that some scientists believe that parrotfish should possibly not be on the menu at all. If you like the taste, a good option would be to try another close relative, such as the wrasse or scaly fish, or perhaps farmed barramundi or grey mullet. **STS**

Gilthead Bream

The sweet, delicate, white flaky flesh of the gilthead bream is sometimes likened to that of sea bass, although in Mediterranean countries the flavour is considered to be far superior. It is considered the most prized of the bream family. Found in the wild, in shallow water over sand or mud, where it mainly feeds on molluscs and crustaceans, it can tolerate brackish conditions in river estuaries but migrates to deeper water to spawn in winter. It is also one of the most important saltwater farmed fish, especially throughout the Mediterranean.

The gilthead has a round deep body that is flattened on the sides, making it easy to fillet. The back of the fish is a dark grey-blue and it has a silver belly. It has a golden spot on each cheek, and a bright golden bar runs across the forehead between the eyes, hence its common name.

Gilthead bream require scaling prior to filleting, although care needs to be taken to trim the sharp fins, particularly the dorsal and rear fins first, as they can inflict a nasty wound if touched. The whole fish is delicious grilled, stuffed, or baked. **STS**

Taste: *Parrotfish flesh is white and soft in texture with the subtle flavours of herbs. Fillets are best grilled to create a seared and seasoned exterior.*

Taste: *The fish can be filleted, but the best flavour is obtained from cooking it whole, on the bone. The cheek, or "pearl," is the sweetest and most delicate morsel of all.*

Golden Kingklip

A member of the eel family, the golden kingklip is found in deep waters off the coasts of Chile, Argentina, South Africa, New Zealand, and Australia, where it burrows in the sand and mud. Also known locally as golden conger, pink ling, and conqria dorado, it is particularly popular in Latin America. Golden kingklip (*Genypterus blacodes*) has an orange-pink, eel-like body that tapers to a point at the tail and can grow to over 5 feet (1.6 m) in length and up to a weight of 55 pounds (25 kg).

Golden kingklip can be found fresh, frozen, or smoked. It is high in protein, rich in calcium, iodine, and iron, and has high levels of Omega-3 and Omega-6 oils. In South Africa, where it is known as *koningklip* in Afrikaans, it is often used along with other local fish, such as *geelbek* and *katokel*, to make excellent pickled and curried fish, a culinary process for which its firm, mild flesh is well suited. Golden kingklip is a versatile fish for the kitchen—excellent for oven-baking, poaching, grilling, and frying. Its texture also makes it ideal for adding in chunks to a flavoursome fish stew. **HFi**

Taste: *The pink to white flesh of golden kingclip is free of bones and has a sweet, light flavour. The mild-flavoured flesh has a firm, moist texture.*

Lamprey

A very primitive fish that mostly survives by clamping itself to other fish and sucking their blood, the lamprey is slimy, muscular, and unprepossessing. It is also very good eating, too much so for one Norman king of England, Henry I who, according to legend, died in 1135 after eating too many of them.

Out of fashion and rarely found in Britain, it is still consumed with gusto in Portugal and in Galicia, northern Spain. Arbo, or "Villa da Lampreas" (Village of Lampreys), holds a spring festival in its honour. Lamprey has protected status in many European countries because of over-fishing and pollution.

In size they can grow to over 3 feet (1 m) long and they would doubtless be more popular were it not for their rather repellent appearance, allied to the difficulty of preparing them. The live fish has to be bled first and the outer slime has to be removed before cooking. In the classic *lamproie à la bordelaise* (Bordeaux is perhaps the only part of France where lamprey is still enjoyed), chunks of lamprey are stewed in red wine with Bayonne ham and the reserved blood is used to thicken the sauce. **MR**

Taste: *The texture of lamprey is quite chewy, closer to monkfish or lobster than other seafood. Its meaty flavour is similar to eel, but with a pleasantly earthy aftertaste.*

Black Scabbard Fish

The black scabbard (*Aphanopus carbo*) is a sinister-looking fish with large eyes, needle-like teeth, and a long, elongated body resembling a scabbard. Although widely found in the northeastern Atlantic from Iceland to the Canary Islands, this fish is inextricably linked with the Portuguese island of Madeira, where it is known as *espada preta*, not to be confused with the *espada branca* (white scabbard) which is also fished off Madeiran shores.

Captured mainly by Câmara de Lobos fishermen, the fish measures about 3 ¼ inches (1 m) long and can live from four to ten years. Due to its deep-water habitat it is a dark fish with big eyes, different from the scabbard fish captured in mainland waters and requiring careful handling because of its sharp teeth. Madeiran fishermen first encountered the inky-black fish in the fifteenth century when they were line-catching mackerel. Because black scabbard lurk at depths of around 3,280 feet (1,000 m), where nets are next to useless, fishermen had to develop special hooks and very long lines—usually 5,250 feet (1,600 m) long—to increase their chances of catching them. Their work is one of the deepest types of deep-sea fishing in the world.

The fin-less fish are marketed whole, but minus their stomachs, which are forced out of their mouths by pressure as they are hauled up from the depths. The firm-textured fish has a fatty layer under the skin and is served simply fried or grilled; in Madeira, it is also paired with fruits, such as banana or passion fruit, to add sweetness to its fine white flesh. The fish is also available smoked. *Espada* should not be confused with *espetada*, a popular Madeiran dish of grilled beef skewers. **STS**

Taste: *The flesh of black scabbard fish is sweet, rich, meaty, and buttery, and comes easily off the bone. The delicate skin cooks away and need not be removed.*

Despite its looks, the deep-sea black scabbard is surprisingly delicious. »

Red Snapper

Red Mullet

Red snapper is one of the most popular white fish on the market and in many countries of the world "white fish" simply means red snapper. Lightly spiced and baked in banana leaves, or blackened with Cajun spices, red snapper goes perfectly with the flavours of its tropical origins.

Red snapper is a member of the huge Lutjanidae family of fish, of which there are over 200 species worldwide, with colours varying from light pink to deep rosy red. Warm, tropical oceans around the world are home to these striking species of fish, which feed on crab, squid, shrimp, and small fish. Species that have a red or pink skin include Bourgeois, Malabar, Vara Vara, yellow tail, and B-line snapper and many of these have regional names depending on the locality in which they were landed. Most commercial red snapper is harvested in the Gulf of Mexico and Indonesia.

Red snapper is a versatile fish, superb filleted, stuffed, or baked whole. And it is, of course, fantastic grilled whole, especially wrapped in a banana leaf to seal in the beautiful flavour. **STS**

Crimson coloured and often streaked with gold, red mullet (*Mullus surmuletus* and *M. barbatus*) are among the most treasured of Mediterranean fish, although they are also found in the Atlantic. They are easily recognized by their colour, which can change from red to pink both while the fish is alive and on the slab. Romans during the first century CE were fascinated by this phenomenon and frequently kept the fish in captivity for observation.

There are other species of red mullet throughout the world, such as *Upeneus sundaicus,* which lives in Australian waters. Outside Europe, red mullet is often known as goatfish. Mediterranean red mullet supplies are currently under pressure and it is best to avoid eating immature fish, less than 9 inches (22 cm) long, and fish caught during the spawning season from May to July.

Red mullet is usually cooked whole (the liver is considered a delicacy), either grilled, fried, or oven-baked *en papillote.* For a perfect taste of summer, simply grill over hot coals with some olive oil and fresh herbs; it needs little other adornment. **LW**

Taste: *Red snapper has a firm texture and a sweet, nutty flavour. It suits seasonings from all round the world, from chillies to herbs, including basil and rosemary.*

Taste: *Firm in texture and delicate but satisfying in flavour, the taste of this elegant fish is sometimes compared to crab, on which the red mullet feeds.*

In the tropics, red snapper may be barbecued with
◉ *fresh herbs and other seasonings on a banana leaf.*

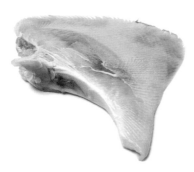

Skate

Unlike many classic dishes that have been given a facelift over the last few years, poached skate served with *beurre noisette*, parsley, lemon, and capers has—thankfully—remained unchanged on most restaurant menus. The parts of this fish most commonly eaten are the wings (fins), although skate "nobs" (cuts from the muscle on the back and head) are sometimes available.

As with many popular fish, there have been concerns over the sustainability of some skate species. Unfortunately, skate (some of which are threatened) and ray (some of which are still plentiful) are difficult to tell apart on the fishmonger's slab: their skin, which is the distinguishing feature, is removed prior to sale. Skate are slow growing, taking five to ten years to mature , and only lay a small number of eggs. They are therefore vulnerable to over-fishing. In common with other cartilaginous fish they excrete urea through the flesh and if not stored correctly will smell of ammonia. Avoid purchasing such fish (and, indeed, any seafood smelling of ammonia) as it is an indication it has deteriorated past consumption. **STS**

Taste: *The delicate textured flesh of the wings lies in strands over a web-like cartilage and can be steamed, roasted, or fried. The unique flavour includes a hint of aniseed.*

Looped over poles, skate dry on the beach at Ericeira, Portugal. »

Turbot

Halibut

Supremely prized in Europe and Asia for its firm, white flesh, turbot (*Psetta maxima*) is almost circular in shape, with a mottled skin that, instead of scales, is studded with knobbly spots that look like nail-heads. Part of a small family of left-eyed flatfish, turbot ranges from the Black Sea, through the Mediterranean to the North Atlantic coast of Iceland. It is farmed in Europe, Chile, Norway, and China.

Turbot have been known to grow to over 3 feet (1 m) in length, but the normal adult size is about half that. Avoid eating turbot from the North Sea where it has been over-fished. In other areas, choose line-caught fish or those caught in dolphin-friendly nets. Given its exploitation, it should not be caught during spawning, between April and August.

Mid-sized turbot are best, weighing 4 ½ to 6 ½ pounds (2–3 kg), and fillets from the top of the fish yield the plumpest flesh. The thickest part of the fins is regarded as a delicacy, having an unusual gelatinous texture. Turbot is frequently steamed and served with rich sauces, such as lobster or hollandaise. It is also excellent fried or grilled. **LW**

Once popularly eaten on holy days, halibut used to be spelled "holibut." Indeed, the word "holy" forms part of its name in several languages. The largest flatfish in the sea, halibut (*Hippoglossus hippoglossus*) has both eyes on the right side of its body. Found in the cool, temperate waters of the Atlantic, halibut can grow to a whopping 8 feet (2.3 m) in length and weigh in at over 650 pounds (295 kg). Not quite so hefty, the Pacific halibut (*H. stenolepis*) lives in waters from California through Alaska to northern Asia, and is less vulnerable to over-fishing than its Atlantic cousin.

In many parts of Scandinavia, halibut has always played a strong part, both fresh and dried, in the national diets. In western Europe, it has been less popular, at times only eaten when nothing else was available. Immortalized in a poem by William Cowper in 1784, it was not until the twentieth century that halibut's star began to rise in England.

Fillets or steaks of halibut are often poached in *court bouillon* and served with a good sauce such as hollandaise, but it is a fish suited to all cooking methods, especially baking and grilling. **LW**

Taste: *The bright white flesh is rich and moist with the bite of a fleshy sautéed mushroom. It has a supremely refined flavour. Even the skin, nail-heads and all, is thought tasty.*

Taste: *Not unlike turbot but less expensive, halibut has a fine, but firm, texture with few bones and a clean, delicately sweet flavour that requires little seasoning.*

Halibut fillets cook on the barbecue within ten minutes per inch (2.5 cm) of thickness. »

Cod

Monkfish

Cod is the king of the Gadidae group and is loved in many countries around the world. However, its enduring popularity has also led to its downfall, as Mark Kurlansky chronicled in his moving book *Cod: A biography of the fish that changed the world*.

As there is such demand for it, cod stocks have been over-exploited for many years. Limited supply, especially from the North Sea, has pushed up market prices. There are, however, sustainable quantities available from the waters around Iceland and the Arctic and, additionally, cod is now being successfully farmed in northern Europe and is of excellent quality.

The best part of the cod is the thickest section around the loin or the top part of the fillet. Cod can be salted, dried, and smoked. It lends itself to most cooking methods and can be baked, grilled, fried, or poached. Cod is still top of the league tables with fish fryers. Although the newspaper of yesteryear has been replaced by greaseproof paper, deep-fried cod in crispy batter and chunky chips, doused in salt and malt vinegar is a British institution. **STS**

In his classic *North Atlantic Seafood*, food writer Alan Davidson noted that monkfish (*Lophius pescatorius*) has a variety of local names: "belly fish and goose fish (because it stuffs itself), allmouth (North Carolina) and the cognate 'lawyer' (parts of New England) and bellows fish." Its other name, anglerfish, points to a dangling fleshy-lipped spine above its voracious jaws that it uses as a bait to lure its prey. This odd-looking fish has a number of seaweed-like fringes around its head that, along with its mottled skin, make it an expert in camouflage.

It is a grotesque fish, related to sharks, that can grow up to 6 feet (2 m) long. With a cartilaginous spine, but no bones other than those of its fins, it is meaty and firm-fleshed, highly regarded by some culinary cultures. Until a generation ago, it was considered by British cooks to be a cheap substitute for lobster or scampi, because of its colour and texture. In Italy, *coda di rospo* (monkfish tail) is fried, grilled, and baked. Cooked through, it can be dry, bland, and chewy, but when it is done to a turn, it lives up to its name of "poor man's lobster." **MR**

Taste: *The chunky white fillets cook to a pure white with large open flakes and a delicate and distinct flavour that resonates with the highlights of its diet of small shellfish.*

Taste: *The texture of monkfish tail changes according to its size, but is always dense and quite juicy. It only becomes dry with over-cooking. The taste is light but sweet.*

Gulls feast on offal from gutted cod and other fish
◐ *caught off the coast of Newfoundland, Canada.*

Chilean Sea Bass

Swordfish

Chilean Sea Bass is the name, in the United States, for Patagonian toothfish or icefish, and is so called because the Chileans were the first to market it there. The fish is a favourite among U.S. chefs because the fillets are pure white, succulent, and very tasty, lending themselves to a myriad of flavour combinations. It is very popular on the West coast of the United States where it is most commonly sold ready prepared as steaks or thick dense white fillets, and is either pan-fried or roasted.

The fish feeds largely on squid and prawns, which goes some way to explain its wonderful flavour. It is found in the cold deep waters of the southern Atlantic, southern Pacific, Indian and southern oceans around the continental shelves. The average weight of a commercially caught fish is 20 pounds (about 9 kg) with large adults occasionally exceeding 440 pounds (200 kg). They can reach a length of 8 feet (2.3 m). The fish is endangered by over-fishing, although the Marine Stewardship Council has certified as sustainable a South Georgia fishery in the South Atlantic. **STS**

A predator at the top of the food chain, this mighty blue-grey fish with its dramatic bill, or "sword," cuts a dash in fish markets the world over. Found globally, the swordfish (*Xiphias gladius*) generally migrates between temperate or cold waters in summer and warmer waters in winter. It can reach up to 13 feet (4 m) in length, including its sword, which it uses to slash or stun its prey.

The swordfish has been an easy target for the harpoon since classical times as it often basks near the water's surface. Today, it is under huge fishing pressure: many swordfish stocks are unmanaged and over-fished. Catches include immature swordfish, as well as a bycatch of other species such as marine turtles. Swordfish populations need to be managed internationally; those in the North Atlantic are recovering well due to the efforts of U.S. authorities.

Swordfish is popular in most world cuisines, especially in Sicily, where the fishermen are renowned for their skill in catching them. Marinated swordfish steaks are delicious char-grilled. In Turkey, thin slices of smoked swordfish are a delicacy. **LW**

Taste: *The flavour is stronger and more robust than other white textured fish, although it is often cooked and treated in the same way as cod.*

Taste: *Slightly pink, compact, and juicy, swordfish has a veal-like texture. Its flavour is mild and meaty, but not as fishy as tuna. Cook till the flesh is opaque, but still moist.*

A swordfish adorns the side of a pirogue, a West African flat-bottomed fishing boat. ❯❯

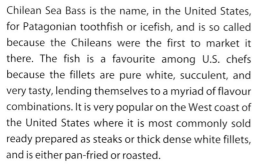

Sea Bass

One of the most highly prized fish in Europe, the sea bass (*Dicentrarchus labrax*) is found all the way from Norway to West Africa. It is a beautiful, streamlined silver fish with a pointed head, which grows to a maximum length of 40 inches (1 m) and a maximum weight of 26 pounds (12 kg).

Although a saltwater fish, the bass has a penchant for fresh water. Most young bass spend their early lives in estuaries and return home from time to time even when mature. According to the poet Horace, gourmets in ancient Rome used to say they could tell the difference between a sea bass caught in the sea at the mouth of the Tiber and one caught between the bridges of the city. (The satirist Juvenal claimed the bass that lurked between the bridges fed on the city's sewage.)

Trawlers target spawning and pre-spawning fish, so if line-caught bass are not available pick the smaller fish that are farmed in salt lagoons and sea cages throughout the Mediterranean and beyond. Simply roast or grill whole with herbs, and serve with a dash of olive oil and lemon juice. **LW**

Striped Bass

Early settlers highly praised the taste and flavour of this American species of bass, regarding it as an excellent proposition for the table and never tiring of its delicate flavour. The pearl in the cheek was, in particular, savoured as it is sweet and especially flavoursome. Striped bass (*Morone saxatilis*) remains highly popular today, and is thought by many to be best served lightly fried and garnished with lemon.

There are several species of bass found in the United States, so called because they resemble the popular European sea bass in shape and size. They have slightly deeper bodies than the European species and are commonly known there as striped sea bass, rock, and rockfish. They are found in both fresh and salt water: like the salmon, they breed in fresh water. The body of the bass is long and silver with dark stripes running from the gills to the base of the tail. It is thought to live up to thirty years, and it can grow to 6 ½ feet (2 m) in length and more than 110 pounds (50 kg) in weight. Highly regarded as a sport fishing species, striped bass are also farmed in Turkey, Mexico, Iran, and Ecuador. **STS**

Taste: *The thin, crisp silver skin of sea bass splits open to reveal firm, fragrant, flavourful flesh—like ultra-soft, ultra-moist chicken breast with a sticky bite.*

Taste: *In its raw state the flesh has a grey translucency that cooks to firm, meaty, white fillets. It has a fine rounded flavour not dissimilar to sea bass.*

People shop for fish in Bologna, Italy; serving
⊗ *sea bass at Passover is an Italian-Jewish tradition.*

Blue Marlin

Famed as the "big fish" in Ernest Hemingway's novella *The Old Man and the Sea*, the blue marlin (*Makaira nigricans*) is one of the most impressive ocean dwellers. It is distinguished by a powerful, long, spear-shaped jaw or bill, and is known to attain 14 feet (4.3 m) in length and to weigh up to 1 ton (910 kg). With its vivid, deep-blue colouring fading to a silvery-white flash across its flanks and belly, the blue marlin is a spectacular creature. It is found in the tropical and temperate waters of the Atlantic, Pacific, and Indian oceans, where it can be readily identified by the pronounced dorsal fin running along the full length of its back.

The blue marlin is thought to use its long, spear-shaped upper jaw, or bill, to slash through dense schools of fish, before returning to eat its stunned and wounded victims. The predator fish prefers the warmer temperatures of surface waters, feeding on pelagic species such as mackerel, but it also eats squid and is known to dive deep to obtain them.

The blue marlin's spectacular size and appearance, coupled with its legendary capacity to fight hard when hooked, have made the species a popular game fish, much coveted by sporting fishermen and trophy hunters. The firm flesh is also used in Japan for sushi and sashimi.

As with other long-lived, top-level ocean predators, warnings of high mercury levels in the meat are attached to consumption of blue marlin. The fish is slow-growing and slow to reproduce, and conservationists are concerned that the population is in decline. An excellent alternative is mahimahi, a smaller fish but one that has a similar, densely textured flesh and rich flavour. **STS**

Kanpachi

In Japan, kanpachi is known as an "ascending fish," which means that its name changes according to its size and age. Kanpachi is the Japanese name for the most mature stage of *Seriola dumerili*, or greater amberjack, when it is over 4 feet (1.2 m) long. The fish is found in the Indo-Pacific, Mediterranean, Caribbean, and along the South and North American east coasts. Its name comes from the yellow (amber) streaks that run down its sides, and a close relative, *Seriola lalandi*, is known as the yellowtail amberjack. Kanpachi is a deep-sea fighter that will test the will and strength of the most experienced of fishermen. It is a carnivore that feeds on smaller fish and can achieve a length of 6 ½ feet (2 m) and weigh 198 pounds (90 kg).

In Japan and elsewhere, kanpachi is often commercially farmed; the fish are fed a special diet to optimize the flavour of the meat, which is popularly used for sushi. Wild adult fish caught in the spring or summer at about half their fully mature size (called *shiogo* or *akahana* in Japan) are considered best for this purpose. Reputedly, the fish is best eaten before it is three years old and not in the autumn (after the spawning season), when it has developed an unpleasant odour.

Kanpachi is an extra lean, dense fish. Kanpachi fillets can be 1 inch (2.5 cm) or more thick and can be served as carpaccio. In the United States, kanpachi from the Gulf of Mexico is sometimes known as Gulf tuna and the fillets are usually grilled or fried. In Japan, however, it is most commonly used in sushi, especially *nigiri*, a type of sushi made with rice and raw fish. Sushi chefs in Japan undergo extensive training to learn to make *nigiri*. **SH**

Taste: *The steaks of this fish are firm and dense with a similar flavour to swordfish. It is easily over-cooked and generally suits char-grilling as a method of cooking.*

Taste: *The pale white flesh is firm and creamy and melts in the mouth. Stronger in flavour than flounder, grouper, or snapper, it has a slight taste of the sea, but is still mild.*

The writer and sports fisherman Ernest Hemingway ◖ described the blue marlin as a formidable foe.

Hake

Hake is a deep-swimming member of the cod family found in the Atlantic and northern Pacific oceans. The European hake (*Merluccius merluccius*) ranges from the Mediterranean to Norway. One North American species is the silver hake (*Merluccius bilinearis*), so called because it has a silvery sheen when freshly caught. Adult hake grow to a length of 40 inches (1 m) and weigh up to 11 pounds (5 kg). The fish is available fresh—whole or as fillets, steaks, or cutlets—and frozen, salted, and smoked.

Hake is much loved on the Iberian Peninsula, where it is known to the Spanish as *merluza* and the Portuguese as *pescada*. It was introduced to Iberian cuisines by the Basques, who call it *legatz*. It often appears in casseroles with other types of fish, as well as shellfish such as lobster, prawns, and mussels. In France, hake is known as *saumon blanc*.

Hake has few small bones and is easy to prepare. The lack of bones makes it suitable for fish soups, stews, and casseroles, and the flesh's subtle, delicate flavour makes it a successful substitute for any recipes that specify cod or other white fish. **FR**

Taste: *Hake's lean flesh is soft and creamy in texture. It is white to pink in colour, and flakes easily. The delicate and unobtrusive flavour lends itself well to light poaching.*

Freshly landed hake is packed on ice in Peterhead, Scotland. »

Black Cod

Black cod, which gained fame through renowned chef Nobu Matsuhisa's Black Cod and Miso, is fast becoming a popular and sustainable alternative to the over-exploited Atlantic cod. This sleek fish is more blue-grey than black, and like many other species, it has a string of regional names, including butterfish (United States and Australia), candlefish (United Kingdom), and coal fish (Canada). But be careful: confusingly, many of these names can also refer to other species, making it easy to buy the wrong fish. True black cod has a firm, meaty texture, although there is a fibrous element to frozen fillets.

It is caught in the cold and very deep waters of the Pacific Northwest, from as far south as Baja California through to the Bering Sea. Canadians tend to fish it in traps that not only preserves the quality of the fish, but has also virtually eliminated the by-catch of smaller fish and therefore helps sustainability. To experience black cod at its best, buy it fresh; much of the fish caught for the European market is frozen on landing and then subsequently transported. **STS**

Taste: Black cod has a strong and unique flavour, which complements the flavours of wasabi, miso, and shoyu particularly well.

Bluefin Tuna

The most highly prized species of fish in Japan, bluefin tuna is considered a must for the very best platter of sashimi, due to its fine quality and delicate but rich oils. The Japanese have a distinct preference for the belly area, or *otoro*, due to its high oil content, whereas in the West, bluefin tuna is filleted, and the lean loin section along the back is the favoured cut.

Northern bluefin tuna is the most valued of the tuna family, used primarily for sashimi; tuna steaks and canned products come from other members of the family. They are the largest of all the tuna species, adults being typically 6 ½ feet (2 m) long when caught, but they can reach in excess of 13 feet (4 m). The largest recorded specimen weighed a massive 1,500 pounds (680 kg), although adults usually average around 550 pounds (250 kg).

In Japan, where it is a particular delicacy, a single giant bluefin tuna fetches an astronomical price. The fish's high status has put enormous pressure on stocks and the northern bluefin is under threat from over-fishing. A more sustainable option is the excellent yellowfin tuna. **STS**

Taste: Bluefin tuna has a similar texture to fillet beef, but with a subtle, understated flavour. It is very lean and has large, open flakes.

Old and new nets for tuna fishing dry in the sun on Isola San Pietro, Sardinia, Italy. »

Rollmop

These sweet and sour delicacies take their distinctive name from the German word *rollen*, which means "to roll." Herring fillets (complete with skin) are first marinated, then rolled around a pickle—usually an onion or a gherkin—before the whole thing is secured with a small wooden stick. Rollmops are popular in many northern European countries, notably Germany, Scandinavia, the Czech Republic, Slovakia, and parts of Scotland—and have even made their way to South Africa. The recipe for the marinade varies from country to country, but usually consists of white wine or cider vinegar, water, onion, peppercorns, mustard seeds, salt, and sugar.

The development of rail transport during the first half of the nineteenth century meant herrings could easily be carried inland from the ports of the North Sea and the Baltic Sea, and so a method of pickling evolved. The results became particularly associated with Berlin, where they had a starring role in the displays of ready-to-eat foods that adorned old Berlin pubs. They still have a reputation as a hangover cure. **LF**

Fugu

Fugu is a spiny fish with a habit of blowing itself up into a round ball if threatened, hence its popular name—blowfish. It is a renowned delicacy in Japan, where it has been eaten for centuries in spite of (or perhaps because of) the fact a lethal toxin is found in its gut, liver, ovary, and skin.

Tingling lips are a normal reaction. But if anything more than a minute amount is eaten the poison attacks the nervous system, leading to creeping numbness, followed by the clatter of chopsticks as the diner loses his grip… However, preparation of the fish in restaurants has been licensed since 1949, and deaths almost always occur as a result of untrained preparation at home.

The gourmet's Russian roulette that is a fugu dinner is always an occasion. The flesh is served as sashimi, cut in wafer thin slices and ostentatiously presented on a huge platter in overlapping slices resembling a flower. It is eaten with a dipping sauce of soy sauce, sudachi citrus, spring onion, grated daikon radish, and red pepper. A one-pot dish of fugu and vegetables usually follows. **SB**

Taste: *Soft, with a glossy appearance and a silky, melting texture, rollmops have a sweet-and-sour flavour. They are particularly good with dark rye and sourdough breads.*

Taste: *The sashimi is light and astringent and the cooked fugu rich and meaty. Many say, however, that its taste is surpassed by the thrill of the experience.*

The Shinsekai blowfish restaurant in Osaka, Japan, attracts diners with a large model of the fish. »

Cantabrian Boquerone

Collioure Anchovy

A superstar among anchovies, the Cantabrian Sea on the northern Atlantic coast of Spain has long been considered the world's best source for these silver-skinned gems.

Rather than being preserved in swathes of salt as many anchovies are, Cantabrian boquerones are usually packed in olive oil or a light cure of oil and vinegar. The fish tend to be plumper and meatier than their Mediterranean cousins, and have a delicious, full flavour. Fresh anchovies deteriorate fast and so processing must take place within hours of landing the catch. The anchovies are trimmed and filleted by hand before being salted, washed, and packed in olive oil or oil and vinegar.

Unfortunately, their popularity comes at a price. Despite regulations governing fishing in the area, reserves have plummeted and, at the time of writing, a total ban has been placed on anchovy fishing in the Cantabrian Sea, so that stocks are allowed to replenish naturally. However, anchovies cured in the Cantabrian-style, although prepared elsewhere, are still available. **LF**

The delicate texture of freshly caught anchovies makes them poor travellers and it is for this reason that they are usually canned, salted, cured, or marinated. Collioure, a small Mediterranean fishing port in the Roussillon region of France, is widely held to produce the ultimate salted anchovy—plump, flavour-packed, and with a unique aroma.

Anchovy fishing was well developed in Collioure by the nineteenth century, although the salt-curing of fish there dates back to the Middle Ages. Today, despite cheaper competition from producers like Morocco, several salting houses in Collioure continue to prepare their fine product, which now has PDO status. Local women, known as *anchoïeuses*, hand pick the freshly caught fish, which are cleaned, gutted, and sandwiched between layers of salt in vats. They are then left to mature for at least 100 days.

Collioure anchovies are made from the *Engraulis encrassicholus* species of anchovy. Populations of European anchovies are fluctuating and the fishing season currently runs from April to May, and again from September to October. **STS**

Taste: *Cantabrian boquerones are meltingly tender and silky in texture. They have a mouth-watering flavour with a hint of sweetness and are not in-your-face fishy.*

Taste: *Collioure anchovies have dark brown, firm textured fillets. They have a distinctive, slightly perfumed scent of mountain ham, and a salty, rich, lingering taste.*

Roque Anchois is just one of the establishments in Collioure, France, that specialize in anchovies. ❯❯

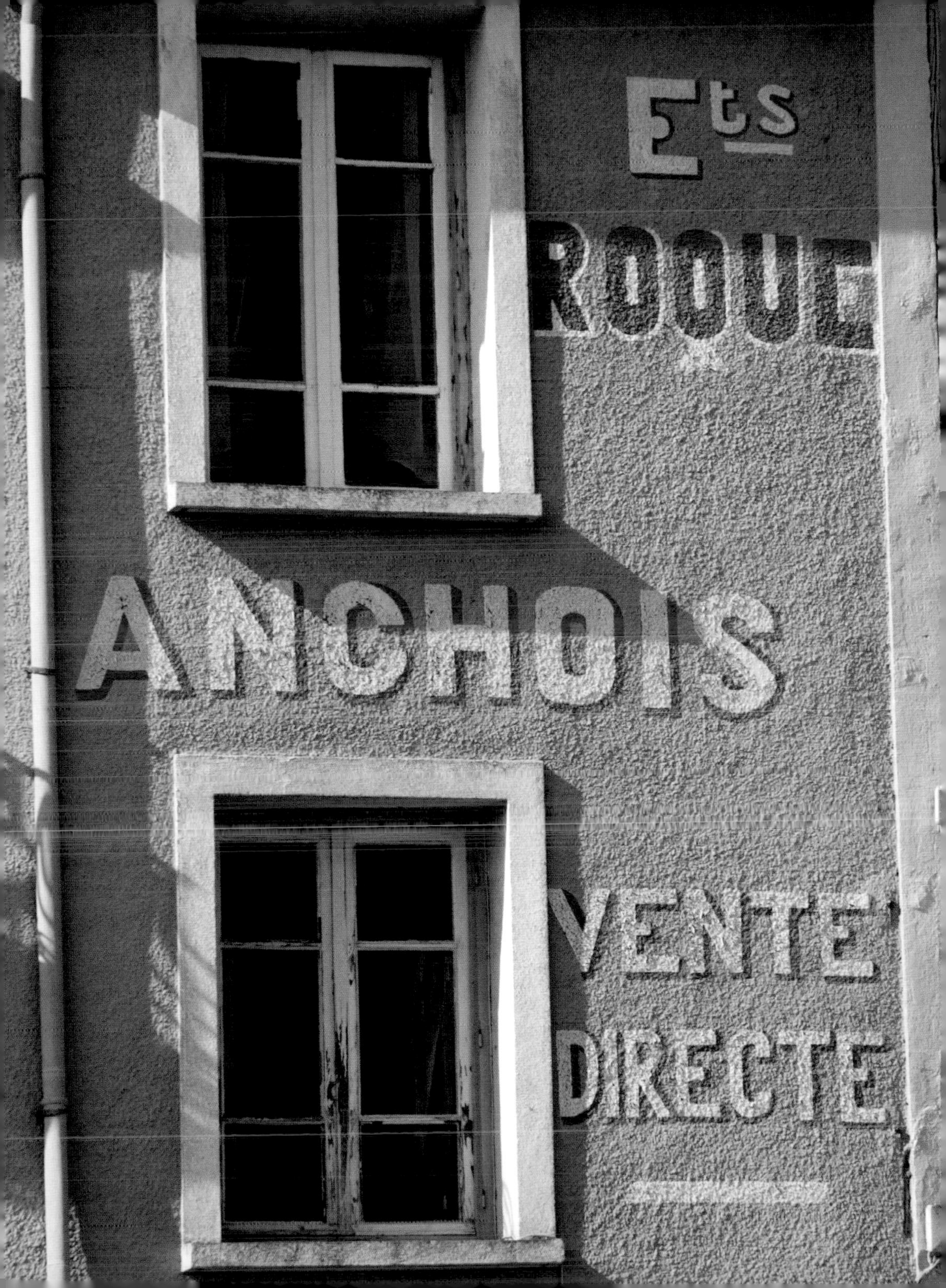
Ets
ROQUE
ANCHOIS
VENTE
DIRECTE

Seki Aji

A speciality of the southern island of Kyushu, seki aji, or horse mackerel, is caught in the Bungo Suido channel, where the strong currents of the Pacific Ocean meet the sheltered water of the inland sea. This results in strong tidal currents that lower the fat content of the fish, because it has to swim so hard against them, and gives it a mildness of flavour esteemed throughout Japan. Seki aji is an example of what the Japanese call *hikari mono*—shiny things— such as herring and mackerel. Although eaten as sashimi, it is always washed and marinated in vinegar before serving. As well as helping to preserve the fish, this also firms up the flesh and makes slicing it easier.

Seki aji is caught only by the traditional pole and line method, using a single hook, and not with nets. This practice, together with the local technique of *ikejime*—a method of draining the blood from the fish very quickly—preserves the flavour.

Eaten as sashimi, often with grated ginger and onion, seki aji also goes well with the citrus yuzu. Local dishes include *matsuoka zushi*, when it is served as *nigiri sushi* then wrapped in a bracken leaf. **SB**

Taste: *Somewhat milder than mackerel with a sweet and fresh taste, seki aji has a slightly crunchy, pinkish flesh with a mild fattiness.*

Isle of Man Kipper

Kippers are a form of smoked herring. The process was adopted in nineteenth-century Britain after John Woodger decided to borrow a technique that was being used to cure salmon—and also finnan haddock. The fish were split, brined, hung in a smokehouse on wooden rods or "tenters," and cold smoked. This method was once widespread along the northeast coast of England but has now almost died out, except at Craster in Northumbria and off the west coast of the Isle of Man.

During the twentieth century kippers were a common breakfast dish. Their popularity was due partly to the abundance of the catch, partly to the fact that processing was industrialized; however, their quality suffered as herring in poor condition were cured and coloured with coal tar dyes. To make Manx kippers, normally sold in pairs, the fattest, freshest herring are smoked over oak chippings. The best way to cook them is in simmering water. To remove the many tiny bones, lay them skin uppermost, peel that off, then rub butter over the flesh and pull it away from the backbone. **MR**

Taste: *The rich flavour from the oak smoking is key to a good kipper, but so is the freshness and oiliness of the fish. A kipper should be succulent, never "fishy," and not too salty.*

Kippers take on their distinctive rich colour and flavour during their time in the smokehouse. »

Maatjes Herring

Surströmming

A herring is referred to as a "virgin" when it has produced neither sperm nor eggs: it has the unique privilege of becoming a virgin again after spawning. The word "maatje"—used to describe the delicious new season herring of the Netherlands—is derived from the term for a virgin, *maagd*.

Each year at the end of May, when the fish are in peak condition (with a minimum 16 per cent fat content), the season begins. In the past, the first barrel of fish landed was offered to the Queen. Today, it is auctioned and sold for charity in the port of Scheveningen as part of the *Vlaggetjesdag* (Flag Day) festivities. From then, until July, maatjes herring are known as *hollandse nieuwe*.

Although there are recipes for cooking maatjes herring, the Dutch like to eat the fillets raw, from street stalls. They may be sampled either simply sprinkled with a little salt or with the addition of chopped raw onion, maybe on a slice of bread. The key to quality is their freshness. They should be eaten within hours of catching and filleted to order before oxidation begins to mar the taste. **MR**

Neither the name, which means "sour herring," nor the pungent, clinging smell, reminiscent of a mix between rotten eggs and sewage, deters the faithful from this traditional Swedish delicacy. In northern Sweden, devotees celebrate its annual premiere, traditionally on the third Thursday in August, with outdoor parties and orgies of consumption.

Until recently a staple in some parts of Sweden, surströmming is made with fermented (not rotten) herring. In the old days, quite possibly from as early as the fifteenth century, fermentation was an alternative to curing with salt or smoke. Today the treatment is most popular in northern Sweden, where most surströmming is produced on the island of Ulvön. A little over a million cans are produced each year, and although a growing number make their way abroad to countries such as Japan, many palates remain unconvinced of its appeal.

Surströmming is eaten with almond potato, finely chopped onion and a type of flatbread known as *tunnbröd*. It is preferably accompanied by beer and *snaps* (schnapps), but some prefer milk. **CC**

Taste: *The flesh is white and soft, with all but the tiniest bones removed, and the skin is a bright gunmetal blue. It has a sweetish, seaweedy taste allied to a touch of oiliness.*

Taste: *Surströmming has an unusual sweet, but mildly salty taste, with an overpowering pungency reminiscent of a well-matured cheese, that lingers on the palate.*

Maatjes herrings have been packed into wooden
⊗ *barrels for centuries; salted herring was a ship's food.*

Gravlax

In the past, salmon was an important staple for Scandinavians. It could be caught in large quantities as the fish, which live in salt water, migrated up rivers and streams each spring to spawn. Yet in the mountainous north, where transportation was difficult, preserving Atlantic salmon was vital, and the most popular method seems to have been fermentation using a small amount of salt. The fish was buried in a *grav* (grave) or hole in the ground, hence the name gravlax.

This process became professionalized in Jämtland, now in central Sweden, as early as 1348. During the seventeenth century it grew into a method closer to that we know today: a sweet cure using salt, sugar, and dill.

Known as gravlax or gravad lax in Sweden, and gravlaks in Norway and Denmark, in mainland Scandinavia farmed salmon is used for this preparation as stocks in the Atlantic and the Baltic are under pressure. Whatever the name, this form of salmon remains an essential element of any Scandinavian smorgasbord. **CC**

Taste: *Gravlax should be served with a dill and mustard sauce. The texture is soft, slightly sticky, and almost melts in the mouth. It tastes salty, sweet, and distinctly of dill.*

Balik Smoked Salmon

Balik is the brand name for a style of mild cured smoked salmon. It is produced in Switzerland using Norwegian farmed fish, although the makers insist that its roots belong to Tsarist Russia. Except that salmon and other freshwater fish were then generally smoked with resinous rather than hardwoods, the old Russian techniques mirror those practised in Britain, where whole cured sides of salmon are laid out and thin slivers are carved on the slant leaving only the skin behind.

A Tsar Nikolaj® fillet—Balik's flagship product—is skinless. The thin membrane over the flesh is pared away, as is the meat forming the belly flap, leaving a single strip of boneless, lean, pink salmon. This is then cut into vertical slices about ⅓ inch (1 cm) thick. Balik, which also manufactures cuts of salmon similar to gravlax, has gained international renown by having its products sold at the chain of Caviar House bars located in airports, alongside other luxury items such as caviar and Champagne. Balik smoked salmon is presented on special boards on which the fillets have been carved. **MR**

Taste: *As the cure is so mild and has not really penetrated the flesh, Balik is not dissimilar to Japanese raw fish. It has a smooth, melting texture with a rich and quite oily flavour.*

Smoked Trout

Smoked Hilsa

Although fish was once smoked to preserve it, today the process is used to impart flavour. There are two types of smoked trout, hot smoked and cold smoked. Hot smoked trout, the more common, is fully cooked by the smoking process, whereas cold smoked trout is a "cured" product, using cool smoke to leave it still, to some degree, raw. Hot smoking is carried out in a kiln, using various hardwoods; oak gives a strong taste, beech is milder. Hickory is popular in the United States, whereas in parts of northern and eastern Europe juniper is used.

The ready availability of farmed rainbow trout has standardized quality. The fish is ideally suited to the smoking process, having a high percentage (around 20 per cent) body fat. At its best, smoked trout is prepared whole, the skin insulating the flesh against the heat and preventing it drying out, but fillets of larger fish may also be handled in this way. Served as a starter, hot smoked trout has a natural affinity with creamed horseradish, which modulates its oiliness. In Scandinavia, it is often accompanied by a glass of ice cold *snaps* (schnapps). **MR**

Hilsa (*Tenualosa ilisha*) is a silvery tropical fish that spends much of its life in the sea, but in late February it leaves the Bay of Bengal and migrates inland to lay its eggs in rivers across the Indian subcontinent, leading many to think of it as a freshwater fish.

Fish is integral to Bengali food and it is cooked in a dazzling variety of ways. But the fish Bengalis prize above all is hilsa, which is also known as *ilish* or *elish*. Hilsa is the national fish of Bangladesh (East Bengal) and many fish lovers there and in West Bengal, especially the capital Calcutta, consider smoked hilsa the best way to savour this oily fish.

Bengali cuisine is characterized by its sweet and spicy mixture of flavours, in which mustard, whether from the seeds or the oil, figures prominently. Smoked hilsa is often prepared with a paste of ground mustard seeds, salt, mustard oil, and turmeric, then wrapped in banana leaves, and cooked with rice. Along with dishes such as railway mutton curry, smoked hilsa is a traditional Anglo-Indian delicacy that is still found on many Indian restaurant menus with a retro twist. **CK**

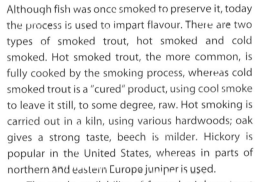

Taste: *Trout are lightly flavoured, but they absorb the aromas of brining and smoking. The texture is quite firm and the meat will flake when teased with a fork.*

Taste: *Smoked hilsa has a delicate texture and aroma. Extremely sweet, juicy, and tender, it delivers a pungent, spicy kick. A very bony fish, it is usually served boned.*

Smoked Eel

Once popular with the Maori of New Zealand, smoked eel is eaten all around the world today, but is probably most highly prized in the Netherlands.

Eels living in European rivers and lakes travel to the Sargasso Sea, a calm patch of the Atlantic rich in sargasso seaweed, on an extraordinary journey to spawn. The best time to catch them is just before they start to migrate, when they are at their fattest and largest. They should be kept alive until the moment they are processed in order to retain their taste and succulence.

Once killed, the eels are gutted and brined or dry salted before being hot smoked in a kiln over hardwood, typically oak or beech. To eat the eels, known as *gerookte paling*, the Dutch peel away the golden, oily skin and eat the flesh directly off the bones. In less atavistic circumstances they may eat the fillets with a creamed horseradish sauce, as do their neighbours in northern Germany and Scandinavia. European eel populations are currently under intense pressure and fishing of wild stocks is strictly regulated by the industry. **MR**

Smoked Mackerel

The smoking of fish to enable long-term storage goes back thousands of years. Fishermen may well have accidentally discovered the effects of smoking fish when drying their catch over a fire. However, since the advent of refrigeration, fish tend to be smoked for their enhanced flavour and texture rather than for preservation.

The oily-fleshed, torpedo-shaped mackerel is perfectly suited to smoking as a culinary treatment and responds to it incredibly well. Mackerel is typically hot smoked, which helps give the fish its characteristically flaky texture. (In general, cold smoking tends to impart the flavours of smoking without affecting the nature of the fish's flesh, because no actual cooking takes place.)

Smoked mackerel is usually sold in vacuum packs or canned in oil; the best brands use extra virgin olive oil. One very special product to look out for is the Beech Smoked Mackerel from the Spanish company Don Reinaldo; softly smoked and packed in olive oil, they offer smoked mackerel at its irresistible best. **LF**

Taste: *Smoked eels are oily, smoky, and rich, almost fatty, under the skin. Their texture is firm and compact—they should not flake—and their taste should not be fishy.*

Taste: *Smoked mackerel has a full, but rounded, almost buttery flavour with a light, balanced smokiness. Its moist, juicy texture comes from the fish rather than the oil.*

Gutted mackerel are suspended directly over the heat of the smokehouse to ensure that they cook. »

Tallinn Kilud

Small, silvery, and piquant, kilud are the celebrated preserved Baltic sprats (*Sprattus sprattus balticus*) that hail from Estonia. They are a particular speciality of Tallinn, the capital city. Too small to be filleted, kilud come with head and guts intact, packed tightly into small cans and spiced with up to twenty spices, including nutmeg, cloves, cinnamon, and black pepper. Each of the bright blue pocket-sized tins traditionally contains a bay leaf.

Salted sprats have long been a staple food in Estonia. The poorer people who lived further inland would come to the coast to trade their grain for fish, which would be salted and cured in huge wooden barrels. Modern methods of preparing kilud are thought to be based on those used as long ago as the sixteenth century, when the sprats enjoyed a reputation for being especially sweet. With the advent of canning, the legend of the Tallinn kilud was born; the cans carry a picturesque image of the medieval skyline of Old Tallinn, which inspired the phrase "sprat-can skyline," an expression now used to describe the view of Tallinn from the sea. **LF**

Taste: *Deliciously sweet, with warm spicy overtones, kilud have an overall softness with the pleasant, slightly crunchy texture of tiny yielding bones.*

The Tallinn skyline, familiar to
⊘ *all purchasers of canned kilud.*

Arbroath Smokie

Smoked Snoek

The dramatic seascape dominates the east coast of Scotland, and for centuries the villages that scatter the cliff tops and the harbours were built on fishing, most often of haddock. Like other smoked fish, Arbroath Smokies (PGI) originated as a method of preservation in the days before refrigeration.

Arbroath Smokies are unusual in two ways: the fish are smoked whole, complete with bones, and they are smoked in pairs. The haddock are gutted, beheaded, and dry-salted for two hours to draw out excess moisture from the skin. Then they are tied in pairs, hung over wooden rods, and washed to remove the salt before smoking over oak or beech. The method was first developed in the village of Auchmithie in the early nineteenth century, but the fish acquired its name as people moved to the larger town of Arbroath further south.

The best way to eat an Arbroath Smokie is "hot off the barrel"—still warm from the smoking process. Otherwise it may be split open and the bone removed before being eating cold or warmed with a chunk of butter in the cavity. **CTr**

Smoked snoek is considered a South African national treasure in much the same way as Parma ham (prosciutto di Parma) is for Italians. It is important, however, not to confuse smoked snoek with its inexpensive cousin, salt snoek.

A cousin of the mackerel, snoek (*Thyrsites atun*) is found in the temperate waters of the southern hemisphere. It should not be mistaken for a type of bass found in the Gulf of Mexico known as snook. In New Zealand and Australia, it is called barracouta, but is not related to the fierce barracuda (though, in the seventeenth century, some of the men of Jan van Riebeeck, the founder of Cape Town, apparently lost their fingers to the fish). Highly popular in South Africa, snoek has even made its own contribution to Cape slang: "Slat my dood met 'n pap snoek," which literally translates to "kill me with a soggy snoek."

Snoek can be cooked in numerous ways. In South Africa, smoked snoek is usually made into pâtés and spreads, but it is also served flaked with tomatoes and peppers in a type of kedgeree dish called *smoor-snoek* (smothered snoek). **HFi**

Taste: *The texture is soft, melting, and flaky. The fresh fish flavour is nicely balanced with a touch of salt and rich smoke. Each component should enhance the other.*

Taste: *Salty in taste, but wonderfully textured because of partial drying and smoking, smoked snoek flakes off the astounding number of vicious-looking bones quite easily.*

Bombay Duck

Although the name conjures up a creature of the feathered variety, Bombay duck (*Harpadon nehereus*) is in fact fish, not fowl. Also known as bummalow, it is found in Asian waters, especially in the estuaries and coastal waters of India, including those around Mumbai (formerly Bombay).

In India, the fish is sometimes served fresh, but the vast majority of it is filleted, salted, and dried in the hot sun. After drying, the fish has an incredibly powerful smell. One story connects its name to during the British Raj when the fish was transported by train and the compartments would reek of it. Brits nicknamed the odour "Bombay dak," after the train

Die-hard Indian food fanatics consider Bombay duck a culinary delight, especially when it is ground and sprinkled over curries. Once commonly served at Indian restaurants in the United Kingdom until the European Union banned it because it was not factory made, it is now available again.

To prepare Bombay duck, fry it for a few minutes and serve hot with poppadoms or a curry. It can also be made into a pickle. **LF**

Taste: *Dried bombay duck has a rather brittle texture that crumbles in the mouth and a love-it-or-loathe-it piquancy, with salty overtones of which anchovy lovers will approve.*

Salt Cod

In Portugal, it is known as *bacalhau*; in Italian *baccalá*; in Spain *bacalao*; in France *morue*; in English, it is simply salt cod. Whatever the language, with modern technology and refrigeration, salting foods in order to preserve them is no longer a necessity, although for hundreds of years, salting and drying was the main method used for preserving fish. But, because salting actually changes the flavour and texture of the fish so superbly, salt cod now belongs in the luxury league.

Over-fishing in the North Atlantic has driven cod stocks to near collapse, so prices have rocketed. It is possible now to find salted Pacific cod and some processors have started to substitute other species of fish such as ling, haddock, and pollack.

Supermarkets in Portugal and Spain have whole counters selling huge flat pieces of salt cod. It looks rather shrivelled and unappetizing, but after soaking for between one and two days, it can be used in a number of fabulous recipes; it makes a great match with good olive oil. It is superb in crisp batter and irresistible in garlic-laced *brandade de morue*. **LF**

Taste: *Reconstituted and cooked, salt cod has a firm but moist, flaky texture and gloriously gutsy, savoury flavour with faintly brackish overtones.*

Mosciame del Tonno

Bottarga di Muggine

This mouth-watering Italian speciality is made from strips of tuna that have been salt cured and sun-dried following ancient methods used by the Phoenicians and subsequently continued by the Romans. Drying in the coastal breezes adds a wonderful depth of flavour to the fish, turning it a rich, red brown colour. In Spain, it is called *mojama*; dolphin dried in a similar way is known as musciame.

Mosciame is thought to have originated in Liguria, although it is now linked with Carloforte, an island off the south of Sardinia. It was introduced by Ligurian fishermen who settled there in the 1700s. The tuna loins are first cleaned and then cured in sea salt. After rinsing, they are hung out to dry in the Mediterranean sun and air, causing the tuna to dehydrate and lose up to half its weight.

Mosciame looks very like the cured Italian beef bresaola, and it is often served in much the same way—in paper thin slices, drizzled with extra virgin olive oil and a squirt of lemon. Also delicious grated into pasta or salads, mosciame is sometimes used in the traditional Genoese dish *cappon magro*. **LF**

Bottarga di muggine is the roe of the female grey mullet. The finest comes from the salty waters of Lake Cabras, in western Sardinia. Sometimes referred to as "the poor man's caviar," this is a fantastic creation in its own right and deserves to be recognized as such.

The roe, which is extracted in one whole piece, is cleaned and salted before being lightly pressed, then washed and dried in the sun. The resulting product is shaped like a long tear drop about 4 to 7 inches (10–18 cm) long and is golden amber in colour. Traditionally enclosed in wax and sold in pairs, today bottarga di muggine is more likely to be vacuum-wrapped in plastic.

After removing the thin surrounding membrane, the bottarga can be cut into wafer thin slices and dressed with good extra virgin olive oil and lemon juice. But, possibly the most delicious and typical way of serving it is to shave or grate it over freshly cooked spaghetti. Ideally, bottarga di muggine should not be bought ready-grated, and it should never be cooked. **LF**

Taste: *Extremely lean and tender, mosciame responds well to good olive oil. It has a pronounced, almost meaty flavour like cured ham, but with subtle fishy overtones.*

Taste: *Bottarga di muggine has a delicately briny, but not overly fishy flavour that opens up on the palate, energizing the taste buds and hinting gently of spice.*

Beeswax is traditionally used to preserve the freshness of the cured roe—bottarga di muggine. ❯❯

Monkfish Liver

A traditional delicacy in Japan, where it is called *ankimo*, this alluring ingredient is beginning to appear in a growing number of kitchens—both in homes and restaurants—around the world. Naturally rich, monkfish liver achieves a silky, melt-in-the-mouth texture when cooked, which has earned it the nickname of the "foie gras of the sea."

The typical monkfish liver weighs in at over 1 pound (450 g). Before cooking, it is often lightly seasoned and marinated—traditionally salted and soaked in sake or mirin—then wrapped into a cylinder and steamed or simmered. Sometimes the liver is battered and deep-fried, to be served with layers of minced or sliced tuna meat. It lends itself best to presentations that include light, fresh, crisp flavours that complement the liver's richness, while allowing its delicate taste to prevail. Presentations initially tended towards "fusion" treatments in which the liver was sliced in small portions and paired with ponzu sauce, perhaps also with seaweed salad or shredded daikon. More recently, U.S. and European chefs have favoured preparations similar to those for duck or goose foie gras.

At the time of writing, monkfish populations are under threat from over-fishing for the huge Chinese and Japanese markets and, latterly, also the European and North American markets, where demand is increasing specifically due to greater appreciation of the liver, rather than the meat. To conserve world stocks, all forms of the fish are best avoided. A ten-year plan to rebuild New England and mid-Atlantic monkfish stocks was implemented in 1999, and in time will hopefully result in better controlled, sustainable fisheries. **CN**

Taste: *The rich texture of classic foie gras pairs with the fresh, briny flavour of simply steamed shellfish, creating a delicacy that more than justifies its gourmet status.*

Potted Shrimp

Potted shrimps are identified with Morecambe Bay, a treacherous expanse of inter-tidal mudflats off the Lancashire coast in England. The small brown shrimps are netted by fishermen who cook their catch by dropping them briefly into boiling seawater to guarantee freshness. (People who live around Morecambe Bay believe that shrimps taste sweeter and juicier when simmered in fresh rather than salted water, but this is a privilege only available to those who go shrimping for their own account, rather than buy a commercial product.) When the tide recedes from the vast area of mud it is possible to catch the shrimps without a boat, and a handful of local fishermen drive tractors over the flats at low tide trailing nets through the shallow water.

The "potting" stage of the process is done on land. First the small crustaceans are chilled. The head and carapace are pulled off and the flesh is squeezed and twisted out of the tail. Removing the flesh is a labour-intensive operation because no machine can do the work; a good picker extracts no more than 1 pound (700 g) of meat in an hour.

The shrimp meat is then packed in pots with butter, seasoned with pepper and nutmeg, then coated with a second layer of clarified butter that insulates the food from the air, helping to preserve it. Shrimps cost more than butter, and so the higher the proportion of tails in the product, the better the quality will usually be.

Potted shrimp is eaten with hot brown toast or crusty brown bread, sometimes served with a wedge of lemon, or in cucumber sandwiches in which the potted shrimp takes the place of butter. It is also served as a starter with green salads. **MR**

Taste: *The sweet shellfish taste balances the salty, iodine flavour and the fattiness of the butter. Spices add an extra piquancy. Potted shrimp taste best eaten with hot toast.*

In Morecambe Bay, England, shrimp are cooked as soon as they are caught to preserve their freshness. »

Taramosalata

Icre

The stridently pink, fishy slurry sold very cheaply in European supermarkets is a travesty of this subtle and delicious meze. The custom of eating mezes is rooted in Greece, Turkey, and Lebanon, and taramosalata is to be found in all three countries, though it is most commonly associated with Greece.

Historically the salted, cured roe used to make taramosalata was from the grey mullet. Carp roe has also been used, but both these have become scarce and so more expensive, leading to widespread use of cod roe instead. The roe is pounded with olive oil, lemon, a small quantity of finely chopped onion (but never garlic), and either bread or mashed potato, which makes it go further and softens the very strong tasting roe.

Now available all year round, taramosalata was traditionally a Lenten fasting food, as it contains no meat or dairy products. Properly made, its colour varies from pale pink to pink tinged with coral. It is often served as an appetizer, or with alcoholic drinks, as the Greeks consider it decadent to drink without eating something at the same time. **AMS**

Today we think of caviar as a Russian contribution to the world's list of gourmet foods, but history suggests it was the Chinese who first made caviar-not with sturgeon roe, but with the eggs of the river fish carp. Genghis Khan took Chinese caviar with him when he invaded Russia, but sturgeon soon gained supremacy as the roe of choice because of its attractive colour.

Although taramosalata made with cod roe has become a national dish in Greece, it has long been produced in southeastern Europe using carp roe. Carp plays an important part in Balkan cuisine, especially in Romania, where their version of taramosalata has the unfortunate name (at least to English language-speakers) of *Icre de crap* (the latter word being Romanian for carp). After removing the membrane on the carp roe, it is salted, and left until the roe turns orange. It is then pounded with fresh breadcrumbs and blended with oil so that it emulsifies with the roe. Seasoned with lemon juice, salt, and sometimes finely chopped onion, it is eaten on crackers or rye bread for a tasty snack. **WS**

Taste: *Often served decorated with black olives, taramosalata is eaten in its home countries simply with bread which enables appreciation of its delicate taste.*

Taste: *Icre has a soft, creamy texture and a delicate fishy flavour that is less salty and strong than commercial taramosalata. Naturally cured, it has a warm orange hue.*

In the eastern Mediterranean, taramosalata and
❦ other meze dishes are commonly enjoyed al fresco.

Kazunoko

Salmon Roe

The salted and preserved eggs harvested from the ovaries of female herring, kazunoko is an expensive delicacy in Japan, where it is known as "yellow diamonds." Although available throughout the year, especially in sushi shops, it is during New Year festivities that most kazunoko is sold, as it is an essential part of the New Year cuisine known as *Osechi ryori*. The ingredients used to make *Osechi ryori* are chosen for their symbolism; the abundance of eggs (one ovary may contain 100,000 of them) in kazunoko symbolizes prosperity and fertility, both of which are hoped for in the coming year.

There are two types: hoshi kazunoko is slightly harder as it is more dried than salted, and shio kazunoko is more salted than dried, and therefore softer. Both should be soaked in water before using, to remove some of the saltiness, although ready-to-eat versions are also available. In sushi shops, it is served thinly sliced as a topping for *nigiri zushi*, or marinated in a mixture of sake, mirin, dashi, and soy sauce. Kazunoko will keep refrigerated for a couple of weeks, and freezes well. **SB**

A brilliant, deep, glassy orange and bursting with sweet, rich salmon fish oil, these impressive eggs are not for the faint-hearted. But anyone who enjoys caviar will love them.

Salmon roe eggs are juicy and inviting, and are used extensively as a stand-alone hors d'oeuvre or to finish canapés and *nori maki* sushi. Eggs harvested from the Pacific species of chum or dog salmon are considered to be the finest, although other salmon roe can also be used.

After gutting the "hen" (female) fish, workers remove the eggs, each of which resembles a pea in size. The eggs are rinsed and tenderly separated from the delicate membrane that holds them in place, before being packed in a salt solution.

Like caviar, salmon roe is best served simply, so that it can be seen and admired. Soured cream and blinis make a fantastic accompaniment, it stands out beautifully on canapés, and in Japan it is most often used as an outstanding decorative finish to sushi. In Japan, the orange coloured spheres were once favoured as fish bait. **STS**

Taste: *Kazunoko is crunchy, hard, salty, and satisfyingly savoury; comparable to a crunchy bottarga, but with a touch more bitterness.*

Taste: *The flavour is a mix of honey, the sea, and the rich oils of raw salmon. The initial mouthfeel is a soft yielding ball that with one bite releases the oil-rich fish contents.*

The red colour of salmon roe, here on sale in Kyoto, contributes to the visual appeal of Japanese cuisine. »

Crab Roe

The decadent unctuousness of crab roe has earned it luxury status throughout Asia, where it is used to garnish steamed dumplings and seafood dishes, enrich soups and sauces, or is simply enjoyed au naturel, scooped out of the cooked crab shells. (When present, male crab milt is often referred to as roe in Asian restaurants, probably because "crab sperm" does not sound quite as appealing.)

Shanghai cuisine's seasonal hairy crabs (named for their furry claws) are beloved for their abundant sticky orange roe. In Hong Kong, a particular crab species is named yellow oil crab.

Around South East Asia, large mud crabs are the most popular source of roe. One unusual southern Chinese dish cures raw mud crab in a bath of soy sauce and spices for a couple of days; the marinating process transforms the roe into a vivid vermilion paste. In the Philippines, the roe of small crabs is a delicacy known as *taba ng talangka*. It is cooked with garlic and calamansi juice and eaten with rice. In the southern United States, crab roe appears in she-crab soup, a cross between a bisque and a chowder. **CTa**

Wasabi Tobiko

Wasabi tobiko, the processed eggs of the flying fish, is becoming increasingly popular outside of Japan for its striking appearance and versatility. Tobiko comes in various colours and flavours, including bright green wasabi flavour, dark green with a jalapeno kick, and black flavoured with squid ink. Tobiko is popular as a topping for *gunkan maki*, or "battleship sushi," where ingredients are placed on top of an oblong of rice and held in place with nori seaweed. Farmed capelin roe (*masago*) from Iceland and Denmark is sometimes passed off as tobiko.

Tobiko is valued more for its texture than its flavour. In its natural state it has a pale yellow colour and is rather tasteless, but perhaps its best quality is its resilience. Hard and crunchy, these tiny eggs, smaller than caviar, do not fall apart when handled. The eggs are first removed from the fish and washed in a centrifuge to free them from their membrane. They are then frozen and sent for further processing. The eggs are salted and, in the case of ordinary tobiko, coloured orange, or with wasabi tobiko, coloured vivid green and flavoured with wasabi. **SB**

Taste: *Roe flavours vary, but have in common a pure, sweet distillation of crab character and umami, melded with the tongue-coating richness of every kind of yolk.*

Taste: *Crunchy and refreshing as the small, loose eggs burst open in the mouth, they have a salty sweetness and a hint of brininess, followed by the heat of wasabi.*

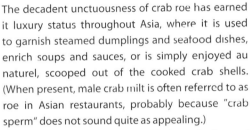

A crab boat laden with crab pots and their bright marker buoys approaches Newfoundland, Canada.

Beluga Caviar

A king's ransom is the price paid for this exceptional and exquisite caviar—the lightly salted roe of female sturgeon from the Caspian and Black Seas—and it must be the ultimate luxury food. Although other countries now produce fine caviar, Russian and Iranian caviar retain their historically high status. Beluga caviar comes from the grandest, oldest, largest, and rarest sturgeon (*Huso huso*). The Beluga sturgeon takes twenty years to reach maturity, hence the hefty price tag on the roe.

Beluga eggs are steely grey in colour and larger than sevruga or osciotr (osetra), both of which come from other species of sturgeon, and with beluga make up the caviar "holy trinity." The eminence of caviar has led to all three species being severely over-fished, especially in the Black Sea; those in the Caspian Sea are now protected. Caviar d' Aquitaine makes a sustainable and delicious alternative. Beluga caviar is best served simply, with thin toast or with blinis and sour cream. Caviar should never be served with a metal spoon or from a metal bowl, as they alter the taste of the eggs. **STS**

Caviar d'Aquitaine

Think of the origins of caviar and most will pinpoint Russia, Iran, and the Caspian Sea. However, since the first half of the twentieth century caviar produced from wild sturgeon caught in the estuaries of the Gironde and Aquitaine has fast gained recognition.

Exploitation and destruction of habitat are increasingly bringing many species to the brink of extinction. But, there is now an excellent, guilt-free caviar coming from Aquitaine where the Siberian baeri sturgeon is being farmed very successfully. The baeri sturgeon thrives in the warmer French waters. In Siberia, sturgeon take between fifteen and twenty years to reach maturity, whereas in Aquitaine it takes half the time.

The young male sturgeon are identified using ultrasound technology. They are culled at the age of three to four years and then sent to the wet fish trade as exceptional sturgeon fillets. Meanwhile, the females are nurtured until their eggs are considered to be a sufficient size and quality to harvest. The eggs have a deep grey colour and release a pale yellow oil when pressed. **STS**

Taste: *Soft and creamy in texture, the oil in the centre of the eggs delivers a hint of walnut. Premium caviar labelled "Imperial" is from the largest, lightest-coloured eggs.*

These cans of Russian caviar cans are colour-coded: red for sevruga, yellow for osetra, and blue for beluga.

Taste: *The caviar from Aquitaine is perfumed with a light, delicate, almost smoky flavour with a long lingering taste of cream cheese, likened by some to a ripe Brie.*

Mantis Shrimp

The marine equivalent of the praying mantis, this peculiar crustacean is so called because of its enlarged pair of grasping forelimbs. Fast moving and difficult to catch, mantis shrimp can grow to about 8 inches (20 cm) in length. Solitary creatures, they burrow themselves into the sand or live in crevices in reefs and rocks.

There are around 400 species of mantis shrimp, which vary from nondescript shades of brown and grey to glowing neon colours. Known as "thumb splitters" by divers, mantis shrimp aggressively use their incredibly strong claws to either smash or spear their prey. They have even been known to crack aquarium glass.

Mantis shrimp are best eaten when their ovaries are full and the flesh is firm. They are popular in Mediterranean countries, especially Italy's Romagna region, where they are simmered, peeled, and dipped in a seasoned batter before being fried. They can also be stewed or used in fish soups. In Japan, where they are known as *shako*, mantis shrimp often appear on sashimi menus. **STS**

Arctic Prawn

As the name would suggest, these crustaceans take their distinctive essence from the icy and unpolluted waters of the far north. Also known as northern or deep-water prawns, they are harvested in the Arctic—particularly around Canada and Greenland—but also in the North Atlantic and North Pacific.

The low temperatures mean that *Pandalus borealis* grows much more slowly than its relatives in warmer climates. The prawns take five or six years to reach maturity, which intensifies the flavour of the meat and improves its texture. There have been concerns regarding over-fishing, and efforts began in the 1990s to stabilize stock levels. Controls and licensing have delivered results, but the impact of global warming on cold water stocks remains to be seen.

Arctic prawns are enjoyed around the northern hemisphere, especially in Scandinavia, where they are traditionally eaten cold at midsummer with an aquavit chaser. These sweet, versatile crustaceans absorb flavours easily and lend themselves to simple, fresh, unfussy Scandinavian dishes, as well as retro favourites such as prawn cocktail. **AME**

Taste: *Their sharp shells make them tricky to open, but the tail meat well rewards the effort: fine in texture and superbly sweet in flavour, it is more like lobster than shrimp.*

Taste: *The Arctic prawn is smaller, juicier, sweeter, and more succulent than many of its relatives, the texture less stringy and more meaty, with a satisfying density.*

The insect-like appearance of the mantis shrimp's
❹ tail accounts for its alternative name of sea locust.

Marron

Probably the best eating crayfish in the world, the marron's only natural habitat is in and around the Margaret River in western Australia. Both *Cherax tenuimanus* ("hairy" marron) and *Cherax cainii* ("smooth" marron) exist in the wild in a very limited area, so recreational fishing is tightly controlled, but farming has made this luxury more available. Farmed marron thrive in Australian waters, especially around Kangaroo Island: the best are exported alive, and frozen is not recommended.

The name, from the local Aboriginal language Nyungar, means something equivalent to "bread" or "food." The world's third largest crayfish, with a weight of up to 4 pounds (1.8 kg), and a high meat-to-shell ratio, marron are dark brown in colour when mature, but turn an incendiary vermilion when plunged into hot water.

The tail meat is best served simply, as medallions with a good mayonnaise or aïoli, lemon, and freshly ground pepper; a deft chef can leave the meat of the whole claw intact. The hepatopancreas or "mustard" is prized for its sweetness and consistency. **RH**

Taste: *Marron flesh is a stark white, tinged red at the edges. The sweetly perfumed flavour offers mild hints of vanilla and nut. The claw meat is particularly stunning.*

Pattes Rouges Crayfish

These make a fantastic addition to a seafood platter, but take care not to leave live crayfish unguarded in the refrigerator, as these feisty little crustaceans will find their way out of the bowl and into anything else they fancy. Pattes rouges crayfish, also known as signal crayfish, originate from the western United States. Take care when handling them too, as they have a punchy nip.

These crayfish can grow up to about 6 inches (15 cm) in length. They look like small lobsters, but are in fact freshwater crustaceans and can survive for long periods of time out of water. This allows them to move between waterways across land. Crayfish are solitary animals and will eat anything from plants to meat, including smaller crayfish. Alive, they have greenish-brown bodies, with large claws, and a deep orange under-shell. As a mini lobster, their body is wide, but short at the tail. The claws reveal a very small morsel of meat, but generally it is only the tail that is eaten. (The claws can make magnificently flavoured shellfish stock, so should be kept.) **STS**

Taste: *Once you have managed to crack open the shell, which can be tricky as it is not brittle, the meat in the tail is beautifully sweet and succulent.*

Wooden crayfish traps; the crayfish are lured inside by a variety of baits. »

Corryvreckan Langoustine

The Corryvreckan "whirlpool"—which lies between the west coast of Scotland and the Inner Hebrides—is the second largest in Europe. Below the surface, tidal currents converge around a pillar of rock that juts from a seabed broken by a deep pit, the result of which is a maelstrom.

The langoustines that inhabit these cold and strenuous waters, at depths of up to 660 feet (200 m), grow to an extraordinary size. Whether known as scampi, Dublin Bay prawns, or simply (in Scotland) prawns, most of the langoustines that are caught off the coasts of Europe are fished with nets at a weight of about 1 to 1 ½ ounces (25–40 g). Off Corryvreckan, where they are captured in traps like lobsters, they can reach as much as 1 pound (450 g) in weight.

Like other crustaceans, *Nephrops norvegicus* must be cooked fresh out of the water and from live to be eaten at their best. Those prepared in seawater and seaweed at the Crinan Hotel in the tiny port of the same name where they are landed are the finest of all. Live langoustines are shipped around the world in tubes, but are never quite so delicious. **MR**

Taste: *Only the tail of the Corryvreckan langoustine is usually eaten. The firm meatiness coupled with the sweetness of the tail meat are utterly unique.*

Langoustines that survive the turbulent seas below
the Corryvreckan whirlpool grow to an impressive size.

Audresselles Lobster

Beloved of French and Dutch aristocrats since the sixteenth and seventeenth centuries, the Audresselles lobster encapsulates the very finest elements of the European lobster. Known in France as *homard bleu*, the exquisite "royal" Audresselles is found off the coast of Brittany.

An uncooked European lobster can vary a little in colour, depending on its habitat, however, the Audresselles lobster is renowned for its stunning dark Prussian blue shell fading to a cream underside, and white freckles along the side of the tail shell and carapace. It is also famed for the sweet flavour of its meat and was once the highlight at banquets.

Lobster meat is always served cooked, whether it be in lobster thermidor or simply boiled for a salad. The meat also makes excellent bisques. The claws are of a particularly delicate nature and it is worth hunting for the meat in the small legs, too, because it is sweet and succulent. When buying a cooked lobster it is important to check the body feels solid and that the tail is tucked tightly under the body, because this shows the animal was cooked fresh. **STS**

Taste: *Audresselles lobster encompasses everything good about seafood. The tail meat has a fibrous, dense texture with a sweetness of flavour that is hard to beat.*

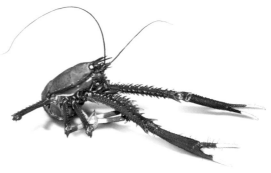

Moreton Bay Bug

Neither the name nor the appearance of the Moreton Bay bug are calculated to appeal to dinner guests: it looks rather like an alien trilobite, or a creature out of *Jurassic Park*. Yet this delicious type of lobster yields a sweet, versatile flesh that is equally good boiled, barbecued, or incorporated into a variety of sauces.

Biologically *Thenus orientalis*, the Moreton Bay bug is found off Australia's northern coast, as well as in the Indian Ocean and western parts of the Pacific. It goes by a range of names, but takes its Anglo-Saxon name from the bay outside Brisbane. Along with its good, but less good, cousin the Balmain bug (*Ibacus peronii*), it often appears as a by-product of prawn and scallop trawling.

Commonly found in local fish markets already cooked to a vibrant orange, the tail meat is the only edible part. The green meat from uncooked bugs has excellent applications in sauces, ravioli, or other dumplings. Tossed with ginger and Chinese greens or sautéed in butter and served over fresh egg fettuccine, Moreton Bay bug meat is sublime. **RH**

Taste: *Freshly cooked Moreton Bay bug is firm and sweet with background notes of ozone and nutmeg, much enhanced by cooking on an open grill.*

Squat Lobster

Squat lobster can be a confusing title since it is used fairly indiscriminately around the world to describe many kinds of crustaceans that look like lobster, but are not. So North Americans often call langoustines this, and stubby, clawless slipper lobsters are also referred to as "squats." True squats are members of the Galatheidae family that includes over seventy species, few of which are fished commercially.

Galathea squamifera thrives off the northwest coast of Scotland and the Orkney Isles. It was overlooked for years because of the flourishing langoustine fishery. Caught in creels, about the size of a crayfish, up to nearly 2 inches (4 cm) long, it contains little meat in the tail, but this is well worth prising out of the shell. Chestnut brown or red and blue in its natural habitat, it turns reddish-orange when boiled. It is only at its very best when cooked from live. The most efficient way of preparing them is to make a bisque with the carapace and serve the shells separately. Because the fishing industry has only begun to exploit squat lobsters, they are considered to be a sustainable species. **MR**

Taste: *It takes two or three squat lobster tails to make a mouthful, but their taste and texture has the characteristic crustacean flavour: very sweet, quite juicy, and chewy.*

Lobster creels wait on the quayside at Stromness, the second-largest settlement in the Orkney Isles. »

MADE IN MAINE.

Maine Lobster

Pitu

Cool ocean water and plenty of rocky shoreline helped cement the iconic relationship between Maine and its beloved lobster (*Homarus americanus*).

Although the first recorded Maine lobster catch was in 1605, it is believed humans consumed the crustacean long before then. Once so abundant it was considered poor man's food, today lobster is a dish of luxury, often served on special occasions. There is some debate over the sustainability of lobster though, prompting lobstermen to establish conservation methods and minimum size limits. It is one of the few foods still sold live in U.S. markets.

Most lobster is sold in its hard-shell form, though soft-shell lobster can be found. Some claim soft-shell lobsters produce sweeter meat and are easier to break open. Generally boiled, steamed, or grilled, meat from the tail is white in colour. Its bite is more firm and dense than the tender claw and knuckle meat, but both have a deeply rich flavour. Though usually a dark brownish colour, rare blue, yellow, or even two-toned lobsters have been caught—all turn bright red when boiled. **CLH**

With its impressive pair of claws, its exceptional meat, and its remarkable size, the pitu, or camarão, is the king of freshwater prawns. It frequents the rivers and estuaries of Latin America, but is most commonly associated with Brazil. The pitu's colour varies depending on where it is fished. At times almost translucent, it can range from terracotta to cinnamon-brown. It is also referred to as *puti*, *canela*, and *camarão verdadeiro* (real prawn).

This prawn is more mildly flavoured than its marine cousins and can reach up to a length of 10 ½ inches (27 cm) and a colossal 14 ounces (400 g) in weight. Its meat is wonderfully delicate and is perfectly cooked after only a short time, when it changes to a pinky colour. It is commonly found in traditional stews such as *moquecas* and *escaldados*.

When Portuguese colonizers first landed on the Bahian coast of Brazil during the 1500s, pitu was one of the foods that the indigenous people brought them as a gift. A staple of the Brazilian dining table for centuries, it is gaining increasing popularity among the country's top chefs. **AL**

Taste: The sweetest, most succulent meat is found in the tail and claws. Maine lobster can be dressed lightly with mayonnaise for a summertime favourite—the lobster roll.

Taste: Similar to a lobster in flavour, the pitu is fantastic when grilled. Only a few drops of Sicilian lime and a drizzle of extra virgin olive oil are needed to bring out its qualities.

These buoys in Ellsworth, Maine, enable fishermen to locate their traps and collect their harvest.

Dungeness Crab

Yellow Oil Crab

The Dungeness crab (*Cancer magister*) is one of the most iconic foods of North America's Pacific Coast. This large, plump crab with sweet, delicious meat is sustainably harvested from California to Alaska, but takes its name from a tiny spot on the shores of Washington State, Dungeness. The town was named after a promontory on the south coast of England by the eighteenth-century explorer Captain Vancouver.

What sets Dungeness apart from other crabs is its size—typically around 2 pounds (900 g). One crab is ideal for a single serving, and both the body and legs are packed with meat. Most crab-lovers prefer to enjoy Dungeness in its simplest form: steamed or boiled and eaten straight from the shell, warm or cold. Many like it plain, untouched by melted butter, mayonnaise, or cocktail sauce. In-shell crab portions can be quickly stir-fried with seasonings such as ginger, garlic, and spring onions for added flavour, or added to a pot of *cioppino*, the Mediterranean-style seafood stew from San Francisco. The meat can be used in countless dishes from the classic crab Louis salad to the ubiquitous crab cakes. **CN**

In these days of global cuisine, when ingredients from all over the world seem to be available practically everywhere, those rare, truly seasonal foods are all the more special. Yellow oil crab is available for only a few months each year, from May to August, and to taste it you will have to travel to Hong Kong or southern China.

Yellow oil crabs are female mud crabs that are literally sunburnt. The scorching heat and high humidity melts the roe of the crabs into a yellow oil that permeates their entire bodies down to the tips of their golden claws. Wild crabs are considered by connoisseurs to be the best because the rich, yellow roe is said to be sweeter than that of farmed crabs. Farming, however, extends the season from just two weeks to up to three months.

The crabs must be cooked carefully so the roe does not spill out of the body. They are usually steamed (plain or with rice wine) or simmered as a *congee* or soup (a decadent version is made with shark's fin). Some chefs remove the crab roe and make it into dumplings or cook it with noodles. **KKC**

Taste: *There is a delicacy to Dungeness crab meat that includes a tender texture. The sweet meat has only the subtlest hint of briny sea flavour when steamed or boiled.*

Taste: *Yellow oil crab roe is as rich and soft as room-temperature butter. After harvesting, the crabs only live a few days so restaurants require they be ordered in advance.*

Moleche

Visit Venice in spring or autumn and the little crabs known as moleche will be a common sight at the famous Rialto market, and *moleche frite* (fried moleche) will feature on the menu of every self-respecting restaurant. Crisp on the outside but capturing the essence of the sea within, these are a delicacy well worth pursuing.

The crabs, known in English as "green crabs" or biologically as *Carcinus mediterraneus*, are at a stage in their life cycle when they are changing shells and are so soft that it is possible—and, more than that, utterly delightful—to eat them whole. They are harvested in nets between February and late April or early May, then again in October and November, along the natural channels in the lagoons of Venice.

Typically these tiny delights are soaked in beaten egg, dusted with flour, and deep fried. The act of soaking appears to purge them of their excess brine and gives a glorious crisp finish. In the Murano region, the legs are generally removed before cooking, whereas in Venice the crabs are more often than not both served and eaten whole. **LF**

Taste: *Salty, crunchy, succulent, all at once briny and sweet, moleche should be devoured hot immediately after serving with a generous squeeze of lemon.*

Hairy Crab

Shanghainese hairy crabs are rarely found outside Hong Kong and China. And anyone who does achieve this will pay a premium for doubtful quality. Like other types of crabs, hairy crabs should be cooked alive, and the quality deteriorates the longer they are out of the water.

Hairy crabs are distinguished by the long, fine hairs on their claws. They are eaten primarily for their abundant roe, rather than for the small amount of meat. What is eaten from a male crab is in fact its sexual organs and sperm. Male "roe" is softer and creamier than that of the females.

Yang Cheng Lake in Jiangsu province is the best source for hairy crabs due to the quality of the water, which gives them lighter hair and sweeter meat. The lake produces only a small percentage of the crabs on the market. Unscrupulous sellers give their crabs, sourced from other lakes, a quick dip in Yang Cheng Lake and claim it as their crabs' provenance. Genuine producers are fighting back with methods such as laser tatoos, but the counterfeiters copy these tactics as quickly as they are created. **KKC**

Taste: *These deliciously sweet, succulent crabs are traditionally eaten steamed, with a dipping sauce made from Shanghainese brown vinegar and shredded ginger.*

Stone Crab

These flat-bodied, oval-shaped crabs with extremely hard claws prized for their meat began their rise to culinary fame in 1921 when Joe Weiss, who owned a small fish shack on Miami Beach, was asked to cook a bag filled with them by a marine researcher. Weiss tossed them in a pot of boiling water, then served them chilled with mustard sauce, coleslaw, and hash brown potatoes. And so a Florida tradition was born.

Found mainly off the Atlantic coast from North Carolina to Florida and around into the Gulf of Mexico, stone crabs are believed by scientists to be right-handed since the claw on the right side is usually the largest. These crabs have the ability to regenerate their claws. For this reason, the crabs caught usually have one claw carefully removed and are then put back into the water to grow a new one. They can regenerate claws up to three or four times.

Stone crabs are usually cooked soon after harvesting; they are sold frozen but freezing can make the meat tough and stringy. Best eaten chilled, they are delicious with melted butter, but are also perfect in any dish calling for crabmeat. **SH**

Goose-necked Barnacle

Unsurprisingly, the goose-necked barnacle gets its name from its resemblance to the head or neck of a goose. In Spain, where it is known as *percebe*, there is an annual festival devoted to it in Galicia. It is also prized in parts of Latin America, and grown commercially in Canada.

A type of crustacean, the goose-necked barnacle lives on rocks and flotsam in the ocean inter-tidal zone. It has a foot that attaches the barnacle to the rock, a long soft body like the neck of a goose, and a hard shell at the top. To feed it needs the motion of the sea to bring it nutrients, and so only survives where there is considerable current or wave action.

Goose-necked barnacles are much sought after as a delicacy in several Mediterranean countries. They can be eaten raw but they are usually steamed in their shells over a seafood stock and then served immediately. This simple recipe best preserves their sublime, clean taste. The soft body has a thick skin that is easily removed after cooking by pulling the hard shell and the skin with a nail. Be prepared for squirting juices; it can be a messy affair! **STS**

Taste: *Paired with Champagne or sparkling wine, stone crab claws are a true delicacy. The sweet, flaky meat has a slight saltiness and taste of the sea.*

Taste: *Often served in clusters, algae and all, goose-necked barnacles taste similar to lobster or crab claws. But, the texture is quite different—moist, soft, and chewy.*

Stone crabs are as much a part of summer on the Florida Keys as boats and sunshine.

Telline de Camargue

Tartufo di Mare

One of the most delicious small clams in the world, the telline (*Donax trunculus*) is just one of the many native gourmet wonders of the Camargue region of France. These little delights are found just beneath the surface of the wet sand along the shoreline of the Mediterranean coast, particularly the stretch between Arles and Montpellier. They became one of the gourmet "finds" of the 1960s and have been heavily marketed in the region ever since.

The traditional method of harvest is a carefully regulated art that takes place in the morning: a net mounted onto a frame is strapped to the *tellinier*, who works back and forth along the shore gathering the molluscs in each sweep. Once harvested the tellines are soaked in water for between twelve and twenty-four hours before being served.

Popular in risotto and pasta dishes, Tellines de Camargue are traditionally enjoyed raw, cooked *à la Provençal*, or garnished with the powerful parsley and garlic mix *persillade*. A steaming bowl of tellines cooked *en persillade* can contain up to fifty little shells per serving. **STS**

One might be forgiven for staying with the rather romantic Italian name of tartufo di mare, or truffle of the sea, for this fabulous variety of shellfish; its other commonly used name is warty clam!

Tartufi di mare are similar in shape to common *vongole*. They have a chunky, solid-looking shell that is beige to brown in colour, with a distinctive covering of prominent, concentric warty ridges. The species *Venus verrucosa* is found in temperate water in parts of the Atlantic and Mediterranean; it is considered a particular delicacy in the provinces of Puglia and Friuli and around the Gulf of Naples. Like all bivalve molluscs, the clams should only be consumed during months that contain an "r" because in the summer months they are breeding. Today many of the waters around Italy are subject to a closed fishing season in late summer, therefore allowing fish stocks to replenish naturally.

Frequently served raw, tartufi di mare are exquisite when prepared in pasta sauces, often in a similar way to the classic *spaghetti alle vongole*. They also perform well in risottos and salads. **LF**

Taste: *With a sweet delicate flavour and a subtle taste of the sea, these molluscs are relished by locals and tourists alike. These are an absolute must for shellfish aficionados.*

Taste: *Tartufi di mare are silky soft in texture and pleasantly brackish on the tongue, suggesting hints of fresh sea air without being overpoweringly fishy.*

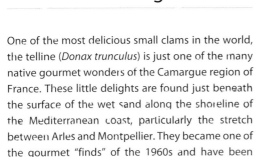

Fresh tellines are offered for sale at
⊗ *a fish market in Aix-en-Provence, France.*

STEWKEY

STIFFKEY

1975

Stewkey Blue Cockle

Littleneck Clam

The North Norfolk village of Stiffkey—once pronounced "Stewkey"—is perhaps as famous for its disgraced vicar, as for its seafood. (Harold Davidson was defrocked in 1932 for consorting with Soho prostitutes and died after being mauled by a lion.)

Stiffkey's harbour silted up towards the end of the nineteenth century and the muddy edges of the village became an excellent breeding ground for cockles with a distinctive grey-blue shell. Stewkey blues (*Cerastoderma edule*) were originally only those harvested from Stiffkey, but is now a generic term for all Norfolk cockles.

Until shortly after World War II, the women of the village harvested cockles throughout the year. Cockling is heavy and dangerous work, as the tide comes in very fast, and the Stiffkey women had Amazonian reputations. Traditionally, the cockles were boiled and eaten with vinegar, and were a popular treat for day trippers. Indeed, they can still be bought like this a little further along the coast at Wells-next-the-Sea. They can also be used instead of clams in dishes such as *spaghetti alle vongole*. **AMS**

Each coast of the United States stakes a claim to its own littleneck clam. The one on the Atlantic coast is not a distinct species. Instead, it is the smallest of the region's hard-shell clam species known as the quahog (*Mercenaria mercenaria*).

This clam is also referred to as the Little Neck clam. It is named after Little Neck Bay on Long Island in New York, which was once the region's most popular source for half-shell clams. In raw bars along the eastern seaboard, littlenecks sit perched on beds of ice, raw on the half-shell ready for slurping. It is also a favourite for the baked-clam treat clams casino, steamed with white wine, or tossed with pasta and fresh herbs.

Not quite as highly prized, the Pacific coast has the common littleneck, or native littleneck (*Protothaca staminea*). Found along the sandy shores from California to Alaska, this littleneck has a chewier texture and is usually cooked—steamed, roasted, or in a chowder. Both Atlantic and Pacific littleneck clams are farmed today, a recommended choice of sustainability watchdogs. **CN**

Taste: *The plump, fishy, succulence of Stewkey blues is best experienced by cooking them in wine, garlic, salt, and pepper until they open. Then eat them immediately.*

Taste: *The tenderness of wild Atlantic littlenecks makes them ideal for eating raw on the half-shell. They are sweet and scrumptious, with a briny hint of Long Island waters.*

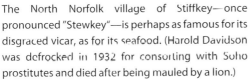

This sign at the Norfolk village of Stiffkey helpfully also supplies the original pronunciation of the name.

Toheroa

This iconic New Zealand speciality is regarded as one of the finest tasting fish, but one you are unlikely to taste fresh. *Paphies ventricosum*, a member of the clam family, is famed for having a highly developed digging tongue, and is native to only a few beaches on both the North and the South Islands. Fresh water from lagoons in the dunes results in an inshore concentration of plankton, food for the toheroa.

Toheroa can grow up to 6 inches (15 cm) long and live in the soft sands between high and low tide; their position is only detectable by a blowhole. At the least disturbance they frantically dig themselves deeper and many a hunter has been defeated by their amazing speed. Disease and over-harvesting in the past, particularly for the canning industry (there were three toheroa canning factories in New Zealand at one time), have resulted in strict prohibition of toheroa-gathering for most seasons: the last season was one solitary day in 1993. An exception is made for Maori who have traditional fishing rights, that is, who have proven toheroa is basic to their lifestyle—yet even they have limits on how many they can gather, may dig only with their hands or wood (no metal), and must gather toheroa that are at least 4 inches (10 cm) long. When permitted, New Zealanders flock to dig for the succulent creatures. In the 1950s, toheroa fritters fried in oil were a popular dish.

The smaller, more prolific tua tua clam is used as a substitute, particularly for toheroa soup. It is good, but does not equal the real thing, and also lacks the distinctive green colour deriving from the plankton in the toheroa gut. Khaki-green toheroa soup was the traditional start to the Christmas meal in New Zealand and has a wonderfully delicate flavour. **GC**

Taste: *Generally chopped and made into soups, pâtés, or fritters, the meat is a grubby green and has a rich flavour, like that of mussels but creamier and more pronounced.*

Geoduck

One of the strangest creatures to be eaten from the sea, the geoduck (pronounced gooey-duck), *Panopea abrupta*, is the world's largest burrowing clam. A slow-growing clam, it is among the longest-living creatures in the world, living for over 100 years in some cases. Its name is thought to derive from a Native American word meaning "dig deep." Indeed, this oversized clam can burrow more than 3 feet (1 m) into the sand. The average weight of a geoduck is around 2 pounds (0.9 kg), although it can weigh as much as 7 pounds (3 kg). The most striking aspect of the clam's appearance is the thick, long, ivory-coloured neck or siphon, which protrudes outside the hinged shells.

The geoduck is indigenous to Pacific waters from northern California to southeast Alaska, with the largest harvest coming from Washington's Puget Sound. With geoduck meat highly esteemed in Asian cuisines, particularly those of Japan, Taiwan, and China (where it is called the "elephant trunk clam"), there is a profitable market in live geoducks shipped to those countries. In the regulated market, geoducks are harvested at twelve years old by divers who use a directional water jet, called a "stinger," to wash away the sediment and reveal the lurking clam, which is lifted out. Wild harvesting of geoduck is increasingly closely regulated, which has led to a marked growth in geoduck aquaculture.

In Japan, the firm, sweet neck meat is prized for use raw in sushi or sashimi, blanched and served with a dipping sauce, or stir-fried. The dried meat is used in China for broths. In the United States the neck meat is used in chowders, whereas the more tender body meat is simply pan-fried. **CN**

Taste: *Meat from the neck (siphon) of the geoduck is typically eaten raw. It has a firm, almost crisp texture and briny sea flavour. The body meat is richer and more tender.*

Given that the long neck is eaten, a geoduck provides much more meat than most clams. »

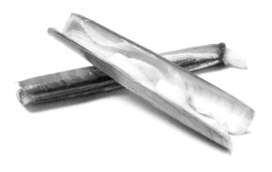

Razor Clam

Date-mussel

Increasingly popular in the United Kingdom, the European razor clam (*Ensis ensis*) has only recently begun to be commercially exploited. It is found from Norway to the Atlantic coasts of Spain, as well as parts of the Mediterranean.

It is a burrowing bivalve mollusc with an elongated narrow shell shaped like a cut-throat razor, hence the name. Both halves of the shell are curved, with a smooth olive-green or brown outer surface. The inner surface is white with hints of purple. The large muscular edible part known as the "foot" almost entirely fills the shell.

When carefully cooked this sweet and textured mollusc has a flavour somewhere between scallop and lobster meat. The long strand of flesh that is extracted from the shell resembles a peeled lychee both in appearance and texture. Cooked from live, razor clams can be steamed open over a ginger-infused stock or grilled with a generous helping of garlic butter; over-cooked, they become a chewy disappointment. Other popular recipes include clam chowder, fritters, and pasta sauces. **STS**

The most highly prized of molluscs, this tiny member of the mussel family takes eighty years to grow to a length of 4 ¾ inches (12 cm). Long, dark, and cylindrical, it looks similar to the fruit of the date palm, hence its name. It is also known as date-shell.

Native to the Mediterranean, the European date-mussel (*Lithophaga lithophaga*) secretes a liquid acid that enables it to soften and then bore into limestone rock and coral where it lives. Its destructive powers were displayed for all to see when the columns of a Roman temple at Puzzuoli, long submerged in the Bay of Naples, were brought to the surface by an earthquake.

Because the date-mussel tunnels through rock, harvesting it disturbs the habitat of other marine life. This slow-maturing mollusc has become so sought after that it is now endangered. Restaurants have had to take it off their menus and any harvesters of illegal date-mussels risk prosecution. Trade has shifted from western Europe, where its collection has been banned or limited, to northern and Eastern European countries. **WS**

Taste: *Razor clam meat has a sweet, succulent seafood flavour. Although the whole clam is generally eaten, the stomach contents should be avoided.*

Taste: *Similar in flavour and texture to a mussel, it is usually eaten raw. In many countries, especially Italy, it is mixed with other shellfish in soups and added to risottos.*

Mont St. Michel Mussel

Mussels grown on *bouchots* (wooden pillars) in France have long been a well-loved shellfish, whether it is those from Île de Ré where the mussels are roasted over flaming pine needles or those that are harvested from the northern Brittany coast, and Mont St. Michel in particular, and cooked in cider and cream. It is the Mont St. Michel mussels (AOC), however, that command the highest prices and have an exceptional reputation among chefs.

The mussel is a bivalve mollusc, with two bluish-black shells and a pointed wedge-shape at one end. Mont St. Michel mussels are relatively small but the succulent cream and orange flesh provide a satisfying mouthful compared to smaller, more traditional shellfish such as cockles. Mussels are best enjoyed from autumn through to spring because they spawn in the warmer months and the flesh becomes thin.

Traditional recipes such as *moules marinières* and *moules frites* are arguably still the best. Some say that female mussels are better than the pale creamy male, but this is personal taste! **STS**

Green-shelled Mussel

These delectable shellfish were known as green-lipped mussels until interfering officials observed it is the shells, not the creatures themselves, that glisten emerald green. Traditionally New Zealanders ate the huge, blue-shelled mussel, a daunting culinary task to those used to smaller, European molluscs. The more elegant, green-shelled mussel, *Perna canaliculus*, became a commercial export crop because it was closer to European expectations.

There has been much discussion, but little proof, of the health-giving properties of green-shelled mussels. However, this has sensibly been superseded by greater interest in their flavour. They come in two flesh colours, an important distinction if you are a mussel on the prowl—the orange ones are boys, the cream are girls. Like blue-shelled mussels, they are sometimes served with vinegar and raw onion, but this overwhelms their delicacy. In New Zealand, they can be purchased cool, wet, and alive from dedicated dispensers in almost every supermarket. Exports tend to be on the half-shell and have "added-value" flavourings or sauces. **GC**

Taste: *Mont St. Michel mussels are at their best when the weather has been very cold. Steamed open, the shells reveal large, meaty mussels with a sweet and juicy flavour.*

Taste: *Best enjoyed simply steamed, where the melting texture of all but the lips tastes elegantly sweet and creamy, with a distinct, tangy aftertaste of the sea.*

Spéciale Gillardeau

Sydney Rock Oyster

Oysters are an iconic food. They have a clean simplicity of taste that expresses the essence of the sea, with elements that reflect the unique area where they are grown, just as a wine reflects its *terroir*.

The French take their oysters very seriously, and have a labelling system with a complexity to match. Gillardeau oysters belong to an elite subset of fines de claire oysters, known as *spéciales de claire*. They are named for the celebrated family of oyster farmers that produces them.

Gillardeau oysters are sent to market in wet wooden baskets, often with seaweed to keep them damp and cool. As with all oysters, it is important they are alive when opened for consumption. If the shell is open, it should close when tapped at the hinge end. If it does not, the mollusc is dead and should be discarded. As living things, oysters must never be sealed in airtight containers, and should not be allowed to get too cold. They are best stored at the bottom of the refrigerator, with the more bowl-shaped half of the shell at the bottom, and a damp cloth over the tray. **STS**

Endemic to Australia, these bivalve molluscs have been commercially cultivated since the 1870s. They breed in saltwater and estuarine habitats along the coasts of Victoria, New South Wales, and Queensland, and at Albany in western Australia.

Compared to other oysters, the Sydney rock (*Saccostrea glomerata*) is medium sized. They reach harvesting size in about three years, but selective breeding trials have developed a "super Sydney rock" that can be harvested in two years. Although they are the most common edible oysters in Australia, they command a high price because of the strict environmental conditions surrounding production.

Sydney rocks are plump and briny with a sweet and creamy taste. They have a starring role on the Sydney dining scene, which is awash with bijou oyster bars and classy seafood restaurants, and many a hesitant diner has been tempted to try a Sydney rock as their first oyster. Although most oysters are eaten raw, they are also magnificent in recipes such as oyster mornay or vichyssoise for those who cannot stomach them live. **SCS**

Taste: *A strong marine flavour without the metallic zing that many associate with oysters. Crush them in the mouth to maximize the nutty aftertaste and briny tang.*

Taste: *Chewed or not, these oysters are sweet on the front palate, then salty with a rich aftertaste. Their delicate characteristics are best enjoyed when served au naturel.*

A farmer checks a rack of Sydney rock oysters on the Hawkesbury River, New South Wales. ❯❯

Hiroshima Oyster

Kumamoto Oyster

Aptly nicknamed "milk of the sea," Hiroshima oysters (*Crassostrea gigas*) can grow up to 10 inches (25 cm) long, and are said to contain more glycogen, iron, and phosphorus than those from other areas. Together, Japan, Korea, and China produce 90 per cent of the world's oysters, but with consumers in Japan concerned over the quality of imports, Hiroshima oysters are increasingly prized.

The oyster is celebrated throughout Hiroshima, and nearby Miyajima hosts an oyster festival each year, where visitors can taste Hiroshima oysters fresh on the half-shell with a selection of dressings such as sudachi citrus and soy sauce, or the Hiroshima speciality *dote nabe*—a one-pot stew, cooked at the table, of oysters, tofu, and vegetables simmered in a miso-based broth.

Oysters are also used to make *kaki meshi* (oyster rice) and *gunkan maki* (battleship sushi), in which soft runny ingredients are placed on top of an oval of sushi rice, encased and supported by a "wall" of nori seaweed. *Kaki furai*—breaded and deep-fried oysters—are eaten all over Japan. **SB**

The Kumamoto oyster (*Crassostrea sikamea*) has a niche market all of its own. However, it is also a stark reminder of the consequences of over-fishing.

Taking its name from the large bay on the southernmost Japanese island of Kyushu, this small Pacific oyster is a wonderful delicacy. But, although they are now grown around the world, they are extinct in their place of origin, Kumamoto Bay. In the United States, they are farmed in Humboldt Bay, California, but take a number of years to grow to a marketable size, making them one of the most costly oysters on the restaurant menu. They are only available in small quantities and are in high demand for their fabulous taste.

Kumamoto oysters have a sweeter, more delicate taste than other Pacific oysters. One reason for their popularity, especially in the United States, is that they are considered to be an excellent year-round oyster remaining firmer and meatier in the warmer months than other species. Their deep shell retains liquor beautifully, making them ideal for serving on the half-shell. **STS**

Taste: *A giant among oysters, the Hiroshima oyster is creamy, shiny, and supple, with a velvety, milky, yet slightly minerally taste. The texture is firm.*

Taste: *Delicately salty, this is an excellent "first timer," the perfect introduction to the joys of eating live oysters. The meat is firm, with a sweet taste, and fills the shell well.*

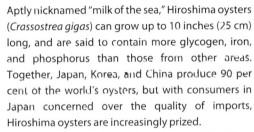

Japanese oyster farmers work beds outlined by buoys near the Amakusa Islands, Kumamoto.

Bay Scallop

Diver King Scallop

Native to the Atlantic coast of the United States—and so emblematic of the East Coast that the scallop is the state shell of New York State—bay scallops (*Argopecten irradians*) grow in shallow coastal waters from New England as far south as Florida. As with other scallops, the edible part is the adductor muscle that opens and closes the iconic shell.

There is still some wild harvest of bay scallops in the northeastern United States, although scallop farming is on the increase, and a large proportion of bay scallops sold in the United States actually originate with Chinese aquaculture operations. Most are shelled immediately upon harvest: scallops in their shells—while harder to come by—are infinitely more rewarding.

Scallop aquaculture throughout the world has gained a green light from watchdogs for its low environmental impact. Incredibly versatile, bay scallops adapt well to most cooking methods. Their small size means that they cook in a flash. Sweet little nuggets of maritime meat, they can tempt even finicky eaters. **CN**

The magnificent diver king scallop (*Pecten maximus*) is caught in the relatively deep waters of the eastern Atlantic from Norway to the south of Spain, and also around the Azores. As the name suggests, these shellfish are harvested by hand by divers who will select the biggest ones available to get the highest market value. Dredged scallops are also available; they are usually much cheaper because they are of variable size and can contain sand and grit from the dredging process.

Seared in a hot pan so that they are brown on the outside but barely cooked in the centre, diver king scallops are a most delicious shellfish and they quite literally melt in the mouth. In Europe, both the white adductor muscle meat and the orange/cream tongue or coral (roe) is eaten, whereas in the United States the white muscle is favoured and the roe is usually discarded.

Popular in both classic and contemporary cuisine, mouth-watering recipes include the heavenly *coquilles St. Jacques a la Parisienne* and seared scallops in a saffron *beurre blanc*. **STS**

Taste: *Eaten raw, their texture is tender but toothsome, and their flavour slightly buttery and sweet. They are best cooked simply—sautéed with butter and lemon.*

Taste: *Sweet, succulent, and rich, the intense flavour of the meat takes on a certain nuttiness when seared in butter. Avoid over-cooking to preserve the delicate texture.*

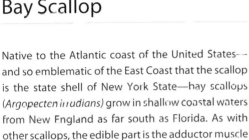

Scallops cook quickly, either on the grill as here or barbecued on skewers with other ingredients.

Baby Squid

Prized along the Mediterranean coast of Europe, these tiny members of the cephalopod family are oval little creatures that measure 1 ¼ to 2 ½ inches (3–6 cm) long. Mother Nature judiciously furnished them with pearly translucent bodies because they swim near to the surface of the water and are prone to attack from below.

They are firm and slightly flattened in shape, with eight arms and two long tentacles, and their soft exterior surrounds a central body cavity with a bony cartilage that is removed before cooking. This provides a perfect natural receptacle for stuffing, although baby squid are also delicious grilled, marinated, fried, frittered, or served in salads.

In Spain, baby squid are known as *chipirones* and are a highly valued delicacy. *Chipirones "Los Peperetes"* are poached baby squid that have been canned in olive oil—a particularly delicious treat not to be missed. Succulent and delectable, they are caught in Galician estuaries and, like other baby squid, pair wonderfully well with good olive oil and lemon juice. **LF**

Taste: *Tender, juicy, and sweet, with a smooth, silky texture, baby squid taste subtly of the sea but are never overly "fishy" in flavour.*

Ika

The Japanese love squid. While there are many species of ika in oceans across the world, and squids of their various kinds are valued from Korea to the Mediterranean, half of the world's catch is consumed in Japan. The most popular species are *surume ika* (Pacific flying squid), *yari ika* (spear squid), and *kaminari ika* (cuttlefish). All ika have a central bone inside the body cavity that is easy to remove.

Different species are suited to different recipes and are prepared in a variety of ways, notably raw in sashimi, deep-fried in tempura, and grilled in teriyaki. Light cooking preserves the soft texture; over-cooking renders it chewy.

Ika somen is a speciality of the town of Hakodate. Raw ika is sliced into long, fine strips that resemble *somen* noodles. These are then eaten like noodles, with a raw quail egg, some wakame seaweed, and a soy-based dipping sauce. Whole raw squid are sometimes stuffed with sushi rice to make *ika zushi*. *Ikayaki* are whole grilled squid basted in a sweet soy sauce and grilled teriyaki-style—a popular festival food in summer. **SB**

Taste: Ika somen *is slightly sticky while being smooth and velvety, with a mild, creamy, but not fishy taste.* Surume ika *is rich, sweet, chewy, and deeply satisfying.*

Squid are laid on a rack to dry; in Asia, dried squid is used in many recipes as well as eaten as a snack. »

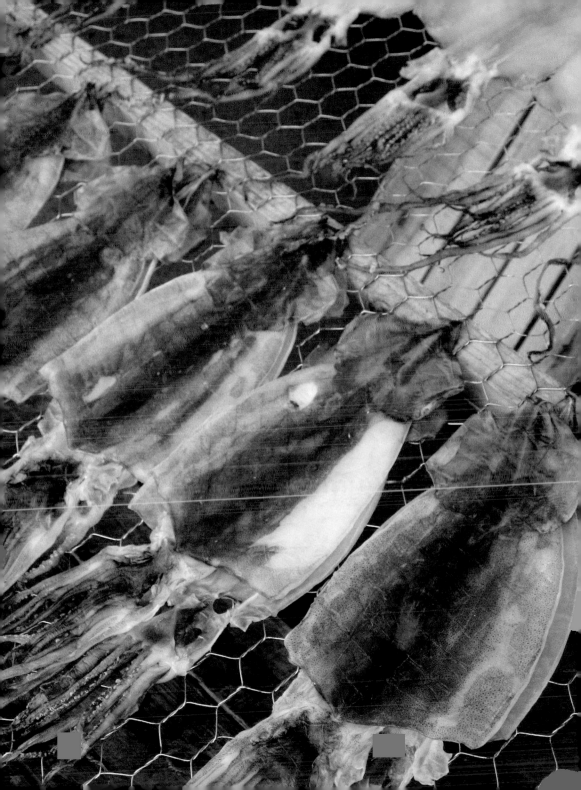

Octopus

There are hundreds of different species of octopus, enjoyed by some cuisines, rejected by others. Unlike cuttlefish and squid, the tentacles rather than the body make for better eating.

Although it is a solitary animal, octopus is still more abundant in the Mediterranean than squid, which helps to explain why so many recipes for cooking it exist. Baby octopus is delicious fried whole as in the Italian *fritto misto*, but larger ones may need prolonged simmering before they become tender. Slices marinated with lemon juice and olive oil are a typical meze. Stewing octopus in its own ink is as popular in Greek island cooking as around the Iberian coast.

While the sight of Greek fishermen tenderizing octopus by beating them against the side of a boat can seem repulsive—although the animal is already dead—it stands little comparison to the Japanese habit of eating octopus as sashimi while still alive enough to wriggle. John Ashburne observes that "The sensation, as the suckers attach to the roof of your mouth, is impossible to convey." **MR**

Akashi Tako

Akashi tako (*Octopus vulgaris*) is eaten enthusiastically by the Japanese who, unlike most of the rest of the human race, are not repelled by its eight legs and strange appearance, but find it positively cute. But this does not stop them eating it—sometimes alive.

A nutrient-rich diet of shrimp, plankton, and crab, along with a fast-moving current, is said to make the tako caught in Akashi the best in Japan. The importance of the octopus to the town is apparent, with octopus nets and clay pots in shop windows and tentacles hanging to dry in the sun. The local fish market Uo no Tana (meaning fish shelf) displays its fresh fish on wooden planks under running water, and has become a tourist attraction.

Rich in protein, low in fat, and high in amino acids, tako can be eaten raw but is more usually lightly boiled; it is also traditionally tenderized by kneading the flesh in finely grated daikon pulp. Popular ways of eating Akashi tako are in *takosu*—thinly sliced boiled tako served in a sweet vinegar, combined with cucumber and sometimes miso, and *takonikomi*—simmered in sweet soy sauce. **SB**

Taste: Octopus offers a whole range of different textures. Thin slices may be rubbery or chewy; whole fried baby octopus is crisp. Large tentacles with suckers are meaty.

Taste: Akashi tako is creamy, soft, and velvety with a light chewiness and a mild sweet taste of the sea. It is particularly good battered and served as akashiyaki.

Japanese takoyaki consists of pieces of octopus grilled in a pancake mixture with ginger and spring onion. »

Sea Urchin

As prickly as hedgehogs, these round, spiky balls litter the floors and rocks of all the world's oceans, concealing a rounded body with neither head nor tail. Like starfish, sea urchins are echinoderms, and their bodies are symmetrical across five axes. Their edible parts, therefore, are also five in number: roe-like yellow to orange lobes that form the creatures' gonads.

Across the numerous culinary cultures of the globe that appreciate sea urchins, there is a general consensus that they are best eaten raw. In Japan, *uni* is eaten as a sushi and there are several grades available in the fish markets. The most sought after are bright golden and firm; the paler ones are softer and less sweet.

While the same degree of refinement is not found in the West, sea urchins are still considered a luxury and, particularly in the Mediterranean, are becoming scarce as a result of over-consumption. Most species are not currently farmed: Canadian fisheries are generally acknowledged as the most sustainable source of the wild delicacy. **MR**

Sea Cucumber

Also known as the sea slug, the sea cucumber's name seems an appropriate one for this ugly creature that slowly crawls the ocean floor in search of food. In Chinese cuisine, it is boiled, salted, and dried before sale, a treatment that turns it ash grey and makes it capable of being stored almost indefinitely: it has to be cleaned, rehydrated, and cooked for hours before it is tender enough to eat.

Like many Chinese delicacies, sea cucumber is appreciated not for its taste but for its texture: this is gelatinous, slightly chewy, and extremely distinctive. Because of its high cost, it is a popular inclusion on Chinese banquet menus, when it is often braised in a superior stock flavoured with rice wine, ginger, soy sauce, and oyster sauce. Populations are endangered in many parts of the world, although Australia operates sustainable sea cucumber fisheries.

Very different sea cucumbers are eaten in Spain, especially around Barcelona, where they are known as *espardeñas* or *espardenyes*. Small, white, and tender, they provide a completely different eating experience from their Pacific cousins. **KKC**

Taste: The taste is always of the sea but never "fishy." It varies across the species, from an intensely salty, seaweedy explosion of the ocean to sweeter, creamier flavours.

Taste: Chinese sea cucumber has a neutral taste that absorbs the flavours it is cooked with. Spanish sea cucumber tastes mild with a chewy, squid-like texture.

The Japanese term uni *refers to the edible portion of a sea urchin; here, more than 100 are displayed.*

Violet

Despite its name, this curious creature is not a flower but an edible sea-squirt (*Microcosmus sulcatus*). So little valued is it in English-speaking cultures that its name is French, and pronounced as such. On the Mediterranean coast, where it is prized, it is also called *figue de mer* (sea fig) or *uovo di mare* (sea egg).

The barrel-shaped adults are attached to underwater rocks, piers, boats, and the sea bottom. The violet feeds by siphoning seawater through its body and using a basket-like internal filter to capture plankton and oxygen; gnarled in appearance, it is the size of a large oyster. It projects two siphons, one for inhaling and one for exhaling seawater. Although the exterior looks shell-like, it is actually leathery.

To reach its edible parts, you must slice the violet in half through the middle, a process that reveals a yellowy mush, similar in appearance to scrambled egg (some may find its appearance off-putting). The yellow pulp has a strong salty flavour with a tang of iodine. The pulp is spooned out and may be eaten raw or alternatively cooked in a soup. Smaller violets have a sweeter flavour than the larger specimens, which have a stronger tang of iodine.

Violets are especially popular in Provence, France, and stalls that offer them as an expensive shellfish snack are still found intermittently in the side streets of Marseille. While occasionally added to the famous fish stew, bouillabaisse, they appear more often as part of a *plateau de fruits de mer*.

Different varieties of sea-squirt are prized in Chile, Korea, and Japan, where they are considered to be a delicacy and served raw. Salted and seasoned sea squirt is especially popular in Korea as a side dish and is widely available in bottles and jars. **MR**

Taste: *Oyster lovers might well like the salty, iodine tang of violets, but their soft, mushy texture makes them an acquired taste for those who prefer firm seafood.*

Squid Ink

As the name would suggest, this viscous ebony ink comes from squid, which, like their fellow cephalopods cuttlefish and octopus, have eight arms and two tentacles arranged in pairs. More relevantly, they have no shell or bone on their exterior, so are very susceptible to attack from predators.

Instead of providing external armour for the squid's self-defence, nature has endowed the squid with the ability to discharge a thick stream of black liquid that clouds the water. This diversion tactic is thought to confuse predators, and at the same time the ink cloud alerts other members of the same species and provides them with cover for escape.

Squid ink is entirely edible and delicious to boot; it adds a wonderful tang of the sea and a unique, eye-catching black tint to sauces, pasta, and rice dishes. In Hokkaido, Japan, a summer squid festival takes place, and among the many savoury squid dishes there is also on sale a squid ink ice cream, *ikazuri aisukurimu*. An ice-cream stall near the famous Tsukiji fish market in Tokyo also sells greyish-black, soft, whipped squid ink ice cream. In Europe, the ink is the defining ingredient in the famous Spanish black rice dish *arroz negro*, and is a popular ingredient in Catalan cuisine in rice and pasta dishes. It features prominently in Italian cuisine, where it is a particular favourite for colouring and flavouring pasta that is then served with shellfish. Squid ink risotto is a traditional Venetian dish. The ink is also good in sauces, the slight downside being that it tends to colour everything it touches—including teeth.

Fresh squid ink should be used immediately or refrigerated for a short time in a non-porous bowl as, like squid, it will begin to smell if left to stand. **LF**

Taste: *Squid ink adds a pleasing salty punch to sauces and a restrained fishy flavour and appealing colour to pasta dough. Look for the natural sac inside fresh squid.*

Italian pasta nero takes its black colouring from squid ink mixed in with the pasta dough before cooking. »

Dried Shrimp

One of the "eight treasures" in the savoury, glutinous rice stuffing that is eaten at celebratory meals in China, and a key element in the Brazilian fritters known as *acarajé*, dried shrimp are appreciated not only in China, and the many nations influenced by Chinese cuisine, but in many parts of Latin America, the Caribbean, and Africa.

They are made with fresh ocean prawns that are salted, shelled, and dried, which concentrates their flavour and reduces their size. The dry, curled results are tiny: although some (the most expensive) can be as large as 2 ½ inches (6 cm), most range in size from smaller than a grain of rice to ¾ inch (2 cm). A bright colour, whether pink, orange, or somewhere in between, is critical: faded shrimp are tired. The odour should be clean, with no trace of ammonia.

As their flavour is so intense, dried shrimp are used in small quantities. In Chinese cooking, they are generally rinsed before use to rid them of any clinging shells then rehydrated in rice wine or water. The soaking liquid absorbs the flavour of the dried shrimp and can be added to the dish. **KKC**

Taste: *Do not let the size of dried shrimp fool you: they may be small, but their taste is powerful. The flavour is salty, sweet, and briny: like packaged essence of the sea.*

Dried Abalone

There are many factors that make dried abalone a pricey ingredient. The univalve grows very slowly; harvesting them is dangerous and difficult; and processing, which involves salting, cooking, and drying, can take months and shrinks them to less than one-fifth of their original weight. Cooking is also time-consuming, and requires skill, patience, and quality ingredients if the abalone is to take on a texture connoisseurs would describe as silky and tender, but resilient and just slightly chewy.

The high price also reflects the endangered status of wild abalone; it has almost been fished to extinction in many countries, including Japan, which is generally seen to be the best source for top quality abalone. However, it is being successfully farmed in California and in southern Australia, and Tasmania has a sustainable wild abalone fishery geared specifically to the Japanese market.

Cooking dried abalone takes a few days. It has to be soaked, heated, and cooled several times to rehydrate it. It is then simmered in stock made with pork bones, chicken, and other ingredients. **KKC**

Taste: *Fresh abalone has a fresh, delicate flavour. Dried abalone is quite different—intense and rich, with a well-balanced, sweet, and salty flavour.*

Jellyfish

Jellyfish was almost certainly first eaten by someone facing starvation. Whoever thought of laboriously processing the fresh, jelly-like blob—which, incidentally, is not a fish, but a marine invertebrate—into something edible had a lot more time on their hands than food in their belly. But jellyfish is now a delicacy—although a fairly inexpensive, everyday one compared to bird's nest, sea cucumber, and the still genocidally popular shark's fin. Like these it is eaten almost entirely for its texture.

The tentacles, with their stings, are first discarded, as are the innards, then the body is cleaned, soaked, salted, and dried. Jellyfish can be bought either dried or rehydrated. The dried version needs soaking overnight in several changes of water to remove excess salt.

On the cold platters served at Chinese banquets, jellyfish is sliced so it resembles a tangle of thick, translucent golden noodles, then dressed with soy sauce, sesame oil, and dried mustard powder. In Japan, it is known as *kurage* and often appears as an ingredient in the salads known as *sunomono*. **KKC**

Taste: *The texture of jellyfish combines chewy and crunchy in a way that is highly unusual. Not everyone appreciates it, however: it has been compared to rubber bands.*

Turu

A delicacy exclusive to those who visit or live in the Amazon rainforest, this freshwater mollusc has a taste somewhere between oyster and sea urchin. A species of *Teredo*, the turu lives underwater and feeds on the dead wood of fallen trees.

It is undoubtedly the turu's appearance that has led to its failure to gain acceptance in mainstream Brazilian cuisine. It is a long, fat, milky-coloured creature, the thickness of a finger, with the head of a bivalve—albeit one with sharp teeth on its shell—and the body of a worm. It can grow up to 16 inches (40 cm) in length, and it takes great skill to extract it from its riverine residence.

Methods for preparing the turu are many. The simplest, and perhaps the tastiest, resembles an Andean ceviche. After cleaning and gutting, the raw turu is seasoned with lime, salt, and chilli and left to "cook" in the acidity for a few minutes. It is also often cooked quickly over heat in its own juice to retain its remarkable tenderness, which releases a lot of liquid that is thickened with cassava flour. Similar species are enjoyed in mangrove swamps elsewhere. **AL**

Taste: *The turu's aroma belies its freshwater origin. The taste resembles other, more popular bivalves, not only the oyster, but also mussels and clams.*

Conch

"Conch" is a generic name used for the many kinds of large, single-shell molluscs found in tropical waters around the globe. However, it is the Queen conch (*Strombus gigas*), with its graceful, pointed shell, and iridescent rosy pink interior "lips," that is sought out by seafood gourmets. The name of conch may seem unprepossessing compared with the flamboyance of the shell, but it becomes even less so in Florida, the Bahamas, and some other Caribbean islands, where it is more bluntly pronounced "konk."

Inside the shell is a large, snail-like mollusc. This creature lives on sandy, sea-grass beds and among the coral reefs of warm shallows, growing to a length of 12 inches (30.5 cm) on a diet of aquatic plants. A slow-moving animal, it is easily harvested by fishermen who can sell both the shellfish and the beautiful shell. For centuries, the molluscs have been prized in the Caribbean, where they are a common source of food, and where their shells are also used for horns, as containers, to make fish hooks, and as ornaments. Today, however, there are major concerns that *Strombus gigas* is being exploited at a rate that is unsustainable worldwide.

Despite this, conch is a hugely popular food in the Caribbean and its surrounding countries. In order to tenderize the meat of this large mollusc, the flesh is often beaten (as with octopus) or marinated in lime juice to tenderize it. It can be grilled whole as a steak or diced and turned into fritters, chowders, or gumbos. It can also be eaten raw in salads, cooked in a tasty stew with red kidney beans, marinated in wafer-thin slices with lime juice as ceviche, or tossed with onions, tomato, and fresh coriander along with a good measure of lemon or lime juice. **WS**

Taste: *Conch meat needs tenderizing or steeping in an acidulated, usually lime juice-based, marinade. It then has a mild brininess and sweet flavour similar to clams.*

Great heaps of conch shells are left by fishermen
of the Netherlands Antilles in the Caribbean.

Frog

It is not just the French who enjoy eating frogs. Outside Europe, particularly in Thailand, sacks of live frogs are a feature of food markets, where they are prepared on the spot and eaten whole in a green curry. In the West, it is usually, though not exclusively, the legs that are consumed. Frogs' legs have been eaten in France since medieval times, particularly during the fasting period of Lent.

In the Italian region of Pavia (Lombardy), frogs' legs are eaten in risottos, frittatas, and tomato stews. In one celebrated recipe, whole frogs are stuffed with spinach. In French regional cuisine, they are preferred sautéed in butter with garlic and parsley. The menus of famous French chef Escoffier euphemistically referred to frogs as *nymphes*. In one of his recipes, *Chaud-froid a L'Aurore*, poached nymphs' legs are steeped in a fish sauce, then layered in a bed of Champagne jelly. The French colonial influence means that frogs also feature in the cusines of Louisiana in the United States and French-speaking parts of the West Indies.

It is often assumed that frogs are caught in the wild, but they are increasingly being farmed in Asia and the Americas. Commercial frog ponds were quite common in France during the nineteenth century, and the region of Dombes, in particular, is famous for its frogs. Over-exploitation combined with the loss of the frog's natural marshy habitat, means that *Rana esculenta* is now a protected species in France. The frogs that appear on French restaurant menus are now generally Asian bullfrogs, imported from South East Asia. There are, however, major animal welfare concerns regarding the international trade in frogs' legs. **MR**

Taste: *The flavour of frogs' legs is often compared to chicken, but the slightly gelatinous texture is actually more akin to young farmed rabbit.*

Akita Hinai-jidori Chicken

Guinea Fowl

Described as "the ultimate free-range chicken," Akita Hinai-jidori birds are reared on small, organic farms with clover pastures and mountain streams, and fed throughout the breeding period on apples, vegetables, and tomatoes. This special chicken is the result of crossbreeding the Hinai-dori, which is native to the mountainous Akita prefecture of Japan, with the Rhode Island Red (*Gallus domesticus*) from the United States. A similar quality chicken has been developed since 1991 in California by Dennis Mao for the Los Angeles restaurant market.

In Japan, the chicken is famed for being served raw, sashimi-style. For this preparation, the chicken needs to be exceptionally fresh (that is, alive on the same day it is served) and not previously frozen. Tokyo restaurants also serve the liver, gizzard, and brain of this esteemed bird. In the Wakayama prefecture, the chicken is seasoned with sea salt and then grilled over *binchōtan*, a traditional oak charcoal. The exceptional breast meat is also delicious grilled and served simply sliced with steamed vegetables. **CK**

Originally thought to be from Guinea in West Africa, these resilient birds have been domesticated and bred throughout the world. Guinea fowl were introduced into China in the seventeenth century and are referred to in India as Chinese fowl.

Having been raised in captivity as far back as 2400 BCE by ancient Egyptians, guinea fowl are today found in the United States in various colours and breeds. In South Africa, they mostly still roam wild, which contributes to the quality of the dark meat, and low fat (around 5 per cent) and cholesterol levels. High in protein and a good source of vitamin B_6, selenium, and niacin, the meat does benefit from some form of barding such as bacon. The delicate meat gives a moist, succulent poultry dish, but care should be taken not to over-cook it.

Males mate for life and young guineas are called "keets." Since it is difficult to distinguish between young males and females by appearance alone, the tell-tale, two-syllable call of the female, sounding like "buckwheat," helps those in the know. Guinea fowl eggs are nutritious but difficult to come by. **HFi**

Taste: *Akita Hinai-jidori chicken yields lean, moist meat with a creamy, firm texture, and a natural chicken flavour. Its renowned quality and flavour make it ideal for sashimi.*

Taste: *Prepared in the same way as chicken, but with reduced cooking times on account of the smaller weight, the meat is rich and gamey with plump poultry juiciness.*

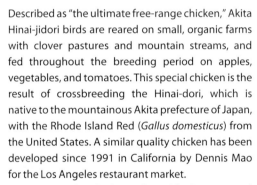

The magnificent vulterine guinea fowl, with its striking blue plumage, is found wild in northeast Africa. »

Volaille de Bresse

Red Grouse

In translation, "Bresse chicken" implies a single product, but the French name covers three equally fine types of poultry: *poulet*, a smallish bird that weighs around 3 pounds (1.4 kg), *poularde*, which weighs 4 to 5 pounds (1.8–2.3 kg), and *chapon*, a capon, or neutered male, that may tip the scales at as much as 9 pounds (over 4 kg). All are covered by an *Appellation d'Origine Contrôlée* and it is the capon, here as elsewhere a luxury for the festive season, that fetches the highest price by weight.

A Bresse chicken must not only come from the Bresse region, near Lyons, but must also belong to the eponymous breed whose pedigree was established early in the twentieth century. There are three separate strains, with white, grey, and black feathers, but all have the distinctive blue feet.

The *poulet* is a supreme spit-roasting bird, succulent, tender, and well flavoured. It is the base of many chicken sauté dishes, especially those associated with *cuisine lyonnaise*. The *poularde* is often braised—in one famous *poularde en demi-deuil* recipe, with truffles under the skin. **MR**

Unique to the British Isles, the red grouse (*Lagopus lagopus scoticus*), which is a subspecies of the willow grouse, lives on moorland, where it feeds almost exclusively on heather. Smaller than the black grouse, it is reddish-brown, with a plump body, and a hook-tipped bill. These wild game birds cannot be successfully commercially reared. Their habitat is managed by gamekeepers and the birds can only be shot during the grouse hunting season that begins on the 12th of August, if their population is high enough. Wet weather during the first two weeks of May, when the chicks hatch, or diseases such as stronglyosis can greatly deplete their numbers.

When preparing grouse, the cook needs to identify whether the bird is young or old because older birds are tougher. The easiest way to do so is to hold the bird by its lower beak and if it snaps, it is young, whereas if it does not, it is old. Young birds are good for roasting and braising whereas older ones are best kept for the casserole. Grouse is often paired with sweet flavours, such as a parsnip mash or wild fruit sauces. **MG**

Taste: *The flavour of Bresse poultry is neither strong nor bland; it is fine and delicately flavoured, with toothsome flesh and thin, crisp skin when carefully roasted.*

Taste: *The unique flavour of red grouse begins on the palate with a rich gamey taste that gives way to the subtle sweetness of heather and the scent of wild herbs.*

The start of the hunting season for red grouse in the United Kingdom is known as the Glorious Twelfth. ❯

Imperial Peking Duck

Challans Duck

Except for pork, animal fat is in short supply in the Chinese diet but fattened duck helps to fill the gap. Semi-wild ducks are used to control small land-crabs that can devastate rice paddies, but the Chinese accidentally discovered they also ate rice.

The Imperial Peking duck breed dates from the Ming Dynasty (1368–1644). Grain being shipped by boat to the capital, Peking, was inevitably spilled on riverside wharves and ended up in the stomachs of the waterside ducks. Peasants, noticing that these ducks grew inordinately fat, began to rear them in cages and force-feed them to develop an even plumper bird, perfect for roasting. Now popular in England and the United States, large Imperial Peking ducks can weigh up to 12 pounds (5.4 kg) and may carry a third of their body weight in fat.

One of the most famous duck dishes is Peking duck. The recipe involves pumping the bird with air and then hanging it up to dry. The characteristic crispy mahogany skin associated with the dish is achieved by coating the duck in a syrup and soy sauce mixture before roasting. **MR**

Close to the Atlantic coast in the heart of the Breton marshes, Challans is a region where wild-fowling has always flourished. According to folk history, Challans ducks are a cross between wild birds and ones that were introduced from Holland during the seventeenth century. By the nineteenth century, under the name of *canard nantais*, they were sent (from Nantes railway station, hence the name) to Paris, where they were much admired.

The reputation of the duck owes much to the renowned Parisian restaurant La Tour d'Argent. It created a recipe for a pressed duck in which the sauce was thickened with the duck's blood. The restaurant has kept a record of every duck sold and who ate it for over a century: the Prince of Wales (the future King Edward VII) ate No. 328 in 1890. Since then the figure has passed the million mark.

In the Loire valley, nearer its home, Challans duck is eaten simply roasted with fresh peas. Those in the know say the female of the species (*la canette*) is tastier than the male; however, both carry plenty of subcutaneous fat over the breast. **MR**

Taste: *The tender, fatty flesh of roasted Imperial Peking duck provides a perfect foil to the crispness of the skin, creating a tantalizing balance of sweet and salty flavours.*

Taste: *Served in thin slices with a sauce of cherries, blackcurrants, or orange, the light, gamey flavour of tender duck contrasts beautifully with the fruit.*

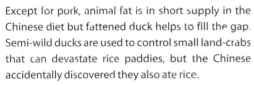

A window display of duck roasted in a mixture of soy and syrup identifies a restaurant in Shanghai, China.

Kelly Bronze® Turkey

Although around 90 per cent of the turkeys reared in the United Kingdom are industrially produced in barns containing up to 20,000 birds, all Kelly Bronze® turkeys range free in woodland and pastures. At the beginning of the twentieth century, British turkeys, although bred for size, were much slimmer than they are now: they looked, when roasted, like angular giant pheasants. However, these breeds were superseded by modern "double-breasted" varieties—often so encumbered by their unnaturally bloated bosoms that they can only be bred using artificial insemination.

In 1984 an Essex farmer, Derek Kelly, revived an old strain of Bronze turkey that combined the yield of meat found on large-breasted breeds with the depth of flavour associated with traditional poultry husbandry. Today Kelly's son, rears his flock semi-wild in woodland, without additives or drugs. Kelly Bronze® turkeys take twice as long as most commercial birds to mature. They are plucked by hand and left to hang for up to a fortnight in order to develop their characteristic gamey taste. **MR**

Taste: *The smell of a roasted Kelly Bronze® is clearly gamey, like partridge. The breast meat is moist but denser than a chicken's and the leg is similar in texture to young lamb.*

Bourbon Red Turkey

Benjamin Franklin once argued that the wild turkey might make a better symbol of America than the bald eagle, and the bird retains a prominent place in U.S. culture. It is not only the beloved centrepiece of November's Thanksgiving celebration but the pride of many holiday feasts—in several European countries as well as in the New World.

Turkey has been an important food source in the Americas for thousands of years: it is thought to have first been domesticated as early as the second millennium BCE. The Bourbon Red, a bird of dark rich mahogany colour with white feather accents on the wings and tail, arrived on the scene relatively late, in Bourbon County, Kentucky, where it was established in the late nineteenth century. The breed was valuable during the first half of the twentieth century but lost favour over the years with breeders who preferred larger-breasted birds. But recent efforts to conserve heritage foods have helped return attention to the Bourbon Red and other varieties that are less buxom but often have more distinctive flavour than their modern cousins. **CN**

Taste: *The Bourbon Red turkey, like many heritage breeds, offers a more richly flavoured meat. Roasted whole, the crisp golden skin contrasts with the juicy meat beneath.*

On their respective Thanksgiving Days, U.S. and Canadian families enjoy a roast turkey dinner. »

Squab

Pigeons have been bred for the table since ancient times, when their meat was valued as a delicacy to be enjoyed by pharaohs, emperors, and kings. The art of raising pigeons for the table began in ancient Egypt, where pigeon stew featured on the menu.

A member of the Columba family and known as *pigeonneau* in France, a squab is any young pigeon on the point of leaving the nest; true squabs have never flown. It must be around four weeks old and weigh less than 14 oz (400 g). The young flesh is plump, delicate, and quite fat, but the fat is under the skin and renders down in cooking making it one of the most easily digestible of all meats, unlike either domestic poultry or wild game birds.

The best way to cook a squab is to split it open and fry it in extra virgin olive oil or butter, or a mix of both. It can also be stuffed and roasted whole, when the breast needs protection with bacon or fat. The delicacy of the meat calls for the simplest of preparations. Squab pie is a traditional dish, although it sometimes contains mutton or pork rather than pigeon. **LW**

Quail

This dainty game bird is beloved both by the hunter and the epicure. It is also known across the world as blue quail, bush quail, and mountain quail. Despite being rather dumpy—seeming almost to strain itself when taking off—the quail is a migratory bird, its long wings enabling it to cross high mountains and seas. It has a distinctive call of three sharp notes that has led to a nickname in England of "wet-my-lip."

Quail is reared commercially in Europe for its meat and its eggs, which are also considered a delicacy. This highly regarded bird (*Coturnix coturnix*) belongs to the same family as the partridge and has a similar appearance, although it is much smaller. In parts of the United States, the terms quail and partridge are interchangeable.

Like most game birds, quail is best prepared simply to appreciate its sweet gamey flavour. Cooked *en papillote*, with the cavity stuffed with a few fresh herbs and garlic or cloves, quail is superb. As the parcel is opened the full fragrance of this delicate bird meets your olfactory senses, preparing you for the luxurious feast within. **LW**

Taste: *What little meat there is on these young birds is perfect: half duck, half chicken, it is dark, flavourful, and extremely tender. Prepare in the same manner as chicken.*

Taste: *Pleasing in shape, taste, and colour, quail meat is rich, uniquely fragrant, soft, and moist. When roasted the skin is crisp and juicy, like crackling on pork.*

Quail is best simply prepared; here it is served grilled on skewers with a tahini and lemon sauce. »

Toulouse Goose

Greylag Goose

The most commonly reared breed of large grey goose in France, the Toulouse (also known as *L'oie grise des Landes* or the Grey Landes goose) is often used for the production of foie gras. It can weigh up to 20 pounds (9 kg) after fattening, but will normally reach maturity at about 12 pounds (5.4 kg).

Although classified as poultry and therefore white meat, goose has dark-coloured flesh and the flavour is stronger and more pungent than most poultry. The Toulouse goose is central to the cuisine of southwest France. The meat is often reserved for *confit d'oie* (goose meat preserved in its own fat), which is a basic ingredient of the white bean and Toulouse sausage stew, cassoulet, but it has other uses. Accompanied by potatoes sautéed in goose fat, garnished with diced black truffles (*à la sarladaise*) it is a speciality of Périgord. The neck can also be stuffed with a forcemeat and braised.

The Toulouse goose is considered to be the best meat bird in Europe and is frequently roasted whole at Christmas, although in France turkey is the more popular choice. **MR**

According to the historian Livy, a flock of noisy geese at Capitoline Hill alerted Rome to invading Gauls in 390 BCE. Geese were first domesticated in Egypt, and both the Egyptians and the Romans prized them for their liver. The greylag goose (*Anser anser*)—the ancestor of domestic geese in Europe and North America—is bigger and bulkier than other grey geese, and can weigh up to 11 pounds (5 kg).

A migratory bird, it is found in parts of northern Europe and Eurasia stretching across to Russia. Its plumage is pale grey with a white belly, and it has a large, orange bill. During the breeding season it is found in fens, marshes, lakes, and damp moorland. The draining of marshland has led to the decline of the greylag goose in Europe.

Goose is common Christmas fare in parts of Europe, although it vies with turkey in popularity. In the United Kingdom, it was once traditionally eaten at Michaelmas. British cookery doyenne Mrs. Beeton recommends cooking it with a glass of port or wine to which mustard, salt, and cayenne pepper have been added. In China, goose is often air-dried. **CK**

Taste: *The dark-reddish flesh of goose has a strong farmyard flavour. Baked in the oven, the fatty skin turns crisp giving a unique contrast with the melting meat.*

Taste: *Greylag goose meat is very rich in flavour and lean, with most of the fat concentrated in the skin. Tart, fruit sauces offset the fattiness of roast goose meat.*

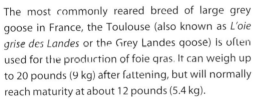

The Toulouse goose is the prime choice for roasting whole, but its fat is also valued for its use in cooking.

Partridge

Of the many varieties of partridge, the two most esteemed for the table in Europe are the common grey partridge (*Perdrix perdrix*) and the red-legged partridge (*Alectoris rufa*). Both have been introduced to the United States, although the chukar partridge (*Alectoris chukar*), which is native to Turkey, is most popular on game farms.

As with other game birds, modern farming methods are affecting the creatures' natural habitat, although the birds are reared extensively for sport shooting. The grey partridge can be found all over Europe as far north as Sweden and Russia, and in parts of Asia; the red-legged partridge is found mainly in Spain, Portugal, and southwest France. Both are small plump birds that are strikingly good to eat, although the red-legged partridges are fleshier and milder in flavour. Young partridges require little or no hanging, and are best cooked simply, either roasted or grilled; their flesh is full of flavour and easily digestible. Older birds are very flavoursome indeed. They should be hung for three or four days and cooked long and slowly. **LW**

Pheasant

According to legend, Jason and the Argonauts brought the pheasant back with them when they returned from the Caucasus with the fabled Golden Fleece; from Greece it went to Rome; and from Rome to Europe. Today, this important and most hunted game bird is found as far east as Siberia and China. A huge population of common pheasant (*Phasianus colchicus*) is sustained artificially in Europe and the United States; in the latter, it is also known as the ring-necked pheasant or Chinese pheasant.

The male pheasant is magnificently handsome, but it is the smaller, plainer hen that chefs seek out for her plump, tender meat. Traditionally, pheasant is hung by the neck for up to ten days before being cooked to heighten the flavour and texture. Young pheasants are wrapped in bacon or larded to keep the meat moist and then roasted. Older birds are sautéed in butter, and then cooked slowly in wines, spirits, and rich stocks. Fruit is often used in the cooking to offset the meat's gamey flavour. Many chefs prefer to cook the breast portion on its own using the rest for pâtés, terrines, and pies. **LW**

Taste: *It is tantalizing to be presented with this plump little bird. The flesh is moist and mildly gamey, rather like the taste and texture of liver especially when served pink.*

Taste: *Pale, lean, and firm, pheasant has the most delicate meat. The breast is creamy yet crumbly with a hint of walnut; the darker leg meat is more sinewy, but still succulent.*

Pheasants need hanging before plucking because having lived in the wild their meat is tougher. »

Gadwall

Widely distributed across Europe, Asia, and North America, the gadwall (*Anas strepera*) is a grey dabbling duck that feeds in both saltwater and freshwater marshland. At the end of summer it leaves its breeding ground in the Arctic Circle to overwinter in southern Europe.

The gadwall is often mistaken by both shooters and butchers for a mallard because it has similar feathers and is a similar size (albeit a bit smaller), but the main distinguishing factor is its white rear wing feathers, which are visible in flight. Gadwall are shot by shooters who either wait at the tide edge for the birds to fly past or sit alongside where the birds are feeding. The gadwall is considered to be one of the easiest ducks to shoot as it tends to fly in a straight line and is more trusting than other wild ducks. It is commonly seen in large flocks, which makes it easier to shoot in bigger numbers.

The first mention of its name is found in *Merrett's List of Birds* (1666) but its exact origin is uncertain. Said by some to be derived from *quedul*, the onomatopoeic Latin word for quack, the gadwall also has a number of local variants and is known variously as the grey duck, rodge, or sand widgeon.

Gadwall is akin to most forms of farmed duck, but being wild it is naturally leaner than its farmed counterpart. It has a coarse-grained meat that works well with traditional duck sauces such as orange. The lack of fat means that the gadwall is best roasted and larded with bacon, or cooked in the classic French style, with turnips, or even boiled in a *court bouillon* and then roasted in a hot oven to keep the flesh moist. Roast gadwall are also excellent stuffed with a veal and wild mushroom forcemeat. **MG**

Taste: Gadwall has a flavour very similar to mallard. Like most duck, it has a pleasant covering of fat under the skin, which is tasty when cooked to a crisp.

Duck breasts are best sautéed over a high heat, long enough to seal the outside but so that the inside is pink.

Teal

The teal (which belongs to the genus *Anas*) is a small, wild dabbling duck, much prized by wildfowlers. The European teal (*Anas crecca*) is partly migratory, overwintering in southern Europe in the wetlands and marshes that form their preferred habitat. The male of the European teal is a handsome bird, with a chestnut head and a broad green eye patch, while both the male and female show bright green wing patches when in flight. There are several species of teal in North America, including *Anas carolinensis*, the green-winged teal, and *Anas discors*, the blue-winged teal. A gregarious bird, the teal arrives at wintering sites in large flocks.

Teal are considered one of the most difficult of wild ducks to shoot, due to their small size and their ability to change direction quickly and unpredictably while flying. Unlike other ducks, they do not respond to calls or to decoys, which adds to their sporting challenge for hunters.

When it comes to eating this flavourful but small wild bird, at least one teal per person is required. They are often eaten as a starter, but when prepared as a main course they are served on a large plate, sometimes with up to three teal per person. The bird's exceptional flavour comes in part from the generous levels of fat found on it. However, the meat is fine-grained and appears to be completely smooth when cut. On the whole, teal, like most wild duck, are enjoyed best when they are served pink, as they can dry out and toughen if cooked for too long. Excellent when cooked with aromatic spices or flavourful herbs, teal can be cooked in a variety of ways, from simply wrapping in bacon and roasting to grilling, frying, or braising with wine. **MG**

Taste: The rich, buttery flavour of teal comes from the fat that the bird acquires on its diet of barley, samphire seeds, and grasses, which contribute to its wonderful flavour.

Golden Plover

Sometimes referred to, rather unfairly, as "poor man's partridge," the golden plover (*Pluvialis apricaria*) spends its summer on breeding grounds in the Arctic Circle and migrates south for the winter. Many gourmands consider the flavour of this small game bird to be superior to that of the French partridge. The bird is so named because of the golden spots that adorn its plumage.

The golden plover lives predominantly on inland, freshwater marshy areas and is seldom encountered in the salt marsh. It uses its short beak to unearth and eat grubs and small water-borne invertebrates. Golden plovers commonly fly in large groups. When a group is shot at from below, the shooter can mistakenly think he has downed the whole group because the birds descend rapidly on hearing the sound of the shot.

Tradition had it that plovers "live on air" and therefore they were among the relatively few gamebirds served without having been drawn—in other words, with their guts intact. A golden plover usually provides just about enough meat for one person. Quickly roasted, the birds were often served on toast—famously, golden plover on toast featured on the dinner menu of the *Titanic*. The breast meat is noted for being covered by a large amount of tasty fat, which makes it particularly juicy, particularly in early summer when the birds fatten themselves for the breeding season.

The first eggs of the season were once offered to the ruling British monarch and reached very high prices. They were also much sought after to prettify fashionable set pieces made of aspic, their colour and shape being said to resemble large opals. **MG**

Taste: *The meat is lighter than that of a snipe, but would not fall into the category of a dark meat like pigeon. It has a delicate flavour, less liverish than most marsh birds.*

Ptarmigan

A member of the grouse family, the ptarmigan (*Lagopus mutus*) is larger than the famous red grouse and can be found in high, snowy, mountainous terrain in Arctic and sub-Arctic countries around the globe. In North America, it is known as the rock ptarmigan. Its thick feathers, which, unusually, extend down over its feet, ensure that it can survive in these cold regions. The ptarmigan burrows into the snow for shelter and to escape predators, such as the Arctic fox. Famously, its plumage alters with the seasons to enable it to blend in with its surroundings. In the winter, when the landscape is covered by snow, the plumage turns pure white, but once the snow has melted the bird develops a mottled, brown plumage, affording it perfect camouflage in the barren rocky terrain.

An edible gamebird, the ptarmigan has long been valued equally for eating and hunting, and pursuing it is a popular sport in those parts of the world where it lives. The flavour of the meat depends on the mountain food, such as shoots, leaves, berries, and insects, that has been available to the bird, but is compared to the rich taste of red grouse or hare. Restaurants often serve ptarmigan with sweet potatoes or a port jus because the sweetness brings out the exceptional flavour of the bird. The liver and hearts are often mashed into a pâté and served as a starter with bread cooked in goose fat. Carpaccio of ptarmigan is a real delicacy, served thinly sliced and dressed with capers, a touch of olive oil, and lime juice. In Iceland, ptarmigan is highly regarded, especially when well hung, and is popular as a Christmas dish accompanied by redcurrant jelly and pickled red cabbage. **MG**

Taste: *Similar to red grouse, the dark meat of ptarmigan is rich and full of flavour. It can combine the smell of heather, the scent of juniper berries, and a hint of Iberian ham.*

The ptarmigan is native to the Canadian Arctic and is still hunted and eaten by Inuit people. ❯

Snipe

Woodcock

As one might expect from a bird that lent its name to a sharpshooter, this little creature is extremely hard to target as it zigzags at high speeds through the wetlands and waterways where it winters. It is noted and prized by hunters in Europe, North America, and beyond; while the season varies from country to country, it can generally be shot from the latter part of summer to late winter or early spring.

Less popular now than during their nineteenth-century heyday, snipe are still held in high regard by many chefs and gastronomes. Both because they are tricky to hunt and because of their tiny size, they tend to be sold mainly by specialists: most weigh only 4 ounces (115 g), with only a third of that weight as meat. Like woodcock, they are traditionally cooked with the entrails left in, and sometimes using their own beak as a skewer: they are often served with toast, brioche, or bread cooked in goose fat so the diner can spread the entrails on them as a pâté, which is excellent accompanied by a glass of port. Snipe should never be hung for too long or over-cooked, as they will become incredibly tough. **MG**

Prized wherever it is found, from Scandinavia and northern Asia through to Italy and southern Spain, the Eurasian woodcock is valued not only for its taste but, particularly in Britain, as a test of the hunter's skill. It roosts in the trees and bushes of wetlands by day, flying out to feed through the night, and uses its long beak to probe the marshy ground for grubs and worms. Like snipe, woodcocks' fast, twisting flight makes them very difficult to shoot. In Britain and Ireland, it is considered a sign of great sporting prowess to shoot two woodcock with two shots one from each barrel of the gun.

Woodcocks are valued not only for their meat but for their entrails: they are always cooked with them in, although the gizzard is removed. In France, they are seasoned with lemon juice, salt, and spices, and combined with brandy and foie gras or fatty bacon; in the Italian *beccacce alla norcina*, they are made into a delicious stuffing with sausages, butter, herbs, and, when in season, black truffle. In Britain, the entrails are eaten on toast. American woodcock are smaller but also highly prized. **MG**

Taste: *Prized for the rich, light meat on the breast, the flavour of snipe is unique: the best comparison is to that of woodcock. Enjoy the smooth, creamy entrails on toast.*

Taste: *Woodcock meat is darker than snipe, with a rich, lightly gamey flavour. The entrails are surprisingly mild: creamy, rich, and smooth, with slightly liverish notes.*

Although snipe does not yield much meat,
⊗ it is still prepared as a delicacy by many top chefs.

Tinamou

Shy and solitary, the tinamou is a bird native to the tropical lowlands of Latin America. In the 1800s it was marketed in Europe as the South American quail until it became rare in the wild. The size of a plump chicken, it does look a little like a quail. There are forty-seven species of tinamou; some are hunted for sport in Argentina, but the Argentine tinamou (*Rhychotus rufescens*) is also popular for the table.

Low in fat and high in protein, the bird is famed for its tender meat, attributed to the fact that it rarely flies, preferring to walk. The meat has a curious opalescent quality, so the tinamou is highly regarded as a table bird. In the wild the tinamou lives an average of five years, but in captivity it reaches its mature weight at twelve to sixteen weeks, and is best eaten at thirteen weeks when its meat is most tender. The breast meat is ideal served as a starter, when it is battered and pan-fried, but it is also a good meat for use in stews flavoured with tomatoes and garlic.

The tinamou's eggs are edible and taste similar to chicken eggs. However, they are most prized for their glossy, green, turquoise, purple, or red shells. Several females may lay eggs in one nest, or one female may lay eggs in several nests. In either case, it is a male tinamou that builds the nest and sits on the eggs, and later tends the chicks. It is the female tinamou that courts the male.

Attempts by enthusiasts to introduce the tinamou into the European repertoire of game birds came to nought when it was discovered that the bird flew only very reluctantly. Its tolerant behaviour towards other birds had led many to believe it would be a successful companion to the pheasant. **CK**

Taste: *The incredibly tender, white flesh of the tinamou is semi-opaque in appearance. It has a mild, gamey flavour and can be prepared in the manner of partridge.*

Tinamou can be prepared in a similar way
🗙 *to quail and partridge such as pan-fried in butter.*

Paca

The paca (*Agouti paca*) is a large, brown, white-spotted rodent found in forests, swamps, and jungles from east central Mexico and Cuba southwards to northern Paraguay, Brazil, and Argentina. Resembling a guinea pig in appearance, an adult can weigh up to 30 pounds (14 kg). Pacas are, despite their rather rotund appearance, remarkably fast on land and in the water; they are generally nocturnal animals.

The paca's tender meat is regarded as an exquisite delicacy, so much so that it was considered to be a gourmet food fit for Queen Elizabeth II of the United Kingdom, who was served paca when she visited Belize on a royal tour in 1985. Unusually for a forest animal, the flesh and skin can be almost white; in flavour and texture they are like chicken.

In the wild, pacas mainly survive on fruits and seeds, but they are hunted by farmers because they eat crops such as corn, yam, cassava, and sugar cane. Some governments have banned paca hunting because the animal has been over-culled in some areas. Attempts have been made to raise it in captivity, although the meat of the domesticated animal is said to be inferior.

In its region of distribution, the meat is cooked in various ways. In Panama, it is grilled on a skewer, or roasted after being marinated in a black pepper sauce. In Mexico, it is boiled unskinned, or it is barbecued over hot coals and eaten with tortillas and a spicy salsa. Indigenous Latin American peoples often smoke the flesh of the paca, which preserves it from deterioration, while the Guyanese stuff the paca's stomach with a pudding of meat and grain before roasting it. **CK**

Taste: *Paca has beautifully tender meat that cuts very easily and simply melts in the mouth. In flavour, it is a cross somewhere between chicken and pork.*

Hare

These beautiful, intelligent creatures, from the *Leporidae* family, feature in folklore and myth from the Hindu *Panchatantra* to *Aesop's Fables*. Hare was the most common game animal in Greek and Roman times, whereas in England their exuberant behaviour over the mating period is responsible for the expression: "mad as a March hare."

Various species of hare are found worldwide, from Europe, China, and India to Africa, the Americas, and Australasia, and the line between rabbit and hare is fairly blurred, although hares, unlike rabbits, have never been domesticated. Generally, hares (a category into which Europeans would place the Californian jackrabbit) are larger than rabbits with long ears, the eponymous hare lip, and strong hindquarters. A young hare is known as a leveret until it is a year old, at which point its lip becomes more pronounced and its smooth coat turns wiry.

Hare should be hung for six days to develop its flavour and texture, head downwards over a bowl to catch its blood for later use in the cooking pot. **LW**

Taste: The meat is lean and dry, the flavour strong—half chicken, half venison. Young hares are best roasted or jugged. Older specimens reward lengthy cooking.

Rex du Poitou®

While the name Rex du Poitou® would not have been familiar to epicures even a generation ago, it is gaining currency today. It refers to a strain of rabbit that was bred by French geneticists to have a commercial value not only for its Orylag fur but for its excellent meat.

In France, rearing rabbits in cages for the table is traditional in the countryside. The meat is sweeter and more tender than that of wild rabbits, and the creatures can reach up to 5 pounds (2.3 kg) in weight, much larger than most of their wild peers.

The Rex du Poitou®, now a registered trademark, began to make an impact on the food world in 1996, when it won the Coq d'Or prize for the best French food product awarded by the *France Gourmande à Domicile* guide. Since then the meat has become more readily available and is sold in Paris at a premium. Farming is carried out on an artisanal scale and the Rex du Poitou® remains an exclusive meat comparable to, say, Bresse chicken. It has been featured by several Michelin-starred chefs and is growing in popularity. **MR**

Taste: Smooth-textured Rex du Poitou® has a plump, fleshy appearance. Its mild taste is less gamey than wild rabbit. Unlike other farmed rabbits, it does not dry out when cooked.

The mild sweet flavour of rabbit meat is enhanced here by marinating the legs in olive oil, garlic, and thyme. ❯❯

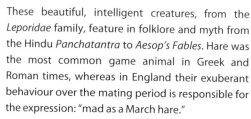

Moose

The largest member of the deer family, the moose, or European elk (*Alces alces*), can weigh up to 1,500 pounds (680 kg). Found in the far north of Europe and Asia, it has played an important role in Scandinavia as a source of protein since the Stone Age, and is known as "king of the forest" in both Norway and Sweden.

For many Swedes and Norwegians moose hunting is one of the highlights of the year. When the season begins, hunters from all walks of life gather—in northern Sweden, schools and factories actually close for the day. Yet despite this active hunting tradition and culture, which sees over 100,000 animals shot each year, the region maintains the world's most dense population of moose.

Thanks to its natural diet of leaves and twigs, moose is lean and full of minerals and vitamins. This healthy meat is not only served as fillets and steaks, but widely used in the form of minced meat. The Swedish astronaut Christer Fuglesang treated his astronaut colleagues to some dried moose meat on his first trip into space. **CC**

Taste: *Moose meat is less gamey than much other venison, and in fact is not unlike beef in its flavour and appearance, although leaner, with a fresher flavour.*

Roe Deer

One of the smaller species of deer, the roe deer (*Capreolus capreolus*) has long been regarded as providing the finest venison. It feeds on a rich diet of shoots, leaves, roses, herbs, and berries that contributes to its exceptionally delicate flavour. Unlike most other deer species, roe deer can be hunted all year round in almost all northern European countries where it lives, ensuring sport for the hunter and fine food for the gourmand.

Also found in Asia Minor and the Caspian coastal regions, roe deer have reddish bodies, a grey face, and a white rump patch. They are shy animals, solitary except for when mating, and live in dense forest and woodland. They are not farmed or seen in parks and need traditional stalking. Wild roe deer has to be hung for at least a week before cooking.

Roe deer provides a fantastically tasty meat, more tender than most other venison. The lean meat simply requires frequent basting when roasting. Neck fillets and rumps can be pan-fried. Roe deer venison is particularly good served with root vegetables and a robust gravy. **MG**

Taste: *The fillets have an incredibly smooth texture, that is like cutting through butter. The subtle flavour is almost like cured meat, but with the venison taste still remaining.*

Roe deer are known to produce the best venison; in this preparation the steaks are coated in a pepper crust. ❯❯

Reindeer

Springbok

This majestic Arctic animal has been a source of meat for the Sami, who inhabit the Sami region, which runs through Norway, Sweden, Finland, and Russia, for as long as it has lived alongside humans. Traditionally, they use every single part of the animal: the meat, blood, and internal organs are eaten; the fur is used for clothing and shoes; the bones and antlers are transformed into knives and decorative objects. Today the Sami ranch them in huge herds, with the help of snowmobiles and sometimes even helicopters.

While greatly reduced in numbers, the reindeer is not endangered. It grazes freely, making a very ethical choice of food. It is lower in fat than beef or pork, making it a healthy choice. Today, it is seen as a delicacy in many parts of Scandinavia, and is most commonly served simply sautéed. Many Sami still cook it according to the old recipes, cutting thin slices from a frozen joint or shoulder, then sautéing in its own fat. It also commonly appears in soups or stews, with the bones forming the base of the broth, as well as dried, or smoked. **CTj**

A national symbol during white minority rule, and a mascot of many sporting teams, the springbok is also a South African delicacy. A smallish antelope, *Antidorcas marsupialis*, its name means literally "jumping buck," because of its tendency to leap straight into the air when excited. During the displays known as "pronking" it can reach many times its own 30 inch (75 cm) height.

The springbok forages for grass in large herds in dry, inland regions, meaning that its meat is entirely organic and free of chemical fertilizers and growth hormones. It leads a highly active lifestyle, and is adapted to survive both drought and low food availability. Its meat is high in protein, low in fat, and finely textured.

The extremely low fat content means that the meat was traditionally viewed as dry, and larger cuts should always be well larded and cooked with care. Cooked, it is often used for pies, terrines, and pâtés, like other venison. Locally it may be salted, spiced, and dried to make biltong or the dried sausage known as *droëwors*. **ABH**

Taste: *Reindeer has a clear gamey taste, not dissimilar to venison, but with a sweeter, smoother finish. It is lean and tender, especially when roasted slowly and not overdone.*

Taste: *Springbok is subtly gamey and is enhanced by the use of garlic and spices during cooking. Its dense texture benefits from partnering with sweet-and-sour flavours.*

Versatile reindeer meat is used in dishes ranging from soups to stews; it is excellent pan-fried and served rare.

Ostrich

Tuscan Wild Boar

Mostly solitary animals when wild, ostriches are once again being farmed in large ranches, as they were during the nineteenth century. By the early twentieth century, their fashionable feathers were ranked fourth on the list of South African exports after gold, diamonds, and wool.

A diet of seeds, leaves, flowers, and insects and strong legs that can produce a speed of 40 miles (65km) per hour both contribute to the oxygen-rich, blood-red meat, which is between 2 and 3 per cent fat, about 26 per cent protein, and low in cholesterol. Because of its low fat content, the meat may appear dry if not correctly cooked.

Steaks, fillets, and neck are the most popular cuts of meat, but almost the entire bird can be used, even the stomach. Schnitzels, goulashes, burgers, pâtés, and biltong are but a few of the dishes made using ostrich meat. Ostrich oil, high in Omega-3, 6, and 9 and also non-comedogenic (does not block pores), is used to produce an excellent soap. Feathers and leather, as well as tourist ostrich rides, continue to contribute to a growing industry. **HFi**

The rolling hillsides and woodlands of Tuscany have always been abundant in game, not least the brawny *cinghiale*, or wild boar. Its meat has a wonderfully intense depth of flavour that is helped by a diet rich in naturally foraged roots, herbs, acorns, chestnuts, mushrooms, and sometimes even truffles, so it comes as no surprise that it has long been a speciality in the region. All manner of recipes have been handed down through the generations and various cuts form the base for some of Italy's finest sausage, prosciutto, and salami products. The meat of wild boar has a deeper, more pronounced essence than that of domestic pigs, and the sausages and cured meat products generally have a more robust flavour and aroma.

The hunting season takes place during the winter months, and Tuscan wild boar respond well to slow cooking in some of the province's gutsy red wines, making rich, powerful stews and casseroles. A favourite with locals and tourists alike is *pappardelle al sugo di cinghiale*, or pappardelle pasta with a rich wild boar sauce. **LF**

Taste: *With a pleasant meaty flavour and a distinct difference from other game, ostrich meat can be used as a healthy alternative to beef in most recipes.*

Taste: *Wild boar has a deep red hue and an intense taste. The meat is aromatic without being overly gamey. The flavour is full-bodied with a sweet but piquant edge.*

Cinghiale porchetta *(roast wild boar) makes a tasty snack served on crusty rustic bread in Tuscany.* ❯❯

Sucking Pig

Sucking or suckling pig—a piglet slaughtered so young that it has fed only on its mother's milk—is considered a delicacy in many countries. Spanish and Chinese cuisines value the animal highly, and In the Philippines, a place where these two cultures meet, the piglets are flavoured with tropical herbs, spit-roasted over charcoal, and sold as *lechón baboy*. (The La Loma district of Quezon City has a special reputation for its sucking pigs.) In Portugal, sucking pig—*leitão assado*—is closely identified with the town of Mealhada, where it is stuffed with garlic and lard and baked in brick ovens.

Yet everywhere it is eaten the *pièce de résistance* is the skin. Carefully handled, it takes on a rich mahogany colour and a texture so brittle that it cracks when pressed. The flesh, naturally bland, white, and sweet, absorbs the flavours of both the stuffing and, over an open fire, smoke. But although the name implies a tiny creature, there are wide differences between a three-week-old animal weighing less than 11 pounds (5 kg) and one more than twice its weight and age. **MR**

Gloucester Old Spot Pork

A generation ago, Gloucester Old Spot pigs from the West of England were in serious danger of extinction. They have recovered partly as a reaction against factory farming, partly on merit. Popular at the turn of the twentieth century, they were also referred to as orchard pigs or cottager's pigs, folksy names that probably described the humble environments where they were reared.

For a period the "Old Spot" was the most valuable British pig, but it fell from favour partly because it had more fat on it than was fashionable, partly because modern crosses could be produced more economically. Yet in the serious business of cooking, it performs far better than its replacements. The fat need not be excessive with good husbandry, just sufficient to protect and baste the joint. The lean meat has intramuscular fat and shrinks less than other pork when roasted.

The belly has thick layers of fat and lean. A handicap in the past, this is now considered an advantage to produce a joint with excellent flavour. The Old Spot also makes an excellent bacon pig. **MR**

Taste: *The cracking skin on a well-roasted sucking pig is as crisp as caramel on a fresh toffee apple. Under it, the meat is beautifully creamy and lightly gelatinous.*

In the Philippines, spit-roasted sucking pigs are eaten
 *on special occasions, often with a liver-based sauce.*

Taste: *The texture of Old Spot is more open than factory-farmed pigs. The fibres of the meat are tastier, softer, and juicier. The fat delivers a rich taste of pork dripping.*

Aveyron Lamb

The Aveyron is a region of France on the edge of the Massif Central renowned for its Roquefort cheese, made with milk from Lacaune sheep. In recent years, its farmers have combined together to create high quality lamb, Agneau Allaiton d'Aveyron, by evolving a Lacaune meat breed.

The young lambs are kept in barns from birth and fed exclusively on their mothers' milk for the first two months. They then remain enclosed until slaughter, receiving additional cereals in their diet; the ewes graze on pasture during the daytime, which enriches their milk.

The objective of this husbandry is to produce a kind of meat that parallels the finest veal, whose texture and taste depend on a diet centred on milk. It produces a carcass of a size that is sought after by chefs in particular, but which has the characteristic tenderness, colour, and taste of spring lamb, which is smaller and only available for a limited season. Untypically, starred gastronomic restaurants are happy to put this lamb's offal—particularly liver—and secondary cuts on their menus. **MR**

Taste: *When roasted or grilled, the underdone joints of Aveyron lamb have a pale pink colour. They are very juicy with the sweetness that is characteristic of spring lamb.*

Gower Salt Marsh Lamb

The Gower Peninsula on the south coast of Wales is characterized by its sandy bays, farmland, and salt marshes. Because the marshes lie at sea level, the vegetation—cordgrass, sea lavender, and sorrel—is impregnated with the brackish, iodine aromatics of seawater. Sheep grazing here produce lambs whose meat has a distinct flavour from that of the surrounding hillsides. It has always paired well with the local seaweeds known as laverbread (*Porphyra*) that are cooked and then fried in small cakes

Until recently, lambs reared in the area were marketed without any attempt to distinguish them from other livestock. However, early in the millennium two sheep farmers started a small cooperative to promote their meat: at the time of writing it handles about 1,500 lambs each year.

There are other sheep that benefit from a similar diet. In the Orkneys, off the north coast of Scotland, a semi-wild breed on the island of North Ronaldsay provides excellent meat; in northern France, on the flats around Mont St. Michel *mouton de pré salé* has enjoyed a similar reputation. **MR**

Taste: *Leaner and darker than meat from the Welsh hills, Gower Salt Marsh lamb has a taste that is closer to a yearling than a young lamb, but sweet and juicy.*

Strong flavours like rosemary and anchovy season lamb well; here pungent caraway seeds are used. ❯

Fat-tailed Sheep

A striking example of selective breeding, the fat-tailed sheep appeared around the fourth millennium BCE. Today, the many different varieties account for around a quarter of the world's sheep population.

The astonishing tail of the fat-tailed sheep is a large, portable lump of fat that can weigh over 25 pounds (12 kg) and is, like the camel's hump, an energy storehouse for the animal. The appearance of the tail varies according to the breed, ranging from a wide flap to a broad, pendulous tail; some are so long that they drag along the ground. Fat-tailed sheep are common in Africa, the Near and Middle East, northern India, Mongolia, and western China.

Mentions of the fat from fat-tailed sheep as an ingredient occur in early Arabic cookery books. As far back as the Middle Ages, recipes for clarifying this fat, *alya*, colouring it, and using it as a cooking ingredient in desserts, pastries, and savoury dishes were already popular. Travelling through Persia at this time, Marco Polo described the tails as "fat and excellent to eat." The smell of the fat being rendered is rank, but the flavour is noted for its delicacy, partly accounting for the fragrance of many Iranian, Syrian, and Lebanese dishes. The Lebanese use the fat in a dish called *qawarma*, in which minced lamb is preserved in fat from the tail of the fat-tailed sheep. A traditional food of Lebanese mountain tribes and once a staple of the winter months, *qawarma* is increasingly seen as a delicacy.

An important aspect of the fat-tailed sheep's continuing popularity is that the meat is lean, since most of the fat of the animal is localized in the tail. In the Lebanon, the lean meat is used in *kibbeh nayeh*, while the liver is eaten raw. **MR**

Taste: *Eaten as halal meat, fat-tailed sheep are bled and not left pink when cooked. The meat is firmer and meatier than European lamb. The fat is mild rather than tallowy.*

Goat

Goats are thought to have been domesticated alongside sheep around 10,000 years ago in southwest Asia. The domestic goat (*Capra hircus*) is probably descended from the wild *Capra aegagrus*. The long history of domestication has yielded many breeds of goats, reared for their milk, meat, and hair. Goats are valued for their ability to thrive in harsh environments and to traverse difficult terrain.

Although goats are reared for their meat as well as their milk in many countries—including sub-Saharan Africa, southern Asia, southern Europe, Latin America, and the Caribbean—the meat, especially from the adult male "billy goat," has an unfavourable reputation for being scrawny and tough. The meat from young goats (kids) is preferred by many for being the most tender and mild in flavour. In Mediterranean countries roast kid is a traditional festive dish.

Curried goat is the de facto national dish of Jamaica, where the animal was probably introduced by the Spanish. The spices with which the goat is seasoned there are in part based on indigenous produce, whereas the recipe's origin may owe more to immigrant labour from the Indian subcontinent. Traditional flavourings for Jamaican curried goat are the fierily hot Scotch Bonnet pepper and fragrant allspice berries. Its popularity has spread across the Caribbean and through the West Indian diaspora.

Goat's milk, with its small, easily digested fat particles, is a popular drink in many parts of the world. In countries with a dairy tradition, such as the United Kingdom, it is also increasingly used to make cheese, easily distinguished from other cheeses by its bright white appearance. **MR**

Taste: *Long, slow cooking tenderizes goat meat. Lean and similar in colour to mutton, it is strongly flavoured without the tallowy taste that is associated with mutton.*

Free-ranging goats, such as these on a Norwegian hillside, search widely for food and yield lean meat. »

Villsau Mutton

Isard

The ancient breed of sheep known locally as Villsau (wild sheep) or Gammel Norsk Sau (old Norwegian sheep) live and graze mainly around the cold and windy western coast of Norway. Although bred for meat, they spend their lives outdoors in freedom, using the natural resources of the rugged landscape to supply food and shelter all year round. It is this diet, rich in wild shrubs, heathers, herbs, grasses, and even seaweeds, that helps give Villsau mutton its unique and spectacular flavour.

Although small in stature, the Villsau's hardy way of life results in a distribution that is very different to that of more standard breeds. Their fatty tissue is concentrated around the internal organs—hence their round bellies—and the marbling of fat on the flesh between the muscle fibres is very fine, making the meat extremely tender. The meat of the Villsau sheep is often used in the traditional Nordic delicacies *pinnekjøtt*, a dish prepared from salted, dried ribs which are then steamed over birch twigs, and *fenalår*, cured leg of mutton. Both dishes are traditionally served at Christmas time. **LF**

The Pyrenean chamois (*Rupicapra pyrenaica*), known as isard in French, is a mountain antelope that inhabits both the French and Spanish sides of the Pyrenees and was so popular among gourmets that it had almost been hunted to extinction by the 1960s. The establishment of the first national parks has enabled the population to recover; hunting is still strictly controlled, although isard are now bred commercially. Isard inhabit rocky high pastures, feeding on grass, lichens, and the young shoots of trees and bushes, which give it the delicate flavour for which it is so highly prized.

Modern chefs prefer younger isard as the meat is more tender and the flavour less gamey. It is often served simply grilled over embers. Mature isard can be treated similarly to venison. In the Spanish region of Catalunya, isard is traditionally marinated for hours in red wine with rosemary, sage, and thyme and then prepared in a stew. The stock is made with the bones and the sauce is enriched with a small amount of chocolate. Isard is good partnered with chestnuts, apples, and mushrooms. **RL**

Taste: *Soaked and steamed until falling off the bone, Villsau mutton has a tender texture and a rich flavour with hints of herbs and grass and a whisper of saltiness.*

Taste: *Lean and firm in texture, the subtle gamey flavour has aromatic nuances of mountain herbs, which distinguish it from the less complex flavours of kid goat.*

Piedmont Veal

Limousin Veal

Veal has long been prized in European gastronomic culture for its tender eating qualities and sweet flavour. In Piedmont, northern Italy, a specific strain of cattle has evolved that has become world renowned for the fantastic quality of its meat. Broad-shouldered and chunky, the *razza piemontese* is a gentle giant of a breed with characteristic double muscling that means it produces lean, concentrated meat with less fat and gristle than normal. A diet rich in natural grasses creates a unique flavour.

Veal was first introduced as a way for the dairy industry to make use of surplus male calves and did not take long to catch on. Today the rosy, relatively mature veal of Piedmont, raised without antibiotics or hormones, has become the basis of various regional specialities. *Carne cruda all'Albese* (or *carne cruda*) is a dish of raw veal, hand-chopped using two knives, then dressed in a simple mixture of extra virgin olive oil and lemon juice, seasoned with salt and black pepper. Occasionally it might be served with shavings of Parmesan; in the autumn fresh truffle makes a decadent embellishment. **LF**

The calves that will produce Limousin veal (PGI) are raised in much kinder conditions than many of their peers: *sous la mère* (with their mothers), and nourished on their mothers' milk. They are raised in the Limousin region of west central France, which centres on the city of Limoges, hence their name.

The title, however, can be confusing. "Limousin" cattle are a prime beef breed. But "Limousin" veal may come from other breeds provided it is reared in the region and according to the criteria laid down in the PGI. The French Label Rouge quality mark lays down that the veal should be reared to between ninety and one hundred and sixty days' old, that it should only be given food supplements during the last two months before slaughter and that the carcass should weigh no more than 375 pounds (170 kg).

The flesh of Limousin veal is paler than that from calves reared by agro-industrial methods, and more succulent because fat from the mother's milk is deposited in the muscle fibres. During cooking, this meat retains its body whereas lesser veal tends to shrink and dry out. **MR**

Taste: *Raw Piedmont veal is succulent and juicy with savoury, grassy notes; cooked, its flavour remains more meaty than milk-fed veals, yet is still tender and juicy.*

Taste: *The prime cuts of Limousin veal—loin, ribs, and cushion—are lightly but cleanly flavoured, with a juicy, firm texture when grilled or fried.*

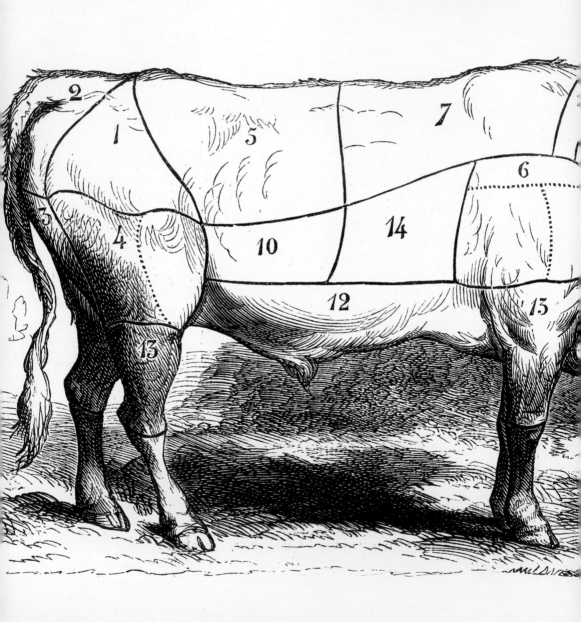

Aberdeen-Angus Beef

The most widely known breed of Scottish cattle originated in the early nineteenth century. A pioneer breeder, Hugh Watson from Kelllor in the county of Angus, developed a strain of cattle that William McCombie from Tillyfour in Aberdeenshire bred closely—hence the name Aberdeen-Angus. The breed's success came from its strong genes: its characteristic black colour, hornlessness, rapid growth, and excellent meat are all easily inherited.

Adaptability has helped keep the Aberdeen-Angus at the top of the table of beef breeds. Today worldwide there are over fifty million Aberdeen-Angus type cattle, and the breed is still developing to produce cattle that fit the current trend for larger, leaner meat such as Charolais and Limousin but with better flavour. The results have fat marbled through their meat. Although available worldwide, most still believe the breed is finest in Scotland, thanks to the climate and husbandry. Wherever it is produced, Aberdeen-Angus carries a certification trademark, which guarantees quality and allows breeders to command a premium. **CTr**

Taste: *Aberdeen-Angus is distinctive by its dense texture and deeply coloured fat. Cooked it has a broad flavour and good texture. Its density also makes it excellent eaten raw.*

An 1855 French illustration informs
beef buyers of the cuts available.

Bison

What is often referred to as buffalo or American buffalo is, in fact, bison (*Bison bison*). This woolly, humped member of the Bovidae family, is only a distant relative of the African buffalo and the Asian water-buffalo. Bison was a mainstay of the diet of the Native Americans and the pioneers who settled on the western plains of the United States and Canada. At one time, millions roamed the plains, but over-hunting reduced their numbers to about 1,500 by the late 1800s. Since the late twentieth century, however, there has been a revival of interest in bison as a source of flavoursome meat; herds are now managed and there are around 2,000 bison producers in the United States.

Bison produces lean, tender meat, higher in iron and lower in fat than most beef. Chefs have eagerly embraced the more costly cuts, like tenderloin, strip, and rib-eye. Care must be taken not to over-cook bison—cook slowly on a low heat. Less tender cuts need braising. Cattle and bison have been cross-bred to produce a new meat known as "beefalo" in the United States and "cattalo" in Canada. **SH**

Taste: *Bison has a deeper red colour than beef with no marbling. Not in the least gamey, it tastes similar to good beef, but slightly sweeter, richer, and fuller in flavour.*

Kobe Beef

What foie gras is to liver, Kobe beef is to steak. It comes from any of several related breeds of native Japanese cattle, known collectively as Wagyu, and so the terms Wagyu and Kobe have been used almost interchangeably. However, the export of Wagyu cattle from Japan to around the world has led the Japanese to protect the denomination Kobe beef so that it can now only be applied to home-grown meat.

The cost and the folklore surrounding Kobe cattle's husbandry have given it epic status. The diet of grain and beer, allied to regular massage—which both tenderizes the beef and relaxes the bullock—is said to turn Wagyu cattle into a uniquely fatty animal. (Incidentally, the meat is low in cholesterol.) All this is true, but the central difference relates to the breeds themselves. They are genetically disposed to produce a much more intramuscular marbling than any Western beef cattle. When seared, the surface of a Kobe beef steak caramelizes rapidly and crisps. It should be eaten rare or blue. Otherwise the benefit of texture and taste will leech out, leaving it dry and uninteresting. **MR**

Taste: *The marbled fat sets Kobe beef apart. It creates a velvety feel, rather than the juiciness, say, of an Aberdeen-Angus steak: the light taste lingers on the palate.*

For centuries the Japanese have been selectively breeding cattle for their high level of fatty marbling. ❯

ACHAT DE CHEVAUX

Horsemeat

Rattlesnake

The concept of eating horse is abhorrent to many Anglo-Saxons "who would rather eat the rider than the horse" but is relatively common in Belgium, France, Austria, Iceland, Italy, Japan, and parts of Canada. While much horsemeat comes from breeds such as carthorses, which might otherwise have become extinct except for their role as food, any kind of horse can be sold for its flesh.

Proponents claim that horsemeat is healthier than beef: it is leaner, and contains fewer calories and less fat. Specialist butchers may take more care in handling the carcass, and, because horses are generally reared on a small scale, there are few of the problems linked to factory farming practices.

The difference between beef and horsemeat is in the tenderness. Nearly all cuts of the latter can be eaten by rapid cooking rather than the slow cooking necessary for tougher joints of beef. Connoisseurs of steak tartare claim that horsemeat is essential to the recipe and the name of the dish itself may have connections to mounted Tartar warriors: horsemeat remains a significant part of the Mongolian diet. **MR**

Snakes elicit reactions of fear in most Western minds. Those anxieties might best be traded with visions of gourmet delight, as have the residents of America's arid southwestern deserts on discovering rattlesnake to be a flavourful source of food.

Ranchers in the U.S. southwest have adopted the western diamondback rattlesnake (*Crotalus atrox*) as an exotic food. The species is quite thick and meaty, with the skinned snake fillets almost always remaining on the bony skeleton. The meat flakes off more easily after cooking, but is usually served up with the numerous pin-like bones intact.

Rattlesnake is available fresh, frozen, and canned in various sauces and smokes, which can overpower the flavour of the meat. Dried and smoked forms of rattlesnake are also traded in the southern U.S. states and Mexico. Care is advised with sourcing uncooked meat as it may carry harmful parasites. Rattlesnake is most commonly deep-fried in a cornmeal coating much like catfish. The canned meat is used in a wide array of recipes ranging from dips to barbecue. **TH**

Taste: *High levels of glycogen in the meat explain why horsemeat tastes sweeter than beef. Its texture is tender enough to fry. Novices prefer eating it rare, or even raw.*

Taste: *More like a strong white fish with gamey overtones than the archetypal comparison to chicken, the chewy texture has been compared to alligator.*

An old Parisian sign advertises horsemeat. Special shops were set up to ensure the quality of the meat sold.

Mississippi Alligator

Kangaroo

Mississippi alligator, or American alligator, is native to Mississippi and southeastern areas of the United States. Primarily found in marshes and freshwater swamps, the high demand for its skin and meat put it on the endangered list in the 1960s and it remains a species of concern. The alligator population has since recovered with the help of captive habitats. These farms meet the demand for alligator products without depleting the species.

Eating alligator is nothing new. Native Americans were smoking and eating alligator when Spanish explorers came to Florida in the 1600s. Because alligators are large, they provide a variety of cuts of meat, both tender and more tough. Alligator takes well to marinades and can be fried or grilled. Often the tougher cuts are simmered in a stew.

Alligator jambalaya with hot sausage, tomato, rice, green pepper, garlic, and other seasonings is a popular dish, as is spicy alligator sausage. Restaurants along the U.S. Gulf Coast serve grilled or fried alligator tail. Spicy Creole and Cajun seasonings go particularly well with this meat. **SH**

Kangaroo has long been a favourite meat among Australian Aborigines, but the idea of eating an animal from the national coat of arms (as well as a fondness for the TV character, Skippy) has been enough to stop many non-indigenous Australians from even trying it. Less squeamish Aboriginal Australians would, and still do, shoot or spear and gut their catch, singe its hair, scrape it off, then bury the animal under earth and hot coals for cooking. The generic term "kangaroo" encompasses several species including wallabies and wallaroos, all marsupials native predominantly to Australia. White settlers ate the meat, which is the same colour as liver, in the early years of the colony because it was much cheaper than imported salt pork and was often the only fresh meat available.

An increase in beef and mutton production saw kangaroo meat disappear from the table and be relegated to pet food status until the late 1970s. As interest in native foods grows, so too does the demand for kangaroo, which is a versatile meat as well as low in fat (2 per cent) and cholesterol. **SCS**

Taste: *Alligator meat is a firm-textured white meat that tastes like chicken, only with a richer, slightly fishy flavour. Depending on how it is cooked, it can have a swampy taste.*

Taste: *Kangaroo should be lightly cooked and well rested to preserve moisture. Young meat tastes very like beef and becomes pleasantly gamey and venison-like over time.*

Five of the forty-eight species of Australian kangaroo— prepared here as kebabs—are harvested for meat. ❯❯

Escargot de Bourgogne

There are many edible varieties of snail, from infant *petit gris* to the giant African land snail that can grow up to 10 inches (25 cm) long, but few have any special appeal. Their attraction lies in the extraction of an unusual meat that was, historically, kept for times when food was scarce. Medieval monasteries added snails to the menu during Lent; sailors carried them onboard ship; and purged on rosemary, they are a traditional component of paella.

The French are voracious eaters of snails, devouring some 40,000 tons per year. Today, the snail most often eaten in France is the common garden snail (*Helix aspersa*) which is mainly imported from farms abroad. Until quite recently, the escargot de Bourgogne (*Helix pomatia*)—a close relative of the common garden snail—was synonymous with a traditional style of French cuisine and figured on every bistro menu. But it is a species that does not like to be farmed, and the modern-day scarcity of wild snails in France means that the dish escargots de Bourgogne is increasingly rare.

Although subtly flavoured, the snails require a good deal of preparation. Gathered alive, they are purged to eliminate plant toxins and grit. This is achieved either by starving them for five to seven days, or by keeping them in a shaded place, such as a bucket, for around two weeks and feeding them herbs. They are then drowned, blanched, and simmered, before they are ready for a final cooking. In the classic recipe, the snails are put back in their large, pale shells with a *beurre d'escargot*—a parsley and garlic butter—and baked in a very hot oven. This high cholesterol dish tastes delicious and is a traditional New Year's specialty in France. **MR**

Taste: *Escargots de Bourgogne have an indefinable meatiness. They are chewy, but owe their fame as a delicacy to the garlic butter, which should be bubbling.*

Although snails are in many cultures a protein source of last resort, the French have elevated their status.

Bee Larva

Eating insects is a strange concept for Westerners, although many different cultures around the world from Asia to Central America have eaten them both as a staple and a delicacy. Humans often turn to insects when there is a scarcity of fish and meat, and alternative sources of protein are needed.

Bee larvae are eaten in Mexico and the Far East. In Japan, China, Thailand, and Vietnam they are usually served as an appetizer, sometimes together with the honeycomb. The yellow larvae look similar to fat maggots or mealworms and are very delicate. They can be eaten live, fresh from the hive, but they are also prepared in a number of different ways. Fried in oil with a little salt and pepper, perhaps a touch of chilli, the larvae take on a crispy texture.

For a sweeter taste, bee larvae are fried with soy sauce and sugar, while in Mexico they are sometimes seen served covered in chocolate. In Japan, bee larvae, *hachinoko*, are sold preserved and canned in soya-bean oil. The Chinese marinate the larvae with onion, lemongrass, and coconut cream. Once they are fully marinated, the larvae are wrapped in linen, steamed for twenty minutes, and served with boiled rice or noodles.

When societies become more urbanized, their eating habits change and there develops a growing dependency on fast food and Western ingredients. In such circumstances, people come to associate their insect consumption with underdevelopment and the past. In Japan, bee larva consumption is said to be declining among the young, while the old still appreciate the nostalgia of their *hachinoko*. Insect secretions such as honey remain almost universally popular, however. **CK**

Taste: *Raw, live bee larvae wriggle, and have a milky, honey taste. When fried, the larvae have a crunchy, crisp texture with a subtle flavour of honey.*

Giant Water Beetle

Thai people are fairly adventurous when it comes to food. Tucking into a bowl of authentic *pad thai* noodles is only touching the tip of the Thai culinary iceberg. Insects such as roasted, spiced crickets and fried bamboo worm larvae are also regular fare. However, it is the giant water beetle (*Lethocerus indicus*)—known as *maeng daa*—that locals devour with a passion. The beetle is considered a delicacy and is prized for its subtle "fishy" flavour.

The water beetle, which can reach almost 4 inches (10 cm) in length, is particularly valued in the rural Isaan region of northeast Thailand. At night locals use lights and vibrations to attract the best specimens which inhabit Thailand's watery rice fields. Such is the demand for the giant water beetle, that it is now being farmed.

Water beetles are best prepared fresh as the taste deteriorates fast. They can be stir-fried with straw mushrooms, spring onions, chilli, and garlic, or ground into a paste with chilli and eaten with sticky rice. But the most popular method of cooking is to deep-fry them whole. Cracking into one takes practice. First the legs are removed and the exoskeleton is prised open to access the meaty interior. The body holds a flaky meat the consistency of tinned tuna and the head contains a gelatinous mix of parts. Beetles laden with eggs—the consistency of tiny caviar—are a particular delicacy.

In the Canton province of China giant water beetles are dropped into boiling, salted water then seasoned with a little oil. In the Far East, insects are often eaten for medicinal purposes, but no health benefits have been ascribed to the giant water beetle. They are eaten solely for culinary pleasure. **TH**

Leaf-cutter Ant

Leaf-cutter ants are so called because they use their jaws to cut away portions of leaves to be carried to their nest. Perhaps surprisingly, the ants are appreciated as a food item, particularly in Brazil's Amazon basin. They are at their best at the beginning of the rainy season when females leave the nest in huge numbers, moving sluggishly enough to be easy prey. They are caught by the basket load, and eaten either raw or roasted with salt. Their taste is nutty and highly appreciated.

In Brazil, the leaf-cutter ant now has an extensive urban following, too, with trays of the cooked ants being hawked through the streets of São Paulo. One of the country's most famous authors, Monteiro Lobato, who was born at the end of the nineteenth century in the Paraíba valley, called leaf-cutter ants the peasant's caviar, the ultimate delicacy for someone from that upstate region. Passed on from generation to generation, the ancient legacy is still alive in the valley today. It is customary to eat ants between the months of September and November, when they grow wings and leave their nests to mate. Only females are eaten, known as *içá* or *tanajura*.

Care is needed in preparing the insect for eating. The head, thorax, legs, and wings are removed, and the back is pan-fried in oil until crispy. The result is best when pork fat, rather than vegetable oil, is used for this process. Once fried, the *içá* is dusted with cassava or corn flour and is ready to serve. Many ant fans crush this mixture with a pestle to obtain the famous *paçoca de içá* (*içá* mixture). Some São Paulo chefs have compared the taste of leaf-cutter ants to that of a strongly flavoured home-made butter, as it consists of pure protein. **AL**

Taste: *Water beetle tastes like whitefish that stayed out all night. Even when prepared with chilli the mild, shrimp flavour shows through with nutty overtones.*

Taste: *After frying, well-toasted leaf-cutter ant is intensely crunchy in the mouth and leaves behind a taste similar to a strong butter.*

*Fried until crispy, the giant water beetle
is Thailand's number one edible insect.*

Veal Sweetbread

Lamb's Kidney

The term "sweetbreads" covers two internal organs: the thymus gland in the throat and the pancreas near the stomach. Of these, the latter attracts more gastronomic interest. When raw, it is rounded, but of irregular shape, off-white to pink in hue, and not dissimilar to a blancmange—at least at first blush. When cooked it becomes firmer and more smooth.

Until the latter part of the last century, the pancreas was soaked, blanched, trimmed, and pressed before being braised in a sauce and served as an intermediate course—after the hors d'oeuvre and the fish, but before the main roast. Now chefs prefer to trim and then roast the sweetbreads, basting them with butter, and leaving them still juicy in the middle. They are popular on the menus of luxury restaurants. A speciality of Alain Ducasse, arguably France's most highly regarded chef—pasta with sweetbreads, coxcombs, cock's kidneys, truffles, lobster, and a cream sauce—gives a sense of how this simple ingredient may be presented, although in Argentina and Uruguay you will find them grilling on the traditional *asado*. **MR**

A lamb's kidneys will reflect the age at which the creature was slaughtered: they may be anything from a few weeks to ten months old. In Spain, where baby, milk-fed lamb is grilled over an open fire, the kidneys are a tiny pink delicacy. But the devilled kidneys that were once served from silver chafing dishes as part of the great British breakfast, like the skewered kebabs that are still part of everyday Turkish street food, are generally rather larger.

Fully developed, lamb's kidneys weigh over 1 ounce (25 g). They have a characteristic shape: rounded on the surface and slightly turned in on the side. Just cooked through, or slightly underdone, a kidney is juicy and tender. Overdone, it becomes unpleasantly hard and rubbery, yet returns to softness after prolonged cooking, as in the British steak and kidney pie (and steak and kidney pudding), where its taste and texture improve on the more usual ox kidney. Because older kidneys have an assertive taste, they are often combined with sauces enriched with sherry, Madeira, port, or mustard, with which they have a natural affinity. **MR**

Taste: *Smooth and tender, sweetbreads make an able and attractive catalyst for other ingredients. Consumed solo, neither their scent nor their taste is especially marked.*

Taste: *Kidneys should have a rich, fresh, meaty taste when cooked, ranging from the delicacy of young pink flesh to the dark, velvety flavour of fully developed organs.*

The filling for steak and kidney pie is cooked separately in order to judge when the meat is tender. ❯❯

Bull's Testicle

The Montana Testicle Festival, held each year in the United States, is most definitely not for everyone, but those who attend always say they "had a ball." The culinary focus there is breaded and deep-fried bull's testicles, commonly referred to as Rocky Mountain oysters or "cowboy caviar."

Although talking about testicles, no less eating them, may offend some twenty-first-century sensibilities, people have been eating animal testicles for many centuries. Not surprisingly, they have aphrodisiac associations. Testicles from sheep (lamb), bulls, calves (sometimes called prairie oysters), pigs, buffalos, turkeys, and roosters have long been considered a delicacy, often a seasonal one, eaten during the spring after male animals have been castrated so they can be retained and raised for meat. In North America, the tradition of eating "Rocky Mountain oysters" is found in those parts of the country that have a history of cattle ranching.

As is apparent, there are many culinary euphemisms for testicles. "Stones" was the historic word for testicles in England. The term "fry" is often used to denote testicles, as in lambs' fry or bull's fry. In France, the term *animelles* is used for testicles from sheep and other animals.

In Spain and Portugal, testicles, known as *criadillas* and *criadilhas* respectively, are considered a delicacy, cut into strips and fried, sometimes flavoured with garlic and parsley. They can also be sautéed, stewed, or served with a variety of sauces. Although North Americans, the British, and the French have become squeamish about this meat, others parts of the world, such as the Middle East and the Philippines, serve it regularly. **SH**

Lamb's Brain

Long accounted a rich delicacy, lambs' brains are very much a food lover's food. In the United States, where animal internal organs may still be lumped together as "variety meats," and the United Kingdom, where animal disease, notably BSE (bovine spongiform encephalitis) has made consumers nervous and the government cautious, they are generally not tolerated. In other parts of the world, however, including Hungary, Turkey, much of the Middle East, Italy, and France they remain a popular, indeed esteemed, food.

Low in fat and rich in iron, the two joined, pale pink lobes contain more than the minimum daily requirement for an adult of vitamin B_{12}. Preparation involves washing the brains, removing membranes and blood vessels, soaking, and washing once more.

In France, lambs' brains are cooked in a wide variety of ways: poached in a *court bouillon* then pan-fried with browned butter and capers; *en matelote*, where they are poached then served with onions, mushrooms, and a red wine sauce; or served as the sophisticated *beignets de cervelle*, brain fritters with a herb mayonnaise. In *tartare de cervelle* they are poached, then combined in a patty with capers, cornichons, hard-boiled eggs, and mustard mayonnaise. In Italy, lambs' brains are eaten in dishes including *cervella alla Napolitana*, baked with olives, capers, and breadcrumbs, and *cervella fritta alla Milanese*, where they are blanched, cut into morsels, breaded, and fried until golden-brown. In Lebanon, Jordan, Syria, Hungary, and elsewhere in the former Ottoman Empire, they are fried and served cold as a salad with olive oil, lemon juice, and often seasoned with parsley and spices. **MR**

Taste: *Testicles resemble chicken in that they take on the flavour of the sauce served on the side. Basically they are bland, with a chewy, sometimes gristly texture.*

Taste: *Brains have a very faint aroma compared to most meats and the taste is mild and delicate. The texture may be soft or curd-like, depending on the duration of cooking.*

A food stall vendor in Marrakesh prepares traditional baked lamb's head and brain. ❯❯

Calf's Liver

Ox Cheek

Food cultures that put a high value on offal consider calf's liver a luxury. Calf's liver figures all over central Europe in Jewish Ashkenazi cuisine and forms the basis of a famous Venetian speciality, *fegato alla veneziana*, strips of liver sautéed with onions cooked until sweet, and of *foie de veau à la lyonnaise*, another liver-and-onion pairing. The flavour of onions is thought particularly to enhance that of the liver.

Although similar on paper, these dishes reflect different culinary approaches. Italians cook their offal right through, whereas the French tend to prefer it a little underdone. Both ways are delicious because calf's liver has a texture and taste that responds to rapid pan-frying. Liver is rich in iron and minerals—a 4 ounce (115 g) slice supplies the daily requirement for vitamins A, B_2, B_{12}, and folate—which helps to account for its depth of flavour.

Even from a young calf the liver's taste is upfront, though it is milder than most lamb's or pig's livers. It should be rosy pink, with a fine grain. The finest comes from animals fed with mother's milk. The quality also depends on skilled butchery. **MR**

The tangle of muscle and sinew around the jaw of an ox works harder than any other part of its body. By its nature it is a tough meat that requires long cooking—a fact that also, counter-intuitively, explains its delights. For a long time, the ox cheek was a cheap cut of meat. French tripe butchers sold it for the poor man's *pot au feu*; Victorian household manuals recommended it as an indulgence for the industrious poor. Inside the cheek is a muscle—the masseter—that weighs about 8 ounces (200 g) and it is this that is increasingly attracting top chefs. Like the shin of beef, it combines lean meat with collagen, a connective tissue that becomes tender after prolonged cooking. In classic dishes such as a *daube de boeuf* or *boeuf bourguignon*, these nuggets of ox cheek give unique richness and body to the sauce in which they are simmered.

France led the ox cheek revival, thanks to the large, hefty cattle breeds developed from working animals. Both their heads and the muscles within them are larger than those on breeds like the Aberdeen-Angus. **MR**

Taste: *Calf's liver should have a clean, distinctive taste that is much sweeter than other forms of liver, allied to a smooth, almost melting texture and a pleasant smell.*

Taste: *The texture of a slow-cooked piece of ox cheek is tender, gelatinous, and succulent. It has a strong beefy taste, perhaps less pronounced than oxtail.*

Pig's Trotter

Bone Marrow

Until the second half of the twentieth century, pig's trotters were treated as rustic food. They might be braised slowly for up to ten hours and coated in breadcrumbs or dished up with a split pea soup. They were used by charcutiers to prepare the jellies that decorated their terrines. Then, with the advent of nouvelle cuisine, pig's trotters took on a new lease of life when chefs began to turn them into a luxury product. The trotters were braised, boned, filled with cream mousselines, sweetbreads, and truffles, then reformed and dished up with wine sauces.

The trotter itself contains little flesh, but the outer pig skin is gelatinous and tender when cooked. It has to be carefully scraped before it can be stuffed. In Cantonese cuisine, pig's trotters are a speciality, often eaten at the start of New Year celebrations for good luck. Traditionally, they are blanched in water from springs in the Bai Yun mountain and served crisp-skinned with a sweet-and-sour sauce. Also popular in Hong Kong, they are eaten smoked or accompanied by a ginger and black vinegar sauce. **MR**

Archaeologists believe that in prehistoric times our cannibal ancestors enjoyed eating the marrow from their victims' bones. More recently, beef marrow bones wrapped in a white napkin were presented at the tables of the wealthy together with a silver scoop for removing the warm, rich, jelly-like fat.

Bone marrow is high in monounsaturated fat and protein. Its function in the body is to produce blood cells. But not all bones contain marrow: some are almost solid. Marrow is found in the limbs, especially in the leg bones. To obtain it, the whole bone can be cut into short lengths and roasted, or the raw bones can be sawn up before the marrow is extracted and poached.

In the Italian dish *osso buco* a sliced shin of veal is braised with the marrowbone; in French classic cuisine a garnish of poached marrowbone was essential to the composition of an *entrecôte bordelaise*. Italians have a high regard for beef bone marrow, and many recipes insist on it being used alongside butter at the start of a risotto. It is also present in a variety of bean soups. **MR**

Taste: *Simply braised, pig's trotters have little to offer, but as a base they actually attract other flavours, enhancing them by helping them to stick to the palate.*

Taste: *The taste of marrow, rather like that of a good beef dripping, is smooth and subtly meaty, but never "red." The texture is fragile, like a lightly set junket, and quite greasy.*

Sheep's Head

Sheep's head is a delicacy that harks back to the days when truly no part of an animal was wasted, although it is still enjoyed by several cultures.

In Norway and Iceland, one sign of autumn was traditionally the treat of smoked sheep's head. This was offered when the sheep were brought down from the hills where they had been fattening over the summer. Some sheep would be culled, according to demand, and the rest used for both their wool and meat through the winter.

Icelanders still enjoy singed sheep's head at Thorablott, the spring festival renowned for unusual food consumption. In Scotland, boiled sheep's head broth was the traditional Saturday night fare for dutiful Christian ministers sitting down to write the Sunday sermon, and would also be served cold the next day for dinner (the recipe in *The Cook and Housewife's Manual*, published in 1828, begins with the instruction, "Choose a large, fat head"). In Italy, fewer people are partaking of the dish, although it appears on the menus of traditional restaurants, such as those in Little Italy in New York City.

In the Middle East, however, sheep's head remains popular, appearing at celebratory banquets where the split roasted head is typically served with the eyes. In Iraq, it is slowly cooked into a meat broth with the stomach and feet for the traditional dish *pacha*, while in both Kazakhstan and Kyrgyzstan boiled sheep's head is consumed during the elaborate ceremonial feast of *Beshbarmak*. In the ceremony, the head is offered as mark of great respect to the honoured guest. Brains and tongues are mostly served with the head. Kazakhs offer the ears to young men to encourage attentiveness. **BF**

Taste: *Grilled, the flavour of the meat is that of mutton. The cheek meat may have more texture when grilled (as opposed to slowly stewed). Brains, if served, are buttery.*

Tripe

Usually from an ox or calf, although also from sheep or deer, tripe is a hold-all term for the stomach, or, to be accurate, for the four separate stomachs that together form a production line to digest the ruminant's food. The first (the rumen) holds the food that is swallowed. This food is regurgitated, chewed again, and swallowed as cud to pass via the second, honeycombed stomach (the reticulum) into the third (psalterium), and ultimately the fourth (abomasum). Each tripe has its own texture and taste. All require scrubbing to make them edible.

Tripe forms the basis of warming soups in cuisines from Jamaica to Turkey. The four different tripes, simmered together slowly for up to ten hours with calf's foot, onions, and carrots, produce the Normandy speciality of *tripes à la mode de Caen*. (Veal tripe is generally considered the finest for this dish.) In the Spanish *callos a la madrileña*, tripe is stewed with ingredients including spicy chorizo sausage and morcilla. In England, honeycomb tripe eaten with onions and a white sauce was once a pauper's food, and is still a nostalgic dish in the north.

During the 1960s a chain of tripe restaurants took northern England by storm. They were run by United Cattle Products and were known as UCPs. More than 150 outlets, mainly in northwest England, were characterized by serving tripe in unexpectedly refined surroundings. Sparklingly clean tablecloths were used, and the food was served by silver service. The business was not to survive the arrival of fast foods, however, and in the 1970s it was sold, eventually to be bought by Wimpy. Tripe is still considered a working-class food in England, but elsewhere it tends to be seen as a regional food. **MR**

Taste: *Stewed together, the flavour of the four tripes is rich, gelatinous, and robust. The texture of tripe depends on which one is used and how it is prepared.*

In France, tripe was traditionally prepared at a triperie. It is especially enjoyed in Normandy and Auvergne. ❯

TRIPERIE

Fraise de Veau
Pieds-veaux·agn·porc
Paté de tête

Tripes < maison
cuites-crue

museaux cuits

Foie Gras de Canard

Cramming ducks with maize, to fatten their livers until the organs weigh about 1 pound (450 g) each, produces the luxury that is known the world over as foie gras de canard. On small farms in southwest France, the ducks are left to grow and range freely most of their lives. It is only during the last two or three weeks that they are force-fed the diet; cruelty lies in the abuse of the system where industrial manufacturers produce foie gras from caged birds.

Experts can distinguish different styles of this luxurious delicacy. Those from the Landes south of Bordeaux are more creamy or silky; from Bearn in Gascony, they are rustic, with a farmyard flavour. Eating a thin sliver of raw, fresh foie gras is the ultimate way of appreciating its taste and texture, but low-slow cooking under vacuum, usually after marinating in Madeira, port, Armagnac, and/or truffle juice, produces the smooth, intensely perfumed terrines that establish the reputations of chefs. Strict legislation protects the use of the name and terms such as parfait, mousse, or pâté on foie gras products indicate added ingredients. **MR**

Taste: *More than its taste, the texture of foie gras is unique: unctuous, smooth, melting, velvety, and creamy. The taste of liver is never strong or overly assertive.*

An old Sarlat shop sign signals the availability of foie gras and truffles in the French Dordogne.

Hungarian Goose Liver

According to historians, Egyptians in pharaonic times were the first to fatten their geese and produce the bloated but delicious livers now known as foie gras. The technique spread across Europe during the Middle Ages, probably by way of Jewish communities, and to nowhere more than Transdanubian Hungary, where rearing geese for their livers is an art form. The birds are bred for their large size, the variety of corn is specially selected for its influence on the fattening process, and the drinking water is mixed with a solution of white clay. Overeating raises the level of fat in the blood, from where it transfers to the liver. (Hungarians prefer the Oroshaza goose, which can supply fattened livers that weigh over 2 pounds (900 g) each.)

In Hungary, roasted goose liver, *sült libamáj*, is often soaked in milk before cooking, coloured in hot goose fat, and seasoned with paprika. The liver is an omnipresent ingredient on Hungarian restaurant menus, dished up fried, used as a stuffing, accompanied by fruit, sweetened with honey, or simply served on bread with peppers. **MR**

Taste: *The liver taste is mild, but has a faint metallic zing in the raw state that disappears with cooking. The texture is similar to that of duck's liver, but seems more compact.*

Confit

This apparently decadent food—meat gently slow-cooked in its own rendered fat until melting and then stored in the fat, which acts as a seal—in fact originated with the most pragmatic of purposes: to preserve meat against the coming winter. The word "confit" is a French term that denotes preservation, and this is an ancient way of preserving food, associated particularly with the southwest region of France. The process tenderizes the meat used—usually goose, duck, or pork—and in sterilized jars (or canned) the meat keeps for several months.

Goose meat is particularly suited to confit. Slow-grown geese, especially those that have been used for foie gras, lay down large amounts of fat, not only underneath their skin, but also inside their carcass, around the vital organs. The leg thigh is highly prized, while wings are valued for their tenderness. Other delicious savoury confits are made using game, rabbit, turkey, and offal ranging from gizzards to tongues. Chefs are now creating versions using less traditional fatty meats, such as lamb and oxtail. When served cold in France, a confit is traditionally accompanied by a bitter salad of dandelion or endive to cut through the fattiness.

A confit is often added as an ingredient to flavour another dish. Confits of both goose and duck are optional but much-employed ingredients of cassoulet, a French dish made with haricot beans and assorted meats, and the Alsatian *choucroute garnie*. The confit technique can be found elsewhere in the world, too; in the Lebanon, for example, *qawarma*, a traditional winter food of Lebanese mountain tribes, consists of minced lamb preserved in fat from the tail of the fat-tailed sheep. **MR**

Taste: *The taste and texture of a confit depends on its end use. In a stew, it may fall off the bone. Roasted, the skin should be crisp, and the meat unctuous and melting.*

Cooked and then covered in a sealed jar with its own
❹ *fat, which acts as a preservative, confits keep well.*

Qalaya

This preserved meat, sometimes written as *khlea* or *khelea*, forms a key part of Lebanese, Moroccan, and Algerian cuisines. Before the days of refrigeration, peoples of the eastern Mediterranean and North Africa prolonged the life of meat in a similar way to the French confit. The long, slow cooking in fat softens the meat's texture and retains its flavour.

The meat most commonly used is beef, which is cut into manageable pieces and rubbed generously with salt and garlic. It is then rubbed again with a mixture of spices—coriander seeds, ground cumin, paprika, dried mint, and occasionally saffron—before being left to marinate in a crock in the cool air, or overnight. The meat is then taken out to dry in the hot summer sun. The qalaya is not left out at night because dampening in the cool dew hastens putrefaction. The meat is now ready for cooking.

The marinated pieces of meat are then fried until crisp in either mutton or beef fat, often with the addition of olive oil. After cooling, the meat is placed in jars and covered completely with melted fat from the pan. The sealed jars are stored until the meat is required for a meal, when the contents are lifted out, the fat scraped off, and excess salt rinsed away.

Qalaya is added as a flavouring for tagines, couscous, and stews. It is sometimes used with beans, lentils, barley, and pumpkins.

With the cost of fresh meat in the Maghreb becoming ever steeper, many families are now obliged to buy their qalaya ready-made from nearby souks, but purists prefer the taste of the real thing: qalaya made in the home. For many, however, the cost of a year's supply of home-made qalaya represents a considerable financial outlay. **WS**

Taste: *Warm and spicy, with the rich, earthy taste of mutton and the fire of chilli, qalaya evokes the vivid aromas and flavours of the souk.*

Rillette

Pâté de Campagne

These delicious examples of charcuterie originate in the late Middle Ages: the name is derived either from an old French word for an ear (*rille*) or, possibly, from the term for a strip of fat (*reille*). Essentially, slow-cooked pork—sometimes combined with other meats—is stewed in its own natural dripping until the fibres of the meat are tender enough to flake into the juices by hand. Cooled, the mixture forms a soft, spreadable emulsion, roughly two parts of lean to one of fat.

The two iconic styles of rillettes are those of Tours and Le Mans. Rillettes de Tours, from the Loire valley, are darker and smoother, taking their colour from the searing they undergo at the outset of cooking. (For the sister recipe *rillons*, chunks of lean pork, stewed until crusty, are left to set in the cooled dripping.) Rillettes du Mans are paler, but contain small pieces of pork. Both versions owe their quality to the individual charcutier's skill. The art lies in blending the flecked meat with its reduced cooking juices and the dripping, which will have absorbed the flavour from the seasoning. **MR**

Leaving aside its rustic title, pâté de campagne, is the Adam and Eve of an endless line of French pâtés and terrines. It is a balanced blend of the darker and lighter meats and the harder and softer fats, usually with the addition of some pig's liver that gives it a softer, almost spreadable texture. Minced, or better still chopped, blended with pickling salt, herbs, and spices, sometimes marinated with wine or finished with cognac or armagnac, it may be baked, steamed, or simmered in a bain-marie. Found in every French market and charcuterie, its quality reflects the traditional craftsmanship of its maker. In contrast with the anaemic pâtés de campagne that are sold both outside France and by some multiples inside it, it is a hearty, nourishing tribute to free-range pigs that have been reared slowly and extensively.

By adding game in place of the lean pork a pâté de campagne can be changed into a partridge, hare, or wild boar version. The basic difference between a pâté de campagne and one baked in pastry—en croûte—is that the latter rarely includes liver and is, in consequence, harder. **MR**

Taste: *Typically prepared from sows that have given birth to just one litter, rillettes are always delectably rich and fatty, but should taste of the finest artisan pork.*

Taste: *The aroma of fresh pâté de campagne is both meaty and spicy. The robust flavours should blend into a harmonious whole with no one ingredient dominant.*

A stall sells rillettes at a farmers' market. They are ⊗ usually served cold, spread on slices of bread or toast.

Nduja

This fabulous, peppery hot, spreadable salami comes from Calabria, the part of Italy at the toe of the big boot. Made with pork meat, fat, and salt, it has a very high content of Calabrian red chilli pepper (or *peperoncini*)—hence the vivid scarlet colour and the kick. Bizarrely, this fiery red chilli explosion is also supposed to have aphrodisiac properties.

The term nduja apparently derives from the French speciality *andouille* which is believed to have been introduced there in the Middle Ages during a period of French supremacy. The seasoned pork is forced into natural pig casings and then smoked over aromatic wood, before being left to mature for several months.

Fantastic as part of an antipasti offering, nduja makes great party food and a versatile and delicious seasoning aid. It can be scooped straight out of its casing and spread over bread, or eaten just as it comes. Stirred into pasta sauces it adds oomph and body, although one favourite Calabrian way to serve it is to heat it in little terracotta pots and keep it warm over a candle to use as a dip. **LF**

Taste: *Moist and meaty, hints of smoke and a spicy zing dance deliciously over the tongue. Fans of fiery food will love it. Add a little ricotta to temper the heat a touch.*

The Calabrian chillies used to spice nduja dry out in the warm open air. »

Chorizo Ibérico de Bellota

Chorizo Riojano

Along with the fabulous Jamòn Ibérico de Bellota and Lomo Ibérico de Bellota, Chorizo Ibérico de Bellota comes from the unique breed of bristly, black-footed pig known as Cerdo Ibérico. Ibérico pigs wander free in an area known as the *dehesa*, a bio-network of eye-catching beauty spanning Spain's Aracena and Extremadura regions. There an abundance of oak and cork trees can be found and the pigs gobble greedily at the acorns until they reach the stipulated weight for slaughter.

Whereas *jamòn* is made from the legs of the pig and *lomo* is whole tenderloin, chorizo is made from selected cuts of the remaining meat. In keeping with the whole Ibérico de Bellota production philosophy, the chorizo is hand crafted. The pork meat is seasoned with salt, garlic, herbs, and paprika; the latter gives it the smoky flavour and rich red colour typical of chorizo. The mixture is then forced into natural casings and cured for two months.

Chorizo Ibérico de Bellota should be served in thin slices, at room temperature. It is typically served as a tapa dish. **LF**

Spain classifies its fantastic range of artisan chorizos into the regions from which they were traditionally made. Chorizo Riojano (IGP) is a speciality of La Rioja in northern Spain. Handmade, using prime quality pork, salt, paprika, and garlic, Chorizo Riojano is a soft-cured sausage suitable for cooking and is traditionally used to add a smoky, peppery depth to soups, stews, and paellas. Like most chorizo, it is available in sweet (*dulce*) or hot (*picante*) versions.

Chorizo, in its present form, does not have as long a history as most other Spanish sausages and cured meats. Pimentón, the Spanish version of paprika produced from pimentos or capsicums, did not arrive on the scene until the sixteenth century. Prior to this, chorizos were a fairly pale affair. Originally the pimentón was added to help prevent the pork from spoiling, but it is now hard to imagine chorizo without its signature paprika flavour.

Chorizo Riojano is encased in natural skins, in either a string or as a characteristic horseshoe shape. It can be grilled, boiled, sautéed, barbecued, or added to give a kick to numerous cooked dishes. **LF**

Taste: *Unctuous and meaty with a glorious flavour that is a skilful balance of piquancy and sweet smokiness. The rich marbling of fat surrenders beautifully on the tongue.*

Taste: *Chorizo Riojano has a complex, full flavour and juicy texture. It has prominent garlic notes and a well-balanced smokiness, enlivened with a distinct piquancy.*

Chorizo is sold hanging in strings along with other dry-cured sausages and meats throughout Spain. ❯❯

Salchichón de Vic

Felino Salami

When it comes to cured pork products, the Spanish really know their stuff and Salchichón de Vic is a fine example of their expertise. Pepper speckled and temptingly rich, it is made from prime cuts of pork from pigs raised on a natural diet and cured in the abundant, undulating landscape of La Plana de Vic, an area between Spain's Catalan Pyrenees and the coast that benefits from altitudes of 1,310 to 1,970 feet (400–600 m). This superb microclimate plays a key role in the salchichón's exquisite flavour.

Lean pork meat is mixed with back bacon and seasoned with salt and pepper, then macerated for a minimum of forty-eight hours before being forced into natural hog casings. The salchichón is then hung to allow the characteristic flavours to develop and the meat to dry out. The typical finished product is about 3 inches (7 cm) in diameter and between 20 and 24 inches (50–60 cm) long, although a smaller version can be found. Production is limited to twenty-eight villages and Salchichón de Vic carries an IGP certificate to ensure that strict criteria governing all aspects of manufacture are adhered to. **LF**

Felino salami is so highly regarded in Italy that it even has its own museum, esconced inside the eighteenth-century cellars of Felino Castle in the province of Parma. However, the production of salami in Felino can be traced back earlier than that, to the fifteenth century. It is made from pork taken from native Italian pigs, using proportions of 75 per cent lean meat to 25 per cent fat, minced and blended with salt, pepper, and little else. It is then forced into pig intestine and left to hang, where it develops its distinctive shape: long, with a slightly bulbous end.

While salami contains a high percentage of salt to aid preservation, the area's microclimate allows the salami to mature in conditions that enhance the flavour and texture without the need for very heavy salting. Ideally, salami should be stored in the fridge, but removed several hours before eating to allow its full flavours to come to the fore. It should be cut into slices no thicker than a peppercorn, at an angle of 60°, to appreciate the optimum flavour. **LF**

Taste: *Full flavoured with a well-balanced mixture of fat to meat, Salchichón de Vic delivers deep savoury notes and a prolonged aftertaste. Serve thinly sliced.*

Taste: *Thinly sliced and served at room temperature, Felino salami is tender and succulent. Garlic tends not to be used in the seasoning, producing a delicate, sweet edge.*

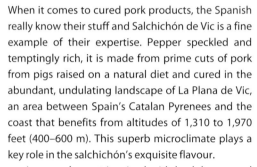

After maturing for at least a month, Felino salami assumes its characteristic white-grey exterior. ❯❯

Chinese Sausage

The so-called "wind-dried" meats are an important feature of the Chinese winter diet. Long strings of reddish *lap cheung* (Chinese sausage)—a kind of sweet and salty salami made from pork—and *yuen cheung* (liver sausage) were traditionally made at home during the winter months, when the air was cool and breezy enough for the sausages to be hung outside to dry without fear of spoilage. Like other Chinese cured meats, they are now made year-round on a large scale by vendors who specialize in them. A base of pork meat, pork liver, or both is lubricated with pork fat, and flavoured with rice wine, five spice powder, soy sauce, and sugar.

Chinese sausages are always cooked before being eaten. One of the easiest and best methods is to steam them on top of rice: the delicious fat in the sausages renders out and adds flavour to the rice. The sausages can also be steamed on their own, then sliced, and fried until crisp. They are often served accompanied by bitter greens because the strong flavours of the vegetables balance the fatty richness of the meat. **KKC**

Taste: *Flavour varies depending on the choice of spice mix: some are quite sweet, while others more savoury. No fillers such as bread are used in Chinese sausages.*

An array of Chinese sausages await purchase at New Year. ❯

Kabanos

Kabanos (plural kabanosy) is a firm, long, finger-thick sausage. Its low moisture content means it keeps indefinitely without refrigeration and so became the preferred food of travellers, hunters, and soldiers in Eastern Europe who could, quite literally, tuck the stick-like sausages under their belts.

Kabanosy are made from a combination of diced lean and fatty pork, seasoned with salt, pepper, garlic, caraway, and sometimes a pinch of ground allspice. A small amount of saltpetre is added to cure the mixture, which is left to blend overnight in a cool place before it is stuffed into thin sheep's casings and hung up to air-dry in the breeze. Next, the sausages are slowly smoked to a nice reddish-brown, and air-dried once again for several days until they weigh roughly about half of what they did before processing.

Their longevity—a product of this smoking and drying—means kabanosy are still favourites of Polish and Ukrainian campers, hikers, anglers, and hunters today: however, they are equally at home at elegant banquets and family celebrations. **RS**

Taste: *Hearty and meaty, the texture of kabanosy varies from firm but supple to quite dry and brittle. The flavour is vigorous, with peppery, garlicky, and smoky notes.*

Linguiça

This smoked pork sausage is seasoned with paprika, onions, garlic, herbs, and spices, to provide a flavour that is distinctly Portuguese. Although linguiça is not dissimilar to the milder types of Spanish chorizo, the Portuguese have been making pork and blood sausages for centuries. The meat is coarsely ground, mixed with the other ingredients, and forced into natural hog casings. The sausages are then smoked.

Linguiça have travelled pretty much anywhere the people of Portugal have settled. As a result, they have become very popular in areas with a high quota of Portuguese immigrants, most notably Brazil, but also places as diverse as New England and Hawaii, where linguiça are usually referred to simply as "Portuguese sausage."

Linguiça sausages are found in *caldo verde*, the Portuguese national stew of potatoes and greens, and in *cozido à Portuguesa*, another hearty stew of beef shin, pork, winter vegetables, and smoked sausages. They can also be grilled over charcoal, fried, or used on any of the myriad occasions a spicy, gutsy, country sausage is required. **LF**

Taste: *Fried in good oil and served hot, linguiça has a gutsy but not overly spicy flavour that is both savoury and smoky with piquant overtones.*

Linguiça, made according to an old recipe, is one of many traditional meats found at Portuguese markets. »

Saucisson d'Arles

Arles is a popular Provençal tourist destination so it is only to be expected that a local speciality should be dressed up with its very own myth. According to a nineteenth-century poet: "An Indian prince visited Arles and found so many beautiful girls there that he lost his head. His arms and limbs dropped off too, leaving behind his torso in a silver gown . . ."—the Saucisson d'Arles. More prosaically, the combination may have been invented about 1655 by a charcutier called Godart who is known to have sold a Bologna *socisol*. Whether the current recipe bears any relation to his sausage is uncertain, however.

Saucisson d'Arles is a dry, cured sausage, like Italian salami but concocted from a mixture of pork, donkey, and bull beef, and seasoned with red wine and *Herbes de Provence*. The donkey meat is what sets it apart, but today it is questionable whether this magic ingredient still finds its way into the mix. Putative Saucisson d'Arles is sold by stallholders at the local market, but the most reliable source for this delicacy is Bernard Genin, a local charcutier who sells it from his shop, La Farandole. **MR**

Taste: *Unsmoked and dried for three weeks, Saucisson d'Arles is a classic example of the French-style saucisson sec. Thinly sliced, it makes an ideal baguette-filler.*

The well-known Provençal sausage looks much like salami. »

Soppressa del Pasubio

Soppressata di Calabria

Mount Pasublo is part of the Prealps or "Little Dolomites" in northern Italy. A strategic site during World War I, it is now an area of great natural beauty, popular not only with hikers and bikers but with the pigs whose meat makes the elegantly textured salami known as Soppressa delle Valli del Pasubio.

Although carefully raised on a diet rich in chestnuts and potatoes, the pigs are substantially free to roam, devouring wild roots and herbs, and drinking from streams rich in natural minerals. This wonderful pattern of eating gives their meat a very distinctive and delicious flavour.

A carefully balanced mixture of finely chopped pork meat and fat is seasoned with salt and pepper, then forced into natural casings. It matures for anything from five months to over two years in cool, dry cellars, acquiring its downy layer of natural white mould. Soppressa del Pasubio is fabulous served thinly sliced as an antipasto offering, but in the Veneto area is often presented as a main course, cut into slightly thicker slices and served atop chunks of golden, grilled polenta. **LF**

Many regions of Italy have their own version of soppressata, but perhaps the most famous is Soppressata di Calabria (DOP), a wonderfully piquant pork salami. It must be made in Calabria from the meat of pigs born in southern Italy— specifically Calabria, Sicily, Basilicata, Apulia, and Campania—and slaughtered in Calabria.

Traditionally, prime cuts of pork shoulder and belly are chopped and seasoned with a mixture of peppercorns, fennel seeds, and chilli pepper—a relatively high yet balanced ratio of added fat gives the salami a superb melting quality. The seasoned meat is encased in a natural hog casing, then pressed between weights into a flattened cylinder before its final curing phase.

There has been a tradition of cured meats in Calabria since the ancient Greeks appeared on the scene, but the first confirmed written reference did not appear until the seventeenth century. A century or so later, the legendary lover Giacomo Casanova was apparently converted to its charms while travelling through Calabria. **LF**

Taste: *Soppressa del Pasubio has a perfectly balanced meat to fat ratio and a firm, dense texture; the flavour is intense and lively without being overly spicy.*

Taste: *Thinly sliced Soppressata di Calabria has a well rounded, warm, piquant flavour and succulent velvety texture that sets it apart from inferior, leathery imitations.*

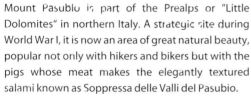

The spectacular scenery of Mount Pasubio is home to the pigs whose meat make a renowned local salami.

 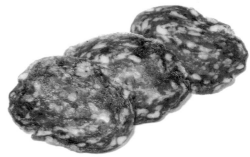

Finocchiona Salami

This full-flavoured, even pungent Tuscan speciality is made from pork that is seasoned with garlic, peppercorns, fennel seeds (or *finocchio*), and often Chianti wine. It has been a traditional local delicacy for so long that its origins are lost.

One legend has it that a thief at a fair close to the town of Prato stole a salami and concealed it in a stand of wild fennel. When he collected it, he discovered the salami had absorbed the essence of the herb and taken on a superb flavour. Another story claims that wine-makers added the seeds to their wine in order to help sell it. Fennel seeds have a slightly numbing effect on the taste buds, and so when potential customers called by to sample the wines, they would be offered finocchiona to inoculate their palates against poor quality wine.

There are two types of finocchiona: a firmer variety known simply as finocchiona and a younger, softer variety known as sbriciolona. Macelleria Falorni produce a true gastronomic finocchiona, made to exceptionally high standards from the meat of a semi-wild Tuscan pig known as Cinta Senese. **LF**

Taste: *Flavoursome, moist finocchiona salami has a piquant zing balanced with a whisper of fennel. Sliced thinly, it is particularly good with unsalted Tuscan bread.*

Salami di Cinghiale

Salami di cinghiale is one of the true kings of Italian cured meats. The best examples are made with the thigh meat of wild boars, which is usually mixed with pork shoulder and then seasoned with salt and pepper. Sometimes extra seasonings such as garlic, chilli, and red wine are added. The mixture is forced into natural hog casings and cured in conditions that can vary according to the climate of the region in which the salami is produced. Although generally regarded as a Tuscan speciality, salami di cinghiale is also produced elsewhere in Italy, including in Umbria and Sardinia.

The diet of the wild boar typically consists of chestnuts, beech nuts, acorns, herbs, roots, mushrooms, and occasionally even truffles. This richly diverse diet lends the meat an incredible, intense quality and the cured salamis produced from it tend to have a delicious, robust flavour.

Salami di cinghiale makes perfect eating when sliced and served as part of an antipasti course washed down with a gutsy red wine. It is also fabulous added to pasta sauces and stews. **LF**

Taste: *Salami di cinghiale has a satisfyingly chewy texture with an intense flavour displaying subtle gamey, nutty, and sweet nuances opening out to a gentle piquancy.*

A specialist butcher's shop in Umbria proudly displays cured meat products including salami di cinghiale. ❱

Rügenwalder Teewurst

Thüringer Leberwurst

This soft, pink sausage is believed to have originated in 1834 in the small Baltic town of Rügenwalde (now part of Poland). Made from finely minced pork, bacon, and beef packed into short reddish-brown skins, teewurst are smoked over beechwood before being left to mature for seven to ten days.

Smooth-textured due to a fat content of between 30 and 40 per cent, teewurst (meaning "tea sausage" in German) probably gets its name due to the ease with which it can be spread on rye bread, crackers, and toast for a teatime snack. It also makes a tasty addition to herby stuffings for goose, chicken, and other poultry, or boned, rolled joints of pork.

In 1927 the companies producing Rügenwalder teewurst were awarded a PDO, but by the end of World War II they had been forced to flee their homeland. Moving west, they established new businesses in the then Federal Republic of Germany. Today it is only teewurst makers who were originally based in Rügenwalde that are allowed to display the protected seal of origin; others must label their produce "Rügenwalder-style teewurst." **WS**

A close relative of teewurst, leberwurst is another popular cooked German sausage and one that is soft enough to spread. Like teewurst, leberwurst is made all over Germany and Austria, with each region having its own particular recipes.

Thüringer Leberwurst (PGI) is one of the most highly regarded and gained its Protected Geographical Indication in 2003. It is produced in a region of central eastern Germany that is renowned for the quality of its foods, especially its meat and sausage products; Thüringen also makes excellent rotwurst and rostbratwurst.

In German leberwurst means "liver sausage." Although most are made using cooked pork liver, goose, calves', and lamb's liver can also be included. Different flavourings and seasonings are added to the minced offal, including onions, chives, spices, and sometimes even apple, with the texture of the finished sausage being fine or coarse. The sausages can also be plainly cooked or smoked. Leberwurst is ideal spread on rye bread or crispbreads for breakfast, or indeed at any time of day. **WS**

Taste: Teewurst is so soft it can be spread with a knife. It has a rich, creamy texture and the savoury flavour of smoked ham spiked with pepper and other warm spices.

Taste: Leberwurst has a strong and savoury flavour, offset by the warmth of onion and pepper. The depth of the flavour depends on the type of liver used in the recipe.

Sausages such as teewurst and leberwurst create an attractive display in a German butcher's shop.

Merguez

Just as the colour red can indicate danger in daily life, the bright hue of these small, thin link sausages indicates at a glance that they are not for the faint-hearted: the colour stems from the addition of the hot chilli paste harissa. Merguez are particularly associated with Algeria and Tunisia, but have been favoured by Arabs around the world since at least the thirteenth century, and are a versatile ingredient in North African and Middle Eastern cooking. As Islam prohibits the consumption of pig products, they are made with lamb, mutton, or beef, never pork.

About 3 to 4 inches (7–10 cm) long, merguez sausages may be spiced with a veritable Aladdin's cave of flavourings. Although harissa is the best-known ingredient, other common choices include preserved lemons, aniseed, cinnamon, sumac (for tartness), and even dried rose petals. They are usually sold fresh for grilling to serve alongside couscous or to be eaten on their own as a snack, although they may be sun-dried and stored in olive oil. Fresh or dried sausages are also included in tagines and stews. **BLeB**

Mititei

A Romanian word meaning "small things," mititei is also the name of one of Romania's traditional dishes. Mititei are spiced, grilled meat balls or rolls that are usually made from minced beef, but they can also be made from a mixture of beef and pork, or beef and mutton. According to legend, mititei were invented at a Bucharest restaurant called La Lordachi, which was renowned for its sausages. The story goes that one busy evening the kitchen ran out of sausage casings and so converted the sausage mixture into small balls instead. These were then grilled, and so mititei were born.

The meat is combined with onion, garlic, olive oil, salt, pepper, and bicarbonate of soda, which plumps up the meat. Paprika is often added, though other seasonings such as thyme, caraway, marjoram, allspice, cumin, chilli, or cloves can also be used. The kneaded mixture is shaped into small rolls and refrigerated for several hours, before being grilled until brown. Mititei are best served with pickles or mustard in a bread roll alongside a cold beer. They also good with potatoes or a rice pilaf. **CK**

Taste: *Always spicy and flavoursome, merguez have a dense texture that makes them ideal for barbecuing or pan-frying. They pair well with lentils and couscous.*

Taste: *Mititei are juicy and tender with a piquant, spicy garlicky flavour, that varies according to the seasonings used. Do not use too lean a meat or the rolls will dry out.*

Spicy merguez sausages await grilling at a Moroccan
◉ *market; they are also popular in France and Belgium.*

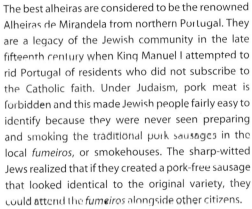

Alheiras de Mirandela

Jésus de Morteau

The best alheiras are considered to be the renowned Alheiras de Mirandela from northern Portugal. They are a legacy of the Jewish community in the late fifteenth century when King Manuel I attempted to rid Portugal of residents who did not subscribe to the Catholic faith. Under Judaism, pork meat is forbidden and this made Jewish people fairly easy to identify because they were never seen preparing and smoking the traditional pork sausages in the local *fumeiros*, or smokehouses. The sharp-witted Jews realized that if they created a pork-free sausage that looked identical to the original variety, they could attend the *fumeiros* alongside other citizens.

Alheiras sausages are made from a wide variety of meats such as veal, duck, chicken, turkey, and rabbit; they do not usually include pork. To create this Portuguese speciality, a seasoned mixture of meats is mixed with bread, garlic, and paprika. The casings are stuffed in such a way that the sausages make a "u" shape, and they are then smoked slowly over several days. Typically, alheiras are fried in olive oil, and served with a fried egg and vegetables. **LF**

How this sausage acquired its name is unknown; perhaps it was seen to resemble a baby Jesus wrapped in swaddling clothes. The Morteau part is simple to explain: Morteau—"dead water"—is a town in the mountainous Jura region of France.

Jésus de Morteau (AOC) is an example of agricultural synergy. Pigs are fed with whey from cheese-making (Tomme de Comté is the local speciality), a diet that produces the rich pork that is the base of the sausage. Diced meat from the shoulder and neck is blended with a little fat from the back, the butcher's personal choice of seasoning is added, and it is piped or filled into a natural casing with a distinctive wooden peg at one end. Then the sausage is smoked in the traditional Jura chimneys—*tuyés*—over resinous coniferous wood.

Sold raw or cooked, Jésus de Morteau adds body to hearty peasant recipes, simmered in a wine-flavoured *court bouillon* and served with potatoes or lentils. In a *gratinée de Morteau*, slices of cooked sausage are coated in sauce, topped with Comté, and glazed in the oven or under the grill. **MR**

Taste: *Alheiras de Mirandela is a truly sassy sausage. A distinct smokiness and the obvious presence of garlic complements the well-defined and appealing texture.*

Taste: *Jésus de Morteau has a spicy, cured taste overlaid by the flavour of resinous wood smoke. It is dense with a firm texture that reflects it high proportion of lean meat.*

The finest alheiras (smoked sausages) come from northern Portugal.

Andouille de Vire

As early as the fifteenth century, the French cookery tract *Le Mesnagier de Paris* described an andouille as intestines packed inside an intestine. It is distinguished from its little sister, the andouillette, by its size. The baby is usually eaten fresh off the grill; the grown-up is served finely sliced and cold.

Unlike andouilles from other parts of France, which may include sheep or cow tripe, the Andouille de Vire from lower Normandy is prepared exclusively from pork chitterlings (intestines). These are washed, brined, seasoned, and packed into a large pork casing. The best artisanal versions are then cold-smoked over beech chippings for about one month. At the end of this they are simmered for six hours in water or a broth, shrinking from 5 pounds (2.3 kg) to just over 1 pound (450 g) in weight. Left to mature, the outer surface develops a dark skin, almost black, while the interior is pale pink and appetizing.

The Andouille de Vire's integrity is protected by a charter from the local craftsmen who make the product. A genuine example is recognized by the length of cord embedded in its outer surface. **MR**

Taste: *The Andouille de Vire tastes clean, fresh, and only a little smoky. Slices should look meaty, without the spiralled appearance of some French tripe sausages.*

Zampone di Modena

Zampone is an Italian pork sausage made from ground pork, fat, and rinds seasoned with spices and encased in a boned pig's trotter. There are two types: an uncooked, authentic one that requires overnight soaking and careful, slow simmering for four hours, and a pre-cooked, vacuum-packed type that needs no more than twenty minutes gentle cooking. Both versions are served hot, in slices, traditionally with lentils at celebrations.

Legend has it that zampone was created in the early sixteenth century in a town called Mirandola, near Modena, when Pope Julius II, otherwise known as the Warrior Pope, invaded the town. The story goes that the townspeople slaughtered all the pigs to prevent them falling prey to the enemy, and so needed to preserve as much as they could. Today Zampone di Modena carries a PGI certification.

Zampone is generally eaten rind and all; when cooked, it has a glutinous, melting consistency. For those who are not keen on trotters' more unctuous qualities, Cotechino di Modena is an almost identical product that is encased in sausage skin. **LF**

Taste: *Deeply flavoured and aromatic, Zampone di Modena's tender, gelatinous, almost gummy, rind gives way to a uniform succulence throughout.*

The uniqueness of Zampone di Modena is that the filling is stuffed into a pig's trotter rather than a casing. ❯❯

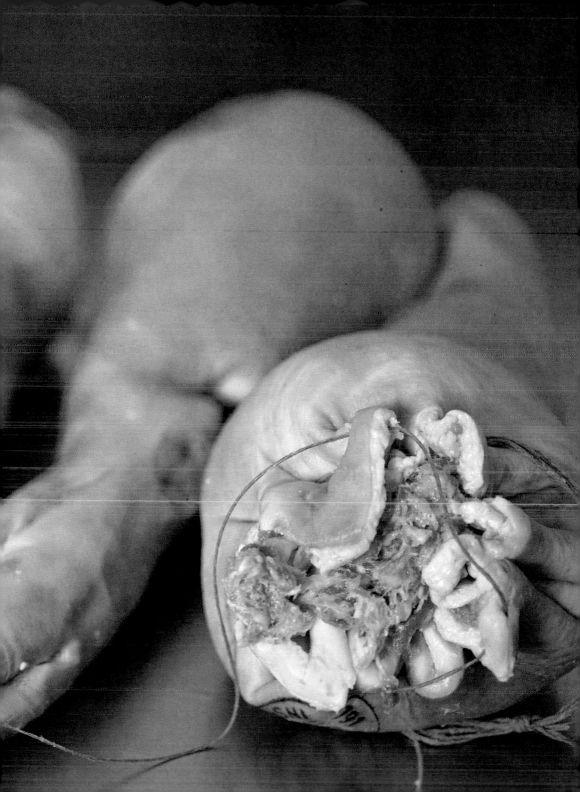

St. Gallen Bratwurst

Thüringer Rostbratwurst

Close to the German border in eastern Switzerland, the beautiful provincial city of St. Gallen is renowned for its colourful oriel windows, its lace embroidery, and for its take on the famous German bratwurst sausage. Bratwurst is made from pork or veal, or sometimes a mixture of both. St. Gallen bratwurst usually consist of finely ground veal that is seasoned, depending on the recipe, with spices such as ginger, nutmeg, coriander, and caraway. These pale, gently spiced sausages are available pre-cooked and fresh, the latter requiring grilling or sautéing.

Made all over Germany, bratwurst is usually named after the place with which it is associated, and St. Gallen is justly proud of its own particular version of this German institution. People can be seen walking all over the historic centre eating hot, juicy bratwurst fresh from street stalls with the bread known as *buerli*. Local company Gemperli's make theirs with a mixture of veal, pork, bacon, and milk. St. Gallen bratwurst are delicious grilled and served with hot mustard, fried onions, and rösti. They are also excellent partnered with a rich, onion gravy. **FP**

Among Germany's numerous sausages, such as bierwurst, bockwurst, knackwurst, and weisswurst, bratwurst from the state of Thuringia is the one with the longest pedigree. References to it go back to the start of the fifteenth century and there are records of fines set for selling poor merchandise, such as rancid beef or meat infested with parasites, dating from 1432. With 365,000,000 pieces sold each year it is among the nation's favourites. In Thuringia itself, each person consumes an average of sixty bratwursts a year.

It is made from pork belly that is first minced and then slowly chopped to obtain a fine, compact mixture that is piped into natural casings. With no additives other than salt and spices it is a pure meat sausage. Sausages are between 6 and 10 inches (15–25 cm) long. Thüringer rostbratwurst are roasted or more commonly grilled after being scored with diagonal cuts to help them cook more evenly. They are usually eaten smeared with mustard. As a snack, they are sold between a bread roll with the sausage poking out at both ends. **MR**

Taste: Firm and lean, St. Gallen bratwurst have a mild veal taste, accented by light spices, which expands on the taste buds. Grill or fry to best seal in the flavour and juices.

Taste: As it contains no preservative and is sold soon after manufacture, Thüringer rostbratwurst is a fresh-tasting, lightly seasoned sausage, with a dense but juicy texture.

Rostbratwurst are usually served grilled; sweet German mustard complements their mild flavour. ❯

Weisswurst

Weisswurst is a tasty, traditional white sausage made from well-seasoned veal and pork meat that started life in Munich and is now famous all over Bavaria. According to legend, it was created more than 150 years ago, when a young butcher to a Munich inn was making veal sausages and found to his horror that the skins for the casing had run out. In a bid to satisfy the customers, the quick-thinking butcher substituted a thinner hog casing. Concerned that the skin would burst if fried, he cooked the sausage in boiling water. The result was greeted with great enthusiasm, and to this day weisswurst is taken to the table in a pot containing its cooking water.

By tradition, weisswurst is a breakfast dish. The sausage is popped out of its skin and the meat sucked out and eaten with Bavarian sweet mustard and a pretzel, all washed down with white German beer. The sausages are very perishable and are best made fresh every morning. In Bavaria, the saying goes that weisswurst should never be allowed to hear the church bells' noon chime, hence they are eaten for the first meal of the day. **LF**

Taste: *This parsley-speckled speciality reveals a juicy, well-balanced combination of lean to fat, with a full meaty flavour that offers hints of lemon and spices.*

Figatellu

Figatellu (figatelli is its plural form) is a traditional form of Corsican charcuterie, a long, thin, dark-coloured sausage, of which the main ingredient is pig's liver. It is chopped or minced together with lean pork, mixed with red or rosé wine, made from the local Niellucciu grape, and seasoned with garlic and sometimes cloves, before being funnelled into sausage skins. It is then gently smoked for up to five days. Grilled over charcoal, it is eaten between slices of *pain de campagne* bread with *pulenta* (polenta) or a chestnut purée.

The tradition of killing a pig at the start of winter, the *tumbera*, is still practised in Corsican villages, particularly in the northern region of Castagniccia, which takes its name from the chestnut woods growing there. Although often described as black, the island breed is in fact a long-snouted animal with a pink coat and mottled black spots that still roams semi-wild, feeding on chestnuts and acorns. It is used for other cured meats—*prisuttu* (ham), *coppa* (loin), *lonzu* (fillet), and *panzetta*—whose names reflect their Italian mainland parentage. **MR**

Taste: *Due to its high blended liver content, figatellu has a texture and taste similar to blood sausage, enhanced with a smokiness from being charred over an open fire.*

Loukanika

Cumberland Sausage

This long, thin sausage from the Greek islands is traditionally made between mid-November and New Year's Day when the farmers slaughter their hogs. The name comes from the Latin *lucanicus*, which is believed to have been a sausage eaten by the Lucanian people who occupied the area of southern Italy now known as Basilicata in the fifth century BCE, and where a long, coiled, chilli-spiked pork sausage called *lucanica* is still popular today.

Loukanika has a high meat content, often a mixture of pork and lamb, although flavourings vary according to where the sausages are made. Cooks on the island of Simi, for example, put in lots of garlic, whereas those from Cyprus prefer coriander, cumin, or oregano. The seasoned meat mixture is stuffed into casings and the resulting sausages soaked in red wine before being smoked. Fresh loukanika are also made.

Loukanika can be fried or grilled and served as part of a mezze platter or with vegetables as a main course. They can also be casseroled with gigantes beans, potatoes, tomatoes, and peppers. **WS**

Instantly recognizable in a butcher's shop window, Cumberland sausage is less easy to pin down with regard to its origin. Its appearance a long tube of chopped or minced pork filling a natural casing of pig intestine coiled into spirals—is unique for an English sausage. What its ingredients are and how it is seasoned is another matter.

Locals in Cumbria, northwest England, say it used to be made with pork from the Cumberland pig, a fatty, lop-eared breed that died out in the 1960s. It is still made from pork, though, as is usual with many British sausages, it may contain up to 20 per cent rusk. (Some Cumberlands have a 98 per cent meat content.) A generation ago, butchers minced the pork coarsely. Now the best sausages, prepared with meat from Rare Breed pigs, are chopped by hand. In either case the coarseness of the mixture implies that only better quality cuts are used.

The seasoning varies from butcher to butcher, but the predominant taste comes from the blend of black and white pepper. Plans are afoot to try and get this regional sausage protected PGI status. **MR**

Taste: *Rich and meaty, the flavours of loukanika depend on individual sausage-makers. Smoked loukanika have a drier texture than fresh, with a hint of woodsmoke.*

Taste: *Usually fried or grilled, Cumberland sausage has a stretched, plump outer skin that is almost crisp and a peppery pork taste. The texture is succulent and chewy.*

Kaszanka

This hearty blood sausage, studded with buckwheat groats, is known as kaszanka in Poland; in North America, where it was introduced during the influx of Poles over a century ago, it is known as kiska. Kaszanka fanciers on both sides of the Atlantic are prepared to pay top money for it.

Like other blood sausages, kaszanka was traditionally prepared at pig-butchering time in early winter, when the frugal folk of yesteryear ensured that absolutely nothing was wasted. Blood spoils and coagulates very quickly, so blood sausage is found in many cultures where pigs are reared.

The Polish kaszanka is distinguished by the addition of buckwheat, as well as onion and spices. Together with hog's blood it contains cooked and coarsely chopped pork rinds, lungs, jowls, and trimmings, and golden-brown nuggets of fatback pork, fried until crunchy. The mixture is seasoned with salt, pepper, marjoram, and sometimes allspice, then packed into large pig intestines and boiled or baked. Some aficionados insist that the sausage is best when steamed. During cooking, a straw is inserted into the sausage to test it for doneness. If the straw is dry, the sausage is deemed to be cooked enough; if it is wet, more cooking is required.

Kaszanka can be eaten cold or hot, on its own or accompanied by mustard, prepared horseradish, or gherkin. Some people like it refried and smothered in onions, while others reheat their kaszanka in boiling water. Hot kaszanka served with mustard, a slice of rye bread, and a stein of beer is traditional street food and market-day fare in Poland. Like all blood sausages, kaszanka has a limited shelf life and is best eaten within three weeks of manufacture. **RS**

Taste: *The dusky groats blend with the meat and blood into a rich, hearty harmonious whole, with fragrant marjoram providing the chief flavour accent.*

Kaszanka sausages provide a welcome hot snack at a busy Krakow winter market.

Botifarra Dolça

Botifarra dolça is a curious, cylindrical, Catalonian sausage characterized by the addition of lemon and sugar or honey. It exists in two forms: raw, and dried, the latter being air-dried for no more than twenty-five days. Cinnamon may also be added to the pork mixture. The sausage meat is stuffed into natural skins and simmered gently in water that also contains lemon and sugar or honey.

Rumoured to come from a Moorish recipe, botifarra dolça has its origins in medieval cookery, when honey and sugar were more frequently used in savoury dishes. This was an alternative method of preserving meat to salting, drying, or storing it in lard. Botifarra dolça is found only around Girona and the Alto Ampurdan region of northern Catalonia, particularly around the three villages of Salitja, Sant Dalmai, and Vilobi d'Onya, which host an annual festival that celebrates the botifarra dolça. Production of the sausage is so localized that it is virtually unknown elsewhere in Catalonia.

The flavour combinations of botifarra dolça are so unexpected to the modern palate that chefs struggle to know when to use it. By tradition it should be prepared as a main course, accompanied by stewed apples or potatoes, but due to its sweetness (the skin caramelizes on cooking), it is often served erroneously as a pudding, often with sweet fried bread. A happy compromise is to offer it with an aperitif, when the aromatic sweetness of the sausage can satisfy initial pangs of hunger. Botifarra dolça is said to have been one of Salvador Dali's favourite foods, and in his honour the longest botifarra dolça in the world was made and measured just outside his birthplace. **RL**

Taste: *Botifarra dolça has the savoury presence of a pork sausage overlaid with clear notes of caramelized honey and light, warm cinnamon undertones.*

Morcilla Dulce

Morcilla de Burgos

Blood sausage, otherwise known as black pudding, is a traditional food popular the world over. Its production goes back centuries, and even earns a mention in Homer's *Odyssey*: "As when a man besides a great fire has filled a sausage with fat and blood, and turns it this way and that, and is very eager to get it quickly roasted . . ."

Morcilla dulce is the Uruguayan sweet version of blood sausage, made from pig's blood with orange peel, walnuts, and sometimes raisins. In a nation that is said to boast more livestock than people—thanks to its vast grassy interior—locals eat a lot of meat grilled, fried, barbecued, or roasted. Along with grilled beef and lamb, morcilla dulce forms the staples of Uruguay's highly popular *parilladas*, or grill rooms, which serve mixed grills cooked over hot wood coals. It is also served at *asados*, or barbecues. Many of Uruguay's national dishes are indebted to European influences, in particular Spanish and Italian cuisine, and morcilla dulce is most likely to have its ancestry in the morcilla blood sausage made throughout Spain. **CK**

Black pudding buffs will love Morcilla de Burgos— the rather delicious blood sausage from Burgos in the Castilla y León region of northern Spain. Morcilla is one of the most typical products in Spanish gastronomy and Morcillas de Burgos is generally considered the best that Spain has to offer.

The sausage was created as a by-product of the ritual of *la matanza*—the slaughter of pigs that has customarily taken place all over Spain during late autumn or winter. Whole families gather together, and the fattened pig is slaughtered and butchered to provide food for the winter months. No part of the pig is wasted—and that includes the blood, which is cooked until it thickens and congeals. In the case of Morcilla de Burgos, spices and seasonings are added for flavour, together with rice to give texture and bulk. The mixture is then forced into the cleaned guts or intestines of the pig.

Morcilla de Burgos is often served sliced and lightly fried as a tapa dish, but it is also used as an ingredient in stews and cooked bean dishes. Anyone travelling to Spain should give it a try. **LF**

Taste: *Morcilla dulce has a complex, crumbly texture that melts in the mouth while delivering a sweet and spicy tang of citrus, and a hint of nuttiness.*

Taste: *Served sliced and hot, dark juicy rice-speckled Morcilla de Burgos oozes bold, lip-smacking flavours that are traditionally highly savoury.*

The age-old tradition of the matanza *(pig slaughter) still takes place in Spanish villages during fiestas.* »

Oak Smoked Back Bacon

Bacon is meat from the side of the pig cured with dry salt or steeped in brine. For many centuries it was a staple food for peasant families, who would keep their own pig and use the cured bacon (smoked and unsmoked) to flavour otherwise bland dishes during the winter months.

After maturing, bacon can be cold-smoked at around 104°F (40°C), popularly over oak or beech wood. Oak smoked bacon is a firm favourite in the United Kingdom and is enjoyed for its earthy yet mellow flavour that will complement rather than overpower accompanying ingredients. It leaves a predictably smoky finish on the palate and the meatier back rashers are particularly succulent.

Oak smoked bacon is extremely moreish; it is an iconic sandwich filling and a popular addition to salads and pasta dishes. High in protein, bacon is also at the heart of the cooked English breakfast, where it might accompany black pudding, sausages, eggs, and a grilled tomato. The "fry up" is of relatively recent origin: in Victorian times Britons were more likely to eat cold meat at breakfast time. **GM**

Taste: *Salty, smoky, and more intense in flavour than ham, smoked bacon provides a comforting taste sensation. It should be sweet as well as smoky and linger on the palate.*

Grilled simply, the quality of oak
Ⓚ ***smoked back bacon shines through.***

Peameal Bacon

To be Canadian is, for many, to understand that bacon comes in two forms: the popular "strip" or "streaky" bacon that forms part of the traditional cooked breakfast popular throughout the British Isles and the pink, juicy, cornmeal encrusted loin known from Newfoundland to British Columbia as peameal bacon.

Unlike imitations presented as Canadian bacon, true peameal bacon is never smoked. Sold both as the boned, rolled loin and, more commonly, in substantial slices that can reach up to ¼ inch (0.5 cm) thick, peameal bacon is trimmed of fat, brined, then coated in a yellowish jacket of cornmeal. This meal was once made from crushed, dried yellow peas, hence the name, but the precise origins of peameal itself remain unknown.

Although sold raw, the classic preparation, as ubiquitously seen in Toronto's St. Lawrence Market, is fried and stacked in the middle of a fresh kaiser bun. Mustard is occasionally offered, but spurned by traditionalists. Alternate preparations include peameal roasts and barbecue-grilled slices. **SBe**

Taste: *Lean, salty, somewhat sweet and faintly nutty tasting, peameal bacon is almost impossible to dry out, thus yielding a consistently moist and juicy meat.*

Guanciale

Hangikjöt

Guanciale is a speciality bacon product that originated in central Italy and is made from the single piece of meat that lies between the throat and the cheek or jowl (*guancia* in Italian) of the pig. As with many Italian cured meats, its history goes back many centuries, and curing methods are still based on traditional recipes. The meat is covered in a mixture of salt, pepper, sugar, and spices, and dry cured for a month. It is then hung for another month before it is ready to be used. Guanciale is the bacon featured in the classic Italian pasta dishes *pasta alla carbonara* and *pasta all'amatriciana*, although many people mistakenly believe that pancetta—belly bacon— has always been used. It is quite a fatty bacon, but the fat renders down as the meat cooks.

Today, guanciale is produced in many areas of Italy, and each regional variation has its own character. Guanciale from Calabria tends to be spicy and fiery, whereas guanciale from Le Marche is sometimes lightly smoked. Tuscan guanciale is more mellow and aromatic. Guanciale has a particular affinity with fish, pulses, and dark green vegetables. **LF**

Hangikjöt, or "hanging meat" as the word translates, is a smoked Icelandic speciality that is now typically made from lamb, but has in the past also been made from mutton and sometimes even horsemeat.

The salting and smoking of meat as a method of preservation in Iceland stretches back to techniques practised among the Nordic peoples in the eighth century. Short summers and long winters meant that it was necessary to conserve food for sustenance during the colder months. What gives hangikjöt such a distinct flavour and aroma is the fact that it is traditionally smoked for up to five days over dried sheep dung; however, this is sometimes mixed with juniper or birch wood shavings.

Although sometimes served as a topping for bread or the thick pancakes known as *skonsur*, hangikjöt is not generally eaten on a daily basis. It is considered a delicacy that is usually offered as part of the Christmas Eve festivities, when it is served hot or cold, accompanied by cooked potatoes with a creamy, béchamel-style white sauce, peas, and pickled red cabbage. **LF**

Taste: *Sliced into lardons and cooked, richly flavoured guanciale adds glorious flavour and distinct savoury notes to accompanying ingredients.*

Taste: *Salty, with a pronounced smokiness, and delicious savoury flavour that kick-starts the gastric juices, hangikjöt has a unique, all-pervading, smoky aroma.*

Icelandic sheep are herded to pasture; the legs, thighs, and sides of lamb are ideal for smoking as hangikjöt. ❯

Yunnan Ham

As with some other types of ham such as Black Forest in Europe and Smithfield in the United States, Chinese Yunnan ham is salted, smoked, and air-dried, and some countries prohibit its importation because it is technically considered raw. Smoking and curing the meat reduces its water content and intensifies the flavour. It can be eaten raw (sliced as thinly as Smithfield ham because it is tough in thicker slices), but often it is added in small quantities to other ingredients to add its sweet-salty richness to the dish. The bones are prized for flavouring broths.

Yunnan ham is expensive, although much cheaper than its European and U.S. cousins, and a little goes a long way. It can be purchased in chunks or slices, with or without the bone. Some houses in Yunnan (and in Hunan, where a similar ham is made) will have a ham hanging from the ceiling rafters so pieces can be carved off and used as needed. Sometimes mould will appear, but if the ham has been properly cured, the mould can be scraped off and the ham underneath used as usual. **KKC**

Taste: *Yunnan ham is beautifully balanced with sweet, smoky, and umami flavours. It is smooth-textured, slightly moist, and a little chewy.*

Smithfield Ham

The little town of Smithfield in Virginia calls itself "the ham capital of the world," and Smithfield ham is one of the more famous of the family of salt-cured and (often) smoked country hams that have deep roots in the southern United States. Commercial production in Smithfield is said to date back to 1779. Smithfield hams gained their distinctive character from the hogs' traditional diet, which was rich in local Virginia peanuts.

Production is strictly regulated. The hams are dry cured with salt, smoked long and slow over hickory wood (often with fruit wood as well), and aged for at least six months. Smithfield connoisseurs often prefer hams that have cured for a year or more, intensifying their flavour and character.

Smithfield ham is almost always cooked before serving. First, it is soaked in water for a day or more, then scrubbed, and simmered in water until tender, when it can be prepared in a myriad ways: rubbed with brown sugar and baked whole or sliced, pan-fried, and served, Southern-style, with red-eye gravy and buttermilk biscuits. **CN**

Taste: *Even after soaking and simmering in water, the dominant taste of this ham is salt. Serve it thinly sliced, or use it to flavour dishes like potato soup or sautéed greens.*

The lengthy process of curing and ageing Smithfield ham in the right conditions contributes to its high price. »

Bradenham Ham

Black Forest Ham

Probably the rarest of British hams, Bradenham has crossed several counties in its peregrinations. Although known as early as the 1780s, when some believe it came from Buckinghamshire, it was granted a Royal Warrant much later, in 1888. By then it was being made in the neighbouring county, at the Royal Wiltshire Bacon Factory, Calne.

A long-cut haunch, taken from a fat bacon pig, Bradenham had an unlikely tar-coloured surface, which came from immersion in a concentrated brine cure that included both juniper and coriander, but most importantly, molasses. The hams were dried for five to six months before they were considered mature, then soaked for up to three days, and poached at a low temperature.

In the late twentieth century, production of Bradenham ham moved to Yorkshire. This factory later shut down and the food was in danger of extinction. However, the recipe, slightly modified, has survived in the form of Dukeshill Shropshire Black Ham, while London's Fortnum & Mason sells an organic version known as "Black Ham." **MR**

When it comes to the ham hall of fame, the mouth-watering speciality known as Black Forest ham (PDO) is up there with the best. The name carries a protected designation of origin certification, which means any ham bearing that label and sold within the European Union must come from a designated area within the Black Forest in the south of Germany.

Black Forest ham is made from prime legs of pork that are hand-rubbed with salt, herbs, garlic, and spices such as coriander and juniper berries, although exact recipes are usually handed down through generations and are often closely guarded secrets. The mixture draws out the moisture from the meat, which is then smoked in special smoke chambers over brushwood gathered from the fir trees of the Black Forest. This process gives the hams a unique and delicious flavour. As a finishing touch, they are sometimes dipped in beef blood to give the outer surface a deep brown or black colour.

Typically served thinly sliced as a starter or snack, Black Forest ham also appears on breakfast tables in Germany, and in cooked dishes. **LF**

Taste: *Bradenham ham has a noticeable sweetness. A firm, meaty ham, the current versions are less fatty than it once was, in line with current food trends.*

Taste: *Black Forest ham has a deep, complex flavour that delivers a pronounced but not overpowering saltiness, which then gives way to well-balanced smoky aromatics.*

Pig farming has long been associated with the Black Forest, and wild boar are still found there. ❯

Culatello di Zibello

Coppa Piacentina

Culatello di Zibello (DOP) is a mouth-watering artisan prosciutto named for the town of Zibello, in Parma, Italy. Records show that it was being produced in the area as long ago as the fifteenth century.

It is made from the large back muscle of the rear legs of pigs that must be bred, raised, and slaughtered within a specified region around the River Po. The river contributes to notoriously heavy winter fogs that contrast with the warm summer weather and create a unique humidity. This permeates the surrounding plains and, as the meat ripens in the moist, cool atmosphere after slaughter, it grows sweet and delicious.

Very soon after the pigs are slaughtered, the hind legs are skinned and boned, and the small, lean front muscle is removed. The meat is hand-salted, then trussed to create its typical pear shape. It is then left to rest. Some days later the meat is massaged to help the salt penetration. Another period of resting follows before the hams are bound in pigs' bladders and left to mature in cellars for at least a year. **LF**

Coppa Piacentina (DOP) is an exquisite cured pork product which uses meat taken from the upper neck part of *suino pesante italiano*, a particular breed of pig reared around Piacenza in Italy. With its temperate climate and lush vegetation, the area has proved an ideal environment for pig farming.

The production of Coppa Piacentina is believed to have started during Roman times but centuries later, in the farmhouses of the Po valley, curing and maturing techniques were perfected that have produced some of Italy's finest cured meats. Since 1997, Coppa Piacentina has carried a *Denominazione di Origine Protetta*, which strictly governs the region in which the pigs are raised and the processes through which the meat is cured and matured.

The pork is covered with a mixture of salt and local aromatics, then left to dry for seven days before being rubbed down by hand, wrapped in pig intestine, and left to cure for at least six months. It is typically served in paper-thin slices which need little more than a drizzle of extra virgin olive oil and perhaps a squeeze of lemon. **LF**

Taste: *Culatello di Zibello has a glorious pink colour and a fine marbling of fat that melts on the tongue to give a superbly structured balance of salty, sweet, spicy, and nutty.*

Taste: *Coppa Piacentina has a deep red colour with a light veining of fat. The full but balanced spicy, grassy aroma gives way to a toothsome, subtle sweetness.*

Culatello di Zibello, instantly recognizable by its distinctive trussed pear shape, cures in a Parma cellar.

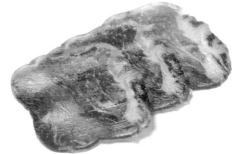

Jamón Ibérico de Bellota

Lomo Ibérico de Bellota

Connoisseurs consider Jamón Ibérico de Bellota the king among cured hams. It is produced in Spain, and comes from a bristly, black-footed, acorn-munching pig known as cerdo Ibérico that roams freely in the *dehesa*, an incredible area spanning over two million hectares of the Aracena and Extremadura mountains. The *dehesa* boasts a diverse ecosystem of cork and oak trees, wild herbs, grasses, and aromatic plants, and this provides the biggest part of the animals' diet.

Bellota is the Spanish word for acorn and during the pre-slaughter fattening period the pigs must reach a specified weight on a diet of foraged acorns and grasses alone; to make the grade, their body weight must increase by at least one third. The resulting fat layer penetrates into the muscle fibres, giving the finished hams a fine, yellowy white marbling and an incomparable flavour. What adds to the magic of this extraordinary ham is that half of this fat is monounsaturated—the type found in extra virgin olive oil, rather than the artery clogging kind more often associated with pork products. **LF**

Just like the superb Jamón Ibérico de Bellota, Lomo Ibérico de Bellota comes from the distinctive breed of stubbly, black-footed pig known as cerdo Ibérico. Prior to slaughter, the pigs have a diet rich in *bellotas*, the acorns that have dropped from the abundant oak trees of the *dehesa*, a protected ecosystem in Spain's Aracena and Extremadura mountains.

Lomo is created using an entire section of the tenderloin that has been dry cured for three months after being rubbed with an enticing mixture of olive oil, garlic, salt, herbs, and spices—usually oregano, nutmeg, and Spanish pimentón. An artisan-produced speciality, it is very different from the more mainstream Spanish sausages—such as salchichón and chorizo—as it is not a mixture of meat, but a whole piece of loin in a natural skin casing. For this reason, it shows off the handsome swirl of yellow-white fat that is so characteristic of Ibérico de Bellota to beautiful effect.

It is typically served thinly sliced, and alone, as a tapas dish; it has such a fabulous flavour there is little need for any accompaniment. **LF**

Taste: *To capture its true essence, eat the ham unadorned and at room temperature. It has an exquisite nutty flavour, savoury-sweet aroma, and melt-in-the-mouth texture.*

Taste: *Eaten at room temperature, the richly flavoured, dark red meat has organoleptic qualities. Both salty and sweet, it has an intense flavour and silky smooth texture.*

Ibérico pigs roam freely in southern Spain. Jamón Ibérico
❸ *must come from pigs that are 75 per cent Ibérico.*

Pancetta

Serrano Ham

Pancetta is produced all over Italy. It is pork belly that has been salted then left to rest for anything between eight and fifteen days, depending on the type of pancetta being produced and, naturally, the weight. Cracked black pepper and spices such as cloves, nutmeg, juniper, and cinnamon are added to the basic salting mixture to enhance the natural flavour. In central Italy, fennel seeds and garlic are sometimes added. (Some varieties are also smoked.)

Pancetta usually has a dark, fleshy pink colour with streaks of white fat, and is traditionally rolled, but sometimes flattened. Pancetta Piacentina (DOP), is produced exclusively in the province of Piacenza, and has a deep red colouring. Pancetta di Calabria (DOP) is produced only in Calabria and is left to cure for at least thirty days. The meat is rosy, with layers of white fat, and is dusted with chilli powder.

Pancetta is usually served thinly sliced or in lardons. It is used in much-loved pasta dishes, such as *spaghetti carbonara* and *pasta all'amatriciana,* and is often used in *soffrito* (the Italian equivalent of the French *mirepoix*) as a base for flavouring. **LF**

Air-cured ham from white-foot pigs is produced in several of the mountainous areas of Spain. Some of the best serrano hams are said to come from Trevélez in the Sierra Nevada and Teruel in Aragón.

Traditionally, hams were ripened in cool, dry mountain sheds called *secaderos*. Nowadays, the meat is cured in high-tech *secaderos* in controlled conditions, monitored by the *Denominacíon de Origen* (DO) inspectors. Serrano hams are first salted for about two weeks to draw off excess moisture, then washed and hung to dry. Finally they are air-cured, usually for between one and two years, during which time they can lose up to 50 per cent of their weight. They are not smoked during the curing process, nor are any artificial flavourings or colourings permitted. Serrano hams contain less moisture than their French and Italian counterparts and the natural curing process gives rise to a unique aroma and flavour.

Cut into thin slices, it is usually served as a tapa but can also be incorporated into soups and other dishes, for example croquettes with ham. **JAB**

Taste: *Pancetta has a subtle sweetness that comes through the mouth-watering, salty tang of the meat. Cooking further enhances its intense savoury notes.*

Taste: *Deep pink in colour, the ham has a salty tang and a sweet flavour, which increases the longer the ham has been cured. It must be eaten at room temperature.*

The low moisture content of Serrano ham—Spain's celebrated meat product—adds to its intense flavour. ❯

Prosciutto di San Daniele

Prosciutto di San Daniele is a mouth-watering cured ham from the town of San Daniele in the beautiful Friuli region of northern Italy. The hams benefit from fresh mountain winds and warm Adriatic Sea breezes, which combine to create the ideal microclimate for curing. The high altitudes and dry air give the hams a wonderful, unique flavour and texture.

Salting and drying is a method of preservation that goes back to ancient times and Prosciutto di San Daniele is still made along those same lines. The thighs of Italian-bred pigs are trimmed and hand massaged weekly with a dry salt cure for a period of one month, before being washed and air-dried for between one and two years. During the drying period, the hams lose up to 30 per cent of their original weight. Prosciutto di San Daniele carries a DOP certificate, which ensures that the hams meet strict criteria governing each stage of production.

Sliced wafer thin and served as antipasti with bread, the ham makes a superb accompaniment to juicy fruits such as melon and sun-ripened figs and is particularly delicious with pasta. **LF**

Taste: *Reddish pink in colour, with a pronounced, deliciously savoury aroma and glorious silky smooth texture, prosciutto di San Daniele melts in the mouth.*

Two digits stamped on prosciutto di San Daniele identify the ham-maker. ❯❯

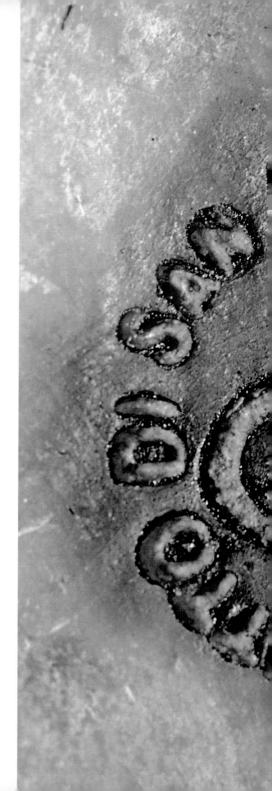

Jambon d'Ardenne

Spalla Cotta di San Secondo

A sixteenth-century engraving by Peter Brueghel the Elder illustrates the virtue Prudence with peasant women preparing hams to be salted. In the Ardenne, the wooded region that extends across the borders of Belgium, France, and Luxembourg, hams were a central part of the rural economy. The pigs would forage in the woods in spring and summer, before being slaughtered and cured for ham in winter.

Famous hams are still produced in the region, from carefully reared pigs, and the use of the name is protected. The best Belgian jambon d'Ardenne is prepared not only by salt-curing but by smoking. The curing mix always includes salt and juniper— "poor man's peppercorns"—and often garlic, shallots, and other spices. The hams are smoked over beech and oak from the Ardenne and allowed to ripen slowly. Although jambon d'Ardenne is normally eaten raw, it may also be desalted and poached to produce cooked hams that can afterwards be baked in pastry. This developed from the habit of serving a ham baked in sourdough at the *kermesse*, or carnival, before Lent. **MR**

The region of the pig par excellence lies north of Parma, Italy, embracing the towns of Brescello, Colorno, Zibello, Busseto, Polesine Parmense, and, specifically, San Secondo. There, during the last week in August, the annual *fiera della spalla* (fair of the pork shoulder) is celebrated. Spalla cotta (boiled pork shoulder) is produced in relatively small quantities and traditionally eaten in the summer, often with the local red wine, fortanina. The meat is salted and seasoned with pepper, cinnamon, and garlic prior to ageing for six weeks and then boiling.

The composer Giuseppe Verdi was a discerning gourmet and he often served spalla to his publisher Giulio Ricordi. In two letters, one dated 1872 and the other 1890, Verdi describes how to prepare the meat. "Put it in lukewarm water for about twelve hours, which will remove the salt. Then put it in cold water and boil it over a low heat, so that it does not break up, for about three and half hours. To check when it is cooked enough, stick a toothpick in the meat and if it goes in easily, the shoulder is cooked enough. Leave it to cool in its own broth and serve." **HFa**

Taste: *When raw, the smokiness dominates Belgian jambon d'Ardenne. Cooked on the bone it is firm-textured and quite salty, with complex, well-developed flavours.*

Taste: *Spalla is a particularly fragrant and very tender ham with a delicate warm spiciness. It is at its best served lukewarm, in thick slices.*

Spalla cotta, a speciality of the Parma lowlands, is found in delicatessens deboned and ready to serve. »

Tiroler Speck

Speck is a delectable, juniper-flavoured, cured ham produced in the Alto Adige, an area often referred to as the South Tyrol because it lies to the south of the Austrian and Swiss Alps. An area of stunning natural beauty, it combines alpine landscapes with clear mountain air, and provides the ideal microclimate in which to cure Tiroler speck (PGI).

Like other cured hams, speck grew from the need to preserve meat for the winter months and it has been made since the fifteenth century in Italy and Austria. The specially selected legs are deboned and trimmed before being immersed in herbs and spices including salt, pepper, rosemary, juniper berries, bay, and pimiento, for about three weeks. The whole process is carried out by hand, and the hams are turned regularly to ensure the flavours are evenly absorbed. The legs are then cold smoked and left to mature in controlled temperatures and humidity levels for about twenty-two weeks.

Tiroler speck is more like German ham than Italian prosciutto. It is excellent with crusty bread and a glass of wine, but is also good in salads. **LF**

Taste: *Thinly sliced Tiroler speck has a mouth-watering, melt-in-the-mouth quality with slightly herby, savoury notes that are balanced with a soft smoky edge.*

The Tyrol offers perfect conditions for curing ham. »

Bresaola dell'Ossola

Bresaola is the name given to an air-dried meat product that is mostly made in the Valtellina area of Lombardy in northern Italy from raw leg cuts of beef that are salted, spiced, and then hung to dry.

Its lesser-known but exceptionally distinctive and delicious cousin, bresaola dell'Ossola, comes from neighbouring Piedmont. While the name may be similar, bresaola dell'Ossola utilizes salt veal rather than beef, flavoured with a marinade of white wine, sugar, pepper, thyme, rosemary, bay leaves, cinnamon, and cloves. Following the ancient practice of preserving meat to eat throughout the year, bresaola dell'Ossola is traditionally made during winter. The veal is trimmed of fat, marinated, and sheathed in natural intestine, before being hung up to cure in a cool, well-ventilated atmosphere.

At the end of the curing process, the meat has an appealing deep red hue and a gloriously piquant aroma. It is high in protein, low in fat, and rich in iron. Typically it is served in paper-thin slices, at room temperature or very slightly chilled, as part of the antipasti course. **LF**

Bündnerfleisch

Bündnerfleisch is a dry-cured beef from the Swiss canton of Grisons whose origins lie in the alpine inhabitants' desire to preserve the best parts of their cattle to eat during the winter. Bündnerfleisch has also become a registered brand name, and is guaranteed as genuine only if marked with the label "zertifizierte GGA ABCert (SCES 038)."

Free from fat and sinew, it is made from the fascia (connective tissue) of beef and seasoned with salt, spices, and alpine herbs. The meat is layered in containers and stored for three to five weeks at near to freezing point, with the layers rearranged weekly to ensure even seasoning. The meat is then washed in wine before being kept for another five to ten days at a low temperature before the drying phase, which can take up to anything from five to seventeen weeks at temperatures of a maximum of 64°F (18°C). Bündnerfleisch's rectangular shape comes from it being pressed during the drying phase to distribute the moisture. It is usually eaten thinly sliced, sometimes with a light oil and vinegar dressing, or diced and added to soups, fondues, and raclette. **CK**

Taste: *When thinly sliced, the tender texture of bresaola dell'Ossola has a melting quality and the rich flavour is redolent of the distinctive aromatics in the marinade.*

Taste: *Bündnerfleisch has a delicate texture and a deep, rich, full-bodied flavour with a hint of the Swiss Alps suggested by the subtle herb and spice seasoning.*

The maturing period of bresaola dell'Ossola gives
❮ ***the lean meat its characteristic deep red colour.***

Pastirma

What bresaola is to Italians, pastirma is to Turks. Air-dried beef, though sometimes made with buffalo meat, it is eaten across the region that once formed the Ottoman Empire. Legend attributes its creation to Turkish horsemen who carried meat in their saddlebags, which became pressed as they rode. Historians believe that it was already being eaten in Byzantium (present-day Istanbul) when it was the capital of the Greek-speaking Roman Empire. Also known as *bastirma*, the Greeks call it *pastourmá*.

Since the seventeenth century, when it was praised in Evliya Çelebi's *Book of Travels*, the finest pastirma has been linked to Kayseri in Central Anatolia. Unlike bresaola, which is normally prepared with boned sirloin, up to twenty-six different joints of meat are used for the preparation. After boning, the beef is scored, salted, washed, and air-dried. During the process it is rubbed with a spicy paste of paprika, garlic, cumin, and fenugreek (*çemen*). Early in its maturation, the outer surface is reddish, but this turns brown with ageing. Sliced finely, it is eaten raw, but it is also lightly grilled or added to bean stews. **MR**

Taste: *Freshly cured pastirma is like a spicy carpaccio with a paprika taste that is typical of Turkish food. The flavours tend to mellow and become rounder as the meat dries out.*

Mocetta

This exquisite cured meat comes from Val d'Aosta in Italy, a diverse and wonderful Alpine region that incorporates rugged mountains, glaciers, forests, and rivers. Originally, it was made from the leg meat of local wild goats, but now the animals are one of a number of protected species that roam the Parco Nazionale del Gran Paradiso. These days, mocetta is usually made from the meat of domesticated adult cattle, although at certain times of year venison is sometimes used.

The legs are usually prepared for curing by hand: the meat is trimmed of fat and the veins and sinews are removed. The legs are then cured in a mixture of aromatic mountain herbs and left to mature for anything from one month to a year. Dark and delicious, mocetta is typically sliced into thin strips and served as an antipasto dish, either simply on its own or with a drizzle of extra virgin olive oil. Although it can work well as a filling for ravioli, it is not generally seen as a meat to cook with; subjecting mocetta to heat will destroy its delicately balanced flavour and texture. **LF**

Taste: *Lean and tender, mocetta has a fine texture and saltiness that gives way to a well-balanced gamey flavour. It combines well with walnut oil and dark rye breads.*

Alpine cattle are now used to make the cured meat mocetta, which once came from the leg of a wild goat. »

Smoked Ox Tongue

In an epic, sixteenth-century, Rabelaisian banquet of over 100 dishes, wedged between "calves fry" and a "cold roast loin of veal," the giant hero, Pantagruel, manages to find space for some smoked ox tongue.

Pickling ox tongues in brine and then smoking them, mirrors the process of making bacon. Adding nitrite, or in the past saltpetre, to the cure gives the tongue the vivid red colour that accounts for its Gallic name *langue à l'écarlate*. The technique of curing and smoking it has been practised from the eastern frontiers of the former Ottoman Empire to the western edge of Europe and thence to the Americas. Jewish cookery also has many recipes for "corned" ox tongue.

In French cuisine, it is more often served hot with a rich sauce. But, it is sold cold in the northern town of Valenciennes, where charcutiers prepare *langue de boeuf Lucullus*, sliced smoked tongue held together with layers of foie gras. Smoked tongue is popular in the Czech Republic where it often features on menus either hot or cold as a starter and is sometimes served with a plum sauce. **MR**

Taste: *The ox tongue itself has a firm texture, whereas the root is much softer. The smoke adds a piquancy to a taste that is reminiscent of corned beef.*

Zebra Biltong

When the Boer pioneers set out from the Cape of Good Hope on their Great Trek into the interior during the 1830s, they needed provisions to last on their journey. The salted, dried meat they produced from their cattle and from game they hunted on their way came to be known as biltong.

While most commonly made from beef today, during the hunting season biltong is also made from venison and other game such as ostrich, giraffe, and, more rarely, Burchell's zebra. The meat is rubbed with a salt mixture that generally contains crushed coriander seeds, vinegar, and sugar, often along with saltpetre (potassium nitrate). It is hung in a draught to air-dry. Once dry, it is rubbed again, then returned to dry further.

Good quality biltong should be dark and dry on the outside, but translucently red on the inside when cut into thin slivers. If kept dry, it will remain good for months without losing its flavour. In days of yore, it was wrapped in muslin once dry and hung inside a chimney for its flavour to be further enhanced by smoke. **ABH**

Taste: *Biltong has a pungent, gamey scent and a savoury, salty tang. Zebra biltong has additional flavour, while the inner meat has an unusually deep red hue.*

Biltong hangs to dry in the South African wind. When dried in the sun, biltong becomes extremely hard. »

Llama Charqui

Llama charqui is cut, pressed, salted, and dried llama meat. It is made in South America, where the llama roams across the high plains of the Andean mountains in Chile, Brazil, Peru, and Bolivia, and where the animal has long been prized for its wool, leather, manure, and as a pack animal.

Llama charqui's origins lie with the Incas—the word *charqui* is from Quechua, the ancient Inca language. This has been anglicized to become jerky, the term now widely used for various forms of dried meat The Incas stored rations in *tambos*, or inns, along the trails that stretched across their empire, such as the one leading to Peru's magnificent ruined city of Machu Picchu. The control of dried llama meat was essential to the success of the Inca civilization, which depended on a regular supply of protein to feed its growing urban population. After the Spanish conquest of the Andean peoples in the sixteenth century, the llama population declined drastically, and with it the consumption of llama meat. However, dried llama meat still provides nutrition for weary travellers, and continues to be traded in the coastal regions.

In South America beef, sheep, and alpaca are also dried in the air and sun to make charqui. The slave populations of Latin America were largely fed upon dried meat and fish, so both have remained part of the culinary heritage over a wide area.

Eaten in flat, thin slices, llama charqui is high in protein and withstands storage for a long period of time. Indigenous peoples such as Bolivia's Aymara still make it, and the Aymara eat a traditional dish called *olluco con charqui* made from small, potato-like tubers cooked with llama charqui. **CK**

Taste: *Flaky sheets of llama charqui have a pleasantly chewy texture. The flavour is both salty and spicy with a rich gamey undertone.*

Suovas

The nomadic Sami people have been preparing suovas, the smoked meat of the Scandinavian reindeer (*Rangifer tarandus*), since ancient times. The Sami are an indigenous people living in Sapmi, an area that spans the northern regions of Norway, Sweden, Finland, and Russia. Their language and culture were shaped by the bitterly cold, harsh environment in which they live. The reindeer is central, indeed essential, to the Sami people's culture and cuisine. Historically the Sami people were nomadic, following the reindeer herd as they migrated annually to the mountains. Many traditional Sami foods, therefore, including suovas, had to remain edible for a long period of time. With winter lasting 200 days of the year in Sapmi, reindeer meat has always been a vital mainstay.

The reindeer herds are now domesticated to a very large extent, however, they still roam free on the open plains of the tundra and graze on a natural diet of grass, herbs, and lichen, so their meat is lean and full of vitamins and minerals.

Suovas means "smoke" in Sami. After salt-drying for at least three days, the meat is duly smoked in the kåta, a cone-shaped, closed timber hut, over a fire of alder, birch, or juniper wood lit directly on the hut floor. The rising smoke cures the meat, a process that lasts for around twelve hours, and it hangs for an additional day to cool down slowly.

After curing, the meat can be eaten either as it is or grilled; it has a delicate but distinctive flavour. This simple food is well known as a gastronomic experience and appears regularly on the menu at the prestigious Nobel Prize dinner. As a starter, thin slices of suovas are served with lingonberry jelly. **CC**

Taste: *The burgundy-red meat is aromatic in taste and extremely tender. The smokiness does not dominate the fine and distinct gamey flavour of the reindeer.*

During the lengthy Sami winter, reindeer meat for suovas has to dry in very cold temperatures. »

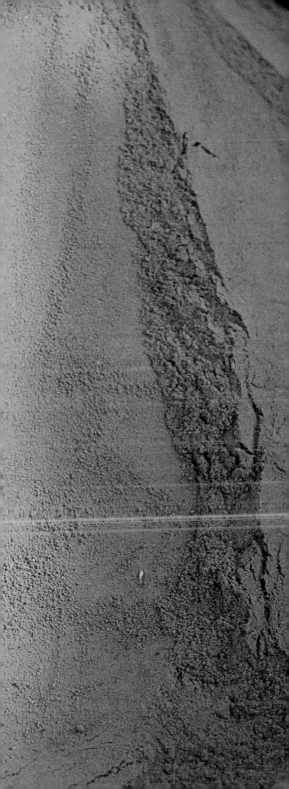

Coriander Leaf

Chervil

One green herb in the garden has become a base flavour in many of the world's cuisines: coriander leaf (cilantro to North Americans). In fact, some estimates rank it second only to basil in volume worldwide. *Coriandrum sativum* in its various forms appears in the records as far back as ancient Egypt but the leaves have risen and fallen in popularity— perhaps because of a predisposition in some diners to taste a soapy character in the leaves. Yet kitchen use in ancient Greece and Rome, and during the Middle Ages, is well documented and a resurgence in modern times has confirmed their culinary merit.

Stacked in bunches next to flat-leaf parsley in a shop, the leaves can be hard to distinguish from their neighbours, but one gentle rub and sniff soon differentiates the two. The larger, lower leaves of the plant are best in the kitchen whereas the wispy growth on the bolting stalks is less pungent and therefore less useful. Served raw in spring rolls and fresh salsas, the full brunt of the flavour is obvious. When cooked into curries or soups, it is often added last to preserve the pungent aromatics. **TH**

If tarragon is a pillar of French herb society, chervil is easily the grande dame of the ball. More intriguing and complex than common parsley, it delivers finesse where more boisterous herbs would simply overpower, yet achieves a unique signature. Even in the garden it looks dressed for polite society with its fern-like fronds and delicate white flowers.

Anthriscus cerefolium sits comfortably next to dill and parsley in the Umbelliferae family and the foliage resembles a cross between the two. The rather scrawny roots are occasionally consumed as a vegetable but the main culinary benefit lies in the young green leaves. The Roman scholar Pliny praised their gentle, cheerful, and warming effects. Because the taste dissipates quickly with heat, the crafty French began infusing chervil into vinegar to preserve the character for cooking. Even with the fresh herb, addition towards the end of cooking is advised. An ideal potency for eggs and fish, chervil adds the right notes of flavour and a brilliant burst of green. It also balances perfectly with chives, parsley, and tarragon in the French blend *fines herbes*. **TH**

Taste: *The herbaceous character of parsley comes with bold citrus overtones and a slightly sharp character. The aromatics are a blend of pepper and mild rosemary or pine.*

Taste: *Faint fennel and liquorice flavours come in slowly behind parsley impressions with very mild pepper tones. Fresh chervil is infinitely preferable to dried.*

Wild chervil (cow parsley) originated in the Middle East; it is used in Japanese vegetarian cookery. ❯❯

Rosemary

Dill

A rosemary bush left to its own devices can overtake whatever parcel of land it inhabits. A single brush against its rounded needles, thick with the aroma of pine and camphor, might suggest a similarly overpowering tendency on the palate, but this gnarly old man of the garden can become a gentle giant of the kitchen. *Rosmarinus officinalis*, has spawned countless myths and legends. It has been grown to attract friends, used in funeral ceremonies, and valued as a symbol of remembrance: modern research has shown antimicrobial effects which support more mundane historic uses as a disinfectant.

The tender new leaves are preferable to older stalks, but even thick stems can be used as skewers on the barbecue to impart flavour. In Spain, bees forage fields of blue rosemary flowers to produce a scented honey. When using fresh leaves, chop small amounts finely or use high heat to temper the pungency of entire branches. When paired with other strong components, like garlic or sage, on a roasting spit of lamb, rosemary will hold its own but the firing will calm the intensity greatly. **TH**

A field of new dill is quietly seductive when first encountered. The light green fronds wave in the most gentle of breezes and invite touch with their delicate leaves. Iran, Turkey, and many European nations have fallen in love with this wisp of a plant and use it in the most delicate, springtime cookery.

Easily cultivated, *Anethum graveolens* shoots a tall, fibrous stalk upwards before seeding. The delicate leaves that branch off this centre are tender, feathery, and surprisingly tart when eaten fresh. Later in the year, however, dill offers more intensely sour flavours as the seeds develop and its alter ego comes forth: strong, robust, and ready to add a potent culinary punch.

In native northern climates, dill was embraced early and is now the quintessential flavouring for cold water fish such as salmon. Many Scandinavian cooks use it to brighten sauces based on cream or yoghurt almost as other cuisines use salt. Further south, potatoes, cabbages, and other brassicas are peppered with ground dill seed in the robust cuisines of Central and Eastern Europe. **TH**

Taste: *Strong cedar comes through in the aroma and flavour. The palate is slightly oily, with notes of pine, camphor, sage, and hints of pepper. Avoid dried versions.*

Taste: *The fresh leaf is subtly sour with a green herbaceous character. Dried versions are less complex. The seeds are stronger with suggestions of liquorice and fennel.*

In the Middle Ages dill was used in medicines and witchcraft; it was believed to have special powers. »

Moroccan Mint

Holy Basil

Fresh green mint is perhaps the purest distillation of spring. The sheer exuberance of the season seems embodied in this prolific perennial that can overtake garden space almost overnight. Although easily grown worldwide, nowhere else has this buoyant leaf found the fame it receives in Morocco.

Most Moroccan growers have planted heirloom seeds gathered from previous crops for generations, leading to great individualistic pride in each farm's production, not to mention uncertainty as to which cultivars and hybrids of spearmint (*Mentha spicata*) and peppermint (*Mentha piperita*) are being produced. What is clear, though, is that the arid soil and intense heat of the North African *terroir* produces leaves that set a global standard for quality and pungency.

Yoghurt stirred with mint complements almost any tagine and the mandatory couscous will have at least been steamed over vegetables simmering in a broth seasoned with mint. Fresh mint is also brewed with Chinese green "gunpowder" tea and copious amounts of sugar, and then served in small glasses in the ceremony that welcomes every guest. **TH**

This bushy, aromatic plant, known botanically as *Ocimum sanctum*, is revered all over India under its local name of tulsi. Whether bright green (*Rama tulsi*) or purplish (*Krishna tulsi*), the divine prefixes underline their sacred place in the Hindu home. The plants are regarded as the earthly manifestation of the Hindu Supreme Being Vishnu and their leaves are traditionally offered to him during prayers. Often offerings to him are returned to the devotee after worship with *tulsi* leaves as a benediction. The woody roots of the plant are also used to make rosary beads.

Yet for all its cultural significance, in India tulsi is used medicinally and spiritually rather than in the kitchen. However, in Thailand, where it is called *kaphrao*, its leaves sit alongside Thai basil and lemon basil as one of the trinity that underpins the national cuisine. Both "red" and "white" leaves are used in traditional curries and stir-fries, most famously *phat kaphrao*, and holy basil is so associated with Thailand in South East Asia that its Lao name (confusingly) means "Thai basil." **RD**

Taste: *Bright, sharp menthol notes and a long-lasting flavour are common to all species. The citrus and pepper scent and zing reveal themselves in varying intensities.*

Taste: *The leaves release a strong aniseed aroma and the juice has a peppery, almost mentholated flavour that is clove-like. It needs to be thoroughly cooked into a dish.*

In parts of India, holy basil is also sold as a tea, which is believed to relieve stress and impart energy. »

French Tarragon

Lemon Thyme

Known as "the dragon herb," genuine French tarragon is a demanding plant. It refuses to grow from seed, must have precisely the soil it asks for, and will deaden the tongue if chewed directly. Perhaps unsurprisingly, it was used as a medicine in ancient times.

Artemisia dracunculus, a perennial that rarely flowers, will form a bushy mass of slender leaves over the hot summer months and recover well from even nearly constant harvesting. It has migrated and naturalized across Europe and North America, propagated by cuttings and division. A relative known as "Russian tarragon" grows from seed but lacks flavour and has little value in the kitchen; an unrelated species called "Mexican tarragon" has similar but less complex tastes and should not be considered a substitute for the genuine article.

French cuisine best uses its namesake tarragon, adding it to bean and lentil dishes, béarnaise sauce, light vinegars, and classic herb blends like *fines herbes*. Beyond French borders, the herb appears in the fish and egg dishes of Scandinavia. **TH**

Thyme really needs little improvement to gain status in the kitchen. Savoury notes complement meats and sauces well with balanced hints of herbaceous sweetness. Mother Nature, however, is never one to rest on her laurels and gives us yet another permutation of thyme, with the distinctive essence of citrus: lemon thyme.

Thymus citriodorus looks almost identical to ordinary thyme although it is usually variegated with leaves of pale yellow and green. Although naturalized widely across Europe and North America, lemon thyme is rarely grown commercially and almost never sold dried. What makes lemon thyme special is the strong citrus aroma that swells up from the foliage with only the slightest touch. The aroma crosses into the flavour, albeit not quite so intensely, and without the acidity of lemon juice.

The light flavours of the fresh herb are perfect for fish and seafood. While roasting and high heat will destroy the lemon character, gentler processes like steeping into cream sauces or a quick sauté will preserve the special essences of lemon thyme. **TH**

Taste: *Mint, anise, and liquorice all merge with a mild numbing effect when tasting true French tarragon. All leaves, fresh or dried, should be a brilliant green.*

Taste: *Like ordinary thyme, the leaves are camphorous and sweet, but with a pronounced citrus aroma. The lemon character infuses or evaporates quickly with heating.*

In summer, the variegated lemon thyme shrub has tiny pinkish flowers that are attractive to bees. »

Chive

Where garlic, onions, or shallots are too strong, or where cooking is not required, chives provide a featherweight alternative. Hundreds huddle together in the herb garden, waving in the breeze like some sort of land-based sea anemone. Delicate, brilliant green tubular stalks reach upward and ultimately burst forth striking purple-pink blossoms.

Chives are just one of many things that Marco Polo supposedly brought back from his journey to the Far East, but evidence suggests they were cultivated in Europe long before his travels. A related species, *Allium tuberosum*, known as "garlic chives" or "Chinese chives," is indeed native to Asia and, as the name suggests, exhibits a stronger flavour in both its flat leaves and its white flowers.

Of all the kitchen herbs, *Allium schoenoprasum* is the easiest to cultivate. The edible flower exhibits all the flavour of the stem but with more pepper, although it is the stem that provides such a delicate accent to many European cuisines. Compound butters, eggs, and soufflés are all flavoured with fresh chives. **TH**

Taste: *Fresh chives have a mild onion character and a delicately grassy taste. Although moist and papery thin, their pleasant texture comes close to a crunch.*

Chives are farmed commercially both for their stems and flowers. »

Kinome

Japanese efficiency lets nothing go to waste, and the prickly ash bush that provides sansho (in Japan) and Sichuan peppercorn (in China) as a spice is no exception to this rule. The young leaves of *Zanthoxylum piperitum*, and sometimes of other related species, are pressed into service as both flavouring and garnish, thanks to a mesmerizing combination of spice and citrus.

The leaves must be young and tender to be used as an ingredient: they provide a vibrant lime-meets-pepper character along with some of the signature shock to the palate that Sichuan peppercorns offer. In older growth, the texture is tough and the flavours dissipated. Individual leaves have a bright green colour and wrinkled, serrated edges, and most commonly appear in markets as intact fronds on the stem or packaged leaves carefully plucked from the branch. Dry versions are nearly nonexistent and of little or no value to the chef. Preparations in Japanese cookery range from a fine shredding of leaves as a garnish in soups and sushi to flash frying in oil or using as a base for a paste. **TH**

Taste: *The citrus aroma is mirrored in taste along with pepper, mint, and mild chilli on the palate. Slight numbing of the tongue is apparent when the leaves are served raw.*

Mitsuba

Of all the cuisines in the world, Japanese is probably the most artistic. Every element is placed with care and intent to emphasize the delicate nature of the craft, like a single long stem of mitsuba, tied into a decorative knot as a garnish.

Cryptotaenia japonica, sometimes called Japanese chervil, Japanese parsley, honewort, or trefoil, shoots forward long, spindly stalks up to 18 inches (45 cm) in length, terminating in a flat trefoil leaf. Both the leaves and stalks are edible with the latter turning a delicate pale green as the plant matures. Farmers sometimes cover the stalks with soil or straw as they grow, or cultivate the entire plant in darkness to blanch it, producing nearly white stems and foliage known as *kirimitsuba*. The plant seeds easily, and seeds are sprouted as an edible.

Mitsuba's flavour is easily destroyed by heat so most recipes call for its use raw or as an addition at the end of cooking, like the leaves that typically float atop a bowl of miso soup. Mitsuba leaves and sprouts can impart a light, chlorophyll-laden taste to sushi rolls, salads, and noodle dishes. **TH**

Taste: *Mitsuba has a delicate flavour, reminiscent of parsley with faint connotations of chervil and celery leaf. Harvest fresh only hours before use.*

Mitsuba leaf stalks resemble coriander stems, although the flavour is much milder. »

Shiso Leaf

Nature has delivered to the Japanese an herb almost ideally suited to their cuisine. Shiso—perilla in the United States—has a bold flavour but is not so strong as to leave an otherwise balanced plate off kilter; the palm-sized serrated leaves, in hues of brilliant purple and intense green, could be considered art all on their own.

Although grown in Korea, China, Burma, and much of South East Asia, *Perilla frutescens* reaches much of the world painstakingly harvested as individual leaves and packaged with true Japanese elegance for export at a price. For the less particular chef who can suffer imperfect leaves, the plant, which is an annual in the mint family, can be grown from seed, and will yield edible flowers as a bonus. The seeds are also edible—fresh, dried, or pressed to extract their potent oil.

Both the leaves and seeds impart their unique flavour to pickles and marinades or are pounded into regional spice mixes. The large ornate leaves may be fried in tempura or included as part of sushi service; in Korea they are used as a wrap for food. **TH**

Kaffir Lime Leaf

If there is a signature flavour that sums up South East Asian cooking, it is most certainly kaffir lime leaf. Any food stall of merit in the region will have a stash of fresh leaves on hand, if not a nearby tree for regular harvests. Pounding them into fresh green curries with coriander, chillies, and lemongrass is a daily chore that is a cornerstone of the cuisine.

The bifurcated double leaves, the knobbly, almost juiceless fruit, and the long, spindly branches give an indication that *Citrus hystrix* offers something different from the citric norm. It is the thick, fresh leaves with their singular, pungent taste that are most commonly used in the kitchen, whether infused into stocks or chopped into dishes. They are sometimes found dried, but the process turns them pale, and they should be used only as a last resort.

A technique common in Thailand is to flavour sea salt with chopped kaffir lime leaves, in sealed jars to preserve the aroma. Kaffir lime leaf also makes a notable appearance in Vietnamese *pho*, a gently simmered broth that marries the taste with lemongrass and white pepper. **TH**

Taste: *Shiso leaf has strong citrus aromas much like grapefruit, which soften on the palate, accompanied by decidedly green herb tastes of chive and mint.*

Taste: *Kaffir lime leaves must be steeped or torn to release their flavour, which is reminiscent of tart lime zest. The aroma is strong and distinctive.*

In addition to its culinary uses, the kaffir lime is an attractive bush with fragrant white flowers. ❯❯

Lovage

Lovage cannot decide whether to be a herb, a spice, or a vegetable. For chefs who have discovered its flavours, perhaps the correct answer is all three.

In Roman times, the likes of Apicius called for *Levisticum officinale* widely in cookery, while Galen, more prosaically, recommended it as a cure for wind. The foliage resembles celery leaf in both shape and taste and can be harvested regularly from the hollow, ribbed stalks which easily reach 5 feet (1.5 m) in height. Both stalks and roots can be used as a vegetable; the leaves may be used as a herb or added to salad; the seed-fruits that ripen on the umbel of yellow flowers can be collected and dried as a spice, much like fennel.

The flavours of lovage in its different forms are well suited to an enormous variety of dishes; the leaves in salads, the seeds in pickles, and the stalks simmered into soups, for example. For fans of the flavour, one traditional rustic Italian preparation calls for stalks and roots sautéed as a vegetable to be spiced with ground seeds, making a trilogy of lovage on a single plate. **TH**

Taste: *Celery leaf flavour dominates. The stalks are like pleasantly bitter cabbage; the roots are dill-like; the seeds are mildly sweet; and the leaves have a light bitterness.*

Fields of lovage are common to Europe, where the shrubs grow equally well in sun or shade.

Neapolitan Parsley

Often known as "celery-leafed parsley," this giant member of the parsley family can grow up to just over 3 feet (1 m) in height, with stems so thick they may be eaten like celery. Like the well known flat and curly-leafed parsleys, and the lesser known Hamburg (root) parsley, Neapolitan parsley (*Parsley Gigante di Napoli*) is one of the *Petroselinum crispum* species, and a member of the celery (Umbelliferae) family.

It is not to be confused with the more common flat leafed variant that is often known as Italian parsley, and is also a key ingredient in many Middle Eastern cuisines. Neapolitan parsley looks very different. Its large, broad, glossy green leaves are smooth with indented edges.

Neapolitan parsley has long been grown in the areas around Naples and is particularly prized in southern Italy. The leaves have a lovely aroma and are much appreciated for their pungent flavour. The stems are generally eaten in much the same way as celery: added to soups and sauces or blanched and served as a vegetable. It has a particular affinity with salty and blue cheeses, beef, and fish. **LF**

Taste: *The sweet aroma and fresh but pungent flavour display well-defined essences of parsley that are gently enhanced by distinct celery-like eating qualities.*

Rau Ram

Curry Leaf

Originally a wild perennial that tends to spread voraciously throughout any warm undergrowth it can find in the South Asian tropics, rau ram is one of the most interesting herbs found in the lush greenery of Vietnam. Despite this vigorous growth, it rarely escapes to kitchens outside the region.

Also known commonly as Vietnamese coriander and Cambodian mint, *Polygonum odoratum* has slender pointed green leaves that are almost as valuable for their characteristic aroma as they are for their flavour. This has led to wider cultivation as an essential oil crop in Australia and India, and is contributing to wider availability as a fresh leaf herb outside the South Pacific. Dried leaves have almost no culinary value.

Malaysia, Thailand, and Indonesia all use rau ram, but Vietnam embraces the leaf most heartily as fresh spice, salad green, and culinary ingredient. Rau ram is such an integral component of laksa that it is known as laksa leaf in Malaysia. In addition to being added to soups, it can also be wrapped into spring rolls or pounded into fresh curry pastes. **TH**

Despite its English name, and European botanical name, the curry leaf has nothing to do with either Europe or that beloved British condiment, curry powder. *Murraya koenigii* takes its title from a pair of eighteenth-century European botanists, Johann Andreas Murray and Johann Gerhard König, but has an indispensable role in Sri Lankan and South Indian kitchens under its respective names of *karapincha* and *karuveppilai*. Recent research has indicated that the curry leaf may be beneficial for diabetics.

Although used in north India and in northern Thailand, too, the curry leaf tree is emblematic of South India. Here most homes grow at least one for the leaves that are plucked fresh for the day's menu. Daily a distinct citrusy yet pungent smell wafts through homes as curry leaves and spices sputter in heated oil. In the cuisine of southern India, the leaves temper staple vegetarian food; in Sri Lanka, they add bite to dry meat dishes. They perk up traditional soups (*rasam*), lentils (*sambhar*), and vegetable stews, plus coconut chutney, pickles, and even buttermilk. **RD**

Taste: *The peppery taste of fresh coriander meets sweet spearmint in rau ram. These flavours are complemented by mildly bitter components much like celery root.*

Taste: *Fried when fresh, the edible leaves release a spicy-citrusy aroma and a peppery flavour. Freeze or refrigerate rather than drying to preserve their subtle characteristics.*

The colours and aromas from the numerous bowls of spices make a most attractive market stall. ❯❯

Boldo Leaf

Smyrna Bay Leaf

Markets in the remote Andes of Chile and Peru are tiny bastions of economic opportunism. Merchants there can shift from selling parkas to potatoes within a week depending on what becomes available. One of the more frequent wares to arrive on their stalls is a native leaf called boldo.

While the leaves are the principal flavouring element of the evergreen tree *Peumus boldus*, which looks much like a large bay laurel, it also produces small green berries that are dried and consumed much like peppercorns. It is now cultivated more widely around the Mediterranean, particularly in North Africa, mainly for medicinal uses, although chefs are slowly discovering uses in the kitchen.

In its native regions, boldo is used both as an addition to slowly simmered dishes and as a wrapper to infuse flavour into grilled meats. Larger leaves are discarded after cooking but tender young leaves can be shredded finely and consumed directly after wilting from the cooking heat. Boldo leaf is also brewed as a tisane by itself or added to the classic South American herb tea, *yerba mate*. **TH**

Bay leaf is a foundation of flavour across most modern cuisines. Its perfume can underpin more complex creations but, as with most foundations, you need to seek out the strongest base material you can find. With bay, that means a trip to Turkey, specifically the hills around the port of Izmir (formerly Smyrna) where the conditions are tailor-made to produce the perfect leaf.

Through the long Turkish summer the bay trees soak in the sunlight; in autumn, drying conditions perfectly concentrate the flavour. Batches of leaves are combed by hand to select the specimens that will become the top grade. Free of blemishes and still slightly pliable, these are intensely fragrant when fresh and remain so for up to a year.

Turkish bay seems able to remind cooks just why *Laurus nobilis* has gained such culinary prominence. Where more pedestrian sources seem weak and pallid, Smyrna produces a deep, rich character that could be a reference point for even the most demanding chefs: it is as likely to appear in classic French stocks as in trendy American meat rubs. **TH**

Taste: *Like a blend of bay and mint, yet slightly more bitter on the palate, the larger fresh leaves have a strong resinous odour that cooks away slowly.*

Taste: *Smyrna bay leaves have the strong herbaceous tastes of thyme and the bitterness of celery. An intense aroma, camphorous and sweet, wafts from fresh sources.*

Bay trees thrive in hot conditions and produce tough evergreen leaves that are usually dried in the shade. »

Lemongrass

Pandan Leaf

At a distance, clusters of lemongrass (*Cymbopogon citratus*) in their native habitat look deceptively plain. Long skinny leaves of an unassuming green fan out from the stem, yet release at a single touch a profuse lemon aroma that has made this pungent plant a staple of kitchens across South East Asia.

In Thailand, Laos, and Vietnam, cooks pulverize lemongrass in tall mortars, combining it with garlic, kaffir lime leaf, and other herbs to create a thick curry paste that is integral to their cooking. Island cultures of the South Pacific also cultivate the crop with great success and include it in their cuisine.

Although the leaves have some use in teas and medicinal applications, the fibrous stalks and slight bulb at the base of the perennial hold the bulk of flavour. Woody and tough, they are commonly macerated in oils and other spices and removed after infusion. (Similarly, a bundle can be tied and simmered in stock to impart the essence.) More rarely, the outer layers of fresh cuttings are separated to reveal tender young shoots in the centre that can be finely chopped and added directly to dishes. **TH**

One of the mysterious nuances of flavour that highlights South East Asian cuisines, this floral leaf has a taste and aroma so subtle one could almost consider it sneaky. *Pandanus amaryllifolius*, sometimes referred to by its family name of screwpine, is cultivated from Thailand to New Guinea for its fragrant leaves. Blade-shaped fronds up to 2 feet (60 cm) in length spread out from a central trunk and are harvested almost year round. When fresh, the leaves are crushed, torn, or even tied into knots before adding to simmering pots to help release their signature taste. In regions where fresh is not available, they may be sold frozen, blanched, infused in water, or as a paste.

Most common in Malay, Thai, and Indonesian cuisines, pandan is commonly found in rice dishes and is often married with coconut. It perfumes sweet treats from ice creams and cocktails to the classic Malay pandan cake, which attains its green colour from the leaves. It also pairs well with chicken and fish, either infused into the region's simmering stews or used as wrappers to flavour the meats. **TH**

Taste: *The aroma can be stronger than genuine citrus, while the flavour is a rich lemon without the acidity. Hints of camphor and mint are present in the freshest sources.*

Taste: *Pandan has a floral character that is like a cross between mild jasmine and vanilla. Frozen leaves are often sold as wrappers but have little flavour remaining.*

Lemongrass can often be seen growing along ◀ *the edges of bogs or shallow water gardens.*

Sweet Marjoram

Trying to navigate the complex family tree of marjoram is like trying to seat bickering relatives at a holiday table without starting an argument. Lamiaceae, commonly known as the mint family, includes potent siblings like oregano and exotic cousins such as shiso, but it is marjoram, especially the sweeter varieties of *Origanum majorana*, which occupies the role of peacemaker and mediator.

Marjoram is one of the herbs that can easily anchor a garden with almost no effort, whether it be a country acreage or an urban window box. Perennial tendrils of numerous cultivars offer repeated harvests throughout the year. Sweetness seems to diminish from the moment of picking, and fresh is generally superior to dehydrated forms, so growing pots near the kitchen is recommended.

Marjoram marries with tomatoes famously: albeit not so potent as oregano, it provides both a savoury and sweet foil for their acidity. All the cuisines that ring the Mediterranean have embraced the herb either alone or in concert with some of its more rambunctious family members. **TH**

Taste: *Most species start with grassy flavours and finish with mild pepper. Anise, sage, and lemon notes appear mid-palate but tend not to linger as with stronger herbs.*

Greek Oregano

Greece is a nation with a long, proud history, and its gardens and wilderness seem to honour the past. Oregano, a popular herb since at least the fifth century CE, still flourishes amid ancient stones and hillsides. Unsurprisingly, given this long history, the Greeks benefit not only from their sandy soils and ocean influences but from specific beneficial species, sometimes sold overseas as "wild oregano." The types known as *hirtum* and *kaliteri* gain most favour among locals, but when even individual cultivars from small producers are transported abroad, something is lost that cannot be duplicated.

Fortunately for the chef, bundles of the herb are dried and exported widely. Since the herb owes its flavour and scent to a high content of essential oils, this process does not do irreparable harm and dry sources are still good in the kitchen. Classically paired with tomatoes and other acidic ingredients, Greek oreganos can withstand culinary pressure. Fresh pickings work well with rosemary and lemon, while dried bunches can simmer at length without being completely destroyed by the heat. **TH**

Taste: *With deeper herbaceous character than ordinary oregano, the notes of liquorice, bay, pepper, and fennel can be individually identified on the palate.*

Greek oregano is a decorative addition to any herb garden and produces pinky purple blossoms. »

Dalmatian Sage

Lemon Myrtle

Of all the herbs in the kitchen, sage is perhaps the most powerful workhorse. But for the best and most complex version of this bold leaf you must seek out crops from the unique coastal region known as Dalmatia. The balance of sun and sea there elevates the taste well above ordinary garden varieties.

Sage has been credited with a wide range of healing powers over the centuries; however, its impact today is culinary. In Croatia, its earthy depths of flavour blossom to new heights thanks to the mists of the Adriatic Sea. Analysis of essential oils shows that the unique microclimate and historical cultivars have mutated ordinary sage into a herb that is mellower and slightly sweeter than the other *Salvia* species. The tender fresh leaves may be used whole but more commonly are dried then rubbed to remove the stems and create a soft, cotton-like down.

Prized across Europe, Dalmatian sage appears in sausages and cured meats to the north and in pastas and herb blends to the south. Like all sages, it makes a perfect foil in herb butters and stronger sauces for roast meats. **TH**

Despites its delicious aromatics, this versatile east coast Australian flavouring is hardly a herb: the parent plant is a rainforest giant that can grow up to 65 feet (20 m) tall. However, in the plantations where cleared rainforest is being reforested, the trees are managed rather like tea.

This traditional Australian ingredient forms the basis of possibly the most widely used Australian flavouring (lemon myrtle sprinkle). It tastes similar to a blend of lemongrass, lime, and lemon oils—all popular flavours on their own—and it is often used instead of, or to enhance, these commodity ingredients. Lemon myrtle sprinkle is well used in both sweet and savoury applications and its popularity is growing internationally. It appears in herbal teas, bakery goods, beverages, and nutritional supplements as both a functional ingredient and flavouring. In the kitchen, it is most appropriately used as a finishing herb in a similar way to coriander (*cilantro*) and basil. Citral, the active essential oil, boils shortly above blood temperature, so the flavours are best infused into warm foods. **VC**

Taste: *Mild pine flavours sneak through grassy base notes, hinting at rosemary and peppercorn. Use fresh leaves or find dried versions that do not crumble to the touch.*

Taste: *The palate is predominantly lime with a late hint of menthol complemented by mild acid, faint anise, and green tea. Initial sweet notes of lemongrass oil.*

Salvia *is a small shrub native to Europe; its spiky flower* ❮ *is vivid purple in colour and most distinctive.*

Filé

Myriad scents permeate the air of Cajun bayous—from the smoke of andouille sausage to the brine of fresh shrimp—but sassafras trees cast a more delicate aroma. Locals dry and grind the multi-lobed leaves of this tree into filé, the powder they use as both flavouring and thickening.

When rubbed, most parts of *Sassafras albidum* will deliver at least a hint of the citrus-meets-earth aroma that first attracted chefs. This scent comes primarily from an essential oil that contains safrole, a substance which, although carcinogenic in large quantities, has appeared in everything from root beer to curative tonics.

Although the powdered leaf is industrially produced for the kitchen, it is small local producers who rub the carefully dried leaf into the delicate fluff most prized by Cajun and Creole chefs for finishing soups and stews. Most notable of these is gumbo, a slow simmer of fresh seafood, okra, and sausage thickened with filé. Experienced chefs stir the powder into a hot dish at service rather than simmer directly for fear of overly mucilaginous results. **TH**

Taste: *Used sparingly and away from direct heat, filé lends a unique base note to dishes. Hints of lime and overtones of sage tinge the palate and—when fresh—the aroma.*

Herbes de Provence

The *garrigue*, with its scented hillsides overgrown in flowers and herbs, is the wilderness at the heart of Provence. In the past—and still for some today—it was part of the culinary folk culture to pick bundles of fresh herbs from the *garrigue* and leave them to dry in the sun. During the 1960s, therefore, "Herbes de Provence" came to mean a blend of dried herbs and lavender, harvested in the south of France.

Since 2003 a French Label Rouge denotes a blend that contains 26 per cent each of savory, rosemary, and oregano, 19 per cent thyme, and 3 per cent basil, a mix that is adapted to char-grilled foods and also to some classic Provençal daubes and sautés. Unlike the original blends, however, these are cultivated herbs, with controlled levels of essential oils that are dried mechanically, rather than by the sun, and others, not covered by the quality denomination, may be equally or even more interesting. Seasoned Pioneers produces a version that mixes wild savory, thyme, and fennel seed with marjoram, rosemary, and lavender, which is close to the earliest Herbes de Provence concept. **MR**

Taste: *The scent of Herbes de Provence is in-your-face fragrant, with contrasting sweet and harsh aromas. They bring the perfumes of the garrigue to cooking.*

This classic blend is famous worldwide and is particularly popular packaged in traditional sacks. ❯❯

Bird's Nest

While it was almost certainly extreme hunger that drove the first person to eat bird's nest, it took great skill and imagination to turn it into a delicacy.

The nests are made by a species of swiflet that build their nests on the high walls of caves. Instead of building their nests from twigs, feathers, and grass, as other birds do, these swiflets, which are native to South East Asia, use a gummy substance that has been variously identified as a regurgitated seaweed or the bird's own saliva. It hardens as it dries and helps the nests adhere to the sheer, cave walls. Harvesting is perilous as it involves scaling the high, slippery cave walls, but some entrepreneurs are enticing swiflets into empty buildings to build their nests, making collection much easier.

Bird's nest is considered highly nutritious and is central to the classic Chinese dish, bird's nest soup. As it is so easy to digest, it is often given as a tonic to the elderly. Whole nests that are almost entirely free of feathers and other foreign matter are the most highly prized, but even the broken nests are extremely expensive. **KKC**

Taste: *Bird's nest is virtually tasteless—it takes on the flavour of the ingredients it is cooked with. The nests are soaked and cleaned before being made into desserts and soups.*

A man collects nests for bird's nest soup in Thailand. »

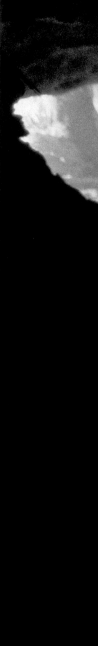

Horseradish

Wasabi

For cooks, horseradish is one of the hardest ingredients to work with. When grated raw, this white potent root causes the eyes to run far worse than the most pungent onion, as the volatile oils that deliver the intense horseradish "hit" are released into the air. These dissipate with exposure: the finer horseradish is ground, and the sooner it is used after preparation, the hotter its taste will be. (It also discolours quickly once cut, unless brushed with lemon juice or vinegar.)

The edible root of the plant *Armoracia rusticana*, horseradish is used in all European cuisines, but is probably most popular in northern, eastern, and central Europe. In Britain it is rarely used, apart from in a cold sauce that is traditionally served with roast beef, but in Germany and Austria in particular, it appears in different sauces or grated by itself as an accompaniment to a range of meat and fish dishes. Mixed with cream, it is the ideal partner for hot smoked fish such as eel or trout. Shredded and combined with apple, it serves as a spicy relish for cold meats. **MR**

Traditionally served as a fiery condiment to sushi and sashimi, this knobbly green root, or rhizome, is sometimes known in the West as Japanese horseradish. The largest producer of the precious fresh root in Japan is the Izu peninsula, where the mild climate and high annual rainfall create the perfect conditions for wasabi growing, and plants grown here are said to have the finest flavour.

Clean, flowing water is essential to the wasabi root's growth, which makes for a rare and expensive product. Demand far exceeds supply and most of the ready-prepared wasabi pastes and powders on the market are based on horseradish. Cultivation has, however, begun in the United States and Canada.

The heat of wasabi comes from the substance allyl isothiocyanate that is released when the root is grated. The best restaurants in Japan bring a grater made of sharkskin (its closely serrated surface creates a fine pulp) to the table to grate it immediately before eating, as the pungency of fresh wasabi decreases after only fifteen minutes. Wasabi pairs well with beef, raw fish, rice, and seafood. **SB**

Taste: At first taste, horseradish has a flavour that is similar to hot mustard, but with a fresher, raw element. Texture depends on how finely it is shredded or grated.

Taste: Fresh wasabi has a creamy, fragrant, and peppery, yet crisp, vegetable taste with a touch of sweetness. It is surprisingly milder than the horseradish-based products.

Although wasabi is largely grown for its root, the leaves and stems are also harvested and processed. »

Spring Ginger

Ginger is well known for its sharp, almost hot bite. The large twisted hands are peeled of their rough leathery skin to reveal fibrous yellow flesh that howls with intensity. Yet this boisterous, gnarly root was once the tender delicacy known variously as "young," "spring," or "green" ginger.

China and Australia produce the most spring ginger. The new growth of *Zingiber officinale* appears in China during March and April, and in Australia during September and October, and looks very different from older versions. It has pale, translucent, edible skin, tender flesh, and pink protruding shoots that would otherwise become the stems of a new plant. This form of ginger is delicate enough to create the best grades of stem ginger, the version sold in syrup as a delicacy, and the candied variety known as crystallized ginger. In Japan, spring ginger is also the basis for *amazu shoga*, the thinly sliced, pink, pickled ginger served with sushi and sashimi. In Chinese cuisines, the young root is often shredded like a vegetable for use in salads and spring rolls. **TH**

Taste: *The sweet essence of ginger is very present, despite the absence of heat. Only look for fresh young ginger in the spring and avoid any with signs of green growth.*

Myoga

The plump, pink, immature flower buds of a member of the ginger family, picked before they open, just on the verge of emerging from the soil, make a very special vegetable. In Japan, they are eagerly sought after when the season begins, despite the belief that eating myoga makes one forgetful.

It was probably the Chinese who introduced *Zingiber mioga* to Japan, where it grows wild in damp, mountainous areas to the north. There the shoots are covered with a natural mulch of thick vegetation, which shields them from the light, meaning the buds are pale. In cultivation, they are grown under substances such as sawdust to achieve the same effect. The Japanese harvest is strictly seasonal, although growers in New Zealand and Australia are beginning to fill the gap in the market.

Myoga is eaten raw, usually very finely sliced as a garnish or part of a salad, or finely chopped as an ingredient in dipping sauces. Not only the buds but the young stems, called *myogatake*, may be pickled: they are often served alongside grilled fish, much as spring ginger shoots might be. **SB**

Taste: *Crisp and juicy, as crunchy as celery, myoga has none of the heat of true ginger, but is strongly aromatic. An attractive trace of bitterness makes it quite unique.*

Galangal

Any South East Asian market on the planet will have a giant pile of fresh ginger. If you look to one side of this old favourite, you will most likely find one of its lesser known cousins, galangal, which is just as essential to their culinary sensibilities. It was widely used in Europe during the Middle Ages, only later falling into disuse as ginger became more available.

While a number of different rhizomes are sometimes sold as galangal, there are two varieties that matter—lesser and greater galangal (*Alpinia officinarum* and *Alpinia galangal* respectively). As they are named for size, not potency, it is lesser galangal that is the hotter of the two. The flesh of greater galangal is a light creamy yellow covered by a translucent skin whereas lesser galangal has reddish skin and flesh of a darker, more amber hue. Both are fibrous, much like common ginger.

Most southern Pacific cuisines use galangal extensively. The roots can be shredded for salsas and marinades or ground into a paste as part of a curry. Fresh forms are preferred but dried galangal may be used in stock and soup seasonings. **TH**

Taste: *A cross between ginger, pepper, and mild mustard in flavour, the impression is similarly hot with hints at horseradish and citrus.*

Turmeric Root

Fresh turmeric, shredded or pounded, adds a much more vibrant flavour to any dish than the cooked, dried, orange powder found in most spice racks. Thinner and darker than its common ginger cousins, one scratch of the thin skin reveals the bright flesh within, which will deeply colour anything it touches, including the cook's fingers.

Fresh *Curcuma longa* draws its intensity from the curcumin in the root, a compound that has been studied extensively in recent years, although the dried version also has many culinary uses. A large part of the crop, however, is destined for commercial dye, both in and out of the food industry; K. T. Achaya, in *A Historical Dictionary of Indian Food* (1998), records its use as a depilatory in India.

In its homeland of South East Asia, fresh turmeric is used widely, particularly in Thai cookery, where it is treated not dissimilarly to its cousin ginger. It is also used fresh in season in many parts of India, although the vegetarian Jains forbid it to be consumed since it grows underground and might therefore contain life forms. **TH**

Taste: *Fresh turmeric has intense, mustard-like overtones and a light peppery character. Dried forms exhibit these flavours when fresh but are prone to lose potency over time.*

Gilroy Garlic

In California, the land of big surf and movie stars, laidback attitudes apply to almost every aspect of life. Not so in the small valley of Gilroy, just south of San Francisco, where garlic is a serious obsession. Annual summer festivals attract thousands with Miss Garlic pageants, garlic marathons, vendors hawking everything from garlic sashes to garlic juice, and veritable parades of people in garlic-shaped hats. Pickled, smoked, as a base, or as a topping, garlic is incorporated into every food imaginable—even ice cream.

Where less desirable garlic can be bitter and flat in taste, Gilroy offers crops that seem to sing a medley taken straight from the California sun. Their sweetness and heady aroma dominate the palate, while their depth of flavour and richness of colour excels. Numerous varieties of *Allium sativum* ranging in colour from pure white to pale purple are grown for harvest and Gilroy processors offer it in forms from fresh peeled whole cloves to dehydrated powders. The bulbs work wondrously in the myriad cuisines where garlic is essential. **TH**

Taste: *Notably more pungent than other sources, Gilroy garlic can be sharp, almost hot, when eaten raw. The sweetness blossoms when roasted.*

An old-fashioned mural advertises Gilroy garlic. »

GILROY
FRASSETTI BROS
JIMMY HIRASAKI
B &T FARMS
GARLIC WORLD
CAPITAL
OF THE WORLD

Borage

Crowned with a handful of star-shaped purple flowers, and covered in tiny hairs—almost as if it were wearing a poorly knitted sweater—borage stands in many gardens like a tall, fuzzy soldier. In Europe it was once known both as a herb and as a vegetable, and credited with the capacity to relieve depression and impart courage. It was one of the first crops to reach the New World in the fifteenth century and is still widely cultivated in Spain.

The crisp, clean taste of raw borage leaves and flowers make them popular additions to salads. The leaves can also be blended into cold sauces, most famously, perhaps, the German spring blend of seven herbs, *Frankfurter Grüne Sosse* (Frankfurt green sauce), or cooked as a vegetable, as in the Italian *pottaggio alla rustica*, where they are parboiled and combined with olive oil, garlic, anchovies, salt, pepper, and wild fennel. The mature stalks have a mild bitterness much like cabbage or celery root when cooked, but still manage to maintain some of their fresh flavours. Hairs toughen with age and should be removed when possible. **TH**

Taste: *Curiously similar to cucumber in flavour, there are also hints of sweet mint and coriander leaf in all parts of borage. The candied stalks taste a little like liquorice.*

The sun rises over a field of borage
◉ *in Wiltshire Downs, England.*

Lavender

From pantry to apothecary, lavender seems to evoke something deep and lusty in the mind, yet with playful, floral accents on the surface.

The French have historically adapted the heady tastes in the kitchen by including lavender flowers in Provençal herb blends and adding them to roasting meats. More recently in the New World, the coastal climates of the Central Pacific have hosted a burgeoning agribusiness with new cultivars entering the market in a wide range of potencies and flavour profiles, amid all the farmers' market pleasures that are a cliché of Mediterranean climes.

Numerous subspecies of *Lavandula officinalis* are easily cultivated in home gardens but care should be taken with drying that concentrates the essential oils. Some people will register an unpleasant soapy taste if the essence is too strong or too much is added to a dish. Uses range from sweet and savoury pastries to saucissons or jellies, whereas bakeries sometimes preserve whole flowers in sugar. When cooking, infuse flowers in cream or stock to temper potency. **TH**

Taste: *The intense savoury character that underlies the floral scent is accented with faint pine and cedar flavours. Subtle sweetness is found only in fresh spring growth.*

Bolivian Rainbow Chilli

New Mexico Chilli

The colour blue does not tend to suggest edibility. When it is accompanied by a full spectrum of other hues—red, orange, green, purple, and yellow—often on the same plant, and at the same time, wise gourmets tread gently. With the Bolivian Rainbow, this caution is well-placed. The searing heat of its vibrant fruit could stop almost anyone in their tracks.

After a dramatic bright purple flowering, small green peppers appear. They will ultimately mature to orange, then red, having turned purple, blue, or yellow, for the intervening period. The leaves, too, may morph from an intense green colour into aubergine hues. Never more than 2 inches (5 cm) long, the shiny, tulip-shaped peppers are evenly strung on the foliage of the naturally bushy parent plant, a botanical colour explosion that has made the pepper almost as popular an ornamental plant as it is an edible one.

Like most heirloom varieties of chilli, the Bolivian Rainbow is usually seen in the old cuisines of Central and South America where it is used sparingly in citrus-themed sauces and fresh salsas. **TH**

In the red deserts of New Mexico there is practically a civil war over who grows the most flavourful chillies—Chimayo to the north or Hatch to the south—and precisely what it is that makes them so distinguished. Scientists at New Mexico State University are studying these and other capsaicin questions, yet both villages serve up distinctive versions of *Capsicum annuum* with a flair that seems to engulf the entire culture at harvest time.

Local farmers arrive at regional festivals as if to a culinary rodeo, in a ragtag fleet of pickup trucks and tractors with huge burlap sacks of chilli pepper bounty coloured a rainbow of reds, oranges, yellows, and greens. Festooned in cowboy hats and snakeskin boots, they seem to come as much for bragging rights as the featured produce.

Small farmers extract the most from optimal growing conditions, and, whether fully ripened red or the prized new green chillies, the flavours have a brilliance and complexity not found elsewhere. Roadside stalls offer the braids of fresh or dried chillies known as *ristras* (strings) in most shapes or sizes. **TH**

Taste: *Fruit are ripe when dark red. Behind the intense heat, residual flavours suggest sweet plum. Even when under-ripe the heat is considerable: treat with respect.*

Taste: *A full range of heat can be found married to characteristic plum, apricot, and cranberry flavours. Colour indicates ripeness but all are equally useful.*

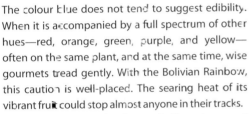

Teardrop-shaped and vividly coloured, the chillies ❰ *resemble a string of Christmas tree lights.*

Habanero Chilli

Chipotle Chilli

With all chillies, it is important to understand the difference between heat and flavour. Mild, fruity types—like Ancho chillies with their notes of plums and raisins—have a very different place in the kitchen to sharp, hot species. But only the related Scotch Bonnet chillies can even come close to Habanero for delivering nature's hottest punch.

The chemical compound capsaicin registers as heat on the human tongue, and it is measured on a scale developed by Wilbur Scoville around a century ago: the hottest chillies run to around 300,000 Scoville units, and both Habaneros and Scotch Bonnets register near this point. While removal of the interior webbing and seeds can lessen the intensity, the flesh alone still packs considerable heat.

Despite the heat, Habaneros develop unique flavours as the walnut-sized fruits ripen from green to orange. Even small amounts can deliver spice to salsas and cooked sauces. The severe heat is also used in bottled condiments that combine the flavours with everything from vinegar to carrots. Use great care when handling all varieties. **TH**

When fairly pedestrian chillies like jalapeños meet vast quantities of charcoal and smoke, they take on a new life and a new name: chipotles, shrivelled nuggets of heat and flavour that can transform even the most mundane dishes into dining that somehow expresses the essence of barbecue. Depending on the region, base chilli, and smoking time, either the larger, brown *ahumado* or the smaller, deep crimson *morita* will emerge from days of smoking and drying.

Smoke, heat, and chillies have a natural affinity that takes little effort to cultivate, and can generate obsessive enthusiasm among fans, spawning legions of hot sauces, barbecue rubs, salsas—even sweets. Chipotles are sold either as smoke-dried whole pods or preserved in a tomato-based *adobo* sauce. Both will offer the deep barbecue tastes but the former seem more pungent, whereas the latter offers the benefit of the infused sauce. Heat levels vary widely, mirroring the range seen in the parent chillies, but tinned versions are typically milder. When using dried chipotles, the seeds and stems should be removed to avoid bitter tastes. **TH**

Taste: *Sharp citrus notes manage to escape from behind the dangerous heat, with essences ranging from apricot to lime. Drying accentuates a mild smoky character.*

Taste: *The flavour of chipotle is almost pure smoke, which eliminates almost all of the original vegetal, sweet chilli flesh tastes. The heat can vary from mild to severe.*

An age-old scene of smoking chipotles. Aztec markets sold smoked chillies five centuries ago. ❯❯

Barberry

There are not many cranberry bogs in Iran. But if chefs want a tart red berry to add punch to stews or rice dishes, they reach for barberries (*zereshk*): it is these that crown the top of *shirin polow*, the fruity pilaf known as "the king of Persian dishes."

The tiny berries cluster under round, waxy leaves protected by sharp thorns: they ripen to a deep red and are sun-dried by processors, which concentrates their tartness many times. Their many species were once to be found growing wild all over Europe and North America, where their high pectin content made them popular in jams and jellies.

Unfortunately barberries can host a fungus known as wheat rust, which can decimate grain crops. This led to extensive eradication efforts in Europe and North America—most notably in the early twentieth century—and, although rust-resistant strains of wheat have been developed, wild barberries remain rare on those continents. In Asia, the berries are still cultivated as an inexpensive tart component for soups, stocks, and desserts. They may be powdered and used as a spice. **TH**

Taste: *Dried barberries are extremely tart and sour but regain a slight sweetness when rehydrated and cooked. The tiny seeds can be gritty if not cooked thoroughly.*

Amchur

In deconstructing the flavour of almost any fruit, the tastes and textures that define it are to be found hiding behind layers of sweetness. Mango creates so much activity on the palate that it begs such an exercise for sheer curiosity. Conveniently, therefore, chefs across India took the sour green fruit and dried them in the sun, creating amchur.

Long slices or fine powder made from dried green mangoes can be found in almost any Indian market. Commercial varieties, which can be spelt in a number of ways or simply sold as "mango powder," can occasionally include preservatives and colouring agents. Whole unripe fruits are also sold in growing areas and home chefs can manufacture their own amchur with simple sun-drying, although care should be taken to avoid mould and bacteria.

Like fresh green mangoes, amchur is used in dishes across India. It acts in much the same way as citrus and tamarind: it is not only a souring agent but a mild tenderizer and, as such, is used in marinades for meat and fish. Starchy vegetables also benefit from the lift sour amchur adds to regional sauces. **TH**

Taste: *Simultaneously sweet and sour, the taste is reminiscent of mild tamarind and bitter melon. The texture is always fibrous and sometimes tough.*

Black Lime

It was probably a happy accident in the desert that first gave the culinary world black limes. Where fresh citrus can be sparse or distant, necessity becomes the mother of invention and nothing is wasted, not even the heat of the day. Traded over long distances, black limes are perfectly preserved for the trip and have scattered themselves among the cuisines of North Africa and the Middle East.

Persian limes, *Citrus latifolia*, are briefly brined and then dried in the intense sun until the exterior turns a pale tan colour. Inside, the process leaves them almost hollow and completely black. Here they transform from fruit to pungent spice: the dried peel and inner flesh retain their original piquant flavour but have become intense with processing.

Moroccan tagines and Middle Eastern lamb stews will often call for whole black limes to be tossed in for the full cooking time to add acidity throughout the dish. Ground, the tart powder can be used as a table condiment in place of salt or included in dry rubs and more complex spice blends as a souring agent. **TH**

Taste: *A dry, tart character is concentrated well beyond normal citrus levels but has little lingering taste or aroma. Black limes can be cracked and simmered or ground fine*

Bush Tomato

Although Australian Aborigines once made this fruit flourish in fired ground, today the knee-high, prickly bushes sprout along the edges of dirt tracks. The term bush tomato, which is colloquial Aboriginal and dates back many years is used in Australian cooking to denote one member of the Solanaceae, *Solanum centrale*, which is generally picked by hand as dried, blueberry-sized fruits that are pale to dark tan in colour.

Alongside another fifteen Solanum species, the bush tomato was a staple food for Aborigines in central Australia, who also call them "desert raisins." They make an exceptional chutney that transforms the classic bruschetta into the colloquially popular "bushetta." Always look for at least 3 per cent bush tomatoes in the ingredients.

The fruit have a very strong taste that can morph from strong to unpalatable quite quickly. For the forager, bush tomatoes growing in rocky ground in association with mulga (*Acacia aneura*) are a lot more bitter than those growing in sand: the bitterness can generally be balanced with a little salt. **VC**

Taste: *When picked dry, these are pungent berries with a flavour that resembles caramel without the sweetness, somewhere between tamarillo and beef stock powder.*

Fennel Seed

Fennel seeds are a culinary chameleon. The aroma is savoury, like liquorice, yet when bitten they deliver a surprising sweetness. Almost as confirmation of this dual life, they appear in many of the world's most balanced spice blends, notably Chinese five spice and panch phoron, and seem able to bend to the will of whichever dish they inhabit.

In India, where they are known as *saunf*, they appear not only in curries but coated with sugar and served as a breath freshener at the end of meals. In Europe, where they are still used occasionally in sweets, they play a starring savoury role as the key spice in many sausages and cured meats.

Used widely in both cuisine and medicine since ancient times, this easy-growing perennial has since spread across most of the globe. The seed fruits form on broad umbels after a brilliant yellow flowering late in the season. They are ridged and distinctly green in hue when at their freshest, but mute to pale yellow or even brown with age. They are perfect candidates for dry toasting before use, which amplifies both their sweet and savoury aspects. **TH**

Taste: *Characteristically dominated by liquorice and anise, the freshest fennel has considerable sweetness in the finish. Stale samples will have a noticeable bitterness.*

Fennel grows wild and in abundance
❸ *on the arid Sardinian landscape.*

Fennel Pollen

Plants are wonderful machines. They pump the pure essence of their environment up from the earth, blend it with sun and rain, and distil all this goodness into their growing efforts. The most aromatic parts of this endeavour usually land in the flowers to lure insects, but something much larger than a bee has discovered the flavour benefits of fennel pollen.

The spice originated in Italy, where sausage-makers wanted a lighter impression of fennel for their wares. Opportunistic farmers found that it was the pollen and anthers that held the most interesting tastes. Harvested by hand and meticulously processed, this magic dust packs considerable punch and some have compared its potency and price with saffron. Although it is traditionally collected in only a few areas of Italy, the profit potential has given rise to new producers in the western United States and wider global availability.

The aroma of fennel pollen is almost as valuable as the flavour. When added at the very end of cooking—or even at the table—and gently stirred into warm dishes, it delivers a heady waft. **TH**

Taste: *This amber and green mottled powder is light, fluffy, and extremely potent. The sweetness is closer to anise than fennel, and there are subtle bites of clove.*

Hungarian Paprika

The Habsburg kings certainly got several things right. Soaring architecture aside, it was during their era that paprika was introduced: the sweet pepper spice destined to become the "red gold" of Hungary.

For a few weeks in late autumn, the valley around Kalocsa becomes a hive of activity with the arrival of crates of fresh brilliant red peppers. They are destined to be dried and ground by local processors whose techniques have passed down through the centuries. Some focus on using only the most tender flesh whereas others concentrate on balancing the flavours found in different batches. They produce a bewildering range of varieties and grades, ranging from honey sweet to noticeably hot, with a sheer cultural focus and dedication to taste that outclasses the rest of the world.

Besides the well-known Hungarian *goulash*, a paprika-laden stew, the crimson powder is key to several regional sausages and meat rubs, too. Care should be taken to find the freshest versions just after harvest because shelf life diminishes over the year leading up to the next season. **TH**

Taste: A base of sweet pepper can be pronounced or tempered with savoury heat. The aroma of this intensely coloured powder is a key indicator of freshness.

Pimentón de La Vera

Smoked paprika, or pimentón, made from ground red chilli peppers, is one of the essential ingredients in Spanish cooking, used in everything from chorizo to soups, from octopus to fried eggs. There are different intensities of flavour depending on the variety of pepper used—from sweet and mild (*dulce*), to bittersweet or medium hot (*agridulce*), and hot (*picante*). The seeds are always removed so pimentón is never as hot as the original chilli.

It seems that within a generation of Christopher Columbus's first voyage to the New World, chillies were established in Extremadura, Spain. Today the descendants of those original peppers are cultivated throughout that region, in the alluvial soils along the river in La Vera. Each autumn the small round peppers are harvested manually, then placed in special drying houses where they are smoked over oak wood for about two weeks and hand-turned every few hours. They are then carefully stone-ground to create Pimentón de La Vera, a regional speciality that has been granted a *Denominación de Origen* (DO) in recognition of its unique quality. **JAB**

Taste: With an intoxicating smoky aroma, almost sweet flavour, and silky texture, pimentón adds colour, depth of flavour, and a variable degree of spiciness to any dish.

Even the spiciest smoked paprika is not as fiery as its vivid red colour would suggest. »

Fresh Green Peppercorn

Peppercorns add punch to almost every cuisine and the familiar dried kernels are an essential flavour on the modern palate. They grow, like miniature grapes dangling from the vine, in dense bunches under wide, waxy green leaves in subtropical climates. Picked and utilized while green and immature, the fresh berries of the peppercorn plant, *Piper nigrum*, will deliver a flavour unlike any other.

Village markets sell the smooth green berries, still clustered on a vine around 4 to 8 inches (10–20 cm) in length. Because they spoil so quickly, many nations brine or pickle them in an attempt to ship them overseas. Yet preservation tends to mute the bright character of fresh fruit and the flavour is often overshadowed by vinegar and salt. Even air-dried and freeze-dried versions fail to deliver the incomparable taste of the spicy fresh fruit.

Thai cuisine has embraced the use of fresh green peppercorns in curries and other piquant sauces. The French have also taken up the banner of both fresh and preserved versions but transportation difficulties tend to limit their global availability. **TH**

Taste: *Green peppercorns offer a sunny interpretation of pepper with little lingering on the palate. Strong herbs like rosemary and tarragon can be perceived in the aroma.*

Tellicherry Peppercorn

Peppercorns could be called the most important spice of all time. They have been the drive behind exploration, the focus of conquests, and the basis of trading empires: they remain a culinary essential.

Highly prized for its black pepper production is Tellicherry, a mountainous coastal region in southwest India. In the high, cool air, green berries are allowed to mature to the largest size achievable before they begin to ripen and turn scarlet, and are then plucked by hand. Oxidization turns them black; drying gives the characteristic dimpled texture; they are then sorted and graded. The auction houses here are some of the oldest in the world and their time-honoured techniques serve as a guarantee of quality.

Sarawak in Malaysia and Muntok in Indonesia are particularly famed for their white peppercorns. These have had their outer husks removed before drying, producing a spice that lacks initial bite but lingers longer on the tongue. Although ripe red peppercorns are sometimes sold, either brined or freeze-dried, these should not be confused with the pink peppercorn, a wholly different species. **TH**

Taste: *The freshest black peppercorns have a heat in the finish much like chillies and complex aromatics that range from clove to allspice. White versions are more mellow.*

Today peppercorns are plentiful and inexpensive.
◑ *In the fifteenth century they were a rare luxury spice.*

Pink Peppercorn

Christmas trees decked in holly do not usually spring to mind in the blazing heat of South America or the Indian Ocean. Yet the Brazilian pepper trees that flourish in both regions, covered in emerald foliage with clusters of tiny pink berries, easily conjure the name "Christmas berries" by colour alone.

Despite their name and appearance, species of *Schinus terebinthifolius* are not related to true peppercorns and gentle crushing reveals the differences quickly. Not a hard solid but rather a paper-thin shell around an inner seed, the berries disintegrate into flakes with little effort. (Some classify the species as mildly toxic, so care should be taken before random harvesting.)

Réunion Island is a French overseas territory and chefs there adopted pink peppercorns into their refined culinary art as beautiful dots of delicate flavour in true French tradition. The flavour is amazingly sweet, with only hints of their namesake peppercorn pungency. This makes them a natural addition to lighter sauces and delicate seafood but also a perfect table condiment. **TH**

Sichuan Peppercorn

Spices easily manage to convey taste and aroma but it is a much rarer feat to evoke an actual physical response. The heat of chillies is a well-known example of this, but so too is the remarkable Sichuan peppercorn, which has the unique effect of numbing the tongue when eaten directly.

The precise relationship between the Japanese spice known as sansho and the Chinese spice known as Sichuan peppercorns has been the subject of much debate, intensified by regional sensitivities. Both are made from the seed pods of the prickly ash bush, *Zanthoxylum piperitum*, or sometimes other *Zanthoxylum* species; both share a flavour profile; the only difference is that sansho is a more refined version than many Sichuan peppers. When buying, choose sources free of stems, seeds, and flecks of fruit.

The flavour and texture of Sichuan peppercorns is essential to classic Chinese five spice powder and substitutions never quite match the original. As its name suggests, the fiery cuisine of Sichuan embraces the spice, utilizing it in hot and spicy dishes such as *ma po tofu*. **TH**

Taste: *Pink peppercorns should be bought whole. They taste sugary sweet when eaten directly. There are mild camphor notes and a very faint peppery bite in the finish.*

Taste: *All the zest of lime is mixed with the aromatics of cardamom, the heat of pepper, and the feeling of chillies in a crescendo that climaxes in the unique numbing effect.*

The attractive berries of pink peppercorns do
❰ *not give off their sweet aroma until crushed.*

Sumac

Colourful piles of ground spices populate Middle Eastern bazaars, but visitors may be perplexed as to the source of the burgundy powder that tastes of salty lemons and cranberries. This spice is actually the ground fruit of the sumac shrub and has become the ultimate condiment from Istanbul to Morocco.

Wild crops of the clustered, tiny, berry-like fruit spring up all around the Mediterranean but *Rhus coriaria* is most readily embraced in Arabic kitchens. Sumac is rarely found whole, although where chefs demand freshness some merchants will grind to order. Older berries become moist, so salt is required during grinding, resulting in tiny flakes. Occasionally the berries are pressed to form a potent juice that is used sparingly, like vinegar.

Used pure or in spice mixes like *zaatar*, sumac can often replace lemon or lime as the souring element in recipes. When rubbed on lamb or stirred into hummus, the bright flavour lifts otherwise heavy cuisine just as citrus might. The tart character lends itself to yoghurt-based sauces and combines well with olive oil as a topping for flatbreads. **TH**

Ajowan

With its dry, arid flavour it is appropriate that ajowan (or ajwain) flourishes in desert lands: it can stand intense heat both in the climate and the kitchen. Set against the searing chilli pastes of northeast Africa, its pungent taste and tarry aroma survive where lesser flavours, such as cumin, might disappear.

Trachyspermum ammi produces seed-like fruits shaped like a squat cumin seed with a characteristic hair-like "tail." The fruits are beige to brown with slight green hues in fresher sources. Produced and sold in Africa, the Middle East, India, and South Asia, they have yet to attain global popularity, probably because of their overwhelming taste. The key flavour in the seeds is thymol, also present in the herb thyme, which is sometimes extracted from the crop for use in toothpaste and digestive aids.

Most chefs will toast or fry the seeds to temper the intensity into a mellower savoury taste. Nan or poppadoms benefit from a small measure of ajowan which will relax in the high heat of baking. Also called Ethiopian cumin, ajowan appears in their famous berbere spice paste. **TH**

Taste: *The fresh spice is tart and puckering with hints of tamarind. Low heat preserves its intensity best but larger measures hold up to grilling and baking.*

Taste: *Somewhere between caraway and celery seed in taste, the thymol can create a domineering thyme flavour. The off-putting tarry aroma is lessened by cooking.*

The berries of some species of North American sumac
❸ *trees were once used to make a lemonade drink.*

Aleppo Pepper

Caraway

Aleppo, a plateau city in northwest Syria, has a secret that has escaped the fortress walls. The surrounding valley produces a mild fruity chilli pepper that many regard as the perfect balance of sweet, sharp, and heat. The microclimate benefits from the Mediterranean trade winds and has transformed what could otherwise be an uninteresting pepper into something brilliant and sublime.

Ancient trade routes first deposited the pepper locally in the late sixteenth century but over time the local crop proved more mellow and interesting than original plantings. Often imitated in parts of nearby Turkey, the genuine article from Aleppo still offers an elusive taste that is only mildly hot and distinctly sweet. Even the crimson colour seems oddly unique when compared to more pedestrian peppers.

Aleppo pepper was often sold ground with some salt added as a preservative, a practice that continues today. A dish of Aleppo pepper at the table for sprinkling over roast vegetables, hummus, or oiled flatbread will exemplify what has made the subtle flavour so popular across the Middle East. **TH**

An unassuming brown colour with little aroma, you would never suspect some of the flavour antics caraway manages later in life. Even in the fields, the plants are reluctant to show their true intent. The feathery greens that look much like their relatives fennel and carrot take two whole years to produce their "seeds" (technically, fruit). The Netherlands, Germany, and Poland remain important producers of good quality caraway, and significant crops also come from the central plains of Canada.

The tiny seeds are curved and ridged, and do not immediately release their pungent taste. Toasting dry or heating in oil solves this problem and most uses include this as a necessary step. Distillers have long used *Carum carvi* to flavour spirits, most notably brennivin in Iceland. More mildly, the seeds add an accent to cheeses and even feature as a flavour note in preserved fish. In the hands of bakers, caraway helps define bold rye bread. It is a classic addition to sauerkraut and potatoes and is frequently credited as a digestive. More infrequently, the roots of the plant are enjoyed as a vegetable. **TH**

Taste: *Mild heat follows light fruit notes akin to apricot and cranberry. The ground form is a minuscule flake rather than a fine powder, and makes an excellent condiment.*

Taste: *Caraway has a dry, woodsy, anise-led character. Uncooked, it displays considerable bitterness and a lack of sweetness; intense heat alleviates these characteristics.*

The caraway plants produce their delicate white flowers in their second year of growth. »

Allspice

Restaurant perfection in the Caribbean is often little more than a grass hut and a fire pit perched on the beach. Tourists and locals sit side by side waiting to see what the chef can concoct from the local market offerings of the day. Whether fish or chicken, tomatillos or plantains, it is a sure bet that everything will be laced with the local favourite: allspice.

Native to the islands and a staple of Central and South American cuisine as far back as the Mayan Empire, the deceptively plain brown berries of *Pimenta dioica* hold a sharp jolt that awakens the taste buds. Commercial cultivation began in Jamaica, and once Spanish traders brought it to the Old World in the seventeenth century, comparisons with cloves and peppercorns began.

Paired with the local Jamaican chillies, allspice is most famous in "jerk," a piquant rub that is applied to fish, pork, and chicken before they are roasted over coals. Across the Atlantic, the spice became popular in mulling wines when paired with cinnamon, cardamom, and orange peel, and appears in recipes for steak sauces and other table condiments. **TH**

Coriander Seed

Coriander is a remarkable plant for the chef. Every part from its spindly roots to the tips of the leaves is consumed in some form or fashion. The seed-fruits that appear in late summer after a proliferation of white flowers ultimately become the basis for everything from curry to pickles.

The botany of *Coriandrum sativum* is unsettled at best with various cultivars grown for seed crops categorized by shape, size, and region. European and African versions are round and lightly ridged with Indian species being smoother and oval shaped. Biblical references and ancient husks found in the archaeological digs of Egypt show some form of coriander seed was cultivated for thousands of years.

Coriander seeds have entrenched themselves in almost every world cuisine. The rich gamut of foods using coriander seeds encompasses Indian spice blends, European sausages, American corned beef, and Asian curries. Often described as "warming," the citrus aroma is nearly as important as the subtle taste, and the prized "white" beers of Belgium rely heavily on that aromatic. **TH**

Taste: *Strong aromatics are obvious, similar to clove but with slightly less potency and bite. Peppercorn notes infuse with menthol and cinnamon hints.*

Taste: *Freshness is key to getting a good citrus aroma and taste from coriander seeds. Newly crushed seeds should exude considerable aroma. Sift out any residual husks.*

⊗ *Roadside stalls sell freshly cooked jerk meat as well as the jerk seasoning itself.*

Guatemalan Cardamom

India has been associated with the bold flavour of cardamom, a member of the ginger family, for thousands of years. Sweet and pungent in aroma, the prized sticky black seeds of the so-called "Queen of Spices" are encased in brilliantly green pods. Somewhat surprisingly, a New World country now rivals India as the world's largest producer of *Elettaria cardamomum*—Guatemala.

In the Middle East, cardamom has long had a symbiotic relationship with coffee. An aromatic brew of the two—known as *kahwe hal* in Arabic—welcomes guests in every home. Guatemala is a key producer of both cardamom and coffee beans, which thrive in the tropical conditions of the highlands, and plantations often mix the two crops. That New World crops can withstand this time-honoured combination half a world away speaks to the impressive way in which Guatemala has entered the cardamom market.

Green cardamom can flavour savoury stews, curries, and pilafs, as well as sweet dishes and hot drinks. Use sparingly, as a little goes a long way. **TH**

Taste: *Top quality cardamom pods have a strong aroma of menthol and ginger. Simultaneously sweet and spicy on the palate, seeds are best preserved in their own pods.*

Cinnamon

Just beyond the tree line of Sri Lankan beaches the faint aroma of cinnamon tempts spice traders and gourmands alike. Plantations peppered about the southern coasts produce this unique spice, frequently imitated but never equalled by its more boisterous and severe cousin from overseas, cassia.

The shrub-like trees, *Cinnamomum zeylanicum*, send out willowy thin branches that are peeled of their bark, known as "quills," and rolled into fragrant bundles. Bark peeling approaches an art form, and the trade traditionally passes down the generations. Practised hands use simple rod-like tools to loosen and cut the inner layers of bark, which are sun-dried, graded, and rolled into final shape. Auctions usher bundles of cut "sticks" into the spice trade destined for ports worldwide.

Praised by Egyptian embalmers and Roman emperors alike, true cinnamon has a myriad of uses. Not merely a staple of sweet pastry, it blends into savoury dishes equally well. Sticks can perfume rice or curry exquisitely and are essential in classic chai or mulled wine. **TH**

Taste: *True cinnamon exudes a delicate floral aroma, with sweetness and pepper-like heat. It is best infused gently to release essential oils and preserve the aromatics.*

One of the first spices to be used in the Mediterranean, cinnamon was initially only added to savoury dishes. »

Anardana

In the Middle East, the heat of the desert often creates as much as it consumes. Reasonable conjecture would say this was the case with anardana, dried pomegranate seed, a spice whose origins are lost in the suns of the past but whose pleasantly tart and bitter taste has stood the test of time. Wild species from the Himalayas are purported to give the best results because the fruit is so sour.

The juicy, crimson pomegranate segments, known as arils, are separated and laid out in the sun on large tarpaulins. Over five to ten days, their colour changes from the brilliant red of the fresh fruit to a dull purple, almost black, and their firm shape withers to a dark smudge around the central seed. Masses of the sticky dried seeds are collected and used as a souring agent both whole and ground.

In its native land, anardana is often sun-dried at home: because of its residual moisture, the quality can falter quickly. Most popularly found in chutneys and sauces, anardana is also used in baking, blended into a variety of spice mixes, and as a souring agent in curries and soups. **TH**

Taste: *The pronounced tartness, very much like dried sour cherries, is immediate, alongside bitter components from the inner seed. Anardana should never be completely dry.*

Juniper

Open a bottle of gin and inhale. Imagine those same aromas beside the sun-drenched Mediterranean. Now picture hillside cascades of spiked green foliage on twisted trunks and dusty blue berries scattered about. Finally wrap that scent around slow-roasted lamb from wood-fired rotisseries and you have the wonderful juniper of Italy's Amalfi Coast.

Perhaps because some junipers are mildly toxic, or perhaps because the fruits take more than a year to ripen from green to dark purple, the culinary species, *Juniperus communis*, is often overlooked. Not so in the south of Italy, where it has been popular since medieval times, when common folk discovered the potent flavour of the berries.

Paired with similarly strong tastes such as rosemary and garlic, juniper can withstand the intense heat of the grill, the long roasts of the oven, or the pungency of game. Pounded together with peppercorn and allspice, it makes a perfect trilogy of savoury, sharp, and sweet. Crushing a few berries in a gin cocktail adds a bright lift that echoes the original distillation. **TH**

Taste: *Dry and arid on the tongue, the scent is distinctly grassy and slightly sharp like cloves. Some subtle bay character shows through. Look for whole, smooth berries.*

The juniper berries are sorted and checked by hand for their suitability for use in gin. ❯❯

Saffron

If you were to plant a few acres of pale purple crocuses, bet your annual salary on the weather, hire hundreds of workers to spend hours plucking the smallest bits from between the petals by hand, then risk the whole lot by drying it over a fire where one mistake could consume the whole affair... Well, you would be wasting your time, of course. Experts already do this in the course of bringing saffron, the most expensive of spices, to a wider audience.

This insane risk tends to breed a fair bit of national pride among the successful growers. Along with La Mancha in southern central Spain, Kashmir leads the pack in both product quality and bragging rights, but notable productions also come from Pakistan and Iran.

Although saffron can command extortionate prices even when sold in typically tiny portions, the stigma of the *Crocus sativus* are so potent that only a few pennies worth are needed per dish. Saffron is embraced in the cuisine of the key growing areas, whether as curries or paella, but has been an exotic delicacy outside their shores for centuries. **TH**

Taste: *Arid on the palate when sampled directly, the taste has a deep savoury undercurrent reminiscent of bay but with a persistent floral aroma akin to lavender.*

Traditionally entire families were involved in the harvest. ❯❯

Vanilla Pod

The perfume of vanilla envelopes the senses with floral sweetness and conjures images of the tropical forests from which it comes. A stroll through the island plantations of Madagascar is itself a sensory paradise as the large green vines blossom with the orchids that will give way to bunches of seed pods.

Vanilla planifolia thrives not only in the tropical humidity of its native Latin America but also in Africa and Tahiti. Only the very best pods are destined for the kitchen. The long, green fruit are cured slowly with careful drying, twisting, and massaging. Over a period of months they acquire a rich, black colour and shrink to about a third of their original size. Second only to saffron in price, the highest quality "beans" are shipped around the globe to anxious pastry chefs waiting to unlock their scent and taste.

The moist, plump pods need airtight storage. After splitting lengthwise, the inner pith with its numerous minuscule seeds can be scraped into mixtures to gently infuse. The tougher outer husk still holds plenty of flavour that can be preserved in sugar for later use. **TH**

Taste: *Pods should never be brittle. The rich, floral aroma and taste lean towards sweetness and can have overtones of orange or sherry.*

After harvest, the vanilla beans are spread
⊘ *out to dry beneath the Tahitian sun.*

Star Anise

The dried fruits of *Illicium verum*, commonly known as star anise, are perfect little rust-coloured stars, with a polished seed nestled inside each elegant carpel. They form in the middle of the year, after the evergreen tree's prodigious light pink or yellow flowering, and impart a flavour and scent that quite simply defines southern China.

Ancient Chinese herbalists utilized star anise long before modern pharmaceutical companies began harvesting the crops for shikimic acid to use in medicines. But recent battles against bird flu have led to shortages of the crop destined for the kitchen. Culinary star anise is almost exclusively cultivated in southern China, with sporadic production elsewhere in South East Asia; the trees take years to mature, which further hinders efforts to expand cultivation.

Chinese five spice powder relies for its impact on star anise, as do many infused liqueurs such as pastis. Whole stars are often included in dishes that require long, slow braising and meld their intensity with meat harmoniously. Buy whole, intact stars as a sign of top quality and grind only as needed. **TH**

Taste: *Star anise derives its liquorice flavour from the aromatic compound anethole. A strong liquorice element with anise-like sweetness is obvious in the aroma.*

Annatto Seed

Some things in nature beg investigation, tempting us with unusual foliage, deep colours, or unique aromas. For the Mayan priests who used it as a colourant in ceremonials, annatto offered all these. It was probably no accident that the brick-coloured seeds that nestle within the pods of *Bixa orellana* quickly made their way from pigment to palate.

Handling the raw seeds turns fingertips red so many Central American cuisines impart not only the colour of annatto but, just as importantly, its flavour by means of an oil infusion. Further north in Mexico, notably in the Yucatan Peninsula, the seeds are used to make a paste known as *achiote*. The taste can create a curious dry sensation on the tongue but the colour it gives to a dish lives up to its parent's nickname, "the lipstick tree."

The complex *mole* sauces of Mexico often include annatto but it can also stand alone as the main seasoning for pit-roasted pork. In coastal regions of Central America, fish are frequently sautéed using only annatto oil. Further inland, it flavours root vegetables and cooked grains. **TH**

Taste: *Earthy and savoury in taste with a pleasantly mild bitterness, the aroma is of sandalwood or cedar. The red pigment releases easily by abrading or steeping in oil.*

Mahlab

The ingenious bakers of the Middle East and Turkey saw a quite literally golden opportunity in a small, wild cherry that grows across the region. Not in the fruit, as one might expect, but in the kernels at the centre that, when dried to a golden brown colour in the sun, become the spice mahlab.

Prunus mahaleb, or St. Lucy's cherry, is a large, shrub-like tree that is cultivated almost exclusively for mahlab spice production. The deep-red fruit is cast off as bitter and inedible, and the stones are split to reveal the soft, inner seed. This will harden as it dries to form an almond-shaped spice with delicate ridges. Many alternative spellings are found on the labels of Middle Eastern markets but all indicate the same aromatic spice: occasionally processors can miss discoloured seeds or other debris so a quick inspection is worthwhile.

The freshly ground seeds are added to breads and pastries, most famously the celebratory Easter breads of Armenia and Greece. As a fine powder, mahlab thickens stews of lamb and grain, and flavours the Middle Eastern cheese nabulsi. **TH**

Taste: *A nutty aroma gives way to bitter notes that hint at celery seed and bitter orange. Mahlab loses flavour easily so it is best to buy whole kernels with a consistent colour.*

Asafoetida

Black Cumin

Growing in the dusty fields of India, giant fennel looks like it has seen better days. Spare leaves and wiry branches seem to barely hold together and about the only thing worse than the look of the plant is the overwhelming stench of the sap, a foul-smelling veil that hides a culinary treasure.

At harvest time, farmers slit the plant until it exudes a deep amber sap. This coagulates into a thick resin that is malleable at first but soon hardens into brittle chunks that exhibit the aroma of sulphur. Slow to dissolve in normal cooking, the dried sap garners a litany of colourful pseudonyms including "Devil's Dung" and "Fetid Sap" but is more commonly known as hing powder to local chefs, who utilize its pungency to flavour dishes in the same way that Western chefs use garlic.

Whether sautéed in oil or flashed with the heat of a tandoor oven, asafoetida requires an intense heat to dissipate the acrid aroma and leave more mellow tastes and smells behind. Also grown in Iran, Iraq, Pakistan, and Afghanistan, it plays a supporting role in many Indian and South Asian dishes. **TH**

When going in search of this gentle expression of common cumin, the first thing to know is that it is not the completely unrelated nigella seeds often sold as black cumin. Nigella seeds (*Nigella sativa*) are black and angular, about the size of mustard seeds, while true black cumin (*Bunium persicum*) is crescent-shaped, and slightly longer and thinner than its common cumin cousins.

Black cumin's colour is, indeed, almost black, tending towards dark brown, while the seeds have the distinct aroma of dried grasses. The plant originates in the wilds of Iran, Pakistan, and northern India, where its scarce nature has earned it the name "royal" cumin. Limited supply means that the black stuff costs about triple the price of the more common "white" cumin. Due to its subtle sweetness, black cumin is preferred in the milder dishes of its native regions, especially when little or no heat is present in the spicing as with, for example, lamb korma. Ordinary cumin can be substituted in dishes, but a better solution would include a small measure of fennel seed to duplicate the sweetness. **TH**

Taste: *Asafoetida tastes like sautéed garlic with mildly bitter notes of caraway or fennel. The smell (sulphur, rotten eggs, and dirty socks) is nothing if not distinctive.*

Taste: *Black cumin is like a sweeter version of common white cumin with some slightly mild bitterness in the taste and aroma much like celery or thyme.*

Grains of Paradise

A merchant standing in fourteenth-century Venice literally had the world on his doorstep. With the rise of the city-state's importance as a trade centre, all manner of exotica was landing daily. The merchant's task was to create a market for such wares and, in an early example of marketing, "Grains of Paradise" was coined as the name for these pungent little seeds.

Given the popularity and cost of peppercorns, not much effort was needed to convince chefs to try *Aframomum melegueta*, although elaborate tales of the dragons, elephants, or even Eden to be found at their source helped spur on sales. Almost pyramidal in shape, they arrived in pods about 2 inches (5 cm) in length with fibrous outer husks, so could easily withstand the overland journey from West Africa to the Adriatic coast.

Yet by the eighteenth century their popularity was in decline, and they had been displaced by peppercorns. Yet, as if to prove the value of a great name, grains of paradise have recently undergone a resurgence of popularity among modern chefs. Traditionally, they are used to flavour meats. **TH**

Taste: *Fair peppery heat is mixed with essences of ginger, camphor, and cardamom on the palate. They are best ground only when needed to preserve their aromatics.*

Blade Mace

Anyone lucky enough to live near a nutmeg grove knows that it is not merely the familiar nutmeg kernels that offer flavour. Inside the peach-like fruit of *Myristica fragrans*, lacy tendrils of a brilliant scarlet clutch the seed pod tightly in their web. Harvest these strands and you have blades of mace, a spice that captivates the taste buds every bit as well as its partner, nutmeg.

Nutmeg and mace provided the flashpoint for the spice races that initiated the Age of Exploration, as traders sought a route to the spice's native Banda Islands, Indonesia. Dutch, Portuguese, and English forces fought for supremacy until finally the crops began to spread across the tropics.

Blades of mace have the consistency of tough leather, however, they lose both this and their colour fast, drying to a brittle pale orange in a matter of days. For this reason, most mace is processed into a fine powder for global export but the prized whole blades can be found closer to the modern growing regions of Indonesia, Sri Lanka, and parts of the Caribbean. **TH**

Taste: *Fresh blades offer a completely different experience from the pale impression powdered varieties provide. The flavour is similar to nutmeg, yet sharper and more intense.*

Arils freshly stripped from the nutmeg fruit are laid out to dry before being processed as mace. ❯❯

Cubeb Pepper

Clove

As if to echo the tangled climbing vines that produced it, cubeb pepper had a long and convoluted path to follow before it reached the tables of medieval Europe. Traced backwards through Venice via the Arabs, across Africa, past India and China, and ultimately to Indonesia, it is no wonder the pepper had an uphill climb.

Sometimes termed "tailed pepper" because of an identifying stem on the dried black berries, *Piper cubeba* originated in tropical Java, from where it was unwilling to stray. This made access to the spice difficult and it was ultimately supplanted by the more easily cultivated common peppercorn. Although popular in Indonesian cookery, cultivation is limited. Minuscule productions, blending with inferior *Piper* species, relegation to medicinal tinctures, and use in cigarettes make cubeb even more unpopular. The few culinary footholds cubeb has found are in Arabic spice mixes like ras-el-hanout and in complex recipes for distilled gin alongside juniper. But the taste is different enough to warrant exploration no matter what route you must follow to find a supply. **TH**

So potent is the taste and scent of cloves that these tiny, unopened buds once divided the globe, as Spain, Portugal, Holland, and England rushed to reach their origins in Indonesia. Cloves were traded as far back as Roman times, via trails that snaked overland through Arabia and India. But these early supply lines were expensive and risky, so the naval powers of the fifteenth century sought an overseas route to the famed "spice islands" and beyond.

Until modern times *Syzygium aromaticum*, the evergreen tree that produces the clustered young buds that will dry into cloves, was cultivated only in Indonesia. Since then it has spread to Sri Lanka, Zanzibar, and Madagascar, among others. Just after the buds turn a dull pinkish hue, they are collected and dried to a darker bronze. (In the freshest batches, the rounded tip is several shades lighter and unmarked by age or travel.)

Used whole, they infuse well and are seen in everything from rice to mulled wine. Ground, their gamut ranges from Indian spice mixes to European sausages and pastries. **TH**

Taste: *Pepper meets ginger and allspice on the palate in a combination that is not as strong as common peppercorn. Cubeb has a bite similar to cloves in flavour and aroma.*

Taste: *Similar to allspice but with more sweetness and peppery character, the strong aroma is matched with a slight numbing effect from the intense oils.*

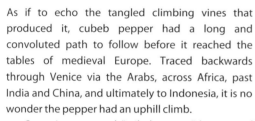

Growing on Mount Lawu, central Java, clove trees are used to make kretek, a type of Indonesian cigarette. »

Fleur de Sel de Guérande

Salt pans on the Atlantic west coast of France supply the unrefined, damp, grey sea salt that chefs and bakers love for their cooking. A small fraction of this brackish harvest, like cream on top of milk, is Fleur de Sel (French for "flower of salt"). This is the fine crystal crust on the surface of the drying salt water that will only form if the wind blows from the right quarter. Freshly scraped off the surface, it may be a frosty flamingo pink, but it turns a dull off-white within a day. It has to mature for a year before it is ready for the table.

Refined salt (pure sodium chloride) tastes bitter to a trained palate, whereas unrefined salt contains a cocktail of minerals including iron, magnesium, and potassium. Cooks used to working with the latter put less into their recipes than they would of the refined product. Although chefs tend to prefer the unrefined, grey Guérande salt for cooking, the costly Fleur de Sel is handled with discretion, a final sprinkling on a finished dish to lift its flavour. In any Michelin-starred restaurant it is the condiment left on the table for customers to serve themselves. **MR**

Taste: *Crisp, crusty, crunchy grains of Fleur de Sel taste obviously of salt, but individual crystals melt on the tongue and linger, rather than giving an aggressive hit.*

Workers rake coarse salt into piles
◈ *from the man-made salt marshes.*

Maldon Salt

Maldon lies at the tail end of the Blackwater Estuary in Essex, amid open water, mudflats, and salt marshes. Here salters harvest the brackish tidal water and transform it into crystalline flakes of salt.

The process starts with seawater collected twice a month, when the new moon and the full moon bring the highest tides, and, assuming there has been no rain, the water will be most salty. Stored in tanks, it settles into three layers: the salter only draws off the water sandwiched between the less salty top and the silt that sinks to the bottom. Simmered for a day in square, shallow pans, the liquid becomes a breeding ground for crystals. As the water evaporates, hollow, pyramid-shaped grains of salt, some microscopic, a few as large as postage stamps, form crazy patterns.

Unlike most table salt, Maldon retains significant traces of potassium, calcium, and magnesium. Chefs claim they need less Maldon salt to season food than common table salt. The Spanish chef Ferran Adrià has ordered consignments of the largest crystals to make them into a crunchy, crystalline "ravioli." **MR**

Taste: *The flakes of Maldon salt are brittle like miniature cornflakes and crumble when lightly crushed. The taste seems to be more lively on the tongue than grain salt.*

Smoked Sea Salt

Something primeval stirs us to crave smoke around our food, and everything from chillies to cheese has taken a pass through smouldering embers to tempt our taste buds further. It seems natural, then, that porous sea salt crystals—which can absorb flavours like a sponge—would ultimately inhale the essence of the fire.

Smoked versions of salt have appeared almost anywhere there is an ocean and a forest, but thankfully modern times have refined the process greatly. In one method, cool smoke is generated and infused into the surface of salt crystals without melting. Another technique distils seawater over fires to produce delicate, crystalline forms completely permeated with smoke. In the United States, the diversity of woods available for the barbecue has seen salts smoked over everything from alder to mesquite; the Danes ascribe their method to the Vikings and use an exotic combination that includes cherry and juniper to impart deep smoke character. Both the smoke and the salt itself contribute to the finished flavour. **TH**

Taste: *Smoke intensity and residual wood flavours vary based on production sources. Colours range from charcoal to mottled amber and crystal sizes are similarly diverse.*

Kala Namak

Naming confusion seems to be normal sport when translating from East to West. A particularly glaring example of this comes with kala namak, or black salt, which is neither black nor a salt. Actually a mined mineral blend from India, the colour is more grey or brown than jet, and sodium chloride is only one component of its complex make-up.

Hues of grey, pink, and beige can all be found in samples depending on their precise source and refinement. The aroma and taste can be off-putting to the uninitiated, recalling hard-boiled eggs and sulphur, but even modest heat tempers these components into a pleasantly earthy mix.

Kala namak is often blended with yoghurt sauces and cooked into various chutneys. *Chaat masala*, a pungent spice blend commonly sprinkled on snacks in India, is dominated by black salt and asafoetida and certainly not for the faint of heart. In the fusion style, pure kala namak can be used as a simple dusting on fresh fruit with no cooking at all for maximum impact. When powdered, humidity can sometimes lead it to clump. **TH**

Taste: *The scent is suitably volcanic, with aromas of asafoetida, sulphur, and garlic leading to a salty, sometimes metallic edge on the palate.*

Unrefined kala namak is sludge-like and is extracted from volcanic lakes using a special tool. »

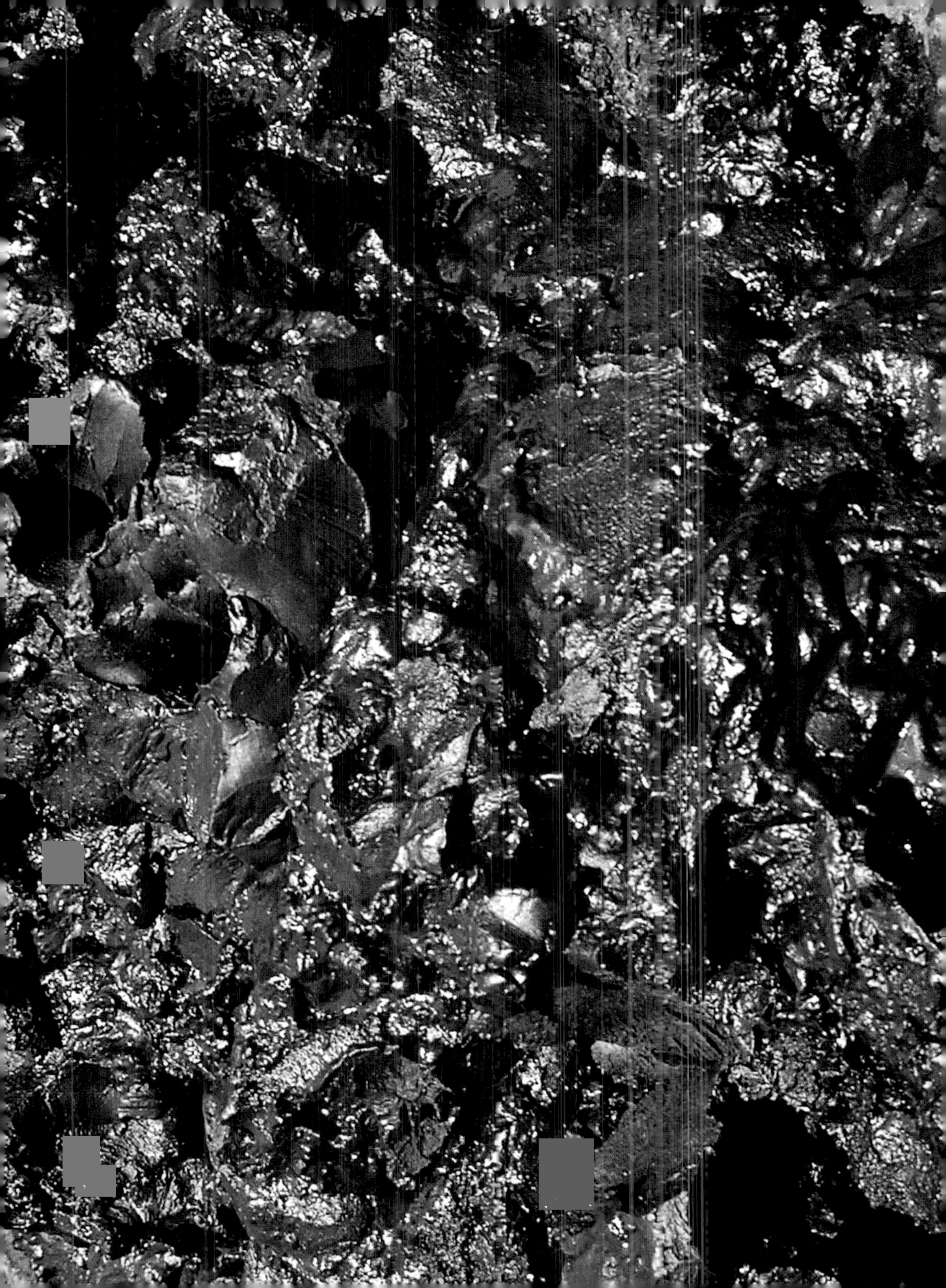

Panch Phoron

The number five occurs in spice mixes with a regularity that suggests an underlying pattern. According to one theory, the four key elements of taste—sweet, sour, bitter, and salt—are experienced in different places on the tongue. The fifth taste is a union of the five, a mysterious balance on the palate.

Panch phoron is a great achievement of the Bengali chefs of eastern India, a visually curious seed mix that generally comprises black or brown mustard, fenugreek, fennel, nigella, and cumin, perhaps with wild onion or celery seed as one element. These flavours developed as a natural bridge between the foods of South East Asia and India and add perfect depth to the largely vegetarian cuisine around Bengal. Roasted dry or fried in butter, panch phoron most often starts the potato and lentil dishes of Bangladesh with its blossoming aroma and the sound of searing seeds leaping from the pan. The intense heat of cooking opens and unifies otherwise closed flavours within the ingredients. Grinding is only advised after this stage; home chefs can easily mix their own using equal parts of each seed. **TH**

Taste: *Mustard seeds add sharp heat and fennel yields sweetness. Nutty and grassy flavours fill in between these extremes to completely engage the palate.*

Curry Powder

The mere mention of curry powder and its hundreds of interpretations will earn you a heated debate. This almost entirely inauthentic spice blend takes its name, like the dish it refers to, from the Tamil word *kari* and the Canarese word *karil*, both of which mean a sauce or relish served with rice. Although in India prepared powders are almost nonexistent and both chefs and home cooks use pure ingredients from the start, a dried ground mix was the simplest way for the British colonial power to transport a flavour back from the East and for tentative European cooks to begin to work with it.

Yet accepting the shortcut and forgiving history, well-crafted curry powders can have merit. The permutations from a typical base of coriander seeds, peppercorns, turmeric, and ginger are endless. Cardamom, cinnamon, chillies, mustard seeds, and fennel are just a few examples of spices that round out formulas from countless vendors. Twenty ingredients is the norm, not an exception, and this flavourful head start in the kitchen can introduce an exotic culinary world in only one jar. **TH**

Taste: *Sometimes hot from peppercorns and chillies, fresh batches usually feature mild citrus tastes on top of deep savoury character, with considerable regional variations.*

Chinese Five Spice

Garam Masala

Ancient Chinese secrets are sometimes hard to uncover but a recipe for classic five spice powder is thankfully more forthcoming. Long ago, master chefs mixed fennel seeds, cassia, cloves, star anise, and Sichuan peppercorns into a blend strong on both flavour and aroma. Walk into any Chinese community and you will smell these melded essences, one of the greatest culinary formulas of all time.

Five spice has come to unify China's many distinct cuisines, and is ubiquitous in kitchens from Beijing to Xiamen. Although exact proportions vary, it is generally accepted in Chinese culture that five spice is a balancing act on the tongue. Warm and cool, bitter and sweet, yin and yang—all seem to blend harmoniously.

After centuries of flavouring the full range of Chinese dishes, from roast meats to simmered rice, the authentic formula has made its way to star in fusion cuisines in urban centres around the globe, whether sprinkled over prawns on a Brisbane beach or enlivening dessert cakes in New York. Multifarious different versions are available across Asia. **TH**

Like most creations of the Indian subcontinent, garam masala transports you to another world of flavour. The term means "hot mix" but most versions vary around a central theme of cinnamon, cardamom, cumin, and peppercorn to obtain a balance between sweet and savoury tastes with relatively little by way of heat. Born of the spice bounty of India, a well-balanced masala will tickle the palate on many fronts, leaving behind an imprint of each component in delightful combination.

In India, pre-packaged spice blends are virtually nonexistent, although local merchants will prepare blends to order; in expat communities and in the West, ready-made concoctions crop up quite regularly. Whichever formula is used, they are ideal for rubs on roast meats and vegetables where the high heat will bloom the spices into an aromatic frenzy. Similarly, a garam masala blend can be worked into dough for flatbread and naan where cooking will finish the melding of flavours. Some Western chefs use blends to add a spicy surprise to sweeter desserts like flan or chocolate torte. **TH**

Taste: *Best ground fresh for maximum aromatic impact. Liquorice base notes meld with sweet top notes, accented with the slightly numbing effects of Sichuan pepper.*

Taste: *Sweet cinnamon and cardamom dominate the coriander base but sharp peppery and grassy notes often intrude. Other pungent components are clove or mace.*

Berbere

Ethiopia may not be a world centre of cuisine but it does manage to make the most of what its surroundings offer. A long history of independence, especially compared to some of its less stable neighbours, has ingrained a rich culinary history unique on the continent. Rich stews, called *wats*, are served with local *injera* flatbread and all is spiced by their own signature spice blend, berbere.

A base of fiery chillies is pounded with spices that can include ginger, fenugreek, cumin, cloves, rue, allspice, cardamom, and ajowan, most typically from regional sources and sometimes roasted to add flavour. Made at home, the mix usually forms a paste from the moisture of fresh chillies or added oil, onions, garlic, or shallots. Packaged versions appear as either a preserved paste or a dry powder that can be rehydrated with oil or water before use.

Despite its incredible heat, berbere is also found on the table as a condiment. In chicken and beef *wats*, the blend also becomes a rub for roasted meats and easily flavours the vegetarian dishes based on lentils and grains in Ethiopian cuisine. **TH**

Taste: *Searing heat is typical of most recipes, but the spice combinations can bring out aromatics, especially cardamom's camphor notes and ajwain's tarry pungency.*

Ras-el-Hanout

There is no greater mystery in the spice world than ras-el-hanout, the famed spice blend that populates the bazaars and markets of Algeria, Tunisia, and Morocco. Stall vendors lie in wait to expound the virtues of their own recipe, most probably handed down through generations and steeped in secrecy.

The name means "head of the shop" and spice merchants often strive to show their prowess by finding the most exotic ingredients. Grains of paradise, cinnamon, peppercorns, and rose petals are just the beginning: some blends contain over thirty ingredients. Some of the oddest additions include long pepper pods and edible beetles.

The blend's complexity and inherent balance make it ideal for seasoning and transforming simple ingredients such as beans or couscous into culinary delights. The huge variety of recipes ranges from pungent to mild. Like garam masala, the ingredients offer a wide variety of accent flavours, and, while most are suitable for roasting (especially lamb and aubergine) or simmering, experimentation with individual batches is essential. **TH**

Taste: *The best ras-el-hanout provides a balance on the tongue that marries savoury with sweet, yet punctuates this pairing with a peppery bite and a floral scent.*

Conical-shaped mounds of spices create an arresting sight at a Marrakesh bazaar. »

Shichimi Togarashi

Harissa

The Japanese art of balancing form and function is perhaps best seen in their cuisine. Every ingredient is carefully chosen to harmonize with others within a dish. This equilibrium is found everywhere from sushi to yakisoba and the spice blends they employ are no exception, not least of which is shichimi togarashi (also known just as togarashi).

Seven flavours combine in this mix: recipes vary but often include chilli, orange peel, sesame seeds, seaweed, hemp seeds, Japanese pepper, and poppy seeds. Careful portions allow each taste to shine through in a progression that starts on one end of the tongue and works around to key each component of taste. What the Japanese strive for is the magical combination of all tastes that sums up as greater than its parts and togarashi delivers just that. The spices lend depth and intensity, and since balance exists within the blend, it can be added almost anywhere. Noodles, fish, and even grilled beef can all take a dose of togarashi well. Coarsely ground, even its appearance seems artistic with a rainbow of colours blended in perfect unison. **TH**

As if the sands of North Africa were not hot enough, the locals have developed a blistering hot spice paste that punctuates almost every food on local menus. Entrenched for centuries in the cuisines of Morocco, Tunisia, and beyond, a shrinking culinary world has made harissa a common staple in many Western groceries and delis.

Hot red chilli, garlic, coriander, salt, and caraway serve as the base: variations further incorporate citrus, oil, cumin, and—increasingly in Western pre-packaged versions—tomato, alongside a cornucopia of spices. Toasting of some ingredients is common and adds extra dimensions to the spectrum of tastes behind the dominant chilli heat.

The kebabs and tagines that traditionally benefit from harissa's punch have inspired Anglo barbecues and stews with otherwise mundane roots to new heights. Adventurous chefs looking for convenient exotica have opened jars of the red paste and wrestled, sometimes in vain, to tame this fiery beast from Africa: it finds uses as diverse as an accent for roasted vegetables, or as a rub for meats and fish. **TH**

Taste: *Recipes range from mild to hot but most have a base of sesame and other seeds, with a slightly numbing peppery impact from mild chillies and sansho in the finish.*

Taste: *The chillies are sharp and hot but other robust flavours manage to emerge. Garlic adds another twist, while in caraway versions the woodsy taste shines through.*

Vendors in Morocco sell jars of harissa paste alongside fresh kebabs flavoured with the spicy blend. ❯❯

Hazelnut Oil

Walnut Oil

Hazelnut oil is a relative newcomer to the range of culinary oils. It was developed in France in the 1970s and inventive chefs have been using it ever since. In Europe, the nuts used for oil come from France, Italy, or Turkey. In the United States hazelnuts are grown mainly in Oregon, where it is the official state nut.

The hazelnut is also known as a "filbert" or "cobnut." One theory of the origin of the former name is that it comes from St. Philibert, a seventh-century French abbot, whose feast day falls in August, in the middle of the nut gathering season.

After the nuts are harvested they are sorted by hand and kept at a temperature of around 40°F (4–5°C) to prevent spoilage until they are crushed with millstones. The crushed pulp is roasted to enhance the flavour and then cold pressed to release the oil. This is mixed with any free run oil from the roasting process. Hazelnut oil is high in monounsaturated fatty acids rather than the polyunsaturates found in walnut oil and so has a longer shelf life. However, it is best served uncooked as it can become slightly bitter when heated. **JR**

This wonderfully rich and well-flavoured oil, made from roasted nuts, was first developed for culinary use in France in the nineteenth century. Before this, walnut oil was pressed from unroasted nuts and used mainly as a treatment for wood—most famously, perhaps, for Stradivarius violins.

The walnut tree is native to Asia but now grows in Europe (particularly France), Turkey, China, and California, which accounts for two-thirds of the world's nuts. The finest walnuts for oil come from the Dordogne region of France where the predominant variety is Le Grandjean.

Most walnut oils from France are unrefined virgin oils, cold pressed from dry nuts which have been lightly roasted. A similar process is used in California but often the oil is extracted with solvents to give a refined oil with no odour or taste. This is mixed with some virgin walnut oil to give a well-flavoured walnut oil that is cheaper than virgin oil. Walnut oil does not have long-lasting qualities; once opened it should be kept in the refrigerator and used within three months. **JR**

Taste: Nut oils generally taste of the nuts from which they are made and hazelnut oil is no exception. The aromas are strong but subtle, and the flavour is attractively toasty.

Taste: The rich, toasty aroma of walnut oil is very good when drizzled over warm vegetables or fish. It also goes well in salad dressings and added to stir-fry dishes.

The walnut kernels are commonly ground into a paste, which is then poured into a press to extract the oil. ❯❯

Italian Extra Virgin Olive Oil

Of all the olive-growing nations, Italy offers the widest spectrum of flavour in its extra virgin olive oils. Almost every province makes olive oil, and nearly every region has its own unique microclimate and cultivates its own varieties of olive tree, both of which affect the flavour, colour, and aroma of the oil. Italy also produces a higher ratio of extra virgin olive oil—the cold-pressed result of the first pressing of the olive—than anywhere else.

Although it is one of the smallest producing areas, Tuscany has gained an excellent reputation for its extra virgin oils. Many of these come from estates owned by a single family: they tend to be quite robust with plenty of bitterness and pepper.

In the southern Tuscan town of Seggiano, set on the slopes of Monte Amiata, film director Armando Manni organically farms the local Olivastra olive. He produces the acclaimed extra virgin oils, *Per Me* (For Me) and *Per Mio Figlio* (For My Child), which are probably the most expensive in the world. These indulgent oils should be saved for finishing and flavouring dishes, or enjoying simply with bread. **JR**

Taste: *Armando Manni extra virgin olive oils are light and sweet, but still have the immense depth of flavour typical of classic Tuscan olive oils*

Spanish Estate Olive Oil

Spain is the largest producer of olive oil in the world, and usually accounts for more than half the world's olive oil. Most is produced by small farmers working together in large cooperatives. However, the very best Spanish extra virgin olive oils usually come from large estates that are often still family owned. The single unit enables great care to be taken with every aspect of cultivation and production. The olives are harvested as single varietals and processed on the estate. The resulting oils are only ever blended with others from the same estate.

The major producing area is Andalusia in the south. Here the olive groves stretch as far as the eye can see under an overbearing sun, producing the sweet and intense oils characteristic of Cordoba and Granada. One of the top estates in this area belongs to the Núñez de Prado family, which owns 160,000 trees in total. The other important area for export oils is Catalonia in northern Spain. This region is widely planted with Arbequina olives, which produce more delicate oils: lightly nutty in character with a touch of apples and sweet herbs. **JR**

Taste: *Núñez de Prado extra virgin olive oil has intense flavours of lemons, melons, and tropical fruit. Despite light pepperiness, it is so sweet that it can be used in desserts.*

Olives being milled in Andalusia, the world's biggest olive oil-producing region. ❯❯

Greek Monastery Olive Oil

The ancient Greeks revered the olive and in later times Greek monasteries, which have always had their own olive groves, played a very important role in ensuring the continuity of olive oil production throughout Greece. While some monasteries, like the ones at Mount Athos and Karpenisi, keep the oil for their own use in holy services and in their kitchens, others, such as the monastery at Toplou on the island of Crete, produce olive oil on a commercial scale.

Olive trees are to be found everywhere in Greece and fourteen regions benefit from a Protected Designation of Origin, but it is the mountainous regions of the island of Crete and of the Peloponnese that are best known for olive oil. The main variety pressed for olive oil is the Koroneiki; the more famous Kalamata is used almost exclusively for table olives. Production is based on numerous small farms and large single estates are rare. Farmers sell their produce to privately owned mills or belong to local cooperatives, which sell to secondary cooperatives that blend and market the oil. **JR**

Taste: *Some oils are delicate with soft salad leaves and apple fruit in their flavour tones, whereas others are more robust with notes of dried grass and nutty almond skins.*

Olive oil from the Toplou monastery is entirely organic. »

Argan Oil

The argan tree, *Argania spinosa,* grows only in the southwestern part of Morocco and is in decline. Over the last century more than a third of the argan forest has disappeared so UNESCO has added the argan tree to the World Heritage list of plants at risk.

Local Berber women have extracted oil from the fruit of the argan tree for centuries but it remains largely unknown outside its home territory. The fruit looks rather like a large, round olive but the oil comes only from the kernel, which is encased in a nut with an extremely hard shell.

Until recently everything was done by hand. After removal from the shell the kernels were toasted and ground to a flour, then mixed with water to make a dough from which the oil was extracted. This was a lengthy process and producing one litre of oil could take twenty hours.

Today mechanical presses similar to those used for olive oil are being installed to crush and grind the kernels to extract the oil. This speeds up the process considerably and improves the quality of the oil as it removes the need for water. **JR**

Taste: *Its light roasted flavour is reminiscent of toasted hazelnuts. Good for cooking and flavouring, it makes an interesting salad dressing mixed with lemon juice.*

Hemp Oil

The hemp plant—*Cannabis sativa*—has been grown in Asia and the Middle East for more than five millennia, a period during which cultivation has spread east to China and west to Europe and North America. Although some varieties have provided a valued high for many cultures, the type pressed for oil is not among them and is perfectly legal. The most dominant use of hemp seed has probably been in the production of rope.

Hemp seeds have been a valued food in many countries. Before sunflower oil, hemp oil was the basic cooking oil of Russia and parts of Poland. The cold pressed hemp oils developed at the end of the twentieth century take the delicate flavour of hemp to a new level.

Rich in polyunsaturated fatty acids, particularly Omega-6 and Omega-3, hemp oil has real nutritional benefits. Unfortunately essential fatty acids are very unstable, making hemp oil extremely susceptible to heat and to light. It should be packed in dark bottles and stored in the fridge; it should never be used in high temperature cooking. **JR**

Taste: *Cold pressed hemp oil has a sweet, delicate flavour, reminiscent of pine nuts, with a slightly vegetal element. It is best used in salad dressings and cold preparations.*

Toasted hemp seeds are eaten as snacks in China, and are increasingly popular elsewhere. »

Mustard Oil

Almost any seed can be pressed to exude a flavourful oil and Indian cooks have long extracted mustard seed oil to use in cooking. Mustard seeds are still processed, mainly in Asia and on the Indian subcontinent, for use as a cooking oil (and a topical rub in Ayurvedic medicine). The raw oil preserves the compounds that give mustard its characteristic "hot" taste: it is very pungent with a distinct aroma.

Heating mustard oil brings out a nutty, subtly sweet character that is ideal for vegetarian cuisine, especially in the stir-frying of mustard's brassica cousins like cauliflower. Bengali cuisine uses the oil in dishes such as the classic fish curry, *maacher jhol*. Similar treatments of potato dishes are seen widely across Bangladesh and most of coastal Indochina.

Recently, in the West, the erucic acid content of some types of mustard oil has led to health concerns. Although found naturally in many brassicas, erucic acid is classified as dangerous both in North America and in Europe, and is banned for food uses in high concentrations. As a result, mustard oil can sometimes be difficult to source. **TH**

Avocado Oil

The avocado takes its name from an Aztec word, and it was in Mexico that Westerners first encountered the large, pear-shaped fruit growing in abundance on the exuberant trees that still flourish there.

Today avocados are cultivated in many parts of the world including the United States, where they are a major crop on the coastal mountain ranges of southern California. But it is only in recent years that the flesh of the fruit has been pressed for oil. The first oils were made in California as part of an effort to use up less than perfect fruit. Avocados are now grown specifically to press for oil not only in California but countries such as Australia, New Zealand, Israel, and Chile.

Cold pressed avocado oil is considered healthy because it is very rich in monounsaturated fatty acids. It is also immensely useful in culinary terms, thanks to a very high smoke point, which means cooks can work at extremely high temperatures without it deteriorating. The thick, velvety texture, usually paired with a wonderful deep green colour, makes it one of the more attractive oils to use. **JR**

Taste: *The oil is sharp and bright with the bitterness and heat expected from mustard. A high cooking heat pleasantly mellows both the flavour and the aroma.*

Taste: *Cold pressed avocado oil is full and fruity with a definite taste of avocado. Some brands have flavour tones of globe artichokes, celery, spinach, or bay leaves.*

Lord Shiva is said to have had his food cooked in mustard oil rather than the more common ghee.

Single Estate Grapeseed Oil

Pumpkin Seed Oil

A by-product of the naturally occurring grape marcs that are left over after the fruit is pressed for winemaking, grapeseed oil is a versatile vegetable oil. As the oil is cholesterol free and rich in vitamin E and essential fatty acids, it is especially valued for its health properties. Its mild flavour does not overpower delicate foods as some oils are prone to do and it has a high flashpoint, which means that it is particularly good for frying at high temperatures.

To make the oil, grape seeds are separated from the marcs and dried gently in rotary driers to avoid any degeneration in the resulting oil due to heat. They are subsequently crushed to extract the oil, which is then filtered before bottling. The quality of the oil largely depends on the raw material; oil content can be anything from 6 to 20 per cent according to the grape variety and a good yield is needed to produce a first-rate product.

In Italy, grapeseed oil is the third most commonly used fat after extra virgin olive oil and butter. It is good for dressing salads and vegetables, such as mange-tout and asparagus, as well as sautéing. **LF**

Although pumpkins originated in Central America it was the Austrians of Central Europe who developed pumpkin seed oil. A mutant variety of pumpkin, *Cucurbita pepo* var. *styriaca,* produces seeds without the stringy skins of other pumpkin seeds, and sometime during the early eighteenth century the Austrians started to extract oil from them.

Today fields of these pumpkins slowly ripen in the warm summer sunshine. At harvest time they are cut open and the seeds picked out of the pulp. Traditionally the whole family would work together but today this is more often done by machines. The seeds are cleaned, dried, ground, and finally toasted, in a crucial process that is the subject of much secrecy. Variation of a degree or two in temperature or a small change in timing can result in quite a different flavour.

The best Austrian pumpkin seed oil has PDO status and must be entirely Styrian in origin. It is high in polyunsaturates and must be kept in a cool, dark place. It is so susceptible to light that the oil in a salad dressing will coagulate in sunlight. **JR**

Taste: *Grapeseed oil has an attractive pale green colour and a light, fresh flavour with vaguely nutty nuances. Its "neutrality" makes it ideal for use with delicate flavours.*

Taste: *Pumpkin seed oil is a dark green-brown in colour, with a sweet, distinctive flavour of toasted nuts. It is good in cold cookery but it can also be heated for a short time.*

Rapeseed Oil

Rape (*Brassica napus*) is a member of the cabbage family, which was not widely cultivated until the last few decades of the twentieth century. Canadian breeders then developed a new variety called Canola that was nutritionally more acceptable than earlier varieties and is now grown across Europe for its seeds. These are crushed and processed at high temperatures to produce a clear, bland cooking oil which may be labelled rape, rapeseed, or Canola oil.

In 2005 British farmers began to experiment with cold pressing their rapeseed and developed a new product with much more flavour than the original oil. This cold pressed rapeseed oil is marketed with an emphasis on its health benefits. Made up predominantly of monounsaturated fatty acids, it is also rich in Omega-3 and Omega-6 polyunsaturated essential fatty acids. It is often described as "extra virgin" or "virgin," but these words have no official meaning in relation to rapeseed oil. There are now around ten brands of cold pressed rapeseed oil from France and the United Kingdom. More are expected to join them in the future. **JR**

Sesame Oil

The origins of this oil, pressed from the seed of the sesame plant—*Sesamum indicum*—stretch back a very long way. Some sources claim that the Chinese were using sesame oil in their lamps as long ago as 5,000 BCE. Others believe that sesame seeds first originated in India or Africa and that they were taken to China at a later date. Early references can be found to the use of the oil in Babylonia and Arabia. A charming story suggests that the "open sesame" of the *Arabian Nights* reflects the fact that the sesame pod bursts open quite suddenly when the seeds are ready to be released.

In fact, there are two types of sesame oil: a dark, amber-coloured oil that is very popular in Chinese cooking and a lighter, pale beige oil which is used in Indian cuisine. The darker oil is pressed from roasted sesame seeds and is ideally added as a flavouring. It should not be used for cooking at high temperatures as it burns quite easily. The lighter coloured oil is cold pressed from uncooked sesame seeds. It has a light, delicate flavour and can be used for sautéing and dressings. **JR**

Taste: *Cold pressed rapeseed oils are generally light and nutty, often with a vegetal tone reminiscent of cabbage, broccoli, or fresh peas. They are viable for all culinary uses.*

Taste: *Dark sesame oil tastes of toasted nuts and seeds with a hint of burnt chocolate. The light oil smells similar to fresh sesame seeds and has a delicately vegetal taste.*

Goose Fat

A mature goose of any breed popular today can lay down 2 pounds (900 g) of soft fat around its internal organs, or even more. Rendered down, this fat is used for cooking in the same way as lard. While once closely identified with the Jewish cuisine of Central Europe, goose fat is now more commonly associated with southwest France. It is a key ingredient in *rillettes d'oie,* potted goose, all forms of confits, and, very often, the Béarnaise *garbure*, the cabbage-based soup-stew simmered in an earthenware pot.

In nutrition and diet, *graisse d'oie* has been linked to what is known as the French paradox: the question of why, despite a high-fat diet, cardiovascular disease in France has been historically low. Goose fat is rich in monounsaturated and polyunsaturated fatty acids. The British, too, once valued goose fat for its health-giving properties—they spread it on working men's vests in winter as a protection against respiratory diseases. Roast goose has always been a popular festive dish and Anglo-Saxon cooks know that goose fat makes absolutely the best roast potatoes. **MR**

Red Palm Oil

This vibrantly coloured oil is to African cooking what extra virgin olive oil is to Mediterranean cuisines. As with the finest olive oils, red palm oil adds its own unique colour and flavour to a dish and contains just as many health-giving properties.

Extracted from the fibrous pulp of the grape-sized fruit of the African oil palm tree, red palm oil—not to be confused with white palm oil, which is produced by crushing the fruit's inner kernel—is non-hydrogenated and transfat-free. The distinctive flame red colour comes from the oil's high levels of beta-carotene and lycopene, the powerful antioxidants that make carrots and tomatoes immune-boosting superfoods.

Also known as *zomi*, red palm oil adds a strong and unique flavour to many traditional West African dishes such as *ndolé* (a bitterleaf soup that is the national dish of Cameroon), *egusi* (a Nigerian meat and fish soup), and *moi-moi* (a steamed cake made with black-eyed beans). Today, most red palm oil is bought ready-made, but traditionally African cooks prepare their own. **WS**

Taste: *Although goose fat absorbs other flavours, it is never bland. The rich farmyard taste lingers on the palate, adding to any ingredient with which the fat is combined.*

Taste: *Foods such as chicken, seafood, or potatoes will be tinged a rich, golden-red when fried or sautéed in red palm oil, absorbing its nutty, sweet, and slightly creamy flavour.*

Workers are housed on an oil palm plantation in the rainforest. »

Varietal Red Wine Vinegar

Corinthian Vinegar

The Greek doctor Hippocrates first extolled the virtues of vinegar in writing some time around 400 BCE but its cleansing, healing, and preservative properties were well known in biblical times. Its origin was probably the result of a happy accident, as suggested by the name, which comes from the medieval French words *vin aigre* (sour wine).

Vinegar is formed when the naturally occurring bacterium *Acetobacter xylinum* gets to work on the alcohol in an alcoholic liquid and converts it to acetic acid. For the very best wine vinegars this process is long and slow. Grape juice is allowed to ferment into wine and then matures for some months before acetification with a carefully prepared bacterial culture. The vinegar itself then matures for a further period of months or even years.

The better the base wine the better the mature vinegar will be. The finest examples come from single varietal wines produced in the famous red wine regions of the world: in Piedmont, Cesare Ciaconne produces outstanding varietal vinegars from Barolo and Barbera. **JR**

Corinthian vinegar is made from Zante currants—the small, intensely flavoured, dried fruit of Black Corinth grapes grown in the Peloponnese peninsula of southern Greece.

The word "currant" comes from the Old French term, *raisins de Corauntz* or "raisins of Corinth." For centuries, production of the fruit was centred around Corinth, however, trade shifted to the island of Zante in the sixteenth century. Production of the vinegar is based on an ancient method of making sweet wine from raisins. The grapes are harvested and left out in the sun to dry. The semi-dried fruit is then pressed, and the resulting juice along with the must (the skins, seeds, pulp, and stems of the grapes) is gently boiled for hours until greatly reduced. The mixture is then strained and the juice is transferred to wooden barrels and left to age.

Full-flavoured, dark, and fruity, Corinthian vinegar works well with roasted and grilled meats and vegetables, or stirred into savoury dressings and sauces. Like balsamicos, it is also good drizzled sparingly over fruit and ice cream. **LF**

Taste: *Varietal red wine vinegars give wonderfully fruity flavours reminiscent of blackcurrants, raspberries, plums, and cherries. They are mellow and harmonious.*

Taste: *An intense vinegar with a complex sweetness that softens the vinegar's innate sharpness; it has a delicate fruity flavour and a clean aftertaste.*

Sherry Vinegar

Sherry wine has been produced in Jerez de la Frontera deep in the southwestern corner of Spain since the sixteenth century and maybe even before that. In those days vinegar was the inevitable result of poor winemaking practices and was given to family and friends for cooking. Today formal regulations govern production.

There are two basic types of sherry. One grows a form of yeast on it called "flor" and one does not. The latter is known as "raya" and it is this wine that goes on to become Oloroso sherry and which is fermented to make the most popular sherry vinegar. Raya is poured into oak casks and placed in the full heat of the sun while the wine turns to vinegar. The vinegar is then left to mature in a solera system for anything from two to twenty-five years. This means that only a third of the vinegar in the oldest barrels is taken each year for bottling. These barrels are then filled up with vinegar from the following year and so on down the line until new vinegar goes into the youngest barrels. Fruitier than other wine vinegars, it gives a real lift to dressings, bastes, and sauces. **JR**

Taste: *Sherry vinegar retains the taste of full Oloroso sherry with its balsamic and dried fruit flavours. It has a light acidity but is much sweeter than other wine vinegars.*

Aceto Balsamico Tradizionale

Written records of this famous condiment start in the mid-nineteenth century, although then its creators made it only for family and friends. Today Modena is defined as the producing region by a DOC, although this elite artisanal product should not be confused with the much newer "balsamic vinegar of Modena," which is largely factory made and may include caramel and preservatives.

Traditional balsamic *aceto* (in many countries, it is not technically classed as a vinegar due to its low levels of acetic acid) is made from the juice or must of local grape varieties, reduced by cooking to a very sweet liquid that is placed in small wooden barrels with a starter of regular vinegar. After the first year, a small amount of liquid is taken out and placed in a second cask: the first barrel is topped up with new concentrated grape must. Over the years a series of barrels of different woods—oak, mulberry, chestnut, cherry, and juniper—are built up, each barrel holding a mixture of vinegars of varying ages. No vinegar may be released from the system until it is at least twelve years old. **JR**

Taste: *Penetrating aromas of mixed dried fruits like raisins, apricots, and prunes. The flavour tones are rich and mellow, the liquid smooth, sweet, and velvety thick.*

Tarragon Vinegar

Cider Vinegar

Tarragon, *Artemisia dracunculus,* has been known as "the dragon" in different times and places. The thirteenth-century Arab botanist Ibn Baithar knew it as *turkhum* perhaps for its strong, at times numbing flavour, but more likely because of its serpentine roots: its botanical name is Latin for "little dragon."

Tarragon, however, is associated most of all with France, and it was the French who were the first to produce tarragon vinegar on a commercial scale. The base vinegar for this product is often made in an acetator. Here white wine is placed in an 8,000 gallon (30,000 litre) vat, the vinegar producing bacteria are added, and warm air is filtered through the vat to raise the temperature and aid the conversion of alcohol to vinegar. The process takes a couple of weeks: the resulting liquids are flavoured with natural extracts or chemicals to simulate the taste of tarragon. The very best tarragon vinegars are made by a much slower method, similar to that used to make varietal vinegars. Once the white wine vinegar is ready, sprigs of French tarragon are infused either in the vat or in the bottle. **JR**

In regions like England and northern France, where apples have been cultivated for at least two millennia, and most likely fermented into alcohol for almost as long, cider vinegar has a history as ancient and unwritten as that of wine vinegar. Like wine vinegar, it is formed when naturally occurring bacteria get to work on the alcohol in a base liquid—here cider—and convert it to acetic acid.

Today much commercial cider vinegar is made in large quantities under controlled, industrial conditions then pasteurized to inactivate the enzymes and kill off any microorganisms. However, a number of smaller producers still favour slower, more traditional methods similar to those used for good red wine vinegar. Unpasteurized and free from preservatives, these vinegars may be fermented from sweet apples, cider apples, or a mixture of the two. They are excellent in salads, salsas, bastes, and pickles, when a sharp vinegar kick is not required. Cider vinegar has a reputation as a healthy food and even an effective medicine. However, there is no scientific evidence of any medicinal value. **JR**

Taste: *It should have a strong aroma of tarragon with a spicy, gingery note but not too sharp. Excellent with chicken, it also makes a good vinaigrette with walnut oil.*

Taste: *Apple is, not surprisingly, the predominant note in both the aroma and taste of cider vinegars, which are often mellowed by tones of light honey or maple.*

Somerset in England is well known for its age-old traditions of growing and pressing cider apples. »

Verjuice

Verjuice comes from the French *vert jus* or 'green juice" and was the name given to the sour juice pressed from unripe fruit. In other countries, there are similar products such as *agresto* in Italy, *argraz* in Spain, *hosrum* in Lebabon, and *abghooreh* in Iran.

In winemaking regions such as France, grapes were the fruit in question, but crab apples, plums, gooseberries, and bitter oranges have been used elsewhere. Some experts believe that verjuice was known in Roman times but the first written reference to it appears in 1375 in a recipe book belonging to Taillevent, the master cook of French king Charles V.

Verjuice gradually fell out of favour as lemons became more widely available but has enjoyed something of a comeback during the latter part of the twentieth century. Maggie Beer, the Australian chef and food writer, led the way, and other producers in Australia, South Africa, California, and parts of Europe followed. Grapes are picked very early in the season, pressed, and the juice is then stabilized and bottled immediately. Occasionally the juice is left to ferment before bottling. **JR**

Taste: *Verjuice has the acidity of vinegar and the tartness of lemons but it is softer on the palate. It can be used whenever a dash of lemon juice or vinegar is specified.*

Unripe grapes are removed from the vines to thin ◷ *out the crop at the beginning of the season.*

Raspberry Vinegar

Raspberry vinegar probably began as a home-made product in those temperate areas where raspberries grew easily. In Yorkshire, it was served with the traditional pudding before the meat. However, there are few historical references to raspberry vinegar before the last century. Commercial production began in France and it was chefs there who popularized its use in the 1980s and early 1990s.

The best raspberry vinegars are made by infusing the fresh fruit in a good quality wine vinegar for about a month. At the end of this period the vinegar is filtered off and sometimes a few fresh berries are placed in the bottle with the vinegar. The list of ingredients of any decent raspberry vinegar should feature raspberries. The words "natural ingredients" usually mean that the vinegar has been made by adding essences or extracts, rather than the fruit itself. Real infusions taste better and are quite easy to do at home.

Mix with a good, easy-going extra virgin olive oil to dress avocados or combine with blue cheese to make a dip for chicory spears. **JR**

Taste: *Good raspberry vinegar tastes of sweet, ripe raspberries with a lightly acidic kick. The flavours should linger in the mouth.*

Shanxi Extra Aged Vinegar

Chinese aged vinegars have a richness, concentration, and complexity that can rival some Italian aged balsamicos and, like their Italian equivalents, are used sparingly as the best are very expensive. They are also extremely difficult to find outside China: usually only mass-produced versions are available elsewhere, which, like supermarket balsamic vinegar, only hint at the complexity of the aged versions.

While vinegars can be made from many different ingredients—notably grapes, fruits, and grains—in China, they are made primarily from glutinous rice mixed with other grains. Shanxi aged vinegar (and a similar type made in Jiangsu province) starts off as all Chinese vinegars do. The grains are cooked to produce a liquid that is fermented; bacteria then convert the alcohol into acid. While regular vinegars are bottled immediately, both Shanxi and Jiangsu aged vinegars undergo a controlled exposure to the elements for months, even years, which concentrates the liquid and tempers its acidity. In fact, the acidity of the best kind is so low that in some markets they cannot be legally classed as vinegars. **KKC**

Mochi Gome Su

The key ingredient in *tamago-su*, a potent Japanese folk remedy, is the vinegar made from brown rice and credited with many health-giving properties. As revered as Modena's balsamic vinegar, the best mochi gome su comes from Japan's Kyushu island, where it is made in a thousand-year-old process.

The process begins when steamed brown rice is mixed with a rice that has been treated with the same *Aspergillus* mould used to make miso and soy sauce. After several weeks the liquid is mixed with a mother vinegar and spring water, and transferred to clay crocks, which some producers bury in the ground. When it is a rich, dark vinegar it is diluted again and left to mature for up to ten months. This lengthy process creates amino acids that enhance both the flavour and the health benefits of the vinegar: it is said to stimulate the appetite, aid digestion, and prevent cholesterol build-up.

Brown rice vinegar balances saltiness in foods and its antiseptic qualities are used to marinate fish. Its delicate sweetness is perfect in dressings, mixed with oil or miso, and added directly to food. **SB**

Taste: *Coloured a brown so dark it is almost black, Shanxi extra aged vinegar is sticky, thick, sweet, and only mildly acidic, with intense, complex flavours.*

Taste: *Exceptionally mild, with a light flavour and underlying sweetness, mochi gome su is much less acidic than most vinegars (although not as sweet and viscous as balsamic).*

Commonly brown rice vinegar is used to season rice when making sushi. ❯❯

Moutarde de Dijon

Dijon, Burgundy's capital, has been famous for its *moutardes* since the early eighteenth century. Shops once sold them by the ladleful and rival artisans vied with each other to devise the latest fashionable flavours: nasturtium, caper and anchovy, and lemon. Some mustards made eyes water, whereas others tasted sweet and aromatic. Today, the Maille shop in Dijon still creates exotic mustards, such as raspberry and champagne, but the yellow, pungent but not overpowering, moutarde de Dijon is the real focus of attention.

Dijon mustard is made from brown or black mustard seeds. When crushed, the seeds are odourless and almost tasteless, but moistening triggers a chemical reaction that gives the kick. Dijon mustard was created in the 1850s in a recipe that substituted verjuice (unripe grape juice) for vinegar, leading to a less acidic, smoother tasting mustard. Freshly ground, the paste is noticeably hot. Within a day it carries a real punch. Eaten fresh like this—the Maille shop sells it from a pump—moutarde de Dijon has a unique zing. **MR**

Moutarde de Meaux

Moutarde de Meaux is often described as a mustard that has been prepared *à l'ancienne* (in the old way). Sold in earthenware pots with cork stoppers and a red wax seal, it looks very much a traditional product. Monks initially cultivated and prepared mustard in France, but J. B. Pommery, a company who made millstones, claim to have a recipe for the mustard dating to 1632. Although it has been much imitated around the world, the product has kept its unique identity.

Like its close cousin from Dijon, moutarde de Meaux uses brown mustard seeds, *Brassica juncea*, but the manufacturing process is different. Instead of discarding the husks they form an integral part of the recipe. The seeds are soaked in verjuice, salt, and spices, then they are crushed and blended with the husks that have been sieved and added back to the mixture. Today, most mustard seeds are imported from Canada rather than grown in central France.

A gastronomic mustard favoured by chefs around the world, moutarde de Meaux is best eaten simply, as a relish to accompany grilled meat. **MR**

Taste: *Dijon mustard is strong enough to seem sharp, its aroma powerful enough to tickle the back of the nose, and its texture smooth without seeming floury.*

Taste: *Milder than Dijon mustard, but still quite spiky when fresh, it is also more vinegary. The texture is intentionally gritty because of the mustard bran.*

Grey Poupon mustard has been produced since 1777 and is still sold in the Rue de la Liberté in Dijon.

Bavarian Sweet Mustard

Mostarda di Frutta

Eating sausage without mustard is regarded as unthinkable in Germany. And Bavarian sweet mustard—brown in colour, mild and sweet in flavour—is considered the only worthy accompaniment to Munich's celebrated white veal sausage, *weisswurst*. In fact, it is even known as white sausage mustard in Germany.

Bavarian sweet mustard was invented in the mid-nineteenth century by Johann Conrad Develey. He opened a mustard factory in Munich that adopted the best principles of artisan production. Constantly trying to create new flavours, Develey spotted a gap in the market for a sweet mustard. He experimented with the traditional mustard mix, adding spices and sugar that had been caramelized. The mixture went through various changes, until brown sugar and roughly ground mustard seeds proved to be the winning ingredients.

As well as being the quintessential partner to *weisswurst*, Bavarian sweet mustard is also eaten with another southern German specialty, *leberkäse* (a liver meatloaf), and knuckle of pork. **LF**

This wonderful concoction of fruits preserved in grape must and spiked with mustard originates from northern Italy. Its beginnings can be traced back as far as Roman times, when gourmets combined honey, mustard, vinegar, and oil in quest of the perfect balance of sweet, sour, and spice.

Mostarda di frutta, or fruit preserved in grape must and spices, was traditionally a country food that originated as a pragmatic means of preserving whatever was left over after the harvest. However, it seems to have acquired some status during the Middle Ages, when sugar was an expensive luxury. A base of grape must or sweetened water was used to cook fruits such as apricots, cherries, pears, plums, and figs. The fruit was then removed and the sauce was seasoned with mustard and vinegar before being simmered until it thickened to an almost jam-like consistency. Today the fruit is usually candied first and then bottled in the spicy syrup. Traditionally, this unique relish is eaten with game, cheese, and cured or boiled meats—in particular *bollito misto*. **LF**

Taste: *Sweet Bavarian mustard has a grainy texture and soft piquancy with predominantly sweet overtones. It is wonderful as a spread, particularly on dark rye breads.*

Taste: *Mostarda di frutta delivers bold, fruity flavours against a wine-rich backdrop. The spice is balanced by a pleasing sweetness: the definitive sweet and sour.*

Mostarda di frutta is a particular delicacy of the city of Cremona in Lombardy, Italy. »

Kimchi

Cwikla

For thousands of years, Koreans have taken pickling to the limit with kimchi (or kimchee). Countless variations play around the themes of spice, colour, and composition, with piquant flavours that put Western pickles to shame. At least one kimchi appears alongside rice at every Korean meal, and there is a museum in Seoul devoted to the subject.

Asian cabbage is cleaned, salted, and stacked in large pots to age for a few days to yield the most basic versions of kimchi. More complex recipes add spices such as chillies, garlic, and paprika, other vegetables such as cucumber or radish, or shrimps and other seafood: whole stuffed cabbage heads are known as *tongbaechu*. Traditionally, earthen pots were used to promote ageing and fermentation, either in buried chambers or outside the home in the back garden to benefit from the climate of each season: "summer" kimchis are typically fermented only for a short time. Today, specialized refrigeration is now available and, while many homes continue the ritual of kimchi preparation, modern demand has given rise to myriad pre-packaged versions. **TH**

Although the origin of this tangy pickled beetroot relish is buried in time, the first recorded recipe for cwikla was provided by the sixteenth-century writer Mikolaj Rej, sometimes known as the "father of Polish literature." Rej's recipe called for oven-baked beetroot, sliced thin and seasoned with horseradish, fennel, and vinegar. Nowadays, the beetroot is usually diced or grated and caraway is the more common flavouring. A splash of red wine can be added. Unfortunately, many commercially available brands of cwikla have the somewhat less appetizing texture of a nondescript mashed purée.

Naturally, the individualistic Poles usually have their own idea on how fine or coarse, how mild or potent, and how tart or sweet their "national" relish should be. The mellower (lower horseradish and vinegar content) version may be regarded as a salad, whereas the more potent variety is more of a piquant condiment. Either way, nothing brings out the flavour of the sausages, hams, roasts, pâtés, jellied pork knuckles, and other cold meats that reign supreme at the Polish table better than cwikla. **RS**

Taste: *Despite considerable salt, most kimchi has a well-balanced taste that preserves the essence of each component. Heat can range from nonexistent to severe.*

Taste: *With a deep ruby-red colour and grainy texture, the faint sweetness of the marinade mellows the earthy beetroot flavour.*

Earthenware kimchi pots absorb the climatic conditions outside a temple in South Korea.

Piccalilli

Its name has an exotic, even Italian ring, but piccalilli is a venerable, English mixed vegetable preserve. The first half of the word no doubt derives from "pickle" and food historians suggest that the second may be a contraction of "chilli." The added tag "Indian pickle," along with the inclusion of mango in some early recipes, such as Hannah Glasse's from 1759, suggests that it may have been an Anglo-Indian invention.

During the Victorian era it appeared alongside large joints of cold beef, mutton, and ham served in Gentlemen's clubs and is still, despite changes to modern eating habits, eaten as a part of cold meals. Today piccalilli is a pickle consisting of some mix of cauliflower florets, green beans, gherkins, and other vegetables preserved in a thickened vinegary sauce and coloured with turmeric to give it a bright mustard colour. It may be spiced with ginger or chilli and mustard. While modern proprietary brands tend to be acetic, domestic versions can be distinctive and far more subtly flavoured. It is more than likely to be found in a pub. **MR**

Mango Chutney

Despite its culinary and etymological origins in India, chutney owes much of its fame to word-of-mouth advertising from travellers and colonists who passed through the subcontinent. There are countless chutney recipes containing ingredients ranging from aubergine to coconut, but few are better known than those featuring under-ripe mango.

Mango chutney has become a standard partner to Indian fare the world over. Domestic versions are made fresh daily using the produce that is seasonally available, whereas foreign sources come preserved in brand-name jars. Although the former tend to be spicier and balance the natural sweetness of the fruit with vinegar and savoury vegetables such as onion, the latter are made sweeter for foreign tastes, by adding tamarind and palm sugar.

Mango chutney is often eaten with poppadoms as an appetizer, but it can also be used to cool hot curries or to pep up blander dishes such as rice or dal. It also goes well with some cheeses. Innovative chefs have taken the chutney into yet another realm, as a pastry filling and as a glaze for roast meats. **TH**

Taste: *The vegetables keep their original shape and are crunchy, never soggy, but have absorbed the flavour of the vinegar. The spicy yellow sauce should not be harshly acid.*

Taste: *The sweetness of the mango is balanced by the naturally tart notes of vinegar and citrus. Spice flavourings commonly include chilli, peppercorns, turmeric, and clove.*

Mango and other chutneys are popularly sold from roadside stalls in Madagascar, Africa. ❯❯

Gari

Once a word known only to sushi aficionados, "gari"—thinly sliced ginger root pickled in sweet vinegar—is beginning to reach a wider audience. Ginger neutralizes strong fishy flavours and gari is commonly eaten alongside sashimi and sushi, to cleanse the palate between courses.

Gari is an indispensable part of the sushi shop ritual, but sushi shops themselves are a relatively new phenomenon. Centuries ago, fish was packed with rice to preserve it: the rice fermented giving the fish a sour taste, and was thrown away, while the fish was eaten. Over time, this grew into sushi—rice was mixed with vinegar to replicate the sour taste, and was itself eaten. A type of pressed sushi developed first and then, in the nineteenth century in Edo (now Tokyo), finger style sushi (*nigiri-zushi*) gained popularity, and this is probably when gari was introduced to the experience.

To make gari, thinly slice fresh ginger, sprinkle it with salt and leave it for an hour or so until it gives off water. Pat dry and pour over a warm mixture of three parts vinegar and two parts sugar. **SB**

Taste: Sweet, hot, and refreshingly sour, crunchy gari is a perfect palate cleanser. Japanese pickled ginger ranges in colour from pinkish to yellowish.

Preserved Lemon

Moroccans are ingenious chefs. A prime example of their creativity can be seen in their technique of making preserved lemons with little more than salt, water, lemons, and time. The fruit matures into a completely unexpected taste and texture that helps define North African cuisine.

Preserved lemons are available to buy from stores and markets, but most chefs will have a jar maturing on the pantry shelf at any given time. The process is very straightforward and involves little more than stuffing whole lemons liberally with salt, packing them into glass jars, and covering with water. After roughly a month of ageing at room temperature, the texture of the peel softens and becomes chewy. Most jars last only as long as it takes the next batch to be aged.

Lamb tagines and curries are often laced with preserved lemons to add a tart lift to otherwise heavy fare. They are served on their own in tiny bowls as a flavourful accent with the evening meal or as a sort of palate cleanser between the courses of more elaborate dinners. **TH**

Taste: Tart, slightly sweet, and pleasantly bitter, the texture of preserved lemons is soft and pliable but should not be mushy. Rinse or dilute with fresh water as desired.

Lemons can be easily preserved at home using a good quality, coarse sea salt. »

Katsuobushi

In the famous Nishiki food market in Kyoto, Japan, an old-fashioned, red enamel, rotating drum churns out freshly-shaved katsuobushi for sale by the bagful. The cured fillet of the skipjack tuna, *Katsuwonus pelamis*, katsuobushi is at the heart of dashi, the flavourful stock that underpins all Japanese cooking.

The drying process is unique to Japan and dates back more than three centuries. Skipjack fillets are simmered and the bones removed, before being hot-smoked for up to two weeks, then trimmed and sun-dried. Next they are cured using the mould *Aspergillus glaucus*, until they are as hard as wood and rich in the umami flavour. The dried fillets can then be shaved into fine flakes, or *kezuribushi*.

Besides dashi (best produced by a fast infusion of freshly shaved katsuobushi in boiling water), very fine shavings can be used as a garnish for vegetables and fish, or mixed with soy sauce and eaten with rice. The flavour disappears rapidly on exposure to air, and the fragrance of freshly shaved katsuobushi is far superior to prepackaged flakes. **SB**

Taste: *The finely shaved flakes seem to dance upon the food they garnish, but they take some chewing. The aroma is smoky, and the taste is of the ocean.*

Cured skipjack tuna at Tokyo's Nisihiki market. The fish is finely shaved into katsuobushi using a special tool.

Shiokara

Originally produced as a way of preserving fish during the winter, shiokara is the salted and fermented guts of fish, most usually squid and cuttlefish, although regional variations are made with the innards of sardines, bonito, and mackerel. Pickling in Japan is almost always a salt-based procedure, rather than a vinegar one, and the process produces amino acids that are beneficial to health and full of flavour. Shiokara is used to flavour dishes, as well as eaten as an accompaniment to rice.

In Nagasaki, on the southern island of Kyushu, shiokara is made with the locally caught anchovies, *katakuchi iwashi*, or, in the local dialect, *etari*. After the catch, the whole anchovies are scaled, washed in sea water, packed under layers of salt, and covered in rice straw, which contains microbial flora and aids fermentation. Unfortunately, *etari* stocks in the area are declining, although efforts are being made to revive them.

Similar salted and fermented fish products are found throughout Asia, such as Thailand's nam pla and Vietnam's nuoc mam. **SB**

Taste: *Shiokara is strong, salty, and highly savoury with a slight bitterness that lingers in the mouth. It has a pleasantly chewy and slippery texture.*

Doubanjiang

An essential flavouring in the cooking of China's Sichuan province, this thick, richly flavoured paste with its reddish-brown hue is based on fresh red chillies, salt, and fermented broad beans: an unusual ingredient, since most other Chinese bean pastes are made only from soya beans. It is produced in various areas of Sichuan, but the best is said to come from the town of Pixian, near the capital, Chengdu.

Although it is made from just a few ingredients, doubanjiang can have very different levels of heat and flavour. It all depends on the long and careful process of fermenting and ageing: each step can take anywhere from a few months to two years, or even longer. In older pastes, the heat level decreases and the complexity increases as age mellows and softens the chillies.

Unlike other chilli bean pastes, doubanjiang is almost always used as a flavouring ingredient, in the same way as garlic, ginger, and rice wine. It is rarely used on its own as a dipping sauce. In English, doubanjiang is usually labelled "spicy [or hot] chilli bean paste" or "spicy [or hot] broad bean paste." **KKC**

Coconut Milk

The coconut tree (*Cocos nucifera*) has a plethora of uses across the tropics where it grows. The fronds can roof a hut, the fibrous husks can mulch a garden, and hollowing out the trunk provides a ready-made canoe. In just one meal, the fruit can yield a drink, flavour a soup or curry, and make a sweet dessert.

Coconut milk is not the water found inside the coconut. It is produced by infusing the shredded white flesh of the fruit with boiling water; the liquid is then strained from the pulp through a cloth. Using less water in the infusion produces a thicker liquid known as coconut cream. This is not to be confused with the product sold commercially, which needs reconstituting with hot water. For the freshest taste, coconut milk can easily be extracted at home.

In the South Pacific, coconut milk is a staple used in everything from *thom kha gai*, a classic Thai chicken and coconut soup, to modern fusion treatments of Australian shrimp curry. In India, coconut milk is made into sweets like *burfi* and simmered into curries. New World chefs are also aware of its delights, using it to concoct exquisite rice puddings and cream pies. **TH**

Taste: *Good doubanjiang has a spicy yet mellow complexity that is delicious with meats and complements subtler ingredients, such as fish, without overwhelming them.*

Taste: *Good coconut milk is silky smooth with a deep aroma. Older or inferior versions will be chalky in texture. Shake tinned versions before opening to redistribute fats.*

Coconut milk is freshly prepared on the shores of Tuamotu, French Polynesia. »

Cassareep

A trip to the local market of any Caribbean island is a true adventure of sight and sound. The cacophony of parrots and stall hawkers is matched with an equally heady mix of colours and smells, amid which the dull brown cassava root looks almost out of place.

Known locally as yuca or manioc, cassava is grown both in the Caribbean and in West Africa as a staple dietary starch and is, curiously, the parent of tapioca. To make cassareep, grated cassava is pressed or squeezed to release the juice, then mixed with raw sugar and spices such as cinnamon or clove. This is simmered and reduced to a moderately thick consistency with a pungency and sweetness that varies considerably between recipes.

The real value of cassareep is in the kitchens of the Caribbean and along the northeastern coasts of South America. There it is synonymous with the many versions of the classic "pepperpot," a regional stew made from pork, chicken, onions, and chillies gently simmered with the syrup. Less commonly, cassareep is the basis for more elaborate chilli or fruit sauces used with both meats and seafood. **TH**

Taste: *Cassareep tastes like the bitter elements of molasses. Rather unpleasant when consumed directly, its complexity adds a unique layer of flavour to pepperpot.*

Once the tough, brown skin of cassava is peeled, the crisp, white flesh grates easily to make cassareep.

Umeboshi

In Japan the appearance of the first ume blossom signals the start of spring, a moment enshrined in poems, paintings, and festivals. When the fruits appear in June it is time to make umeboshi, the brine-cured, sun-dried fruit that has been an indspensable part of the Japanese diet for centuries.

Beloved of the seventeenth-century feudal lord and gourmet Mito Komon, these highly acidic delights are still a daily feature of the Japanese table. Ume fruits (*Prunus mume*), despite their alternative names of Japanese apricots or Japanese plums, are acid and bitter when raw, and toxic when unripe. Their characteristic colour comes from red shiso leaves, which also add flavour and minerals.

The flavour of umeboshi marries well with green vegetables, and oily fish simmered in an umeboshi broth is particularly fine. One single plum on top of white rice resembles the Japanese flag, thereby gaining this food a symbolic as well as nutritional place in the hearts of the Japanese. A purée of the flesh of umeboshi, *bainiku*, adds piquancy to dressings and sauces. **SB**

Taste: *Small umeboshi can be crunchy and tart but larger ones can be soft, juicy, and fruity. All are exceptionally salty and acidic, with a palate-cleansing zestiness.*

Mayonnaise

The origin of the word "mayonnaise" has long been controversial. Some food historians suppose it to be a corruption of *bayonnaise* (from Bayonne in southwest France) or linked to an Old French word for egg yolk, *moyeu*. It is generally accepted, however, that its earliest spelling—*mahonnaise*—ties it to the capital of the Balearic island of Minorca, Mahón.

A simple, seasoned, emulsified sauce made from egg yolk and olive oil, it may have evolved from mortar and pestle emulsions such as aïoli into the whisked sauce that was fashionable by the early nineteenth century. Over time, the sauce has added a wide palette of variations such as flavouring with vinegar, mustard, or lemon juice and the use of different oils. Science has demystified the process by putting mayonnaise under the microscope to show how the droplets of oil and yolk coalesce. Modern electric blenders allow its making in under a minute.

At its simplest and best, prepared with egg yolks from free-range chickens and a golden extra virgin olive oil that is soft and sweet, rather than harsh and overly green, it stands the test of time. **MR**

Aïoli

The eighteenth-century Provençal poet Jean-Baptiste Germain, wrote a poem about a divine fish stew, *la bourrido dei dieoux*, in which he memorably described a perfect aïoli: "Venus made it so stiff for him, / That the pestle stood upright in the mortar." Erect pestles and love goddesses aside, however, the couplet gives an indication as to how the garlic and olive oil sauce that is the "national" dish of Provence should be. Like many other sauces, it is made into an emulsion—the difference here is that this is done in a mortar. First the garlic is crushed, then it is mixed with egg yolk, and finally the oil is added, drip by drip.

In nineteenth-century farmhouses, aïoli was made in large quantities—the pestle was attached to the ceiling by a cord so that the cook's arms did not become too tired blending in the oil. In winter it was eaten with vegetables, but restaurants today present it with fish, salt cod, or the *bourride* to which it plays the same supporting role as *rouille* does to bouillabaisse. Neighbouring Catalans usually omit the egg and call their sauce *allioli*. **MR**

Taste: Creamy, smooth, and unctuous, fresh mayonnaise should be light and well-aerated, too. The taste should reflect a perfect balance between the oil and the egg.

Taste: Aïoli should be thick and unctuous almost to the point where a spoon will stand up in it. The fresh flavour of garlic should be softened by a gentle Provençal olive oil.

Aïoli is traditionally made using olive oil and garlic, although some recipes add egg as an emulsifier. ❱

Tartare Sauce

Banana Ketchup

In its modern incarnation, tartare sauce is a hybric containing elements of a seventeenth-century sauce remoulade, and a nineteenth-century derivative of mayonnaise. It has nothing to do with the Mongolian Tartars who overran China in the thirteenth century and its link to the raw, chopped steak tartare may be either incidental or accidental.

The earliest remoulades were a kind of broth mixed with anchovies, capers, onions, garlic, anc parsley. The first English recipe for tartare sauce using mayonnaise, capers, and herbs was published by Eliza Acton in 1845—forty-one years after the first printed reference to mayonnaise. Since then this piquant sauce has become an omnipresent partner to fried fish, initially in aspirational, French-inspirec cooking, but more recently in pubs and fish and chip shops. Overly acidic manufactured versions skimp on the capers, cornichons, spring onions, and fresh parsley that give the recipe interest.

In France, the sauce is traditionally preparec with a hard-boiled egg-yolk, sometimes with the chopped white added to it. **MR**

Since the eighteenth century ketchups based on various ingredients have seen highs and lows of popularity. In the Philippines, and from the South Pacific into Indonesia and the Caribbean, it is mashed bananas that mutate the now-classic pairing of ripe tomatoes and exotic spices into an experience worthy of the most intrepid gourmand.

Although most likely invented in imitation of the tomato version, banana ketchup vastly expands both its sweet and heat dimensions. It uses little or no tomato purée, relying instead on locally available fruits, vegetables, vinegar, a litany of spices, and, of course, fresh bananas, but is generally coloured red, either naturally or artificially.

Variations on the theme vary as widely as the culinary cultures that create them, and each region will add its own local twist to the recipe. Wherever they are, they gain favour as a principal ingredient in barbecues, as additions to soups and stocks, and as a condiment on a huge variety of dishes from noodles to *lumpia*, the spring rolls of the Philippines and Indonesia. **TH**

Taste: *The smoothness of the mayonnaise contrasts with the texture of the diced vegetables. It should taste herby and only a little sharp without eclipsing the olive oil flavour.*

Taste: *Curiously reminiscent of tomato ketchup in colour and consistency, but sweeter and with more spice. The banana flavour, surprisingly, can even be hard to spot.*

The buds of the Mediterranean caper shrub are 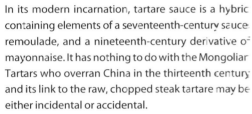 *picked before they open and are then pickled.*

Mole

Throughout the thirty-one states of Mexico, there are countless culinary opinions, which makes the task of defining authentic tastes challenging. No more so than in the case of the classic sauce mole.

Many misconceptions about this elusive group of sauces exist. For example, while many do contain chocolate, it is not always a defining ingredient. (The bitter dark chocolate used enriches the mole sauce rather than sweetens it.) However, what seems to define mole is a complex formula, rich in chillies, that takes careful, often long preparation. The most famous mole sauces come from Oaxaca and Puebla, where current recipes are thought to first originate.

Recipes can call for twenty or more ingredients, including seeds, nuts, raisins, allspice, cinnamon, and several different chillies. The ingredients, often roasted, are ground up, sometimes with oil, and then simmered in a stock. In one popular dish, poultry is cooked in a dark brown *mole poblano* sauce until it almost falls off the bone. Another incarnation is *mole verde*, a green sauce made with tomatillos that is perfect with roast pork. **TH**

Taste: *Most versions are complex enough to redefine the flavours of the component ingredients. Rich and smoky, mole often has chocolate and chilli undertones.*

A Mexican woman offers mole in tortilla at the family altar. »

Hummus

A Middle Eastern meze table without a bowl of hummus is like an Arabian night without a tale. This simple dish of mashed or puréed chickpeas, usually now flavoured with tahini, garlic, lemon juice, salt, and often olive oil too, was originally an inexpensive, vegetarian protein source. Today it is enjoyed by rich and poor on a daily basis throughout the Arab world, as well as in Israel, Turkey, Greece, and Cyprus. It is a national food for many countries, several of which claim credit for its creation, and most of which compete for the best recipe.

Available in supermarkets and delis around the globe, hummus is easy to make. Both texture and flavour profile vary from region to region, depending on the balance of ingredients and how they are blended: Syrian versions often include herbs and spices. Hummus is served with a variety of garnishes, often in combination with each other: olive oil, whole chickpeas, parsley, coriander, paprika, cumin, and anardana (pomegranate seeds) are just a few of the adornments that find their way onto the plate. It may also be used as a sandwich filling. **BLeB**

Taste: *The best-made hummus has the key notes of tahini, garlic, and lemon juice blended so no single flavour dominates. Texture ranges from smooth to chunky.*

Hummus is traditionally served as one of the small appetizer dishes that make up meze.

Tahini

Hummus, baba ghanoush, and tarator would all be much lesser culinary treats if they lacked the subtle, earthy flavour of this creamy paste. Although not usually eaten on its own in its natural state, tahini is an essential flavouring element in many traditional Middle Eastern dips and sauces. In Israel, it is thinned with water and drizzled over just-fried falafel and hot kebabs; in Lebanon, it is made into a simple lemony sauce that is served with fresh fish. It even finds its way into some of the many different recipes for halva, a sweet confection that appears in many guises in every country of the Middle East.

The versatile paste is laboriously extracted from sesame seeds in a process that involves crushing, grilling, milling, and two periods of soaking. The paste, which is sold in jars in Middle Eastern food shops, delis, and some supermarkets, is thick and varies in colour from light to dark beige; aficionados favour the lighter ones, which come from earlier pressings, but either quality adds a depth of flavour to other ingredients. Tahini is known in Arabic, and sometimes in English, as tahina. **BLeB**

Taste: *Rich, thick, and smooth, tahini paste has a pronounced, earthy sesame flavour that combines well with lemon juice and other sharp flavours.*

Genoese Pesto

Essentially a pounded blend of herbs and other flavourings, pesto must be one of the oldest sauces in the world. It is probably also one of the most copied—with, on occasion, some of the worst results. The real McCoy was a Genoese invention, a delicious concoction that highlighted the magical flavour of the sweet, fragrant leaves of the local Ligurian basil. (Today much of Italy's commercial pesto production is centred around the village of Pra in Liguria, an area noted for its basil farms.)

Genoese pesto has always been made using a pestle and mortar: the word comes from the Italian verb *pestare*, which means "to crush." Garlic, pine nuts, salt, olive oil, and cheese—customarily a mixture of Pecorino and Parmigiano Reggiano—are the only components apart from basil.

Fresh, handmade Genoese pesto is one of the world's true delights, best stirred into hot pasta, soup, or slathered over warm focaccia as it is in its home region. Although pairing it with hot or warm ingredients accentuates its flavour, cooking would kill its essence: fresh crushed basil. **LF**

Taste: *Heady with sweet, perfumed basil, the subtle suggestions of garlic combine with a creaminess helped by slightly buttery pine nuts and balanced by salty cheese.*

The regular harvesting of basil promotes generous new growth.

Pâté di Carciofi

Artichokes are an utterly sublime vegetable that belongs to the thistle family, but, like so many superlative foods, they are seasonal. In Italy, where artichokes have long been especially valued, the age-old art of conservation comes to the rescue in the form of Pâté di Carciofi, a glorious pâté with a texture similar to tapenade, usually made simply from artichokes, extra virgin olive oil, white wine vinegar, salt, and garlic, and sometimes herbs. There are versions available containing ground almonds, Parmigiano Reggiano cheese, and even truffles.

Pâté di Carciofi—also referred to as Crema di Carciofi—is always available from good food stores and delis. It is especially popular in Sicily and Apulia, two of Italy's major artichoke growing areas. A versatile spread, it creates a fabulous topping for bruschetta and crostini, makes a tasty sandwich filling and, stirred into hot pasta, makes a stunning yet simple sauce. It is easy enough to make at home too, either by using fresh artichokes in season, or by puréeing good quality artichokes that have been preserved in extra virgin olive oil. **LF**

Taste: *Depending on the recipe, Pâté di Carciofi will display a balance of smooth, grassy, and buttery characteristics, along with a gently muted sweetness.*

Tapenade

Ancient Roman cooks had a recipe for crushed olives—*epityrum*—that they mixed with cumin, coriander, rue, mint, and oil. It pre-dates tapenade by almost two millenia. What it lacks, however, is capers. The Provençal word for a caper tree—*tapeno* or *taperié*—gave its name to a caper sauce *tapenado* that has since evolved into what is known as tapenade today—the flavoured blend of crushed olives, extra virgin olive oil, anchovies, and capers. (Somehow anchovies joined the mix along the way.) Not exactly a dip, a paste, or a sauce—it is really all three depending on how it is used. It may be spread on toast, offered as a dip with raw celery, or served as an accompaniment to grilled fish.

Both green Picholine and black olives can be made into tapenade, although black olives from Nyons in the Drôme are ideal. The capers themselves are the buds from the tree, picked before they flower, and pickled in salt or vinegar. Making tapenade with an electric blender takes only a few moments today, but its texture and taste seem to improve when it has been ground slowly by hand in a mortar. **MR**

Taste: *Tapenade can be smooth, coarse, or granular. Its dominant flavour is of olives, but the anchovies and capers should also contribute their distinctive notes.*

Ajvar

In the Balkans, at the end of the autumn harvest, a delicacy arises from the surplus that rivals mustard and mayonnaise in versatility: ajvar. Most kitchens will hold a jar of this blend of red peppers and aubergine, whether home-made or pre-packaged, to use as a spread or condiment.

Recipes blossom from this simple base into more complex affairs featuring small amounts of squash, tomatoes, onions, and garlic. Traditionally the ingredients are hand-prepared, stripping off skins and seeds, then simmered together slowly to preserve their flavours. Wood fires are often used to impart mild smoke notes, but spicing and heat are never overpowering. The brilliance of ajvar is the ingenuity that sees individual ingredients married into a blend that is greater than the sum of its parts.

Texture varies from smooth to chunky and, while almost always a brilliant fresh red, some versions can be green or amber depending on the vegetables involved. Perfect on sandwiches and antipasti, ajvar can also be tossed with warm pasta or used as a dip with pitta bread. **TH**

Taste: *The sweetness of pepper flesh is accented by the mild bitterness of aubergine. There are "mild" and "hot" varieties, as well as some with a stronger smoked taste.*

Baba Ghanoush

It is not for nothing that this popular Middle Eastern dish is known as "poor man's caviar." The intriguing combination of smoky aubergine blended with tahini, garlic, lemon juice, and salt create a tasty dip or spread that belies its simple ingredients.

The origins of this essential meze dish are lost in the mists of time and culinary folklore, although medieval Arabic manuscripts indicate that the passion for aubergines dates back to at least the thirteenth century. It appears in many guises throughout the region, sometimes under its alternative name of moutabel, and in Ottoman times it was said that the women of the harem prepared it to win the Sultan's favour. A Lebanese version omits the tahini, making a less indulgent dish; in parts of Syria, yoghurt replaces the tahini.

The essential smoky flavour comes from grilling the aubergine over hot coals or baking it in a very hot oven until it simply collapses, making the flesh easy to blend with the other ingredients. It is served chilled or at room temperature with pitta or other kinds of flatbread. **BLeB**

Muhammara

Smoky, slightly textured, and red, a glowing mound of muhammara awaits the invasion of a triangle of crisp flat bread to escort it to an eager mouth. Less well-known than its meze cousins hummus and baba ghanoush, this roasted red pepper dip originated centuries ago in Aleppo, within the borders of modern-day Syria, where the spice routes of the Mediterranean, and Turkish and Armenian culinary traditions influenced its zesty complexity.

Muhammara is made by grinding scorched and skinned red peppers with oil, walnuts, lemon, garlic, cumin, and pomegranate molasses. The local piquant Aleppo pepper adds a spicy, but subtle kick. This lush, highly favoured purée makes a stronger statement than other meze dips and is equally good as an accompaniment to grilled meats or fish. In western Turkey, it is sometimes known as *acuka*, whereas in the Lebanon mint leaves are occasionally added to the exotic mixture and it is spread on toast. The flavour of muhammara is best when it has been prepared a few hours in advance and served at room temperature. **RH**

Taste: *Grilled, rather than baked, aubergines give a more pronounced smoky flavour, which is complemented by the tang of lemon juice and garlic. The texture should be light.*

Taste: *Tantalizing complex, the slightly nut-textured mouthfeel of muhammara bursts with a smoky sweetness levelled out by the tartness of the pomegranate and lemon.*

Bumbu Kacang

In Indonesia, the special peanut sauce, known locally as bumbu kacang, is used on everything from chicken satay to rice noodles.

While peanut sauces are common throughout South East Asia, this elaborate version gains fame by the inclusion of shrimp paste and chilli, whether chopped fresh or via prepared *sambal oelek*, a paste made of chilli and garlic. Soy sauce, citrus juices, ginger, kaffir lime leaves, and even fruit chutneys further round out the taste of bumbu kacang, offering a cascade of flavours, layer upon layer. The peanuts are usually roasted fresh in most recipes, with the newly expressed oil contributing to the end consistency. Palm sugar, garlic, and onions balance the heat of the chilli and bring further complexity. Purists refrain from overcooking the sauce and rely on time to meld the flavours into their final form.

Satays of any kind are traditionally accompanied by bumbu kacang, as is *gado-gado*, the famous salad of Indonesia, but the sauce appears elsewhere for both table and kitchen use throughout the archipelagoes of South East Asia. **TH**

Taste: *Freshly prepared bumbu kacang is simultaneously salty, sweet, and sour on top of an intense, roasted peanut flavour. Flavour accents vary according to the recipe.*

Yeast Extract

The dark brown, savoury paste, known to millions as Marmite, is made from the yeast that is a by-product of the brewing industry. Marmite is a British brand owned by the food giant Unilever and has been spread on bread and toast for over a century. The name refers to a French cooking pot, pictured on the label, which was perhaps chosen because the colour, appearance, and aroma of Marmite vaguely resemble the juices produced by pot-roasting beef. The brand trades on its "love it or loathe it" image.

The process of converting waste yeast into a protein-rich paste was discovered by the German scientist Baron Liebig. Salt added to the yeast triggers a process known as autolysis whereby the biological cells self-destruct. To complete the recipe, the outer husks of yeast cells are removed and the remaining "sludge" is blended with a similar vegetable extract, natural flavourings, and added vitamins.

Marmite is made under licence in New Zealand, but to a different recipe which includes sugar, giving it a less assertive flavour. The rival brand Vegemite is much loved in Australia. **MR**

Taste: *A little goes a long way because it is sticky, sharp, and salty. The taste is heightened by the naturally occurring umami in it, caused by the protein's breakdown.*

Yeast is skimmed off the top of Guinness before it is passed to vats for maturing at the brewery in 1953. »

Yellow Bean Sauce

Hoisin Sauce

The ancient Chinese discovered that fermenting different types of beans was a way to both preserve them as well as enhance their flavour. Yellow bean sauce gets its name not from the colour of the finished product—which is actually brown—but from the Chinese name for the main ingredient—*huang dou* or yellow soya beans.

Yellow bean sauce is made by first soaking the soya beans, then cooking them, and letting them ferment before adding rice wine and sugar. The fermented beans are then aged before being mashed and mixed with other ingredients. Depending on the producer and the region where it is made, the salty sauce can be chunky, smooth, sweet, or spicy. In Vietnam, where it is known as *nuoc tuong*, lemongrass, coconut, ground peanuts, chilli, and garlic are usually included in the sauce.

Yellow bean sauce is popular in Chinese and Thai cookery. It can be mixed with other ingredients to make a dipping sauce or condiment, or incorporated into cooked dishes. It works well with fish and seafood, as well as chicken and beef. **KKC**

In China, hoisin sauce is used in much the same way as ketchup is in the West—although, fortunately, a little more sparingly. It may be used as a dipping sauce straight from the jar or bottle, added judiciously during cooking to add depth and complexity, or mixed with other ingredients to make a coating for barbecued meats—hence its occasional name of "barbecue sauce."

One of the better-known Chinese condiments, hoisin sauce is made from fermented soya beans, vinegar, salt, sugar, garlic, chilli, and five spice powder, thickened with starch and coloured with food colourings. It is often served with Peking duck—the laboriously prepared whole duck with golden, crisp skin and moist, succulent flesh—but in China the traditional accompaniment is thinner and less sweet, yet also based on fermented soya beans.

Although some of the cheaper Chinese restaurants have hoisin sauce on the table for diners to use at will, any talented Chinese chef would be every bit as horrified by this notion as a French or American counterpart. **KKC**

Taste: *Thick, glossy, and brown, yellow bean sauce varies in texture. The saltiness of the sauce should be balanced by the flavour of the other ingredients added to it.*

Taste: *Hoisin sauce should always be used sparingly—a little goes a long way. The best versions are beautifully balanced with salty, sweet, and spicy flavours.*

Oyster Sauce

XO Sauce

Even in the bad old days of experimental fusion cooking, when chefs were haphazardly adding all sorts of Asian ingredients to their food, oyster sauce never really made the culinary leap from East to West. Commercial oyster sauce—the kind that is sold on supermarket shelves—is made by cooking oyster extract with other ingredients such as soy sauce, sugar, cornflour, caramel colouring, and preservatives. But a few artisans in Chinese seaside villages or Hong Kong's New Territories still make it the traditional way. They harvest oysters and cook them according to secret family recipes, without any of the industrial additives. You might have to go to the source to buy these small-batch sauces, but it is worth every step of the journey.

While oyster sauce is at times used as a dipping sauce, it is more often used in small quantities to flavour dishes. It goes well with eggs, noodles, vegetables, and meats such as beef and chicken but should be used with care in seafood dishes so as not to overwhelm the delicate flavours. A vegetarian version is made from mushrooms. **KKC**

Although it has its namesake in XO cognac, XO sauce contains no alcohol. The name is meant to evoke a luxurious, expensive, and very special product, something with a status and cost equivalent to the fine cognac that is a cult item in China. XO sauce was invented in Hong Kong during the 1980s and its popularity spread quickly. Many chefs claim credit for its creation, but what is certain is that it was originally made only at the top Cantonese restaurants, and these places still produce the best: most restaurants that make it sell their own recipe in jars on the premises.

The essential ingredients in XO sauce are dried scallops, oil, chillies, and garlic. It can also contain dried shrimp, dried Chinese ham, and salted fish. It is usually used in small quantities, often as a dipping sauce with dim sum. The sauce shines in simple preparations. It is delicious tossed with noodles; paired with finely chopped spring onions it makes a delectable topping for fresh oysters. As it is relatively expensive, XO sauce is a popular gift in Christmas and Chinese New Year hampers. **KKC**

Taste: *Authentic, small-batch oyster sauce has a strong, pure, oyster flavour. Despite the unappealing colour, this is a different creature from the factory-made ingredient.*

Taste: *The best brands contain larger quantities of dried scallops, which are more expensive than other ingredients. The intense, chunky sauce is salty, spicy, and oily.*

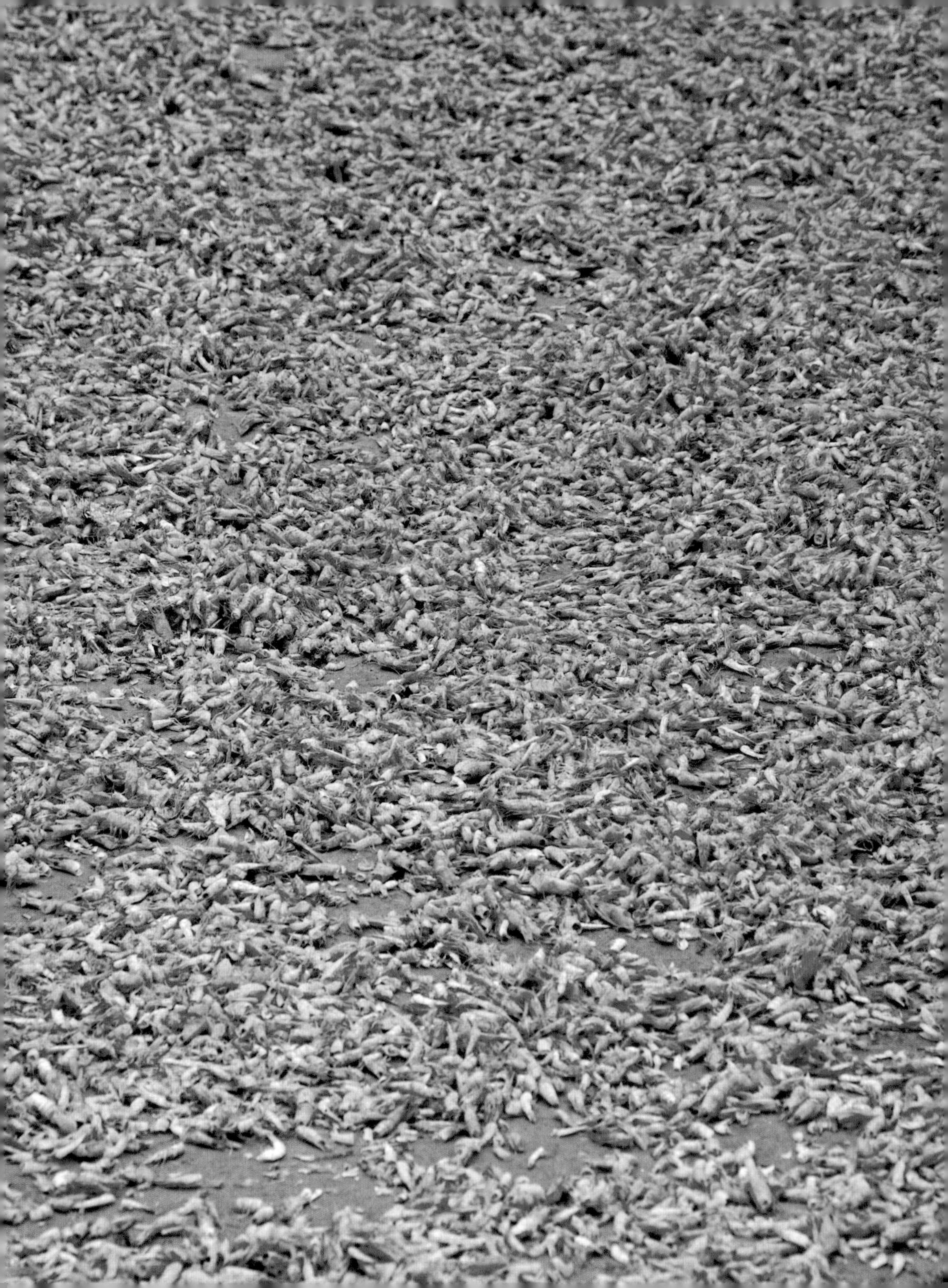

Terasi

Foul-smelling and rotten, Indonesian terasi, a paste made from shrimps that have been left to ferment, can entirely overwhelm the uninitiated. Yet, like garlic or asafoetida, this unappealing ingredient can utterly transform a dish, as the aroma of rotting shrimp thankfully dissipates, leaving behind a taste that puts common fish sauce to shame.

The shrimps turn a mahogany colour during fermentation and are often sun-dried, pulverized, and pressed into blocks before packaging It is also sold in jars as a thick paste, sometimes capped with wax or oil as a preservative, and more rarely as a powder. Salt is always added, but other ingredients vary from producer to producer. Connoisseurs seek out artisan producers who use the very smallest shrimp, and ferment them the longest.

In Indonesia, the chilli paste sambal is mixed with shrimp paste and other ingredients like tamarind and vinegar to produce the hot sambal terasi. Elsewhere in South East Asia terasi, or its siblings such as Malaysian *belacan* or Thai *kapi*, are added to hot oil before starting meat or vegetable sautés. **TH**

Taste: *Terasi tastes like an extremely concentrated fish sauce but leaves, surprisingly, far less aroma than the raw paste would suggest. Use fluid paste in tiny amounts.*

Sheto

Situated on the west coast of Africa and the beneficiary of great ocean bounty, Ghana has put its own unique twists upon the culinary influences spread by seafaring traders over the centuries. Sheto is one of the distinctive hot condiments found across Africa and locals will argue to the death about the origins and recipe permutations of their own beloved pepper sauce.

Pronounced "shee-toe," it partners two foods found in abundance locally, dried chillies and dried shrimps. These are blended with other ingredients such as ginger, garlic, and tomato paste into a salted oil base much like the harissa found elsewhere in Africa. Made from only dried ingredients, it can keep for months; versions featuring fresh chillies, herbs, and vegetables require quicker consumption.

Sheto is used to flavour many dishes. *Waakye,* simply rice and beans cooked in the local fashion, is almost always heightened with a dose of sheto. Similarly, starchy *fufu* balls made from cassava or yam can be dipped in shito and peanut stew can have a few spoonfuls stirred in to give extra kick. **TH**

Taste: *Hot chilli and rich salty shrimp flavours are prominent but accented by other additions. Improves with age as the flavours meld and slightly mellow.*

Small shrimps are laid out to dry in the sun.
◐ *The colour of the paste varies from village to village.*

Tamari Shoyu

Shiro Shoyu

Traditionally made soy sauce, or shoyu, in the style made many centuries ago, when soy sauce first arrived in Japan from China, makes up only 1 or 2 per cent of Japan's entire production. There are only a handful of families who continue to make it the old way.

One such is the Aoki family in Aichi, who still handcraft tamari shoyu to their original, 500-year-old recipe, using multiple, complex fermentations over a period of two years. They soak soya beans in spring water, then steam and crush them. Aspergillus spores and roasted barley flour are added, before the whole is left to incubate for three days, transforming into a fluffy mass of mould-covered beans. This is dried and mixed with sea salt and water to make a mash called *moromi*, which ferments in century-old cedar kegs, over two summers, as enzymes, yeasts, and bacteria break down the proteins and carbohydrates. It seems that the microorganisms and natural oils in the wood of the cedar casks are crucial to the sauce that is ultimately pressed from the mash. **SB**

A white soy sauce, shiro shoyu is the product of a process that reverses the usual ratio of wheat and soya beans, using only 20 per cent soya beans and 80 per cent wheat. (The Shichifuku company in Aichi make an organic shiro shoyu using an even higher ratio, of 90 per cent wheat and only 10 of soya beans.) Soy sauce has been used in the Orient for centuries, and was brought to Japan by Buddhist monks from China in the thirteenth century, but it was only around 400 years ago that wheat was used in its preparation—before then it was made only with soya beans. Using such a high proportion of wheat gives the sauce a much lighter amber colour and a sweet mellow flavour.

In Japan, shiro shoyu is used mainly for cooking, not as a dipping sauce, and it is especially prized when the cook wants to preserve the natural colour of an ingredient. It is popular in the cuisine of Kyoto when the natural colour of vegetables, such as the *Kyo ninjin* red carrot and white daikon, must be displayed to their best advantage. It is also used in the delicate, steamed egg custard, *chawan mushi*. **SB**

Taste: Tamari shoyu has the prized umami taste. With its thick, viscous texture and rich savoury, but mildly salty taste, it is ideal both for dipping sauces and for cooking.

Taste: Sweet, mellow, and lightly smoky, while still being salty, shiro shoyu has a background muskiness of wheat. The colour darkens with age, but does not affect the flavour.

Kecap

Nuoc Mam

Soy sauce, Asia's most famous culinary export, is believed to have its roots in the sixth century when Buddhists in China developed a salty, grainy paste as a meat substitute. Popular in all oriental cuisines, styles of soy sauce vary widely from country to country, and Indonesia's kecaps are quite unique.

Kecap manis is sweet, thick, dark, and syrupy from the addition of palm sugar. If unavailable, it can be made by simmering a Chinese or Japanese dark soy sauce with sugar, star anise, and garlic, or replaced in recipes with a blend of molasses, dark soy sauce, and vegetable or chicken stock. Kecap asin is lighter, thinner, and saltier than its manis cousin. Kecap manis needs the richness of beef and lamb to balance its strong flavour, whereas kecap asin is more versatile and complements dishes where retaining the fresh flavour and colour of the food is necessary, such as chicken or seafood dishes.

One theory links kecap to ketchup, a generic word used to describe sauces and condiments long before it became synonymous with a well-known brand of tomato sauce. **WS**

In South East Asia, where fermented fish sauces play a similar role to the soy sauces of Japan and China, Vietnam's nuoc mam is probably the most sublime, and the most revered. A warm, rich brown in hue, its finely-nuanced flavour is the foundation for many dipping sauces; when used in cooking, its natural glutamates and other proteins enhance the overall taste profile of a dish without domineering it.

Nuoc mam is made by layering fresh anchovies and sea salt in wooden or earthenware vats and letting them ferment for several months to a year. The first, most treasured tapping of the vats is sold as nuoc mam nhi, an "extra-virgin" nuoc mam. Later "pressings" are based on what remains from the first tapping, and labels often—but not always—bear a rating expressed in degrees, which is a guide to quality. Higher grades have undergone less dilution and are suitable for table use. Lower grades are reserved for cooking. Phu Quoc, a Vietnamese island whose surrounding waters teem with especially prized anchovies is famous for its nuoc mam, which now has protected appellation status. **CTa**

Taste: *Dark, thick, and almost treacly in consistency, kecap manis packs a powerful sweet-savoury punch. Lighter, saltier, kecap asin can season all kinds of dishes.*

Taste: *Top grade nuoc mam has an intensely marine savour that is never pungent or harsh. Its saltiness is balanced by caramel notes and a natural sweetness.*

Chimichurri

The Argentines, purveyors of some of the world's best beef, allow very little else to come into contact with their sublime steaks. Chimichurri is the notable exception. Across South America there are countless recipes for this blend of herbs, spices, vinegar, salt, and olive oil, which varies not only by region but according to each chef's secret recipe. In Argentina, fresh parsley, garlic, oregano, and chillies form the basis of the blend; in other parts of Latin America, coriander is a popular ingredient; tea, lemon, honey, mint, and other herbs may also feature.

Most think this herb-packed sauce originated with the gauchos, who roamed the fertile grasslands that are now in Argentina, Uruguay, and Paraguay during the nineteenth century. Some folk tales attribute its name to a corruption of the name of a European immigrant—maybe Jimmy McCurry or Jimmy Curry—who concocted the sauce using vinegar to tenderize the lean beef of the highlands. Whatever the truth of the matter, the taste clearly reflects the manifold flavours brought by the wave of arrivals from different European nations. **IA**

Taste: *Chimichurri has a vibrant flavour, the piquancy of which depends on the vinegar content. Its green herb freshness works nicely as a condiment to grilled steak.*

Gauchos traditionally ate chimichurri with their steak. »

Sunflower Seed

Sunflowers (*Helianthus annuus*) have a long history. Indigenous Americans were eating the energy-rich seeds of these bright flowers thousands of years ago. When sixteenth-century explorers brought the seeds back to Europe, the plants were at first grown only for decoration. However, when Peter the Great (1672–1725) brought the flowers to Russia, their arrival coincided with an edict banning the eating of oily plants on fast days: sunflowers, as a new introduction, were omitted from the list and so their seeds gained popularity. Today, sunflower oil is still the most important cooking oil in Russia, while plants are extensively cultivated in North America.

Sunflower seeds are a popular snack, particularly around eastern Europe. They can be purchased with or without the stripy hull, salted or unsalted, roasted or plain, from street vendors or at farmers' markets. While for many the ritual of cracking the salty hull with one's teeth, extracting the smooth seed, and spitting out the shell is a big part of the fun, the hulled seeds also make a fine addition to breads, biscuits, muffins, muesli, or granola. **SH**

Taste: *Plain sunflower seeds are crunchy and slightly oily with a lively, nutty taste that is overwhelmed by too much salt. The roasted seeds have a richer, toastier flavour.*

Sunflowers are known for their ability to grow to great
❮ heights; the heads can contain up to 2,000 seeds.

Pumpkin Seed

People have been eating pumpkin seeds since pumpkins were first cultivated probably more than 7,000 years ago. And for good reason. These flat, green seeds with a yellow-white hull are extremely nutritious and tasty. Spanish conquerors very likely learnt of them from the Aztecs and then took them back to Europe.

Today, since pumpkins are grown everywhere except for Antarctica, the seeds are available and eaten throughout the world. Most are consumed either raw or toasted as a snack food, but they also play a role in cooking. Called *pepitas* in Spanish, they are an ingredient in Mexican *moles*, derived from an ancient Aztec recipe made from pumpkin seeds, tomatillos, and other ingredients and served with chicken or duck.

Tossing them in olive oil and soy sauce before toasting is another way to make a delicious snack. Pumpkin seeds can also be turned into a delicious pesto. They are frequently used by vegetarians, who add them to salads and baked goods and use them ground in soups, stews, and casseroles. **SH**

Taste: *Pumpkin seeds have a chewy texture and a nutty flavour with just a hint of pumpkin. If some pumpkin pulp is left on before toasting, the pumpkin taste is stronger.*

Wattleseed

For nearly a century Australians have celebrated Wattle Day by wearing a wattle-blossom as a show of patriotism. There are many hundreds of varieties of this Australian acacia, from scrambling woody shrubs to tall trees, but all are recognized by their clusters of golden (or sometimes pink) flowers.

For thousands of years, Australian Aborigines in different groups around the country collected, cleaned, parched, and milled the seeds from around 120 varieties, baking the coarse flour into nourishing seed cakes, high in protein and unsaturated fats. However, as wheat flour became increasingly easy to come by, this practice became rare.

The humble wattle's fortunes were changed forever when, in 1984, Australian Vic Cherikoff accidentally over-roasted a unique species, creating the modern-day product known as wattleseed. The result of this happy accident is now available as a ground seed product, a liquid extract, and a paste, and is used around the world in ice cream, cream, chocolates, spreads, butters, breads, pancakes, biscuits, beverages, and other savouries. **VC**

Taste: *The short chocolate palate offers ongoing coffee notes but without the bitterness and with a nutty finish. Cream or milk unmasks these subtler flavours well.*

Lotus Seed

Somewhere or other in Asia, almost every part of the lotus plant is eaten. The rhizome is consumed in myriad ways; in Thailand, Vietnam, and parts of India, the stems and young leaves are valued vegetables; older leaves are used as wrappings; even the petals may be used as a garnish, or even eaten. The seeds are also beloved. They are sometimes eaten fresh out of hand but are more versatile when dried: in Vietnam they are often cooked in soups and stews.

In China, dried lotus seeds are used in sweet preparations. A thick sweet lotus paste is used to fill buns, particularly the mooncakes that are eaten during the Mid-Autumn Festival and the buns, shaped like a peach to symbolize long life, that are traditionally served at birthday parties. Candied, they are a traditional part of *cheun hup*—the box of sweets presented to visitors over Chinese New Year.

When buying dried lotus seeds, tiny holes indicate the presence of bugs. Seeds that are too yellow are too old; seeds that are too white have been bleached. **KKC**

Taste: *Lotus seeds have a starchy, subtly sweet flavour. They are delicious when roasted, which enhances the sweetness and gives them a flavour similar to corn.*

Lotus seeds can be seen growing in the top of curious, bowl-shaped pods. »

Pine Nut

Macadamia Nut

These small, creamy, ivory-coloured seeds also known as pine kernels, have been appreciated for their exquisite flavour since prehistoric times. The ancient Greeks and Romans knew and loved pine nuts: they are one of the foods archaeologists discovered in the ruins of Pompeii.

Although all of the numerous varieties of pine trees around the world produce seeds, only some are edible. Of these, the seeds of the Mediterranean (or Italian) stone pine, *Pinus pinea*, are particularly prized for their pronounced nutty flavour. It can take up to twenty-five years for a pine tree to crop, and seven years for the cones to mature sufficiently to release their seeds, so they are naturally expensive.

An essential ingredient in the exquisite Italian basil sauce pesto, pine nuts are paired with raisins and spinach in many Mediterranean cuisines. They are also fabulous added to salads and vegetables. They are high in monounsaturated fats (the good kind) and rich in protein, which does mean that they tend to go rancid quite quickly; they are best stored in the fridge. **LF**

Australian Aborigines have been eating macadamia nuts for millennia, gathering them from the tree they called *kindal kindal*. The Western culinary world, however, discovered them comparatively late. It was not until 1857 that two botanists came upon the trees in a Queensland rainforest and recorded the nuts' existence. Baron Ferdinand von Mueller described the tree botanically and Dr. Walter Hill named it after the pharmacist Dr. John Macadam.

Despite the difficulty in cracking their rock-hard shells, the nuts' qualities were soon recognized and small-scale commercial cultivation began. The Hawaiians made the first large-scale commercial planting in 1882, sparking an industry that now accounts for around 90 per cent of world production. *Macadamia integrifolia* and *M. tetraphylla* are the main edible species found in the wild and have been widely hybridized for agricultural use.

Most nuts are eaten plain or salted but they can be made into biscuits, cakes, confectionery, and ice cream. Small quantities of macadamia nut butter are also produced. **SC-S**

Taste: *Raw pine nuts have a soft, milky texture and a sweet, buttery flavour. Light toasting without fat releases a more prominent nutty flavour, inviting aroma, and crisp texture.*

Taste: *Mellow-flavoured and buttery, macadamias are best eaten unadorned with, at most, a little salt. Less brittle than harder nuts, they nonetheless have a satisfying crunch.*

The torpedo-shaped Italian nut is easily distinguished from the Chinese nut, which is more triangular.

Ginkgo Nut

Baobab Seed

The ginkgo tree is considered a living fossil, the last surviving species of a type that ruled the earth around 200 million years ago. Today the nuts—technically seeds—that appear during autumn are an important part of Chinese vegetarian cuisine.

Ginkgo biloba trees are either male or female, and pollination has to take place before the female bears seeds. Sadly for ginkgo-loving humans, many of whom would relish the thought of harvesting the abundant seeds of the female tree, there is a big drawback to having a ginkgo tree in your backyard: the soft pulp around the seed has a highly pungent, unpleasant smell, and gives off a sticky substance. Fortunately, ginkgo is cleaned before being sent to market. The smelly exterior is removed leaving a pristine, easy-to-crack, beige shell around the edible core, which is also sometimes removed for ease.

In China, ginkgo seeds are used in the well-known and appropriately named vegetarian dish, "Buddha's delight." In Japan, they frequently appear alongside other elements in the savoury custards known as *chawan mushi*. **KKC**

The monumental baobab tree (*Adansonia digitata*) provides one of the most striking silhouettes on the landscapes of Africa and Australia: its vast trunk sprouts tangled, root-like branches that look as if the tree has been planted upside down. Indeed, legend has it that the tree was uprooted by the gods and replanted after it complained about its appearance.

Taken from the elongated, velvet pods borne by the large, white pendulous flowers of the tree, baobab seeds are covered in a powdery white pulp that is rich in citric and tartaric acid, as well as having high levels of vitamin C, calcium, iron, and dietary fibre. The tart fruit pulp of the seeds is used to make a refreshing, astringent drink, which locals use to treat fever and diarrhoea. The pulp can substitute for cream of tartar and is also used in powder form to thicken sauces. The seeds are ground to make a creamy butter and a soft porridge.

The baobab tree offers vital shelter, food, and water (its trunk stores large quantities), among many other things. With so many valuable uses, it is no wonder it is also known as "the tree of life." **HFi**

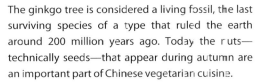

Taste: *Ginkgo nuts are waxy, tender, and slightly chewy; the flavour is like chestnuts, especially when roasted or grilled. Avoid canned, peeled, or vacuum-packed versions.*

Taste: *Encased in a hard brown shell, the seeds are coated in a powdery pulp, which has a mildly sour, light lemony taste. The seeds can be eaten raw or roasted.*

The ginkgo tree is the official tree of Kumamoto; it can often be found planted in avenues around the city.

Cashew Nut

Toasted and salted, the cashew nut's wonderful combination of delicate flavour, tangy salt, and smooth but crunchy texture has made them one of the world's favourite appetizers. Yet they have many other uses, too. Native to the coast of Brazil, the cashew tree, *Anacardium occidentale*, was exported by Portuguese colonizers first to Africa, then to Asia; it has since reached Australasia as well. Its curved nut is part of the cuisine of many countries, including India, Indonesia, China, and Vietnam.

In Brazil, the cashew nut has a staggering range of uses. Fresh cashews star, with egg whites and other additions such as shrimp and coconut, in the delicious *frigideira de maturi*; they can also be a part of the Bahian fish stew *moqueca*. The nuts are also used in baking and sweet-making; ground and crushed, they decorate the rim of ice cream goblets; and they are at the heart of cashew butter, a tasty spread used in a similar way to peanut butter. In South China, India, and Vietnam, cashews appear in many savoury dishes; in Indonesia they are part of the spicy fruit salad known as *rujak*. **AL**

Marcona Almond

Marcona almonds are cultivated throughout the Mediterranean provinces of Spain, from Catalunya down to Murcia. They were probably introduced to the region by the Moors in the thirteenth century but it was only during the twentieth century that they became widely cultivated when demand for dried fruits and pâtisserie products grew worldwide. The most highly prized marcona almonds are harvested in the mountainous regions of Alicante.

The marcona almond is a short, oval almond appreciated for its sweet flavour and high levels of fat. Various traditional almond products in Spain can only be made with marcona almonds if they wish to comply with quality standards of their respective PDOs. In Spain, marcona almonds are widely used for making traditional Christmas specialities such as *turrón de Jijona*. Similar to Middle Eastern *halva*, the main ingredients of *turrón* are almonds and honey.

Almond growers assess the quality of marcona almonds by eating them raw, straight out of the shell, as heating them allows some of the essential oils to escape. **RL**

Taste: *With a flavour between hazelnut and pistachio, the toasted cashew nut can win over most palates. It is also enticing when mixed with chocolate in sweets or truffles.*

Taste: *The sweet, buttery flavour of the marcona is evident when the nuts are drizzled in olive oil and lightly roasted. Fabulous with a little salt and a dry sherry.*

Almonds ripen on the tree; they can be harvested once the shell has split open to reveal the nut. »

Iranian Pistachio

Wild Green Hazelnut

The green, moreish nuts, brought to earth by Adam according to an Islamic legend, are indigenous to Iran and their name derives from the Persian *pesteh*. In their native soil, they grow to be larger than elsewhere. *Pesteh khâm* are the plain kind and *pesteh shoor*, the roasted salted ones.

The outer shell of a pistachio nut is hard. When the fruit reaches ripeness the shell starts to gape. Referred to as "laughing" in Iranian, the opening reveals the kernel, covered in a reddish skin. This is an indication of the freshness of the nut because it turns darker over time. Iranian pistachios have pale-green flesh, which is probably the reason behind the artificial green colour of "pistachio" ice cream. The colour of Iranian pistachios distinguishes them from Californian varieties, which are yellowish, but not those from Turkey, which are equally good to eat.

In classic Persian cooking raw pistachios are ground up, combined with cinnamon, green cardamoms, and saffron to flavour basmati rice dishes. It is an ingredient of the Persian *toot*—a nut paste bonbon served as a New Year treat. **MR**

In spring, the furry catkins of the wild hazelnut, less obtrusive than other hedgerow blooms, tell country dwellers all over Europe and North America where they will find nuts in August and September. Unlike blackberries and elderberries, crab apples and rosehips, a reminder is needed: the nuts themselves will be very well hidden underneath the leaves.

Sometimes called *filberts*—probably because St. Philibert's Day, August 20, traditionally marked the beginning of the season—green hazelnuts are a true wild delicacy. Larger, cultivated varieties, notably Kentish cobnuts, can also be bought green, but the pleasure of finding and eating your own lifts them to another level.

In nineteenth-century England, many regions of the country gave children a holiday on Holy Cross Day—September 14—so that they could go nutting. While hazel twigs were traditionally used as dowsing rods and the nuts used in love divinations, the main reason for collecting the nuts was always to eat them as fresh as possible. They lose their succulence in less than a week. **AMS**

Taste: *In texture, fresh pistachio is less brittle and less moist than an almond, but quite oily. Its taste is unique, and is at once recognized regardless of how it is served.*

Taste: *Green hazelnuts are crisp, milky, and sweet in the way that a raw pea is, but with a savoury twist. They are not that "nutty," but still as delicious as any ripe nut.*

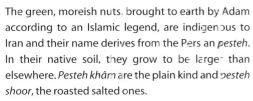

Pistachio nuts command high prices; they cost three or four times as much as other nuts.

Grenoble Walnut

Chestnut

When it comes to walnuts, the milky, magical nuts of Grenoble in the southeast of France are the crème de la crème. They were introduced to the region by the Romans and now carry an AOC certificate, which sets strict criteria for their production.

Walnuts are among the oldest tree-grown foods known to man—archaeologists uncovered petrified walnut shells dating back 8,000 years. The ancient Romans and Greeks thought that they so closely resembled the human brain, they must have special properties. They believed walnuts could cure headaches, but while there is little evidence to prove this theory, walnuts are now recognized as a so-called superfood because they are highly nutritious.

September heralds the new season for walnuts; the freshly picked walnuts are an unquestionable treat. As the season moves on, the nuts are kiln-dried and so the shells harden and the flesh develops vaguely bitter characteristics, although pronounced bitterness signals a rancid nut. It is possible to restore the newly picked flavour and texture by soaking the shelled kernels in milk overnight. **LF**

Throughout history, chestnuts have obligingly succumbed to canning, candying, drying, flour making, and more, but one of the simplest and most splendid ways to enjoy them is freshly roasted. Hot roasted chestnuts are one of the truly great joys of late autumn and early winter, especially when bought fresh from the glowing braziers of street vendors on crisp days during the run up to Christmas; the glorious aroma wafting through the air is almost as enjoyable as eating the actual nut itself.

On the tree, chestnuts are encased inside a green prickly burr. When the ripe burrs fall to the ground it can be opened to reveal the familiar brown-shelled nuts. A quick tip: if cooking them at home, cut slits in the shells beforehand to make them easier to open.

Chestnut flour is another seasonal speciality well worth trying. It is usually available for only a short period each year because of its limited keeping qualities, and is typically used in cakes, pasta, gnocchi, fritters, and batter. **LF**

Taste: *Grenoble walnuts have a delightful light crunch and an effortless chewiness. The tender, quite succulent kernel has a sweet milky flavour and mild nutty taste.*

Taste: *Inside its robust brown armour, the chestnut yields soft, faintly floury and deliciously sweet flesh; roasting brings out rich, nutty but slightly floral nuances.*

Traditionally, chestnuts were roasted on an open fire in a special perforated roasting pan. »

Pecan

Brazil Nut

Pecans take their name from the Algonquian word *paccan*, and were used by Native Americans for many thousands of years. Pecans were growing in Georgia, generally the largest pecan-producing state in the United States, long before the first settler arrived. They were mainstays in the local diet—especially during the winter months—and eaten out of hand or ground into a thickener for stews.

Today there are more than 1,000 varieties of pecan. Although they are also grown commercially in Mexico, Australia, South Africa, and parts of Latin America, they remain most associated with the United States: *Carya illinoinensis* is native to parts of the southern United States and northern Mexico.

Pecans may be eaten raw, used in batters for waffles and pancakes, turned into pecan butter, or included in stuffings for turkey, chicken, or duck. They are most often used, though, in various desserts, most famously the all-American tart known as pecan pie. Spiced pecans are often served as an appetizer, while sugared pecans appear on wedding buffet tables in the southeast United States. **SH**

In the Brazilian Amazon, the enormous tree called *Bertholletia excelsa* is known as the "forest ceiling" for good reason. It can grow to as much as 200 feet (60 m) tall, with a trunk more than 10 feet (3 m) in diameter. The fruit it bears—known as the *ourico*—can weigh up to just under 4 ½ pounds (2 kg). Inside the fruit, like jewels in a casket, nestle up to twenty-four seeds surrounded by hard, almost triangular shells—Brazil nuts.

Indigenous tribes have used Brazil nuts as the basis of their diet for centuries, but it is only relatively recently that they have gained importance in the rest of Brazil and elsewhere. They are harvested wild in the virgin rainforest from fruit that have fallen the long drop to the forest floor: in fact, the tree requires virgin rainforest to grow, since it relies on specific orchids and bees to pollinate it, and on animals known as *agoutis* to extract the seeds from its fruit.

Rich in selenium, Brazil nuts make a tempting addition to sweets, cakes, and ice creams, and are scrumptious coated in good quality dark chocolate. They are also fantastic toasted, whole or in slices. **AL**

Taste: *Pecan nuts are crisp, but not hard. Light to mild tasting, they have a rich, buttery flavour that is similar to a walnut yet without its bitterness.*

Taste: *Nothing beats eating Brazil nuts whole and raw. They have a pleasant, smooth crunch combined with a measured sweetness and a gentle oiliness.*

Brazil nut trees provide welcome shade from the searing heat of the Amazon rainforest. ❯❯

King Coconut

Coco de Mer

The king coconut (*Cocos nucifera*) is native to Sri Lanka, where it is known as *thembili* or *weware*, although it has also been introduced to India, Fiji, Indonesia, Malaysia, and the Philippines. The coconuts are frequently sold at the roadside, and the water of fresh, tender, young, green coconuts is prized as a refreshing drink called *kurumba* to combat the oppressive heat. Sellers cut off the top of the coconut and buyers drink the tender coconut water through a supplied straw.

The soft, spongy, and tangy kernel is eaten straight from the split nut by scooping it out with a spoon or using a piece of nut shaved from the shell. King coconut is widely used in cooking. Coconut milk—made from grated coconut meat and warm water—is added to curries, and coconut meat can be grated on salads or ground and mixed with red chillies and lime, and then heated to make *sambals*. It is also used as an ingredient in sweet dishes such as *halapes,* made from coconut meat and jaggery, and *kiri bath*, a thick rice pudding made with the creamy part of coconut milk. **CK**

Native to just two islands in the Seychelles's 115-island archipelago—Praslin and its near neighbour Curieuse—coco de mer is the prehistoric nut of a variety of fan palm. The nut is the largest seed in the world and can weigh up to 50 pounds (22 kg).

The mature nuts are, famously, an almost perfect representation of the lower torso of a rather shapely lady, so it comes as no surprise that they caused much comment among sailors and early explorers who found them floating in the sea. If that were not enough, both male and female trees are needed to produce the nut. Legend tells how at certain times of the year the enormous trees uproot themselves from Praslin's dense Vallée de Mai forest and make their way down to the beach to mate.

Inevitably the distinctively shaped nuts are in high demand as souvenirs, which has forced the Seychelles government to place strict controls on the 7,000 or so remaining trees. The government, has registered each tree and issues every harvested nut with an individual ID number to deter the black market trade. **WS**

Taste: *King coconut water has a very refreshing, sweet, mild flavour; the coconut meat has a tangy flavour and a soft, spongy texture.*

Taste: *The milky jelly inside can be scooped out and eaten as a soft pudding similar to Turkish delight. The flesh has a hint of mint and some consider it a powerful aphrodisiac.*

The coco de mer tree not only produces giant nuts, but also grows extraordinarily large palm leaves . »

Puy Lentil

Lentilles Vertes du Puy were the first French legume to enjoy AOC status. These small green lentils are farmed in a unique area of the Massif Central in south-central France that surrounds the village of Puy-en-Velay and benefits from a special microclimate, referred to as the "Foëhn effect."

In summer, the mountains to the southwest trap the cloud formations brought by the prevailing winds. The result is a high level of sunshine and clear skies in the zone, which generates extra heat that serves to stress the plants, which duly sweat out moisture. The plants then develop seeds (lentils) that are small, with lower protein levels and thinner skins than similar varieties—an evolutionary defect that becomes a gastronomic advantage. In cooking, the lentils soften more readily and are sweeter and less starchy than most other varieties.

Although featured by star chefs as a garnish, Puy lentils are best eaten as a simple rustic food, cooked with onions, garlic, herbs, and the local dry-cured *ventrèche* bacon, or combined with a mustard-flavoured vinaigrette into a *salade de lentilles*. **MR**

Urd

This small, oval, richly nutritious bean is one of India's most highly valued pulses. Also known as urad, black gram, urid beans, and matpe beans, urd have been cultivated since ancient times and are believed to be a relative of the mung bean. The seed of a trailing, very hairy annual herb, the beans grow in slim, cylindrical pods. Although native to southern Asia, they have now been planted in other tropical areas, mostly introduced by Indian immigrants.

Urd are a staple in the Punjab, where they are known as *maanh*. There they are often cooked with red kidney beans for a contrast of colour and texture. In northern India, Muslims cook them whole; in the south the beans are skinned and ground to a flour for making wafe-like *dosas*, crisp *papads*, and steamed *idlis*, while across the subcontinent they are hulled, split, and eaten as urad dhal. Naturally low in fat, high in fibre, and protein rich, urd have a dull, black skin covering the creamy-yellow beans inside. With their skins on, they are often sold as "black lentils," whereas split and with their skins removed, they are labelled as "white lentils." **WS**

Taste: *Properly cooked Puy lentils should not be hard and gritty, nor mushy or floury. The taste has a delicate hint of sweetness that blends with the ingredients around it.*

Taste: *More gelatinous than either mung beans or other varieties of lentil and split pea, whole urd have a comfortingly creamy texture and a rich, earthy flavour.*

Lentils grow in flat, delicate pods in Puy-en-Velay,
France; they were introduced there by the Gauls.

Tiger Nut

Tiger nuts (*Cyperus esculentus*) are not really nuts at all, but small tubers. They look a little like crumpled peanuts. In Spain, they are more commonly known as chufa nuts and are the principal ingredient in one of Spain's most famous drinks, *horchata de chufa*, a refreshing summery concoction made from ground chufa nuts mixed together with sugar and water and often embellished with cinnamon and lemon.

The plant is known to have been cultivated since ancient times, with evidence of its use having been found in early Egyptian tombs. It is thought that the Moors introduced the plant to Spain, where Valencia in particular was found to provide an ideal growing environment. The plants have subsequently flourished there.

Once they are harvested, the tubers are dried over the course of several months, after which they can be stored for a number of years. They can be reconstituted by a period of soaking and then boiling, which nudges out a subtle sweetness that is not as pronounced in the dried nut. **LF**

Taste: *Chewy on the outside, soft and milky on the inside, tiger nuts have a delightful flavour that can be compared to a young hazelnut, with hints of almond and coconut.*

In Spain, cafes sell the popular drink horchata de chufa. »

Purple Rice

Also known as black glutinous or red rice, this native of Thailand is the Rolls Royce of the rice world. It's inappropriately named, though, as the grains contain no gluten and are black or rust-red rather than purple. When raw, the grains can best be described as looking like brown rice that has been burnt. However, as they cook, colour seeps out, staining the whole grain and giving the cooked dish a uniform indigo hue.

Although purple rice is gluten free it does contain two kinds of starch, amylose and amylopectin, and the more amylopectin the grains contain, the stickier they are when cooked.

The rice is most commonly eaten as a feast day dessert in south east Asia, in the form of a sticky pudding. The grains are first soaked for several hours or overnight to shorten their cooking time and then steamed for around forty-five minutes, rather than boiled. As the colour leaches out, it dyes the inside of the bamboo steamer (and the hands of the cook) a vivid purplish-black and whilst this will not wash away, it does fade quite quickly. **WS**

Taste: *Purple rice has a natural, subtly sweet flavour but many cooks add extra sugar according to personal taste. Purple sticky rice pudding is served hot with coconut milk.*

Wild Rice

Not actually a rice, but an aquatic grass, wild rice (*Zizania aquatica*) is native to North America. It has been eaten since prehistoric times and was a staple in the diets of the early inhabitants of North America. Native Americans call it *manomin* or "good berry." It is also known as Canadian rice, squaw rice, water oats, and marsh oats. In French, it is *riz sauvage*.

In its natural state, wild rice grows along lake and river banks in the Great Lakes region, which includes the Canadian provinces of Ontario and Quebec and eight U.S. states. A slightly different species is also native to ecologically similar habitats in Asia. Cultivated wild rice is grown in flooded fields or paddies in Minnesota, California, and elsewhere.

Aromatic kernels of wild rice have a black-brown hue and open like a butterfly when cooked. The quality of the rice depends a great deal on how carefully it is harvested. Long, slender, unbroken grains are the best and the most costly. Lumberjacks once ate wild rice mixed with honey as a hot cereal, similar to oatmeal. Today, it is used in pilafs, stuffings, salads, soups, and many other dishes. **SH**

Taste: *Wild rice blends well with other ingredients. It has a firm texture and a nutty, grassy taste. Some varieties have an earthy flavour somewhat like wild mushrooms.*

The wild rice plants grown in Texas have been declared an endangered species. »

Buckwheat Groat

Despite its name, buckwheat (*Fagopyrum esculentum*) is not a cereal like wheat or barley. Belonging to the same family as rhubarb and sorrel, it is native to Siberia and northern China. Crusaders brought it to Europe during the Middle Ages.

Buckwheat is commonly ground into dark, gritty flour that can be used to make anything from pancakes to noodles. It has dark, roughly triangular seeds that when left whole are known as "groats." These can be hulled, cracked, or even sprouted and used as a green vegetable in salads. Raw groats can be used as a seasoning, but their bitter flavour means that they are usually hulled and toasted in oil for a few minutes before being used in cooking.

Buckwheat groats can be added to pilafs, soups, and stews. Russian and Polish immigrants introduced buckwheat groats to the United States, where they are known as kasha. They are used as a filling for the fried or baked snacks known as knishes or served with noodles and vegetables as varnishkes. In Eastern Europe, however, kasha refers to a number of cooked grains including buckwheat. **CK**

Taste: *Raw buckwheat groats are rather bitter. Toasted they have a sweet, nutty earthy flavour and are plump and tender in texture. They make an ideal stuffing.*

The buckwheat from meadows in Japan is used mainly in noodles. »

Pearl Barley

Barley was once a staple, the most important European food grain, but it has been supplanted by wheat and is now used primarily for making beer.

To turn the grains into pearl barley, the outer husks are discarded and the kernel is polished This process, known as pearling, produces fine, medium, or baby "pearls" that can be left whole, flaked, cut (grits), or ground into flour. Containing about 80 per cent starch, it looms large in vegetarian cooking. However, it also has its place in European regional cuisines. *Orzotto,* a barley equivalent of risotto, is popular throughout northern Italy. In Russia, it occurs in both savoury and sweet *kasha,* grain dishes that are midway between porridge and pudding. In Scotch broth, a traditional soup-stew, partly pearled barley (pot barley) adds both body and texture

The flour does contain some gluten, the protein that gives elasticity to bread, but a barley loaf requires the addition of some wheat flour to the dough for it to rise satisfactorily. Scalded pearl barley is also the basis of the popular cordial lemon barley water. **MR**

Freekeh

Since ancient times this highly nutritious wheat grain has played an important part in Middle Eastern cuisines, particularly those of Jordan, Lebanon, and Syria. The wheat is harvested while still young, soft, and green and the stalks are then roasted and smoked over open wood fires to preserve the nutritional value and "green" taste before being hulled. In the past, tiny stones would sometimes creep in among the wheat and threaten the teeth of unsuspecting diners, but modern harvesting and processing methods keep dentists' bills to a minimum.

High in fibre, low in carbohydrates, and with a low GI, freekeh (pronounced "free-ka") can replace rice or couscous in salads, stuffings, vegetarian burgers, breads, or pilafs, but in Middle Eastern homes one of the most popular ways to serve it is in a stew. Whole-grain freekeh is quite coarse and dark greeny-brown and needs to be simmered for around forty-five minutes in water or stock to tenderize it. Cracked grain freekeh is browner and blander and requires a shorter cooking time. **WS**

Taste: *Grains of pearl barley have a chewy texture allied to an almost slippery surface. The taste is relatively bland but it soaks up the flavours of accompanying ingredients.*

Taste: *The cooked grains have a slightly smoky, rich— almost meaty—flavour and add a pleasingly nutty texture to both hot and cold dishes.*

Ripened barley ready for cutting by
⊗ *a loch in the lowlands of Scotland.*

Polenta

Couscous

Polenta is a cornmeal grain that has become very fashionable outside Italy, even though it was traditionally a food favoured by the poor. When meat and fresh foods were scarce during World War II, it became a principal part of the Italian diet in many regions, but in fact it had been an important staple in the north of Italy for hundreds of years. In the Fruili and Veneto regions, it was more popular than bread.

The name polenta is taken from the Latin *pulmentum*, which was the mainstay of the Roman legionnaires' diet. *Pulmentum* was made from an ancient variety of wheat, with the grain toasted on hot stones. When Christopher Columbus introduced corn into Europe in the fifteenth century, the abundant rainfall in the north of Italy meant that the new crop flourished.

Polenta was cooked over the fireplace, with a stream of the golden grains poured into boiling water and stirred for forty-five minutes until it formed a thick yellow mass. It was then served with cheese, or a small amount of meat if it was available. **LF**

It is a sign of the times that couscous granules, which have required slow and careful steaming to render them tender and edible since at least the thirteenth century, are now available in quick-cooking varieties that soften within minutes in boiling water. The tiny dried dough balls that were traditionally handmade from freshly ground whole grains are now mass-produced global comfort food.

Durum wheat couscous is still a staple of its home territory, the Maghreb, where the steamed grains are served in many guises, just like rice. Couscous is best known in the dish that bears its name: the grains are steamed over a spicy stew in the top of a two-tier, perforated vessel called a *kiskis* in Arabic but better known in the West by its French name *couscoussier*. The stew is eventually served on top of the soft grains that have cooked in its steaming juices.

Generic, uniform grains are readily available in Western supermarkets, but in the Middle East and in Middle Eastern food stores overseas, there is more variety, and dry grains can range in size. **BLeB**

Taste: *Polenta has a granular texture and bland flavour in its basic form. However, with strong cheese or other ingredients it is wonderful served with stews and sauces.*

Taste: *The slightly sweet, but neutral flavour of couscous makes it an ideal backdrop for highly spiced meat and vegetable mixtures. Leftover grains make excellent salads.*

Handmade, ceramic tagines are used to cook the stews traditionally served with couscous. ❯

Fregola Pasta

Tajarin

Although it is often mistaken for a type of grain because of its coarse appearance, fregola is a golden wheat pasta speciality that comes from Sardinia. It is similar in some ways to couscous, and in fact is sometimes referred to as Sardinian couscous. Both products consist of fine pellets of pasta created when durum wheat (semolina) and water are rubbed together; the name fregola comes from the Italian verb *fregare*, which means "to rub." Little known outside Sardinia until relatively recently, fregola is becoming increasingly popular because, unlike couscous, it is lightly toasted after being dried and therefore takes on an exquisite nutty flavour. The beads of fregola are larger than couscous, too.

Little is recorded about the arrival of pasta fregola on the culinary scene; some Sardinians are adamant that fregola was their own creation, but it is more likely it was first introduced to Sardinia when Genovese navigators returned from the last crusade.

Fregola is incredibly versatile. Often served in soups and broths, most notably with clams, it can also be used as a substitute for couscous. **LF**

Tajarin (pronounced ta-ya-reen) is a wonderful speciality pasta that originated in the Langhe, a hilly area in Piemont, northern Italy. It is similar to fine tagliatelle, with long flat strands that are usually no wider than ⅛ inch (2 mm). It has a glorious flavour and beautiful golden colour. In Italy, it is easy to buy special eggs, with strikingly yellow yolks, for pasta making: these eggs come from hens that have been fed with a particular dye. The colour of tajarin, however, is pronounced because it contains a far higher proportion of egg yolks than more common varieties of egg pasta.

Traditionally tajarin was always home-made, and mixed and cut by hand. All but the wealthiest of women would have been taught the art of creating it as a matter of course.

Alba is the principal town in the Langhe and is famous for its exquisite white truffles. Tajarin has a wonderful affinity with them; the combination is unforgettable. Fresh white truffles grated over butter-tossed tajarin, or tajarin with truffle butter, must surely be on the menu in heaven. **LF**

Taste: *Served unadorned, pasta fregola has a moist, pleasantly chewy bite and an appealing nutty taste. It will also happily absorb other flavours.*

Taste: *Tajarin has an elegant, faintly eggy richness and exhibits superb buttery nuances. Cooked until al dente, its texture is velvety but with a graceful robustness.*

Alba market is famous for the fresh white truffles that partner tajarin pasta so well. ❯❯

Durum Wheat Spaghetti

There are two basic types of pasta that Italians eat and have made famous around the world; fresh egg pasta and dried pasta. Neither is seen as better in the eyes of the Italians; each kind simply serves a different purpose.

Dried pasta is made from durum wheat flour; *durus* being the Latin word for "hard." A law passed in Italy in 1967 states that all dried pasta, including that which contains egg, must be made with durum wheat; it is the high gluten content that gives the pasta its distinctive texture and bite when cooked. Pasta made outside Italy is often made with other types of flour and hence can never be cooked al dente as pasta should.

As with most traditional Italian foods, the exact beginnings of pasta are disputed. Many give Marco Polo the credit for bringing it across from China; the Chinese were eating noodles as long ago as 2000 BCE. On the other hand, frescoes found in ancient tombs near Rome show people making flour and water pastes, although it is believed the dough may have been baked on flat stones rather than boiled. **LF**

Taste: *Good dried pasta should not simply be a vehicle for sauce, but should have a voice of its own, with a subtle, almost nutty flavour and pleasing toothsome texture.*

Tortelli di Zucca

Not to be missed, tortelli di zucca are gorgeous little Italian pasta parcels with a pumpkin-based filling. The ingredients combined with the pumpkin will vary from region to region, but perhaps the most famous tortelli di zucca are those from Mantua, (or Mantova as it is known in Italy). In Mantua, the pumpkin used to make the filling is usually a local variety known as *Marina di Chioggia*. It is cooked and mixed with crushed amaretti biscuits, grated Parmesan cheese, and *mostarda*, a wonderful savoury-sweet conserve typical of the area made from fruit and mustard oil. The intriguing piquant but syrupy *mostarda* complements the sweet flesh of the pumpkin beautifully. Tortelli di zucca is sensational tossed with melted butter and sage, but occasionally a tomato and bacon sauce is offered as an alternative.

Tortelli di zucca is eaten throughout the autumn and winter, but it is traditionally always served as part of the feast on Christmas Eve. As with all things Italian, each family will have its own secret classic recipe, handed down through generations from mother to daughter. **LF**

Taste: *Tortelli di zucca parcels have a buttery, vaguely sweet, pleasantly salty filling with a delightful smack of mustard fruits, enhanced by a wrapping of egg-rich pasta.*

The art of making perfect fresh pasta for tortelli parcels requires great attention to detail. »

Kisoba Noodle

Japanese soba noodles are buckwheat noodles—but because pure buckwheat flour does not bind together well, most soba noodles are in fact made with a combination of buckwheat flour and wheat flour. However, aficionados believe that the best taste comes from noodles made with buckwheat alone. These pure noodles are known as kisoba.

Soba noodles are something of a paradox in Japan. They are a sustaining everyday food, available on every station platform, but also a sacrosanct food, associated with shrines and temples. It is at the shrines and temples that kisoba will most often be served, from the specialist noodle shops that are usually found there.

Purists eat them entirely on their own, cold and without any dipping sauce, in a style known as *mori soba* (*mori* means "to heap"). However, they are usually served with a little dried nori on top and a small cup of soy sauce-based broth in which to dip them, and from which they are noisily slurped. Such slurping is thought polite, and it is said that taking in air while eating kisoba enhances the flavour. **SB**

Taste: *Rich and earthy with a delicate, satisfying sweetness of flavour. When cooked al dente, kisoba has a firmness akin to wholewheat pasta.*

Sanuki Udon Noodle

Sanuki udon are thick, wheat flour noodles that originate from the Sanuki (now known as Kagawa) prefecture in Japan. The area does not have enough rainfall for extensive rice cultivation, and so wheat and wheat noodles have become a speciality.

Sanuki noodles are famed for their strong body and chewy texture, as well as their smoothness, which gives an attractive *nodogushi*—the feeling as the noodles slips down the throat. The other crucial factor in their appeal is the ratio of salt and water used when they are made, which changes according to the season; 1:3 is considered optimum in summer, making them saltier than in winter, when a ratio of 1:6 is preferred.

Udon noodles have always been popular in western Japan, although in the east buckwheat noodles have traditionally been preferred. However the 2002 publication of an enormously successful Sanuki Udon travel guide (*Osorubeki Sanuki Udon*—"Magic of Sanuki Udon") led to a boom in popularity. Specialist shops have now sprung up in Tokyo, nationwide, and even overseas. **SB**

Taste: *Silky smooth with a chewy texture. The slightly salty, bread-like taste complements the delicate dashi and soy sauce flavour of the broth they are cooked in.*

Fen Si Noodle

Laksa Noodle

Fen si is better known in English as glass noodles, cellophane noodles, or mung bean noodles. Their resemblance to glass or cellophane is more apparent after they have been rehydrated—the wh teish, pliable, slightly wrinkled noodles then become smooth and translucent.

The noodles do not have any particular taste of their own, but they have a pleasantly tender "bite" and absorb the flavour of whatever they are cooked with. They are made from the famously versatile mung bean, which is ground into a smooth paste and then shaped and dried.

Usually sold in convenient packages perfect for home cooking, the tidiest way to separate a large bundle of noodles into smaller portions is to pull it apart while still in its bag. This stops the small pieces that break off from flying everywhere. They are then easily prepared for cooking by soaking them in hot water for about ten minutes. Although less common, dry (unhydrated) noodles can also be fried, which makes them puff up slightly and turn white and crunchy. These are usually used as a garnish. **KKC**

Modern-day laksa noodles are intimately linked to the "Nonya" cuisine, a hybridized form of regional Chinese and Malayan cookery styles.

Round, slippery, and made from rice, laksa noodles are the basis of spicy soups that are eaten as snack meals. They are classic street food, sold by hawkers at all hours, right or day. These soups may be thick and curry-like, containing bean curd and prawns and seasoned with *rempah*, a paste made from chillies, candlenuts, and fermented fish paste, or the broth can be paler, similar in texture to hot and sour Thai soups.

Laksa has also been adopted by fusion cooks working in Australia and New Zealand, who have added their personal imprint. Many local recipes exist, but the broth usually includes coconut milk and chilli. The island of Penang, for instance, is famed for its *assam laksa*, which contains shredded mackerel and is flavoured with tamarind, galangal, lemongrass, and mint. Instead of the traditional laksa noodle, some cooks prefer rice vermicelli or even wheat-based noodles. **MR**

Taste: *Although they have no real taste themselves, fen si's texture and consistency make them a popular base for a wide range of Asian dishes, from soups to spring rolls.*

Taste: *In a curry-style laksa, the noodles are almost coated by the sauce and the dish can be eaten without a spoon, but the more soupy laksas have the texture of a broth.*

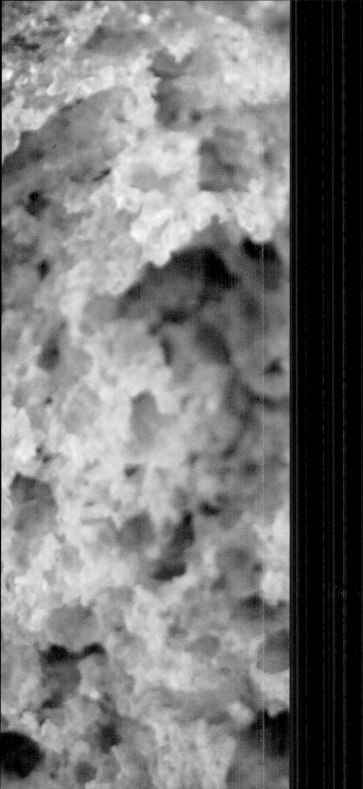

Bakery

Cornish Pasty

Samosa

The Cornish pasty, as its name suggests, does indeed originate from Cornwall, the most southwestern county of England. This substantial filled pastry was once a traditional, regional, working man's food but is now widely produced and consumed. Easily portable, pasties were historically eaten for lunch by Cornish tin and copper miners. Legend has it that the thick pastry crimp characterizing the Cornish pasty was used as a convenient handle by miners. The miners' wives were said to mark their husband's initials on their pasties when they made them.

Pasties range in shape from oval to semi-circular and are generally made from shortcrust pastry. Meat pasties are the best known, filled with chopped (not minced) beef skirt or chuck steak, swede, onion, and potato, and simply flavoured with salt and plenty of pepper. There are several variations, however, including cheese and potato, cheese and leek, and egg and bacon. To make a pasty, the filling ingredients are added uncooked, sealed in the uncooked pastry, and baked. Ideally, Cornish pasties should be eaten warm from the oven. **JL**

Of all South Asia's myriad snacks, this filled, fried or baked pastry parcel is probably the best-known. A popular street food in India, Pakistan, Bangladesh, and Sri Lanka, it is also found around the world, reflecting the South Asian diaspora. It is one of a large "family" of filled pastries eaten in many regions, such as the Middle East's *sambusak*.

Traditionally, samosas are triangular in shape, varying, however, considerably in size, from dainty bite-sized morsels, served at drinks parties, to large, substantial creations. Key to its popularity is its versatility; this is a food with many forms. Fillings range enormously—potato with ginger and garlic, cauliflower, spiced lamb mince, minced fish, or chicken—and can be mild, fragrant with aromatic spices, or formidably hot, laced with green or red chilli. A crisp, flaky pastry coating is characteristic, but the pastry can also vary in texture. In South Asia, samosas are often served with a fresh mint or coriander leaf chutney. Production varies from domestic or small-scale to large-scale industrial, making both frozen and ready-cooked samosas. **JL**

Taste: *A pasty at its best has a fine layer of crumbly, golden-brown pastry wrapped around a peppery and moist, meaty filling of steak, potato, onion, and swede.*

Taste: *It is the contrast of textures that makes samosas so satisfying—the fine, crisp, golden pastry coating gives way to a deliciously spiced vegetable or meat filling.*

Deep-fried samosas, also known as patties or curry puffs, are popular across South Asia. »

Empanada

Believed to have been unassumingly created in Galicia, Spain, when finely chopped meat or fish was wrapped in two layers of pastry, the empanada is one of Spain's most popular culinary contributions to Hispanic America. Taking the shape of a *media luna* (half moon) and traditionally sealed one at a time, empanadas can be oven-cooked or fried. Although their size and fillings vary, they are generally enjoyed as a starter, snack, or quick meal.

The pride of the national cuisines of Bolivia, Colombia, Peru, Uruguay, Venezuela, and Mexico, the empanada has, however, found its richest expression in Argentina. Popular both at home and in bars and restaurants, Argentina has its own particular pastry recipe using wheat flour and beef fat. Among the fillings, nothing beats beef chopped with a knife and mixed with fresh seasoning, spices, chilli, boiled egg, and olives, all fried in beef fat. Versions with chicken, white corn, ham, and cheese are equally delicious. The empanada even makes an appearance as a dessert, for example filled with the country's famed *dulce de leite* (sweet milk syrup). **AL**

Tamale

This Mexican, Central American, and South American delicacy dates back at least to the time Columbus discovered the New World and quite possibly much earlier. Tamales may have been made when prehistoric peoples began processing corn with ashes or slaked lime. This process softens the corn, making it easier to both grind and digest. To make a tamale, the corn dough is then wrapped in corn husks or banana leaves and steamed or baked.

Plain tamales can be made very simply, but they are often mixed with other ingredients, including spices, vegetables such as squash and beans, meats such as beef, pork, and chicken, and fish. Tamales are commonly served plain, but they are delicious eaten with a savoury and spicy sauce. They can even be served as desserts: *tamales de dulce* or sweet tamales are filled with sugar, jams, fruits, or nuts.

A basic tamale recipe includes *masa harina* (dough flour), salt, fat (most often lard), and a liquid such as chicken broth, milk, or water. Although tamales can be eaten on any occasion, they are traditionally served at Christmas celebrations. **JH**

Taste: *Though tasty when fried, it is best to eat empanadas fresh from the oven, made with a juicy filling and crunchy pastry. Heavenly with a few drops of chilli sauce.*

Taste: *Plain tamales boast a sweet corn taste and a soft, spongy texture. Always best warm, flavoured tamales should showcase the flavourings of the other ingredients.*

Kulebiaka

Melton Mowbray Pork Pie

The naming of this rich Russian pie is often disputed. Does it derive from *kulebyachit*, to knead with the hands (the pastry part is a kind of brioche), or does it come at one remove from the German *kohlebacken*, which means to bake with coals? Etymology apart, it gained prominence at the turn of the twentieth century as coulibiac, when it joined the repertoire of international haute cuisine.

The standard version is a large salmon *pâté en croûte* filled with hard-boiled eggs and rice flavoured with dill. Auguste Escoffier's *Guide Culinaire* (1903) insisted that it should include vesiga, a sturgeon's spinal marrow. In Russian cookery, though, there are many different kinds. At its simplest, it can be filled with cabbage, but this can be substituted with meat, mushrooms, or other combinations of savoury ingredients. In effect, it is the big brother of the smaller Russian patties known as *pirozki*, that can be both simple street food or delicacies fit for a Tsar. Kulebiaka is normally shaped in a rectangular parcel for easy slicing, although some fanciful interpretations resemble a sucking pig. **MR**

The first printed recipe for the pork pie apparently appeared in an English court cookbook in the fourteenth century. It is a raised pie in which a hot water crust encloses a ball of simply seasoned chopped or minced pork, and its easy portability perhaps explains its popularity among huntsmen.

Pork pies have long been associated with the Leicestershire market town of Melton Mowbray, and producers there—among them Dickinson & Morris, which bakes 4,000 pies a week, and the award-winning Nelsons of Stamford—take pride in the Melton Mowbray difference. After the pastry has been pressed into shape using a wooden implement called a dolly, it is filled with seasoned, chopped, fresh pork—which will be grey after cooking—then sealed. The pies are baked without hooped supports, producing the characteristic saggy sides. As the pie cools, the meat contracts, leaving a space between pastry and filling. This is filled with jelly made from pigs' trotters, which is poured into one of two holes cut into the lid of the pie. This was originally done to prolong the life of the pie. **ES**

Taste: *The kulebiaka pastry should be crisp and buttery. The moist, thick strip of wild salmon fillet contrasts with a creamy layer of eggs and rice with dill notes.*

Taste: *Crisp, dark, lard-rich pastry makes a delicious casing for a firm pork filling with a slight spiciness from the seasoning of white pepper.*

Injera

Injera is so central to Ethiopia and Eritrea's way of life that the standard daily greeting is "Have you eaten injera today?" This spongy, pancake-like flatbread is the staple food that lays the foundation for every meal. It is prepared daily and can take up to three days to be ready to cook. Injera is usually made from ground tef, a grain native to Ethiopia and the country's most important cereal crop. However, it can also be made using ground barley, corn, sorghum, or wheat. A mix of flour, water, salt, and sometimes yeast are left to ferment for up to three days. The batter is then cooked on a clay plate known as a *mogogo*, which is placed over a fire or on top of a special electric plate.

Injera is served with most meals and traditionally accompanies another Ethiopian classic dish, *wat,* a spicy meat or vegetable stew. An injera is laid down, rather like a plate, and then *wat* is spooned on top. Additional injera is served and small pieces of this are torn off and used to scoop up the *wat.* Once the food is eaten, the "plate"—having soaked up all the tasty juices—is also eaten. **SBI**

Tortilla

When the Spanish conquistadors landed on Mexican shores in the sixteenth century, they discovered corn, or maize, a crop that had been cultivated for several millennia by the Aztec and Maya peoples, possibly as far back as 1,000 BCE. Considered a gift of the gods, maize was a staple food of these ancient peoples, and legend has it that tortillas, known as *tlaxcalli* in the indigenous Nahuatl language, were invented by a peasant for a hungry king.

Corn was often soaked in lime and then ground up into a paste or dough called *masa*. It would then be flattened and cooked on both sides over a hot griddle. The Spanish named them tortillas or "little cakes." Whereas homemade corn tortillas are the most authentic and tasty kind, wheat or flour tortillas evolved when Mexicans moved north in the 1700s into what is now Texas, Arizona, and California, where corn was not as plentiful as wheat.

Tortillas are used to sop up food, but they can also be combined with meats, cheeses, chilli sauces, and vegetables. They are also used to make burritos, quesadillas, and enchiladas. **JH**

Taste: *Light, airy, and spongy in texture, injera has a tangy, sour flavour. Its fundamentally bland taste is ideal for absorbing the spicy, strong flavours of other foods.*

Taste: *Proper tortillas only contain cornmeal or wheat flour, water, and salt. Corn tortillas should have a chewy, slightly dense texture and a slightly sweet but mild taste.*

Tortilla dough is shaped by hand and then slapped straight onto a hot griddle to cook. »

Pane Carasau

This delightful Sardinian flatbread is so wafer-thin that it is also known as *carta di musica*, from the term for the paper on which music was written. An ancient bread, it was eaten in great quantities by shepherds who had to live in the mountains with their grazing flocks for many months. They wrapped it in cloth and tucked it easily into their bags. It was light to carry on their long and solitary journey, and formed an invaluable staple in their limited diet. The bread's crisp, dry texture gives it fantastic keeping qualities; stored away from moisture, it will make excellent eating after many, many months.

Explorers and hermits aside, pane carasau's longevity is possibly less likely to be tested these days, but it remains remarkably delicious and versatile. It can be nibbled at just as it is, or drizzled with olive oil and oven baked for added crunch. It can be moistened with water and rolled around a filling, used as pasta would be in a makeshift lasagne, or star in the wonderful Sardinian recipe *pane frattau,* moistened with stock and topped with tomatoes, pecorino, and a poached egg. **LF**

Taste: *Usually found in feather-light discs, pane carasau is pale parchment in colour. It has a pleasant, slightly grainy texture and a subtle salty crunch.*

The dough blows up into a bubble in the oven and is then split in two. »

Barbari

Nan

This traditional Persian bread can be found all over Iran, freshly baked and piled high in bakeries ready to be taken home for the next meal. Its full name is *nan-e-barbari*, meaning bread of the Barbars—a people who live near the eastern borders of Iran in Afghanistan—and it is said that it was the Barbars who introduced barbaree to Iran.

There are many regional breads in Iran, but as well as barbari, there are three other national flatbreads: *sangak*, *lavash*, and *taftun*, and bakeries tend to specialize in making an individual bread. Barbari is the second most common type of flatbread. It can be made from white or wholemeal flour and is made into long, oblong shapes about 1 inch (2.5 cm) thick and lightly baked to a pale, golden colour.

The baker marks grooves down the length of the dough before it is baked. Traditionally, this is done in a domed brick oven heated by coals, and it bakes very quickly—in about five minutes. Barbari is most often eaten at breakfast and is popularly served with the feta-like cheese *tabriz*. **SBI**

The word "nan" is actually a Persian word, meaning bread, although it is now used in India, Pakistan, and Afghanistan, and into central Asia. Most people in the West, think of nan as the leavened bread commonly served in Indian restaurants. The bread's distinctive teardrop shape comes from the flattened dough, which is cooked stuck to the side of a clay tandoor oven, being stretched downwards during baking. Yoghurt and milk are often added to give volume to the dough. Nan can be plain, brushed with ghee, or sprinkled with seasonings such as sesame seeds. They are sometimes stuffed; *keema* nan is stuffed with minced meat, whereas *Peshwari* and *Kashmiri* nan are filled with nuts and raisins.

There are, however, numerous other examples of nan breads. Uzbekistan makes *goshtli nan*, which is stuffed with minced meat, *shirmay nan*, which is made with chickpeas, and a bran bread, *jirish nan*. Iran makes a sweetened nan called *nan-e-shir*. In its various incarnations, nan is a staple food at meals throughout central and South Asia and is usually torn into pieces and used to scoop up the food. **SBI**

Taste: *Crisp, golden, and often sprinkled with salt or sesame seeds on the outside, barbari is soft and tender when you break into it.*

Taste: *Tastes and textures vary, but a classic plain nan, such as that found in India, has a light smoky flavour, is crisp on the outside, and tender in the centre.*

Stretched nan dough is smacked against the clay walls of the oven, and a lid put in place to retain heat. ❯❯

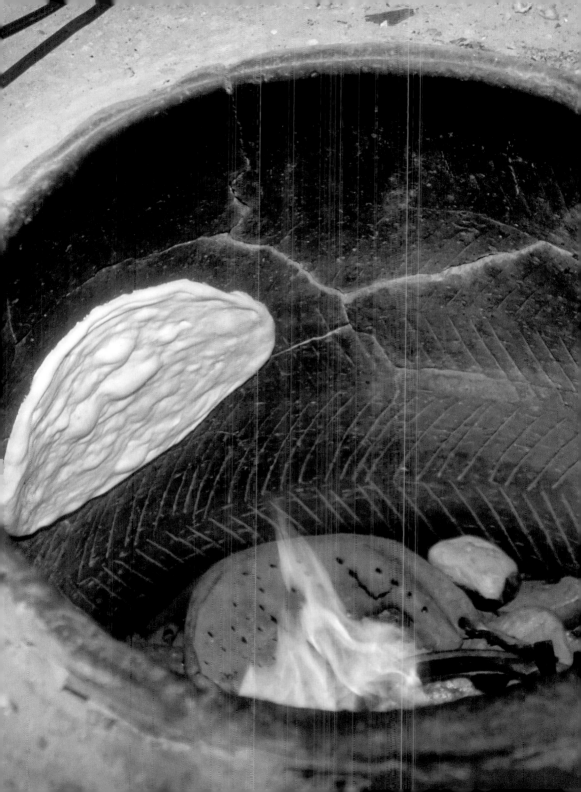

San Francisco Sourdough

Pain au Levain Naturel

Nearly as well known a symbol of San Francisco as the Golden Gate Bridge, sourdough bread began its rise to fame in 1849 when the influx of "gold rushers" brought a subsequent increase in bakeries. To bake leavened bread, in this era before the invention of bakers' yeast, "starters" were used. A fermented mixture of flour and water was saved from making one batch of bread and used to start off the next. Leavened bread was most likely discovered by accident by the Egyptians thousands of years ago.

Bakers who came to San Francisco found that when they baked their bread, it had a different and unidentifiable taste. Some say it was the San Francisco fog; others suspect it was wild yeast from the nearby grape-growing region that changed the flavour. They called it sourdough and the name stuck.

Although there are many bakeries making sourdough in San Francisco and elsewhere, the original San Francisco sourdough was made by the Boudin family from France. The legendary bakery still makes sourdough bread from a starter derived from the one made in 1849. **SH**

Pain au levain is delicious, gutsy sourdough bread made with a fermented starter rather than commercially made yeast. It is believed that the Egyptians inadvertently gave us the first leavened bread as long ago as 2,300 BCE when they discovered that dough left uncovered for several days began to rise (as a result of being infected with airborne yeast spores.) They baked the batch of dough regardless, and it produced a wonderful light bread.

Although manufactured yeast allows bread to rise in one to two hours, naturally leavened breads take many hours. When the starter is mixed with whole grain flour and salt, carbon dioxide is produced and fermentation continues. The slow rising of the dough creates a loaf with good old-fashioned flavour.

The name Poilâne is synonymous with pain au levain naturel. In 1932 Pierre Poilâne opened a bakery in Paris and made bread using stoneground flour, natural fermentation, and a wood-fired oven. Slowly but surely, he transformed what was essentially a rustic sourdough bread into an authentic luxury product, which is still sold all around the globe. **LF**

Taste: *Sourdough bread has a slightly sour yet wheaty taste, which makes it great for dipping into seafood stew. It has a chewy crust and a firm texture.*

Taste: *Dense, chewy, and flavoursome with a thick, golden crust, pain levain au naturel has a pleasant sour taste that goes well with both savoury and sweet.*

The Poilâne bakery's trademark is a curly initial "P." It is carved into each loaf at the bakery in Paris. »

Pain de Campagne
Pain Poilâne
3,87 le kg

Pane di Altamura

Soda Bread

Pane di Altamura (DOP) is a fabulous crisp and fragrant bread with a distinctive straw-coloured crumb. It is made in the Alta Murgia region of Apulia in Italy from the milled grain of specified varieties of durum wheat according to strict criteria.

It is a leavened bread made with a fermented starter using methods that may reputedly be traced back at least as far as the first century BCE, when the Roman poet Horace praised the local bread in his "Satires." Traditionally, it was made, kneaded, and fashioned into large loaves at home then taken to public ovens to be baked. Each individual loaf would be stamped with the initials of the head of the family, so that it would be easily identified after it had been baked.

Like many breads customarily produced in the hills and mountains of Italy, Pane di Altamura has good keeping qualities: an essential requirement for the peasants and shepherds who lived and worked in remote farms across the hills of Alta Murgia. Just before eating, it was dipped briefly into boiling water and dressed with olive oil and salt. **LF**

A staple of the Irish table and an indicator of a good meal to come, soda bread's history is surprisingly short. Bicarbonate of soda, which reacts with sour milk or buttermilk to lift the bread, became available in Ireland only in the early-to-mid nineteenth century. Early breads would have been baked over the fire in a lidded cast-iron pot or bastible.

Soda bread is traditionally shaped in rounds and "blessed" by cutting a deep cross through the centre. Many cooks also prick each of the four resulting segments with the tip of their knife, in order to "let the fairies out" lest the bread be jinxed.

The finest soda bread is made with Irish flour—it can be either white or a combination of brown and white—which is famously soft. The bread should be eaten on the day it is made. Although it is quick to make (no kneading is required), fresh soda bread is a sign of a generous host.

Variations of soda bread tend to include relatively expensive ingredients, such as dried fruit (to produce what is known as "spotty dog") or chocolate. Small soda scones are also made. **ES**

Taste: *Pane di Altamura has a delicious crisp crust and a well-balanced, uniform crumb. Good extra virgin olive oil and salt draw out the unique flavours of the wheat.*

Taste: *Soda bread is best eaten barely warm, with salted Irish butter. It has a compact but not heavy crumb and a crisp crust. The sour milk or buttermilk lends a faint acidic tang.*

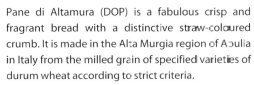

Pane di Altamura should be stone-baked and its crust should be a minimum of 3 mm thick.

Challah

Butterzopf

Challah is the traditional Jewish Shabbat (Sabbath) bread. The challah is made from a slightly sweetened dough made with many eggs and white flour, which is then braided, glazed, and sprinkled with sesame or poppy seeds before being baked.

Two loaves of challah are served at each of the three Shabbat meals, with prayers said over the bread. The loaves represent the double portion of *manna*, which is said to have fallen from heaven on the sixth day while the Israelites were in the wilderness, providing them with food both for that day and the Sabbath day that followed.

For certain festivals or celebrations, challah may be formed in different shapes. For Rosh Hashanah (Jewish New Year), the loaf may be shaped into a round or crown. Small individual challah rolls, known as *boulkas*, are often served at weddings and are shaped into rounds, braids, or spirals.

Classic Shabbat breads belonging to the Sephardi tradition include jam-filled *mouna* from the Algerian community, and the coiled, steamed breakfast bread, *kubaneh*, from the Yemen. **SBI**

Similar in appearance to challah, butterzopf is a type of braided butter loaf from Switzerland. It originates in the dairy pastures of the Emmental valley in the Canton of Bern in west central Switzerland. It is also known simply as "züpfe" or "zopf." The latter name comes from the distinctive shape of the bread and means "braid." Butterkopf is usually eaten for breakfast or brunch on Sundays, along with butter, fruit preserves, or cheese.

Butterzopf is sold in bakeries, although it is also commonly made at home. The rich bread is made from zopf flour that is 90 per cent white wheat flour and 10 per cent white spelt flour. Butter, milk, egg, salt, and yeast are the other ingredients. A dash of kirsch, sultanas, nuts, sunflower seeds, or chips of dark chocolate are occasionally added to the dough.

The dough, which is made with hot melted butter, is left to rise to double its size before being divided into two or four strands that are braided together. It is then left for thirty to sixty minutes under a cloth. Before baking, the dough is brushed with egg yolk to produce its shiny, golden crust. **CK**

Taste: *Soft, sweet, and tender, challah is not dissimilar to French brioche in taste and texture, although the sprinkling of seeds on top gives it a slightly different taste.*

Taste: *Butterzopf bread has a very rich, white bread flavour with a light inner texture and a crispy crust. It is ideal eaten warm from the oven with jam or honey.*

Kosher challah, as sold by this Jewish bakery
⊘ in France, is made without dairy ingredients.

Ciabatta

Focaccia

Ciabatta is one of the most well known of all the Italian breads outside Italy. In translation it simply means "slipper," a name the bread earned because it looks just like a flat, elongated slipper. It has a crisp crust and a chewy, often holey texture.

As is so often the case in Italy, recipes for ciabatta vary from region to region, however, most are made with wheat flour and a fermented dough starter called a *biga*, a rising agent that has been used in Italian baking for thousands of years. Breads made with *biga* generally share a characteristically moist, permeable texture and a deliciously pronounced flavour. Ironically, what has now become a highly fashionable bread was once a food of the poor. After World War II, a shortage of grain meant that white dough was reserved for the most prosperous people. But the odds and ends of dough that were left over from the bread-making were stretched into slipper shapes—and the ciabatta was born.

Ciabatta is best served warm alongside good Italian cheese or cured meats, but it can also be enjoyed alone with good extra virgin olive oil. **LF**

Like ciabatta, this traditional Italian bread is becoming known worldwide. Yet focaccia arrived on the scene even before the oven did. A precursor of pizza, it is one of Italy's most ancient breads, and is thought to have originated with the Etruscans. The earliest focaccia were unleavened flatbreads made from flour, water, and salt. This simple composition meant they could be cooked using any available heat source at the time—most often in the hearth of domestic fires. The dough was flattened over a stone slab and cooked under the hot ashes, hence its Latin name *panis focacius* (hearth bread).

Over the centuries recipes for focaccia have become more elaborate. Today yeast is commonly added, the basic dough includes olive oil, and loaves are often baked with herbs, bacon, cheese, or other ingredients. In its homeland, focaccia is probably most closely linked to Genoa, on the Italian Riviera, where it is known as Pizza Genovese and topped with thinly sliced sautéed onions. Around Bologna it is known as *crescentina*; in Tuscany and parts of central Italy, it becomes *schiacciata*. **LF**

Taste: *Artisan ciabatta has a crisp golden crust, a pleasantly chewy but porous centre and a subtly yeasty aroma, almost reminiscent of Champagne.*

Taste: *The best known focaccias have a golden, dimpled, slightly salty crust and a soft centre. However, texture varies according to region and flavours vary with ingredients.*

Before baking, slits are sometimes cut into the focaccia dough and stuffed with herbs or other ingredients. »

Hardough

This classic bread—most frequently associated with Jamaica—is the most popular bread within the Caribbean islands. Made from white flour, the plain white bread is baked in loaf tins or sometimes shaped into plaits and has a dense, chewy texture, a slightly sweet flavour, and is surrounded by a soft, pale-golden crust. Outside of the Caribbean, you will find hardough in countries such as the United Kingdom and the United States where there are large Caribbean populations.

The loaves are sold whole and are delicious cut into chunky slices. Hardough is popular for its firm texture, which does not crumble nor become soggy when spread with butter or served with wet foods such as soups or stews. It should be noted that wheat is not a staple crop of the Caribbean and most wheat is imported into the region to be ground and then used in bread and other products.

Caribbean bun also has a dense texture, but is slightly stickier and darker in colour due to the addition of molasses, allspice, and moist dried fruit—all of which contribute to its distinctive flavour. **SBI**

Limpa Bread

Limpa bread is the dark, sweet, deliciously aromatic bread that is also known as Swedish rye bread. It is flavoured with molasses, anise, or fennel seed and orange peel. There are two types: *vort limpa*, which is typically made with light rye flour and *Stockholm limpa*, which is made from a blend of white and rye flours and is often brushed with butter after baking to give it an appealing soft, well-flavoured crust.

Little has been written about the origins of limpa bread, but rye goes back thousands of years. On the whole, the ancient Greeks and Romans gave rye a wide berth and it became synonymous with poverty. The grain thrived in Scandinavia and Eastern Europe, however, and has long been valued in culinary terms.

Swedish cuisine has been built largely on the need for preserving and storing. Brief summers and long dark winters meant that pickles and preserves were customarily made and rye bread was baked slowly into loaves that could be stored for long periods. The ironic thing is that limpa bread is so delicious that there seems little chance its capacity for storage will be put to the test. **LF**

Taste: *Hardough is firm and moist, with a dense texture that makes it great for sandwiches, or served alongside traditional Caribbean dishes such as fish or soup.*

Taste: *Fragrant, dark, treacly, and satisfyingly sweet, limpa bread has a dense chewiness and a wonderful composed spiciness. Try it with butter and lingonberry jam.*

A family prays before breaking bread in this 1909 stained-glass window in the Tiska Kyrka, Stockholm. »

Gestiftet v. Fredrik Althaus u. seiner

Pumpernickel

Roggenvollkornbrot

Pumpernickel is a type of wholegrain rye bread that originated in Westphalia, Germany. An unusual bread with a dark colour and dense texture, when sliced it has a similar appearance to small, heavy-duty cork tiles, yet is surprisingly delicious. It has a particular affinity with luxury fish products such as caviar and smoked salmon and, as such, is often served as a base for these delicacies in hors d'oeuvres.

Unlike some imitation breads that are coloured with molasses or caramel, traditional pumpernickel gets its dark, almost black colour from a chemical browning reaction. It happens as a result of the long, slow cooking of the bread, which can be baked or steamed for anything up to twenty-four hours.

Rye flourished in the sandy soils of Westphalia; it was ground into course meal and made into dough that was mixed in hollowed-out tree trunks and trampled by barefoot labourers until pliable. The hefty loaves weighed in excess of 110 pounds (50 kg) and were baked in huge ovens. Machinery has now taken over where the feet left off, but the bread's unique properties have remained the same. **LF**

Roggenvollkornbrot is a German whole grain rye bread that is made with a sourdough starter. It is a highly nutritious bread with a heavy, dense texture and pronounced sour flavour. It is regarded as a very acquired taste, but complements sweet foods such as jams and honey and makes a wonderful base for canapés with oily fish toppings, such as smoked salmon and eel, and is superb with caviar. Roggenvollkornbrot is considered good bread for anyone trying to lose weight because it is slow to digest and so is particularly filling and satisfying.

Although there are numerous delicious types of bread in Germany, rye breads have long been top of the popularity polls. Like pumpernickel, good artisan-baked roggenvollkornbrot gets its dark colouring from a chemical reaction that occurs naturally in some foods when they are heated. It is the same process that causes the change in the colour of bread when it is toasted. The inferior industrially made varieties are usually baked for a much shorter time and so the flavour and colour is enhanced by caramel syrup and sugar beet. **LF**

Taste: *With faint hints of bitter chocolate and slightly sour overtones, German pumpernickel has a big, bold, gutsy flavour that marries well with salty ham, oily fish, and beer.*

Taste: *Roggenvollkornbrot has an earthy aroma and sour flavour, balanced by a vaguely sweet aftertaste. Splendid with oily fish, creamy cheeses, and sweet preserves.*

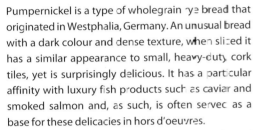

Rye breads are common in northern European countries because rye grows well in cooler latitudes.

Rúgbraud

Rich in molasses and crumbly in texture, rúgbraud is an Icelandic dark rye bread. What makes "hot spring bread" unique is that it is traditionally cooked inside steam boxes in the burbling, spouting geysers that dot Iceland's bleak lunar-like landscape.

Icelandic cuisine has evolved out of the skills and resourcefulness of its people. With its shortage of natural light and harsh environment, not much can be grown on the land and fresh food is hard to come by. At one time, fuel was also in short supply. Icelanders therefore developed methods of drying, pickling, and fermenting foods that would last them through the relentless winters. Ingeniously, they also harnessed the geothermal power generated by vents in the volcanic soils to cook their food.

Once a fundamental part of the Icelandic diet, rúgbraud (also known as thunder bread) continues to be enjoyed today. Icelanders typically serve rúgbraud with salted butter, fish, and potatoes, but it is also good with cheese, pickled herring, and cured meats. The steaming process also provides an unusual spectacle for visiting tourists. **LF**

Taste: *Rather like traditional pumpernickel in appearance and texture, rúgbraud has sweet, slightly burnt toffee overtones that hint of bitter chocolate.*

The geothermal power of geysers is used to steam Icelandic rúgbraud. »

Pane Siciliano

Kavring

Pane Siciliano is a delicious Sicilian speciality bread made with a high percentage of semolina flour and often scattered with sesame seeds. Although little is documented about the origins of pane Siciliano, the scattering of sesame seeds over bread is nothing new. The decorated tomb of an Egyptian noble dating back around 4,000 years or so portrays a baker going about his trade, adding sesame seeds to his bread dough. The ancient Greeks were known to have used sesame seeds in bread, but some believe that the tradition of sesame bread in Sicily came about through Arab influence.

Typically eaten at breakfast or lunch with anything from jam to hams or cheese, pane Siciliano is one of the most popular breads in Sicily and has been prepared for centuries to traditional recipes by the women of Sicilian households. The different forms have interesting names such as *occhi di Saint Lucia* (eyes of St. Lucia) and *corona* (crown), but perhaps the most popular is a serpentine-like configuration with a final straight piece of dough being laid along the entire length of the centre. **LF**

Kavring is the collective name for many different kinds of Swedish soft breads that are good to store and can be kept fresh for a long time. Kavring breads even improve if left to mature for a few days.

In Sweden, where the climate limits harvesting to a relatively short period in the warmer season, finding ways to store food was an important issue. The longevity of kavring made the bread an important staple in the Swedish diet, and the difference between life and death for some.

In medieval times kavring was baked from rye, the dominant crop at the time, but is now baked with any flour. Scalding part of the rye flour and adding sourdough gives the bread a moist feel and slightly acidic flavour. It is also characterized by its spices such as cumin, aniseed, or bitter orange. Baking the bread twice to create a hard crust stops the bread from drying out; this baking method also gives it a unique dense consistency. The blend of sourdough and wholemeal flour allows the body to absorb minerals more effectively. Kavring is a central part of the Christmas smorgasbord. **CC**

Taste: *Bite into aromatic pane Siciliano and the soft golden crust gives way to a delightful crunch of sesame seeds that yield a creamy, almost peanut-like flavour.*

Taste: *Black syrup gives the bread a slight toffee-like taste and the hard crust a pleasant toasted tone. Delicious with pâté or skagenröra, a dill, shrimp, and mayonnaise mix.*

Crown-shaped loaves of Sicilian bread are distributed for the feast of San Paolo in Sicily.

Bammy

In the 1990s the widespread availability and popularity of bread made from wheat flour threatened to relegate Jamaica's national flatbread to an "old-time" dish. Fortunately, bammy lovers revived the dish and agricultural authorities stepped in to support the cassava farmers and their industry.

Bammy is said to have originated with the Arawak Indians who once inhabited the West Indies. They harvested the tuberous edible root from the cassava plants, which grow in hot climates including the Caribbean, South America, and West Africa. It was found to be a natural ingredient for making flatbreads.

Cassava is the source of tapioca, which is used as a thickener and to make puddings. Because the different varieties of cassava contain varying levels of toxic substances, the tuber must be peeled, washed, and cooked before eating. To make bammy, the cassava is grated and the liquid is pressed from it. Then it is seasoned with salt, formed into a flat cake, and deep-fried, pan-fried, or baked. Once cooked, it is served with butter as the traditional accompaniment to fried fish or other fried foods. **SH**

Taste: *The texture and flavour are quite bland. The taste is slightly sweet, a little bready, and resembles hash brown potatoes. It picks up a little of the flavour of the oil used.*

A mobile vendor sells bammy to a hungry stallholder in Jamaica. »

Bagel

A Jewish bread originating in central Europe, bagels have an uncertain history. Polish statutes from 1610 are said to contain records that bagels were presented to women who had given birth. However, there is no doubt that, two centuries later, Eastern European Jewish immigrants brought bagels to the United States and Canada. With their relatively large Jewish populations, New York City and Montreal soon became the bagel capitals of North America.

This round yeast bread with the hole in the middle is one of the few breads that is cooked twice. In New York City, where all bagels were once handmade, the dough is first dropped into rapidly boiling water and then baked in a moderately hot oven. In Montreal, bagels, or beugels, are smaller and have larger holes. There the dough is dropped into honey-flavoured boiling water and then baked in a wood-fired oven. Usually the bread is finished off with a sprinkling of sesame or poppy seeds.

Bagels are traditionally eaten with a "shmear" of cream cheese and some sliced lox (smoked salmon), red onion, tomato, and capers. **SH**

Bialy

Slathered with butter and washed down with hot lemon tea or coffee, these warm, flavourful onion rolls are a breakfast favourite of many New Yorkers. They look similar to a bagel with a diameter of up to 6 inches (15 cm), but, instead of a hole in the middle, they have a depression that is filled with a delicious diced onion mixture, often containing poppy seeds and a little crushed garlic.

In *The Bialy Eaters* (2000), food writer Mimi Sheraton tried to retrace the bialy's journey from the Polish city of Białystok to Manhattan. In the old country, the bialy (a Yiddish word) was a Jewish speciality, known as *Białystok kuchen*. However, when Ashkenazi Jewish immigrants brought it with them to the United States at the beginning of the twentieth century, the name was shortened to bialy. The Jewish bakers who remained in the Polish city perished in the Nazi camps of World War II. In today's Poland, the closest equivalent to the bialy is the *cebulak*, a type of onion cake. Bagel bakery owner Harry Cohen is said to have been the first to market bialys in the United States. **RS**

Taste: *Plain bagels are pleasantly sour and taste like dense, slightly moist bread. Montreal bagels are sweeter than New York bagels and usually have seeds.*

Taste: *The bialy is not boiled before baking, so is lighter and less chewy than a bagel, although still with a touch of chewiness. The flavour is subtly yeasty.*

Crumpet

A popular delicacy served for afternoon tea, recipes for these traditional English griddle cakes date to the eighteenth century, but their origins reach back beyond that. Predecessors of the crumpet are thought to have been the fourteenth-century crompid cake and the buckwheat griddle cake, known as a crumpit, which appeared from the seventeenth century. It has also been associated with the Welsh pancake, *crempog*, and the Breton buckwheat pancake, *krampoch*.

Crumpets are made from a yeasted batter. Once the batter has been left to ferment, invariably baking powder (or a mixture of bicarbonate of soda and cream of tartar) is added to the batter just before cooking. Unlike the similar pancakes, pikelets, which are popular in the north of England and are also cooked on the griddle, crumpets are cooked inside a ring to give them their round shape. The cooked crumpet is golden and flat on its underside with a deeply holed top, which gives it its distinctive texture. Crumpets are always toasted before eating, and are delicious eaten hot and oozing with butter. **SBI**

English Muffin

Distinct from the cake-like muffins of the United States, English muffins are unsweetened round pats of yeast dough enriched with milk and butter and cooked on a griddle to produce a disc that is crisp and flat on its top and bottom, but spongy and yeasty in the middle. They feel more like a bread than their holey relatives, crumpets and pikelets.

Home-made muffins can be eaten fresh from the griddle, but shop-bought examples are warmed by toasting on both sides. They are traditionally split into half around the circumference with the fingers, due to the belief that cutting with a knife will make them heavier. They are usually spread with butter, and also form the base of the breakfast dish eggs Benedict, topped with bacon or ham, poached eggs, and hollandaise sauce.

Muffins enjoyed their heyday in the nineteenth century. Muffin men would walk the streets with a basket of warm muffins advertising their wares with the ringing of a bell. Their popularity is confirmed by the words of the nursery rhyme, which asks "Have you seen the muffin man?" **ES**

Taste: *Crumpets have a plain, slightly salty flavour. Their real appeal lies in their spongy texture. Served toasted, they are best slathered with butter and sometimes jam.*

Taste: *English muffins have a crisp top and bottom, and a soft, fairly damp crumb. Spread with salted butter, they are one of the simplest treats of the English table.*

Croissant

Although there are earlier culinary references to "croissants," the first recipe for the croissant we know today only emerged as recently as 1906 and the huge growth in popularity of this fabulous pastry appears to have been a twentieth-century sensation.

This classic, crescent-shaped French pastry is made from a yeast-based dough, which is rolled and layered to incorporate butter. Because of the cost of butter, many bakers use cheaper substitutes such as margarine, so you will find that most bakeries in France offer two types of croissants: croissant and croissant au beurre. The former tends to be breadier, whereas the latter is much richer and, as one would expect, more buttery. A popular habit among bakers is to bend the butterless croissant into a distinctive curve, while straightening out the croissant au beurre so as to distinguish clearly between the two.

You will also find croissants stuffed with different sweet and savoury fillings. The classic sweet-filled croissants are almond croissants, whereas savoury croissants might be filled variously with fillings such as cheese, spinach, or ham. **SBI**

Taste: *Golden, buttery croissants should be crisp and flakey on the outside and wonderfully soft and tender on the inside, with a texture that can be almost pulled apart.*

The unusual crescent shape is part of the pastry's appeal. »

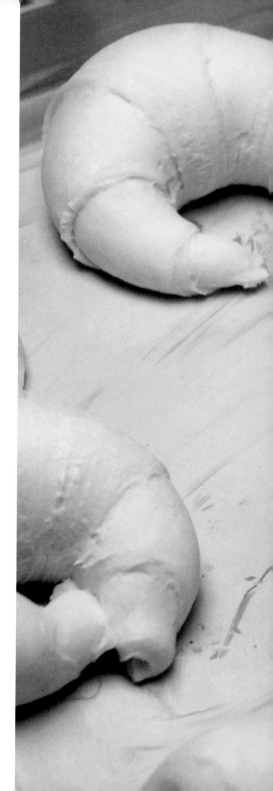

Brioche

This delectable treat from the French bakery had arrived in Paris by the seventeenth century, and the word "brioche" has been in use since at least the fifteenth century. The yeasted bread is enriched with butter, eggs, and milk and a little sugar to create a wonderfully soft, crumbly texture. The butter ratio is very high—often half to three-quarters butter to flour—and the bread is usually kneaded three times, as opposed to twice as in ordinary bread-making

One of the best known varieties is the brioche à tête, which is cooked in a fluted pan with sloping sides and has a little brioche ball nestled on top. Brioche Nanterre is made up of balls of dough arranged along the bottom of a loaf pan, whereas the similar brioche Parisienne has balls of dough arranged in a circle. A speciality brioche comes from the village of St. Pierre-d'Albigny. Flavoured with saffron or anise, it is known as the hand of St. Agatne, which refers to the severed hand of the patron saint of young mothers and wet nurses. As well as these more interesting loaves, you can also find plain loaves and simple brioche rolls. **SBI**

Pan de Coco

Every Caribbean island and Latin American country has its own unique style of coconut bread. According to some, pan de coco dates from the arrival of the Garifuna people, a cultural mix of Africans and West Indians who have lived along the coastline of Belize and Honduras since the eighteenth century. One hundred years before, their forebears escaped from slavery to settle and live on St. Vincent as free men and women, intermarrying with the island's indigenous people. They later resisted British efforts to establish a slave plantation on St. Vincent and eventually settled in Belize and Honduras.

A profusion of local coconuts suggests that early pan de coco, cooked over glowing coals, became a survival food for the new settlers. Today's loaves are still served at nearly every meal but are baked in conventional ovens and are commonly made using only flour, coconut milk, grated fresh coconut, and yeast or baking powder However, in remote areas, basic recipes still exist for making flatbreads from just coconut milk and flour. These breads are baked on a hot iron skillet in a similar way to corn tortillas. **WS**

Taste: *Brioche has a deliciously tender, golden crumb and a slightly sweet flavour. In France, it is popularly served for breakfast or at teatime with coffee or hot chocolate.*

Taste: *Pan de coco is a simple bread with a crisp, brown crust and a moist, pale quite heavy, crumb—perfumed and flavoured with the sweet creaminess of fresh coconut.*

A perfectly formed brioche à tete, topped with its characteristic small dough ball.

Malt Loaf

Kugelhopf

This quintessentially British treat is a yeasted loaf usually made from wheat flour and barley malt, traditionally about the size of a small brick, with a dark colour and dense texture, and studded with juicy sultanas. The bread is fairly soft, so it is best cut with a serrated knife, pulled gently across the grain, so as not to squash the loaf as you cut into it.

The dark colour and dense texture come from the addition of malt extract and treacle, which also give the bread its delicious flavour. Malt extract is a dark brown, syrupy concentrate obtained from malt. Barley grains are germinated, dried, and ground; the ground malt is then "mashed" in hot water to make brewer's wort, and the malt extract is obtained from this by process of evaporation in a partial vacuum.

Although the history of malt loaf is unsure, it is thought that the habit of adding malt extract to bread began towards the end of the nineteenth century. Malt was then incredibly popular as an ingredient because of its reputation as a tonic and restorative, and appeared in malted cocoa, malted preserves, malted jellies and, of course, malt loaf. **SBI**

There are many variations of this enriched, yeasted cake-bread that is baked all the way from the Alsace region of France through parts of Germany and Poland and into Austria. Its name varies too, according to region; it tends to be known as kugelhopf in the western part of its range and gugelhupf in the east. It is held in great esteem and in the tiny village of Ribeauville in Alsace, there is even a fete held every summer in its honour.

The defining feature of a kugelhopf is its shape, produced by the tin in which it is baked—a high, round, fluted pan with a central funnel. The resulting cake is tall and ring-shaped, not dissimilar to a bundt cake. It is frequently dusted with icing sugar to highlight the fluted pattern and sometimes decorated with slivered almonds.

Kugelhopf contains eggs, butter, and sugar as well as yeast and flour and in that respect is similar to the French brioche, but it is also often flavoured with lemon peel and raisins. In the Alsace, there are also savoury versions made with bacon, lard, and fromage frais or cream cheese. **SBI**

Taste: *Despite an uninspiring appearance, malt loaf has a chewy, almost fudgy texture. Fruity, but not too sweet, this teatime treat or snack is usually eaten sliced and buttered.*

Taste: *Sweet kugelhopf has a taste and texture like well-flavoured brioche. The less common, savoury version still has a tender, enriched crumb but flecked with bacon bits.*

A copper mould signals that kugelhopf can be bought from this baker in Ribeauville, Alsace. »

Bara Brith

One of the best-known Welsh fruit breads, bara brith literally means "speckled bread." The dried fruit, usually currants, raisins, or sultanas and candied peel, with which the bread is packed is frequently soaked in tea before adding to the bread, which gives it a very moist texture. Traditionally, bara brith was always yeasted, although modern versions are often leavened with raising agents such as baking powder or bicarbonate of soda, which affects the finished flavour and texture.

In Wales, there are many different variations of this bread in shops, bakeries, and in the home, and most families will have their own closely guarded recipe. But bara brith is not just confined to Wales and the British Isles. As far away as Argentine Patagonia there are versions of this moist Welsh bread, where it was introduced by Welsh settlers who arrived in Chabut province from 1865. There it is known as *torta negra*, meaning black cake, but despite its change in name and the distance it has travelled, *torta negra* still bears a striking resemblance to the original bara brith. **SBI**

Paasiaisleipa

As with other Easter breads from around the world, rich paasiaisleipa from Finland is full of everything that has traditionally been eschewed during the Christian fast of Lent. The dough is enriched with eggs, butter, and milk and flavoured with cardamom, orange and lemon rind, nuts, and dried fruit, which are kneaded into the dough. This is then traditionally baked in a milk pail to give the loaf a sloped, cylindrical shape. (Modern recipes suggest using a round cake tin instead of a milk pail.)

Paasiaisleipa's roots are thought to hark back to pre-Christian times. Cylindrical breads have a long history in pagan celebrations: some theories suggest their phallic shape made them important in spring festivals; others believe the shape to resemble the long skirt of a woman, a symbol of fertility.

Paasiaisleipa takes pride of place at the centre of an Easter buffet, piled high with home-baked breads, alongside rich spring butter, creams, and cheeses, and one of the oldest Finnish Easter dishes known as *mämmi*—a mixture of molasses, water, and rye flour flavoured with raisins and orange peel. **SBI**

Taste: *Bara brith is a moist, lightly spiced loaf with a fairly dense, fruit-packed texture. Although it is delicious buttered, some purists believe it should be served plain.*

Taste: *Lightly spiced, with a citrus tang, this bread is not unlike panettone. Slightly cakey, it has a brioche-like taste and texture.*

Lussekatter

Birnbrot

The Christmas season would not be Christmas for Swedes without lussekatter, the sweet, yellow saffron buns, whose name means "St. Lucy's cats." Still celebrated in homes, churches, schools, and concert halls across Scandinavia with processions led by a white-clad girl wearing a crown of candles, St. Lucy's Day was marked by the Swedish gentry as early as the eighteenth century. Lussekatter are believed to have originated during this period from a Germanic forerunner known as *dövelskatter*, or "devil's cats," named after an evil figure that used to follow St. Nicholas and spank naughty children.

Lussekatter are baked with yeast, flour, milk, egg, butter, sugar, raisins, and a generous amount of expensive saffron, used specifically because of its exclusivity. The dough is traditionally formed in patterns and shapes that date back centuries, notably crosses, sheaves, "priests' hair," "swaddled baby," and "golden cart." The pig is as associated with Christmas in Sweden as the turkey is in the United States and Britain, and so the most popular kind today is the S-shaped "Christmas-pig." **CC**

This dense fruit and nut bread is popularly served throughout Switzerland for Christmas and, although it contains many different dried fruits, its name literally means "pear bread." The rustic loaf has peasant origins, but these simple beginnings belie its delicious flavour. Packed with dried pears, prunes, dates, figs, sultanas, and raisins, which give the bread a wickedly dark colour when you cut into it, the bread also contains candied orange and lemon, pine kernels, nuts, and kirsch and the dough is flavoured with spices, vanilla, and a little sugar.

The fruits and nuts are combined with a dough, then encased in a thin layer of plain dough to make a densely packed loaf. The bread has remarkable storage qualities and traditionally it is made in large quantities before Christmas so there are enough loaves to last until Candlemas (2 February).

Birnbrot has been likened to the Christmas spice cake *berawecka*, which originates from the Alsace region of France. The French cake is similar in flavour and texture, except that it is baked without an outer covering of plain, enriched bread dough. **SBI**

Taste: *Best eaten warm, fresh out of the oven, lussekatter are slightly sweet with a wonderful scent and taste of saffron. They are usually served with tea or coffee.*

Taste: *This heavy, chewy, spiced bread is naturally sweet from all the fruit it contains. It should be cut into thin slices and served either plain or thinly spread with butter.*

Stollen

Originating in Germany, this classic bread cake has become almost ubiquitous in many parts of the world as traditional Christmas fare. The origins of stollen have been traced back to the city of Dresden in the Middle Ages, although it should be noted that the early versions of stollen were not the luxurious treat that we know today. The stollen of the Middle Ages was made to a much more austere recipe, with a dough made only from flour, oats, and water—in line with church doctrines that did not allow the use of richer ingredients over the Christmas period.

Today's stollen, however, is a veritable treat. The yeasted dough is enriched with eggs, butter, milk, sugar, and spices into which currants, sultanas, and candied peel are kneaded. Almonds are sometimes finely chopped and added to the dough, and sometimes ground to a marzipan-like paste and rolled into the bread to give it a moist, sweet centre. The loaf is then shaped into an oval or oblong with tapering ends to represent the form of the baby Jesus wrapped in swaddling clothes—hence stollen's sometime name of Christstollen. **SBI**

Taste: *Stollen offers a perfect not-too-sweet bread base, packed with dried fruit and topped off with a dusting of icing sugar. It is quite rich and dense, so serve in thin slices.*

Panettone

Gloriously scented and enriched with butter, eggs, sugar, raisins, and candied fruit, panettone is essentially *the* Italian Christmas cake, traditionally eaten over the festive period and New Year. It is made like a bread, using a fermented starter to raise the dough, and acquires its characteristic dome shape as it hangs upside down to cool.

The legends behind panettone are as rich as the cake, although all agree that panettone was first made in Milan, and most Italians like to believe its name was originally *pan di Toni* (Toni's bread). One story has it that a young Milanese nobleman fell in love with Toni, the daughter of a local baker. He bluffed his way into the kitchen masquerading as an apprentice and won her heart by creating a huge, dome-shaped confection. Another fable tells of Toni, a young kitchen boy working in the court of Ludovico il Moro, a duke of Milan during the Renaissance. When the chef ruined the Christmas dessert, Toni saved the day with a bread he had made from leftover dough and enriched with eggs, fruit, and butter, impressing the duke immensely. **LF**

Taste: *Panettone has an outwardly firm texture, which gives way to a soft, exquisitely buttery centre studded with fruit, and flaunting tempting vanilla overtones.*

The distinctive light texture of panettone comes from proving the dough for an unusually long time. »

Blini

Scots Pancake

To the Russian poet Alexander Kuprin (1870–1938) blinis were "yellow gold and hot like the sun, the symbol of sublime days, rich harvests, harmonious marriages and healthy children." Today these pancakes are so popular that in St. Petersburg a chain of fast-food blini restaurants has been dubbed "Blindonalds" by the local population.

Traditionally made with buckwheat flour and known as red or *krasnyj* blinis, other ground grains such as millet and barley can also be used. Modern recipes favour a mix of buckwheat and ordinary wheat flour to give a lighter, less brittle result.

Blinis can be served piled up with fillings layered between or stuffed and rolled. The range of fillings is as wide as the cook's imagination and could be caviar, soured cream, hard-boiled egg, chopped herring, honey, jam, or fruit. As with all pancakes, blinis are best eaten as soon as they are made and guests in a Russian home would be allowed to sit in the kitchen with the hostess ready to enjoy her labours the moment the lightly puffed dough clouds were flipped off the hot, cast iron griddle. **WS**

The simplicity of making these little pancakes belies their versatility. Also known as "drop" or "dropped" scones in England and in some parts of Scotland, Scots pancakes are traditionally sweet and made with plain flour, cream of tartar, bicarbonate of soda, sugar, eggs, and milk. The resulting batter is then dropped onto a griddle, which is a hot metal plate set over an open fire. As the pancakes begin to bubble they are ready to be turned over; this usually takes about a minute on each side because Scots pancakes are thicker than other varieties.

They are a popular dish to make for unexpected guests because the batter can be made and cooked very quickly, and the pancakes served warm with butter and jam. A savoury version can also be made with brown flour or buckwheat and without sugar. It is similar to a blini and can be served with crème fraiche and smoked salmon or other savoury additions.

Scots pancakes are easy to find ready-made, but because of the simple recipe and the fact that they are most delicious fresh from the griddle, they are best made at home. **CTr**

Taste: *With the robust, nutty taste of buckwheat, blinis should be eaten warm, before they become tough, and be slightly puffed like a thicker version of the French crêpe.*

Taste: *Scots or Scotch pancakes are more of a vehicle for other foods, not having great flavour in themselves, but the texture is light and spongy with a sweet aftertaste.*

Hopper

In the tropical splendour of Sri Lanka they are called hoppers; in Kerala, Southern India, *appams*, but both are the same rice flour pancake, fried in a kind of wok and eaten for breakfast. They are made from a light dough that is fermented overnight with a little palm toddy. Once it has risen like a sponge, it is thinned with coconut cream. To make each one, a little batter is poured over a heated round, cast-iron pan (*cheena chatti*) and baked so that it is crisp and curling at the edges and still fluffy in the middle. It is eaten in many ways, with hot sambals, chill relishes, grated coconut, or curries. The favourite way in the subcontinent is with a fried egg sunny-side up. Like pancakes, hoppers can be consumed in quantity and Sri Lankans would have little difficulty in polishing off half a dozen while watching a cricket match.

The name "hopper," an Anglo-Indian invention, derives from the Tamil *appam*, used to describe a fried snack. *Iddiappams* or string hoppers are a related snack-cum-breakfast food, also made from rice flour, but formed like a string by being forced through a mould and steamed. **MR**

Arepa de Choclo

Visitors to Venezuela will not have to travel far before they find a bar or small *arepera* restaurant serving these sweet corn cakes. Made from yellow arepa meal (*masarepa* or *masa harina*)—a gluten-free flour ground from starchy cooked corn, which should not be confused with cornmeal, cornflour, polenta, or hominy grits—arepas de choclo were originally a food staple of the poor but have now become a national dish. Before technology stepped in, preparing arepa meal was time-consuming. Dried corn kernels had to be soaked in water and lime to remove their skins, then cooked, drained, dried, and ground between two stones. Traditionally sweetened with an unrefined, brown loaf sugar called *papelón*, modern recipes simply call for sugar.

Arepas de choclo are eaten at any time of day as a snack, appetizer, or accompaniment to a meal instead of bread. They can be fried, baked, or griddled, eaten plain, or with *queso fresco* and chopped chillies added to the mix. They can also be split and sandwiched with slices of chicken, meat, or strong cheese, or topped with guacamole. **WS**

Taste: *Brittle at the edges, almost lace-like, hoppers become progressively softer towards the centre where they are almost spongy. They have a mild taste of rice.*

Taste: *Best eaten warm, so the golden outside is crusty and the inside light and soft. The freshly cooked ground corn kernels give a creamy texture and extra sweetness.*

Bath Oliver

In the mid-eighteenth century, Dr. William Oliver was the most fashionable physician in ultra-fashionable Bath—the spa town to which England's rich and famous flocked as a retreat from the smell and squalor of London. Bath's sulphurous mineral waters had been famous since Roman times, but the eighteenth century brought a renewed focus on their health benefits, and Dr. Oliver apparently created these fairly plain, unsweetened biscuits to be taken with the waters. Today, of course—but for the chocolate-coated versions, which were allegedly John Lennon's favourite biscuit—they are mostly eaten with cheese.

The plain Bath Olivers have been continuously in production since Dr. Oliver's death in 1764. The story goes that he bequeathed to his coachman, a Mr. Atkins, the recipe for the famous biscuit, together with a sack of flour, and a large sum of money. Mr. Atkins promptly set up a baking business and became rich on the proceeds. The production rights have since been transferred several times, and the biscuits are no longer made in Bath. **AMS**

Oatcake

The unique crumbly texture of the Scottish oatcake has made it known across the world. Developed in the seventeenth century, when oats took over from barley as Scotland's staple food grain, it was quick and easy to make in front of the open fire: a simple mix of meal and water blended into a paste and baked on the hot hearthstones. Historical references are many. The fourteenth-century French chronicler Jean Froissart noted how Scottish soldiers mixed meal with water and seared it over the fire to produce a "biscuit." The English diarist Dorothy Wordsworth observed in 1803 that they were "kneaded with cream and were excellent." (Today warm lard is more traditional than cream.)

Commercial oatcakes are usually made with wheat flour to hold them together. They have retained their popularity as they make as good an accompaniment as bread to many dishes, and are seen as healthier because of their low gluten content and the perception that they absorb cholesterol. They can be eaten with oily fish, cheese, jams, butter, and honey, as well as with soup. **CTr**

Taste: *These mild biscuits are slightly soft, rather than crisp, with a fine grain. The texture and smooth, almost creamy flavour make them an ideal partner to cheese.*

Taste: *Commercial oatcakes tend to be smoother with a nutty crunch. Homemade versions can be very thin and brittle, with a fuller flavour and delightful toasty edge.*

People enjoy the healing waters of Bath—home of the famous biscuit—in this eighteenth-century illustration.

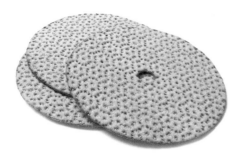

Knäckebröd

Matzo

Thin, hard flatbreads have been baked in Sweden since the sixth century, when they were originally based on barley, then the dominant grain. For the last thousand years, rye has been the grain of choice, although versions are made using wheat, barley, and oats. Knäckebröd has remained remarkably popular, both in its homeland and abroad, where it is generally known as crispbread.

Recipes and styles vary from region to region, but when making knäckebröd a dough of flour, water, yeast, and salt is rolled out into thin, flat rounds. A special rolling pin creates the distinctive cratered texture, and a large hole is made in the middle before the bread is baked at a high temperature. After baking, numerous breads are then hung on a long wooden rod to dry, using the hole in the middle. This method gives the bread its distinctive dry feel, as well as the long shelf life, which was a necessity in older days. Today knäckebröd is rarely baked at home but is a central feature of any Swedish smorgasbord. It also comes in smaller rectangular shapes. **CC**

Derived from the Hebrew word *matzah*, flat brittle matzo is the traditional Jewish unleavened flatbread baked for Passover—or Pesach as it is known in the Jewish calendar. Matzo is symbolic of the flight from slavery in Egypt, when there was no time for leavened bread, and every year unleavened matzo is eaten for the eight days of Passover.

It is the only flour product that can be eaten during Passover. Guidelines on preparation are strict and once the flour has been mixed with water, no longer than eighteen minutes may pass before the baked matzo is removed from the oven. To make sure the production of the matzo has adhered to these regulations for Passover, the packaging is always marked "kosher for Pesach."

Other matzo products include matzo meal, which can be used for making cakes and biscuits, as well as the Jewish classic recipe *knaidlach* (matzo balls for serving in chicken soup), and binding ingredients in dishes such as *gefilte* fish (fish balls) and *latkes* (potato pancakes), and matzo farfel, which is lightly crushed matzo. **SBI**

Taste: *Knäckebröd should be crisp and hard. It is neutral in taste, sometimes with a faint smoky note. It is served as a sandwich with cheese, sausage, or pickled herring.*

Taste: *Crisp, dry matzos come in large oblong sheets, creamy coloured and speckled with brown. They are extremely versatile and taste rather like water biscuits.*

The mother of a Jewish family breaks wrapped matzo in a fourteenth-century Hebrew manuscript. »

אַחַת מִשֶּׁדֶּשֶׁהַמַּצּוֹת אֲ

אֲשֶׁר כֶּסֶל וּמֹעֲאוֹתָהּ

לְשַׁתַּיִם וּמִנֶּחֱצְיָהּ כַּן

שַׁתַּיִם שְׁלֵמוֹת וְחַצְתֶם

הַמַּצָּה וְיְחֻנְּסֵל שְׁנֵי

Nürnberger Elisenlebkuchen

Basler Leckerli

The first traditional German Christmas biscuits known as lebkuchen are thought to have been baked by monks in Franconia, Germany, during the thirteenth century, but the most famous variety is from Nürnberg and dates from 1395. Since 1808, the very best lebkuchen has been Elisenlebkuchen (PDO), and one of Nürnberg's most celebrated Elisenlebkuchen bakeries is the Lebkuchen Schmidt.

Unlike other gingerbreads, this elite biscuit contains little or no flour, the most important ingredients being nuts (hazelnuts and/or almonds) and a special spice blend. Each bakery adds its own characteristic blend and the mix of spices used is a jealously guarded secret. Some ancient recipes use honey instead of sugar; the forerunner of today's lebkuchen was known as honey cake and can be traced back to the Egyptians, Greeks, and Romans.

Elisenlebkuchen can be baked as plain rounds decorated with whole nuts and dusted with icing sugar, cut into decorative shapes and iced, or set on wafers and covered with a glistening layer of smooth dark chocolate. **WS**

Since the mid-fourteenth century these spicy honey biscuits have been baked to celebrate every festive occasion in Basel, Switzerland. The first recipes were devised by local spice merchants.

Lebkuchen-makers plied their trade in the markets of Strasbourg, Nürnberg, and Memmingen and it was to escape the fierce competition from them that a self-employed baker moved to Basle and opened a small shop selling leckerli. The sugar-glazed biscuits proved popular with the Basel elite and a new craft established itself, the first mention of leckerli appearing in the city's council records of 1720. Today one of the leading producers is the Läckerli-Huus, establ shec in 1903.

As well as ready-made biscuits, the original shop also stocked candied lemon and orange peel, nuts, honey, spices, and kirsch, so customers could bake their own. Similar in texture and flavour to *panforte di Siena*, leckerli can be stamped out using a special cutter or simply cut into bars with a knife. *Lecker* means delicious in German and the biscuits are a powerhouse of complementary flavours. **WS**

Taste: *A range of spices including cinnamon, coriander, nutmeg, clove, allspice, cardamom, and ginger adds a warm spicy glow to the soft and crumbly Elisenlebkuchen.*

Taste: *The honey gives a mellow flavour, candied peels add the tang of citrus, almonds give a nutty crunch, and cinnamon provides the warmth of exotic spice.*

Heart-shaped lebkuchen bearing a huge
❸ *variety of messages are widely sold in Germany.*

Amaretto di Saronno

Amaretti—"little bitter ones"—are perhaps the most famous of all Italian biscuits. As with most Italian recipes, there are regional specialities from all over the country, each reflecting the customs, traditions, and tastes of their district. Styles range from soft and sugary to hard and crunchy, and most contain both sweet and bitter almonds.

Yet of all the multifarious amaretti, those from Saronno in Lombardy are best known. The Lazzaroni brand is found the world over and the biscuits have a history almost as colourful as the papers they are wrapped in. Legend would have it that, almost three centuries ago, the Cardinal of Milan paid a visit to the town. To honour him, two young lovers, Giuseppe and Osolina, created bittersweet biscuits made from sugar, apricot kernels, and egg whites, and wrapped them in pairs as a symbol of their love. The cardinal blessed the couple, who went on to marry; their recipe has remained a secret ever since.

Amaretti are served with coffee, dessert wines, and liqueurs. Crumbled, they are used in Italian desserts. They enjoy a special affinity with peaches. **LF**

Taste: *At first bite, Amaretti di Saronno are crunchy and sweet, but the texture soon becomes chewily soft. They have an almond flavour, reminiscent of fine marzipan.*

The act of unwrapping amaretti to take with coffee 🎯 *is enjoyed as much as the biscuits themselves.*

Brandy Snap

These crisp, lacy, wafer-thin biscuits that literally "snap" as you bite them are traditional English treats. They are made from a mixture of butter, golden syrup, sugar, and flour flavoured with ginger. The mix is melted in a pan, then dropped on to baking sheets and baked. As the mixture cooks, it spreads out to create the dimpled texture that is so distinctive. While still warm and soft, the biscuits are lifted off the tray and rolled around a spoon handle to make hollow tubes. Once cooled, they can be eaten as they are or filled with whipped cream.

Along with "fairings," brandy snaps were sold at English fairs, and were sometimes sold flat rather than rolled. Despite their name, brandy snaps are not always flavoured with brandy. It is thought that earlier recipes used brandy, but that the ingredient was dropped because it was so expensive and had a minimal effect on the taste. Other early versions of the biscuits were made with treacle.

Today, you may also find brandy snaps shaped into baskets rather than tubes, creating edible containers in which desserts can be served. **SBI**

Taste: *The texture of sweet, buttery brandy snaps is between a biscuit and a toffee-like wafer that melts in the mouth and crackles around the teeth. Delicious with tea.*

Appenzeller Biber

Florentine

Known for its elaborate embroidery and delicious cheeses, the Appenzell canton of Switzerland is also home to an addictive pastry. Appenzeller biber (or Appenzeller Baerli-Biber) is a special gingerbread filled with almond paste.

The gingerbread was first baked several centuries ago, and today it is still made in bakeries throughout the region. Although the gingerbread shares similarities with the German lebkuchen, Appenzeller biber is unique in that it starts with a layer of dough pressed into a decorative mould (often of a bear). This dough is then topped by a layer of marzipan or homemade almond paste, and finished with another layer of dough.

The gingerbread often has honey in it, sometimes has liqueur, and always has spices, but the exact amount of spices and exactly which spices depend on the baker. Most often it has ginger, cinnamon, and nutmeg, and sometimes rosewater is also added. It can come in the form of large cakes known as *fladen*, but is also served as cookies known as *biberli*, traditionally served as a Christmas treat. **JH**

The word "florentine" is commonly used in reference to the city of Florence, and frequently to describe dishes containing spinach. However, with regard to these delicate, sweet little biscuits, this is not the case. Their exact history and provenance appears to have been lost in the mists of time but what is certain is that they are not specific to the city of Florence, but are popular all over Europe and beyond.

The bottom of these rich, chewy nut biscuits is made of flaked almonds and candied fruit and usually coated in chocolate marked with distinctive wavy lines. They make a popular *petit four* (a collective term for any number of pretty little cakes and biscuits such as macaroons and meringues).

There are countless variations of florentine when it comes to the combination of fruits and nuts and the coating of chocolate—whether it be dark, milk, or white. The classic florentine uses flaked almonds, but you will find versions made with pistachio nuts, walnuts, and others. Again, the candied fruit used is as varied as the candied fruits available—whether citrus, apricot, pineapple, mango, fig, or cherry. **SBI**

Taste: *The gingerbread has a dry, cake-like texture and is not overly sweet, which goes nicely with the very sweet almond paste filling. Perfect with good hot chocolate.*

Taste: *Florentines are irresistibly, moreishly sweet, chewy, and mouth-watering. Whether served after dinner with coffee or for afternoon tea, one is never quite enough.*

For the hungry passer-by, few sights are more enticing than sweetmeats in an Italian pasticceria. »

Shortbread

Although similar styles of biscuit are made elsewhere, shortbread has become synonymous with Scotland. It appeared in 1736 in the first Scottish cookery book, Mrs. McLintock's *Recipes for Cookery and Pastry-work*: she made her recipe with flour, butter, and "barm" (yeast). Ninety years later, when Meg Dods wrote *The Cook and Housewife's Manual*, it had become the sweet food it is today.

Shortbread has a distinctive crumbly texture and is made using three main ingredients—flour, butter, and sugar. The dough is rolled out, cut into shapes, and baked in a slow oven until golden coloured. While today's manufacturers sometimes add chocolate and ginger, and use ground almonds and different flours in their base recipe, the round style that breaks into triangular pieces known as "petticoat tails" tends to include no additions except perhaps caraway seeds, which purists consider the traditional method. As with any tourist treat, quality varies widely, and shortbread made with fats other than butter is best avoided. Walkers of Aberlour in Scotland produce fantastic petticoat tails. **CTr**

Chocolate Chip Cookie

The North American cookie is generally richer and chewier than an English biscuit, and has been made under that name since at least the beginning of the eighteenth century, and probably much longer. But the chocolate chip cookie—the most famous cookie of all—was invented only during the 1930s.

Ruth Graves Wakefield and her husband bought the Toll House Inn in the town of Whitman, Massachusetts, in 1930. Ruth did the cooking, and she became known locally for her desserts. While experimenting with an old cookie recipe for Butter Drop Do, she chopped up a bar of semi-sweet chocolate into tiny bits, and added it to her cookie dough. The pieces did not melt, but held their shape, softening slightly to a creamy texture.

A large manufacturer of baking chocolate astutely acquired the rights to her recipe, and printed it on their packaging. Then they created "chips" of chocolate specifically for her recipe. Today Nestlé owns the Toll House Cookie trademark. Other homemade chocolate chip cookies are marketed commercially in a range of shapes and sizes. **SH**

Taste: *The thin petticoat tail has a crisp, almost brittle, yet buttery texture with a sweet flavour. The thicker biscuit is denser but still with the distinctively rich flavour.*

Taste: *The texture of chocolate chip cookies can vary from crisp, even crunchy, to deliciously chewy. The taste is nutty and chocolaty with brown sugar notes.*

Chocolate chip cookies were airlifted to U.S. front-line troops in the Gulf to boost morale. »

Liège Waffle

Also known as *gauffres*, waffles are one of Belgium's best-known culinary inventions. The Liège waffle, created in the town of Liège, should be described in terms of how it differs from its better known counterpart: the Brussels waffle. The Brussels waffle is the rectangular waffle made from a yeasted batter cooked in a waffle iron, then served with toppings such as icing sugar, whipped cream, strawberries, or chocolate sauce and usually served on a plate with a knife and fork. It was this waffle that was introduced to the United States and has become ubiquitous there as a breakfast food, whereas in Belgium it remains a snack food to be enjoyed at any time.

In contrast, the Liège waffle is smaller and has a more rounded shape. The batter is made without yeast and the resulting golden waffle has a denser texture and sweeter flavour, with a caramelized burnt sugar coating that is produced as a result of adding small lumps of sugar to the batter. Liège waffles are sold by street vendors and from small shops all over Belgium and they are simply wrapped in paper and eaten in the hand as a snack. **SBI**

Madeleine de Commercy

It was famously the recollection of eating a madeleine that sparked Proust's *À la Recherche du Temps Perdu*, and these scallop-shaped little sponge cakes are indeed delicious. But opinions differ as to their precise origin. Some say the recipe came from a convent of St. Mary Magdalene in Commercy during the eighteenth century, when nuns made cakes and sweets, and sold them to support themselves. When the French Revolution led to the abolition of convents and monasteries, the nuns sold the recipe to village bakers for a handsome fee.

Another story centres on a different Madeleine, a young servant girl, who made them for the Duke of Lorraine in the eighteenth century. He was so impressed with them that he gave some to his daughter Marie, the wife of Louis XV, who subsequently took them to Versailles where they were a huge hit. Others credit Jean Avice (1754–1838), a celebrated pastry chef, with their distinctive shape. Whatever their beginnings, their delicate flavour can be appreciated with tea and coffee, or alongside creamy desserts and sweet wines. **LF**

Taste: *Liège waffles are best eaten while still warm to fully enjoy their crunchy outside and fluffy inside. They are naturally sweet, so there is no need for extra toppings.*

Taste: *The madeleine's crisp, lightly browned edges rise into a golden dome of springy, closely textured crumb that is light, moist, and buttery with hints of lemon and vanilla.*

Traditionally, madeleines are baked in scallop-shaped moulds. ❯❯

Scone

Brownie

Although they can be large, savoury, made with soda bread dough, or cooked like pancakes, the popular notion of scones in their British home is now the small, slightly sweet, but very simple baked item served mainly with tea. The word is originally Scottish and there is a strong tradition of scone-making in that country: like other similar Scottish goods, they would originally have been cooked on a heavy metal plate known as a "girdle" or "griddle."

The most common recipe today is based on white flour, baking powder, and butter, with eggs and milk. The dough is cut into thick rounds or, sometimes, triangles and baked in a hot oven. Sweet scones served with clotted cream and jam form part of the cream tea, a delicious ritual observed happily by tourists in Devon and southwest England, where it originated, and increasingly in the quainter corners of other counties. Like other plain mixtures, scones take happily to additions, such as dried fruit, grated cheese, or a crunchy sugar topping, but restraint should be exercised. Scones go stale fast and should be eaten soon after baking. **ES**

This square bar of dark, rich, chocolate indulgence is not as dense as fudge, nor as light as a cake, yet strikes the perfect balance of texture between the two. Nuts, particularly walnuts, often add crisp notes to the blend but, as so often with popular U.S. recipes, embellishments are endless: anything from crumbled toffee to dried fruit or chocolate chips may be added to the mix.

The word "brownie" was used in reference to various confections before it became firmly attached to the food it denominates today. The cookery teacher and writer Fannie Farmer is credited with printing the first modern brownie recipe in the 1906 edition of her *Boston Cooking School Cook Book*. It gained popularity in the United States as an easier alternative to home-baked cakes and pies for mothers who were becoming increasingly time-pressed as the twentieth century gained pace: they are still popular packed in a lunch bag or a picnic basket, or served at a casual dinner. Topping with ice cream and chocolate sauce or caramel sauce creates the ever-popular brownie sundae. **CN**

Taste: *A fresh scone should be light and not too crusty, with a soft texture more like soda bread than cake. Simply serve split and spread with butter. Its plainness is a virtue.*

Taste: *The brownie is all about its rich chocolate flavour. Texture is a matter of personal taste. Some like brownies chewy and dense, whereas others prefer them lighter.*

Scones with clotted cream and jam are always served as part of an English cream tea.

Berliner Doughnut

Dating back to at least the early 1800s, the Berliner doughnut goes by different names in different regions of Germany. Outside of Berlin it is known simply as Berliner, but in Berlin itself it is better known as *Berliner pfannkuchen* or *pfannkuchen*, which means Berlin pancake, or pancake.

Whatever its name, a Berliner doughnut is essentially a classic jam doughnut made from a sweet yeast dough that has been deep-fried in oil, filled with jam or plum sauce, then usually dusted or rolled in sugar. Other recipes include custard-filled varieties, or a type of doughnut known as *fastnachts*, which are traditionally served on Shrove Tuesday. These differ from Berliners in that they are round or diamond-shaped and made from a yeast-raised potato dough; classically they are sprinkled with sugar and served with syrup.

Since 1961, the Berliner doughnut has been inextricably tied to the U.S. President J. F. Kennedy, after he famously tried to say, "I am a citizen of Berlin." But instead he said, *"Ich bin ein Berliner,"* which translates as "I am a doughnut." **SBI**

Mooncake

Mooncakes are as central to the Chinese Mid-Autumn Festival as lanterns, candles, and gazing at the full harvest moon. Traditionally these round or square pastries were simple: a thin, slightly sweet pastry moulded around a rich filling generally made of lotus seed paste. Along the line, a whole salted egg yolk was added to symbolize the moon.

Today mooncakes are more varied, as top hotels and restaurants from Beijing to Singapore vie to create exotic (and expensive) new versions. Some bakeries add four or more salted egg yolks in their recipes, while fillings can include red bean paste, nuts, seeds, salted ham, durian paste, mashed taro, and even bird's nest. "Snowy" mooncakes have a wrapper of sweetened rice flour paste; ice cream mooncakes come in various flavours with a core of mango sorbet to stand in for the egg yolk.

Mooncakes allegedly played a role in the overthrow of the Mongol Yuan Dynasty that ruled China in the fourteenth century. Messages outlining plans for the revolts were hidden in mooncakes, which were given as gifts to supporters. **KKC**

Taste: *Soft, golden Berliner doughnuts are a treat indeed, oozing with jam as you bite into them. They are best when fresh, so be sure to seek out a bakery with a good turnover.*

Taste: *Mooncakes are smallish but they are rarely eaten whole because of their rich filling. Instead, they are cut into wedges, the better to appreciate the "moon" at the centre.*

In 2007 a mooncake weighing 13 tons was baked in China; it incorporated ten of these smaller cakes. »

Baba

Italy, the Ukraine, and Poland (where it is known as *babka*), all claim to be the originators of baba, the sweetened, cylindrical shaped cake. Baba means old woman or grandmother (*babka* is its diminutive—little old granny), and the cake's name is said to come from its tapered shape, which resembles the full skirts once worn by peasant women.

While the shape of baba is Slavic in origin, the recipe seems to have travelled around Europe, gaining various culinary influences along the way. Recipes vary from simple yeast-raised cakes and fruited breads to its alcohol-laden incarnation as the celebrated *baba au rhum*, a development that took place in France (perhaps thanks to an exiled Polish king who may have taken *babka* there in the eighteenth century).

Iced or sugar-dusted babas are traditional Easter fare in Russia and Poland. Their luscious golden dough may be scented with saffron and studded with plump raisins, and the white icing dripping down the sides is often sprinkled with slivered almonds, although the original baba was plain. **RS**

Taste: *Light, porous, and buttery, with yeasty undertones, baba sometimes has a subtle hint of saffron, vanilla, almonds, or rum, depending on the flavourings used.*

A cylindrical mould gives baba its distinctive shape, but ◎ the cake can also be baked in small individual rounds.

Honey Cake

This traditional Hungarian confection known as *mézeskalács* is more of a biscuit than a cake. Today, the highly decorated honey cakes, which are rather like gingerbread, are sold not only all over Hungary but also across central Europe, and they make a popular token of friendship or love.

The earliest honey cakes date back to before the fourteenth century. They were made of a soft dough of warmed honey, sugar, and flour pressed into intricate moulds frequently carved with religious characters, indicating that the cakes were probably used as offerings to saints on special occasions. Later moulds depicted images of outlaws, animals, and dancing couples. The shapes of the moulds were so beautiful that no further decoration was needed.

Today, the honey cakes are cut, not cast, into a shape, then decorated with icing and elaborate decorations. Red is a popular colour and mirrors are often used within the cake decorations. To this day, the most favoured shape is the heart, and honey cakes bearing the words *szívküldi szívnek* ("from a heart to a heart") can often be found. **SBI**

Taste: *Honey cakes are very similar in taste and texture to gingerbread, although with a lighter, more honeyed taste. They are often treated as an object of admiration.*

Maid of Honour

These golden-coloured, almond-flavoured, dainty English curd tartlets have a venerable history. As their name suggests, they are associated with royalty. Legend links them with the Tudor monarch Henry VIII, who is said to have first come across the tarts when he met Anne Boleyn and other maids of honour eating them. Such was Henry's fondness for the tarts that he insisted the recipe be kept secret within Richmond Palace. Another version of the story links them to the royal palace of Hampton Court.

Historically the tarts have a long association with the town of Richmond in Surrey, where a local shop was famous for its maids of honour during the eighteenth century. Today the tradition of making the tarts is maintained by a charming bakery and tea shop called Newens, situated by Kew Gardens. The connection between the Newens family and making maids of honour goes back to the mid-nineteenth century, when Robert Newens served an apprenticeship at the Richmond shop, before setting up his own business baking the tartlets and offering them on his own premises. **JL**

Tarte Tatin

This legendary French caramelized apple upside-down tart is the subject of much culinary folklore. In one story of its origins, Stephanie, one of the two Tatin sisters who ran the Hotel Terminus in Lamotte-Beuvron in the Loire Region, accidentally placed the apples in a tart dish before she had lined it with pastry. She then layered the pastry on top of the apple and proceeded to cook it, inverting it when serving. Another version simply credits the Tatin sisters with producing particularly fine examples of a tart traditionally made in the region.

Whatever the truth of the matter, tarte tatin is a culinary treat of such importance to the French that their restaurants are assessed on their ability to make it successfully. For a classic tarte tatin, sliced dessert apples are first fried with butter and sugar, then topped with pastry and baked in the oven; the result is turned upside-down to reveal caramelized apple on a fine, golden pastry base. The tart is served warm from the oven. Variations exist, using fruits such as pineapple, pear, or quince instead of apple, but made according to the same principles. **JL**

Taste: *This little, open tart has a crisp puff-pastry case containing a sweet, almond-flavoured curd filling. The tart is at once moist and slightly crumbly.*

Taste: *The bitterness of the caramel contrasts deliciously with the sweetness of the apple, enhanced by the melting buttery richness of the pastry*

The Newens family tea shop, famed for its maids of
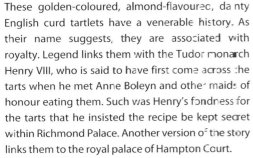 *honour, moved to its current location in Kew in 1887.*

MRS. RORER'S
NEW COOK BOOK

Devil's Food Cake

A chocolate lover's delight, this cake became popular in the United States in the early 1900s. Although there are different versions of the recipe and the cake's first creator is unknown, a recipe for devil's food cake first appeared in *Mrs. Rorer's New Cook Book* in 1902. Other recipes soon followed. The cake acquired its reddish-brown colour from the mix of bicarbonate of soda and cocoa in the recipe, which has led it to sometimes be confused with Waldorf Astoria cake or red velvet cake. Purists still make it with cocoa, but only alkalized European cocoa will do as natural cocoa will not make the cake rise.

Whatever recipe is used, devil's food cake is made from chocolate layers topped with white or chocolate icing to produce a "sinfully" delicious cake. The cake may have gained its name for its contrast to the light, airy, and white angel food cake, known in the United States by about 1870.

Devil's food cake is wonderful topped with a scoop of vanilla ice cream and a glass of ice-cold milk or dark, rich coffee. Many believe it tastes better after being refrigerated for a day. **SH**

Taste: *Devil's food cake has a rich, chocolate taste and a tender, moist crumb. Because cocoa is used, it is only moderately sweet, but with slightly bitter undertones.*

Mrs. Rorer's book distills the experience she ◐ *gained in her Philadelphia cookery school.*

Dobos Torte

A contemporary of Auguste Escoffier, Josef Dobos became equally famous outside his native Hungary as his fellow master baker did outside France. Born into a family of chefs in 1847, Dobos became particularly renowned for the extravagant layered cake he created in 1887.

Gourmets gasped at the five or more extra-thin layers of sponge—each individually baked—that were sandwiched with rich butter cream and sometimes topped with a layer of crisp sugar caramel. The Dobos torte was an instant sensation and, thanks to its appearance at the 1896 Millennium Exposition, it became a Hungarian institution.

Dobos shrewdly designed packaging sufficiently robust to send his masterpiece abroad. But, when the market was flooded with inferior imitations, he decided to release his secret recipe; when he retired in 1906, he donated it to the Budapest Pastry and Honey-bread Makers' Guild. In 1962, Hungary's pastry chefs celebrated the anniversary of the creation of his classic cake by parading a giant-sized Dobos torte through the streets of Budapest. **WS**

Taste: *The thin vanilla sponge layers of Dobos torte have a characteristic dryness, providing the perfect foil for the melt-in-the-mouth chocolate butter cream icing.*

Sacher-Torte

Sacher-Torte is a chocolate cake to die for that hails from Vienna, Austria. It has two glorious tiers of rich, intensely flavoured chocolate sponge, sandwiched together with apricot jam, and swathed in a glossy chocolate coating. The cake was invented in 1832 by Franz Sacher, a sixteen-year-old apprentice working in the kitchens of Prince Metternich, the legendary Austrian diplomat. When Metternich ordered a grand dessert for distinguished guests and the head cook was taken ill, Sacher stepped in to create a splendid chocolate cake. To this day, Sacher-Torte continues to be baked to the original, well-guarded recipe.

In 1876 Sacher's son Eduard opened the Hotel Sacher in Vienna, and an authentic Sacher-Torte must carry the official hotel seal on the face of the cake, made in chocolate. Cakes to carry away are packed in a gold-cornered wooden box, bear the registered trademark "Hotel Sacher Wien" on the lid, and have a wood engraving of the Hotel Sacher Wien inside the cover. The box is then gift-wrapped in Bordeaux-coloured paper and decorated with a Biedermeier design. **LF**

Taste: *Dense but deliciously yielding, the sublime cocoa-rich crumb and silky glaze are complemented by a tangy apricot fruitiness. Serve with clouds of whipped cream.*

Sacher-Torte is still made at the Hotel Sacher today. »

Café~Garten

Baumkuchen

Black Forest Gateau

A speciality of German bakers for over 200 years, the German word "baumkuchen" literally means tree cake. The name refers to the layers of golden rings that are revealed when the cake is cut into, which are not dissimilar to the rings of a tree trunk.

This unusual effect is produced by a labour-intensive cooking method. A thin layer of batter is brushed over a spit and baked until golden. (This would once have been over a wood fire, but today it is usually over a grill.) Another layer of batter is then brushed on top of the cake and cooked, and so the process is repeated, with ten to twenty layers of batter, until a full cake has been created. For special occasions, chefs bake very large cakes weighing 100 pounds (45 kg) or so. The finished baumkuchen is usually covered with a sugar or chocolate glaze.

In Luxembourg, where it is known as *baamkuch*, baumkuchen has become a traditional dish for special celebrations, in particular weddings. Other national variations include the Polish *sekacz* with its distinctive finger-like protrusions that make the cake look rather like an ice formation. **SBI**

Known as *Schwarzwälder Kirschtorte* in its homeland of Germany, which literally translates as Black Forest cherry cake, this wonderfully indulgent dessert is popular the world over, and became something of an iconic dessert in the 1970s.

The gateau is constructed from several thin layers of chocolate cake, which are frequently sprinkled with the cherry liqueur kirsch, and sandwiched together with stoned, cooked, sweetened sour cherries and whipped cream. The whole cake is then decorated with more whipped cream and chocolate shavings, and perhaps more cherries. The sharpness of the cherries set against the richness of the cream and the dark bitterness of the chocolate, plus that indefinable punchy kick provided by the kirsch, should all come together to make a slice of Black Forest gateau an utterly luxurious taste sensation.

The history of this dessert is elusive, but it is generally dated to 1930s Berlin. In Germany, you will find very few variations on the classic recipe, but in Austria you may find it made using rum. **SBI**

Taste: *The long, slow cooking of baumkuchen, along with the ground nuts used in the batter, gives it a very distinctive taste and texture. Serve it in slices with coffee.*

Taste: *A slice of genuine Black Forest gateau should be a truly sublime experience, with a perfect balance of flavours. It is worth searching out high and low.*

A boy carrying a pretzel and a baumkuchen
❸ *traditionally signals a bakery in southern Germany.*

Fruit Cake

There are many types of fruit cake in Britain, and most of them are good. Made with dried fruit, nuts, and candied citrus peel, these sturdy creations have been linked with celebrations for three centuries or so. Perhaps because of the ingredients—which were once huge luxuries and remain relatively expensive even today—they are usually served at weddings and Christmas. They can be kept for months or even years, during which time the flavour is believed to improve—hence the old practice of reserving the smallest tier of a wedding cake to eat at the christening of the couple's first child.

Although a fruit cake will never be light, they have always been leavened. They probably began as fruit breads, leavened with yeast, during the Middle Ages, with eggs replacing yeast as a raising agent in the eighteenth century and baking powder added after that. Its solidity makes it ideal for decoration; a layer of marzipan is applied to protect the cake, and stop the traditional white icing from being stained by the fruit. An alternative decoration is a topping of glacé fruits and nuts. A moist texture is prized. **ES**

Taste: *Recipes vary greatly, but the fruit cake eaten at Christmas, for example, is dark and dense. Brandy, nuts, candied peel, and dried fruit can all emerge in the flavour.*

Madeira Cake

Despite the name, this confection does not originate from the island of Madeira, but is a traditional English cake from the nineteenth century. Moist and closely textured but buttery rich, it is most often flavoured with lemon peel, and usually baked in the shape of a loaf. The link with Madeira is that it was originally served with a glass of this celebrated fortified wine, with which it pairs fantastically well.

Combining wine with cake was a practice enjoyed by upper-class English ladies, arising from their habit of waking late and subsequently taking breakfast late. Dinner was usually an early evening meal, and so a light, stopgap affair was needed to keep hunger pangs at bay: a sort of precursor to the meal that later became recognized as lunch. (The working class already had an established bread and ale habit, but the leisurely lifestyle of the rich meant it took a while to catch on.) When eventually lunch became an accepted meal of the day, the custom developed of offering a slice of cake and a drink (be it wine or tea) to visitors who called in the middle of the morning or in the afternoon. **LF**

Taste: *A golden soft outer layer gives way to a dense, moist interior. Although the cake typically contains lemon peel, the prevailing flavour is that of vanilla and butter.*

Potato Apple Cake

Cheesecake

This is an ancient dish with ancient roots, but no less charming for it. Mashed potatoes mixed with butter, ginger, and flour are kneaded to a soft dough, then shaped into farls (a round shape scored into triangles) or a loaf, and layered with apples, sugar, and more butter. It is then cooked on the griddle until golden in colour, with the apples tender and the butter and sugar melted to a succulent sauce.

Potato apple cake is a classic dish to serve on Halloween—the eve of the Christian celebration of All Saints Day. Halloween can be seen as an amalgamation of Christian, Celtic, and Roman traditions. Samhain is an ancient Celtic festival celebrated annually at the end of October. By 43 CE, the Roman Empire had conquered most of the Celtic regions and the Roman festival of Pomona, whose symbol was an apple, became incorporated into the festivities of Samhain. The eve of All Saints Day used to be a day of strict abstinence and traditional fare tended to consist of meatless dishes favouring potatoes; this unusual potato apple cake soon became a favourite at this time. **SBI**

Of all the variations on this American classic, the New York style cheesecake reigns supreme. That is not to say that cheesecake is a New York invention—not in the least. Similar custardy, cheese-based sweet cakes had been introduced to the city by immigrants from Europe, and it is possible that a similar dish was enjoyed in ancient Rome. But it was in the hands of New York City cooks that cheesecake became the denser, creamier product it is today.

The classic cheesecake recipe sees a blend of cream cheese, eggs, and sugar sitting atop a crust, commonly made from digestive biscuits. But this simple formula offers almost a blank slate for the creative cook. Although cream cheese is classic for the New York version, cheesecake may be made with ricotta cheese, sour cream, or cottage cheese replacing some or all of the cream cheese; the base may be of pastry or biscuit crumbs; the cheese topping may be flavoured or decorated in endless ways, sometimes with fruit. Savoury variants include a blue cheese cheesecake that may be served either as a starter or in place of a cheese course. **CN**

Taste: *Potato apple cake is a sweet-savoury griddle cake. It is best served hot in wedges drizzled with thick cream, if you like, and accompanied by steaming cups of strong tea.*

Taste: *New York style cheesecake has a rich, slightly tangy dairy character from the cream cheese, with moderate sweetness and a subtle flavour from vanilla or lemon zest.*

Pashka

This creamy, moulded confection of curd cheese, lemon zest, nuts (usually almonds), and dried fruits was created by Russian Orthodox Christians to eat as a dessert at the end of Lent. The name comes from *Pascha*, the Hebrew word for Passover.

Pashka is similar to an unbaked cheesecake but without the crust. Curd cheese is used to celebrate the first rich milk of spring. The curd cheese is sweetened, softened with cream, and sharpened with lemon, before the nuts and fruit are added and the finished mixture spooned into a perforated mould. (Traditionally, the mould is pyramid shaped and leaves an imprint of the orthodox cross on the surface of the pashka.) It is then pressed and left for twelve to twenty-four hours to give the whey time to drain from the curds.

When ready to serve, the pashka is unmoulded onto a plate and nuts or fruit are sometimes used to form the initials "XB"—meaning "Christ is risen"—on the side. At Easter pashka is traditionally served with *kulich*, a tall, iced fruit bread similar to an Italian panettone, and coloured hard-boiled eggs. **WS**

Taste: *The tangy curd cheese and lemon zest give a slight sourness and perfectly temper the creaminess of this wonderfully rich dessert. Serve in small portions.*

Pavlova

A large, thick disc of swirled meringue that is soft and marshmallow-like in the middle, the pavlova is like life itself to both New Zealanders and Australians, who compete for ownership of what is in both countries an iconic national delicacy. Perhaps the most misused of all culinary terms, a pav is not a pav unless it has that ethereal soft layer in the middle, produced by the addition of vinegar, cornflour, or both to the egg whites and sugar that would otherwise create a crisp meringue.

The name commemorates the fluffy tutus of the Russian ballet dancer Anna Pavlova, who toured Australasia in 1926 and 1929. The question of which nation first celebrated her in pâtisserie is vexed, but Professor Helen Leach delivered a paper at Tasting Australia 2007 showing that a recipe for pavlova appeared in New Zealand as early as 1929.

Today, specialist shops sell several sizes of pavlova, and imaginative chefs come up with elaborate contemporary versions of the classic dessert, featuring roasted peaches, orange flower water, loganberries—even chocolate. **GC**

Taste: *The mouth experience of pavlova is a rich, changing swirl of mousse-like meringue and whipped cream accented by the crisp crust and sharp fruit topping.*

A signed portrait of prima ballerina Anna Pavlova on stage at the Imperial Palace in 1912. »

Torta di Castagne

Torta Caprese di Mandorle

Chestnuts have long flourished along the Apennines. The ancient Greeks ate them boiled or roasted; the Romans made them into flour and turned them into a type of bread; today, more than 300 different types of chestnut grow all over Italy.

Torta di castagne is a traditional northern Italian chestnut cake that seems to have originated in the town of Pontestura in Piedmont. The first written reference dates back to 1800, when the town's bakers were making and selling the cakes at Easter time. (They would also cook cakes prepared at home by families with no suitable oven of their own.)

The basic ingredients are puréed chestnuts, butter, eggs, sugar, and, nowadays, vanilla, but any number of ingredients can be added, depending on the preferences of the cook. Typical additions might include citrus peel, amaretti, cocoa, nutmeg, and usually some form of alcohol such as marsala or rum. The egg whites are whipped separately before adding to the cake, which helps give the cake its light texture. It is best served in thin slices alongside coffee, the perfect foil for its gratifying richness. **LF**

Dark, dense, and utterly divine, Torta Caprese di Mandorle could well make you fall head over heels in love at first slice. Although the Italians produce some fantastic chocolate, by tradition they are not particularly big on chocolate cakes. However, this glorious exception confirms that quality comes first and foremost over quantity. It really is a stunner.

Torta Caprese takes its name from Capri, the beautiful island in the Bay of Naples where it is a speciality. The cake is made with the best quality bitter chocolate, butter, eggs, ground almonds, and, in some recipes, the vaguest suggestion of flour. Sometimes a splash of strega liqueur is added and it is decorated with a stencil image of the island and a lone palm tree. It is best sampled in the wonderful pastry shops of Capri or in Naples alongside the dock where the ferries leave for the island.

Little is recorded about the true origins of the cake. Locals say it was the result of a happy accident when a forgetful baker omitted baking powder and flour from his mixture. Whatever its provenance, the cake makes essential eating. **LF**

Taste: *Torta di castagne has a dense but moist texture that is never cloying or heavy; the chestnuts add a nutty, sweet creaminess to the other ingredients.*

Taste: *Ground almonds, and little or no flour, give a dense moistness to the cake. The deep flavour is rich with the essence of cocoa, but with no obvious nuttiness.*

Torta Caprese is the obvious choice at coffee time for visitors relaxing in Capri. »

Linzer Torte

This classic fruit tart originated in Linz in Austria and recipes for Linzer torte can be found dating back to the seventeenth century. In the earlier recipes, butter, almonds, sugar, flour, and spices were used and little has changed in the intervening years. It was clearly a favourite tart in baroque times and has lasted in popularity through to modern times.

The round Linzer torte is distinctive in appearance with a golden lattice top and fruit filling oozing through. The golden, crumbly pastry is usually made with ground almonds, butter, sugar, flour, and egg yolks; it is rolled out, spread with a sweet redcurrant or blackcurrant preserve, then topped with a lattice made with more rolled pastry. It is crumbly, without being dry, with a lovely moistness added by the layer of fruit in the centre.

Although a redcurrant preserve is the traditional filling for Linzer torte, you will find other fillings as well. Raspberry is a particularly popular alternative. Likewise, almonds are the classic nut used in the pastry, but you will also find plenty of variations made with other nuts such as hazelnuts. **SBI**

Taste: *Linzer torte is delicious in its very simplicity: a rich, nutty, pastry with fruit preserve. It is best served mid-morning or mid-afternoon, perhaps with a little cream.*

The Old City of Linz is lined with bakeries and other specialist shops. »

Treacle Tart

Tarte aux Fraises

A traditional English dessert, comforting in its simplicity, treacle tart dates back to Victorian times. Popular nursery fare, it also features on the menus at gentlemen's clubs and old-fashioned British restaurants. These days the name is the source of some confusion, as "treacle" in England refers to black treacle or molasses, the dark, sticky, strongly-flavoured sweet by-product of sugar processing. Treacle tart, however, is usually sweetened with golden syrup or pale treacle, another by-product of the sugar industry. The market for golden syrup or "goldie" in England was recognized by business man Abram Lyle, who began canning and selling the sweet, sticky syrup in 1885.

Treacle tart draws on a thrifty tradition of using basic ingredients to make a treat. The classic recipe mixes fresh breadcrumbs with a generous amount of golden syrup and a touch of lemon juice and grated lemon peel. This sticky filling is then spread into a shortcrust pastry case and baked until set. Some versions add cream or eggs to the filling, and often the tart is decorated with a pastry lattice. **JL**

With its bright, scarlet berries, the classic French strawberry tart is a delectable sight, one that is seen in the windows of pâtisseries in villages and cities throughout France. This pretty creation is one manifestation of France's rich and varied tradition of fruit tarts. A simple concept, the secret of a truly great tarte aux fraises rests with the quality of the ingredients used and the care taken in its making.

There are numerous variations on the theme. The pastry, for example, may be a simple shortcrust or a richer pâte sucrée, enriched with egg yolks and sweetened with sugar. Either way, the pastry should be rolled out very finely and used to make a pre-baked pastry case. In some versions, whole strawberries are simply arranged in the pastry case, then glazed with redcurrant jelly. A more indulgent tarte aux fraises, however, sees the addition of a layer of *crème pâtissière* spread over the base of the tart. This pastry cream is a thick, creamy-textured custard, made from eggs, sugar, butter, flour, and milk, the latter infused with a vanilla pod. The cream contrasts beautifully with the fresh strawberries. **JL**

Taste: *One of the pleasures of treacle tart is its distinctive texture, as the stickiness of the filling melts away into a yielding, buttery sweetness with a hint of lemon.*

Taste: *The flavour of ripe, sweet strawberries should dominate, combined with the rich, vanilla-scented crème pâtissière and the crisp, fine texture of the pastry.*

The distinctive packaging of Lyle's Golden Syrup, used in treacle tart, has changed little since 1885.

Apple Strudel

Belgian Frangipane Pastry

Most closely associated with German and Austrian cuisine, but enjoyed all over central Europe, the delight that is apple strudel is made from layer upon layer of wafer-thin sheets of pastry, wrapped around a tender filling of apples and sultanas. In traditional recipes, the pastry is wrapped around the filling to make a long sausage shape, then twisted into a horseshoe before baking. The word "strudel" comes from the German for "whirlpool," reflecting the swirling layers that characterize this dessert.

The pastry with which strudels are made is all-important, and the making of it is judged an art form. Similar to filo, strudel pastry is made from flour, eggs, butter, and water. It must be kneaded until smooth and elastic and left to rest. The dough is then rolled and stretched by hand over a large table until so thin as to be almost transparent. Then, and only then, is it ready to be made into a strudel.

Apple strudel is the best loved of all strudels, but other fillings are extremely popular, too. Cherry strudel is an absolute classic, and you will also find savoury versions filled with, for example, spinach. **SBI**

Variations of frangipane have been enjoyed for centuries—with recipes dating back to seventeenth-century France. However, although frangipane pastries can be found all over Europe, the Belgian version is not to be missed. Usually baked as individual tartlets, the crisp golden pastry shell is filled with sweet frangipane—a mixture of ground almonds, butter, and sugar combined to make a sweet, tender filling. The pastry may then be finished off with a striped pattern on top, or a swirl of icing.

Other popular frangipane tarts include the French *amandine*, which is popular sprinkled with slivered almonds and brushed with a translucent glaze. The *galette des rois* (cake of kings) is a larger French frangipane tart. Similar to a *pithivier*, it is traditionally baked for the festival of Epiphany, when Christians celebrate the visit of the three wise men to the newborn baby Jesus. Often made of puff pastry, the case is usually filled with frangipane, then topped with another disc of pastry and a bean or charm is hidden inside. The lucky person who finds the bean is crowned "king" for the day. **SBI**

Taste: *Apple strudel is sweet, but not too sweet, with a sharp filling and a delicate pastry jacket. It may be eaten hot or cold, and is a popular choice for serving with coffee.*

Taste: *These sweet, crisp, delicious pastries are utterly moreish. The combination of nuts, sugar, and butter in the frangipane is rich, but not too sweet or overpowering.*

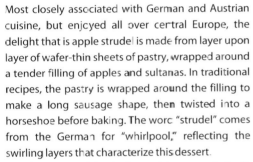

Apple strudel comes with a liberal serving of
ⓚ *whipped cream in this restaurant in Mosel, Germany.*

BOURBONNEUX
ses MACARONS

BOULANGERIE PATISSERIE

PATISSIER.BOULANGER.CONFIS

Éclair

Danish Pastry

The origins of these choux pastry confections filled with cream and topped with icing or chocolate are vague, suggesting that they have evolved over time into the delicacy that we know today. Certainly—according to the *Oxford English Dictionary*—the word can be traced back to 1861.

The classic éclair is made of choux pastry piped into a finger shape and baked until hollow in the centre. In France, you will find two types: *éclairs au chocolat*, filled with a chocolate-flavoured *crème pâtissière* and topped with chocolate icing, and a coffee version with a coffee-flavoured filling and coffee icing. The English version, in contrast, is usually filled with whipped cream and topped with melted chocolate. A similar choux-based pastry is the profiterole: round choux buns filled with cream and topped with chocolate sauce, which are usually served as a dessert. Another confection found in France is the *religieuse* (nun). Flavoured with coffee or chocolate, a *religieuse* consists of two filled choux buns topped with icing, a smaller one sitting on top of the other to resemble a little fat nun. **SBI**

Although associated with Denmark, the "Danish" pastry is not one hundred per cent Scandinavian. In its homeland, it is called *wienerbrød*, which means "Viennese bread," whereas in Austria it is known as *Kopenhagener*. According to one story, when Danish bakers went on strike during the mid-nineteenth century, Austrian bakers migrated to the country to work bringing with them recipes for a pastry known as *plundergebäck*. When the Danes returned, they refined the Austrian recipes, creating pastries with ever more and ever finer layers of dough and butter.

Today Danish pastries come in many shapes and sizes. (A large pastry shaped like a pretzel is known as a *kringle*, and is the official sign for bakeries in Denmark.) Fillings include custard, jam, and, most typically *remonce*—butter creamed with sugar, and nuts or cinnamon. They are often topped with icing. For Danish families it is a Sunday tradition to have pastries at breakfast. It is almost a rite of passage for young people to knock on the back door of the local bakery for freshly baked pastries on their way home in the early hours from a night out. **CTj**

Taste: *This truly indulgent pastry is light in texture yet rich, sweet, and creamy in the mouth. Éclairs are wonderful bought fresh from a pâtisserie.*

Taste: *Biting into a piece of freshly baked Danish pastry is a very sweet experience. The texture is fluffy and crispy, with the buttery softness of the remonce in the middle.*

Superb éclairs are available from French pâtisseries
❮ *such as this impeccable example in Montmartre, Paris.*

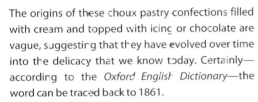

Mince Pie

In Britain, these small, sweet pies are synonymous with Christmas—although they are not usually served as part of the Christmas Day meal, but kept in a tin as an offering for visitors during the festive season. The most famous of these is Father Christmas, for whom children often leave a mince pie and a glass of sherry on Christmas Eve.

Mince pies owe their existence to a medieval pastry called a chewette, which was first made with meat and spices, then later with the addition of dried fruit. Today they are made with a base and lid of shortcrust or puff pastry, and filled with mincemeat—a mixture of dried fruit, spices, grated apples, citrus, nuts, and perhaps a little brandy. The mincemeat is traditionally based on beef suet: the last remnant of the old, meat-based recipes. Although meat had fallen from popular use by the nineteenth century, *petits pâtés de Pézenas,* the sweet meat pastries from Herault in the Languedoc, are similar to earlier mince pies. Local lore has it that the recipe derives from a visit to Pézenas by the British colonial general Robert Clive in 1768. **ES**

Taste: *Much depends on the mincemeat, which should be dark and fruity with notes of cinnamon and ground ginger, and the pastry, which should be crumbly.*

Pastéis de Nata

These creamy, buttery, little pastry tarts, dusted with cinnamon and icing sugar, are emblematic of Portugal and the wonderful Portuguese way with pastry. They can be found in pastry shops and cafés across the country, and wherever the Portuguese gather around the globe.

As with a number of other traditional pastries and sweetmeats, it is thought that it was nuns who originally created pastéis de nata: in this instance, the sisters at the Mosteiro dos Jerónimos (the Hieronymite monastery) in Belém, near Lisbon, some time around the turn of the eighteenth century. In the capital they were, and still are, more likely to go under the name of pastéis de Belém, after their original home, and in 1837, a little shop called Casa Pastéis de Belém opened its doors. This was the first place outside the convent to sell the much-loved cakes and to this day locals and tourists alike still travel to the shop to enjoy them fresh and warm from the oven: velvety rich custard encased in layers of buttery, crisp puff pastry, topped with a delicate powder of cinnamon and sugar. **LF**

Taste: *Best eaten warm, pastéis de nata yield melt-in-the-mouth layers of crisp yet buttery puff pastry, which give way to a glorious silky, sunshine yellow custard.*

Gerbet Macaroon

Millefeuille

These colourful, flavoured sweetmeats—almond and egg white biscuits stuck together in pairs with a near-infinite variety of fillings—are a Parisian pâtisserie that originated during the Belle Époque. Their name links them to the Ladurée family that owned a celebrated Salon de The in the capital's Rue Royale—a business that is still flourishing today.

Although popular since their creation, they owe their current form to the celebrated pastry chef Pierre Hermé, who worked for Ladurée as a young chef, but started experimenting with the recipe after he went to work at Fauchon, the most famous food shop in Paris. Until Hermé began developing his own recipes, gerbets were smooth and dry on the outside and a little chewy: a thin butter cream or ganache held the pairs together. He transformed the range of fillings, adding fruit, nuts, and a galaxy of textures and tastes. His signature gerbet—"Ispahan"—is scented with rose water and filled with fresh raspberries, but each year he brings out a new range of gerbets in much the same way as a fashion house brings out a new collection. **MR**

The French name of this classic, indulgent pastry literally means "a thousand leaves," reflecting the numerous wafer-thin layers of puff pastry contained in just one heavenly slice. This name is not far off the mark when one considers that a typical sheet of puff pastry has 729 layers and a millefeuille can consist of two or more layers of pastry.

This confection is usually rectangular in shape and made up of three sheets of crisp, golden puff pastry with a layer of rich, creamy filling spread between each one. The top is dusted with icing sugar before the pastry is sliced gently into smaller, individual millefeuille. The filling is made of whipped cream, or sometimes *crème pâtissière*, with fruit.

In France, there is an oval-shaped millefeuille known as a "Napoleon," which is made of two layers of pastry sandwiching a creamy, almond filling. (However, in the United States this name applies to all kinds of millefeuille.) A caramel-coated version is known as *Szegedinertorte*, after the Hungarian town of Szeged, which some attribute to the birth of the original millefeuille. **SBI**

Taste: *The surface of each macaroon should be crisp; the inside should be moist and chewy, having been left, ideally for twenty-four hours, to absorb moisture from the filling.*

Taste: *Crisp, buttery pastry contrasts delightfully with the soft, luscious cream, which oozes out from between the layers. Fruit cuts across the rich creaminess of the filling.*

Güllaç

Found in every local bakery during the month-long Muslim festival of Ramadan, this Turkish confection dates back to the Ottoman Empire. Records suggest that güllaç was served at the circumcision ceremony of the sons of Suleiman the Magnificent, who ruled the empire from 1520 to 1566. Some say that güllaç is an early version of baklava, the classic sweetmeat made of layers of filo pastry, nuts, and sugar syrup.

Sweet and milk-based, it consists of layers of güllaç leaves (thin wafers made of corn starch, wheat flour, and water) that have been soaked in milk, sugar, and ground nuts. Although walnuts are the traditional choice, they tend to colour the milk so almonds are often favoured to produce a snowy-white hue. Güllaç can be flavoured with rose water or vanilla and is often decorated with vibrant red pomegranate seeds and pale green pistachio nuts. This distinctive confection is traditionally brought out after the *iftar*—the evening meal served to break the day's fast. Although güllaç can be bought, homemade is best, and güllaç leaves can be purchased at most Turkish grocers. **SBI**

Taste: *Intensely sweet with a milky richness, güllaç is distinctly lighter than other similar classics, such as baklava, and is ideal for completing the Ramadan meal.*

Gaziantep Baklava

Gaziantep, the largest city in southeast Turkey, can claim to be the country's gastronomic capital. It is also the spiritual home of the syrupy, nutty, flaky pastry: baklava. Across the Middle East and the Balkans, baklava changes its character: sometimes larger, sometimes drier, sometimes sweeter, sometimes more sticky. In Gaziantep, each piece is small, moist, and packed with the finest pistachios grown in the surrounding countryside. Above all, its pastry, rolled out with a long, tapering, pear wood pin, is unequalled in its fineness. The pastry, referred to as *yufka*, is transparent and thinner than the thinnest strudel pastry; when baked it becomes a pile of brittle layers. After they are taken from the oven, boiling syrup is poured over them and they separate into leaves.

The origin of the pastry is not clear but it may have evolved from the flatbreads layered with nuts that were eaten by nomads living in the region that was once Kurdistan, where Gaziantep lies. Indeed, the best pastry shops in Istanbul today are owned and run by Kurds. **MR**

Taste: *Baklava is a complex mixture of textures and tastes. The crisp buttery upper layers give way to the moister lower ones, blending with a filling of pistachios and syrup.*

After baking, baklava pastries are cut into individual portions for display to customers. »

Sbrisolona

Vatrushka

Sbrisolona, which is also known as sbriciolona, is a delightfully crisp, buttery cake from Mantua, in Lombardy, northern Italy. The name means "crumbly," and that is exactly what this cake-cum-cookie is. Too brittle to be cut with a knife, sbrisolona is generally broken into pieces and often served with coffee or sweet dessert wines such as Malvasia or Vin Santo. Although it is enjoyed throughout the year, it is a particular favourite at Christmas time.

Sbrisolona was traditionally a frugal affair: a treat for the poor, based on inexpensive, easily available ingredients. Typically a sweetened mixture of cornmeal and hazelnuts, shortened with lard, it was a far cry from the rich cakes the wealthy enjoyed. Yet the hazelnuts were replaced by almonds and butter took the place of lard, giving the cake an entrée to Mantua's upper class. A recipe for the indulgent version of sbrisolona appeared in Pellegrino Artusi's landmark recipe book *La Scienza in Cucina e l'Arte di Mangiar Bene*, which was first published more than one hundred years ago and is still highly regarded today. **LF**

Vatrushki are sweet cheese pastries that are a classic of the Slavic cuisine and are particularly associated with Russia and the Ukraine. Their name comes from the word *vatra*, which means "fire" or "fireplace" in various Slavic languages including Czech, Polish, Ukrainian, Serbian, and Croatian.

Typically, vatrushki are made from a yeasted wheat flour dough enriched with butter, eggs, and sugar rather like brioche, shaped into a flattened round that is pinched up and then filled with *tvorog* —a kind of farmer's curd cheese similar to German quark or Italian ricotta. The *tvorog* filling is usually sweetened, often simply with sugar or honey, or flavoured with vanilla or lemon rind. The filling may have raisins added and you may also find jam vatrushki, although these are less common. Every family tends to have their own recipe and tradition.

Savoury vatrushki are also delicious; the dough of these is usually made of wheat and rye flour and the filling flavoured with onion. A similar pastry is the Siberian *shangi*, made with sourdough and a simple potato and sour cream filling. **SBI**

Taste: *Wonderful served next to creamy zabaglione, sbrisolona has a fabulous crisp texture and rich buttery flavour. Beyond the almond edge are hints of lemon zest.*

Taste: *Sweet, tender vatrushki resemble rustic-style, cheese Danish pastries and are typically served with strong black Russian tea. Savoury vatrushki are served with soup.*

Vatrushki are popular as a quick snack bought from vendors such as this one in Warsaw, Poland. »

CUKIERNIA

GESLER

Pączek

Pączek + Coca-

Struffoli di Napoli

Mochi

Fans of the sweet, sticky, and sublime should stop right here. Struffoli di Napoli are little golden balls of fried dough that are drenched in honey. Especially popular at Christmas time when they are found piled high in mounds on restaurant tables, struffoli is a speciality of southern Italy, particularly Naples.

The Greeks probably introduced the antecedent of struffoli to the Italians; the name comes from the Greek "strongulos," which means "rounded." Central Italy has its own version of struffoli, known as *cicerchiata*, which also feature chopped almonds and candied fruit. Fried sweets such as these are descended from *frictilia*, which were popular at Carnival time in ancient Rome.

For years, struffoli were prepared by nuns in convents and were given as gifts to the aristocracy in thanks for charitable deeds. Today, they are sold in pastry shops, though many people still make their own, following old family recipes. Each home has its own special tweaks and touches, but apparently the secret is to make the balls as small as possible so that each one gets an ample coating of honey. **LF**

In *A Diplomat in Japan* (1853–64), Sir Ernest Satow described these glutinous rice cakes "prepared and decorated in proper fashion with a Seville orange and fern." And o-mochi (the honorific is commonly used for this sacred food) remain an indispensable part of the New Year celebrations even today, displayed alongside a satsuma orange in the family seasonal alcove.

Making mochi is a winter ritual, traditionally performed by man and wife, and an exercise in trust as she deftly turns and wets the steamed glutinous rice in a large wooden tub before her husband brings the large wooden mallet crashing down to pound it. Mochi is an essential item at the New Year breakfast, eaten in a hot soup called *zoni*. Its glutinous texture, however, calls for careful chewing—many old people end their lives choking on the New Year mochi, and numbers are duly reported in the newspapers next day. Dried mochi keeps a long time, and is sold in individually wrapped pieces—simply grill or simmer in soup to soften. It is always satisfyingly filling. **SB**

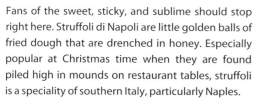

Taste: *Each mouthful of struffoli combines the sticky, sweetness of honey with soft, light dough. Recipes vary, but can include chewy peel and crunchy nuts.*

Taste: *The taste and texture of freshly pounded mochi, with a little soy sauce and wasabi, is unforgettable. Sweet and sticky, it forms an appealing golden crust when toasted.*

One after the other, Japanese men pound glutinous rice with mallets to make mochi. »

Sweetmeats

Crystallized Ginger

Amid the barren expanses of inland Queensland, Australia, fields of green fronds flourish in the shade of long black tarpaulins. The crop enticing farmers to carve out a living in this rugged climate is ginger.

The hardy rhizome that flourishes under these extreme conditions produces particularly pristine "hands"—or clumps of roots—that reach their best when sweetened and transformed into crystallized versions. The rhizomes are peeled, chopped, or sliced into a variety of shapes, then cooked briefly in sugar syrup. This mellows the hot nature of ginger, creates a candy-like texture, and partially preserves the root. Once dried, the pieces are typically rolled in sugar: occasionally, they are packed in the cooking syrup and sold as "stem ginger." The potency and sweetness depends on factors ranging from the age of the roots at harvest to the preparation and recipe.

Crystallized ginger is worked into countless desserts from ice cream to chocolates but can also be eaten out of hand like sweets. This expression of ginger works especially well in classic treats such as gingerbread and ginger biscuits. **TH**

Taste: *Peppery flavours echo the fresh ginger origins but the process sweetens the rhizome considerably. A mild heat remains—an almost fruity variant on the ginger theme.*

Candied Citrus Peel

Once associated primarily with domestic baking and cake decorating, candied citrus peel is now commonly considered a luxurious sweet treat. Eating deliciously chewy and succulent orange peel that has been carefully candied and dipped in dark chocolate, for example, is a truly divine experience.

Candied fruit peel is perhaps one of the oldest confections in the world; the ancient Egyptians, Chinese, and Arabs all candied fruits using honey, which was later substituted with sugar. By the sixteenth century, candied citrus peel was being sold as sweets. Some were preserved in syrup and known as "wet sucket," whereas simply dried and coated with sugar they were called "dry sucket." Up until the twentieth century, this is largely how most people encountered citrus fruits. Candied citrus peel remains popular across the world from Europe to Asia.

Oranges, lemons, grapefruits, and citron all make excellent candied peel. In Italy, the whole fruit is candied to make a stunning shop display. Candied citrus peel also features in Italian confections such as cassata, panettone, and panforte. **LF**

Taste: *Tender, with a delightful crunchy sugar coating, the best candied peel will retain the essence of the fruit and have a juicy tang without any bitterness.*

Marron Glacé

These famed specialities from the Ardeche area of France are essentially sweet chestnuts preserved in a particularly strong sugar syrup, which also adds the typical fine, flaky glaze of all glacé fruits. But these are not the chestnuts you might roast on an open fire. They are a particular variety: the marron has only one chestnut per shell, whereas better known varieties have two, hence the satisfying, compact presentation of marrons glacés.

The heightened sweetness dictates both what you can and cannot do with them; preservation rather overpowers the nutty flavour of the basic marrons so using small pieces in, say, an ice cream or in a creamy cake filling only works if they dominate the mixture. Generally marrons glacés should be enjoyed just as they are, absorbed and savoured slowly after a meal with coffee, a liqueur, or brandy. If allowed to sit in brandy or rum for some time, much of the sugar dissolves out and you then have a chestnut-flavoured liqueur and an alcoholic chestnut with bigger flavours. Broken pieces in syrup are sometimes sold quite cheaply. **GC**

Taste: *Their firm texture is made smooth and unctuous by the sugar syrup content. Best enjoyed slowly, so the sweetness dissipates, leaving vestiges of chestnut flavour.*

Ameixas d'Elvas

Ameixas d'Elvas (DOP)—sugar-coated, dried plums from the town of Elvas in eastern Portugal—are an unbelievably luscious speciality. The green-amber coloured fruit used—similar to a greengage—is thought to be among the elite of all dessert plums.

The Portuguese have been candying plums since the fifteenth century. They were originally produced by nuns from convents in the Elvas area, as a luxury food confined to the wealthy. Production moved on to dedicated producers, and since the nineteenth century their delights have been enjoyed by a growing international audience. Today, Ameixas d'Elvas carry a DOP certificate, protecting the production methods. Harvested between June and August, the plums are boiled gently, first in water, and then again in a sugar and water mixture. They are then left to soak in the syrup before being dried in the sun or special chambers.

Ameixas d'Elvas are wonderful served after dinner with liqueurs. In Portugal, they are often eaten with an egg custard-style dessert known as *sericaia,* a magical combination. **LF**

Taste: *Succulent, juicy, and very sweet, Ameixas d'Elvas hold on to the fruit's fresh plummy tang. This is superbly contrasted by the slight crunch of the sugar coating.*

Titaura

Made with the pulp of Lapsi fruit, titaura originates from Nepal. Lapsi trees need a cold climate to grow and hence most titaura is made during the winter months. Lapsi is boiled and the pulp extracted is then sun-dried; it is seasoned with sugar, salt, and spices. Most households in Kathmandu make it at home, and it is also sold at almost all food and beverage shops in Nepal. Young, old, rich, and poor, titaura does not have any social or economic boundaries, but it is most popular with children, teenagers, and women.

The sweetmeat is unique to Nepal; however, countries like Bhutan, India, and Tibet tend to import it on demand. Titaura is made and sold in all shapes, sizes, and flavours. It comes in dried or gravy-like varieties in salty, sweet, sour, and chilli flavours. Shapes vary from round or square, to rectangular or even long thin strips. In Kathmandu, Ratna Park is famous for housing a number of stores dedicated to selling titaura. Most Nepalese living abroad tend to stock up before leaving the country, and titaura makes a popular gift when travelling. **TB**

Taste: *To an untrained taste bud, the sweet variety is still quite spicy. Titaura contains Nepalese spices and is mostly tangy due to the Lapsi fruit, somewhat like gooseberry.*

Women trade all kinds of sweets in Maktinath, Nepal. »

Liquorice Drop

Whereas some countries such as the United Kingdom prefer liquorice to be sweet, in Scandinavia and the Netherlands it is usually eaten salty. "Drop" is the Dutch word used for hundreds of liquorice sweets that come in all shapes and sizes; the consumption of which can almost be classed as a national addiction. The liquorice plant is a legume that looks like a purple flowered bean. Its straggling, woody roots contain a sweet compound called glycyrrhizin. Mixed with water they are pulped, boiled, and processed into a syrupy extract that is poured into moulds. The result is block-drop. This can then be reprocessed to make liquorice sweets that are hard and toffee-like, gummy or soft, sweet or extra salty.

Alongside Boerderijdrops (farmyard animals) and Katjes (cat-shaped drops), highly salty Haring drops are perennial favourites. The name describes their fishy shape and the salt dusting gives them an immediate salty hit. Doctors have been known to prescribe them for patients with low blood pressure, and drops are sold by chemists in the Netherlands as well as in shops and supermarkets. **MR**

Maple Candy

Before the United States and Canada were first settled as colonies, the First Nations (Canada) and Native Americans knew what it meant when the "sap was running." At this time maple trees were ready to be tapped to provide a source of sweetener for the year ahead. The sap was boiled down into syrup but some of it was cooked even longer so that it crystallized and formed a "sugar" to be stored in blocks. Since it was late winter and early spring, snow may have been on the ground. When droplets of hot syrup hit the cold snow, jack wax or maple in the snow—a toffee-like confection—would form.

Maple in the snow can still be found in areas where sugar maples are tapped, but commercial maple candy is a bit more sophisticated. The maple sap is heated to the crystalline stage; then it is whipped and poured into moulds, often shaped like maple leaves. Since it can also be made from maple syrup, it is available year-round. This is a soft candy and the most popular. Maple sap or syrup, however, is also turned into a hard candy and into a fudge-like candy, sometimes known as Ohio maple cream. **SH**

Taste: *Liquorice drops have a chewy texture that is similar to wine gums. The salty coating helps salivation and enhances the natural liquorice taste.*

Taste: *Maple candy is made from different grades of syrup: the darker the syrup the richer the taste. The best candy is not overly sweet and tastes like brown sugar.*

Children sample maple syrup cooled in snow at the Elmira Maple Syrup Festival in Ontario. »

Doncaster Butterscotch

Buttermint

Butterscotch is a smooth, caramel-like sweet made by boiling butter and sugar syrup together with cream. It is essentially a type of toffee but boiled for longer so that it becomes hard and crunchy rather than chewy like traditional pulled toffees.

The first written records appear in 1817, when an enterprising confectioner and grocer called Samuel Parkinson in the town of Doncaster in the north of England began to make a brittle toffee; before long, his invention became one of its most famed exports, and the town was synonymous with butterscotch. In 1851, when Queen Victoria opened the famous St. Leger horse race, she was presented with a tin of Parkinson's butterscotch and the company gained royal approval. In 1893, the business was sold and by 1977 production had halted. Twenty-six years later, however, a Doncaster businessman came upon an old box in a cellar that contained one of the old St. Leger tins. His wife took a fancy to the tin and Parkinson's Butterscotch was resurrected, apparently using the original recipe she had found, neatly folded, in the tin. **LF**

A traditional wedding reception confection in the United States, buttermints have long been made at home by sweet-makers. They were perfected for commercial production though in 1932 by U.S. sweet-maker Katherine Beecher. Her company was acquired by another sweet manufacturer in 1974, but the Beecher buttermints are among the many brands sold throughout the world today.

Manufactured from butter, cream, peppermint flavouring, and icing sugar, buttermints are sometimes also called party mints, after dinner mints, pastel mints, and wedding mints. They come individually wrapped, often with custom logos, and in a variety of colours, including pale green, yellow, and pink. Some are filled with liquorice or various flavours of jelly. Sometimes confused with flat mints or a hard candy also called buttermints, true buttermints are small and pillow shaped, although slightly larger ones can be found. Also consumed as a breath freshener, buttermints are sugary and quickly melt in the mouth leaving a lingering mint flavour. **SH**

Taste: *Smooth and creamy, Doncaster butterscotch has a gloriously addictive buttery-sweet caramel flavour and a pleasantly crunchy texture that will delight toffee fans.*

Taste: *Buttermints taste like peppermint with a hint of butter. They are sweet and creamy and leave a refreshing coolness in the mouth.*

Vichy Mint

These distinctive octagonal white pastilles with an invigorating mint flavour were invented in 1828. A local pharmacist in the famous spa town of Vichy in central France discovered a method of extracting minerals from the town's thermal waters, created by volcanic activity in the nearby Massif Central. He then mixed the minerals with sugar and natural peppermint to produce a mint pastille that was used as a cure for heartburn.

Vichy mints were doubtless also enjoyed for their singular, fresh minty taste. They were particularly popular throughout the nineteenth century and were a favourite of the Empress Eugenie, wife of the Emperor Napoleon III. Emblazoned with the name of their place of origin, the mints remain much in demand today, and it is said that eating eight of the pastilles daily is as beneficial to one's health as a course of spa treatments. The mineral-rich water is also used to prepare *carrots à la Vichy*, a dish of thinly sliced carrots cooked in the spa water with butter and sugar, and garnished with chopped parsley. **FP**

Chicle Gum

Chewing gum may be the bane of the modern pavement, but the confection's roots go back centuries to the Mayans and Aztecs. Chicle is the resin that comes from the sapodilla trees native to Central America. In the Mayan language, the chewing gum made from chicle, lake-asphalt, and oily yellow grease obtained by crushing the axin insect was known as *tzictli*, and in Spanish the word for chewing gum remains *chicle*.

Mexican general Antonio López de Santa Anna was the one who came up with the idea of commercial chewing gum. It was taken up by a U.S. businessman, Thomas Adams, in 1869, who added sugar and flavourings to make chewing gum.

However, chicle as the base for chewing gum soon disappeared as companies opted for cheaper synthetic alternatives that could feed the growing demand in the 1950s and 1960s. But gum based on chicle is still available from Mexico. The resin is filtered and stirred to remove impurities, resulting in a white elastic substance that is moulded into a compact block that is used as the gum base. **CK**

Taste: *Vichy mints have a clean, fresh flavour with a slight peppermint heat and are smooth and pleasingly chalky as they dissolve in the mouth. A mint of distinction.*

Taste: *Chewy, sticky, elastic texture, with a subtle taste, although the flavour depends on what may have been added to the base gum, such as clove or peppermint.*

Lowzina

Ur, the ancient name for modern Iraq, is the oldest country on earth and it was here, in this crescent-shaped land spanning the mighty Euphrates and Tigris rivers, that the almond tree become one of the first food crops to be cultivated. The almond tree is now grown all over the world for its creamy, oval-shaped nut, which plays a part in practically every cuisine. Back in its homeland of Iraq, the almond has retained its popularity and is used in many everyday dishes as well as celebratory foods such as lowzina.

Lowzina b'Shakar, to give the sweetmeat its full Iraqi name—*shakar* means grateful in Arabic, and is also an Arabic name—is a diamond- or triangular-shaped white sugar confection made with almonds and flavoured with rose water, lemon juice, and the warm-scented spice, cardamom. The rose water and lemon juice are first boiled with water and sugar to make a concentrated syrup. When it has reached the correct consistency and has been allowed to cool, freshly ground almonds and cardamom—either seeds from cardamom pods or the powdered spice—are stirred in. The mixture is then spread out in a shallow tray and left until it is firm enough to cut into pieces, while remaining quite soft.

This special sweetmeat is reserved for special occasions such as weddings, when the lowzina is covered with delicate sheets of the finest gold leaf and sent by the family of the bride as a gift to their relatives and friends. Edible gold is a popular enhancement of celebratory dishes all over Asia, from Turkey to Japan. Although the gold used to make it is genuine, the sheets are so fine that their cost is not prohibitive. Asian celebratory dishes may also be sprinkled with edible gold dust. **WS**

Peppermint Rock

Alongside bawdy postcards and crazy golf, this garish confection embodies the traditional British seaside holiday. Sold in coastal resorts, it comes in sticks displaying, in cross-section, the name of the town where it was bought. Traditionally, people taking their holidays by the seaside would bring home sticks of peppermint rock as gifts for those not fortunate enough to be able to accompany them.

As a reminder of home, rock-making travelled to the antipodes, where the unique confection can be found in Sydney and in Tasmania. Peppermint rock has also been made since 1859 in Gränna, Sweden, where it is called *polkagris* after the polka dance. In Gränna, rock-making began as a one-woman operation, but now tourists flock to see it being made in a number of bakeries.

Every child's query—"How do the words get inside the rock?"—can best be answered by watching the hot, heavy, sometimes dangerous work that goes on at a traditional rock shop. Sugar, glucose, and an anti-foaming agent are boiled together, with some of the mixture set aside and coloured for use as the outside layer. The rest is flavoured, cooled, and worked to form the core. The lettering is added by interleaving long bars of coloured sugar (each cross-section is a letter) with white to create a long strip with letters running through it that can be wrapped around the core of the rock. The outer layer is added, resulting in a large cylinder that is then stretched to form sticks.

Made in Scotland, Edinburgh rock is a slightly different confection. Soft and crumbly, it melts in the mouth and comes in many flavours. It is the original rock but does not enjoy the same popularity. **ES**

Taste: *Soft and creamy, lowzina has a delicate nuttiness. Its sweetness is balanced by the warm spice of cardamom, the exotic perfume of rose water, and a hint of citrus.*

Taste: *Hard, minty, and very sweet, if crunched too keenly peppermint rock can break into shards that hurt the soft tissues of the mouth. This is, of course, all part of the fun.*

Classic peppermint rock has a bright pink coating, but now many other colours and flavours are available. ❯❯

Pear Drop

Pear-shaped, like a droplet, pear drops are among the old-fashioned, British, boiled sweets that were traditionally sold loose, by the quarter pound (115 g), from rows of large jars behind a sweet shop counter. Nostalgia has seen a resurgence in their popularity during the early twenty-first century but as the local newsagent gives way to the convenience store, fans are more likely to find their fix online.

Pear drops are made with sugar, glucose syrup, water, and citric acid. The sugar mixture is boiled, flavoured, and coloured, then cut, shaped, and rolled in caster sugar to give a slightly rough coating. The finished sweets are usually pinkish red, yellow, or a mixture of the two, and vary in shape from flat and elongated to stubby and squat. They are flavoured either with jargonelle pear essence or the less appealing pentyl acetate.

Like the sour sweets known as acid drops, pear drops evolved from boiled sugar recipes that date to the seventeenth century, and which used acid fruit juices to ensure that the boiled sugar syrup stayed hard and clear on cooling. **ES**

Jelly Bean

Jelly bean lovers around the world may have the Turks and the French to thank for this many-flavoured, all-American confection. The chewy centre possibly derives from Turkish Delight, while the hard outer shell may have been inspired by French sugared almonds. The name jelly bean first appeared in 1861, when an advertisement recommended sending them to soldiers fighting the American Civil War.

Traditional jelly beans, egg-shaped and about the size of a red kidney bean, were sold first as Christmas sweets then, from the 1930s, as Easter sweets. They came in just a few flavours, mostly fruit, although liquorice has always been popular. It was, of course, a U.S. company that produced the first "gourmet" jelly bean in 1976. Smaller than traditional jelly beans, Jelly Belly® beans are richer in flavour and have taste and colour inside and out. Today there are more than fifty varieties of Jelly Belly® beans available, including strawberry cheesecake, margarita, and a watermelon version with a green shell and a red chewy centre. **SH**

Taste: *For fans, sucking the sugar off these hard sweets is a genuine pleasure. The taste is sweet, sour, and synthetic—of pear flavouring, rather than pear.*

Taste: *Gourmet jelly beans are chewy, quite sweet, and more intensely flavoured than traditional beans. They create a tangy mouthful of shamelessly artificial pleasure.*

Ronald Reagan sent Jelly Belly® beans into space in 1983. This portrait was made in tribute. ❯❯

Fondant

Genoa has a long-standing reputation for producing cool candy creations. In the eighteenth century, Antonio Maria Romanengo began producing elegant candied fruits and sugar-coated *dragées*. When Parisian confectioners opened shops later that same century, Romanengo was suitably inspired to expand his repertoire. Fans included such eminent members of society as Giuseppe Verdi and Prince Umberto, whose wedding feast in 1868 featured an impressive array of Romanengo's sugary goodies.

The fondants are considered with particularly high regard and the process of making them is complex. A syrupy solution is made by dissolving sugar and glucose syrup in water, and boiling. The liquid is worked with a spatula into a crumbly solid, then kneaded until smooth and left overnight to stand. The consistency of the fondant makes it an ideal coating for small fresh fruits and the acidity of the fruit combined with the extreme sweetness of the fondant makes the confection even more special. For sightseers in Genoa, a visit to the ornate premises of Pietro Romanengo is a must. **LF**

Taste: *Sweet, soft, sugary, smooth, melting fondants launch the taste buds on a path towards paradise—only a hard-edged dentist could possibly resist.*

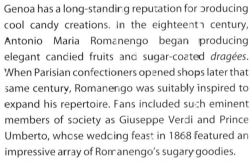

Rolls of fondant sweets await cutting into bite-sized pieces at a confectioner's shop in Istanbul, Turkey.

Rasgulla

For centuries Indians have been cooking down milk to keep it from souring, and along the way they invented their own distinctive range of sweets. A fresh, crumbly curd cheese, known as *chhena*, is used in a number of Indian confections including rasgulla. These are soft, porous balls of curd cheese and semolina that have been boiled and soaked in a sugar syrup, often infused with rose water. Rasgulla can also be dry and stuffed with nuts and fruit.

Believed to originally hail from Puri in the east coast state of Orissa, where they are used as temple offerings, rasgulla are also considered a typical Bengali dessert. They are popular throughout the subcontinent on occasions such as weddings, birthdays, and Hindu festivals like Diwali. A variation on rasgulla, *rasmalai* are made with a sweetened, screwpine-infused milk rather than a sugar syrup.

Rasgulla are highly perishable and need to be eaten quickly. They are also available tinned. Any place in the world with an Indian community is sure to have its own Indian sweet shop where aficionados can stock up on these dumpling delights. **TB**

Taste: *Rasgullas are light and spongy with a slightly squeaky texture. Generally sweet and milky, with a refreshing hint of rose, flavours depend on the recipe.*

Marshmallow

Candyfloss

Food mythology attributes the invention of marshmallows to the ancient Egyptians but the word was first used to describe a sweetmeat in the nineteenth century. Then they were prepared using an extract from wild marshmallow plants. Today, their spongy texture most often comes from gelatine. The basic ingredients of a marshmallow are sugar, syrup, and flavourings, which can include chocolate, strawberry, or vanilla, or, in the case of the celebrated chef Pierre Gagnaire, additions such as rose or rosemary. These are whipped with gelatine and starch, then baked, cut up, and rolled in a fine dusting of icing sugar and cornflour.

Marshmallows feature in the game "Chubby Bunny" where children fill their mouths with them then try and pronounce a difficult sentence. This pastime is not as harmless as it sounds, and at least two victims are known to have choked to death. Americans have found more culinary uses for marshmallows than the rest of the world: they occur in many cake and cookie recipes, as well as in the celebrated Rocky Road ice cream. **MR**

No more, no less than spun sugar, prototype candyfloss was probably an Italian invention of about 1400. However, it did not become the fairground attraction it is today until 1897 when two sweet-makers, William J. Morrison and John C. Wharton, patented a machine that would cook the sugar with added flavour and colour and then, using centrifugal force, push the melted mixture through a screen to create a dense sugar cocoon.

This fluffy, sugary mass was introduced to the world at the Paris Exhibition of 1900 as fairy floss. An instant hit, it soon made its way to the United States where it was sold to thousands of visitors at the St. Louis World Fair of 1904. It became an archetypal fairground treat and stallholders quickly learnt to spin the candyfloss onto beech sticks or into cardboard cones. The attraction in terms of profit would not have been lost on these traders. Though inextricably tied to popular food culture, the candyfloss machine has been adopted by the Spanish über-chef Ferran Adrià who features candyfloss in his gastronomic recipes at his el Bulli restaurant. **MR**

Taste: *The marshmallow's appeal lies in its texture. Heated over the embers at a barbecue, the crisp skin sits on a layer of hot syrup atop a centre that is both fluffy and chewy.*

Taste: *The first mouthful is the best, because the fine strands crackle as the mouth gets to grips with them, while the sugar sticks to the lips. The taste is sweet and synthetic.*

Modern marshmallows are pink and white like the wild
◖ *marshmallow flower once used in their manufacture.*

Turkish Delight

Qum Sohan

This soft, jewel-like sugar bomb became popular among the people of Turkey—who knew it as lokum—around the turn of the nineteenth century. The Turkish confectioner Hadji Bekir, who arrived in Istanbul from Anatolia in 1776, is often credited with its invention. Some claim that the sultan was so enamoured of the sweetmeat he deemed Hadji Bekir the palace's chief confectioner.

Until refined sugar reached Turkey at the end of the nineteenth century, their sweets had been a sticky mix of honey or dried fruit and wheat flour. Lokum transformed the culinary scene. It earned world fame from the 1830s when an English traveller brought a sample of "Turkish Delight" back home. The author C. S. Lewis played up the sweet's alluring properties by giving it an important role in *The Lion, the Witch and the Wardrobe* (1950). The child Edmund becomes so intoxicated by Turkish Delight that he betrays his siblings in an effort to get more.

Today, the fifth generation of Bekir's family runs Ali Muhiddin Hadji Bekir confectioners in Istanbul. It exports Turkish Delight around the world. **DV**

The holy city of Qum situated 96 miles (155 km) south of the Iranian capital Tehran, is famous for three things. As the centre of Shi'ite Islam, it has more sacred shrines than anywhere else in Iran, its local carpet-makers weave beautiful, handmade silk rugs that are prized by collectors around the world, and its bakers sell sohan, an irresistible honey and nut confection. Similar to peanut brittle, aficionados agree that the very best sohan comes from Qum.

Iranian people adore their cakes and pastries and their collective sweet tooth is legendary. As Qum has a patisserie on virtually every street corner and side of the bazaar, cooks seldom take the trouble to make sohan at home. Flat and rectangular in shape, sohan is made from an aromatic dough of honey, sugar, butter, saffron, cardamom, and nuts, usually a mixture of toasted almonds and locally grown pistachios. Less sickly than most Iranian sweets, Qum sohan is eaten with morning coffee or afternoon tea or with other sweetmeats after a meal. With great "crunch appeal," sohan is addictively delicious once you have first tasted it. **WS**

Taste: *The sugar-dusted jelly collapses into a sticky paste in the mouth. Rose water provides a heady fragrance and floral taste. Lemon, mint, and nuts are common additions.*

Taste: *Qum sohan is buttery and crunchy with the tantalizing scent of cardamom and saffron, the mellow sweetness of honey, and the warmth of toasted nuts.*

Turkish delight and other mouth-watering
❸ *sweetmeats are piled high at a bazaar in Istanbul.*

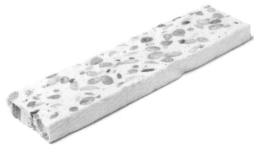

Turrón de Jijona

Montelimar Nougat

Turrón di Jijona (IGP) is a soft nougat made in a small town close to Alicante in the Valencia region of central Spain. Made from ground Marcona almonds, egg whites, sugar, and honey, it has a similar texture to peanut butter. There is also a hard version—turrón de Alicante—that is similar to peanut brittle.

To make turrón de Jijona, whole almonds are shelled and peeled before being roasted in special drums. The honey is heated with the almonds; the mixture is bound by eggs whites and then cooled. The mixture is then milled before being transferred to cauldrons; there it is further cooked while at the same time being kneaded, until it takes on its characteristic smooth consistency and golden hue. The best-quality turrón de Jijona, labelled "Suprema," must contain 60 per cent almonds.

Turrón is an old confection, believed to have been introduced to Spain over 500 years ago by the Arabs. It is traditionally eaten at Christmas. There is a museum dedicated to its history at the factory where the El Lobo and 1880 brands, the finest examples of this distinctive nougat, are made. **LF**

An aristocrat of confectionery, the nut-studded nougat of Montelimar, France, has roots in ancient recipes from Greece and the Eastern Mediterranean, where honey and nuts were traditionally cooked together. Such ideas then came to the Mediterranean coast of Provence, perhaps with the Romans. When almond trees were grown inland in the seventeenth century, Montelimar created nougat.

There are several methods of manufacture: long-cooked syrup of honey with almonds and pistachios is whisked into whipped egg whites, or honey and egg whites are slowly cooked and nuts are added at the end. It is the proportion of one ingredient to the other that is the touchstone, said to be 28 per cent almonds and 16 per cent honey. The final temperature reached by the mixture gives either soft or hard nougat. Such variations as using a lavender honey, and Sicilian or Greek pistachios, support the claims of superiority by one maker over another, but all agree that only the very finest local almonds can make true *nougats de Montelimar*, with their lingering tastes and gratifying flavours. **GC**

Taste: *Sugary, soft, and with a pleasantly sandy texture, turrón de Jijona has superb honeyed qualities that sweep over the taste buds, with a light caramel aftertaste.*

Taste: *Honey adds unique richness to the bland background, so, slowly chewing or sucking nougat gives a greater flavour spectrum than expected.*

Good confectioners ensure that nougat is fresh for the customer by slicing it only a little at a time. ❯❯

Kaju Katli

Sparkling silver leaf often anoints the dense, fudgy richness of these ground cashew sweets. One of the vast constellation of sticky Indian treats (*mithai*), kaju katli, and its various derivations, is made in the south of India in Kerala and Tamil Nadu, and in the west in the Goan and Gujarati regions. In the north, almonds are often used as a substitute for cashews.

Crushed, softened, raw cashews are ground with palm sugar syrup flavoured with cardamom and rose essence until a thick spreadable paste is formed. The oil-rich, emollient mass is spread out, cut into diamond shapes, and adorned with edible silver leaf. During festivals like Diwali, gold leaf may replace the silver.

Used more as a gesture of hospitality than an end of meal palate refresher, in India sweets are symbolic of welcome. An essential part of all celebrations, they serve an important function in a country with a large vegetarian population. Nuts, cow's milk, and sugar formed into rich sweets will not offend any of the major religions practised in India, so make the perfect gift. **RH**

Habshi Halwa

Connoisseurs of Indian cuisine consider habshi halwa to be one of the country's great dessert delicacies. Halwas are a specific type of Indian sweet. They are a type of thick pudding, made with caramelized milk, sugar, ghee, and wheat flour, and of the different varieties, habshi halwa is considered the *shezhada*, or crown prince, of halwas. Though habshi halwa shares its name with a Middle Eastern dessert made of sesame paste, the Turkish candy is nothing like this Indian treat.

Nuts, especially almonds, cashews, or pistachios are always mixed into the smooth, almost polenta-like consistency of the pudding, and sometimes raisins are also added. Cardamom, mace, nutmeg, and even saffron can also be used to enhance the flavour. Some versions are very sweet, whereas others offer only a small taste of sugar.

Halwa is traditionally served more often during the winter months, from September to March, than summer months in India, but in the United States and the United Kingdom, it is made year-round in Indian sweet shops. **RD**

Taste: *Kaju katli has a soft but slightly grainy unroasted nut taste and is not as sugary as some Indian sweets. The pale nuts absorb the flavours of rose and cardamom.*

Taste: *Silky textured habshi halwa is almost unctuous on the tongue, with layers of sweetness and just a little bit of spice. The boiled nuts in the halwa add a gentle crunch.*

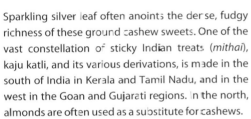

Kaju katli is just one of several types of sweetmeat ❰ *sold at this beautifully presented stall in India.*

Pista Burfi

Burfis (or barfis) are popular Indian sweets that are synonymous with most special occasions in the country. Although it originated in India, today the sweet is also part of tradition and culture in Pakistan, Nepal, and Bangladesh. In India, it is a common tradition to give sweets to family, friends, and neighbours for special festivities like Diwali, and no *mithai* box is complete without burfi. At weddings, burfi is exchanged between the families of the bride and groom as a gesture of good will.

Made from real silver, the silver coating on burfis is shaped into edible leaf, which is used in many other Indian sweets, too. Indeed, its excessive use in India sees tons of silver churned every year to make it.

Burfis are expensive delicacies made from condensed milk, which is cooked with sugar, water, clarified butter, ground pistachio, and powdered milk until it makes a thick paste. The mix is then spread out and, once cool, can be cut into diamond shapes or squares and decorated with silver leaf or *varak* to give it shine. The sweetmeat comes in different flavours, such as coconut or cashew. **TB**

Taste: *Pista burfi has a sweet and creamy taste. The pistachio gives it a slightly nutty and heavy texture. The silver leaf lends the sweet a cool and metallic taste.*

Confectioners are among the busiest traders in Delhi. »

Cornish Fudge

Honeycomb Toffee

For a substance that tastes so timelessly sweet, fudge is a surprisingly recent arrival. The creamy, chewable blend was first made by female college students in the United States during the 1880s. Other possible ancestors include Scottish tablet—a hard blend first recorded in the early eighteenth century—or the Mexican nut fudge *penuche*. Some Indian sweets also have a character similar to fudge.

Confectioners in many countries boil fudge from sugar, milk, and butter. Fudges where the mixture is cooled before being beaten will be softer and creamier than those manipulated while the mixture is still hot, which tend to be harder and grainier. Fudge is often flavoured with vanilla, chocolate, coffee, fruit, and nuts, and then coated with chocolate.

Fudge is probably most commonly associated with Cornwall, where a hard, grainy fudge (or tablet) along the old Scottish lines, was traditionally popular. Soft styles, often based around clotted cream, now dominate the tourist market. This cream, a Cornish speciality, gives a benign creaminess and pale colour to the finished fudge. **ES**

Honeycomb toffee, also known as cinder toffee in England, puff candy in Scotland, and sponge candy in parts of the United States, is one of those confections that has to be tasted to be able to appreciate it. Nostalgically part of the childhood years of many people in the United Kingdom, it is still one of the most popular confections there.

Toffee first became popular in the 1800s when sugar and treacle, a molasses-like syrup, became inexpensive enough to be made into a treat. Honeycomb toffee is simply a regular toffee to which a little bit of vinegar and bicarbonate of soda has been added. These ingredients, which do not affect the taste, give the toffee a light, airy texture, like a honeybomb.

In New Zealand, honeycomb toffee is an integral part of hokey pokey ice cream, whereas in Britain it is enjoyed coated in chocolate in the form of the popular Cadbury's Crunchie bar. Confectioners in the United States, especially in Buffalo, New York, make a similar treat called sponge bar: caramelized crisp candy dipped in creamy milk chocolate. **SH**

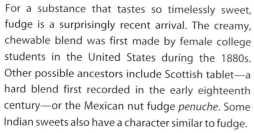

Taste: *Cornish butter tablet is firm, granular, and crumbly at the edges. Fudge is much softer, with a more obvious creaminess. Both are terrifyingly, magnificently sweet.*

Taste: *Sugary with a foam-like texture, honeycomb toffee is extremely crunchy at first bite before melting in the mouth. The flavour is of molasses and light butterscotch.*

Soft Caramel

Salt Caramel

Soft caramels occupy a delicious place between hard toffee and soft butterscotch or buttercrunch, a U.S. speciality. Their origins seem to be in Western Europe and Britain, with different countries adding twists according to national preferences. The essential ingredients are those of toffee, butter, and sugar, to which are added milk or cream. By varying the type of butter, by using white or brown sugars, and by varying the proportions of milk and cream or using just one of these, a different texture and flavour is easily made. Like toffee, you first make a light butter/sugar caramel, and once the milk or cream is added the mixture is cooked only to the firm-ball stage.

Caramels are specially good with high cocoa fat dark chocolates, as these add both acidity and a touch of bitterness, thus presenting a fuller and more gratifying mouth experience. The rich sweetness of soft caramels is the perfect complement to almost every fruit and citrus flavouring, and exploring the choice can become a life-long pleasure. **GC**

These sweetmeats are also known as salted caramels or sea-salt caramels, if such salts are used. Like all caramels, their basis is a hard toffee of butter and sugar, but this mixture is softened and extended by the addition of milk or cream. They are also cooked only to the firm-ball stage, at a much lower temperature than toffee.

Their origin is thought to be a French custom of sometimes making caramels with salted rather than unsalted butter (*caramels au beurre salé*). In these the salt taste is subtle and sweetness still dominates. The sudden worldwide popularity of salted caramels is perhaps generated by the better availability of single-origin salts and of super-special *fleur de sel*, salt naturally crystallized by the wind on wave tops and collected by hand. As the world celebrates the increasing choice of salt caramels, so chefs have explored deeper. They now offer salt caramels with chocolate and such flavours as lemon, orange, coffee, or lavender, and with every type of salt, from the flat white crystals of English Maldon to the pink salts of Hawaii and Australia's Murray River. **GC**

Taste: *Buttery sweetness and a satin-smooth texture give way to the touch of bitterness provided by the caramelization of the sugar; there should be no graininess.*

Taste: *A sweet and satiny taste dissolves into one of salt. The salt increases our ability to taste flavours, heightening the characteristics of the caramel and other ingredients.*

Single Estate Chocolate

Milk Chocolate

The first taste of single estate chocolate can be a shock to the unaccustomed palate. Unlike mass-market chocolate, usually made from a mix of traded cocoa beans, serious chocolatiers will purchase or partner with plantations to make chocolate that can be sold as single estate chocolate. At this elevated level, chocolate becomes rather like wine: the variety of bean, the *terroir* in which it grows, and the treatment of the pods from the cacao tree—from which cocoa and chocolate are derived—all hugely affect the finished product.

The artisan French chocolatier Bonnat was probably the first to produce a single estate chocolate, in 1996, but the idea really took off when another French company, Valrhona, began making their Gran Couva in 1998. Today, there are many good examples, perhaps most famously Amedei's Chuao, from a legendary Venezuelan plantation accessible only by boat. Michel Cluizel makes Los Anconès, from the Dominican Republic, and Maralumi from Papua New Guinea, which is—unusually—also available as a milk chocolate. **MC**

A delight for young and old alike, milk chocolate is the approachable face of chocolate. Milk softens the bitterness and strong flavours that can be found in many cacao beans. The scientist, and founder of the British Museum, Sir Hans Sloane first came up with the idea of adding hot milk to chocolate drinks while travelling in Jamaica at the end of the seventeenth century. Solid milk chocolate arrived in 1879, when Daniel Peter added Henri Nestlé's newly invented milk powder to cocoa butter and ground cacao beans and began a famous Swiss tradition. Swiss milk chocolate, like British and U.S. milk chocolate, tends to be very sweet: too much so for purists.

In recent years there has been a trend for high strength milk chocolate. The French chocolatier Valrhona has produced what is recognized as one of the best milk chocolates: their Jivara contains 40 per cent cocoa solids, more than some mass-market dark bars. The French artisan chocolate maker Bonnat and the Italian company Slitti have both experimented with milk chocolate containing cocoa solids of 65 per cent or more. **MC**

Taste: *Flavours such as tobacco, berries, grass, and citrus are common. The chocolate should have a good melt and mouthfeel; the "length" can last as long as forty minutes.*

Taste: *Good milk chocolate melts well and is never greasy: it strikes a delicate balance between creamy dairy and the tart notes often found in cacao beans.*

Untouched, bricks of chocolate pass from moulds
 *along a conveyor belt in the Valrhona factory.*

Cocoa Bean

The essence of chocolate, cocoa beans grow in pods on the tropical tree. *Theobroma cacao*, the name of which so appropriately means "food of the gods." For the Aztecs, the beans were so precious they were used as currency. The drinks made from them were reserved—as one would expect of liquid gold—for the emperor and aristocracy. After early reticence, the conquering Spanish began to experiment with cocoa: *mole poblano*, the rich chilli-cocoa sauce, is probably an early example of this. When cocoa reached Europe, it was the Italians who led the way, using the new spice in savoury dishes, and creating some of the earliest chocolate sweets.

More recently, chefs have utilized the textures and flavours afforded by cocoa beans, which are often crushed or chopped into "nibs." These can be added to balsamic vinegar to make a salad dressing or sprinkled on ice cream; they can add thickness to a sauce or texture to a cake. Nibs are available from companies such as Scharffen Berger in the United States, while the Italian company Domori produces Kashaya, beans roasted specially for eating. **MC**

Taste: *Eating a whole cocoa bean can be rather like eating a bitter chocolate almond. The flavours tend to be pungent and untamed, while quality is very obvious.*

Cocoa beans dry in the sun at a farm near
the town of Assin Adadientem, Ghana.

Dried Fruit in Chocolate

The simplest of chocolate centres, dried or candied fruit coated with chocolate makes a moreish, mouth-watering delight. Candied orange peel is a favourite among chocolatiers; the bite and texture of the peel and the slow melt of the chocolate create a multi-level taste sensation. Some products, however, may use low grade chocolate or, even worse, a substitute made with vegetable fat. Although preserved, candied and dried fruits will lose flavour as they age, so it is best to eat the chocolates freshly made.

Most fruits have been combined with chocolate at one time or another, but some of the most interesting are prunes soaked in vodka, cherries in kirsch, and *chinotto*—whole baby citrus fruits from Italy. Candied orange or lemon are classic choices and usually come in thin strips.

Bucking the Belgian trend for sweetness in chocolates, Brussels chocolatier Laurent Gerbaud imports dried kumquats from China and coats them in Domori chocolate from Italy. His square bars sprinkled with sun-dried Persian cranberries are to die for, if not strictly speaking chocolate-coated fruit. **MC**

Taste: *A high percentage dark chocolate like Valrhona will work best with the tartness of candied orange, bringing out the citrus notes and adding depth of flavour.*

Truffle

Lübecker Marzipan

The chocolate lover's favourite, this classic mix of chocolate cream filling, crisp chocolate coating, and a dusting of cocoa powder creates a wave of delight when popped in the mouth.

Created as imitations of the highly prized fungi, chocolate truffles probably originated in France around the start of the twentieth century, following the invention of modern, solid chocolate. Fillings vary from hand-rolled, fresh chocolate and cream ganaches with a shelf life of only a few weeks to industrial mixtures dominated by vegetable fat, sugar, and preservatives. Some of the best examples are found in Paris from chocolatiers like Jean-Paul Hévin or Pierre Hermé. New World artisans such as Fran's of Seattle also make excellent truffles.

Although "champagne" truffles are endlessly popular and perceived as luxurious, they are rarely made with real Champagne. Instead Marc de Champagne, a young brandy from the same region, is substituted, or worse still, artificial flavourings. Working with real champagne is a difficult art. Rare exponents include London's Paul A. Young. **MC**

Intensely almondy and utterly divine, Lübecker marzipan (PGI) is considered to be the finest in the world. Produced in the pretty Hanseatic town of Lübeck in northern Germany, the town also claims to be the inventor of the almond confection, but it is more likely to have first originated in the Orient.

The delicacy arrived in Europe by way of Venice, during the time of the Crusades and was introduced to Spain, Portugal, and Germany. Marzipan, at its simplest a ground paste of almonds and sugar, was initially regarded as a medical remedy and made by chemists. By the fourteenth century, it had found its way onto the table of aristocratic diners as a luxurious dessert. With the discovery of the New World and the introduction of sugar into Europe, marzipan began to be produced by confectioners who transformed basic marzipan into an elegant art form, sculpting the paste into all manner of shapes.

Marzipan-makers in Lübeck, such as the companies Niederegger and Carstens, make a dark chocolate-coated marzipan that is wonderful eaten with a dark roasted coffee after dinner **LF**

Taste: *As you bite into the chocolate shell, cocoa powder falls on the tongue and the soft, creamy filling inside melts. The chocolate flavour floods out as the textures combine.*

Taste: *Lübecker marzipan has a pleasant, lightly grainy texture and a delicious almond aroma. The flavour is not overly sugary, but delivers a balanced sweetness.*

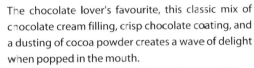

The cocoa powder coating of chocolate truffles contrasts with their smooth texture and sweetness.

Creole Praline

A popular sweet souvenir of New Orleans, pralines (pronounced prah-leens in that city) actually originated in France, reputedly during the seventeenth century. There the confection was made by sugar coating almonds. However, New World tastes and ingredients subverted that tradition, and New Orleans made Creole pralines one of its many culinary claims to fame. They are made throughout the city often in storefront windows. Tourists line up to watch the women stirring the big vats of light corn syrup, sugar, milk, butter, vanilla extract, and pecans, then dropping the mixture by the spoonful onto waxed paper to harden and cool. The result is a sugary, fudge-like confection that looks very like a biscuit.

Although true Creole pralines are made in the New Orleans way, pralines come in different varieties and may be made with brown sugar, maple syrup, or other sweeteners. Commercial producers have even added flavourings like chocolate and banana to their recipes. The best and the most authentic, however, are made the old-fashioned way. **SH**

Taste: *Creole pralines have a flavour and texture not unlike a light biscuit: a slight crunch gives way to a creamy fudge. The nutty flavour of the pecans offsets the sugary taste.*

Praline

Legend has it that in 1671, an angry chef spilled boiling sugar over almonds a clumsy kitchen boy had dropped on the floor. Short of a dessert for his master—the Maréchal du Plessis-Praslin—the chef served the sugared almonds, which were a great success. The latter part of his master's name is said to be the origin of the word "praline."

The name initially referred to single almonds covered in caramelized sugar, but over time it also came to refer to a ground mixture that could be used in cakes and pastries. After solid chocolate was invented, this was often added to the nut mix, which duly became a popular filling for chocolate bonbons. So much so, confusingly, that in countries such as Belgium, all filled chocolates are known as pralines.

The best praline is prepared by hand using freshly roasted nuts. In Europe, almonds or hazelnuts are almost always used; pecans and pistachios are popular in the United States. The use of peanuts by newcomers such as New York's Chocolat Moderne makes a scrumptious treat, but would be frowned upon back in Europe. **MC**

Taste: *The strong, nutty, toasted flavour, combined with slightly burnt sugar, makes praline a moreish delight. It is even better when coated with dark chocolate.*

Ganache Chocolate

For the connoisseur, chocolates filled with ganache are the ultimate expression of the chocolatier's art. In the freshest, most skilfully made examples, the combination of chocolate, cream, and sometimes a little butter create a semi-liquid filling that allows the chocolate's natural flavour to flow over the tongue in a sensual wave of pleasure. Ganache can be the perfect base for combining traditional and exotic flavours with chocolate: the best will be infused by hand from natural ingredients. Examples worth trying include cinnamon, chili, as well as more unusual flavours, such as the Japanese citrus yuzu, or the Swedish liquorice-flavoured ganaches.

The recipe for ganache was invented in the mid-nineteenth century, but fell out of fashion in the twentieth century until Robert Linxe founded La Maison du Chocolat in Paris during the 1970s. The French are still the true masters of ganache, with Paris, Bayonne, and Lyon—where the legendary Bernachon house is based—among the most prolific areas. The art of ganache has recently spread to North America, Scandinavia, and London. **MC**

Taste: *Textures vary from soft and buttery to firm as fudge. A good ganache will really open up the flavour notes of the chocolate and deliver a clear aftertaste.*

Gianduja

Perhaps the perfect combination of chocolate and nuts, gianduja pairs chocolate with the famous *Tonda gentile* hazelnuts from the Langhe in Piedmont. The British, however, can take some credit for this Italian invention. Naval blockades during the Napoleonic wars helped create cocoa shortages across Europe that lasted for much of the first half of the nineteenth century. Inventive chocolate-makers in northern Italy began adding ground paste made from toasted local hazelnuts to their chocolate, extending what little cocoa they had and creating a new tradition in the process. They named their creation after the comic carnival character and mask that represents Piedmont.

One of the first commercial producers was Pierre Paul Caffarel, who perfected his recipe in 1865 and began selling it in the famous "upturned boat" shape, wrapped in gold foil paper. Others followed, including Ferrero, whose gianduja-filled Rocher is now ubiquitous but a pale imitation of the original recipe. Venchi's gianduja sticks, elegantly disguised as cigars, are popular with connoisseurs. **MC**

Taste: *The best gianduja has a crisp, toasted nut flavour, a silky smooth texture, and a pleasant chocolaty-ness without the cloying sweetness of mass-produced versions.*

Chocolate Spread

Dulce de Leche

Whether loading a knife with mountains of rich, thick chocolate to spread on hot buttered toast or getting caught red-handed with the spoon in the jar, chocolate spread has a child-like appeal that many adults never manage to shake off.

Although chocolate has been spreadable for quite some time—over two centuries—chocolate spread itself is a relatively recent invention. Cocoa shortages caused by rationing during World War II led the Ferrero company in northern Italy to begin producing a version of gianduja—a blend of ground local hazelnuts and chocolate—by adding vegetable fat. Around twenty years later they marketed an improved version, and the Nutella brand was born.

Most chocolate spreads on the market imitate the Nutella recipe, but are often overly sweet and use hydrogenated vegetable fat: even organic brands rely on a high proportion of vegetable fat. However, many good quality chocolatiers—among them Venchi and Paul A. Young—produce higher quality chocolate spreads, which are often freshly made and have a short shelf-life. **MC**

This ambrosial "milk jam" is nothing short of an obsession in South America, particularly in Argentina and Uruguay, around the River Plata. It is a source of great national pride for both countries, although neither has a DOC classification. (In 2001, Argentina unsuccessfully tried to get UNESCO to recognize dulce de leche as part of its national patrimony.)

Essentially a slow-boiled mix of cow's milk and sugar, often enhanced with a little vanilla and bicarbonate of soda, the origins of dulce de leche are nebulous. Popular Argentine legends suggest it was discovered by accident in the early nineteenth century when a maid left sweetened milk on the stove, only to come back and find it transformed into a thick and creamy mixture. It is also closely related to a number of caramelized milk goodies—such as the dessert known as *manjar blanco*, which is popular in Peru, Chile, and Colombia, and the French *confiture de lait*. South Americans apply it to all kinds of desserts—from pancakes to cakes and ice cream. It is the traditional filling for the South American biscuit sandwich known as *alfajor*. **IA**

Taste: *The best chocolate spreads should balance a good chocolate flavour with toasty notes from the nuts. The texture should be thick without being waxy in the mouth.*

Taste: *This thick, milky, brown sauce is wonderfully sweet, silky smooth, and glossy, with a milky flavour. It lacks the intensity and burnt notes found in sugar caramels.*

Green Walnut Gliko

Black Butter

There are many types of gliko, the delicious Greek speciality known as "spoon sweets": wonderful preserves made from fruits or nuts that are often harvested while slightly under-ripe, and conserved in thick, sweet syrup. Green walnut gliko is just one variety, but it is considered very special because it is made from the famous walnuts of Arcadia, on the Peloponnesian Peninsula in Greece. The walnuts are harvested while they are young and still sheathed in a downy green jacket, before the inner shell has formed. The sugar syrup in which they are preserved is often spiced with cinnamon and cloves.

There has long been a tradition of preserving nuts and fruits in syrups; the ancient Greeks were particularly fond of combining nuts with honey. The name "spoon sweets" evolved because the preserves were offered on small spoons, usually as a sign of welcome and hospitality, although legend attests that the habit of taking a spoonful from one dish ensured that the sweetmeats were safe to eat and not poisoned. Small-scale artisan production means it is still possible to enjoy these wonderful treats. **LF**

The English "black butter" should not be confused with the French *beurre noir*, burnt butter that is dished up with skate. It is a form of syrup made by boiling apples that was popular during the Regency period and is still made today on the Channel Island of Jersey. It was made at the novelist Jane Austen's home and, in a letter to her sister Cassandra in 1808, she described eating a pot of it: "Though not what it ought to be; part of it was very good."

Before its agriculture was dominated by the cultivation of new potatoes, Jersey was covered in orchards. Cider is still pressed at La Mare Vineyards and Distillery in the centre of the island. Black butter is made by boiling and crushing apples (traditionally with sweet cider and spices, liquorice especially) until they reduce to a sticky, dark brown mass. Left to mature, the syrup's colour deepens to that of molasses. Young Jersiaise farmers hold an annual black butter-making party—*la séthée d'nièr beurre*—when the apples are boiled slowly for most of the night over an open cauldron. The recipe itself most likely evolved from a medieval apple sauce. **MR**

Taste: *Glossy and smooth with a uniquely alluring bite, the syrup-soaked walnuts display exotic notes enhanced by the gentlest intimation of warm spice.*

Taste: *Black butter may have a faintly smoky aroma mixing with the sweetness of apples. Its taste is a moreish combination of toffee and fruit that lingers on the palate.*

Amardine

Membrillo

Across the Middle East dried fruits are a staple part of the local cuisine, but sweet and succulent as many of them are, none can match the glistening orange opulence of Syria's apricot leather, or amardine.

Each July the new season's crop of ripe apricots is harvested, the best fruit coming from the orchards around the town of Malatya on Syria's northern border, where the soil and climate suit the unpredictable apricot tree perfectly. The fruit is carefully transported to the leather-maker's workplace where it is gently crushed and then tipped into large vats to be simmered with a little water until pulpy. The pulp is pushed through a sieve to remove the skins and stones and the thick purée sweetened before being cooked down to a paste. Shallow oblong trays are greased with olive oil, the apricot paste is poured into them and the trays left on a sunny rooftop for forty-eight hours until the paste has dried out. The amardine is then removed and cut into sheets, for sweet-toothed customers to snack on, use to make drinks and desserts, or add to lamb and vegetable stews. **WS**

Memorillo is a wonderful amber-pink coloured Spanish preserve in the form of a firm paste, the type often referred to as "fruit cheese." It is made from the pulp of the fruit the Spanish call membrillo (quince). The quince (*Cydonia oblonga*) is too hard and acerbic to be eaten raw, but when sweetened and cooked for several hours, the pulp softens and takes on a glorious fire-red colour and a flavour of apples and pears.

Quinces are high in pectin, a compound that helps to set fruit pulp, and this makes them well suited to preserving. Membrillo paste was in fact the original "marmalade" (rather than the orange conserve we usually associate with the word today).

Membrillo is characteristically served with slices of manchego, Spain's deliciously spirited sheep's milk cheese; the combination of sweet quince with piquant manchego is magical. As its reputation spreads internationally, membrillo is increasingly being eaten alongside other hard cheeses, too. The preserve also has a particular knack for cutting rich and fatty foods such as lamb and duck and will melt happily into divine glazes and simple sauces. **LF**

Taste: *The chewy amardine sheets have a concentrated fruity flavour and are sweet enough to satisfy even the most intense sugar craving.*

Taste: *Sweet and delicately flowery, with a superb, compact jelly-like consistency, membrillo makes the most wonderful partner for salty and savoury foods.*

In a market sheltered from the heat of Aleppo, Syria,
❮ vendors sell many preserved rather than fresh foods.

Lekvar

Lemon Curd

European plums have been cultivated since ancient times. The first trees probably grew in central and southeastern Europe, where each year much of the harvest is turned into a thick fruit butter called lekvar. The first written reference to this jam-like conserve can be traced back to 1350, but today some East European villages still hold a festival where plums are puréed and slowly simmered in big copper pots until thick enough to spread on bread.

Lekvar is traditionally packed into small wooden barrels lined with waxed paper, from which the fruit butter is then scooped out with a wooden paddle. As plums contain a natural preservative, lekvar has a long shelf life, so the barrels can be shipped around the world. Today, however, it is more common to see it packed in jars and sitting on delicatessen or supermarket shelves alongside the jams.

Lekvar is a popular filling for pastries such as *pierogies* and the croissant-shaped Austrian *kipfels*. The prune butter is also used as one of the fillings for *hamantashen*, the traditional triangular pastries eaten at the Jewish festival of Purim. **WS**

The most luxurious of custard-style tart or pie fillings, (although it is also now used as a spread), lemon curd is a direct descendant of the lemon creams and orange butters of Hannah Glasse's eighteenth-century *Art of Cookery*. It is made from only lemons, eggs, butter and sugar, and so does not keep for more than a few weeks even if pasteurised—it must be kept refrigerated. Much commercially available "lemon curd" is a travesty of the real thing, being thickened with cornflour and a little dried egg. While these keep well without refrigeration, they are not worth eating.

Limes and Seville oranges are also used to make these custards, and some gourmets would rate orange curd above lemon curd. In all cases, it is necessary to cook the mixture over a very low heat, in order to stop the mixture curdling. Hannah Glasse's lemon cheesecakes were filled with the mixture and then baked—a far cry from a modern cheesecake. Her most extravagant recipe called for two lemons, half a pound each of sugar and butter, twelve egg yolks and eight egg whites! **AMS**

Taste: *The long, slow process of boiling down the plum purée gives lekvar butter an intense prune-like flavour, so a little goes a long way if you are spreading it on bread.*

Taste: *Lemon curd can be spread on scones as well as used in puddings. It is a much better filling for lemon meringue pie than one thickened with cornflour.*

Homemade lemon curd is best made in small amounts because it does not keep well. »

Seville Orange Marmalade

The qualities that make the Seville orange ideal for marmalade are almost exactly those that mar its viability as an eating orange: its thick, rough skin encases a pulp that is extremely sour, even bitter, and chock full of seeds.

Bitter oranges (*Citrus aurantium*) probably first originated in China and India but by the twelfth century the Moors had brought both oranges and irrigation technology to southern Spain. There, despite Andalusia's arid climate, the fruit began to flourish: bitter oranges took their generic name, Seville, from the region's capital.

Although the name derives from a Portuguese quince paste called *marmelada* and the oranges come from Spain, modern marmalade is a very British affair, and appears on the national culinary list along with roast beef, Yorkshire pudding, and fish and chips. Most stories concur that marmalade took its current form—a transparent spreadable jelly enriched with pieces of peel—during the eighteenth century in Scotland: some attribute its creation to James Keiller of Dundee. **LF**

Taste: *Fruity and jelly-like with an intense bittersweet orange tang and chewy slivers of peel, Seville orange marmalade is a perfect topping for hot buttered toast.*

A Victorian marmalade factory in Seville, Spain. »

Rowan Jelly

Fig Jam

A West Country name for the bright vermilion orange berries that cluster on a rowan tree is "poison berries." And the rowan tree or mountain ash (*Sorbus aucuparia*), that grows wild in Europe and northern Asia, does indeed bear a toxic fruit. When raw, it contains parasorbic acid, but cooking converts this into the harmless, easily digested sorbic acid.

Berries ripen in autumn but are not ready to be harvested before the first frosts. In their raw state they are bitter and astringent, which does not bother the birds that seem to crave them. Made into a sweetened jelly, they develop an unusual, almost citric flavour that retains more than a hint of their initial bitterness.

The fruit is very low in the setting agent pectin and recipes for rowan jelly suggest combining it with an equal quantity of crabapples to achieve a proper set. Whole clusters of berries are stewed until soft and the juice they render is boiled with sugar. In Britain, where there is a tradition of eating jellies with meat, rowan jelly is served alongside mutton or, especially, venison. **MR**

The Mediterranean produces some of the world's best figs. Fig trees there bear two crops: the first flush comes in June or July, the second from the end of August. The latter produces the juiciest, sweetest fruit, perfect for the best jams. The many varieties of fig that grow divide into "white," which (confusingly) have green or yellowish outer skins and "black" ones, which are dark purple. Both are suitable for jamming and recipes abound, featuring extra ingredients such as vanilla, walnuts, and lemon juice. A Spanish *mermelada de higo* is no different, in essence, from an Italian *confettura di fichi*. (Note, however, that the delicious Sicilian preserve *fichi d'India* is made from prickly pears.)

As experienced jam-makers know, setting depends on the amount of pectin in fruit. Figs can be tricky in this regard as they can set without it, but not always. The Tuscan town of Carmignano near Florence, famous for its dried figs, makes jams too, using the local varieties: Dottato, Verdino, Brogiotto Nero, and San Pietro. Italians eat fig jam with white meats and cheese, such as Gorgonzola. **MR**

Taste: *The set jelly, similar to redcurrant jelly, is clear, bright, and orange in colour. Both colour and flavour make it comparable to a unique form of marmalade.*

Taste: *Dense, brightly coloured, and grainy in texture from the seeds, fig jam should smell sweet, fruity, and fragrant. The flavour should be rich, intense, and persistent.*

Sour Cherry Jam

Sour cherry jams are made with an infinite number of variations throughout the Balkans, in Turkey and Iran, and as far east as Russia. Each culinary culture has seized on the contrast between the sweetness of the sugar, or honey, used for preserving and the tartness of the fruit. Greek *víssino glikó* is essentially the same recipe as Turkish *vişne reçeli*, in which juice from the stoned cherries (morello or similar) is mixed with sugar and boiled. The fruit is cooked in the light syrup, left overnight to stand, and boiled again until the syrup thickens. It can then be stored like a jam. The result though is different from some jams, in that cherries are low in pectin but will keep their shape. Elena Mclokhovets, doyenne of nineteenth-century Russian cooking, recommended *vishni i chereshni*, in which the *vishni* (sour cherries) were cooked together with *chereshni* (sweet ones).

These preserves are not intended for eating with bread but are taken in small quantities as a spoon sweet. In Persia, the syrup may be poured over a glass of crushed ice and sipped as a sherbet (*sharbat-e albaloo*), a prototype of the modern sorbet. **MR**

Taste: *The syrup's colour will reflect the variety of cherry used: dark or bright red. The taste of fruit is not dominated by the sugar and retains a memory of its original sourness.*

Damson Jam

Damsons produce a quintessentially English jam. In the Middle Ages these small blue-purple plums were also called "Damascenes," which reveals their link to Damascus in Syria. However, they belong to a native European species (*Prunus instititia*), which includes the rounder bullace plum and the wild, astringent sloe. Even when perfectly ripe, damsons are sour and their popularity as a country garden fruit rests entirely on their suitability for jamming.

In Cumbria, England, Damson Saturday was celebrated each year up to the outbreak of World War II. Carts and trailers brought loads of semi-wild and cultivated fruit to be sent to the jamming factories in the neighbouring county of Lancashire. A traditionally poor rural area, the income often helped to pay the rents of tenant farmers.

Nowadays damson jam is mainly the preserve of hobby cooks. It is naturally rich in pectin, sets well, and has more body than other kinds of plum jam. The fruit is not usually stoned before cooking, but the stones rise to the surface of the pan during boiling and can be removed with a slotted spoon. **MR**

Taste: *Damsons make a dark purple, almost black, jam. The high proportion of skins gives a sense of texture and body. The taste is of wild plums, powerful and dense.*

Plum Slatko

Wild Beach Plum Preserve

Plum slatko is a fruit preserve from Bosnia-Herzegovina. In neighbouring countries it is also made from fruits such as strawberries, raspberries, blueberries, and cherries. Typically made at home, a spoonful of slatko would traditionally be served in a special cup to guests on special occasions. Commercial production of the preserve, based on the traditional recipe and using the local blue Pozegaca plums has, however, begun in Bosnia-Herzegovina's Upper Drina valley, spearheaded by local women keen to reinvigorate the economy, replant old plum orchards, and create new ones.

The second crop of plums, harvested in mid-September, is used to make slatko. The plums are peeled and pitted, and placed in a mix of water and lime juice to firm up their flesh. They are then boiled in a clear sugar syrup flavoured with lemon slices. Cloves, walnuts, and almonds are sometimes added.

Plum slatko is usually eaten with young cheeses, *kaymak*, Turkish coffee, or goat's milk tea, although it also makes an excellent topping for ice cream, pancakes, and waffles. **CK**

Prunus maritima or beach plums grow wild in sand dunes and by the roadside on the east coast of North America. Explorer Henry Hudson found them when he landed in 1609 on what is now Long Island, New York, but Native Americans had been eating them long before Hudson and other Europeans arrived.

A member of the rose family, beach plums have fragrant white blossom and produce crimson to blue-black fruit, although a variety native to New England produces yellow fruit. Early settlers to New England and other areas where beach plums grow turned the fruit into jams, jellies, and preserves. No large-scale commercial enterprise lasted long though, because beach plums continually defy attempts to cultivate them successfully. Thus, the production of commercial beach plum preserves remains for the most part a cottage industry.

Wild beach plum preserves and jellies are hard to find outside the plant's native habitat. Some producers do, however, provide mail order service and the product can be found through gourmet and speciality food shops online. **SH**

Taste: *Slatko has a light, creamy consistency with a delicate sweet flavour that is reminiscent of Turkish rose-petal preserves.*

Taste: *Raw wild beach plums have an astringent flavour and can be sweet or very tart. The preserves, however, strike a balance and have some ordinary plum flavours.*

Beach plum's showy flowers resemble cherry blossom. The shrub produces cherry-sized fruit. »

1001 FOODS
YOU MUST TRY BEFORE YOU DIE

GENERAL EDITOR FRANCES CASE

PREFACE BY GREGG WALLACE

A Quint**essence** Book

First published in Great Britain in 2008 by Cassell Illustrated
A division of Octopus Publishing Group Limited
2–4 Heron Quays, London E14 4JP
An Hachette Livre UK company

A CIP catalogue record for this book is available from the British Library

ISBN: 978-1-8440-3612-7
QSS.KFOO

This book was designed and produced by
Quint**essence** Publishing Limited
226 City Road
London EC1V 2TT

Project Editor	Victoria Wiggins
Editor	Fiona Plowman
Assistant Editors	Rebecca Gee, Frank Ritter
Editorial Assistant	Helena Baser
Art Editor	Dean Martin
Commissioned Photography	Rob Lawson
Designer	Gaspard de Beauvais
Picture Researcher	Sunita Sharma-Gibson
Editorial Director	Jane Laing
Publisher	Tristan de Lancey

Colour reproduction by Pica Digital Pte Ltd., Singapore.
Printed in China by SNP Leefung Printers Ltd.

Contents

Preface
By Gregg Wallace

For someone like me, who has spent nearly all his working life handling fresh produce, this book is delightful. Listed in these pages are quite simply the best food products from around the globe. Nobody, no matter how clever or well travelled, could claim to know all the culinary wonders of the world—even a television "ingredients expert" like myself!

Of course, a book of this scale and magnitude could not possibly work without illustrations. My time as a judge on the BBC TV show *MasterChef* taught me just how difficult it is to explain taste and smell. No writer finds it easy to describe perfectly the appearance of a particular French goat's cheese, or an incredible-looking fruit like the mangosteen. The photographs in this book are beautiful, and I admire the book's attempt to bring flavour and aroma to the page.

I have a personal love of food history. It is not something I suppose many people consider, but every food originates somewhere. The golden age of European exploration brought to Old World dining tables a treasure trove of new flavours, textures, and sights. *1001 Foods* is packed full of wonderful anecdotes and the history behind many familiar and not so familiar ingredients. I am always boring my children and dinner guests with food histories, and this book has more than doubled my knowledge.

As a greengrocer, I found the sections on fruits and vegetables especially fascinating. I would like to boast that I recognized each and every fruit and each and every vegetable, but I didn't. I loved the descriptions of produce that I know very well, and found it nearly impossible to disagree with the writers. But this book also does a terrific job of filling in the gaps in my knowledge, particularly in the complex world of aromatics. As I write this, I'm scratching my head and trying to think of a comparable work. I am lucky to have a kitchen full of cookery books from around the world, and I will be putting this book alongside my *Larousse gastronomique* and Alan Davidson's *Oxford Companion to Food*. Like those two works, I expect *1001 Foods* to age beyond its years through frequent thumbing.

I have had this book with me now for just over a week and I can't help turning through the pages to see what has been written about the foods I am preparing for each mealtime. Reading it, I've found myself pondering the possibility of a Herculean but divine journey of exploration across the world, sampling each of the 1001 ingredients as I go. This is surely a wild dream, but a hugely pleasant one none the less. And even if I never manage this journey of gastronomic discovery, what I will undoubtedly do, the next time I travel, is make a list of the favoured products of my destination. In fact, as I look through the book, I realize just how many gems I have missed on previous travels. There is only one thing for it—I am going to have to revisit those countries with *1001 Foods* tucked into my suitcase. Owning this book is a must for anyone who enjoys cooking or eating well. Wherever you go in the world, or however you cook, the cornerstones are good ingredients. Nothing can be achieved without them and any attempt made at good cooking will be a struggle.

Allow me a little indulgence here. Because there is so much included in the book's pages, everyone is going to have their favourite chapters. Of course, my major interest is fruit, vegetables, and herbs—all of which are brilliantly described—but the coverage of preserved meats has filled me with special admiration. Food preservation is a subject dear to my heart. In order to survive, every race of people had to learn ways of preserving slaughtered beasts. As well as providing tremendous detail of the dried and salted meats that are familiar to me, this book whetted my appetite for meats I never even knew existed.

Anyone who has watched the BBC TV show *MasterChef* will know what a sweet tooth I have. I fell in love with *1001 Foods* as soon as I realized it had devoted a whole chapter to confectionery and sweetmeats. Sweets play a huge part in our childhoods and some people, like me, never lose their passion for them. I cannot believe I went ski-ing in Scandinavia last winter and had no idea I could have bought myself a big bag of salted, fish-shaped liquorice crops. I am now also on a mission to get my hands on the Iranian honey-and-nut combo known as Qum schan. And I am horrified that honeycomb toffee has been available in Britain for years, and I've never tried it. As soon as I've finished writing this, I am going to put "honeycomb toffee" into a search engine and order myself a packet.

This is a truly beautiful book—full of information and filled with treats you will not have tried. I'm now on a mission to try as many as I can.

Surrey, England, 2008

Introduction
By Frances Case, General Editor

Food is not only an essential part of our lives, but also a source of great joy. In the words of the eighteenth-century gastronome Jean-Anthelme Brillat-Savarin (who himself has a cheese named after him), "The discovery of a new dish confers more happiness on humanity, than the discovery of a new star." Today, there is a growing passion for food around the world, and for food from all over the world.

With the food in supermarkets becoming less recognizable as food and containing all sorts of odd chemicals we would not expect to find on the kitchen shelf—from nitrites and stabilizers to trans fats and glutamates—we want to get closer to the land, closer to our heritage. This explains the surge in popularity of growing our own fruit and vegetables, buying organic, traceable foods, and the belief that "less is more": the fewer ingredients a supermarket-bought meal contains, the better.

Responsible eating is hip. We are concerned about the risk to the environment of food production and the air miles required to transport foods from overseas. Farmers' markets are springing up in every major city from San Francisco to London, with urban markets priding themselves on offering things grown within a few miles of where they are sold. Restaurants such as London's Konstam go further, promoting the fact that they source all their ingredients within the city's limits.

Another concern is sustainability, especially as more people have access to gourmet and unusual ingredients than in previous generations. The sustainability of seafood is a hot topic, and this book warns of foods that we should not eat from the wild—at least until their stocks recover. Some are already almost impossible to find. Over-fishing of certain sea creatures has decimated stocks, and climate change is already having an impact on marine ecosystems.

Take toheroa, the iconic, fast-burrowing New Zealand shellfish, or elvers, the Anglo-Spanish delicacy of baby eels, collected from the Sargasso Sea. Even tuna and cod are under threat, and one of the saddest things about researching this book was reading about delicacies that no longer exist because they have been made extinct in the wild over the last decade: like the giant catfish of the Mekong, famed for its delicacy and exterminated because of it. Of the world's fish stocks, 76 per cent are over-exploited, and many are severely depleted: scientists now agree that we must find a radical new approach to farming the seas, to ensure the health of our oceans for future generations.

Regionality provokes strong passions, especially when it comes to foods. Many European cheeses are made on or around the mountains where herds of cows, goats, or sheep are bred, and which also form national boundaries. European Union (E.U.) product laws exist to protect such traditional foods and ensure that substandard products do not enter the market and damage their reputation. *Appellation d'origine contrôlée* (AOC) guidelines governing traditional production methods were drawn up as far back as the fifteenth century, and are strictly enforced. For example, a patriotic debate rages over whether Vacherin, a mountain cheese matured in spruce, is French or Swiss, with both sides laying claim to the name and insisting that their Vacherin is the authentic one; a similar dispute occurs over Emmentaler and Emmenthal. Over forty French cheeses have been granted the AOC label, and even lentils from Le Puy-en-Velay carry it.

For any country, shared heritage means shared food, and national delicacies that might seem unpalatable to some are often based on a plentiful supply of a particular animal or vegetable. The Scandinavians, for example, have a passion for moose, and it is no coincidence that Sweden has the largest moose population in the world. Many Polish dishes are based around cabbage and potatoes, both of which grow in abundance in the region. There is a natural balance between supply and demand.

Cookery shows on television are now hugely popular. The chefs who present them are bona fide celebrities who can increase sales of a particular ingredient by 300 per cent by using it in a recipe. Martha Stewart, Delia Smith, Nigella Lawson, Wolfgang Puck, and Anthony Bourdain are household names in many countries. Their programmes attract huge audiences. Nigella Lawson's most recent series, *Nigella Express*, peaked with 3.5 million viewers per episode in the United Kingdom. The Food Network cable channel is distributed to 90 million U.S. households. We now spend more time watching cooking on television than we do actually preparing food in our kitchens—and probably more time reading about it, too.

For this book we have assembled an international team to reflect the cuisines and delicacies specific to each continent and country. Despite this, we are bound to have trodden on some national toes. Pavlova, for example, is the national dish of both Australia and New Zealand, a matter not necessarily known to both nations. So, to any Ukrainians finding their national dish described as Polish, any Lithuanians whose Sunday special has been attributed to Estonia, and any Norwegians feeling that their cuisine has been hijacked by the Swedes, I offer my sincere apologies.

Selecting the 1001 foods featured in this book has not been easy. We have tried to include a mix of affordable and unusual ingredients, alongside luxury items—a difficult balancing act. Each foodstuff we chose to include had to justify its place in the list of greats: there are hundreds of types of mushroom, so which ones deserve to be included, and why? Some of the tastes in here will provoke strong personal reactions—sulphurous truffle will not necessarily be to everyone's taste, any more than stinky-sweet surströmming (fermented Baltic herring), but one is considered a delicacy by more people than the other. Luxurious, indulgent foods, such as single estate chocolate, oysters, and lobster, sit alongside less celebrated ones, such as the delicacy of hop shoots— without question the most expensive green food on earth.

We have included a fantastic range of fruits and vegetables, from "superfoods" such as pomegranate and edamame to everyday heroes such as fennel, peppers, and shallots. (Our terms, as Jeffrey Steingarten magnificently remarked in *The Man Who Ate Everything*, are culinary, not botanical, so you will find tomatoes in the vegetable chapter, along with their companions in the salad drawer.)

1001 Foods encourages you to branch out and explore, broadening your palate, with tasting notes that should give you an idea of what you are getting into. Some of the foods may not be easy to track down, and some are extraordinary: miracle berries, so sweet that lemons taste like sweets for minutes after you have eaten them; turu, the Amazonian tree worm that tastes of oysters; and yellow oil crabs, the Shanghainese speciality of female crabs so sunburnt that their roe has melted and turned to buttery oil. Other foods are simply marvellous examples of the familiar, the best of their kind, such as Azores pineapples, lovingly grown under glass as they once were for the grand houses of Europe; heritage Blenheim apricots; and Cox's Orange Pippin apples. The focus of this book is on taste, not texture, although we do include some iconic, texture-led Chinese delicacies—jellyfish, sea cucumber, and bird's nest.

Food myths and lore are intrinsically tied to the appeal of certain delicacies, from the aphrodisiac properties of oysters and asparagus to fact-based claims made about certain foods. Popeye munched on spinach to maintain his bulging muscles, and most of us will benefit—perhaps not to the same extent—from eating more of this iron-rich vegetable. We wanted to make this a global guide, with offerings from all seven continents, but Antarctica proved stubbornly resistant (any readers on a research station, please write in).

1001 Foods is about foods and their tastes, rather than the dishes you can make from the ingredients. There's a book of "1001 Dishes" to be made, but this is not it: so, while curried goat or lobster thermidor are dishes everyone should try before they die, you will not find them here. Neither is this book a simple dictionary of ingredients. Every food in here has been selected because it is special in some way—whether iconic to a nation (or the world), simply delicious, part of a fascinating story, unique, or unusual. We love seasonal foods: the Christmas breads and cakes were hard to choose between, and I wish we had discovered the Finnish pastries *jouluotttu* before we finalized the list.

I would like to thank our wonderful team of contributors, who produced fantastic copy, often to ludicrously tight deadlines. Special thanks to Michael Raffael, whose passion for cheese and patient exploration of the finer points of E.U.-cheese law went well beyond the call of duty, and to C. L. Jackson and her team at the Seafood Training School, a charitable company promoting awareness of fish in both the public and the industry. Tony Hill imparted an incredible knowledge of spices, and was willing to find, buy and taste absolutely anything. Special thanks also to Beverly LeBlanc, for her Americanizing, practicality, and ability to perform miracles; Shirley Booth, for her unswerving enthusiasm for and knowledge of all things Japanese; Anne-Marie Sutcliffe, for covering both Mani and Greece; Rob Lawson, for his fantastic photography; Suzanne Hall, for her enthusiasm for all things that grow; and Victoria Wiggins and Fiona Plowman, for keeping the whole project on the road against considerable odds. Personally, I would also like to thank Victor Sutcliffe, Howard Case, Frances Voss, Michelle Jeffares, and Zachary Sutcliffe, for putting up with me during the book's production, for parts of which we oh-so-ironically subsisted largely on takeaways.

The main goal of this book is to encourage you to try new foods, broaden your palate, and discover new favourites. You may not enjoy everything you taste—the Sardinian cheese casu marzu immediately springs to mind—but you will certainly have fun experimenting.

Foods Index

Acknowledgments

Appetit/Alamy **650** Steve Atkins Photography/Alamy **652** Rob Walls/Alamy **654** Pat O'Hara/CORBIS **655** Jignesh Jhaveri/StockFood UK **657** blickwinkel/Alamy **658** Vibrant Pictures/Alamy **661** Photolibrary **663** Simon Grosset/Alamy **664-5** Owen Franken/CORBIS **666** Eill Bachmann/Alamy **671** Bob Sacha/Corbis **673** Lindsay Hebberd/CORBIS **674** Hemis/Alamy **677** CHRIS LEWINGTON/Alamy **681** Jeremy Horner/Corbis **683** Sergio Pitamitz/CORBIS **685** JUPITERIMAGES/Agence Images/Alamy **687** Felix Stensson/Alamy **688-9** Paul Cowan/Alamy **691** WoodyStock/Alamy **692** World Religions Photo Library/Alamy **697** Edward Parker/Alamy **701** Mark Bolton Photography/Alamy **702** ZenShui/Laurence Mouton/Getty Images **705** Andrea Matone/Alamy **706** Russell Kord/Alamy **709** AA World Travel Library/Alamy **710** Radius Images/Alamy **713** Danita Delimont/Alamy **715** Bon Appetit/Alamy **717** Fabian Gonzales Editoria/Alamy **719** Iconotec/Alamy **720** Wolfgang Kaehler/Alamy **723** Owen Franken/CORBIS **724** cesare dagliana/Alamy **726-7** Danita Delimont/Alamy **728** foodfolic/Alamy **730** Richard Bickel/CORBIS **735** Burt Hardy/Getty images **738** dbimages/Alamy **742-3** Javier Etcheverry/Alamy **744** Goss Images/Alamy **746-7** Photolibrary **748** Photolibrary **751** Photolibrary **752** Vincenzo Lombardo/Getty Images **754** Frederick Fearn/Alamy **757** Nature Picture Library/Alamy **758** Photolibrary **761** foodfolio/Alamy **763** Jacques Jangoux/Alamy **764** Alison Wright/Corbis **765** Photolibrary **766** Holt Studios International Ltd/Alamy **770-1** DAVID NOBLE PHOTOGRAPHY/Alamy **775** Joel Sartore/National Geographic/Getty Images **776-7** JTB Photo Communications, Inc./Alamy **778** David Cairns/Alamy **781** Nova Pomortzeff/Alamy **783** Photolibrary **785** Walter Cimbal/StockFood UK **788-9** Photolibrary **791** Neil McAllister/Alamy **792** Cynthia Brown/StockFood UK **795** Woman Making Tortillas **796-7** Nick Haslam/Alamy **799** Photolibrary **801** Owen Franken/CORBIS **802** Cubolmages srl/Alamy **804** Robert Holmes/CORBIS **807** Cubolmages srl/Alamy **809** The Art Archive/Corbis **810** Photolibrary **812-3** Bob Krist/CORBIS **814** Cubolmages srl/Alamy **816-7** Cris Haigh/Alamy **820-1** Istock **822** Alan Richardson/Getty Images **825** imagebroker/Alamy **829** Cristofani/ANSA/Corbis **832** Victoria Art Gallery, Bath and North East Somerset Council/Bridgeman Art Library **835** The Art Archive/British Library **836** Amazing Images/Alamy **838** Jo Kirchherr/StockFood UK **841** Anne-Marie Palmer/Alamy **843** Tsgt. H. H. Deffner/Department Of Defense (DOD)/Time Life Pictures/Getty Images **845** Iconotec/Alamy **846** Adam Woolfitt/CORBIS **849** Zhang Wenxui/ChinaFotoPress/Getty Images **850** Alberto Moretto/StockFood UK **852** Travelshots.com/Alamy **856-7** Photolibrary **858** imagebroker/Alamy **859** Gaby Bohle/StockFood UK **863** Mansell/Time Life Pictures/Getty Images **865** Travel-Ink/Chris Stock **865-7** Photolibrary **868** Redfx/Alamy **870** Frances M. Roberts/Alamy **872** Barry Lewis/Corbis **877** IML Image Group Ltd/Alamy **879** john normar/Alamy **881** john lander/Alamy **882-3** Photolibrary **886-7** Michael S. Lewis/CORBIS **889** Bill Brooks/Alamy **893** Manor Photography/Alamy **895** David Paul Morris/Getty Images **896** Rebecca Erol/Alamy **898** keith burdett/Alamy **900** OJPHOTOS/Alamy **903** J-Charles Gèrard/Photononstop **904** Photolibrary **906-7** John Birdsall/Alamy **910** Jean Pierre Amet/BelOmbra/Corbis **912** Olivier Asselin/Alamy **914** Photolibrary **920** Bill Lyons/Alamy **923** Jonathan Little/Alamy **924-5** Mary Evans Picture Library/Alamy **929** Photolibrary **930** Rogan Coles/Alamy **935** Arco Images GmbH/Alamy **941** JTB Photo Communications, Inc./Alamy

Additional commissioned photography by:
Masami Bornoff **254**
Craig Fraser **377, 414**
Kenzaburo Fukuhara **198, 345, 370, 438, 718**
John Hollingshead **39, 46, 108, 121, 750**
Ricardo Lagos **45, 132, 353**
Simon Pask **180, 208, 246, 253, 254, 254, 264, 311, 328, 330, 357, 359, 360, 353, 367, 369, 372, 381, 386, 396, 400, 410, 414, 422, 443, 445, 455, 458, 474, 514, 529, 533, 553, 592, 790, 820, 823, 853, 866, 869, 873, 875, 876, 878, 836, 890, 897, 905, 909, 940**
Gerson Sobreira **39, 45, 67, 92, 98, 354, 437, 465, 641, 937**
Jeremy Sutton-Hibbert **92, 96, 105, 214, 221, 224, 400, 404, 453, 458, 470, 510, 610, 632, 634, 717, 740**

We would like to express our gratitude to the following:

The Ice Box, New Covent Garden Market, London

Editors: Phil Hall
David Hutter
Felicity Jackson

Indexer: Kay Ol erenshaw

Food Sourcing: Masami Bornoff
Wendy Sweetser

Artworking: Don Ward
Chris Taylor

Image Libraries

Alamy — Maria Kuzim

Corbis — John Moelwyn-Hughes

Getty — Hayley Newman

Photolibrary — Tim Kantoch

StockFood — Kathy Sinclaire

Picture Credits

20-21 Photolibrary 22 Numb/ Alamy 23 Michael Freeman/CORBIS 24 Istockphoto 25 Getty Images/StockFood UK 26 Corbis, Photolibrary 28 Istockphoto 29 Ilan Rosen/ Alamy 30 D. Hurst/Alamy 31 Photolibrary 32 Photolibrary 34 Foodcollection/StockFood UK 35 Roland Krieg/StockFood UK 37 Olaf Doering/Alamy 38 Photolibrary 39 Paul Williams/Alamy 40 AfriPics.com/Alamy 42 Photolibrary 47 STR/AFP/Getty Images 48 CSIRO Australia 48 Flávio Coelho/StockFood UK 49 Christine Sohns, Photolibrary 51 LOOK Die Bildagentur der Fotografen GmbH/Alamy 52 Jon Arnold Images Ltd/Alamy 56–7 Martial Colomb/Getty Images 58 Pawan Kumar/Reuters/Corbis 60 Istockphoto 60 AGStockUSA, Inc./Alamy 62 MERVYN REES/Alamy 64 Photolibrary 66 Steven Lee/Alamy 67 Gerson Sobreira/Terrastock 68 Photofrenetic/Alamy 71 Edwin Remsberg/Alamy 73 Peter Titmuss/Alamy 74 Profimedia International s.r.o./Alamy 76 Luca Tettoni/Corbis 78 Gerson Sorbreira/Terrastock 79 Schieren, Bodo A./ StockFood UK 80 The Art Archive/Dagli Orti 83 Photolibrary 85 Photolibrary 86 FoodStock/Alamy 88 J.Garcia/photocuisine/Corbis 90 Paul Collis/Alamy 92 Gerson Sobreira/Terrastock 95 Zach Holmes/Alamy 97 Walter Pietsch/Alamy 99 Nigel J. Dennis; Gallo Images/CORBIS 101 Photolibrary 102 ricardo junqueira/Alamy 104 Beaconstox/Alamy 107 adam eastland/Alamy 110 PhotoStock-Israel/Alamy 113 Asia/Alamy 115 Paulo Fridman, Corbis 116 Cephas Picture Library/Alamy 118 Gerhard Bumann/StockFood UK 119 Bob Sacha/Corbis 120 Jonathan Blair/CORBIS 123 Yogesh More/Alamy 125 blickwinkel/Alamy 126-7 Photolibrary 129 FoodPhotography Eising/StockFood UK 130 Tony Arruza/CORBIS 133 Phil Degginger/Alamy 134 Photolibrary 139 Photolibrary 140 Scenics & Science/Alamy 143 Natural Visions/Alamy 146-147 dbimages/Alamy 148 Robert Harding Picture Library Ltd/Alamy 151 Ulrich Doering/Alamy 155 Stockbyte/Alamy 156 Gunter Marx Photography/CORBIS 157 MIXA Co., Ltd./Alamy 158 J. Schwanke/Alamy 162 The Garden Picture Library/Alamy 163 Stefan Braun/StockFood UK 165 J.Garcia/ photocuisine/Corbis 167 Photolibrary 168 Sebun/Getty Images 169 MIXA Co., Ltd./Alamy 170 Ulana Switucha/Alamy 172 Tim Hill/Alamy 173 Clynt Garnham/Alamy 175 Bryn Colton/Assignments Photographers/CORBIS 176 Julian Nieman/Alamy 178 Istock 179 Photolibrary 182 TOM MARESCHAL/Alamy 185 Photolibrary 187 David Boag/Alamy 191 Bob Krist/CORBIS 192 julian marshall/Alamy 194 Thomas R. Fletcher/Alamy 195 Photolibrary 197 Alberto Moretto/StockFood UK 199 Photolibrary 200 Picture Box/StockFood UK 202 Photolibrary 203 Rodrigo Aliaga Ibargüen/Fotolibra 204 Photolibrary 209 Chao-Yang Chan/Alamy 211 CHARLES JEAN MARC/CORBIS SYGMA 212 Arco Images GmbH/Alamy 215 Greg Vaughn/Alamy 217 Stockbyte/Alamy 219 Photolibrary 220 ASTRID & HANNS-FRIEDER MICHLER/SCIENCEPHOTO LIBRARY 221 WILDLIFE GmbH/Alamy 222 MIXA Co., Ltd./Alamy 223 Jeremy Hoare/Alamy 225 Nic Hamilton/Alamy 226 Marc O'Finley/StockFood UK 226 Ottomar Deiz/ StockFood UK 227 Stan Kujawa/Alamy 228 Herbert Lehmann/StockFood UK 229 Foodcollection.com/Alamy 230 Michael S. Yamashita/CORBIS 235 Craig Lovell/Eagle Visions Photography/Alamy 237 blickwinkel/Alamy 238 PhotoAlto/Alamy 241 Bernd Euler/StockFood UK 242 David R. Frazier Photolibrary, Inc./Alamy 244 Peter Widmann/Alamy 245 Rodrigo Aliaga Ibargüen/Fotolibra 247 Karin Lau/Alamy 249 Aqua Image/Alamy 250 john lander/Alamy 251 FoodPhotogr. Eising/StockFood UK 257 JTB Photo Communications, Inc./Alamy 258-9 Photolibrary 260 Photolibrary 262 Iain Masterton/Alamy 265 wronaphoto/Alamy 266 Bob Krist/CORBIS 269 Jason Hosking/zefa/Corbis 271 Joan Vendrell Marcé/Alamy 275 Bob Krist/Corbis 279 Bon Appetit/Alamy 280 Franz-Marc Frei/Corbis 282 Adam Woolfitt/CORBIS 285 Cephas Picture Library/Alamy 287 Hemis/Alamy 289 Kevin Galvin/Alamy 291 Adrian Sherratt/Alamy 293 LOOK Die Bildagentur der Fotografen GmbH/Alamy 295 Bon Appetit/ Alamy 296 Photolibrary 301 Ingolf Pompe 22/Alamy 303 Robert Harding Picture Library Ltd/Alamy 304 Cubolmages srl/Alamy 307 Huw Jones/Alamy 309 Michael Maslan Historic Photographs/CORBIS 310 Martin Ruetschi/Keystone/Corbis 314 Hemis/Alamy 317 Cephas Picture Library/Alamy 321 Panoramic Images/Getty Images 322 Michael S. Yamashita/CORBIS 327 Allison Dinner/StockFood UK 329 PSL Images/Alamy 332 Iconotec/Alamy 334 jack sparticus/Alamy 337 CuboImages srl/Alamy 339 Atlantide Phototravel/Corbis 341 Reino Hanninen/Alamy 342 Anna Stowe Travel/Alamy 343 A&P/Alamy 343 birdpix/Alamy 347 China Photos/Getty Images 348-9 Photolibrary 350 J Marshall - Tribaleye Images/Alamy 352 The Art Archive/Gianni Dagli Orti 354 Photolibrary 355 piluhin/Alamy 356 john lander/Alamy 357 Bon Appetit/Alamy 358 allOver photography/Alamy 361 Steven J. Kazlowski/Alamy 362 Tanya Zouev/StockFood UK 364 Michael Busselle/CORBIS 365 FoodPhotogr. Eising/ StockFood UK 366 Garry Gay/Alamy 368 Mark Bassett/Alamy 370 Ashley Mackevicius/StockFood UK 371 Simon Reddy/Alamy 373 terry harris just greece photo library/ Alamy 375 Tony Arruza/CORBIS 377 WILDLIFE GmbH/Alamy 379 Mikael Utterström/Alamy 380 Nikolai Buroh/StockFood UK 383 B.A.E. Inc./Alamy 387 Amos Schliack/ StockFood UK 388 canadabrian/Alamy 391 Robert Estall photo agency/Alamy 392 Douglas Pearson/Corbis 394 Corbis 396–7 Simon Price/Alamy 399 CuboImages srl/ Alamy 396 Brigitte Krauth/StockFood UK 397 Visual&Written SL/Alamy 401 Phillip Augustavo/Alamy 402 Steven Morris/StockFood UK 403 Per Karlsson - BKWine.com/ Alamy 405 Doug Houghton/Alamy 406 Bon Appetit/Alamy 411 Werner Otto/Alamy 412-3 Yadid Levy/Alamy 416 CuboImages srl/Alamy 417 Alain Caste/StockFood UK 419 Gerry McLoughlin/Alamy 420 Eric James/Alamy 423 FoodPix/Alamy 424 Rolf Hicker Photography/Alamy 426 Ulana Switucha/Alamy 428 Foodcollection.com/Alamy 429 Bon Appetit/Alamy 430 Shutterstock 431 Ulana Switucha/Alamy 432 Peter L Hardy/Alamy 435 orkneypics/Alamy 436 Jeff Greenberg/Alamy 438 Lew Robertson/ StockFood UK 439 Photo Agency EYE/Alamy 440 Andy Newman/epa/Corbis 441 Lew Robertson/StockFood UK 441 Photolibrary 442 Tony May Images/Alamy 445 David Hobart/Alamy 447 Michael T. Sedam/CORBIS 451 an Waldie/Getty Images 452 Michael S. Yamashita/CORBIS 453 Riviere Rauzier/StockFood UK 454 Henrik Freek/ StockFood UK 457 john lander/Alamy 459 B&Y Photography/Alamy 460 MIXA Co., Ltd./Alamy 461 J.Riou/photocuisine/Corbis 461 Frans Lanting/Corbis 463 Inspirestock Inc./Alamy 465 Gerson Sobreira - Terrastock 466 Nik Wheeler/Corbis 468-9 Photolibrary 471 Photolibrary 473 Shenval/Alamy 474 Jon Arnold Images Ltd/Alamy 475 Bon Appetit/Alamy 477 Food Image Source/StockFood UK 479 Debi Treloar/StockFood UK 480 Tim Graham/Alamy 481 Tim Hill/Alamy 482 Brigitte Krauth/StockFood UK 482 Teubner Foodfoto/StockFood UK 483 Jack Hobhouse/Alamy 484 Jochen Tack/Alamy 487 Bryan & Cherry Alexander Photography/Alamy 488 Peter Johnson/CORBIS 490 Photolibrary 492 Brigitte Krauth/StockFood UK 492 Brigitte Krauth/StockFood UK 493 Peter Medilek/StockFood UK 495 Winfried Heinze/StockFood UK 496 Per Magnus Persson/StockFood UK 499 BRIAN HARRIS/Alamy 500 Michael Freeman/CORBIS 503 Dierdre Rooney/Photolibrary 505 Photolibrary/ Digital Vision 508-9 Mary Evans Picture Library/Alamy 511 Chloe Johnson/Alamy 512 Glenn Harper/Alamy 515 FoodPhotogr. Eising/StockFood UK 516 Sandro Vannini/CORBIS 518 Peter Widmann/Alamy 521 Winfried Heinze/StockFood UK 523 Kevin Foy/Alamy 527 Trevor Hyde/Alamy 528 Glenn Harper/Alamy 530 Tim Hill/Alamy 532 John Ferro Sims/ Alamy 534-5 CuboImages srl/Alamy 537 Joe Tree/Alamy 539 Jacques deLacroix/Alamy 540-1 Peter Adams/zefa/Corbis 543 Travelshots.com/Alamy 544-5 Michael Freeman/CORBIS 546 Iugris/Alamy 549 Shenval/Alamy 550 Photolibrary 552 Robert Fried/Alamy 554 M. Fonseca Da Costa/StockFood UK 557 Photolibrary 559 JoeFoxBerlin/Alamy 560 MELBA PHOTO AGENCY/Alamy 562 Crispin Rodwell/Alamy 565 Alberto Paredes/Alamy 566 Winfried Heinze/StockFood UK 567 Radius Images/Alamy 569 Dave G. Houser/Corbis 570 Bon Appetit/Alamy 571 Karen Kasmauski/Corbis 572 DK Images 573 Arco Images GmbH/Alamy 574 Bob Sacha/Corbis 576 mike disney/Alamy 579 Photolibrary 580-1 allOver photography/Alamy 582 Bon Appetit/Alamy 582 Bon Appetit/Alamy 583 Rough Guides/Alamy 586-7 Gareth McCormack/Alamy 588 Edith Gerlach/StockFood UK 590 FoodPhotogr. Eising/StockFood UK 591 Gareth McCormack/Alamy 593 Brian Seed/Alamy 595 Genevieve Vallee/ Alamy 596-7 Photolibrary 599 Kathy Collins/Getty Images 601 blickwinkel/Alamy 603 Pep Roig/Alamy 605 Photolibrary 606 TH Photo/StockFoto UK 608-9 Arco Images GmbH/Alamy 610 MIXA Co., Ltd./Alamy 611 Teubner Foodfoto//StockFood UK 613 Chris Dennis/Alamy 614 INTERFOTO Pressebildagentur/Alamy 617 sébastien Baussais/ Alamy 618 DEA/A. MORESCHI/Getty Images 619 Powered by Light/Alan Spencer/Alamy 620 Eising. FoodPhotogr/StockFood UK 620 Westend61/Alamy 621 IStock 622 Bon Appetit/Alamy 624 TH Foto/Alamy 625 blickwinkel/Alamy 626 Shutterstock 629 Neil Sutherland/Alamy 630-1 Michael Freeman/CORBIS 633 amana images inc./Alamy 636-7 Deborah Dennis/Alamy 638 David Noton/Getty Images 640 Shutterstock 643 Photolibrary 646 Organics image library/Alamy 647 Istock 649 Bon

morcilla dulce, 564
Rügenwalder teewurst, 551
St. Gallen bratwurst, 558
Salchichón de Vic, 538
saucisson d'Arles, 544
Thüringer leberwurst, 551
Thüringer rostbratwurst, 558
weisswurst, 560
Zampone di Modena, 556
see also salami
savory, 621
sbrisolona, 878
scabbard fish
black, 378
scallion (spring onion), 193
scallop
bay, 455
diver king, 455
Sclerocarya birrea, 41
schiacciata (focaccia), 806
scone, 847
scorzonera, 207
screwpine (pandan leaf), 627
scuppernong, 93
sea buckthorn, 36
sea cucumber, 461
sea urchin, 461
seed
baobab, 755
lotus, 750
pumpkin, 749
sunflower, 749
wattleseed, 750
sekacz, 859
seki aji, 404
serendipity berry (miracle berry;
miracle fruit), 36
sfusato amalfitano, 106
shallot
Jersey ("false shallot"), 189
sheep
fat-tailed, 504
head of, 526
sheto, 739
shichimi togarashi, 682
shiitake, 231
shiokara, 717
shiro shoyu, 740
shisamo, 367
shiso leaf, 612
shortbread, 842
shrimp
dried, 464
mantis, 429
potted, 418
shungiku, 169
Sicana ororifera, 98
skate, 382
skyr, 267

slatko
plum, 928
snail
escargot de Bourgogne, 517
snakeskin fruit (salak), 60
snapper
red, 381
snipe, 489
snoek
smoked, 414
sofrito, 607
Solanum centrale, 645
Solanum melongena, 149
Solanum quitoense, 82
sole
Dover, 384
lemon, 385
som-ma-fai (wampee), 53
sorbet
lemon, 938
sorrel, 163
sorubim
spotted, 353
soup
bird's nest, 630
egusi, 255
miso, 248
ogbono, 255
potage cressonnière, 161
sour cherry, 44
toheroa, 446
spaghetti
durum wheat, 784
spalla cotta di San Secondo, 582
Spanish lime (mamoncillo), 43
Spanish plum (red mombin), 50
spinach
arrowhead (arrowleaf spinach), 166
wild (uzouza leaf), 169
Spinacia oleracea, 166
Spondias dulcis, 53
Spondias purpurea, 50
springbok, 497
spugnola (morel), 231
squab, 478
squash
butternut, 154
silk, 153
spaghetti (noodle squash), 154
winter melon, 157
squid
baby, 456
ika, 456
ink from, 462
Stachys affinis, 213
star anise, 667
"star fruit" (carambola), 70
steak tartare, 513
stem lettuce (celtuce), 171

sterlet, 354
stollen, 828
stracchino, 336
strawberry
alpine, 33
Mara des Bois, 33
strawberry guava, 70
strudel
apple, 871
struffoli di Napoli, 880
sudachi, 105
sugar, muscovado, 936
sugar cane, 114
sugardilly (sapodilla), 79
sült libamáj, 529
sumac, 655
sun peach (golden kiwi fruit), 69
suovas, 594
superfood
açaí, 39
sea buckthorn, 36
walnut, 760
"Surinam cherry" (pitanga), 45
surke (Tartous shanklish), 320
surströmming, 407
sushi, 395, 422, 425
"swamp cabbage," 131
sweetbread
veal, 520
sweetcorn
Silver Queen, 142
sweet potato, 210
swordfish, 390
syrup, maple, 931
Syzygium leumannii, 39

T
Tabasco sauce, 745
tafelspitz, 206
tahini, 729
Tahitian quince (ambarella), 53
tajarin, 782
tamale, 792
tamarillo, 82
tamarind, 122
Tamarindus indica, 122
tamari shoyu, 740
tapenade, 732
taramosalata, 421
Taraxacum officinale, 177
taro (taro root; eddo), 214
tarragon
French, 604
tart
treacle, 869
tartare sauce, 725
tarte aux fraises, 869
tarte tatin, 853
tartufo di mare, 443

Kashta

Salep Ice Cream

As a former part of the Ottoman Empire, the Lebanon shares some of its culinary heritage with Turkey. Known as *kaymak* in Turkey, kashta or kishta is a thick white cream that often tops rich pastries. The finest quality is prepared with buffalo milk, but the Lebanese dairies that make it for the pastry shops use cow's milk. They dissolve milk powder in untreated milk and simmer it very gently for several hours (the process is similar to that used to make Cornish clotted cream) until a white, elastic membrane forms on the surface. This is drawn to the back of the tray and the simmering continues until several more layers of skin form. These are then raked off and the kashta is ready to eat.

Although it contains over 50 per cent fat, it is sometimes eaten by itself sweetened with honey, but it is more often an ingredient in desserts and pastries. At Abdul Rahman Hallab, a famous Tripoli patisserie founded in 1881, it is used as a filling for a rice-flour sweet called *halawet el riz*. Flavoured with rose water or orange flower water, it decorates a range of pastries also known as kashta. **MR**

Imagine the rhythmic thud of wood against metal, deadened by chilled, elastic ice cream. Elastic? In Turkey the 300-year-old method of creating thick ice cream by mixing milk and sugar with salep—a flour made from the dried ground tuber of wild orchids—was developed as a way of retarding the melting process and creating a magnificent texture. The polysaccharide (bassorin) in the tuber acts as a thickening agent to produce a dense, chewy, ice cream. This is then hung on hooks, stretched, shaped, dipped into shards of pistachios and eaten, all without dissolving into a puddle.

The name salep comes from an Arabic term meaning "fox testicles," a graphic description of the appearance of the ovoid root tubers of the orchid, and a hint at salep's alleged reputation as an aphrodisiac. Called *salepi dondurma*—dondurma is the Turkish word for ice cream—it was first made in the town of Kahramanmara in southeastern Turkey. It continues to be made throughout Turkey, Syria, and the Lebanon (where it is known as *bouza bi haleeb*) in traditional ice cream parlours. **RH**

Taste: *Kashta has the texture of a smooth, thick white pomade that holds its shape on a spoon. Its rich, milky taste is neutral and absorbs other flavours very well.*

Taste: *Salep ice cream has a chewy, nougat-like texture and sometimes needs eating with a knife and fork. It has a sweet, nutty taste and an earthy fragrance.*

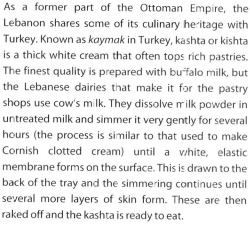

A vendor in Bursa, Turkey, uses long paddles to stretch salep ice cream and keep it workable. ❯

Dibis

Blackstrap Molasses

For thousands of years, humans have cultivated dates, and for almost as long, they have used them to create a sweet syrup. This is believed to be the "honey" of the "land of milk and honey" that Moses led the Israelites to after their enslavement in Egypt.

That syrup, known as dibis, is today perhaps the most popular date product produced in the Middle East. Also known as date syrup and date honey, this thick-as-molasses sweetener is used to flavour pastries, spooned onto bread instead of jam, and mixed with tahini as a spread (dibis w'rashi). It can also be drizzled onto ice cream or yoghurt, used in place of maple syrup on pancakes, and added to warm or cold milk for a sweet treat. Sometimes, date syrup is also used to soften and preserve dates.

While most dibis is factory made, traditionally it was produced at home by extracting and then boiling down the juice. In villages, the production of date syrup has been used to celebrate special occasions such as the birth of a child or the birthday of the Prophet Muhammad. In such instances, it is poured on a cooked dough known as *asseeda*. **JH**

Sugar is a complex beast. Modern industrial refining processes work hard to deconstruct it into individual components to meet contemporary tastes, but some of the most interesting parts of raw sugar are what is left at the end: blackstrap molasses.

In a curious sort of reverse engineering of cane sugar juice, refined white sugar crystals are removed with each of several boiling stages. After the third such boiling, the results are thick and viscous. Sulphur is occasionally added to aid processing but typically in amounts small enough to leave the flavour unaltered. Light, dark, and blackstrap molasses have similar qualities and uses to light, dark, and black treacle found in the United Kingdom.

Blackstrap found its way into the peasant foods of the southern United States where refined sugars were expensive. Recipes commonly call for molasses in lieu of other sweeteners. Perhaps most famously, slow-cooked baked bean recipes of Boston rely on molasses for depth of flavour. Modern cane sugar producers now recognize blackstrap's value and capture it as a premium product. **TH**

Taste: *Thick and viscous, dibis is darker in colour than most honeys, and its sweetness is tempered by acidity and what some would perceive as a slightly bitter flavour.*

Taste: *Blackstrap molasses is certainly sweet, but with decidedly bitter components not found in other sugars. Mineral tastes are noticeable when sampled directly.*

Before being turned into molasses, raw sugar cane is shredded and the juice extracted at the sugar mill. ❯❯

Maple Syrup

Beech Honeydew

In late winter and early spring, across New England, the northern American states, and Canada's eastern provinces, warmer daytime temperatures spur the sugar maple (*Acer saccharum*) into life and stimulate its sap flow. A single tree can produce several gallons a year. A thin, clear liquid in its natural state, with only a faint sweetness, when the sap is boiled down it becomes the thick, sweet syrup beloved for topping pancakes and waffles, making maple walnut ice cream, or glazing carrots. A special treat is "maple in the snow" made by further reducing the syrup before drizzling it on fresh snow: the syrup sets into a chewy, toffee-like confection.

Syrup grading is a complicated subject, and each region has different standards. All, however, rely on the colour, which may range from light to dark amber, as a primary yardstick. The flavour intensity echoes the colour: lighter syrups have a more delicate maple flavour whereas darker syrups are more pronounced. Vermont's maple syrups are especially prized for their higher viscosity, but generally "best" is a matter of personal taste. **CN**

The ancient black and red beech trees growing in New Zealand's pristine southern wilderness host two aphids that part-process their aromatic sap. The sweet liquid they produce is known as honeydew, and bees that feed on this, rather than on the more common flower nectar, produce a unique honey. Marketed as "beech honeydew," it is the nation's largest honey export, and is very popular in Germany.

The make-up of honeydew honeys is very different from flower honeys. Their mineral content is higher; they have fewer simple fructose and glucose sugars and more complex sugars, meaning they are much less likely to crystallize. These complex sugars—oligosaccharides—are thought to help the human gut promote beneficial bacteria, and studies suggest honeydew honeys offer greater antioxidant and antiseptic properties than manuka honey.

Beech honeydew has a distinctive dark colour, partly because it is stored in darker combs closer to the brood nest in the hive and partly because it contains a residue of sooty moulds from the forest, a typical marker of genuine honeydew honeys. **GC**

Taste: *Sweetness is the distinguishing characteristic of maple syrup, but beyond that intense first impression, a maple, almost smoky flavour lingers on the palate.*

Taste: *There is a definite earthy tang of the forest in this malty, intense, amber to golden honey. It is used in European folk medicine, in cooking, and as a spread.*

Tapping maples for their sap is an expensive process;
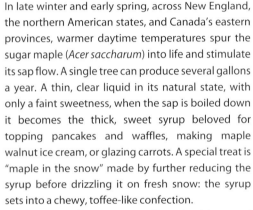 *inferior imitations are made with cheaper ingredients.*

A Bone of Contention

ALSO BY SUSANNA GREGORY
FROM CLIPPER LARGE PRINT

A Plague on Both Your Houses

A Bone of Contention

Susanna Gregory

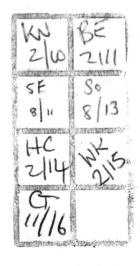

W F HOWES LTD

This large print edition published in 2008 by
W F Howes Ltd
Unit 4, Rearsby Business Park, Gaddesby Lane,
Rearsby, Leicester LE7 4YH

1 3 5 7 9 10 8 6 4 2

First published in the United Kingdom in 1997
by Little, Brown and Company

A CIP catalogue record for this book is available
from the British Library

ISBN 978 1 40741 950 3

Typeset by Palimpsest Book Production Limited,
Grangemouth, Stirlingshire
Printed and bound in Great Britain
by MPG Books Ltd, Bodmin, Cornwall

FSC
Mixed Sources
Product group from well-managed
forests and other controlled sources
Cert no. SGS-COC-2953
www.fsc.org
© 1996 Forest Stewardship Council

To Bob and Phyl

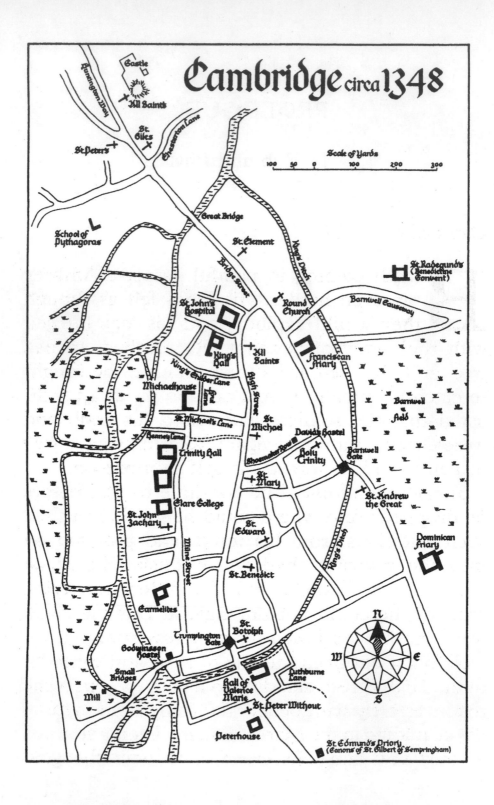

PROLOGUE

Cambridge, 1327

Breath coming in painful gasps, d'Ambrey ran even harder. His lungs felt as though they would explode, and his legs burned with the agony of running. He reached an oak tree, and clutched at its thick trunk as he fought to catch his breath. A yell, not too far away, indicated that the soldiers had found his trail, and were chasing him once again. Weariness gave way to panic, and he forced himself to move on.

But how long could he continue to run before he dropped? And where could he go? He pushed such questions from his mind, and plunged on into the growing shadows of dusk. His cloak caught on a branch, and, for a few terrifying seconds, he could not untangle it. But the cloak tore, and he continued his mindless running.

He burst out from the line of trees and came on to the High Street, skidding to a halt. At sunset the road was busy with people returning home after a day of trading in the Market Square. People stopped as they saw him. His green cloak with the gold

1

crusader's cross emblazoned on the back was distinctive, and everyone knew him.

He elbowed his way through them towards the town gate, but saw soldiers there. He could not go back the way he had come, so the only option was to make his way along the raised banks of the King's Ditch. The King's Ditch was part fortification and part sewer. It swung in a great arc around the eastern side of the town, a foul, slow-moving strip of water, crammed with the town's waste and a thick, sucking mud washed from the Fens. There had been heavy rains with the onset of autumn, and the Ditch was a swirling torrent of brown water that lapped dangerously close to its levied banks.

D'Ambrey scrambled up the bank, mud clinging to his hands and knees and spoiling his fine cloak. He saw the soldiers break through the trees on to the road, pushing through the people towards him, and turned to race away from them along the top of the bank. But it was slippery, and moving quickly was difficult. The soldiers spotted him, and were coming across the strip of grass below, beginning to overtake him.

It was hopeless. He stopped running, and stood still. His cloak billowed around him in the evening breeze, blowing his copper-coloured hair around his face. The soldiers, grinning now that their quarry was run to a halt, began to climb up the bank towards him. Knowing he was going to die, he drew his short dagger in a final, desperate attempt to protect himself.

He heard a singing noise, and something hit him hard in the throat. He dropped the dagger and raised his hands to his neck. He felt no pain, but could not breathe. His fingers grasped at the arrow shaft that was lodged at the base of his throat. The world began to darken, and he felt himself begin to fall backwards. The last thing he knew was the cold waters of the Ditch closing over him as he died.

CHAPTER 1

September 1352

'What, again?' asked Matthew Bartholomew incredulously, watching Brother Michael for some sign of a practical joke.

Michael rubbed his fat, white hands together with a cheery grin. 'I am afraid so, Doctor. The Chancellor requests that you come to examine the bones that were found in the King's Ditch by the Hall of Valence Marie this morning. He wants you to make an official statement that they do not belong to Simon d'Ambrey.'

Bartholomew sighed heavily, picked up his medical bag from the table and followed Michael into the bright September sunshine. It was mid-morning and term was due to start in three days. Students were pouring into the small town of Cambridge, trying to secure lodgings that were not too expensive or shabby, and conducting noisy reunions in the streets. Although Bartholomew did not yet have classes to teach, there was much to be done by way of preparation, and he did not relish being dragged from his cool room at

5

Michaelhouse, into the sweltering heat, on some wild-goose chase for the third time that week.

As he and Brother Michael emerged from the College, Bartholomew wrinkled his nose in disgust at the powerful aroma wafted on the breeze from the direction of the river. Cambridge was near the Fens, and lay on flat, low land that was criss-crossed by a myriad of waterways. To the people who lived there these were convenient places to dispose of rubbish, and many of the smaller ditches were continually blocked because of it.

The summer had been long, hot and dry, and the waterways had been reduced to trickles. People had made no attempt to find other places to rid themselves of their rubbish, and huge blockages had occurred, growing worse as summer had progressed. The first autumn rains had seen the choked waterways bursting their banks, flooding houses and farms with filthy, evil-smelling water. The situation could not continue, and, for once, the town and the University had joined forces, and a major ditch-clearing operation was underway. The University was responsible for dredging the part of the King's Ditch that ran alongside the recently founded Hall of Valence Marie.

Michael headed for the shady side of the road, and began to walk slowly towards Valence Marie. The High Street was busy that Saturday, with traders hurrying to and from the Market Square with their wares. A ponderous brewery cart was stuck in one of the deep ruts that was gouged into

6

the bone-dry street, and chaos ensued when other carts tried to squeeze past it. A juggler sat in the stocks outside St Mary's Church, and entertained a crowd of children with tricks involving three wizened apples and a hard, green turnip. His display came to an abrupt end when a one-eyed, yellow dog made off with the turnip between its drooling jaws.

'Have you seen these bones that have been dredged up?' Bartholomew asked, striding next to the Benedictine monk.

Michael nodded, plucking at Bartholomew's tabard to make him slow down. Bartholomew glanced at him. Already there were small beads of perspiration on the large monk's pallid face, and he pulled uncomfortably at his heavy habit.

'Yes. I am no physician. Matt, but I am certain they are not human.'

Bartholomew slowed his pace to match Michael's ambling shuffle. 'So why bother me?' he asked, a little testily. 'I am trying to finish a treatise on fevers before the beginning of term, and there is a constant stream of students wanting me to teach them.'

Michael patted his arm consolingly. 'We are all busy, Matt – myself included with these new duties as Senior Proctor. But you know how the towns-people are. The Chancellor insisted that you come and pronounce that these wretched bones are from an animal to quell any rumours that they belong to Simon d'Ambrey.'

'Those rumours are already abroad, Brother,' said Bartholomew, impatiently. 'If the towns-people are to be believed, d'Ambrey's bones have been uncovered in at least six different locations.' He laughed suddenly, his ill-temper at being disturbed evaporating as he considered the ludicrous nature of their mission. 'As a physician, I can tell you that d'Ambrey had about twenty legs, variously shaped like those of sheep and cows; four heads, one of which sprouted horns; and a ribcage that would put Goliath to shame!'

Michael laughed with him. 'Well, his leg-count is likely to go up again today,' he said. 'You may even find he had a tail!'

They walked in companionable silence until Michael stopped to buy a pastry from a baker who balanced a tray of wares on his head. Bartholomew was dissuaded by the sight of the dead flies that formed a dark crust around the edge of the tray, trapped in the little rivers of syrup that had leaked from the cakes. Voices raised in anger and indignation attracted their attention away from the baker to a group of young men standing outside St Bene't's Church. The youths wore brightly coloured clothes under their dark students' tabards, and in the midst of them were two black-garbed friars who were being pushed and jostled.

'Stop that!'

Before Bartholomew could advise caution, or at least the summoning of the University beadles – the law-keepers who were under the orders of Brother Michael as Proctor – the monk had surged forward, and seized one of the young men by the scruff of his neck. Michael gave him a shake, as a terrier would a rat.

Immediately, there was a collective scraping sound as daggers were drawn and waved menacingly. Passers-by stopped to watch, and, with a groan, Bartholomew went to the aid of his friend, rummaging surreptitiously in his medicine bag for the sharp surgical knife he always kept there. Two scholars had already been killed in street brawls over the last month, and it would take very little to spark off a similar incident. Bartholomew, although he abhorred violence, had no intention of being summarily dispatched by unruly students over some silly dispute, the cause of which was probably already forgotten. His fingers closed over the knife, and he drew it out, careful to keep it concealed in the long sleeve of his scholar's gown.

'Put those away!' Michael ordered imperiously, looking in disdain at the students' arsenal of naked steel. He gestured at the growing crowd. 'It would be most unwise to attack the University's Senior Proctor within sight of half the town. What hostel are you from?'

The young men, realising that while student friars might be an easy target for their boisterous teasing, a proctor was not, shuffled their feet uneasily, favouring each other with covert glances. Michael gave the man he held another shake, and

Bartholomew heard him mutter that they were from David's Hostel.

'And what were you doing?' Michael demanded, still gripping the young man's collar.

The student glowered venomously at the two friars and said nothing. One of his friends, a burly youth with skin that bore recent scars from adolescent spots, spoke up.

'They called us cattle thieves!' he said, blood rising to his face at the mere thought of that injustice. Bartholomew suppressed a smile, hearing the thick accent which told that its owner was a Scot. He glanced at the friars, standing together, and looking smug at their timely rescue.

'Cattle thieves?' queried Michael, nonplussed. 'Why? Have you been stealing cows?'

The burly student bristled, incensed further by an unpleasant snigger from one of the friars. Michael silenced the friar with a glare, but although his laughter stopped, Michael's admonition did little to quell the superior arrogance that oozed from the man.

'It is a term the English use to describe the Scots,' muttered the student that Michael held. 'It is intended to be offensive and spoken to provoke.'

Bartholomew watched the friars. The arrogant one stared back at him through hooded lids, although his companion blushed and began to contemplate his sandalled feet so he would not have to meet Bartholomew's eyes.

Michael sighed, and released the Scot. 'Give your names to my colleague,' he said peremptorily, waving a meaty hand towards Bartholomew. He scowled at the friars. 'You two, come with me.'

Bartholomew narrowed his eyes at Michael's retreating back. Being Fellows of the same college did not give Michael the right to commandeer him into service as some kind of deputy proctor. He had no wish to interfere in the petty quarrels that broke out daily among University members between northerners and southerners; friars and secular scholars; Welsh, Scots, Irish and English; and innumerable other combinations.

The Scots gathered around him, subdued but clearly resentful. Bartholomew gestured for them to put away their daggers, although he kept his own to hand, still concealed in his sleeve. He waited until all signs of glittering steel had gone, and raised his eyebrows at the burly student to give his name.

'Stuart Grahame,' said the student in a low voice. He gestured to a smaller youth next to him. 'This is my cousin, Davy Grahame.'

'My name is Malcolm Fyvie,' said the student Michael had grabbed, a dark-haired man with a scar running in a thin, white line down one cheek. 'And these two are Alistair Ruthven and James Kenzie. We are all from David's Hostel. That is on Shoemaker Row, one of the poorer sections of the town. You would not want Scotsmen in Cambridge's more affluent areas, would you?'

11

Ruthven shot Fyvie an agonised glance, and hastened to make amends for his friend's rudeness.

'He means no offence,' he said, his eyes still fixed on the resentful Fyvie. 'David's is a very comfortable house compared to many. We are very pleased to be there.'

He looked hard at Fyvie, compelling him not to speak again. Bartholomew regarded the students more closely. Their clothes and tabards were made of cheap cloth, and had been darned and patched. Ruthven knew that antagonising the Proctor and his colleagues would only serve to increase the fine they would doubtless have to pay for their rowdy behaviour that afternoon. They were probably already being charged a greatly inflated price for their lodgings, and did not look as though they would be able to afford to have the fine doubled for being offensive to the University's law-keepers. Ruthven's desire to be conciliatory was clearly pragmatic, as well as an attempt to present himself and his fellows as scholars grateful for the opportunity to study.

'Is David's a new hostel?' asked Bartholomew, choosing to ignore Fyvie's outburst. There were many hostels in Cambridge, and, because the renting of a house suitable for use as a hall of residence was largely dependent on the goodwill of a landlord, they tended to come and go with bewildering rapidity. New ones sprung up like mushrooms as townspeople saw an opportunity to make money out of the University – a bitterly resented presence in the small Fen-edge town. Many of the hostels did not survive for more than a term – some buildings were reclaimed by landlords who found they were unable to control their tenants, while others were so decrepit that they, quite literally, tumbled down around their occupants' ears.

'It was founded last year,' said Ruthven helpfully, seizing on the opening in the conversation to try to curry favour. 'There are ten students, all from Scotland. The five of us came last September to study, and we hope to stay another year.'

'Then you should avoid street brawls, or you will not stay another week,' said Bartholomew tartly.

'We will,' said young Davy Grahame with feeling. His cousin gave him a shove one way and James Kenzie the other, and Bartholomew immediately saw which of the five were in Cambridge to study and which were hoping to enjoy the other attractions the town had to offer: brawling, for instance.

'Have you arranged masters and lectures?' asked Bartholomew. Ruthven and Davy Grahame nodded vigorously, while the others looked away.

'Is there anything you wish me to tell the Proctor?' Bartholomew asked, knowing who would answer.

Ruthven nodded, his freckled face serious. 'Please tell him that it was not us who started the brawl. It was those friars. They think that their habits will protect them from any insults they care to hurl.'

'But it takes two parties to create a brawl,' said Bartholomew reasonably. 'If you had not responded, there would have been no incident.'

Ruthven opened his mouth to answer, but none came.

'We don't have to listen to such insults from those half-men!' said Kenzie with quiet intensity.

'You do if you want to remain in Cambridge,' said Bartholomew. 'Look, if you have complaints about other students, take them to your hostel principal; if he cannot help, see the proctors; if they cannot assist you, there are the Chancellor and the Bishop. But if you fight in the streets, no matter who started it, you will be sent home.'

'No!' exclaimed Kenzie loudly. The others regarded him uncomfortably. He glanced round at them before continuing in more moderate tones. 'It would not be fair. We did not start it – they did.'

'People in this town do not like the Scots,' agreed Fyvie vigorously. 'Is it our fault that they choose to fight us?'

'Oh, come now,' said Bartholomew wearily. 'The Scots are not singled out for any special ill-treatment. That honour probably falls to the French at the moment, with the Irish not far behind. Go back to David's and study. After all, that is the reason you are here.'

Before Fyvie could respond, Ruthven gave

Bartholomew a hasty bow, and bundled his friends away towards Shoemaker Row. Bartholomew watched them walk back along the High Street, hearing Ruthven's calming tones over Kenzie's protestations of innocence, and Fyvie's angry voice. Ruthven would have his work cut out to keep those fiery lads out of trouble, Bartholomew reflected. He rubbed a hand across his forehead, and felt trickles of sweat course down his back. The sun was fierce, and he felt as though he were being cooked under his dark scholar's gown.

On the opposite side of the street, Michael dismissed the student friars with a contemptuous flick of his fingers, and sauntered over to join Bartholomew. The friars, apparently subdued by whatever Michael had said to them, slunk off towards St Bene't's Church. The plague, four years before, had claimed many friars and monks among its tens of thousands of victims in England, and the University was working hard to train new clerics to replace them. The would-be brawlers were merely two of many such priests passing through Cambridge for their education before going about their vocations in the community.

The large number of clerics – especially friars – at the University was a continuing source of antagonism between scholars and townspeople. Much of the antipathy stemmed from the fact that clerics – whether monks and friars in major orders like Brother Michael, or those in minor orders like Bartholomew – came under canon law, which was notably more lenient than secular law. Only a month before, two apprentices had been hanged by the Sheriff for killing a student in a brawl; less than a day later three scholars had been fined ten marks each by the Bishop for murdering a baker. Such disparity in justice did not go unremarked in a community already seething with resentment at the arrogant, superior attitudes of many scholars towards the people of the town.

'I suppose the friars said the Scots started it,' said Bartholomew with a grin at Michael, as they resumed their walk up the High Street.

Michael nodded and smiled back. 'Of course. Unruly savages trying to start a fight, while our poor Dominicans were simply trying to go to mass.' He pointed a finger at the friars as they disappeared into the church. 'Remember their names, Matt. Brothers Werbergh and Edred. An unholy pair if ever I saw one, especially Edred. I am surprised the Dominican Order supports such blatant displays of condescension and aggression.'

'Well, perhaps they will make fine bishops one day,' remarked Bartholomew dryly.

Michael chuckled. 'I will go to David's Hostel later today,' he said, 'and see their Principal about those rowdy Scots. Then I will complain to the Principal of Godwinsson Hostel about those inflammatory friars.'

Bartholomew nodded absently, walking briskly so that Michael had to slow him down again, so

16

that they – or rather the overweight Michael – would not arrive too sweat-soaked at the Hall of Valence Marie.

As they approached the forbidding walls of the new College, Michael turned to Bartholomew and grimaced at the sudden stench from where the King's Ditch was being dredged. Years of silt, sewage, kitchen compost, offal, and an unwholesome range of other items hauled from the dank depths of the Ditch lay in steaming grey-black piles along the banks. The smell had attracted a host of cats and dogs, which rifled through the parts not already claimed by farmers to enrich their soil. Among them, spiteful-eyed gulls squabbled and cawed over blackened strips of decaying offal and the small fish that flapped helplessly in the dredged mud.

Bartholomew and Michael turned left off the High Street, and made their way along an uneven path that wound between the towering banks of the King's Ditch and the high wall that surrounded Valence Marie. Because Cambridge lay at the edge of the low-lying Fens, the level of the water in the Ditch was occasionally higher than the surrounding land; to prevent flooding, the Ditch's banks were levied, and rose above the ground to the height of a man's head.

Away from the High Street, the noise of the town faded, and, were it not for the stench and the incessant buzz of flies around his head, Bartholomew would have enjoyed walking across the strip of scrubby pasture-land, pleasantly shaded by a line of mature oak trees.

'You have been a long time, Brother,' said Robert Thorpe, Master of the Hall of Valence Marie, as he stood up from where he had been sitting under a tree. There was a hint of censure in his tone, and Bartholomew sensed Thorpe was a man whose authority as head of a powerful young college was too recently acquired for it to sit easily on his shoulders. 'I expected you sooner than this.'

'The beginnings of a street brawl claimed my attention,' said Michael, making no attempt to apologise. 'Scots versus the friars this time.'

Thorpe raised dark grey eyebrows. 'The friars again? I do not understand what is happening, Brother. We have always had problems with warring factions and nationalities in the University, but seldom so frequent and with such intensity as over the last two or three weeks.'

'Perhaps it is the heat,' suggested Bartholomew. 'It is known that tempers are higher and more frayed when the weather is hot. The Sheriff told me that there has been more fighting among the townspeople this last month, too.'

'Perhaps so,' said Thorpe, looking coolly at Bartholomew in his threadbare gown and dusty shoes. As a physician, Bartholomew could have made a rich living from attending wealthy patients. Instead, he chose to teach at the University, and to treat an ever-growing number of the town's poor, preferring to invest his energies in combating

18

genuine diseases rather than in dispensing placebos and calculating astrological charts for the healthy. His superiors at the University tolerated this peculiar behaviour, because having a scholar prepared to provide such a service to the poor made for good relations between the town and its scholars. Bartholomew was popular with his patients, especially when his absent-mindedness led him to forget to charge them.

But tolerance by the University did not mean acceptance by its members, and Bartholomew was regarded as something of an oddity by his colleagues. Many scholars disapproved of his dealings with the townspeople, and some of the friars and monks believed that his teaching verged on heresy because it was unorthodox. Bartholomew had been taught medicine by an Arab physician at the University of Paris, but even his higher success rate with many illnesses and injuries did not protect him from accusations that his methods were anathema.

Thorpe turned to the obese Benedictine. 'What word is there from the Chancellor about our discovery?' he asked.

'Master de Wetherset wants Doctor Bartholomew to inspect the bones you have found to ensure their authenticity,' said Michael carefully. What the Chancellor had actually said was that he wanted Bartholomew to use his medical expertise to crush, once and for all, the rumours that the bones of a local martyr had been discovered. He did not want

19

the University to become a venue for relic-sellers and idle gawpers, especially since term was about to start and the students were restless. Gatherings of townspeople near University property might well lead to a fight. The Sheriff, for once, was in complete agreement: relics that might prove contentious must not be found. Both, however, suspected that this might be easier said than done.

The Hall of Valence Marie had been founded five years previously – by Marie de Valence, the Countess of Pembroke – and the Chancellor and Sheriff were only too aware of the desire of its Master to make the young Hall famous. The bones of a local martyr would be perfect for such a purpose: pilgrims would flock to pray at the shrine Thorpe would build, and would not only spread word of the miraculous find at Valence Marie across the country, but also shower the College with gifts. The Chancellor had charged Michael to handle Thorpe with care.

Thorpe inclined his silver head to Bartholomew, to acknowledge the role foisted on him by the Chancellor, and walked to where a piece of rough sacking lay on the ground. With a flourish, Thorpe removed it to reveal a pile of muddy bones that had been laid reverently on the grass.

Bartholomew knelt next to them, inspecting each one carefully, although he knew from a glance what they were. Michael, too, had devoured enough roasts at high table in Michaelhouse to know sheep bones when he saw them. But

Bartholomew did not want to give the appearance of being flippant, and was meticulous in his examination.

'I believe these to be the leg bones of a sheep,' he said, standing again and addressing Thorpe. 'They are too short to be human.'

'But the martyr Simon d'Ambrey is said to have been short,' countered Thorpe.

Michael intervened smoothly. 'D'Ambrey was not that small, Master Thorpe,' he said. He turned to Bartholomew. 'Am I right? You must remember him since you lived in Cambridge when he was active.'

'You?' asked Thorpe, looking Bartholomew up and down dubiously. 'You are not old enough. He died a quarter of a century ago.'

'I am old enough to remember him quite vividly, actually,' said Bartholomew. He smiled apologetically at Thorpe. 'He was of average height – and certainly not short. These bones cannot be his.'

'We have found more of him!' came a breathless exclamation from Bartholomew's elbow. The physician glanced down, and saw a scruffy college servant standing there, his clothes and hands deeply grimed with mud from the Ditch. He smelt like the Ditch too, thought Bartholomew, moving away. The servant's beady eyes glittered fanatically, and Bartholomew saw that Master Thorpe was not the only person at Valence Marie desperate to provide it with a relic.

'Tell us, Will,' said Thorpe, hope lighting up his

21

face before he mastered himself and made his expression impassive. 'What have you found this time?'

They followed Will across the swathe of poorly kept pasture to the Ditch beyond. A swarm of flies hovered around its mud-encrusted sides, and even Bartholomew, used to unpleasant smells, was forced to cover his mouth and nose with the sleeve of his gown. The servant slithered down the bank to the trickle of water at the bottom, and prodded about.

'Here!' he called out triumphantly.

'Bring it out, Will,' commanded Thorpe, putting a huge pomander over his lower face.

Will hauled at something, which yielded itself reluctantly from the mud with a slurping plop. Holding it carefully in his arms, he carried it back up the bank and laid it at Thorpe's feet. His somewhat unpleasant, fawning manner reminded Bartholomew of a dog he had once owned, which had persisted in presenting him with partially eaten rats as a means to ingratiate itself.

Holding his sleeve over his nose, Bartholomew knelt and peered closely at Will's bundle.

'Still too small?' asked Michael hopefully.

'Too small to belong to a man,' said Bartholomew, stretching out a hand to turn the bones over. He glanced up at Thorpe and Michael, squinting up into the bright sun. 'But it *is* human.'

Bartholomew and Michael sat side by side on the ancient trunk of an apple tree that had fallen against the orchard wall behind Michaelhouse. The intense heat of the day had faded, and the evening shade, away from the failing sunlight, was almost chilly. Bats flitted silently through the gnarled branches of the fruit trees, feasting on the vast number of insects that always inhabited Cambridge in the summer, attracted by the dank and smelly waters of the river. That night, however, the sulphurous odours of the river were masked by the sweeter smell of rotting apples, many of which lay in the long, damp grass to be plundered by wasps.

Bartholomew rubbed tiredly at his eyes, feeling them gritty and sore under his fingers. Michael watched him.

'Have you not been sleeping well?' he asked, noting the dark smudges under the physician's eyes.

'My room is hot at night,' Bartholomew answered. 'Even with the shutters open, it is like an oven.'

'Then you should try sleeping on the upper floor,' said Michael unsympathetically. 'The heat is stifling, and my room-mates sincerely believe that night air will give them summer ague. Our shutters remain firmly closed, regardless of how hot it is outside. At least you have a flagstone floor on which to lie. We have a wooden floor, which is no use for cooling us down at all.'

He stretched his long, fat legs out in front of him, and settled more comfortably on the tree trunk. 'It will soon be too cold to sit here,' he added hastily, seeing Bartholomew's interest quicken at the prospect of a discussion about the relationship between summer ague and night air. Fresh air and cleanliness were subjects dear to his friend's heart, and Michael did not want to spend the remainder of the evening listening to his latest theories on contagion. 'The nights are drawing in now that the leaves are beginning to turn.'

Bartholomew flapped at an insistent insect that buzzed around his head. 'We could try an experiment with your room-mates' notion about night air,' he said, oblivious to Michael's uninterest. 'You keep your shutters closed, and I will keep mine open—'

'Strange business today,' Michael interrupted. He laughed softly. 'I felt almost sorry for that greedy dog Thorpe when you told him his precious bones could not belong to that martyr he seems so intent on finding. He looked like a child who had been cheated of a visit to the fair: disappointed, angry, bitter and resentful, all at the same time.'

Bartholomew sighed, regretful, but not surprised, that Michael was declining the opportunity to engage in what promised to be an intriguing medical debate. 'I suppose Thorpe wants to make money from d'Ambrey's bones as saintly relics,' he said.

Michael nodded. 'There is money aplenty to be made from pilgrims these days. People are so afraid that the Death will return and claim everyone who escaped the first time, that they cling to anything that offers hope of deliverance. The pardoners' and relic-sellers' businesses are blossoming, and shrines and holy places all over Europe have never been so busy.'

Bartholomew made an impatient sound. 'People are fools! Relics and shrines did not save them the last time. Why should they save them in the future?'

Michael eyed his friend in monkish disapproval. 'No wonder you are said to be a heretic, Matt!' he admonished, half-joking, half-serious. 'You should be careful to whom you make such wild assertions. Our beloved colleague Father William, for example, would have you hauled away to be burned as a warlock in an instant if he thought you harboured such irreligious notions.'

Bartholomew rubbed a hand through his hair, stood abruptly, and began to pace. 'I have reviewed my notes again and again,' he said, experiencing the familiar feeling of frustration each time he thought of the plague. 'Until the pestilence, I believed there were patterns to when and whom a disease struck. But now I am uncertain. The plague took rich and poor, priests and criminals, good and bad. Sometimes it killed the young and healthy, but left the weak and old. Some people say it burst from ancient graves during an earth-quake in the Orient, and was carried westwards on the wind. But even if that is true, it does not explain why some were taken and some were spared. The more I think about it, the less it makes sense.'

'Then do not think about it, Matt,' said Michael complacently, squinting to where the last rays of the sun glinted red and gold through the trees. 'There are some things to which we will never know the answers. Perhaps this is one of them.'

Bartholomew raised his eyebrows. 'It is encouraging to see that Michaelhouse supports a tradition of enquiring minds,' he remarked dryly. 'Just because an answer is not immediately obvious does not mean to say that we should not look for it.'

'And sometimes, looking too hard hides the very truth that you seek,' said Michael, equally firmly. 'I can even cite you an example. My Junior Proctor, Guy Heppel, lost the keys to our prison cells yesterday. I spent the entire period between prime and terce helping him search for them – a task rendered somewhat more urgent by the fact that Heppel, rather rashly, had arrested the Master of Maud's Hostel for being drunk and disorderly.'

'You mean Thomas Bigod?' asked Bartholomew, between shock and amusement. 'I am not surprised you were so keen to find the keys! I cannot see that a man like Bigod would take kindly to being locked up with a crowd of recalcitrant students.'

'You are right – he was almost beside himself

with fury once he awoke and discovered where he was. But we digress. I searched high and low for these wretched keys, and even went down on my hands and knees to look for them in the rushes – no mean feat for a man of my girth – and do you know where they were?'

'Round his neck, I should imagine,' said Bartholomew. 'That is where he usually keeps them, tied on a thong of catgut or some such thing.'

Michael gazed at him in surprise. 'How did you know that?'

Bartholomew smiled. 'He had me going through the same process last week when he came to see me about his cough.'

'Is it genuine, then, this cough of his? I thought he was malingering. The man seems to have a different ache or pain almost every day – some of them in places I would have imagined impossible.'

'The cough is real enough, although the other ailments he lists – and, as you say, it is quite a list – are more imagined than real. Anyway, when I told him he must have lost his keys in the High Street, and not in my room, he almost fainted away from shock. He had to lie down to calm himself, and when I loosened his clothes, there were the keys around his neck. I was surprised when he was appointed your junior. He is not the kind of man the University usually employs as a proctor.'

'All brawn and no brain you mean?' asked Michael archly, knowing very well how most

27

scholars regarded those men who undertook the arduous and unpopular duties as keepers of law and order in the University. 'Present company excepted, of course. But poor Guy Heppel has neither brawn nor brain as far as I can see.'

'Why was he appointed then?' asked Bartholomew. 'I cannot see how he could defend himself in a tavern fight, let alone prevent scholars from killing each other.'

'I agree,' said Michael, picking idly at a spot of spilled food on his habit. 'He was a strange choice, especially given that our Michaelhouse colleague, Father William, wanted the appointment – he has more brawn than most of the University put together, although I remain silent on the issue of brain.'

'That cough of Heppel's,' said Bartholomew, frowning as he changed the conversation to matters medical. 'It reminds me of the chest infection some of the plague victims contracted. It—'

Michael leapt to his feet in sudden horror, startling a blackbird that had been exploring the long grass under a nearby plum tree. It flapped away quickly, wings slapping at the undergrowth. 'Not the Death, Matt! Not again! Not so soon!'

Bartholomew shook his head quickly, motioning for his friend to relax. 'Of course not! Do you think I would be sitting here chatting with you if I thought the plague had returned? No, Brother, I was just remarking that Heppel's chest complaint is similar to one of the symptoms some plague

28

victims suffered – a hacking, dry cough that resists all attempts to soothe it. I suppose I could try an infusion of angelica . . .'

As Bartholomew pondered the herbs that he might use to ease his patient's complaint, Michael flopped back down on the tree trunk clutching at his chest.

'Even after four years the memory of those evil days haunts me. God forbid we should ever see the like of that again.'

Bartholomew regarded him sombrely. 'And if it does, we physicians will be no better prepared to deal with it than we were the first time. We discovered early on that incising the buboes only worked in certain cases, and we never learned how to cure victims who contracted the disease in the lungs.'

'What was he like, this martyr, Simon d'Ambrey?' interrupted Michael abruptly, not wanting to engage in a lengthy discussion about the plague so close to bedtime. Firmly, he forced from his mind the harrowing recollections of himself and Bartholomew trailing around the town to watch people die, knowing that if he dwelt on it too long, he would dream about it. Bartholomew was not the only one who had been shocked and frustrated by his inability to do anything to combat the wave of death that had rolled slowly through the town. The monk flexed his fingers, cracking his knuckles with nasty popping sounds, and settled himself back on the tree trunk. 'I have heard a lot about

Simon d'Ambrey, but I cannot tell what is truth and what is legend.'

Bartholomew considered for a moment, reluctantly forcing medical thoughts from his mind, and heartily wishing that there was another physician in Cambridge with whom he could discuss his cases – the unsavoury Robin of Grantchester was more butcher than surgeon, while the other two University physicians regarded Bartholomew's practices and opinions with as much distrust and scepticism with which he viewed theirs.

'Simon d'Ambrey was a kindly man, and helped the poor by providing food and fuel,' he said. 'The stories that he was able to cure disease by his touch are not true – as far as I can remember these stories surfaced after his death. He was not a rich man himself, but he was possessed of a remarkable talent for persuading the wealthy to part with money to finance his good works.'

Michael nodded in the gathering dusk. 'I heard that members of his household were seen wearing jewellery that had been donated to use for the poor. Personally, I cannot see the harm in rewarding his helpers. Working with the poor is often most unpalatable.'

Bartholomew laughed. 'Spoken like a true Benedictine! Collect from the rich to help the poor, but keep the best for the abbey.'

'Now, now,' said Michael, unruffled. 'My point was merely that d'Ambrey's fall from grace seems to have been an over-reaction on the part of the town. He made one mistake, and years of charity were instantly forgotten. No wonder the towns-people believe him to be a saint! It is to ease their guilty consciences!'

'There may be something in that,' said Bartholomew. He paused, trying to recall events that had occurred twenty-five years before. 'On the day that he died, rumours had been circulating that he had stolen from the poor fund, and then, at sunset, he came tearing into town chased by soldiers. He always wore a green cloak with a gold cross on the back and he had bright copper-coloured hair, so everyone knew him at once. As the soldiers gained on him, he drew a dagger and turned to face them. I saw an archer shoot an arrow, and d'Ambrey fell backwards into the Ditch.'

'It is very convenient for Thorpe that his body was never found,' observed Michael.

Bartholomew nodded. 'A search was made, of course, but the Ditch was in full flood and was flowing dangerously fast. There were stories that he did not die, and that he was later seen around the town. But I have seen similar throat wounds since then on battlefields in France, and every one proved fatal.'

'I still feel the town treated d'Ambrey shamefully,' mused Michael. 'Even if he were less than honest, the poor still received a lot more than they would have done without him.'

'I agree,' said Bartholomew, with a shrug. 'And,

as far as I know, it was never proven that he was responsible for the thefts. Just because his relatives and servants stole from the poor fund did not mean that d'Ambrey condoned it, or even that he knew. After his death, his whole household fled – brother, sister, servants and all – although not before they had stripped the house of everything moveable.'

'Well, there you are then!' said Michael triumphantly. 'His family and servants fled taking everything saleable with them. Surely that is a sign of their guilt? Perhaps d'Ambrey was innocent after all. Who can say?'

Bartholomew shrugged again, poking at a rotten apple with a twig. 'The mood of the townspeople that night was ugly. D'Ambrey's family would have been foolish to have stayed to face them. Even if they had managed to avoid being torn apart by a mob, the merchants and landowners who had parted with money to finance d'Ambrey's good works were demanding vengeance. D'Ambrey's household would have been forced to compensate them for the thefts regardless of whether they were guilty or not.'

'So d'Ambrey paid the ultimate price, but his partners in crime went free,' said Michael. 'A most unfair, but not in the least surprising, conclusion to this miserable tale. Poor d'Ambrey!'

'No one went free,' said Bartholomew, sitting and leaning backwards against the wall. 'The town nominated three of its most respected burgesses to pursue d'Ambrey's family and bring them back for trial. Although the d'Ambreys had gone to some trouble to conceal the route they had taken, they were forced to sell pieces of jewellery to pay their way. These were identified by the burgesses, who traced the family to a house in Dover. But the evening before the burgesses planned their confrontation with the fugitives, there was a fire in that part of the town, and everyone died in it.'

'Really?' asked Michael, fascinated. 'What a remarkable coincidence! And none of the fugitives survived, I am sure?'

Bartholomew shook his head. 'The town erupted into an inferno by all accounts, and dozens of people died in the blaze.'

'And I suppose the bodies were too badly charred for identification,' said Michael with heavy sarcasm. 'But the requisite number were found in the d'Ambrey lodgings, and the burgesses simply assumed that the culprits were all dead. D'Ambrey's family must have laughed for years about how they tricked these "most respected burgesses"!'

'Oh no, Brother,' said Bartholomew earnestly. 'On the contrary. D'Ambrey's household died of asphyxiation and not burning. None of the bodies were burned at all as I recall. D'Ambrey's brother and sister had wounds consistent with crushing as the house collapsed from the heat, but none of their faces were damaged. The bodies were brought back to Cambridge, and displayed in the

Market Square. No member of d'Ambrey's household escaped the fire, and there was no question regarding the identities of any of them.'

'I see,' said Michael, puzzled. 'This body-displaying is an addendum to the tale that is not usually forthcoming from the worthy citizens of Cambridge. Do you not consider these deaths something of a coincidence? All die most conveniently in a fire, thus achieving the twofold objective of punishing the guilty parties most horribly, and of sparing the town the bother and cost of a trial.'

Bartholomew flapped impatiently at the insects that sang their high-pitched hum in his ears. 'That was a question raised at the time,' he said, 'although certainly not openly. I eavesdropped on meetings held at my brother-in-law's house, and it seemed that none of the burgesses had unshakeable alibis on the night of the fire.'

'What a dreadful story,' said Michael in disgust. 'Did any of these burgesses ever admit to starting the fire?'

'Not that I know of,' said Bartholomew, standing abruptly in a futile attempt to try to rid himself of the insects. 'They all died years ago – none were young men when they became burgesses – but I have never heard that any of them claimed responsibility for the fire.'

'So, dozens of Dover's citizens died just to repay a few light-fingered philanthropists for making fools of the town's rich,' said Michael, shaking his

34

head. 'How unpleasant people can be on occasions.'

'We do not know the burgesses started the fire,' said Bartholomew reasonably. 'Nothing was ever proven. It might have been exactly what they claimed – a fortuitous accident, or an act of God against wrongdoers.'

'You do not believe that, Matt!' snorted Michael in amused disbelief. 'I know you better than that! You suspect the burgesses were to blame.'

'Perhaps they were,' said Bartholomew. 'But it hardly matters now. It was a long time ago, and everyone who played any role in the affair died years ago.' He sat again, fiddling restlessly with the laces on his shirt. 'But all this is not helping with our skeleton. Did you have any luck with the Sheriff this afternoon, regarding to whom these bones might belong?'

'Do bones belong to someone, or are they someone?' mused Michael, rubbing at his flabby chins. 'We should debate that question sometime, Matt. The answer to your question is no, unfortunately. There are no missing persons that fit with your findings. Are you sure about the identification you made? The age of the skeleton?'

Bartholomew nodded slowly. 'After you had gone to the Chancellor, I helped Will dredge up the rest of the bones and the skull. I am certain, from the development of the teeth and the size and shape of other bones, that the skeleton is that of a child of perhaps twelve or fourteen years.

I cannot say whether it was a boy or a girl – I do not have that sort of expertise. There were no clothes left, but tendrils of cloth suggest that the child was clothed when it was put, or fell, into the Ditch.'

'Could you tell how long it had been there?' said Michael. 'How long dead?'

Bartholomew spread his hands. 'I told you, I do not have the expertise to judge such things. At least five years, although, between ourselves, I would guess a good deal longer. But you should not tell anyone else, because the evidence is doubtful.'

'Then why do you suggest it?' asked Michael. He leaned forward to select an apple on the ground that was not infested with wasps, and began to chew on it, grimacing at its sourness.

The blackbird he had startled earlier swooped across the grass in front of them, twittering furiously. Bartholomew reflected for a moment, trying to remember what his Arab master had taught him about the decomposition of bodies. He had not been particularly interested in the lesson, preferring to concentrate his energies on the living than learning about cases far beyond any help he could give.

'All bones do not degenerate in the same way once they are in the ground, or in the case of this child, in mud. Much depends on the type of material that surrounds them, and the amount of water present. These bones had been immersed in the thick, clay-like mud at the bottom of the Ditch, and so are in a better condition than if they had been in peat, which tends to preserve skin, but rot bone. But despite this, the bones are fragile and crumbly, and deeply stained. I would not be surprised if they had been lying in the Ditch for twenty or thirty years.'

'So, we might be looking for a child of fourteen who died thirty years ago?' asked Michael in astonishment. 'Lord, Matt! Had he lived, that would make him older than us!'

'I could be wrong,' said Bartholomew. He stood and stretched, giving such a huge yawn that Michael was compelled to join him.

Michael tossed his apple core into the grass. 'Simon d'Ambrey died twenty-five years ago,' he said thoughtfully. 'Perhaps even at the same time as this child. Can you tell how this child met its death?'

'Again, I cannot be certain,' said Bartholomew, rubbing his eyes tiredly. 'But there is a deep dent on the back of the skull that would have compressed the brain underneath. Had the child been alive when that wound was delivered, it would have killed him – or her – without doubt. However, if the body has lain in the King's Ditch for thirty years, the damage may have been done at any time since by something falling on it. So, this child may have been knocked on the head and disposed of in the Ditch; he may have fallen and hit his head; or he may have died of some disease and his body disposed of in the Ditch and the skull damaged later.'

Michael disagreed. 'Not the latter. Why would anyone need to hide a corpse of someone who had died in a legitimate manner? And surely someone would miss a child if it had had an accident and fallen in the river? The only likely solution, I am sorry to say, is the first one. That the poor thing was killed and the body hidden in the Ditch.'

Bartholomew shook his head, smiling, and slapped his friend on the shoulders. 'You have become far too involved in murder these last few years,' he said. 'Now you look for it where there may be none. How do you know the child was not an orphan, or that his parents simply did not report him missing? You know very well that a death in a large, poor family is sometimes seen as more of a relief than a cause for grief, in that it is one less mouth to feed – especially with girls. Or perhaps he was one of a group of travellers, who had passed out of Cambridge before he was missed? Or perhaps he was a runaway from—'

'All right, all right,' grumbled Michael good-humouredly. 'Point taken. But you were in Cambridge as a child. Did any of your playmates go missing with no explanation?'

Bartholomew leaned down to pick up his medicine bag. 'Not that I recall. It was a long time ago.'

'Oh, come now, Matt!' exclaimed Michael. 'You are not an old man yet! If you are right in your hunch about the time of this child's death, he may well have been a playmate of yours. Older than you, perhaps, but you would have been children together.'

Bartholomew yawned again. 'I can think of none, and I did not play with girls, anyway, which means I only have knowledge of half of the juvenile population. You should ask someone else. And now it is late, and so I will wish you good night.'

He turned to walk back through the orchard to the College, leaving Michael to his musing. He cut through the kitchens, his leather-soled shoes skidding on the grease that formed an ever-present film over the stone-flagged floor. The great cooking fires were banked for the night, and the kitchens were deserted. A door, concealed behind a painted wooden screen, led from the kitchen to the porch where Michaelhouse's guests were received before being ushered to the hall and conclave above. Bartholomew walked through the porch, and across the beaten earth of the courtyard to his room in the north wing.

The last rays of the sun were fading, and the honey-coloured stone of Michaelhouse's walls was a dark amber. Bartholomew paused, and glanced around at the College, admiring, as he always did, the delicate tracery on the windows of the north and south wings where the scholars slept. The dying sunlight still caught the bright colours of the College founder's coat of arms over the porch, a cacophony of reds, blues and golds. He yawned yet again, and gave up the notion of reading for an hour by the light of a candle before he slept – all that would happen would be that he would fall asleep at the table and candles were far too expensive a commodity to waste, not to mention the possibility that an unattended candle might fall and set the whole College alight.

His mind wandered back to the grisly display of asphyxiated corpses in the Market Square some twenty-five years ago, the result of another careless candle if the burgesses were to be believed. Then, he pushed thoughts of murder and mayhem to the back of his mind, opening the door to his small, neat room. He lay on the bed, intending to rest for a few moments before rising again to wash and fold his clothes, but he was almost immediately asleep, oblivious even to the sharp squeal of a mouse that the College cat killed under his bed.

Alone in the orchard, Michael chewed his lip thoughtfully. Bartholomew had a sister who lived nearby, whose husband was one of the richest and most influential merchants in the town. Edith was some years older than her brother. She had married young, and Bartholomew had lived with her and her new husband until he went to the school at the Benedictine Abbey in the city of Peterborough to the north. Perhaps Edith, or her husband, Sir Oswald Stanmore, might remember something about a missing child.

Michael saw the Stanmores the following day on his way back from church. It was a fine Sunday afternoon, and the streets thronged with people. Gangs of black-gowned students sang and shouted, eyed disapprovingly by the merchants and tradesmen dressed in their Sunday finery. Edith and her husband looked happy and prosperous, walking arm-in-arm down Milne Street to the large house where Stanmore had his business premises. Although Stanmore worked in Cambridge, he preferred to live at his manor in Trumpington, a tiny village two miles south of the town. It was unusual to see him and his wife in Cambridge on a Sunday, and Michael strongly suspected that the merchant had been conducting some covert business arrangement when he should have been paying attention to the words of the priest at mass. Edith, a lively soul who enjoyed the occasional excursion into the town from the village, would not have noticed what her husband was doing, and would have been more interested in catching up with the local gossip from the other merchants' wives.

Edith had the same distinctive black hair and pale complexion of her brother, a stark contrast to Stanmore's slate-grey hair and beard. She wore a dress of deep crimson, and she carried a blue cloak over one arm, one corner of it trailing unheeded along the dusty road. With a smile, the monk recognised that she apparently had the same careless disregard for clothes as her brother, whose shirts and hose were always patched and frayed. He headed towards her, dodging past a procession of Carmelite friars heading towards St Mary's Church, and jostling aside a pardoner with unnecessary force. Michael did not like pardoners.

Edith hugged Michael affectionately, making the usually sardonic, and occasionally lecherous, monk blush. Oswald Stanmore admonished her for her undignified behaviour in the street, but his words lacked conviction, and they all knew she would do exactly the same when she next met Brother Michael.

Stanmore, ever aware of the latest happenings in the town from his extensive network of informants, asked Michael about the skeleton that had been found. Michael told them briefly, and asked whether they were aware of any missing children during the last twenty or thirty years.

'Thirty years!' exclaimed Edith. 'Has this body lain in the Ditch so long?'

Michael shrugged indifferently. 'No, no. I am just keen to ensure we do not confine ourselves to looking recently, when the child may have died much earlier.'

Stanmore scratched his chin as he wracked his brains. 'There was old Mistress Wilkins' daughter,' he said uncertainly.

Edith shook her head. 'Reliable witnesses saw her

alive and married to a farm lad over in Haslingfield village a few weeks after she disappeared. What about the tinker's boy? The one who was said to have drowned near the King's Mill?'

Now Stanmore shook his head. 'His body was found a year later. And anyway, he was too young – four or five years old. There was that dirty lad whom Matt befriended, who told us he was a travelling musician, and led the local boys astray for a few weeks.' He turned to Edith. 'It may well be him; he would have been about twelve. He set the tithe barn alight and then ran away. What was his name?'

'Norbert,' said Edith, promptly and rather primly, her mouth turning down at the corners in disapproval. 'I remember him well. We had only just arrived in Trumpington, and Matt immediately struck up a friendship with that horrible boy. It hardly created a good impression with my new neighbours.'

Stanmore gave her hand an affectionate squeeze, and spoke to Michael. 'After the barn fire, we locked this Norbert in our house, so that the Sheriff could talk to him about it the next day. But somehow he escaped during the night.'

'Poor Norbert!' said Bartholomew, coming up silently behind them, making them all jump. 'Still blamed for burning the tithe barn, even though he had nothing to do with it.'

'So you insisted at the time. But he fled the scene of the crime, and that was tantamount to

43

admitting his guilt,' said Stanmore, recovering his composure quickly.

'He fled because he knew that no one would believe his innocence,' said Bartholomew. 'And because I let him go.'

There was a short silence as his words sank in. Michael smothered a grin, and folded his arms to watch what promised to be an entertaining scene.

'Matt!' exclaimed Edith, shocked. 'What dreadful secrets have you been harbouring all this time?'

Bartholomew did not reply immediately, frowning slightly as he tried to recall events from years before. 'I had all but forgotten Norbert's alleged crime.'

'Alleged?' spluttered Stanmore. 'The boy was as guilty as sin!'

'That was what everyone was quick to assume,' said Bartholomew. 'No one bothered to ask his side of the story and then make a balanced judgement. That was why I helped him to escape.'

'But we locked the priest with him in the solar!' said Stanmore, regarding Bartholomew with patent disbelief. He turned to Michael, who quickly assumed an air of gravity to hide his amusement. 'Norbert was only a child, and even though he had committed a grave crime, we did not want to frighten him out of his wits. We also thought the priest might wring a confession from him.' He swung back to Bartholomew, still uncertain whether to believe his brother-in-law's claim.

'How could you let him out without the priest seeing you?'

'The priest was drunk,' said Bartholomew, smiling. 'So much so, that the cracked bells of Trumpington Church and their unholy din could not have roused him. I waited until everyone was asleep, took the solar key from the shelf outside, and let Norbert out. After, I relocked the door, and Norbert disappeared into the night to go to his sister, who was a kitchen maid at Dover Castle.'

'But this is outrageous!' said Stanmore, aghast. 'How could you do such a thing? You abused my trust in you! And those bells are not cracked, I can assure you. They just need tuning.'

Edith suddenly roared with laughter, and some of the outrage went out of her husband. 'All these years and you kept your secret!' she said. She reached up and ruffled her brother's hair as she had done when he was young. 'Whatever possessed you to risk making my husband look foolish in front of his neighbours?'

Bartholomew looked at Stanmore thoughtfully for a moment before answering. 'I am not the only one who knows Norbert was innocent. I suppose I still should not tell, but it was such a long time ago that it cannot matter any more. It was not Norbert who fired the tithe barn: it was Thomas Lydgate.'

'Thomas Lydgate? The Principal of Godwinsson Hostel?' said Michael, halfway between merriment and horror.

Bartholomew nodded, smiling at the monk's reaction. 'I suspect he did not set the building alight deliberately, but you know how fast dry wood burns. I suppose he had no wish to own up to a crime that might make him a marked man for the rest of his life, and Norbert was an ideal candidate to take the blame, since he was an outsider, and had no one to speak for him.'

'But how do you know this?' asked Stanmore, still indignant about the wrong that had been perpetrated against him in his own house. 'Why are you so certain that Norbert did not commit the crime and Lydgate did?'

'Because Norbert and I saw Lydgate enter the barn when we were swimming nearby; we saw smoke billowing from it a few moments later and someone came tearing out. Naturally curious, we crept through the trees to see who it was. We came across Lydgate, complete with singed shirt, breathing heavily after his run, and looking as though he had seen the Devil himself. If you recall, it was Lydgate who raised the alarm, and Lydgate who first blamed Norbert.'

'But what if Lydgate followed Norbert and killed him to ensure he would never tell what he had seen?' mused Michael, suddenly serious. 'It is perfectly possible that the bones in the Ditch belong to your Norbert. From what you say, he was the right age, and all this appears to have happened about twenty-five years ago.'

'Impossible!' said Bartholomew. 'I received letters

from Norbert in Dover a few weeks later to tell me that he had joined his sister, and he wrote to me several times after that, until I went to study in Paris. He has made a success of his life, which is more than could be said had the Trumpington witch-hunters laid their vindictive hands on him.'

'And how could you receive letters without my knowledge?' demanded Stanmore imperiously. 'This is nonsense! How could you have paid whoever brought these messages, and how is it that my steward never mentioned mysterious missives from Dover? Not much slips past his eagle eyes!'

Edith shuffled her feet, and looked uncomfortable. 'Letters from Dover, you say?' she asked. 'From someone called Celinia?'

Stanmore rounded on her. 'Edith! Do not tell me you were a party to all this trickery, too!'

'Not exactly,' said Edith guiltily, looking from her husband to her brother.

'Not at all,' said Bartholomew firmly. 'Norbert's sister was called Celinia. I imagine she wrote the letters, since Norbert was illiterate, and she signed her own name so that no one would know the letters were from him. Celinia is an unusual name, and Norbert knew I would guess that the letters were from him if she signed them. Edith simply assumed I had found myself a young lady. She did not ask me about it, so I did not tell her.'

'Extraordinary!' said Michael gleefully. 'All this subterfuge in such a respectable household!'

'Really!' said Stanmore, still annoyed. 'And in my own house! The villagers were not pleased that Norbert had evaded justice while in my safekeeping, and neither was the Sheriff when he found he had made the journey for nothing. Thank God Norbert was not caught later to reveal your part in his escape, Matt!'

'Well I never!' drawled Michael facetiously, nudging Bartholomew in the ribs. 'You interfering with the course of justice, and Lydgate an arsonist! Did you confront him with what you had seen?'

'Are you serious?' queried Bartholomew. 'Since Lydgate was not above allowing a child to take the blame for his crime – for which Norbert might well have been hanged – it would have been extremely foolish for me to have let him know that I had witnessed his guilty act. No, Brother. I have carried Lydgate's secret for twenty-five years and none have known it until now except Norbert.'

'I still cannot believe you took the law into your own hands in my house in such a way,' said Stanmore, eyeing his brother-in-law dubiously. 'What else have you done that will shock me?'

Bartholomew laughed. 'Nothing, Oswald. It was the only serious misdemeanour I committed while under your roof . . . that I can remember.'

Stanmore regarded Bartholomew with such rank suspicion that the physician laughed again. He was about to tease Stanmore further, when he saw the Junior Proctor, Guy Heppel, hurrying along the street towards them, his weasel-like face creased with concern.

When Heppel reached them, he was breathless, and there was an unhealthy sheen of sweat on his face. He rubbed his hands down the sides of his gown nervously.

'There is another,' he gasped. 'Another body has been found in the King's Ditch next to Valence Marie!'

CHAPTER 2

Bartholomew and Michael hurried towards Valence Marie, while Guy Heppel panted along behind them. Bartholomew glanced round at the Junior Proctor, noting his white face and unsteady steps.

'Another skeleton?' he asked.

Heppel shook his head, but was unable to answer, and clutched at his heaving chest pathetically. Bartholomew wondered anew why the Chancellor had chosen such an unhealthy specimen to serve as a proctor, especially since he might be required to control some of the more unruly elements in the University with physical force. Bartholomew doubted if Heppel could control a child, let alone some of the aggressive, self-confident young scholars who roamed around the town looking for trouble. Not only was Heppel's appointment a poor choice for the University and the town, it was a poor choice for Heppel himself. Bartholomew studied him hard.

Heppel was a small man, with a peculiarly oblong head. His face was dominated by a long, thin nose that always appeared to be on the verge

50

of dripping, and underneath it rested a pair of unnaturally red lips. He had no chin at all, and his upper teeth pointed backwards in his mouth in a way that reminded Bartholomew of a rodent. Bartholomew supposed Heppel's hair was dark, but the Junior Proctor always wore a woollen cap or a hood, even in church, so that his head was never exposed to the elements.

'Does that physic I gave you help your cough?' Bartholomew asked, concerned by Heppel's pallor.

'This is no time for a medical consultation,' said Michael briskly, pulling on his friend's arm. 'You can do that when no more bodies claim your attention.'

'I am a physician, not an undertaker,' said Bartholomew, pulling his arm away irritably. 'My first duties are to my patients.'

'Nonsense, Matt,' said Michael. 'Your first duties are to your University and to me as Senior Proctor. Your second duties are to your patients – one of whom may well be waiting for you to unravel the mystery of his death.'

Bartholomew stopped dead in his tracks and gazed at Michael. 'I can assure you, Brother, that the University, with all its treachery and plotting, is not more important than my patients. If I thought that were ever the case, I would resign my Fellowship and abandon teaching completely.'

'No, you would not,' said Michael with total assurance. 'You like teaching, and you believe you play a vital role in training new physicians to replace those that died during the plague. You will never leave the University – unless you decide to marry, of course. Then you will have no choice. We cannot have married masters in the University. Although, I suspect there is no danger of that: you have been betrothed to Philippa for more than three years now, and you have done virtually nothing about it. Of course, there is always that whore of yours.'

'What?' asked Bartholomew, bewildered by the sudden turn in the conversation. 'What are you talking about?'

Michael poked him playfully in the ribs with his elbow. 'Do not play the innocent with me, Matt! I have seen the way you look at that Matilde, the prostitute. You should watch yourself. If Father William sees you ogling like a moonstruck calf, you will not need to worry about where your loyalties lie, because you will be dismissed from your Fellowship faster than you can lance a boil.'

'But I have not . . . he cannot . . .'

Michael laughed. 'If being tongue-tied is not a sign of your guilt, I do not know what is! Come on, Guy. We cannot be standing around all day listening to Dr Bartholomew describe his secret lust for the town's most attractive harlot.'

Bartholomew grabbed Heppel's sleeve as he made to follow Michael. 'Ignore him,' he ordered, scowling after the monk's retreating back. 'Did you take that physic I gave you?'

Heppel nodded vehemently, coughing into a

strip of linen. 'Every drop. I was going to ask you for more because it was beginning to have an effect. Of course, when the pains in my chest had eased, the ones in my stomach and head started.'

'In your stomach and head,' echoed Bartholomew thoughtfully, wondering which of the herbs in his medicine had adversely affected his patient.

'And then there are my legs,' continued Heppel, lifting his gown to reveal a skinny limb swathed in thick black hose. 'They burn and ache and give me no rest.' He rubbed his hands vigorously down the side of his gown in a peculiar nervous habit Bartholomew had noticed before. 'And my ears ached last night. I think Saturn must have been ascendant. And I have an ulcer on my tongue, and my little finger is swollen.'

'Anything else?' asked Bartholomew dryly, now certain his medicine could not be to blame for Heppel's impressive list of maladies.

Heppel gave the matter some serious thought. 'No, I think that is all.'

'Right,' said Bartholomew, thinking that patients like Heppel were exactly the reason why he had no desire to treat the wealthy. The cure, he was sure, would be for Michael to allocate the Junior Proctor extra duties, so that he would not have time to dwell on every twinge in his body and imagine it to be something serious. Perhaps exercise and fresh air might help, too, although Bartholomew's attempts to suggest that bizarre remedy to patients in the past had met with a gamut of reactions ranging from patent disbelief to accusations that he was in league with the Devil.

'As I said, I think Saturn was ascendant last night,' said Heppel helpfully. 'I was born when Jupiter was dominant, you see, and there was a full moon.'

'Good,' said Bartholomew, unimpressed. 'I shall tell Jonas the Poisoner . . . I mean the Apothecary, to make you an infusion of angelica mixed with some wine and heartsease. I think when your cough eases, these other symptoms will disappear, too.'

'But angelica is a herb of the sun,' protested Heppel. 'I need a herb of the moon to match the time when I was born. And I must have something to counteract the evil effects of Saturn.'

Like most physicians, Bartholomew did not particularly like patients who claimed a knowledge greater than his own – especially when that knowledge was flawed. He bit back his impatience, recalling his Arab master's insistence on listening to every patient with sympathy and tolerance, regardless of how much nonsense they spoke.

'Angelica is gathered in the hour of Jupiter,' he said reluctantly, not particularly wanting to engage in what might be a lengthy discussion of herb-lore with Heppel when Michael was waiting. 'You say you were born when Jupiter was dominant, and angelica is very effective against the diseases of Saturn. Heartsease, of course, is a saturnine herb.'

Considering the conversation over, he made to

walk on. Heppel scurried after him, and tugged at his tabard to make him stop.

'I think I shall require a complete astrological consultation,' said the Junior Proctor. 'Herbs of Saturn and Jupiter will not help my ears.'

Bartholomew sighed. In his experience, the planet that governed a particular herb made little difference to whether it healed a patient or not, and, over the years, he had gradually abandoned astrological consultations as a tool to determine the causes of a person's malaise. It was a decision that made him unpopular with his fellow physicians, and often resulted in accusations of heresy. But there was no denying that he lost fewer patients than his colleagues, a remarkable achievement given that most of his clients were less well-nourished and more prone to infections than the wealthier citizens the other physicians doctored.

'Just take the medicine,' he said to Heppel impatiently. 'And Saturn most certainly does control diseases of the ears, so the heartsease will work.' He did not add that if, as he believed, Heppel's ears ached only in his imagination, then Saturn could quite happily explode with no ill-effects to the organs under discussion.

'All right, then,' said Heppel dubiously. 'But I will have my astrological consultation next week if your concoction does not work.'

Not from me, thought Bartholomew. Complete astrological consultations were time-consuming affairs, and while Bartholomew conducted the occasional one to ensure he still remembered how, he was certainly not prepared to do one at the beginning of term with corpses appearing in the King's Ditch every few hours. Thoughts of the King's Ditch made him look away from Heppel for Michael. The fat monk was puffing towards him.

'What happened to you?' Michael demanded. 'There I was, regaling you with a list of the prostitute Matilde's physical virtues, when I saw Father William staring at me. Then I saw that you were nowhere to be seen, and I had been strolling up the High Street talking loudly to myself about a whore! Really, Matt! You might have more regard for my vocation. I am a monk, chaste and celibate!'

'You might have more regard for it yourself,' said Bartholomew, smiling at the image of Michael being caught in the act of airing some of his less monkish thoughts by the austere Father William. 'You should not be filling your chaste and celibate mind with thoughts of prostitutes – especially on a Sunday.'

'I was trying to help you,' retorted Michael pompously, eyeing him with his baggy green eyes. He smoothed down the lank brown hair that grew around his perfectly circular tonsure. 'Now, Matthew, if you can spare a few moments away from your unseemly, lustful imaginings, a dead man awaits us at Valence Marie – assuming the poor fellow has not turned into the dust from whence he came in the interim.'

He turned abruptly, and stalked away, glancing around to ensure that Bartholomew and Heppel followed him. The dark grey stone of St Botolph's Church came into view, and Valence Marie stood a few steps away, on the far side of the King's Ditch. They walked quickly along the small path that ran between the College and the Ditch to where Robert Thorpe stood, wringing thin hands.

'This way, gentlemen,' he said, clearly relieved at their eventual arrival. Without further ado, he ushered them over to the patch of scrubby grass near where the small skeleton had been retrieved the day before.

'More bones?' asked Bartholomew, curious at the man's obvious agitation.

Thorpe flung him a desperate glance and gestured that he should look over the raised rim of the Ditch and into the water that trickled along the bottom. Puzzled, Bartholomew scrambled up the bank, while Michael followed more warily. Heppel declined to climb, and went to stand in the shade of one of the old oak trees, scrubbing his hands against his tabard. Bartholomew watched him, intrigued. The garment was shiny where the material had been rubbed so often, and Bartholomew wondered whether Heppel might have some itchy skin complaint that caused him to move them so.

Turning his attention back to the Ditch, he was greeted by the sight of a body floating face down in the shallow water, its arms raised above its head, almost as if it were swimming. Blood from a wound in its head stained the water in a pink halo around it.

Bartholomew turned questioningly to Thorpe, who had remained where he was, and obviously had no intention of scaling the bank.

'He was found about an hour ago by one of the servants,' Thorpe called. 'I immediately sent word to the Chancellor, and he, presumably, sent the Junior Proctor to fetch you.'

Bartholomew slipped and skidded down the inside of the muddy bank and tried to haul the body over on to its back. It was so stiff that the task proved difficult, and Michael was obliged to clamber down into the smelly water to help. Their eyes met as Bartholomew wiped away some of the thick, black mud to reveal the face.

'Which one is it?' asked Michael, holding his sleeve over his nose against the smell rising from the Ditch.

'James Kenzie, I think,' replied Bartholomew, wracking his brains to try to recall the names of the five young Scots from David's Hostel he had encountered the day before.

'I saw the Principal of David's yesterday, and he agreed to be responsible for the good behaviour of those five unruly undergraduates for the rest of the term,' said Michael, shaking his head as he looked down at the student. 'It looks as though he did not keep them out of trouble for long.'

He helped Bartholomew to pull the corpse out

of the water and up on to the rim of the Ditch, away from the clinging mud that sucked at their feet and stained the hems on their gowns with an oily blackness. Bartholomew began a preliminary investigation.

'He has been dead a good while,' he said, pulling at one of Kenzie's arms. 'See how stiff he is? Of course, the heat will accelerate such stiffness; it would not be so if it were winter now.'

'I am not one of your students, Matt,' said Michael tartly. 'Just tell me what I need to know and keep the lectures for the ghouls that enjoy them.'

Bartholomew grinned at him, but completed his examination in silence. Eventually, he sat back on his heels and looked thoughtfully at the body.

'I think it likely that he died last night,' he said, 'nearer dusk than dawn. He was killed by the wound to the top of his head, which has stoved in his skull. You can see that splinters of the skull have penetrated the brain. He must have been put in the water after his death because his mouth is empty. Had he drowned, he probably would have inhaled mud and water from the Ditch as he tried to breathe air. I will make a more thorough examination later, if you wish.'

'I do,' said Michael. 'So, are you saying he was murdered? He did not just die from a fall?'

Bartholomew just managed to stop himself from running his mud-coated hand through his hair as he surveyed the Ditch and its surroundings.

On one side of the Ditch were the high walls of Valence Marie, meeting the narrow stretch of poorly tended pasture on which Thorpe and Heppel now waited. Although this strip of land belonged to Valence Marie, it was not fenced off, and access to it was possible from the High Street at one end, and Luthburne Lane at the other. On the opposite side of the Ditch was an untidy line of houses, most wattle and daub, and all frail, dilapidated and mainly abandoned. The plague had struck hard at those people who had lived in cramped, crowded conditions, and Bartholomew knew that only a handful from these hovels had survived.

'Yes, he was murdered,' he said, having considered the possibilities. 'I would say it was not possible to sustain a wound like this, on the top of his head, from a fall. I suspect Kenzie was hit with a heavy instrument, and his body was brought here or left where it fell – the current in the Ditch is not strong enough to move something as heavy as a corpse at the moment. Either way, I am certain he was dead when he entered the water.'

'Was he drunk? Are there signs of a struggle?'

Bartholomew inspected the young man's hands, but his finger-nails were surprisingly well-kept, and there was no sign that he had clawed or attacked his assailant. His clothes, too, were intact, and Bartholomew saw only the mended tears he had noted the previous day.

'I would say he had no idea his attacker was

behind him. Or that he knew someone was behind him, but felt no need to fear. As to drink, I can smell only this revolting Ditch on him. Perhaps he was drunk, but if so, the water has leached all signs of it away.'

He looked suddenly at Michael as if to speak, but then thought better of it and turned his attention back to the body.

'What is it?' asked Michael, catching his indecision.

Bartholomew frowned down at the body. 'Remember I told you that the skeleton we found also had an indentation on the back of its skull? Possibly hit on the head and dumped in the Ditch?'

'Of course,' said Michael. 'But you said there was not enough evidence to prove that the child was murdered, and you seem sure that Kenzie has been. What are the differences?'

Bartholomew rubbed his chin absently, leaving a black smudge there from the mud on his hand. 'The child lay dead in the Ditch for many years, providing ample time for damage to occur to the skull after death; Kenzie has been dead only a few hours. Also, Kenzie's wound bled copiously as you can see from his stained clothes. Wounds do not bleed so if inflicted after death, but we do not have such evidence for the skeleton. I did not say the child was not murdered, only that I cannot prove it.'

'But let us assume he was,' said Michael

thoughtfully. 'It is surely something of a coincidence that the body of a murdered child is discovered one day, and the very next, a man is killed in the same manner. You think there might be a connection?'

Bartholomew grimaced. 'Yes, I do. But that is the essence of why I was reluctant to speak. If I am right about the length of time the skeleton has been in the Ditch, Kenzie would not even have been born when the child died.'

'But you could be wrong, and the skeleton is only a few years dead. That would mean that there might be some connection between the two victims.'

'Not even then, Brother,' said Bartholomew. 'Kenzie is a Scot and not local. He has only been here for twelve months at the very most. How could there be a connection?'

'Can you not tell more from this child's bones?' asked Michael.

Bartholomew looked at him for a moment, and then laughed. 'Despite the fanciful teachings of an Oxford astrologer who maintained in a lecture I once attended that the Scots are a "cruel, proud, excitable, bestial, false and underhand race who must therefore be ruled by Scorpio", it is not possible to tell one of them from an Englishman from bones alone, Scorpio or otherwise!'

'Oxford University supports that?' said Michael, astonished. 'No wonder their Scots are always rioting and looting its halls and colleges.'

62

'It is only the claim of a single scholar,' said Bartholomew. 'And doubtless Scottish astrologers have cast an equally unflattering national horoscope for the English. But we are digressing from our task.'

'So the child might have been born a Scot,' mused Michael, looking back at Kenzie's body, 'but there is no way to prise that information from his bones?' Bartholomew nodded, and Michael gave a sigh of resignation. 'I have a feeling this might be more difficult to resolve than I first thought. If the link between these two bodies spans many years, we might never know the truth.'

'There are some things to which we will never know the answers,' said Bartholomew in an exaggerated imitation of Michael's pompous words to him in the orchard the night before. 'Perhaps this is one of them.'

Michael shot him an unpleasant look. 'If you value peaceful relations between town and gown, Matt, you had better hope not,' he said primly. 'The students might riot if they believe one of their number has been murdered – especially if we cannot provide evidence that the culprit was not a townsman.'

Bartholomew shook his head impatiently. 'That would be an unreasonable assumption on their part. Kenzie's killer might just as easily be one of his four friends from David's Hostel.'

'And since when has reason ever prevented a riot?' demanded Michael in a superior tone. 'You know as well as I that the mood of scholars and townsfolk alike is ugly at the moment. It seems to me that Kenzie's death might provide the perfect excuse for them to begin fighting each other as they so clearly wish to do.'

Bartholomew regarded him soberly. The fat monk was right. Over the last month or so, he had noticed a distinctly uneasy atmosphere in the town: it had been the subject of discussion at high table at Michaelhouse on several occasions. Optimistically – overly so in Bartholomew's opinion – the Master and Fellows hoped that the tension would ease once term began, and most students would be forced to concentrate on their studies.

Michael climbed to his feet clumsily, wincing at his stiff knees, and called down to Thorpe. 'Why did you take so long to discover the body, Master Thorpe? Doctor Bartholomew says this man might have died as early as yesterday evening.'

Thorpe shrugged elegantly. 'It is Sunday,' he replied. 'No one is dredging the Ditch today, and the body might well have remained undiscovered until tomorrow, but, by chance, our scullion, Henry, noticed the body when he came to dispose of some kitchen scraps.'

Bartholomew sighed. There was little point in dredging the Ditch if scullions were not prepared to dump their kitchen waste elsewhere. In a year or two, the town would be facing the same problems all over again.

'I heard that their other servant – that little fellow, Will – claims to have seen more bones in the Ditch on the other side of the High Street,' said Michael in an undertone to Bartholomew, drawing the physician's mind away from the litany of diseases he believed owed their origins to dirty water. 'Master Thorpe will doubtless move the workmen to look for martyr relics in more fertile ground tomorrow.'

'What are you two muttering about?' said Thorpe uneasily, taking a few steps up the bank towards them.

'We are wondering whether you know this man who died on your property last night,' Michael called back pleasantly. 'Will you come to see?'

Very reluctantly, Thorpe scrambled towards them, and looked down at Kenzie's body. He gave it the most superficial of glances, and then looked a second time for longer.

'It is not a student of Valence Marie,' he said, his voice halfway between surprise and relief. 'I do not believe I have met him before. He is a student, though. He is wearing an undergraduate's tabard.'

'Thank you, Master Thorpe,' said Michael, regarding the scholar with a blank expression. 'I might have overlooked that, had you not pointed it out.'

Thorpe nodded, oblivious to the irony in Michael's voice, and turned to make his way back down the bank, swearing when he slipped and fell on one knee. Heppel hurried to help him, and Bartholomew heard him regaling the Master of Valence Marie with an infallible remedy for unsteadiness in the limbs that could be procured from powdered earthworms and raw sparrows' brains.

'If Thorpe is foolish enough to take that concoction, then he deserves all the stomach cramps he will get,' he muttered to Michael, watching Heppel warm to his subject.

'Thorpe might be a coward for not coming immediately to see if the corpse was a member of his own college, but he is no lunatic. Can you tell me any more about Kenzie's death before we move the body to the church?'

'Only one thing.' Bartholomew took one of Kenzie's hands and pointed at the little finger. There was a thin, but stark, white band on the brown skin, showing where, until recently, a ring had been worn.

'The motive for his murder was theft?' asked Michael, staring down at the young man's hand.

Bartholomew shrugged. 'Possibly. You should ask Kenzie's friends whether the ring was valuable and whether they know if he was wearing it when he died. But, assuming he died during the night, the killer would need eyes like an owl to detect a ring on his victim's hand in the dark before he struck. There was no moon last night.'

'Perhaps he killed first and looked later,' said Michael. 'Although a young man who is so obviously a student in patched clothes is hardly likely to render rich pickings to justify so foul a crime.'

Bartholomew gave a brief smile without humour. 'We both know that people have been killed for far less than a ring in this town.'

The sun was casting long shadows across the High Street by the time they had ordered Kenzie's body to be taken to St Botolph's Church, and spoken to the servant, Henry the scullion, who had discovered the corpse. He could tell them nothing, other than to say that he had seen no one matching Kenzie's description hanging around the Ditch the day before.

'I must go to David's Hostel before someone else tells this young man's friends what has happened,' said Michael, squinting at the sun, a great orange ball in the cloudless sky. 'Come with me, Matt. I would be happier if there were two of us judging the reactions of Kenzie's compatriots when we give them the news of his death.'

Bartholomew started to object – he had planned to work on his treatise on fevers while there was still sufficient daylight in which to write – but Michael was right. If there had been some kind of falling out between the five friends that had resulted in the death of one of them, it would be better if there were more than one observer for guilty reactions. Neither Michael nor Bartholomew put much faith in Guy Heppel's powers of observation.

'You look tired, Guy,' said Michael solicitously

to the Junior Proctor who trailed along behind them. 'Tell the Chancellor what has happened and then go home to rest.'

'I do feel weary,' said Heppel, stretching out a white hand to the monk's arm to support himself, as if even admitting to his weakness had suddenly sapped the remaining strength from his limbs.

'Shall I order you a horse to take you there?' asked Michael, eyeing the hand on his arm with disapproval. 'After all, it might be almost a quarter of an hour's walk by the time you retrace your steps from the Chancellor's office to your room in the King's Hall.'

Heppel seriously considered the offer, while Bartholomew turned away to hide his smile. 'I think I can manage to walk,' Heppel said eventually.

Michael and Bartholomew watched him walk away, a slender figure whose overlarge scholar's tabard hung in dense, cumbersome folds.

'You are supposed to be compassionate to your fellow men, Brother,' said Bartholomew. 'Not add to his already impressive list of ailments by telling him he looks ill.'

'The man is a weasel,' said Michael, unrepentant. 'And I do not believe him to be as self-obsessed as he appears. He heard every word of what you told me about Kenzie's corpse, and will report it all faithfully to the Chancellor.'

Bartholomew was confused. 'You think Heppel is spying on you for de Wetherset?'

Michael gave a short bark of laughter. 'De Wetherset would not dare – especially with an agent of Heppel's mediocre talents. But de Wetherset had some reason for appointing him over Father William, and it would not surprise me to learn that Heppel is his nephew or some other relative.'

'If that is true, then you will never find out from de Wetherset,' said Bartholomew with conviction. 'He is not a man to allow himself to be caught indulging in an act of flagrant nepotism.'

'True,' said Michael. 'But at least Heppel will be out of our way when we visit David's Hostel. The last thing we want as we gauge reactions to the news of Kenzie's death is Heppel offering special potions to ease grief.'

They began to walk along the High Street to Shoemaker Row. The intense heat had faded with the setting of the sun, but the air was still close and thick with the smell of the river and the Ditch. Carts rattled past them, hurrying towards the Trumpington Gate and the villages beyond before darkness fell and the roads became the domain of robbers and outlaws. Although it was Sunday, and officially a day of rest, the apprentices were active, darting here and there as they ferried goods to and from their masters' storehouses along Milne Street and the wharves. Bartholomew ignored the noise and bustle, and thought back to his encounter with the David's students the day before.

'Two of the Scots – Ruthven and Davy Grahame – seemed well-disposed to study,' he said. 'But the others gave the impression they would rather be anywhere other than making a pretence of scholarship in Cambridge.'

'Really?' asked Michael thoughtfully. 'What else would they rather be doing, do you think? Fighting? Rioting? Whoring?'

'Very possibly,' said Bartholomew. 'The one you grabbed by the collar is called Fyvie. He has something of a temper, and is perhaps over-sensitive to insults to his nation, whether real or perceived. He is unwise to wear his emotions so openly: it is asking for someone to taunt him into starting a brawl.'

He jumped as the doors of St Mary's Church were flung open with a crash and troops of noisy, yelling scholars came out, jostling and shoving each other. One of them was leading a chorus in Latin, the words of which made Bartholomew exchange a look of half-shock and half-amusement with Michael. Bartholomew smothered a smile when he noticed how much over-long hair was bundled into hoods, and bright clothing was hastily covered with sober scholars' tabards, as the students recognised Michael, the Senior Proctor. He also noticed that one of his own students, Sam Gray, was singing the bawdy Latin chorus as loudly as he could, and saw that he had his tabard wrapped around a girl he had obviously smuggled into the church.

The University, partly because of the large numbers of friars and monks in its ranks, and partly to protect the local female population, forbade its students any dealings with women. In some ways, the rule was a wise one, for it went at least some way in preventing potentially dangerous incidents involving outraged husbands, fathers and brothers. Yet, with hundreds of hot-blooded young men barely under the control of their masters, the rule was often impossible to enforce. If a headstrong and disobedient student – like Sam Gray – decided to embark on a relationship with a woman, there was little that could be done about it. Gray could be 'sent down' from the University in disgrace, but the plague meant that student numbers were low, and the University wanted to increase, not decrease them. The students were only too aware that the University's colleges and hostels were sufficiently desperate for their fees that they were prepared to overlook a good deal to keep them.

Gray saw Bartholomew, and his jaw dropped in horror. He hastily disentangled himself from the girl in a feeble attempt to make it look as though she were with someone else. Bartholomew favoured him with a reproving stare, and was gratified to see that Gray at least had the grace to look shame-faced. Fortunately for Gray, Michael's eyes were still fixed on the singer, who, seeing he had the un-wanted attention of the Senior Proctor, slunk away through the churchyard. Once their leader had gone, the other students dispersed rapidly under Michael's authoritative glower, some with almost comical furtiveness.

'The students are always rowdy at the beginning of term,' said Michael, walking on. 'But I detect more than just rowdiness in them now. They seem dangerous to me, Matt. I have a feeling it would take very little to ignite them into doing something quite serious. I only hope one of those Scottish lads confesses that he has killed Kenzie. If these students think the townspeople have killed a scholar, they will riot for certain.'

'All former differences forgotten in the common cause,' mused Bartholomew. 'That only yesterday saw the beginnings of a brawl between the Scots and the friars will not prevent them fighting side by side against the townsfolk.'

They turned off the High Street into Shoemaker Row. David's Hostel was a half-timbered building, the rough plaster crudely covered in patchy white limewash that was stained with black rivulets running from some internal rot. The ends of the great wooden beams that formed the basic structure of the house were frayed and flaking, and bright orange fungus sprouted from the side of one window. Michael rapped officiously on a door that was new and strong, in contrast to the rest of the house, and waited.

Eventually, they heard footsteps, and the door was dragged open by a servant. He gave them a querying smile, and introduced himself as Meadowman the steward. He added shyly that Bartholomew had once treated him for river-fever, although Bartholomew could not honestly say that there was anything familiar in the steward's homely face. Meadowman conducted them along the corridor, and into a spacious room at the back of the house, which served as dining room and lecture hall. Beyond the room was a kitchen, where a scullion crashed about noisily, preparing the next meal.

'Ivo!' called Meadowman, warning the scullion to silence his clattering while David's was the subject of a proctorial visit. The noise stopped, and Ivo's greasy head poked around the door to study the august personage of the Senior Proctor with undisguised curiosity.

'Greetings, Father Andrew,' said Michael, pushing past Bartholomew to stride into the room. Sitting at a large table with an open book in front of him was an elderly friar who smiled serenely as Michael entered. He had watery blue eyes, and his unlined, honest face reminded Bartholomew of a saintly hermit he had once met on a remote Spanish island. Also gathered around the table were several students, all wearing neat, black scholars' tabards, despite the heat.

As Bartholomew was introduced to Father Andrew, he had the distinct impression they were interrupting a lecture. He glanced at the book and recognised it as Porphyry's *Isagoge*, a basic under-graduate introduction to the philosophy of Aristotle.

'You will see David's Hostel has taken your warning seriously about our students' behaviour, Brother,' said Father Andrew in a voice that was soft and lilting with the accent of southern Scotland. 'We have been reading philosophy today, even though it is Sunday and term does not begin until the day after tomorrow. The Principal, Master Radbeche, will continue with Aristotle's *Praedicamenta* immediately after mass in the morning.'

'Master Radbeche?' asked Bartholomew, impressed. 'I had no idea Master Radbeche was Principal here.'

The old friar smiled. 'We are lucky to have such a notable scholar in our midst. Without wishing to sound boastful, there is no one who understands Aristotle like Master Radbeche.'

'Indeed not, Father,' said Michael. He cast a disparaging glance at the students. 'And it is unfortunate that his students do not seek to uphold his reputation and that of his hostel with scholarship and gentle behaviour.'

Bartholomew looked around the room. The fiery-tempered Fyvie sat staring morosely at the table, although whether his ill-humour resulted from the unwelcome proctorial visit or from being made to listen to Porphyry's dry text, Bartholomew could not determine. The cousins, Davy and Stuart Grahame, sat together at the end of the table, Davy with a quill in his hand and a pile of parchment scraps in front of him for making notes. Ruthven sat next to Father Andrew where he had evidently been peering over the friar's shoulder. Perhaps Father Andrew's reading had been too slow for him, and he was trying to read ahead. Three other students sat near the empty fireplace on stools, which were arranged in such a way that Bartholomew wondered whether they might have been playing dice out of Father Andrew's line of vision.

'Where were you all last night?' asked Michael, not wasting time on further formalities.

There was a startled silence until Father Andrew found his tongue.

'Why do you ask, Brother? Has there been more trouble in the town? I can assure you that after you spoke to the Principal yesterday, we kept all our students here. The front door was locked at seven o'clock last night, and no one left until mass at five this morning.'

'You said there were ten students at David's,' said Bartholomew to Ruthven. 'Where are the others?'

'Well,' said Ruthven slowly, casting a quick, nervous glance at Fyvie that neither Bartholomew nor Michael missed. 'There are the five of us from Edinburgh whom you met yesterday, and then there are the three Tarbert cousins from the Isles.' He gestured to the trio of students near the fireplace. 'We all have been here studying as you can see. Robert of Stirling is upstairs suffering from an ague, and his brother John is with him. That is all of us.'

Not exactly, thought Bartholomew, watching the faces of the others intently as Ruthven spoke. Fyvie sat motionless, his eyes fixed unblinking on the table. Davy Grahame held his quill with trembling hands, while his cousin flushed such a deep red, that the colour seemed to reach as far as his throat. However smooth Ruthven was trying to be, the others were very much aware that their comrade was missing, and might even know why.

'I can vouch for these young men,' said Father Andrew, waving his hand round at his charges. 'We have been here all day, and even took our meals here – despite the fact that Ivo, our scullion, has much still to learn about cooking. The students have not been out of the building at all. Robert of Stirling and James Kenzie are ill upstairs, and John is looking after them. The others are all here as you can see.'

'What about last night?' said Michael. He looked at the four students who sat round the table. 'I think some of you know why we are asking.'

Father Andrew's expression was one of confusion, and he looked at his students in bewilderment. 'Tell the Proctor you were all here,' he said, looking at each one in turn. When none of them spoke up, his shoulders sagged suddenly in weary resignation. 'What are you hiding?' he asked in a tone that indicated he would tolerate no lies or half-truths. 'What have you done this time to bring shame upon David's Hostel?'

There was a silence during which the four looked from one to the other, knowing that they would have to tell what they knew, but none wanting to be the one to begin. Finally, Ruthven spoke.

'James Kenzie is gone,' he said miserably.

'James Kenzie is ill upstairs,' protested Father Andrew. 'I saw him asleep in his bed only a short while ago.'

'You saw his rolled up blankets,' said Ruthven apologetically to Father Andrew. 'Jamie is not here. He has gone.'

'Gone where?' demanded Michael.

'We do not know. We would have looked for him today, but we have been kept here studying. We did not wish to make a fuss and draw attention to the fact that he is absent, but now we are worried about him. We decided this afternoon that if he has not returned by nightfall, we would tell the Principal and Father Andrew.'

'Why wait?' asked Michael, unconvinced. 'Surely it would be better to tell them sooner, rather than later, if you are worried about your friend?'

Ruthven looked away, chewing on his lower lip in agitation.

Davy Grahame took a deep breath. 'Jamie has a woman,' he blurted out.

Father Andrew's jaw dropped in shock, and he regarded Davy Grahame aghast.

'Davy!' exclaimed Fyvie, starting to his feet. 'You did not have to tell them that!'

'Yes, I did,' said the younger Grahame, his firm tone of voice forcing Fyvie to sit again. 'I am worried. Supposing those two friars came across him last night and had him harmed? The Proctor might be able to help him.' He turned to Michael. 'Jamie has had a lover since last term.

He occasionally slips out before the door is locked at night, and one of us makes up his bed to look as though it is occupied. He then joins us at mass at first light, and walks back with us to the hostel. Last night, it was more difficult than usual, because Father Andrew was with us constantly after he learned of our quarrel in the street yesterday. Anyway, Jamie feigned illness and said he was going to bed early. He must have slipped out while we were eating our supper. But this morning he did not appear at mass, and we have not seen him since. Do you know where he is?'

The others looked eagerly at Michael, and Bartholomew did not envy the fat monk his next task.

'I am afraid I do,' said Michael quietly. 'He is in St Botolph's Church.'

'St Botolph's?' echoed Fyvie, puzzled. 'What is he doing there?'

'Then why does he not come back?' demanded Stuart Grahame belligerently. 'We have been worried sick about him all day. He must surely know that! Why has he not sent word?'

'He will not be coming back,' said Michael, trying to be gentle.

Fyvie and Ruthven stared at him in disbelief, while Davy Grahame, quicker on the uptake than his elders, brought his hands quickly to his mouth in shock. Father Andrew's face was pale as the meaning of Michael's words became clear to him.

'Not coming back?' said Stuart Grahame. 'Why

ever not? He has not decided to become a friar, has he? Has he been hurt in this love affair and sworn to forsake the world?' He stood abruptly. 'Let me see him. I will talk some sense into the fool!'

'Sit down, Stuart,' said Davy Grahame in a soft voice. 'Brother Michael is telling us that Jamie is dead.'

'What?' The colour drained from Stuart Grahame's face and he sat down suddenly with a jolt, as if his legs had turned to jelly.

'But he cannot be dead, Davy!' he said unsteadily. 'We saw him yesterday evening!'

Davy ignored him. 'How did he die?' he asked, looking from Michael to Bartholomew, his expression one of dazed horror. 'Where?'

'Quickly,' said Bartholomew, 'and without pain. Near the King's Ditch at Valence Marie. Can you think of anyone who would want to harm him?'

'He was killed by another?' asked Father Andrew, appalled. 'You mean murdered?'

Michael nodded, and calmly blocked the door as Stuart Grahame suddenly lurched towards it. 'Those friars!' the Scot yelled. 'The friars killed him!'

Michael took him firmly by the elbow and led him to sit at the table again, where Father Andrew put a comforting arm around his shoulders. The biggest, oldest and toughest of the Scots began to weep uncontrollably. The others looked away, Ruthven scrubbing surreptitiously at his eyes with the back of his hand.

79

'We will speak to the friars, of course,' said Michael. 'But at the moment, we need you to think of reasons others might have for wishing Kenzie harm. We can start with his woman.'

Fyvie shook his head as if he were trying to clear it. 'She would not kill him – she loved him dearly! Her name is Dominica and she is the daughter of the Principal of Godwinsson Hostel.'

Ruthven seized Michael's sleeve. 'Tread carefully, though. She is a kindly girl, but her father is not well-disposed towards Scots. You could ruin her by indiscretion.'

The indiscretion was James Kenzie's, thought Bartholomew, if he had picked a lover whose father was so adverse to his nationality. But Ruthven's caution was obviously meant well – a final act of friendship in attempting to protect the reputation of his dead comrade's lover.

Michael appraised him coolly. 'We will not be indiscreet,' he said, 'although I trust no other of you is so flagrantly breaking the University's rule about women?'

Vigorously shaken heads met his inquiry, and Michael relented. 'Do you have anything more that might help us? Were you all here last night as you claim?'

Ruthven, still white-faced, answered. 'Yes. Father Andrew was with us until it was time for the door to be locked, but Jamie had already left by then. We told Father Andrew that Jamie was ill and was resting upstairs in bed, like Robert of Stirling. Father Andrew saw us all to our dormitory, and can vouch that we all accompanied him to mass this morning. The Principal stayed here with the two students from Stirling and Jamie . . . or so he thought.'

Father Andrew nodded. 'Seven students were with me at mass: these seven,' he said, gesturing at Kenzie's four friends and the trio by the fireplace. 'I thought Jamie was ill. Until now.' He looked sternly at the subdued students. 'You have been extremely foolish in aiding your friend to slip out at night, and you very possibly have contributed to his death. Think on that before you break more University rules.'

'I want to go home!' wailed Stuart Grahame suddenly. His younger cousin rushed to his side in an attempt to quell the tears. 'I do not like this violent town!'

'Did Jamie have a ring?' asked Bartholomew, watching Davy comfort his distraught kinsman. 'One that he wore on his little finger?'

For a moment there was silence, except for Stuart's soft weeping, and then Davy spoke up. 'Yes, he did. And although he never said so, I had the feeling that Dominica gave it to him. Why? Do you have it? I doubt it was valuable.'

Bartholomew shook his head. 'It was missing, and so we must consider theft as a possible motive for Jamie's murder. In the dark, it would have been difficult to tell whether or not something was valuable, and a thief might have stolen it believing it was worth more than it was.'

'Have there been others in his family to die violently?' asked Michael, addressing Ruthven.

'Of course there have,' said Ruthven, as surprised by the question as Michael was by the answer. 'At home we need constantly to defend our lands and property, sometimes from the English and sometimes from our neighbours. And, on occasions, we attack others. Of course Jamie has relatives who have died violently.'

'I see,' said Michael, bemused. 'But that is not what I meant.'

'He wants to know whether there is any possibility that the skeleton unearthed yesterday is related to Jamie,' said Davy. The student shrugged at Michael's surprise. 'You said Jamie died in the King's Ditch at Valence Marie, and rumour has it that a skeleton was found in the same location yesterday. It does not take three terms of Aristotle to guess why you posed such a question.'

'Of course Jamie is not related to those bones,' said Ruthven, bewildered. 'Why should he be? Do you know who the skeleton is?'

Michael shook his head. 'I am merely trying to ensure that I overlook nothing. As Davy has just noted, Jamie and the skeleton were found in the same area within a few hours of each other.'

Davy frowned. 'We have only been studying here for a year. Jamie was the first of his family to acquire learning – he constantly joked that he was the first of his clan to step on English soil without intending to steal the cattle. The skeleton cannot be any of his forebears.'

'What will happen to us?' asked Ruthven in a low voice, as Michael prepared to leave.

'You will remain in the hostel, and you will not leave it unless you are in the company of a master,' said Michael. 'If I hear that any of you has disobeyed me, I will arrest you at once.'

He turned abruptly and left the room, waiting for Father Andrew and Bartholomew to follow him into the corridor. As Father Andrew closed the door behind them, they heard Stuart Grahame begin to cry again, while Fyvie and Ruthven's voices immediately rose in a clamour of questions and self-recriminations.

Father Andrew shook his head wearily, and leaned against the door. 'I am so sorry, Brother. I had no idea they would be so stupid as to assist one of their number to spend nights out with his paramour. I should have realised that they would not be subdued as easily as they pretended to be. Do you know who killed Jamie? Was it these friars they mentioned, the ones with whom they brawled yesterday?'

'We do not know yet,' said Michael. 'His killer may have been a friend. Can you be certain that all four were here last night?'

Father Andrew nodded. 'I saw them into the dormitory. I was still furious with them – if we Scots are seen brawling in the streets, the townspeople may take reprisals. You probably noticed our new door? We were forced to buy that when our last one was kicked to pieces following an argument between the Principal and a baker about underweight loaves. People here still resent the Scots' victory over the English at Bannockburn in 1314, you know – some of the older townsmen were even in King Edward the Second's army at the time. Anyway, suffice to say that our intention is to remain aloof from conflict at all costs. It would not do if our landlord refused to rent us this building next year because we had earned a reputation for fighting.'

Michael gave him a sympathetic smile. 'I appreciate that maintaining a distance from brawls might prove difficult for these fiery lads,' he said. 'And I appreciate your efforts in attempting to control them. The continued good reputation of your hostel is even more reason why we must resolve James Kenzie's death as quickly as possible. We should take a quick look at his belongings to see if he left some clue regarding the identity of his killer. Where did he sleep?'

Father Andrew led the way up a narrow wooden staircase to the dormitory. Bartholomew saw that, as was the case in many hostels, the dormitory was converted into a common room during the day, when the straw mattresses that served as beds were rolled up and stacked against one wall. The room was reasonably tidy, although there was a strong smell of dirty clothes. Two large chests stood at one end of the room in which the students could store their few belongings.

Two mattresses were still out. A young man tossed feverishly on one, while another student sat anxiously at his side. The other mattress held nothing more than cunningly bundled clothing. Father Andrew clicked his tongue in disapproval.

While Michael conducted his search of the upper floor, Bartholomew went to the ailing student and rested his hand on the boy's forehead. It was burning hot, but the bed was heaped with blankets. The room was stuffy, too, and a quick glance around told Bartholomew that the poor lad was provided with nothing to drink to ease his fever. He sent for fresh water, and set about making him more comfortable. He prescribed a potion to ease the ague, and showed the student's anxious brother how to keep him cool. Dismissing Father Andrew's grateful thanks with a nod, he went to join Michael who was waiting at the door.

'Well, neither of them is the culprit,' said Bartholomew in a low voice, indicating the two lads in the dormitory. 'One would have been too sick, and the other has not left his brother's side.'

'And the mullions on the windows are so close together that I doubt even a slender student could squeeze through,' whispered Michael. 'The other room on the upper floor is where the masters sleep, and has similarly narrow windows. There is no back door: *ergo*, the only way out is through the front. And Kenzie was the only one who has been absent since last night, if we can believe what we have been told. I would guess they have been honest with us.'

He and Bartholomew left the hostel with relief, still conscious of Stuart Grahame's wails of grief, and the voices of his friends trying to offer him comfort.

'Well?' said Bartholomew. 'What now? It looks as though none of Kenzie's friends killed him. Do we go to see the friars?'

'We do indeed,' said Michael, his expression serious. 'Because, for one thing, I still have not spoken to their Principal about their behaviour in the High Street yesterday, and for another thing, they are members of Godwinsson Hostel, where Kenzie's lover is also the Principal's daughter.'

Godwinsson's door was answered by a gangling Welshman called Huw, who conducted them into a small, but comfortable, solar that glowed red with the last of the setting sun. The windows were glazed, an extravagance that had not been considered necessary for most of the house, which had only shutters to exclude winter winds and summer flies.

Bartholomew began to prowl restlessly as they waited for the Principal to see them. The steward had explained that Principal Lydgate lived with his wife in the adjoining house, while the students and other masters lived at the hostel proper. Godwinsson was a more pleasant house than

David's – it was larger, cleaner, and did not smell of burning cabbage.

'It is odd how Lydgate's name has occurred so often of late,' said Michael, speaking mainly to distract Bartholomew, who was becoming impatient. 'First, two of his students are involved in a disturbance of the peace; then you reveal his childhood secret; and finally, it is his daughter who was receiving the attentions of the murdered man.'

'Lydgate was no child when the barn was fired,' said Bartholomew. 'He was at least eighteen: almost as old as Kenzie. But we should not speak of this, especially here. It will do no good to unturn such a stone, and he would probably deny it anyway.'

'Deny what, Bartholomew?'

Bartholomew jumped at the sound of Lydgate's voice so close behind him. The Principal of Godwinsson had not entered by the same door through which Bartholomew and Michael had been shown, but from a second door in the opposite wall that Bartholomew had assumed was a cupboard. Glancing through it, he could see that it connected Lydgate's family house next door with the hostel. Had this been the route James Kenzie had used to meet Lydgate's daughter: either him to sneak to her room, or her to slip out to him?

'We are here to investigate the death of a student from David's,' said Michael, recovering from his surprise faster than Bartholomew, who was wondering, uncomfortably, how much of their conversation Lydgate had overheard.

'A student of David's is no concern of mine,' said Lydgate, shifting his small, hard blue eyes from Bartholomew and fixing them on Michael.

'The brutal murder of a member of the University should be the concern of every scholar,' Michael retorted superiorly. 'Especially now, in this climate of unease.'

'Who has been murdered?'

Bartholomew thought he had detected a shadow in the interconnecting corridor between the two houses, and so the unannounced entry of Lydgate's wife into their conversation did not startle him as Lydgate's had done.

'A David's student, Mistress,' said Michael, bowing politely to her. 'He was last seen alive yesterday evening at seven o'clock, and was found dead this afternoon.'

'Not one of our boys?' asked Cecily Lydgate. She sniffed dismissively. 'Then this has nothing to do with us.' She went to her husband, placing a proprietary hand on his arm. With undisguised irritation, he shrugged it off.

Bartholomew remembered the marriage of Cecily to Thomas Lydgate some twenty years or more before. It was not a love match, but a union designed to bring together two adjoining manors in Trumpington. When both fathers had died, Lydgate sold the Trumpington land within a week, and bought himself a pair of handsome houses in the town centre.

The physician studied Cecily Lydgate with

interest. Although she had lived in the town for many years, he had seldom seen her. She had servants who did her shopping, and daily trips to church and the occasional outing to a fair or a banquet apparently satisfied any ambitions she had for entertainment outside her home. Lack of exercise and fresh air, however, were beginning to take their toll, for although her clothes were evidently made of cloth that was expensive, they did little to disguise the plumpness underneath. A fiercely starched wimple kept every hair from her face, making her eyes appear bulbous and her teeth too large.

By contrast, her husband had aged well, and still retained his hulking figure, although it was beginning to turn to fat around his waist. His hair remained jet black, with no traces of grey, and his clean-shaven face made him appear much younger than his wife, although Bartholomew knew they were the same age. Bartholomew had had nothing to do with Lydgate since his own studies had taken him to Peterborough, Oxford, and Paris, but dislike for the man, suppressed for many years, began to resurface, as fresh and crystal clear as when he had wronged Norbert.

Michael, uninvited, sat on the best chair in the room, and indicated, with an insolent flick of his hand, that Lydgate and his wife should sit on a bench opposite him.

Lydgate declined, and went to stand with his back to the last sunlight that streamed in dark gold rays through the window. A clever move, Bartholomew noted, for it was difficult to see his face with the light behind him.

'So, Brother. You have told me a David's scholar is dead. What would you have me do about it?' Lydgate asked coldly.

'Yesterday he was seen quarrelling in the street with two friars who live here,' said Michael, easing himself back comfortably in his chair, and folding his hands across his stomach.

Lydgate's response was aggressive. 'Rubbish,' he said, with a contemptuous toss of his head. 'Whoever claimed to have seen this was lying to you.'

'Really?' said Michael, with a pleasant smile. 'Then you will have no objections to us speaking to Brothers Edred and Werbergh.'

'I most certainly do have objections,' said Lydgate vehemently. 'You have no authority to come here harassing my students on the word of some lying townsman.'

'Oh? And who do you think has been lying to us, Master Lydgate?' probed Michael softly, raising his eyebrows and tapping one hand gently on the other.

'Labourers or guildsmen, they are all the same,' said Lydgate. He walked to the door and hauled it open to indicate that the interview was over. When Michael and Bartholomew did not move, Lydgate made an impatient gesture with his hand. 'I am a busy man. That is all, gentlemen.'

'I do not think so, Master Lydgate,' said Michael, standing to stroll casually across the room and close the door. 'You see, the witnesses you are so certain were lying are Doctor Bartholomew and me.' His tone lost its silkiness. 'I want to speak to Brothers Werbergh and Edred, and I want to do it now. And I can assure you that the authority I own was invested in me by the Chancellor from the King himself. If you do not consider the King's authority sufficient to answer my questions, tell me so, and I will relay the message to His Majesty myself.'

Disconcerted by Michael's sudden force of will and by the none too subtle threat of treason, Lydgate hurriedly sent his steward to find the friars, and fought to regain moral superiority by bluster.

'I will complain to the Chancellor about your attitude,' he said hotly. 'The King's authority does not give you the right to be offensive.'

Cecily Lydgate joined in with her nasal whine. 'You have been most rude.'

Michael rounded on her fiercely. 'How so, Madam? By requesting to speak to two men who were seen quarrelling with a student the day before he was brutally murdered? Do you have something to hide from me?'

'No! I . . .' protested Cecily, flustered. 'I have done nothing . . .'

'Then kindly refrain from meddling in University affairs, Madam,' said Michael in his most icy tones.

91

'Neither the Chancellor nor the King will be pleased if they hear that Godwinsson proved unhelpful – obstructive even – during the course of my inquiries into the foul murder of a member of the University.'

By the time Huw had ushered the friars into the solar, Lydgate and his wife were sitting side by side on the bench, while Michael stood in front of them, allowing his own considerable bulk to dominate them, as Lydgate had attempted to do to him.

'Where were you last night?' Michael snapped at the wary friars. 'Ah! Do not look at each other for the answer! Where were you? Come on, come on. I do not have all day!'

'Here,' ventured Werbergh, watching Michael fearfully.

'Here!' sneered Michael. 'Doctor, would you take Brother Werbergh into the corridor and ask him for his movements since his quarrel in the street yesterday? I will talk to Brother Edred here, and then we will see whether their accounts tally.'

Bartholomew took Werbergh's arm before he had the chance to exchange the slightest of glances with the sullen Edred, and guided him outside, closing the door behind them. Huw the steward scuttled away from where he had evidently been listening through the keyhole.

Werbergh looked terrified, which was no doubt what Michael had intended. Bartholomew waited in silence for Werbergh to bare his soul.

The physician had learned from Michael that uncomfortable silences frequently served to make people gabble, and, in gabbling, they often revealed more than they intended.

'After we . . . after you saved us from the Scots, Edred and I went to St Botolph's Church for vespers. We came straight home then, because the Senior Proctor told us to. We had to go out in the evening for compline, and after that I came back here. I walked home with Mistress Lydgate. You can ask her. She likes one of us to take her arm when she goes to church. Prefers us to her husband, I would say,' he added, with a sly grin at Bartholomew.

'What are you saying, Brother?' asked Bartholomew coldly, not liking the way in which the pale-faced friar was trying to ingratiate himself by tale-telling.

Werbergh began to talk quickly again, Bartholomew's hostility making him more nervous than ever. 'Mistress and Master Lydgate are not the loving couple they seem, and she prefers younger scholars to his company.'

'What has this to do with where you were last night?' asked Bartholomew, making no attempt to hide his disgust at the friar's transparent obsequiousness. Any fool could see that relations between the Lydgates were far from rosy, and Bartholomew resented Werbergh's attempt to distract him from his inquiries by plying him with malicious gossip. Mistress Lydgate could seduce

93

all the young scholars she pleased, and it would be none of Bartholomew's business – unless she set her sights on any of his own students, but they were all perfectly capable of looking after themselves in that quarter, probably far more so than Bartholomew would be.

The student shook his head miserably, his attempt to distract Bartholomew in tatters. 'I escorted Mistress Lydgate to her house and then followed the other students here. It was already getting dark, so most of us went to bed.'

'And what of Edred? Where was he?'

Werbergh licked dry lips. 'I did not notice where he was. We do not go everywhere together, you know,' he added with a spark of defiance. 'But I have been with other people from the moment we returned from our quarrel with the Scots until now. You can check.'

'Do you have any idea why we might be asking you this?' asked Bartholomew, watching the student carefully.

Werbergh shook his head, but two pink spots appeared on his cheeks, and the way in which his eyes deliberately sought and held Bartholomew's was more indicative of guilt than honesty.

'It is surely against the rules of your Order to lie?' said Bartholomew softly.

Werbergh's eyes became glassy, and the redness increased. 'Yes,' he said finally, tearing his gaze away, and studying his sandalled feet instead. 'I can guess why you are asking me these questions.

But I was afraid such an admission might make you assume my guilt. You think Edred and I may have stolen his ring.'

'Ring?' echoed Bartholomew, taken off-guard.

Werbergh looked at him with an expression of one who has played cat-and-mouse for long enough. 'The Scottish student's ring,' he said wearily. 'He was waiting for us when we came out of compline. He accused us of stealing his ring while we were pushing at each other in the High Street.' He paused for a moment, oblivious to Bartholomew's confusion. 'He was very upset; I almost felt sorry for him. We professed our innocence, and he left quietly.' He looked up and met Bartholomew's eyes a second time, but this time with truthfulness. 'That is why you have come, is it not? Because he has accused us of stealing his nasty ring?'

'It is not,' said Bartholomew. 'James Kenzie was murdered last night. And if what you say is true, you may have been the last ones to see him alive, with the exception of his killer.'

Blood drained from Werbergh's face, leaving him suddenly white and reeling. Bartholomew, genuinely concerned that the friar might faint, took his elbow and sat him on a chest. Werbergh stared ahead of him blankly for a moment, before looking up at Bartholomew with eyes that were glazed with shock.

'You would not jest with me on such a matter?' he asked in a whisper. He studied Bartholomew's face. 'No. Of course you would not. What can I tell you? The Scot had been waiting in the churchyard, and he beckoned Edred and me to one side. Mistress Lydgate saw, I think. He sounded more hopeful that we might give his ring back to him, than angry that we might have stolen it. When we denied having it, he left. As I said, I felt almost sorry for him, even though he was so offensive earlier. He was alone – at least, I saw no one with him. I did not see anyone following him when he left.' He screwed up his face in what Bartholomew assumed was a genuine attempt to remember anything that might help. Eventually, he shrugged, and shook his head. 'That is all I can recall, I am afraid. We had a stupid argument in the street, but I did not wish any of the David's men dead because of it.'

The solar door flung open and Michael stalked out, the Lydgates and Edred, whose face was tear-stained, on his heels. Bartholomew bowed to Mistress Lydgate, and followed Michael, leaving Werbergh to make good his escape from his Principal by scuttling off in the other direction. Bartholomew was aware that Lydgate was pursuing him and Michael along the corridor and down the stairs to the front door, but was surprised to find his shoulder in a grip that was so firm it was almost painful. He spun round quickly so that Lydgate was forced to let go.

'I resent this intrusion into my affairs, Bartholomew,' said Lydgate in a low hiss. 'I have connections in the University. If I find you have been meddling in things that are not your concern, you will live to regret it.'

Had Lydgate overheard them talking about the burning of the tithe barn, Bartholomew wondered, as he met Lydgate's hostile glower with a cool stare of his own? Or was he merely referring to the rather insalubrious connection of two of his students with a murder victim?

'Leave well alone, Bartholomew,' Lydgate whispered with quiet menace when Bartholomew did not answer, and pushed the physician roughly towards the door.

Bartholomew slithered out of his grip, and thrust Lydgate away from him. The two stared at each other for a long moment of undisguised mutual loathing, before Bartholomew turned on his heel and strode after Michael. Lydgate watched him go and then closed the door. He leaned against the wall and his eyes narrowed into hard, vicious slits.

CHAPTER 3

In a small, secluded garden behind the Brazen George tavern later that evening, Michael sat at a wooden table with a large goblet of fine red wine in front of him, and watched Bartholomew pace back and forth in the gloom. The physician's hard-soled shoes tapped on the flagstones of the yard, and he tugged impatiently at his sleeve when it snagged on a thorn of one of the rose bushes that added their heavy scent to the still air of the night.

'We should not be here, Michael. You are a proctor and a monk. It would not be good for you to be seen in a tavern, especially drinking, and even more especially on a Sunday.'

Michael leaned back against the wall, where the stones still held the warmth of the day. 'We will not be disturbed, and, for your information, I conduct a good deal of business here on behalf of the University and the Bishop.'

Bartholomew gave a huge sigh, and came to sit next to Michael on the bench. He took a sip of the ale Michael had bought him, and then another. 'This ale is not sour!' he exclaimed in surprise.

He peered into the heavy pewter goblet, and realised the beer was clear enough to allow him to see the bottom.

Michael laughed. 'There are advantages to conducting business outside Michaelhouse.' He sipped appreciatively at his rich red wine. 'You should venture out more, Matt. You have become far too used to that foul concoction brewed at Michaelhouse for your own good health.'

They were silent for a while, listening to the beadles in the street outside calling out the curfew, and, in the distance, the excited yells and shouts of people who were apparently enjoying some kind of celebration. The garden was dark, and the taverner had provided them with a lantern that they shared with hundreds of insects. Michael flapped them away from his wine.

'I had a letter last week,' began Bartholomew casually. 'Philippa, to whom I was betrothed, has married someone else.'

Michael was taken aback. Philippa had been the sister of a former room-mate of Bartholomew's, and had become betrothed to the physician after the plague. Some time ago, Philippa had declared herself bored with life in Cambridge and, seduced by the descriptions of fairs, pageants and feasts in her brother's letters, had set off to sample the delights of London. Three months had stretched to six, and Michael realised he had not seen Bartholomew's attractive fiancée since early summer of the previous year. The monk had not given her long absence a second thought. Neither had Bartholomew, apparently.

'Perhaps, since neither of you made the effort to visit the other during the time she was away, this would not have been a marriage made in heaven,' said the monk carefully, uncertain of his friend's feelings on the matter. 'You would not want to end up as a couple like the dreadful Lydgates.'

Bartholomew studied him in the darkness. 'I suppose not. Philippa married a merchant. She wrote that, at first, she thought that she would not mind being the wife of an impoverished physician, but realised that in time she might come to resent it. Then she said I would have taken rich patients to please her, and we both would have been unhappy.'

'You always paid more attention to your patients than to her,' said Michael, thinking in retrospect that Bartholomew might well have had a lucky escape. 'I cannot say I am surprised by her decision.'

'Well, I was!' said Bartholomew earnestly. 'I did not expect her to shun me quite so suddenly.'

'She has been gone more than a year; that is hardly sudden,' Michael pointed out practically. 'Women are like good wines, Matt. They need to be treated with care and attention – not abandoned until you are ready for a drink.'

Despite his melancholy mood, Bartholomew smiled at Michael's blunt analogy. 'And what would you know of women, monk?'

'More than you, physician,' replied Michael complacently. 'I know, for example, that since she was betrothed to you, it is illegal for her to wed another. You could take her to court.'

Bartholomew raised his eyebrows. 'And what would that achieve? I would acquire a wife who despised me on two counts: my poverty, and the fact that I wrenched her away from the husband of her choice.'

Michael shrugged. 'Then it is best you put the whole affair from your mind. And anyway, if you had married, you would have had to give up your Fellowship at Michaelhouse and your teaching. You like teaching, and you are good at it. Think of what you have gained, not what you have lost.'

'I would have lost the opportunity to investigate murders,' said Bartholomew morosely. 'And the chance to meet such charming people as the Lydgates, Edred and Werbergh.'

Michael chuckled. 'Such characters are not exclusive to the University, Matt. You would have encountered people just like them elsewhere, too. You might even have had to be pleasant to them, if they were your patients and you wanted them to pay you.'

Bartholomew grimaced with distaste at the notion. 'I miss her,' he persisted. 'I lie awake at night and wonder whether I will ever see her again.'

Michael eyed him soberly. 'So that is why you have been looking so heavy-eyed over the last few days. But if you do see her again, Matt,

101

she will be someone else's wife and unavailable to you, so put such thoughts out of your mind. Perhaps you should consider becoming a monk, like me.'

'How would that help?' asked Bartholomew listlessly. 'It would make matters worse. At least now I am not committing a sin by thinking about women. If I were a monk, I would never be away from my confessor.'

'Oh really, Matt!' said Michael in an amused voice. 'What odd ideas you have sometimes! You are capable of great discretion, and that should be sufficient to allow you to choose your secular pastimes as and when you please. A monastic vocation would suit you very well.'

Bartholomew regarded him askance, wondering what kind of monk would offer a jilted lover that kind of advice. He took another sip of the excellent ale, and pondered whether he would ever know Michael well enough not to be surprised by some of his opinions and behaviour.

Michael took a noisy slurp of wine, and refilled his cup from the jug on the table. He stretched and yawned.

'It is getting late,' he said. 'We should be considering Godwinsson Hostel and its shady inhabitants, not discussing your sinful desires for another man's wife. Lydgate, Cecily, Werbergh and Edred – what an unpleasant group of people to be gathered under one roof.'

'Two roofs,' said Bartholomew, forcing his

thoughts away from Philippa. 'I forgot to ask about Kenzie's lover, Dominica. Did you?'

'I learned a little,' said Michael. 'But what did your nasty little friar tell you?'

Michael listened with growing interest as Bartholomew repeated his conversation with Werbergh, and gave a low whistle when he had finished.

'Well,' he said, 'one of them is lying. Edred's story coincides with Werbergh's until after compline. Then he says he walked back to the hostel in the company of Werbergh, but makes no mention of Mistress Lydgate.'

'Well, he would not,' said Bartholomew. 'He could scarcely claim his Principal's wife as an alibi with her sitting there and likely to denounce him as a liar. But neither story fits,' he continued thoughtfully. 'If Werbergh offered his arm to Mistress Lydgate, and Edred claims that he returned to the hostel with Werbergh, then all three must have been together. Edred makes no mention of Mistress Lydgate, while Werbergh makes no mention of Edred. Mistress Lydgate must surely have noted that it was she and not Edred who walked with Werbergh back to the hostel. Something is not right here, Brother.'

He could hear the rasp of Michael's nails against his whiskers as he scratched his chin in the darkness. 'And Edred did not mention Kenzie asking for his ring, even after I told him the lad had been murdered, and that I would appreciate any information he might have. I had a feeling he was not being honest with me.'

'Either Edred is remarkably stupid not to guess that Werbergh would tell me about meeting Kenzie, or it did not happen,' reasoned Bartholomew. 'Or Edred is hiding evidence of what he considers a minor incident, because he is involved in one that is more serious. I am inclined to believe Werbergh was generally truthful, which means that Edred is the one telling lies.'

'Edred and Cecily Lydgate both,' said Michael thoughtfully. 'If Werbergh is telling the truth and he walked home to Godwinsson with Cecily, then why did she not denounce Edred as a liar when he claimed *he* was with Werbergh? Something untoward is going on in that hostel. Give me the honest poverty at David's any day over the thin veneer of civilisation at Godwinsson.'

'So what about Dominica?' asked Bartholomew. 'What did you manage to find out about her?'

'Very little, I'm afraid,' said Michael. 'Only that on the night of Kenzie's murder she was staying with relatives – much against her will if I read correctly the set chin and determined looks of Mistress Lydgate the elder. Dominica is still with them. Which means that wherever Kenzie went last night, it was not Dominica's room, because she was not there.'

'Not necessarily,' said Bartholomew watching the bats flit around the garden. 'Perhaps that is exactly where he went, expecting to find her.'

'And instead found an angry father and a dragon of a mother,' said Michael. 'Which means that they killed him, and dumped his body in the Ditch to avoid suspicion falling on them.'

'That seems too easy,' said Bartholomew. 'There is something not right about all this.'

'Why should it not be easy?' asked Michael with a shrug. 'The Lydgates are hardly over-endowed with intelligence, and neither is Edred if he could not come up with a better story than the one he spun me – knowing that Werbergh would not support his alibi if pressed for the truth.'

Bartholomew sighed. 'I suppose you are right, but we cannot do anything about it, because we have no proof. All we know is that lies have been told.' He stood, feeling suddenly chilly in the cool night air. 'Perhaps the evidence we need will appear tomorrow. Lord save us! What was that?'

A tremendous crash, followed by yells and screams, shook the ground and made the leaves on the trees tremble. Flickers of orange light danced in the street outside, and the shouting suddenly increased dramatically.

The landlord of the Brazen George came hurrying into the garden, his face tight with fear.

'I know you do not like to be disturbed, Brother,' he said apologetically, 'but I thought you should know: the students are rioting. They have tied ropes to Master Burney's workshop and hauled the whole thing down. Now they are trying to set it on fire.'

★　　★　　★

Bartholomew and Michael raced out into the street. The rickety structure, the upper floor of which had been Master Burney's tannery, now lay sprawled across the High Street with flames leaping all over it. Bartholomew knew that Burney, a widower since the plague, slept in the workshop, and started towards the roaring flames. Michael caught his arm and hauled him back.

'If Burney was in there when it fell, you can do nothing for him now,' he choked, eyes watering from the smoke.

Bartholomew saw that Michael was right: the searing heat from the flames was almost unbearable, even at that distance. He screwed up his eyes against the stinging fumes, and surveyed the wreckage. A tangle of limbs protruded from under a heap of smouldering plaster. Michael let out an appalled gasp and gripped Bartholomew's arm to point them out.

'Mistress Starre's son,' Bartholomew shouted, recognising the huge frame of the simple-minded giant among the twisted remains. 'I heard he died recently.'

'What are you talking about?'

'This building belongs to the Austin Canons of St John's Hospital,' Bartholomew yelled over the crackle of burning wood. 'They use the lower storey as a mortuary since they believe the smell from the tannery above will dispel the unhealthy miasma emanating from the corpses. The bodies you see were probably dead already – I know young Starre was.'

'Does their theory hold any validity?' asked Michael before he could stop himself. They should not be considering medical matters now, but attempting to order the rioting students back to their hostels and colleges – and if that failed, seek sanctuary somewhere before they became the victims of a town mob themselves. Fortunately for him, Bartholomew's attention was elsewhere.

'The fire is spreading!' he yelled, and Michael looked to where he was gesticulating wildly, seeing smoke seeping from the roof of the house next door. Seconds later, there was another dull roar, and a bright tongue of flames shot out of one of the windows.

'Mistress Tyler lives there with her daughters!' Bartholomew whispered, his horrified voice all but lost in the increasing rumble and crackle of the flames, greedy for the dry wood of the house.

'No. She lives next door. And anyway, look,' said Michael, indicating behind him with a flick of his head. Bartholomew saw with relief the frightened faces of the Tyler family huddled against the wall of the Brazen George opposite, clutching what few belongings they had managed to grab as they fled for safety.

Students were everywhere, flitting like bats in the dancing light of the flames in their dark tabards. Michael was shouting to them to put out the flames, but while some obeyed, others amused themselves by hurling missiles at the horn windows of the Brazen George. Townspeople, woken by the din, began to pour into the street, and small skirmishes began between them and the scholars. Backing up against the wall next to the terrified Tyler family, Bartholomew saw a group of apprentices kicking a student they had seized and knocked to the ground, while a short distance away, a group of University men were poking at a fat merchant and his wife with sharpened sticks.

A group of three students ran past, shouting to each other in French, but one, seeing the pretty face of the eldest Tyler girl, called to his friends and they came back. They seized her arms, and were set to make off with her, the expressions on their faces making their intentions perfectly clear. Mistress Tyler ran to the defence of her daughter, but stopped short as one of them jabbed at her stomach with a knife.

Bartholomew hit the student's arm as hard as he could, knocking the dagger from his hand, and wrenched the girl away from the others. With a quick exchange of grins, the French students advanced on him, drawing short swords from the arsenal they had secreted under their tabards. Bartholomew drew the small knife that he used for surgery from the medicine bag he always carried looped over his shoulder.

Seeing the tiny weapon compared to their swords, the students began to ridicule it in poor English. While one's attention strayed to his friends, Bartholomew leapt at him, inflicting a minor wound on his arm. The student gave a yell of pain and outrage, forcing Bartholomew to jerk backwards as a sword whistled towards him in a savage arc. Suddenly, the students were not laughing or jeering, but in deadly earnest, and Bartholomew was aware of all three taking the stance of the trained fighter. He knew he would not win this battle, armed with a small knife against three men experienced in swordsmanship. And then what would happen to the Tyler women?

'Run!' he yelled to them, not taking his eyes off the circling Frenchmen.

But the Tyler women had not managed to live unmolested on the High Street, with no menfolk to care for them since the plague, by being passive. Seeing Bartholomew's predicament they swung into action. The eldest hurled handfuls of sand and dust from the ground, aiming for the Frenchmen's eyes, while the mother and two younger daughters pelted them with offal and muck from a pile at the side of the road.

Bartholomew staggered backwards as one student, a hand upraised to protect his face from the barrage of missiles, lunged forwards. As Bartholomew stumbled, his foot slipped on some of the offal that the Tylers were hurling, and he had to twist sideways to avoid the stabbing sword that drew sparks from the ground as it struck. He continued to roll, so that he crashed into the legs of the second swordsman, and sent him sprawling to the ground. The third had dropped his weapon, and was rubbing at his eyes, where one of the handfuls of dust had taken a direct hit.

The second Frenchman grabbed Bartholomew around the neck, preventing him from rising. Bartholomew, struggling desperately to prise the arm away from his throat as he felt it begin to cut off his breath, realised that he had dropped his knife. The first student, his hand still raised to protect his eyes, advanced on the physician smiling evilly, assured that his quarry would now be easily dispatched. Bartholomew lunged forward with every ounce of his strength, and succeeded in breaking the hold that had pinned him to the ground. He scrambled to his feet, but found himself up against a wall with nowhere to move. The two Frenchmen moved apart by unspoken agreement, effectively eliminating any chance of escape.

Without warning, one of them dropped to his knees, his sword falling from his hand as he scrabbled at his back. His face wore an expression of shock that would have been comical in other circumstances. Then he pitched forward, and Bartholomew saw his own knife firmly embedded between the man's shoulder-blades, and Mistress Tyler standing behind him, her face white with shock and anger.

The third Frenchman, his eyes raw from the dust he had rubbed from them, called for the other one to come away, his voice becoming more urgent when he perceived their friend's fate. The student ignored him, and advanced on Bartholomew, his sword whistling in a series of hacking sweeps. Bartholomew, seeing defence was useless, dived at him when he was off-balance from a particularly vigorous thrust. Both men fell to the ground in a frenzy of flailing arms and legs, and Bartholomew's hands fumbled for the Frenchman's throat. Ignoring the pounding of fists on his chest and arms, he began to squeeze as hard as he could.

He was dimly aware of the other man coming to his friend's rescue, and heard the Tylers renew their assault on him with any missiles they could find. There was a heavy thud as he fell. The student Bartholomew held was almost unconscious now, and Bartholomew forced himself to release him. The man flopped on to his side, concerned only with dragging sweet air down his bruised throat, while his friend crawled towards him.

Breathing heavily himself, Bartholomew grabbed Mistress Tyler's arm and hauled her from the street into the small alley that ran down the side of the Brazen George, trusting the daughters would follow. In the comparative peace, the five of them regained their breath, the girls holding on to each other for comfort. Mistress Tyler was the first to recover, while Bartholomew leaned against a tall fence, hoping he would not disgrace himself by being the only one to allow his shaking legs to deposit him on the ground.

Although Oswald Stanmore had been to some trouble to teach his young brother-in-law the rudiments of swordplay, archery and boxing,

Bartholomew had not taken easily or happily to such training, preferring to seek out the company of Trumpington's rector, and ply him with an endless barrage of questions about natural philosophy and logic. Occasionally, however, Bartholomew wished he had paid more attention to Stanmore's lessons – the learning he had acquired over the years would not save him from a sword thrust, and Cambridge seemed to be growing ever more dangerous, with murders and riots at every turn.

He winced as a student friar tore past the top of their alleyway, screaming like an infidel. Students and townsfolk alike ran this way and that, most in small groups for safety. Distant yells indicated that the riot was spreading to other parts of the town, and the dark night sky was glowing orange in at least two places, suggesting that fires were not confined to the High Street. Several riderless horses galloped by, adding to the mayhem. Bartholomew wondered how the Sheriff would manage to control such widespread disorder with troops that had been sorely depleted during the plague and never replaced. Bravely, Mistress Tyler seized on a brief lull in the chaos to peer into the High Street, starting backwards when a shower of sparks danced across the road towards her.

'The fire is more or less out,' she called over her shoulder. 'But there are people inside our house – probably looting, although they will find precious little to take.' She put her arms around the elder girls' shoulders, while the youngest clung to her skirts. 'This is my treasure,' she whispered shakily. 'I will not risk it to save a few sticks of furniture.'

'Shall I try to drive the looters out?' asked Bartholomew, wondering whether his aching limbs would allow it, and regretting his offer the moment it was made.

Mistress Tyler looked at him aghast. 'Of course not! You have done enough for us already by rescuing my Eleanor from those French devils. But if you will do us a final kindness, Doctor, and escort us to my cousin's house, we would much appreciate it.'

Bartholomew agreed readily enough, but wondered whether his presence – a single, unarmed man – could do much to protect the Tyler women from further assault. He felt something pressed into his hand, and met the clear, grey eyes of Eleanor as she returned his knife to him, sticky and glistening black with blood. She must have retrieved it before following her mother to the alley. He was grateful, knowing that his knife found in the back of a corpse might well have been considered sufficient evidence to hang him for murder in one of the hasty and vengeful trials that often followed such disturbances, regardless of the fact that he was innocent.

He gave her a wan smile, and followed the women down the alley. They reached Shoemaker Row, where they kept to the shadows, avoiding the groups of apprentices that ran this way and that armed with a wicked assortment of weapons. At the Franciscan Friary, the stout doors were firmly closed: the friars obviously intended to keep well clear of the mischief brewing that night, and to protect their property from harm. One priest, braver or more naïve than his fellows, stood atop the gate, exhorting the rioters to return to their homes or risk the wrath of God. Few heeded his words, and he was eventually silenced by a well-aimed stone.

Finally, having pursued a somewhat tortuous route to avoid confrontations, Mistress Tyler stopped outside the apothecary's house.

'Is Jonas the Poisoner your cousin?' asked Bartholomew, using without thinking the usual appellation for the apothercary, following an incident involving confusion between two potions many years before.

'His wife is,' answered Mistress Tyler. She took Bartholomew's arm and, when the door was opened a crack in response to her insistent hammering, she bundled him inside with her daughters.

While she told her fearful relatives of their near escape, Bartholomew allowed himself to be settled comfortably in a wicker chair, and brought a cup of cool wine. As he took it, his hands shook from delayed fright, so that a good part of it slopped on to his leggings. Mistress Tyler's middle daughter – a young woman almost as pretty as her elder sister – handed him a wholly inadequate square of lace with which to mop it up. She was unceremoniously elbowed out of the way by Eleanor, and dispatched to fetch something larger, overriding Bartholomew's embarrassed protestations that it was not necessary.

'I did not thank you,' said Eleanor, smiling at him as she refilled his cup. 'You were more than kind to come to our rescue – especially given that you are clearly no fighting man.'

Such a candid assessment of his meagre combat skills was scarcely an auspicious start to the conversation, but he decided her comment was not intentionally discourteous. 'We were more evenly matched than the Frenchmen imagined,' he said, acknowledging the Tylers' own considerable role in the skirmish. 'And I should thank you for not running when I told you to.'

'Yes, or you would have been dead by now for certain,' she said bluntly. Bartholomew took a sip of wine to hide his smile, certain she was oblivious to the fact that many men would have taken grave exception to such a casual dismissal of their martial abilities.

She looked thoughtful. 'You are a scholar: tell me why the students are so intent on mischief this term. They are always restless and keen to fight, but I have never known such an uneasy atmosphere before.'

'We have discussed this at Michaelhouse several times, but we have no idea as to the cause,' he answered, setting his cup down on the hearth before he could spill it again. 'Should you discover it, please let us know. We must put a stop to it before any more harm is done.'

The middle daughter returned with water and a cloth with which to wipe up the slopped wine, and a slight, somewhat undignified tussle for possession of them ensued between the two sisters, a struggle that ended abruptly when the bowl tipped and a good portion of its contents emptied over Bartholomew's feet. Quickly, he grabbed the rest of it before they drenched him further. Across the room, Mistress Tyler tried to see what was happening.

'Hedwise, give the doctor more wine,' she called, before turning her attention back to the persistent questioning of her anxious relatives.

'No, thank you,' said Bartholomew hastily, as Hedwise tried to pour more wine into a cup that was already brimming. He did not want to return to Michaelhouse drunk.

Hedwise looked crestfallen, and Eleanor smiled enigmatically. 'Fetch some cakes, Hedwise. I am sure Doctor Bartholomew is hungry after his ordeal.'

The last thing Bartholomew's unsteady stomach needed was something to eat. He declined, much to Hedwise's satisfaction, and she settled herself on a small stool near his feet, still clutching the wine bottle so that his cup could be refilled the instant he took so much as a sip. Eleanor knelt to one side, leaning her elbows on the arm of his chair.

'When the weather is good, I sit outside to work – you know our family makes lace for a living –

and students often talk to me. I will ask around to see if I can discover the cause of this unease for you.'

'Me too,' said Hedwise eagerly.

'It might be better if you were to stay inside,' said Bartholomew, concerned. 'Supposing those French students return?'

'Oh, they will,' said Eleanor confidently. 'They have been pestering me for weeks.'

'And me,' said Hedwise.

Eleanor ignored her. 'Our mother was forced to speak to their Principal about them.'

'Which hostel?' asked Bartholomew, feeling a strange sense that he already knew the answer.

'Godwinsson,' the women chorused.

'Do you know Dominica?' Bartholomew asked, looking from one to the other. 'The daughter of Master Lydgate, the Principal?'

Eleanor smiled, her teeth white, but slightly crooked. 'Dominica is the only decent member of that whole establishment. She was seeing a student, but her parents got wind of it. They sent her away to Chesterton village out of harm's way.'

Hedwise giggled suddenly. 'They think she has chosen a student from their own poxy hostel, but the reality is that she has far too much taste to accept one of that weaselly brood. It is another she loves.'

'Her parents do not know the identity of her lover?' asked Bartholomew, surprised.

'Oh, no!' said Eleanor. 'But they would do anything to find out. They even offered money to their students to betray their fellows. A number of them did, I understand, but when stories and alibis were checked, the betrayals were found to be false, and stemmed from spite and malice, not truth.'

'What an unpleasant place,' said Bartholomew in distaste, recalling his own brief visit there – only a few hours ago, although it felt like much longer. 'Do you know who Dominica's lover is?'

'Dominica tells no one about her lovers, for fear their names would reach her father,' said Eleanor. 'She is clever though, never meeting in the same place twice, and ensuring there are no predictable patterns to her meetings.'

Had Dominica chosen the King's Ditch to meet Kenzie then, Bartholomew wondered, and the Scot had been killed as he waited for her to appear? If Dominica chose a different location each time she and Kenzie met, then she might well have been reduced to using a place like the shadowy oak trees near Valence Marie if the relationship had lasted for any length of time.

Feeling water squelch unpleasantly in his shoes, Bartholomew stood to take his leave of the Tylers and Jonas, declining their offer to stay the night. He wanted to return to Michaelhouse and sleep in his own bed.

Eleanor reached out to take his hand. 'We will worry about you until we see you again, Doctor Bartholomew. Visit us, even if it is only to say you arrived home safely.'

'Oh, yes,' said Hedwise, forcing her way between

Bartholomew and her sister. 'Come to see us soon.'

Mistress Tyler looked from her daughters to Bartholomew as she ushered him out of the door, first checking to see that it was safe. She touched his arm as he stepped into the street. 'Eleanor and Hedwise are right,' she said. 'You must visit us soon. And thank you for your help tonight. Who knows what might have happened to us had you not come to our aid.'

Bartholomew suspected that they would have thought of something. The Tyler women were a formidable force – resourceful and determined. Eleanor caught his hand as he left, and it was only reluctantly that she released him into the night.

The streets were alive with howling, yelling gangs. Some were scholars and some were townspeople, but all were armed with whatever they had been able to lay their hands on: a few carried swords and daggers, a handful had poorly strung bows, while others still wielded staves, tools, and even gardening equipment. Bartholomew, his own small knife to hand, slipped down the noisy streets hoping that his scholar's tabard would not target him for an attack by townspeople. There was little point in removing the tabard, for that would only expose him to an assault from scholars.

Here and there fires crackled, although none were as fierce or uncontrolled as the one that had destroyed Master Burney's workshop. In places, window shutters were smashed, and from one or two houses, shouts of terror or outrage drifted, suggesting that looting had begun in earnest. Bartholomew ignored it all as he sped towards Michaelhouse. He could do very little to help, and would only get himself into trouble if he interfered.

He felt someone grab his arm as he ran, pulling him off balance so that he fell on one knee. He brought his knife up sharply, anticipating another fight, but then dropped it as he recognised Cynric ap Huwydd, his Welsh bookbearer. Cynric was fleet of foot and possessed of an uncanny ability to move almost unseen in the night shadows; Bartholomew supposed he should not have been surprised that the Welshman had tracked him down in the chaos.

Cynric tugged Bartholomew off the road, and into the shadows of the trees in All Saints' churchyard.

'Where have you been, boy?' Cynric whispered. 'I have been looking for you since all this fighting started. I was worried.'

'With Mistress Tyler's family at Jonas the Poisoner's house. Is Michaelhouse secure? Are all our students in?' asked Bartholomew, peering through the darkness at the man who, although officially his servant, would always be a friend.

Cynric nodded, looking through the trees to where a large group of students was systematically destroying a brewer's cart with stout cudgels. The brewer was nowhere to be seen, and his barrels of ale had long since been spirited away.

'All Michaelhouse students are being kept in by the Fellows – some by brute force, since they are desperate to get out and join in the looting. Only two are missing as far as I can see: Sam Gray and Rob Deynman.'

'Both my students,' groaned Bartholomew. 'I hope they have had the sense to lie low.' He coughed as the wind blew thick, choking smoke towards them from where a pile of wreckage smouldered. 'As should we. We must get home.'

Cynric began to glide through the shadows, with Bartholomew following more noisily. They had to pass the Market Square to reach Michaelhouse, and the sight that greeted them reminded Bartholomew of the wall paintings at St Michael's depicting scenes from hell. For a few moments he stood motionless, ignoring the rioters who jostled him this way and that. Cynric, ever alert to danger, pulled him to one side, and together they surveyed the familiar place, now distorted by violence.

Fires, large and small, lit the Market Square. Some were under control, surrounded by cavorting rioters who fed the flames with the proceeds of looting forays; others raged wildly, eating up the small wooden stalls from which traders sold their wares in the daytime. The brightly coloured canvasses that covered the wooden frames of the stalls, flapped in the flames, shedding sparks every- where, and causing the fires to spread. Bartholomew saw one man, his body enveloped in fire, run soundlessly from behind one stall, before falling

121

and lying still in his veil of flames. Bells of alarm were ringing in several churches, occasionally drowned by the wrenching sound of steel against steel as the Sheriff's men skirmished with armed rioters.

Here and there, people lay on the ground, calling for help, water or priests. Others wandered bewildered, oblivious to the danger they were in from indiscriminate attack. A group of a dozen students sauntered past, singing the Latin chorus that Bartholomew had heard sung outside St Mary's Church the previous day. One or two of them paused when they saw Bartholomew and Cynric but moved on when they glimpsed the glitter of weapons in their hands.

Bartholomew saw the voluminous folds of Michael's habit swirling black against the firelight. Two of his beadles were close, all three laying about them with staves, as they fought to break up a battle between two groups of scholars – although, in their tabards and in the unreliable light of the fires, Bartholomew wondered how they could tell who was on whose side. He took a secure hold on his knife, and went to help Michael, Cynric following closely behind him.

He was forced to stop as one of the stalls in front of him suddenly collapsed in a shower of sparks and cinders, spraying the ground with dancing orange lights. By the time he was able to negotiate the burning rubble, he had lost sight of Michael. Then something thrown by a passing apprentice hit him on the head, and he sprawled forward on to his hands and knees, dazed. He heard Cynric give a blood-curdling yell, which was followed by the sound of clashing steel. With a groan another stall began to collapse, and Cynric's attackers were forced to back off or risk it falling on them. Once away, they obviously thought better of dealing with Cynric, a man more experienced with arms than any of them, and went in search of easier prey. Bartholomew crawled away from the teetering stall, reaching safety moments before the whole thing crashed to the ground in a billow of smoke that stung his eyes and hurt the back of his throat. Cynric joined him, his short sword still drawn, alert for another attack.

'The whole town has gone mad!' said Cynric, looking about him in disgust. 'Come away, boy. This is no place for us.'

Bartholomew struggled to his feet, and prepared to follow Cynric. Nearby, another wooden building, this one used to store spare posts and canvas, began to fall, the screech of wrenching wood almost drowned in the roar of flames. With a shock that felt as though the blood were draining from his veins, Bartholomew glimpsed Michael standing directly in its path as it began to tilt. He found his shouted warning would not pass his frozen lips, and was too late anyway. He saw Michael throw his arms over his head in a hopeless attempt to protect himself, and the entire structure crashed down on top of him.

Bartholomew's knife had slipped from his nerveless fingers before Cynric's gasp of horror brought him to his senses. Ripping off his tabard to wrap around his hands, he raced towards the burning building. Oblivious to the heat, he began to pull and heave at the timber that covered Michael's body. Three scholars, on their way from one skirmish to another, tried to pick a fight with him, but when he whirled round to face them wielding a burning plank they melted away into the night.

Bartholomew's breath came in ragged gasps, and he was painfully aware that his tabard provided inadequate protection for his hands against the hot timbers. Next to him, Cynric wordlessly helped to haul the burned wood away. Bartholomew stopped when part of a charred habit appeared under one of the beams, and then redoubled his efforts to expose the monk's legs and body. But Michael's head was crushed under the main roof support; even with Cynric helping Bartholomew could not move it.

Bartholomew sank down on to the ground, put his face in his hands and closed his eyes tightly. He listened to the sounds of the riot around him, feeling oddly detached as he tried to come to terms with the fact that Michael was dead. Bells still clanged out their unnecessary warnings, people yelled and shouted, while next to him the pop and crackle of burning wood sent a heavy, singed smell into the night air.

'This is not a wise place to sit,' called a voice from behind him.

Bartholomew spun round, jaw dropping in disbelief, as Michael picked his way carefully through the ashes.

Cynric laughed in genuine pleasure, then took the liberty of slapping the fat monk on the shoulders.

'Oh, lad!' he said. 'We have just been digging out your corpse from under the burning wood.'

Michael looked from the body that they had exposed to Bartholomew's shocked face. Bartholomew found he could only gaze at the Benedictine, who loomed larger than life above him. Michael poked at the body under the blackened timbers with his foot.

'Oh, Matt!' he said in affectionate reproval. 'This is a friar, not a monk! Can you not tell the difference? And look at his ankles! I do not know whether to be flattered or offended that you imagine such gracile joints could bear my weight!'

Bartholomew saw that Michael was right. In the unsteady light from the flames, it had been difficult to see clearly, and the loose habits worn by monks and friars tended to make them look alike. Bartholomew had assumed that, because he had seen Michael in the same spot a few seconds before, it had been Michael who had been crushed by the collapsing building.

He continued to stare at the body, his thoughts a confused jumble of horror at the friar's death and disbelief that Michael had somehow escaped. He felt Michael and Cynric hauling him to his feet, and grabbed a handful of Michael's habit to steady himself.

'We thought you were gone,' he said.

'So I gather,' said Michael patiently. 'But this is neither the place nor the time to discuss it.'

When Bartholomew awoke in his room the next day, he was surprised to find he was wearing filthy clothes. As he raised himself on one elbow, an unfamiliar stiffness and a stabbing pain in his head brought memories flooding back of the previous night.

'Michael?' he whispered, not trusting which of the memories might be real and the others merely wishful thinking.

'Here,' came the familiar rich baritone of the fat monk from the table by the window.

Bartholomew sank back on to his bed in relief. 'Thank God!' he said feelingly. He opened his eyes suddenly. 'What are you doing here? What happened last night?'

'Rest easy,' said Michael, leaning back on the chair, and closing the book he had been reading. When Bartholomew saw the chair legs bow dangerously under the monk's immense weight, he knew he could not be dreaming. He eased himself up, and swung his legs over the side of the bed. There was a bump on the back of his head, and his hands were sore, but he was basically intact. He pulled distastefully at his shirt, stained and singed in places, and smelling powerfully of smoke.

'I thought it best to let you sleep,' said Michael.

'We virtually carried you home, Cynric and I. You should lose some weight, Doctor. You are heavy.'

'The rioting?'

Michael rubbed his face, and for the first time Bartholomew noticed how tired he looked.

'There was little we could do to stop it,' said Michael. 'As soon as we broke up one skirmish, the brawlers would move on to another. We have some of the worst offenders in the Proctors' cells, and the Sheriff informs me that his own prison is overflowing, too. We even have three scholars locked up in the storerooms at Michaelhouse. But even with at least twenty students – and masters too, I am sorry to say – under arrest and at least twice as many townspeople, I feel that we still do not have the real culprits. There is something more to all this than mere student unrest. I am certain it was started deliberately.'

'Deliberately?' asked Bartholomew in surprise. 'But why?'

Michael shrugged wearily. 'Who knows, Matt?'

Bartholomew stood carefully, took off his dirty shirt, and began to wash in the water Cynric left each night.

'Were many killed or injured?'

Michael shrugged. 'I do not know yet. Once I realised how little we were doing to bring a halt to the madness, I decided to seek sanctuary in Michaelhouse until it was over. I suspect my beadles did the same, and there was scarcely a soldier to be seen on the way home. When you are ready, I will go out with you to see.' He nodded towards the gates, firmly barred against possible attack. 'It has been quiet since first light, and I expect all the fighting is over for now. Your skills will doubtless be needed.'

Bartholomew finished washing in silence, thinking over the events of the night before, blurred and confused in his mind. From beginning to end, for him at least, it had probably not taken more than two hours – three at the most. He hoped he would never see the town in such turmoil again. He found clean clothes, and shared a seedcake – given to him by a patient in lieu of payment – with Michael, washed down with some sour wine he found in the small chamber he used to store his medicines.

Michael grimaced as he tasted the wine and added more water. 'How long have you had this?' he grumbled. 'You might do a little better for those of us you consider to be your friends. Did you buy this, or did you find it when you moved here eight years ago?'

Bartholomew, noting the bottle's dusty sides, wondered if Michael's question was not as unreasonable as it sounded. He glanced out of the window. The sun was not yet up, although it was light. The College was silent, which was unusual because the scholars usually went to church at dawn. Michael explained that most of them had only just gone to bed – the students had milled around in the yard, fearful that the College would come under attack, and the Fellows had been obliged to stay up with them to ensure none tried to get out. The Master, prudently, had ordered that no one should leave the College until he decided it was safe to do so.

'You might not believe this,' Michael began, breaking off a generous piece of the dry, grainy seedcake for himself, 'but I heard some scholars accusing townspeople of murdering James Kenzie.'

'What?' said Bartholomew in disbelief. 'How can they think that? Our main suspects at the moment are the scholars of Godwinsson!'

'Quite so,' said Michael, chewing on the seedcake. 'But a rumour was put about that he had been killed by townsfolk. As far as I can tell, that seems to have been why the riot started in the first place. Meanwhile, the townspeople are claiming that the death of Kenzie was revenge for the murder – by scholars – of the child we found in the Ditch.'

'But that child has been dead for years!' cried Bartholomew. 'And there is nothing to say it was killed by a scholar.'

'Indeed,' said Michael. 'But someone has used the child's death, and Kenzie's, for his own purposes. There is something sinister afoot, Matt – something far more dangerous than restless students.'

'But what?' asked Bartholomew, appalled. 'Who could benefit from a riot? Trade will be disrupted and if much damage has been done, the King will grant the burgesses permission to levy some kind of tax to pay for repairs. No one will gain from this.'

'Well, someone will,' said Michael sombrely. 'Why else would he – or they – go to all this effort?'

Each sat engrossed in his own thoughts, until Bartholomew rose to leave.

'Are you sure you are up to going out and throwing yourself on the mercy of the town's injured?' Michael said in sudden concern. 'There are sure to be dozens of them and you are the town's most popular physician.'

Bartholomew waved a deprecatory hand. 'Nonsense. There is only Father Philius from Gonville Hall, Master Lynton of Peterhouse, the surgeon Robin of Grantchester, or me from which to choose. Philius's and Lynton's services are expensive, while Robin has a mortality rate that his patients find alarming. It does not leave most people with a huge choice.'

Michael laughed. 'You are too modest, my friend.' He grew serious again. 'Are you certain you feel well? You were all but witless last night.'

Bartholomew smiled. 'It was probably the shock of seeing you rise from the dead,' he said. His smile faded. 'It was not one of my more pleasant experiences. I lost my knife and tabard,' he added illogically.

'Cynric has your knife,' said Michael. 'It is not a good idea to leave an identifiable weapon at the scene of multiple murders you know. The Sheriff might find it and feel obliged to string you up as an example, despite the fact that he seems to consider himself your friend. We brought your tabard back but it was so damaged we had to throw it away. So get yourself another weapon, don your spare tabard, and let us be off.'

Bartholomew followed Michael across the yard of Michaelhouse, breathing deeply of the early morning air as he always did. Today, the usually clean, fresh wind that blew in from the Fens was tinged with the smell of burning.

Surprisingly, given the violence of the night's rioting, only eight people had been killed. The bodies had been taken to the Castle and Bartholomew promised the harassed Sheriff that he would inspect them later in the day to determine the cause of death for the official records. But there were many injured, and Bartholomew spent most of the day binding wounds, and applying poultices and salves. Some people were too badly hurt to be brought to him, and so Bartholomew traipsed from house to house, tending them in their homes. He was just emerging from the home of a potter who had been crushed by a cart, when he met Eleanor Tyler. Shyly, she handed him a neat package that rattled.

'Salves,' she explained. 'I thought you might need extra supplies today, given the number of people I hear have been injured. I packed them up myself in Uncle Jonas's shop.'

'Thank you,' said Bartholomew, touched by her

thoughtfulness. 'That was kind, and I have been running low.'

She glanced at the potter's house with its sealed shutters. 'Will he live?'

Bartholomew shook his head. 'Father William should be here soon to give him last rites.'

She took his arm and led him away. 'I am sure you have done all you can for him but now you should look to your own needs. You look pale and tired and you should rest while you eat something. My mother has made some broth and we would be honoured if you would come to share it with us.'

'That would be impossible,' he said somewhat ungraciously, as he tried to extricate his arm. 'I have another six patients to visit, and I cannot just abandon them.'

'No one is asking you to abandon them,' she said, taking a firmer grip on his sleeve. 'I am simply advising you that if you want to do your best for them, you should rest. Uncle Jonas says it is dangerous to dispense medicines unless you are fully alert, and you cannot be fully alert if you have been working since dawn.'

'Eleanor, please,' he objected, as she pulled him towards the High Street. 'I am used to working long hours and none of the medicines I will dispense are particularly potent.' In fact, most of his work had involved stitching wounds and removing foreign bodies, work usually considered beneath physicians and more in the realm of surgeons.

They were almost at Eleanor's home, still marked

with streaks of soot from the fire of the previous night. Mistress Tyler and her other two daughters were scrubbing at the walls with long-handled brooms, but abandoned their work when they saw Bartholomew. Before he could object further, he was ushered through a small gate to an attractive garden at the rear of the house. While the two older daughters pressed him with detailed questions about the town's injured, Mistress Tyler and the youngest child fetched ale and bread.

'I heard that Michaelhouse's laundress – Agatha – drove away a group of rioters from the King's Head virtually single-handed,' said Hedwise with a smile. Hedwise, like her older sister, had rich tresses of dark hair and candid grey eyes. She was slightly taller than Eleanor and had scarcely taken her eyes off Bartholomew since he had arrived.

'What was Agatha doing at the King's Head?' asked Bartholomew. 'She lives at Michaelhouse.'

'The King's Head is her favourite tavern,' said Eleanor, surprised. 'Did you not know? She can often be found there of an evening, especially when darkness comes early and there is nothing for her to do in the College. She says if Michaelhouse will not buy her any candles so that she can see to sew, then she will take her talents elsewhere.'

'Agatha?' asked Bartholomew, bemused. 'I had always assumed she went to bed after dark. I did not know she frequented taverns.'

'You see how these scholars fill their heads with books to the exclusion of all else?' asked Eleanor of Hedwise. 'Doctor Bartholomew probably has no idea about how Agatha earns herself free ale in the King's Head!'

'And I do not wish to,' he said hastily, embarrassed. The notion of the large and formidable woman, who ruled the College servants with a will of steel, dispensing favours to the rough male patrons of the King's Head was not an image he found attractive.

Eleanor and Hedwise exchanged a look of puzzlement before Hedwise gave a shriek of shocked laughter and punched him playfully on the arm. 'Oh, Doctor! You misunderstand! Agatha mends torn clothes for free ale. She is very good.'

'I see,' said Bartholomew, not sure what else he could say after what, in retrospect, indicated that he had a low opinion of the moral character of Michaelhouse's most powerful servant. He hoped the Tyler women were discreet, for Agatha was not a woman to suffer insults without retaliating in kind.

Eleanor dispatched her sister to help Mistress Tyler with the broth. Hedwise left Bartholomew and Eleanor alone with some reluctance, glancing backwards resentfully as she left. As soon as she was out of sight, Eleanor rested her hand on his knee.

'I hear Michaelhouse is due to celebrate its foundation next week,' she said.

'Yes, next Tuesday,' he said, grateful for the

change in conversation. 'It is the most important day in the College calendar, and is the only time that its Fellows are allowed to bring ladies into the hall. We are each allowed two guests.'

'I know,' said Eleanor, smiling meaningfully, still gripping his knee.

Bartholomew looked at her, not certain what he was expected to say. He continued nervously. 'Our founder, Hervey de Stanton, provided a special endowment for the occasion, so that there will always be money to celebrate it. The Founder's Feast and the Festival of St Michael and All Angels the following Sunday – St Michael is the patron saint of Michaelhouse – come close together.'

'So, who have you invited to this feast?' asked Eleanor, raising her eyebrows.

'I had been planning to ask my sister and her husband, but I left it too late and they accepted an invitation from one of the commoners instead. So, I have invited no one.' It would have been pleasant, he thought ruefully, to have taken Philippa. The mere thought of her long, golden hair and vivacious blue eyes sent a pang of bitter regret slicing through him. He looked away.

'I am free on Tuesday,' said Eleanor casually. 'And I have never been to a Founder's Feast before.'

'Would you like to come?' asked Bartholomew doubtfully, wondering why a lively and attractive woman like Eleanor should want to sit through a long, formal dinner, with lengthy Latin speeches that she would not be able to understand, attended by lots of crusty old men whose aim was to eat enough to make themselves ill the following day and drink sufficient wine to drown a horse.

'Yes, I would,' she said happily, her face splitting into a wide grin. 'I would be delighted!'

'Good,' said Bartholomew, hoping she would not be bored. 'It begins at noon.'

Mistress Tyler arrived with the broth, and Eleanor's hand was withdrawn from his knee. Bartholomew ate quickly, concerned that he had already been away too long from his patients. It was excellent broth, however, rich and spicy and liberally endowed with chunks of meat that were edible. The bread was soft and white and quite different from the jaw-cracking fare made from the cheapest available flour that emerged from the Michaelhouse kitchens. Perhaps Michael had been right in the tavern the previous night, and Bartholomew did need to venture out of College more and sample what the world had to offer. Including the company of women, he decided suddenly.

As he took his leave, one of Jonas the Poisoner's children came to say that his father was inundated with requests for medicines after the riot, and that he needed Eleanor's help.

'You have some knowledge of herbs?' asked Bartholomew, impressed.

'She sweeps up,' said Hedwise with disdain.

'I do not!' Eleanor retorted, glowering at her sister. 'I have a good memory, and Uncle Jonas says I am indispensable to him in his work.'

'Then you had better go to him,' said Hedwise archly. 'I shall accompany Doctor Bartholomew to see his next patient.'

'There is no need for that,' said Bartholomew, not liking the way Eleanor's look had turned to something blacker.

Hedwise took his arm. 'Shall we be off, then? I shall return later,' she called to her family as she opened the garden gate and bundled him out.

'Do not be too long,' Eleanor shouted after her. 'You still have the pig to muck out, and I have that potion for the rash on your legs that you asked me to fetch from Uncle Jonas. You should apply it as soon as possible before it becomes worse.'

Hedwise laughed lightly and, Bartholomew thought, artificially, as she closed the gate behind her. 'Eleanor likes to jest, although mother is always berating her for being overly vulgar. But I have watched Uncle Jonas very carefully in his shop, and if I can be of service to you this afternoon, I shall be happy to oblige.'

'What about the pig?' asked Bartholomew, desperately trying to think of a way to reject her offer without hurting her feelings. It was not that he did not want her company, but some of the sights he had seen that morning had been horrific and he had no wish to inflict them on young Hedwise Tyler.

'The pig will manage without me for an hour or two,' said Hedwise, 'and I am sure I can do more good by assisting you than by dealing with that filthy animal.'

'Perhaps another time, Hedwise,' said Bartholomew gently, 'although I do appreciate your offer and the fact that you are prepared to subject yourself to some unpleasant experiences in order to help me.'

She looked away and, to his horror, he saw that her eyes brimmed with tears. At a loss, he offered her a strip of clean linen from his bag with which to wipe her eyes.

'I so seldom leave the house,' she said in a muffled voice. 'Eleanor, being the eldest, is always the first to go on errands and the like, while I have to stay at home with the pig.'

Bartholomew's discomfort increased, so, uncertain what to say, he said nothing. She gave a loud sniff.

'I never go anywhere,' she continued miserably. 'I have not even been to the Festival of St Michael and All Angels at St Michael's Church.'

'Oh, I could take you to that,' he said, relieved he could at least suggest something positive. 'It is the Sunday after next, although I cannot see that you would enjoy it – Michael's choir is going to sing, you see, and they are not what they were before the plague. Afterwards, Michaelhouse

138

provides stale oatcakes and sour wine in the College courtyard. If it rains, we just get wet because the Franciscans outvote everyone else that the meal – if you can call it that – should be held in the hall. The Franciscans do not approve of townspeople in the hall except at the annual Founder's Feast.'

He realised he had not made the offer sound a particularly appealing one, and sought for something to say in the Festival's favour. Hedwise did not give him the chance.

'How wonderful!' she exclaimed, tears forgotten. 'Oh, thank you!'

'You can bring your mother,' he said, recalling that her elder sister had already inveigled an invitation to the Founder's Feast. He did not want Mistress Tyler thinking he was working his way through her entire family. Hedwise, however, had other ideas.

'Oh, no,' she said briskly. 'Mother will not want to sit in a damp church all day. But I will be delighted to accompany you. Just the two of us.'

'And a hundred other people,' he said. 'The church is always full for the Festival. Of course, it might not be so well attended if people hear the choir in advance. But if you have second thoughts about wasting a Sunday, you must tell me. I promise you I will not be offended if you find something better to do.'

'I can think of nothing better to do than to spend a Sunday with you at the Festival,' she announced.

She gave him a huge grin and slipped away, dodging deftly out of the path of a man driving an ancient cow to the Market Square. A little belatedly, Bartholomew began to wonder what he had let himself in for.

CHAPTER 4

Bartholomew's fears for Hedwise's well-being were unfounded as it happened, and most of the cases he saw the afternoon after the riot comprised minor injuries, rather than serious wounds. He tended a merchant who had gashed his hand on glass when he tried to protect his home from looters, and then set off along Milne Street to where a baker with eyes sore from smoke awaited him. On his way, he was accosted by a shabby figure in dark green, with protuberant blue eyes and a dirty, unshaven look. His hands, Bartholomew could not help but notice, were black with dried blood.

'Good afternoon, Robin,' he said, involuntarily stepping backwards as the surgeon's rank body odour wafted towards him.

'I hear you have been stitching and cutting,' said Robin of Grantchester in a sibilant whisper, pursing his lips and looking at Bartholomew in disapproval. 'Chopping and sewing.'

'Yes,' said Bartholomew shortly, walking on. He did not have the time to engage in a lengthy discussion with the surgeon about the techniques he used, despite the fact that Bartholomew thought the man could use all the help he could get: Robin of Grantchester was not noted for his medical successes. The surgeon scurried after him.

'Surgery is for surgeons,' hissed Robin, sniffing wetly. 'Physicking and reading the stars is for physicians. You are taking the bread from my mouth.'

Bartholomew heartily wished that were true, and that Robin would pack up his unsanitary selection of implements and look for greener pastures in another town. The more Bartholomew observed the surgeon in action, the more he was convinced that his grimy hands did far more harm than good, and shuddered to think of anyone being forced to pay him for any dubious services he might render. The fact that Robin always demanded payment in advance because of his high mortality rate did little to endear him to Bartholomew.

'My job is slitting and slicing,' said Robin venomously.

'Hacking and slashing, more like,' muttered Bartholomew, wondering whether the man had been drinking. His eyes were red-rimmed and he seemed unsteady on his feet.

'You are not a surgeon. You have no right,' persisted Robin. 'I do not profess to read the stars or inspect urine. Keep to your profession, Bartholomew, and I will keep to mine. I shall complain to the master of Michaelhouse if you continue to poach my trade.'

'Complain then,' said Bartholomew carelessly, knowing that Master Kenyngham would do nothing about it. 'I am duty bound to do whatever it takes to ensure the complete recovery of my patients. If that involves a degree of surgery, then so be it.'

'You can call me to do it,' said Robin, wiping his runny nose with a bloodstained finger. 'The other physicians do so, and I insist you do not poach my work.'

'All right,' said Bartholomew, stopping outside the sore-eyed baker's house. 'I promise you I will ask any patient I operate on whether they would rather have you or me. Will that suffice?'

Robin saw it would have to, and slunk away down a dark alley, his canvas sack of saws and knives clanking ominously as he went. Before Bartholomew could knock at the baker's door, he was hailed a second time, and turned to see Adam Radbeche, the Principal of David's Hostel and the man responsible for Father Andrew and his unruly Scottish students.

Radbeche was a distinctive-looking man, with a shock of carrot-coloured hair that reminded Bartholomew of a scarecrow. The Scot was a well-known figure in the University, famous for his brilliant interpretations of the works of Aristotle, and Bartholomew was pleased that Radbeche's scholarship had been rewarded by an appointment to Principal – even if it were only to the small, anonymous David's Hostel. Students and masters from the same part of the world tended to gather together, so it was not unusual that Radbeche had attracted fellow Scots to his establishment.

The philosopher's hand was bandaged; he explained that he had been burned while assisting a neighbour to extinguish a fire. The students had also helped to bring the fire under control, but, Radbeche said, at least three times he had counted them all back in again, so Bartholomew was inclined to believe that the Scots had played no part in the rioting. He led Radbeche across the road to sit on the low wall surrounding the little church of St John Zachary – decommissioned since the plague had taken most of its parishioners, and now with weeds growing out of its windows and its roof sagging dangerously.

While Bartholomew inspected and re-dressed the burned hand, Radbeche informed him that the ailing student Bartholomew had treated the day before at David's was recovering well. When Bartholomew waved away the offer of payment, impatient to attend the baker who had emerged from his house and was blinking at him anxiously, Radbeche suggested instead that he might like to borrow a medical book by the great Greek physician Galen. Bartholomew was surprised.

'Galen? But you have no medical students.'

Radbeche smiled. 'It was a gift from a man who could not read and who purchased the first book that matched the price he was willing to pay. It is the only book we own, actually. We borrow what we need from King's Hall or the Franciscan Friary.'

'Which book by Galen do you have?' asked Bartholomew with keen interest.

144

Radbeche seemed taken aback. '*Prognostica*, I believe.' He saw Bartholomew's doubtful look at his ignorance, and shrugged. 'I am a philosopher, Doctor. I have no interest in medical texts – even if they are all we have!'

Despite the fact that the University was a place of learning, and students were obliged to know certain texts if they wanted to pass their examinations, books were rare and expensive, and each one was jealously guarded. Michaelhouse only possessed three medical books and Bartholomew was delighted by Radbeche's generous offer. He gave the Principal a grateful grin and made his farewells so that he could attend to the agitated baker.

Later, as he was returning to Michaelhouse for more bandages, Bartholomew saw the untruthful Brother Edred limping up the High Street. Moments after, his colleague Brother Werbergh slunk past sporting a bruised eye, looking very sorry for himself.

Justice in Cambridge was swift and brutal, and, before evening, four men alleged to have been ringleaders in the rioting were hanged on the Castle walls as a grim warning to others who might consider breaking the King's peace. Other rioters were released when heavy fines had been paid, with warnings that next time, they too would be kicking empty air on the Castle walls. Whether the hanged men really were the ringleaders of the riot was a matter for conjecture. While Bartholomew

145

imagined they might have been in the thick of the fighting – perhaps even urging others to do damage and harm – the evidence that they were the real instigators was, at best, dubious.

As the shadows began to lengthen, and the heat of the day was eased by a cooling breeze, Bartholomew finished his work. Sam Gray and Rob Deynman, the two students who had been missing from Michaelhouse the night before, had helped him with the last few visits. Deynman had shown an aptitude for bandaging that Bartholomew never realised he had; this offered some glimmer of hope that his least-able student might yet make some kind of physician.

'Where were you two last night?' asked Bartholomew as they walked home together.

The students exchanged furtive glances and Bartholomew, tired and hot, felt his patience evaporating. His students sensed it too and Gray hastened to answer.

'We were at Maud's Hostel. I know we are not supposed to frequent other hostels,' he added quickly, seeing Bartholomew's expression of weary disapproval. 'But Rob's younger brother is there, as you know.' He cast Bartholomew a sidelong glance. Bartholomew, struggling to teach Rob Deynman – not the most gifted of students – had seen within moments that the younger brother made Rob appear a veritable genius and had refused to teach him at Michaelhouse. The younger Deynman, therefore, had secured himself a place at Maud's, an exclusive establishment with a reputation for rich, but slow, students.

'It was my brother Jack's birthday,' said Deynman cheerfully, 'and we were invited to celebrate at Maud's. By the time the wine ran out and we were ready to leave, the riot had started. The Maud's Principal advised us to stay.'

'Very wise,' said Bartholomew, wondering whether the idea to stay was truly the Principal's, or, more likely, Gray's. Gray, with his loaded dice and silver tongue, would profit greatly from an evening among the wealthy, but gullible, students at Maud's. Deynman, slow-witted and naïve, was often an innocent foil to Gray's untiring and invariably imaginative ploys to make money by deception. Still, Bartholomew was grateful that they had had the sense not to stray out on to the streets when the town was inflamed – whatever their motive. He was fond of Gray and Deynman, and had been relieved when they had reported to him unharmed earlier that day.

'Just the man I wanted to see,' came a soft voice from behind him, and Bartholomew felt his spirits sink. Guy Heppel, the Junior Proctor, sidled closer, smiling enthusiastically from under a thick woollen cap. He held out a hefty pile of scrolls to Bartholomew. 'I have all the information you will need to conduct a complete astrological consultation on me. Would now be a convenient moment?'

'No,' said Gray, before Bartholomew could think of a plausible excuse. 'There is a new moon tonight, you see, and Doctor Bartholomew, being born under the influence of Venus, is never at his best when the moon is new. You would be better off trying him next week.'

Heppel nodded in complete and sympathetic understanding. 'Then I shall do so,' he said, rubbing his free hand up and down the sides of his gown in the curious manner Bartholomew had noticed earlier. 'It is just as well you are indisposed, I suppose. The Chancellor has ordered me to march around the town with the beadles to warn scholars that anyone caught out after the curfew will spend the night in our cells. So, it is all for the best that you cannot entice me from my duties to spend the time with you on my consultation. When I finish announcing the curfew, I intend to go home to King's Hall and spend the evening by the fire.'

'Fire? In this weather?' asked Bartholomew before he could stop himself.

Heppel looked pained. 'For my chest,' he explained. 'You understand. And I find a fire so much better for reading after dark. Much better than a candle, don't you think?'

Since candles were expensive and firewood more so, Bartholomew had seldom had the opportunity to find out.

'I heard your brother-in-law's premises were attacked last night,' Heppel added as he rolled up his sheaf of parchments. 'I hope no damage was done.'

Bartholomew had not given his family a single thought that day, assuming that if any of Oswald Stanmore's household had been harmed they would have summoned him. He decided he should pay them a visit, reluctantly banishing from his mind the attractive alternative of a wash in clean water and a quiet supper in the orchard. He rubbed his hand through his hair wearily, nodding to Heppel as he took his leave.

'Thank you for getting me out of that, Sam,' he said when the Junior Proctor had gone. 'The last thing I feel like doing now is thinking about astrology. Did you make it all up?'

'Of course I did,' said Gray, surprised by the question. 'I certainly did not learn it from you, did I, bearing in mind your antipathy to the subject?'

'I have taught you some astrology,' said Bartholomew indignantly, 'including how to do consultations of the kind Heppel has in mind. In fact, you can do his next week and I shall listen to see how much you have remembered.'

Gray sighed theatrically. 'Never do a master a favour, Rob,' he instructed Deynman. 'It is seldom appreciated and often dangerous.'

'I will do Master Heppel's consultation,' offered Deynman enthusiastically. 'I recall everything you said about Venus and Mars.'

Bartholomew seriously doubted it, and had reservations about letting Deynman loose on anyone, even for something as non-invasive as a consultation about astrology. He might well

149

inform Heppel that he only had a few days to live, or that a strong dose of arsenic would increase his chances of living to be a hundred years old. While Deynman's outrageous interpretations of planetary movements provided Bartholomew with an endless supply of amusing anecdotes with which to horrify Michael, it would scarcely be appropriate to inflict him on real patients.

Tiredly, Bartholomew sent his students back to Michaelhouse with orders not to go out again and went to find his brother-in-law. Soldiers were very much in evidence on the streets, sweating under their chain-mail, and armed to the teeth. Heppel and his group of beadles were marching around the town proclaiming that all scholars must be in their hostels or colleges by seven o'clock, and that any who were not would be summarily arrested. The Sheriff's men were issuing similar warnings to the townspeople.

It seemed to be working: the streets were emptier than usual. People had laboured all day in the sweltering sun to restore order to the town and, with luck, would be too exhausted for rioting that night. Burned wreckage had been moved into a large pile and other rubbish swept away. Bartholomew saw some of it being carted off in the direction of the King's Ditch, and wondered if, after all the dredging efforts by both town and University, the Ditch was to be blocked again so soon. He also wondered at the wisdom of collecting all the partly burned wood into a large pile in the Market Square: even to the most naïve of eyes, it looked like a bonfire waiting to be lit.

Stanmore's business premises were protected by a high wall and sturdy gates. No harm had come to them that Bartholomew could detect, although the house next door had been attacked and looted. Stanmore employed a small number of mercenaries to protect his ever-increasing trade and it would be a foolish man who would risk targeting his property. Bartholomew, with an ease born of familiarity, walked across the yard and ran lightly up the wooden stairs to the fine solar on the upper floor. Bartholomew had always liked the room Stanmore used as an office. A colourful assortment of rugs were scattered across the floor and it always smelled of parchment, ink and dyed cloth.

Stanmore sat at a table near the window, dictating a letter to his secretary. The merchant dismissed the clerk as Bartholomew poked his head round the door, then greeted his brother-in-law warmly. He sent for wine, and gestured that Bartholomew should sit on one of the cushioned window seats where he would be fanned by the breeze.

'Guy Heppel told me your premises had been attacked,' said Bartholomew, sipping at some fine red wine. He glanced down at it, noting how clear it was and the richness of its colour. He decided Michael was wrong after all – if Bartholomew acquired a taste for good wine, clear ale and edible food, he would starve to death at Michaelhouse.

'Guy Heppel was mistaken,' said Stanmore, sitting opposite him and offering him an apple from a large dish. 'I had my men posted on the walls with arrows at the ready; the rioters prudently went elsewhere – next door among other places.'

'Do you have any ideas about why the town is in such turmoil?' asked Bartholomew. Stanmore's wide network of informants meant that he was often party to information inaccessible to University men and it was always worth asking what he had heard.

Stanmore shook his head slowly. 'Ostensibly, the riots were about the death of that student and the skeleton in the Ditch,' he said, 'but I cannot believe they were the only reasons. The whole town has been growing increasingly uneasy during the past two weeks or so. A student was killed by an apprentice last month in a street fight and his death did not provoke such a violent reaction.'

'Michael was thinking along the same lines this morning,' said Bartholomew. 'However, neither of us can imagine why anyone should want to instigate such chaos.' He rubbed a hand through his hair, staring down at the wine in his cup. 'Damage was done to both town and University property and there were arrests on both sides. It is difficult to see what anyone might have gained – scholar or townsperson. Do you have any ideas yourself?'

Stanmore blew out his cheeks. 'None that I can prove,' he replied. 'But Master Deschalers's house next door was systematically sacked last night – not looted on the spur of the moment, but carefully burgled and only items of the greatest value taken. Oh, things were broken and thrown around to make it look as if it had been sacked, of course. But the reality was that nothing was stolen except that which was most valuable and easily spirited away.'

'You think someone caused a riot to burgle Deschalers's house?' asked Bartholomew, startled.

Stanmore made an impatient sound. 'Of course not, Matt! But it would not surprise me if you discovered Deschalers's was not the only house looted last night. If several such burglaries took place, then someone might have benefited considerably.'

Bartholomew regarded him soberly, and finished his wine. 'If the word is spread that the riots were started to allow burglars to operate, then sensible people will hide their valuables. It might deter thieves from sparking off another night of chaos to do it again.' He set the cup down on the window-sill and stood.

'True,' said Stanmore, following Bartholomew down the stairs to see him out. 'And the threat of burglary might be enough to keep people off the streets. Who would be foolish enough to leave their homes, knowing that they were being enticed out deliberately?'

'I doubt it was the wealthy merchants, with houses worth looting, who were out rioting last night,' said Bartholomew, looking backwards at him. 'It was the apprentices and the poor people with little to lose. I do not think burglars would start a riot to steal a few cracked plates and a handful of tallow candles.'

'Times are hard, Matt,' said Stanmore primly. 'Since the Death, there is a shortage of everything – including plates and candles. Such items are valuable these days.'

'If you were poor, would you burgle Deschalers's mansion or Dunstan the Riverman's hovel?' asked Bartholomew. 'If caught, you would be hanged in either case.'

'True enough,' admitted Stanmore. 'Suffice to say I am glad I am not in the Sheriff's shoes today. I would not know where to start investigating all this.'

Bartholomew glanced up at the dusky sky, and swore softly. 'The Sheriff! Damn! I promised him I would go to the Castle and examine the bodies of those who died last night.'

'Better hurry, then,' said Stanmore, ushering him out of the gate. 'The curfew is early tonight, and I would not break it if I were you.'

Bartholomew walked briskly away from Stanmore's house towards the Castle. The land on which Cambridge stood was flat, but at the northern end, there was a small rise on which William the Conqueror had chosen to build a wooden keep in 1068. The small rise became Castle Hill, and the wooden keep had developed into a formidable fortress with a thick curtain wall and several strong, stone towers.

As he walked, Bartholomew saw the streets were virtually deserted, and cursed himself for agreeing to examine the bodies that day. He did not feel safe walking alone along streets that usually thronged with people, nor did he like the fact that the only people he did see were heavily armed.

'Matthew!' came a voice from the shadows. 'You should not be out so late. The curfew bell will sound in a few moments, and you are heading in entirely the wrong direction.'

'Good evening, Matilde,' said Bartholomew, turning with a warm smile to the woman who emerged from the house of one of the town's brewers. 'You should not be out, either.'

As soon as he had spoken, he realised how stupid his words were. Matilde was a prostitute, and the hours of darkness were, presumably, when she conducted much of her business. Known as 'Lady Matilde' because, according to popular rumour, she had once been a lady-in-waiting to a duchess but had been dismissed for entertaining one too many gentlemen in her chambers, she had come to Cambridge to ply her trade in peace. Unlike the other prostitutes, Matilde was well-spoken, and her manners were gentle. Bartholomew had never asked her whether the story were true – not because he thought she might not tell him, but because he liked her aura of mystery and enigma.

Matilde was, to Bartholomew's mind, the most attractive woman in Cambridge. She had long hair that reached her knees in a glossy veil, and a small, impish face that was simultaneously beautiful and mischievous. He found he was staring at her and had not heard a word she had been saying.

'I am going to the Castle,' he said, trying to mask the fact that he had not been paying attention. 'Can I escort you somewhere?'

'I have just told you that I am going home,' said Matilde, laughing at him. 'Have you not been listening to me?'

'Sorry,' said Bartholomew, beginning to walk towards The Jewry – the part of the town that had once been inhabited by a little community of Jews before their expulsion from England some sixty years before – where Matilde lived. It was on his way, and would not be an inconvenience. 'I have had a long day, Matilde, given the number of people who were injured last night.'

She gave him a sympathetic look, and they walked for a while in silence. Bartholomew was aware that he was dirty and dusty, but that she smelled clean and fragrant. Her hair shone, even in the faint light of dusk. Next to her the Tyler sisters paled into insignificance, like distant stars compared to the sun. Not for the first time in their friendship Bartholomew wished that she had chosen a different profession, and that he might ask her to accompany him for walks by the river, or even to the Founder's Feast. He was surprised when she replied, realising with a shock that he must have spoken the invitation aloud.

'I do not think that would be a good idea,

Matthew,' she said. 'What would Master Kenyngham say when he saw you had invited a courtesan to dine at his college?'

Master Kenyngham would not know a courtesan if one appeared stark naked at his high table, thought Bartholomew, but his colleague Father William would, and then there would be trouble. But Bartholomew was tired, he was missing Philippa more than he thought possible, and he was about to go and inspect corpses in the dark for the Sheriff. He decided he did not care what Father William might say, and since the invitation had apparently been issued, he could hardly withdraw it.

'Please come,' he said. 'It is the only occasion in the year that Michaelhouse provides food fit for eating, and the choir are going to sing some ballads.' He hesitated. 'If you have heard them in church, that might put you off. But apart from the singing and the speeches, the day might be quite pleasant – much more so than the Festival of St Michael and All Angels will be.'

'I heard that you have already invited Eleanor Tyler to the Founder's Feast,' said Matilde. 'Are you sure that my presence will not be awkward for you?'

He gazed at her in astonishment. He had totally forgotten his invitation to Eleanor – not that it mattered, since he was allowed two guests – but it was remarkable that Matilde should know.

'She has been telling anyone who will listen that she is to be the guest of the University's senior physician for Michaelhouse's Founder's Feast,' said Matilde, smiling at his confusion. 'It is quite the talk of the town.'

'It is?' asked Bartholomew, bemused. 'To be honest, I think she more or less invited herself. I suppose she wanted to see the College silver, or hear the music.'

'That is what you think, is it?' asked Matilde, eyes sparkling with merriment. 'Oh, Matthew! You are a good man, but I do not think this University of yours is teaching you very much about life!'

'What do you mean?' asked Bartholomew, slightly offended. 'I have travelled as far as Africa and the frozen lands to the north, and I have seen great cathedrals and castles, and the aftermath of wars, not to mention—'

'That is not what I meant,' said Matilde, still smiling. 'I do not doubt your experience or your learning. You just seem to know very little of women.'

'I know enough,' said Bartholomew, although his recent experience with Philippa made him suspect Matilde was right. 'Some of my patients are women. But will you come? To the Founder's Feast?'

Matilde reached up and touched his cheek. 'Yes, I will. Although if you have second thoughts in the cold light of day, you must tell me. I will not be offended.'

Bartholomew had said as much to Hedwise Tyler after he had invited her to the Festival of St Michael and All Angels. His head reeled. Had

Philippa's rejection of him addled his mind? In the course of a single day, he had issued invitations to three separate women, one of whom was a prostitute, to visit Michaelhouse. While he might be expected to get away with one, three would certainly catch the eye of the fanatical Father William, not to mention the other Fellows. The best Bartholomew could hope for was that his colleagues would have some sort of collective fainting fit, only recovering their wits when the day was over and the women safely off the College premises. His mind still whirling, Bartholomew made his way to the Castle on the hill.

The Castle had the air of being in a state of siege. There was no soldier, inside or out, who was not fully armoured and armed. Archers lined the curtain walls in anticipation of an attack, and the great gates that normally stood open were closed, the wicket door heavily guarded. Bartholomew saw that there was a guard near the portcullis mechanism, ready to release it at a moment's notice. It was no secret in the town that the chains that held the portcullis needed to be replaced – such chains were yet another item impossible to buy since the plague – and it was generally believed that if the portcullis were lowered, the chains would not be strong enough to allow it to be raised again. Sheriff Tulyet, Bartholomew realised, must be anxious indeed if he were considering using it.

Bartholomew was allowed through the barbican,

and then into the Castle bailey. Soldiers milled around restlessly, some preparing to leave on patrol, others returning. Every one of the towers that studded the curtain wall seemed to be a focus of frenetic activity. Ancient arms were being dragged out of storage to substitute for those that had been lost or damaged the night before; fletchers and blacksmiths laboured feverishly in the failing light to meet the Sheriff's demands for repairs and replacements.

The bodies Bartholomew had been asked to examine were in one of the outbuildings in the bailey. The building was little more than a shack; inside it was dank, airless and stiflingly hot. Bartholomew felt the sweat begin to prickle on his back after only a few seconds. There were no windows, and the Castle clerk who had been assigned to record Bartholomew's evidence brought a lamp so they would be able to see what they were doing.

'Five bodies were recovered from the burned houses on the High Street,' said the clerk as he sharpened an ancient quill. 'But they were all reclaimed by the Austin Canons from St John's Hospital on the grounds that they were already dead. The Canons use a house on the main street as a mortuary.' He paused in his sharpening, favouring Bartholomew with a look that indicated fervent disapproval.

'They think the smell from the tannery above might negate any ill-effects the odours from the bodies might produce,' said Bartholomew.

'I know what they think,' snapped the clerk. 'They were at great pains to explain it all to me when I complained. My wife's sister lives next door.'

Bartholomew stared at him. 'The building was burned to the ground last night. I hope . . .' He wondered what he could say. The clerk came to his rescue.

'The fire spread the other way, thank the Lord.' He crossed himself automatically, testing the tip of his quill for sharpness at the same time with his other hand. 'But she does not like living next to corpses. It is all very well for the Canons to say there are no ill-effects, but how would they know?'

Bartholomew suspected the clerk had a point, and had argued with the Canons at the time that the stench from the tannery probably masked dangerous odours, rather than neutralised them. But debating the point with the clerk would lead nowhere. He gestured for the man to kindle the lamp and lead him to the bodies that awaited their attention.

For a moment, both men stood together staring down at the neat row of sheeted figures that lay on the beaten-earth floor. Then, anxious to complete his task as soon as possible, Bartholomew knelt next to the first one, and drew back the rough cover. Memories surged forward unbidden as he found himself looking into the face of the French student he had fought, and whom Mistress Tyler had stabbed. He made a pretence at searching for other wounds, glad that the clerk's mind was on his writing, but feeling as if guilt must shine from every pore in his body. He muttered that the cause of death was due to a single stab wound in the back, covered the body, and moved on thankfully to the next one.

If anything, this was a worse encounter, for it was the corpse of the friar he had mistaken for Michael. He found his hands were shaking, and blinked the sweat from his eyes. For a moment he thought he might faint, and had to close his eyes tightly before he could regain control of himself.

'Have you identified this friar?' he asked, partly for information, but mainly because he wanted to hear the clerk's voice in this room of death.

'Brother Accra from Godwinsson,' said the clerk, consulting a list.

Godwinsson again! 'How can you be sure?' Bartholomew snapped, rattled. He continued a little more gently. 'His skull is crushed beyond all recognition.'

'He was identified by a scar on his knee,' said the clerk, apparently oblivious to Bartholomew's outburst. 'Principal Lydgate and a Brother Edred were the witnesses. They both claimed there was no doubt.'

Bartholomew covered the friar's mangled head with its blanket, and braced himself for the next one. It was the potter he had tended that morning. He glanced along the row of bodies and saw that there were nine, and not eight after all.

'This man is dead from crushing injuries caused by a cart,' he told the clerk. 'I saw him alive this morning, but did not think much to his chances.'

The fourth body was so badly burned that Bartholomew could not recognise the features. A sudden picture of old Master Burney came into his head as he remembered the tannery workshop collapsing in the High Street. Other visions flitted through his mind too: the Market Square alive with fire, and someone staggering across it as the flames leapt up his body until he fell. Bartholomew peered more closely at the corpse in the dim light, but there was nothing familiar in the hairless, blackened head. He moved on.

Of the next four, one was a student, and the others townsmen. All had died of knife wounds, great gaping red slashes that had splintered the bone beneath. The last was the body of a woman with long fair hair. Bartholomew was appalled to see that she had been much misused. Her face was battered beyond recognition, and she had been raped. He told the clerk who did not write it down.

'Better to write that she died from a head injury, Doctor. That is what you say killed her?'

Bartholomew frowned at him across the gloomy room. 'The wound to her head was the fatal one,' he said, 'but she has also been raped. What purpose is there in suppressing the truth?'

'The purpose is to prevent grounds for another riot,' said a voice from behind them. Bartholomew turned to see Richard Tulyet, the Sheriff, leaning against the door frame.

Tulyet, small, slight and efficient, gazed in distaste into the outbuilding and waited for Bartholomew to come out. The clerk remained behind to finish making a record of Bartholomew's findings, his pen scratching away in the small circle of light thrown out by the lantern.

'The townspeople might revolt again if we tell them one of their womenfolk was raped before she was murdered,' Tulyet said, closing the door and turning to look across the bailey. He made a sound of impatience as one of his men dropped a sword. The soldiers were nervous, and one of the sergeants strutted round them, yelling in a vain attempt to boost their courage. 'The town will automatically assume that the crime was committed by students, regardless of the truth.'

'I understand that,' said Bartholomew. 'But when her family comes to claim the body they will see for themselves what has happened. You do not need to be a physician to see how she was misused.'

'We have already considered that,' replied Tulyet. 'And so we are not releasing the dead to their families. The University will bury the students; the town will bury the others. In that way, no one will see the bodies, or attempt to instigate another riot to avenge them.'

'And that woman's attackers will go unpunished,' remarked Bartholomew disapprovingly. 'Perhaps they might commit such a crime again when the fancy takes them. Why not? No one bothered to investigate the first time.'

'Would you have me risk another riot and nine dead to avenge a rape?' asked Tulyet coldly.

'Yes I would,' Bartholomew returned forcefully. 'Because if you do not word will get round that any vile crime can be committed, and you will do nothing about it lest it interfere with the King's peace. Then, Master Tulyet, you will have a riot masking crimes that will make last night's business seem tame.'

Tulyet turned from him with a gesture of impatience. 'You scholars think you can mend the world with philosophy,' he said. 'I am a practical man, and I want to prevent another riot – whatever the cost.'

'And if your cost is too high?' demanded Bartholomew. 'What then?'

Tulyet tipped his head back, looking up at the darkening sky. Some of the anger went out of him and he grimaced. 'Perhaps you are right, Matt. But what would you have us do?'

Bartholomew contemplated. 'Make discreet inquiries. Find out who last saw her alive and with whom.' He gripped Tulyet's mailed arm, his expression earnest. 'You should at least try, Dick. Supposing some of the townspeople saw her raped and murdered and are expecting at least some attempt to catch the culprit? The last thing the town needs is a retaliation killing.'

'Is that not what last night was about anyway?'

asked Tulyet, leaning against the dark grey stone of the curtain wall, and scrubbing at his fair beard. 'Scholars seeking to avenge the death of James Kenzie and townsfolk the poor child in the Ditch?'

'Oswald Stanmore does not think so,' said Bartholomew. 'And neither does Brother Michael. Both believe the riot to be part of some other plot.'

Tulyet's interest quickened. 'Really? Do they know what?'

Bartholomew shook his head. 'No. But both arrived at the same conclusion independently of each other: that the riot was a means, not an end in itself.'

Tulyet took his arm and guided him to his office in the round keep that loomed over the bailey. He glanced around before closing the door, ensuring that they could talk without being overheard. 'I have been thinking along the same lines myself,' he said, his expression intense. 'I cannot understand why the town should have chosen last night to riot – I do not see Kenzie's death or the discovery of the skeleton as particularly compelling motives to fight. It has been scratching at the back of my mind all day.'

Bartholomew rubbed at his temples. 'When Brother Michael and I found Kenzie murdered, it went through our minds that the students might riot if they believed he had been killed by a townsperson. We went to some trouble to keep our thoughts on the matter to ourselves. But neither of us anticipated that the scale of the rioting would be so great. It was terrifying.'

Tulyet puffed out his cheeks, and gave him a rueful smile. '*You* were terrified! Imagine what it felt like to be the embodiment of secular law – for scholar and townsperson alike to single out for violence and abuse! These are dangerous times, Matt. Since the plague, outlaws have flourished and it is difficult to recruit soldiers to replace the ones we lost. Violent crime is more difficult to control and the high price of bread has driven even usually law-abiding people to criminal acts. But all this does not answer our basic question: what was the *real* cause of last night's violence?'

'Perhaps the way forward is to investigate the crimes that were perpetrated under its cover: for example the rape of that woman, and the burglary at Deschalers's home,' suggested Bartholomew.

'Those among others!' said Tulyet with resignation. 'I have had reports of three similar lootings – where only what was easily carried and of the highest value was stolen – and there are the nine deaths to consider.'

'Do you think one of those nine is at the heart of all this?' asked Bartholomew.

Tulyet shrugged. 'I think it unlikely. The only one of any standing or influence was the young friar from Godwinsson.'

Bartholomew told him about the visit he and Michael had paid to Godwinsson Hostel and the possible roles of the student friars, Edred and Werbergh, in Kenzie's death.

'Godwinsson,' mused Tulyet. 'Now that I find interesting.'

He went to a wall cupboard and poured two goblets of wine, inviting Bartholomew to sit on one of the hard, functional benches that ran along the walls of his office. Once his guest was settled as comfortably as possible on the uncompromising wood, Tulyet perched on the edge of the table. He swirled the wine around in his goblet, and regarded Bartholomew thoughtfully.

'We should talk more often,' he said. 'Not only are two of the dead from last night students of Godwinsson – a friar and a Frenchman – but this morning, the Principal of Godwinsson told me that his wife is missing.'

'So, Mistress Lydgate has flown the nest,' mused Michael, leaning back in his chair and smiling maliciously. 'Well, I for one cannot blame her, although I would say the same if it were the other way around, and Lydgate had taken to his heels.'

'A most charitable attitude, Brother,' said Bartholomew mildly. 'It is good to see that compassion is not dead and gone in the Benedictine Order.'

Tulyet was sitting on the chest in Bartholomew's room at Michaelhouse sipping some of the sour wine left from breakfast. Because it was dark, and therefore after the early curfew imposed following the riot, Tulyet had escorted Bartholomew back

168

to Michaelhouse. The streets had been silent and deserted, but Bartholomew had been unnerved to detect a very real atmosphere of unease and anticipation. Doors of houses were not fully closed and voices whispered within.

'This is an unpleasant brew,' said Tulyet, looking in distaste at the deep red wine in his goblet. 'I would have expected better from Michaelhouse.'

'Then you must go to the Senior Fellow's chamber,' said Michael. 'He is the man with the taste, and the purse, for fine wines, not a poor Benedictine and an impoverished physician. But tell us about Mistress Lydgate. What happened at Godwinsson last night?'

Tulyet shrugged. 'Master Lydgate was out all night and discovered his wife was missing when he returned this morning.'

'Why was the Principal of a University hostel abroad on such a night?' demanded Michael. 'Why was he not at home, ensuring his students kept out of mischief, and protecting his hostel? And more to the point, why is he bothering you about his missing wife?'

Tulyet shook his head. 'It just slipped out. He came to the Castle this morning to identify a couple of the people killed last night. He was in quite a temper, and ranted on to me for some time about the audacity of his students to get themselves killed when it was so inconvenient for him. When I asked him what he meant he

169

blustered for a while. Eventually he revealed that his wife had left him.'

'And where did he say he was last night, instead of locking up his wife and students?' asked Michael.

'I was told, begrudgingly – for I was assured his whereabouts were none of the Sheriff's concern – that he had been dining at Maud's Hostel and had remained there when he saw how the streets seethed with violence.'

'Maud's?' asked Bartholomew, pricking up his ears. 'Two of my students claimed they stayed at Maud's last night. I can ask them to verify Lydgate's alibi.'

'Can you indeed?' said Tulyet, fixing bright eyes on Bartholomew. 'Master Lydgate will not be pleased to hear that. It is no secret that the Master of Maud's – Thomas Bigod – is not kindly disposed to secular law, and would never confirm or deny an alibi to help me. Bigod recently lost title to a wealthy manor in the secular courts, and is said to have missed out on a fortune because of it. He holds me, as the embodiment of secular law in the area, responsible for his misfortune.'

'He is none too fond of University law, either,' said Michael gleefully. 'Guy Heppel arrested him the other night for being drunk and disorderly. Unfortunately, he ended up being our guest for longer than necessary because Heppel lost the keys to the cells.'

Tulyet roared with laughter and clapped his

hands. 'Excellent! I wish I could have seen that! Heppel, for all his physical frailty, knows how to give a man his just deserts. Bigod has been a thorn in my side for months, using every opportunity to thwart the course of law and justice.'

'And I imagine Lydgate is only too aware of Bigod's antipathy to you,' said Bartholomew, 'which is why Lydgate chose him to provide an alibi.' He went to the door and told a passing student to fetch Gray and Deynman.

Tulyet stroked his fair beard thoughtfully. 'All this is most interesting. I told Lydgate to liaise with the University Proctors regarding his dead students' remains. He became abusive and said he did not want you near them because he was not convinced of your competence. I was rather surprised.'

'Well, I am not,' said Michael. 'Master Lydgate and I have had cause to rub shoulders once or twice recently, and the experience was not a pleasant one for either of us. The man is little more than a trained ape in a scholar's gown.'

'What makes you think he is trained?' asked Bartholomew.

'I heard he bought his way through his disputations when he was a student here,' said Tulyet. 'Is that true?'

'I would imagine so,' replied Michael, not in the least surprised by the rumour. 'I doubt he earned his degree by the application of intellect. Perhaps that is another reason why he did not want the

Proctors looking too carefully into his affairs. Anyway, we certainly did not part on the most amicable of terms – he probably overheard us discussing the burning of the tithe barn yesterday, and resents his ancient crime being resurrected after so long.'

'What title barn fire?' asked Tulyet curiously. 'No fires have been reported to me.'

'It happened a long time ago,' said Bartholomew, fixing Michael with a reproving look for his indiscretion.

'Not the one at Trumpington twenty-five years ago?' persisted Tulyet, not so easily dissuaded. 'I remember that! It was the talk of the town for weeks! An itinerant musician is said to have started it, but he escaped before he could be brought to justice. My father was Sheriff then. Are you saying that Lydgate was involved? Was it Lydgate who let the culprit go?'

'No, Matt did that,' said Michael, laughing. 'Lydgate's role in the fire was a little more direct.'

'It was all a long time ago,' repeated Bartholomew, reluctant to discuss the matter with the 'embodiment of secular law'. He began to wish he had never broken his silence in the first place, and certainly would not have done had he known that the investigation into Kenzie's death would bring him so close to Lydgate and his Godwinsson students.

'Lydgate was the arsonist!' exclaimed Tulyet, laughing. 'Do not worry, Matt. I will keep this matter to myself, tempting though it would be to mention the affair at a meeting of the town council. But even the prospect of Lydgate mortified is not cause enough to risk another riot. If town and gown will fight over some ancient skeleton, they will certainly come to blows if the Sheriff accuses a University principal of arson!'

'That is true,' said Michael. 'But anyway, you can see why Master Lydgate is not exactly enamoured of the Senior Proctor at the moment. I can understand why he would rather keep me at a distance.'

'I also heard,' said Tulyet, reluctantly forcing his mind back to the present, 'that Mistress Lydgate's chamber was ransacked. A sergeant, who chased a Godwinsson student into the hostel after he was seen looting, told me her room was chaotic.'

'Really?' said Michael. 'I wonder why.'

'Hasty packing, I should think,' said Bartholomew. 'She probably did not know how long she had before her husband returned and gathered everything she could as quickly as possible.'

At that moment, Gray and Deynman knocked and entered, looking at Michael and Tulyet with such expressions of abject guilt that Bartholomew wondered uneasily what misdemeanours they had committed that so plagued their consciences.

'Who was at Maud's with you last night?' he asked.

'Master Bigod will vouch for us both,' began Gray hotly.

'And so will all the other students. I swear to

you, we did not leave there, even for the merest instant!'

Bartholomew was amused at Gray's indignation – the student regularly lied or stretched the truth to get what he wanted, and there was an element of outrage in Gray that he was not believed when he was actually being honest. 'There is no reason to doubt you,' he said to mollify him. 'It is not your doings that concern us now, but someone else's. Can you remember who was there?'

Deynman relaxed immediately and began to answer, although Gray remained wary: Deynman's world was one of black and white, while Gray was a natural sceptic.

'All the Maud's students were there,' Deynman began. 'They all like my brother Jack and wanted to celebrate his birthday.'

Bartholomew did not doubt it, especially since the wealthy Deynmans were known to be generous and would have provided fine and plentiful refreshments for Jack's birthday party.

'How many?' asked Bartholomew.

'There are eight students including Jack,' said Deynman, screwing up his face in the unaccustomed labour of serious thought. 'We were all in the hall. Then there were the masters. There was one who does logic, another who teaches rhetoric, and the Principal, Master Bigod, who takes philosophy for advanced students.'

Bartholomew saw Michael smile at the notion that any of the students of Maud's were advanced and imagined that Master Bigod probably had a very light teaching load.

'Were there others?' asked Bartholomew. 'From different hostels or colleges?'

'No,' said Deynman with certainty. 'Jack invited me because I am his brother, and I invited Sam. There were no others.'

'During the time you were there, did anyone else visit? Did any master or student leave to see about the noise from the rioting?'

Deynman shook his head. 'We all ran to the window when we heard that workshop falling, but Master Bigod ordered the shutters closed and the doors barred immediately.' He grimaced. 'I started to object because it was hot in the hall and the open windows provided a cooling breeze. He told me I could leave if I did not like it.'

'But you told me he insisted you stayed once the riot had started,' said Bartholomew, looking hard at Gray. Gray shot his friend a weary look, and Deynman, suddenly realising that he had been caught out in an earlier lie, flushed red and became tongue-tied.

'What were you doing that made leaving so undesirable?' Bartholomew persisted. He eyed the full purse that dangled from Gray's belt. 'Cheating at dice?'

Gray gave Deynman an even harder glare and Bartholomew knew he had hit upon the truth. It was not the first time Gray had conned money from the unsuspecting with his loaded dice.

'We are getting away from the point,' said Tulyet impatiently. 'Did anyone else visit Maud's at any point last night, for however brief a time?'

Gray and Deynman looked at each other. Deynman's brows drew together as he tried to recall, while Gray appeared thoughtful.

'We were merry by dusk,' he said, 'but some time later, there was a knock on the door. I remember because Master Bigod was called out and he missed the end of one of my stories. It was a woman who came. She glanced into the hall, saw us all sitting round the table and withdrew hastily. She spoke for a few moments to Bigod before leaving. I heard the front door open and close again.'

'What was this woman like?' asked Tulyet. It was clearly not Lydgate.

'Small and dumpy with a starched white wimple that made her look unattractive,' said Gray unchivalrously.

'About fifty years old? With expensive, but ill-hanging clothes?' asked Michael, exchanging a glance with Bartholomew.

Gray nodded. 'Exactly! You must know her. That is all I can tell you, I am sorry. There were no other interruptions to our evening after she had gone. And there were no others in the hall with us. Master Bigod stayed up all night. I think he was afraid his students might disobey his orders and go out if he went to bed.'

Bartholomew dismissed them, and Gray cast a

furtive glance at Michael before he left. Michael dutifully studied the ceiling in an unspoken message that the illegal dicing would be over-looked this time. Deynman beamed at him before following Gray out.

'So,' said Michael when the door had been closed and the students' footsteps had faded away. 'The visitor was Mistress Lydgate, but Thomas Lydgate was not there.'

'This is all most odd,' said Tulyet, rubbing at the bridge of his nose with a slender forefinger. 'Lydgate claims Bigod as an alibi but does not set foot in Maud's that night. Meanwhile, his wife, who has reached the end of her tether and is running away, does visit Bigod.'

'It will be no good us questioning Bigod,' said Michael, taking a careful sip of his wine. 'He will refuse to answer you, Dick, on the grounds that he does not come under the jurisdiction of secular law. And he certainly will not speak to me after Heppel's escapade with the cell keys. I suppose you could try Lydgate again – tell him you have witnesses prepared to swear he was not at Maud's as he claims, and see what he says.'

Tulyet sighed. 'I could. But I am not inclined to do so. I have more than enough to do without wasting my time on lying scholars. I need to concentrate on preventing another of these distur-bances.'

'That should certainly be your first priority,' agreed Michael. 'And mine, too. Good luck to

177

Cecily for fleeing that ignoramus of a husband. They are both better off without each other. But I am more concerned with Kenzie's killer at the moment. It is not pleasant to think of him free and laughing at us while the town is ripped to pieces about our ears by feeble-witted people filled with self-righteous rage.'

Tulyet picked up his goblet but put it down again with a shudder before he drank. He stood, peering out at the night through the open window shutters. 'I must be away,' he said. 'It is vital the patrols are seen tonight if we are to prevent more mischief. It has been most interesting chatting to you both. As I said earlier, the University and the town should talk more often. I am certain my crime rates would drop if we did.'

'Do you have any information at all about the woman who was raped?' asked Bartholomew as he walked with the Sheriff across the yard to the gate.

Tulyet shrugged. 'Very little. She was called Joanna, and she was a prostitute. Perhaps she was out plying her trade and got more than she bargained for.'

'That is an outrageous thing to say!' exclaimed Bartholomew. 'Because she is a prostitute does not give someone the right to rape her!'

Tulyet eyed Bartholomew in the darkness. 'I forgot,' he said. 'You have championed the town prostitutes on other occasions. Well, I am in sympathy with your point, Matt, but I need to concentrate on preventing further riots. I cannot spare the men to look into this Joanna's death. One of my archers says he saw Joanna in the company of some French scholars after the riot erupted. Tell Brother Michael it is a University matter and persuade him to investigate.'

He took the reins of his horse from the waiting porter and watched Bartholomew unbar the gate so that he could leave. As he led his horse out of the yard, he caught Bartholomew's arm. 'But if you do look into this death be tactful, Matt. It would be unfortunate if incautious inquiries sparked off another riot.'

Making certain that the gate was firmly closed and barred, Bartholomew strolled back across the courtyard to intercept Michael, who was heading towards the kitchens for something to eat before he, too, went to patrol the streets with his beadles. Bartholomew told the monk about Joanna but met with little enthusiasm.

'Dick Tulyet is right, Matt. There were many grievous crimes committed last night – nine dead and countless injured – which is why we cannot allow it to happen again. It is a terrible thing that happened to this whore, but it is done, and there is nothing we can do about it now.'

'We can avenge her death,' Bartholomew replied, disgusted that Michael should take such a view. 'We can find out who misused her and punish them for it.'

'But we have no idea who it may have been,' said Michael with a patent lack of interest.

'Tulyet said she was last seen with French scholars. French scholars tried to make away with Eleanor Tyler last night. Perhaps they had already committed one such crime.'

'Well, if so, then they are punished already,' said Michael dismissively, 'for you told me yourself that one already lies dead in the Castle, stabbed by Mistress Tyler. And you are being unfair. There are a lot of French scholars in the University; there is no reason to assume the Godwinsson trio are to blame.'

Bartholomew ran a hand through his hair and considered. 'There are not that many French students here. You could supply me with a list, since the University keeps records of such things. Then I could make some inquiries.'

'I will do no such thing,' said Michael firmly. 'First, it might be dangerous. Second, you are not a proctor and have no authority to investigate such matters. And third, even enquiring might strike the spark that will ignite another riot. No, Matt. I will not let you do it.'

'Then I will make inquiries without your help,' said Bartholomew coldly, turning on his heel and stalking back towards his room.

Michael hurried after him and grabbed his arm. 'What is the matter with you?' he asked, perplexed. 'I know you dislike violence, so why are you so intent on subverting the attempts of the Sheriff and the University to prevent more of it?'

Bartholomew looked at Michael and then up at the dark sky. 'The dead woman had hair just like Philippa,' he said.

Michael shook Bartholomew's arm gently. 'That is no reason at all,' he chided. He blew out his cheeks in a gesture of resignation. 'You are stubborn. Look, I will help you, but not tonight. I will get the list tomorrow and we can look into this together. I do not want you doing this alone.'

Bartholomew hesitated, then gave Michael a quick smile and walked briskly across the rest of the yard to his room. Michael was right: it was far too late to begin inquiries into Joanna's death that night and, anyway, he was weary from his labours with the injured all that day. He had surprised himself by revealing to Michael the overwhelming reason why he felt compelled to avenge Joanna and supposed he must be more tired than he guessed. Bearing in mind his ill-conceived invitation to Matilde as well, he decided to retire to bed before he made any more embarrassing statements. Thinking of Matilde reminded him of Philippa and he was disconcerted to find that the image of her face was blurred in his mind. Was her hair really the same colour as Joanna's? On second thoughts, he was not so sure that it was. He reached his room, automatically extinguishing the candle to save the wax. He undressed in the darkness and was asleep almost before he lay on the bed.

Michael watched his friend cross the yard and then resumed his journey to the kitchen. He knew from experience that he would be unable to prevent Bartholomew doing what he intended, and that it would be safer for both of them if Michael helped rather than hindered him. He gave a huge sigh as he stole bacon-fat and oatcakes for his evening repast and hoped Bartholomew was not going to champion all fallen women with fair hair like Philippa.

In an attempt to keep the scholars occupied and off the streets, term started with a vengeance the following day. All University members were obliged to attend mass in a church; lectures started at six o'clock, after breakfast. The main meal of the day was at ten, followed by more teaching until early afternoon. Since the plague, Michaelhouse food, which had never been good, had plummeted to new and hitherto unimaginable depths. Breakfast was a single oatcake and a slice of cold, greasy mutton accompanied by cloudy ale that made Bartholomew feel queasy; the main meal was stewed fish giblets – a favourite of Father William – served with hard bread. Michael complained bitterly and dispatched one of his students to buy him some pies from the Market Square.

When teaching was over for the day Bartholomew and Michael were able to meet. A light meal was available in the hall but when Bartholomew heard it was fish-giblet stew again – probably because it had not been particularly popular the first time round – he went instead to the kitchens, Michael in tow.

'And what is wrong with my fish-giblet stew?' demanded Agatha the laundress aggressively, blocking the door with her formidable frame, arms akimbo. 'If it is good enough for that saintly Father William, then it should be good enough for you two layabouts.'

'Father William is not saintly!' said Michael with conviction. 'If he were, he would not eat the diabolical fish-giblet stew with such unnatural relish!'

'What do you mean?' demanded Agatha, looking from Michael to Bartholomew with open hostility. 'There is no unnatural relish in my fish-giblet stew, I can tell you! I only use the finest ingredients. Now, off with you! I am busy.'

Agatha determined, and in a foul temper, was not a thing to be regarded lightly, and Bartholomew was fully resigned to returning to his room hungry. Michael, however, was less easily repulsed, particularly where food was concerned.

'Everything you cook is delicious, Madam,' he said, attempting to ease his own considerable bulk past hers. She was having none of that and stood firm. Michael continued suavely, standing close enough so that he would be able to shoot past her the moment a gap appeared. 'And the fish-giblet stew is no exception. But a man can have too much of a good thing, and, in the interests of my immortal soul, I crave something a little less fine, something simple.'

Agatha eyed him suspiciously. 'Such as what?'

'A scrap of bread, a rind of cheese, a wizened apple or two, perhaps a dribble of watered ale.'

'All right, then,' said Agatha reluctantly after a moment's serious consideration. 'But I am busy with the preparations for the Founder's Feast next week, so you will have to help yourselves.'

'Gladly, Madam,' said Michael silkily, slipping past her and heading for the pantry. Agatha glared at Bartholomew before allowing him to pass, and he wondered what he could have done to upset her. Usually, she turned a blind eye to his occasional forays to the kitchens when he missed meals in hall. He wondered whether the Tyler women had told her that he believed she had dispensed amorous favours to the rough men in the King's Head to earn free ale.

While she gave her attention to a mound of dead white chickens that were piled on the kitchen table, he took a modest portion of ale from the barrel in the corner. Michael clattered in the pantry, humming cheerfully. Just when the monk had taken sufficiently long to make Agatha start towards the source of the singing with her masculine chin set for battle, Michael emerged, displaying two apples and a piece of bluish-green bread. Agatha inspected them minutely.

'Go on, then,' she said eventually. 'But that is

all you are getting, so clear off and keep out of my way.'

She gave Bartholomew a hefty shove that made him stagger and slop the ale on the floor. He had darted out of the back door before she noticed the mess, lest she was tempted to empty the rest of the jug over his head. Michael followed more sedately, heading for the fallen apple tree in the orchard. He plumped himself down, turning his pasty face to the sun and smiling in pleasure. His contentment faded when he saw the ale Bartholomew had brought.

'There is wine by the barrel in the kitchens!' he cried in dismay. 'All for the Feast. Could you not have smuggled us some of that?'

'With Agatha watching?' asked Bartholomew, aghast. 'Suicide is a deadly sin, Brother!'

'She has always liked you far better than the rest of us,' said Michael, reproachfully. 'You have only to hint and she will willingly give you whatever you want. If I were in such a powerful position, Matt, I would not squander it as you do. I would ensure you and I dined like kings.'

'She did not give the impression that she liked me just now,' said Bartholomew. 'She was positively hostile.'

'So I noticed,' said Michael, peering into the ale jug in disgust. 'What have you done to annoy her? Whatever it is, you are a braver man than me. I would not risk the wrath of Agatha!'

He stood, shaking his large body like some

bizarre oriental dancer. Bartholomew was not in the least bit surprised when a large piece of cheese, a new loaf of bread, a sizeable chunk of ham, and some kind of pie dropped from his voluminous habit into the grass at his feet. The monk tossed the two apples and the moudly crust away in disdain.

'Never eat anything green when there is meat to be had,' he advised sagely. 'Green food is a danger to the stomach.'

'And which medical text did this little pearl of wisdom come from?' asked Bartholomew, ripping a piece of bread from the loaf. It was nowhere near as fine as that he had eaten in Mistress Tyler's garden, but, even though it was hard and grey and made with cheap flour, it was an improvement on what he usually ate.

'You put too much store in the written word,' said Michael complacently. 'You should rely more on your instincts and experience.'

Bartholomew thought about Matilde's jibe the night before, and how she had laughed at his lack of experience with women. For the first time that day he considered the predicament he had landed himself in with his invitations.

'What is on your mind?' asked Michael, eyeing him speculatively as he broke the cheese in two, handing Bartholomew the smaller part. 'Something has happened to worry you. Is it this Joanna business?'

'Yes. No.' Bartholomew shrugged. 'Partly.'

'I always admire a man who knows his own mind,' said Michael dryly. 'You are not having second thoughts about taking that Tyler woman to the Founder's Feast, are you?'

Bartholomew gaped at him. 'How did you know that?' He corrected himself. 'Is there anyone in the town who does not know?'

Michael gave the matter serious thought, cramming a slice of ham into his mouth as he did so. 'Father William, I should imagine, or he would have mentioned the matter to you with his customary disapproval. He would ban all women from the Feast, if he could.'

'What is wrong with women in the College for a few hours?' demanded Bartholomew, standing and pacing in agitation. 'They might give it a little life and make us see the world in a different perspective.'

'That is exactly what William is afraid of,' said Michael, chuckling. 'I am all for it, myself, and I would have them in for a lot more than a few hours. Sit down, Matt. This ham is delicious and you will not appreciate it striding up and down like a hungry heron.'

Bartholomew flopped on to the tree trunk, taking the sliver of ham Michael offered him. With his other hand, the monk crammed as much bread into his mouth as would fit and then a little more. Within a few moments, he was gagging for breath, forcing Bartholomew to pound him hard on the back.

'Eat slowly, Brother,' admonished Bartholomew mechanically. He had long since given up hoping that his advice would be followed. 'It is not a race and I promise to take none of your share.'

'You are not still pining after that Philippa, are you?' asked Michael when he had recovered his breath. 'Pining will do you no good at all, Matt. You need to go out and find yourself another one, if you decline to take the cowl. I suppose Eleanor Tyler is acceptable, although you could do a good deal better.'

'I also invited Matilde to the Feast,' Bartholomew blurted out. He stood again and resumed his pacing.

Michael's jaw dropped, and Bartholomew would have laughed to see the monk so disconcerted had he not been so unsettled himself.

'Matt!' was all Michael could find to say.

Bartholomew picked up one of Michael's discarded apples and hurled it at the wall. It splattered into pieces and some of it hit the monk.

'Steady on,' he objected. 'Does this uncharacteristic violence towards fruit mean that you are pleased or displeased by your appalling indiscretion?'

'Both,' said Bartholomew. 'Pleased because I think her a fine woman, and displeased because I am afraid of what the other Fellows might say to offend her.'

'They offend her?' gasped Michael. 'She is a

prostitute, Matt! A whore! A courtesan! A harlot! A—'

'All right, all right,' said Bartholomew uncomfortably. 'I understood you the first time. But the invitation has been issued, so I can hardly renege.'

'Is this worth your Fellowship?' asked Michael. 'Your career?'

'On the one hand you tell me to go out and get a woman and on the other you tell me the ones I choose are inappropriate.'

'I recommended a discreet friendship with a respectable lady, not a flagrant dalliance with a prostitute *in the College*! And to top that, you even have a spare waiting on the side in the form of Eleanor Tyler.'

'Two spares, actually,' said Bartholomew. 'I have invited Hedwise Tyler to the Festival of St Michael and All Angels.'

This time he did laugh at the expression on Michael's face. Eventually Michael smiled too.

'It's all or nothing with you, isn't it? You never do things by halves. Perhaps I can have a word with the steward about the seating plan to see if a little confusion can be arranged. The last thing you want is a whore on either side of you. They might fight.'

'Eleanor Tyler is not a whore,' objected Bartholomew.

Michael sighed. 'No, she is not, although she is horribly indiscreet. Half the town knows that you have invited her to the Feast. Lord knows what

189

she will say when she learns the identity of your second guest.'

It was something Bartholomew had not considered before. Michael was right – any respectable woman would baulk at the notion that she formed one of a pair with a prostitute.

Michael finished his repast, and led the way back through the kitchens towards the courtyard, still chuckling under his breath at Bartholomew's predicament.

'Out of my way, you two,' said Agatha sharply. 'I cannot have you under my feet all the time. I have a feast to organise, you know.'

'Yes, we do know,' said Michael. 'We have been invited.'

'And some of you have invited all manner of hussies,' said Agatha, fixing Bartholomew with an angry glare. 'Eleanor Tyler indeed! How could you stoop so low? I had expected better of you!'

So that was it, Bartholomew thought. Agatha disapproved of Eleanor Tyler. He exchanged a furtive glance with Michael and wondered what the robust laundress would find to say when she discovered whom he had asked as his second guest. Still fixing him with a steely glower, Agatha continued.

'That young woman is bragging to half the town about how she wrung an invitation from you to our Feast. She has all the discretion of a rutting stag!'

From Agatha, this was a damning indictment

indeed. Seeing she had made her point, the laundress bustled Bartholomew out of the kitchens and began bellowing orders at the cowering scullions.

'What is wrong with Eleanor Tyler?' asked Bartholomew of Michael, a little resentfully. 'She is attractive, intelligent, witty . . .'

'Yes, yes,' said Michael impatiently. 'It is perfectly clear that you are smitten with the woman. But beware! Do not imagine that you will be allowed to render free services to poor patients if you marry either of the Tyler women. You will only be able to take wealthy clients who will pay you well enough to keep them in the lap of luxury.'

'Oh, really, Brother! I have invited them to a feast, not proposed marriage! Being crushed into a church, and then a hall, with dozens of other people can scarcely be considered romantic, can it!'

Michael pursed his lips primly and did not deign to reply.

While they had been in the orchard, Michael had sent Cynric to the Chancellor's office with a request for a list of all the French students in residence. The book-bearer was waiting with it in Bartholomew's room.

'You were right, Matt,' said Michael, scanning the list. 'There are only fourteen French scholars currently registered at the University. Of these, three are in Maud's, and have alibis in Gray and Deynman; three are in Godwinsson, although we

191

know that one of them is now dead; two are in Michaelhouse – the only students missing from here were Gray and Deynman, so that lets them off the hook; one is in Peterhouse—'

'I know him,' interrupted Bartholomew. 'He cannot walk without the aid of crutches and his health is fragile. He cannot be involved.'

'There is one at Clare Hall,' continued Michael, 'but he is a Benedictine, who is at least seventy and would certainly not be out on the streets in the dark, let alone abduct and rape a young woman. Then there are two at St Stephen's, and two at Valence Marie.'

'So, the only possible suspects are the two at Valence Marie, the two at St Stephen's and the two surviving students at Godwinsson,' said Bartholomew.

Michael regarded him thoughtfully. 'I wonder if there are connections in any of this,' he said. 'We have Godwinsson and David's scholars quarrelling in the street, after which one of them is killed near Valence Marie; the same student of David's is having an affair with the Principal of Godwinsson's daughter, his identity unknown to her parents; French scholars from Godwinsson try to attack Eleanor Tyler, and one of them is killed in the process; and the Principal of Godwinsson wrongfully claims that he has been at Maud's all night. Meanwhile, his wife really did visit Maud's after the riot began; a skeleton is found at Valence Marie; and the dead prostitute is last seen with

French scholars, which must have been those from Valence Marie, Godwinsson or St Stephen's.'

Bartholomew considered. 'There is nothing to suggest this skeleton can be linked with any of the other events.'

'Except that we have agreed that it is a strange coincidence that Kenzie should die so near where the skeleton had been found the day before, and in an identical manner.'

'We agreed no such thing!' said Bartholomew, startled. 'I said there was insufficient evidence to show that they died in the same way, although it is possible that they did.'

Michael flapped a flabby hand dismissively, before standing and stretching his large arms. 'I would like to make two visits this afternoon. I want to ask the Scottish lads at David's more about Kenzie, and then I want to have another word with those unpleasant Godwinsson friars. While we are there, we can drop a few questions about their part in the riot, and about the French louts that tried to kill you. If our inquiries proceed well, I might even ask a few questions of Lydgate himself – if he really was up to no good while the riot was in full swing, I doubt he has the brains to cover his tracks sufficiently to fool someone of my high intellectual calibre.'

'And on the way, we can stop off at St Stephen's and Valence Marie and see about these Frenchman, thus making the best possible use of the brilliant skills at detection you have just claimed,' said Bartholomew with a smile, ignoring Michael's irritable sigh.

The nearest hostel was St Stephen's, where the Principal told them, with some ire, that he had received a letter from France informing him that the two students he had been expecting would not be coming because of a death in the family. His anger seemed to result chiefly from the fact that bad weather had delayed the letter by more than a week, and he would have problems in finding students to fill their places now that most scholars were already settled in lodgings. There was no reason to doubt the authenticity of the letter, so Bartholomew's list of suspects was narrowed to those French students registered at Godwinsson Hostel and those at the Hall of Valence Marie.

The next visit was to David's, where the young Scots told Bartholomew and Michael that Kenzie had been becoming increasingly agitated about his affair because Lydgate was so intent on preventing it. Kenzie and Dominica had been forced to invent more and more ingenious plans to see each other, and they had begun to run out of ideas – much as Eleanor and Hedwise Tyler had suggested the night of the riot.

When Michael asked for more information about the missing ring, the students were unable to add anything, other than that they all believed Dominica had given it to Kenzie. It had been silver, they said, with a small blue-green stone.

Ruthven, clearly embarrassed, revealed reluctantly that Kenzie had often waxed lyrical about Dominica's blue-green eyes, while playing with the ring on his finger.

As they made their way from David's to Godwinsson, Michael turned to Bartholomew.

'The last time we visited Godwinsson, Lydgate threatened you,' he said. 'I think you should wait outside.' He raised a hand to quell Bartholomew's objections. 'Lydgate does not like you, and nothing will be gained from antagonising him with your presence in his own home. Wait outside: listen at the window if you would, but stay out of sight. I will ask about the Frenchmen for you.'

Despite his misgivings, Bartholomew knew Michael was right, and as the fat monk knocked loudly on Godwinsson's front door, he slipped down a filthy alleyway by the side of the house and into the yard at the back. He glanced up and saw that, as last time, the window shutters in the solar where Lydgate had received them were flung open. The glazed windows also stood ajar to allow a breeze to circulate inside.

A sound from what he presumed to be the kitchen startled him, and he realised he was being foolish in prowling so openly around Godwinsson's back yard. There was a decrepit lean-to shed against the back of the house, a tatty structure that would not survive another winter. Its door was loose on decaying leather hinges and the roof sagged precariously. Heart pounding, Bartholomew slipped inside just as someone emerged from a rear door to pour slops into a brimming cesspool in a far corner of the yard.

The shed was stiflingly hot, and full of pieces of discarded wood and rope. Bartholomew picked his way across it until he was on the side nearest the solar. The warped wood created wide gaps in the walls that allowed him to see out, and, as long as Michael and Lydgate did not whisper, Bartholomew thought he should be able to hear much of what was happening in the solar without being seen.

He heard Huw, the Godwinsson steward, show Michael into the room as before and saw the monk lean out of the window to look into the yard as he waited for Lydgate. Bartholomew was about to signal to him when the kitchen scullion came out with another bowl of slops. Alarmed, Bartholomew jerked backwards, realising too late that sudden motion was more likely to give away his hiding place than his raised arm, half-hidden in shadows.

'You will find nothing of interest there, Brother,' came Lydgate's voice, clear as a bell, moments later. Bartholomew saw Michael's head withdraw and the scullion glance up at the window, distracted momentarily from his task. 'Unless you like cesspools.'

'Which brings me to your hostel, Master Lydgate,' came Michael's unruffled reply. 'I would like to see two of your students: the two French lads.'

'Why?' asked Lydgate. 'They have not been brawling with the Scots.'

The scullion in the yard gave his bowl a final scrape and returned to the kitchen.

'How do you know?' said Michael. 'Reliable witnesses saw them brawling with one member of the University and four defenceless women.'

Despite his tension, Bartholomew smiled at Michael's description: defenceless was certainly not a word that could truthfully be applied to the resourceful, independent Tyler women.

'How can you be sure of that?' snapped Lydgate. 'The night was dark and it was difficult to be certain who was who in the darkness with all those fires burning.'

'So you were out, too,' said Michael. It was a statement and not a question. Bartholomew could almost see Lydgate spluttering with indignation at having been so deftly fooled into admitting as much.

'My whereabouts are none of your concern!' Lydgate managed to grate finally. 'But for your information, I have people who can say where I was, whose word is beyond doubt.'

'But not in Godwinsson, Master Lydgate? To protect your family and students?' Michael continued smoothly.

'I was out!' Lydgate almost shouted.

'As were your students without you here to control them, it seems.'

Bartholomew heard the creak of floorboards and

guessed that Lydgate was pacing to try to control his temper. 'All Godwinsson students were here. The other masters will testify to that.'

'I am sure they will,' said Michael, his tone ambiguous. 'Now, I would like to speak with these French students.'

As he spoke, the kitchen door opened again, and two students were ushered out by Huw the steward and the scullion. Speaking in low voices, and taking care to stay close to the walls where they would not be observed from the solar window, the students made for the alleyway that led to the road. Bartholomew pressed back into the shadows as they passed, although they were so intent on leaving that they did not so much as glance at the open shed door. Bartholomew was not surprised to hear them speaking French.

He watched them disappear up the alley before opening the door to follow. As the sunlight flooded into the gloomy lean-to, something glinted on the ground. Bending quickly to retrieve it, Bartholomew found a small, silver ring. Although there was no blue-green stone, there were clasps to show where such a gem might once have been. The ring was dirty, and its irregular shape indicated that it had been crushed, perhaps by someone stamping on it. He looked around quickly to see if he could see the stone, but there was no sign of it on the hard, trampled earth that formed the floor.

Slipping the ring into his pocket, Bartholomew

left the shed and made his way quickly up the alley. As he emerged, he glimpsed the two students disappearing round the corner into the High Street. He ran after them, oblivious to the startled face of Huw the steward, who had come to the front of the hostel to watch their escape. Huw's surprise changed to artifice, and he rubbed at his whiskers, eyes glittering.

Bartholomew followed the two Frenchmen along the High Street towards the Market Square. It was more drab than usual: the colourful canopies that usually shielded the traders' wares from sun or rain had been burned during the riot. Here and there, skeletal frameworks had been hastily erected to replace those that had been lost, a few of them crudely covered with rough canvas, but for the most part, the traders were reduced to piling their goods on the ground. Ash and cinders had been trampled into the beaten earth, and, to one side of the Square, a great mound of partially incinerated wood still loomed up where it had been piled the day before, waiting for someone to remove it and dump it all in the river.

It was nearing the end of the day, and, with the curfew fast approaching, the tradesmen's battle to sell the last of their wares was becoming frantic. Stories about how Cambridge had erupted in a welter of flame and violence had spread through the surrounding countryside, and many rural folk had elected not to risk coming to the town to buy supplies. Trade was poor so that potential customers were not permitted to escape easily; hands grabbed and pulled at Bartholomew as he tried to pass. Suddenly he could not see his quarry. Impatiently shrugging off a persistent baker, he dived down one narrow line of stalls, emerging at the opposite end of the Square. There was no sign of the French students. Bartholomew sagged in defeat, sweat stinging his eyes from the late-afternoon heat.

Suddenly, he spotted them again, surfacing from a parallel line of stalls eating apples. They walked at a nonchalant pace towards Hadstock Way. Bartholomew followed them a little further, although he now knew exactly where they were going. Without knocking, and with an ease born of a long familiarity, the two students casually strolled into Maud's Hostel.

There was nothing more Bartholomew could do without Michael's authority as Proctor, so he retraced his steps back to Godwinsson. He stopped to buy something to drink from a water-seller, but the larvae of some marsh insects wriggling about in the buckets gave him second thoughts. He remembered the foul wine he had shared with Michael and Tulyet, and went into the booth of a wine-merchant to buy a replacement. He purchased the first one that caught his eye, opened it, and took a large mouthful in the street.

'Not the best way to enjoy good wine,' came Michael's voice at his shoulder. 'But then again, judging from the wine you keep, what would you know of such things? Where have you been?'

He took the bottle from Bartholomew and took a hearty swig himself, nodding appreciatively at its coolness, if not its flavour.

Bartholomew told him what had happened, while Michael listened with narrowed eyes.

'Lydgate told me that the French students were at church,' he said. 'I thought it was a likely story. I learned little, I am afraid. Brothers Edred and Werbergh are taking part in a theological debate at the School of Pythagorus, and so were not available to talk to me. Since Lydgate knows I can check that excuse easily, he is probably telling the truth about that, at least. I will have to come back and speak to them later.'

Valence Marie was nearby, so they went there next, although Michael was reluctant. There was no porter on the door, no one answered their knocking, and they were forced to go inside to find someone to answer their questions. But the College appeared to be deserted. Putting his head round the door to the hall, the thought crossed Bartholomew's mind that, had he been a thief, he could have made off with all the College silver, which lay carelessly abandoned on the high table.

He shouted, but there was no reply. They left the hall and went to the Ditch at the side of Valence Marie where the skeleton had been found, but there was no one there either. Bartholomew flapped irritably at the haze of flies that buzzed around his head, disturbed from where they had been feasting on the foul-smelling muck that lined both sides of the near-empty canal. At the very bottom of the Ditch was a murky trickle that would turn into a raging torrent when the next heavy rains came. With a sigh of resignation, Bartholomew saw some unidentifiable piece of offal move gently downstream. Despite the cost and inconvenience of the dredging operations, people were still disposing of their waste in the waterways. They had learned nothing from the last time the Ditch had been blocked with rubbish and then flooded, causing some to lose their homes.

'We will have to return tomorrow,' said Michael, breaking into a trot in a vain attempt to escape the haze of flies that flicked around his head. 'The place is abandoned.'

The King's Ditch ran under the High Street and emerged the other side. Bartholomew always felt that, despite the distinct elevation in the road, the High Street did not have a bridge as much as the King's Ditch had a tunnel: its fetid, black waters slid through a small, dark hole, and oozed out into a pool on the other side. He crossed to the opposite side of the High Street, and stood on tiptoe to look over the wall that screened the western arm of the Ditch from the road. Here was a different story: the bank was alive with activity, but it was all conducted in total silence.

A dozen or so students stood in a line looking

down into the Ditch, the monotony of their black tabards broken by the occasional grey or white of a friar's habit. A gaggle of scruffy children had also gathered to watch the proceedings; even their customary cheekiness had been subdued by the distinct aura of gravity that pervaded the scene.

'What are they doing?' Bartholomew whispered to Michael.

They edged closer, and saw Will and Henry, the Valence Marie servants, poking about in the vile trickle of water, watched intently by Thorpe, who stood with his Fellows clustered about him. Thorpe looked up and saw Bartholomew and Michael.

'Ah!' he announced, his voice almost sacrilegious in the self-imposed silence of the scholars. 'Here are the Senior Proctor and the physician. I am impressed with your speed, gentlemen. It has only been moments since I dispatched a messenger to the Chancellor's office to ask you to come.'

'Oh Lord, Michael!' exclaimed Bartholomew under his breath. 'Thorpe has found himself some more bones!'

Reluctantly, he moved towards Thorpe and his findings. The only sounds were Michael's noisy breathing behind him and the muffled rumble of carts from the High Street. As he walked, the students moved aside so he could pass, their faces taut with anticipation.

He met Thorpe's eyes for a moment, then looked down into the Ditch to where Will and Henry crouched in the muddy water. A distant part of Bartholomew's mind noted that the piece of offal he had observed shortly before had made its way downstream, and was now bobbing past Will's legs. It served to dissolve the feeling that he was attending some kind of religious ceremony, attended by acolytes who generated an aura of hushed veneration. He wondered how Thorpe had managed to effect such an atmosphere, disliking the way he felt he was being manipulated into complying with it. He saw that the mood of the onlookers was such that, even if they had discovered a donkey in the black, fly-infested mud, they would revere it like the relics of some venerable saint.

'What have you found this time, Master Thorpe?' he asked, his voice deliberately loud and practical.

Thorpe favoured him with a cold stare, and answered in subdued tones that had the scholars furthest away moving closer to hear him.

'We have discovered a relic of the saintly Simon d'Ambrey,' he said, clasping his hands in front of him like a monk in prayer. 'There can be no doubt about it this time, Doctor.'

He met Bartholomew's gaze evenly. Without breaking eye contact, he gestured to the Ditch, so that Bartholomew was the first to look away. Something lay on the cracking mud, carefully wrapped in a tabard to prevent the swarming flies from alighting on it. Bartholomew, aware that he was being watched minutely, clambered down the bank to examine it, while Michael, curiously silent, followed.

Bartholomew picked up the tabard and gave it a slight shake, causing what was wrapped inside it to drop out. There was a shocked gasp from the watching scholars at this rough treatment of what they already believed was sacred. Michael bent next to him as he knelt, and hissed furiously in his ear.

'Be careful, Matt! I do not feel comfortable here. These scholars are taking this nonsense very seriously. I imagine it would take very little for them to take on the role of avenging angels for any perceived insult to their relic. I do not wish to be torn limb from limb over a soup bone.'

Bartholomew glanced up at him. 'This is no soup bone, Brother.' He looked back at the mud-encrusted object that had tumbled from the tabard. 'This is the hand of a man, complete with a ring on his little finger.'

CHAPTER 5

Michael pretended to look closer at the grisly object that lay on the bank so he could whisper to Bartholomew without being overheard.

'Hell's teeth, Matt! We have been desperate to avoid a situation like this! Now there will be gatherings of people to see the thing, and fights between town and gown will be inevitable. Are you sure this hand belongs to a man? Can you not say it is that of a woman?'

Bartholomew shook his head. 'It is far too big. You are stuck with this, I am afraid. These are the bones from a man's hand without question, and any other physician will tell you the same. Unfortunately, the thing even *looks* like a relic with that ring on its finger. What do you want me to do?'

Michael sat back on his heels, and watched Bartholomew wipe away some of the mud from the sinister hand. 'Take it to St Mary's Church,' he said. 'The Chancellor will be able to control access to it more easily there, and the beadles will be able to break up any gathering crowds.'

Bartholomew re-wrapped the hand in the tabard

and called out to the servant, Will, who was still grubbing about in the ooze of the Ditch.

'Have you found anything else?'

Will shook his head. 'We shall continue to look, though, sir. The rest of the skeleton must be here somewhere since we have the hand.'

Bartholomew exchanged a brief glance of concern with Michael. Above them, the scholars muttered approval. Clutching the precious relic, Bartholomew began to climb back up the bank, followed by a puffing Michael.

'With your permission, Master Thorpe,' Bartholomew began, 'I will take this to St Mary's Church where I can examine it more closely . . .'

'You most certainly do not have my permission,' said Thorpe brusquely. He reached out his hand for the bones. 'It was found by Valence Marie scholars, and it will stay on Valence Marie land.'

Michael intervened smoothly. 'It will be treated with all reverence at St Mary's,' he said. 'If this really is a sacred relic, then it should be in the most important church of the University for all to see. The Chancellor will want to verify it himself. And doubtless the Bishop of Ely will want to see it, too.'

'It does not belong to the University or your Bishop, Brother,' said Thorpe with quiet dignity. 'It belongs to Valence Marie. We found it, and with us it will stay.' He looked around him, appealing to the watching scholars. Michael's fears had been justified and Bartholomew could detect that the atmosphere had undergone a rapid transition from reverent to menacing. Thorpe was a shrewd manipulator of crowd emotions.

Michael stepped forward as Thorpe tried to grab the bones from Bartholomew. 'It would be prudent to allow Doctor Bartholomew to examine them more closely, Master Thorpe, so that he can attest that they are genuine.'

'I need no such examination to convince me of the relic's authenticity,' said Thorpe, pulling himself up to his full height, and looking down his long nose at the monk. 'If you wish to satisfy your heathen curiosity, Brother, you may do so. But you will do so here, at the Hall of Valence Marie.'

Michael began to speak, but stopped as one or two scholars stepped forward threateningly. Bartholomew thought he heard the sound of someone drawing a dagger from its leather sheath, but could not be certain. The situation had become ugly: the scholars were convinced that Valence Marie now possessed a valuable relic and were prepared to go to extreme lengths to keep it. Bartholomew could already see the glitter of anticipated violence in the eyes of some students, their demeanour making it clear that if Bartholomew and Michael wished to leave the Ditch at all, it would not be with the bones.

Thorpe leaned forward and took the relic from Bartholomew's unresisting hands. He held the parcel in the air, and turned towards his scholars.

'The bones of a martyr have been entrusted to

us,' he announced in a strong, confident voice. There was a growl of approval. 'There will be many who will want to come to see them, and we must allow them to do so. But we have a sacred trust to ensure that they will always rest at Valence Marie!'

There was a ragged cheer. Some of the scholars began to follow Thorpe as he led the way back along the bank of the Ditch to his college. Others remained with Bartholomew and Michael, and formed a tight escort that almost immediately began to jostle and shove them.

Michael spoke rapidly in Latin to Bartholomew, trusting that his low voice and the speed of his words would render him incomprehensible to the students surrounding them. One or two moved closer to try to hear what he was saying, but most ignored him, their attention fixed on the silvery head of Thorpe leading his procession, and carrying his precious bones.

'We are in a fix, Matt. Examine the wretched thing, but say nothing of what you find. It seems Thorpe has already convinced them that they have the hand of a martyr – whether it is true or not.'

Bartholomew staggered as a hefty student crashed into him, almost knocking him over. With difficulty, he refrained from pushing him back, but almost fell again as someone gave him a hard shove from behind. He felt Michael's warning hand on his shoulder, and did nothing.

They reached Valence Marie, where Thorpe laid his bundle gently on the high table and unwrapped it. He called for water, and began to clean away the remaining mud. Underneath the filth, the bones gleamed yellow-white, and the ring on the little finger glittered in the golden rays of the early evening sun that lanced through the open windows. When Thorpe held up the relic for the scholars to see, there were murmurs of awe; one student even dropped to his knees, crossing himself.

Michael stepped forward, but Bartholomew's arms were seized before he could follow. Michael glanced round at the sounds of the ensuing scuffle.

'Might we examine the hand now that it is clean, Master Thorpe?' he asked politely. 'Then we will tell the Chancellor of your discovery.'

'There is no need for a medical examination,' said Thorpe, eyeing Bartholomew disdainfully. 'It is perfectly apparent what we have here.'

'But you said that any who wished to see it should be allowed to do so,' Michael pointed out. 'Does that courtesy not apply to Fellows of Michaelhouse?'

Thorpe was silent for a moment as he considered. He was aware that if he refused to allow the Chancellor's representatives to examine the bones, rumours doubting their authenticity would surely follow. But he was also aware that a negative verdict by the University's senior physician could be equally damning, as it had proved to be with the bones of the child. He rose to the occasion.

'You may examine the hand, as Fellows of

Michaelhouse,' he said magisterially. 'But we will permit no unseemly treatment of it. No touching.'

Bartholomew was released reluctantly, stumbling as he tripped over a strategically placed foot. He heard one or two muffled snorts of laughter coming from the students.

'I see Michaelhouse has little to learn from the manners of the scholars of Valence Marie,' he remarked coolly to Thorpe, ignoring the way the Master's mouth tightened into a hard line. Out of the corner of his eye, he saw Thorpe glare a warning at the offending students, whose sniggering ceased instantly.

The now-cleaned bones lay on the muddy tabard. Bartholomew leaned forward to move them slightly but was not in the least surprised to feel Thorpe's restraining grip on his wrist. He was aware of the scholars edging towards him, mutters of anger and resentment rippling through their ranks.

'You are invited to look, but I said you are not to touch,' Thorpe said firmly.

Bartholomew pulled his arm away, peering closely at the hand. Although the bones appeared bright and clean, they were still joined together, mostly by brownish sinews. Thus they were not merely a disconnected collection of small bones, but a complete skeletal hand. He moved into a different position and inspected the ring. Finally, he straightened. Michael prepared to leave, but Thorpe blocked their way.

'Well?' he asked, his eyes flicking from one to the other.

Bartholomew shrugged. 'It is the hand of a large man,' he said simply.

'It is the hand of a martyr,' said Thorpe loudly, so that the hall rang with his words. 'Why else would it be wearing a ring so fine?'

Why indeed? wondered Bartholomew and followed Michael out of Valence Marie, into the fading rays of the evening sun. He took a deep breath and began to walk quickly back along the High Street towards Michaelhouse, suddenly longing to be safe inside its sturdy walls. For once, Michael did not complain about the rapid pace, obviously as eager to put as much distance between himself and Valence Marie as Bartholomew.

After a few moments, when Michael was satisfied that they were not being followed by a crowd of resentful, antagonistic Valence Marie scholars, he repeated Thorpe's question. 'Well?'

Bartholomew slowed his pace fractionally and looked at Michael. 'You saw I was prevented from conducting a proper investigation but I can tell you two things. First, however much those Valence Marie servants root around in the mud, I will wager anything you please that no more of the skeleton will ever be found; and second, the hand does not belong to the martyred Simon d'Ambrey, unless he was considerably bigger than I recall and he died fairly recently.'

Michael stopped dead, but then glanced uneasily

behind him and began walking again. They had reached St Mary's Church, near which the Chancellor had his offices. Michael took Bartholomew's arm and dragged him into the wooden building where Richard de Wetherset sat poring over documents in the fading daylight. He was a solid man, whose physical strength had largely turned to fat from a lifetime of sitting in offices. He had iron-grey hair and a hard, uncompromising will. Although Bartholomew appreciated de Wetherset's motives were usually selfless, and that he put the good of the University above all else, Bartholomew did not like the Chancellor, and certainly did not trust him. The Junior Proctor was with him, sitting on a stool and signing some writs, shivering in the pleasant breeze that wafted in from the window and snuffling miserably.

De Wetherset scowled as Bartholomew and Michael entered, none too pleased that he was being interrupted while there was still daylight enough to be able to read the last accounts of the day's business transactions. As Michael told him what had happened, the Chancellor flushed red with anger, his documents forgotten.

'This is the worst possible thing that could have happened,' he said, his voice low with barely restrained anger. 'What does that fool Thorpe imagine he is doing? He is putting the fame and wealth of his college above the peaceful relations of the University with the town. There will be a riot for certain when this gets out: the town will demand this wretched hand for itself, and Valence Marie will refuse.'

He sat back in his chair, the muscles in his jaws bulging from his grinding teeth as he considered the University's position.

Heppel watched him anxiously. 'We must prevent another riot at all costs.'

'You are right. We must inform the Sheriff immediately lest the townspeople start to gather outside Valence Marie.'

De Wetherset stood abruptly and sent a clerk to fetch one of the Sheriff's deputies. He sat again, indicating that Bartholomew and Michael should take a seat on one of the benches that ran along the wall opposite the window. 'Did you examine this confounded relic?' he asked.

'Not as completely as I would have wished, but enough to tell me that the "confounded relic" no more belongs to a man twenty-five years dead in the King's Ditch than does my own,' Bartholomew replied. The Chancellor, not in the least surprised, gestured for him to continue.

'The hand was severed from the arm. There are cut marks on the wrist bones where the knife grazed them. And, think of the skeleton of the child, also in the Ditch for some years. It was stained dark brown by the mud. The bones on the Valence Marie hand are almost white, and I think it doubtful that they have been in the Ditch for any length of time. And finally, some care was taken to leave the sinews in place so that the collection of bones would be identifiable as a hand. Except for the little finger. There, the sinews must have broken or come loose, because the finger is held in place by a tiny metal pin almost hidden by the ring.'

'A pin?' exclaimed Heppel in astonishment. 'Are you suggesting, therefore, that someone planted this hand for Thorpe to find?'

Bartholomew ran his hand through his hair. 'It is possible, I suppose. It is equally possible that he planted it himself. But all I can tell you for certain is that the hand was taken from a man – a man larger than any of us, and whether alive or already dead I cannot say – and boiled to remove the flesh. When one of the fingers came loose, it was repaired expertly with a pin.'

Michael looked at him in concern. 'Another murder victim? Or someone desecrating the dead? How do you know that the bones were boiled?'

'Come now, Michael,' said Bartholomew. 'You have gnawed on enough roasted joints to know the answer to that. The bones of the relic are whitish-yellow, a colour they are unlikely to keep when embedded in the black mud of the King's Ditch, and they have a freshness about them that suggests careful preparation. You must have noticed how easily the mud washed off when it was cleaned. Moreover, think about the choice of relic: a hand is manageable, and easily prepared – ring and all. It is not so repellent as, say, a skull but more inspiring than a thigh-bone or a rib. I am willing to wager anything you please that no other parts will be found until there is a market for them.'

'And these bones belonged to a man larger than us?' asked de Wetherset, frowning. 'None of us is exactly petite!' He glanced at Heppel, swathed in a thick cloak against nasty draughts, and wiping his long, thin nose with a pale, white hand. 'Well, some of us are not.'

Bartholomew held up his own hands. 'The fingers were at least an inch longer than mine and the bones were dense and thick. I suspect a large hand was deliberately chosen to make it impossible for us to dismiss it as that of a woman.'

'Is it possible that Master Thorpe did all this?' wondered Heppel in revulsion. 'Selected a large corpse, stole its hand and boiled it up?'

Michael scratched his chin thoughtfully. 'He was desperate to find a relic in the Ditch and was most disappointed when Matt kept pronouncing that his finds were animal bones. Valence Marie is a new college and will benefit greatly from having a venerated relic on its premises, especially after the expense of dredging the Ditch in the first place.'

'Or perhaps someone is using Thorpe's desperation to play a cruel trick on him,' mused de Wetherset. 'It would not be the first time one scholar made a fool of another.'

'Or a townsman made a fool of the University,' pointed out Bartholomew.

De Wetherset glared at him for a moment, but then

accepted his comment with a resigned nod. 'The real question is what are we to do?'

'Go to see Thorpe yourself, ask to see the hand and then point out the bright, new pin,' said Bartholomew promptly. 'He can hardly refuse to allow you to examine his relic, can he?'

De Wetherset agreed reluctantly and rose. 'Are you sure about this pin?' he asked. 'I would not wish to be made a fool of either.'

'You will see it,' said Bartholomew, 'especially if you pick the hand up.'

As de Wetherset went to confront Thorpe, accompanied by a nervous Guy Heppel and two beadles, Bartholomew and Michael walked home. It was almost dark, and the curfew was in force. The streets were virtually deserted but, with relief, Bartholomew detected none of the atmosphere of anticipation he had sensed the night before. Doors were firmly closed, and although voices came from some of the houses, most were silent and in darkness. Dawn came early and the summer heat was exhausting for people who worked hard for their meagre livings. The Statute of Labour had been passed the year before, an edict that made it illegal for people to seek better-paid work by leaving their homes. The Statute had decreed that wages should remain at the pre-plague levels, despite the fact that food prices had soared since then. Unrest and bitter resentment festered, although the labourers were far too exhausted from scratching paltry livings from the land to do much about their miserable conditions.

'Thorpe was very masterly at manipulating the emotions of his scholars,' said Michael thoughtfully. 'I wonder if he could apply that talent to incite a mob to riot.'

Bartholomew raised his eyebrows, and nodded. 'There was one other thing neither of us mentioned to de Wetherset,' he said.

Michael nodded as they knocked on Michaelhouse's gates to be allowed in. 'I thought you had noticed,' he said. 'The ring on the relic had a blue-green stone, just like the colour of Dominica's eyes.'

The next day dawned in a golden mist that was soon burned away by the sun. By the main meal at ten o'clock, it was so hot that Bartholomew had to tend to two students who were sick and dizzy from dehydration. As a special dispensation, and, because he had no wish for his scholars to be fainting around him as he ate, the Master announced that it would not be necessary to wear tabards in the College during lectures or meals until the evening. The austere Franciscans pulled sour faces at the slackening of discipline, although Bartholomew found the Master's announcement eminently sensible.

By noon, the heat was so intense that Bartholomew, teaching in the College conclave, found it difficult to concentrate, and was very aware that his students were similarly afflicted. The conclave was a small room at the far end of the hall, and Bartholomew preferred teaching there than in the hall itself, where he had to compete for space with the other Fellows. The conclave, however, was bitterly cold in the winter when the wind howled through gaps in its windows, and unbearably hot in the summer when the sun streamed in. He tried blocking the sunlight by closing the shutters but that made the room unpleasantly stuffy. With the shutters open, the occasional breath of breeze wafted in, but students and master melted in the sunlight.

Gray drowsed near the empty fireplace, Deynman's attention alternated between the insects in the rushes and picking at a hole in his shirt, and even Tom Bulbeck, Bartholomew's best student, appeared uninterested. The topic of the day was Galen's theories about how different pulse rates related to the heavenly spheres – a subject that even Bartholomew found complex and overly intricate. Finally, he gave up, and, pulling uncomfortably at his sweat-soaked shirt, allowed the students their liberty for the rest of the day, accompanied with strict rejoinders about obeying the curfew.

Bulbeck hovered as the others left. Bartholomew smiled at him encouragingly.

'Even the great physician Bernard Gordon, who taught at Montpellier, found it difficult to distinguish between subtle variations of pulse beats,' he said, assuming Bulbeck was concerned that he was taking too long to grasp the essence of Galen's hypothesis.

Bulbeck gnawed at his lower lip. 'It is not that,' he said. He hesitated, aware that Gray and Deynman were waiting for him near the door. He made up his mind. 'It is this notion of heavenly bodies. I know you are sceptical of the role played by the stars in a patient's sickness – and the little I have seen of medical practice inclines me to believe you are right. So why must we waste time with such nonsense? Why do you not teach us more about uroscopy or surgery.'

'Because if you want to pass your disputations and graduate as a physician, you will need to show that you can calculate the astrological charts that can be used to determine a course of treatment. What I believe about the worth of such calculations is irrelevant.'

'The medical faculty at Paris told King Philip the Sixth of France that the Death was caused by a malign conjunction of Saturn and Jupiter,' said Gray brightly from the doorway.

'I know,' said Bartholomew. 'And this malign conjunction was said to have occurred at precisely one o'clock on the afternoon of 20 March 1345. The physicians at the medical school of Montpellier wrote *Tractatus de Epidemia*, in which they explained that the reason some areas were worse affected than others was because they were more exposed to evil rays caused when "Saturn looked upon Jupiter with a malignant aspect".'

'But you do not believe that,' pressed Bulbeck. 'You think there is some other explanation.'

Bartholomew thought for a moment, uncertain how much to tell his students of his growing dissatisfaction with traditional medicine. He had been accused of heresy more times than he could remember for his unorthodox thinking, and was ever alert to the possibility that too great an accumulation of such charges might result in his dismissal from the University. In the past, he had not much cared what his colleagues thought about his teaching, assuming that the better success rate he had with his patients would speak for itself. But he had moderated his incautious attitude when he realised that his excellent medical record would be attributed to witchcraft if he were not careful, and then his hard work and painstakingly acquired skills would count for nothing.

'No, I do not believe that heavenly bodies were entirely responsible for the plague,' he said eventually. 'And I do not think that consulting a patient's stars will make much difference to the outcome of his sickness. I have found that my patients live or die regardless of whether I consult their stars to treat them or not.'

'Father Philius at Gonville Hall believes astrology is the most powerful tool that physicians have,' said Gray, leaning nonchalantly on the door frame. 'He says treatment without astrological consultation is like treating a patient without seeing him at all.'

'I am well aware of Philius's views,' said Bartholomew irritably. 'I have debated them with him often enough. But Philius will be at your disputations, Tom, and if you cannot convince him that you know your astrology, you will not pass, even if you are the best physician the world has known since Hippocrates.'

Bulbeck looked despondent, and Bartholomew recalled how he had felt when his Arab master in Paris had insisted that he learned astrology, even though he had not believed in its efficacy. So Bartholomew had learned his traditional medicine, and answered questions about poorly aligned constellations in his disputations. But he had also learned Ibn Ibrahim's unorthodox theories on hygiene and contagion, and so his patients had the benefit of both worlds.

Despite his scepticism, he was aware that the patient's mental state played an important role in his recovery. On occasion, Bartholomew's treatments had failed because a person had genuinely believed he could not be cured as long as Bartholomew had failed to consult the planets. Guy Heppel, the Junior Proctor, would probably prove to be one of them; the physician knew that he would have to relent in the end, and at least make a pretence of studying the man's astrology if he ever wanted to pronounce him well. He said as much to Bulbeck, who looked more glum than ever.

The student trailed out of the conclave and followed his friends through the hall. By the time he had reached the yard, however, Bartholomew saw he had already thrown off his gloom and was arguing loudly with Gray about how much a physician could justifiably charge for an extensive astrological consultation. Bartholomew realised that if he let Gray loose on Heppel's stars as he had planned, he would have to ensure the Junior Proctor was not charged a month's wages for the dubious privilege.

Bartholomew wandered back to his own room, which was not much cooler than the conclave. He spent most winter nights trying to invent new ways of keeping warm and now it seemed as though he would also have to invent means to stay cool in the summer.

He sat at the table and sharpened a quill to begin working on his treatise on fevers, but no sooner had he written a few words than his eyelids grew heavy and he began to doze. He was awoken when Davy Grahame arrived to deliver the book by Galen that the Principal of David's had promised to lend him. Bartholomew was to keep it for as long as he wanted, said Davy, and then enquired with ill-concealed envy about the fine collection of philosophy and theology texts at Michaelhouse. Bartholomew showed him where the books were chained to the wall in the hall, and left him happily browsing through them.

Bartholomew returned to his room, then pushed open the shutters to allow what little breeze there was to circulate. Abandoning his treatise, he sat again at the small table and opened the Galen.

He smiled when he saw it was not the *Prognostica*, as Master Radbeche had thought, but the *Tegni*. He wondered whether anyone from David's had ever bothered to look at the book at all. But Bartholomew did not mind Radbeche's mistake. It was a luxury to have a book to read in the comfort of his own room, as opposed to begging an uncomfortable corner in another college, or listening to someone else reading aloud.

Unfortunately, David's Hostel's cherished tome was not a good copy of the *Tegni*, and the scribe's writing was difficult to decipher. But, a book was a book, and far too valuable a commodity to be judged harshly. Bartholomew began to read, slowly at first as he struggled with the ill-formed letters and frequent errors, but then faster as he became familiar with the clerk's idiosyncratic style, delighting in the richness of the language and the purity of Galen's logic.

Absorbed in his book, Bartholomew did not know Michael was behind him until a heavy hand dropped on his shoulder. He leapt from his chair, then slumped back again, clutching his chest and glaring at the chuckling Michael.

'Most sensible masters have decided no learning can be achieved in such heat,' said Michael, hurling himself on to Bartholomew's bed, which protested with groans from its wooden legs. 'I sent my lot away before noon. They are supposed to be thinking about the doctrine of *creatio ex nihilo*, although I doubt that much creation theology is running through their minds at this precise moment.'

'Mine are supposed to be learning about stomach disorders caused by dangerous alignments of the stars,' said Bartholomew, standing and stretching. 'Although I would rather tell them not to waste their time, and advise people not to drink from the river instead. It would save their prospective patients a good deal of suffering, and, in many cases, effect a quick cure.'

'You are mistaken, Matt,' said Michael. 'You may be happy to treat those who live in the hovels along the river banks, but your students will want to treat the rich, whose lips would never deign to touch river water. Keep your heretic thoughts to yourself and let the fledgling physicians learn about the astrology of the wealthy who will expect more of them than advice about water.'

Bartholomew opened his mouth to argue, but he knew that Michael was right. He fetched the wine he had bought the day before and poured some for Michael, who drank it quickly and held out his cup for more.

'Have you seen de Wetherset since last night?' Bartholomew asked, settling back on his chair and sipping distastefully at the warm wine.

Michael nodded, pouring himself a third cup. 'Apparently Thorpe has this damn hand in a glass case, all wrapped round with satin. De Wetherset thinks the box is so elaborate that it must have been made in advance, which suggests to me that Thorpe is in the process of perpetrating some massive fraud, not to mention the question of where the hand came from in the first place. De Wetherset pointed out the pin, but Thorpe maintains it must have become lodged there at some point during its twenty-five year sojourn in the river. He even intimated that the pin was put there by divine intervention, to prevent the sacred bones from falling apart!'

He gave a snort of laughter, and looked to see if there was more wine in the bottle. 'De Wetherset could do nothing to convince Thorpe the thing was a fake and it is too late now in any case. The rumours are abroad that a saintly relic is in Valence Marie, and they are amassing a veritable fortune by charging an entrance fee to see it.'

'It will all die down,' said Bartholomew. 'Give it time.'

'We do not have time,' snapped Michael suddenly. 'Thorpe is a fool to make Valence Marie such a centre of attention with the town so uneasy. It will be an obvious target if there is another riot. And the damn thing is a fake! I would be charitable and suggest it got into the Ditch by chance if it were not for the ring and the pin.'

'The ring,' mused Bartholomew. He felt around in his pocket, and pulled out the broken one he had found at Godwinsson. 'Is this Kenzie's ring, do you think? Did he lose it when he was skulking around Godwinsson waiting for Dominica to

226

appear? Or is Kenzie's ring now adorning the severed hand in Valence Marie?'

Michael swilled the dregs of the wine around in the bottom of his cup before draining it in a gulp. 'We could ask the Scottish lads to have a look at the one at Valence Marie,' he said. 'They might recognise it.'

'Would that be wise? Can we trust them not to start some rumour that Kenzie's severed limb is in Valence Marie? Then we might really have a problem on our hands. So to speak.'

'They might have a point,' said Michael.

Bartholomew shook his head firmly. 'Impossible. First, Kenzie's hands were not big enough to be the one at Valence Marie – believe me, I would have noticed if someone of Kenzie's height had hands the size of that skeleton's: it would have looked bizarre to say the least. Second, Kenzie was not wearing his ring when he was killed – he was asking Werbergh and Edred if they had it before he died.'

'Perhaps he found it after he had his conversation with Werbergh and Edred, and *was* wearing it when he was murdered,' said Michael with a shrug.

'I suppose he might,' said Bartholomew after a moment, 'although there is the ring I found in Godwinsson. That might have been the one Kenzie lost.'

Michael made an impatient click with his tongue. 'The ring you found is probably nothing to do with all this. It might have been in that derelict shed for weeks – even months – before you picked it up. There could be all sorts of explanations as to why it was there – not least of which was that it was thrown away precisely because it is broken. When I looked out of the window, I saw a scullion emptying waste there. The whole yard is probably a repository for rubbish.'

'It certainly smelled that way,' said Bartholomew, grimacing. 'But regardless of whether Kenzie did or did not have his ring when he died, the hand at Valence Marie does not belong to him. I will stake my reputation on it.'

'Well now,' said Michael, regarding his friend with an amused gleam in his eye. 'It is not often you are so absolutely unshakeable over the deductions you make from corpses. You usually insist on a degree of leeway in your interpretations. So, I suppose I will have to believe you. But I am not the issue here – the David's students are. And we have a problem: the David's lads are the only ones who might recognise the ring as Kenzie's, and yet we cannot risk them identifying it as his, because a riot would follow for certain.'

'Dominica would recognise it if, as Kenzie's friends suppose, it was a gift from her,' said Bartholomew.

Michael wrinkled his nose disdainfully at the notion. 'And how would we get the permission of her parents to let her come?' he said.

The sun went behind a cloud briefly, cooling the room for an instant, before emerging again and beating down relentlessly on the dried beaten earth of the courtyard.

Bartholomew leaned forward and thought. 'Let us assume she did give Kenzie the ring,' he said. 'Where would she have got it from? I doubt she had the money to go out and buy it herself. Therefore, she must have owned it already – it had probably been given to her by her parents. I am certain that Lydgate and his wife know exactly what jewellery their daughter owns, especially valuable pieces. If Lydgate or Cecily go to see this hand, they might recognise the ring.'

'That is even more outrageous,' said Michael. 'You are even less likely to get Lydgate to view this hand than his daughter. He would refuse outright if we asked. Sensible Cecily, meanwhile, has not yet returned to her husband, and if she has any intelligence at all, she never will. And not only that, neither of them knows that Kenzie was their daughter's lover, remember?'

Bartholomew was thoughtful for a moment. 'Your last point is irrelevant – it does not matter whether they know the identity of Dominica's lover or not for them to be able to identify the ring.'

'*Your* point is irrelevant,' Michael flashed back. 'Even if Lydgate can identify the ring as Dominica's, he would not tell us about it. And, as I said, sweet Cecily is still away. Lydgate has not exactly been scouring the countryside for his loving spouse; I have the feeling that he is as relieved to be apart from her as she, doubtless, is happy to be away from him.'

'I cannot make any sense out of all this, but one thing is patently clear.' Bartholomew fiddled with the laces on his shirt. 'If the ring on Valence Marie's relic really is the one that Kenzie lost – and I do not believe he miraculously found it after speaking with the Godwinsson friars only to die without it a few hours later – then the link between Kenzie and the fraud relating to this relic is beyond question.'

'I do not deny that,' said Michael. 'It is the nature of the link that eludes me.'

Both were silent as they reconsidered the few facts they had, until Bartholomew stood, and began to drag on his tabard.

'In all the excitement of finding that disgusting hand, we forgot the reason why we were at Valence Marie in the first place,' he said. 'We still need to talk to the French students about the rape and murder of Joanna.'

'We have managed to make enemies of the Principals of Godwinsson and Valence Marie both,' said Michael. 'I doubt very much if Thorpe will cooperate with you. He will assume you are still trying to prove his relic a fake – and after our experience earlier, I would be happier if you stayed well away from Valence Marie and their nasty bones.'

Bartholomew hesitated, recalling vividly the unmistakeably hostile atmosphere at Valence

Marie. After a moment, he brightened. 'You are right about Thorpe, but there are others. One of the Fellows there is Father Eligius, and he is one of my patients. We have always been on friendly terms. He will help me if I ask.'

Michael eyed him dubiously. 'I know Eligius, too, and he looked to me like one of those most convinced of the hand's authenticity. He appeared positively fanatical. I cannot see that he would help you if he thought the outcome might be the discovery that the relic is a fake – regardless of your motives for asking the questions. And I cannot see him abandoning loyalty to his fellow members of College to allow you to prove some of them committed murder.'

'I will try anyway,' said Bartholomew, picking up his bag from the floor. He slipped the Galen into it so he would have something to read if Eligius kept him waiting. 'I have patients to see. I can try Eligius afterwards.'

'Try if you must,' said Michael, leaning back on the bed and closing his eyes, 'but be careful. I would go with you, but it is too hot, I am tired from patrolling last night, and I have no reason to believe you will be successful in discovering the murderer of this woman.'

Bartholomew shrugged off Michael's apathy and left the College for the High Street. Two of the more seriously injured riot victims still needed his attention, and he wanted to see Mistress Fletcher, one of the first people he had treated in

Cambridge, now dying of a disease of the lungs despite all his efforts. He tapped lightly on her door and climbed the narrow wooden stairs to the upper chamber where she lay in her bed. Her husband and two sons sat with her, one strumming aimlessly on a badly tuned rebec. They stood as Bartholomew entered and Fletcher moved towards him.

'Please, Doctor,' he said. He gestured at his wife lying on the bed, her breathing a papery rustle. 'She needs to be bled.'

Bartholomew experienced a familiar feeling of exasperation at the mention of bleeding. It was an argument he had had with many of his patients, most of whom believed bleeding would cure virtually anything. He looked down at the sick woman with compassion, and his resolve hardened. She was dying anyway and invasive treatments now would merely serve to make her last few days miserable. He had brought a strong pain-killer that would help her through to the end without too much discomfort. He sent one of her sons for a cup of watered wine then crumbled the strong powder into it. Kneeling next to her, he helped her sip it until she had drunk it all. She lay back, the potion already easing the pain in her chest, and smiled gratefully.

'We could call Robin of Grantchester,' said Fletcher. 'He bleeds people for a penny, and applies leeches for two pennies.'

'It is very cheap,' added one of her sons hopefully.

'I am sure it is,' said Bartholomew, determined that the unsanitary surgeon would never set his blood-encrusted hands on poor Mistress Fletcher while he had breath in his body to prevent it.

The sick woman made a weak gesture and her husband bent to hear her. 'Please let Doctor Bartholomew treat me as he sees fit. He has already eased my chest. I want no leeches and no bleeding.'

Her husband stood again, awkwardly. 'I am sorry,' he said to Bartholomew. 'But this is difficult for us. I would do anything to give her a little more time.'

'She does not want it,' said Bartholomew gently. 'Not like this.'

Fletcher gazed down at his wife and said nothing. Seeing his patient asleep, her breathing less laboured than it had been, Bartholomew took his leave.

The street was almost as deserted as it had been the previous night: there were few who cared to venture out into the burning heat of the mid-afternoon sun. After only a short distance, the tickle of perspiration begin to prick at Bartholomew's back and he felt uncomfortably hot. He removed the tabard and shoved it into his bag. Guy Heppel could fine him for not wearing it, but the comfort of shirtsleeves would be worth it.

After visiting the two riot victims, Bartholomew walked towards Valence Marie, hoping to waylay Father Eligius as he left Valence Marie to attend terce at St Botolph's Church. Bartholomew was subdued because of his helplessness in treating Mistress Fletcher. He wondered what it was that caused wasting sicknesses in the chest and how they could be prevented. The more patients he saw and experience he gained, the more he realised how little he knew; the lack of knowledge depressed him.

When Father Eligius told him Valence Marie's French students had left that morning for London, Bartholomew grew even more dispirited. He walked past the town boundary, making his way across the meadows that led down to the river behind the Church of St Peter-without-Trumpington Gate. Reaching a cluster of oak trees, he stopped, dropped his bag, and sat with his back against one of the sturdy trunks. He squinted up into the branches, where the breeze played lazily with green leaves beginning to turn yellow. It was cooler in the meadow than in the town and the air smelled cleaner. It was also peaceful, with just the occasional raucous screech from a pair of jays that lived in one of the oaks and distant high-pitched chatter from children playing in the river to break the silence.

He thought about Kenzie, a young Scot who had had the misfortune to fall in love with a woman whose father would never accept him, and who was forced to keep his relationship secret. So who had killed him? Was it Dominica's angry father? Was it her mother? Since it did not take a great feat of strength to brain a man from behind, Bartholomew knew that a woman could have slain Kenzie as easily as a man. Perhaps Cecily's guilt was the real reason for her sudden flight from home. Were the killers the friars from Godwinsson, who were the last people known to have seen Kenzie alive? Was his death a random killing by someone intent on theft? And if so, was it Kenzie's ring that adorned Valence Marie's relic? But why had the two French students been ushered out of Godwinsson when Michael had asked to speak to them? Perhaps they were the murderers, and not the friars at all.

And what of poor Joanna? She had been buried at dawn that morning in a cheap coffin paid for by the town, like the other town victims of the riot. Bartholomew had attended the funerals after mass at St Michael's, but he had been the only mourner for Joanna. While the family and friends of the other victims stood around the graves in St Botolph's churchyard, Bartholomew had stood alone, watching the verger shovel dry earth on top of Joanna. He wondered whether her friends and family even knew that she was dead. If no one had cared enough to attend her funeral, certainly no one cared enough to avenge her murder. Michael had said it was none of the University's affair, and anyway, the University was not in the business of hunting down its students for a crime on a victim that no one claimed; and Tulyet had neither the time nor the manpower.

Bartholomew stretched his legs out in front of him, and closed his eyes. Godwinsson, David's, Valence Marie and Maud's. All four seemed to be interconnected somehow with the murders of Kenzie or Joanna. And the dead child? Somehow he had been overlooked in all this. He had been buried the day before, his bones bundled up in a dirty sheet and thrust into a shallow grave in St Bene't's churchyard. A small mound of brown earth marked the site now, but in a few weeks it would be gone, and he would be forgotten again, just as he had been all those years before.

That thought brought a picture of Norbert into his mind, and Bartholomew smiled. It had been his only serious act of disobedience in Stanmore's household but one that he still felt was just. Did Lydgate know that Bartholomew had finally revealed his long-kept secret? Although the crime was twenty-five years old, there were still many who would remember it, and the hunt that had taken place for Norbert the following day. Bartholomew winced. That had been an unpleasant day for him, wondering whether vengeful villagers would return with Norbert captive to reveal who had let him escape.

Bartholomew wondered what he should do next. Should he follow the advice of Michael and Tulyet, and forget Joanna? The French students at Valence Marie had gone, so the only way forward was for him to talk to the two at Godwinsson. He knew their names and their faces, which meant he would not have to ask to see them through Lydgate. He stood up and reached for his bag, determining upon a course of action. The ailing Mistress

Fletcher lived close enough to Godwinsson to allow Bartholomew to be nearby a good deal without arousing suspicion. He could even see Godwinsson from the windows on her upper floor. Starting tomorrow, he decided he would stay with Mistress Fletcher until he saw the Frenchmen leave, then follow until they reached a convenient place for him to confront them.

He retraced his steps through the meadow towards the High Street. Absorbed in thoughts of Mistress Fletcher's lungs and in ways to find Joanna's killer, he was so engrossed that he walked past Matilde without noticing her. It was only when she repeated his name, a little crossly, that he came out of his reverie and saw her.

'You are in a fine mood today,' she said, noting his grave face as he turned. 'I thought you were pretending not to know me!'

He smiled then. 'Oh no! Never that.'

But many men would, he knew. There were few who would converse openly with one of the town prostitutes in the middle of the High Street, at least, not during daylight hours. There were even fewer who would invite one to the most auspicious College event of the year, risking instant dismissal from their fellowships. He thrust that thought to the back of his mind, and listened to Matilde's amusing account about how a number of stray cats had raided the Market Square fish-stall while its owner had slipped away to view the relic at Valence Marie.

It occurred to Bartholomew, as he talked with Matilde, that she might very well know Joanna, the murdered prostitute with hair like Philippa. Bartholomew had no idea how many prostitutes worked in Cambridge, but he did know that they had an unofficial guild and held meetings during which they exchanged information and advice. When he asked her, Matilde looked taken aback.

'I know of no sister called Joanna,' she said. Bartholomew smiled to himself; he had forgotten Matilde referred to the other prostitutes as sisters. 'What did this Joanna look like?'

Bartholomew was at a loss for words. Joanna's face had been so battered that to describe it was impossible. He remembered in vivid detail the wounds she had suffered during the rape, and the savage blow to her head that had killed her, but telling Matilde that would get him nowhere. 'She was tall and had long, fair hair,' he said lamely.

Matilde spread her hands. 'None of the sisters is called Joanna,' she repeated. 'I thought perhaps you may have been referring to one or two ladies in the villages who ply their wares here occasionally, but none of them has long, fair hair. Why do you want her? Perhaps I can help.'

Realising how her words might be interpreted, she blushed. Bartholomew, seeing her embarrassment also looked away, feeling the colour mounting in his own cheeks. After a brief silence they looked at each other again, and smiled, so that the uneasy atmosphere was broken.

'Joanna was killed in the riots,' he said. 'I wondered whether you might know her.'

Matilde looked shocked. 'No sister was foolish enough to be out when the riots were on, Matthew,' she said. 'All those men prowling around in gangs? Heavens, no! We may have been overwhelmed by business, but none of it would have been paid for. As soon as we saw what was happening, we put out the word that any sensible woman should remain indoors.'

'Do you know what all this rioting was about? Michael, Sheriff Tulyet, my colleagues at Michaelhouse, and even my brother-in-law, are at a loss as to why there is such an atmosphere of disquiet in the town.'

Matilde did not answer immediately, but looked away down the High Street. Bartholomew stared at her, admiring yet again her delicate beauty. She wore a plain blue dress that accentuated her lithe figure, and her unblemished skin, glossy hair and small, white teeth bespoke of health and vitality. She was also one of the few people Bartholomew knew who always seemed to have clean hands, and one of fewer still who did not have a perennial crust of dirt beneath her finger-nails. When she finally started to answer, Bartholomew found he had been so absorbed in looking at her, that he had all but forgotten what he had asked.

'In our profession,' she began, 'your hear things. Recently, I have been hearing a great deal.' She turned to look at him. 'I trust you, Matthew, which is why I will tell you what I know, although you must understand that I am breaking one of my own rules by breaching the confidence of a client. I would not do it for anyone else.'

'Are you sure you should?' Bartholomew asked. He found himself wishing yet again that she was not a prostitute and was angry at himself. Philippa's sudden rejection of him must have affected him more than he had originally appreciated; he felt he was becoming like Brother Michael, full of secret lusts!

Matilde, unaware of the conflict within him, peered at him earnestly. 'Are you well, Matthew? You look pale.' At his nod, she continued. 'I have heard that the death of the Scottish student and the discovery of the child's bones were used to start the riot. Rumours said that both had been murdered and students and townsfolk alike were goaded with accusations of cowardice because they had done nothing to avenge them. The rumours started among the stall-holders in the Market Square, who are notorious as sources of gossip.'

Bartholomew rubbed his chin. So it seemed that Stanmore, Tulyet and Michael had been right after all – there was more to the riots than met the eye. Rumours had been deliberately started in a place where they would be sure to spread and inflame.

Matilde watched him. 'You had already guessed that much,' she said. 'I can see in your face you are not surprised. I heard that the rumour that the Scot was murdered by a townsman came from

Godwinsson Hostel and the Hall of Valence Marie.'

Bartholomew stared at her. Godwinsson and Valence Marie yet again!

Matilde smiled, showing her even teeth. 'There! Now I have told you something you did not already know.'

Before he could stop himself Bartholomew asked, 'Was the person who told you all this responsible for starting the rumours? He must be, or how else would he know?'

Matilde pursed her lips. Bartholomew knew she was resentful that he should ask the name of her client when she had already overstepped her own personal code of conduct by talking about him in the first place.

'The riot was started in order to hide something else,' she continued, ignoring his question. 'Two acts were committed that night and the riot was contrived to hide them.'

'What two acts?' asked Bartholomew, nonplussed. 'The burglary of Deschalers's property? The burning of the Market Square?'

'I do not know,' said Matilde. 'I am only repeating what I have been told. The riots were contrived to mask the true purpose of two acts. Those were the exact words of my client.'

They talked a little more, before they parted to go separate ways. Bartholomew was mystified. He wished he knew the identity of Matilde's client, so that he could discover what these two acts were that necessitated such bloodshed and mayhem to mask them. The burglary at Deschalers's house had not been masked: several of Stanmore's apprentices had heard the house being ransacked and had seen dark-cloaked figures running away from the scene of the crime. Could one of the acts be the death of the woman called Joanna? But why? Bartholomew distinctly remembered her clothes. They were of good quality but not luxurious, suggesting that she had been comfortable but not rich. So, why would anyone need to spark off a riot to harm her? If she had committed some offence, it would have been far easier to have dispatched her in a dark alley with a knife.

Matilde was scarcely beyond earshot when Bartholomew was accosted by Eleanor Tyler, her dark hair bundled into a white veil and her grey eyes narrowed against the sun.

'Eleanor!' he exclaimed in genuine pleasure. 'Good evening!'

'Not so good,' she muttered, looking down the street to where Matilde picked her way gracefully through the ever-present rubbish and waste.

'Why? What has happened?' asked Bartholomew, concerned. 'Is your mother ill? One of your sisters? Hedwise?'

Eleanor pulled a sulky face at him and glanced back to where Matilde now stood talking to one of Stanmore's seamstresses. Eleanor's meaning suddenly struck home to Bartholomew. Did she believe he had been making arrangements for an assignation with Matilde?

'Matilde is a friend,' he began, wishing her to know the truth before it went any further. He hesitated. What more could he say without being offensive about Matilde – especially since it would not be long before Eleanor learned that Matilde was to be his other guest at the Founder's Feast?

'I heard you have a liking for her,' said Eleanor coldly.

'It is not like you imagine,' said Bartholomew, not certain that he was telling her the entire truth.

'You mean you do not engage her professional services?' said Eleanor bluntly. 'All very well, but it does your reputation no good to be seen chatting with her so confidently in the High Street. And now, since I am talking to you, my reputation is also being damaged.'

Bartholomew stared at her in disbelief. 'I hardly think—'

'For a man who has spent so much time travelling and seeing the world you have learned very little.' She raised her hand to silence his objections. 'I am not saying you have not learned your medicine. Indeed, you are generally regarded as the best physician in Cambridge, although you should know that many say your methods are dangerous, and disapprove of the fact that you are regularly seen in the streets talking to beggars, lepers – and now prostitutes!'

'But many of these are my patients—'

'And,' she continued, overriding him a second time, 'you should know that this woman – Lady Matilde, as you doubtless call her – should not be trusted. She makes up stories about her clients. See her if you must, but I would warn you against it for your own good.'

With that, she turned on her heel and stalked away, leaving Bartholomew bewildered in the middle of the High Street. A shout from a farmer with a huge cart saved him from being trampled by a team of oxen and, regaining his composure, he was suddenly angry. He hardly knew Eleanor Tyler and felt she had no right to talk to him about Matilde in the way she had. A veritable fountain of responses came into his mind, in the way that they usually did when the situation for using them had passed.

Then his anger faded. What did it matter? Eleanor had called him naïve. Perhaps he was – Matilde and Michael had both told him as much recently. It was clear that Eleanor strongly disapproved of Matilde and he should see her outburst for what it was: a simple, and not entirely surprising, dislike of prostitutes. He wondered whether Eleanor imagined she had some kind of claim on him following the invitation to the Founder's Feast. The thought also crossed his mind that his innocent discussion with Matilde might well give Eleanor cause to decline his offer, and then at least he would only have one woman to explain away to his chaste-minded colleagues.

He looked back to where Matilde was still speaking with the seamstress. Seeing him watching them, they both waved; self-consciously, he waved back. He hoped Eleanor's words were nothing more than jealousy, because he felt Matilde's information might prove helpful to Tulyet and Michael if it were true. But if Matilde were known to be untrustworthy, her clients might feed her false information, so her claim that the riot had been started to hide two acts might be meaningless. Yet she had appeared to consider carefully before breaking the confidence of her client. But then perhaps she preceded all her gossip with this show of reluctance. He dismissed the whole affair from his mind impatiently, realising that mulling over what Matilde and Eleanor had said meant that he was merely raising yet more questions to which he had no answers. He decided to tell Michael what Matilde had revealed, but to advise him to use the information cautiously.

As he walked past St Bene't's Church, the doors opened and the students who had been to sext filed out. Since this was not one of the religious offices the students were obliged to attend, only those that wanted to pray were there. Thus it was a subdued crowd that emerged, in contrast to the high-spirited one he had seen three days before.

He saw a familiar figure and darted after him, stopping him dead in his tracks with a firm grip on his arm.

'You are hurting me!' whined the terrified

Werbergh, looking in vain for help from his Godwinsson cronies. They, however, had more sense than to interfere in the dubious affairs of their untrustworthy colleague, and quickly melted away, leaving the friar and Bartholomew alone. Panic-stricken, Werbergh began to struggle, whimpering feeble objections about his rough treatment.

'Let me go! You cannot lay hands on a priest! I am one of God's chosen! I will tell Master Lydgate that you have been molesting a man of God!'

Bartholomew gave a small, humourless smile. 'Men of God do not lie. And you were not wholly honest with me, Brother Werbergh.'

Werbergh squirmed in Bartholomew's grip. 'I told you everything that happened. Please!'

'But when I discussed what you had told me with Brother Michael, your story and Edred's did not tally. You said you returned to Godwinsson with Cecily Lydgate after compline the night Kenzie was murdered, but Edred – with Cecily listening – claimed to have accompanied you. One, or both, of you is lying. What have you to say?'

Werbergh stopped struggling, his head and shoulders sagging. 'I told you the truth,' he insisted. 'I *did* go to compline with Edred and I *did* walk back with Mistress Lydgate. The Scot – Kenzie – *did* ask us if we had stolen his ring the night he was killed. But I suppose I did not tell you everything,' he added with a fearful glance at

Bartholomew. 'That is to say, I only told you what I know to be true and what I understand.'

'Oh, for heaven's sake!' said Bartholomew, exasperated. 'Stop twisting words and tell me something honest.'

People on the High Street were beginning to notice them, wondering why he was holding the friar's arm so uncomfortably high. Bartholomew's tabard was in his medicine bag, so he looked like a townsperson abusing a student. He relaxed his hold on Werbergh to one that looked more natural, before some scholars took it into their heads to rescue the friar.

'I omitted only one thing,' said Werbergh miserably, looking up at Bartholomew. The physician in him noted the friar's shaking hands and unhealthy pallor. Werbergh was not a man at peace with the world or himself. 'I think Edred probably did steal the ring. I did not see him do it, but he has done it before. He jostles people, and afterwards, they discover that something is missing. I do not know how he does it. Anyway, he jostled the Scot, but it misfired and we ended up in that silly argument in the street.'

Bartholomew released Werbergh completely, watching him as he rubbed his arm. 'Anything else?'

'I was coming to see you anyway,' said Werbergh, glancing up and down the street nervously. 'That is why I was in the church – I was praying for guidance. I had just decided to come to talk to you and there you were, like an avenging angel.'

He looked at Bartholomew with glistening eyes, and Bartholomew wondered whether he had been drinking.

'I think Edred stole the ring. I think he knows more about Kenzie's death than he is telling,' said Werbergh in a rush. 'He was also gone all night when the riot was on and I believe he was out fighting. Perhaps he has a taste for violence; when I asked him where he had been the next day, he gave me this black eye.'

Bartholomew remembered Werbergh's bruised face the day after the riot and saw that his cheek remained discoloured. Edred had been limping. So what had the other duplicitous friar been doing?

'And where were you when the town was ablaze, Brother Werbergh?' Bartholomew asked.

'In Godwinsson, virtually alone,' said Werbergh unhappily. 'I have no taste for rough behaviour. I imagined I might get hurt if I went out fighting.'

'What about the French students at Godwinsson? Were they out that night?'

Werbergh, once he had started informing on his colleagues, was more than ready to continue. 'Of course. They love fighting, and they boast that they are good at it. Two came back later and said that their friend had been killed.'

'Did they say anything about what they had done that night?'

'Oh, yes. They spoke in great detail about the tremendous fight they had had with ten townsmen all armed with massive broadswords. They say they were lucky to survive but that Louis had been treacherously stabbed in the back before being overwhelmed.'

So, the Frenchmen's pride had been injured, Bartholomew thought, and they were unwilling to admit that Louis had been killed by a woman. Perhaps it was better that way. He did not like to think that the Godwinsson students might take revenge on the Tyler household for his death. Werbergh could tell him nothing more and Bartholomew let him go, watching him thoughtfully as he weaved his way through the throngs of tradesmen making their way home.

CHAPTER 6

Thunder rolled again, distantly. And another silver fork of lightning illuminated the darkened courtyard of Michaelhouse. Bartholomew sipped the sour ale he had stolen from the kitchens and watched through the opened shutters of his room. The night was almost dripping with humidity, even in the stone-walled rooms of the College and, from low voices carried on the still air, Bartholomew knew he was not the only person kept awake by the heat and the approaching storm.

He thought about Mistress Flecher. She would find the night unbearable with her failing lungs. She would be unable to draw enough air to allow her to breathe comfortably and would feel as though she were drowning. He considered going to visit her, perhaps to give her a posset to make her sleep more easily, but distant yells and the smell of burning suggested that a riot of sorts had broken out in some part of the town. The streets would be patrolled by the beadles and the Sheriff's men and he had no wish to be arrested by either for breaking the curfew.

Sweat trickled down his back. Even sitting in his room sipping the brackish ale was making him hot. He stood restlessly and opened the door, trying to create a draught to cool himself down. The lightning came again, nearer this time, lasting several moments when the College was lit up as bright as at noon. In the room above, he heard Michael's heavy footsteps pacing the protesting floorboards, and the muttered complaints of his room-mates for keeping them awake.

While the evening light had lasted, Bartholomew had read his borrowed book, then had fallen asleep at the table with his head resting on his arms. He had woken stiff and aching two hours later, his mind teeming with confused dreams involving Philippa, Matilde and Eleanor, and wild collections of bones arising from the King's Ditch.

Philippa. He thought about her now, humorous blue eyes and long tresses of deep gold hair. He had not realised how much he missed her until he knew she would not be returning to him. He wondered how he had managed to make for himself a life that was so lonely. A creak from the room above made him think of Michael, a Benedictine monk in major orders. Bartholomew often wondered, from his behaviour and attitudes, how seriously the monk took his vow of chastity. But Michael had deliberately chosen such a life, whereas Bartholomew had not, although he might just as well have done. He wondered whether he should take Michael's advice and become a friar or a monk, devoting himself entirely to his studies, teaching and patients. But then he would never be away from his confessor, because he liked women and what they had to offer.

He went to lie down on his bed to try to sleep, but after a few minutes, rose again restlessly. The rough blanket prickled his bare skin and made him hotter than ever. He paced the room in the darkness, wondering what he could do to pass the time and divert his mind from dwelling on Philippa. Since candles were expensive they were not readily dispensed to the scholars of Michaelhouse, and Bartholomew had used the last of his allowance that morning to read before dawn. When the natural light faded, most reading and writing ceased and the scholars usually went to bed, unless they took the considerable risk of carousing in the town. Then Bartholomew realised that he did have a spare candle, given to him in lieu of payment by a patient. He had been saving it for the winter, but why not use it now, to read the Galen, since he could not sleep?

He groped along the single shelf in his room, recalling that he had left it next to his spare quills. It was not there. He wondered if perhaps Cynric had taken it, or Michael. But that was unlikely. It was more probably Gray, who had taken things from Bartholomew without asking before. He took another sip of the warm ale, and then, in disgust at its rank, bitter flavour, poured it away out of the window.

'The Master has forbidden the tipping of waste in the yard. At your own insisting, Doctor,' came the admonishing tones of Walter, the night porter, through the open window. Bartholomew was a little ashamed. Walter was right: Bartholomew had recommended to Kenyngham that all waste should be tipped into the cesspool behind the kitchen gardens, following an outbreak of a disease at Michaelhouse that made the bowels bleed. Bartholomew had been proven correct: the disease had subsided when the scholars were not exposed to all kinds of unimaginable filth on their way from their rooms to meals in the hall.

'What do you want, Walter?' Bartholomew asked testily, setting the empty cup on the window-sill. 'It is the middle of the night.'

Walter's long, morose face was lit by a flicker of lightning and Bartholomew saw him squint at the brightness. Both looked up at the sky, seeing great, heavy-bellied clouds hanging there, showing momentarily light grey under the sudden flash.

'A patient needs you. Urgent.' It was no secret that Walter resented the fact that Master Kenyngham had given Bartholomew permission to come and go from the College during the night if needed by a patient. Such calls were not uncommon, especially during outbreaks of summer ague or winter fevers.

Walter glanced up at the sky again. 'You will probably get drenched when this storm breaks,' he added, in tones of malicious satisfaction.

Bartholomew looked at him in distaste, confident

that Walter would be unable to make out his expression in the darkness of his room.

'Who is it?' he asked, reaching for his shirt and pulling it over his head, grimacing as it stuck unpleasantly to his back. He tucked it into his hose, and sat on the bed to put on his boots. Walter was right about the rain and Bartholomew had no intention of tramping about in a heavy downpour in shoes. He knew well what sudden storms were like in Cambridge: the rainwater would turn the dusty streets into rivers of mud; in the mud would be offal, sewage, animal dung and all manner of rotting vegetation. Wearing shoes would be tantamount to walking barefoot.

Walter rested his elbows on the window-sill and leaned inside, lit from behind by another flash of lightning.

'Mistress Fletcher,' he said. 'Does she have a son? It was not her husband who came.'

'Yes, she has two,' said Bartholomew, his stomach churning. Surely it was not time for her to die already? Perhaps the wetness of the air had hastened her end. He hoped the storm would break soon and that in her last moments she would breathe air that carried the clean scent of wet earth.

Bartholomew saw his door open, and Michael stepped inside, clad in his baggy black robe with no cowl or waist-tie, while the wooden cross he usually wore around his neck had been tucked down the front of his habit. Michael had explained that it had once caught on a loose slat of his bed

254

and all but strangled him in his sleep; now he slept with it inside his habit out of harm's way. He looked even larger than usual. Without the trappings that marked him as a monk, Bartholomew thought, he looked like one of the fat, rich merchants who lived on Milne Street.

'I heard voices,' Michael said. 'What has happened?'

'Mistress Fletcher needs me,' Bartholomew answered, struggling with his second boot. The hot weather seemed to have shrunk them somehow. Or perhaps his feet were swollen.

Michael shook his head. 'There were the beginnings of a riot tonight, Matt. It is not safe for you to go out.'

'Who was rioting?' Bartholomew asked, pulling harder at his boot.

'Some apprentices set light to that big pile of wood in the Market Square. The Sheriff's men put it down fairly easily, but I am sure small groups of youths looking for trouble are still roaming around, despite the patrols.'

The boot slid on at last and Bartholomew stood. He indicated his tabard folded on the room's single chest. 'Then I will leave that here and, if I meet any apprentices, they will think I am a townsperson.'

Michael sighed. 'They will see a lone man and will attack regardless of whether you are town or gown,' he said. 'Wait three hours until the curfew is lifted.'

Bartholomew shook his head. 'She might not be alive in three hours. She needs me now.'

Michael gave a resigned sigh. 'Then we shall go together,' he said. 'From the sound of it, she will be more in need of my skills than yours anyway.'

Bartholomew gave him a grateful smile in the darkness, and followed him into the yard. Once out, he realised how comparatively cool it had been in his room after all. The heat lay thick, heavy and still in the night air. It was slightly misty, where the fetid ditches and waterways were evaporating into the already drenched air. The smell was overpowering. Lightning cracked overhead, followed immediately by a growl of thunder. Quickly, Bartholomew led the way out through the wicket gate, up St Michael's Lane and into the High Street. Mistress Fletcher lived on New Bridges Street, almost opposite Godwinsson Hostel. On the way they had to pass the leafy churchyards of St Michael's, St Mary's, St Bene't's and St Botolph's, all stretching off into a dark abyss of overgrown grass and thick bushes.

As they reached St Bene't's the lightning flickered again and, out of the corner of his eye, Bartholomew thought he saw something glint briefly. He paused, peering into the gloom to try to make out what he had seen. Michael plucked at his sleeve.

'Let's not dally here of all places,' he said anxiously, then stopped short as someone came hurtling out of the row of trees running along the edge of the churchyard. He was knocked to his knees and someone leapt on his back with considerable force, pushing him flat on the ground. He was aware that Bartholomew had been similarly attacked and was angry with himself for not insisting that they were both armed before going out. Usually, the sight of Michael, monk and Senior Proctor, was enough to ward off most potential acts of violence, but he was not wearing his full habit tonight because of the heat.

He began to squirm under the weight of the man on top of him, and felt a second person come to help hold him down.

'Shame on you! Attacking one of God's monks!' he roared, a tactic that had worked successfully in the past. A snort of laughter met his words, indicating he had not been believed. He struggled again but his arms were pinned to his sides. The sound of a violent scuffle to one side told him in an instant what was happening. The message had been sent to lure Bartholomew out of the College. Michael had not been expected, and the two men holding him down were doing no more than that: he was not being harmed or searched for valuables, simply being kept from going to the aid of his friend.

The knowledge enraged him and he began his struggles anew, yelling furiously, hoping to raise the alarm. A heavy, none-too-clean, hand clamped down over his mouth, and he bit it as hard as he could. There was a cry of pain and the hand was removed to be replaced by a fistful of his own loose gown, rammed so hard against his face that he could scarcely breathe. He heard a shrill howl coming from the skirmish to his right and guessed that Bartholomew, unarmed or not, was putting up quite a fight.

'Where is it?' came a hissed question, more desperate than menacing.

Michael heard the fight abate and Bartholomew ask, 'Where is what?'

Loud cursing by an unfamiliar voice suggested that Bartholomew had taken advantage of the lull to land a heavy kick. Michael, dizzy from lack of air, renewed his own efforts to escape but stopped when he felt the cold touch of steel against his neck.

'Tell us, or we will kill him.' On cue Michael felt the blade move closer to his throat.

'I do not know what you want!' Bartholomew sounded appalled. 'He is a monk. Kill him, and you will be damned in the sight of God!'

Michael mentally applauded the threat of hell fires and eternal damnation to get them out of their predicament, but his brief flare of hope faded rapidly when he realised Bartholomew's ploy had not worked.

'This is your brother-in-law, Oswald Stanmore,' the voice hissed again, the knife pricking at Michael's throat. 'He is a merchant, not a monk!'

Michael closed his eyes in despair. In the daylight, his habit would be unmistakeable, tied

258

and cowled or not, but in the dark it was just a robe. He strained against his captors again, but weakly because of the burning in his lungs, protesting at the lack of air. Any moment now he would black out.

He was dimly aware that Bartholomew was still fighting but the noise did not induce the people who lived in the houses opposite the churchyard to come to their rescue. But why should they? They were likely to be harmed, and almost certain to be arrested for breaking the curfew.

'No!' someone yelled.

Then followed: 'Fool!'

Someone grabbed a handful of Michael's hair and wrenched his head up, and he saw a knife flash in the darkness. He closed his eyes again tightly and tried to remember the words of the prayers for the dying.

Abruptly and unexpectedly, he was released. The weight that had been crushing him lifted, and the handful of material that had been slowly suffocating him dropped away. For a moment, all he could do was suck in great mouthfuls of air. He scrabbled at his throat to see if it had been cut and he was bleeding to death, and felt instead the wooden cross that must have fallen out of his habit when his head had been pulled back. He looked up and down the High Street, glimpsing several dark shadows moving some distance away, and then they were gone. The road was deserted and as still as the grave.

Slowly, he crawled to Bartholomew. The first heavy drops of rain began to splatter in the dust, breaking the silence as they fell harder and faster. He pulled himself together and rolled Bartholomew on to his back, giving him a rough shake that made him open his eyes. After a moment Michael stood, reeling from his near strangulation, and hauled Bartholomew to his feet.

'Bring him here.'

Michael saw Mistress Tyler standing in the doorway to her house a short distance away, and they staggered towards her. The rain was coming down in sheets; by the time they reached her door they were drenched.

Wordlessly, Michael pushed past her into the small room beyond and Bartholomew sank gratefully on to the rush-strewn floor. Eleanor kindled a lamp, exclaiming in horror as she recognised them when the room jumped into brightness. Mistress Tyler dispatched her for wine, and bundled the younger girl away to bed.

'The commotion awoke us but we would have been able to do little to help,' said Hedwise, wringing her hands. 'We would have tried, though, had we known it was you, even if it had only been throwing stones from the window.'

'It is better that you stayed out of it,' said Michael. 'I doubt you would have been able to help and you may have brought reprisals upon yourselves. Did you ask us here without knowing who we were, then?'

Mistress Tyler nodded. 'We saw only two men attacked and needing help.'

Michael was impressed, certain that such open charity would not be available to anyone from Michaelhouse, especially if the morose Walter were on gate duty. He turned back to Bartholomew, and saw a large red stain on the front of his shirt. He took a strip of linen from Eleanor, bundled it into a pad, them pushed it down hard, as he had seen Bartholomew do to staunch the blood-flow from wounds.

Bartholomew looked at him in bewilderment. 'What are you doing?'

'Stopping the bleeding,' Michael answered assertively. Now the first shock of the attack was over, he was beginning to regain some of his customary confidence; the terrifying feeling of helplessness he had experienced when he was being suffocated was receding.

Bartholomew sat up, pushing Michael's hands away. 'What bleeding?' he asked, holding his head in both hands as it reeled and swam at his sudden movement.

'You are bleeding,' answered Michael, applying his pressure pad again firmly.

Bartholomew shook his head and instantly regretted it. He hoped he was not going to be sick in Mistress Tyler's house. He saw the red stain on his shirt but knew it was from no injury of his own. At some point in the struggle Bartholomew had scored a direct hit on one man's nose, and blood had splattered from him on to Bartholomew as they fell to the ground together.

Michael gazed at Bartholomew's shirt with wide eyes, looking so baffled that Bartholomew would have laughed had his head not ached so.

'Did you not check there was a wound first?' asked Bartholomew, his voice ringing in his head like the great brass bells at St Mary's Church.

Michael shrugged off this irrelevance. 'If the blood is not yours, what ails you?'

'A bump on the head,' Bartholomew replied.

'Is that all?' Michael sighed. 'Then we should stop pestering Mistress Tyler and return to Michaelhouse.'

'Stay a while,' insisted Eleanor, returning from the kitchen with a bottle and some goblets. 'At least wait until the rain stops.'

'And take a little wine,' said Mistress Tyler, filling a cup and offering it to Bartholomew. 'You look as though you need some.'

Michael snatched it and drained it in a single draught. 'I did,' he said, handing the empty goblet back with satisfaction. 'I was almost suffocated, you know.'

'We saw,' said Eleanor, with a patent lack of interest in Michael's brush with death. She knelt next to Bartholomew and offered him another goblet. 'Drink this, Matt. It is finest French wine.'

'He needs ale, not wine,' said Hedwise scornfully,

appearing on his other side with a large tankard of frothy beer. 'I brewed this myself.'

'Rubbish!' snapped Eleanor, thrusting her goblet at Bartholomew. 'Everyone knows that wine is the thing for sudden shocks. Ale will do him no good at all.'

'With respect,' said Bartholomew, pushing both vessels away firmly, 'I would rather drink nothing.' He felt queasy and the proximity of alcoholic fumes was making his stomach churn. He struggled to stand, hindered more than helped by the sister on either side of him.

'Are you ready?' asked Michael archly, when the physician had finally extricated himself from their helpful hands.

Bartholomew nodded and followed Michael towards the door.

'See you next Tuesday,' said Eleanor, beaming as she opened it for him.

'And I shall see you the following Sunday,' said Hedwise, raising her chin in the air defiantly as she glowered at her sister.

Sensing an unseemly disagreement in the making, Mistress Tyler hauled them both back inside and closed the door quickly. Bickering voices could be heard through the open window.

Once they began to walk along the High Street, Bartholomew wished he had stayed longer. Walking made him dizzy and he wanted to lie down. He lunged across the road to retrieve his medicine bag that had been upended and searched during the fight. Michael took his arm and guided him away from some of the deeper potholes, some rapidly filling with rain.

'You are in for one hell of a day at the Founder's Feast,' remarked Michael unkindly. 'That Eleanor has set her sights on you and she will be none too pleased when she sees she has a rival for your affections.'

'Eleanor has done nothing of the sort,' muttered Bartholomew, rubbing his eyes to try to clear them. 'She is probably just interested in hearing your choir.'

Michael shook his head firmly. 'You want to watch yourself, Matt, dallying mercilessly with all these ladies. If you are not careful, you will end up like Kenzie – murdered in the King's Ditch. There is nothing as venomous as a woman betrayed.'

'Oh, really?' asked Bartholomew. 'Over the last four years or so, I have seen a good deal more venom expended by the men of the town than by the women.'

'We should be considering what has just happened, not discussing your love life,' said Michael, suddenly serious, perhaps because he knew Bartholomew was right. 'What did those men want from you? Did you know them? It seems that Walter was right when he did not recognise the messenger as one of Mistress Fletcher's family. We were foolish to have walked into such an obvious trap.'

Bartholomew put his hand to his head in an

effort to stop it spinning and closed his eyes. That was worse. He opened them again.

'They thought you were Oswald Stanmore,' he said, leaning heavily on Michael.

Michael caught him as he stumbled. 'Watch where you are going! I imagine my dark robe misled them.'

'They were from Godwinsson,' Bartholomew said, trying to concentrate on the way ahead, them wincing as a flash of lightning lanced brightly into his eyes. The rain was pleasant though, drenching him in a cooling shower and clearing the blurring from his eyes.

'Godwinsson? How could you see that in the dark?' queried Michael in disbelief.

'You should not ask me questions if you do not think I can answer them,' Bartholomew retorted irritably. 'There were lightning flashes and I saw their faces quite clearly. One was Huw the steward, and another was the servant I saw emptying the slops while I was hiding in Godwinsson's back yard – Saul Potter, I think he is called. And one of the ones who fought you was Will from Valence Marie – the fellow who keeps digging up bones.'

'That puny little tyke?' exclaimed Michael. 'Are you certain?'

Bartholomew nodded cautiously, his hand still to his head. 'And the one demanding to know where "it" was I think may have been Thomas Bigod, the Master of Maud's.'

Michael whirled around. 'Now I know you must

be raving! Why would Master Bigod attack us in the street? Or rather, attack you, since I think this whole business has nothing to do with me – it was to you the message was sent. What did you say to Father Eligius when you went to Valence Marie this afternoon that has set the servant after you so furiously? Did you press him too hard about the Frenchmen?'

Bartholomew could not imagine he had said anything to Eligius, or anyone else, to warrant such a violent attack. 'I simply asked him if he knew where I might find his college's French students. He told me that they had gone to London.'

Michael looked sceptical. 'Just when term is beginning? It is an odd time for students to be leaving the University to say the least. Did you tell Eligius why you wanted them? Did you mention the relic and offend him by your rejection of it?'

Bartholomew skidded in something slippery. 'He would not have noticed if I had. He was too absorbed in his own devotion to the thing. It was difficult to persuade him to discuss anything else.'

Michael was silent, concentrating on steering himself and Bartholomew clear of the more obvious obstacles that turned the High Street into a dangerous gauntlet of ankle-wrenching holes, treacherously slick mud, and repellent mounds of substances the monk did not care to think about.

'But what about Master Bigod?' he said eventually. 'I cannot imagine why he would be out in the rain ambushing his colleagues.'

Bartholomew frowned, trying to concentrate. 'I may be mistaken – I did not see his face because it was hidden by a hood. But I am sure I recognised his voice. He is from Norwich, and his accent is distinctive, not to mention the fact that his voice is unusually deep.'

'Well, what do you think he wanted?' asked Michael, still dubious.

Bartholomew shrugged. 'I have no idea.' He stopped abruptly, turning to face Michael. 'Unless it could be that broken ring I found.'

Michael scratched his chin, the rain plastering his thin brown hair to his scalp, making his head seem very small atop his large body. 'It may have been, I suppose.'

'I think I may have broken the arm of one of our attackers: I was holding it when I fell and I heard it crack. He was wielding a knife, trying to stab me, and Bigod called for him to stop. I struggled and he missed, striking the ground instead – I heard it scrape the ground next to my ear. I suppose the sight of the blood on my shirt led Bigod to assume it was mine. I decided to play into their belief that I was dead so they would leave, but one of them, that Saul Potter I think, kicked my head.' He rubbed it ruefully. 'A tactical error on my part.'

'I do not think so, Matt,' said Michael soberly. 'They were certainly going to slit my throat. They

267

only desisted at the last moment because they realised I really was a monk and not just Oswald Stanmore.'

Bartholomew tried to work out what the servants of Godwinsson and Valence Marie could possibly want from him. Or Master Bigod from Maud's. It proved their institutions were connected in some way. But how? To the murder of the child and James Kenzie? To the rape and murder of Joanna? To the mysterious movements of Kenzie's ring? Or to the 'two acts' that Matilde said the riot was instigated to hide?

Thinking was making him feel light-headed and he felt his legs begin to give way. They had reached St Michael's Church. He lurched towards one of the tombstones in the church-yard and held on to it to prevent himself from falling.

'I think I am going to be sick,' he said in a whisper, dropping to his hands and knees in the wet grass.

Feeling better, he was helped to his feet by Michael. 'May the Lord forgive you, Matthew,' the monk said with amusement. 'You have just thrown up on poor Master Wilson's grave.'

When Bartholomew woke, he sensed someone else was in the room with him. He opened his eyes and blinked hard. Above him the curious face of Rob Deynman hovered.

'At last!' the student said, his voice loud and

unendearingly cheerful. 'I was beginning to think you would sleep for ever.'

'So I might, had I known I would wake to you,' Bartholomew muttered unkindly, sitting up carefully.

'What was that?' Deynman said, putting his ear close to Bartholomew in a grotesque parody of the bedside manner that Bartholomew had been trying to instil into him. Not receiving a reply, he pushed Bartholomew back down on the bed and slapped something icy and wet on his head with considerable force.

'God's teeth!' gasped Bartholomew, his eyes stinging from the violence of Deynman's cold-compress application.

'You just lie there quietly,' Deynman yelled, hauling the blanket up around Bartholomew's chin with such vigour that it all but strangled him. Bartholomew wondered why Deynman was shouting. He was not usually loud-voiced.

'Where is Michael?' he asked.

Deynman favoured him with an admonishing look. 'Brother Michael is asleep, as are all Michaelhouse scholars. Tom Bulbeck, Sam Gray, and I – we three are your best students – are the only ones awake.'

'Not for long if you keep shouting,' said Bartholomew, feeling cautiously at his head. Someone had bandaged it, expertly, and only a little too tight.

Deynman laughed. 'You are back to normal,' he said. 'Crabby!'

Bartholomew stared at him in disbelief. Cheeky young rascal! 'Where is Sam?' he demanded coldly.

'Gone for water,' said Deynman, still in the stentorian tones that made Bartholomew's head buzz. 'Here he is.'

'Oh, you are awake!' exclaimed Gray in delight, entering Bartholomew's room and setting a pitcher of water carefully on the table. He knelt next to Bartholomew and peered at him.

'What is Deynman doing in my room?' Bartholomew demanded. 'What time is it?'

Gray sent Deynman to the kitchen for watered ale, and arranged the blanket in a more reasonable fashion.

'You should rest,' Gray said softly. 'It is probably somewhere near midnight and you have been ill for almost two days. We wondered whether you might have a cracked skull but now you seem back to normal, I think not. But your stars are sadly misaligned.'

'Two days?' echoed Bartholomew in disbelief. 'That cannot be right!'

But even as he said it, vague recollections of moving in and out of sleep, of his students, Michael and Cynric, hovering around him began to flicker dimly through his mind.

'Easy,' said Gray gently. 'The kick Brother Michael said you took in that fight must have been harder than you realised. And, as I said, your stars are not good. You were born when Saturn was in

270

its ascendancy and the conjunction of Mars and Jupiter on Wednesday—'

'Oh really, Sam!' exclaimed Bartholomew irritably. 'You do not have the slightest idea when I was born. And if you had been to Master Kenyngham's lecture last week, you would know there was no conjunction of Mars and Jupiter on Wednesday.'

Gray was not easily deterred. 'Details are unimportant,' he said airily. 'But you were attacked on Wednesday night and it is late on Friday.'

'Two days wasted,' said Bartholomew, his mind leaping from his neglected teaching to the inquiries he had been pursuing with Michael.

'We have not been idle,' said Gray, not without pride. 'While Deynman stayed with you, I read the beginning of Theophilus's *De urinis* to the first- and second-year students, while Tom Bulbeck read Nicholas's *Antidotarium* to the third, fourth and fifth years.'

Bartholomew regarded him appraisingly. 'It seems I am no longer needed,' he said, complimenting Gray's organisational skills.

Gray looked at him sharply to see if he were being facetious, but then gave a shy grin. 'I would claim it was all down to my talent for teaching but the students were only malleable because you were ill,' he said in an rare moment of honesty. 'Had you left me in charge and went drinking in the taverns all day, it would have been a different matter. We were all concerned for you. After all, since the plague, there is just you, Father Philius and Master Lynton who teach medicine. What would happen to us if you were to die?'

'Nicely put,' said Bartholomew.

'We have had to turn away hoards of anxious women who came to enquire after you,' announced Deynman, loud enough to be heard in every college in Cambridge as he returned with the watered ale. Tom Bulbeck slipped in behind him and came to squat next to Gray, inspecting his teacher anxiously. Deynman, choosing to ignore Gray's gesture to keep his voice down, continued with his oration.

'These ladies have been very persistent; we had a difficult job keeping them out of the College.'

'Oh?' said Bartholomew cautiously. 'Which ones came?'

'Which ones!' echoed Gray admiringly. He gave Bartholomew a conspiratorial wink. 'And all this time we thought you were destined to take the cowl, like Brother Michael. Now we find out you have a whole secret life that is positively teeming with some of the loveliest females in town.'

'I have nothing of the kind,' snapped Bartholomew testily. 'I simply invited one or two young ladies to the Founder's Feast.'

'And one to the Festival of St Michael and All Angels,' added Deynman helpfully. 'And she was the prettiest of them all.'

All? thought Bartholomew in horror. How many of them had there been? He sincerely hoped one of them had not been Matilde. Bulbeck, more sensitive to his teacher's growing discomfort than his friends, put him out of his misery.

'It was just the four Tyler women and your sister, Edith,' he said. 'They were concerned about you. And Agatha, of course.'

'That is no woman,' declared Deynman.

'You should keep your voice down,' advised Bartholomew. 'Or she might hear you and then I will not be the only one with a cracked head.'

The three students exchanged fearful glances, and Deynman crossed himself vigorously. Bartholomew smiled. He was beginning to feel better already. He was not at all surprised that the kick had rendered him insensible, especially given the sensations of sickness and dizziness he had experienced on the way back to Michaelhouse. He thanked his mis-aligned stars that astrology had been the subject of his recent discussion with his students, and not trepanation, or he might have awoken to find Gray had relieved him of a chunk of skull rather than simply predicted his horoscope. Dim memories began to drift back. Had Michael accused him of vomiting on Master Wilson's grave? If that were true, he really ought to do something to atone for such an act of sacrilege. When the pompous Master Wilson had died during the plague, he had made a deathbed demand that Bartholomew should oversee the building of his fine tomb. Three years had passed, and, apart from ordering a slab of black marble, Bartholomew's promise remained unfulfilled.

When he opened his eyes again, it was early morning and daylight was beginning to glimmer through the open window. On a pallet bed next to him, Gray slumbered, fully clothed, his tawny hair far too long and very rumpled. Bartholomew sat up warily, and then stood. Apart from a slight ache behind his eyes, he felt fine. So as not to wake Gray, he tiptoed out of his room, taking the pitcher of water with which to wash and shave. Then he unlocked the small chamber where he stored his medicines. Pulling off the heavy bandage he fingered the lump on the back of his head. He had felt worse, although not on himself.

He went back to his room for clean clothes, tripping over the bottom of Gray's straw mattress. The student only mumbled and turned over without waking. Bartholomew wondered at the usefulness of having him in a sick-room if he slept so heavily, but then relented, knowing he was a heavy sleeper himself. It was not the first time Gray had kept a vigil at Bartholomew's bedside, and he knew he should not be ungrateful to his student, whatever his motives for wanting his teacher hale and hearty.

Outside, the air was cool and fresh. The rain of two nights ago seemed to have broken the unbearable heat and the breeze smelled faintly of the sea, not of the river. Bartholomew looked at the sky, beginning to turn from dark blue to silvery-grey, ducked back inside to his room for his bag – noting that someone had thought to dry it out after the heavy rain – and walked across the yard to the front gates. Then he made his way to St Michael's Church. The ground was sticky underfoot, and here and there puddles glistened in the early light. He reached the church and walked furtively to Master Wilson's grave, relieved to see that nothing appeared to be amiss.

In the church, Fathers William and Aidan, Franciscan friars and Fellows of Michaelhouse, were ending matins and lauds. Bartholomew sat at the base of a pillar in the cool church and let Father William's rapid Latin echo around him. William always gave the impression that God had far better things to do than to listen to his prayers, and so gabbled through them at a pace that never failed to impress Bartholomew. However, if Bartholomew would ever be so rash as to put his observation to William, the friar would scream loudly about heresy and they would end up in one of the interminable debates that William so loved.

Aidan favoured Bartholomew with a surprised grin, revealing two large front teeth, one of which was sadly decayed. While Aidan fiddled about with the chalice and paten on the altar, William gave Bartholomew one of his rare smiles and sketched a benediction at him in the air. On the surface, Bartholomew and William had little in common and argued ceaselessly about what was acceptable to teach the students. Any display of friendship between them was usually unwillingly given, although beneath their antagonism was a mutual, begrudging respect.

In pairs and singly, Michaelhouse's scholars began to trickle into the church, and Bartholomew took up his appointed place in the chancel. Master Kenyngham arrived and gestured to the Franciscans to begin prime. The friars started to chant a psalm, and Bartholomew closed his eyes, relishing the way their voices echoed through the church, slow and peaceful. Roger Alcote, the Senior Fellow, stood next to him and enquired solicitously after his health. Bartholomew smiled at the fussy little man: he had no idea he was so popular among his colleagues – unless, like Gray, they knew that they would have a serious problem trying to find a replacement Regius physician to teach medicine at Michaelhouse.

During the morning's lectures, his students were uncommonly considerate, keeping their voices low, even during an acrimonious debate about the inspection of urine to determine cures for gout. Bartholomew was amazed to learn that they had been instructed to keep the noise down by Deynman of all people, which was especially surprising given his uncharacteristic loudness during the night. Apparently, he had thought Bartholomew might be deaf because the bandage had covered his ears. Bartholomew wondered what it was like to see the world in such black and white terms as Deynman.

When teaching was over for the day, Bartholomew sent for the town's master mason. While he waited, he read his borrowed Galen: although Radbeche's message had been that Bartholomew might use it as long as he liked, to be in possession of a hostel's one and only book was a grave responsibility, and he wanted to return it to them as soon as possible.

When the mason arrived, Bartholomew handed him the small box that contained the money Wilson had given him for the tomb. The mason opened the box and shook his head, clicking his tongue.

'Three years ago this would have bought something really fancy, but since the plague everything costs more – tools, wages . . . Even with the stone already bought, I can only do you something fairly plain.'

'Really?' said Bartholomew, his spirits lifting. 'Master Wilson wanted an effigy of himself with a dozen angels, carved in the black marble and picked out in gold.'

The mason sucked in his breath and shook his head. 'Not with this money. I could do you a cross with some nice knots at the corners.'

'That sounds reasonable,' said Bartholomew and a deal was struck. He did not know whether to feel relieved that the hideous structure Wilson had desired would not now spoil the delicate contours of the church, or guilt that his intransigence had meant that Wilson's tomb-money had so devalued.

As he pondered, Michael sought him out, his face sombre. 'Mistress Fletcher died yesterday,' he said. He squeezed Bartholomew's shoulder and then went to sit on the bed. 'I went to her when word came that she was failing. She had fallen into a deep sleep in the afternoon and did not wake before she died some hours later. There was nothing you could have done and she would not have known whether you were there or not.'

Bartholomew looked away and said nothing. They sat in silence for a while. Michael played with the wooden cross around his neck, and Bartholomew stared out of the window into the sunny yard. He watched some chickens pecking about in the dirt and saw Deynman chase a hungry-looking dog away from them. Deynman spied Bartholomew gazing out of his window and waved cheerily. Absently, Bartholomew waved back.

'Damn Bigod!' he said in a low voice. 'I promised her I would be there.'

Michael did not reply. Bartholomew stood up, knocking something from the window-sill as he did so. As he stooped to retrieve it, he saw it was the candle he had been looking for the night he and Michael had been attacked. Pangs of guilt assailed him when he remembered thinking that Gray might have taken it. He replaced it on the shelf, wondering who had moved it in the first place. Cynric, perhaps, when he was cleaning.

Michael stood, too. 'I am going to talk to Tulyet about your notion of persuading Lydgate to look at the ring on Thorpe's skeleton,' he said. He raised his hands in a gesture of defeat. 'We have Kenzie murdered; a recently dead hand claimed to be a relic; riots possible every night and we do not know why; your raped and murdered prostitute;

278

the attack against you in the night; and the child's skeleton. All unsolved mysteries, and I can think of no way forward with any of them. Tulyet will help us because he is as baffled as we are and I can think of nothing else to do.'

Bartholomew picked up his bag. 'I had planned to sit with Mistress Fletcher and watch Godwinsson at the same time. The French students were bound to go in or out sooner or later and I was going to follow them and question them about Joanna.'

'Forget them for now,' said Michael. 'We know where to find them.' He hesitated, then sat again, fiddling with the wooden cross that hung round his neck. Bartholomew waited, sensing the monk had something to say. He put the Galen in his bag, then perched on the edge of the table. Michael gave a heavy sigh.

'Two days ago, when you were indisposed, I went to see Master Bigod of Maud's Hostel. He denies totally the charge that it was he who attacked us in the street. I asked to see Will at Valence Marie but was told he was visiting a sick sister in Fen Ditton, and had been gone since the night the relic was found. Then I went to Godwinsson and, in the company of Guy Heppel, put the fear of God into Huw, their steward, and that scullion Saul Potter who you said kicked you. Do you know what I discovered?'

Bartholomew shook his head, setting his bag down on the table while he listened to Michael.

'Nothing!' spat Michael in disgust. 'Not even

the tiniest scrap of information. Huw and Saul Potter claim they spent the evening cleaning silver, and went to bed by eight o'clock. I collared other Godwinsson servants, and they confirmed that the hostel was locked up and everyone was asleep long before the church clock struck nine. It was past midnight before we were attacked.' He turned to the physician. 'Are you certain that it was Will, Huw, Saul Potter and Bigod you recognised?'

Bartholomew thought back to the attack: Huw swearing at him in Welsh, Saul Potter's piggy eyes glittering as Bartholomew had torn away his hood, and Bigod demanding to know where something was.

'I injured one as we fell – his hand broke,' he said, the memory dim. 'Did any of the men you spoke to have injuries? What about Will from Valence Marie? Perhaps he left Cambridge to hide the fact that he was wounded.'

Michael looked pained. 'Damn! Your memory has played us false! You told me originally that the man had broken his arm, not his hand, and you said Will had been holding me down, not fighting with you. I inflicted no broken bones – although I certainly bit someone fairly hard – and so Will cannot be in hiding to cover his wounds.'

He banged his fist on the table in frustration. 'I wondered at the time whether you might not have been rambling. You were weaving all over the road like a drunk. When I went haring off to confront Bigod and the others, I had no idea your injury was so serious. Gray warned us you might lose some memory after he consulted your stars. I should have waited.'

'Stars!' spat Bartholomew in disgust. 'I *do* remember Bigod, Huw, Saul Potter and Will there. Others too. The lightning lit up their faces.'

Michael looked sceptical. 'How many were there?'

Bartholomew thought, struggling with the blurred images that played in his mind. 'Will and two others fought with you, while Huw, Saul Potter and Bigod fought with me.'

One of the Benedictines in the room above began to sing softly as Michael shook his head. 'Wrong again, Matt. Only two had been allocated to me; one sat on my back, while the other held my gown over my face and almost smothered me. But there were five men fighting you. I saw them. I had been taken by surprise and was knocked to the ground before I could react. You had more time to defend yourself and were able to fight harder. Do you remember any words they spoke?'

For a brief moment, Bartholomew considered not answering, feeling foolish and vulnerable at his lapse in memory. 'I heard Huw speak in Welsh, and Bigod asked me where something was,' he said reluctantly.

'I heard no Welsh,' said Michael, 'and I heard every word that was spoken, lying as I was immobilised. Damn! Should I apologise to Bigod for accusing him wrongly? The servants I do not care about but the Principal of a hostel is another matter.'

'I am certain I saw those four,' persisted Bartholomew. 'And I heard and felt the sharp crack of a bone breaking . . .'

He stopped, aware that Michael was regarding him unconvinced.

'I suspect I saw a good deal more than you, since I was pinned helplessly on the ground for several minutes while you fought,' said the monk. 'The faces of our attackers were very carefully concealed – I saw nothing. And I am sure they would not have left us alive had they the slightest suspicion that they might have been identified. Yet you claim to have recognised four of the seven. It must have been your imagination that led you to name Bigod, Will, Saul Potter and Huw. I can come up with no other explanation than that these were professional outlaws hired to collect something from you.'

'But what?' asked Bartholomew, uncomfortable at the way in which Michael was so blithely dismissing his recollections. 'And why me, not you? You are just as deeply involved in all this business as me – perhaps more so, since you are the Senior Proctor.'

'Perhaps it has nothing to do with "this business", as you put it,' said Michael. 'I have given the matter considerable thought. The attack was most definitely aimed at you, since you were the one who was lured out on the pretext of a medical emergency; I was merely incidental. No one knows you have that ring you found at Godwinsson,

282

except me, so it cannot be that – unless you were seen picking it up. The only answer I can come up with is that these men were hired by a patient of yours to get something . . .'

'Such as what?' interrupted Bartholomew in disbelief. 'Medicine? Most people know I prescribe medicine perfectly willingly and do not need to be ambushed for it.'

'Perhaps you took something in lieu of payment that someone wants back,' suggested Michael. 'You are often given all manner of oddments when people have no money.'

'Exactly!' said Bartholomew. '"Have no money." Which means that they also would not be able to afford to pay outlaws to get whatever it was back again. And I hardly think seedcakes, candle-stubs and the occasional pot of ink warrant such an elaborate attack. Anyway, as Gray will attest, I often overlook payment when a patient is in dire need.'

'Yes, yes,' said Michael testily. 'But I can think of no other reason why you alone should be enticed out of college and searched for something. You have some rich patients – they are not all beggars.'

'But they pay me with money,' said Bartholomew. 'And the motive for the attack was not theft, because neither of us was robbed.'

Michael was becoming impatient. 'Perhaps your misaligned stars have led you to forget something obvious. Some transaction with a patient?'

'I have not!' said Bartholomew angrily. 'And my stars are not misaligned!'

A distant screech of raucous laughter from the kitchens spoke of the presence of Agatha. For a frightening instant, Bartholomew, who had heard the laugh often, thought that it sounded alien to him. Gray's physical diagnosis had been right: it was only to be expected that some of his faculties might be temporarily awry following a hefty blow to the head. Perhaps a clearer memory of the fight would emerge in time. Then again, perhaps it would not.

But Bartholomew knew that his stars had nothing to do with the fact that his memories were dim. Ironically, it seemed as though his reluctant adherence to teaching traditional medicine would backfire on him, if Gray was telling all and sundry that his master's stars augured ill. People would treat anything he said with scepticism until he, or better yet, Gray, showed that his stars were back in a favourable position. He almost wished he had been discussing trepanation rather than astrology, after all.

Bartholomew was torn between doubt and frustration for Michael's dilemma. The more he thought about it, the more he was certain that the men he had named were their attackers, but the details remained hazy. He rubbed his eyes tiredly.

'You should rest,' said Michael, watching him. 'And I must go to see Tulyet.'

Checking that the Galen was in his bag, Bartholomew followed Michael out of his room. He felt claustrophobic in the College, and wanted to be somewhere alone and quiet, like the meadows behind St Peter-without-Trumpington Gate. Ignoring Michael's silent glances of disapproval that his advice about resting was being so wilfully dismissed, Bartholomew walked purposefully across the courtyard, and up St Michael's Lane. Less decisively, he wandered along the High Street and began to notice things he had not seen before: there was a carved pig on one of the timbers of Physwick Hostel; one of the trees in St Michael's churchyard was taller than the tower; Guy Heppel had a faint birthmark on one side of his neck.

'I am delighted to see you up and about,' breathed the Junior Proctor, sidling up to him. He rubbed his hands up and down his gown in his curious way. 'I was most concerned to hear your stars are so unfavourable.'

'Thank you,' said Bartholomew shortly. 'But I can assure you that they are becoming more favourable by the hour.'

Heppel looked surprised at his vehemence. 'I am glad to hear it. I was hoping to have my astrological consultation from you soon. My chest is a little better with that angelica you gave me, but now I have a stiffness in my knees. I almost went to Father Philius at Gonville Hall when you were ill – I am told he does an adequate job – but now you are well again, I am glad I waited. Brother Michael informs me you are by far the best man in Cambridge for stars.'

Bartholomew's eyes narrowed and he walked away, leaving Heppel somewhat bewildered. He had not gone far when he saw Matilde. She approached him shyly and smiled with genuine pleasure.

'Agatha told me you were better,' she said. 'I was worried.'

'My stars are badly aligned, apparently,' he said, turning to glower at the retreating figure of Guy Heppel, who was still rubbing his hands up and down the sides of his gown.

'They have certainly put you in an ill-humour,' she said wryly. 'Or was that the doing of the Junior Proctor?'

'It was the doing of Brother Michael, telling people I am good at astrological consultations. If he spreads that tale around, I shall never be able to do any work.'

Matilde smiled. 'Then you should tell Heppel that his stars will augur well if he devotes himself to music, and persuade him to join Michael's choir. Heppel sings like a scalded cat and it will serve Michael right.'

Bartholomew regarded her doubtfully. 'Are you sure a scalded cat would not serve to improve Michael's choir? I cannot imagine it could be any worse than it is. It used to be quite good but he has not spent the time needed on it because of his extra duties as Senior Proctor.'

'Time has nothing to do with it, Matthew. It is not lack of practice that has made the choir what it is, but Michael's policy of providing bread and ale after each rehearsal. For many folk, it provides the only decent meal they have in a week.'

'I wondered why so many people were so keen to join,' said Bartholomew. 'I knew it had nothing to do with their appreciation for music.'

'Even so, I am looking forward to hearing it on Tuesday.' She looked at him anxiously. 'Unless you have changed your mind, or you feel too unwell, that is.'

'No, of course not,' he said quickly, although his predicament with his two guests had completely slipped his mind. He forced himself to smile. 'Just remember to bring something to stuff in your ears.'

After he had left Matilde, he met Oswald Stanmore, who asked whether his stars had improved. Bartholomew regarded him coolly and silently cursed Gray's enthusiasm for the subject. Puzzled by the uncharacteristic unfriendliness, Stanmore changed the subject and told him about a fight in Milne Street the night before between the miller's apprentices and students from Valence Marie. Bartholomew barely listened, preoccupied with how he might neutralise Gray's diagnosis. Stanmore put up his hands in a gesture of exasperation when he saw his brother-in-law was not paying him any attention, and let him go. The merchant then strode to the small building where his seam-stress worked. She was there talking to Cynric, who had been courting her slowly and shyly for more than a year. Stanmore beckoned him over, and within moments Cynric was slipping along Milne Street behind Bartholomew.

The sun was hot but not nearly as strong as it had been. White, fluffy clouds drifted across the sky affording temporary relief and there was a breeze that was still relatively free of odours from the river. Bartholomew continued to walk, acknowledging the greetings of people he knew but not stopping to talk to them. He passed St Bene't's Church, where he and Michael had been attacked, and reached St Botolph's. Glancing across the churchyard to where Joanna and the other riot victims were buried, he saw a figure emerge from where it had been standing behind some bushes. Curious, and with nothing else to do, Bartholomew climbed over the low wall and walked towards the back of the church. He peered out round the buttresses and saw that as he had thought, the person – cloaked and hooded, even in the hot sun – was standing by Joanna's grave.

Bartholomew abandoned stealth and approached the mourner openly. The figure turned to see who was coming and then looked away. It was a man of Bartholomew's height, taller even. Bartholomew drew level and was about to address him, when the man spun round and shoved Bartholomew so hard that he fell back against the wall of the church.

Then he raced off along the path back towards the High Street. Bartholomew's feet skidded on wet grass as he fought to regain his balance. But as the man ran his hood fell away from his face and Bartholomew, for the briefest of moments, was able to recognise him.

Bartholomew tore after him but on reaching the High Street saw that the man had disappeared into the mass of people walking home from the market. As he looked up and down the road in silent frustration, he saw that Cynric had materialised next to him.

'Did you see him?' Bartholomew gasped. 'It was Thomas Lydgate, standing at Joanna's grave-side.'

Cynric looked at him perplexed. 'You are still addled, lad,' he said gently. 'There was no one here other than you.'

CHAPTER 7

Bartholomew was growing exasperated, while Michael and Cynric listened to him with a sympathetic patience that only served to make him feel worse. He rubbed his head and flopped down into the large chair next to the kitchen hearth from which Agatha oversaw the domestic side of the College.

'So, you say you saw Lydgate at Joanna's grave,' said Michael. 'And that Lydgate is her father.'

'Not quite,' said Bartholomew tiredly. 'I think Joanna must be Dominica and it is she who lies in the grave.'

'But Joanna is a prostitute,' said Michael. 'How can she be Dominica?'

Was Michael trying to force him to give up his theory by being deliberately obtuse? Bartholomew wondered. Michael was not usually so slow to grasp the essence of his ideas. He rubbed the back of his head again, trying to ease the nagging ache there, and tried again. 'Joanna is not a prostitute known to Matilde,' he said. '*Ergo*, I believe Joanna was not a prostitute at all. I think someone deliberately misled Tulyet with a false name, and that

290

Joanna's real identity is Dominica, whom no one has seen since she was sent to these mysterious relatives in Chesterton.'

'But she was sent to them before the riots, to keep her away from her lover – *before* you think she was killed,' said Michael. 'She is probably still there with them. In Chesterton.'

'Then check. I will wager you anything you like she will not be there,' said Bartholomew. 'Her death the night of the riot explains the curious actions of her parents. Cecily went to Maud's, and stayed briefly talking to Master Bigod. Perhaps she was asking him if he had seen Dominica. Why else would a respectable lady, who seldom leaves her house anyway, be out on the night of massive civil unrest? Meanwhile, Thomas Lydgate was missing all night, and gave a false alibi to Tulyet. He was probably also searching for her. The next day he and Edred went to the Castle to identify the friar who died, whom I thought was you' He faltered. That memory at least was burned indelibly into his mind.

'And you think that while Lydgate and Edred were at the Castle, they also had a look at this Joanna and satisfied themselves it was Dominica?' finished Michael.

Bartholomew nodded. 'Why else would Lydgate be at her grave?'

He saw Michael and Cynric exchange glances, but was too tired to be angry with them. Cynric had not seen Lydgate, but that did not mean he had not been there. Because Michael doubted

Bartholomew's memory over the events of two nights ago, the monk was prepared to doubt him now. How long would he continue to doubt? A few days? Weeks? For ever? Bartholomew rubbed his eyes, trying to clear his blurred vision.

He wondered how Cynric had happened to be so close to hand all of a sudden, appearing at the church so fortuitously? It occurred to him that Cynric must have been following him. Probably not from Michaelhouse, but from Milne Street, where he had been alerted by Stanmore. Gray's insouciant diagnosis – made when the student did not have the most basic information necessary to allow an accurate prediction – was impinging on every aspect of Bartholomew's life. If only he had been teaching something else that week! He wondered whether he could bribe his fellow physician Father Philius to provide a more favourable astrological reading. But Philius and Bartholomew opposed each other on virtually all aspects of medicine, and Philius would probably seize on the notion that his colleague was unbalanced with the greatest of pleasure.

Michael was speaking, and Bartholomew realised he had not heard anything the monk had said. When he asked him to repeat it, Michael stood abruptly.

'I was saying that there might be all manner of reasons why Lydgate might visit Joanna's grave. Perhaps she was his personal prostitute, which might be why Matilde did not know her – it would mean she remained exclusive to him and did not tout for business on the streets. Perhaps he thought he was at the grave of his friar and not Joanna's at all. And if you persist in your theory that Dominica was Joanna, who do you think raped and killed her? It would hardly be the French students of Godwinsson!'

Bartholomew was too weary to try to reason it all out. 'Did you speak to Tulyet about asking Lydgate to identify the ring?' he asked, partly for information, but mostly so that he would not have to answer Michael.

The monk nodded. 'He advises – and on reflection. I believe he is right – that we should ease up on our inquiries into Kenzie's death until the town is more peaceful. Inflaming a man like Lydgate by suggesting his daughter's ring is on Valence Marie's relic will serve no purpose other than to risk more violence.'

'So the next time I wish to murder someone, all I need to do to make sure I get away with it is to start a riot,' said Bartholomew bitterly. 'It is a good thing to know.'

Michael sighed theatrically. 'We are simply being practical, Matt. I would rather one murderer went free than another nine innocents – including someone like your Joanna – die in civil unrest. But we should not be discussing this while you are incapable of drawing rational conclusions. You should rest and perhaps the planets will be kinder to you tomorrow.'

Cynric agreed. 'You look tired, boy. Would you like me to see you to your room?'

'I am not one of Oswald Stanmore's seamstresses,' said Bartholomew, trying not to sound irritable when Cynric was attempting to be kind. 'I do not think I am likely to be accosted by ruffians while walking from the kitchens to my room.'

'You never know,' said Michael, smiling. 'You might be if Father William has caught wind of all your dalliances with these women!'

Bartholomew trailed across the courtyard to his room as the last orange rays of sun faded and died, still feeling helpless and angry. He took a deep breath, scrubbed at his face, and went over to the chest for the pitcher of water that usually stood there. It was on the floor. He frowned. He never kept it on the floor because he was likely to kick it over when he sat at the table. He looked around more carefully. The candle he had replaced on the shelf that morning now lay on its side, and one of his quills was on the floor. He picked it up thoughtfully, and looked in the chest. He was tidy in his habits and kept what few clothes he owned neatly folded, but the shirts in the chest had been moved awry.

He took the key from his belt to the tiny chamber where he kept his medicines, and tried to unlock the door. It was open already. He entered the room cautiously and peered around in the gloom. Several pots and bottles had been moved, attested by the stain marks on the benches. When he crouched to inspect the lock, there were small scratches on it that he was certain had not been there before, suggesting that someone might have picked it.

Locking the door carefully, he went back to his room. Only he had the key to the medicines room, on the grounds that he necessarily kept some potions that, if administered wrongly, might kill. Gray and Bulbeck were allowed in, Deynman was not, for his own safety. Could Gray or Bulbeck have entered the medical store while he was ill? It was possible, although neither of them was likely to rummage through his chest of clothes: they had no earthly reason to do so since Bartholomew probably owned fewer clothes than either of them, and those he did own were darned and patched and could scarcely be coveted items, even to impecunious students.

So, the only logical conclusion was that someone else had been in his room and the medicines store. Could this person have been looking for the object Bigod was so keen to have? Bartholomew thought again. He knew that either Gray, Bulbeck or Deynman had been with him the whole time he had been ill, so the first opportunity for anyone else to search his room would have been that day, either while he was teaching, or when he had gone out later. He frowned and rubbed the back of his head. He had been unable to find the candle stub the night of the thunderstorm; the notion crossed his mind that his room must have been searched before he was attacked, too.

He saw a shadow on the stair outside and saw

Michael pause to glance in at him, before going upstairs to his own room. 'What is the matter?' asked the monk. 'What are you doing?'

'I think my room has been searched,' Bartholomew replied. 'Several bottles have been moved in the store-room, and the water pitcher . . .' He stopped when he saw the expression on Michael's face.

'Good night, Matt,' Michael said and climbed the stairs to his room.

A light rain was falling when Bartholomew awoke the next morning, the clouds after the previous clear days making dawn seem later than it was. Bartholomew had slept well, feeling better than he had done for days as he washed, shaved, dressed and walked briskly across the courtyard towards the gates. Walter eyed him speculatively.

'Where are you going?' he demanded rudely.

Bartholomew was nonplussed. Where did Walter think he was going? Where did scholars usually go at this hour in the morning? Then it struck him. It was Sunday and the morning service was later on Sundays. Something in Walter's gloating look made him reluctant to admit his mistake and give the porter proof that he was mentally deficient as well as astrologically lacking.

'I am going visiting,' he replied briskly, lifting the bar from the gate himself since Walter apparently was not going to do it for him. 'As I often do on Sundays.'

'In the rain?' queried Walter. 'Without a cloak?' Suspicion virtually dripped from his words.

'Yes,' said Bartholomew, opening the gate and stepping out into the lane. 'Not that it is any of your affair.' He closed the gate, and then opened it again moments later, catching Walter halfway across the yard. 'And I do not need Cynric to follow me,' he shouted.

He walked quickly towards the river, following a sudden desire to be as far away from Michaelhouse as possible. There was a thick mist swirling on the dull waters, rolling in from the Fens. He began to walk upstream, thinking that he would visit Trumpington and have breakfast with Stanmore and Edith. Abruptly, he stopped. They would be as bad as the scholars of Michaelhouse: they would see him arriving early, having walked to them in the rain, and would doubt his sanity.

So, downstream then, he thought, and struck out enthusiastically along the towpath that led behind the Hospital of St John. Once he saw a spider's web encrusted with more tiny drops of water than he thought it would have the strength to hold and stopped to admire it. Further on, past the Castle and St Radegund's Convent, he came face to face with a small deer, which stared at him curiously before bolting away into the undergrowth. After a while he came to the village of Chesterton, where Dominica Lydgate, the unfortunate daughter of the Master of Godwinsson, was supposed to be staying with her mysterious relatives.

The bell in the church was beginning to toll for the early morning service. Bartholomew waded across the river, still shallow from weeks of dry weather, and made his way through a boggy meadow towards it. He opened a clanking door and slipped inside as the priest began to say mass. One or two children regarded him with open interest and Bartholomew wondered how he must appear to the congregation: cloakless, tabard dripping wet, shoes squelching from fording the river. One child reached up and patted his bag, giggling afterwards with her sister at her audacity. Bartholomew smiled at them, increasing their mirth, until a nervous mother moved them away.

The Chesterton priest apparently had better things to do with his morning than preaching, for he raced through the mass at a speed that would have impressed Father William. The quality of his Latin, however, was appalling, and once or twice he said things that Bartholomew was certain he could not mean. As he intoned his unintelligible phrases, he eyed his few parishioners with what was so obviously disdain that Bartholomew was embarrassed.

After the brief ceremony, the priest stood at the door to offer a limp hand and a cold nod to any who paused long enough to acknowledge him. Bartholomew loitered, taking his time to finish his prayers, and then pretending to admire the painted wooden ceiling. When he was certain everyone else had left, he headed for the door.

The priest nodded distantly at him, and almost jostled him out of the building so that he could lock the door.

'Nice church,' said Bartholomew as an opening gambit. The priest ignored him and began to stride away. Bartholomew followed, walking with him up the path that led to the village – a poor collection of flimsy cottages clustered around a square, squat tower-house.

'Have you been here long?' he asked politely. 'It seems a pleasant village.'

The priest stopped. 'I do not like scholars in my church,' he growled, eyeing Bartholomew with open hostility.

'I am not surprised, given your atrocious Latin,' Bartholomew retorted. Since the polite approach had failed, Bartholomew considered he had little to lose by being rude in return.

'What do you want here?' said the priest. 'You are not welcome – not in my church and not in the village.'

He made as if to move on but Bartholomew stood in front of him and blocked his path. 'And why would that be?' he asked. 'On whose orders do you repel travellers?'

'Travellers!' the priest mocked, looking hard at the tabard that marked Bartholomew not only as a scholar of the University of Cambridge but as one of its teachers. 'I know who you are. Doctor Bartholomew.'

Bartholomew was startled when the priest gave

his name. The man looked smug when he saw Bartholomew's astonishment.

'They said you would come,' he said. 'You or Brother Michael. You will find nothing to interest you here.'

'I wish the answers to two questions,' said Bartholomew, 'and then I will go. First, where is the house where Dominica Lydgate is supposed to be staying? And second, who told you to expect us?'

The priest sneered and started to walk away. 'You will learn nothing from me, Bartholomew. And do not try to cow me with threats because I know you have been ill and your stars are unfavourable. I was a fighting man once, and could take you on with one hand behind my back.'

Could you indeed? thought Bartholomew. 'Perhaps you might like to repeat that to the Bishop when I bring him here to celebrate mass with you next week. The Bishop is also a fighting man, especially after hearing bastard Latin in his churches.'

The man turned back, and Bartholomew saw him blanch. 'The Bishop would not come here,' he said, but his voice lacked conviction. Although he could not be sure that a scholar like Bartholomew would have sufficient influence with the Bishop of Ely to induce him to visit Chesterton, he was certainly aware that the Bishop could have him removed from his parish in the twinkling of an eye. It was clear the priest was not popular with his parishioners and it seemed unlikely that any of them would speak in his favour.

Bartholomew shrugged. 'You will know next week,' he said, and began to walk back the way he had come. He heard the priest following him and turned, uneasy with the man so close behind.

The priest sighed and looked out towards the meadows. 'First, Dominica was in the tower-house, but she is no longer here. Second, this manor is owned by Maud's Hostel, so I need not tell you on whose instructions we are bound to silence.'

The man's arrogance had evaporated like mist; Bartholomew suddenly felt sorry for him in his shabby robes and dirty alb.

'Who lives in the tower-house?' he asked.

'That is your third question,' said the priest, some of the belligerence bubbling back. 'It belongs to Maud's, and Mistress Bigod lives there. Now, please leave.'

'What relation is she to Thomas Bigod, the Master of Maud's?' asked Bartholomew before he could stop himself. He looked apologetically at the priest, who grimaced.

'Since I have already told you what I was expressly forbidden to reveal, what can other questions matter?' he asked bitterly. 'Mistress Bigod is Thomas Bigod's grandmother.'

'His grandmother? Thomas Bigod is no green youth, so she must be as old as the hills. Does she live there alone?'

'She has a household of servants and retainers,' said the priest. 'And she is probably eighty-five or eighty-six now. I have given her last rites at least four times over the past two years.'

Bartholomew reflected. So much for the Lydgates' claim that Dominica had been staying with relatives. She had been left in the care of a kinswoman of none other than the surly Master of Maud's Hostel – a man whose name seemed to crop up with suspicious regularity whenever Bartholomew and Michael discovered something odd. The last time Bartholomew had encountered Master Bigod had been when the man had tried to rob him on the dark street during the thunderstorm.

The priest was growing restless. He was keen to be away from the person to whom he had been forbidden to speak, but was still afraid that Bartholomew might have the influence to persuade the Bishop to visit Chesterton's church. The physician promised not to reveal the source of his information, although it would not be difficult for anyone to guess, given that several villagers had watched him speak with the priest, and gave his word never to mention Chesterton and miserable Latin in the same breath to another living soul. The priest remained uneasy but there was little Bartholomew could do to convince him further that he had far better things to do than to hang around in Ely waiting for an audience with a busy bishop, who would not be interested in a remote and unimportant parish anyway.

Finally tearing himself away, Bartholomew walked towards the untidy collection of shacks that comprised the village, but left quickly, unnerved by the hostility that brooded in the eyes of the people he met. A short distance away, certain he was not observed, he found a suitable vantage point, and settled in the long grass to watch the tower-house for any indication that Dominica might still be there. There was little to see, however, and he soon grew chilled from sitting still.

Perhaps around ten o'clock, the church bell rang for mass again. The occupants of the tower-house evidently preferred the later sitting, for a large number of people trudged through the drizzle to the dismal church. In the midst of them, carried in a canopied litter, was the old lady. Bartholomew's professional eye could detect no signs of senility, no drooling or muttering. If anything, she seemed to exercise a rigid control over her household, and her sharp, strong voice wafted insistently to where Bartholomew listened.

When the church doors had been closed to block the draughts, probably on the old lady's orders, Bartholomew left his hiding place and made for the tower-house. He skulked around the outbuildings, attentive for signs that someone had remained behind, but heard nothing. It seemed Mistress Bigod's entire household was obliged to attend the ten o'clock service: the tower-house and its stables and sheds were deserted. He walked quickly into the yard and looked up at the keep. It was a simple structure, based on the Norman way of building: a flight of steps outside led up to the main entrance on the middle floor; the upper floor had glazed windows and was probably the old lady's private apartments; the lower floor was virtually windowless and was doubtless used for storage.

Climbing the stairs, Bartholomew found that the heavy, metal-studded door was shut but not locked. He pushed it open and walked lightly into the large room that served as a hall. He glanced around quickly but there was nothing much to see: trestle-tables had been set up ready for the midday meal and trenchers laid at regular intervals along them.

Quelling his nervousness, Bartholomew tiptoed across to the narrow spiral staircase in the far corner and ascended to the upper floor. This was divided into two smaller rooms, each with a garderobe passage and a fireplace. One room was unmistakeably masculine, and a scholar's tabard thrown carelessly over a chest indicated that Thomas Bigod probably used it when he visited his grandmother. Bartholomew's heart began to thump, as his fear of being caught grew with each door he opened. But there was nothing in the hall, or the chambers above, of remote interest to him, and no sign that Dominica had been kept there.

He crept back down the staircase to the hall. At the far end, opposite the hearth, was a screen, behind which stood a long table for the servants to use when preparing meals – like many houses, the kitchens were in an outbuilding to reduce the ever-present risk of fire. Under the table was a trap-door with a ladder that led to the lower floor. The basement was lit by narrow slits, and smelled musty and damp. The dankness suggested that it was not used for storage and was usually empty. A quick glance round told Bartholomew there was nothing to see whatsoever, that he should give up his wild notion of locating where Dominica had been and leave the tower-house before he was apprehended.

Suddenly he became aware of voices and froze in horror. Surely the mass could not be over yet, bad and fast Latin notwithstanding! He felt his stomach churn in anticipation of being discovered, realising that he had been foolish to enter the tower-house alone. What if Bigod found him? His henchmen could easily knock him on the head, dump him in the river and no one would ever know what had become of him. And even if Bigod did baulk at cold-blooded murder, Bartholomew would be hard-pressed to explain to the Sheriff what he was doing prowling around the house of someone he had never met while she was at church.

He fought down his panic. The voices were not coming closer. In fact, they seemed to be emanating from underneath him. Cautiously, he peered around in the gloom until he saw a second trapdoor leading to another chamber – like a bottle-dungeon below ground level that he had once seen in a castle in France. He eased the trapdoor up a fraction, noting that the hinges were well oiled, and that the wood was new. The voices came clearly through the gap now. A woman's voice, remonstrating with a man. Dominica?

He eased the trapdoor up a little more, so that he could see down into the lower storey. What he saw was not a bottle-dungeon, deep and dark and rank-smelling with offal, but a well-lit, pleasantly decorated room. A wooden ladder led up to the trapdoor and there were no locks to seal it from without. This arrangement was obviously not to keep someone prisoner but to allow its occupant to come and go at will. He glanced around the chamber in which he knelt. Piles of rushes were heaped around the walls and a heavy-looking chest stood nearby. Doubtless the rushes could be spread and the chest dragged across the trapdoor to hide it, should the underground chamber need to be kept from prying eyes.

The speakers were out of sight; Bartholomew looked down at the tapestries on the walls and the rich woollen rugs on the floor with astonishment. Delicate silver drinking vessels stood in a neat line across a table draped with a lace cloth; the remains of what had probably been a fine breakfast sat in a tray nearby. By changing position, Bartholomew saw that the underground chamber housed two compartments. The second was probably a bedroom.

The voices suddenly grew louder as the speakers moved into the room immediately below Bartholomew. Thomas Bigod's distinct accent wafted up first, accompanied by the unpleasant nasal wheedling of Cecily Lydgate. So that was where she had been hiding from her husband, thought Bartholomew, mystified.

Bigod put his foot on the bottom rung of the ladder to climb up it, as, in the same instant, voices came from the hall above. Lowering the trapdoor in panic, Bartholomew looked round desperately for somewhere to hide. There was only one possible place and he was relieved beyond measure to find the chest was empty. He had just managed to close the hefty lid with unsteady hands when, simultaneously, he heard footsteps on the ladder from the hall and Bigod pushing open the lower trapdoor.

Inside, the chest was airless and pitch black. Bartholomew dared not try to lift the lid a fraction, lest it make a noise and give him away. His heart was thumping so much that he wondered if it were shaking the chest. He closed his eyes, took a deep breath and tried to concentrate on what was being said in the basement outside.

Bartholomew deduced, from her characteristic whine, that Cecily Lydgate had followed Bigod up the ladder. Did that mean that she was with Dominica in the hideous underground boudoir? Bartholomew strained his ears but with the chest sturdily made, it was difficult to hear much at all.

'Edred did,' he heard Cecily say, 'with Thomas.' Which Thomas? Bartholomew wondered: her husband Thomas Lydgate or Thomas Bigod?

'. . . . relic is in Valence Marie.' Bigod again,

talking about the skeletal discovery that would make Valence Marie rich.

Bartholomew tried to ease the lid open to hear better, but felt the hinges judder and knew it would squeak if he tried to raise it further.

'Thomas does not know yet . . . Werbergh has been told not to tell him . . .' Cecily's whine. She must be referring to her husband now, since she was referring to a Godwinsson student. Bartholomew determined to talk to the untruthful Brother Werbergh again as soon as possible – if he ever escaped from his predicament.

There was a long pause, during which Bartholomew thought he heard the trapdoor being lowered into place, and Cecily, in childishly giggling tones, bid Bigod farewell as she went back down to her underground hideaway. Bartholomew was so tense that his palms were slippery with sweat and stung where his nails had dug into them; his shoulders and neck ached. If Bigod were to pull the chest across the trapdoor to hide it now, Bartholomew's weight would surely betray him! Or perhaps Bigod would just snap shut the sturdy lock that hung on the side of the chest, and leave him there. That thought made the saliva dry up inside Bartholomew's mouth and he felt as if he could not breathe. He bit his lower lip hard and tried to control his rising hysteria.

'Dominica dead . . .' came Bigod's Norfolk-accented voice, a few moments later. So Dominica was dead after all, and he had been right. He wondered if the identity of her killers was what Werbergh was not to tell Thomas Lydgate. Unless it was Thomas Lydgate who had killed her, with Edred. But that seemed unlikely, for if so, why would Lydgate then risk going to his daughter's grave?

'And the next riot will be on Thursday night,' came a new voice, loud and clear, with a note of finality. The voice was familiar but Bartholomew could not place it.

He heard footsteps climbing the ladder to the hall, then the chamber was silent. Cautiously, he pushed up the lid of the chest, his stomach flipping over for an unpleasant moment when it stuck. There was a low, but very audible, groan from the protesting hinges as it rose and Bartholomew was glad he had not tried to raise it when Bigod and his co-conspirators were in the room. He listened carefully. Cecily was now safely ensconced within her underground chamber with the trapdoor closed. Some of the rushes had been scattered, so that, unless someone knew where to look, the lower trapdoor was concealed from casual observers. The upper trapdoor remained open.

It had been closed when Bartholomew had entered the basement. Was someone planning to come back? Were the servants and the old lady back from mass yet? He listened, but could hear nothing. Just as he was about to climb out, the trapdoor darkened and someone began to descend the ladder, whistling as he came. Bartholomew swore softly to himself, ducked inside the chest, and eased the lid back down. This time, to give himself some air and to allow him to see and hear what was happening, he groped around for something to wedge between the rim of the chest and the lid. His fingers closed on the handle of an old pottery jug that had been lying in the bottom of the chest with sundry other bits of rubbish: some rags screwed up into balls, a rusty knife, and some flowers withered to a crisp brown.

Legs paused in front of the chest, and Bartholomew reached silently for the rusty knife, bracing himself for the lid to be thrown open. What would he do if it were? His legs were numb from crouching and he doubted whether he would be able to react fast enough to prevent the man from raising the alarm. Bartholomew held his breath, feeling sweat begin to form on his face and back.

With a small thump, something landed on the chest. The man had tossed something on to it. Bartholomew released pent-up breath slowly: someone would hardly put something on the lid if he intended to open it. He forced himself to relax and watched as the man began to walk around the chamber. The man began to whistle again. Bartholomew saw him wrench an old sconce from the wall with a creak of ancient metal and try a new one for size. It evidently did not fit, for there was an irritable pause in the whistling and one or two grunts could be heard as force was applied.

The man came back to the chest and Bartholomew heard the clink of metal. It had been his tools he had put there. A few moments later, there came the sound of metallic rasping as something was filed into shape. The sconce was tried again, but to no avail. The man advanced on the chest once more, then sat on it heavily.

A loud snap exploded in Bartholomew's ears as the pottery handle broke under the man's weight. Bartholomew heard him curse and stand to inspect the chest. By now, Bartholomew almost wished he would be discovered, just to end the unbearable tension. The lid had been forced down over the broken handle, which was now wedged firmly between the lid and the side of the chest. With horror, Bartholomew saw the man's fingers curl under the lid as he attempted to prise it open.

Fortunately for Bartholomew, the attempt was a half-hearted one; with a grunt, the man gave up and sat down again, forcing the lid to jam further shut with his weight. The whistling was resumed, accompanied by filing in time with the rhythm of the tune. It seemed to go on for ever. Bartholomew eased himself into a slightly more comfortable position and waited.

After an age, a voice drifted down into the chamber. The workman called back, and Bartholomew heard them share a joke about the eccentricity of a mistress who wanted new sconces fitted in rooms that nobody used. At last, the man seemed happy with the sconce's fitting, and his whistle receded as he climbed the ladder. There was a deep thump as the upper trapdoor was dropped into place and then there was silence.

Taking a deep breath, Bartholomew pressed his back to the lid of the chest and pushed. Nothing happened. He tried again but the lid was stuck fast. Bartholomew felt his heart begin to pound and his mouth go dry. What could he do? He could hardly call for help! He took several deep breaths and concentrated on using every ounce of his strength in forcing the lid to open. Just when it seemed the task was impossible, and he was on the verge of giving up in despair, it flew up with a tremendous crash that reverberated all around the small chamber. Bartholomew winced at the noise and stood shakily, his legs wobbling and burning with cramp and tension. And came face to face with Cecily Lydgate.

As Cecily opened her mouth to scream, Bartholomew raised his hands in a desperate gesture to beg her silence, and saw that he still clutched the rusty knife that had been at the bottom of the chest. In the light from the lamp in the new sconce – that Cecily had evidently been in the process of lighting – he saw that it was not rusty at all, but thickly coated in dried blood.

Cecily saw the knife, too, and the scream died before it reached her throat. She looked at Bartholomew with a rank fear that sickened him.

Unsteadily, he climbed out of the chest and walked towards her. His blood began to circulate again, sending unpleasant buzzing sensations down his arms and legs. He longed to be away from this dank cellar and its vile secrets.

'What will you do with me?' Cecily asked, her bulging eyes flicking from Bartholomew's face to the knife in his hand.

'Nothing, if you do not shout,' Bartholomew replied, wondering how he could extricate himself from the situation without harm to either of them.

They were both silent while Bartholomew moved his weight from foot to foot to try to speed up the process of easing his cramp.

'Master Bigod's retainers are looking for you outside,' she said finally.

Bartholomew grimaced. 'Because the villagers told them I had come?'

Cecily nodded, her eyes fixed on the knife. 'But they will not think to look here. My husband said you were clever.'

Not a great compliment from one whose intellect Bartholomew did not rate highly. He said nothing, but closed the chest so he could sit on it. Cecily stayed where she was.

'Why are you here, Mistress?' he asked, gesturing around the gloomy basement. 'It can scarcely compare with your handsome house in the town.'

Her pale grey eyes suddenly filled with tears that dropped down her wrinkled cheeks. 'I am safe here.'

'Safe from whom?' asked Bartholomew, although he had already guessed at the answer.

'Safe from him. From Thomas.'

'Do you think your husband would harm you?' Bartholomew asked. He was not surprised she was afraid: Lydgate seemed to be a man who might resort to violence if it suited him.

'He killed Dominica!' she said in a sudden wail, muffling her face in one of her wide sleeves. Bartholomew cast a nervous glance up at the trap-door. If she carried on so, someone would come to investigate. He thought about her accusation. Could it be true? Lydgate had no alibi for the night that Dominica had died. Indeed, he had worse than no alibi: he had given one that had proven to be false. Could Lydgate have killed his daughter? Was his appearance at her grave remorse, rather than grief? He glanced at the knife in his hand, some of the dried blood staining his palm, and wondered whether it had been used on Dominica. He almost cast it away from him in disgust, but if he were unarmed, Cecily would certainly raise the alarm.

Once the matter was out in the open, Cecily began to talk with evident relief. 'As soon as the riots started most of the students left, spoiling for mischief. I was grateful Dominica was safe, away from the town. Then Edred came back, breathless and limping and said he had seen her in the company of a man near the Market Square. Thomas was furious. He knew she had been seeing

314

a student but she would not tell us which one. Thomas set out into the night, and I followed, hoping to find her first so that I could warn her.'

She paused, wiping first her eyes, then her nose, on the ample material of her sleeves. 'I went to all the places where I thought she might be – her friends, a cousin, the church. And then I saw Thomas, standing with his dagger dripping, and Dominica lying there with her clothes all drenched in blood. There was a man there, too, also dead – her lover, I presume. Thomas did not see me. I ran to Maud's, and Thomas Bigod ordered one of his servants to bring me here.'

'Is this where you kept Dominica before she died?' Bartholomew asked, gesturing to the underground chamber and trying to force his bewildered mind to make sense of the details.

'Yes, with the chest across the trapdoor. But she got out when a servant brought her food. The servant claimed she stabbed him but I do not believe Dominica could do such a thing.'

Bartholomew and Cecily simultaneously looked at the bloodstained knife. Cecily's hands flew to her throat. But the poor girl had been kept a prisoner in the painted dungeon, so who could blame her for using violent means to escape? Bartholomew thought Dominica must have disposed of the knife in the chest before she left.

Bartholomew did not doubt that Cecily believed the story she had related to him, but was what she saw really what had happened? He had seen no stab

315

wounds on Dominica – assuming she was Joanna, of course – and so if Lydgate had killed her, it had not been with his blood-dripping knife. But two students had died from knife wounds that night, although, whatever Cecily might believe, neither of them could have been Dominica's lover because James Kenzie had been murdered the night before. And who had raped Dominica? Surely not Lydgate!

Bartholomew was certain that Lydgate might kill given the right circumstances – for a short while he had given serious consideration to the possibility that Lydgate might have killed Cecily, and was only claiming she had left him to explain her sudden absence. And he definitely had something to hide, or why would he be so hostile to Michael and his inquiries, and give Tulyet a false alibi? Bartholomew recalled Tulyet saying that Cecily's room had appeared to have been ransacked. When he asked her about it, thinking she would confirm his suspicion that she had done it herself in her haste to pack up a few belongings, she denied that she had returned to the hostel after seeing the dead Dominica. In fact, she was horrified.

'Did you see it?' she cried. 'Did they take anything?'

'What do you mean? Who?'

'Those thieving students, of course! They all know I have one or two paltry jewels in my room, and they must have been looking for them! Did they get them?'

'I have no idea; I did not see your room. But

your husband would have noticed whether anything was missing, surely?'

She calmed down somewhat. 'That is true. He would not let a stone lie unturned if he thought we had been relieved of any of our meagre inheritance.'

Her reactions seemed a little more fervent than a 'meagre inheritance' should warrant, and Bartholomew wondered what riches the Lydgates had secreted away in their house. If Dominica had silver rings with blue-green stones to give away to casual lovers, then their fortune was probably substantial. But there seemed no point in pursuing that line of thought any further, so he let it drop.

'Has Bigod lost something, or want something he does not have?' he asked instead, thinking about the attack on him in the High Street and hoping Cecily might be able to shed some light on it. He fiddled with the knife in his hands. 'Something important?'

'Such as what?' she asked, her voice unsteady as she fixed her eyes on the blood-stained weapon.

'Such as a ring?' Bartholomew suggested.

She looked confused. 'Dominica lost a ring. Well, it was my ring, really, but she took it without asking and then lost it.'

'With a blue-green stone?' Bartholomew asked.

Cecily's eyes narrowed and Bartholomew saw her fear mingle with suspicion. 'How do you know that? Did Thomas tell you?'

Bartholomew shook his head slowly, but decided there was nothing to be gained by telling this embittered woman that her daughter had given the ring to her lover, whose identity Cecily still did not know. He thought for a while, information and clues tumbling around in his mind in a hopeless muddle, while Cecily watched him like a cornered rat.

'When Brother Michael asked Edred where he had been the night James Kenzie – the Scot from David's Hostel – was murdered, you did not contradict him when you knew he was lying,' he said after a few moments. 'You knew Edred did not return to Godwinsson with Werbergh because Werbergh accompanied you. Why did you not expose him?'

Cecily wiped her nose again. 'When Huw, our steward, said you wanted to see us, Thomas told me to say nothing, even if I heard things I knew were not true. He said you and the Benedictine wanted to destroy our hostel and that unguarded words might help you to do it.'

Bartholomew supposed her answer made sense. 'Who knows you are here, besides Master Bigod?' he asked.

'No one,' said Cecily, surprised by the question. 'It would be too risky to trust anyone else.'

'Then who was Bigod speaking with just now? He mentioned that there would be a riot on Thursday.'

'There was no one here except Thomas Bigod and me,' she said, genuinely bewildered. 'You must have imagined it, or perhaps he was speaking to a servant. None of them know I am hiding here.'

Bartholomew knew he had imagined nothing of the sort, but then recalled that the voice he had half-recognised had joined the conversation after he had heard Cecily return to her bottle-dungeon. He looked down at the knife in his hand.

'So, what do we do now?' he wondered aloud. 'If I leave you here alive, you will raise the alarm and Bigod will come after me. If I bind and gag you, you will tell them I was here when they release you, and they will have little problem in hunting me down in the town.'

Her eyes flew open, wide with terror. 'No! I will help you escape! I will create a diversion that will allow you to slip away, and I will tell them nothing!'

Bartholomew raised his eyebrows at this unlikely proposition. 'Did you love your daughter, Mistress?' he asked.

She blinked, confused by the sudden change in direction. 'More than she believed,' she answered simply.

'Would you like to see her killer brought to justice?'

Her eyes glittered. 'More than you can possibly imagine.'

'Then you must trust me, and I must trust you. I do not think your husband killed Dominica.' He quelled her stream of objections with a steady gaze. 'I do not doubt what you saw but I examined what I believe was Dominica's body and there was no knife wound on it. She was killed by a blow to the head. Whoever's blood was dripping from your husband's knife, it was not Dominica's. I suspect Dominica was already dead when Lydgate found her. Perhaps the blood came from the body of the man you said was next to her. Last night, I saw Lydgate at what I think is Dominica's grave . . .'

'She is buried then? Where?'

'St Botolph's Church. I will show you where when this is over. Officially, she is recorded as a woman called Joanna and no one wants to investigate why she died lest it spark another riot. But I will try to find her killer, Mistress.'

Her face was chalky white as she tried to come to terms with the new information. 'Why?' she asked eventually. 'What makes you want to avenge my Dominica?'

Bartholomew was unable to find an answer. He could hardly say her hair reminded him of Philippa's. In truth, he did not know why finding her killer had become important to him. Perhaps it was merely because he had been told not to. He shrugged.

Oddly, this unpleasant, vindictive woman seemed to accept that his motives were genuine without further explanation. She nodded, and came to perch next to him on the chest. Bartholomew let the knife clatter to the floor. An understanding had been reached. They sat silently for a while, until Cecily spoke.

'Since I have been here, I have asked myself

again and again why Thomas should have killed Dominica. She was the only person he has ever truly loved – we both did. If it had not been for her, I suspect Thomas and I would have embarked upon separate lives many years ago. Although I saw him standing over her with the knife, a part of me has always been reluctant to accept that Thomas would destroy the most important thing in his life, and this is why I am prepared to accept your reasoning. Perhaps it was not Dominica's blood I saw on the weapon, but that of her lover laying next to her. I am sure Thomas would have no compunction in slaying *him*.'

'Perhaps,' said Bartholomew carefully.

'But even if Thomas is innocent of Dominica's death, I fear him still,' said Cecily, her expression a curious mixture of defiance and unease. 'How can I be sure that you will not tell Thomas where I am?'

'Why would I? I do not like him.'

'You do not like me either.'

That was certainly true. 'But if I informed your husband of your whereabouts, you could have your own revenge by telling Bigod that I overheard part of his conversation.

She nodded, appreciating his point. 'So, we have a bargain,' she said. 'I allow you to leave unmolested and keep from Master Bigod that you were hiding here, while you do not tell anyone where I am, and will investigate the death of my daughter. It seems evenly balanced, would you not say?'

Bartholomew agreed cautiously. 'Evenly enough. But when I return to Michaelhouse, I will write a letter to Thomas Lydgate telling him of our conversation and of your whereabouts. I will seal it, and leave it with a trusted friend with orders that in the event of my unexplained death or disappearance, it is to be given to him.'

Anger glittered in her eyes for a moment and then was gone. She nodded, begrudgingly accepting his wariness. 'Then be careful, Doctor Bartholomew. Do not disappear or die in your investigations. Although I am well hidden here, there is only one way out, and I do not relish the idea of being trapped in this dungeon if Thomas were to discover my whereabouts.'

'Nor would I,' said Bartholomew with a shudder. 'What an unpleasant place. Could Bigod not have found you somewhere more conducive?'

Cecily looked away, and Bartholomew detected an unsteadiness in her voice when she spoke. 'I wondered whether he might allow me to share the chamber he has on the upper floor but he insists this one is safer for me. I am grateful for his help but I sense I am more of a hindrance to him than a welcome guest. I am not sure I would have fled to him had I known he would recommend I stay here. It reminds me too much of Dominica.'

Personally, Bartholomew would have asked Bigod to lend him some money and left the area for good had he been in Cecily's position, but he imagined she was probably afraid to stray too far from the place where she had lived all her life. Bartholomew was unusual in that he had travelled quite extensively: most people did not if they could help it, considering it an unnecessary risk.

Cecily looked at the open trapdoor in the floor and gave a short, bitter laugh. 'This place was never intended to be a prison, you know. Before this house came into the possession of the Bigod family, it was owned by Jewish merchants. They built this secret chamber during the events that led to their expulsion in 1290, intending it to be a refuge if they were ever attacked. But it has become a prison now. First for Dominica and now for me. And both, ultimately, because of Thomas.'

One part of Bartholomew's mind had been listening for sounds from the hall above. It had been silent for some time now. Cecily saw him glance up at the trapdoor, and nodded.

'On Sundays, the old lady likes a tour of her manor. The entire household is obliged to be in attendance and the whole affair might take several hours. Go now, Bartholomew. To the north of the house, behind the stable, you will find a path that leads to the river without passing through the village. Wait! Take this!'

She held out her hand. A silver ring lay there, with a blue-green stone. He looked at her bewildered. How many of these things were there?

'There were two,' she said, as if reading his thoughts. 'Lover's rings and identical, except for the size.' She gave a wry smile. 'I am not a fool,

Bartholomew. I know why Dominica claimed she lost one ring and clung so dearly to the other. And you mentioned that Master Bigod may have been looking for a ring – perhaps Thomas asked him to look for the one Dominica says she lost.' She dropped the ring in Bartholomew's palm. 'I took that from her the night I sent her here. I have worn it since her murder. Take it. It might help you find the foul beast who killed her – perhaps this lover of hers that she went to such extremes to conceal from us. Who knows? Perhaps he may be foolish enough to wear her ring still, and now you will be able to recognise it from its fellow.'

Bartholomew put the ring into one of the pouches in his medicine bag. He climbed the ladder, and opened the trapdoor a crack. Cecily waited below. She was right: the hall was abandoned. He clambered out, and helped her to follow. In the gloom, he glimpsed her face, white and shiny with tears. She looked away, embarrassed. He left her behind the service screen and slipped stealthily across the hall towards the door.

'Hey!'

Bartholomew froze in horror as a group of men entered the hall. He ducked under one of the trestle-tables, but it was an inadequate hiding place at best, and his heart pounded against his ribs in anticipation of being dragged out. The men were not servants, but mercenaries, probably the ones who, according to Cecily, had been looking for him earlier.

'Just stop that!' came the voice again, loud in indignation as a conical helmet bounced on the floor. The speaker stooped to retrieve it, so close that Bartholomew was treated to a strong waft of his bad breath. It was all over now! It had to be!

A piercing scream tore through the air, and all eyes were drawn to the screen at the end of the hall. Bartholomew rubbed ran a hand through his hair wearily. It had not taken Mistress Lydgate long to renege on their agreement. But what else could he have done? He could not have killed her in cold blood, and locking her in the underground chamber would only have given him a few hours at most until Bigod came to seek him out. Perhaps he should have done just that and fled Cambridge for London or York. Now he was about to be dispatched by Cecily instead – not by her own hand it was true, but the outcome would be the same.

The screamed petered out. 'A rat! A rat!' came a wavery voice.

The soldiers looked at each other and grinned or grimaced, depending on their tolerance.

'A rat!' muttered the one whose helmet had been knocked from his head. 'Blasted woman.'

'There it goes! After it!' Cecily screeched. 'Oafs! Catch it!'

With rebellious mutterings, the men shuffled in the direction she was pointing up the spiral stair, until the hall was empty. Bartholomew emerged, still shaking, from his hiding place and slipped out of the door. As he left, he raised his hand in a silent salute of thanks to Cecily, who gave him a weak smile, and followed the men up the stairs.

Outside, the yard was empty; Bartholomew easily found the path Cecily had told him to take. He forced his stiff legs into a trot, continuing to run until he reached the river. He splashed across it, his haste making him careless, so that he missed his footing on one of the slippery rocks in the river bed and fell. Coughing and choking, he regained his feet and continued across, grateful he did not have the copy of Galen in his bag as he had done for the past few days. The water was very cold and the path had led him to a deeper part of the river than where he had crossed that morning.

He scrambled up the opposite bank, and crashed through the undergrowth until he reached the path that led to Cambridge. He began to race along it, hoping that the vigorous movement would restore some warmth to his body, but then slowed. He should be more careful. Bigod was also likely to use this path if he intended to return to town. Perhaps he was already on it, and Bartholomew had no wish to run into him. He stopped and listened intently, but heard nothing except for the dripping of leaves from the morning's rain, and the soft gurgle of the river. Cautiously, he began to move forward again, stopping every few steps to listen. Voices carried on the still air forced him to hide in the dripping undergrowth twice, but the only travellers on the path on a wet Sunday afternoon were three boys returning from a fishing trip, and a small party of friars bound for a retreat in the woods.

The light was beginning to fade when the high walls of Michaelhouse came into view. He tried the small back door that led into the orchard, but it was firmly barred. The Master, wisely, was taking no chances of unwanted visitors in his grounds while the town was in such a ferment of unrest. Bartholomew knocked on the front gates to be allowed in, ignoring the interested attention of the day porters as he squelched across the yard to his room.

'Matt! Where have you been?' demanded Michael, standing up from where he had been reading at Bartholomew's table. 'What a state you are in! What have you been doing?'

'What are you doing here?' Bartholomew responded with a question of his own, slinging down his bag and beginning to remove his wet clothes.

'Waiting for you! What does it look like? Where were you?'

'Out walking,' said Bartholomew non-committally. He had not yet considered how he would tell Michael what he had discovered without breaking his promise to Cecily to keep her whereabouts a secret.

'Out swimming more like!' retorted Michael, looking at Bartholomew's sopping clothes and dripping hair. 'What have you been doing?'

Bartholomew swung round to face him, irritated by the monk's persistent prying. 'Do you think the Proctor should know the comings and goings of all?'

Michael looked taken aback by his outburst, but then became angry himself. 'Walter said you left before dawn to go walking in the rain with no cloak. What do you expect me to think? We know about your badly aligned stars. I was worried.'

Bartholomew relented. 'I am sorry. I did not mean to cause trouble. But there is no need for all this concern, from you or anyone else. You are constantly demanding my expertise as the University's senior physician, so listen to me now – there is nothing wrong with me. Gray has never yet made the correct calculations for an astrological consultation – quite aside from the fact that he does not have the necessary information about me even to begin such a task. And you know I doubt the validity of astrological consultations, anyway. I cannot imagine why you are so ready to believe Gray over me.' He went to the water jug, but it had not been refilled that day. 'Where is Cynric?'

'Looking for you,' Michael said waspishly. 'And keep your voice down if you must hold such unorthodox views, or Father William will hear you, and then you will be in trouble.' He sat down again. 'Have you been looking into the death of that prostitute? I thought you may have gone to see Lady Matilde, but she said she has not seen you since yesterday, while the Tyler women complain bitterly that they have not set eyes on you since the night you were attacked. What have you been doing? You have certainly been up to more than a walk. Will you tell me?'

Bartholomew shook his head impatiently. He was tired and needed to think first, to work some sense into the jumble of information he had gathered before passing it to Michael. Such as the identity of the man whose voice was familiar, who had decreed that there will be a riot on Thursday.

'Then go to bed, Matt!' said Michael, throwing up his hands in exasperation. 'We will talk again in the morning.'

He left, and Bartholomew slipped his hand into his medicine bag, withdrawing the ring that Cecily Lydgate had given him. He looked at it for a moment, before feeling in the sleeve of his gown for the broken ring he had found at Godwinsson. He put them together. They were almost identical, except for the missing stone and the size. What did that tell him? That the light-fingered friar Edred had stolen Kenzie's ring and ground it under his heel in anger when he realised it belonged to his Principal's wife? That Kenzie had lost it while he waited in Godwinsson's shed like a moonstruck calf, hoping for a glimpse of his lover through the windows of her house? That Kenzie had somehow found his ring, only to have it stolen again after his death, and placed on the skeletal hand at Valence Marie? But Werbergh had said that Kenzie had come to him and Edred to ask if they had it. Werbergh believed Edred had taken it, and the fact that Kenzie was prepared to risk a confrontation with the friars to ask for it led Bartholomew to deduce that he could not have been wearing it when he died.

Bartholomew rubbed the bridge of his nose. He was tired, and the time spent crouching in the chest had taken a greater toll on him than he realised. He washed away the smell of the river as best he could in the drop of water left from the morning, and lay down on the bed, huddling under the blankets. He was on the edge of sleep when he remembered he had left the rings on the table. Reluctantly, he climbed out of bed, and dropped them both back into the sleeve of his gown. It was not an original hiding place but one that would have to do until he found a better one.

He was asleep within moments. Michael waited until his breathing became regular then stole back into the room. He smiled when he saw Bartholomew's gown had been moved slightly, and slipped his hand down inside the sleeve. It would not be the first time that his friend had used the wide sleeves of his scholar's gown to hide things. He froze as Bartholomew muttered something and stirred in his sleep, although Michael was not seriously worried about waking him. There were few who slept as heavily as the physician, even when he was not exhausted from a day's mysterious labours.

The rings glinted dimly silver in Michael's palm. He stopped himself from whistling. The broken one he had seen already and had dismissed as something of little importance. But it was important now, with a second, virtually identical, ring beside it. He looked to where Bartholomew slept and wondered how he had come to have it. He shrugged mentally letting the rings fall back inside Bartholomew's sleeve. He would ask him tomorrow, when he told him that there had been more trouble at Godwinsson Hostel that day, and that Brother Werbergh lay dead in St Andrew's Church.

CHAPTER 8

In the Parish Church of St Andrew, Werbergh lay on a trestle-table behind the altar. A tallow candle spluttered near his head, adding its own odour to the overpowering scent of cheap incense and death. Michael had been told that Werbergh's colleagues had agreed to undertake a vigil for him until his funeral the following day, but the church was deserted.

It was late afternoon, the day's teaching was completed, and the students had been given their freedom. Orange rays slanted through the traceried windows making intricate patterns on the floor, although the eastern-facing altar end of the church was gloomy. Bartholomew picked up the candle so that he could see the body better, while Michael wedged himself into a semicircular niche that had been intended to hold a statue before the church-builders had run out of money.

Someone had been to considerable trouble to give Werbergh a modicum of dignity during his last hours above ground. His hair had been brushed and trimmed and his gown had been carefully cleaned. Bartholomew inspected the friar's

332

hands and saw that they, too, had been meticulously washed and the nails scrubbed.

'Where was he found?' Bartholomew asked.

Michael regarded him in the dim light. 'Tell me what you discovered yesterday and I will tell you about Werbergh.'

Bartholomew dropped Werbergh's hand unceremoniously back on the table. 'I will be able to tell you little of any value if you do not provide me with the necessary details,' he said irritably. 'In which case, we are both wasting our time.'

Michael stood. 'I am sorry,' he said reluctantly. He gave a sudden grin, his small yellow teeth glinting in the candlelight. 'But it was worth a try.'

Bartholomew raised his eyebrows and returned his attention to Werbergh's body.

'He was found dead in the wood-shed in the yard of Godwinsson yesterday afternoon,' said Michael. 'Apparently, he had been looking for a piece of timber that he might be able to make into a portable writing table. Huw, the Godwinsson steward, said he had been talking about the idea for some weeks. The shed is a precarious structure and collapsed on top of him while he was inside.'

Bartholomew thought of his own visit to the ramshackle shed in Godwinsson's back yard. It had definitely been unstable but he had not thought it might be dangerous, and certainly not dangerous enough to kill someone who went inside.

'When did you first see the body?'

'Lydgate sent word to the Chancellor as soon

as it became clear that Werbergh was in the rubble. No one thought to look until he was missed some hours later. Why do you ask?'

Bartholomew picked at the tallow that had melted on to the table. 'So, Werbergh has been dead for at least an entire day. I would expect the body to be stiffer than it is, given the warm weather.'

Michael came to stand next to him as Bartholomew began a close inspection of the body. The physician ran his hands through Werbergh's hair, then held something he had retrieved between his thumb and forefinger. Michael leaned forward to look but shook his head uncomprehendingly.

'It is a piece of dried river weed,' said Bartholomew, dropping it into Michael's outstretched palm. He forced his hands underneath the body while Michael looked increasingly mystified. Bartholomew explained.

'Feel here, Brother. The body is damp underneath.'

'It looks to me as though his friends may have washed his habit,' said Michael, indicating Werbergh's spotless robe. 'Perhaps they washed it in the river so it would be clean for his funeral. People do launder clothes there, you know, despite what you tell them about it.'

'Give me time,' said Bartholomew. 'I need to inspect the body without the robe. Can we do that? Will it give offence?'

'Oh, doubtless it will give offence,' said Michael

334

airily, 'especially if you can show that our friar's death is not all it seems. Examine away, Matt, with the Senior Proctor's blessing, while the Senior Proctor himself will guard the door and deter prospective visitors. After all, there is no need to risk offending anyone if your findings are inconclusive.'

He ambled off to take up a station near the door, while Bartholomew began to remove Werbergh's robe. The task was made difficult by the fact that the table was very narrow. Eventually though he completed his examination, put all back as he had found it and went to join Michael, slightly out of breath and hot from his exertions.

Michael was not at the door, but outside it, engaged in a furious altercation. Bartholomew shrank back into the shadows of the church as he recognised the belligerent tones of Thomas Lydgate, poor Werbergh's Principal. Bartholomew had never heard him so angry, and, risking a glance out, saw the man's face was red with fury and his eyes were starting from his head. The physician in Bartholomew wanted to warn him to calm down before he had a fatal seizure, but he hung back, unwilling to become embroiled in the dispute.

'You have no right!' Lydgate was yelling. 'The man is dead! Can you not leave him in peace even for his last few hours above ground?'

'Like your students have done, you mean?' asked Michael innocently. 'The ones you told me would keep a vigil over him until tomorrow?'

Lydgate's immediate reply was lost in his outraged spluttering, and Bartholomew smiled to himself, uncharitably gratified to see this unpleasant man lost for words.

'If I hear that you have let that witless physician near him, I will complain in the strongest possible terms to the Chancellor and the Bishop.' Lydgate managed to grate his words out and Bartholomew imagined his huge hands clenching and unclenching in his fury. 'I will see you both dismissed from the University!'

'Why should you object so strongly to Doctor Bartholomew examining your student's body, Master Lydgate?' asked Michael sweetly. 'You have no reason to fear such an examination, surely?'

Once again came the sounds of near-speechless anger. 'There are rumours that he is not himself,' Lydgate managed eventually. 'I would not wish his feeble-minded ramblings to throw any kind of slur on my hostel!'

'Can a slur be thrown, or should it be cast?' Michael mused. Bartholomew smiled again, knowing that Michael was deliberately antagonising Lydgate. 'But regardless of grammatical niceties, Master Lydgate, I can assure you that my colleague is no more witless than you are.'

Bartholomew grimaced, while Lydgate appeared to be uncertain whether Michael was insulting him or not. He broke off the conversation abruptly and pushed past Michael towards the door. Bartholomew edged behind one of the smooth, round pillars and waited until Lydgate had stormed through the church to the altar before slipping out to join Michael. Michael took his arm and hurried him to a little-used alley so that no one would see them emerge from the churchyard.

'So, you think I am as witless as Lydgate, do you?' said Bartholomew, casting a reproachful glance at the fat Benedictine.

'Do not be ridiculous, Matt,' Michael replied. 'Lydgate is a paragon of wit compared to you.' He roared with laughter, while Bartholomew frowned, wondering whether there was anyone left in Cambridge who was not intimately acquainted with the alignment of his stars – even Lydgate seemed to know all about them. Michael saw his expression and his laughter died away.

'Witless or not, I would sooner trust your judgement than that of any other man I know,' he said with sudden seriousness. 'Even that of the Bishop. And as for your stars, I have far more reason to trust your judgement in matters of physic than Gray. If you say you are well, why should I doubt you?'

Bartholomew smiled reluctantly. Michael continued.

'So I am inclined also to believe you over the matter of the identities of our attackers, despite my reservations the day before yesterday when you gave me answers that I thought conflicted with what you had said earlier. What you say makes no sense, but that is no reason to assume you were mistaken. We will just have to do more serious thinking.'

Bartholomew was more relieved than he would have thought possible. Some of his irritability began to dissipate and he found himself better able to concentrate on Werbergh.

'So,' said Michael cheerily, 'tell me what your witless mind has seen that the genius of Lydgate has sought to hide.'

'The evidence is crystal clear,' began Bartholomew. 'I judge, from the leakiness and swelling of the body, that Werbergh has been dead not since yesterday morning, but a day or two earlier. He probably died on Friday night or Saturday morning. At some point, he was immersed in water, although he did not die from drowning. His robe is still damp, the skin is slightly bloated which is consistent with his body being in water after death, and in the hair on one arm I found more river weed. Although there are marks on the body that are consistent with the shed collapsing on him, the fatal wound was a blow to the back of the head – like Joanna, Kenzie, and possibly the skeleton of the child.'

Michael's face was grave. 'You believe Werbergh was murdered then?'

'Well, it was certainly not suicide.'

'Could the wound have been caused by the falling shed?

'It could,' said Bartholomew, 'but in this case it was not. There is no doubt that the shed collapsed, or more likely was arranged to fall, on Werbergh:

there are wounds where slivers of wood can be found, but they were inflicted some time after he died. The injury to the back of his head was caused by something smooth and hard – the pommel of a sword perhaps, or some other metal object – and has no traces of wood in it. Had that wound been caused by the falling shed, I think it would have contained splinters, given the fact that the timber was so rotten.'

Michael scratched at his cheek with dirty fingernails, his face thoughtful. 'Well, this explains all too clearly why Lydgate did not want you to examine Werbergh. Few would know these signs, or think to look for them, if the death appeared to be an accident.'

'Do you think Lydgate killed him?' asked Bartholomew. 'His actions are certainly not those of an innocent man.'

'They most assuredly are not,' agreed Michael. 'But if we try to report our findings to the Chancellor now, Lydgate will claim you are incompetent to judge because of your unfavourable stars.' He resumed scratching his cheek again. 'So, we will keep this knowledge to ourselves. And thinking he has managed to fool us might lead the killer – whether it is Lydgate or someone else – into making a mistake. I spoke to the Godwinsson scholars yesterday and all had alibis for the alleged time of Werbergh's death, but now we need to know what they were all doing on Friday night, not Sunday.'

'Kenzie first and now Werbergh,' said Bartholomew. 'I wonder where those Scottish lads were on Friday night. Perhaps they grew tired of waiting for justice and took it into their own hands to avenge Kenzie's death.'

'True,' said Michael, nodding slowly as he ran through the possibilities in his mind. 'Since Master Lydgate seems to have an aversion to you, I will go alone to chat informally to the scholars of Godwinsson, to see if I can find out what was afoot on Friday night. Meanwhile, how would you like to visit David's to see how our Scottish friends are?'

Bartholomew shrugged assent. Michael rubbed his hands together and then clapped Bartholomew on the back. 'We will outwit whoever is responsible for these crimes, my friend, you and I together.'

Despite the cooler weather of the last two days, David's Hostel was stifling. The shutters were thrown open but the narrow windows at the front of the house allowed little air to circulate: the large windows at the back allowed the sun to pour in but faced the wrong direction to catch the breeze. Bartholomew imagined that the decrepit building, although unhealthily hot in the summer, would be bitterly cold in the winter.

Meadowman, the David's steward, showed Bartholomew into the large room that served as the hostel's hall, while Fyvie hurried away to fetch the Principal. Davy Grahame and Ruthven were seated at the table with a large tome in front of them, while the older Grahame played lilting melodies on a small pipe in a corner with one or two other students.

Through the window, Bartholomew could see the brother of the student who had been ill. He was stripped to the waist and was splashing around happily with a brush and a bucket of water. From the envious eyes of some of the others, Bartholomew could see that cleaning the yard and escaping from academic studies was regarded more as a privilege than a chore. Ivo the scullion clattered about noisily in the kitchen as usual, and Meadowman went back to polishing the hostel pewter.

Robert of Stirling, the brother of the student cleaning the yard, rose when he saw Bartholomew and began fumbling in the scrip tied around his waist. Shyly he offered Bartholomew a silver coin, muttering that it was for the medicine he had been given. Bartholomew, who could not recall whether he had been paid or not, waved the money away with a shake of his head. The student pocketed his coin again hurriedly, giving Bartholomew a quick grin.

'Have you found Jamie's murderer yet?' he asked, the smile fading.

Bartholomew was aware that, although no one had moved, everyone in the room was listening for his answer.

'Not yet,' he said. What more could he say? They were really no further forward than they had been when he and Michael had first imparted the news of Kenzie's death to his friends several days before. And now there was a second death, similar to the first.

He looked up as Father Andrew entered. The friar's benign face was slightly splattered with ink, and his hands were black with it. He noticed Bartholomew's gaze and smiled apologetically.

'I am having problems with a new batch of quills,' he explained in his soft, lilting voice. 'I am a theologian, Doctor, and I am afraid such practical matters as cutting quills elude me.'

Bartholomew returned his smile, and Andrew perched on a stool next to him, clasping his stained hands together.

'Ivo!' he called to the noisy scullion. 'We have visitors, boy! Meadowman, can you not give Ivo a task he might complete more quietly?' He turned to Bartholomew. 'David's is severely limited in whom it can afford for servants,' he said in a low voice, so he would not be overheard and hurt Ivo's feelings. 'Meadowman is efficient enough but our scullions must be supervised constantly. But enough of our problems. What can we do for you, Doctor?' A smile crinkled his light blue eyes as he saw Ruthven and Davy Grahame return to their reading and he nodded approvingly at their diligence. 'I am afraid Master Radbeche is out at the moment but I will help you if I can.'

'I am afraid we are making little headway in this business concerning James Kenzie,' said

Bartholomew. 'I really came to ask if there was anything else you might have heard, or remembered, since the last time we met that might help.'

The smile left Andrew's eyes and his face became sad. 'Poor Jamie,' he said softly. 'He would never have made a good scholar but he was a decent lad: truthful and kind. It was a terrible thing that he died such a death. His parents will be devastated.' He shook himself. 'But my eulogies will not help you catch his killer. In truth, I have thought of little else during these last few days, but I have been unable to come up with the merest shred of information that could be of use to you. I did not know he had a secret lover, and I certainly did not know it was Dominica Lydgate, or I would have dissuaded him immediately.'

'Why?' asked Bartholomew. 'Did you not like her?'

Andrew shook his head vehemently. 'You misunderstand,' he said. 'I have never met her. But I can see no future in a relationship between a poor student and the daughter of a wealthy principal. I would have dissuaded him for his own ultimate happiness. It is not for nothing the University has strict rules about women!'

'Who do you think might have killed Jamie?' Bartholomew asked.

Andrew spread his hands. 'I wish I knew. As it is, I do not even know why. You asked his friends about a ring Jamie was supposed to have had. Perhaps he was killed for that, if his killer assumed it was of value. I cannot imagine what he was

343

doing near the Ditch at Valance Marie, but maybe that is not a safe place to be of an evening. Perhaps a group of apprentices were looking for trouble and killed him for simple mischief.'

'Do you think it possible that he may have been killed by students from another hostel?' asked Bartholomew. 'For example the friars with whom he argued the day before he died?'

Andrew spread his inky hands again. 'It is possible, I suppose, but it seems an extreme reaction on the part of the friars. Students of different hostels are always quarrelling with each other, but such altercations seldom result in murder – at least, not cold-blooded, premeditated slaying; we all know they kill each other in the heat of the moment.'

Although they were pretending to be doing other things, Bartholomew knew that the students were listening intently.

'Do you think the friars killed Jamie?' he asked Stuart Grahame.

Stuart Grahame looked up and flushed red at the sudden attention. 'I did to begin with,' he said, 'but not now. The friars would have been more likely to have killed me or Fyvie, since we were the ones who reacted the most strongly to their insults. Jamie did not antagonise them enough so that they would want to kill him.'

And how much would that be? Bartholomew wondered. He watched the others carefully but could see nothing in the wide, guileless eyes of Davy Grahame that suggested guilt, while Ruthven nodded wisely at Stuart Grahame's words, so that Bartholomew suspected that Grahame was merely repeating Ruthven's own logic. Fyvie, however, stared moodily at the rushes and his face revealed nothing.

'And what do you think, Fyvie?' asked Bartholomew, watching him intently.

Fyvie said nothing for a few moments, and then stood. He loomed over Bartholomew, who would have felt threatened had Father Andrew not been present. He slowly pointed a finger at the physician.

'I have no reason to dismiss anyone from my list of suspects,' he said. 'Perhaps Stuart Grahame is right about the friars and perhaps he is not. But who else had a reason to kill him?'

Who indeed? thought Bartholomew. If Werbergh had been telling the truth about Kenzie appearing at the church to ask if the friars had stolen his ring, then Edred might well have been presented with the perfect opportunity to follow and kill him. His motive might simply have been that he did not want the Scot to be alive to accuse him of theft. The more Bartholomew considered it, the more the evidence seemed to stack against Edred.

They all jumped as water hit one of the window shutters with a crash, splattering in over the sill and spraying Ruthven and Davy Grahame. The two students ducked away, grinning at each other as they shook droplets from their hair and wiped their faces with their sleeves. From the yard, there was a gale of laughter and a moment later the smirking face of the student who had been working there appeared. His mischievous delight vanished when he saw David's had a visitor.

'John!' admonished Father Andrew. 'Where are your manners, lad?'

'Have you got him?' asked John of Bartholomew, leaning earnestly through the window. 'Is that why you are here? To tell us you have caught Jamie's murderer?'

'He has not,' said Father Andrew. 'Go back to your chores, John, and no playing with the water or I will tell your brother to take over your duties.'

While John reluctantly went back to his cleaning, the friar spoke gently to Fyvie, urging him to sit down. 'Perhaps Jamie's murder was a random crime. Many deaths occur without a reason. You must brace yourself for the possibility that his killer may never be caught, despite the best efforts of the Senior Proctor and his colleagues.'

Fyvie looked up at him and then his glower abated somewhat. 'I am sorry,' he wailed suddenly, making Bartholomew start nervously. 'But we are cooped up here day and night, not allowed to go out unless we are accompanied, and all the while Jamie's murderer is laughing at us! I am not saying I wish to kill the man myself,' he said, with an apologetic glance at Father Andrew, 'but I do wish to bring him to justice.'

The friar patted his arm consolingly. 'The Proctor is doing all he can. Meanwhile, you would not wish to upset your family by becoming embroiled in things you should not.'

He sighed and called to the open window. 'There is no need to eavesdrop, John. Come in if you insist on listening.'

John's begrimed face appeared immediately, and he leaned his elbows on the window-sill.

'A shed collapsed on Brother Werbergh yesterday morning,' said Bartholomew somewhat abruptly.

Students and master looked at each other in confusion. 'Is Brother Werbergh one of the Godwinsson friars with whom our students argued?' asked Andrew. Bartholomew nodded. 'Is he badly hurt?'

'He is dead,' said Bartholomew.

There was a deathly silence. 'Is that why you are here?' asked Andrew. 'To see where David's Hostel students were at the time of his death?' His eyes became sad. 'You might have been a little more straightforward with us, Doctor. I assure you, we have nothing to hide, and you have no need to resort to this trickery. Yesterday morning, you say? We were either at church or here.'

'What about Friday and Saturday?' Bartholomew asked.

'You said he died yesterday,' Andrew pointed out. 'But it makes no difference. Since this dreadful business began we have kept our students here, or out under supervision. As I told you earlier we cannot afford to be seen brawling, or we will lose our hostel. Either I, or the Principal, can vouch for every one of our students at any time since. And I can assure you that none of them has fooled us with rolled-up blankets this time.'

Bartholomew rose to leave. 'I am sorry to have wasted your time, Father,' he said, 'but these questions needed to be asked – to clear your names from malicious gossip if nothing else.'

Andrew's mild indignation abated somewhat. 'I am sorry, too. Doctor. We have nothing to be ashamed of, so we do not resent your inquiries. We will answer any questions that will bring Jamie's killer to justice.' He rubbed at the ink on his hands. 'Have you finished with our Galen yet? Although we have no medical students at David's, a book is a valuable thing, and we would like it back soon.'

Bartholomew, who had been under the impression from Principal Radbeche that there was no immediate urgency for him to finish with it, was embarrassed that he had taken his time to read it. He offered to return it immediately. Andrew gave Bartholomew an apologetic smile.

'It is the only book we own outright,' he said again. He gestured at the tomes that were piled on the table. 'These others are borrowed from King's Hall. While I am delighted that you have found our Galen useful, I would feel happier in my mind knowing it is back here.' His grin broadened, and his voice dropped as he leaned towards Bartholomew so the students could not overhear. 'I show it to the illiterate parents of prospective students, so they know that we are serious about learning. Even though our book is a medical text, it serves an important function at David's!'

Bartholomew said he would send Gray round with the book as soon as possible. He offered his hand to Father Andrew, who clasped it genially before settling down at the table to read with Ruthven and Davy. Robert of Stirling leapt to his feet to see him out and Bartholomew followed him along the stuffy corridor. The student removed the bar from the gate, all the while gabbling about the attack several weeks before in which the old door had been kicked down. Bartholomew sensed the lad was chattering to hide his nervousness.

As Bartholomew stepped past him, Robert took his arm, casting an anxious glance back down the corridor. He made as though to speak but then closed his mouth firmly. Sweat beaded on his upper lip and he scrubbed at it irritably with his shirt-sleeve.

'What is wrong?' Bartholomew asked, wondering whether Robert had fully recovered from his fever. Perhaps he needed more medication and was afraid he would not have enough money to pay for it.

'Jamie's ring,' the student blurted out. 'I admired it. My father is a jeweller, you see. I know about good stones.' His words were jerky and he gave another agitated glance down the corridor.

'If it will put your mind at ease, I will tell no one we have spoken,' said Bartholomew gently, giving the nervous student a reassuring smile.

Robert swallowed hard. 'I persuaded Father

Andrew to take me and my brother John to see the relic at Valence Marie on Saturday,' he said. He paused again and Bartholomew forced himself to be patient. 'Jamie's ring was on that horrible thing!' Robert's words came in a rush.

'I noticed the hand wore a ring similar to the one Jamie is said to have owned,' said Bartholomew carefully. One thing they could not afford was for Robert to claim Kenzie's ring was at Valence Marie: Valence Marie would start a fight with David's for certain. 'It is not necessarily the same one.'

'It *is* the same!' said Robert, his voice loud, desperate to be believed. Bartholomew grew anxious and wondered how he might dissuade Robert from his belief.

'Easy now,' he said. 'I will ask Brother Michael to inspect the ring, and—'

'You do not understand!' interrupted Robert, shaking off Bartholomew's attempt to placate him. 'I am not telling you it is similar. I am telling you it is the same one.'

'How can you be sure?' asked Bartholomew with quiet reason. 'I have seen at least one other ring identical to the one at Valence Marie myself recently.'

Robert looked pained. 'You recognise different diseases,' he said. 'I recognise different stones. My father is a jeweller, and I have been handling jewels since I was old enough not to eat them. It was the same ring, I tell you!'

His point made, he became calmer, although he kept casting anxious glances towards the hall.

'Why did you not tell me this when you were in the hall with the others?' asked Bartholomew.

Robert shook his head violently and fixed Bartholomew with huge eyes. 'I could not explain how I know,' he whispered.

Bartholomew was puzzled. 'But you said your father is a jeweller. Is that not explanation enough?'

Robert lowered his gaze. 'No one but you knows that. John told a lie when we first arrived two years ago. We have been living it ever since. We cannot reveal that we are the sons of a merchant.'

Bartholomew shook his head, nonplussed. Many merchants' sons studied in Cambridge and he was unaware that any of them faced serious problems because of it. Looking at Robert's dark features, he suddenly realised the physical similarity between him and the Arab master with whom he had studied in Paris. In a flash of understanding, it occurred to him that Robert and John might be Jewish, that their father was a money-lender rather than a jeweller. In France, the Jewish population had been accused of bringing the plague, and the situation was little better in England. If Bartholomew's supposition were true, he did not blame Robert and John for wishing to keep their heritage a secret.

Robert continued. 'Master Radbeche and Father Andrew think my father owns a manor near Stirling.'

'They will not learn otherwise from me,' said Bartholomew. 'But this matter of Jamie's ring . . .'

Robert became animated again. 'It is his ring!

There is no doubt! I pretended to examine the hand closely but really I was looking at the ring.'

Bartholomew felt in the sleeve of his gown. 'But what about this?' he asked, handing the ring Cecily had given him to Robert. Robert took it and turned it around in his fingers, smiling faintly.

'Ah, yes, lovers' rings. I wondered if Jamie's might be one of a pair. But this is not the ring he had.' He gave it back to Bartholomew. 'He had the gentleman's; this is the lady's.'

Bartholomew showed Robert the other ring, the one he had found on the floor of Godwinsson's shed. The shed that killed Werbergh, he thought, although obviously Werbergh could not have been looking for the ring, since he was already dead when he was put there.

Robert was talking, and Bartholomew forced his thoughts back to the present. 'This would once have held a stone about the same size as the ones in the lovers' rings, although the craftsmanship on this is very inferior. See the crudeness of the welding? And the arms of the clasp are different sizes.' His nervousness seemed to abate as he talked about something he knew. 'This is a nasty piece. I would say it belonged to a whore, or someone who could not afford anything better. In fact, I would go as far as saying there was no stone at all, but perhaps coloured glass.'

He looked up, dark brown eyes meeting Bartholomew's. 'I cannot say how Jamie's ring came to be on that horrible hand, but it is his without a doubt. The matching ring you have is the other half of the pair; I imagine you got it from Dominica. The third ring is nothing – a tawdry bauble. Do you think they might have some connection to why Jamie was killed?'

Bartholomew slipped them back into his sleeve and shrugged. 'The one on the relic definitely does. You have helped considerably by telling me what you have, and I promise you, no one will ever know where I came by the information. Perhaps you will return the favour by keeping your knowledge of the matter to yourself.'

Robert looked at Bartholomew as though he were insane. 'I feel I have risked enough just talking to you. I will not tell another soul – not even my brother John. John does not share my interest in precious stones, and found the hand sufficiently repulsive that he did not look at it long enough to recognise Jamie's ring.'

Bartholomew felt in his bag, pulling out a small packet. 'Take this. It is a mixture of herbs I give babies when they are teething and will do you no harm. If anyone should ask why you have been talking with me for so long, tell them you still feel feverish and wanted some medicine.'

The student gave Bartholomew a grin and took the packet. 'I should go,' he said, with another glance over his shoulder. 'I am glad I could help. I want you to catch Jamie's killer.'

As Bartholomew left, he heard Robert slide the bar into place behind the door, and frowned thoughtfully. Assuming Robert was not mistaken, Kenzie's ring on the hand found at Valence Marie lent yet more evidence to the fact that Thorpe's relic was a fake: if Kenzie had worn the ring a few days before, there was no legitimate way the bony hand could have been wearing it for the last twenty-five years. Bartholomew walked slowly, his head bent in concentration. Will, the Valence Marie servant, might have been near the place where Kenzie had died. Had he discovered Kenzie's body, stolen the ring, and then decided to adorn the hand with it?

Bartholomew sighed. He was back to a question he had asked before: who else would recognise the ring? Kenzie would have done, certainly, but he was dead. Dominica, assuming Bartholomew was right in his assumption that she was Joanna, was also dead. Thomas and Cecily Lydgate would know it, especially Cecily. Had Kenzie been killed just so that the ring could be put on the hand for the Lydgates to see? It seemed a very elaborate plot and there was nothing to say that the Lydgates would ever go to view the hand. Also, it necessitated a high degree of premeditation: Kenzie was killed several days before the relic appeared, and it was surely risky to kill for a ring, then just toss it into the Ditch on a skeletal hand in the hope that it might be found by the dredgers.

Try as he might, Bartholomew could make no sense of it all. Only one thing was clear. His left sleeve had a small tear in it that he had been meaning to ask Agatha to mend. Because of this, he had been careful to put the two rings into his right sleeve the night before. But when he had shown the rings to Robert, they were in his left sleeve. Although the hiding place was perhaps an obvious one, there was only one person who might guess that he would use it. Bartholomew frowned again, wondering why Michael had searched not only his gown the previous night as he slept, but also his room the day before.

The day of the Founder's Feast dawned bright and clear. All the scholars of Michaelhouse rose long before dawn to help with the preparations for the grand occasion. Agatha, who had not slept at all the night before, bellowed orders at the frantic kitchen staff and at any scholars who happened to be within bawling range. Bartholomew smiled when he saw the dignified Senior Fellow, Roger Alcote, struggling irritably across the courtyard with a huge vat of saffron custard, trying not to spill any on his immaculate ceremonial gown.

'Sam Gray!' yelled Agatha from the door of the kitchen, loud enough to wake half of Cambridge. Gray's tawny head appeared through the open window shutters of his room, looking anxious. 'Run to the Market Square and buy me a big pewter jug for the cream. That half-wit Deynman has just cracked mine.'

'How can he have cracked a pewter jug?'

called Gray, startled. 'They are supposed to be unbreakable.'

Bartholomew heard Agatha's gusty sigh from the other side of the courtyard. 'That is what I always thought but Deynman has managed it. So, off to the market with you. Now.'

Gray rubbed his eyes sleepily. 'The market stalls will not be open yet.' he called. 'It is still dark.'

'Then go to the metal-smith's house and wake him up!' shouted Agatha, exasperated. Even the wily Gray knew better than to disobey a direct order from Agatha, and he scuttled away, running his fingers through his hair in a vain attempt to tidy it. Meanwhile, Agatha had spotted Bartholomew who, with Father William, was draping one of Alcote's luxurious bed-covers over the derelict stable that teetered in one corner of the yard.

'And what do you think you are doing?' she demanded in stentorian tones to Father William. He looked taken aback, apparently considering that the purpose of their task was obvious to any onlooker.

'Father Aidan said he thought these crumbling walls were an eyesore and he suggested we cover them.' He shook his head in disapproval. 'All vanity! We should be saving our guests from the eternal fires of hell, not pandering to their earthly vices by disguising ramshackle buildings with pieces of finery!' He gave the bed-cover a vicious tug as though it were personally responsible for Father Aidan's peculiar recommendation.

'I meant why are you forcing Doctor Bartholomew to help you?' she roared. 'He should not be cavorting about with you when his stars are bad.'

Bartholomew closed his eyes in despair, wondering yet again how much longer Gray's diagnosis would continue to haunt him. Still, he thought, trying to look on the positive side, at least his recent accident had meant that Agatha had forgiven him for inviting Eleanor Tyler to the Feast, and he was now back in her favour. When he opened his eyes again Father William was regarding him uneasily.

'I can finish this, Matthew,' he said. 'You go to your room and lie down.'

'I am perfectly healthy,' Bartholomew snapped, pulling the bed-cover into place with unnecessary roughness. 'In fact, much more so than you.'

'Me?' asked William, surprised. 'How can you tell that?'

'You keep rubbing your stomach and you are as white as snow. Did you eat that fish-giblet stew that has been making an appearance at every meal since last week?'

William winced and looked away queasily. 'It tasted much stronger than usual and I should have known not to eat it when some of it spilled and the College cat would not touch it.'

Bartholomew stepped back, satisfied that the unsightly, tumbledown stable would not now offend the sensibilities of Michaelhouse's august guests. Of course, some of them might well wonder why a bed-cover was draped over one of the buildings in the yard, but that question could be dealt with when it arose.

'I can give you some powdered chalk mixed with poppy juice. That should settle it down. But if you take it you must avoid drinking wine today.'

'I was not planning to indulge myself in the sins of the flesh,' said William loftily. 'A little watered ale is all I shall require at the Feast. And I certainly shall not be eating anything.'

'Good,' said Bartholomew, setting off towards his room, Father William in tow. He stopped abruptly. 'Oh, Lord! There is Guy Heppel. I hope he has not found another body in the King's Ditch.' It crossed his mind, however, that investigating such a matter might be a perfect opportunity for him to extricate himself from the delicate situation he faced with his two female guests that day.

William snorted. 'That canal is a veritable cemetery! I cannot see that either the town or the University will be keen to dredge it again after all it has yielded this time.'

He watched Heppel making his way delicately across the uneven yard, holding his elegant gown high, so that it would not become fouled with the mud, some hard and dry but some sticky and thick, that covered it.

'That man is a disgrace! To think he was appointed over me to keep law and order in the town!' William drew himself up to his full height and looked down his nose as the Junior Proctor approached. 'And I think he wears perfume!'

Heppel arrived, breathless as always. He was apparently to be someone's guest, perhaps Michael's, for he wore ceremonial scarlet and a pair of fine yellow hose. Uncharitably, Bartholomew could not but help compare the skinny legs that were thrust into them with those of a heron.

'Thank the Lord you are awake,' said Heppel to Bartholomew in relief. 'I must have this astrological consultation before I enjoy the pleasures of your Founder's Feast today. After the last one I attended, I was ill for a week. I must know whether my stars are favourable, or whether I should decline the invitation.'

Father William gave a sudden groan and clutched at Bartholomew to support himself. 'Oh, I do feel ill. Matthew,' he whispered hoarsely. 'I think I might have a contagion.'

'A contagion?' squeaked Heppel in alarm, moving backwards quickly. 'What manner of contagion?'

'One that is both painful and severe,' said William, holding his stomach dramatically. 'I do hope its miasma has not affected Matthew. You might be better waiting a while for this consultation, Master Heppel, in case he passes it to you.'

Heppel took several more steps away, and shoved a vast pomander to his nose.

'Saturn is still ascendant,' said Bartholomew, thinking he should at least try to ease Heppel's obvious concern for his well-being. 'So take a small dose of that angelica and heartsease I gave you and eat and drink sparingly today. That should see you safely through the ordeal. And avoid anything that might contain fish giblets.'

'Are fish giblets under the dominion of Saturn, then?' asked Heppel, puzzled and taking yet another step backwards as William reeled.

'Yes,' said William before Bartholomew could reply. 'Say a mass before you come to the Feast, Master Heppel, and pray for me.'

Heppel bowed briskly to Bartholomew and William and walked out of the yard a good deal more quickly than he had walked in. Bartholomew took Father William's arm, although the ailing friar made a miraculous recovery once Heppel had been ushered out of the front gate by the porters.

'Did you smell it?' William growled to Bartholomew. 'Perfume! Like a painted whore! And God knows whores have no business in a place of learning!'

Bartholomew swallowed hard and hoped Michael had ensured that Matilde was not seated anywhere near Father William at the Feast. He unlocked the little storeroom where he kept his medicines and mixed a draught of chalk and poppy syrup. William gulped it down and pulled a face.

'God's teeth, Matthew, that is a vile concoction! You should give a dose to that reprehensible Heppel. That would stop him coming after you for his astrological consultations.'

'Remember,' Bartholomew warned as the friar left. 'No wine.'

'I am not one of your dull-witted students, Matthew,' said William pompously. 'I only need to be told something once for it to sink in. No wine.' He looked Bartholomew up and down disparagingly. 'I do hope you are going to change into something a little more appropriate. You look very scruffy this morning.'

'But wearing fine clothes would be indulging in the sins of the flesh,' Bartholomew pointed out to the man who professed to have no wish for material goods and to care nothing for appearances.

Aware that he had been caught out in an inconsistency, Father William pursed his lips. 'You have my blessing to indulge yourself today, Matthew. After all, we cannot have Fellows of other colleges thinking that Michaelhouse scholars are shabby, can we? I, of course, as a lowly friar, own no fine clothes, but Agatha washed my spare habit specially for the occasion. Unfortunately, it shrank a little and is now a lighter shade of grey than it should be, but it is spotlessly clean.'

'Are you telling me that this is the first time it has ever been washed?' asked Bartholomew, disgusted. 'You have had the same two habits since before I became a Fellow here and that was eight years ago!'

'Grey does not show the dirt, Matthew. And anyway, I was afraid laundering might damage them. I am well aware of your peculiar notions about washing, but I personally believe that water has dangerous properties and that contact with it should be avoided at all costs.'

'So I see,' said Bartholomew, noticing, not for the first time, that the friar's everyday habit was quite stiff with filth. He imagined there was probably enough spilled food on it to keep the College supplied for weeks.

'Well, I must go and prepare the church for prime,' said William. He raised a hand to his head. 'The burning in my stomach has eased but I feel a little giddy. Is it that potion you gave me?'

'It might be,' said Bartholomew. 'Of course, it might equally well be the terrifying notion of wearing a clean habit. You will need to take another dose, probably just before the Feast. I will leave it for you on my table, so you can come to get it when it is convenient. Only take half of it, though. The rest is to be drunk before you go to bed.'

William nodded and was gone. Alone, Bartholomew washed and shaved and donned a clean shirt and hose, although both were heavily patched and darned. Cynric slipped into the room with Bartholomew's ceremonial red gown that he had painstakingly brushed and ironed. Bartholomew took it reluctantly, guessing that Cynric had been to some trouble to render it so smart. The physician was careless with clothes, and knew it would be only a matter of time before something spilled on it or it became crumpled.

'It should be a fine day,' said Cynric, nodding to where the sky was already a clear blue. 'I hope you have a good time with that Eleanor Tyler.'

His good wishes did not sound entirely sincere and Bartholomew glanced at him, puzzled. 'First Agatha and now you. What is wrong with Eleanor Tyler?'

'Nothing, nothing,' said Cynric hastily. He hesitated. 'Well, she is a touch brazen, boy, if you must know the truth. And she is after a husband. With no father to negotiate for them, those Tyler daughters are taking matters into their own hands. That is what makes them brazen.'

But not as brazen as a prostitute, Bartholomew thought, wondering what Cynric would say when he found out about Matilde. It crossed his mind that Cynric, Agatha and even Father William, might excuse his choice of guests on the grounds that his stars were misaligned, assuming, of course, that they did not discover that the invitations were issued long before he was hit on the head.

The day was already becoming warm as the scholars assembled in the yard to walk to the church for prime. Bartholomew found he was uncomfortable in his thick gown, and warned Cynric that watered ale might be required at some point of the proceedings if someone fainted. Master Kenyngham, the gentle Gilbertine friar who was head of Michaelhouse, beamed happily at his colleagues, blithely unaware of Gray scampering late into his place near the end of the procession.

Agatha approached Gray nonchalantly, and a large pewter jug exchanged hands, even as the line of scholars began to move off towards the church.

Michael walked next to Bartholomew, behind the Franciscans, his podgy hands clasped reverently across his ample stomach. He wore his best habit, and the wooden cross that usually hung around his neck had been exchanged for one that looked to be silver. His thin, brown hair had been trimmed, too, and his tonsure was, as always, perfectly round and shiny.

'You look very splendid today, Brother,' Bartholomew remarked, impressed by the fact that, unlike everyone else, the monk had escaped being involved in the frantic preparations that morning.

'Naturally,' said Michael, raising a hand to his hair. 'A good many important people will be at this Feast, not to mention your gaggle of hussies. I must make a good impression.'

'Did you ask the steward to make sure Matilde was not near William?' asked Bartholomew anxiously.

The monk nodded. 'Eleanor will be next to Father William. Matilde will sit between you and our esteemed Senior Fellow, Roger Alcote.'

'Are you insane?' Bartholomew cried. The Franciscans looked round to glower at him for breaking the silence of the procession. He lowered his voice. 'Alcote will be worse than William, if that is possible, and William will be horrified to find himself next to Eleanor!'

'That cannot be helped,' said Michael primly. 'You should have considered all this before inviting a harem to dine in our College.'

The church was gloomy in the early morning light but candles, lit in honour of the occasion, cast wavering shadows around the walls. The procession made its way up the aisle and filed silently in two columns into the chancel, Fellows in one and students in the other. The body of the church was full of townspeople and scholars from other colleges. Eleanor Tyler was standing at the front and gave Bartholomew a vigorous wave when he saw her. Michael sniggered unpleasantly and then slipped away to join his choir.

'What in God's name is Father William wearing?' hissed Roger Alcote from Bartholomew's side. 'Has he borrowed a habit from Father Aidan? It is far too small for him – you can virtually see his knees! And the colour! It is almost white, not grey at all!'

'He washed it,' explained Bartholomew, smiling when he saw William's powerful white calves displayed under his shrunken habit. 'He said he thought that water might be dangerous to it, and, from the state of it, I would say he was right!'

Michael cleared his throat, and an expectant hush fell on the congregation.

'Let us hope he has chosen something short,' muttered Alcote, as Michael raised his hands in the air in front of his assembled singers. 'Or we may find we have fewer guests for the rest of the day than we had anticipated.'

His uncharitable words were not spoken lightly. As one, the congregation winced as the first few notes of an anthem by the Franciscan composer Simon Tunstede echoed around the church. What Michael's singers lacked in tone was compensated for by sheer weight of numbers, so that the resulting sound was deafening. Michael gesticulated furiously for a lowering of volume but his volunteers were out to sing for their supper and their enthusiasm was not to be curtailed. The lilting melody of one of Tunstede's loveliest works was rendered into something akin to a pagan battle song.

The door of the church opened and one or two people slipped out. Bartholomew saw his sister standing near the back of the church, her hand over her mouth as she tried to conceal her amusement. To his horror, he saw Eleanor Tyler had no such inhibitions and was laughing openly. Next to her, Sheriff Tulyet struggled to maintain a suitably sombre expression, while his infant son howled furiously, unsettled by the din. Only Master Kenyngham seemed unaffected, smiling benignly and tapping his hand so out of time with the choir that Bartholomew wondered if he were hearing the same piece.

To take his mind off the racket, Bartholomew looked at the space that had been cleared for Master Wilson's tomb. The mason had said the whole contraption would be ready before the end of autumn, when Wilson's mouldering corpse could be removed from its temporary grave – recently desecrated by Bartholomew – and laid to its final rest under his black marble slab. The notion of exhuming the body of a man who had perished in the plague bothered the physician. Some scholars believed that the pestilence had come from graves in the Orient, and Bartholomew had no desire to unleash again the sickness that took one in every three people across Europe. He decided that he would exhume the grave alone, wearing gloves and mask, to reduce the chances of another outbreak. Anyone who felt so inclined could come later and pay their respects – although he could not imagine that the unpopular, smug Master Wilson would have many mourners lining up at his grave.

When the long Latin mass was over, the scholars walked back to Michaelhouse and prepared to greet their guests in the courtyard. There was a pleasant breeze – although it had blown the bed-cover hiding the stable askew – and the sun shone brightly. Agatha's voice could be heard ranting in the kitchens, almost drowned out by the church bells. The gates were flung open and the guests began to arrive.

One of the first was Eleanor Tyler, who flounced across the courtyard, looking around her speculatively. She looked lovely, Bartholomew thought, dressed in an emerald-green dress with her smooth, brown hair bound in plaits and knotted at the back of her head. She beamed at Bartholomew and took his arm. Her face fell somewhat when she saw a patched shirt-sleeve poking from under his gown.

'I thought you were all supposed to be wearing your best clothes,' she said, disappointed.

'These are my best clothes,' protested Bartholomew. 'And they are clean.'

'Clean,' echoed Eleanor uncertainly, apparently preferring grimy finery to laundered rags. But her attention was already elsewhere. 'Why is there a bed-cover on that old wall?' she asked, pointing to Bartholomew and William's handiwork. 'If it is being washed, you might have taken it in before your guests arrived.'

'Your choir put their hearts and souls into that anthem by Simon Tunstede,' remarked Bartholomew as Michael came to stand next to him. 'It must have been heard fifteen miles away in Ely Cathedral.'

Michael winced. 'More like sixty miles away in Westminster Abbey! Once their blood is up, there is no stopping those people. My only compensation is that my guest, the Prior of Barnwell, told me he thought it was exquisite.'

'But he is stone deaf,' said Bartholomew, startled. 'He cannot even hear the bells of his chapel any more.'

'Well, he heard my choir,' said Michael. 'Here he comes. You must excuse me, Madam.' He bowed elegantly to Eleanor, lingering over her hand rather longer than was necessary.

Eleanor's indignation at the monk's behaviour was deflected by the magnificent spectacle of the arrival of Sheriff Tulyet and the Mayor, both resplendent in scarlet cloaks lined with the softest fur, despite the warmth of the day. Sensibly, Tulyet relinquished his to a servant, but the Mayor knew he looked good and apparently decided that sweating profusely was a small price to pay for cutting so fine a figure. Master Kenyngham approached, smiling beatifically, and introduced himself to Eleanor, asking her if she were a relative of Bartholomew's.

At that moment, Bartholomew spotted his sister and her husband, and excused himself from Eleanor's vivid, and not entirely accurate, description of how Bartholomew had saved her on the night of the riot. Kenyngham, Bartholomew noted, was looking increasingly horrified; he hoped Eleanor's account of the violence that night would not spoil the gentle, peace-loving Master's day.

'Matt!' said Edith Stanmore, coming to greet him with outstretched arms. 'Are you fully recovered? Sam Gray tells me your stars are still poorly aligned.'

Bartholomew raised his eyes heavenwards. 'I am perfectly well, Edith.' He fixed his brother-in-law with a look of reproval. 'And I have no need of Cynric following me everywhere I go.'

Stanmore had the grace to look sheepish. 'This is Mistress Horner,' he said, turning to gesture towards an elderly woman who stood behind him. Mistress Horner was crook-backed and thin, wearing a dowdy, russet dress that hung loosely from her hunched figure. A starched, white wimple framed her wind-burned face, although her features were shaded by a peculiar floppy hat. A clawed, gloved hand clutched a walking stick, although she did not seem to be particularly unsteady on her feet. Bartholomew had not seen her before and assumed she must be someone's dowager aunt, wheeled out from some musty attic for a day of entertainment. He bowed politely to her, disconcerted by the way she was staring at him.

Stanmore caught sight of the Mayor standing nearby, and was away without further ado to accost him and doubtless discuss some business arrangement or other. Edith was watching her brother with evident amusement.

'You have met Mistress Horner before,' she said, her eyes twinkling with laughter.

'I have?' asked Bartholomew, who was certain he had not. He looked closer and his mouth fell open in shock. 'Matilde!'

'Shh!' said Matilde, exchanging a look of merriment with Edith. 'I did not go to all this trouble so that you could reveal my disguise in the first few moments. What do you think?'

She smiled up at him, revealing small, perfectly white teeth in a face that had evidently been stained with something to make her skin look leathery, while carefully painted black lines served as wrinkles. Bartholomew was not sure what he thought; there was no time anyway because Eleanor had arrived to reclaim him, and the bell was chiming to summon the scholars of Michaelhouse and their guests into the hall for the Feast. His heart thudded painfully as he escorted Eleanor and Mistress Horner through the porch, in the way that it had not done since he was a gawky youth who had taken a fancy to one of the kitchen maids at his school. He heard his sister informing Eleanor, who was not much interested, that Mistress Horner was a distant relative.

When they reached the stairs, Eleanor grew impatient with Mistress Horner's stately progress, and danced on ahead, eyes open wide at the borrowed tapestries that hung round the walls of Michaelhouse's hall, and at the yellow flicker of several hundred candles – the shutters were firmly closed to block out the daylight, although why Michaelhouse should think its guests preferred to swelter in an airless room to dining in a pleasant breeze, Bartholomew could not imagine. On the high table, the College silver was displayed, polished to a bright gleam by Cynric the night before. Bartholomew solicitously assisted his elderly guest towards it, alarmed when Father William stepped forward to help. Matilde, however, was completely unflustered and accepted the friar's help with a gracious

371

smile that she somehow managed to make appear toothless.

Despite the fact that there were perhaps four times as many people dining in College than usual, only one additional table had been hired for the occasion. The scholars and their guests were crammed uncomfortably close together, particularly given that the day was already hot, and hundreds of smoking candles did not make matters any easier. Squashed between Eleanor on the one side and Matilde on the other, Bartholomew felt himself growing faint, partly from the temperature, but mainly from anticipating what would happen if Matilde's make-up should begin to melt off, or Eleanor Tyler display some of the indiscretion that his friends seemed to find so distasteful. He reached for his goblet of wine with an unsteady hand and took a hefty swallow. Next to Eleanor the misogynistic Father William did the same, sweat standing out on his brow as he tried to make himself smaller to avoid physical contact with her.

Father Kenyngham stood to say grace, which was perhaps longer than it might have been and was frequently punctuated by agitated sighs from behind the serving screen, where Agatha was aware that the food was spoiling. And then the meal was underway. The first course arrived, comprising a selection of poultry dishes.

Eleanor clung to Bartholomew's arm and chattered incessantly, making it difficult for him to eat anything at all. Father William was sharing a platter with the voluptuous wife of a merchant that Father Aidan had invited, and was gulping at his wine as his agitation rose with the temperature of the room. Bartholomew could only imagine that the College steward, who decided who sat where, must have fallen foul of William's quick tongue at some point, and had managed his own peculiar revenge with the seating arrangements. Meanwhile Roger Alcote, another Fellow who deplored young women, was chatting merrily to the venerable Mistress Horner and was confiding all kinds of secrets.

'I hear you have had little success in discovering the killer of that poor student – James Kenzie,' said Eleanor, almost shouting over the cacophony of raised voices. She coughed as smoke from a cheap candle wafted into her face when a servant hurried by bearing yet more dishes of food.

'We have had no success in finding the murderers of Kenzie, the skeleton in the Ditch, or the prostitute, Joanna,' said Bartholomew, taking a tentative bite of something that might have been chicken. It was sufficiently salty that it made him reach immediately for his wine cup.

Further down the table Father William did the same, although, unlike Bartholomew, the friar finished his meat, along with another two cups of wine to wash it down. Bartholomew was concerned, knowing that wine reacted badly with poppy juice, as he had warned that morning. So much for William's claim that he only needed to be told something once, thought the physician. He tried to attract the friar's attention, but then became aware that Eleanor had released his arm and was regarding him in a none-too-friendly manner.

'Why are you bothering with this whore?' she demanded, loud enough to draw a shocked gasp from Alcote, two seats away. 'No one in the town cares about her, so why should you?'

'I feel she was badly used,' said Bartholomew, surprised by the venom her voice.

'So were the other eight people who were killed in the riot, but none of them has a personal crusader searching for their killers.'

'But they all had someone who cared about them at their funerals,' Bartholomew pointed out. 'Joanna had no one.'

'That was probably because she was unpopular,' said Eleanor coldly.

'Did you know her then?' asked Bartholomew, startled.

'Of course not! She was a whore!'

Bartholomew glanced uneasily at Matilde, but if she was paying any attention to Eleanor, she did not show it. Her head was turned in polite attention towards Roger Alcote, who had recovered from his shock at the mention of whores and was informing her, in considerable detail, about the cost of silver on the black market.

Bartholomew wondered how Alcote knew about such matters, but realised that Alcote was not the wealthiest of Michaelhouse's Fellows for nothing.

'You must desist with this ridiculous investigation,' Eleanor announced firmly. 'This harlot's killer is long gone and you will only waste your time. Not only that, but think how it looks for a man of your standing and reputation to be fussing about a prostitute!'

'Because she was a prostitute does not give someone the right to kill her,' reasoned Bartholomew quietly.

'No, it does not, but you are wrong in applying yourself so diligently to her case. Why can you not look into whose cart crushed that poor potter instead – he was a good man and well-liked. Or what about the scholars who were slain? That friar from Godwinsson, for example.'

'I do not think I will be able to make much progress with Joanna's murder anyway,' said Bartholomew in a placatory tone, reluctant to discuss the matter with Eleanor if she was going to be hostile. It was none of her business and she had no right to be telling him what he could or could not do in his spare time. 'I have discovered nothing at all, except that the two Frenchmen from Godwinsson are the most likely suspects, and they are never at home.'

'Are you mad?' asked Eleanor in horror. She dropped her voice to a whisper when Alcote leaned forward to gaze disapprovingly at her. 'My mother killed their friend to save you! Have you not considered that your prying might force them to reveal her as the killer? And then she will be hanged, and it will be all your fault!'

She had a point. Eleanor had already told him that the French students had often pestered her while she sat outside to sew, and the surviving pair would know exactly who had killed their friend. In fact, Mistress Tyler was probably fortunate that they had not retaliated in some way already, although the fact that the students had told all and sundry that they were attacked by a crowd of well-armed townsmen seemed to indicate that they were prepared to overlook the matter in the interests of appearances.

'All right,' he conceded. 'And as I said, I think there is little more I can do anyway.'

Eleanor gazed at him sombrely for a moment, before turning her attention to the portion of roast pheasant in front of her.

'Thank you,' she said, as she ripped the bird's legs off. 'But we should not spoil this wonderful occasion by quarrelling, Matt. Pass me some of that red stuff. No, not wine, addle-brain! That berry sauce.' She took a mouthful, and quickly grabbed her goblet. 'Pepper, flavoured mildly with berries!' she pronounced, fanning her mouth with her hand. 'That is spicy stuff!'

Father William evidently thought so too, for Cynric stepped forward to refill his cup three times in quick succession. By the time the second course arrived, the friar was distinctly red in the face, and was considerably more relaxed than he had been when the Feast had begun.

'I advised you to drink no wine, Father,' Bartholomew whispered to him behind Eleanor, who was giving her entire attention to stripping the pheasant to the bone with her teeth. 'It does not mix well with the medicine you took.'

'Nonsense,' said William expansively. 'I feel in excellent health. Try some of this meat, Matthew, lad. I do not have the faintest idea what it is, but what does that matter, eh?'

He elbowed Eleanor hard in the ribs and Bartholomew regarded him aghast. The Franciscan slapped a generous portion of something grey on top of the mountain of gnawed bones on her trencher, and then peered at it short-sightedly.

'That should probably do you,' he said finally. 'Put some flesh on you, eh?'

He gave her another nudge and burst into giggles. Amused, Eleanor grinned at him, and he slapped his hand on her knee, roaring with laughter. Bartholomew groaned.

'Cynric! Do not give him any more to drink. Fetch him some water.'

'I told you this morning, I do not approve of water,' bellowed William jovially. 'Bring me wine, Cynric and bring it quickly! Now, Mistress, I do not believe I have seen you in our congregation

377

very often. I hope you are not bound for the old fires and brimstone of hell, eh?'

William would have fires and brimstone in his stomach the next day if he did not moderate his wine consumption, Bartholomew thought, astonished as the friar brought his face close to Eleanor's and began to regale her with a tale of how he had once sought out heretics in the south of Spain. It was not a pleasant story, nor one that was appropriate for such an occasion, but Eleanor was spellbound, her food forgotten as she listened to the Franciscan's account of what amounted to wholesale slaughter in the name of God.

As dessert was being served, Bartholomew noticed that Father William had not been the only one who had drunk too much too quickly. Alcote, next to Matilde, had the silly, fixed grin on his face that told all those who knew him that he was on the verge of being insensible. With relief, Bartholomew was able to give Matilde his full attention. Like the physician, she had eaten and drunk little, and was one of the few people left in the hall in full control of her faculties. She watched the guests and scholars around her with delight, laughing when the Mayor's fine hat fell into his custard because he was trying to maul Edith Stanmore who sat across the table from him, and enthralled by the way Michael's choir went from appalling to diabolical as they became steadily more intoxicated. When one of the tenors passed out, taking a section of the altos down with him, she turned to Bartholomew with tears running down her cheeks.

'Oh, Matthew! I do not think I have laughed so much in years! Thank you for inviting me. I was uncertain about coming at first – after all, a feast in a University institution attended by a crowd of debauched, drunken men, is not really an occasion respectable women should attend – but now I am glad I came. The sisters will love hearing about all this!'

It was ironic, Bartholomew thought, that one of the most auspicious occasions in the University calendar should be seen in terms as a source of mirth for the town's prostitutes. But looking around him, it was difficult to argue with her. Alcote had finally slipped into oblivion, and was asleep in his chair with his mouth open; Father Aidan, Bartholomew was certain, had his hand somewhere it should not have been on the person of the St Radegund's Convent cellarer who sat next to him; Michael, virtually the only one in the hall still eating, was choking on his food, and was being pounded on the back by a trio of young ladies; Father Kenyngham had blocked out the racket around him and was contentedly reading a book; William was on his feet, unsteadily miming out some nasty detail about his days in the Inquisition while Eleanor listened agog; and in the body of the hall, scholars and guests alike were roaring drunk or on the verge of passing out.

Those that were still able were beginning to leave. Edith gave Bartholomew and Matilde a nod before she picked her way out of the hall, followed by Oswald Stanmore who walked with the unnatural care of those who have over-imbibed. Judging from Edith's black expression, her husband was not in her good graces for enjoying the wine and carelessly abandoning her to the unwanted attentions of the Mayor. Bartholomew would not have wanted to be in Stanmore's shoes the following morning.

'So, did you dress as a grandmother to save your reputation, or mine?' he asked, turning away from the chaos to look at Matilde.

'Both,' she said. 'But mainly yours. It was your sister's idea, actually, although of course her husband knows nothing about it. He thinks I am some distant cousin you invited, and lost interest in me as soon as he learned I had nothing to sell and didn't want to buy anything.'

Bartholomew laughed, then raised an arm to protect her as Father William, now describing some fight in which he had emerged victorious, snatched up a candlestick and began to wave it in the air, splattering wax everywhere and landing the voluptuous merchant's wife on his other side a painful crack on the back of the neck.

'And so I managed to escape from those evildoers, stealing back all my friary's sacred relics to protect them from pagan hands,' he finished grandly, slumping back down into his chair.

'You escaped from these heathens with *all* the relics?' asked Eleanor, impressed. 'All alone, and with no weapon other than a small stick and your own cunning?'

'And the hand of God,' added William, as an afterthought. He wiped the sweat from his face with the edge of the tablecloth. 'The relics are now safe in Salamanca Cathedral. We later returned to the village and charged everyone with heresy.'

'The whole village?' asked Eleanor, eyes wide and round. 'What happened?'

William seized the candlestick again and lurched to his feet. 'There was a fight, of course, but I was ready for them!'

The merchant's wife received another crack on the head as William girded himself up for action. Before he could do any more damage, Bartholomew wrested the object from him and he and Cynric escorted him, none too willingly, to his room. The fresh air seemed to sober the friar somewhat.

'That damned medicine of yours,' he muttered. 'You gave me too much of it.'

Bartholomew looked sharply at the friar. 'Did you take all that I left on the table? You were supposed to have saved some of it for later.'

'Then you should have told me so,' growled William, trying to free his arm from Cynric to walk unattended. 'It was powerful stuff.'

'So was the wine,' remarked Bartholomew. As soon as the friar was on his bed, he began to snore.

Bartholomew turned him on his side and left a bucket next to the bed, certain he would need it later.

Meanwhile, back in the hall, Bartholomew's place had been taken by Sam Gray who was deep in conversation with Eleanor. When the physician offered to walk her home, she waved him away impatiently, and turned her attention back to Gray.

'I will see her home,' Gray volunteered, far more readily than he agreed to do most things. He proffered an arm to Eleanor, who took it with a predatory grin. Side by side, they picked their way across fallen guests, scraps of food and empty bottles, and left the hall.

'Eleanor will be safe enough with him,' said Matilde, seeing Bartholomew's look of concern. 'It is still daylight outside and she is a woman well able to take care of herself.'

'Then, perhaps I can escort you home.'

'No, Matthew. The sisters will be waiting to hear all about this Feast, and they will want to see me in my disguise. I shall go to them now, so that they have my tale before they start work tonight.'

'Why are they so interested?'

'Why should they not be? These men, who lie in drunken heaps, are the great and good of the town, who use us for their pleasures on the one hand, but who are quick to condemn us on the other. The sisters will enjoy hearing about how they have debased themselves. My only regret is that

I have no suitable words with which to describe the choir.'

'I could think of some,' said Bartholomew, looking across to where a few of them were carousing near the screen. Whether they were still singing, or simply yelling to make themselves heard, he could not decide.

'Thank you again,' she said, touching him on the arm. 'You will be busy tomorrow, dealing with all these sore heads and sick stomachs, so go to bed early.'

With this sound advice, she took her leave, making her way carefully across the yard and out of the gates, a curious figure whose matronly attire and walking stick contrasted oddly with her lithe, upright posture and graceful steps. Bartholomew heaved a sigh of relief, aware that a combination of good luck, Matilde's ingenuity and strong wine had extricated him from his delicate situation with no damage done. Wearily, still smiling about the spectacle William had made of himself, Bartholomew headed for his room.

No one at Michaelhouse was awake before sunrise, and the Franciscans, to a man, missed their pre-dawn offices. Father William looked gaunt and pale and roundly damned the perils of over-indulgence. Notwithstanding, he helped himself to a generous portion of oatmeal at breakfast, so Bartholomew supposed that he could not feel too ill.

Before lectures started, Robin of Grantchester

appeared at the gates, informing the scholars of Michaelhouse that he was prepared to offer them a collective discount on any leeching or bleeding that was required. No one took advantage of his generosity, although a number of Fellows and students availed themselves of Bartholomew's services, which tended to be less painful, less expensive, and more likely to work. Unkindly, Bartholomew suggested that Robin should visit the Mayor, who was last seen being carried home in a litter, singing some bawdy song that, rumour had it, Sam Gray had taught him.

Once teaching was finished, Bartholomew found he had a large number of patients to see. A few of them were people suffering the after-effects of the previous night's excesses, but others were ill because food was scarce following the plague, and not everyone could afford to buy sufficient to keep them in good health. The irony of it did not escape the physician.

Michael meanwhile, after a day's break from his duties, announced that he was going to pay another visit to Godwinsson Hostel to try to wring more information from its students about their whereabouts at the time of Werbergh's death. His previous attempt had proved unsuccessful because no one had been at home. Concerned for his friend entering what he considered to be a lion's den, Bartholomew offered to accompany him but Michael waved him away saying that the physician might be more hindrance than help in view of

Lydgate's antipathy towards him. They walked together to the High Street and then parted, Michael heading towards Small Bridges Street, and Bartholomew to St Mary's Church where the Chancellor was paying for his greed over a large plate of sickly marchpanes the day before.

It was late by the time Bartholomew had completed his rounds, and the evening was gold and red. He knew he should return to Michaelhouse, and send Gray to return the Galen to David's Hostel that he had forgotten about the day before, but it was too pleasant an evening to be indoors. There were perhaps two hours of daylight left – time enough for him to walk to the river and still be back at Michaelhouse sufficiently early to send Gray to David's with the book before curfew.

He decided to visit two of the old men who lived near the wharves on the river. Both were prone to attacks of river fever and, despite Bartholomew's repeated advice against drinking directly from the Cam's unsavoury depths, they were set in their ways; because they had been using the river as a source of drinking water since they were children, they saw no reason to change. They were old and each new bout of illness weakened them a little further, especially in the summer months. Bartholomew visited them regularly. He enjoyed sitting between them on the unstable bench outside their house, watching the river ooze past, and listening to tales of their pasts.

A cool breeze was blowing in from the Fens

and the setting sun bathed the river in a soft amber light. Even the hovels that stood in an uneven line behind Michaelhouse looked picturesque, their crude wattle-and-daub walls coloured pale russets and rich yellows in the late daylight.

The two old men, Aethelbald and Dunstan, were sitting in their usual place, their backs against the flimsy wall of their house, and their dim-sighted eyes turned towards the wharves where a barge from Flanders was unloading. They greeted Bartholomew with warm enthusiasm and, as always, made room for him to sit between them on the bench that was never built to take the weight of three.

Bartholomew sat cautiously, ever alert for the sharp crack that would pre-empt the three of them tumbling into the dust. There was nothing more than an ominous creak and, gradually, Bartholomew allowed himself to relax.

They chatted for a while about nothing in particular. Aethelbald was recovering well from his last attack of river sickness, and both claimed that they were now only drinking from the well in Water Street. They told him about a fox that was stealing hens, that there were more flies now than when they were young, and that one of Dunstan's grandchildren was suffering the pangs of his first unrequited love.

The two old men talked while Bartholomew listened. It was not that he found chickens, flies and adolescent crushes fascinating, but there was something timeless about their gossip that he found reassuring. Perhaps it was that what they told him was so unquestionably normal and that there were no hidden meanings or twists to their words. Their lives were simple and, if not honest, then at least their deceptions were obvious ones, and their motives clear – unlike the devious twisting and reasoning of the University community.

Dunstan was chuckling about his grandson's misfortunes in love because, apparently, the lady of his choice was a prostitute.

'Which one?' asked Bartholomew curiously.

'Her name was Joanna,' said Dunstan, still cackling.

Bartholomew stared at him. 'Joanna? But there is no prostitute in the town by that name!'

The two men stared back, their laughter giving way to amused disbelief. 'You seem very sure of that, Doctor,' said Dunstan with a wink at his brother.

Bartholomew was chagrined to feel himself flush. 'I was told,' he said lamely.

Now it was Aethelbald's turn to wink. 'I'm sure you were, Doctor,' he said.

Dunstan saw Bartholomew's expression and took pity on him. 'She is not from these parts. She was visiting relatives here from Ely when she met my lad. She has gone back now.'

'When did she go? What did she look like?' asked Bartholomew, sitting straight-backed on the rickety bench, oblivious to the protesting cracks and groans of its flimsy legs.

The brothers exchanged a look of surprise but answered his questions. 'She went back the morning after the riot,' said Dunstan, 'She was a big lass with a good deal of thick yellow hair.'

Fair hair, mused Bartholomew. Could Joanna have been the body he had seen in the castle after all? Was it Joanna that Cecily had seen dead at the feet of her husband, and not Dominica? He recalled his own experiences of mistaken identity that night in relation to Michael and winced. It was not easy to be certain in the dark, with only the flickering light of uncontrolled flames to act as a torch. Perhaps Cecily Lydgate had seen only fair hair and had jumped to the wrong conclusion. Which would mean that Michael had been right all along and that Dominica and the mysterious Joanna were different people.

'Did you see her after the riot?' Bartholomew asked.

Dunstan shook his head. 'Our lad had a message the morning after, bidding him farewell. That is how we came to know about it. She wrote our lad a note and he cannot read, so he had to bring it here because Aethelbald has some learning – providing the words are not too long, and they are all in English.'

Aethelbald looked proud of himself, and explained that he had spent a year at the Glommery School next to King's Hall and had learned his letters. Bartholomew's thoughts tumbled in confusion. If Joanna, and not Dominica, had been killed during the riot, then why had there been no one except Bartholomew at her funeral service? What of the people she had come to the town to visit?

As if reading his thoughts, Dunstan began telling him about the relatives Joanna had come to see.

'It was that family on the High Street,' he began unhelpfully.

'That family of women,' added Aethelbald. 'A mother and three daughters.'

For the second time in the space of a few minutes, Bartholomew gazed from one to the other of the brothers in bewilderment.

'Mistress Tyler and her daughters?'

Dunstan snapped his fingers triumphantly. 'That's it!' he exclaimed. 'Agnes Tyler.' He was silent for a moment, before he began to chuckle again. 'And, although she said she was delighted to have a visit from her Ely niece, I know for a fact from Mistress Bowman that she did not take kindly to Joanna running some unofficial business from Agnes's home!'

The two old men howled with laughter, then returned to the business of the fox and the chickens, while Bartholomew's thoughts whirled in confusion. Joanna had not been with the Tylers in the riot. Surely Mistress Tyler would not have left her inside the house? He chewed on his lower lip as he recalled the events of that night. He had offered to go back to oust looters from the Tyler home after the fire had died out, but Mistress Tyler had asked him to escort them to Jonas the Poisoner's house instead. If Dunstan was right, then Joanna would still have been in Cambridge and had left the following morning.

But if it had been Mistress Tyler's niece that had been murdered, why were her aunt and cousins not at her funeral service? Was it because they did not know she was dead? But surely that was not possible? The names of the riot victims had been widely published and Tulyet had gone to some trouble to ensure the families of the dead were informed. And even if Mistress Tyler had believed Joanna had already left for Ely, the name Joanna on a list of town dead must surely have raised some question in her mind?

He closed his eyes, seeing again the events of that night: students and townsmen running back and forth, shouting and brandishing weapons; Master Burney's workshop alive with flames and the fire spreading to the Tyler home nearby; Mistress Tyler saying there were looters in the house after the French students' attack had been thwarted. Bartholomew had not seen or heard the looters: he only had Mistress Tyler's word that they had been in her house. And then he thought about the house when Michael and he had recovered from the attack; it had been pleasant, clean and fresh-smelling, and the furniture was of good quality and well kept. There was no evidence that the room had been ill-used or damaged by fire.

He felt sick as the implications began to dawn on him. Had Mistress Tyler left Joanna in the house deliberately, to be at the mercies of the supposed looters? Did that explain why she wanted him to escort her to Jonas's house – even though the family had already shown they were more than capable of looking after themselves, and his presence would not make a significant difference to their chances – to keep him from knowing Joanna was still in the house? And did it explain why Eleanor had been so keen to dissuade him from his investigations when he had told her that he was looking for Joanna's killer during the Feast?

Also, the night he and Michael were attacked, Agnes Tyler had invited them into her house as an act of charity without knowing who they were. Would she have invited them so readily had she known, aware that any signs of looters in the house only a few nights before were essentially invisible? When Eleanor had invited him to eat with them the day after the riot, he had been taken to the garden, not to the house itself. Or was it simply that the Tylers had been to some trouble to eradicate quickly any signs of what must have been an unpleasant episode in their lives?

Slowly, feeling that the frail bench was beginning to give way under their combined weight, he stood to take his leave of the old men. He walked slowly back along the river bank in the gathering gloom, aware that the curfew bell must have already sounded because the path was virtually empty. His thoughts were an uncontrolled jumble of questions and he tried to sort them out into a logical sequence. First and foremost was the revelation that Joanna had existed, while Bartholomew had wrongly assumed that she was Dominica. Second was that Matilde had been certain that Joanna had not been a prostitute, which had misled him: Joanna had not been a prostitute who lived in Cambridge.

He rubbed at his temples as he considered something else. Eleanor Tyler had seen Bartholomew talking in the street with Matilde and had chided him for it. What had she said? That Matilde was not to be trusted, and that she revealed the secrets of her clients. At the time, he had been disturbed more by the slur to Matilde than by what she might have meant. Eleanor's was an extreme reaction but one he had put down to the natural dislike of prostitutes held by many people. But in the light of what he had just learned from Dunstan and Aethelbald, it could mean that she had guessed that he might be asking about Joanna, and wanted to ensure that any information given to him by Matilde would be disregarded.

Matilde had also told him that the riots had been started to hide two acts. Perhaps one of the acts was the murder of Joanna – getting rid of the unwelcome visitor that had been bringing shame to Mistress Tyler's respectable household.

He raised his eyes heavenward at this notion. Now he was being ridiculous! How could Mistress Tyler possibly have the influence, funds or knowledge to start riots? And surely it was not necessary to start a riot merely to be rid of Joanna? Why not simply send her home to Ely?

All Dunstan's information had done was to muddy already murky waters. Now Bartholomew did not even know whether Dominica was alive or not, whereas before he had been certain she had been dead. But he was sure Lydgate had been at the grave. Why? Had he, like Cecily, mistaken Joanna for Dominica in the dark? Was his graveside visit to atone for a life taken by mistake?

The shadow of a cat (or was it a fox?) flitting across the path brought him out of his reverie. He realised that he had been so engrossed in his thoughts that he had walked past the bottom of St Michael's Lane and was passing through the land that ran to St John's Hospital. With an impatient shake of his head, he turned to retrace his steps, quickly now, for the daylight was fading fast, and he did not wish to be caught outside the College by the Sheriff's men or the beadles without a valid excuse.

As he turned, he saw another shadow behind him. This time, it was two- not four-legged and made a far less competent job of slipping unobtrusively into the bushes than the animal. Bartholomew was after him in an instant, diving recklessly into the undergrowth and emerging

393

moments later clutching a struggling student. He hauled him upright to see if he could recognise the scholar's face in the rapidly fading light.

'Edred,' he said tonelessly. He released the Godwinsson friar and watched him warily.

Edred made a quick twitching movement and Bartholomew thought he might dart away. But he stayed, casting nervous glances at his captor.

'Well?' asked Bartholomew. 'Why were you following me?'

Edred's eyes slid away from Bartholomew's face looking off down the river.

'To see where you were going.'

'That is no answer,' said Bartholomew impatiently. 'Did someone tell you to? Master Lydgate?'

The name produced a violent reaction, and Edred shook his head so vigorously that Bartholomew thought he might make himself sick. Bartholomew had seen many soldiers before they went into battle and knew naked fear when he saw it. He took the young friar's arm and escorted him firmly back towards Michaelhouse.

Michael had been waiting at the gates. Relief showed clearly in his face when Bartholomew shouted to be let in. He was surprised to see Edred but said nothing while Bartholomew led the student to the kitchen, and asked Agatha to give him a cup of strong wine. While Edred drank, colour seeped back into his pinched white features. Michael nodded to Agatha to keep her matronly eye on him and beckoned Bartholomew out of earshot in the yard.

Venus was twinkling way off in the dark blue sky and Bartholomew wondered what it was that made it shine first red, then yellow, then blue. When he had been a child, he had imagined it was about to explode and had studied it for hours. He had watched it with Norbert, too, many years before, both wanting to witness what they imagined would be a dramatic event. The last time they had seen it together had been at the gates of Stanmore's house in Trumpington, before Norbert had disappeared into the night to flee to the safety of Dover Castle.

'I was beginning to be worried,' Michael was saying. 'I was back ages ago and I thought you may have run into trouble, given that your attackers are still on the loose. I was about to go out to look for you.'

Bartholomew raised apologetic shoulders and gave his friend a rueful smile. 'Sorry. I did not think you might be anxious.' He ran his fingers through his hair. 'What did you discover at the Hostel from Hell?'

Michael laughed softly at his appellation for Godwinsson. 'Very little, I am afraid. There was some kind of celebration at Valence Marie on Friday night because of finding the relic. The scholars of Maud's and Godwinsson were invited. Some went, others did not, but by all accounts it was a drunken occasion and those that did attend are unlikely to recall those who did not. It will be almost impossible to check alibis for anyone. Just about anybody could have knocked Werbergh over the head and hidden his body. Including Lydgate.'

'Not so for David's Hostel,' said Bartholomew, recalling his visit there two days before. 'Master Radbeche has his students under very strict control – perhaps too strict for such active young men. Anyway, none of them are ever out of the sight of either Radbeche or Father Andrew.'

He had a pang of sudden remorse as he remembered the Galen. He considered sending Gray with it, but it was almost dark and he did not wish to be the cause of his student's arrest by the beadles. Father Andrew would have to wait until morning.

'The only thing I managed to ascertain,' continued Michael, 'was that Edred has not been seen since Werbergh's body was found. And, as I was beginning to wonder whether he might have gone the same way as his friend, you bring him to Michaelhouse.'

Bartholomew told him how he had encountered Edred, and Michael listened gravely. He decided to keep his thoughts about Joanna until later, when he and Michael had the time to unravel the muddle of information together.

When they returned to the kitchen, Agatha had settled Edred comfortably at the large table with some of her freshly baked oatcakes. He looked better than he had done when he first arrived, and even managed a faint smile of thanks at

Agatha as she left the kitchen to go to bed. Bartholomew was aware of a slight movement from the corner, and saw Cynric sitting there, crouched upon a stool, eating apples which he peeled with a knife. He raised his eyebrows to ask whether he should leave, but Bartholomew motioned for him to stay.

Bartholomew sat opposite Edred and leaned his elbows on the table. Michael went to Agatha's fireside chair and the room was filled with creaking and puffing sounds until the fat monk had wriggled his bulk into a position he found satisfactory.

'Why did you steal James Kenzie's ring?' asked Bartholomew softly.

Edred's gaze dropped. 'Because Master Lydgate offered money for the student who returned it to him,' he said, his voice little more than a whisper. 'We were all looking for it, mostly on each other. Then I saw it on the Scot. It was me who started the argument in the street that day. I wanted to get closer to him to make sure it was the right ring.'

He looked down, unable or unwilling to meet the eyes of his questioners.

'How did you steal the ring from Kenzie's finger?' asked Bartholomew, more from curiosity than to help with solving the riddle of Kenzie's death.

Edred shrugged. 'I have done it before,' he said. 'I jostled him and we pushed and shoved at each other. I pretended to fall and grabbed at his hand. When I released it, I had his ring and he did not.'

'A fine talent for a friar,' said Bartholomew dryly.

Edred favoured him with a superior smile. 'It is a skill I learned from a travelling musician in exchange for a basket of apples when I was a child. It is a trick, nothing more.'

'Not to James Kenzie,' said Michael. 'Why did you lie about this when I asked you about it later?'

Edred's eyes became frightened again and he seemed to lose some of the colour from his face. 'Because I took the ring to Master Lydgate and he told me if I ever mentioned to anyone what I had done, he would kill me,' he said.

'So, why are you telling us now?' asked Michael, unmoved by the friar's fear.

'Because he made a similar threat to Werbergh. Werbergh spoke to you,' said Edred, looking at Bartholomew with large eyes, 'and now he is dead.'

'But if you think Werbergh died because he spoke to me,' said Bartholomew reasonably, 'why are you now doing the same?'

'Because I do not know what else to do,' said Edred. Bartholomew had expected him to break down into tears and wail at him, but Edred was made of sterner stuff. He swallowed hard and met Bartholomew's gaze evenly. 'I thought if I told you what I know, you might be able to sort out this mess and offer me some kind of protection.'

Michael sighed. 'It all sounds most mysterious,' he said cynically. 'But let us start at the beginning.

We will consider your protection when we better know what we must protect you against.' He leaned back into his chair again, ignoring the creaking wood. 'Proceed.'

Edred looked from one to the other, his face expressionless. 'Master Lydgate killed Dominica and a servant from Valence Marie that she was with the night of the riot. He also killed Werbergh and James Kenzie. And if he knows where I am he will kill me too.'

CHAPTER 9

In the silence that followed Edred's announcement, Bartholomew was aware of small sounds
in the kitchen: Michael's heavy breathing, a
student laughing in one of the rooms, the purring
of the College cat as it rubbed around his legs.

'How do you know all this?' asked Michael, the
first to regain his tongue.

Edred studied an oatcake, then began to
crumble it in his fingers. 'On the night of the riot,
I was out with some of the other students. I was
only there to administer to those that might need
me, and to try to stop needless fighting,' he said,
looking at Michael.

'Of course you were,' said Michael flatly. 'Pray
continue.'

'Then I saw Dominica Lydgate in the company
of two men. I knew she was thought to be safe in
Chesterton, and so I ran back to Godwinsson to
tell Master Lydgate that she was in Cambridge.'

Bartholomew nodded. That accorded with what
Cecily had told him. He thought of Joanna and
the uncertain light. 'Are you certain it was
Dominica? Could you have been mistaken?'

Edred looked surprised. 'Yes, I am certain,' he said. 'It was Dominica I saw.'

'Did you recognise the men she was with?' asked Michael, looking at the small pile of crumbs on the table from Edred's oatcake.

Edred hung his head and swallowed noisily.

'Come now, Brother Edred,' said Michael firmly. 'You are safe here. Tonight you can sleep in Michaelhouse and tomorrow we will see about getting you away from Cambridge altogether. But only if you are honest with us now.'

Edred nodded miserably. 'I thought I recognised who she was with,' he said, 'although I am still uncertain. I think one of the men was called Will – he is a grubby little man who works at Valence Marie and who has been trawling the King's Ditch for relics recently. The other was his brother, Ned, who died in the riot.'

Bartholomew thought back to the bodies lying in the castle outbuilding. One may well have been Will's brother.

He looked up to find Edred staring at him intently. 'Master Lydgate has killed four people already. My conscience will not allow him to kill again.'

'But what evidence do you have that he has killed these four people?' asked Bartholomew, denying himself the satisfaction of asking the arrogant friar why his conscience only started to prick after four deaths.

Edred began to push the oatcake crumbs into a

heap with his index fingers. 'When I told Master Lydgate I had seen Dominica the night of the riot, he left to find her. He was in a rage such as I have never seen before.' He looked up briefly. 'And, believe me, I have witnessed a fair few of his rages during my time at Godwinsson. Anyway, after he had gone Mistress Lydgate said she was going, too. I did the only thing an honest friar could do and accompanied her.'

Michael and Bartholomew exchanged a wry look in response to the friar's claimed motive. Edred, his attention fixed on his pyramid of crumbs, did not notice.

'We searched for some time and then we found Dominica. But Master Lydgate had arrived before us and Dominica already lay dead. He had also killed Ned. He was standing over the bodies with his dagger dripping. Of Will there was no sign. He must have managed to escape, for I have seen him alive since.'

'But did you actually see Lydgate kill them?' persisted Bartholomew. Although Edred's story corroborated Cecily's, there remained a small thread of doubt in his mind.

Edred gave a short bark of laughter. 'No, I did not. But a man hovering over two corpses with his dagger dripping blood? What else would you imagine had happened? Mistress Cecily was all for rushing forward to Dominica, but I prevented her. Master Lydgate stood over his victims for a while, looked around him as though he expected the Devil to snatch him away, and then slunk off. We had seen enough. Mistress Lydgate asked me to escort her to Maud's and I left her there. By the time I returned to the scene of the murder, Dominica's and Ned's bodies had been removed by the Sheriff's men.'

Michael looked at Bartholomew as he asked his next question. 'Do you know where Cecily Lydgate is now?'

Bartholomew avoided his eyes while Edred continued. 'I cannot say what happened after I left her at Maud's. She did not return to Godwinsson, but apparently someone had made a terrible mess of her room – perhaps when it was searched.'

'Searched for what?' asked Michael.

'Her jewellery, I suppose. It is widely known that she possesses a great deal of priceless jewellery.'

'Was this jewellery missing after her room was searched?' Michael asked.

Edred's mouth lifted at one corner in a disdainful sneer. 'Of course not. She does not keep it on display. It is all hidden away in places known only to her and Master Lydgate.'

'Not Dominica?' asked Bartholomew.

Again the sneer. 'One or two places, perhaps, but not all. The Lydgates are not a trusting couple where their wealth is concerned.'

Around Edred's neck was a delicate golden crucifix that Bartholomew had not seen him wear before. Since Edred seemed to know about

Cecily's hidden treasure, Bartholomew supposed it was not too much of a leap in logic to suppose that Edred had taken the opportunity to ransack her room himself. It would certainly explain why he had taken so long to return to the scene of Dominica's murder – long enough so that the Sheriff had removed the body – after he had seen Cecily safely to Maud's Hostel.

'The day after all this, you went to the Castle to identify the body of the Godwinsson friar who died during the riot, did you not?' asked Bartholomew. 'In the company of Master Lydgate?'

Edred nodded. 'Several students were missing after the riot and Master Lydgate wanted to see whether any of the dead were ours. Two were: the friar and the French student. The friar's head was crushed but we saw the scar on his knee where he was injured at the Battle of Crécy. Or so he always claimed. Master Lydgate insisted on viewing all the dead, although I only looked at ours.'

Bartholomew caught Michael's eye, wondering if he would consider this evidence that Lydgate had been looking for Dominica among the dead. Except that now, Bartholomew was no longer certain whom Lydgate had been seeking – or even which of the women had lain dead in the makeshift Castle mortuary. Edred went back to his pile of crumbs.

'Now, tell us why you also think Lydgate killed

Werbergh?' asked Michael, leaning back in his chair and folding his arms across his considerable girth. 'His death was an accident, was it not? The shed fell on him when he went to find timber to build a writing desk. Why do you think Werbergh was murdered?'

Edred looked pained. 'Because Master Lydgate told us that if we talked to you, he would kill us. Werbergh was seen talking to you and he disappeared, only to reappear dead under the shed.'

'And you think this suspicious?' asked Michael.

Edred gave another of his short, explosive laughs. 'I most certainly do! Oh, it looked convincing enough, and our servants, Saul Potter and Huw, both claimed that Werbergh had told them he was going out to look for wood to build a desk, but it seemed too convenient. A man disappears and suddenly returns only to die in a fluky accident? No! That is too coincidental.'

'But you did not actually see Lydgate kill Werbergh,' pressed Bartholomew. It was a statement and not a question.

'It is not necessary to have seen him plunge the dagger into his victims in order to make sense of the evidence,' retorted Edred, his temper ruffled. He suddenly put his head in his hands, scattering the crumbs. 'I should have known it was a mistake to come to you. Why should you believe me?'

Why indeed? thought Bartholomew. Edred had really given them very little new information, and most was in the form of supposition and conjecture.

But Bartholomew's compassion was aroused when he saw the young man's shoulders shaken by a sob. Edred obviously believed what he was telling them was the truth and was frightened by it.

'And what about James Kenzie?' he asked in a gentler tone. Edred shook his head, unable or unwilling to answer, so Bartholomew answered for him. 'You stole the ring from him during the street brawl and took it to Lydgate to claim your reward. Lydgate was simultaneously pleased to have such a clue regarding the identity of his daughter's lover, but angry when you told him it was a Scot. He is a man who blusters and threatens. He vowed to kill Kenzie, and hurled the ring from the window in his anger. Then he threatened to kill you if you confessed that you had stolen the ring.'

Edred looked at him with a tear-stained face. 'No. It did not happen quite like that. I gave the ring to Master Lydgate and he became furious. But not with the Scot, with me. He said the ring was a fake, a cheap imitation of the original. He accused me of having it made so that I could claim the reward from him. He hurled it to the floor and stamped on it. Then he said that if I ever told anyone what I had done, he would kill me. He said having a friar who was a confessed thief and liar would bring Godwinsson Hostel into disrepute. After he had gone I picked up the ring and I could see that he was right. What I had thought was silver was cheap metal. I flung it through the window in disgust.'

'So the ring you took from Kenzie was a fake?' said Bartholomew thoughtfully. He reached into his sleeve and brought it out. 'Is this it?'

Edred took the broken ring and examined it briefly. 'Yes. That's the wretched thing that brought me so much trouble. I don't know how the Scot came to have it, rather than the original. He came later that night to ask if I had taken it, but since it was already broken, and it had landed me in so much trouble, I told him I had not.'

But what was Kenzie doing with a ring that was a fake? wondered Bartholomew. Dominica had definitely given one of the original pair to Kenzie – Robert had identified it quite clearly as the one at Valence Marie – while the other, the one Dominica had kept, had remained with Cecily. But Kenzie had not worn the real ring in the street brawl, he had worn a cheap imitation. Meanwhile, the real ring was on the finger of the relic at Valence Marie. It made no sense. How did the real ring get from Kenzie to the hand found at Valence Marie?

'So, if Lydgate knew that the ring you had taken from Kenzie was a false one, why do you think Lydgate killed him?' Michael was asking.

'That evening, after I had shown the false ring to Master Lydgate, Dominica was sent away to relatives in Chesterton to keep her from seeing her lover,' said Edred. 'I was restless after the scene with the Scot, and knew I would be unable to sleep, so I stayed out. As I was returning, much

407

later, I saw someone throwing pebbles at Dominica's window. He threw perhaps three or four before he realised he was not going to be answered, and then he stole away.'

'And did you recognise this person?' asked Michael.

'Oh yes, I recognised him by the yellow hose under his tabard, which was obvious, even by moonlight. It was the Scot – James Kenzie you say his name was. A few moments after, I saw Master Lydgate leave the house and follow him up the lane. I went to bed, and the next day, you came to say that Kenzie was murdered. I made the reasonable assumption that Lydgate had also seen Kenzie throwing stones at Dominica's window, guessed him to be her lover, followed him and killed him.'

'Why did you not tell us this before?' asked Michael. 'And why did you lie to us when we asked where you were that night?'

Edred looked frightened again, but also indignant. 'How could I do otherwise? By telling you, I would have admitted to theft and lying, two virtues not highly praised by my Order. I would have been thrown out of the University. And anyway, how could I accuse the Principal of murder? Who would you have believed: the poor, lying thief of a friar who had been seen by the Proctor arguing with the murdered man the day before his death, or the rich and influential Lydgate?'

Michael inclined his head, accepting the young man's reasoning. 'But by hiding your own lesser sins, you have protected the identity of a murderer. And you now say that this murderer has struck thrice more and will do so again.'

Edred looked away. 'I did not know what to do. I did not think you would believe me, because I had already lied to you. But I was afraid, too. The Lydgates know I was absent from the hostel the night of Kenzie's death, and Mistress Lydgate could have accused me of lying when I used Werbergh as my alibi that night. But she did not, and I think she guessed I saw her husband leaving to follow Kenzie. Perhaps she saw me returning through her window. Anyway, the message was clear: if I maintained my silence about what I had seen, so would they.'

It made sense logically, thought Bartholomew, casting his mind back to the information they had been given the day of Kenzie's murder. Edred's story and Werbergh's had not tallied and Bartholomew had wondered whether Edred was lying about the theft of the ring to mask a far more serious incident. The incident had been that he believed his Principal had committed murder. It tallied with Cecily's story, too. She had been told not to contradict anything said to protect Godwinsson from the unwelcome inquiries of Brother Michael. But were Edred's suspicions to be believed? It was all so simple: Lydgate killed Kenzie, then his daughter and Ned from Valence

Marie, then Werbergh, whom he thought might be passing information to Bartholomew and Michael. Was Lydgate a man who could kill four people with such ease? Cecily certainly feared her husband sufficiently to flee from him, so perhaps he was.

'Two more questions,' said Bartholomew, seeing the student's shoulders begin to sag with tiredness, 'and then you should sleep. First, do you know who attacked Brother Michael and me in the High Street?'

Edred shook his head. 'I heard about that from Master Lydgate. He was delighted that you had received your just deserts, but he did not know who would attack you, and neither do I.'

Bartholomew nodded, satisfied with the answer, especially given the very plausible response reported from Lydgate. But that did not mean that Godwinsson was uninvolved. Bartholomew remained convinced that it had been Saul Potter and Huw's voices he had heard that night, despite his hazy memory.

'And second,' he continued, 'where are Godwinsson's French students?'

Edred looked frightened again. 'One was killed in the riot. But when Master Lydgate had the truth from the other two that they had been involved in a brawl with you – and not with ten heavily armed townspeople as they initially claimed – he grew angry. They left to return to France. Huw and Saul Potter helped them escape.'

Escape from their Principal, thought Bartholomew. What a terrible indictment of his violent and aggressive character. No wonder Cecily had left him.

As if reading his thoughts. Edred added, 'He hates you. That is one of the reasons I came. Any man who has earned such hatred from Master Lydgate must surely be the man whom I can trust with my life, and who will protect me from him.'

Bartholomew nodded absently, and indicated for Cynric to show Edred where he might sleep. The Welshman fetched a spare blanket from the laundry and led the weary scholar out of the kitchen towards Bartholomew's room. When they had gone, Bartholomew and Michael sat in silence.

'Do you believe him?' asked Bartholomew after a while.

Michael nodded. 'I am certain he thinks he is telling the truth. But that is not to say I agree with his interpretation of it.'

Bartholomew concurred. 'All his evidence – such as it is – suggests that Lydgate killed Dominica, Kenzie, Ned and Werbergh. But there is something not right about it all, something missing.'

'But what? The motives are there in each case, and the opportunity.'

'I know, but there is something I cannot define that does not fit,' said Bartholomew insistently.

'I would have thought you would have been pleased with Edred's evidence. It adds weight to your theory that Joanna was really Dominica.'

411

'Oh, that,' said Bartholomew dismissively.

Michael leaned forward in his chair, while Bartholomew repeated the conversation he had had with the old rivermen. Michael listened gravely.

'And there is something more, is there not?' he asked when Bartholomew had finished. 'About Mistress Lydgate's disappearance? I know you have another ring like the one on the relic in your sleeve. I found it while you were asleep a couple of nights ago. So, you may as well tell me what else you have learned.'

'Did you search my room?' asked Bartholomew. remembering the moved candle and jug.

'Of course not!' said Michael indignantly. 'And I did not really search for the rings. I just knew where you would hide them.' He paused. 'Are you certain your room was searched?'

Bartholomew nodded. 'Twice. And if it was not you, it must have been those who attacked us, looking for whatever it was they wanted me to give them.'

Michael picked at a spot on his face. 'Perhaps. But tell me what happened on Sunday when you were out. Perhaps the two of us can make some sense out of all these clues.'

Bartholomew hesitated, wondering about his agreement with Cecily regarding her hiding place. But unless he told Michael all he knew, they would never get to the bottom of the mystery and more people might die. Michael was a good friend and

Bartholomew knew he could be trusted with secrets, so he told Michael about his visit to Chesterton. When he had finished, Michael sat back thoughtfully.

'This is an odd business,' he said. 'Is the dead woman Joanna or Dominica? And whichever one it is, where is the other? And did Lydgate really kill all these people? I see no reason to suppose he did not, although, like you, I have doubts niggling in the back of my mind. And now we know there is a riot planned for tomorrow night, we can deduce for certain that the recent civil unrest is not random. I will send a messenger to Tulyet tonight. He might be able to avert trouble if he has warning of what is planned.'

Bartholomew, recalling the scenes of violence and mayhem a few nights before, sincerely hoped so. Michael fingered the whiskers on his cheek, thinking aloud.

'I do not like Bigod's involvement in this affair. You say he was one of those who attacked us – although he denies it – and it is he who secretes Mistress Lydgate away from her husband. His role is even more puzzling when you consider that not only does he provide Cecily with a haven, but that he is Lydgate's alibi for the night of the riot. It is odd, I would think, for someone to be such a good friend to both parties simultaneously – most friends would side with either one or the other.'

Bartholomew frowned in thought. 'I wondered at the time why Cecily chose Bigod, of all people, to flee to that night. He is clearly a loyal intimate of Lydgate. But then she said she had hoped he would allow her to share the upper chamber at Chesterton tower-house with him. It became clear – he is her lover and Lydgate's best friend.'

Michael's eyes were great round circles. 'You never cease to amaze me, Matt,' he said. 'That seems something of a leap of faith, given the evidence you have.'

Bartholomew grinned, accepting Michael's caution. 'I know. But it would explain some of Bigod's actions – he is prepared to risk a good deal by offering Lydgate an alibi for the night of the riot. At the same time, he is willing to hide away the man's wife. And Werbergh told me the first time we visited Godwinsson that Cecily was more interested in students than in her husband.'

'All right, then,' said Michael. 'Let us assume you are correct. But we are not finished with Bigod yet. The conversation you overheard in the basement at Chesterton shows he knows when there is to be a riot. Extending this logically, it can be assumed that he knew about the last riot too, which explains why Maud's students were all safely inside at a birthday party.'

'Of course,' said Bartholomew. 'But the Godwinsson students were out, so it seems Lydgate was not party to Bigod's plans.'

'Maybe,' said Michael. 'I wonder if these "two acts" that Matilde told you about were the murder of Lydgate's wayward daughter and her lover.

Lydgate was out all night, after all, and we have not the faintest idea what he was up to when he was not standing over corpses with dripping daggers.'

Bartholomew rubbed the back of his head, becoming disheartened at the way every question answered seemed to pose ten more. 'But even Cecily has her doubts about Lydgate's role in the murder of Dominica. She is reluctant to believe he would kill the person he loved most.'

'People do the most peculiar things for the most bizarre of motives, Matt,' said Michael in a superior tone of voice. 'But one of the oddest aspects about this whole business is these damned rings. How did one of Whining Cecily's rings find its way on to the relic at Valence Marie? And I wonder who that other person was that you heard in the basement, the one whose voice you could not place. Have you considered who it might be? This is important.'

'Not really,' said Bartholomew, closing his eyes as he recalled the clear tenor. 'It was familiar but I cannot place it at all.'

'Was it someone from Valence Marie?' asked Michael to prompt him along. 'Father Eligius, perhaps. Or that fellow who looks like a toad – Master Dittone? Robert Bingham is ill with ague, so it cannot be him. Or one of the merchants, maybe?'

Bartholomew racked his brains but the identity of the voice eluded him still. 'Cynric is a long time,' he said eventually, standing and looking out of the window.

'Probably looking for a pallet bed,' said Michael, standing also. 'It is too late to do anything tonight. First thing in the morning, I suggest we talk to Mistress Tyler and see if we can discover the whereabouts of Joanna. Then, unpleasant though it might be, I must tackle Lydgate. I do not want you there but I will ask Richard Tulyet to accompany me. Perhaps afterwards, Mistress Lydgate will find it safe to come out of her self-inflicted imprisonment.'

They walked across the courtyard together, Michael still speculating on Lydgate's guilt. Cynric had lit a candle in Bartholomew's room, and the light flickered yellow under the closed shutters. Bartholomew wondered why Cynric was wasting his only candle when he knew his way around perfectly well in the dark. As he turned to listen to Michael, he heard the faint groan of the chest in his room being opened. Michael stopped speaking as Bartholomew darted towards the door.

His attention arrested by Edred's hands in the chest, Bartholomew did not see Cynric sprawled across the floor, until he fell headlong over him. He heard Michael yell, and Edred swear under his breath. Bartholomew struggled to his knees, his hands dark with the blood that flowed from the back of Cynric's skull. Blind fury dimmed his reasoning and he launched himself across the room at the friar with a howl of rage.

Edred's hands came out of Bartholomew's storage chest holding a short sword. It was one Stanmore had given him many years ago that Bartholomew had forgotten he had. Edred swung at him with it, and only by dropping to one knee did the physician avoid the hacking blow aimed at his head. Edred swung again with a professionalism that suggested he had not always been in training for the priesthood. Bartholomew ducked a second time, rolling away until he came up against the wall.

Edred came for him, his face pale and intent as he drew back his arm for the fatal plunge. His stroke wavered as something struck him hard on the side of the head, and Bartholomew saw shards of glass falling around him. Michael was not standing helplessly in the doorway like some dim-witted maiden but was hurling anything that came to hand at Edred.

While the friar's attention strayed, Bartholomew leapt at him, catching him in a bear-like grip around the legs. Edred tried to struggle free, dropping the sword as he staggered backwards. Michael continued his assault and Bartholomew could hear nothing but smashes and grunts. Suddenly, Edred collapsed.

Bartholomew squirmed to free himself from Edred's weight. Michael came to his aid and hauled the unresisting friar to his feet. Edred's knees buckled and Michael allowed him to slide down the wall into a sitting position. Bartholomew scrambled across the floor to where Cynric lay.

The Welshman's eyes were half open and a trickle of blood oozed from the wound on the back of his skull. Bartholomew cradled him in his lap, holding a cloth to staunch the bleeding.

'So, I am to die from a coward's blow,' Cynric whispered, eyes seeking Bartholomew's face. 'Struck from behind in the dark.'

'You will not die, my friend,' said Bartholomew. 'The wound is not fatal: I have had recent personal experience to support my claim.'

Cynric grinned weakly at him and closed his eyes while Bartholomew bound the cut deftly with clean linen, praying it was not more serious than it appeared.

'Matt!' came Michael's querulous voice from the other side of the room. Bartholomew glanced to where the monk knelt next to Edred.

'I have killed him,' Michael whispered, his face white with shock. 'Edred is dying!'

Bartholomew looked askance. 'He cannot be, Brother. You have just stunned him.'

'He is dying!' insisted Michael, his voice rising in horror. 'Look at him!'

Easing Cynric gently on to the floor, Bartholomew went to where Michael leaned over the prostrate friar. A white powder lightly dusted Edred's black robe and the smell of it caught in Bartholomew's nostril's sharply. The powder was on the friar's face too, it clung to the thin trail of blood that dribbled from a cut on his cheek and stuck around his lips. Bartholomew felt for a life-beat in the friar's neck and was startled to feel it rapid and faint. Puzzled, he prised open Edred's eyelids and saw that the pupils had contracted to black pinpricks and that his face and neck were covered in a sheen of sweat.

'Do something, Matt!' said Michael desperately. 'Or I will have brought about his death! Me! A man of the cloth, who has forsworn violence!'

The noise of the affray had disturbed those scholars whose rooms were nearby and they clustered around the door as Bartholomew examined Edred. Gray and Bulbeck were among them, and he ordered them to remove Cynric to his own room, away from the strange white powder that seemed to be killing Edred. He grabbed the pitcher of water that stood on the window-sill and washed the powder from the cut on Edred's face and from his mouth. The friar was beginning to struggle to breathe.

'What is happening? What have you done?' Roger Alcote, still a little pale from the aftermath of the Founder's Feast, forced his way through the scholars watching at the doorway, and stood with his hands on his hips waiting for an answer.

'I threw a jar,' said Michael shakily, backing away from where Edred was labouring to breathe. 'It struck him full in the face and broke, scattering that powder everywhere.' He turned on Bartholomew suddenly. 'What was it? Why do you keep such deadly poisons lying so readily to hand?'

'I do not,' protested Bartholomew. He went to

considerable trouble to keep the few poisons he used under lock and key in his storeroom. He shook his head in disbelief. 'The powder is oleander, judging from its smell. I keep a small quantity locked in the chest in the storeroom but I used the last of it several days ago.'

'So where did it come from?'

Bartholomew ignored Michael's question. More important at that moment was that he did not understand why Edred was reacting to the poison so violently. Edred's breathing was becoming increasingly shallow, and Bartholomew forced his fingers to the back of the friar's throat to make him vomit. He doubted whether it would help, since the oleander had also entered the friar's body through the cut in his head and had probably been inhaled when the jar had smashed, but he had to try. He dispatched Michael to fetch the charcoal mixture he had used successfully against oleander poisoning – although admittedly a very mild dose – in the past, and forced Edred to swallow it. But it was all to no avail. Bartholomew felt the friar's heartbeat become more and more rapid, and then erratic. He tried to ease him into positions where the student might be able to breathe more readily, but he was fighting a lost battle.

'Matt! He is dying!' pleaded Michael. 'Do something else! Make him walk. Let me fetch eggs and vinegar. That worked with Walter last year.' Without waiting for Bartholomew's reply, he thrust himself through the silent group of watching scholars at the door and they heard him puffing across the yard towards the kitchens.

Bartholomew stood and turned to face them. 'It is too late.'

'How did this happen?' asked Master Kenyngham, shocked. 'Who is he? And what is he doing in our College?'

Bartholomew wondered how he could begin to explain, but at that moment Michael returned, his hands full of eggs and a pitcher of slopping vinegar. He sagged when he saw Edred's half-closed eyes and waxen face.

'Is he dead?' he asked hoarsely.

Bartholomew nodded. 'Oleander is a powerful poison. There was nothing I could do.'

Alcote elbowed him out of the way to look at Edred. 'I wonder you ever have any patients, Matthew. You always seem to be losing them. First Mistress Fletcher, and now this friar.'

Bartholomew flinched. While he had a better rate of success with his cures than most of his colleagues, he was only too aware that there were diseases and injuries when a patient's demise was inevitable, no matter what treatment he might attempt. Knowing that his skills and medicines were useless in such cases was the part of being a physician he found most difficult part to accept.

'You did not even consult his stars,' Alcote was saying, kneeling next to the dead man, and preparing to give him last rites.

'He had no time,' Kenyngham pointed out, rallying

to Bartholomew's defence. 'It all happened rather quickly. And how could the man answer questions about his birth-date anyway, when he lay fighting for his last breath?'

Alcote declined to answer, and traced vigorous crosses on Edred's forehead, mouth and chest. The sudden movement created a puff of the white dust and Alcote raised his hand to his mouth as he prepared to cough. Bartholomew leapt forward and dragged him away.

'Wash your hands, Roger,' he said firmly. 'Or you will be discovering first-hand how my medical skills cannot save a man from poisoning.'

Colour drained from Alcote's face and he scurried hastily from the room to act on Bartholomew's advice. Kenyngham ushered everyone out and closed the door behind him.

'There is nothing more to see,' he said to the still-curious scholars. 'Go back to your chambers. Fathers William and Aidan will pray for this man's soul.' He watched them disperse to do his bidding and turned to Bartholomew. 'It is clearly not safe to be in your room with that white poison floating around, so we will deal with the friar's earthly remains in the morning when we can see what we are doing.'

Bartholomew leaned against the door wearily, wondering what nasty turn the investigation would take next, and whether he and Michael would live to tell the tale. Meanwhile, Michael was trying to explain to Kenyngham what had happened.

The placid Gilbertine listened patiently to Michael's brief summary of his inquiries into the death of Kenzie and the involvement of Lydgate, but refused to allow the monk to dwell too deeply on the details of Edred's death. He took the distressed Benedictine firmly by the shoulder.

'No good will come of thinking about the matter before we have made a thorough examination of the facts. You did not seek to kill this man, Michael: it was an accident. And who can say that if you had not thrown the poison jar, this friar would not have slain Matthew? Or both of you? It seems to me he was bent upon some kind of mischief. It grieves me to see such evil in a man of the cloth, but if you are determined to be a proctor you must inure yourself to such matters.'

It was sound advice, although Bartholomew was surprised to hear it from Kenyngham, a man whose gentleness and reluctance to believe ill of anyone sometimes proved a liability to his College.

Kenyngham continued. 'It is too late and too dark to begin inquiries into this mysterious powder now. Sleep in Michael's room tonight, Matthew. I will send a porter to inform the Chancellor of what has happened immediately.'

Bartholomew followed Michael up the creaking stairs. Michael was strangely subdued, and Bartholomew's mind whirled with questions as he lay under the coarse blankets of his borrowed bed. What had Edred been doing? Was his confession

423

merely an excuse to get into the College to search Bartholomew's room? What was so important that he had been prepared to kill? And perhaps more important to his own peace of mind, why had Edred died so quickly and violently from his slight exposure to the oleander powder?

When Bartholomew awoke the next morning, the room was unfamiliar. The wooden ceiling was brightly painted and the bed was lumpy. He raised himself on one elbow, and in a rush the events of the previous night came back to him. Michael snored softly in his own bed, while Gray was on another, his tawny hair poking out from under the blanket. Gray had been concerned that some of the oleander might have landed on Bartholomew and had insisted on staying with him to be on hand lest he began to show symptoms of poisoning. After all, he had added, his blue eyes wide, Master Lynton and Father Philius had full classes already, so who would teach him and his friends medicine if Bartholomew were to die? Trying not to disturb them, Bartholomew stood up as quietly as he could.

Michael, a light sleeper, woke immediately.

Bartholomew pointed to the lightening sky. 'It is time for us to be about our business,' he whispered. 'We have a lot to do today, and there may be a riot tonight.'

Michael swung his large legs off the bed and sat up with a yawn.

Their voices woke Gray, who uncurled himself and watched Bartholomew. 'I will don a mask and gloves and clean the poison from your room,' he offered, rubbing the sleep from his eyes.

Bartholomew thanked him. 'But do not let Deynman help – he is not to be trusted around poisons for his own safety. Ask Tom Bulbeck to assist you. I suppose someone will arrange for Edred to be returned to Godwinsson today?'

Michael shook his head. 'The Master heard from de Wetherset last night after you were asleep. He recommends that Edred be buried discreetly in St Mary's churchyard. He is afraid that the death of a scholar in a college other than his own might start another riot, and I believe he is right. I do not trust Lydgate to be sensible about this and so he shall not be told. Not yet, anyway. Master Kenyngham will call a meeting of all our scholars this morning and order that last night's events are not to be discussed outside Michaelhouse. He will appeal to their sense of College loyalty in dangerous times, and I am sure they will comply.'

'But what did Edred want?' asked Bartholomew, his bewilderment of the night before surging back to him. 'What do I have that causes people to search my room – three times now – and lure us out in the depths of the night to attack us?'

'Medicines? Poisons?' suggested Gray, who had been listening with interest to their conversation.

'I have nothing that Jonas the Poisoner, Father Philius or Hugh Lynton do not have,' said

Bartholomew, 'not to mention the infirmarians at Barnwell Priory and the Hospital of St John's.'

'The rings in your sleeve?' asked Michael, ignoring Gray's look of incomprehension.

Bartholomew shook his head. 'Edred saw me take the broken ring from my sleeve in the kitchen. Why bother to look in my room when he knew where they were?'

'Do you have letters from anyone, or documents?' said Gray, racking his brains.

'Not that I can think of,' said Bartholomew. 'I have records of the treatments given to patients and of medicines dispensed. But these cannot be important to anyone but me.'

'Whatever it was, Edred was prepared to kill for it,' said Michael. 'And he died for it. Are you certain it was the oleander that killed him?' Bartholomew saw the silent appeal in his friend's eyes and looked away.

'I am afraid so. He was most definitely poisoned, and I am sure the white powder that coated him was oleander from one of the jars you threw. His symptoms matched those usual in such cases, although Edred succumbed very rapidly to the poison's effects.'

'But why do you need such a foul powder?' cried Michael, suddenly agitated. 'You are a physician, not a poisoner! And you are usually so careful with toxins, Why did you leave this one lying so readily to hand?'

'I use a diluted form of oleander for treating

leprosy.' said Bartholomew. 'It works better on some forms of the disease than other potions. But it is a very diluted form and, as I said last night, I used the last of it several days ago.'

'You ordered more oleander from Jonas the Poisoner before your stars became so sadly aligned,' said Gray helpfully. 'It came yesterday while you were out. I could not lock it in the store-room because you were out with the key, so I put it on the shelf in your chamber so it would not be lying around too obviously. But it was powerful stuff, this oleander – much more so than the stuff you usually use. It seems to me that this friar died more quickly than he would have done had he been killed with your normal-strength powder.'

At his words, Bartholomew's stomach started to churn with a sudden, vile realisation. He sat down abruptly and looked up at Michael with horrified eyes, 'The Tyler family!' he said in a whisper. 'They are related to Jonas's wife!'

'So? Are you saying that the Tyler women are trying to poison you?' asked Michael, astounded.

'They may have sent me some kind of oleander concentrate, instead of the diluted powder I usually order from Jonas. It would be easy enough to do, given that they would look the same.'

Michael thought for a moment and then sighed, raising his shoulders in a gesture of defeat. 'It is possible, I suppose. They are involved in all this business somehow, through Joanna. Maybe they felt you were coming too close to the truth about her and wanted you out of the way.'

'But I take great care with powerful medicines,' said Bartholomew, thinking uncomfortably of how Eleanor had tried to dissuade him from looking any further into Joanna's death. 'I am unlikely to be poisoned by them.'

'Perhaps they did not want to kill you at all,' said Gray. He stiffened suddenly as a thought occurred to him. 'Not me, either! I swear to you that I did not lay a finger on her! Well, perhaps a little kiss, but she was willing enough for that.'

'What is this?' asked Michael, bewildered.

'Sam escorted Eleanor home after the Founder's Feast,' said Bartholomew. 'Are you sure you did nothing to anger her? Or her mother?'

'Nothing!' cried Gray. 'Honestly! I thought she had set her sights on you but you had put her off somehow during the Feast. I was singing your praises and she told me, rather sharply, to keep them to myself. That's when I decided to make a move. Well, just a kiss. Perhaps they wanted you to dispatch one of your patients for them. That would make sense.'

'But I only use oleander for treating leprosy,' objected Bartholomew. 'And all the lepers I attend are poor, pathetic creatures who have long since ceased to deal with affairs outside their own community.'

'Why should the Tylers know what you use oleander for?' said Michael. 'None of them are physicians or even apothecaries.'

Bartholomew spread his hands. 'We may be wronging them terribly,' he said. He thought back to the events of the previous night. 'Did Edred say anything to you after he was stricken?' he asked, recalling Michael kneeling next to the friar as Bartholomew attended to Cynric, before Michael realised that Edred's sudden collapse was more serious than a jar breaking in his face.

Michael rubbed his cheeks with his hands. 'Nothing,' he said softly. 'Not so much as a whisper.'

Gray stood to pour him a cup of watered wine from the supply on the window ledge. As he flopped back on the bed again, he winced as he sat on something hard. He pulled it from underneath him and shot Bartholomew a guilty glance.

'Master Radbeche's Galen,' said Bartholomew, recognising the rough leather binding. 'I must return that today.'

'I saw it yesterday afternoon when I put the package from Jonas in your room,' said Gray, defensively. 'I thought I might borrow it since you were out. I brought it here to read last night, but I fell asleep,' he finished lamely.

'You should ask before you take things,' said Bartholomew mildly, pleased that Gray was prepared to undertake voluntary reading, but concerned that he should borrow David's Hostel's precious tome without permission.

'It is an interesting text,' said Gray, detecting that Bartholomew's admonition held an underlying note of approval and keen to turn it to his advantage. 'Although I must say that the last chapter was the most interesting of all. And not by Galen,' he said with a laugh.

'How do you know it is not by Galen?' asked Bartholomew. Although Gray was a quick student, he rarely used his intellectual talents to the full and was far too lazy to instigate a debate that would mean some hard thinking. 'Are you so familiar with his style and knowledge of medicine that you are able to detect mere imitation from the master himself?'

'Oh, no!' said Gray hastily, knowing that he would never be able to take on Bartholomew in a debate about the authenticity of Galen. 'But the last chapter is not about medicine at all. Have you not read it? It is a collection of local stories – like a history of the town.'

Michael made a sound of irritation at this irrelevance and drained the wine from his cup. 'So what? Parchment is expensive and scribes often use spare pages at the end of books to record something else so as to avoid waste. If you are surprised by that, Sam Gray, then you are revealing that you have read far fewer books than you should have done at this point in your academic career.'

'I was not surprised by it,' said Gray hotly. 'I was just pointing out to you that the last chapter was considerably more interesting than boring old Galen.'

He scrambled to his feet and brought the book over to Bartholomew. 'Your marker is here,' he said, indicating a point about three-quarters of the way through, where Bartholomew had reached. 'And the interesting chapter is here.'

He opened the book to the last few pages. The text was in the same undisciplined scrawl that characterised the rest of the book, complete with spelling errors, crossings out and ink blots. Gray was right about the content: there was nothing medical about the subject of the last chapter and parts were illustrated with thumb-sized sketches. The drawings were good, and Bartholomew suspected that the anonymous scribe derived a good deal more pleasure from his illustrations than his writing.

'See?' said Gray. 'Here is a bit about how William the Conqueror came in 1068 and ordered that twenty-seven houses should be demolished so that the Castle could be built. And here is a description of the fire that almost destroyed St Mary's Church. My uncle remembers that very well.'

'Does he?' asked Bartholomew, startled. The fire in St Mary's, he knew, had been in 1290, and Gray's uncle was certainly no more than forty years old.

'Oh, yes,' said Gray. 'He often tells the story about how he dashed through the flames to save the golden candlesticks that stood on the altar.'

'So, it runs in the family,' muttered Michael, also aware of the date of the fire. 'That explains a lot.'

'What do you mean?' demanded Gray. 'My uncle is a very brave man.'

'What else is in this history?' asked Bartholomew quickly, before tempers could fray. While Michael's sharp, sardonic wit might best Gray in an immediate argument, Michael would then be considered fair game for all manner of Gray's practical jokes, not all of them pleasant or amusing.

'There is a bit about the hero Hereward the Wake. who fought against William the Conqueror in the Fens,' continued Gray, giving Michael an evil look. 'And a paragraph about Simon d'Ambrey who was shot in the King's Ditch twenty-five years ago and whose hand is in Valence Marie. The whole thing ends with a tale about some Chancellor called Richard de Badew who funded Clare College before the Countess came along and endowed it with lots of money in the 1330s.'

Intrigued, now that the University and not the town was the subject of the text, Michael came to sit next to them, peering at the book as it lay open on Bartholomew's lap.

'The rest of the book is undoubtedly Galen,' said Bartholomew, flicking through it. 'I have read it before, although this is by far the worst copy I have ever seen.'

'It was the book!' exclaimed Gray suddenly, grabbing Bartholomew's arm. 'The attack in the street, your room searched. It was the book they wanted!'

'Whatever for?' asked Bartholomew, unconvinced.

'It is a poor copy of Galen at best and certainly not worth killing for.'

'Not for the Galen. For the bit at the end,' insisted Gray, eyes glittering with enthusiasm. 'Perhaps it contains information about the town that no one knows.'

'Perhaps Hereward the Wake is alive and well and wants to read it,' said Michael, laughing. 'Or maybe this long-dead Chancellor, de Badew.'

'It was no apparition that brained me in the High Street,' said Bartholomew firmly. 'That was Will, Huw, Saul Potter and Bigod. And it was Edred who searched my room.'

He leaned back against the wall and began to study the book with renewed interest. Were the local stories significant, or was the copyist merely using up leftover paper at the end of his book, as Michael suggested? The leather covers of the tome were thick and crude, and inside, an attempt had been made to improve their appearance by pasting coloured parchment over them. Bartholomew ran his fingers down them and then looked closer. He was wrong – the parchment had not been placed there to make the inside cover look neater, but to hide something. He picked at it, uncertain. Michael watched silently. Both were scholars with a love of learning and of the books that contained it. Damaging one of these precious items was an act alien to both of them.

Gray took it from him, and with a decisive move-ment of his hand, ripped the parchment away.

Bartholomew and Michael, as one, winced at the sound of tearing, but looked with interest at what spilled out into Gray's hands. While Gray performed a similar operation with the front cover, Bartholomew and Michael read the documents that had fallen from the back.

Bartholomew felt sick. 'These are copies of letters sent by Norbert to me after he fled to Dover,' he said in a low voice. 'They date from a few weeks after he left, to the last message I had about fifteen years ago and are signed with the name of his sister, Celinia.'

'Who is Norbert?' asked Gray, intrigued.

Bartholomew sighed. 'He was accused of burning the tithe barn at Trumpington when we were children. I helped him escape.'

'And this,' said Michael, waving another document in the air, 'is a list of times and dates suggesting meetings, along with names and addresses. They include Mistress Tyler, Thomas Bigod, Will of Valence Marie, Cecily Lydgate, and the Godwinsson servants Saul Potter and Huw, to name but a few. You were right, Matt. It was Bigod, Will, Potter and Huw who attacked us – for these parchments.'

'Do you think they are involved in starting the riots, then?' asked Gray, his eyes alight with excitement.

Bartholomew turned the letters over in his hands. 'That seems something of a leap in logic, but does not mean that you are wrong. The only thing finding these documents has made clear to me is that Norbert may have returned to the area. Why else would his letters be here?'

Mistress Tyler's house was silent and still. Tulyet's sergeant kicked at the door until it gave way and forced his way in, shouldering aside the splintered wood to stand in the small chamber on the ground floor. Bartholomew peered in. The room was bare except for a heavy chest, a table and some shelves. Tulyet pushed past him and began to climb the ladder that led to the upper chamber where the women had slept. He shook his head in disgust as he descended.

'Gone,' he called. 'And swept so clean that a spider could not hide.'

'This will confound your plans for the Festival of St Michael and All Angels on Sunday,' remarked Michael to Bartholomew leeringly. 'Whom will you ask to escort you now Hedwise Tyler has fled? I doubt you will get away with Matilde a second time. You might be reduced to taking Agatha given that you are so intent on being surrounded by women!'

Bartholomew pretended to ignore him, wondering how such things could occur to the fat monk when the situation was so grave.

'Why clean a house you are abandoning for ever?' he mused, looking around him.

'I will never understand women,' agreed Tulyet. 'What a waste of time!'

'Perhaps not,' said Bartholomew, frowning.

Watched by the others, he began a careful examination of the room. Finally, he stopped and pointed to some faint brownish stains on one of the walls. When he moved some cracked bowls and pots that had been left, there was a larger stain on the wooden floor.

'Cooking accident?' asked Michael, nonplussed.

'Hardly, Brother,' said Bartholomew. 'Only people who do not mind their houses going up in flames cook so close to the walls. This stain is blood. It splattered on the wall and then pooled on the floor.'

'Whose blood?' asked Tulyet, staring at it. 'This Joanna's?'

'Probably,' said Bartholomew, thinking again of Mistress Tyler leading him away from her house the night of the riot. 'There is enough of it to suggest that a serious, if not fatal, wound was inflicted and there was simply too much blood to be cleaned away.'

Michael puffed out his cheeks, and prodded half-heartedly at the stone jars and bowls that had been left. Bartholomew leaned against the door frame and thought. He had been hoping that there had been some mistake, and that they would discover the Tylers' part in the affair was coincidental, or innocent. But how could he hold to that belief now? They had fled the town, taking everything that was moveable with them. He wondered if Eleanor had been given the idea by Father William while at the Feast, since he had regaled her with stories of how he had run away laden with monastic treasures.

Hope flared within him suddenly. Perhaps they had been taken by force; abducted and taken away against their will. The hope faded as quickly as it had come. What abductor would take the furniture with him and sweep the upstairs chamber before making away with his prizes? Not only that, but Bartholomew very much doubted that the Tyler women could be abducted anywhere they did not want to go.

Michael bent to one of the bowls and Bartholomew saw him run his finger around its rim. He held it up lightly coated with a gritty, white powder and raised the finger to his lips to sniff at it. With a bound, Bartholomew leapt at him, knocking Tulyet sideways before slapping Michael's hand away from his face and wiping the powder from his finger with his shirt-sleeve.

Michael looked puzzled. 'How will we know what this is unless we smell it?' he said. 'I have watched Jonas the Poisoner smell and taste his medicines often enough.'

'Then Jonas is a fool,' snapped Bartholomew. 'If, as you believe, that powder is the same kind that killed Edred, it is in a highly concentrated form.'

'But you told me last night that the poison might have worked more quickly on Edred because it entered a wound or because he inhaled it in. A small amount on my hand will not harm me.'

437

'It might,' said Bartholomew. 'Can you feel your finger now?'

Michael rubbed his finger cautiously. 'It is numb. I cannot feel it,' he added with a slight rise in pitch, and his eyes widening with horror.

Bartholomew pursed his lips. 'Go and rinse it off,' he said. 'The feeling will return eventually.'

Tulyet crouched next to the bowl, poking at it with his dagger. 'Is it the same concentrated powder that killed the friar in your room?' he asked, glancing at Bartholomew as Michael hurried from the house in search of water.

'It would seem so,' said Bartholomew. 'Even a small amount has taken the feeling from Michael's fingertip.'

Tulyet stood. 'I will send men after Mistress Tyler and her devious daughters to see what she has to say for herself.' He looked down at the bowls again. 'Although, all we can prove is that she had the same powerful poison in her house that Jonas sent to you.'

'I will go to see if Jonas knows where she might have gone,' said Bartholomew. 'If he has any ideas I will send you a message.'

Wringing and flexing his afflicted finger, Michael followed Bartholomew to the apothecary's shop, while Tulyet went to organise men to search for the Tyler family, although they all knew that they would be long gone.

Jonas's shop was empty of customers, and the apothecary was mixing potions on a wide shelf

438

that ran along one side of the room. He was humming to himself, his bald head glistening with tiny beads of sweat as he applied himself to pounding something into a paste with considerable vigour. His two apprentices were hanging bunches of herbs to dry in the rafters of an adjoining room.

'You sent me a powerful poison, Jonas,' said Bartholomew without preamble, watching the apothecary jump at the nearness of the voice behind him. Colour drained from Jonas's usually pink-cheeked face. He cast a nervous glance at his apprentices and closed the door so that they should not hear.

'Please, Doctor,' he said. 'That matter was finished with a long time ago and I paid dearly for my mistake. Do not jest with me about poisons!'

'I am not jesting about the events of years ago,' said Bartholomew. 'I am talking about the events of yesterday. You sent me oleander so concentrated that Brother Michael's finger is numb from touching a few grains of it.'

Michael held up his finger, an even more unhealthy white than the rest of him. Jonas's eyes almost popped from their sockets. Cautiously, like a bird accepting a much desired crumb, Jonas inched forward to examine Michael's finger. He put out a tentative hand and touched the pallid, puckered skin.

As though he had been burned, he snatched his hand back again.

'Oleander without a doubt,' he said. 'But why were you touching it?'

'That was caused by the same oleander you sent to me for the physic I use for leprosy,' said Bartholomew.

Jonas backed up against the wall, as though faced with a physical threat. 'Not me, Matthew,' he said. 'You know I am careful with such poisons. Have I ever made a mistake in the measurements and doses I send to you? Everything that leaves this shop, even down to the mildest salve, is checked. First by me, then by my apprentices and then by my wife.'

'But nevertheless, this powerful oleander was sent to me,' said Bartholomew persistently. 'Yesterday afternoon.'

Jonas's confusion increased. He pointed to a package on one of the wall shelves. 'There is your order of oleander, Matthew. It is ready but, as I said, all potions leaving my shop are checked. Your order has not yet been checked by my wife, which is why it is waiting.'

Now it was Bartholomew's turn to be confused. 'But you sent my order yesterday.'

Jonas bristled. 'I did no such thing. You can look in my record book if you doubt me.'

Bartholomew exchanged a puzzled look with Michael. 'Were Eleanor or Hedwise Tyler here yesterday?' he asked.

Jonas smiled suddenly. 'Both were here. Eleanor has been most helpful these last few weeks. The outbreak of summer ague has meant that we have been busier than usual and she has been a valuable assistant. She helped to prepare some of the orders yesterday, and even offered to deliver them, so that my apprentices would not have to leave their work.'

The smile slowly faded and he swallowed hard. 'Oh no!' he said, backing away from them. 'You are not going to tell me that Eleanor sent the poison?'

'Does she have access to your poisons?' asked Bartholomew.

'Not access as such,' said Jonas, his small hands fluttering like birds about the front of his apron in his agitation. 'But she was interested in my work and I showed her what was where.'

'I assume you store your oleander in its concentrated form and sell it diluted for medicines?' asked Bartholomew. It was standard practice among apothecaries and there was nothing untoward in it. Jonas nodded. 'Did Eleanor know this?'

'I showed her how I diluted it yesterday,' said Jonas, his hands fluttering even more wildly. 'For you as a matter of fact. You ordered some for the lepers at Barnwell Priory.'

'Do you know Eleanor and her family have gone?' asked Bartholomew.

'Gone where?' asked Jonas, bewildered. 'Not far, surely. She said she would help me this afternoon and I have come to rely on her. And her family is coming for dinner this evening.'

'I do not think so,' said Michael. 'The Tyler house is abandoned and all removeable items gone.'

Jonas shook his head. 'They are coming to eat with us tonight. Meg!' he yelled suddenly, making Bartholomew leap out of his skin. Immediately, there were footsteps on the wooden stairs, and Jonas's wife appeared.

'They say Agnes has left town, Meg,' said Jonas, still wringing his hands. 'I told them that was impossible because she and the family are coming to dinner tonight.'

Meg's eyes grew huge and flitted from Bartholomew to Michael in terror.

'Tell us what you know, Mistress,' said Michael, watching her reaction with resignation.

Meg's fearful eyes danced back to her husband, who smiled at her, encouraging her to support his statement.

'I went round to Agnes's house yesterday afternoon and they had everything piled up in the middle of the room,' she said. 'They made me promise not to mention they were leaving until they had gone.'

'Gone where?' asked Bartholomew. 'And why?'

Meg shook her head. 'I begged them to stay. They are my only relatives here but they were insistent that they should go.'

'Do you know that Eleanor sent me a powerful poison yesterday, in place of the diluted oleander I use for treating leprosy?'

'No!' Meg cried. 'She did not!'

'Oh, but she did, Mistress,' said Michael. 'And I suspect you know far more than you are telling us. Now, we do not have all day, so tell us the truth and hurry up with it.'

Meg's eyes flitted to her husband's horrified face and she burst into tears.

'This oleander has caused the death of someone,' Michael pressed. Jonas's legs gave out and he plopped on to a low bench on top of a bunch of dried mint. Within moments, the herb's pungent odour filled the shop.

'Oh no!' he groaned. 'Who has died? Not that saintly Master Kenyngham? My business will be finished for ever if this gets out!'

Meg wailed louder, so that Michael had to raise his voice to be heard. 'I am sure your part in all this will be overlooked if you tell us what we need to know.'

Meg fought to bring her sobs under control. 'Eleanor said that Doctor Bartholomew had been asking questions about Joanna,' she said, after a few moments of serious sniffing. 'She was terribly distressed because she said she did not want him, of all people, to be the cause of her mother's downfall. I am not sure what she meant. I thought it was Joanna's prostitution and that Eleanor was worried for the good name of her mother's household, but I think now that it was more than that.'

She paused to scrub at her nose with the back of her hand. 'I saw Eleanor in the poisons cupboard yesterday and she told me she was preparing your order of oleander. Later, I remembered that Jonas always keeps the diluted oleander for you in a separate jar, but that Eleanor had been using the concentrated powder.'

'So it is true!' wailed Jonas in horror. 'We did send concentrated oleander to Doctor Bartholomew! This is just too dreadful!'

'Please continue, Mistress,' said Michael, silencing the apothecary with a disdainful glance.

Meg took a deep breath. 'I was appalled that she might inadvertently have sent you the wrong thing, and rushed to her house so we could put all to rights before Jonas found out, or anyone was harmed. Agnes and Hedwise had all their belongings piled in the middle of the floor while Eleanor sat in a corner and wept. They would not tell me what was amiss. I asked Eleanor about the powder but she said it was still on the shelf with the other orders awaiting delivery.'

She gestured to the package above her head with Bartholomew's name written on it, a certain defiance in her eyes. 'And there it is.'

'But she was lying, Mistress,' said Michael harshly. 'Eleanor had already dispatched one package to Doctor Bartholomew – the one she had prepared at home containing the concentrated oleander she had stolen from Jonas. She hoped it would have done its job before he received the real package and became suspicious. And you suspected all was not well by her behaviour.'

'No!' shrieked Meg, weeping afresh. 'I did *not* know. I came home, and there was the package, just as she said it would be. I threw it away and prepared another in its place – with diluted oleander.'

'And do you know what Eleanor's motives were in all this?' persisted Michael, his grim expression making it abundantly clear that he did not believe her for an instant.

'Motives for what?' cried Meg. 'She did nothing wrong! She accidentally used the wrong powder in your order but I discovered her mistake and corrected it before anyone came to harm. I do not know how poor Master Kenyngham died but it was not with anything from our shop!'

Michael said nothing, and regarded her long and hard. Bartholomew had known Jonas and Meg for years and knew they would not risk their livelihood so rashly: he was therefore inclined to believe they were telling the truth. But Eleanor was another matter. Clearly, she had stolen the concentrated oleander and prepared it for Bartholomew in the safety of her own home, as attested by the residues in the bowl Michael had touched. But was Mistress Tyler aware of her daughter's actions? Or Hedwise? Surely, Bartholomew's feeble investigation concerning Joanna could not warrant Eleanor trying to kill him? He decided that he might be wise to stay away from future involvements with women – at least until he had learned a little more about them.

Meg wiped her nose. 'Eleanor told me some days ago that Doctor Bartholomew had some odd notion that Joanna had been murdered during the riot. Of course, nothing of the kind had happened and we all know that Joanna had left because she found Cambridge too violent.'

'So, Joanna is in Ely?' asked Michael. Meg nodded and Michael continued. 'In that case, surely it would be a simple matter to summon her back again and prove that she is alive and well, living a life of sin near the greatest Benedictine House in East Anglia. Why did Mistress Tyler not do that?'

Meg looked bewildered, as though such a notion had not occurred to her before. 'I do not know,' she stammered. 'Perhaps because they were so relieved when she left. Joanna was definitely not the demure and gentle niece we remembered from years ago.' She pursed her lips in disapproval. 'She had become a harlot.'

Bartholomew studied the frightened woman soberly. She did not possess the quick intelligence and courage of her Tyler relatives and Bartholomew was in no doubt that she had believed what she had been told. Meg's crime was nothing more than gullibility. But Bartholomew was now certain that Joanna had played a part in some plot – whether willingly or unwillingly he did not know – and that Eleanor had sent him the poison in order to prevent him coming any closer to the truth. The more he thought about it, particularly in relation to the bloodstains in the house, the more he sensed that there was most definitely something untoward about Joanna's sudden departure, and that Eleanor had taken it upon herself to protect her family from the consequences.

'Did you see Joanna after the riot?' asked Bartholomew, already guessing what the answer would be.

Meg shook her head. 'Agnes said Joanna did not want to help with the clearing up afterwards. It is typical of her. She has become a lazy woman. Agnes saw her off early that morning.'

But Joanna, if Joanna it were, was already dead in the Castle mortuary that morning and Agnes Tyler herself was staying at Jonas's house because her own had been looted.

'Where did Agnes see Joanna?' pressed Bartholomew.

'I do not know,' said Meg. 'She was up early and went off to inspect the damage done to her house. I did not question where they met.'

If they ever met, thought Bartholomew. There was no evidence to suggest that they did, and quite a bit to suggest that they did not.

'One last question,' he said. Meg nodded cautiously, still sniffling. 'Could Joanna write?'

Meg looked taken aback. 'Of course not,' she said. 'Her mother always planned for her to follow in her footsteps and become a dairy-maid at the Abbey. She had no need to learn her letters.'

But Eleanor could write, thought Bartholomew. And someone had written a note, purporting to be from Joanna, to Dunstan's lovesick grandson, perhaps so that her sudden disappearance would not arouse the lad's suspicion, and cause him to go to Ely to find her. If Joanna was illiterate, it was unlikely that she would have written a note – or even bother to dictate one – to a moonstruck adolescent who could not read. Eleanor Tyler's role in the affair was becoming increasingly suspect.

Bartholomew made his farewells to Meg and the agitated apothecary. As he turned to leave the shop the doorway darkened. Against the bright sunlight, a figure stood silhouetted.

'Doctor Bartholomew,' said the hulking shape in a loud, confident voice that dripped with loathing. 'And Brother Michael. I have been searching for you two. We should talk. Meet me at St Andrew's Church at sunset tonight.'

The figure moved away, leaving Bartholomew and Michael staring at the empty doorway.

'Well,' said Michael. 'Do we obey this summons and meet Master Lydgate tonight?'

'A summons from the Devil?' asked Bartholomew dubiously.

CHAPTER 10

In a flaming ball of golden orange the sun began to dip behind the orchard walls, bathing the creamy stone of Michaelhouse in a deep russet-red. Shadows lengthened, or flickered out altogether and in the distance carts clattered and creaked as farmers and merchants made their way home at the end of the day.

Michael stood and stretched. 'Ready?' he said, looking down to where Bartholomew was still sitting comfortably on the fallen tree, his back against the sun-warmed stones of the orchard wall.

Reluctantly, Bartholomew climbed to his feet, and followed Michael through the trees to the back gate. They let themselves out and walked quickly towards the High Street. It thronged with people heading for home. Horses and donkeys drew carts of all shapes and sizes and weary apprentices hastened to complete the last business before trading ceased for the day. One cart had lost a wheel in one of the huge pot-holes, and a fiery argument had broken out between the cart's owner and those whose path he was blocking. A barking dog, children's high-pitched taunting of the carter and a barker's increasingly strident calls to sell the last of his pies, added to the general cacophony.

Bartholomew and Michael ignored the row, squeezing past the offending cart. As they emerged the other side, Bartholomew heard something thud against the wall by his head. Someone had thrown a stone at him! He turned, but Michael's firm hand pulled him on.

'Not a place to linger, my friend,' he muttered. Bartholomew could not but agree. Any large gathering of townspeople, already riled by an incident such as the blockage caused by the broken cart, was not a place for University men to tarry. Bartholomew glanced backwards as they hurried on, glimpsing the owner of the broken cart howling in rage as three or four hefty apprentices tried to shoulder it out of the way.

He paused briefly, frowning at the carter as something clicked into place in the back of his mind, but yielded to Michael's impatient tug on his sleeve. They reached St Andrew's Church without further incident and slipped into its cool, dark interior. Here, the shadows lay thick and impenetrable and the only light was from a cluster of candles near the altar. Michael closed the door, blocking out the noise of the street, while Bartholomew prowled around the church looking for Lydgate.

Bartholomew had not wanted to come to this meeting. He did not trust Lydgate and did not understand why, after so many protestations of dislike, the man should suddenly want to meet them. Inadvertently, his hand went to the dagger concealed under his tabard, which he had borrowed from the ailing Cynric. He rarely carried weapons but felt justified in bringing one to the meeting with Lydgate, although surely even Lydgate would be loath to commit murder in a house of God? But desperate or enraged men would not stop to consider the sanctity of a church. Even the saint, Thomas à Becket, had not been safe in his own cathedral.

The door gave a sudden creak and Bartholomew instinctively slipped into the shadows behind one of the pillars. Lydgate entered alone, pulling the door closed behind him with a loud bang. He stood for a moment in the gloom, accustoming his eyes to the dark after the brightness of the setting sun outside. Michael approached him and Bartholomew left his hiding place to join them.

Before any greetings could be exchanged, Lydgate pointed a finger at Bartholomew.

'You have many questions to answer, Bartholomew,' he hissed belligerently.

Bartholomew eyed him with distaste. It was not an auspicious start. Even the Principal of a hostel had no authority to speak to him so. But nothing would be served by responding with anger, especially with the blustering Lydgate.

'We have much to discuss with you,' he replied as pleasantly as he could.

Lydgate regarded him with his small blue eyes. 'First,' he began, 'where is Edred?'

Michael spoke before Bartholomew could answer. 'Where is your daughter, Master Lydgate?' he asked. 'Is she still with your relatives away from Cambridge?'

Bartholomew looked at him sharply. He did not want Michael to mention Cecily's hiding place at Chesterton, even in connection with something else. Although he did not have an overwhelming respect for Lydgate's powers of reasoning, he did not wish Michael to give him even the most obtuse clue that might betray her.

Lydgate seemed nonplussed at Michael's question, and stood looking from one to the other in confusion, his hands dangling at his sides. How could such a man, a lout with poor manners and worse self-control, ever have become the Principal of a hostel? wondered Bartholomew. The University clearly needed to review its selection procedures.

'She is . . .' Lydgate began. He seemed to remember himself. 'Tell me where Brother Edred is lurking. He did not return home this morning.'

'This morning?' Michael pounced like a cat. 'Why this morning and not last night? Surely, you do not expect your scholars to return at dawn when they should be safely tucked up in bed all night, Master Lydgate?'

Again the confused look. Bartholomew began to feel tired. It was like having an argument about logic with a baby. Lydgate was incapable of subtlety: he was too brutal and impatient. Bartholomew looked at the great hands hanging at Lydgate's sides. They were large, red and looked strong. Had those hands committed all the murders that Edred had claimed?

'We have much information that might be of interest to each other,' said Michael, relenting. 'Let's sit and talk quietly. Come.'

He led the way to some benches in the Lady Chapel. Lydgate sat stiffly, unafraid, but wary and alert to danger. Bartholomew sat opposite him, the hand under his tabard still on the hilt of his dagger. Michael sat next to Bartholomew.

'Now,' the monk said. 'I will begin and tell you what Edred has told us. Then, in turn, you can tell us what you know and together we will try to make sense of it all. Is that fair?'

Lydgate nodded slowly, while Bartholomew said nothing. The beginnings of a solution, or at least part of one, were beginning to form in his mind, and the implications bothered him. They centred around the carter who had been blocking the High Street.

'Edred came to us last night saying he was in fear of his life,' Michael began. 'He claimed you had killed young James Kenzie, then your daughter Dominica and a servant from Valence Marie and finally your student Brother Werbergh.'

Lydgate leapt to his feet. 'That is not true!' he shouted, his voice ringing through the silent church. 'I have killed no one.'

Michael gestured for him to sit down again. 'I am merely repeating what we were told,' he said

453

in placatory tones. 'I did not say we believe it to be true. Indeed, Edred's claims were all based on circumstantial evidence and conjecture, and he had nothing solid to prove his allegations. We arranged for him to sleep in Michaelhouse last night, since he seemed afraid. While Matt's book-bearer made his bed, Edred struck him from behind and began a search of the room. Do you have any idea what he might have been seeking?'

Lydgate shrugged impatiently. 'No. What was it?'

'We are uncertain,' said Michael. Bartholomew was grateful that Michael had decided to be less than open with Lydgate although, hopefully, Michael was providing him with sufficient infor-mation to loosen his tongue.

Michael continued. 'When we caught Edred rummaging, he drew a sword and threatened us. In the ensuing struggle, Edred was killed.'

Lydgate's mouth dropped open, and Bartholomew swallowed hard. The Chancellor and Master Kenyngham had advised against telling Lydgate of Edred's death and Bartholomew wondered whether Michael had not committed a grave error in informing him so bluntly. He sat tensely and waited for an explosion.

He waited in vain. 'You killed Edred?' said Lydgate, his voice almost a whisper. He scrubbed hard at the bristles on his face and shook his big head slowly.

Michael flinched. 'I did not kill him deliberately. Which cannot be said for the murderer of Werbergh.'

'Werbergh?' echoed Lydgate. 'But he died in an accident. My servants, Saul Potter and Huw saw it happen.'

'Werbergh did not die in the shed,' said Bartholomew. 'I hope this will not distress you, Master Lydgate, but I took the liberty of examining Werbergh's body in the church. I think he died on Friday night or Saturday, rather than Sunday morning under the collapsing shed. And he died from a blow to the head, after which he fell, or was pushed, into water.'

Lydgate scratched his head and let his hands fall between his knees. He looked from one to the other trying to assimilate the information.

'How can you be sure?' he asked. 'How can you tell such things? Did you kill him?'

'I most certainly did not!' retorted Bartholomew angrily. 'I was not up and about until Saturday, as anyone in Michaelhouse will attest.'

Michael raised his hands to placate him. He turned to Lydgate. 'There are signs on the body that provide information after death,' he said. 'Matt is a physician. He knows how to look for them.'

Lydgate rubbed his neck and considered. 'You say Werbergh died on Friday night or Saturday? Friday was the night of the celebration at Valence Marie. A debauched occasion, although I kept from the wine myself. I do not like to appear drunk in front of the students. Virtually all of them were insensible by the time the wine ran out.'

'Was Werbergh there?' asked Bartholomew. 'Was Edred?'

Lydgate scowled, and Bartholomew thought he might refuse to answer, but Lydgate's frown was merely a man struggling to remember. 'Yes,' he said finally. 'Both were there. Werbergh was drunk like the others. Edred was not. They left together, late, but probably before most of the others.' He looked from Michael to Bartholomew. 'Do you think this means Edred killed Werbergh?'

Bartholomew ran a hand through his hair. 'Not necessarily. I think he genuinely believed Werbergh had died by your hand sometime on Sunday morning, not from a blow to the head on Friday night.'

'No,' said Michael, shaking his head. 'That is false logic, Matt. He may have killed Werbergh on Friday, but claimed Master Lydgate had killed him on Sunday lest any should remember that it was Edred who accompanied the drunken Werbergh home on the night of his death.'

Lydgate scratched his scalp. 'What an unholy muddle,' he said.

'Unholy is certainly the word for Edred,' said Bartholomew feelingly. 'What was his intention last night? What did he think he could gain by blaming the murders on his Principal?'

'Oh, that is simple,' said Lydgate. 'It is the only thing I understand in this foul business.' He gave a huge sigh and looked Bartholomew in the eye. 'But I do not know why I should trust you. You have already tried to blackmail me.'

Bartholomew gazed at him in disbelief. Michael gave a derisive snort of laughter.

'Do not be ridiculous, Master Lydgate! What could Matt blackmail you about?'

But Bartholomew knew, and wondered again whether Lydgate had overheard him and Michael discussing the burning of the tithe barn during their first visit to Godwinsson.

After a few moments, Lydgate began to speak in a voice that was quiet and calm, quite unlike his usual bluster. 'Many years ago, I committed a grave crime,' he said. He paused.

'You burned the tithe barn,' said Bartholomew, thinking to make Lydgate's confession easier for him.

Lydgate looked at him long and hard, as though trying to make up his mind. 'Yes,' he said finally. 'Not deliberately, though. It was an accident. I . . . stumbled in the hay and knocked over a lantern. It was an accident.'

'I never imagined it was anything else,' said Bartholomew. 'Nothing could have been gained by a deliberate burning of the barn – it was a tragic loss to the whole village. That winter was a miserable time for most people, with scanty supplies of grain and little fodder for the animals.'

'You do not need to remind me,' said Lydgate bitterly. 'I was terrified the whole time that you would decide to tell the villagers who was the real cause of their misery – me and not that dirty little Norbert you helped to escape.'

'You knew about that?' asked Bartholomew, astonished.

Lydgate nodded. 'I saw you let him go. But I kept your secret as you had kept mine. Until the last few weeks, that is, when you threatened to tell.'

'I have done nothing of the sort,' said Bartholomew indignantly. 'The whole affair had slipped my mind and I did not think of it again until the skeleton was uncovered in the Ditch. Edith thought the bones might be Norbert's and I told her that was impossible.'

'How do you know?' asked Lydgate curiously.

'Because I received letters from him,' said Bartholomew. He looked at Michael. 'Copies of which were concealed in a book I have recently read,' he added.

'Then it must be Norbert who, is trying to blackmail me and not you at all! He has waited all these years to claim justice! I see! It makes sense now!' cried Lydgate.

Various things became clear in Bartholomew's mind from this tangled web of lies and misunderstandings. Lydgate must have already been sent blackmail messages when Bartholomew and Michael had gone to speak to him about Kenzie's murder, which was why he had threatened Bartholomew as he was leaving Godwinsson, and why he had instructed Cecily not to contradict anything that was said. And it was also clear that

Lydgate's aversion to Bartholomew inspecting Werbergh's body was not because he was trying to conceal his murder, but because he was keen to keep his imagined blackmailer away from events connected to his hostel.

'Not so fast,' said Michael, his eyes narrowing thoughtfully. 'We must consider this more carefully before jumping to conclusions. We found copies of Norbert's letters in a book. That tells us that he probably kept them to remind himself of the lies he had written, so he would not contradict himself in future letters. Perhaps he always intended to return to Cambridge to blackmail the man who almost had him hanged for a crime he did not commit.'

'Were these blackmail messages signed?' asked Bartholomew of Lydgate.

Lydgate shook his head. 'There have been three of them, all claiming I set the barn alight, and that payment would be required for silence.'

'What about Cecily?' asked Bartholomew. 'Could she have sent the notes? After all, you are hardly affectionate with each other.'

'She did not know it was me who set the barn on fire!' said Lydgate with frustration. 'No one does, except the three of us.'

'But why has Norbert not contacted me?' mused Bartholomew looking puzzled. 'I would have thought he might, given what I risked to save him.'

'Perhaps he is afraid you will not support him,' said Michael. 'How does he know you can still be trusted after twenty-five years?' He rubbed at the bristles on his chin. 'But it does seem that you were right and that Norbert has returned to Cambridge. We find his letters to you and Master Lydgate receives blackmail notes. It is all too much of a coincidence to be chance.'

'So it was Norbert and his associates who attacked us a week ago, looking for the book that contained that vital piece of evidence?' said Bartholomew, standing and beginning to pace, as he did when he lectured to his students and needed to think. He had sometimes carried the Galen in his medicine bag and it had probably been there when his room had been searched. But the night he was attacked, he had left the book behind because it was going to rain and he did not want it to get wet. Norbert and his associates had been unfortunate in their timing.

'And Norbert killed Werbergh?' asked Lydgate. He rubbed at his eyes tiredly. 'Even with my story and your information, it is still a fearful mess. I can make no sense of it. It was all clear to me when I thought Bartholomew was the blackmailer.' He watched Bartholomew pace back and forth, and then cleared his throat. 'One of the notes said Dominica would die as a warning,' he said huskily.

'What is this?' said Michael, aghast again. 'A warning for what?'

'This is painful for me,' said Lydgate. He leaned forward, resting his elbows on his knees, large hands dangling, and his head bowed. 'One note said that if I did not comply and leave money as instructed, my daughter would die. I sent her immediately to Chesterton for safety. During the riot, Edred came back to say she was in Cambridge again. I went out to see if I could find her but it was too late. She already lay dead, her face smeared in blood and her long golden hair soaked in gore and dirt. Ned from Valence Marie lay by the side of her, a dagger in his stomach. I pulled it out. I suppose it might be possible she was just a random victim of the riots, but I am sceptical so soon after I had the letter threatening her life.'

Bartholomew thought of Lydgate's story in the light of what he had been told by Cecily and Edred. They claimed they had seen Lydgate standing over the dead Dominica and Ned, holding a dripping knife. If everyone was telling the truth, then Cecily and Edred had indeed seen Lydgate standing over two bodies with a dagger, but had misinterpreted what they had seen. On the strength of these erroneous assumptions, Mistress Cecily had left her husband, and Edred had applied what he had known of the other deaths to reason that Lydgate had not only killed Dominica and Ned, but Werbergh and Kenzie, too.

Bartholomew rubbed the back of his head. Cecily, Lydgate and Edred all said it was Dominica they had seen lying dead near Ned from Valence Marie. In which case, where was Joanna? Bartholomew was certain she was dead, or the Tyler family would not have gone to such lengths to prevent him from looking too closely into her disappearance. But the more he thought about it, the more convinced he became that the woman with the unrecognisably battered face and long, golden hair was Joanna and not Dominica at all. It had been dark, both during the riot and in the Castle mortuary and that, coupled with the fact that the face had been battered, would have made definite identification difficult, if not impossible. And finally, there was the ominous patch of blood in the Tylers' house.

He glanced at Michael, wondering whether to share his thoughts with Lydgate. The monk had been watching him intently and gave a barely perceptible shake of his head. Michael had apparently guessed what Bartholomew had been reasoning, but thought the evidence too slim to give Lydgate hopes that he might have been mistaken and that Dominica might yet be alive.

'Dominica's name was not among the dead,' said Michael when he saw Bartholomew was not going to speak. 'Why did you not claim her body?'

Lydgate put his head in his hands. 'I did not know what to do,' he said. 'Cecily was gone, and there was no one with whom to discuss it. I decided to let Dominica's death remain anonymous until I had had time to think. You see, the soldiers at the Castle were saying that the woman who had died had been a whore. I did not want to risk Dominica's reputation by claiming that this whore was her. Half the town knew that she had a lover and she would always be remembered as the whore who died in the riots. I had to think before I acted, so I said nothing.'

'You went to her grave, though,' said Bartholomew.

Lydgate fixed his small eyes on Bartholomew. 'Yes. And you found me there. I thought you had come to gloat. You were lucky I did not run you through.'

'Does your wife know about the blackmail notes?' asked Michael.

'I told her I was being blackmailed, but I did not tell her why. She was concerned only for Dominica, and cared not a fig for me or my reputation should all this come out. She ran away from me the night Dominica died and lurks in her underground chamber at Chesterton.'

'You know where she is?' asked Bartholomew, startled.

'Of course!' said Lydgate dismissively. 'My wife is not a woman richly endowed with imagination, Bartholomew. I knew immediately that she would flee to the same place where we had hidden Dominica. And even if I had not guessed, my friend Thomas Bigod would have told me. Bigod has been a good ally to me. He gave me an alibi the night Dominica died and is keeping Cecily safe until such time as we can settle our differences – if we ever bother.'

'Cecily believed you killed Dominica,' said Michael baldly.

Lydgate gave a faint smile. 'So Thomas Bigod

tells me. Silly woman! She can stay away as long as she likes. The house is more pleasant without her whining tongue.'

Bartholomew let all this sink in. Cecily was hiding away, and Lydgate had not been fooled for an instant about her whereabouts. Lydgate had told Cecily that Bartholomew had been blackmailing him, but she had shown no compunction about helping the man she thought was her husband's enemy. To Cecily, Bartholomew had been an instrument to use against her husband. That must have been at least partly why she had helped him to escape from the manor at Chesterton: she believed she was releasing her husband's blackmailer to continue his war of attrition!

Lydgate sighed. 'I knew Dominica was seeing a scholar. The day after I sent her away, I heard him throwing stones at her window. When he saw he would get no response, he left and I followed him. But I am too big and clumsy for such work and I lost him before we reached the High Street.'

Unfortunately for Kenzie, thought Bartholomew. He might still be alive had his killer seen the hulking figure of Lydgate pursuing him.

'All I saw was a man in a scholar's tabard,' continued Lydgate wearily. 'I could not see him well enough to identify him again.'

'It was James Kenzie, the David's student who was murdered,' said Michael.

Lydgate gazed at the Benedictine in mute disbelief, and then slammed one thick fist into the palm of his other hand. 'Of course!' he exclaimed. 'That student was killed the same night I followed Dominica's visitor. No wonder you paid me so much attention!'

Bartholomew and Michael exchanged a look of bemusement, wondering how Lydgate had never put the two together in his mind before. Lydgate did not notice and continued. 'So, Dominica chose a Scot! She knew how to be hurtful. What more inappropriate lover could the daughter of a hostel principal chose than an impoverished Scot?'

'But if you did not kill him, who did? And why?' asked Bartholomew, wanting to get back to the business of solving the murders, away from Lydgate's domestic traumas.

Lydgate looked at him as though he were mad. 'Why, Norbert, of course,' he said.

Bartholomew paced up and down and shook his head impatiently. Lydgate followed him with his eyes. 'But why? Norbert has no reason to kill Kenzie.'

'What about the ring?' asked Michael. 'The lover's ring that Kenzie had lost to Edred that day?'

'Why?' said Bartholomew. 'Why should Norbert want the ring? And if you recall, Kenzie wore no ring when he died. Edred had stolen it earlier – or at least, had stolen the fake.'

Lydgate nodded. 'Edred tried to claim a reward by offering a cheap imitation of Dominica's ring. I grew angry with him and since then he has been sulky with me. That is why he accused me of those murders – as I said, it is the only thing I truly understand in all this muddle.'

'Ah!' said Michael. 'So, the slippery friar changed his allegiance. This begins to make sense. Repulsed by you in his attempts at winning favour, he was recruited by, or turned to, Norbert. It was Norbert who told him to make sure you were blamed for all those deaths by coming to us, and it was for Norbert that Edred searched Matt's room looking for the Galen. I think Edred believed what he told us was true and I think he was afraid of you. But he was working for Norbert all the time!'

It was dark in the church now and the only light came from the candles. There seemed to be little more to be said and Michael and Lydgate stood. As Lydgate stepped forward, he stumbled against Michael's bench. Bartholomew caught him by the arm and prevented him from falling. Lydgate peered down at the bench and grimaced.

'How long have your eyes been failing?' asked Bartholomew gently.

Lydgate glared at him and pulled his arm away sharply. 'That is none of your business,' he snapped, but then relented. 'My eyesight has never been good, but these last three years have seen a marked degeneration. Father Philius says there is nothing I can do. I have told no one except Dominica. It is worse at night, though. Everything fades into shadow.'

As they opened the door of the church, they saw an orange glow in the sky and, very distantly, they could hear shouting and screams carried on the slightest of breezes.

'Oh, Lord, no!' whispered Michael, gazing at the eerie lights. 'The riot has started!'

'My hostel!' exclaimed Lydgate and hurried away into the night without so much as a backward glance. Michael watched him go.

'How did you guess about his sight?' he asked.

Bartholomew shrugged. 'The signs are clear enough. He rubs his eyes constantly and he squints and peers around. When I paced, he spoke to me in the wrong direction. And he failed to see the bench he fell over. He lost Kenzie when he followed him and he, unlike Edred, did not see his bright yellow hose. But even more importantly, he probably did not see Dominica. It was Joanna he saw dead.'

'So, your theory was wrong after all,' said Michael. 'Dominica and Joanna are different.'

'It would seem so,' said Bartholomew. 'The woman's face was bloody, and the street where he found her and the Castle mortuary were dark, where Lydgate admits he cannot see well. The dead woman was probably Joanna after all. But I am not the only one who was mistaken. Lydgate, Cecily and Edred all think Dominica died on the night of the riot. Edred and Cecily only saw a fair-haired corpse from a distance; Lydgate saw her close but has poor vision.'

'So Lydgate went to look at her body at the Castle,' said Michael, 'because he had not trusted his failing eyesight on the night of the riot.'

Bartholomew ran a hand through his hair and then scrubbed hard at his face. Although things were clearer – Joanna and Dominica were not one and the same; he now understood the reason behind Lydgate's hostility towards him; and they finally knew more about the treacherous Edred's actions – there were still many questions that remained unanswered. Where was Dominica? Where was Norbert? Why had Bigod and his cronies elected to organise a riot that night? And why had someone been to such trouble to ensure that Joanna's body had been mistaken for Dominica's? He and Michael sank into the shadows of the church as shouting and running feet began to echo along the High Street. It grew closer, many feet pounding the dust of the road.

'It sounds like an army,' whispered Michael, edging further back.

Torches threw bouncing shadows in all directions as the mob surged past, yelling and calling to each other. Bartholomew recognised some of them as tradesmen from the Market Square. They all carried weapons of one kind or another – staves, knives, scythes, sticks, even cooking pots. Where the torchlight caught the occasional face, Bartholomew saw that they appeared mesmerised. They chanted together, nonsense words, but ones that created a rhythm of unity. Bartholomew had heard that clever commanders were able to create such a feeling of oneness before battles and that the soldiers, whipped up into a frenzy, fought like wild animals until they either died or dropped from sheer weariness. The crowd that surged past Bartholomew and Michael ran as one, chanting and crashing their weapons together. Bartholomew knew that if he and Michael were spotted now in their scholars' garb, they would be killed for certain. No amount of reasoning could possibly work against this enraged mob.

As the last torch jiggled past and the footsteps and chanting faded, Michael crossed himself vigorously, and Bartholomew crept cautiously to the fringe of trees in the graveyard to check that the rioters did not double back.

'That was an evil-intentioned crowd,' he whispered, as Michael joined him. 'There will be murder and mayhem again tonight. Brother. Just as Bigod promised there would be.'

Michael regarded him sombrely. 'That was no random group of trouble-makers,' he muttered. 'That was a rabble, carefully brought to fever-pitch, and held there until it is time to release it.'

'We had better return to Michaelhouse,' said Bartholomew, his voice loud in the sudden silence. The fat monk tried to muffle Bartholomew's voice with a hand over his mouth.

'Hush! Or they will release it on you and me!' he hissed fiercely.

Bartholomew had never seen Michael so afraid before and it did little to ease his troubled mind.

Michael's beadles seemed pathetic compared to the confident mob that Bartholomew had seen thunder past. They looked terrified, too. Each time an especially loud yell occurred, they glanced nervously over their shoulders, and at least two of them were so white that Bartholomew thought they might faint. One took several steps backwards and then turned and fled. Bartholomew did not blame him: the group that had been hurriedly assembled in St Mary's churchyard was pitifully small, and would be more likely to attract the violent attentions of the crowd than to prevent trouble. To one side, Guy Heppel stood in the shadows and trembled with fear. His hands rubbed constantly at the sides of his tabard in agitation.

The Chancellor stalked up and down in front of his frightened army, twisting a ring around on his finger with such force that he risked breaking it.

A sudden shout made several of the beadles shy away in alarm, and all of them jumped. It was Tulyet, his face streaked with dirt, and his horse skittering and prancing in terror. Only Tulyet's superior horsemanship prevented him from being hurled from the saddle.

'At last!' breathed de Wetherset, and smiles of relief broke out on the faces of one or two of the beadles. 'What is the news? Is the mob dispersing?'

Tulyet leaned towards him so that the fearful beadles would not overhear.

'One hostel has been fired, but it seems that most, if not all, of the scholars escaped. St Paul's Hostel is under siege but is holding out. Townsfolk are gathering near St Michael's Church and it looks as though there will be an attack on Michaelhouse soon. And at least three other hostels have been sacked.'

'Are the scholars retaliating?' asked Bartholomew, trying to stay clear of the horse's flailing hooves.

'Not yet,' said Tulyet. He flashed Michael a grin of thanks as the fat monk took a firm hold of his mount's reins, preventing it from cavorting by sheer strength of arm. 'But I have had reports that they are massing. Valence Marie are out and so are King's Hall.'

'What of Godwinsson?' asked Michael, stroking the horse's velvet nose, oblivious to the white froth that oozed from its mouth as it chewed wildly on the bit.

'That is the one that has been fired,' said Tulyet. 'The students are out somewhere.'

'What do you plan to do?' asked the Chancellor. There was a loud crash from the direction of the Market Square, and he winced. It was only a short distance from the Market Square to St Mary's Church, the centre of all University business, and the place where all its records were stored. It would take very little for the townspeople to transfer their aggressions from the market stalls to the obvious presence of the University in Cambridge's biggest and finest church.

Tulyet scrubbed at his face with his free hand. 'I scarcely know where to begin,' he said. 'It is all so scattered. The best plan I can come up with is to remove temptation from the mob's path. I want all scholars off the streets, and I want no action taken to curb the looting of the hostels that have already fallen – if there are no bands of scholars with which to fight, the fury of the mob will fizzle out.'

'It is not the University that precipitated all this,' said de Wetherset angrily. 'The townspeople started it.'

'That is irrelevant!' snapped Tulyet impatiently. 'And believe me, Master de Wetherset, the University will lose a good deal less of its property if you comply with my orders, than if you try to meet the rabble with violence.'

'You are quite right, Dick,' said Michael quickly, seeing de Wetherset prepared to argue the point, his heavy face suffused with a deep resentment. 'The most useful thing we can do now is to urge all the scholars indoors, or divert them from the mob. Heppel – take a dozen beadles and patrol Milne Street; I will take the rest along the High Street.'

Heppel looked at him aghast. 'Me?'

'Yes,' said Michael. 'You are the Junior Proctor and therefore paid to protect the University and its scholars.'

'God help us!' muttered de Wetherset under his breath, regarding the trembling Heppel in disdain. Bartholomew could see the Chancellor's point.

'But do you not think it would be better to lock ourselves in the church?' Heppel whispered, casting fearful eyes from Michael to the Chancellor. 'You said it would be best if all scholars were off the streets.'

'I was not referring to the Proctors and the beadles,' said Michael, placing his hands on his hips. 'It is our job to prevent lawlessness, not flee from it.'

'I did not anticipate such violence when I took this post!' protested Heppel. 'I knew Cambridge was an uneasy town, but I did not expect great crowds of townsfolk lusting for scholars' blood! I was not told there would be murder, or that the students would be quite so volatile!'

De Wetherset swallowed hard, and glanced around him uneasily, as if he imagined such a mob might suddenly converge on the churchyard. Meanwhile, Heppel's fear had communicated itself to the beadles and there were two fewer than when Bartholomew had last looked. Michael raised his eyes heavenward, while Tulyet pursed his lips, not pleased that the University was producing such a feeble response to its dangerous situation.

'The students are always volatile,' said Bartholomew who, like Tulyet and Michael, was unimpressed at Heppel's faint-heartedness. 'Just not usually all at once. And not usually in conjunction with the entire town. However, like the last riot, this is no random occurrence. It was started quite deliberately. And this time, I know at least one of the ringleaders.'

'Who?' demanded Tulyet, fixing Bartholomew with an intent stare. His horse skittered nervously

473

as another volley of excited shouts came from the direction of the Market Square.

'Ivo, the noisy scullion from David's Hostel,' said Bartholomew, thinking about what had clicked into place when the stone had been hurled at him as he and Michael had gone to meet Lydgate. 'He was the man whose cart was stuck on the High Street earlier today. A fight broke out when it blocked the road for others. He threw a stone at us as we passed – it hit a wall, but he was probably hoping to start a brawl between scholars and townsfolk there and then. And then I saw him quite clearly leading the mob past St Botolph's, calling to them, and keeping their mood ugly. He was also one of the seven that attacked Michael and me last week, looking for the book and its hidden documents.'

'Are you certain?' asked Michael, cautiously. 'It was very dark and you have not mentioned Ivo before.'

'Something jarred in my mind when I saw him with his cart,' said Bartholomew. 'He was out of his usual context – the only other times I have seen him have been when he was crashing about in the kitchens at David's, and suddenly, he was in the High Street with a cart, purporting to be an apple-seller. As I thought about it, and listened to his voice, I realised exactly where I had seen and heard him before. It struck me as odd.'

'But this means that David's is involved,' said Michael in disgust. 'And I thought we had settled on Valence Marie, Godwinsson and Maud's.'

'Only one of their servants,' said Tulyet. 'But this makes sense. I saw that fight on the High Street tonight, and I had a bad feeling that my men had not broken it up sufficiently for it not to begin afresh.'

'Enough chattering,' said de Wetherset, his agitation making him uncharacteristically rude. 'Brother, take the beadles and clear the students off the streets. Bartholomew, go to Michaelhouse, and warn them that they may be about to be under siege. Master Tulyet,' he added, peering up at the Sheriff, 'could you try to prevent the looting of at least some the hostels near the Market Square? It is too late for Godwinsson, but perhaps we might save others. Heppel – perhaps you had better wait with me in the church.'

Bartholomew grabbed Michael's arm, and gave him a brief smile before they parted to go in different directions. Michael traced a benediction in the air at Bartholomew as he sped up the High Street and, after a moment's consideration, sketched one at himself. He gathered his beadles together, and set off towards the Trumpington Gate, intending to work his way along the High Street and then back along Milne Street. The Chancellor watched them go and then bundled his frightened clerks and Junior Proctor into St Mary's Church, taking care to bar the door.

Figures flitted back and forth at the junction between St Michael's Lane and the High Street, and there was a good deal of noise. Bartholomew edged closer. One man in particular, wearing a dark brown tunic, yelled threats and jeers towards little St Paul's Hostel that stood at the corner. Bartholomew, watching him, saw immediately what he was doing: St Paul's had only five students and was poor. The man was using it to work his crowd up to fever pitch, at which point they would march on nearby Michaelhouse, bigger, richer, and well worth looting.

Bartholomew ducked down one of the streets parallel to St Michael's Lane and then went along Milne Street, running as hard as he could. On reaching the opposite end of St Michael's Lane, he peered round the corner and began to head towards the sturdy gates of his College. At the same time, a great cheer went up from the crowd and Bartholomew saw them begin to march down the lane.

They saw him at the same time as he saw them – a lone scholar in the distinctive gown of a University doctor. A great howl of enraged delight went up and they began to trot towards him. Bartholomew was almost at Michaelhouse's gates when he faltered. Should he try to reach the College, or should he turn and run the other way? If he chose the latter, it would draw the mob away from Michaelhouse and they might not return. There was sufficient distance between him and the crowd so that he knew he could outrun them – and he could not imagine that such a large body of people would bother to chase him too far along the dark, slippery banks of the river. His mind made up, he did an about-face. A second yell froze his blood. The crowd had divided – perhaps so that one group could try to gain access through the orchard, while the others distracted attention by battering at the front gates. He was now trapped in the lane between two converging mobs.

Both began to surge towards him, their inhuman yells leaving him in no doubt that he was about to be ripped limb from limb. He ran the last few steps to Michaelhouse, and hammered desperately on the gates, painfully aware that his shouts for help were drowned by the howls of the rioters. A distant part of his mind recalled that the surly Walter was on night duty that week and Walter was never quick to answer the door. By the time he realised one of Michaelhouse's Fellows was locked outside, Bartholomew would be reduced to a pulp.

The crowd was almost on him and he turned to face them. The man in the brown tunic was in the lead, wielding a spitting torch. In the yellow light, his features were twisted into a mask of savage delight, revelling in his role as rabble-rouser. Around him, other faces glittered, unrecognisable – nothing but cogs in a violent machine. It was not a time for analysis but in the torch-light Bartholomew recognised the man in brown as Saul Potter, the scullion from Godwinsson.

Bartholomew screwed his eyes closed as tightly

as he could, not wanting to see the violent hatred on the faces of the rioters. Some of them were probably his patients and he did not wish to know which ones would so casually turn against him. He cringed, waiting for the first blow to fall and felt the breath knocked out of him as he fell backwards. He struck out blindly, eyes still tightly closed. He felt himself hauled to his feet and given a rough shake.

'You are safe!'

Finally, Master Kenyngham's soothing voice penetrated Bartholomew's numb mind. The physician looked about him, feeling stupid and bewildered, like Lydgate had been in the church just a short time before. He was standing in Michaelhouse's courtyard, while behind him students and Fellows alike struggled to close the gate through which they had hauled him to safety.

'It was lucky you were leaning against the wicket gate,' said Gray, who was holding his arm. 'If you had been standing to one side of it, we would never have got you back.'

'It was me who heard your voice,' said Deynman, his eyes bright with pride. 'I opened the gate quickly before anyone could tell me not to and we pulled you inside.'

'No one would have told you not to open the gate, Robert,' said Master Kenyngham reproachfully. 'But your quick thinking doubtlessly saved Doctor Bartholomew's life.'

Deynman's face shone with pleasure, and

Bartholomew, still fighting to calm his jangling nerves, gave him a wan smile. Despite Kenyngham's assertion, Bartholomew was far from certain the other scholars would have allowed the gates to be opened for him with a mob thundering down the lane from both directions at once, and even if they had, the merest delay would have cost him his life. Deynman's uncharacteristically decisive action had most certainly delivered Bartholomew from a most unpleasant fate. He made a mental note to try to be more patient with Deynman in the future – perhaps even to spend some time coaching him away from the others.

Bartholomew noticed one or two students rubbing bruises, and eyeing him resentfully. It had not been the mob at which he had lashed out so wildly, but his colleagues and students. He grinned at them sheepishly and most smiled back.

The scholars trying to close the wicket gate against the throng on the other side were finding it difficult. The door inched this way and that, groaning on its hinges against the pressure of dozens of sweating bodies on either side.

'The door!' shouted Master Kenyngham, and Deynman and Gray hurried to assist their friends. 'And ring the bell! Other scholars may come to our aid.'

'No!' cried Bartholomew. Kenyngham looked at him in astonishment, while Bartholomew tried to steady his voice. 'Brother Michael is trying to keep the scholars off the streets in the hope that, with no one to fight, the rioters will disperse.'

He glanced around him. There were perhaps thirty students and commoners at Michaelhouse, and seven Fellows including the Master, as well as six servants and Agatha the laundress. Although there were at least twice that number in the horde outside, Bartholomew thought that with the aid of Michaelhouse's sturdy walls and gates, they could hold out against the rioters. Kenyngham, however, appeared bewildered by the situation and his appalled passivity was doing nothing to improve their chances.

'May I make some suggestions, Master Kenyngham?' Bartholomew asked him urgently. The other Fellows clustered around anxiously.

Kenyngham fixed him with a troubled stare. 'No, Matthew. Michaelhouse has always had good relations with the town and I do not want to jeopardise that by meeting its inhabitants with violence. I will climb on to the gate and try to talk reason to these people. They will leave when I point out the folly of their ways.'

Bartholomew regarded him uncertainly, while the more pragmatic Father William let out a snort of derision and jabbed a meaty finger towards the gate behind which the crowd howled in fury.

'Listen to them, man! That is not a group of people prepared to listen to reason. That is a mob intent on blood and looting!'

'They will be more likely to shoot you down

than to listen to you,' agreed Father Aidan, flinching as a stone hurled from the lane landed near him in a puff of dust.

'Perhaps we could toss some coins to them,' suggested Alcote hopefully. 'Then they would scramble for them and forget about looting us.'

William gave him a pained look. 'Foolish Cluniac,' he muttered under his breath, just loud enough for Alcote to hear. 'What an absurd suggestion! Typical of one of your Order!'

'I suspect that would only serve to convince them that we have wealth to spare,' said Bartholomew quickly, seeing a row about to erupt between William and Alcote.

'You are quite right, Matt,' said Aidan. 'But we must decide what we can do to prevent the mob entering the College. What do you have in mind, Master?'

All eyes turned to Kenyngham, who had been listening to the exchange with growing despondency. 'Do none of you agree with me that we can avert such an incident by talking to these people?'

Alcote yelped as a pebble, thrown from the lane, struck him on the shoulder, and Bartholomew raised an arm to protect his head from a rain of small missiles that scattered around him.

'What do you think, man?' demanded William aggressively. 'Talking would be next to useless – if you could even make yourself heard over the row. For once, Master Kenyngham, all your

Fellows are in agreement. We need to defend ourselves – by force if need be – or that rabble will break down our gates and that will be the end of us.'

Kenyngham took a deep breath. 'Very well. Tell me what you have in mind, Matthew. I am a scholar, not a soldier, and I freely admit to feeling unequal to dealing with the situation. But please try to avoid violence, if at all possible.'

Bartholomew quickly glanced around him again. The students had finally managed to close and bar the gate and were standing panting, congratulating each other, ignoring the enraged howls of the mob outside. But they would not be secure for long. Bartholomew began to bark orders.

'Agatha, take all the servants, and find as many water containers as possible. Fill them from the well and be ready to act if they try to set us on fire. Alcote and Aidan, take a dozen students and make sure the College is secure at the rear. Post guards there. If the crowd breaks through into the orchard, do not try to stop them, but retreat into the servants' quarters. Father William, take the Franciscans to the servants' quarters and gather as many throwable items together as you can: stones, sticks, apples – anything will do. We might have to defend the back if the mob gets into the orchard. The rest of you, collect stones that can be thrown from the wall at the front. Pull down the stable if you need to.'

All, unquestioning, sped off to do his bidding,

while Bartholomew considered the front of Michaelhouse. The gates were sturdy enough, but they would be unable to withstand attack for long if the mob thought to use a battering ram of some kind. He sent Bulbeck and Gray in search of anything that might be used to barricade the door, while he clambered up the side of the gate and on to the wall to look down at the surging mob below.

Michaelhouse had been founded thirty years before by a chancellor of Edward II, who was well aware that his academic institution might come under threat by a resentful local population at some point in the future. Michaelhouse's walls were strong and tall, and there was something akin to a wall-walk around the front.

The mob was eerily quiet; Bartholomew saw Saul Potter in a small clearing in the middle of them giving orders. Despite straining, Bartholomew could not hear what was said, but a great cheer from the crowd as Potter finished speaking made his blood run cold.

'I think we are in for a long night,' he said unsteadily to Kenyngham as he scrambled down. 'They are planning to attack us somehow. We must be ready.'

While Bartholomew and the students hurried to find usable missiles, the mob went ominously silent. Then an ear-splitting roar accompanied a tremendous crash against the gates, which shuddered and groaned under the impact.

Horrified, Bartholomew climbed back up the gate to the top of the wall, where a dozen or so scholars crouched there, each one armed with handfuls of small stones gathered from the yard. Deynman was enthusiastically applying himself to demolishing the derelict stable, and some very large rocks were being ferried to augment the waiting scholars' arsenals. Below, the rioters had acquired a long, heavy pole, and willing hands grabbed at it as it was hauled backwards in readiness for a second strike.

'Aim for the men holding the battering ram,' Bartholomew called to the students, looking down at the seething mass of the mob beneath, searching for Saul Potter. The battering ram had a carved end; he realised with a shock that someone had taken the centre-post from one of the river people's homes. He hoped it had not been Dunstan and Aethelbald's house that had been destroyed in the mindless urge for blood and looting.

The gates juddered a second time as the post was smashed into them, accompanied by another mighty yell from the crowd. Bartholomew saw the head of the post shatter under the impact. One man fell away with a cry as one of the splinters was driven into his side. But the crowd was oblivious to his distress and the great post was hauled back for a third punch.

Bartholomew watched as the scholars pelted the rioters with their stones. At first, their defence seemed to make little difference, but gradually individuals in the crowd began to look up as the shower of pebbles continued to hail down on them. When a hefty rock landed on one man, the crowd wavered uncertainly. Immediately, Saul Potter was among them again.

'Our lads have breached the rear!' he yelled. An uncertain cheer went up. 'Come on, lads!' Saul Potter continued. 'Think of what will soon be yours! Silver plate, jewellery, clothes and all the University's ill-gotten gains. You will not let these snivelling scholars defeat the honest men of Cambridge, will you?'

This time the clamour was stronger. Encouraged, Saul Potter went on. 'These wretched, black-robed scholars do nothing for this town but take our women and make us paupers. Will you let the likes of them get the better of us honest folk?'

There was no mistaking the enthusiasm this time, and rioters began to peel off from the group to head for the back gate. Ordering Gray to keep up the barrage of fire from the front, Bartholomew slithered down from the wall to race to the back of the College, gathering any idle hands as he ran.

Sure enough, the mob had broken through into the orchard and were besieging the servants' quarters. Father William and his Franciscans were doing an admirable job in repelling them with a variety of missiles hurled from the upper floor, but the windows were small and allowed the defending scholars little room for manoeuvre. The crowd's reinforcements were beginning to arrive. On the lower floor, the doors were thick, but nothing like the great gates at the front. They were already beginning to give way under the rioters' kicks, despite Bulbeck's desperate attempts to block them with chests and trestle tables.

'This brings back memories,' came a quiet, lilting voice from Bartholomew's elbow.

'Cynric!' Bartholomew's delight at seeing his book-bearer up again was tempered by the sight of his drawn face under the bandage that swathed his head. 'You should not be here.' He saw Cynric held a small bow and several arrows.

'Just let me fire a few of these, boy, and I promise you I will be away to lie down like the old man I am,' said Cynric.

Bartholomew knew from the determined glitter in the Welshman's eyes that he would be unable to stop him anyway. He moved aside.

'Saul Potter,' he said. 'He is wearing a brown tunic.'

'Oh, I know Saul Potter, lad,' said Cynric, approaching the window and selecting an arrow. 'Agatha told me he was boasting in the King's Head about how he had kicked you witless last week. I was going to pay him a visit anyway. Perhaps I can settle matters with him now.'

Cynric's arm muscles bulged as he eased back the taut bowstring. He closed one eye and

486

searched out his quarry with the other. The Franciscans had ceased their stone-throwing and were watching Cynric intently. Father William moved towards another window and began chanting a prayer in his stentorian tones. The effect on the crowd was immediate. They became still, their voices gradually faltering into silence and all faces turned to the window from where Father William's voice emanated. There was not a man in the crowd who did not recognise the words William spoke: the words spoken by priests when someone was going to die.

Saul Potter began to shout back, but his voice was no match for William's, which had been honed and strengthened by long years of describing from the pulpit the fires and brimstone of hell and the dangers of heresy.

The sound of Cynric's arrow singing through the air silenced William. It also silenced Saul Potter, who died without a sound, the arrow embedded in his chest. Cynric slumped back against the window frame with a tired but triumphant grin. Bartholomew helped him to sit down.

'I have lost none of my skill by living with these learned types,' Cynric muttered proudly. He tried to dismiss the admiring praise of the students who clustered around him, but the physician could see he was relishing every moment. Bartholomew stood to look out of the window again. Deprived of their leader, the crowd was milling around in confusion. Bartholomew made a sign to William, whose teeth flashed in one of his rare smiles. The friar took a deep breath and began chanting a second time.

The meaning was clear. As one, the crowd edged back and then began to run, leaving the body of Saul Potter behind. After a few minutes, Bartholomew took a group of scholars and scoured the orchard for lingerers. But there were none: the mob, to its last man, had fled. He left Father Aidan to secure the back gate and walked back through the orchard with William.

'Is it over?' asked William, the strong voice that had boomed over the mob hoarse with tiredness.

'It is at Michaelhouse,' said Bartholomew. 'But I can still see the glow from the fires in the rest of the town. And Michael is still out there with his frightened beadles.'

William slapped a hand on Bartholomew's back. 'Do not fear for Michael,' he said. 'He is clever and resourceful but also sensible. He will not attempt more than he knows he can achieve.'

They walked in silence, watching torches bobbing here and there among the trees, as the students still searched for hidden rioters. The immediate danger over, Bartholomew felt his legs become wobbly, and he rested his hand on the friar's shoulder after stumbling in the wet grass for the second time.

'I recognised the man Cynric killed,' said William, taking a fistful of Bartholomew's tabard to steady him. 'He is a servant from Godwinsson.'

'Yes,' said Bartholomew. His mind began to drift. He tried to imagine what Norbert might look like now, so that he might find him. He caught the end of William's sentence, and turned to face him in shock.

'I am sorry, Father. Could you repeat that?'

William clicked his tongue irritably, never patient with wandering minds. 'I was telling you, Matthew, that the University seems to be inundated with people who are not all they seem. That Godwinsson scullion was clearly no ordinary servant – it takes skill and experience to manipulate a crowd as he did and anyone with such abilities would hardly be satisfied with a position as scullion. And then I told you about my encounter with Father Andrew of David's. I told you I believe he is no Franciscan. I went to a mass of his last week and he did not know one end of his missal from the other. His Latin was disgraceful. I checked up on him with my Father Prior and learned that the only Father Andrew from Stirling in our Order died two months ago.'

Bartholomew recalled that William had been with the Inquisition for a time, an occupation that must have suited his tenacious mind. If William's suspicions had been aroused, he would not rest until they had been sufficiently allayed.

'What are you saying?' asked Bartholomew, exhaustion making his thoughts sluggish.

William sighed in exasperation. 'I will put it

simply, Matthew, since your mind seems to lack its normal incisive skills. Father Andrew, friar and master of theology at David's Hostel, is an impostor.'

CHAPTER 11

Few Michaelhouse scholars felt like sleeping as the last of the mob disappeared up St Michael's Lane. Bartholomew worked hard to buttress the main gates further and ordered the stones and sticks that the scholars had hurled from the walls to be collected to use again if necessary. Once he was satisfied that as many precautions as possible had been taken against further attack, the scholars relaxed, sitting or standing in small groups to talk in low voices.

Saul Potter's body was brought from the orchard and laid out in the conclave, where Kenyngham insisted a vigil should be kept over it.

'At least he did not die unshriven,' said Alcote maliciously. 'Father William yelled an absolution from the window in the servants' quarters before he was killed.'

Kenyngham crossed himself, his eyes fixed on the body and the arrow that still protruded from its chest. 'I asked that there be no violence,' he admonished, tearing his gaze from the corpse to Bartholomew. 'And now a man lies dead.'

'And you, Master Kenyngham, might have been

lying here instead of this lout had Cynric not acted promptly,' said Agatha hotly. 'You owe your life to Cynric, Father William and Matthew.'

'But surely it could have been managed without bloodshed?' insisted Kenyngham. 'Now we have this man's death on our hands.'

'Nonsense, Master,' said William irritably. 'He brought about his own demise by his rabble-rousing. That mob intended serious mischief and Matthew's organisation of our defences and Cynric's marksmanship saved all our lives – to say nothing of the survival of the College.'

Aidan agreed. 'The College would have been in flames by now and all of us slaughtered, had the rioters gained access,' he lisped, his pale blue eyes flicking restlessly between his colleagues' faces.

'But to shoot an unarmed man in our orchard . . .' began Alcote, enjoying the dissension between the Fellows and seeking to prolong it until he could turn it to his own advantage.

'He was not unarmed!' said William loudly. 'He had a sword and a large dagger that should, by rights, be slitting your scrawny throat at this very moment. After all, you are the only one among us to own anything worth stealing. You would have been their first victim.'

'Hear, hear. And good riddance, too,' put in Agatha, eyeing Alcote with dislike.

Alcote swallowed nervously, disconcerted by the frontal attack from a combination of the forceful personalities of William and Agatha. 'But—'

'No buts,' said William firmly. 'And the man was probably a heretic anyway. At least the last thing he heard were the sacred words uttered by me. Perhaps I was his salvation.'

He glared round at the others, daring them to contradict him and then strode away to organise the students to patrol the College grounds until morning. Alcote slunk back to his room and, through the open window shutters, Bartholomew saw him unlock a chest to begin checking that none of his valuables had gone missing during the affray. Aidan knelt next to Saul Potter's body and began the vigil, while Bartholomew prepared to follow Kenyngham through the hall and down the spiral stairs to the yard. Agatha stopped him.

She poked him in the chest with a thick forefinger. 'Do not allow the Master and that loathsome Alcote to bother you, Matthew, for I am telling you what you did was right,' she said grandly. 'You, Father William and Cynric saved the College tonight. Now, I have business to attend – the kitchens do not run themselves, you know.'

She marched away, large hips swaying importantly as scholars scattered in her path. Bartholomew smiled. Agatha was of the firm belief that she was one of God's chosen because she had not been struck by the plague, and had used that belief to add credence to all manner of wild claims ever since. He supposed he should be grateful that Agatha thought his actions defensible – no Michaelhouse scholar enjoyed being in opposition to the formidable laundress, unless he did not mind clothes damaged in the wash and the worst of the food.

Outside in the yard Kenyngham took a deep breath and gazed up at the stars. 'Tonight saw some foul deeds, Matthew,' he said. 'No matter how Father William and Agatha might seek to justify them, a member of Michaelhouse murdered a townsman. How do you think the citizens of Cambridge will react to that? I, and Master Babington before me, have worked hard to establish good relations between Michaelhouse and the town, and now all is lost.'

'All might have been lost anyway had the rioters gained access to the College,' said Bartholomew. 'I agree that the death of a man in such circumstances is a terrible thing, but better Saul Potter than some of our students, or even one of the rioters. They are probably as much victims of Saul Potter's rabble-rousing as we might have been.'

Kenyngham remained unconvinced. 'This will have repercussions for months to come,' he sighed. 'How can I allow you to continue your good work in the town now? You might be slain in retaliation. Any of us might.'

'I do not think so,' said Bartholomew, stretching limbs that ached from tension and tiredness. 'The riot tonight was no random act of violence but a carefully planned event with Saul Potter at its centre. I do not think the townspeople will mourn

– or seek to avenge – him once his role in all this becomes clear.'

Kenyngham eyed him doubtfully. 'I hope you are right, Matthew,' he said. 'Meanwhile, I must now ensure that none of our students slips away to take their revenge for the attack. And you should determine that Cynric has suffered no harm from all this.'

Bartholomew walked briskly to the servants' quarters to where Cynric slept peacefully. The physician smiled when he saw the book-bearer still held his bow; he imagined that Cynric might expect considerable acclaim as a hero by the students who had witnessed his shot, regardless of Kenyngham's misgivings. Bartholomew sat for the rest of the night listening to the Welshman's easy breathing as he slept, thinking over the events of the past two weeks.

Dawn came, and Bartholomew slipped out of Cynric's room to assess the damage to the gates. With Walter, he ran his hands over the splintered wood, impressed at the quality of workmanship that had withstood the assaults of the battering ram. He walked to the wharves and saw that the mob had demolished the first of the rickety structures that served as homes to the river folk in their hunt for a sturdy post. He knew that the old lady that lived there was away, and was relieved that the rioters had limited their violence to the destruction of a house and not turned it towards the people who lived nearby.

Dunstan and Aethelbald were already up and greeted him with enthusiastic descriptions of the events of the night before. Bartholomew was so grateful to see that they had been left unmolested, he did not even notice Dunstan stooping to fill his drinking cup from the river shallows.

He fetched warmed ale and oat mash for Cynric, then began to pace the yard as he waited for Michael to return. When the scholars, led by Kenyngham, went to a mass of thanksgiving for their deliverance the night before, Bartholomew asked to be excused.

After an hour, the scholars began to trickle back from St Michael's Church and made their way to the hall for breakfast. Bartholomew followed, but had no appetite, and looked up expectantly for Michael each time the door opened. Traditionally, meals were taken in silence at Michaelhouse, or eaten while the Bible scholar read tracts from religious and philosophical texts. But Master Kenyngham was lenient and often allowed intellectual debate at mealtimes, although the language was restricted to Latin. That morning, however, Bartholomew heard English, French, and even Flemish but no Latin, and the subject chosen was far from academic. Kenyngham chose to ignore it, although the Franciscans complained bitterly about the breach in discipline.

Bartholomew picked at the watery oatmeal without enthusiasm, and relinquished his portion of sour, cloudy ale to Father Aidan, who was eyeing it with undisguised interest. Bartholomew had a sudden longing for some of Mistress Tyler's fine white bread and wondered where she was and whether her daughters were safe.

The bell rang for lectures to begin, and Bartholomew tried to concentrate on his teaching. Bulbeck offered to read aloud from Isaac Iudaeus's *Liber urinarum* for the rest of the morning, and with a grateful smile, Bartholomew escaped his duties. The master mason came to report on the progress on Wilson's tomb, and Bartholomew listened patiently but without full attention to the mason's litany of complaints about the stone: it was too hard; it contained crystals that made cutting difficult; and black was a wearisome colour with which to work and really should only be carved in high summer when the light was good.

Bartholomew asked whether the marble slab should be abandoned and a cheaper, but more easily workable, material purchased instead. The mason gazed at him indignantly and claimed loftily that no stone had ever bested a craftsman of his calibre. Perplexed, Bartholomew watched him strut across the yard and then tried to apply himself to his treatise on fevers. So far, he had written five words and crossed each one out, unable to concentrate without knowing the whereabouts of his portly friend.

He had just decided to go in search of Michael himself, when the monk stepped through the wicket gate, commenting cheerily on the damage to the door and humming his way across the yard.

'Where have you been?' demanded Bartholomew, looking him over to assess any possible damages. 'Are you harmed? What of the riot? Why are you so late? I have been worried!'

'Aha!' said Michael triumphantly, pulling his arm away. 'Now you know how I feel when you disappear without telling anyone where you are going. Well, like our friend Guy Heppel, I am not a man for foolhardy bravery. I took one look at those mobs last night and took refuge with my beadles in the first University building I came across. If there were scholars insane enough to be abroad last night, then it would have taken more than me and my men to persuade them back to safety. I spent the night at Peterhouse, safe in a fine feather bed with a bottle of excellent wine to help me sleep. The Master was most hospitable and insisted I stay for breakfast.'

He rubbed at his ample girth with a grin. Bartholomew groaned, feeling exhausted. While he had fretted all night, worrying that Michael might be in the thick of violent fighting, the Benedictine had secured himself some of the most comfortable lodgings in Cambridge.

'Do you have news of what happened?' he asked, thinking that a Peterhouse breakfast must be fine indeed if it could last until so late in the morning. He was sure it had not been watery oatmeal and sour beer.

'I saw the Chancellor on my way here. He and Heppel spent the night cowering in St Mary's Church,' Michael said with a chuckle. 'Courage is not a quality with which us University men are richly endowed, it seems. There was damage, but mostly not major. Only two University buildings came under serious attack: Michaelhouse and Godwinsson, and only Godwinsson sustained any real harm. The students fled to Maud's, so there were no casualties. David's Hostel were out and most of those fiery Scots are currently languishing in Tulyet's prison cells – they were rash enough to attempt a skirmish with his soldiers. Master Radbeche was away and Father Andrew was unable to keep them in when the excitement started, although two of them – John of Stirling and Ruthven – are still at large.'

He paused in his narrative to assure Father William, who was passing them on his way to terce, that he had survived the night intact.

'Several smaller hostels were set alight,' he continued when William had gone, 'but the fires were doused before they did any real harm. The rioters gained access to about five of them, but you know how poor most of these places are. The would-be looters looked around thinking to find riches galore and were lucky to leave with a couple of pewter plates. If hostels own anything of value at all, it is likely to be a book and the mob had no use for any of those.'

'Is the rioting over, then?'

'Oh yes. A rumour spread that Michaelhouse had shot one of the leaders and it fizzled out like a wet candle.'

'I have been thinking most of the night about the evidence we have gathered so far,' said Bartholomew, tugging at Michael's sleeve to make him walk towards the orchard. 'It is beginning to make sense but there is still much I do not understand.'

'Well, I have given it no thought at all,' said Michael airily, grabbing a handful of oatcakes from a platter in the kitchen as they walked through it. As Agatha turned and saw him, he gave her a leering wink that made her screech with laughter. On their way out, Michael looked at the neat lines of containers filled with water, sand and stones, and spare trestle tables stacked against one wall to be pushed against the back door if necessary.

'If you have been thinking as hard as you say, let us hope these precautions will no longer be necessary,' he said. He became sombre. 'We must put an end to this business, Matt.'

Bartholomew led the way to the fallen tree in the orchard and, as Michael sat on the trunk eating his oatcakes, Bartholomew paced in front of him telling him what he had reasoned.

'We need to consider two things,' he said, running a hand through his hair. 'First, we need to establish the significance of these blue-green rings. And second, we must discover the identity of Norbert.'

'What do you mean, discover his identity?' asked Michael through a mouthful of crumbs. He brushed some off his habit, where they had been sprayed as he spoke.

'He has assumed another identity,' said Bartholomew impatiently. 'Father William told me he became suspicious of Father Andrew's credentials after he had attended one of his masses. He investigated him as only an ex-member of the Inquisition knows how, and discovered that the only Father Andrew from Stirling in Franciscan records died two months ago. William believes Andrew is an impostor.'

'That gentle old man?' choked Michael. 'Never! Well, perhaps he might not be Father Andrew from Stirling but I find it hard to believe he is your Norbert.'

'There are, however, four things that suggest Andrew is not all he seems,' Bartholomew continued, ignoring Michael's reaction. He scrubbed at his face tiredly and tried to put his thoughts into a logical order. 'First, he said he comes from Stirling. Now, his students, Robert and John, are also from Stirling, claiming to be the sons of a local landlord. I do not want to go into details, but they are nothing of the kind. The towns and villages in Scotland are small and people know each other. I find it hard to believe that Andrew, if he really is from Stirling, would not know that John and Robert's family are not who they claim.'

'Perhaps he does, but is maintaining silence for the sake of these lads,' said Michael. 'It would be in keeping with his character.'

'It is possible, I suppose,' said Bartholomew, disconcerted that the first of his carefully reasoned arguments had been so easily confounded. He tried again. 'Second, when I last visited, Andrew had been writing in his room. His hands and face were covered in ink, like a child who first learns to write. No real scholar would ever make such a mess.'

'And so, because he does not know how to control his quill, you think he is not a scholar. That is weak, Matt,' warned Michael.

Bartholomew pressed on. 'Third, while all the students have alibis for Kenzie's death and Werbergh's, we did not think to ask the masters. Either Radbeche or Andrew are with the students almost every moment of the day, but where are Radbeche and Andrew when they are not acting nursemaid? We did not think to ask that.'

'That was because we had no cause to ask such a thing,' said Michael with a shrug.

'And fourth.' Bartholomew took a deep breath. 'He was the man at Chesterton tower-house who said there would be a riot last night.'

'What?' exclaimed Michael, leaping to his feet. 'You have not fully recovered your wits, my friend! That is one of the most outrageous claims I have ever heard you make! And believe me, you have made a fair few!'

'I told you the voice was familiar, but that there was something about it I could not quite place,' said Bartholomew defensively.

'And why is it that you have suddenly remembered this fact now?' asked Michael, not even trying to disguise the sarcasm in his voice.

'It is not a case of remembering,' said Bartholomew, controlling his own sudden flare of anger at Michael's casual dismissal of his revelation. 'It is a case of recognition. Andrew speaks with a Scottish accent. Well, when I overheard him in Chesterton making his proclamation about the riot, he did not. He spoke in the accent of an Englishman. It was his voice, I am certain, but I did not recognise it immediately because he usually disguises it.'

'Oh really, Matt!' said Michael, sitting back down again and stretching out his large legs in front of him. 'The late Master Wilson would be spinning in his grave to hear such wild leaps of logic!'

'Logic be damned!' said Bartholomew vehemently. 'It fits, Michael! If you put all we know together, it fits!' He sat next to the monk and gave the tree trunk a thump in exasperation. 'We know David's is involved in this business somehow. Ivo, who pre-empted yesterday's riot with his broken cart in the High Street, works at David's. Kenzie was killed, and he was at David's. And the Galen, containing the letters from Norbert to me, was from David's.'

Michael shook his head slowly. 'I accept your point that Andrew is not who he claims, but I cannot accept that he is Norbert. He is too old for a start.'

'Grey hair and whiskers always add years to a man,' said Bartholomew. 'It is probably a disguise to conceal his true age.'

'Maybe, maybe.' Michael picked up another oatcake and crammed it into his mouth so that his next words were muffled. 'But tell me about the rings. What have you reasoned there?'

'I have deduced nothing new,' admitted Bartholomew. 'But we should reconsider what we do know. There are three rings. Dominica took two of them – the lovers' rings – from Cecily, kept one for herself and gave the other to Kenzie. One of his friends is certain that the ring Kenzie had originally was of great value. But the ring that was stolen from him by Edred was the third ring and a cheap imitation of the others. At some point someone, perhaps Kenzie himself, exchanged them. Kenzie's original ring then appeared three days after his death on the relic at Valence Marie. Cecily took the other half of the pair back from Dominica when she was sent to Chesterton, and gave it to me.' He removed the ring from his sleeve and looked at it, glinting blue-green in the morning light.

Michael took it from him and twisted it around in his fingers. 'So, what you conclude from all this,' he said, 'is that the Principal of Godwinsson's ring has ended up on Valence Marie's relic via a student from David's. And that Father Andrew is at the heart of it all, on the basis of William's records and the fact that Andrew is at the same hostel that owns the Galen. Am I correct?'

Bartholomew leaned forward, resting his elbows on his knees, and closed his eyes. Now he had repeated his arguments to Michael, they sounded weak and unconvincing, whereas during the night they had seemed infallible.

'Dominica,' said Bartholomew suddenly, snapping upright. 'Where is she? If she is not dead, then where is she?'

'She was ruled by a rod of iron by two extremely unpleasant people,' said Michael. 'She saw her opportunity to escape and took it.'

'I do not think so,' said Bartholomew. 'She is still here. In fact, I am willing to wager you anything you please that we will find her at David's.'

'In a hostel?' cried Michael in disbelief. 'You are insane, my friend! Adam Radbeche would never stand for such a flouting of the University rules!'

'Well, in that case, you will have no objection to coming with me to see,' said Bartholomew, rising abruptly and striding off through the orchard. Michael followed, grumbling.

'But where is your evidence?' he panted, struggling to keep up with Bartholomew's healthy pace. 'Where is your proof?'

Bartholomew grinned mischievously. 'I suppose

I have none at all, just a feeling, a hunch if you will.'

Michael made as if to demur, but could see the determination in his friend's face and knew there was little he could do to dissuade Bartholomew from visiting David's. All he could hope to do was to minimise any damage Bartholomew might cause by wild accusations.

The signs of the previous night's rioting were obvious as they hurried along the High Street to Shoemaker Lane, but the damage was mostly superficial and already much had been cleared away. None of the townspeople's houses or shops had been attacked. The rioters had concentrated on University property. Bartholomew was puzzled. If he were to attack the University he would not choose Michaelhouse, one of the largest and strongest of the University's properties, or some small and impoverished institution like St Paul's Hostel. He would pick those places that were known to be wealthy and not particularly well fortified – like Maud's. He would also attack St Mary's Church, since it was perhaps the most prominent of the University's buildings, and look for the University chest where all the valuables were kept. But Michael said that St Mary's had not been touched.

He frowned. The only explanation he could find was that the leaders of the riot did not want to inflict serious damage on the University. In which case, what was their motive? Now the curfew on

506

the townspeople would be imposed more harshly than ever, entry into the town would become more rigidly controlled, and legal trading times would be curtailed. Also, the Sheriff would have to hang some of the rioters he caught as a deterrent to others, and there would be taxes to pay for the damage. After the previous night's riot, the towns-people would suffer more than the University.

He tried to clear his thoughts as they approached David's. Its strong door had been torn from its hinges and there were scratches along the wall where something had been forced along it. There was no reply to Michael's knock, so they entered uninvited. Bartholomew called Radbeche's name, but his voice bounced back at him through the empty corridor.

He hammered on the door at the end of the passageway that led to the large chamber where lessons took place, and shouted again. There was no reply, so he opened it, stepped inside and looked around.

The cosy room at David's, with its ancient, patterned window-shutters and warm smell of cooking food, was deserted. Bartholomew walked slowly to look over the other side of the table. Master Radbeche lay there, his throat cut so deeply that Bartholomew thought he could see bone beneath the glistening blood.

'Is Dominica there?' came Michael's voice from behind him.

'No,' said Bartholomew shortly. Michael elbowed

507

him out of the way impatiently, but let out a gasp of shock when he saw Radbeche's body.

'Oh, Lord!' he exclaimed in a whisper. 'What happened to him?'

'It seems as though someone cut his throat,' replied Bartholomew dryly. 'With considerable vigour, by the look of it.'

'My question was rhetorical, Matt,' said the monk testily. 'As well you know.' He gazed down at the redheaded philosopher. 'Poor Radbeche! What could he ever have done to warrant such violence? The University will be a poorer place without his sharp intelligence.'

He shuddered as Bartholomew began to examine Radbeche's body. The Principal of David's had been dead for several hours – perhaps even before the riot had started, when Bartholomew had been talking with Lydgate and Michael in the church. Bartholomew sat back on his heels and looked around the room. He saw that the small door that led to the kitchen and storerooms was ajar, and picked his way across the floor towards it. The doorknob was sticky and Bartholomew's hand came away stained red with blood. He gritted his teeth against his rising revulsion, took a hold of it again, turning it slowly and pushing open the door. In the kitchen, pans had been knocked from their hooks on the wall and someone had kicked charred logs from the fire across the room. Bartholomew walked to the small storeroom beyond, shoving aside a strip of hanging leather that served as a door.

Alistair Ruthven sat on the floor cradling John of Stirling in his arms. At first, Bartholomew thought they were both dead, since their faces were so white and their clothes so bloodstained. But, slowly, Ruthven turned a stricken face towards Bartholomew and tried to stand.

Bartholomew lifted John off Ruthven and set him gently on the floor.

'Are you injured?' asked Bartholomew, looking to where Ruthven hovered nervously.

Ruthven shook his head. 'I was not here when this happened. John is dead,' he added, looking at his friend on the floor. He suddenly looked about him wildly. 'Who could have done this?' he wailed. 'Master Radbeche and John are dead and I only escaped because I pretended to be dead, too.' His eyes glazed, he stumbled into the hall.

'Stop him!' said Bartholomew urgently to Michael. With a blood-curdling howl, Ruthven dropped to his knees and brought clenched fists up to his head. 'He will become hysterical,' said Bartholomew warningly. 'Take him outside, quickly. And send word for the Austin Canons to come for John.'

With Michael's large arms wrapped around him, Ruthven staggered along the corridor to the street. Bartholomew bent back to John who, despite Ruthven's claim, was certainly not dead. He suspected that a good deal of the blood had probably come from Radbeche, for when he pulled away the lad's shirt to inspect the wound, it was superficial.

John's eyes flickered open as Bartholomew slid a rug under his head, rummaged in his bag for clean linen and set about binding the gash.

'Am I going to die?' he whispered. 'Or am I dead already?'

'Neither,' said Bartholomew, smiling reassuringly. 'This is little more than a scratch. You will be perfectly all right in a day or two.'

'But all that blood!' He swallowed hard and looked at the physician with a desperate expression.

'Lie still,' said Bartholomew gently. 'I think you must have fainted.'

John smiled wanly, his eyes fixed on Bartholomew's face. 'The sight of blood makes me dizzy. It was bad enough seeing Master Radbeche's, but someone came at me in the dark, and then I saw some of my own.'

'So, what happened?' asked Bartholomew, cradling the student's head so that he could sip some water. 'Did you see who attacked you?'

John shook his head, his face suddenly fearful. 'But I think it was Father Andrew. I think he killed Master Radbeche!'

'Start at the beginning,' said Bartholomew, not wanting his jumble of facts to become more confused by John's wild speculations. 'Tell me exactly what happened.'

'I went out at sunset with Father Andrew to buy bread, although Master Radbeche had gone away for the night, and I was surprised that Father

Andrew would leave the others unsupervised. Anyway, Father Andrew met Father William from Michaelhouse, and they started to argue, so he told me to buy the bread on my own.'

If Radbeche was supposed to be away, thought Bartholomew, what was he doing lying dead in the kitchen?

John sipped some more water before resuming. 'It was the first time I had been allowed out alone for so long and so I determined to make the most of it. I met some friends and it was dark by the time I returned. There was a crowd of people outside the hostel, throwing stones and insults up at the windows and two people were stealing the door. I knew the others must have gone out, because they would never have allowed the hostel to come under attack like that without retaliating had they been in. I hid in the shadows of the runnel opposite, and watched.'

He paused again. 'After a while, Father Andrew approached. He addressed the people confidently as though he had done so many times before. The leader of the mob just led them away, like children. I was about to run into the hostel after Father Andrew, when I thought about what he had done: he had given the rioters orders and they had obeyed without question. His voice was different. I am not sure . . .'

'He no longer sounded Scottish?' asked Bartholomew.

'Yes!' exclaimed John. 'That was what was

different! His voice was his own, but he sounded like a someone from here. I always thought his accent was not from Stirling.'

'Then what?' asked Bartholomew gently, helping the student to sit up.

John took a shuddering breath. 'After talking to the mob, Father Andrew went inside David's, but left again moments later. I came in and found . . . Master Radbeche . . . dead with . . . As I stood looking at him I felt a pain in my chest and I looked down and saw . . .' He shuddered and Bartholomew was afraid he might faint again. He eased the student back against the wall and gave him more water.

After a few moments, John began to speak again. 'I fainted and when I came round Alistair Ruthven was with me. He had been with me all night – he could not get out because of the rioters, although I tried to persuade him to leave in case Father Andrew came back. He had escaped by hiding upstairs.'

'But you did not see Father Andrew kill Radbeche,' said Bartholomew, 'or who attacked you.'

'No, but Father Andrew went into the hostel and then came out again. It must have been him!'

Bartholomew shook his head. 'That cannot be possible. You said Father Andrew came from elsewhere when he addressed the mob, and you had noticed that the hostel seemed abandoned.

Radbeche must already have been dead when Father Andrew entered.'

'Then why did he not cry for help when he found Master Radbeche dead?' asked John, regarding Bartholomew with his dark, solemn eyes.

'I did not say that he is not involved, only that he probably did not kill Radbeche while you watched from outside,' said Bartholomew. He sat back and thought.

Andrew had met Father William at sunset. William could well have confronted him about the fact that he knew Andrew was not whom he claimed to be, and so Andrew must have realised that he had to complete whatever business he was involved in quickly. Meanwhile, the Scottish students had probably escaped the hostel as soon as Andrew had left them unchaperoned, taking quick advantage of their sudden chance of freedom, and Radbeche had arrived back to find the hostel deserted. So, either Andrew had killed Radbeche, left and come back again to be seen by John, or another person had done the slaying.

'Perhaps it was Norbert.' Bartholomew spoke aloud without intending to.

'Norbert?' said John, looking at him in confusion. 'You think Norbert might have killed him?'

'Do you know Norbert?' asked Bartholomew in astonishment.

'Well, yes,' said John. 'Not well, of course, him being a servant and newly arrived. But I know him. I cannot say I like him, though – he is surly and rude. And he smells.'

'What does he look like?' asked Bartholomew, wondering whether he would be able to recognise Norbert from a description twenty-five years after their last meeting.

'He is always dirty,' said John, 'and he wears a piece of cloth swathed around his head. We always say he looks like a Saracen, especially because his face is nearly always black with dirt. He usually wears lots of clothes, even in the heat, bundled round him in the way that beggars do in winter. Father Andrew brought him here about a week ago to work in the kitchens. He told us he was a mute and that we should leave him be.'

'How old?' said Bartholomew, feeling excitement rising.

'Perhaps sixteen or seventeen,' came the disappointing answer. 'It was hard to tell with all that dirt. Master Radbeche said if he were to stay, he had to wash, but Father Andrew begged for him to be left alone.'

'I bet he did,' said Bartholomew, a sudden flash of inspiration coming to him. 'Tell me, John, did you ever see James Kenzie's lover, Dominica?'

'No,' said John, his face clouding. 'But he talked about her: fair hair, blue-green eyes.'

'And what were Norbert's eyes like?' asked Bartholomew.

John looked at him with a slack mouth. 'Bluegreen,' he said. 'Startling – the only nice thing about him. But surely you cannot believe . . .' He was silent for a moment, plucking at the edges of his bandage. 'There is probably something you should know.'

'What?' asked Bartholomew warily, sensing he was about to be told something of which he would not approve.

John shot him a guilty glance. 'I did not consider it important before, and anyway, Father Andrew ordered me not to tell.'

'Tell what?' said Bartholomew, spirits sinking.

'A couple of weeks ago, Father Andrew told me that if I were to borrow Jamie's ring, which he said was one of a pair of lovers' rings, he would pray over it that the relationship between Jamie and Dominica would finish. I liked Jamie, and agreed with Father Andrew that he would be better not seeing Dominica any more.'

'And he said that praying over the ring would cause this relationship to end?' asked Bartholomew, surprised. 'How peculiar! It is almost as bad as consulting the stars!'

John looked at him oddly before continuing. 'I borrowed Jamie's ring when he took it off to clean out some drains. Father Andrew kept it for several days and poor Jamie nearly went mad searching for it. When he eventually returned it, I lied and told Jamie I had found it between the floorboards because Father Andrew had made me promise not to tell him what we had done. He said it was for Jamie's own good that he should not know.'

Bartholomew groaned. 'I wish you had told us this a week ago, John,' he said. 'It would have helped us more than you can possibly imagine.'

John's face crumpled with remorse. 'I am sorry! I did not see how it could be important, and I had promised Father Andrew that I would not tell. It is only now, when Father Andrew seems to have been pretending to be something he is not, that I feel free to break my promise.'

'When I last visited David's, Father Andrew said that he did not know Jamie had a lover, and that he certainly did not know it was Dominica.'

'Then he was not telling you the truth. He knew all about Dominica, although I do not know who told him – it was not me.'

'Why did you not tell me that Father Andrew was lying at the time?'

'I did not hear him make any such claim to you. I was cleaning the yard on Monday and only heard the last part of your conversation, while the first time you came, I was with my sick brother upstairs. Believe me, I would have exposed him as a liar had I heard him say he knew nothing about Jamie's romance!'

'Did you tell anyone else about this peculiar plan to pray over the ring?'

'No. Father Andrew ordered me not to. I did not even tell Robert, my brother. He would not have approved of my stealing from Jamie anyway, even if it was for his own good.'

As Bartholomew helped him to sit, the colour

drained from his face as he glimpsed the blood on the front of his shirt. Bartholomew had encountered people who were overly sensitive before, but none of them had been as feeble as poor John of Stirling. No wonder the lad had been insensible half the night! He made the Scot lie down again, his mind whirling with questions and fragmented pieces of information. What confused Bartholomew most was the relationship between Norbert and the disguised Dominica. It was too much of a coincidence that Bartholomew should have found copies of letters written years before, and Dominica just happened to be in the hostel where they had been concealed using the alias of Norbert. He racked his brain for answers, but every solution he could produce seemed flawed in some way.

He thought about Radbeche, who was supposed to have been away, but had returned only to die. Was he involved in the riot somehow? And perhaps most importantly of all, where was Father Andrew now that his hostel was abandoned and his Principal murdered?

It was not long before the Austin Canons from St John's Hospital came to help John away. Michael was waiting for Bartholomew outside and told him that Ruthven had been dispatched to inform the Chancellor that Radbeche had been murdered. Bartholomew was concerned.

'Was it wise to let the lad go on his own? He was deeply shocked by what had happened.'

'I released him into the care of one of Tulyet's sergeants,' said Michael. 'The one whose son you cured of an arrow wound last year. He will look after him, and I thought it best to get him as far away from David's as possible.'

'So, what did he tell you?' asked Bartholomew, still doubtful as to the wisdom of Michael's decision.

'Nothing much,' said Michael. 'As soon as Father Andrew took John off to buy bread, thus leaving the students without a nursemaid for the first time in days, they took advantage of it. All were out of the hostel before Father Andrew had scarce turned the corner, although Ruthven remained behind to study.'

'Ruthven and Davy Grahame are the two who seem most interested in learning,' said Bartholomew. 'The others would rather be away cattle-rustling.'

'You have been reading too much of the rantings of this English astrologer who casts national horoscopes,' said Michael admonishingly. 'Such a bigoted comment is unworthy of you. As I was saying, Father Andrew was barely out of Shoemaker Row when the David's lads were away, looking to enjoy themselves for a night on the town. Shortly afterwards, the riot broke out. Ruthven heard a mob gathering and objects were hurled at the windows. Terrified, he fled upstairs and hid under the pile of mattresses. He is not sure how long he remained there, but he only emerged when all was quiet. He found Radbeche dead and John mortally wounded. He sat with John until he died, and was too frightened to move until we arrived.'

'We should tell him John is not dead,' said Bartholomew. 'He just fainted at the sight of his own blood. Many people are affected in that way, although John's aversion is unusually powerful.'

'Did John tell you anything we did not already know?'

Bartholomew summarised what John had said as they waited for Guy Heppel to arrive and take charge of Radbeche's body. Heppel was, as usual, white-faced and wheezing.

'This is a dreadful business,' he gasped. 'Murders and mayhem. No wonder God sent the plague to punish us if the rest of England is like Cambridge!'

'Are you ill?' asked Bartholomew, concerned by the man's pallor.

'I feel quite dreadful,' replied Heppel, raising a hand to his head. 'I must have that consultation with you as soon as possible. I should not have gone to that Founder's Feast of yours without it, because I have not been myself ever since.'

'Did you eat any fish giblets at Michaelhouse?' asked Bartholomew suspiciously.

Heppel gripped his stomach and flashed him a guilty glance. 'I have always been rather partial to fish livers and you did not tell me why I should avoid them, specifically. You said Saturn was ascendant and that I should take more of the medicine you gave me, but that had nothing to do with fish livers.'

'I told you to avoid them because I knew they were bad.'

'Not because of Saturn?' asked Heppel. 'And not because Jupiter will be dominant later in the week?'

'Jupiter will not be dominant this week,' said Bartholomew, thinking to comfort him. 'Mars will.'

'Mars!' breathed Heppel, sagging against a wall weakly. 'Worse still! Once I see this corpse to the church, I shall return to my room and lie down before I take a serious sickness.'

'See?' demanded Bartholomew of Michael as they set off back towards the High Street, leaving Heppel and two beadles to take Radbeche's corpse to nearby Holy Trinity Church. 'Astrology is nothing but hocus pocus! Heppel imagined himself to be far worse when he thought Mars was dominant. And the truth of the matter is that Mars will be nothing of the sort. I made it up thinking it would make him feel better.'

'You should know better than to mess with Heppel's stars,' said Michael. 'And you don't lie! What has got into you? Have you been taking lessons from Gray?'

'Heppel is an odd fellow,' said Bartholomew, glancing back to where the Junior Proctor had his mouth covered with his pomander as he supervised the removal of Radheche's body. 'Sometimes I wonder whether he is all he seems.'

'Who is in this town? We have old men pretending to be friars, rabble-rousers pretending to be scullions, and Principal's daughters pretending to be boys – not to mention the extremes to which prostitutes will go to slip into colleges.' He cast a sidelong glance at Bartholomew. 'The only people I am sure about are you and me. And even you have been revealing a different aspect of your character over these last few days with your indecent obsessions with all these harlots. You have become like a Mohammedan with his harem.'

Bartholomew sighed heavily. 'I have decided to have done with all that. One, or possibly two, members of my harem, as you put it, tried to kill me, while the other can only talk to me without causing a scandal if she dresses as an old lady.'

'Yes, you have shown an appalling lack of judgement in your choices,' said Michael bluntly. 'But you should not despair. Perhaps I can arrange one or two ladies . . .'

'Here comes Heppel again,' said Bartholomew. 'Now what? I wonder what caused him to leave Radbeche.'

'He has probably found out you have lied to him about Mars, and is coming to accuse you of heresy.'

Heppel's pale face was glistening under its habitual sheen of sweat. 'Master Lydgate is dying,' he gasped. 'A soldier has just informed me that he is at Godwinsson and recommends that you go there immediately before it is too late.'

'Oh, Lord, Matt!' groaned Michael, turning away from the Junior Proctor to hurry towards Godwinsson. 'It is all beginning to come together. Someone's master plan has been set in motion, and it is playing itself out.'

'But we still do not know what this master plan is,' Bartholomew pointed out, keeping pace with the monk. 'And, as has been true all along with this wretched affair, the more information we gather, the less clear matters become. How did Lydgate allow himself to be drawn into it after our discussion last night? It was obvious there was some kind of danger.'

Michael raised his eyebrows. 'As we know, Master Lydgate is not overly endowed with powers of reasoning. Come on. We should not dally if the man is dying.'

Bartholomew glanced behind him to where Heppel was almost bent double, trying to catch his breath, fanning himself with his hand. All Bartholomew's doubts about him bubbled to the forefront of his mind yet again.

'That man is far too unhealthy for proctorial duties,' he commented. 'I still cannot imagine what possessed the Chancellor to make such a choice.'

'Since you ask. Matt, I made inquiries about Guy Heppel while I was at Peterhouse last night.

He is one of the King's spies, planted here to see whether anything subversive is underway.'

'Really?' asked Bartholomew, not surprised to learn that Heppel had another role, but astonished that it was one of such importance.

'After everyone else had gone to bed, I seized the opportunity to glance at one or two documents in the Peterhouse muniments chest – the Chancellor often stores some of his sensitive papers there in order to keep them from certain members of his staff.'

'Such as you?' asked Bartholomew.

'Of course not such as me!' said Michael, offended. 'I am one of his most trusted advisers.'

'Then why did he not tell you about Heppel?'

'I imagine he knew I would find out anyway,' said Michael airily. 'Perhaps he thought it might provide me with an intellectual challenge.'

Bartholomew gave him a sidelong glance, wondering whether he would ever understand the peculiarities of the University administration.

Michael continued. 'It was all there in black and white. Heppel is here as an agent of the King and his mission is to detect why the town is so uneasy this year.'

'I would have credited the King with more common sense than to plant a spy who stands out like a diseased limb,' said Bartholomew. 'Heppel wears his cowardice like a banner – hardly a trait to make him a suitable Junior Proctor.'

'It is not your place to question the King,

Matthew,' said Michael firmly. 'Again, I tell you, watch your words or you will be accused of treason as well as heresy. Ah! Here we are.'

Godwinsson's once-fine building had been reduced to little more than a shell. Its strong timbers were blackened and charred and fire had blown the expensive glass out of the windows. It littered the street below, causing considerable risk to those who walked barefoot. One of Tulyet's sergeants waited for them and directed them to the solar.

Inside the hostel the fine tapestries had gone – those not burned had been ripped from the walls by looters. Chests lay overturned, and anything not considered worth taking had been left strewn across the floor. Even the woollen rugs had been stolen so that Bartholomew's footsteps echoed eerily in the room where sound had once been muffled by the richness of its furnishings.

Lydgate was sprawled on the floor. One arm was draped across his stomach and a thin trickle of blood oozed from the corner of his mouth. Bartholomew grabbed a partly burned rug and eased it under the man's head, trying to straighten his limbs to make him more comfortable. Michael began to drone prayers for the dying, his alert eyes darting around the room suggesting that he was more concerned with clues to find Lydgate's killer than with his eternal rest.

Lydgate started to speak, and Michael leaned towards him, expecting a confession. Bartholomew, respecting his privacy, moved away and went to fetch a jug of water with which he might moisten the man's parched lips.

When he returned, Michael was kneeling on the floor. 'Master Lydgate maintains he has been poisoned,' he said.

Bartholomew stared at him. 'How? By whom?'

Michael flapped a hand towards a cup that lay on the floor. Bartholomew picked it up and inspected it carefully. It had held wine, but there was a bitter smell to it and a grittiness in the dregs. He would need to test it, but Bartholomew thought it was probably henbane. The cup was sticky, which meant that there had been enough time since Lydgate had drunk the wine for it to dry, leaving the tacky residue. Therefore, it was not the same powerful poison that had killed Edred, or Lydgate would never have finished his wine without beginning to feel ill.

'I have things I must say,' Lydgate whispered hoarsely. 'Before I die. I must reveal my killer, bitter though that might be, and I must set certain things straight.'

'Can you give him an antidote?' asked Michael, sensing that Lydgate had a good deal to say, and afraid the man might die before he finished.

Bartholomew shook his head. 'There is nothing I can do. It is too late and there is no antidote that I know.'

'Poisons aren't your strong point, are they?' said Michael, somewhat maliciously.

Bartholomew winced, thinking of Edred. 'Do you know who did this to you?' he asked Lydgate, slipping off his tabard to cover the dying man. 'Was it Norbert?'

'I wish it had been,' breathed Lydgate. 'I wish to God it had been. But, for my sins, it was Dominica.'

'Dominica?' exclaimed Michael. 'I thought she was supposed to be the decent member of the family! Now we find out that she is a poisoner?'

Bartholomew thought quickly. Dominica was certainly alive – John's story proved that – and, if she had been driven to living in the hostel of her dead lover disguised as a servant, then she may very well feel bitter towards the father whose domineering nature had forced her there in the first place. But was she bitter enough to kill him?

'Dominica,' said Lydgate softly. He waved away the potion Bartholomew had made for him to ease his discomfort. 'I feel no pain, only a coldness and a tingling in my limbs. I must make my confession now, before this poison takes my voice. Stay, Bartholomew. You might as well listen, too. My only problem is that I do not know where to start.'

'Try the beginning,' said Michael. He sensed he was in for a lengthy session with the dying Principal, and glanced anxiously out of the window at the sky. He had a great deal to do and knew he should not spend too much time listening to the ramblings of the mortally ill – especially since Lydgate had already named his killer.

Bartholomew also had patients waiting who had been injured during the night's upheavals, and he needed to be with people he could help, not those with one foot and four toes already in the grave.

'Shall I start at the very beginning?' asked Lydgate huskily.

'Well, start at the onset of events that led to your . . .' Michael paused, uncertain which word to use.

'Then I must take you back twenty-five years,' said Lydgate. Michael stifled a sigh, reluctant to sit through another tedious dive into local history, but obliged to do so since the man was making his final confession. Oblivious or uncaring, Lydgate continued. 'I was not entirely honest with you last night. You see, I did not burn the tithe barn, Simon d'Ambrey did.'

Bartholomew had thought he was beyond being surprised by Lydgate, but this latest statement truly confounded him. He wondered whether Lydgate was still in command of all his faculties, that perhaps the henbane had affected his mind.

'But half the town witnessed Simon d'Ambrey's death the day before the barn burned,' he protested. 'Myself included.'

'Then half the town, yourself included, was mistaken,' said Lydgate, a waspish edge to his voice. 'I also witnessed what I thought to be d'Ambrey's death, but we were all wrong. It was not Simon d'Ambrey who died that night at the hands of the King's soldiers, but his brother – the

527

cause of d'Ambrey's downfall. D'Ambrey dedicated his life to preventing injustice, but his brother proved to be dishonest and stole the money intended for the poor. D'Ambrey himself was accused of the thefts and the townspeople were quick to believe the accusations. But it was d'Ambrey's brother who died in the King's Ditch.'

'This news will put a different slant on Thorpe's relic business,' said Michael, inappropriately gleeful given he was hearing a death-bed confession. 'He has the thieving hand of d'Ambrey's brother, a petty criminal!'

'D'Ambrey went from being adored by the townspeople, to being despised as a thief within a few hours,' Lydgate continued softly. 'But he was clever. He led the soldiers to his house and told his brother – the root of all his problems – that the soldiers were coming not for him, but for his brother, and that he should run. He lent him his own cloak as a disguise and then sent him off. Everyone knew d'Ambrey's green and gold cloak and the soldiers spotted it in an instant. They chased after his brother like a pack of dogs. You know the rest of the story. He reached the Ditch, an arrow took him in the throat and he drowned. His body was never found.'

He stopped speaking, and Michael began to fidget restlessly, casting anxious glances at the sun and keen to be about his business.

'But what of Simon?' asked Bartholomew. He wondered how much of Lydgate's story could be true. He, with so many others, had seen Simon d'Ambrey on the bank of the King's Ditch, his cloak billowing around him. He recalled vividly the copper hair whipping around his face as he looked back at his pursuers. Bartholomew thought again. The copper hair was what he remembered, along with the green cloak with its crusader's cross on the back. He had not actually seen the man's face, and he had been a fair distance away watching in poor light, even with a child's sharp eyes. If Simon and his brother looked anything alike, it would have been possible to mistake one for the other in the fading daylight.

Lydgate coughed, and Bartholomew helped him sip some water. After a moment, the Principal of Godwinsson nodded that he was able to continue.

'Simon took the opportunity to escape. He was expecting his brother to be recognised, and a search sent out for him, but that did not happen – his ruse had worked more perfectly than he could have dared hope. Rather than set out imme- diately in pursuit of his fleeing household, and run the risk of meeting the three burgesses who were charged with hunting them down, d'Ambrey hid for a night or two in Trumpington.'

He paused, and Michael cleared his throat noisily. 'An interesting conjecture, Master Lydgate, but we must think about your absolu- tion. Time is short. Do you repent of your sins?'

Lydgate looked at him, some of his old belliger- ence returning. 'You will allow a dying man the courtesy of completing his tale in his own time. Brother,' he whispered harshly. He coughed again, then continued, his voice growing weaker, so that Bartholomew and Michael had to strain to hear.

'At the time, I was betrothed to Cecily. It was not my choice, and hers neither. But the contract was sealed and we were bound by it. The day after d'Ambrey's supposed death, I saw Cecily enter the tithe barn and leave some time later. I went into the barn myself, hoping she might have a lover there. If that were the case, I might yet escape the marriage contract that I did not want. D'Ambrey was there, leaning back in the straw like a contented cat. It was quite clear what they had been doing and, even though it was in my interests to be glad he was Cecily's lover, I was moved to anger by his gloating. He told me how he had escaped, and I knew he would not allow me to leave the barn alive. We fought, but a lamp was knocked over and the barn began to burn. Then he hit his head against a post and I could not rouse him. I panicked and fled.'

Raised voices from outside distracted him momentarily, but they died away, and the house was silent once more. Lydgate continued with his tale, sweat beading on his face. Bartholomew wiped it away.

'I told my father everything. He said the marriage contract would stand anyway, and that I should conceal Cecily's indiscretions unless I wanted to be branded a cuckold. He suggested

530

we accuse Norbert of starting the fire, since using him as a scapegoat, rather than someone else, would precipitate no feuds or ill-feelings among the villagers.'

'Most noble,' retorted Bartholomew, unable to stop himself. 'So Norbert was blamed so that you would not be seen to have an unfaithful wife, and Cecily would not be labelled a whore?' He stood abruptly and paced. 'He was a child, Lydgate! They were going to hang him!'

Lydgate shrugged painfully. 'You saved him.'

'What a dire tale,' said Michael unsympathetically. 'No wonder Norbert has returned to wreak havoc on the town.'

'But no body was found in the barn,' said Bartholomew, trying to rationalise Lydgate's story. The whole event, now he knew the truth of it, had an unsavoury feel, and he did not like the notion that he had protected the identity of a murderer for the last twenty-five years.

'The fire caused such an inferno that metal nails and bolts melted in the heat,' breathed Lydgate, swallowing hard. 'A body would never have been identified from that mess.'

'So, you were responsible for the death of Simon d'Ambrey?' asked Michael. 'Is that the essence of this lengthy tale? I take it you confessed to burning the tithe barn yesterday because you knew that was the crime of which Matt believed you were guilty?'

Lydgate nodded, and then shook his head.

'I became confused. The blackmail notes mentioned the burning of the tithe barn, and hinted at the murder of d' Ambrey while he was trapped in it. I was going to confess to both of them to you last night. Then I realised that you did not know about the murder, only about the fire. I did not see why I should have to confess to that sort of thing when I did not have to, so I just allowed myself to be guided by you, and told you only about the fire.'

'What a mess!' said Michael. 'These notes must have been very carefully worded if you were not certain whether they threatened to expose you for murder or arson.'

Out of the corner of his eye, Bartholomew saw something move. It was a shadow in the interconnecting passage between the two Godwinsson houses. Bartholomew, who had been taken unawares by it once before, was not fooled a second time, and darted forward to seize the person who hid there. Cecily gave a cry as she was unceremoniously hauled into the solar. She stared down at her prostrate husband, several blackened pieces of jewellery dangling from her fingers.

Lydgate saw her and gave a ghastly smile. 'My loving wife! It is not my impending death that brings you home, but your treasure.'

'I thought I should see what I could salvage,' she said coldly. 'Fortunately, I hid most of my belongings well.'

So much for her 'meagre inheritance', her 'paltry jewels', thought Bartholomew, eyeing the fistfuls of treasure in some disgust. No wonder she had been so concerned in Chesterton when she heard her room had been ransacked.

'Do you have everything?' asked Lydgate with heavy irony. 'Or shall I help you look?'

'You might tell me where you kept that silver chain,' said Cecily, before she realised he was not sincere. 'Have you seen that little gold crucifix of my father's? I cannot find it.'

'The last time I saw that, it was being fingered by Brother Edred,' said Lydgate maliciously. 'I imagine he stole it after you ran away. He was always covetous of that cross.'

'Why did you not demand it back?' cried Cecily, appalled.

Lydgate shifted weakly in what might have been a shrug. 'These things are no longer important to me, Cecily. I let him keep it, hoping it might throttle him in his sleep.' His words were becoming indistinct, and speaking was clearly an effort now.

'Your husband has only a short time left,' said Bartholomew, thinking it said very little for the sacred institution of marriage that the Lydgates so hated each other that they were prepared to squander his final moments on Earth arguing about jewellery. 'You might wish to be alone with him.'

'I have been alone with him for twenty-five miserable years. Why should I wish for more? I have things to do, and I have no time to wait around here.' She stuffed her jewels down the front of her dress for safekeeping.

'Then a few moments longer cannot make a difference,' said Bartholomew, gesturing for her to kneel next to him.

'Why should I?' she demanded with sudden anger. 'I have just heard him confess that he murdered the man I loved. All these years, and I knew nothing of this! I lived with a killer! I am glad Dominica poisoned him.'

'I thought you believed Dominica was dead,' said Bartholomew. 'You gave me that ring to help me find her killer.'

'I was mistaken. Poor Dominica was forced to feign her death in order to escape from her brute of a father. I discovered she was alive when she came to see me yesterday morning. My husband discovered she was alive when she and I came to see him together last night – when she gave him wine to help him recover from the shock.'

'And this medicinal wine contained henbane?' asked Bartholomew.

Cecily nodded. 'Justice has been done. She has killed the monster who murdered the man I love.'

'You still love Simon d'Ambrey, even though you believed he died all those years ago?' asked Michael, clearly unconvinced. Lydgate made a sound, that had he been strong enough, would probably have been a snort of derision.

Cecily smiled, caught in an untruth. 'Perhaps not, but I grieved deeply for him for several weeks. And I always knew this pathetic creature was not the father of my Dominica.'

534

'So, Dominica is the daughter of Simon d'Ambrey,' said Bartholomew in sudden realisation. On the floor, Lydgate gave an agonised gurgle. Although he could still hear, the poison had deprived him of coherent speech.

'That cannot be so,' objected Michael. 'Dominica is too young. Kenzie, her lover, was only eighteen or twenty.'

'Dominica was born the same year that Lydgate married Cecily – about six months after d'Ambrey died,' said Bartholomew, his mind working fast. 'Her early birth was the subject of speculation among the villagers for weeks. Dominica is about twenty-four.'

'But she cannot be that old,' said Michael. 'She would have been married off by now.'

'Master Lydgate is wealthy, and so it is unlikely that there will be a shortage of suitors for her hand – regardless of her age,' said Bartholomew. 'John of Stirling said Norbert was sixteen or seventeen. I imagine a young woman covered in dirt to disguise the lack of whiskers, might pass for a lad.'

'How could this oaf ever imagine he was the father of my Dominica?' asked Cecily spitefully. 'Dominica is clever – she fooled us over the matter of her death, and she helped Ivo and Saul Potter plan this riot so that we could be avenged on the man who destroyed our lives.'

'Destroyed your lives?' asked Michael. 'But you have just admitted that you grieved for d'Ambrey for a few weeks only and Dominica, with her secret lovers, has scarcely led a hard life.'

'It was a shame about poor Master Radbeche, though,' said Cecily, ignoring him. 'He was a kindly man.'

'What do you mean?' asked Michael suspiciously. 'You did not kill him, surely? What would you have been doing in David's Hostel in the middle of the riot?'

'Not Cecily,' said Bartholomew wearily. 'Dominica. Poor Radbeche must have caught her without her disguise at David's and so she killed him to ensure his silence.'

'That was my husband's fault, too,' said Cecily, her eyes narrowed spitefully. 'If he had not forced Dominica to take refuge at David's in order to escape from him, then Dominica would not have been forced to kill Radbeche to make certain he did not tell anyone who she really was.'

'I see,' said Michael. 'John told us that poor Radbeche was supposed to have taken a trip last night, but I suppose he heard rumours that there might be rioting and he, like a responsible Principal, returned to take care of his hostel. Of course, by this time, Father Andrew had gone for bread, the students had sneaked out and the hostel was bare – except, unfortunately for Radbeche, for Dominica.'

'And then,' said Bartholomew, easing Lydgate's head to one side as his breathing became more laboured. 'Dominica attacked John of Stirling because he almost caught her in the act of killing Radbeche.'

He saw that Lydgate's last reservoirs of strength were failing fast. Two tears slid from under the dying man's eyelids, and coursed down his cheeks. Michael pressed his hands together and began the words of the final absolution. Outside in the street, there were howls of merriment and smashing sounds, as children realised that throwing the shards of glass against the wall could be fun. The sergeant's voice cut over their laughter, but his tone was friendly, and he obviously thought they were doing no harm. While Michael prayed and Bartholomew bent to tend Lydgate, Cecily slipped away down the stairs and was gone. Michael looked up briefly, but let her go. Bartholomew was grateful, revolted by the malice and bitterness that seemed to taint all members of the Lydgate household.

When Michael had finished his prayers and Lydgate lay dead, Bartholomew followed the monk down the stairs. Instead of turning right to return to the street, they turned left to the kitchens in an unspoken agreement to take some time to think. All was deserted. Bartholomew opened a shutter and surveyed the yard. Against the wall lay a pile of wood – the remains of the shed that had been made to look as though Werbergh had died under it. And it had been Huw and Saul Potter – proven rioters and attackers of Bartholomew in the High

Street – who had insisted that they had seen him enter it.

'Why did you let Cecily go?' asked Bartholomew. 'She might have been able to tell us where Dominica is.'

'I do not think so,' said Michael. 'It seems to me that while Dominica is central to this grand plan, Cecily is wholly unimportant. I think she knows nothing that she has not already told us, and I am not inclined to want to speak any further to someone who is so twisted with bitterness and hatred; such people see the truth through warped eyes. Anyway, Matt, the woman is not quick-witted like your Tyler daughters – she will probably head straight back for her bottle-dungeon at Chesterton, imagining that we will not guess where she is hiding.'

He looked around for a place to sit, but every stool and bench that could be carried away had gone. All that remained was a large table littered with broken pots and jars. He settled for elbowing Bartholomew to one side and perching on the window-sill. Bartholomew opened another shutter and followed suit, gazing gloomily at the looted kitchen.

'You know, we have allowed Lydgate's suspicions to mislead us, Matt,' said Michael, after a moment. 'It is not Norbert we are seeking, but Simon d'Ambrey himself.'

'And how have you reasoned that out?' asked Bartholomew, startled.

'I think he did not die in the barn, as Lydgate said, and that he escaped. He has bided his time, and he has returned to Cambridge to wreak revenge on the town that was so quick to believe ill of him after all his charity. It is he who is behind the riots; it is he who has brought about the death of Lydgate and the destruction of Godwinsson Hostel; and it is he who put the ring – Cecily's ring – on the hand of the skeleton that the town believes is his! That explains why the attacks against the University resulted in little destruction, except at David's and Godwinsson. The attacks appear to be aimed at the University, but they will ultimately damage the town far more.'

'That cannot be right,' said Bartholomew, wearily. 'We have one too many corpses belonging to the d'Ambreys as it is. We have the man who was shot with an arrow on the King's Ditch, the corpse in the burning barn, and the body brought back with the rest of d'Ambrey's household from Dover that I saw displayed in the Market Square years ago. Three corpses for two d'Ambreys – Simon and his brother.'

'No one ever saw this corpse reputedly burned in the barn,' persisted Michael. 'And regardless of what Lydgate said, I am sure he searched for it in the wreckage. I certainly would have done. And Lydgate's suspicions and unfounded conclusions are not the only ones to have misled us. Yours have, too.'

'Mine?' asked Bartholomew cautiously.

'Yes, yours!' said Michael, pursing his lips. 'Tell me again what you saw the day the tithe barn burned all those years ago.'

Bartholomew sighed. 'I saw Lydgate enter the barn while Norbert and I were swimming nearby. A brief while later, I saw smoke issuing from the barn, and Lydgate came tearing out. We followed him through the trees and saw him watch the barn burn for a few moments before he left to raise the alarm.'

'But that is not what you told me a few days ago,' said Michael. 'You said you saw someone run from the barn, you followed him, and then you saw Lydgate. What if the person you saw running from the barn was not Lydgate at all? Just because you came upon Lydgate moments later does not mean that he was the man you saw running. You have made the same assumption that misled Lydgate, Cecily and Edred over Dominica – you saw what you expected to see and not what was actually there.'

Bartholomew stared at him. 'But Lydgate's clothes were singed and he had been running hard.'

'Of course,' said Michael. 'He had just fled a fire. What would you expect? But Lydgate told us he left almost as soon as the lamp was knocked over and the straw caught fire. You saw a man running away after smoke had started seeping from the building. It would have been a couple of minutes at least before the fire had caught hold

540

sufficiently for smoke to start pouring out. And by then, Lydgate was well away. The man you saw was Simon d'Ambrey.'

'But surely Lydgate would have seen him, too,' said Bartholomew, bewildered by the sudden turn in Michael's deductions.

'Not necessarily, not if he were concentrating on his own escape and was in a state of shock over what he had done. And we know Lydgate has never had good eyesight – he told us that himself in St Andrew's Church.'

'And Father Andrew, of course, is about the same age as Simon d'Ambrey would be,' said Bartholomew, rubbing his temples tiredly. 'There is our killer.'

CHAPTER 12

Michael claimed the stench of burning in the hostel had made him thirsty and, reluctantly, Bartholomew went with him to the secluded garden at the Brazen George. The landlord obligingly told three indignant bakers that they had to leave so that Michael and Bartholomew could talk in private, then brought them a large platter of roast lamb smothered in a greenish, oily gravy. Michael scraped the sauce away with Bartholomew's surgical knife, muttering in disgust when he discovered a piece of cabbage lurking in it.

'People who eat things that grow in the dirt will die young, Matt,' he pronounced firmly. 'And there is always the danger that there might be a worm or a slug served up with them.'

'Time is running short. We need to try to sort out some of this mess before it is too late.'

'Very well,' said Michael, his mouth full. 'We had just deduced that the kindly Father Andrew is none other than the villainous martyr Simon d'Ambrey himself. Sit down and eat something, Matt. You will wear yourself out with all that pacing.'

Bartholomew sat next to him and toyed with his food, trying to make some sense out of the mass of fact and theories. Michael carefully trimmed the fat from a piece of meat and ate it, pushing the lean part to one side.

'All right, then. Let me start. Father Andrew is too old to be your Norbert, but Father William has exposed him as a fraud, and there is clearly something untoward about the man: John of Stirling told us that Father Andrew had some kind of hold over the rioters last night, and there were all your suspicions that he was not all he seemed – the way he splattered ink when he wrote, the fact that you think you heard him while you were sneaking around the Chesterton tower-house, and so on. He is clearly up to no good. Meanwhile, we learn from Lydgate that he once roasted a martyr in the barn but, conveniently, no body is ever recovered. With one of those leaps of logic of which you are so fond, it is clear that Simon d'Ambrey escaped the fire in Trumpington, was never shot at the King's Ditch, and now he has returned to take his revenge on the town that so wronged him.'

He leaned back against the wall, pleased with what he had reasoned. Bartholomew rubbed a hand through his hair as his mind still grappled with the complexities of the evidence they had acquired.

'Who can blame him?' Michael added, gnawing on a bone. 'You all behaved abominably. I told you days ago that I thought the town had abused him.'

Bartholomew watched him. 'If all this is true, then d'Ambrey has succeeded in his revenge. The King, whose spy Heppel is probably here because of the growing unrest, will see the town as a hotbed of insurrection and he will clamp down on it hard. He will raise taxes, send more soldiers and shorten trading hours, so that Cambridge will be unable to compete with other market towns. Gradually, her wealth and influence will decline. Perhaps the University might even flounder, and take away another source of income, resented by the town though it may be. And as Cambridge sinks further into poverty – the poverty that d'Ambrey once fought so hard to reduce – he will have had his vengeance on the town.'

'Now this is beginning to come together,' said Michael with satisfaction, scrubbing the grease from his face with the sleeve of his habit. 'Although I cannot yet see where Norbert fits into all this – unless he and d'Ambrey are in it together.'

'They may be,' said Bartholomew thoughtfully. 'But something else became clear to me when the charming Lydgates were baring their souls. I think I now know what the two acts were that Matilde's client told her about.'

'From something the Lydgates said?' asked Michael, frowning. 'I cannot see what.'

'The riots were instigated to mask two acts,' said Bartholomew slowly. 'We thought at first that these acts might be burglaries, such as the one at the house next to Oswald, or perhaps the destruction of the Market Square. But now I think these were just coincidental. The two acts were matters much closer to d'Ambrey's heart: the first was his daughter Dominica's supposed death, and the second involved Will finding a suitable hand to use as a relic.'

'You reasoned this from something the Lydgates said?' asked Michael, unconvinced.

'Only the first one – Dominica's supposed death,' Bartholomew admitted. 'We need to review what we know and it involves Joanna.' Michael raised his eyes heavenwards. 'No, listen to me, Michael! It will make sense if you listen! A short while ago, Joanna, a prostitute from Ely and Agnes Tyler's niece, came to Cambridge. Mistress Tyler was not happy with her guest, because Joanna started some unofficial business from her home, putting her good name at risk – we had that from Jonas the Poisoner's wife and from the old river men. Obviously, Mistress Tyler would not want Joanna's clients calling at her house with three daughters to protect. Meanwhile, Dominica wanted to escape from the Lydgates, and what better way than to pretend she was dead? And Joanna had long, fair hair, like Dominica.'

'Now, just a moment,' said Michael, sufficiently startled to pause in his repast. 'Are you saying that Mistress Tyler plotted to have Joanna's body mistaken for Dominica's?'

545

'Yes,' said Bartholomew earnestly. 'Either she plotted with Dominica herself, or with d'Ambrey, who might well want his daughter back from the man who almost killed him in the tithe barn fire.'

'Why?' demanded Michael. 'Why should a perfectly law-abiding, honest woman like Mistress Tyler plot with a fallen martyr and his murderous daughter to have her niece killed and her body given the identity of another?'

'I have no idea what her motive might be,' said Bartholomew. 'But we know that the Tyler family are involved in something sufficiently sinister to force Eleanor to try to stop me from asking too many questions – and I am sure that something involves Joanna. Eleanor has virtually ordered me to stop investigating Joanna's death twice – once in the High Street and once at the Feast – and even the apothecary's wife suspects their sudden flight had something to do with Joanna.'

'All right,' said Michael grudgingly. 'We will ignore the motive for now – for your convenience – and concentrate on what we know. Continue.' He picked up Bartholomew's knife and began to prod the bones to see if there was any more meat to be salvaged.

'This plan would allow Dominica to be free of the Lydgates and her life at Godwinsson. She could help d'Ambrey in the last stages of his revenge against the town, along with his other faithful friends – Master Bigod, Saul Potter, Huw, Ivo, and so on, the ones whose names were recorded in the hidden documents in the Galen. And afterwards, she could go wherever d'Ambrey might take her.'

'I see,' said Michael. 'So, the plan was to kill Joanna and leave her for Lydgate to find. You told me that her face was battered, which would make her difficult to recognise. Dominica knew her father's eyesight was failing and he would be easy to fool. He was not a man given to reason anyway, particularly when enraged. He would storm off into the night searching for Dominica, see a blur of golden hair and assume his daughter was dead.' He shook his head. 'Unpleasant though it may seem, I suppose it is a just revenge on a man who had tried to kill d'Ambrey twenty-five years ago, and deprived him of seeing his daughter grow up.'

Bartholomew took up the tale. 'Edred must have been in on the deception – he tried to steal the Galen with Norbert's documents in it, so we can assume he was in their pay. Edred was the one who told Lydgate that he had seen Dominica in the streets of Cambridge. Naturally, Lydgate raced out to bring her back, while Edred and Cecily followed. Dominica knew the places Lydgate was most likely to look, so Joanna was killed at one of them by Godwinsson's Frenchmen, who first raped her.'

'No,' said Michael, stopping him. 'She was killed in Mistress Tyler's house – we saw the bloodstains – and then dumped at a place Lydgate would be likely to look. That was why Mistress Tyler would not allow you to try to oust the looters from her house, and why she – a woman who knows how to look after herself and her property – chose to abandon her house and spend the night with Jonas and his wife.'

Bartholomew nodded. It was beginning to make sense. 'Meanwhile, Cecily took the opportunity to run away from her husband, while Edred, after he had helped her, sneaked back and ransacked her room. Lydgate told us he had stolen a crucifix.'

'So, we have reasoned out Matilde's "first act",' said Michael. 'Ah, here comes the landlord with a pie. Apple! Excellent! Carry on, Matt. What of the second act – this relic business?'

'The answers to that have been staring us in the face all the time. Think about where the first riot started – at Master Burney's tannery. Everyone knows that the Austin Canons own the room underneath, and that they use it as a mortuary, thinking the smell of the tannery will eliminate any dangerous miasmas that might come from the corpses.'

'Mistress Starre's son!' exclaimed Michael in sudden realisation, his pie forgotten. 'That feeble-minded boy who was a giant and whom you put into the Canons' care when he was implicated in all that business with the saffron trade a while ago. We saw his body in the wreckage of Master Burney's tannery!'

Bartholomew recalled the tangle of limbs in the rubble after the tannery had collapsed, and remembered that he had even told Michael that Starre was one of the dead. 'There was too much else to be done with caring for the injured for the Canons to have been concerned with a missing hand, although I am sure d'Ambrey and his accomplices ensured that the body was carefully arranged so that the damage looked accidental.'

Michael shook his head in grudging admiration. 'These people are clever. They selected Starre's hand so that there would be no question that it belonged to a man because he was so big.'

'And, of course, there were signs that the hand had been boiled and there was a pin to hold two of the bones together. The hand had not simply been discovered in the King's Ditch – it had been carefully prepared. On top of all this, there was the ring it wore. John of Stirling took the ring Dominica gave to Kenzie at Father Andrew's – d'Ambrey's – request. D'Ambrey must have had an imitation made, which John then gave back to Kenzie, later to be stolen by Edred, thrown into the shed, and found by me. The real ring d'Ambrey must have given to Will of Valence Marie, with which to adorn the skeleton's hand. Cecily said the pair of lovers' rings were hers – perhaps they were a gift from d'Ambrey if he were her paramour.'

'And d'Ambrey could not simply use the one Cecily still had because it was too small to fit over the big hand they had prepared – she had the woman's ring, and they needed the man's.

Dominica's generosity to James Kenzie brought about his death.'

'But it could not have done, Michael. Kenzie had the false ring, remember? And he clearly was unable to tell the difference and did not know the rings had been exchanged, or he would not have gone to Werbergh and Edred in his desperation to have it back.'

Michael sighed. 'Regardless, we had better apprehend this Simon d'Ambrey before he does any more damage. But what about Werbergh's murder? How does that fit into this foul web of retaliation?'

'We will have to work that out as we go,' said Bartholomew, reaching out a hand and hauling Michael to his feet. 'We have wasted enough time already. If we are correct in our deductions, then d'Ambrey's work is almost done here and he will soon be gone.'

'Where are we going?'

'To Valence Marie. That is where this relic purporting to be d'Ambrey's hand is, and that, I am certain, is where d'Ambrey will go sooner or later.'

They left a message with the sergeant to tell Tulyet of their suspicions – neither Bartholomew nor Michael felt there was much point in entrusting the information to the feeble Guy Heppel. Tulyet, Bartholomew knew, would not stop to question their message; he would hasten to Valence Marie and leave explanations until later.

The sun was high as they hurried along the High Street, but it was already beginning to cloud over with the promise of rain. As Michael raised his hand to knock on the great gate, Bartholomew pushed it away. The memory of Radbeche's murder at David's was clear in his mind. He and Michael had been incautious to walk so blithely into David's – Radbeche's killer could easily have been lurking still at the scene of his crime. He wished Cynric were with them, since he would know exactly how to proceed.

Bartholomew pushed open the door and peered round it. There was no porter at the lodge. He drew a surgical knife from his bag, while Michael found a sturdy piece of wood he could use as a cudgel. Bartholomew pushed the door open a little further, and stepped inside. Like the last time they had visited Valence Marie, it was eerily quiet. Bartholomew took a deep breath and began to make his way around the edge of the yard, Michael following.

The hall door was ajar. Standing well back, Bartholomew pushed it open with the tip of his knife and looked inside. It was deserted. Puzzled, he lowered the knife and walked in. It looked as though it had been the scene of a violent struggle. Cups and plates lay scattered on the floor and two of the long tables that ran down the sides of the hall had been overturned. Several tapestries hung askew, wine had pooled on the polished floor. Michael pushed past him, whistling at the mess.

Without warning, something heavy fell on Bartholomew from above. With a cry, he dropped to his hands and knees, the knife sent skittering across the stone floor. The minstrels' gallery! Valence Marie had a small gallery for musicians that was just above the main door; it was from here that someone had dropped down on to him.

Michael spun round with his cudgel, but was knocked backwards by a tremendous punch swung by Master Thorpe himself. Valence Marie scholars poured down the stairs where they had been hiding with howls of fury. Bartholomew attempted to regain his feet but someone leapt on to his back, forcing him to the ground. He tried to scramble forwards to reach his knife but one of the Fellows saw what he was doing, and kicked the blade away so hard that it disappeared under a bench on the opposite side of the hall.

Michael lay on his back, his stomach protruding into the air like an enormous fish, while Thorpe stood over him wringing his fist. Bartholomew began to squirm and struggle with all his might. He felt the man clinging to his back begin to lose his grip. Others came to help but Bartholomew had managed to rise to his knees. As one scholar raced towards him, Bartholomew lowered his head and caught him hard in the middle. He heard a groan as the student dropped to the floor clutching his stomach.

But it was an unequal contest and, despite valiant efforts, Bartholomew found himself in the firm grip of several of Valence Marie's strongest students. Realising that further struggling would merely serve to sap his strength, Bartholomew relented. He glanced nervously at Michael, still lying on the floor.

'What do you mean by entering my hall armed with a knife?' asked Thorpe coldly. 'We saw you sneak into our yard like a thief, without knocking or calling out to announce yourself.' He gave a superior smile. 'So the scholars of Valence Marie decided to give you a welcome you did not anticipate.'

As several students jeered triumphantly, Bartholomew wondered how to explain. He tried to see the faces of the men who held him, to see if Father Andrew were there but he could not move. He tried to think of an answer that Thorpe would accept, but the Master of Valence Marie did not give him the chance to reply before firing another question at him.

'What have you done with our relic?'

'Your relic?' repeated Bartholomew stupidly. 'The skeleton's hand? Has it gone?'

Thorpe looked hard at a small upended box that lay on the floor next to a piece of fine white satin and then back at Bartholomew, pursing his lips. 'I have no doubt that you have taken it. The Chancellor has already instructed me to get rid of it, but who am I to deny the people of Cambridge their heritage? I refused. One of the students thought he might have found more sacred bones, but while we were out to investigate his discovery, our hand was stolen. Then, even as we searched for it, you enter my College, without permission and armed.'

Bartholomew could see why Thorpe was suspicious of him. 'But if we had taken your relic, Master Thorpe, we would not still be here. We would go to hide it.'

Thorpe gestured to his scholars and Bartholomew and Michael were thoroughly searched. Bartholomew's bag was torn from his shoulder and emptied unceremoniously on the floor. Phials and bandages rolled everywhere, and the damaged copy of Galen shaken vigorously, as if it might produce a stolen hand. Bartholomew looked around him quickly. One of the men who held him was the burly Henry, who had been present when the hand was found in the Ditch. Standing to one side was another servant, his arm in an untidy splint. Next to him, not taking a part in restraining Bartholomew, but favouring him with a gaze that was far more frightening than the scholars' rough hands, was Will.

As Bartholomew looked into Will's glittering eyes, cold and unblinking, he knew he was in trouble indeed. Seeing Bartholomew was observing him, the diminutive servant moved his tunic slightly to reveal the long, wicked-looking dagger in his belt. The hand that rested on its hilt had a semicircular mark that Bartholomew immediately recognised as a bite. Michael had bitten one of the men who had attacked them on the High Street the previous

554

week, while Bartholomew knew he had broken the arm of another: Will and the servant who stood next to him.

'Well, you might not have our relic with you,' said Thorpe, oblivious to Will's implicit threat, 'but I know that you, or another of the Chancellor's men, have taken it away. We found this precious thing. It came to us in the knowledge that it would be revered and honoured at Valence Marie.'

To say nothing of its use to amass wealth, thought Bartholomew. 'I really have no idea where it is,' he said. 'And I cannot imagine that the Chancellor would arrange to have it taken by stealth. You do Master de Wetherset an injustice, sir.'

Thorpe clenched his fist again, and Bartholomew thought he was going to strike him. But Thorpe's hand had already been bruised by punching Michael, and he was loath to risk harming himself a second time.

'We will see,' he said. He turned to Will. 'Make sure they cannot escape. Lock them in, and we will go to discuss this with the Chancellor.'

He turned on his heel and stalked out. Bartholomew's arms were pulled behind him and tied securely. Will still regarded him with his curious glittering eyes.

'You go with the Master,' he said to the students, nodding at Thorpe's retreating back. 'Henry, Jacob and I will remain here and guard these two.'

Bartholomew struggled to stand. He thought

quickly, knowing that if he were left alone with Will and his cronies, he and Michael would not live to tell how they knew that the hand of Valence Marie did not belong to Simon d'Ambrey.

'Can your Master not manage his affairs without the entire College at his heels?' he shouted, trying to shame some of the retreating scholars into staying behind. 'Do you find it necessary to follow him around like faithful dogs?'

Father Eligius, one of Bartholomew's patients, hesitated. 'This is an important matter, Matthew. If all Valence Marie's Fellows are present and in complete agreement, it will add weight to our case that this sacred relic belongs here.'

'But there is no sacred relic,' said Bartholomew desperately. 'It is the hand of a recently dead corpse planted in the Ditch by Will and his associates. It belonged to Mistress Starre's son.'

Eligius looked startled, while the other Fellows laughed in derision.

'Will has been a faithful servant since the College was founded,' said Eligius reproachfully. 'Such an accusation does you discredit, Matthew.'

'But it is true!' pressed Bartholomew. 'Think about it! Why should a sacred relic have a pin to hold the bones together? Because it was carefully prepared by Will! And why was it wearing a ring recently stolen from the David's student murdered just outside your walls? And why did Will just happen to have a fine casket lined with satin to use as a reliquary for it?'

'This is nonsense,' said a burly, angry-looking man, whom Bartholomew recognised as Master Dittone, as he ushered the students from the hall. 'I am surprised at you, Bartholomew. I always thought you were a man of integrity. Now I learn that you steal, prowl around other colleges with weapons and make vile accusations against lowly servants who are not in a position to answer back.'

'Do not be too harsh on him,' said Eligius kindly. 'Doctor Bartholomew suffered a grievous wound to the head recently, and his stars are poorly aligned.'

Bartholomew's spirits sank. Would there be no end to the repercussions of Gray's impetuous diagnosis?

'The relic is a fake!' he insisted to the last of the retreating scholars. Dittone shot him a vicious look and, for a moment, appeared as though he would like to silence Bartholomew permanently, there and then. He was edged firmly to the door by Eligius, who then paused.

'Take good care of them, Will,' he said. 'Remember the doctor is unwell and needs to be treated with sympathy. It is not his fault that he was driven to steal the relic but the fault of the devils that possess him.'

'Eligius!' cried Bartholomew as the Dominican friar closed the door behind him. 'Stay with us!'

The door shut with a clank and Bartholomew's words echoed around the silent hall. Will exchanged glances with his friends. Bartholomew began to back away down the hall, while Will, ensuring that the door was locked, drew his dagger and followed.

Bartholomew saw Henry draw his own dagger and lean over Michael, who still lay flat on his back. The students had not tied the monk's hands, but he was insensible. Bartholomew looked around him desperately for some kind of weapon but realised that even a broadsword would be useless to him with his hands bound. He saw Henry hold Michael's head back as he prepared to cut his throat. Henry then watched Will, waiting for an order.

'That hand, Will,' said Bartholomew, hoping to distract them long enough to give him a chance to think of some way to escape. 'It was Starre's, was it not? You took it the night of the first riot.'

Will grinned, but did not stop his relentless advance. 'The first riot gave us plenty of time to acquire the limb of a recently dead pauper, and we did the body no harm. We could not risk you claiming the hand belonged to a woman because it was overly small.'

'But it broke as you boiled it. You had to mend it with a pin.'

Will pulled an unpleasant face. 'I might have known it was you who told the Chancellor that. Fortunately, Master Thorpe was not deterred by so minor a point and it did nothing to diminish his belief in the relic's sanctity.'

'And then, a couple of days later, with the hand

suitably prepared, you pretended to find it in the Ditch. By then, it was wearing the ring that Father Andrew – Simon d'Ambrey, should I say – had given to you.'

Will began to gain on Bartholomew, who continued to speak as he backed down the hall.

'You had even made a fine box for it in advance, lined with satin for it to lie on.'

'What if I did?' asked Will with a shrug. 'But there is nothing you can do about it now and we cannot have you running all over the town claiming that our saintly relic is a fake.'

'But it is a fake,' Bartholomew pointed out.

'Did you take it?' asked Will, still advancing. He fingered his dagger. Jacob, the man with the broken arm, picked up a piece of broken pot in his good hand, and prepared to follow.

'I do not think he did, Will,' he said, 'or he would not have come back.'

'True, I suppose,' said Will grudgingly. 'But he has the book by Galen that Master d'Ambrey so badly wanted back. He will be pleased when I give it to him.'

'We know it was you who attacked us that night,' said Bartholomew. 'You three, with Master Bigod, Huw, Saul Potter, and Ivo from David's Hostel. Jacob's arm was broken then, and you were bitten. And it was probably you who searched my room the first two times.'

'We should have finished you then, in the street, along with that meddlesome monk. But Master

Bigod was too squeamish, damn him, especially when he saw I was about to kill a man of God. Everything was going to plan until you two started to poke about.'

Jacob hurled his piece of broken pot. Bartholomew ducked as it sailed over his head to crash against the wall in a shower of shards. Undeterred, the servant looked about for something else to throw.

'And it was you who burgled those houses,' said Bartholomew, ducking a second time as a pewter jug narrowly missed him. 'Because you knew exactly where and when the riots would break out, you were able to use the opportunity to select the houses of certain rich merchants and steal from them.'

'So what?' said Jacob, leaning down to grab another jug to throw. 'Is it fair that fat merchants should have more wealth than they know what to do with, while the rest of us are starving?'

'You are not starving,' Bartholomew pointed out.

Will gave an unpleasant smile. 'Not now, perhaps, but we have to think of the future, and a man like Simon d'Ambrey always needs funds.'

'I bet he does,' said Bartholomew. 'Funds for paying people to incite riots, funds to have corpses desecrated, funds to assassinate people he does not like.'

Will came nearer, flanked by Jacob. 'I have had enough of this!'

He turned to nod to Henry to dispatch Michael. Seeing him momentarily distracted, Bartholomew propelled himself forward with an almighty yell, crashing into him and knocking him off balance. Will fell into Jacob, who dropped to his knees with a shriek as he cradled his injured arm. Michael's hands suddenly shot out, one grasping Henry's throat, the other the arm that held the dagger. As Henry began to choke with a series of unpleasant gurgles, Bartholomew turned his attention back to Will. Will lunged with his knife and Bartholomew jumped away.

'What is in all this for you, Will?' asked Bartholomew, flinching backwards as Will lunged a second time. 'Why should you risk your livelihood for d'Ambrey?'

'He once paid a surgeon to set my broken leg,' said Will, circling Bartholomew like a dog. 'I have always deeply regretted that I did nothing to help him when he was accused all those years ago. It is a second chance, and I will go with him when he leaves tonight. I will no longer be a mere servant, taken for granted and given the most menial of tasks to perform, but a member of a respectable household, the head of which will be the saintly Master d'Ambrey.'

'But the man has changed!' said Bartholomew, his feet crunching on broken pottery as he ducked away from Will's dagger. 'Saints do not kill and order the desecration of the dead!'

'Shut up!' hissed Will. He darted forward and

caught hold of Bartholomew's tabard to hold him still.

'D'Ambrey must be held to blame for all the deaths that occurred in the riots he inspired,' persisted Bartholomew breathlessly, tearing away from Will's grip as a swipe of the dagger ripped his shirt. 'Including that of your brother. He died in the first riot, I understand.'

He jerked backwards to avoid another furious hacking blow and stumbled over a broken chair. Will was now incensed and his eyes flashed with loathing. Instead of distracting the man, Bartholomew had succeeded in enraging him to the point where any chance of escape seemed hopeless. Off-balance, Bartholomew crashed to the floor, while Will's arm flicked down and under in a swift, efficient movement aimed at the physician's unprotected stomach.

Even as the knife flashed towards him, there was a loud thump, and Will's head jolted forward. Will looked as surprised as Bartholomew, before crumpling into a heap on the floor. Jacob still sat hunched over his injured arm while Henry lay massaging his bruised neck.

Across the hall, Michael sank down on to a bench and closed his eyes. Shakily, Bartholomew climbed to his feet and joined him.

'Thank the Lord you like reading heavy books,' said Michael, pointing to where the Galen lay next to Will. Michael had hurled it in the nick of time.

*   *   *

As Bartholomew approached the door to leave Valence Marie's hall, he froze, and edged back into the shadows. There were voices – Thorpe's and d'Ambrey's, complete with the lilting Scottish accent of Father Andrew. Bartholomew opened the door slightly so he could hear what was being said.

'I am most distressed that the relic has disappeared,' d'Ambrey was saying, wringing his hands and appearing every inch the benevolent old friar. 'Most distressed indeed. I wanted to see it again before I left.'

'You are leaving Cambridge, Father?' asked Thorpe politely, but without interest. He had other things to worry about than an elderly friar who had missed his opportunity to view the relic. But the friar's concern was insistent – as well it might be.

'Do you have an idea of where it might be?' he said. 'Can I help you look for it?'

'You are most kind, Father,' said Thorpe. 'But we will manage. We have already turned the College upside-down in our quest to locate it – you should see the state of our poor hall! I am now on my way to discuss the matter with the Chancellor.'

'I know you will guard that relic and see that it is awarded the honour it deserves,' continued d'Ambrey. Thorpe looked at him sharply. D'Ambrey was overplaying his role, enjoying too much the opportunity to promote himself as the object of reverence.

He realised the danger, and bowed to Thorpe before taking his leave. He was shown out of the main gate by one of the students and Bartholomew saw him glancing this way and that as he walked, as though the hand might appear suddenly in the mud and refuse that lay ankle-deep in the yard. Thorpe dallied, his students milling about him restlessly.

'Has de Wetherset stolen the hand?' whispered Bartholomew to Michael as he watched them. 'Or Heppel?'

Michael shrugged. 'Possibly. What is Thorpe doing? Why does he not leave? We should follow d'Ambrey before he escapes us completely, but we cannot do so with Thorpe prowling around outside. His students are vengeful – they would hang us in an instant if Thorpe gave them his blessing, and even Father Eligius's claims that you are mentally deficient will not save us.'

Bartholomew regarded him sharply. 'Exactly when was it that you recovered your senses from Thorpe's blow?' he asked.

Michael looked uncomfortable. 'I am not sure. But I had to wait for the right moment before I acted.'

'You cut it very fine, Brother,' said Bartholomew, regarding the monk uneasily.

'The truth was that you were doing such a fine job of wringing a confession from Will that I decided to wait a while. He would never have been so verbose had I leapt to my feet and overpowered

Henry. He was bragging to you simply because he thought he was going to kill you, and that you would never be in a position to reveal anything he had said.'

'He almost killed me several times during his confession!' said Bartholomew, aghast. 'How could you put Will's paltry revelations over my life?'

'Come now, Matt!' said Michael impatiently. 'Do not be so melodramatic! I knew what I was doing. I saved your life, did I not? And together we overwhelmed that unwholesome trio there.'

He glanced over his shoulder to where Will, Henry and Jacob sat with their backs to the serving screen, secured there with ropes that had been used to suspend the tapestries from the walls. Henry and Jacob were subdued, but Will was livid. He struggled and heaved against his bonds, making guttural sounds through the bandages with which Bartholomew had gagged him.

Bartholomew turned his attention back to the yard, and gave a start of horror as he saw Thorpe begin to walk towards the hall. His heart lurched in anticipation of being discovered free, and he was momentarily frozen with fear. Sensing his alarm, Will's struggles increased, and Michael grabbed Will's abandoned dagger, racing across to the serving screen to wave it menacingly at the gagged servant before Thorpe heard the noise.

Thorpe drew closer, and Bartholomew looked around in panic, wondering how they might escape. There was no other way out. Bartholomew knew instinctively that if Thorpe discovered they had overpowered his servants, he would give them into the custody of his vengeful students, and that would be their death warrant. As Thorpe's hand reached out to push open the hall door, a scholar emerged from the Master's quarters, carrying a bundle of cloth. Thorpe's hand dropped from the door and he began to walk away. Bartholomew was so relieved, his legs turned to jelly, and he had to lean against the wall for support. Next to Will, Michael dropped the dagger in revulsion.

Bartholomew gave the monk a weak smile. 'Master Thorpe does not want to confront the Chancellor improperly attired,' he explained shakily. 'He was waiting for a student to fetch him his best robe.'

Michael gnawed at his finger-nails. 'We will lose d'Ambrey if Thorpe does not leave soon!'

While they waited for Thorpe to be satisfied with the way his gown fell, Bartholomew crammed bandages and salves back in his medical bag and tucked the Galen into one of the side pockets. Michael fretted at the door. By the time Bartholomew had finished, Thorpe and his entourage had gone and Michael was already across the courtyard and out of the main gates. As they emerged into the High Street, they caught a glimpse of d'Ambrey's grey habit disappearing up the Trumpington Road.

They set off after him, pausing briefly to tell the

guards on the gate that there were three felons secured in Valence Marie, and that Tulyet should follow as soon as possible. After a moment's hesitation, Michael tossed a small child a penny and sent her with a message to the Chancellor and Heppel.

'Wicked waste of a penny,' muttered Michael. 'De Wetherset will be in a business meeting and his clerks will be too frightened to disturb him on our behalf, while Heppel's presence while we apprehend a killer will be more hindrance than help.'

While they had been in Valence Marie the clouds had thickened, and a light, misty rain was falling. It should have been a welcome relief after the heat of the morning, but it served only to increase the humidity. Michael complained that he could not catch his breath; even Bartholomew began to feel uncomfortable. But the rain afforded some advantage, for it provided a haziness in the air that meant that Bartholomew and Michael were able to follow d'Ambrey with less chance of being seen.

They walked quickly and without speaking, alert for any sound that would warn them that d'Ambrey had stopped. One or twice they glimpsed him ahead and, as they went further from the town, Bartholomew began to wonder how far d'Ambrey was going to go. They reached the small manor owned by Sir Robert de Panton, where the land had been cleared for farming, affording uninterrupted views down the road for some distance. D'Ambrey was nowhere to be seen. Michael sagged in defeat.

As they dithered, wondering where d'Ambrey might have turned, they met Sir Robert himself, who told them that he had seen an elderly friar pass along the Trumpington Road just a few moments before. Encouraged, Bartholomew and Michael hurried on.

They continued in silence, the only sounds being Michael's heavy breathing, and their feet on the muddy road. As they began to despair that they might have lost him a second time, a thought occurred to Bartholomew. They were near Trumpington village, where d'Ambrey had almost been incinerated in the tithe barn fire. The new barn had been built closer to the village, so it could be better protected, and the charred timbers of the old one had been allowed to decay. Now, nothing remained, apart from one or two ivy-covered stumps and a clearing in the trees where it had once stood.

Wordlessly, Bartholomew led Michael off the main path to the site of the old barn. He was beginning to think he must have miscalculated, when he heard voices. One was d'Ambrey, speaking with no hint of a Scottish accent. Peering through the trees, Bartholomew saw an unwhole-some creature wrapped in filthy rags, but standing straight and tall and speaking in a firm, clear voice. The murderous Dominica.

D'Ambrey said something, and there were

growls of agreement from others: Huw from Godwinsson, Ivo from David's, and Cecily, who looked sullen. As Bartholomew turned to indicate to Michael that they should withdraw and wait for Tulyet, he heard the unmistakeable click of a crossbow bolt being loaded. He spun round.

'Ruthven!'

Ruthven smiled, and indicated with a small flick of his crossbow that they should precede him into the midst of Simon d'Ambrey's meeting.

D'Ambrey scowled when he saw Ruthven's captives. 'Where did you find these gentlemen?'

'Listening to you from the bushes over there,' said Ruthven with a toss of his head. He poked at Bartholomew with his weapon and indicated that he and Michael should sit on the grass.

'Well, we can do nothing until nightfall, anyway,' said d'Ambrey with a shrug. 'I would like Huw to return to Valence Marie and find out from Will what is happening about my hand.' He turned to Bartholomew and Michael, and smiled. 'Given long enough, I might be made a saint, do you think? Perhaps a fine abbey built around my shrine?'

'I doubt it,' said Michael. 'Although people do seem to worship the oddest things.' He smiled guilelessly back at d'Ambrey, ignoring Bartholomew's warning kick.

D'Ambrey saw Bartholomew's reaction, however. 'I see you seek to caution your friend, lest he moves me to anger, Doctor,' he said. 'You have doubtless seen many forms of madness since you have become a physician. Well, you have no need to look for any such signs in me. I am as sane as you. Angry, perhaps. Betrayed, certainly. And vengeful. But most assuredly not mad.'

He smiled in a way that made Bartholomew seriously doubt it. The only hope for him and Michael, he realised, was that one of the messages that they had left for Tulyet would reach him, especially the one with the guards at the gate. He prayed that the Sheriff would not be waylaid into helping Thorpe search for the missing relic.

D'Ambrey sat on a tree stump and smiled beatifically. Even with his accent and friar-like demeanour gone, Bartholomew felt the man still had a peculiarly saintly air about him.

'You are wondering what made me change,' he said, looking from one to the other of his captives. 'I was loved by the people. My brother and sister adored me. And then my brother betrayed me. He stole the treasure I had collected for the poor and flaunted it by wearing it around the town. People thought I had given it to him and turned against me. I ran to the woman I had always liked best for sanctuary. But she betrayed me too. She told her betrothed where I was and he came to kill me.'

'No!' Cecily rose from where she had been sitting, uncomfortable and bedraggled, on the grass. 'You know I did not betray you! I saw smoke coming from the barn and ran back to warn you,

570

but it was already too late. I thought it was a terrible accident, not murder!'

'But you did not try to look for me after the blaze,' said d'Ambrey, with quiet reason. 'You were quick to assume I was dead.'

'But the barn was an inferno!' wailed Cecily desperately, moving towards him, arms outstretched. 'No one could have survived! Even the nails melted from the heat!'

'And then you married the man who brought about my death,' continued d'Ambrey relentlessly. 'And you allowed him to bring up my daughter as his own child. You did not even keep the rings I gave you. Somehow one of them ended up on a shabby little student at my own hostel and I had to go to all manner of contortions to get it back to adorn my relic at Valence Marie.'

'Dominica gave it to him,' protested Cecily. 'I kept both rings close to my heart for twenty-five years. I only gave one to Bartholomew recently because I thought he might be able to use it to catch Dominica's killer.'

'I did no such thing, father,' said Dominica disdainfully. 'She and Thomas Lydgate were far too mean to give me jewellery to dispense with as I pleased. She is lying!'

'I think you *did* give it to Jamie, Dominica,' said Ruthven uncertainly. 'He said you did.'

'My Dominica has no cause to lie,' said d'Ambrey, somewhat rashly, since it was clear to everyone in the clearing that she had every reason to stretch

571

the truth. Cecily gazed at her daughter in mute appeal, and Bartholomew found he could not watch.

'Those rings belonged to my parents,' said d'Ambrey sternly. 'My father had them made to match my mother's blue-green eyes. They are not baubles to be dispensed to any snotty-nosed scholar who wanted one, especially a lad like James Kenzie, who was so careless. First he let John steal it and then he lost the false one I replaced it with while he was brawling on the High Street.'

'But I kept them safe!' shrieked Cecily. 'I did! Dominica stole them from me to give to her paramour!'

D'Ambrey turned from her and made a quick gesture to Ruthven. There was a swish and a thump. Ruthven was reloading his crossbow with a new quarrel before the shocked Bartholomew could act. Cecily looked at d'Ambrey in horror, her hands clawing at the bolt that protruded from her chest. Her bulbous eyes popped out even further as she sank on to the grass.

Bartholomew made to go towards her.

'Leave her!' d'Ambrey snapped, his gentle tones vanished. 'She deserves to die.'

Bartholomew looked at him in revulsion. 'Why?'

'She has served her purpose,' said d'Ambrey with a shrug. 'I only brought her into the plot at the last minute because she had hidden away her family jewels so well that neither Edred nor Dominica could find them. She kindly brought them – Dominica's inheritance – a few moments ago, although they are a little fire-damaged. But I do not want her slowing us down when we leave tonight. We will need to move fast if we want to escape.'

'I can give her something to ease the pain,' said Bartholomew, reaching for his bag and flipping it open.

'You will leave her alone,' d'Ambrey repeated, looking inside the bag with interest. 'You have my Galen, I see. A little late, perhaps, but I am pleased to have it back.'

Before Bartholomew could reply, d'Ambrey had plucked the tome from the bag, and was sitting with it on his knees. He saw immediately where Gray had torn the covers away and shook his head slowly, fingering the damage with sadness in his face.

'Is this the way scholars treat their books? Would you do this, eh, Ruthven?'

Ruthven came to peer over d'Ambrey's shoulder, looking at the torn cover. 'Was this where the documents were hidden?' he asked.

D'Ambrey nodded. 'I tried several times to get this back,' he said to Bartholomew. 'But if I sent someone to search your room, you would have it in your bag, and when I waylaid you on the High Street, you had left it in your room. And then, when I simply asked you for it, you offered to return it immediately!'

'My father wrote that book,' said Ruthven with pride.

'What was his name?' asked Michael.

'No one you would know, Brother,' said d'Ambrey. 'Just a scholar I helped many years ago. You should empathise, Doctor, for he was a man whose revolutionary medical ideas gave rise to an accusation of heresy. I gave him money to flee to Scotland to safety. He remembered me, unlike so many, and told his son, already a student here, to help me in my revenge against the town.'

'It seems you have engineered quite a plot against the town, Master d'Ambrey,' said Michael, knowing that as soon as d'Ambrey grew tired of them, he and Bartholomew would go the same way as Cecily. They had to try to keep him talking until Tulyet arrived. 'Perhaps you would care to entertain us with the details.'

D'Ambrey looked pleased. 'Shall I start at the beginning, then?' he asked sweetly. At Michael's nod, he settled himself comfortably and beamed around at his audience. 'Well, to take you back twenty-five years, I fled the burning barn and sought safety near the river. I was not the only abandoned soul that night. A lad named Norbert was also fleeing that horrible little village. We joined forces and lived rough for several days. He told me what you had done for him and it did much to cheer me, Bartholomew. We exchanged our plans of revenge – me on the town, him on the village – and he confided his plans to become an archer at Dover Castle.'

'Oh, no!' said Bartholomew suddenly, an uneasy

feeling uncoiling in his stomach. 'It was you! You killed Norbert! It *was* his skeleton we found in the Ditch after all!'

He gazed, horrified, at d'Ambrey, who smiled back at him, unperturbed by his distress. 'I am afraid you are right. But it was all a dreadful mistake. You see, one night, Norbert disappeared, and I assumed that he had gone to fetch soldiers. I was desperate to stop him and caught him near the Ditch where my brother had died. I slipped up behind him and stoved in his skull with a stone. He had just enough breath, before he died, to tell me that he was going to burgle a house to steal me a new cloak for our journey south together. I have been sorry about Norbert ever since,' he finished, looking wistfully at the crushed grass at his feet.

Bartholomew felt sick. The messages he had received had been forged by d'Ambrey, and the copies in the back of the book kept so he would not forget the lies told. Bartholomew had released Norbert from Trumpington, only for him to fall into the hands of a murderer.

D'Ambrey's eyes were guilelessly wide. 'I sent Bartholomew letters – signed with the name of Norbert's sister so as not to get him into trouble with his family – so that he would not fret about the welfare of his young friend. It was a simple act of kindness.'

Bartholomew gazed at him with renewed awe. Such dishonesty surely could not be considered kindness? He wondered afresh at d'Ambrey's sanity. The man sat, still dressed in his friar's habit, smiling benevolently down at them like a beloved old grandfather. Yet he had ordered Cecily's brutal murder without a moment's hesitation.

'And you needed somewhere to hide these letters,' said Michael. 'Where better than the Galen? The book was never used by David's students because none of them were studying medicine. It would have been difficult to hide them otherwise – hostels are notorious for their lack of privacy.'

D'Ambrey nodded. 'You have it, Brother. Scholars are naturally curious and I did not want them poking about in my belongings and finding the letters. The Galen was a perfect hiding place until Radbeche lent it to you! But we digress.' He gave a huge sigh, and continued. 'It was my intention that Norbert's skeleton should be dredged from the Ditch and revered as mine at Valence Marie, assuming it had not washed away. But, ironically, it was you who prevented that, Doctor, by saying it was too small.'

'How could you know your brother's skeleton would not be dredged up?' asked Michael. 'Or his and Norbert's?'

'The Ditch was in flood the night my brother died,' said d'Ambrey. 'His body was washed a long way downstream. When I killed Norbert, the Ditch was low. The water did not cover him, and so I buried him in the mud at the bottom.'

'And then you went to Dover,' said Bartholomew, unsteadily.

'I did indeed,' said d'Ambrey, 'I went in pursuit of my fleeing household – as did the three burgesses from the town. It was easy to follow them, and I disguised myself as a travelling priest.'

Bartholomew closed his eyes in despair. 'And I suppose it was you who started the fire in which all those people died, your household included.'

D'Ambrey smiled. 'It was nothing,' he said modestly. 'An oven left burning in a baker's shop when it should have been doused for the night; a specially prepared pie that would ensure my household slept through any alarms that might have been raised before the fire was underway.'

'Dozens of innocent people died in that blaze,' said Bartholomew, appalled, 'not just members of your household.'

'It could not be helped,' said d'Ambrey. 'And I am sure you will understand my need for revenge after what had happened to me.'

'But how did you manage to make the burgesses believe that your brother was among the casualties?' asked Michael. 'His body was never recovered.'

'Never recovered?' queried d'Ambrey. 'On what grounds do you base such an assumption? Believe me, my brother's body lies in the grave

577

that is marked with his name. I could not allow it to be found when all believed it was *me* who had died in the Ditch that day. Norbert helped me search for it and, when I assumed my disguise as a priest, I hid it in the portable altar I carried on my cart.'

'And then you left his body for the burgesses to find after the fire,' said Bartholomew.

'Exactly. I had to disguise the wound in his throat, but that was easy enough with all that falling timber. The whole affair was expertly brought to a satisfactory conclusion. I even heard later that the worthy burgesses were suspected of starting the fire themselves,' he added with a chuckle.

'But how could you know that the Ditch would be dredged at such an opportune time?' asked Michael, shifting uncomfortably on the sodden ground.

'Think!' said d'Ambrey with chiding patience. 'It was mainly Thorpe who set the scheme in motion in the first place: Will mentioned the money that might be made if the relics of Simon d'Ambrey were to be found by Valence Marie. Thorpe needed little encouragement once that seed was sown. I wonder what happened to that hand . . .'

He thought for a moment before resuming. 'I returned here two months ago and secured myself a place at David's. Ruthven's father sent a letter of recommendation, along with the name of a friar

– recently deceased – whose identity I could assume. It was an excellent idea. After all, who would suspect an elderly Scottish friar? Any lapses in my theological knowledge would merely be put down to my nationality.'

Ruthven looked at him sharply and fingered his crossbow. But d'Ambrey was oblivious to Ruthven's patriotic ire and continued with his tale.

'I had settled in nicely by the time term had started; I had secured the help of people who owed me favours – Will, Henry and Jacob, who now work at Valence Marie; Huw and Saul Potter of Godwinsson; even Master Bigod of Maud's owes me a small favour – you see, I once loaned him the money to pay a hag to rid one of his mistresses of an unwanted child. Bigod was always one for the women, as Cecily will attest.'

He flung a disparaging glance at the writhing woman on the ground.

'You were right, Matt!' whispered Michael, as d'Ambrey stood to peer through the trees for signs of Huw returning with news of the lost relic. 'Cecily and Bigod were lovers! I do not know which one I feel more sorry for!'

So Bigod, like Lydgate, was being blackmailed, thought Bartholomew, watching d'Ambrey resettle himself on the tree stump with his Galen. That Bigod spoke of Dominica's death in the Chesterton basement, however, suggested that he was not party to that part of the plot.

'I sent Master Lydgate little notes,' continued d'Ambrey, 'reminding him that he had fired the tithe barn and hinting about my death. He was meant to be terrified that I had returned from the dead to haunt him. But he, foolish man, did not have sufficient imagination, and settled for a more practical explanation. He thought you were sending them, Doctor. How he justified belief in such a sudden and uncharacteristic move on your part, I cannot imagine. But Lydgate was not a man to allow reason to interfere with his prejudices.'

He fell silent, and the only sounds were the slight swish of wind in the trees, the drip of rain on leaves. Ruthven cocked his crossbow at Michael who was trying to make himself comfortable on the ground, while Dominica, bored by the narration, moved away to talk to Ivo. Horribly aware that as soon as they failed to keep d'Ambrey amused, Ruthven would be ordered to kill them, Bartholomew desperately searched for something to say.

'We know about your two acts,' he said. 'Faking the death of Dominica and producing a hand for the relic.'

'So, Matilde *did* betray me,' he said sadly. 'That cannot go unpunished.'

Bartholomew's stomach churned and he was furious at himself. Putting Matilde in danger was not what he had intended! 'She told us nothing! We reasoned it all out for ourselves!'

'I do not think so, Doctor. You simply do not have the cunning and clarity of mind to best me. No one does.' He frowned down at the soggy Galen. 'So, Eleanor Tyler was right after all about that harlot. She told me she was not to be trusted.'

'Where is Eleanor?' asked Bartholomew.

'Far away by now, I should think. Dominica needed to escape and what better way than by using Mistress Tyler's harlot niece?'

'Why did Mistress Tyler allow herself to become involved in this mess of lies and spite?' asked Bartholomew, not sure that he really wanted to know the answer.

'I was told you had a liking for her daughters, although you would have been kinder to have concentrated your efforts on just one of them rather than two. But Mistress Tyler helped me because she has a dark secret that I concealed for her many years ago.'

'What dark secret?' asked Michael, interested.

'Mistress Tyler killed her first husband,' said d'Ambrey casually. 'It was an accident, you understand. The cooking pot simply fell from her hand on to his head. But it was after months of abuse, and the man was a brute. I hired a physician to say that he died of a fever. So she is indebted to me. Her second husband was a good man and the father of her three girls. He died quite naturally during the plague I understand – no cooking pots involved there.'

'Did you help Mistress Tyler because you felt her crime had a just cause, or so that you could blackmail her later?' asked Bartholomew coldly.

D'Ambrey's smile faded and his eyes became hard. 'You are arrogant, Doctor, just as Lydgate said you were. For your information, I knew Mistress Tyler and her first husband and I judged for myself which was the victim.'

'*That* is arrogant!' exclaimed Bartholomew. 'On what authority do you presume to act as judge over your fellow men?'

There was a tense silence, and even Cecily desisted with her soft moans. Bartholomew thought he had gone too far and had tipped this unstable man across the thin boundary from sanity. He caught Michael's agonised look from the corner of his eye.

D'Ambrey's smile returned, and there was an almost audible sigh of relief from all in the clearing. From the tension of d'Ambrey's associates, Bartholomew judged that displays of temper were probably not unknown from this seemingly gentle man.

'I instructed Mistress Tyler to ensure Joanna remained indoors after the riot had started. She was simply to take her daughters and spend the night with her relatives. It was foolish of those French boys to have attacked Eleanor first, but it was even more foolish of the Tylers to have embarked on a friendship with you, given that you were obsessed with Joanna's death.'

'Did they know what you planned to do to Joanna?' asked Michael.

D'Ambrey shook his head. 'I simply told them to slip Joanna a little something from Uncle Jonas's store to make her sleep, and that she would be removed from their house never to bother them again. Of course, they were unsettled by the idea, but they soon saw sense when I pointed out that the alternative would be Mistress Tyler hanged for her husband's murder, and her daughters left unprotected.'

'Did you tell them to leave the town?' asked Bartholomew shakily.

'I did not, although what else could they have done, especially after foolish Eleanor sought to solve matters by trying to poison you? Silly child! Had she succeeded, Brother Michael would never have let the matter rest until he had discovered the truth and that, of course, would have been dangerous to me. I was relieved when they fled.'

Bartholomew took a deep breath, feeling the sweat prick at his back despite the chill of the rain. 'The second riot was different from the first,' he said, changing the subject with some relief. Despite the fact that he had already guessed that Eleanor had sent him the poison, he did not want to dwell on the matter.

'Godwinsson was to be destroyed,' said Michael, seizing on the opportunity to launch d'Ambrey into explaining another part of his plan, and thus buy them more time. 'And Michaelhouse attacked so that the Sheriff will be forced to take serious measures against the town. You incited both riots. You started rumours in the Market Square, Valence Marie and Godwinsson and they spread like wildfire. Experienced rabble-rousers, like Saul Potter, fanned them to see that they did not die out.'

'Right,' said d'Ambrey, nodding appreciatively. 'You have reasoned all this out very well. The complaints of the University that it has been attacked will be sure to evoke a response from the King. Extra troops will be called in and crippling taxes imposed. That was my plan all along. After last night's riots the Sheriff will be ordered to clamp down so hard on the townspeople – the townspeople that were so quick to believe ill of me after I had dedicated my life to helping them – that the town will be unable to function as a viable trading centre. Gradually, it will decline and the people will sink deeper and deeper into poverty.'

Bartholomew wondered whether d'Ambrey really believed that the people he was so keen to punish were the same ones that had failed to rally to his defence twenty-five years before. Few, if any, of the scholars were the same, since the University was a transient place, and so many of the towns-people had died of the plague that d'Ambrey was lucky to be remembered by anyone at all. Seeing d'Ambrey begin to fidget, Bartholomew continued quickly before he lost interest altogether and ordered them shot.

'Cecily told us that Dominica killed Radbeche. Is that true?'

Dominica smiled at him, distracted from her conversation with Ivo by the mention of her name.

'Yes,' said d'Ambrey. 'I had arranged for Radbeche to be away for the night, but he heard rumours that there might be a riot, abandoned his trip, and hurried home. Meanwhile, those silly Scots escaped as soon as I left the hostel – as I knew they would.' He paused and looked down at the book on his knees. The rain was making the ink run but he seemed oblivious to the damage.

'Unfortunately, when Radbeche came bursting into the hostel crying out that there would be murder and mayhem that night, he saw Dominica – not as Norbert the scullion, but as a woman with long, fair hair. She could not have him telling everyone about that, so she ensured his silence. Scarcely had she wiped the blood from her blade when John walked in.'

'Dominica ran him through, too,' said Ruthven, eager to tell his part in the story. 'But her aim was false in the dark, and I could not bring myself to finish him off, so I stayed with him until he died. My part was finished anyway. All I had to do was to explain to the proctors that the mob had killed Radbeche and John and then ask the Chancellor's permission to return to Scotland to recover from

585

my terrible experience. I was convincing, was I not?'

Bartholomew hoped Michael would not reveal that John was still alive, or d'Ambrey was certain to order his death. But the monk was far too self-composed to make such an error. He assessed d'Ambrey coldly.

'Yesterday afternoon, when you went out with John, Father William left you in no doubt that he would uncover you as a fraud. Your work, therefore, had to be finished today, or you would risk being reviled by the townspeople a second time.'

'People are fickle,' mused d'Ambrey sadly. 'The scholars at David's were fond of me but I do not doubt for an instant that they would denounce me had Father William uncovered my disguise. You are right. I had to finish all my business today.'

Bartholomew wondered how he could have been so misled. The people at Godwinsson – Lydgate, Cecily, Edred and Werbergh – were an unsavoury crowd, but Bartholomew found them easier to understand than the smiling villains at David's. He glanced behind him into the trees, wondering how much longer they would be able to keep d'Ambrey entertained.

'But who killed Kenzie and Werbergh?' asked Michael. His thin hair was plastered to his head, giving it a pointed appearance, and he, like Bartholomew, was shivering – partly from sitting still in the rain, but mostly from the almost unbearable tension of wondering whether Tulyet would arrive in time to save them.

'I imagine Ruthven killed Kenzie,' said Bartholomew, looking hard at the Scot. 'Kenzie had lost his ring – or the fake – and was broken-hearted. Master d'Ambrey decided it was time to rid himself once and for all of the youngster who was not only careless with his belongings, but who had the audacity to fall in love with his daughter Dominica. So, Ruthven went with Kenzie to help him look for his ring, then hit him on the head when he, trustingly, went first along the top of the Ditch in the dark. Correct?'

Ruthven's eyes were fixed guiltily on Dominica.

'James Kenzie was entirely the wrong choice for my Dominica,' said d'Ambrey before the Scot could reply. 'Ruthven agreed to solve the problem before it became overly serious.'

Dominica did not appear to be impressed at this example of paternal care. 'You introduced me to him,' she said accusingly. 'Anyway, I was not planning to marry him. He was just fun to be with and he was imaginative in fooling my parents.'

'Well, Ruthven hit him on the head with the pommel of his dagger,' said d'Ambrey un-remorsefully. 'And then poor Radbeche and I had to keep all our students in so that the University would think we were serious about discipline. It worked brilliantly. You never suspected any of us.'

'Actually, we did,' said Michael.

Dominica shook her head slowly at Ruthven, ignoring d'Ambrey's mild outrage at Michael's claim. 'But Jamie was your friend!'

Ruthven declined to answer and stared at the wet grass, fiddling dangerously with the winding mechanism on the crossbow.

'Very clever,' said Michael, turning back to d'Ambrey. 'Ruthven's alibi for the time of the murder was the man who ordered the murder in the first place.'

Bartholomew wondered whether Dominica might launch herself at Ruthven in her fury, and tensed himself to take advantage of the situation while Ruthven battled with her. He was unprepared for her sudden, dazzling smile. His spirits sank.

'Such loving care! My parents never managed to prevent me from seeing the men of my choice but you two have!'

'Men?' asked d'Ambrey suspiciously. 'There were others?'

'And what of Werbergh?' asked Michael, uninterested in Dominica's romantic entanglements. 'Why was he killed and his death made to look like an accident?'

'Ah yes, Werbergh,' said d'Ambrey, still looking uncertainly at Dominica. 'Werbergh was employed by me as a spy to keep an eye on Lydgate's movements, but he was next to worthless. He was so nervous that it must have been obvious to a child what he was doing. I began to distrust his discretion, so I had Ruthven slip out and kill him as he came back drunk from the celebrations at Valence Marie. Will hid the body near the Ditch, until Saul Potter and Huw were able to make his death look like an accident.'

So that explained why the body had been wet and there were pieces of river weed on it, thought Bartholomew. It also explained why Werbergh had died so long before his accident in the shed, and why Saul Potter and Huw were the ones who said that he had been going to fetch some wood.

'But I do not know what happened to Edred,' said d'Ambrey. 'I sent him to spin a few tales to confuse you and to have a good look for my book, but he never returned. He was playing a double game, passing information to Lydgate as well as to me. He could not be trusted either.'

Bartholomew understood why Edred's fear had been genuine: it was a dangerous game indeed that he had been playing.

D'Ambrey stood. He held the book, now beginning to warp from the rain. 'It is unfortunate you took my letters, but there are few who will understand their importance should they fall into the wrong hands. Now. It is getting dark, and it is time to leave.'

He gave Ruthven a cursory nod, and began to gather his belongings together. Ruthven swung his crossbow up and pointed it at Bartholomew.

'But why wait twenty-five years?' asked Michael, his voice sounding panicky to Bartholomew's ears.

'Why not strike sooner, when those that wronged you were still alive?'

'Oh, I had other things to do,' said d'Ambrey carelessly. 'I travelled a good deal and used my considerable talent for fund-raising to my own advantage. And anyway, I wanted to wait until the time was right. People would have recognised me had I returned too soon, and Dominica would not have been old enough. But that is none of your concern. Ruthven, make an end to this infernal questioning.'

Bartholomew forced himself to meet Ruthven's eyes as the student checked the winding mechanism on his crossbow, and pointed it at him.

The little clearing was totally silent. Even the birds seemed dispirited by the rain, while the group of horses tethered to one side hung their heads miserably.

'Hurry it up,' ordered d'Ambrey. 'We have a long way to go tonight.'

Ruthven took aim.

'Drop it, Ruthven!' came Tulyet's voice, loud and strong from one side of the clearing. Bartholomew's relief was short lived, as Ruthven, after lowering the weapon for an instant, brought it back up again to aim at Bartholomew's chest. There was a whirring sound, and Ruthven keeled over, his loosed crossbow quarrel zinging harmlessly into the ground at Bartholomew's feet. Bartholomew forced his cold legs to move and scrambled upright.

Tulyet's men were suddenly everywhere, advancing on the clearing with their clanking weapons. Huw was with them, held between two men-at-arms, and gagged securely. Hovering at the rear, away from any potential danger, was Heppel, swathed in a huge cloak against the rain.

D'Ambrey looked at them in disbelief. 'What is this?' he cried. 'Where have you come from? You should not be here!'

'So it would seem,' said Tulyet dryly, helping the stiff Michael to his feet. 'I have been listening to you for quite some time now, Father Andrew. Or do you prefer Master d'Ambrey? What you have said, in front of my men, will be more than enough to interest the King.'

'Are you accusing me of treason?' asked d'Ambrey, his voice high with indignation.

'I would consider inciting riots and killing His Majesty's loyal subjects a treasonable offence, yes,' said Tulyet. He motioned to his men and they began to round up d'Ambrey's band of followers. D'Ambrey watched aghast.

'Not again!' he said. 'I have been betrayed again!'

'This time,' said Tulyet, 'you have betrayed yourself.'

D'Ambrey bent slowly to retrieve something from the ground. His action was so careful and deliberate that it seemed innocent. But then he straightened with frightening speed, a knife glinting in his hand. He tore towards Tulyet who had turned to supervise his men. Bartholomew hurled himself forward. He crashed into d'Ambrey, his weight bearing them both to the ground. D'Ambrey began to fight like a madman and, despite his superior size and strength, Bartholomew felt himself losing ground.

Tulyet and his men rushed to help, but it took several of them to drag the spitting, struggling man away, and to secure him in a cart.

'He would have killed me!' exclaimed Tulyet in horror. 'The man is possessed! Is he mad, do you think?'

Bartholomew shivered and not only from the cold. 'It would be convenient to think so,' he said ambiguously.

Tulyet looked uneasily at where d'Ambrey glowered at him. 'Well, I will only be happy when we have him well secured in the Castle prison.'

'Me too!' said Heppel with feeling. 'That man is extremely dangerous and so are his associates!'

'Be careful,' Bartholomew warned Tulyet. 'There are people who consider d'Ambrey a martyr. If it becomes known that you have him in your prison cart, you might well have a riot to free him.'

'Heaven forbid,' said Tulyet with a shudder. 'I hope we have rounded up all the ringleaders of these riots now. With them gone the people will grow peaceful again in time. I plan to send the prisoners to London for trial. We need no more local martyrs here.'

He turned his attention back to his captives,

while Bartholomew went to Cecily. She was past anything he could do, and her breath was little more than a thready whisper. Thinking to make her more comfortable, Bartholomew loosened the tight bodice of her dress, recoiling in shock at what tumbled out into his hands.

There, still with the blue-green ring on its little finger was the hand from Valence Marie. It was warm from being in Cecily's gown and sticky with blood. Bartholomew flung it from him in disgust.

'So, it was you who took it from Valence Marie,' he said softly. 'You slipped into the College when that greedy Thorpe and his scholars were off hoping to find more relics.'

But she was past confirming or denying him. He stared up at the leafy branches of trees that swayed and dripped above his head. When he looked again she was dead, a grimace fixed on her face and her eyes turning glassy.

Tulyet's men came to take her away, while Michael retrieved the hand from the grass. 'I expect the Chancellor would like this,' he said, turning it over in his hand.

'Each to his own,' said Bartholomew, climbing to his feet. He handed Michael the rings from his sleeve. 'Give him these, too. I imagine he will destroy them all together.'

'I cannot think why he would keep them,' said Michael. 'Simon d'Ambrey returning from the dead twenty-five years after half the town saw him die is enough to make him a martyr all over again. The Chancellor will not want bits of him around the town acting as a focus for gatherings.'

'Make sure Thorpe understands that,' said Bartholomew.

'I had news from the King this morning,' said Heppel, pulling his clock more closely around his neck. 'Thorpe, although he does not know it yet, is going to be offered a position as master of a grammar school in York.'

'A grammar school?' echoed Bartholomew. 'That is something of a step down from Master of Valence Marie. Will he accept?'

'Oh, he will accept,' said Heppel. 'One does not decline an offer from the King, you know. Thorpe is too unsubtle to be Master of a College.' He exchanged a knowing glance with Michael, and moved away to talk to Tulyet.

'Is he saying that if Thorpe had managed the matter of the hand with more tact and less zeal, he might still be in office?' asked Bartholomew.

Michael laughed at his shocked expression. 'Undoubtedly,' he said airily. 'And do not look surprised, my friend. You have listened to a most appalling tale over the last hour. You cannot raise your eyebrows at the King – or the Chancellor for that matter – when you have just heard the confessions of the Devil Incarnate.' He began to laugh, and draped an arm over Bartholomew's shoulders. Bartholomew shrugged it off quickly

594

when he saw that it was the one that held the hand.

'What a revolting affair,' he said, moving away from the monk. 'D'Ambrey was supposed to have been saintly, and look how many people have died because of him – Kenzie, Werbergh, Edred, Lydgate, Cecily, Radbeche, Joanna, the riot-dead, not to mention his entire household and a good part of the population of Dover twenty-five years ago.'

'I always said Cambridge used d'Ambrey badly,' said Michael. 'It is a shame he decided to use violence to avenge himself. Had he elected to resume his charitable acts, I think many people might have flocked to him, perhaps even me. He could have been a saint had he chosen to be.'

'I do not think so, Brother,' said Bartholomew. 'Saints do not harbour murderous intentions for twenty-five years, help wives conceal the killings of their husbands, or assist scholars to rid themselves of unwanted pregnancies.'

Michael yawned. 'So you have solved the mystery surrounding Joanna – she was killed to allow Dominica to be free of her parents. But it seems your Tyler women did not know what d'Ambrey intended – at least, not before it happened. They guessed afterwards because they must have found all that blood in their house.'

'I hope they are well away by now,' said Bartholomew.

'But by killing her first husband, Mistress Tyler is as much a murderer as is d'Ambrey!'

'I know, but Mistress Tyler is a good woman. She could have left me to the Frenchmen on the night of the riot, but she chose to stay and help, risking her life and the lives of her daughters. She also invited us in when we were attacked on the High Street without even knowing who we were. It was an act of selfless charity. I hope she reaches London safely and starts a new life.'

But what of Eleanor? he thought. Would her escape from justice encourage her to use murderous means the next time someone did something of which she did not approve? That she had gone so abruptly from being friendly to attempting to kill him left him oddly disoriented. The more he thought about it, the more he hoped their paths would never cross again, and realised that Matilde had definitely been correct when she had accused him of knowing nothing of women. He decided that he would most definitely not embark on any more friendships with them until he had devoted more time to understanding them. Had he done as much years ago, he would not have been jilted by Philippa, and would not have allowed himself to become embroiled in the uncomfortable business at the Feast. Michael's vast yawn interrupted his morose thoughts.

'We were right about the riots,' said Michael, yawning again. 'We thought there was more to them than random violence and we were correct.'

'All the clues that we uncovered piecemeal now fit together,' said Bartholomew, smothering a yawn of his own, brought on by watching Michael. 'I did not think they would ever match up.'

'If you are honest, some do not,' said Michael. 'It was pure chance that Norbert and Kenzie were both killed by wounds to the back of the head, and we saw a connection where there was none. Well, not a direct one anyway. We also thought Bigod was at the centre of the whole business, since you heard him when we were attacked on the High Street. And you heard him discussing the second riot at Chesterton. But he was just following orders.'

They began to walk back through the dripping trees towards Cambridge. Ahead of them was Tulyet's convoy with its prisoners, the wheels of the carts groaning and creaking and the low voices of Tulyet's men drifting on the breeze as they talked among themselves.

'What will happen to d'Ambrey and his associates?' asked Bartholomew.

'Tulyet will send them to London for trial,' said Michael with a shrug, 'but no one will be in any hurry for the facts to emerge. Years will pass, people will die, and one day there will be no records that any such prisoners ever arrived.'

'And the legends of d'Ambrey?'

'Oh, they will fade away in time,' said Michael. 'Have you considered that it may have been people like Will, Dominica and Huw that kept them alive all these years? Now they have gone the stories, too, will melt away to nothing. This incident will not be recorded in the University history and in fifty years or so no one will know the name of Simon d'Ambrey.'

'Talking to you is sometimes most disheartening,' said Bartholomew. 'Everything is to be forgotten, buried in the mists of time, covered up. Unwanted people are sent to places where they will never be heard of again. Events of which the University does not approve do not get written in the University history. What will people think of us in the future when they come to read this great history? That there was no crime, no underhand dealings, no deceits?'

'Not unless human nature undergoes a radical change,' said Michael blithely. 'They will have their own crimes, underhand dealings and deceits, and they will understand that the silence and blanks in our history say as much as the words.'

'That is not particularly encouraging,' said Bartholomew. He remembered Wilson's tomb and compared it to the vanishing pile of earth that marked Norbert's small grave. 'What will people think when they see Wilson's black monstrosity? Will they think that here lies a man that Michaelhouse loved and revered? Or will they know he paid for his own memorial? That vile man will be remembered long after poor Norbert is forgotten. It does not seem fair.'

Michael did not reply, and screwed up his eyes as the wind blew needles of rain into his face. 'Summer is on its way out,' he said. 'I complained about the heat and now I can complain about the cold.'

Bartholomew smiled reluctantly, but then froze as he heard shouting from ahead. A figure darted from one of the carts and disappeared into the thick undergrowth at the side of the road.

'That was d'Ambrey,' he said in a whisper. 'Escaped!'

Tulyet's men tore after him but Bartholomew knew that their chances of finding him were slim. There were so many ditches and dense bushes in which to hide, that all d'Ambrey needed to do was to wait until dark and slip away. Even dogs could not follow a scent through the myriad of waterways at the edge of the Fens.

A ragged cheer rose from d'Ambrey's supporters and Dominica made as if to follow while the soldiers' attention was engaged. She slithered out of the cart and began to run after him. She slumped suddenly and the howls of encouragement from her friends petered away.

'Good shot,' said Michael admiringly to Heppel. The Junior Proctor looked at the small pebbles in his hands in astonishment. Luck, not skill, had guided the missile that had felled Simon d'Ambrey's daughter.

Heppel grasped at Michael for support. 'Oh, Lord! I have just damaged my shoulder with that throw! I should not have tried to embark on heroics.'

'It is a pity you could not have struck d'Ambrey down too,' said Michael, unsympathetic. 'Now this business might end very messily.'

'Especially for Dominica and her associates,' said Bartholomew, looking to where she was being helped back into the cart. She saw Heppel and her eyes glittered with hatred.

'I grabbed these pebbles to hurl at d'Ambrey if he tried to harm me,' said Heppel shakily. 'I can assure you, I had no intention of trying to do the Sheriff's job for him. I was just carried away with the excitement of the moment when I aimed them at Dominica. It most certainly will not happen again. I shall suffer agonies from this shoulder injury for weeks and all because the Sheriff hires poorly trained guards! The King shall hear of this!'

Tulyet had ordered half his men to escort the remaining prisoners to the castle and the other half to search for d'Ambrey. His face was dark with anger and his temper was not improved by Heppel's accusations of incompetence.

'That gentle nature of d'Ambrey's beguiled my men,' he said in a voice that was tight with fury. 'He looks and acts like a friar and he made them feel as though they were escorting their grandfather! He fooled them into relaxing their guard and was gone in an instant!'

'I doubt that you will get him back,' said Bartholomew. 'It is not the first time he has escaped from the jaws of death in this area. History repeats itself.'

'He will be old indeed if he tries again in another twenty-five years,' said Michael.

'But, if there is a next time, he will not fail,' said Bartholomew.

EPILOGUE

Brown leaves rustled on the ground of the churchyard as they were stirred by the breeze. It was already dusk, even though the day's teaching was barely done, and there was an unmistakeable chill of winter in the air. St Michael's Church afforded some protection from the wind, but was damp and cold, and Bartholomew stamped his feet to try to keep them warm.

The mason added a few final taps and stood back to admire his work. The black tomb was in its place in the choir, stark and dismal against the painted wall. In place of the effigy stipulated by Master Wilson was a neat cross, carved into the polished marble with simple but elegant swirls and knots. Bartholomew nodded his satisfaction and the mason left, warning him not to touch the mortar, which was not yet set.

From the vestry, Michael's rich baritone rose as he sang while preparing for compline. Bartholomew went to find him.

'Is it done? Have you atoned for being sick on his grave?' Michael asked, raising a humorous eyebrow. He began thumbing his way through

603

the gospels to find the correct reading for the day.

Bartholomew winced. 'It is done,' he said, sitting on one of the wall benches in the cramped room.

'You have done Michaelhouse a great service – dallying so that Master Wilson's smug face will not sneer for eternity on our scholars from his effigy,' said Michael, peering at the open text in front of him.

Bartholomew was inclined to agree. 'Norbert's will, though.'

Michael regarded him uncertainly.

'I sold d'Ambrey's Galen to Father Philius, the physician at Gonville Hall. Then I gave the money to that mason, so he will carve Norbert's likeness on one of the sculpted heads that will be in St Mary's new chancel. He says he remembers Norbert from the tithe barn incident.'

'You do have a strange sense of justice,' said Michael, amused. 'Still, I suppose Norbert has as much right to his immortality as Wilson.'

He sniffed suddenly. 'I can smell perfume, Matt. Is it you? I thought you had given up on women after your deplorable lack of success with them.'

'Master Kenyngham told me I would find you here.'

Bartholomew and Michael started violently at the sound of Guy Heppel's breathy voice at the door of the vestry. As Heppel moved towards them, the fragrant smell grew stronger and Michael sneezed.

'Are you still in Cambridge?' said the monk, not entirely amiably. 'I thought you had returned to Westminster.'

Heppel smiled, his white face appearing even more unhealthy than usual in the gloom of the late-autumn dusk. He rubbed the palms of his hands on his gown, as if there was something on them he found distasteful. 'I had one or two loose ends to tie up first and I thought I would come to bid you farewell before I left.'

Michael nodded, but Bartholomew eyed him suspiciously. Once d'Ambrey's followers had been dispatched to London, Heppel had dropped all pretence at being the Junior Proctor and had announced himself to be one of the King's most trusted agents. Since then, he had been negotiating with the Sheriff as to how the King's peace might be maintained, trying to balance the King's opportunistic demand for extra taxes to pay for his continuing wars with the French, with the welfare of the people. A compromise had finally been struck, which left the people poorer than before, but less so than they would have been had d'Ambrey's plans come to fruition.

'Farewell, then,' said Michael, turning his attention back to his work. 'You should not tarry too long in this cold church, Master Heppel, or your cough will become worse.'

'My cough?' asked Heppel. He smiled suddenly. 'Oh, that does not bother me any more. Since you have been so busy, Matthew, I availed myself of the services of Father Philius. Once my stars had been consulted, my cough healed most miraculously. I cannot tell you how relieved I am to know my stars are favourable.'

'You mean Father Philius cured you?' asked Bartholomew incredulously.

'Totally,' Heppel said, and beamed. 'You should forget all those heretic notions of hand-washing and herbs, Matthew. Astrology is where the real power of healing lies.'

Michael roared with laughter, his voice echoing through the church. 'Take note, Matt! Astrology is the way forward for modern medicine! Perhaps you are a heretic after all!'

'You may like to know that Master Bigod met with a hunting accident,' Heppel said, changing the subject abruptly.

Bartholomew raised his eyebrows. 'A fatal one, I am sure,' he said.

Heppel regarded him askance. 'Well, naturally! Father Aidan of your own College has been appointed his successor at Maud's Hostel, while Master Thorpe will be settled in his grammar school by now. His successor at Valence Marie will be you, Brother Michael, should you decide to accept such an office.'

Michael inclined his head, his face expressionless. Heppel, disappointed at not getting an answer, continued.

'Given your interest in the business of the prostitute Joanna,' he said, turning to Bartholomew, 'you may also wish to know that the two surviving French students from Godwinsson were apprehended in Paris by the King's agents. They confessed to the girl's murder and are doubtless at the bottom of the River Seine by now. Joanna is avenged, Matthew.'

Bartholomew studied the floor. It gave him no pleasure to learn that yet more people had died in this miserable affair, but at least Joanna could rest easy now her killers had been punished. Heppel was right: loose ends were being tied indeed. Joanna's killers were dead, Thorpe was dispatched to the north, Bigod was dead. The only person to have escaped all this tying up was d'Ambrey himself.

It seemed that Heppel could read his mind. 'You are thinking that d'Ambrey, the cause of all this mayhem, has escaped unharmed. He has not. He lies in his grave as securely as all the rest.'

Bartholomew and Michael stared at him in astonishment.

'That cannot be,' said Michael. 'We saw him escape ourselves. Despite valiant efforts, Tulyet could not find him.'

'That was because Tulyet did not look in David's,' said Heppel, his pinched features lighting into a faint smile as he witnessed their growing incredulity.

'Do not play games with us, Heppel,' said Michael impatiently. 'D'Ambrey would not have returned to David's.'

'But he did,' said Heppel. 'He was found there this morning.'

'This is not possible,' said Bartholomew. 'He has been missing for three weeks now.'

'And that is probably as long as he has been dead,' said Heppel. As Bartholomew stood in what Heppel judged to be a threatening manner, the ex-Junior Proctor moved backwards and continued hastily. 'Late the night that d'Ambrey escaped, as the soldiers scoured the dark countryside, two hostels were boarded up – Godwinsson, irreparably damaged; and David's, which was shabby and unsafe anyway. You yourself, Brother, had seen to it that the surviving David's students were dispersed to other hostels so that they should not be together to inflame each other to riotous behaviour.'

Michael made an impatient gesture with his hand and Heppel hurried on.

'Carpenters were ordered to seal David's that night, so that it would not become a centre for gatherings of d'Ambrey devotees. It was late, they were tired, and perhaps they were a little fearful. The building was not properly searched before they started their work. Yesterday morning, David's Hostel was due to be demolished. As work began, Meadowman, the steward, was instructed to salvage anything that he thought might be reusable or saleable. Inside, he found d'Ambrey. He went straight to the Chancellor and the Chancellor informed me. Sure enough, the body in David's was d'Ambrey's.'

608

'But why did he return to David's?' asked Michael, not at all convinced. 'He could have been out of the country once he had escaped into the Fens.'

Heppel shrugged. 'I can only surmise that he considered it the safest location for him the night he escaped – it would certainly be the last place I would have considered looking for him. The carpenters did a good job of boarding up the hostel but d'Ambrey could have got out had he really wanted. He was found sitting in a chair at the kitchen table surrounded by quills and parchment. There was ink everywhere.'

'Was he planning to write his own version of the events of the last few weeks, do you think?' asked Bartholomew.

Heppel nodded. 'It would seem so, although the parchment in front of him was blank.'

Michael gave a snort of disbelief. 'Was it, now? That I find hard to believe.'

Heppel gave him a cold look. 'The parchment was blank. Anyway, the body was very decayed, and I think he must have died within a day or two of his escape: he had no time to embark on a lengthy treatise before he died. Perhaps the shock of seeing his plans fail so completely made him lose the will to live. Perhaps the stress of that day gave him a fatal seizure. We will never know.'

'Where is he now?' asked Bartholomew.

Heppel smiled pleasantly. 'I thought you might ask that. Come.'

They followed him through the dark church and into the graveyard. Heppel picked his way around the mounds to where Wilson's grave had been, before he had been installed in his permanent tomb in the church. Next to the yawning hole, shivering in the cold, knelt Meadowman, guarding something wrapped in a winding sheet.

Bartholomew crouched next to him and pulled the sheet away to reveal the face. D'Ambrey's beatific, features loomed out at him, and Bartholomew judged that Heppel's estimation of the time of his death was probably right – two or three weeks. He covered the face again and looked up at Heppel.

'So now all the loose ends are tied, and you can return to your King with a complete story,' he said.

Heppel nodded. 'The excavation of Master Wilson's grave was most timely. Now, only the four of us will know it did not remain empty.'

He gestured to Meadowman, who rolled d'Ambrey's body into the yawning hole, where it landed with a soft thump. The steward shovelled the earth back into place, until only a dark mound remained.

'There. It is done,' said Heppel, rubbing his hands on his robe, even though it was Meadowman who had done the shovelling. 'And now I should go. Father Philius tells me my stars are favourable for travelling tonight, so I should take advantage of them.'

'I hope we will not have mysterious accidents,' said Michael, eyeing Heppel distrustfully, 'to ensure our silence on these matters.'

Heppel gave his sickly smile. 'Do not be ridiculous, Brother. You are the Master of a respected College.'

He shook hands with them and melted away into the darkness, Meadowman following.

Bartholomew watched them go. 'So were Thorpe and Bigod,' he said softly.

As Heppel slipped out through the trees of the churchyard on to the High Street, they saw him wiping his hands on the sides of his robe, as if trying to clean them.

HISTORICAL NOTE

In the fourteenth century, the university at Cambridge was an uneasy institution. The townspeople's attitude towards it was ambivalent: it provided employment, spiritual support and a demand for rented accommodation, allowing Cambridge to become an important, prosperous town in the region; on the other hand, it clearly caused resentment among the locals, who objected to the scholars' assumed superiority. Scholars took minor orders in the Church and so offences were dealt with under lenient canon law, rather than the much harsher secular law that applied to the townspeople.

Riots in Cambridge were commonplace. One of the worst occurred in 1381, during which the University was targeted for a vicious attack by the town. Ten years previously, scholars had been indicted for breaking into town houses, assaulting their owners, and stealing fowling nets. Beside the town-gown strife, the University was a battleground within itself. Scholars from East Anglia fought those from the north, and 'foreigners' such as Scots, Welsh, Irish or French, were always considered fair game for attack. A good proportion of the University comprised scholars from the religious Orders, and disputes were common between the mendicant friars (the Franciscans and Dominicans) and monks (like the Benedictines). The friars made themselves especially unpopular with the general body of students by applying to the Pope to grant them exemption from various parts of the curriculum.

The plague of 1348–1349 evinced many changes in England. It is thought that in its wake many people turned to sources of miraculous intervention to plead for deliverance from its return. Relic selling was a profitable business in the Middle Ages, and there were many shrines that were the centres of pilgrimages. Among these were the tomb of Thomas à Becket in Canterbury Cathedral, the shrine of Our Lady of Walsingham in Norfolk and the shrine of St Swithin in Winchester Cathedral, to name but a few. Traditionally, great abbeys and churches grew up around the shrines, built from the benefactions of grateful pilgrims. For an institution to be in the possession of a relic, therefore, would have been lucrative indeed.

Throughout the Middle Ages, the King's Ditch was a stagnant ribbon of foul water that surrounded the settlement, and was used by town and University alike for waste disposal. Parliament met in Cambridge in 1388, and legislation was passed making illegal the use of public waterways as sewers. It was doubtless the state of the notoriously filthy

King's Ditch that prompted such legislation. There was no such person as Simon d'Ambrey, and the King's Ditch was never dredged for relics, although it was doubtless cleaned from time to time. The Master of Michaelhouse in the summer of 1352 was Thomas Kenyngham, and the Master of the Hall of Valence Marie (now called Pembroke College) was Robert de Thorpe.